MANAGERIAL ECONOMICS

Seventh Edition

MANAGERIAL ECONOMICS

Seventh Edition

Mark Hirschey

University of Kansas

James L. Pappas

University of South Florida

THE DRYDEN PRESS   *Harcourt Brace Jovanovich College Publishers*

Fort Worth   Philadelphia   San Diego   New York   Orlando   Austin   San Antonio
Toronto   Montreal   London   Sydney   Tokyo

Acquisitions Editor: Rick Hammonds
Developmental Editor: Michele Tomiak
Marketing Manager: Ted Barnett
Manager of Production: Lynne Bush

Project Management: Elm Street Publishing Services, Inc.
Text and Cover Designer: Rebecca Lemna/Lloyd Lemna Design
Compositor: Weimer Incorporated

ISBN: 0-03-074804-4

Library of Congress Catalog Card Number: 92-22542

Printed in the United States of America
234-039-987654321

Cover Source: H. Yagi / SUPERSTOCK

To Christine, Jessica, and Nicholas—MH
To Bonnie, Kari, and Kristen—JLP

THE DRYDEN PRESS SERIES IN ECONOMICS

Asch and Seneca
Government and the Marketplace
Second Edition

Baker
**An Introduction to
International Economics**

Baumol and Blinder
Economics: Principles and Policy
*Fifth Edition (Also available in
micro and macro paperbacks)*

Baumol, Panzar, and Willig
**Contestable Markets and the
Theory of Industry Structure**
Revised Edition

Berch
**The Endless Day: The Political
Economy of Women and Work**

Breit and Elzinga
**The Antitrust Casebook:
Milestones in Economic Regulation**
Second Edition

Campbell, Campbell, and Dolan
Money, Banking, and Monetary Policy

Claudon and Olsen
Eco Talk

Demmert
**Economics: Understanding
the Market Process**

Dolan and Lindsey
Economics
*Sixth Edition (Also available in micro
and macro paperbacks)*

Eckert and Leftwich
**The Price System and
Resource Allocation**
Tenth Edition

Edgmand, Moomaw, and Olson
Economics and Contemporary Issues

Estey
**The Unions: Structure,
Development, and Management**
Third Edition

Friedman
Milton Friedman Speaks (*Video*)

Gardner
Comparative Economic Systems

Glahe
**Microeconomics:
Theory and Application**
Second Edition

Green
Intermediate Macroeconomics

Gwartney and Stroup
Economics: Private and Public Choice
*Sixth Edition (Also available in
micro and macro paperbacks)*

Gwartney, Stroup, and Clark
Essentials of Economics
Second Edition

Heilbroner and Singer
**The Economic Transformation of
America: 1600 to the Present**
Second Edition

Hirsch and Rufolo
**Public Finance and Expenditure
in a Federal System**

Hirschey and Pappas
**Fundamentals of
Managerial Economics**
Fourth Edition

Hirschey and Pappas
Managerial Economics
Seventh Edition

Hoerneman, Howard, Wilson, and Cole
**CAPER: Computer Assisted Program
for Economic Review**

Hyman
**Public Finance: A Contemporary
Application of Theory to Policy**
Fourth Edition

Johnson and Roberts
**Money and Banking: A Market-
Oriented Approach**
Third Edition

Kaufman
The Economics of Labor Markets
Third Edition

Keating and Wilson
**Fundamentals of
Managerial Economics**

Keating and Wilson
Managerial Economics
Second Edition

Kennett and Lieberman
**The Road to Capitalism: The
Economic Transformation of Eastern
Europe and the Former Soviet Union**

Kidwell and Peterson
**Financial Institutions,
Markets, and Money**
Fifth Edition

PREFACE

In the years since the first edition of *Managerial Economics* was published, the role of managers has become evermore challenging and vital to the long-term success of all organizations. Dynamic change in the economic environment makes it difficult to assess accurately demand and supply conditions, as it increases the need for timely and effective managerial decision making. Widespread volatility in input prices and availability, the rapid pace of technical change, plus the ongoing globalization of the marketplace all combine to make the efficient use of economic resources very difficult. Sound economic analysis has never been more important than it is in the 1990s—regardless of whether the decision-making unit is an individual, household, firm, nonprofit organization, or government agency.

Managerial Economics, seventh edition, is designed to provide a solid foundation of economic understanding for use in managerial decision making. This text offers an intuitive *calculus-based* treatment of economic theory and analysis. A wide variety of examples and simple numerical problems illustrate the application of managerial economics to a wide variety of practical situations. The nature of the decision process and the role that economic analysis plays in that process are emphasized throughout the text.

A key feature of this text is its attempt to depict the firm as a cohesive, unified organization. The basic valuation model is constructed and used as the underlying economic model of the firm. Each topic in the text is then related to an element of the value maximization model. In this process, management is seen to involve an integration of the accounting, finance, marketing, human resources, and production functions. This integrative approach demonstrates that important business decisions are *interdisciplinary* in the truest sense of the word. Students find that the presentation of the business firm as a unified whole, rather than as a series of discrete, unrelated areas, is one of the most valuable aspects of the study of managerial economics.

Although both micro- and macroeconomic relations have implications for managerial decision making, this text concentrates on microeconomic topics of particular importance. Following the development of the economic model of the firm, the vital role of profits is examined. Because the decision-making process often involves conditions of uncertainty, a number of optimization and risk analysis techniques for investment and operating decisions that are subject to risk are also described. Because the demand for a firm's products plays a major role in determining its profitability and ongoing success, demand analysis and estimation are essential areas of study. This naturally leads to a discussion of economic forecasting and methods for assessing forecast reliability. Production theory, cost analysis, and linear programming techniques are then explored as means for understanding the economics of resource allocation and employment.

Another important topic is market structure analysis, which provides a foundation for studying the external economic environment and for examining the pricing practices required for successful management. The role of government in the market economy, including the constraints it imposes on management, requires an examination of regulation and antitrust law. Finally, capital budgeting is shown as the method for introducing marginal analysis into the long-range strategic planning and control process. The capital budgeting process is not only important within firms, hospitals, and all other types of economic organizations but also to society as a whole because it involves the allocation of scarce capital resources.

Managerial Economics, seventh edition, takes a practical problem-solving approach to the study of managerial economics. The text focuses on the economics—not the mathematics—of the managerial decision process. When appropriate, quantitative methods and tools are introduced to give greater insight into the methods of economic analysis and to facilitate the practical use of economics in decision situations. The emphasis, however, is clearly on economic intuition as a useful tool for problem solving.

CHANGES IN THE SEVENTH EDITION

The environment in which managerial decisions are made is constantly changing. Therefore, a textbook must be modified and updated to maintain its value as an educational resource. This revision of *Managerial Economics* contains a number of important additions and refinements. Indeed, every chapter has been updated in response to valuable suggestions provided by students and instructors and to reflect recent developments in the field. The following section highlights some of the most important changes in the seventh edition.

Content

- In response to user suggestions, Chapter 3, *Risk Analysis,* has been completely revised from the previous edition and moved up in the book to allow consideration of decision making under uncertainty early in the course. The discussion of utility concepts prior to the introduction of demand analysis also makes clear the role of economic theory in describing the motivation for consumer demand.
- Chapter 6, *Demand Estimation,* has been expanded and refined to show how the use of basic statistical tools can provide valuable information concerning demand relations. Chapter 6 offers a basic introduction to statistical analysis that is relied upon heavily in the study of production, cost, and market structure relations in later chapters.

- Chapter 8, *Production Analysis and Estimation,* now develops the concept of optimal input combinations by emphasizing the relations among factor productivity, value of output, and resource employment. Practical examples show how these relations are equally valuable in analyzing the production of both goods and services. An introduction to the use of statistical methods for production function estimation has also been added.
- Chapter 9, *Cost Analysis,* has been revised extensively to demonstrate the practical relevance of economic analysis through expanded coverage of topics such as minimum efficient scale, economies of scope, and learning (or experience).
- The analysis of market structure and competitive strategy has also been expanded and streamlined in Chapter 12, *Perfect Competition and Monopoly,* and Chapter 13, *Monopolistic Competition and Oligopoly.* Both price and nonprice (e.g., advertising) methods of competition are carefully examined in perfectly and imperfectly competitive markets.
- Chapter 15, *Government Regulation of the Market Economy,* has undergone a comprehensive revision to offer perspective on recent moves to deregulate and re-regulate various types of private market activity. Incentive regulation is also carefully examined as a new means for achieving social objectives through the cooperation between the public and private sectors.
- Chapter 16, *Capital Budgeting,* has been rewritten to reflect the broad range of issues addressed in the capital budgeting process by firms of all sizes. The use of modern spreadsheet software for capital budget analysis is also more fully explored.

Learning Aids

- Each chapter incorporates a wide variety of simple numerical examples and detailed practical illustrations of key concepts. These features portray the valuable use and real-world implications of covered material. A special symbol, ▶, in the margin indicates the location of these useful learning aids.
- Each chapter also includes three Managerial Applications boxes to show current examples of how concepts introduced in managerial economics are actually used in real-world situations. In the entire text, 48 new Managerial Applications based on articles from *Barron's, Business Week, Forbes, Fortune,* and the *Wall Street Journal* are provided. This feature offers an attractive and popular basis for classroom discussion.
- Each chapter is now accompanied by a new case study that provides in-depth treatment of important concepts. To meet the needs of all instructors and students, many of these case studies are written to allow, but not require, a computer-based approach. These case studies, identified by a computer symbol, ▪, in the margin, are fully self-contained. Both 3.5″ and 5.25″ floppy diskettes for IBM PC® and IBM® compatible computers that contain case study data and detailed solutions are provided to adopters with the *Instructor's Manual.* These case studies are especially helpful to instructors who wish to incorporate the use of basic spreadsheet and statistical software into their courses.

- The text also provides several new regression-based illustrations of chapter concepts using actual company data, or data adapted from real-world situations. These illustrations build on the introduction to the statistical analysis of economic relations given in Chapter 6. Like all aspects of the text, this material is self-contained and intuitive.
- Effective managers in the 1990s must be sensitive to the special challenges posed by an increasingly global marketplace. To increase student awareness of such issues, the text also features a number of examples, Managerial Applications, and case studies that relate to global business topics. A special symbol, 🌐, indicates the location of these effective learning aids.
- More than 300 new end-of-chapter questions and problems are also provided, after having been subject to necessary revision and class testing. Questions are designed to give students the opportunity to grasp basic concepts on an intuitive level and express their understanding in a nonquantitative fashion. Problems cover a wide variety of decision situations and illustrate the role of economic analysis from within a simple numerical framework.

ANCILLARY PACKAGE

Managerial Economics, seventh edition, is supported by the most comprehensive ancillary package available to make teaching and learning managerial economics both easy and enjoyable.

Instructor's Manual   The *Instructor's Manual* offers learning suggestions plus detailed answers and solutions for all chapter questions and problems. As mentioned previously, diskettes for IBM PC and IBM compatible computers that contain case study data and detailed solutions are provided to adopters with the *Instructor's Manual.*

Study Guide   The *Study Guide* furnishes a detailed line summary of major concepts for each chapter, a brief discussion of important economic relations as they are covered in the text, and an expanded set of more than 150 solved problems. This completely new edition has undergone extensive class testing and analysis. Based on the comments of students and instructors alike, this new *Study Guide* is highly recommended as a valuable learning resource.

Test Bank   A comprehensive *Test Bank* is also provided, which offers a variety of multiple-choice questions, one-step, and multi-step problems for every chapter. Full solutions are included. With a selection of more than 500 questions and problems, the *Test Bank* is a valuable tool for exam preparation. The *Test Bank* is also available in computerized form.

ACKNOWLEDGMENTS

A number of people have aided in the preparation of *Managerial Economics,* seventh edition. Helpful suggestions and constructive comments have been received from a great number of instructors and students who have used previous editions. Numerous reviewers have also provided insights and assistance in clarifying difficult material. Among those who have been especially helpful in the development of this edition are Mel Borland, Western Kentucky University; Keith Chauvin, University of Kansas; John Dodge, Calvin College; Peter Frederiksen, Naval Post Graduate School; Gerald Hanweck, George Mason University; Julia Heath, Memphis State University; and C. W. Yang, Clarion University. Special recognition is merited for Christine E. Hauschel, who did extensive manuscript reviewing and problem checking.

The University of Kansas, the University of South Florida, students, and colleagues have together provided a stimulating environment and general intellectual support. We are also indebted to The Dryden Press staff and would like to thank Lynne Bush, Rick Hammond, Michele Tomiak, and Millicent Treloar for their special efforts. Finally, we want to thank our wives, Chris and Bonnie, for their encouragement, support, and assistance.

Every effort has been made to minimize errors in the text. However, errors do occasionally slip through despite diligent efforts to provide an error-free package of text and ancillary materials. Readers are invited to correspond with us directly concerning any corrections or other suggestions.

Finally, it is clear today, more than ever before, that economic efficiency is an essential ingredient in the successful management of private and public sector organizations. Like any dynamic field of study, the field of managerial economics continues to undergo profound change in response to the challenges imposed by a rapidly evolving environment. It is stimulating and exciting to participate in these developments. We sincerely hope that the seventh edition of *Managerial Economics* contributes to a better understanding of the usefulness of economic theory and methodology to managerial practice.

Mark Hirschey
James L. Pappas
September 1992

About the Authors

Mark Hirschey, Ph.D. (University of Wisconsin-Madison), is a professor in the School of Business at the University of Kansas, where he teaches undergraduate and graduate courses in managerial economics and finance. Professor Hirschey is president of the Association of Managerial Economists and a member of several professional organizations. He has published articles in the *American Economic Review, Journal of Accounting Research, Journal of Business, Journal of Business and Economic Statistics, Journal of Finance, Journal of Industrial Economics, Review of Economics and Statistics,* and other leading academic journals. He is editor of *Managerial and Decision Economics* and co-author of *Fundamentals of Managerial Economics,* fourth edition, with James Pappas.

James L. Pappas, Ph.D. (UCLA), is Dean and Lykes Professor of Banking and Finance in the College of Business Administration at the University of South Florida. He is a member of several professional organizations and has served as an officer of the Financial Management Association. Articles by Professor Pappas have appeared in *Decision Sciences, Engineering Economist, Financial Analysts' Journal, Journal of Business, Journal of Finance, Journal of Industrial Economics, Journal of Marketing Research,* and other leading academic journals. He is co-author of *Fundamentals of Managerial Economics,* fourth edition, with Mark Hirschey. Active in executive education, Professor Pappas also serves as Academic Dean of the Graduate School of Banking, offered by the Central States Conference of Bankers Associations and the University of Wisconsin-Madison.

CONTENTS

MANAGERIAL ECONOMICS

Seventh Edition

PART I

INTRODUCTION TO MANAGERIAL ECONOMICS

CHAPTER

THE NATURE AND SCOPE OF MANAGERIAL ECONOMICS

How do managers make good decisions? What pitfalls must be avoided? When are the characteristics of a market, a line of business, or an industry so attractive that entry becomes appealing? When are these attributes so unattractive that growth is not warranted and exit is preferable to continued operation? Why do some professions continue to pay well, while others offer only minimal financial rewards? How do you effectively motivate employees? All of these questions involve important economic issues that pose a continuing challenge to the managerial decision-making process.

The first step in this process is to carefully collect and organize economic information so that a clear basis can be established for managerial decisions. The goals of the organization must then be clearly stated so that suitable managerial objectives can be formulated. Making sure that resources are effectively utilized is the prime consideration. Capital must be obtained and employed; workers need to be trained and motivated; and information systems must be installed to ensure that ongoing performance is accurately reported and monitored. Extensive knowledge and a wide variety of skills are required to complete each of these important tasks so that appropriate decisions can be made. One of the most important requirements for a successful manager is the ability to make good decisions, and one of the most important tools used by successful managers is the methodology of managerial economics.

Managerial economics
Applies economic tools and techniques to business and administrative decision making.

Managerial economics applies economic theory and methods to business and administrative decision making. Because it uses the tools and techniques of economic analysis to solve managerial problems, managerial economics links traditional economics with the decision sciences to develop vital tools for managerial decision making. This is illustrated in Figure 1.1.

The value of managerial economics can be appreciated by examining its prescriptive and descriptive components. Managerial economics prescribes rules for improving managerial decisions. It tells managers how things should be done to achieve organizational objectives efficiently. Managerial economics also helps

FIGURE 1.1 **The Role of Managerial Economics in Managerial Decision Making**

Managerial economics uses economic concepts and decision science techniques to solve managerial problems.

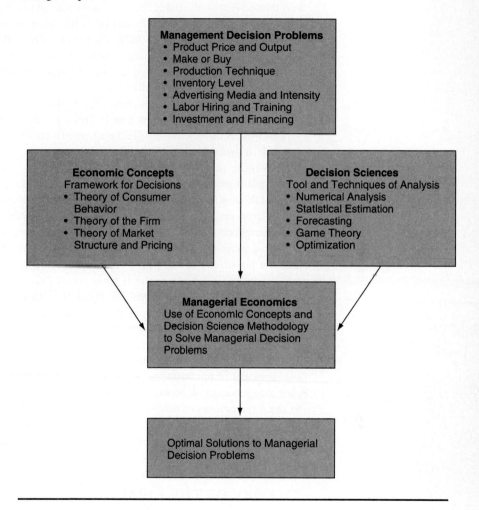

managers recognize how economic forces affect organizations and describes the economic consequences of managerial behavior.

Managerial economics can be used to identify ways to efficiently achieve virtually any of the organization's goals. For example, suppose a small business seeks rapid growth in order to reach a size that will permit efficient use of national media advertising. The firm's managers can use managerial economics to identify pricing and production strategies that will help meet this short-run objective as quickly and effectively as possible. Similarly, managerial economics provides production and marketing rules that will permit the company to maximize net profits once it has achieved its growth objectives.

Managerial economics has prescriptive applications in both the for-profit and not-for-profit sectors. For example, an administrator of a nonprofit hospital strives to provide the best medical care possible given limited medical staff, equipment, and related resources. Using the tools and concepts of managerial economics, the administrator can determine the optimal allocation of these limited resources. In short, managerial economics helps managers arrive at a set of operating rules that aid in the efficient utilization of scarce human and capital resources. Following these rules enables businesses, nonprofit organizations, and government agencies to meet their objectives efficiently.

To establish appropriate decision rules, managers must thoroughly understand the economic environment in which they operate. Managerial economics describes how economic forces affect and are affected by managerial decisions. For example, a grocery retailer may offer consumers a highly price-sensitive product, such as milk, at an extremely low markup over cost—say, 1 or 2 percent—while offering less price-sensitive products, such as nonprescription drugs, at markups of as high as 40 percent over cost. Managerial economics describes the logic of this pricing practice with respect to the goal of profit maximization. Similarly, managerial economics reveals that imposing auto import quotas reduces the availability of substitutes for domestically produced cars, raises auto prices, and creates the possibility of monopoly profits for domestic manufacturers. It does not tell us whether imposing quotas is good public policy; that is a decision involving broader political considerations. Managerial economics only describes the predictable economic consequences of such actions.

With its prescriptive and descriptive components, managerial economics provides a comprehensive application of economic theory and methodology to managerial decision making. Managerial economics is just as relevant to the management of nonbusiness, nonprofit organizations, such as government agencies, cooperatives, schools, hospitals, museums, and similar institutions, as it is to the management of profit-oriented businesses. Although this text focuses primarily on business applications, it also includes examples and problems from the government and nonprofit sectors to illustrate the broad relevance of managerial economics concepts and tools.

THEORY OF THE FIRM

A useful way to begin the study of managerial economics is to consider the broad framework within which managerial decisions are analyzed. A business enterprise is a combination of people, physical and financial assets, and information (financial, technical, marketing, and so on). People directly involved include stockholders, management, labor, suppliers, and customers. Society in general is affected by business because the business community uses scarce resources, pays taxes, provides employment, and produces much of society's material and services output. Firms thus exist because they are useful for producing and distributing goods and services—they are economic entities and are best analyzed in the context of an economic model.

Theory of the firm
The basic model of the business enterprise.

The basic model of business is called the **theory of the firm.** In its simplest version, the firm is thought to have profit maximization as its primary goal. The

MANAGERIAL APPLICATION 1.1

Does Anybody Care about Stockholders?

"Customers are first, employees second, shareholders third, and the community fourth," says Tony Anderson, 56, chief executive officer (CEO) of the H. B. Fuller Company. Shareholders third? What ever happened to value maximization and the concept of running companies the old-fashioned way—for the stockholders? Is this another case of entrenched management operating a company to meet its own agenda rather than that of its owners? Or is the concept of value maximization quite broad and encompass a range of company activities that might at first appear inconsistent with value maximization, but in the long run are quite compatible with shareholder interests? For some insight on these and related questions, it is worth paying attention to what Anderson has to say.

"I'm not your typical *Fortune* 500 CEO," Anderson admits. His company, H. B. Fuller, sells glue—the kind that holds together office furniture, keeps houses erect, and holds magazines such as *Fortune* in one piece. H. B. Fuller sells so much glue in fact that the company is No. 374 and climbing fast on the *Fortune* 500 list. This is despite the fact that the H. B. Fuller Company clearly covets customer satisfaction over quarterly profits, wins praise from environmental groups, and contributes as much as 5 percent of pretax income to charitable organizations. (The corporate average for charitable gift-giving is approximately 2 percent of pretax profits.) From this perspective, it is interesting indeed what such a do-gooder can accomplish. Over the past ten years, H. B. Fuller has returned almost 20 percent per year to investors. In mid-1992, the company's stock sold for more than $70 a share, roughly twice the 1991 price. How does the company do it?

Customer service is the key. It started with Anderson's father, Elmer L. Anderson, 82, a popular and progressive former governor of Minnesota, who bought Fuller in 1941. The senior Anderson encouraged salespeople to be responsive to customer needs, sometimes unlocking plants in the middle of the night to deliver glue to customers who had inadvertently let supplies run dry. Says Tony, the CEO since 1973: "I don't know how to perform for shareholders over the long term unless I do my best for customers."

That sometimes takes dogged determination. H. B. Fuller had sold adhesives to Procter & Gamble for years but to secure a permanent relationship, H. B. Fuller wanted a significant contract to make glue for P&G's disposable diapers in the United States. In 1986, a top salesperson for H. B. Fuller analyzed the needs of the diaper business and four chemists were assigned to come up with a moisture-resistant adhesive supple enough to replace several glues P&G had been using. To show P&G how serious it was, H. B. Fuller started building a $17 million factory in Paducah, Kentucky, three years before the supply contract was signed. While the factory produced little glue during its first year of operation, it is now operating at capacity.

Thinking long term, H. B. Fuller began investing abroad in the early 1960s. By 1991, non-U.S. operations contributed 46 percent of company revenues and 63 percent of profits. Neither revolutions nor earthquakes nor rampant inflation have caused management to shut any of H. B. Fuller's 32 factories in Latin America. In fact, H. B. Fuller management believes that the company owes its Latin American constituents something in return for the hefty profits generated by this part of the business. In Lima, Peru, where malnutrition is widespread, H. B. Fuller is using two huge gluepots temporarily idled by recession to cook soy porridge for 10,000 children per day.

At times, such corporate generosity appears to have its price: H. B. Fuller's profit growth has been somewhat uneven and the company's common stock has been volatile. However, the company's basic operating philosophy is well articulated by its new president and chief operating officer Walter Kissling, 60, the former head of H. B. Fuller's international operations. Kissling argues: "A company exists to make money for its shareholders, but if you have happy customers and employees who support its value system, the payoff to stockholders will work itself out."

Source: Patricia Sellers, "Who Cares about Shareholders?" *Fortune,* June 15, 1992, 122.

Expected value maximization

Optimization of profits in light of uncertainty and the time value of money.

firm's owner-manager is assumed to be working to maximize the firm's short-run profits. Today, the emphasis on profits has been broadened to encompass uncertainty and the time value of money. In this more complete model, the primary goal of the firm is long-term **expected value maximization,** which is now considered the primary objective of business in the economic model of firm behavior.

Defining Value

Value of the firm

The present value of the firm's expected future net cash flows.

Present value

Worth in current dollars.

Since the basis of the economic model is maximizing the value of the firm, the meaning of *value* must be clarified. Many concepts of value are found in economics and business—book value, market value, liquidating value, going-concern value, and so on. The **value of the firm** is the present value of the firm's expected future net cash flows. If cash flows are equated to profits for simplicity, the value of the firm today, or its **present value,** is the value of expected profits or cash flows, discounted back to the present at an appropriate interest rate.[1]

This model is employed throughout this book and can be expressed as follows:

Value of the Firm = Present Value of Expected Future Profits

$$= \frac{\pi_1}{(1 + i)^1} + \frac{\pi_2}{(1 + i)^2} + \cdots + \frac{\pi_N}{(1 + i)^N} \quad \textbf{(1.1)}$$

$$= \sum_{t=1}^{N} \frac{\pi_t}{(1 + i)^t}.$$

Here, $\pi_1, \pi_2, \ldots, \pi_N$ represent expected profits in each year, t, and i is the appropriate interest, or discount, rate. The final form for Equation 1.1 is simply a shorthand expression in which sigma (Σ) stands for "sum up" or "add together." The term

$$\sum_{t=1}^{N}$$

simply means, "Add together as t goes from 1 to N the values of the term on the right." For Equation 1.1, the process is as follows: Let $t = 1$ and find the value of the term $\pi_1/(1 + i)^1$, the present value of year 1 profit; then let $t = 2$ and calculate $\pi_2/(1 + i)^2$, the present value of year 2 profit; continue until $t = N$, the last year included in the analysis; then add up these present-value equivalents of yearly profits to find the current or present value of the firm.

Because profits (π) are equal to total revenues *(TR)* minus total costs *(TC),* Equation 1.1 can be rewritten as

$$\text{Value} = \sum_{t=1}^{N} \frac{TR_t - TC_t}{(1 + i)^t}. \quad \textbf{(1.2)}$$

[1] Discounting is required because profits obtained in the future are less valuable than profits earned presently. To understand this, one needs to recognize that $1 in hand today is worth more than $1 to be received a year from now, because $1 today can be invested and, with interest, grow to a larger amount by the end of the year. If we had $1 and invested it at 10 percent interest, it would grow to $1.10 in one year. Thus, $1 is defined as the present value of $1.10 due in one year when the appropriate interest rate is 10 percent.

This expanded equation can be used to examine how the expected value maximization model relates to a firm's various functional departments and activities. The marketing department of a firm has a major responsibility for sales *(TR)*; the production department has a major responsibility for costs *(TC)*; and the finance department has a major responsibility for acquiring the capital needed to support the firm's investment and operating activities and, hence, for the discount factor *(i)* in the denominator. There are many important overlaps among these functional areas. The marketing department, for example, can help reduce the costs associated with a given level of output by influencing customer order size and timing. The production department can stimulate sales by improving quality and reducing delivery lags. Still other departments—for example, accounting, personnel, transportation, and engineering—provide information and services vital to sales growth and cost control. The determination of *TR* and *TC* is a complex task that requires recognizing important interrelations among the various areas of firm activity. All of these activities affect the firm's risks and thus the discount rate used to determine present values. An important concept in managerial economics is that managerial decisions throughout the firm should be analyzed in terms of their effects on the various determinants of value as expressed in Equations 1.1 and 1.2.

Constraints and the Theory of the Firm

Managerial decisions are often made in light of constraints imposed by technology, resource scarcity, contractual obligations, and government laws and regulations. To make decisions that will maximize value, managers must consider both short-run and long-run implications as well as how various external constraints affect their ability to achieve organizational objectives.

Firms and other organizations frequently face limited availability of essential inputs, such as skilled labor, key raw materials, energy, specialized machinery, and warehouse space. Managers also often face capital constraints that place limitations on the amount of investment funds available for a particular project or activity.

Managerial decisions can also be constrained by contractual requirements. For example, labor contracts limit flexibility in worker scheduling and job assignment, sometimes even affecting whether labor costs are fixed or variable. Contracts often require that a minimum level of output be produced to meet delivery requirements. In other instances, output must meet certain minimum quality requirements. Some common examples of output quality constraints are nutritional requirements for feed mixtures, audience exposure requirements for marketing promotions, reliability requirements for electronic products, and customer service requirements for minimum satisfaction levels.

Legal restrictions that affect both production and marketing activities can also play an important role in managerial decisions. Laws that define minimum wages, health and safety standards, pollution emission standards, fuel efficiency requirements, and fair pricing and marketing practices all limit managerial flexibility.

The role that constraints play in managerial decisions makes the topic of constrained optimization a basic element of managerial economics. Later chapters consider important economic implications of both self-imposed and social constraints. This analysis is important because value maximization and allocative efficiency in society depend on the efficient use of scarce economic resources.

Limitations of the Theory of the Firm

Optimize
Seek the best solution.

Satisfice
Seek satisfactory rather than optimal results.

Some critics question why the value maximization criterion is used as a foundation for the study of firm behavior. Are not managers interested, at least to some extent, in power, prestige, leisure, employee welfare, community well-being, and society in general? Further, do managers really try to **optimize** (seek the best result) or merely **satisfice** (seek satisfactory rather than optimal results)? Does the manager of a firm really seek the sharpest needle in a haystack (optimize), or does he or she stop upon finding one sharp enough for sewing (satisfice)?

It is extremely difficult to determine whether managers actually attempt to maximize firm value or merely attempt to satisfy stockholders while pursuing other goals. How can one tell whether company support of the United Way, for example, leads to long-run value maximization? Are high salaries and substantial stock options necessary to attract and retain managers who can keep the firm ahead of the competition? When a risky venture is turned down, can one say that this reflects inefficient risk avoidance on the part of management? Or does it, in fact, reflect an appropriate decision from the standpoint of value maximization?

It is impossible to give definitive answers to questions like these, and this has led to the development of alternative theories of firm behavior. Some of the more prominent alternatives are models in which size or growth maximization is the assumed primary objective of management, models that argue that managers are most concerned with their own personal utility or welfare maximization, and models that treat the firm as a collection of individuals with widely divergent goals rather than as a single, identifiable unit.

Each of these alternative theories, or models, of managerial behavior has added to our knowledge and understanding of the firm. Still, none can supplant the basic value maximization model of the firm as a foundation for analyzing managerial decisions. Examining why provides additional insight into the value of studying managerial economics.

The theory of the firm states that managers maximize the value of the firm subject to constraints imposed by resource limitations, technology, and society. The theory does not explicitly recognize other goals, including the possibility that managers take actions that benefit parties other than stockholders—perhaps the managers themselves or society in general—and *reduce* stockholder wealth. The model seems to ignore the possibilities of satisficing, managerial self-dealing, and voluntary social responsibility on the part of business.

Given that firms assert the existence of multiple goals, engage in "social responsibility" programs, and sometimes exhibit what appears to be satisficing behavior, is the economic model of the firm an adequate basis for the study of managerial decision making? Based on the evidence, the answer is yes.

Research has shown that vigorous competition in markets for goods and services typically forces managers to seek value maximization in their operating decisions. Competition in the capital markets in which firms acquire the investment funds necessary for current operations, growth, and expansion forces managers to seek value maximization in their financing decisions as well. Stockholders are, of course, interested in value maximization because it affects their rates of return on common stock investments. Managers who pursue their own interests instead of stockholders' interests run the risk of being replaced. Buyout pressure from unfriendly firms ("raiders") has been considerable during recent years. Unfriendly takeovers are especially hostile to inefficient management, which is usually replaced. Further, recent studies indicate a strong correlation between firm profits and managerial compensation—managers have strong economic incentives to pursue value maximization through their decisions.

It is important to remember that managers must consider costs and benefits before they can make reasoned decisions. This also applies to the decision to satisfice rather than to maximize. Before a firm can decide on a satisfactory level of performance, management must examine the costs of such a decision. Would it be wise or profitable to seek out the best technical solution to a problem if the costs of finding this solution greatly exceed resulting benefits? Of course not. What often appears to be satisficing on the part of management can be interpreted as value-maximizing behavior once the costs of information gathering and analysis are considered. Similarly, short-run growth maximization strategies are often consistent with long-run value maximization when the production, distribution, or promotional advantages of large firm size are better understood.

Finally, the value maximization model also offers insight into a firm's voluntary "socially responsible" behavior. The criticism that the neoclassical theory of the firm emphasizes profits and value maximization while ignoring the issue of social responsibility is important and will be returned to later in the chapter. For now, it will prove useful to examine the concept of profits, which is central to the theory of the firm.

PROFITS

To understand the theory of the firm and the role of the firm in a free enterprise economy, one must understand the nature of profits. Profits are such a key element in the free enterprise system that the system would fail to operate without profits and the profit motive. Even in planned economies, where state ownership rather than private enterprise is typical, the profit motive is increasingly used to spur efficient resource use. In the former East Bloc countries, the former Soviet Union, China, and other nations, new profit incentives for managers and workers have led to higher product quality and cost efficiency. Thus, profits and the profit motive play an important and growing role in the efficient allocation of economic resources worldwide.

Business versus Economic Profit

The general public and the business community typically define profit using an accounting concept. This gives rise to a general understanding of profit as the residual of sales revenue minus the explicit accounting costs of doing business. It is the amount available to fund equity capital after payment for all other resources

Business profit
Residual of sales revenue minus the explicit accounting costs of doing business.

Normal rate of return
Minimum profit necessary to attract and retain investment.

Economic profit
Business profit minus the implicit costs of capital and any other owner-provided inputs.

the firm uses. This definition of profit is often referred to as accounting profit, or **business profit.**

The economist also defines profit as the excess of revenues over the costs of doing business. However, inputs provided by the owners, including entrepreneurial effort and capital, are resources that must be paid for as well if they are to be employed. The economist includes a normal rate of return on equity capital plus an opportunity cost for the effort of the owner-entrepreneur as costs of doing business, just as the interest paid on debt and the wages paid to labor are considered costs in calculating business profit. The risk-adjusted **normal rate of return** on capital is the minimum return necessary to attract and retain investment. Similarly, the opportunity cost of owner effort is determined by the value that could be received in an alternative activity. In economic terms, profit is business profit minus the implicit costs of capital and other owner-provided inputs used by the firm. This profit concept is frequently referred to as **economic profit** to distinguish it from business profit.

The concepts of business profit and economic profit can be used to explain why profits exist and what their role is in a free enterprise economy. The concept of economic profit recognizes a required payment for the use of owner-provided inputs. There is a normal rate of return, or profit, for example, that is necessary for inducing individuals to invest funds in one activity rather than investing them elsewhere or spending them for current consumption. This normal profit is simply a cost for capital; it is no different from the cost of other resources, such as labor, materials, and energy. A similar price exists for the entrepreneurial effort of a firm's owner-manager and for other resources that owners bring to the firm. These opportunity costs for owner-provided inputs offer a primary explanation for the existence of business profits.

What explains the difference between the economist's concept of normal profits as a cost of equity capital and other owner-provided inputs and the actual business profits earned by firms? In equilibrium, economic profits would be zero if all firms operated in perfectly competitive markets. All firms would report business profits reflecting only a normal rate of return on equity investment and payment for other owner-supplied inputs. In actual practice, reported profit rates vary widely among firms. During recent years, for example, business profits have ranged from very low in the airline, banking, and savings and loan industries to very high in the office equipment, pharmaceutical, and soft drink industries. Some of this variation in business profits represents the influence of risk premiums necessary to compensate investors if one business is inherently riskier than another, but many firms obviously earn significant economic profits or experience economic losses at any given point in time. Examining several theories used to explain the existence of economic profits provides further insight into their critical role in a market economy and in managerial decision making.

Frictional Theory of Economic Profits

One explanation of economic profits or losses is **frictional profit theory.** It states that markets are sometimes in disequilibrium because of unanticipated changes in demand or cost conditions. Shocks occur in the economy, producing disequilibrium conditions that lead to positive or negative economic profits for some firms.

Frictional profit theory
Abnormal profits observed following unanticipated changes in demand or cost conditions.

For example, the use of automatic teller machines (ATMs) makes it possible for the customers of financial institutions to easily obtain cash, enter deposits, and make loan payments. At the same time, ATMs render obsolete many of the functions that used to be carried out at branch offices and help lead to a consolidation in the industry that still continues. Similarly, a new generation of user-friendly computer software leads to a marked increase in the demand for high-powered personal computers (PCs) and a rapid growth in returns for efficient PC manufacturers. Alternatively, a rise in the use of plastics or aluminum in automobiles might drive down the profits of steel manufacturers. Over time, barring impassable barriers to entry and exit, resources would flow into or out of financial institutions, computer manufacturers, and steel manufacturers, thus driving rates of return back to normal levels. During interim periods, profits might be above or below normal because of frictional factors that prevent instantaneous adjustment to new market conditions.

Monopoly Theory of Economic Profits

Monopoly profit theory
Above-normal profits caused by barriers to entry that limit competition.

A further explanation of above-normal profits, **monopoly profit theory,** is an extension of frictional profit theory. This theory asserts that some firms are sheltered from competition by high barriers to entry. Economies of scale, high capital requirements, patents, or import protection enable some firms to build monopoly positions that allow above-normal profits for extended periods. Monopoly profits can even arise because of luck or happenstance (being in the right industry at the right time) or from anticompetitive behavior. Unlike other potential sources of above-normal profits, monopoly profits are often seen as unwarranted. Thus, monopoly profits are usually taxed or otherwise regulated. Monopoly, a most interesting topic, is discussed at length in Chapters 12, 13, and 15, which consider the causes and consequences of monopoly and how society attempts to mitigate its potential costs.

Innovation Theory of Economic Profits

Innovation profit theory
Above-normal profits that follow successful invention or modernization.

An additional theory of economic profits, **innovation profit theory,** describes the above-normal profits that arise following successful invention or modernization. For example, innovation profit theory suggests that Xerox Corporation historically earned a high rate of return because it successfully developed, introduced, and marketed xerography, a superior copying technology. Xerox continued to receive these supernormal returns until other firms entered the field and drove profits down to a normal level. Similarly, McDonald's Corporation earned above-normal rates of return as an early innovator in the fast-food business. With increased competition from Burger King, Wendy's, and a host of national and regional competitors, McDonald's, like Xerox, has seen its above-normal returns decline. As in the case of frictional or disequilibrium profits, profits that are due to innovation are susceptible to the onslaught of competition from new and established competitors.

Compensatory Theory of Economic Profits

Compensatory profit theory describes above-normal rates of return that reward firms for being extraordinarily successful in meeting customer needs, maintaining efficient operations, and so forth. If firms that operate at the industry's average

Compensatory profit theory

Above-normal rates of return that reward efficiency.

level of efficiency receive normal rates of return, it is reasonable to expect that firms operating at above-average levels of efficiency will earn above-normal rates of return. Inefficient firms can be expected to earn unsatisfactory, below-normal rates of return.

Compensatory profit theory also recognizes economic profit as an important reward to the entrepreneurial function of owners and managers. Every firm and product starts as an idea for better serving some established or perceived need of existing or potential customers. This need remains unmet until an individual takes the initiative to design, plan, and implement a solution. The opportunity for economic profits is an important motivation for such entrepreneurial activity.

The Role of Profits in the Economy

Each of the preceding four theories describes economic profits obtained for different reasons. In some cases, several might apply. For example, a very efficient manufacturer may earn an above-normal rate of return in accordance with compensatory theory, but, during a strike by a competitor's employees, the above-average profits may be augmented by frictional profits. Similarly, Xerox's profit position might be partly explained by all four theories: The company earned high frictional profits while 3M, Kodak, Canon, and other firms were tooling up in response to the rapid growth in demand for office copiers; it has earned monopoly profits because it has some patent protection; it has certainly benefited from successful innovation; and it is well managed and thus has earned compensatory profits.

Economic profits play an important role in a market-based economy. Above-normal profits serve as a valuable signal that firm or industry output should be increased. Expansion by established firms or entry by new competitors often occurs quickly during periods of high profit. Just as above-normal profits provide a signal for expansion and entry, below-normal profits provide a signal for contraction and exit. Economic profits are one of the most important factors affecting the allocation of scarce economic resources. Above-normal profits can also constitute an important reward for innovation and efficiency, just as below-normal profits can serve as a penalty for stagnation and inefficiency. Thus, profits play a critical role both in providing an incentive for innovation and productive efficiency and in allocating scarce resources.

An understanding of how profits affect business behavior provides important insight into the relationship between the firm and society.

ROLE OF BUSINESS IN SOCIETY

As suggested previously, an important element in the study of managerial economics is the relationship between the firm and society. Managerial economics clarifies the vital role of firms and points out ways of improving their contribution to the achievement of social objectives.

The evidence that business contributes significantly to social welfare is clear and convincing. The economy in the United States and several other countries has sustained a notable rate of growth over many decades. The benefits of that

●

MANAGERIAL APPLICATION 1.2
Managerial Ethics

During the mid-1980s, Dennis B. Levine, a managing director of mergers and acquisitions for Drexel Burnham Lambert, Inc., admitted to stealing material nonpublic information from his employer and using it to amass millions of dollars in illegal stock market trading profits. The scandal broadened when the Securities and Exchange Commission found that Levine had cultivated a mutually profitable relationship with Ivan Boesky, a stock market speculator. Levine supplied Boesky with tips concerning pending merger announcements in return for a share of the trading profits Boesky realized. Seeking to minimize his own pending sentence on criminal charges, Boesky implicated a wide range of Wall Street financiers, including Robert Freeman, Martin Siegel, Boyd L. Jefferies, John A. Mulheren, and Paul Blizerian. Eventually, as the full truth became known, Drexel Burnham Lambert, Inc. magnate Michael R. Milken was also implicated. In pleading guilty to criminal charges of stock manipulation, Milken and his associates admitted that they cashed out as investors unwittingly rushed into the junk bond market, and these investors left holding the bag with billions of dollars in losses. Milken and others implicated in this insider trading scandal were forced to give up ill-gotten profits, paid millions of dollars in fines, served time in federal prison, and were barred from the securities business for life.

In additional civil charges that will take years to unravel, the Federal Deposit Insurance Corporation (FDIC) contends that in pioneering the junk bond market, Milken perpetrated history's largest Ponzi scheme. According to the FDIC, an epidemic of inside dealing artificially inflated the value of many junk-bond issues and created an illusion of liquidity. Junk bonds were allegedly "parked" with S&L's to hide true ownership, executives were bribed to buy securities with S&L resources, and the Milken group regularly engaged in self-dealing to profit at their customers' expense. For example, civil suits filed by the FDIC allege that Milken and his confederates regularly shifted funds from one organization to another to illegally hide trading profits.

In several instances, Lincoln Savings and Loan Association was allowed by Drexel to purchase millions of shares of stock in companies as an inducement to buy their high-risk unsecured bonds. Such stock was later transferred by Lincoln to its unregulated parent company at bargain-basement prices that resulted in multimillion dollar profit for the parent. Meanwhile, the regulated subsidiary Lincoln continued to hold high-risk debt that later defaulted at a cost of billions of dollars to the taxpayer.

In reviewing the history of these Wall Street shenanigans, one is tempted to ask, "What the heck is going on here?" Such base, immoral, and unscrupulous behavior clearly cannot be regarded as ethical or consistent with the long-run interests of stockholders. However, while the behavior typified by the Milken scandal is most regrettable and unfortunate, it is important to recognize that such scandals occur only infrequently. Every business day on Wall Street, thousands of transactions, some involving billions of dollars in cash and securities, are made on the basis of a simple phone conversation. One's word is one's bond. If honesty and trust didn't pervade Wall Street, the ability of the securities business to operate would be more than hampered; it would founder. Notice that the Levine/Boesky relationship came to light within only eighteen months of inception. Keeping such a lucrative and intricate scheme hidden was apparently impossible in light of typical industry practice and regulation.

Perhaps the best way of gaining perspective on the conduct of notorious unethical "losers" is to consider the experience of one of Wall Street's most famous "winners"—Omaha's multibillionaire Warren E. Buffett, chairman of Berkshire Hathaway, Inc. Buffet says, "After some early mistakes, I learned to go into business only with people whom I like, trust, and admire." While a company won't necessarily prosper because its managers display admirable qualities, Buffett relates that he has never succeeded in making a good deal with a bad person.

Source: James W. Michaels and Phyllis Berman, "My Story—Michael Milken," *Forbes,* March 16, 1992, 78–100; R. Hutchings Vernon, "The Warren and Charlie Show," *Barron's,* May 11, 1992, 14, 19.

growth have also been widely distributed. Suppliers of capital, labor, and other resources all receive substantial returns for their contributions. Consumers benefit from an increasing quantity and quality of goods and services available for consumption. Taxes on the business profits of firms, as well as on the payments made to suppliers of labor, materials, capital, and other inputs, provide revenues needed to increase government services. All of these contributions to social welfare stem directly from the efficiency of business in serving the economic needs of customers.

The Social Responsibility of Business

Firms exist by public consent to serve the needs of society. Only by executing this mandate will businesses survive and prosper. As the needs and social requirements placed on the economic system change, business must adapt and respond to this changing environment.

If social welfare could be measured, business firms might be expected to operate in a manner that would maximize some index of social well-being. Maximization of social welfare requires answering such important questions as the following: What combination of goods and services (including negative by-products, such as pollution) should be produced? How should goods and services be provided? And how should goods and services be distributed? These are some of the most vital questions faced in a free enterprise system, and they are important issues in managerial economics.

In a free market economy, the economic system produces and allocates goods and services according to the forces of demand and supply. Firms must determine what products customers want, bid for necessary resources, and then offer their products for sale. In this process, each firm actively competes for a share of the customer's dollar. Suppliers of capital, labor, and raw materials must then be compensated out of sales proceeds. The share of revenues paid to each supplier depends on relative productivity, resource scarcity, and the degree of competition in each input market.

Although this process of market-determined production and allocation of goods and services is for the most part highly efficient, there are potential difficulties in a totally unconstrained market economy that can prevent the maximization of social welfare. Society has developed a variety of methods for alleviating these problems through the political system. One possible difficulty with an unconstrained market economy is that certain groups could gain excessive economic power, permitting them to obtain too large a share of the value created by firms. To illustrate, the economics of producing and distributing electric power are such that only one firm can efficiently serve a given community. Furthermore, there are no good substitutes for electric lighting. As a result, electric companies are in a position to exploit consumers; they could charge high prices and earn excessive profits. Society's solution to this potential exploitation is direct regulation. Prices charged by electric companies and other utilities are controlled and held to a level that is thought to be just sufficient to provide stockholders with a fair rate of return on their investment. In theory, the regulatory process is simple; in practice, it is costly, difficult to implement, and in many ways arbitrary. It is a poor but sometimes necessary substitute for competition.

An additional problem can occur in a market economy when, because of economies of scale or other barriers to entry, a limited number of firms serve a given market. If firms compete fairly with one another, no difficulty arises. If they conspire with one another in setting prices, they may be able to restrict output, obtain excessive profits, and reduce social welfare. Antitrust laws are designed to prevent such collusion as well as the merging of competing firms when the effect of the merger would be to lessen competition substantially. Like direct regulation, antitrust laws contain arbitrary elements and are costly to administer, but they too are necessary if economic justice, as defined by society, is to be served.

A further problem relates to workers being exploited under certain conditions. Because of the potential for exploitation, laws have been developed to equalize the bargaining power of employers and workers. These labor laws require firms to allow collective bargaining and to refrain from unfair practices. The question of whether labor's bargaining position is too strong in some instances also has been raised. For example, can powerful national unions such as the Teamsters use the threat of a strike to obtain excessive increases in wages, which may in turn be passed on to consumers in the form of higher prices? Those who believe this to be the case have suggested that the antitrust laws should be applied to labor unions, especially those that bargain with numerous small employers.

A market economy also faces difficulty when firms can impose external costs on society through their production activities. For example, firms can impose costs on others when they dump wastes into the air or water or when they deface the earth, as in strip mining. If a factory pollutes the air, causing nearby residents to suffer lung ailments or other health impairments, a meaningful cost is imposed on these people and society in general. Failure to shift these costs back onto the firm—and, ultimately, to the consumers of its products—means that the firm and its customers benefit unfairly by not having to pay the full costs of its activities. Therefore, the presence of pollution and other externalities may result in an inefficient and inequitable allocation of resources. In both government and business, considerable attention is being directed to the problem of internalizing social costs. Some of the practices used to internalize social costs include setting health and safety standards for products and work conditions, establishing emissions limits on manufacturing processes and on products that pollute, and imposing fines or closing firms that do not meet established standards.

All of these measures—utility regulation, antitrust laws, labor laws, and the direct regulation of products and operations—are examples of actions taken by society to modify the behavior of business firms and to make this behavior more consistent with broad social goals. These constraints have an important bearing on the firm's operations and, hence, on managerial decision making.

What does all this mean with respect to the value maximization model of the firm? Is the model adequate for examining issues of social responsibility and for developing rules for business decisions that reflect the role of business in society? Business firms are primarily economic entities and, as such, can be expected to analyze social responsibility from within the context of the economic model of the firm. This is an important consideration when examining the set of inducements used to channel the efforts of business in directions that society desires.

The World Is Turning to Capitalism and Democracy

Capitalism is based on voluntary exchange between self-interested parties. Given that the exchange is voluntary, both parties must perceive benefits, or profit, for market transactions to take place. If only one party were to benefit from a given transaction, there would be no incentive for the other party to cooperate and no voluntary exchange would take place. A self-interested capitalist must also have in mind the interest of others. In contrast, a truly selfish individual is only concerned with himself or herself, without regard for the well-being of others. As such, selfish behavior is inconsistent with the capitalistic system. Self-interested behavior leads to profits and success under capitalism; selfish behavior does not.

Like any economic system, capitalism has far-reaching political and social consequences. Similarly, democracy has far-reaching economic consequences. What is sometimes not understood is that capitalism and democracy are mutually reinforcing. Some philosophers have gone so far as to say that capitalism and democracy are intertwined. Without capitalism, democracy is impossible. Without democracy, capitalistic systems fail. To better understand the relation between capitalism and democracy, it becomes necessary to consider the fundamentally attractive characteristics of a decentralized exchange economy.

Capitalism is socially desirable because of its decentralized and customer-oriented nature. The menu of products to be produced is derived from market price and output signals originating in free and competitive markets, not from the output schedules of a centralized planning agency. As such, production is freely directed by self-interested producers seeking to meet the demands of individual customers. Resources and products are impartially allocated through market forces. They are not allocated on the basis of favoritism due to social status or political persuasion. Through their purchase decisions, customers are able to influence the quantity and quality of products brought to market. Any producer that is able to meet these demands is allowed to compete.

A freely competitive market gives customers a broad choice of goods and services and gives all producers the opportunity to succeed. As such, capitalism reinforces the individual freedoms protected in a democratic society. In democracy, government does not grant individual freedom. Instead, the political power of government emanates from the people. Similarly, the flow of economic resources originates with the individual customer in a capitalistic system. It is not centrally directed by government.

Competition among producers is also a fundamentally attractive feature of the capitalistic system because it tends to keep costs and prices as low as possible. By operating efficiently, firms are able to produce the maximum quantity and quality of goods and services possible, given scarce productive resources. Even though efficiency in resource allocation is an often recognized virtue of capitalism, the egalitarian nature of capitalistic production methods is sometimes overlooked. Mass production is, by definition, production for the masses. By its nature, capitalism seeks to satisfy a broad rather than a narrow constituency. Competition by entrant and nonleading firms typically limits the concentration of economic and political power. When economic forces tend to reduce rather than increase the number of viable competitors, antitrust or regulation policy is sometimes used to avoid potentially harmful consequences. On balance, and especially when compared to centrally planned economies, competitive processes in a capitalistic system tend to further the principles of individual freedom and self-determination. From this perspective, capitalism and democracy are mutually reinforcing. Strong market forces tend to undermine the economic favoritism that occurs under totalitarian systems of government. Similarly, the democratic form of government is inconsistent with concentrated economic influence and decision making.

In the 1990s, communism and totalitarian forms of government are in retreat around the globe. China has experienced violent upheaval as the country embarks on much-needed economic and political reforms. In the Soviet Union, Eastern Europe, and Latin America, years of economic failure have forced governments to dismantle entrenched bureaucracy and install economic incentives. Rising living standards and political freedom have made life in the West the envy of the world. Against this backdrop, the future is bright indeed for capitalism *and* democracy!

Source: Steven Baker and Elizabeth Weiner, "Latin America: The Big Move to Free Markets," *Business Week,* June 15, 1992, 51–55.

Similar considerations should also be taken into account before applying political pressure or regulations to constrain firm operations. For example, from the consumer's standpoint it is desirable to pay low rates for gas, electric, and telephone services. If public pressures drive rates down too low, however, utility profits could fall below the level necessary to provide an adequate return to investors. In that event, capital would not flow into the regulated industries, innovation would cease, and service would deteriorate. When such issues are considered, the economic model of the firm provides useful insight. This model emphasizes the close relation between the firm and society, and it indicates the importance of active business participation in the development and achievement of social objectives.

STRUCTURE OF THIS TEXT

Objectives

This text should help you accomplish the following objectives:

- Develop a clear understanding of economic theory and methods as they relate to managerial decision making;
- Acquire a framework for understanding the nature of the firm as an integrated whole as opposed to a loosely connected set of functional departments;
- Recognize the relation between the firm and society and the key role of business as a tool for social betterment.

Throughout the text, the emphasis is on the *practical* application of economic analysis to managerial decision problems.

Development of Topics

The value maximization framework offers a useful perspective for characterizing actual managerial decisions and a means for developing rules that can be used to improve those decisions. The basic test of the value maximization model—indeed, of any model—is its ability to explain behavior in the real world of managerial decision making. As basic elements of managerial economics are introduced, it is important to recognize how they relate to real-world practice. This text highlights the complementary relation between theory and practice—theory is used to improve managerial decision making, and practical experience leads to the development of better theory.

Chapter 2 begins by examining basic economic relations. The important role that marginal analysis plays in the optimization process is also introduced. The balancing of marginal revenues and marginal costs to determine the profit-maximizing output level is explored, as are other fundamental economic relations that help organizations efficiently employ scarce resources. All of these economic relations are considered based on the simplifying assumption that cost and revenue relations are known with certainty. In Chapter 3 this assumption is relaxed, and the more realistic circumstance of decision making under conditions of uncertainty is examined. This material shows how optimization concepts can be effectively employed in situations when managers have extensive information about the chance or probability of certain outcomes, but the end result of managerial decisions cannot be forecast precisely.

The concepts of demand and supply are basic to understanding the effective use of economic resources. The general overview of demand and supply in Chapter 4 provides a framework for the more detailed inquiry that follows. In Chapter 5, attention is turned to a detailed consideration of demand relations. The successful management of any organization requires a thorough understanding of the demand for its products. The demand function relates the sales of a product to such important factors as the price of the product itself, prices of other goods, income, advertising, and even weather. The role of demand elasticities, which measure the strength of the relations expressed in the demand function, is also emphasized. Issues addressed in the prediction of demand and cost conditions are explored in Chapters 6 and 7, where demand estimation and the methodology of economic forecasting are considered. Given the sheer size and complexity of modern corporations, a careful statistical analysis of economic relations is often conducted to provide the information necessary for effective decision making. The material provided in these chapters provides a useful framework for the ongoing estimation of important economic relations.

Chapters 8, 9, and 10 examine production and cost concepts. The economics of resource employment in the manufacture and distribution of goods and services is the focus of this material. These chapters present economic analysis as a context for understanding the underlying logic of managerial decisions and as a means for developing improved operating and planning practices. Production analysis and estimation develops and illustrates rules for optimal resource combination and employment levels. This material demonstrates how resources can be combined in a profit-maximizing manner. Cost analysis and estimation focuses on the identification of cost–output relations so that appropriate decisions regarding product pricing, plant size and location, and so on can be made. Chapter 11 introduces linear programming, a tool from the decision sciences that can be applied to many important optimization problems. This technique offers managers highly useful input for short-run operating decisions, as well as information helpful in the long-run planning process.

The remainder of the book builds on the foundation provided in Chapters 1 through 11 to examine a variety of topics in the theory and practice of managerial economics. Chapters 12 and 13 explore market structures and their implications for the development and implementation of effective competitive strategy. The analyses of demand and supply relations are integrated to examine the dynamics of economic markets. Chapter 12 studies perfect competition and monopoly to gain a perspective on how product differentiation, barriers to entry, and the availability of information interact to determine the vigor of competition. Chapter 13 considers "competition among the few" for industries in which monopolistic competition and oligopoly prevail. Chapter 14 analyzes pricing practices commonly observed in business to show how they reflect the predictions of economic theory. Chapter 15 focuses on the role of government in the market economy by considering how the external economic environment affects the managerial decision-making process. The chapter investigates how interactions among business, government, and the public result in antitrust and regulatory policies with direct implications for the efficiency and fairness of the economic system. Chapter 16 examines the final elements necessary for an effective planning framework for managerial decision making. It investigates the capital budgeting process and how firms combine demand, production, cost, and risk analyses to effectively make strategic long-run investment decisions.

SUMMARY

Managerial economics links traditional economics with the decision sciences to develop important tools for managerial decision making. This approach is successful because it focuses on the application of the tools and techniques of economic analysis to practical business problem solving.

- **Managerial economics** applies economic theory and methods to business and administrative decision making.
- The basic model of the business enterprise is called the **theory of the firm.** The primary goal is seen as long-term **expected value maximization.** The **value of the firm** is the present value of the firm's expected future net cash flows, where **present value** is the value of expected cash flows discounted back to the present at an appropriate interest rate.
- Valid questions are sometimes raised about whether managers really **optimize** (seek the best solution) or merely **satisfice** (seek satisfactory rather than optimal results). Most often, especially when information costs are considered, managers can be seen as optimizing.
- **Business profit,** or accounting profit, is the residual of sales revenue minus the explicit accounting costs of doing business. Business profit often incorporates a **normal rate of return** on capital, or the minimum return necessary to attract and retain investment for a particular use. **Economic profit** is business profit minus the implicit costs of equity and other owner-provided inputs used by the firm.
- One explanation of economic profits or losses is **frictional profit theory,** in which abnormal profits are observed following unanticipated changes in product demand or cost conditions. **Monopoly profit theory** asserts that above-normal profits are sometimes caused by barriers to entry that limit competition. **Innovation profit theory** describes above-normal profits that arise as a result of successful invention or modernization. **Compensatory profit theory** holds that above-normal rates of return can sometimes be seen as a reward to firms that are extraordinarily successful in meeting customer needs, maintaining efficient operations, and so forth.

The use of economic theory and methods to analyze and improve the managerial decision-making process combines the study of theory and practice to gain a useful and practical perspective. Although the logic and consistency of managerial economics are intuitively appealing, the primary virtue of managerial economics lies in its usefulness. It works!

Questions

Q1.1 Why is it appropriate to view firms primarily as economic entities?
Q1.2 Explain how the valuation model given in Equation 1.2 could be used to

describe the integrated nature of managerial decision making across the functional areas of business.

Q1.3   Describe the effects of each of the following managerial decisions or economic influences on the value of the firm:

A. The firm is required to install new equipment to reduce air pollution.

B. The firm's marketing department, through heavy expenditures on advertising, increases sales substantially.

C. The production department purchases new equipment that lowers manufacturing costs.

D. The firm raises prices. Quantity demanded in the short run is unaffected, but in the longer run, unit sales are expected to decline.

E. The Federal Reserve System takes actions that lower interest rates dramatically.

F. An expected increase in inflation causes generally higher interest rates, and, hence, the discount rate increases.

Q1.4   It is sometimes argued that managers of large, publicly owned firms make decisions to maximize their own welfare as opposed to that of stockholders. Would such behavior create problems in using value maximization as a basis for examining managerial decision making?

Q1.5   How is the popular notion of business profit different from the economic profit concept described in the chapter? What role does the idea of normal profits play in this difference?

Q1.6   Which concept—the business profit concept or the economic profit concept—provides the more appropriate basis for evaluating the operations of a business? Why?

Q1.7   What factors should be considered in examining the adequacy of profits for a firm or industry?

Q1.8   Why is the concept of self-interest important in economics?

Q1.9   "In the long run, no profit-maximizing firm would ever knowingly market unsafe products. However, in the short run, unsafe products can do a lot of damage." Discuss this statement.

Q1.10   Is it reasonable to expect firms to take actions that are in the public interest but are detrimental to stockholders? Is regulation always necessary and appropriate to induce firms to act in the public interest?

CASE STUDY FOR CHAPTER 1

Boards of Directors Are Revolting

A deep slump in auto sales drove worldwide losses for General Motors, Inc., to a whopping $4.5 billion during 1991. In fact, overseas and non-auto operations trimmed the overall loss; North American auto operations lost a stunning $7.1 billion. Despite an avalanche of new cars and trucks, GM's U.S. market share plummeted from more than 40 percent in 1984 to roughly 35 percent in 1991, and a dangerous hemorrhaging of red ink had erupted with no quick relief in sight. After standing idly by while GM deteriorated badly throughout the 1980s, GM's board of directors had finally seen enough and sprang into motion.

In unprecedented action, the GM board removed Robert C. Stempel from his post as head of the board's influential executive committee during April 1992. The executive committee is the key policy and strategy setting arm of GM's board, and the base from which all key operating and planning decisions emanate. At the same time, the board demoted Stempel's hand-picked president of GM, Lloyd E. Reuss. To replace Reuss as president of GM, the board promoted John F. Smith, Jr., the former chief of GM's international operations. Although the board announced that it would not involve itself in the day-to-day details of running GM, it is clear that Stempel and the entire top management of the company were put on probation. If the earlier plant closing announcements of GM were intended to shake up the troops, these GM board's actions had the undeniable effect of shaking up the generals.

Spearheading the GM board's moves to shake up the company was John D. Smale, the now retired chairman of the Procter & Gamble Company. A 10-year veteran of GM's board, Smale had watched GM's long-term decline without taking action. But by Thanksgiving 1991, Smale had begun talking to GM executives about the company's strategy and management. Other directors set up sessions with outsiders, including Wall Street analysts, looking for some independent input concerning possible solutions to GM's chronic woes. Regular meetings between GM directors began to take place, conspicuously absent from these gatherings was GM's top management, including inside directors.

As the weeks passed, board members became increasingly concerned about GM Chairman Stempel's lack of dramatic action to halt the losses. A career GM veteran, Stempel is a consensus builder with little apparent appetite for radical moves. At the urging of GM's board, Stempel announced a restructuring plan in December 1991 that involved closing 21 plants and eliminating 74,000 jobs. In a second restructuring announcement during February 1992, Stempel sketched out plans to cut duplication and overhead by reorganizing GM's three car and truck divisions into a single North American automotive group by 1996. Although the board supported Stempel in these moves, it balked at the slow pace with which changes were to be implemented. Instead, they installed Smith as president and chief operating officer (COO) with a clear directive to cut costs, especially white-collar overhead. Moreover, the board set a quick timetable for such cost-cutting moves. Clearly, the board wanted immediate action.

Among the factors that led the board to demote Stempel was his unyielding support for Reuss. As chief of the North American unit since 1986, Reuss was directly responsible for the division's enormous losses. Indeed, Stempel's relationship with Reuss may have been the most conspicuous symptom of the executive politics that had come to cripple GM. Without sufficient regard for merit, managers at GM have often gotten ahead as their buddies got ahead. As far back as 1990, when Stempel was named chairman, the board had suggested someone other than Reuss as COO. Yet Stempel insisted on his long-time colleague, and while the board went along with Stempel's wishes, it refused to give Reuss the COO title. With Reuss's operation foundering, GM's sales kept falling short of Reuss's rosy forecasts, and directors began clamoring for his ouster. By Sunday,

April 5, when the board met in Dallas for dinner, outside directors decided that they had seen enough. The next day, in an all-day board session, they forced Stempel's hand. Perhaps ironically, the board revolt took place at the headquarters of GM's Electronic Data Systems unit, the onetime home of outspoken GM critic Ross Perot.

As COO, Smith must build upon the successful turnaround of GM's now highly profitable European unit and move quickly to fix GM's North American car operation. A financial expert, Smith is credited with forcing costs down in Europe and boosting output without adding expensive new plants through innovative labor agreements. Smith has a reputation as being low key but demanding. To fix GM, Smith must slash GM's white-collar staff; the company is thought to have as much as 30 percent to 50 percent too many white-collar workers. While trimming the number of plants, Smith must also boost efficiency by converting manufacturing processes toward a common standard so that one plant can build a variety of car models.

The ultimate success of the board revolt at GM won't be known until the mid-1990s, at the earliest. Yet GM has several hidden strengths that make ultimate triumph likely. GM still has a market-leading position in the United States, significant customer loyalty, and an enviable dealer network. At the low end of GM's product line, Saturn sedans and coupes are proving highly popular with customers and are greatly exceeding initial sales objectives. This is despite limited distribution due to continuing production problems at Saturn's plant. At the high end of GM's product line, solvable production problems at the plant that builds the hot Cadillac Seville and Eldorado have held back deliveries of cars that bring GM profits of more than $10,000 per unit. Once these production problems are resolved, production and profits should begin rolling in. Also helping GM's outlook is the fact that the buoyant stock market of mid-1992 allowed the company to issue additional equity on favorable terms for the first time in over 30 years. These funds will come in handy during the 1990s as GM reinvests in plant, equipment, and new product development.

Although the board revolt at GM shook company management to the core, its effects are not likely to stop there. All across the country, board members and stockholders are asking: Will GM's boardroom rebellion prove contagious? Early evidence at a number of blue-chip companies suggests that it might indeed. At a minimum, top management has been put on notice that outside directors will not sit idly by while corporate performance continues to deteriorate. Captive boards have also been put on notice that stockholders won't tolerate mediocre performance indefinitely.

At IBM, for example, the company's failure to stay ahead of smaller and leaner competitors has brought about a downward spiral in operating performance for what was once a premiere growth company. When the company finally began to realize the potential of powerful personal computers and workstations, its slow-moving bureaucracy failed to respond. Since 1985, IBM has shed more than 60,000 employees, closed plants, and restructured its entire U.S. operations into quasi-independent units, each focusing on a particular market. Investors are clearly disappointed with IBM's negative total return during the late 1980s and early 1990s, and company chairman John F. Akers is on a hot seat. Top management at Digital Equipment Corp. is under similar pressure to perform. Digital's market value dropped by $19 billion between 1989 and 1992, executives bailed out in increasing numbers, and the company suffered its first-ever operating loss in the quarter ending in December 1991. Analysts argue that Eastman Kodak, American Express, and Sears could all benefit from a GM-style boardroom coup. Each of these companies has highly paid top executives presiding over deteriorating corporate performance, an endless series of shakeups and restructuring, and plummeting stock-price performance. One of the most interesting developments to watch during the 1990s is sure to be the manner in which management problems at these and other large companies are corrected.

A. Does the documented ineptness of GM's top management during the 1980s invalidate the value-maximization theory of the firm?

B. Dissatisfied with Chairman and CEO Edward A. Brennan's failure to budge Sears' return on equity past 10 percent, shareholders offered a proxy resolution in 1992 that would split the chairman and CEO posts and install an outsider as chairman. From the shareholder viewpoint, discuss some of the advantages and disadvantages of an "outside" chairman.

C. Shareholders want change where corporate performance is poor, top executive pay excessive, or management unresponsive, even to the point of replacing both insiders and independent directors. However, removing corporate directors by shareholder vote is almost impossible. In annual proxy contests, shareholders are generally offered only one slate of candidates, and they can vote no only by withholding votes from would-be board members. Does this mean that the current shareholder voting process is a wholly ineffectual means of corporate control? How might this process be improved?

D. In addition to casting their vote in annual proxy contests, shareholders "vote with their feet" when they sell the stocks of poorly performing companies. How is this likely to influence inferior performance by top management and the board of directors?

Selected References

Agrawal, Anup, and Gershon N. Mandelker. "Shark Repellents and the Role of Institutional Investors in Corporate Governance." *Managerial and Decision Economics* 13 (January–February 1992): 15–22.

Anderson, Kye. "The Purpose at the Heart of Management." *Harvard Business Review* 70 (May–June 1992): 52–62.

Baucus, Melissa S., and Janet P. Near. "Can Illegal Corporate Behavior Be Predicted? An Event History Analysis." *Academy of Management Journal* 34 (March 1991): 9–36.

De, Sankar. "Diversification Patterns and Long-Term Corporate Performance." *Managerial and Decision Economics* 13 (January–February 1992): 1–13.

Dechow, Patricia M., and Richard G. Sloan. "Executive Incentives and the Horizon Problem: An Empirical Investigation." *Journal of Accounting and Economics* 14 (March 1991): 51–89.

Foulkes, Fred K., ed. *Executive Compensation: A Strategic Guide for the 1990s.* (Boston: Harvard Business School Press, 1991).

Gaver, Jennifer J., Kenneth M. Gaver, and George Battistel. "The Stock Market Reaction to Performance Plan Adoptions." *Accounting Review* 67 (January 1992): 172–182.

Hirschhorn, Larry, and Thomas Gilmore. "The New Boundaries of the 'Boundaryless' Company." *Harvard Business Review* 70 (May–June 1992): 104–115.

Lee, Chu I., Stuart Rosenstein, Nanda Rangan, and Wallace N. Davidson, III. "Board Composition and Shareholder Wealth." *Financial Management* 21 (Spring 1992): 58–72.

Lewellen, Wilbur, Claudio Loderer, Kenneth Martin, and Gerald Blum. "Executive Compensation and the Performance of the Firm." *Managerial and Decision Economics* 13 (January–February 1992): 65–74.

McDowell, Banks. *Ethical Conduct and the Professional's Dilemma: Choosing Between Service and Success.* (New York: Quorum Books, 1991).

Main, Brian G.M. "Top Executive Pay and Performance." *Managerial and Decision Economics* 12 (June 1991): 219–229.

Martin, Kenneth J., and John J. McConnell. "Corporate Performance, Corporate Takeovers, and Management Turnover." *Journal of Finance* 46 (June 1991): 671–688.

Michel, John G., and Donald C. Hambrick. "Diversification Posture and Top Management Team Characteristics." *Academy of Management Journal* 35 (March 1992): 9–37.

Pound, John. "Beyond Takeovers: Politics Comes to Corporate Control." *Harvard Business Review* 70 (March–April 1992): 83–93.

Rosenstein, Stuart, and Jeffrey G. Wyatt. "Outside Directors, Board Independence, and Shareholder Wealth." *Journal of Financial Economics* 26 (August 1990): 175–191.

Taffler, Richard J., and Peter Holl. "Abandoned Mergers and the Market for Corporate Control." *Managerial and Decision Economics* 12 (August 1991): 271–280.

Tiedman, T. Nicolaus. "Being Just While Conceptions of Justice are Changing." *American Economic Review* 82 (May 1992): 280–284.

Trevino, Linda Klebe, and Bart Victor. "Peer Reporting of Unethical Behavior: A Social Context Perspective." *Academy of Management Journal* 35 (March 1992): 38–64.

Williamson, Oliver E., and Sidney G. Winter, eds. *The Nature of the Firm: Origins, Evolution, and Development.* (New York: Oxford University Press, 1991).

Zaleznik, Abraham. "Managers and Leaders: Are They Different?" *Harvard Business Review* 70 (March–April 1992): 126–135.

ECONOMIC OPTIMIZATION

Effective managerial decision making is the process of efficiently arriving at the best possible solution to a given problem. If only one solution is possible, then no decision problem exists. When alternative courses of action are available, the decision that produces a result most consistent with managerial objectives is the **optimal decision.** The process of arriving at the best managerial decision, or best problem resolution, is the focus of managerial economics.

Optimal decision

The choice alternative that produces a result most consistent with managerial objectives.

A major challenge that must be met in the decision-making process is characterizing the relative desirability of decision alternatives in terms of the objectives of the organization. Decision makers must recognize all available choices and portray them in terms of appropriate decision variables, costs, and benefits. The description of decision alternatives is greatly enhanced through application of the principles of managerial economics. Managerial economics also provides tools for analyzing and evaluating decision alternatives. Economic concepts and methodology are used to select the optimal course of action in light of available options and objectives.

This chapter introduces fundamental principles of economic analysis, which are essential to all aspects of managerial economics and form the basis for describing demand, cost, and profit relations. Once basic economic relations are understood, the tools and techniques of optimization can be applied to find the best course of action. Most important, the theory and process of optimization is a worthwhile basis for study given its potential to provide practical insight concerning the value maximization theory of the firm. Understanding optimization techniques is helpful because such techniques offer a realistic means for dealing with the complexities of goal-oriented managerial activities.

MAXIMIZING THE VALUE OF THE FIRM

In managerial economics, the primary objective of management is assumed to be maximization of the value of the firm. This *value maximization* objective was introduced in Chapter 1 and is again expressed in Equation 2.1:

$$\text{Value} = \sum_{t=1}^{N} \frac{\text{Profit}_t}{(1 + i)^t} = \sum_{t=1}^{N} \frac{\text{Total Revenue}_t - \text{Total Cost}_t}{(1 + i)^t}. \qquad \textbf{(2.1)}$$

Maximizing Equation 2.1 is a complex task that involves detailed consideration of future revenues, costs, and discount rates. Total revenues are directly determined by the quantity sold and the prices received. Factors that affect prices and the quantity sold include the choice of products made available for sale, marketing strategies, pricing and distribution policies, nature of competition, and the general state of the economy. Similarly, complex cost relations are also encountered in the production process. Cost analysis requires a detailed examination of the prices and availability of various input factors, alternative production schedules, production methods, and so on. Finally, the relation between an appropriate discount rate and the company's mix of products and both operating and financial leverage must be determined. All of these factors affect the value of the firm as described in Equation 2.1 and must be considered by management.

To determine the optimal course of action, marketing, production, and financial decisions must all be integrated within a decision analysis framework. Similarly, decisions related to personnel retention and development, organization structure, and long-term business strategy must be combined into a single integrated system that shows how any managerial initiative affects all parts of the firm. The value maximization model of the firm provides an attractive basis for such integration. Using the principles of economic analysis, it is also possible to analyze and compare the higher costs or lower benefits of alternative, suboptimal courses of action.

The complexity of completely integrated decision analysis—or global optimization—often confines its use to major planning decisions. For many day-to-day operating decisions, managers typically employ less complicated, partial optimization techniques. Partial optimization abstracts from the complexity of a completely integrated decision process by concentrating on more limited objectives within the firm's various operating departments. For example, the marketing department is usually required to determine the price and advertising strategy that achieves some sales goal given the firm's current product line and marketing budget. Alternatively, a production department might minimize the cost of a specified quantity of output at a stated quality level. In both instances, the fundamentals of economic analysis provide the basis for optimal managerial decisions.

The decision process, regardless of whether it is applied to fully integrated or partial optimization problems, involves two steps. First, important economic relations must be expressed in a form suitable for analysis; that is, the managerial decision problem must be expressed in analytical terms. Second, various optimization techniques must be applied to determine the best, or optimal, solution in light of managerial objectives. In the material that follows, a number of concepts useful for expressing decision problems in an economic framework are introduced. Several economic relations are then employed to determine the firm's optimal price, and output combinations are investigated.

BASIC ECONOMIC RELATIONS

Table
A list of economic data.

Spreadsheet
A table of electronically stored data.

Tables are the simplest and most direct form for listing economic data. When these data are displayed electronically in the format of an accounting income statement or balance sheet, the tables are referred to as **spreadsheets.** When the underlying relation between economic data is very simple, tables and spread-

Graph
Visual representation of data.

Equation
An analytical expression of functional relationships.

sheets may be sufficient for analytical purposes. In such instances, a simple **graph** or visual representation of the data can provide valuable insight. However, in many instances the complex nature of economic relations requires that more sophisticated methods of expression be employed. An **equation** is an analytical expression of functional relationships that offers a very useful means for characterizing the connection among economic variables. Equations are frequently used to express both simple and complex economic relations. When the underlying relation among economic variables is uncomplicated, equations offer a useful, compact means for data description; when underlying relations are complex, equations are helpful because they permit the powerful tools of mathematical and statistical analysis to be employed.

Functional Relations: Equations

The easiest way to examine basic economic relations to gain insight into the economics of optimization is to consider the functional relations incorporated in the basic valuation model. Consider first the relation between output, Q, and total revenue, TR. Using functional notation, a general total revenue relation is stated as

$$TR = f(Q) .\tag{2.2}$$

Equation 2.2 is read, "Total revenue is a function of output." The value of the dependent variable—total revenue—is determined by the independent variable—output. In an equation such as this, the variable to the left of the equal sign is called the **dependent variable.** Its value depends on the size of the variable or variables to the right of the equal sign. Variables on the right-hand side of the equal sign are called **independent variables.** Their values are determined outside or independently of the functional relation expressed by the equation.

Dependent variable
Y variable determined by X values.

Independent variable
X variable determined separately from the Y variable.

Equation 2.2 does not indicate the specific relation between output and total revenue; it merely states that some relation exists. Equation 2.3 provides a precise expression of this functional relation:

$$TR = P \times Q ,\tag{2.3}$$

where P represents the price at which each unit of Q is sold. Total revenue is equal to price times the quantity of output sold. If price is constant at $1.50 regardless of the quantity sold, the relation between quantity sold and total revenue is

$$TR = \$1.50 \times Q .\tag{2.4}$$

The data in Table 2.1 are specified by Equation 2.4 and graphically illustrated in Figure 2.1.

Total, Average, and Marginal Relations

Marginal relation
Change in the dependent variable caused by a one-unit change in an independent variable.

Total, average, and marginal relations are very useful in optimization analysis. Whereas the definitions of totals and averages are well known, the meaning of marginals needs further explanation. A **marginal relation** is the change in the dependent variable caused by a one-unit change in an independent variable.[1] For

---

[1] Appendix 2A provides a comprehensive review of mathematical techniques from basic algebra through differential calculus. Most students will find a review of basic algebra helpful. A basic understanding of calculus is also required to fully appreciate the material covered in the text, and many instructors make modest use of calculus in their courses.

TABLE 2.1   **Relation between Total Revenue and Output;
Total Revenue = $1.50 × Output**

Total Revenue	Output
$1.50	1
3.00	2
4.50	3
6.00	4
7.50	5
9.00	6

FIGURE 2.1   **Graph of the Relation between Total Revenue and Output**

When P = $1.50, a one-unit increase in the quantity sold will increase total revenue by $1.50.

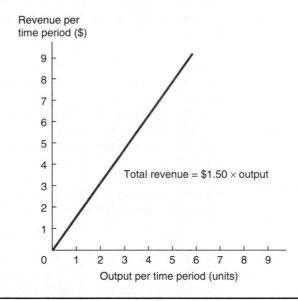

Marginal revenue

Change in total revenue associated with a one-unit change in output.

Marginal cost

Change in total cost following a one-unit change in output.

Marginal profit

Change in total profit due to a one-unit change in output.

example, **marginal revenue** is the change in total revenue associated with a one-unit change in output; **marginal cost** is the change in total cost following a one-unit change in output; and **marginal profit** is the change in total profit due to a one-unit change in output.

Table 2.2 shows the relation among totals, marginals, and averages for a simple profit function. Columns 1 and 2 display the relation between output and total profits. Column 3 shows the marginal profit earned for a one-unit change in output. Column 4 gives the average profit per unit at each level of output. The marginal profit earned on the first unit of output is $19. This is the change from $0 profits earned when zero units of output are sold to the $19 profit earned when one unit is produced and sold. The $33 marginal profit associated with the second unit of output is the increase in total profits (= $52 − $19) that results when

TABLE 2.2   Total, Marginal, and Average Relations for a Hypothetical Profit Function

Units of Output Q (1)	Total Profits π^a (2)	Marginal Profits $\Delta\pi^b$ (3)	Average Profits $\overline{\pi}^c$ (4)
0	$ 0	$ 0	—
1	19	19	$19
2	52	33	26
3	93	41	31
4	136	43	34
5	175	39	35
6	210	35	35
7	217	7	31
8	208	− 9	26

[a] The Greek letter π (pi) is frequently used in economics and business to denote profits.
[b] The symbol Δ (delta) denotes difference or change. Thus, marginal profit is expressed as $\Delta\pi = \pi_Q - \pi_{Q-1}$.
[c] Average profit ($\overline{\pi}$) equals total profit (π) divided by total output (Q): $\pi = \pi/Q$.

output is increased from one to two units. When the marginal is positive, the total is increasing; when the marginal is negative, the total is decreasing. The data in Table 2.2 illustrate this point. The marginal profit associated with each of the first seven units of output is positive, and total profits increase with output over this range. Since the marginal profit of the eighth unit is negative, profits are reduced if output is raised to that level. Maximization of the profit function—or any function, for that matter—occurs at the point where the marginal switches from positive to negative.

Since the marginal represents change in the total, it follows that when the marginal is greater than the average, the average must be increasing. For example, if a firm operates five retail stores with average annual sales of $350,000 per store and it opens a sixth store (the marginal store) that generates sales of $400,000, average sales per store will increase. If sales at the new (marginal) store are less than $350,000, average sales per store will decrease. Table 2.2 also illustrates the relation between marginal and average values. In going from four units of output to five, the marginal profit of $39 is greater than the $34 average profit at four units; therefore, average profit increases to $35. The $35 marginal profit of the sixth unit is the same as the average profit for the first five units, so average profit remains identical between five and six units. Finally, the marginal profit of the seventh unit is below the average profit at six units, causing average profit to fall.

Graphing Total, Marginal, and Average Relations

Knowledge of the geometric relations among totals, marginals, and averages can prove useful in managerial decision making. Figure 2.2a presents a graph of the profit-to-output relation given in Table 2.2. Each point on the curve represents a combination of output and total profit, as do Columns 1 and 2 of Table 2.2. The marginal and average profit figures from Table 2.2 have been plotted in Figure 2.2b.

FIGURE 2.2   **Geometric Representation of Total, Marginal, and Average Relations:
(a) Total Profits; (b) Marginal and Average Profits**

(a) Marginal profit is the slope of the total profit curve; it is maximized at Point *C*. More important, total profit is maximized at Point *E*, where marginal profit equals zero. (b) Average profit rises (falls) when marginal profit is greater (less) than average profit.

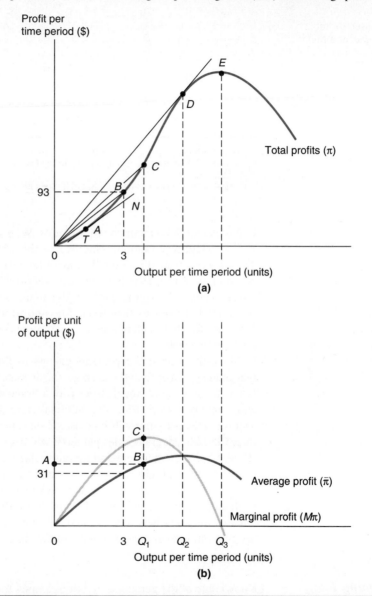

Just as there is an arithmetic relation among the totals, marginals, and averages in the table, so too is there a corresponding geometric relation. To see this, consider first the average profit per unit of output at any point along the total profits curve. Average profit is equal to total profit divided by the corresponding number of units of output. Geometrically, this relation is represented by the slope of a line from the origin to the point of interest on the total profits curve. **Slope** is a measure of the steepness of a line, and it is defined as the increase (or decrease) in height per unit of distance along the horizontal axis. The slope of a straight line passing through the origin is determined by dividing the Y coordinate at any point on the line by the corresponding X coordinate. Using Δ (read delta) to denote change, slope $= \Delta Y/\Delta X = (Y_2 - Y_1)/(X_2 - X_1)$. Since X_1 and Y_1 are zero for any line going through the origin, slope $= Y_2/X_2$; or, more generally, slope $= Y/X$. The slope of the line $0B$ can be calculated by dividing \$93 (the Y coordinate at point B) by 3 (the X coordinate at point B). This involves dividing total profits by the corresponding units of output. *At any point along a total curve, the corresponding average figure is given by the slope of a straight line from the origin to that point.* These average figures can also be graphed directly, as in Figure 2.2b. There, each point on the average profit curve is the corresponding total profit divided by the output quantity.

The marginal has a similar geometric association with the total curve. In Table 2.2 each marginal figure was shown to be the change in total profit associated with the last unit increase in output. This rise (or fall) in total profit associated with a one-unit increase in output is the *slope* of the total profit curve at that point.

Slopes of nonlinear curves are found by drawing a straight line tangent to the curve at the point of interest and determining the slope of the tangent. A **tangent** is a line that touches but does not intersect the curve. In Figure 2.2a, marginal profit at point A is equal to the slope of the total profit curve at that point, which is equal to the slope of the tangent labeled *TAN*. *At any point along a total curve, the corresponding marginal figure is given by the slope of a line drawn tangent to the total curve at that point.* Slope, or marginal, figures can also be graphed directly, as shown by the marginal profit curve in Figure 2.2b.

Several important relations among total, marginal, and average values become apparent when considering Figure 2.2a. Note that the slope of the total profit curve is increasing from the origin to point C. Lines drawn tangent to the total profit curve become steeper as the point of tangency approaches point C, so marginal profit is increasing up to this point. This is also illustrated in Figure 2.2b, where the marginal profit curve increases up to output Q_1, corresponding to point C on the total profit curve. At point C, called an *inflection point,* the slope of the total profit curve is maximized; marginal but not average or total profits are maximized at that output. Between points C and E, total profit continues to increase because marginal profit is still positive even though it is declining. At point E, the total profit curve has a slope of zero and thus is neither rising nor falling. Marginal profit at this point is zero, and total profit is maximized. Beyond E (output Q_3 in Figure 2.2b), the total profit curve has a negative slope, indicating that marginal profit is negative.

In addition to the total–average and total–marginal relations, Figure 2.2b shows the relation between marginals and averages. At low output levels, where

Slope
A measure of the steepness of a line.

Tangent
A straight line that touches a curve at only one point.

the marginal profit curve lies above the average, the average is rising. Although marginal profit reaches a maximum at output Q_1 and declines thereafter, the average curve continues to rise so long as the marginal lies above it. At output Q_2, marginal and average profits are equal, and the average profit curve reaches its maximum value. Beyond Q_2, the marginal curve lies below the average, and the average is falling.

Deriving Totals from Marginal and Average Curves

Just as marginal and average profit figures can be derived from the total profit curve in Figure 2.2a, total profits can be determined from the marginal or average profit curves of Figure 2.2b. Total profit is average profit times the corresponding number of units of output. The total profit associated with Q_1 units of output, for example, is average profit, *A,* times output, Q_1. Total profit is equal to the area of the rectangle $0ABQ_1$. This relation holds for all points along the average profit curve.

A similar relation exists between marginal and total profits. Recall that the total is equal to the sum of all the marginals up to the specified output level. The total profit for any output is equal to the sum of the marginal profits up to that output quantity. Geometrically, this is the area under the marginal curve from the Y axis to the output quantity under consideration. At output Q_1, total profit is equal to the area under the marginal profit curve, or the area $0CQ_1$.

Because average, marginal, and total relations underlie several basic principles of managerial economics, they should be thoroughly understood. The most widely known example of their use is in short-run profit maximization: Marginal cost and revenue curves are derived from average or total figures, and profits are maximized where marginal profit is zero. Since marginal profit equals marginal revenue minus marginal cost, profit is maximized where marginal revenue is equal to marginal cost. This is only one illustration of the use of these concepts; many others are encountered in the study of managerial economics.

It is worth considering the use of elementary calculus to find optimal solutions for economic problems. Calculus concepts help to clarify the relations among marginals, averages, and totals and the importance of these relations in the optimization process.

MARGINALS AS THE DERIVATIVES OF FUNCTIONS

Whereas tables and graphs are useful for explaining concepts, equations are frequently better suited for problem solving. One reason is that the powerful analytical technique of differential calculus can be employed to locate maximum or minimum values of an objective function. In addition, basic calculus concepts are easily extended to decision problems in which the options available to the decision maker are limited by one or more constraints. A calculus-based approach is especially useful for the constrained optimization problems that often characterize managerial decision making.

●

MANAGERIAL APPLICATION 2.1

The Relevance of Theory to Practice

Have you ever been a spectator at a golf, tennis, or racquetball tournament when a particular athlete's play became the center of attention? As people admired the performance, some questions inevitably arose. Have you ever heard people ask, "Where did that athlete study physics?" or "Who was her geometry instructor?" or "Wow, who taught that guy physiology?" Chances are you haven't. Instead, the discussion probably centered on the players' skill, finesse, or tenacity. Natural talent developed through long hours of dedicated training and intense competition is commonly regarded as the chief prerequisite for becoming an accomplished amateur or professional athlete. But if you think about it, an accomplished racquetball player must also know a great deal about angles, speed, and acceleration. Likewise, a successful tennis competitor must fully understand his or her physical limits as well as the competition's.

While success in these sports requires that one understand the basic principles of geometry, physics, and physiology, most athletes develop their "feel" for these subjects on the tennis court, golf course, baseball diamond, or gridiron. In fact, some successful athletes have had little or no formal textbook instruction in these subjects. Their understanding more often is based, for example, on the "applied physics" courses offered daily on the tennis court. What is critical is that these "students" have mastered their subject; how they came about this expertise is often much less important.

Similarly, some very successful businesses are run by people with little or no formal training in accounting, finance, management, or marketing. This is especially true of older executives who came up through the ranks before the post–World War II college education boom. These executives' successes testify to their ability to develop a feel for business in much the same way that the successful athlete develops a feel for his or her sport. Although the term optimization may be foreign to such individuals, the methodology of optimization is familiar to each of them in terms of their everyday business practice. Adjusting prices to avoid stockout situations, increasing product quality to "meet the competition," and raising salaries to retain valued employees all involve a basic, practical understanding of optimization concepts.

The behavior of both the successful athlete and the successful executive can be described, or modeled, as being consistent with the process of optimization. In the case of, say, the tennis player, the pursuit of on-the-court success can be described as being consistent with performance maximization, given his or her skill and other capabilities. In the case of the successful business executive, the day-to-day activities incorporated into ongoing business practice typically are quite consistent with long-term value maximization. The fact that some successful sport and business practitioners learn their "lessons" through hands-on experience rather than in the classroom doesn't diminish the value of the formal educational experience. In the classroom, one can discuss and analyze the basic lessons and themes that emerge in the business practice of successful managers and firms. When described in model form, such as in the value maximization model, the generality of these lessons and themes becomes apparent, thereby enhancing the classroom experience.

The usefulness of economic models and optimization analysis lies in the logical framework they provide for characterizing and *predicting* practical managerial experience. The old saw, "That may be O.K. in theory, but it doesn't work in practice," is plainly incorrect. Useful theory describes and predicts actual business decisions. If a given theory doesn't describe and predict actual practice, it should be rejected in favor of theory and models that actually describe and predict real-world behavior. The reason why economic theory and methodology form the basis for the study of managerial decision making is quite simple—it works. Managerial economics works not just in the classroom but more importantly it works in the everyday "lab" of business practice. There is no conflict between theory and practice. The study of theory is helpful because the task of successful business management is made easier through the careful combination of theory and practical business experience.

Source: Andrew Erdman, "Staying Ahead of 800 Competitors," *Fortune*, June 1, 1992, 111–112.

Concept of a
Derivative

A marginal value is the change in a dependent variable associated with a one-unit change in an independent variable. Consider the general function $Y = f(X)$. Using Δ to denote change, it is possible to express the change in the value of the independent variable, X, by the notation ΔX and the change in the dependent variable, Y, by ΔY.

The ratio $\Delta Y/\Delta X$ is a general specification of the marginal concept:

$$\text{Marginal } Y = \frac{\Delta Y}{\Delta X}. \tag{2.5}$$

The change in Y, ΔY, divided by the change in X, ΔX, indicates the change in the dependent variable associated with a one-unit change in the value of X.

Figure 2.3 is a graph of a function relating Y to X that illustrates this relation. For values of X close to the origin, a relatively small change in X provides a large change in Y. Thus, the value of $\Delta Y/\Delta X = (Y_2 - Y_1)/(X_2 - X_1)$ is relatively large, showing that a small increase in X induces a large increase in Y. The situation is reversed farther out along the X axis. A large increase in X, say from X_3 to X_4, produces only a small increase in Y, from Y_3 to Y_4, so $\Delta Y/\Delta X$ is small. The marginal relation between X and Y, as shown in Figure 2.3, changes at different points on the curve. When the curve is relatively steep, the dependent variable Y is highly responsive to changes in the independent variable, but when the curve is relatively flat, Y does not respond as notably to changes in X.

Derivative

A precise specification of the marginal relation.

A **derivative** is a precise specification of the marginal relation. Finding a derivative involves finding the value of the ratio $\Delta Y/\Delta X$ for extremely small changes in X. The mathematical notation for a derivative is

$$\frac{dY}{dX} = \lim_{\Delta X \to 0} \frac{\Delta Y}{\Delta X},$$

which is read: "The derivative of Y with respect to X equals the limit of the ratio $\Delta Y/\Delta X$, as ΔX approaches zero."[2] This concept of the derivative as the limit of a ratio is precisely equivalent to the slope of a curve at a point. Figure 2.4 presents this idea, using the same curve relating Y to X as shown in Figure 2.3. Notice that in Figure 2.4 the *average* slope of the curve between points A and D is measured as

$$\frac{\Delta Y}{\Delta X} = \frac{Y_4 - Y_1}{X_4 - X_1}$$

---

[2] A limit can be explained briefly. If the value of a function $Y = f(X)$ approaches a constant Y^* as the value of the independent variable X approaches X^*, then Y^* is called the limit of the function as X approaches X^*. This is written as follows:

$$\lim_{X \to X^*} f(X) + Y^*.$$

For example, if $Y = X - 4$, then the limit of this function as X approaches 5 is 1; that is,

$$\lim_{X \to 5} (X - 4) = 1.$$

This says that the value of X approaches but does not quite reach 5; the value of the function $Y = X - 4$ comes closer and closer to 1.

FIGURE 2.3 **Illustration of Changing $\Delta Y/\Delta X$ over the Range of a Curve**

The ratio $\Delta Y/\Delta X$ changes continuously along a curved line.

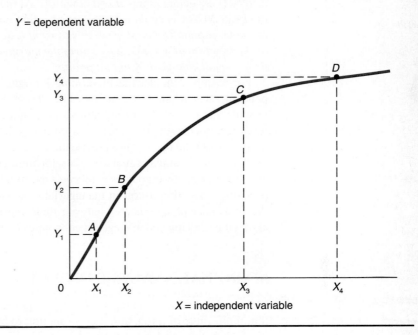

FIGURE 2.4 **Illustration of a Derivative as the Slope of a Curve**

The derivative of Y with respect to X identifies the slope of a curve.

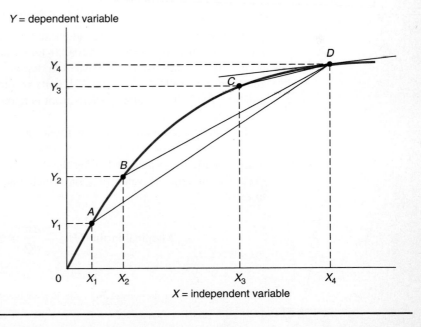

and is the slope of the chord connecting the two points. Similarly, the average slope of the curve can be measured over smaller and smaller intervals of *X,* such as those connecting points *B* and *C* with *D.* At the limit, as ΔX approaches zero, the ratio $\Delta Y/\Delta X$ is equal to the slope of a line drawn tangent to the curve—for example, at point *D. The slope of this tangent is defined as the derivative,* dY/dX, *of the function at point* D; *it measures the marginal change in* Y *associated with a very small change in* X *at that point.*

For example, the dependent variable *Y* might be total revenue, and the independent variable might be output. The derivative *dY/dX* shows precisely how revenue and output are related at a specific output level. Because the change in revenue associated with a change in output is defined as marginal revenue, the derivative of total revenue is a precise measure of marginal revenue at any specific output level. A similar situation exists for total cost: the derivative of the total cost function at any output level indicates marginal cost at that output. Derivatives provide information useful in managerial economics. Illustrations developed in the remainder of the chapter indicate their value for problem solving and for clarifying fundamental managerial economics concepts.

MARGINAL ANALYSIS IN DECISION MAKING

Managerial decision making frequently requires one to find the maximum or minimum value of a function. For a function to be at a maximum or minimum, its slope or marginal value must be zero. The *derivative* of a function is a very precise measure of its slope or marginal value at a particular point. Thus, maximization or minimization of a function occurs where its derivative is equal to zero. To illustrate, consider the following profit function:

$$\pi = -\$10{,}000 + \$400Q - \$2Q^2 . \tag{2.6}$$

Here, π is total profit and *Q* is output in units. As shown in Figure 2.5, if output is zero, the firm incurs a $10,000 loss (fixed costs are $10,000); but as output rises, profit also rises. Breakeven points are output levels where profit is zero and are reached at 29 and 171 units of output. Profit rises as output expands to 100 units of output, where profit is maximized at $10,000, and declines thereafter.

The profit-maximizing output is found by calculating the value of the function at a number of outputs, then plotting these as in Figure 2.5. The maximum can also be located by finding the derivative, or marginal, of the function, then determining the value of *Q* at which the derivative (marginal) is equal to zero.[3]

$$\text{Marginal Profit } (M\pi) = \frac{d\pi}{dQ} = \$400 - \$4Q .$$

---

[3] Basic rules for finding the derivative of a function are found in the appendix to this chapter.

FIGURE 2.5   **Profit as a Function of Output**

Total profit is maximized at 100 units, where marginal profit equals zero. Beyond that point, marginal profit is negative and total profit decreases.

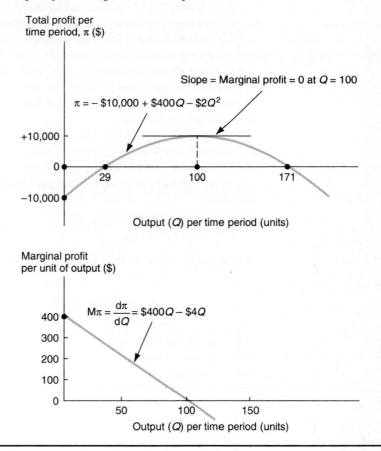

Setting the derivative equal to zero results in

$$\$400 - \$4Q = 0$$
$$\$4Q = \$400$$
$$Q = 100 \text{ units.}$$

Therefore, when $Q = 100$, marginal profit is zero and total profit is at a maximum. Beyond $Q = 100$, marginal profit is negative and total profit is decreasing. Even in this simple illustration, it is easier to locate the profit-maximizing value by using calculus than by using graphic analysis. Had the profit function been more complex, a calculus-based method might have been the only efficient means of determining the profit-maximizing output level.

*Distinguishing
Maximums from
Minimums*

Inflection point

A point of maximum
or minimum slope.

A problem can arise when derivatives are used to locate maximums or minimums. The first derivative of a total function indicates whether the function is rising or falling at any point. To be maximized or minimized, the function must be neither rising nor falling; slope as measured by the first derivative must be zero. Setting the first derivative equal to zero indicates **inflection points,** or points of maximum or minimum slope. Since the marginal value, or derivative, is zero for both maximum and minimum values of a function, further analysis is necessary to determine whether a maximum or a minimum has been located.

This point is illustrated in Figure 2.6, where the slope of the total profit curve is zero at both points *A* and *B*. Point *A* is a point of minimum profits; *B* is the profit-maximizing output.

The concept of a *second derivative* is used to distinguish maximums from minimums along a function. The second derivative is simply the derivative of the original derivative. If total profit is given by the equation $\pi = a - bQ + cQ^2 - dQ^3$, as in Figure 2.6, then the first derivative defines the marginal profit function as

$$\frac{d\pi}{dQ} = M\pi = -b + 2cQ - 3dQ^2 . \qquad (2.7)$$

The second derivative of the total profit function is the derivative of the marginal profit function, Equation 2.7:

$$\frac{d^2\pi}{dQ^2} = \frac{dM\pi}{dQ} = 2c - 6dQ .$$

Just as the first derivative measures the slope of the total profit function, the second derivative measures the slope of the first derivative or, in this case, the slope of the marginal profit curve. The second derivative is used to distinguish between points of maximization and minimization. The second derivative of a function is always *negative* when evaluated at a point of *maximization* and *positive* at a point of *minimization*.

The reason for this inverse relation can be seen in Figure 2.6. Note that profits reach a local minimum at point *A* because marginal profits that have been negative suddenly become positive. Marginal profits pass through the zero level from below at point *A*. The reverse holds at a point of local maximization; the marginal value is positive but declining up to the point where the total function is maximized, and it is negative thereafter. The marginal function is negatively sloped and has a negative derivative at the point of maximization for the total function.

Another example should clarify this concept. Assume the total profit function illustrated in Figure 2.6 is

$$\text{Total Profit} = \pi = -\$3{,}000 - \$2{,}400Q + \$350Q^2 - \$8.33Q^3. \quad (2.8)$$

Marginal profit is the first derivative of the total profit function:

$$\text{Marginal Profit} = \frac{d\pi}{dQ} = -\$2{,}400 + \$700Q - \$25Q^2. \qquad (2.9)$$

Total profit is either maximized or minimized at the points where the first derivative or marginal profit is zero:

FIGURE 2.6 **Locating Maximum and Minimum Values of a Function**

The second derivative of a function is always negative when evaluated at a point of maximization and positive at a point of minimization.

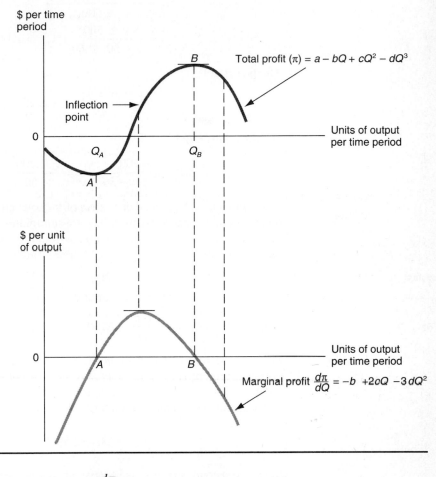

$$\frac{d\pi}{dQ} = -\$2{,}400 + \$700Q - \$25Q^2 = 0. \qquad \textbf{(2.10)}$$

Output quantities of 4 and 24 units satisfy Equation 2.10 and are therefore points of either maximum or minimum profits.

Any equation of the form $Y = aX^2 + bX + c$ is a quadratic, and its two roots are found using the general quadratic equation:

$$X = \frac{-b \pm \sqrt{b^2 - 4ac}}{2a}.$$

Substituting the values from Equation 2.10 into the quadratic equation gives

$$X = \frac{-700 \pm \sqrt{700^2 - 4(-25)(-2{,}400)}}{2(-25)}$$

$$= \frac{-700 \pm \sqrt{490,000 - 240,000}}{-50}$$

$$= \frac{-700 \pm \sqrt{250,000}}{-50}$$

$$= \frac{-700 \pm 500}{-50}.$$

The plus root is

$$X_1 = \frac{-700 + 500}{-50} = \frac{-200}{-50} = 4 \text{ units,}$$

and the minus root is

$$X_2 = \frac{-700 - 500}{-50} = \frac{-1,200}{-50} = 24 \text{ units.}$$

Evaluation of the second derivative of the total profit function at each of these output levels indicates whether they are minimums or maximums. The second derivative of the total profit function is found by taking the derivative of the marginal profit function, Equation 2.9. For example, at output quantity $Q = 4$;

$$\frac{d^2\pi}{dQ^2} = \frac{dM\pi}{dQ} = \$700 - \$50Q.$$

$$\frac{d^2\pi}{dQ^2} = \$700 - \$50(4) = \$500.$$

Since the second derivative is positive, indicating that marginal profits are increasing, total profit is *minimized* at 4 units of output. Total profit at 4 units of output corresponds to point A in Figure 2.6.

Evaluating the second derivative at 24 units of output gives

$$\frac{d^2\pi}{dQ^2} = \$700 - \$50(24) = -\$500.$$

Since the second derivative is negative at 24 units, indicating that marginal profit is decreasing, the total profit function reaches a *maximum* at that point. This output level corresponds to point B in Figure 2.6.

Use of Marginals to Maximize the Difference between Two Functions

Profit maximization
Activity level that generates the highest profit, $MR = MC$ and $M\pi = 0$.

Another example of the importance of the marginal concept in managerial economics is provided by the important and well-known microeconomic corollary that marginal revenue equals marginal cost at the point of **profit maximization.** It stems from the fact that the distance between revenue and cost functions is maximized at the point where their slopes are the same. Figure 2.7, where hypothetical revenue and cost functions are shown, illustrates this point. Total profit is equal to total revenue minus total cost and is, therefore, equal to the vertical distance between the two curves at any output level. This distance is maximized at output level Q_B, where the slopes of the revenue and cost curves are equal.

FIGURE 2.7   **Total Revenue, Total Cost, and Profit Maximization**

The difference between the total revenue and total cost curves is greatest when their slopes are equal. At that point, marginal revenue equals marginal cost, marginal profit equals zero, and profit is maximized.

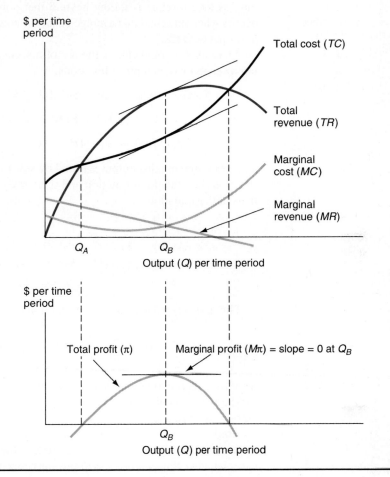

Because the slopes of the total revenue and total cost curves measure marginal revenues (*MR*) and marginal costs (*MC*) where these slopes are equal, *MR* = *MC*.

The reason that Q_B is the profit-maximizing output level can be seen by considering the shapes of the two curves to the right of point Q_A. At Q_A, total revenue equals total cost, a **breakeven point** where profit equals zero is indicated. At output quantities just beyond Q_A, total revenue is rising faster than total cost, so profits are increasing and the curves are spreading farther apart. This divergence of the curves continues as long as total revenue is rising faster than total cost or, in other words, as long as *MR* > *MC*. Once the slope of the total revenue curve is exactly equal to the slope of the total cost curve—in other words, where marginal revenue equals marginal cost—the two curves are parallel and no longer

Breakeven point

Output level at which total profit is zero.

diverging. This occurs at output quantity Q_B. Beyond Q_B the slope of the cost curve is greater than that of the revenue curve (marginal cost is greater than marginal revenue), so the distance between them is decreasing and total profits decline. Marginal revenue equals zero at the point of **revenue maximization,** as long as total revenue is falling beyond that point. **Average cost minimization** occurs when marginal and average costs are equal and average cost is increasing as output expands.

Revenue maximization

Activity level that generates the highest revenue, $MR = 0$.

Average cost minimization

Activity level that generates the lowest average cost, $MC = AC$.

An example should clarify the use of marginal relations. Consider the following revenue, cost, and profit functions:

$$\text{Total Revenue} = TR = \$41.5Q - \$1.1Q^2.$$

$$\text{Total Cost} = TC = \$150 + \$10Q - \$0.5Q^2 + \$0.02Q^3.$$

$$\text{Total Profit} = \pi = TR - TC.$$

The profit-maximizing output is found by substituting total revenue and total cost functions into the profit function and then analyzing the first and second derivatives of that equation:

$$\begin{aligned}
\pi &= TR - TC \\
&= \$41.5Q - \$1.1Q^2 - (\$150 + \$10Q - \$0.5Q^2 + \$0.02Q^3) \\
&= \$41.5Q - \$1.1Q^2 - \$150 - \$10Q + \$0.5Q^2 - \$0.02Q^3 \\
&= -\$150 + \$31.5Q - \$0.6Q^2 - \$0.02Q^3.
\end{aligned}$$

The first derivative of the profit function is marginal profit:

$$M\pi = \frac{d\pi}{dQ} = \$31.5 - \$1.2Q - \$0.06Q^2 .$$

Setting marginal profit equal to zero and using the quadratic equation to solve for the two roots gives the solutions $Q_1 = -35$ and $Q_2 = +15$. Since negative output quantities are not possible, Q_1 is an infeasible output level and can be rejected.

An evaluation of the second derivative of the profit function at $Q = 15$ indicates whether this is a point of profit maximization or profit minimization. The second derivative is:

$$\frac{d^2\pi}{dQ^2} = \frac{dM\pi}{dQ} = -\$1.2 - \$0.12Q.$$

Evaluating this derivative at $Q = 15$ indicates a value of $-\$3$; therefore, $Q = 15$ is a point of profit maximization.

The relevance of marginal revenue and marginal cost relations to profit maximization can be demonstrated by considering the general profit expression $\pi = TR - TC$. Marginal profit, the derivative of the total profit function, is

$$M\pi = \frac{d\pi}{dQ} = \frac{dTR}{dQ} - \frac{dTC}{dQ}.$$

Given that dTR/dQ is, by definition, marginal revenue, *MR,* and that dTC/dQ represents marginal cost, *MC,* it follows that

$$M\pi = MR - MC.$$

Since maximization of any function requires that the first derivative equal zero, profit maximization occurs where

$$M\pi = MR - MC = 0$$

or where

$$MR = MC.$$

In the numerical example described previously, marginal revenue and marginal cost are found by differentiating the total revenue and total cost functions:

$$MR = \frac{dTR}{dQ} = \$41.5 - \$2.2Q.$$

$$MC = \frac{dTC}{dQ} = \$10 - Q + \$0.06Q^2.$$

At the profit-maximizing output level, $MR = MC$; thus,

$$MR = \$41.5 - \$2.2Q = \$10 - Q + \$0.06Q^2 = MC.$$

Combining the terms gives

$$\$31.5 - \$1.2Q - \$0.06Q^2 = 0,$$

which is the same expression obtained when the first derivative of the profit function is set at zero. Solving for the roots of this equation (again using the quadratic formula) results in $Q_1 = -35$ and $Q_2 = 15$, the same values found previously. This confirms that marginal revenue equals marginal cost at the output level where profit is maximized. This example also illustrates that although *MR* must equal *MC* at the profit-maximizing activity level, the converse does not hold. Profits are not necessarily maximized at any point where $MR = MC$, as for example at $Q = -35$ in the current problem.

To conclude the example, Figure 2.8 presents a graph of the revenue, cost, and profit functions. The upper section of the graph shows the revenue and cost functions. At 15 units of output, the slopes of the two curves are equal, and $MR = MC$. The lower section of the graph shows the profit function, and the profit-maximizing output is shown to be 15 units, at which output $d\pi/dQ = 0$ and $d^2\pi/dQ^2 < 0$.

MULTIVARIATE OPTIMIZATION

Multivariate optimization

The process of optimization for equations with three or more variables.

Because many economic relations involve more than two variables, it is useful to examine the concept of **multivariate optimization,** the process of optimization for equations with three or more variables. Demand is often a function of the product's own price, the price of other goods, advertising, income, and other

FIGURE 2.8   **Profit-Maximizing Output Conditions**

Profit is maximized at $Q = 15$, where $MR = MC = \$8.50$, and $M\pi = 0$.

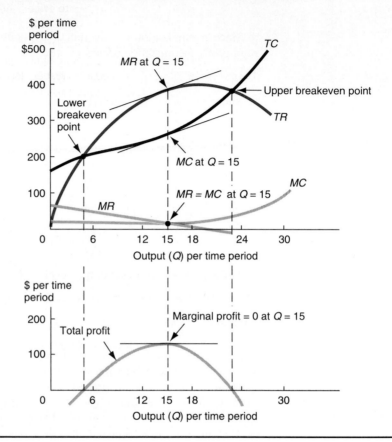

factors. Similarly, cost is determined by output, input prices, the nature of technology, and so on. As a result, multivariate optimization is often employed in the process of optimization.

The Partial
Derivative Concept

Consider the demand function for a product where the quantity demanded, Q, is determined by the price charged, P, and the level of advertising, A:

$$Q = f(P,A). \qquad \textbf{(2.11)}$$

When analyzing multivariate relations, such as Equation 2.11, one is interested in the marginal effect of each independent variable on the dependent variable. Optimization requires an analysis of how a change in each independent variable affects the dependent variable, *holding constant the effect of all other independent variables.* The partial derivative is the concept used for this type of marginal analysis.

Based upon the demand function of Equation 2.11, it is possible to examine two partial derivatives:[4]

1. The partial of Q with respect to price is $\delta Q/\delta P$.
2. The partial of Q with respect to advertising expenditure is $\delta Q/\delta A$.

The rules for determining partial derivatives are essentially the same as those for simple derivatives. The concept of a partial derivative involves an assumption that all variables except the one with respect to which the derivative is being taken remain unchanged. Other variables are treated as constants. For example, consider the demand function facing MacGyver, Inc.:

$$Q = 5{,}000 - 10P + 40A + PA - 0.8A^2 - 0.5P^2, \qquad \textbf{(2.12)}$$

where Q is quantity, P is price (in dollars), and A is advertising expenditures (in hundreds of dollars).

In this function there are two independent variables, P and A, so two partial derivatives can be evaluated. Since A is treated as a constant, the partial derivative of Q with respect to P is

$$\frac{\delta Q}{\delta P} = 0 - 10P + 0 + A - 0 - P$$
$$= -10 + A - P.$$

In determining the partial of Q with respect to A, P is treated as a constant. The partial with respect to A is

$$\frac{\delta Q}{\delta A} = 0 - 0 + 40 + P - 1.6A - 0$$
$$= 40 + P - 1.6A.$$

Maximizing Multivariate Functions

The maximization or minimization of multivariate functions is similar to that for single-variable functions. All first-order partial derivatives must equal zero.[5] Thus, maximization of the function $Q = f(P, A)$ requires

$$\frac{\delta Q}{\delta P} = 0$$

and

$$\frac{\delta Q}{\delta A} = 0.$$

To illustrate this procedure, reconsider the MacGyver demand function, Equation 2.12, given previously:

$$Q = 5{,}000 - 10P + 40A + PA - 0.8A^2 - 0.5P^2.$$

[4] The symbol δ, the Greek letter delta, is used to denote a partial derivative. In oral and written expression, the word *derivative* is frequently omitted. Reference is typically made to the *partial* of Q rather than the *partial derivative* of Q.

[5] Second-order requirements for determining maxima and minima are complex and are not necessary for the types of managerial problems considered in this text. A full discussion of these requirements can be found in any elementary calculus text.

To maximize the value of this function, each partial must equal zero:

$$\frac{\delta Q}{\delta P} = -10 + A - P = 0$$

and

$$\frac{\delta Q}{\delta A} = 40 + P - 1.6A = 0.$$

Solving these two equations simultaneously yields the values $P = \$40$ and $A = \$5,000$.[6] Inserting these numbers for P and A into Equation 2.12 results in a value for Q of 5,800. Therefore, the maximum value of Q is 5,800.

The process involved here can be visualized by referring to Figure 2.9, a three-dimensional graph of Equation 2.12. For positive values of P and A, Equation 2.12 maps out a surface with a peak at point X^*. At the peak, the surface of the figure is level. Alternatively stated, a plane that is tangent to the surface at point X^* is parallel to the PA plane. This means that the slope of the figure with respect to either P or A is zero, as is required for locating the maximum of a multivariate function.

CONSTRAINED OPTIMIZATION

In many decision problems faced by managers, there are constraints imposed that limit the options available to the decision maker. For example, a production manager may be charged with minimizing total cost, subject to the requirement that specified quantities of each of the firm's products be produced. At other times the production manager may be concerned with maximizing output from a particular department, subject to limitations on the quantities of various resources (labor, materials, or equipment) available for use.

The Role of Constraints

Constrained optimization

Decision situations that involve limited choice alternatives.

Managers in several functional areas frequently face **constrained optimization** problems, decision situations with limited choice alternatives. Marketing managers are often charged with the task of maximizing sales, subject to the constraint that they not exceed a fixed advertising budget. Financial officers, in their efforts to minimize the cost of acquiring capital, typically work within constraints imposed by investment financing requirements and creditor restrictions.

Constrained optimization problems can be solved in several ways. Where the constraint equation is not overly complex, it can be solved for one of the decision variables, and then that variable can be substituted for in the objective function that the firm wishes to maximize or minimize.[7] This approach converts the prob-

---

[6] Since $-10 + A - P = 0$, $P = A - 10$. Substituting this value for P into $40 + P - 1.6A = 0$ gives $40 + (A - 10) - 1.6A = 0$, which implies that $0.6A = 30$ and $A = 50(00)$, or $\$5,000$. Given this value, $P = A - 10 = 50 - 10 = \$40$.

[7] This section examines techniques for solving constrained optimization problems where the constraints can be expressed as equations. Some constraints impose only upper or lower limits on the decision maker and, therefore, may not be "binding" at the optimal solution. Constraints of this second, more general, type are properly expressed as inequality relations. In such instances another optimizing technique, linear programming, is used to analyze the problem. Linear programming is the subject of Chapter 11.

FIGURE 2.9 **Finding the Maximum of a Function of Two Variables:**
$$Q = 5,000 - 10P + 40A + PA - 0.8A^2 - 0.5P^2$$

All first-order partial derivatives are set equal to zero to find the maximum of a multivariate function.

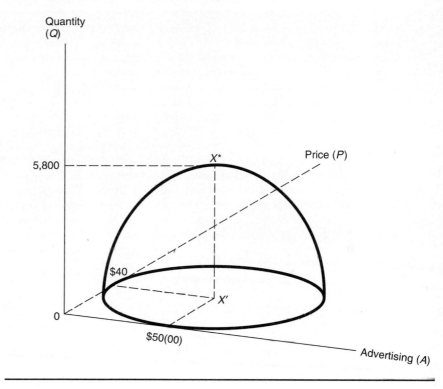

lem to one of unconstrained maximization or minimization, which can be solved by methods outlined previously.

This procedure can be clarified by examining its use in a constrained minimization problem. Suppose a firm produces its product on two assembly lines and operates with the following total cost function:

$$TC = \$3X^2 + \$6Y^2 - \$1XY,$$

where X represents the output produced on one assembly line and Y the production from the second. Management seeks to determine the least-cost combination of X and Y, subject to the constraint that total output of the product is 20 units. The constrained optimization problem is

Minimize

$$TC = \$3X^2 + \$6Y^2 - \$1XY,$$

subject to

$$X + Y = 20.$$

●

M A N A G E R I A L   A P P L I C A T I O N   2 . 2

Entrepreneurship Is Alive and Well

Sometimes it is easy to overlook the fact that firms are made up of people. Firms often are started by a single individual with no more than an idea for a better product or service—the entrepreneur. Taken from the Old French word *entreprendre,* meaning "to undertake," the term entrepreneur refers to one who organizes, operates, and assumes the risk of a business venture. Until recently, there appeared to be little academic or public policy interest in this key function or in the entrepreneur's role in the economy's overall performance. The entrepreneur's skill was simply considered part of the labor input in production. Now, both academicians and practitioners are beginning to better understand the critical role of the entrepreneur, partly because entrepreneurship has become a formal field of study at many leading business schools.

As a catalyst, the entrepreneur brings economic resources together in the risky attempt to meet consumers' needs and desires. This process often leads to failure—in fact, the odds against success are long. Seldom do more than one in ten start-up businesses enjoy even minimal economic success. Even those select few that see their product or service reach a national market find stable long-term success elusive. Once established, they in turn become targets for future entrepreneurs. As entrepreneurs create new opportunities, they destroy the old way of doing things. Thus, entrepreneurship plays an important role in what economist Joseph Schumpeter once called the "creative destruction of capitalism." This is the process of replacing the old with the new, the inefficient with the efficient, and low quality with a superior product.

Given the long odds against success, you might wonder why so many willingly embark on ventures (adventures?) that appear doomed to fail. One reason is that one-in-a-million chance of developing "the" truly revolutionary product or service that will fundamentally change how people live, work, play, or shop. Sam Walton, the founder of retailer Wal-Mart, Inc., made *billions* of dollars bringing brand-name merchandise at bargain prices to rural America—and created thousands of well-paid job opportunities for Wal-Mart "associ-

ates." Even though the opportunity for wealth is surely an important motivation, the impact and recognition that come with creating a truly unique good or service often are equally important to entrepreneurs. Many simply want to "make a difference."

What about the entrepreneur's role from the standpoint of society in general? Clearly, everyone benefits from the innovative products, services, and delivery systems that result from entrepreneurs' efforts. Consider the benefits resulting from the efforts of such entrepreneurs as Thomas Edison, Chester Carlson, and Bill Gates. Their fame and fortune only partly reflect the benefits enjoyed from phonography, electric lighting, photography, xerography, the "graphic desktop," and "user-friendly" computers. Like all entrepreneurs, they have played an important role in determining the types of goods that become available in the marketplace and when they become available.

Evidence of the private and social benefits of entrepreneurs is clearly evident when one considers the rising stars featured on *Business Week's* annual ranking of the 100 best small corporations. Outstanding rates of growth in sales, profits, and employment are unmistakable at such companies as software company Artisoft, Inc., restaurant chain Outback, Inc., and physical therapist National Rehabilitation Centers, Inc. In each case, high rates of return on invested capital suggest the wise use of capital in meeting the needs and desires of consumers.

An important recently recognized form of entrepreneurial activity is called intrapreneurship, in which the entrepreneur works within the overall framework of an existing organization. Many firms, such as titans Merck & Co. and the Du Pont Co., have come to recognize the importance of the intrapreneur. Thus, entrepreneurship plays a key role in both the initial development and ongoing revitalization of firms. The opportunity to earn a normal business profit plus an attractive salary or wage is the realistic objective of every entrepreneur. The hope of above-normal economic profits is the dream that spurs the market-based "bottoms-up" method of economic development.

Source: Tatiana Pouschine and Manjeet Kripalani, "I Got Tired of Forcing Myself to Go to the Office," *Forbes,* May 25, 1992, 104–114.

Solving the constraint for X and substituting this value into the objective function results in

$$X = 20 - Y,$$

and

$$
\begin{aligned}
TC &= \$3(20 - Y)^2 + \$6Y^2 - \$1(20 - Y)Y \\
&= \$3(400 - 40Y + Y^2) + \$6Y^2 - \$1(20Y - Y^2) \qquad \textbf{(2.13)} \\
&= \$1,200 - \$120Y + \$3Y^2 + \$6Y^2 - \$20Y + Y^2 \\
&= \$1,200 - \$140Y + \$10Y^2.
\end{aligned}
$$

Now it is possible to treat Equation 2.13 as an unconstrained minimization problem. Solving it requires taking the derivative of the total cost function, setting that derivative equal to zero, and solving for the value of Y:

$$
\begin{aligned}
\frac{dTC}{dY} &= -\$140 + \$20Y = 0 \\
20Y &= 140 \\
Y &= 7.
\end{aligned}
$$

A check of the sign of the second derivative evaluated at that point ensures that a minimum has been located:

$$\frac{dTC}{dY} = -\$140 + \$20Y$$

$$\frac{d^2TC}{dY^2} = \$20.$$

Since the second derivative is positive, $Y = 7$ is indeed a minimum.

Substituting 7 for Y in the constraint equation allows one to determine the optimal quantity to be produced on assembly line X:

$$
\begin{aligned}
X + 7 &= 20 \\
X &= 13.
\end{aligned}
$$

Thus, production of 13 units of output on assembly line X and 7 units on line Y is the least-cost combination for manufacturing a total of 20 units of the firm's product. The total cost of producing that combination is

$$
\begin{aligned}
TC &= \$3(13^2) + \$6(7^2) - \$1(13 \times 7) \\
&= \$507 + \$294 - \$91 \\
&= \$710.
\end{aligned}
$$

Lagrangian Multipliers

Unfortunately, the substitution technique used in the preceding section is not always feasible. Constraint conditions are sometimes too numerous or complex for substitution to be employed. In these cases, the technique of *Lagrangian multipliers* can be used.

Lagrangian technique
Method for solving constrained optimization problems.

The **Lagrangian technique** for solving constrained optimization problems is a method that calls for optimizing a function that incorporates the original objective function and the constraint conditions. This combined equation, called the Lagrangian function, is created in such a way that when it is maximized or minimized the original objective function is also maximized or minimized, and all constraints are satisfied.

A reexamination of the constrained minimization problem illustrated previously illustrates this technique. Recall that the firm sought to minimize the function $TC = \$3X^2 + \$6Y^2 - \$1XY$, subject to the constraint that $X + Y = 20$. We rearrange the constraint to bring all terms to the right of the equal sign:

$$0 = 20 - X - Y.$$

This is always the first step in forming a Lagrangian expression.

Multiplying this form of the constraint by the unknown factor λ and adding the result to the original objective function creates the Lagrangian expression:[8]

$$L_{TC} = \$3X^2 + \$6Y^2 - \$1XY + \lambda(20 - X - Y). \qquad \textbf{(2.14)}$$

L_{TC} is defined as the Lagrangian function for the constrained optimization problem under consideration.

Because it incorporates the constraint into the objective function, the Lagrangian function can be treated as an unconstrained optimization problem. The solution to the unconstrained Lagrangian problem is *always* identical to the solution of the original constrained optimization problem. To illustrate, consider the problem of minimizing the Lagrangian function constructed in Equation 2.14. At a minimum point on a multivariate function, all partial derivatives must equal zero. The partials of Equation 2.14 can be taken with respect to the three unknown variables, X, Y, and λ, as follows:

$$\frac{\delta L_{TC}}{\delta X} = 6X - Y - \lambda,$$

$$\frac{\delta L_{TC}}{\delta Y} = 12Y - X - \lambda,$$

and

$$\frac{\delta L_{TC}}{\delta \lambda} = 20 - X - Y.$$

Setting these three partials equal to zero results in a system of three equations and three unknowns:

$$6X - Y - \lambda = 0, \qquad \textbf{(2.15)}$$

$$-X + 12Y - \lambda = 0, \qquad \textbf{(2.16)}$$

and

$$20 - X - Y = 0. \qquad \textbf{(2.17)}$$

---

[8] The Greek letter lambda, λ, is typically used in formulating Lagrangian expressions.

Notice that Equation 2.17, the partial of the Lagrangian function with respect to λ, is the constraint condition imposed on the original optimization problem. This result is not mere happenstance. The Lagrangian function is specifically constructed so that the derivative of the function taken with respect to the Lagrangian multiplier, λ, always gives the original constraint. So long as this derivative is zero, as it must be at a local extreme (maximum or minimum), the constraint conditions imposed on the original problem are met. Further, since the last term in the Lagrangian expression must equal zero $(0 = 20 - X - Y)$, the Lagrangian function reduces to the original objective function, and thus the solution to the unconstrained Lagrangian problem is always the solution to the original constrained optimization problem.

Completing the analysis for the example illuminates these relations. To begin, it is necessary to solve the system of equations to obtain optimal values of X and Y. Subtracting Equation 2.16 from Equation 2.15 gives

$$7X - 13Y = 0. \tag{2.18}$$

Multiplying Equation 2.17 by 7 and adding Equation 2.18 to this product gives the solution for Y:

$$
\begin{aligned}
140 - 7X - 7Y &= 0 \\
7X - 13Y &= 0 \\
\hline
140 - 20Y &= 0 \\
140 &= 20Y \\
Y &= 7.
\end{aligned}
$$

Substituting 7 for Y in Equation 2.17 yields $X = 13$, the value of X at the point where the Lagrangian function is minimized.

Since the solution of the Lagrangian function is also the solution to the firm's constrained optimization problem, 13 units from assembly line X and 7 units from line Y is the least-cost combination of output that can be produced subject to the constraint that total output must be 20 units. This is the same answer obtained previously, using the substitution method.

The Lagrangian technique is a more powerful technique for solving constrained optimization problems than the substitution method; it is easier to apply to a problem with multiple constraints, and it provides the decision maker with valuable supplementary information. This is because the Lagrangian multiplier itself has an important economic interpretation. Substituting the values of X and Y into Equation 2.15 gives the value of λ:

$$
\begin{aligned}
6 \times 13 - 7 - \lambda &= 0 \\
\lambda &= \$71.
\end{aligned}
$$

Here, λ is interpreted as the marginal cost of production at 20 units of output. It means that if the firm were allowed to produce only 19 instead of 20 units of output, total costs would fall by approximately $71. If the output requirement were 21 instead of 20 units, costs would increase by roughly that amount.[9]

Since $\lambda = \$71$ can be interpreted as the marginal cost of production, an offer to purchase another unit of output for $100 is acceptable because it results in a $29 marginal profit. Conversely, an offer to purchase an additional unit for $50 would be rejected because a marginal loss of $21 would be incurred. λ can be thought of as a planning variable, since it provides valuable information concerning the effects of altering current activity levels.

Another example provides additional perspective on the usefulness of the Lagrangian method. Recall from the discussion of Equation 2.6 and Figure 2.5 that the profit function,

$$\pi = -\$10{,}000 + \$400Q - \$2Q^2,$$

where π is total profit and Q is output in units, is maximized at $Q = 100$ with $\pi = \$10{,}000$. The impact of constraints in the production process, and the value of the Lagrangian method, can be portrayed further by considering the situation in which each unit of output requires 4 hours of skilled labor, and a total of only 300 hours of skilled labor is currently available to the firm. In this instance, the firm seeks to maximize the function $\pi = -\$10{,}000 + \$400Q - \$2Q^2$, subject to the constraint $4Q = 300$ (since $L = 4Q$). Rearrange the constraint to bring all terms to the right of the equal sign:

$$0 = 300 - 4Q.$$

Multiplying this form of the constraint by λ and adding the result to the original objective function creates the Lagrangian expression:

$$L_\pi = -\$10{,}000 + \$400Q - \$2Q^2 + \lambda(300 - 4Q), \qquad \textbf{(2.19)}$$

with the following partials:

$$\frac{\delta L_\pi}{\delta Q} = 400 - 4Q - 4\lambda$$

and

$$\frac{\delta L_\pi}{\delta \lambda} = 300 - 4Q.$$

Setting these two partials equal to zero results in a system of two equations and two unknowns. Solving provides the values $Q = 75$, $\lambda = \$25$, and, from the objective function, $\pi = \$8{,}750$. The constraint on skilled labor has reduced output from 100 to 75 units and has reduced total profits from $10,000 to $8,750. The value $\lambda = \$25$ indicates that should a one-unit expansion in output become possible, total profits would rise by $25. This information indicates that the maximum value of additional skilled labor is $6.25 per hour, since each unit of output

---

[9] Technically, λ indicates the marginal change in the objective function solution associated with an infinitesimally small change in the constraint. It only approximates the change in total cost that would take place if one more (or less) unit of output were produced.

FIGURE 2.10   **The Role of Constraints in Profit Maximization**

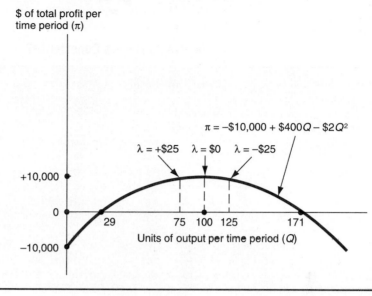

requires four hours of labor. Assuming there are no other costs involved, $6.25 per hour is the most the firm would pay to expand employment.

The effects of relaxing the constraint as progressively more skilled labor becomes available are illustrated in Figure 2.10. If an additional 100 hours of skilled labor, or 400 hours in total, is available, the output constraint would become $0 = 400 - 4Q$, and solved values $Q = 100$, $\lambda = \$0$, and $\pi = \$10,000$ would result. The value $\lambda = \$0$ indicates that skilled labor no longer constrains profits when 400 hours are available. Profits are maximized at $Q = 100$, which is the same result obtained in the earlier unconstrained solution to this profit maximization problem.

In this instance, the output constraint becomes *nonbinding* because it does not limit the profit-making ability of the firm. Indeed, the firm is not willing to employ more than 400 hours of skilled labor. To illustrate this point, consider the use of 500 hours of skilled labor and the resulting constraint $0 = 500 - 4Q$. Solved values are $Q = 125$, $\lambda = -\$25$, and $\pi = \$8,750$. The value $\lambda = -\$25$ indicates that one additional unit of output, and the expansion in employment that results, would *reduce* profits by $25. Conversely, a one-unit reduction in the level of output would increase profits by $25. Clearly, the situation in which $\lambda < 0$ gives the firm an incentive to reduce input usage and output, just as $\lambda > 0$ provides an incentive for growth.

Lagrangian multiplier, λ

The marginal effect on the objective function of decreasing or increasing the constraint requirement by one unit.

To generalize, a **Lagrangian multiplier, λ,** indicates the marginal effect on the objective function of decreasing or increasing the constraint requirement by one unit. Often, as in the previous examples, the marginal relation described by the Lagrangian multiplier provides economic data that help managers evaluate the potential benefits or costs of relaxing constraints. This use of the Lagrangian variable is further examined in Chapter 11, where the linear programming approach to constrained optimization is introduced.

MANAGERIAL APPLICATION 2.3
Do Profits Have a Conscience?

Corporations can be rightly criticized when toxic waste handling and disposal policies result in careless dumping because common safeguards are ignored. Any company policy of firing older, higher-salaried workers to save on retirement and health benefit costs can be similarly criticized for age discrimination. However, by focusing on the higher short-term profits sometimes earned by companies with such socially misguided policies, the broader and highly beneficial role of profits in the economy can be obscured.

Perhaps Karl Marx is most responsible for popularizing the view of the foundations of capitalism as being morally deficient. According to his view, profits and the concept of private property serve no useful social purpose. Rather than regarding profits as reflective of superior operating performance by firms or individuals, Marx had the perspective that profits represent the amount of resources taken out of the economic system and converted from social to private use. Although this viewpoint is losing credibility and support in former Communist bloc countries, it retains some credibility in the West in both government and the private sector. Even in largely market-based economies like the United States, there are those who regard profits as evil. For example, in their 1986 pastoral letter on the economy, U.S. Catholic bishops described the profit motive as a "vexing" moral problem—a view that remains controversial among Catholics and others. The fact that some still regard all profits as immoral suggests that profits and the profit motive remain misunderstood.

It is important to recognize that not all profits, including above-normal or economic profits, are immoral or unwarranted. Firms cannot operate outside the law or outside the common bounds of morality. They must operate within the limits that society imposes. This follows from the fact that the economy is part of the larger political, economic, and moral system. Firms that needlessly pollute or discriminate in their employment practices face the prospect of legal sanctions leading to long-run costs that far exceed any short-run benefits from such action. Apart from the effects of regulation,

market forces themselves often act to correct such abuses. A company that discriminates in its hiring policies will find it difficult to attract and retain valued employees. Any short-term benefits gained through environmental abuse and age discrimination are sure to be more than offset by long-term penalties imposed by consumers, workers, and the government. Profits earned through such antisocial behavior tend to be especially fleeting because all such parties seek their speedy elimination.

By narrowly focusing on the benefits gained by those that earn profits, critics fail to recognize the socially beneficial effects that profits generate. Profits and the profit system play a key role in the long-term betterment of all individuals. For example, profits provide a needed signaling mechanism for the allocation of scarce economic resources. When profits are too high, firms expand or new competitors rush to increase the availability of valued goods and services. When profits are too low, established firms exit or cut back on production so that valued resources can be deployed in higher-valued uses.

Before the time of Adam Smith, an 18th century Scottish political economist and philosopher, human poverty was commonplace. The wealth of nations was measured in terms of the quantity of gold in the monarch's treasury or the amount of precious goods enjoyed by nobility. Smith argued that, in contrast, the wealth of nations is best measured in terms of the level of well-being enjoyed by the common worker.

As in the time of Adam Smith, a country's wealth is still sometimes measured by trade surpluses generated by government policies that focus on export markets rather than on basic domestic needs. Likewise, many still fail to recognize the market economy's demonstrated capacity to lift the poor out of poverty as powerful testimony to the ability of the profit motive to do good. It is perhaps ironic that firms and individuals whose primary objective is to do well (earn profits) end up doing good (cause economic betterment for all) in the process.

Source: Andrew Tanzer and Gale Eisenstodt, "Rich Country, Poor Japanese," *Forbes,* May 25, 1992, 44–45.

THE INCREMENTAL CONCEPT IN ECONOMIC ANALYSIS

The marginal concept is a key component of the economic decision-making process. It is important to recognize, however, that marginal relations are limited for managerial decision making because they measure only the effect associated with *unitary changes* in output or some other important decision variable. Many managerial decisions involve a consideration of changes that are much broader in scope. For example, a manager might be interested in analyzing the potential effects on revenues, costs, and profits of a 25 percent increase in the firm's production level. Alternatively, a manager might want to analyze the profit impact of introducing an entirely new product line, or assess the cost impact of changing the complete system used to produce the firm's current products. In all managerial decisions, the study of *differences* or *changes* is the key element in the selection of an optimal course of action. The marginal concept, while correct for analyzing unitary changes, is too narrow to provide a general methodology for evaluating alternative courses of action.

The incremental concept is the economist's generalization of the marginal concept. Incremental analysis involves examining the impact of alternative managerial decisions or courses of action on revenues, costs, and profit. It focuses on changes or differences between the available alternatives. The **Incremental change** is the total change resulting from a decision. For example, the incremental revenue associated with adding a new item to a firm's product line is measured as the difference between the firm's total revenue with the product and without the product.

Incremental change

Total difference resulting from a decision.

Incremental Profits

Incremental profit

Gain or loss associated with a given managerial decision.

The fundamental relations of incremental analysis are essentially the same as those of marginal analysis. **Incremental profit** is the profit gain or loss associated with a given managerial decision. Total profit increases so long as incremental profit is positive. When incremental profit is negative, total profit declines. Similarly, incremental profit is positive (and total profit increases) if the incremental revenue associated with a decision exceeds the incremental cost. The incremental concept is so intuitively obvious that it is easy to overlook both its significance in managerial decision making and the potential complexity of correctly applying it.

For this reason, the incremental concept is often violated in practice. For example, a firm may refuse to sublet excess warehouse space for $5,000 per month because it figures its cost as $7,500 per month—a price that it paid for a long-term lease on the facility. However, if the warehouse space represents true excess capacity with no current value to the company, its historical cost of $7,500 per month is irrelevant and should be disregarded. The firm would forego $5,000 in profits by turning down the offer to sublet the excess warehouse space. Similarly, any firm that adds a standard allocated charge for fixed costs and overhead to the true incremental cost of production runs the risk of turning down profitable sales.

Care must be exercised to ensure against incorrectly assigning overly low incremental costs to a decision. Incremental decisions involve a time dimension that simply cannot be ignored. Not only must all current revenues and costs associated with a given decision be considered, but any likely future revenues and costs be incorporated in the analysis. For example, assume that the excess warehouse space described earlier came about following a downturn in the overall economy. Furthermore, assume that the excess warehouse space was sublet for a period of one year at a price of $5,000 per month, or a total of $60,000. An incremental loss might be experienced if the firm must later go out and lease additional, more costly space to accommodate an increase in production following a subsequent upturn in economic activity. If $75,000 had to be spent to replace the sublet warehouse facility, the decision to sublet would involve an incremental loss of $15,000. To be sure, making accurate projections concerning the future pattern of revenues and costs is risky and subject to error. Nevertheless, they simply cannot be ignored in incremental analysis.

Another interesting example of the incremental concept involves the measurement of the incremental revenue resulting from introducing a new product to a firm's product line. Incremental revenue in this case would include not only the revenue received from sale of the new product but also any change in the revenues generated by the remainder of the firm's product line. Thus, the incremental revenues would include any revenue resulting from increased sales of another product, where that increase was the result of adding the new product to the firm's line. Similarly, if the new item took sales away from another of the firm's products, the loss in revenue on sales of those products would have to be accounted for in measuring the incremental revenue of the new product.

An Incremental Concept Example

▶

A more detailed illustration of the comprehensive nature of the incremental concept is found in the financing decision that is typically associated with business real estate and plant and equipment financing. Consider a small business whose $100,000 purchase offer recently was accepted by the seller of a small retail facility. The firm must obtain financing to complete the transaction. The best rates it has found are at a local financial institution that offers a renewable five-year mortgage at 9 percent interest with a down payment of 20 percent, or 9.5 percent interest on a loan with only 10 percent down. In the first case, the borrower is able to finance 80 percent of the purchase price; in the second case, the borrower is able to finance 90 percent. For simplicity, assume that both loans require interest payments only during the first five years. After five years, either note would be renewable at then-current interest rates and would be restructured with monthly payments designed to amortize the loan over 20 years. An important question facing the firm is: What is the incremental financing cost of the additional funds borrowed when 90 percent versus 80 percent of the purchase price is financed?

Because no principal payments are required, the annual financing cost under each loan alternative can be calculated easily. For the 80 percent loan, the annual financing cost in dollar terms is

$$\frac{\text{Financing}}{\text{Cost}} = \text{Interest Rate} \times \text{Loan Percentage} \times \text{Purchase Price}$$
$$= (0.09)(0.8)(\$100{,}000)$$
$$= \$7{,}200. \tag{2.11}$$

For a 90 percent loan, the corresponding annual financing cost is

$$\frac{\text{Financing}}{\text{Cost}} = (0.095)(0.9)(\$100{,}000)$$
$$= \$8{,}550.$$

To calculate the incremental cost of the added funds borrowed under the 90 percent financing alternative, the firm must compare the additional financing costs incurred with the additional funds borrowed. In dollar terms, the incremental annual financing cost is

$$\frac{\text{Incremental}}{\text{Cost}} = \frac{90\% \text{ Loan Financing}}{\text{Cost}} - \frac{80\% \text{ Loan Financing}}{\text{Cost}} \tag{2.12}$$
$$= \$8{,}550 - \$7{,}200$$
$$= \$1{,}350.$$

In percentage terms, the incremental cost of the additional funds borrowed under the 90 percent financing alternative is

$$\frac{\text{Incremental Cost}}{\text{in Percentage Terms}} = \frac{\text{Incremental Financing Costs}}{\text{Incremental Funds Borrowed}}$$
$$= \frac{\$8{,}550 - \$7{,}200}{\$90{,}000 - \$80{,}000}$$
$$= \frac{\$1{,}350}{}$$
$$= 0.135, \text{ or } 13.5\%.$$

Careful analysis indicates that the true incremental cost of funds for the last $10,000 borrowed under the 90 percent financing alternative is 13.5 percent, not the 9.5 percent interest rate quoted for the loan. While this high incremental cost of funds is perhaps surprising, it is not unusual. It results because with a 90 percent loan the higher 9.5 percent interest rate is charged on the entire balance of the loan, not just on the incremental $10,000 in funds borrowed.

The incremental concept is important for managerial decision making because it focuses attention on the changes or differences between available alternatives. It also indicates that revenues and costs unaffected by the decision are irrelevant and should not be included in the analysis. This incremental concept is examined in somewhat greater detail in Chapters 8 and 12.

SUMMARY

Effective managerial decision making is the process of finding the best possible solution to a given problem. Both the methodology and tools of managerial economics play an important role in this process.

- The decision alternative that produces a result most consistent with managerial objectives is the **optimal decision.**
- **Tables** are the simplest and most direct form for listing economic data. When these data are displayed electronically in the format of an accounting income statement or balance sheet, the tables are referred to as **spreadsheets.** In many instances, a simple **graph** or visual representation of the data can provide valuable insight. In other instances, complex economic relations are written using an **equation,** or an analytical expression of functional relationships.
- The value of a **dependent variable** in an equation depends on the size of the variable(s) to the right of the equal sign, which is called an **independent variable.** The values of independent variables are determined outside or independently of the functional relation expressed by the equation.
- A **marginal relation** is the change in the dependent variable caused by a one-unit change in an independent variable. **Marginal revenue** is the change in total revenue associated with a one-unit change in output; **marginal cost** is the change in total cost following a one-unit change in output; and **marginal profit** is the change in total profit due to a one-unit change in output.
- A **derivative** is a precise specification of the marginal relation. A **tangent** is a line that touches a curve at only one point.
- In graphic analysis, **slope** is a measure of the steepness of a line and is defined as the increase (or decrease) in height per unit of movement along the horizontal axis. An **inflection point** reveals a point of maximum or minimum slope.
- Marginal revenue equals marginal cost at the point of **profit maximization,** as long as total profit is falling as output expands from that point. The **breakeven point** identifies an output quantity at which total profit is zero. Marginal revenue equals zero at the point of **revenue maximization,** as long as total revenue is falling beyond that point. **Average cost minimization** occurs when marginal and average costs are equal and average cost is increasing as output expands.
- **Multivariate optimization** is the process of optimization for equations with three or more variables. Managers in several functional areas frequently face **constrained optimization** problems, decision situations that involve limited choice alternatives. The **Lagrangian technique** for solving constrained optimization problems is a method that calls for optimizing a function that incorporates the original objective function and the constraint conditions. The **Lagrangian multiplier, λ,** indicates the marginal effect on the objective function of decreasing or increasing the constraint requirement by one unit.
- The incremental concept is often employed as the practical equivalent of marginal analysis. **Incremental change** is the total change resulting from a decision. **Incremental profit** is the profit gain or loss associated with a given managerial decision.

Each of these concepts is fruitfully applied in the practical analysis of managerial decision problems. As seen in later chapters, basic economic relations provide the underlying framework for the analysis of all profit, revenue, and cost relations.

Questions

Q2.1 What key ingredients are crucial to the optimization process?

Q2.2 What is the difference between global and partial optimization techniques?

Q2.3 Why do you think electronic spreadsheets are rapidly growing in popularity as a means for expressing economic relations?

Q2.4 Describe the relation between totals and marginals, and explain why the total is maximized when the marginal is set equal to zero.

Q2.5 Why must a marginal curve always intersect the related average curve at either a maximum or a minimum point?

Q2.6 Would you expect total revenue to be maximized at an output level that is typically greater or less than the profit-maximizing output level? Why?

Q2.7 Does the point of minimum long-run average costs always represent the optimal activity level?

Q2.8 Economists have long argued that if you want to tax away excess profits without affecting allocative efficiency, you should use a lump-sum tax instead of an excise or sales tax. Use the concepts developed in the chapter to support this position.

Q2.9 "It is often impossible to obtain precise information about the pattern of future revenues, costs, and interest rates. Therefore, the process of economic optimization is futile." Discuss this statement.

Q2.10 Distinguish the incremental concept from the marginal concept.

Self-Test Problem

Electro-Optical, Inc., is a small but rapidly growing company that manufactures and markets precision optics, electrical and optical components, and surgical laser systems. Demand and cost relations for a major product produced by the company are as follows:

$$P = \$31,800 - \$50Q$$
$$TC = \$1,000,000 + \$9,000Q + \$64Q^2,$$

where P is price, Q is quantity, and TC is total cost.

A. Set up a table or spreadsheet for Electro-Optical output (Q), price (P), total revenue (TR), marginal revenue (MR), total cost (TC), average cost (AC), marginal cost (MC), total profit (π), and marginal profit ($M\pi$). Establish a range for Q from 0 to 150 in increments of 5 (i.e., 0, 5, 10, . . . , 150). (Note: $TR = \$31,800Q - \$50Q^2$, $MR = \$31,800 - \$100Q$, $AC = \$1,000,000/Q + \$9,000 + \$64Q$, $MC = \$9,000 + \$128Q$, $\pi = TR - TC$, and $M\pi = MR - MC$.)

B. Using the Electro-Optical table or spreadsheet, create a graph with *TR*, *TC*, and π as dependent variables and with units of output (*Q*) as the independent variable. At what output level is total profit maximized? Why?

C. Again using the Electro-Optical spreadsheet, create a graph with *P*, *AC*, *MR*, *MC*, and *M*π as dependent variables and with units of output (*Q*) as the independent variable. At what output level is average cost minimized? Why?

D. Compare your answers to Parts B and C. Discuss any differences.

Solution to Self-Test Problem

A. A spreadsheet for Electro-Optical output (*Q*), price (*P*), total revenue (*TR*), marginal revenue (*MR*), total cost (*TC*), average cost (*AC*), marginal cost (*MC*), total profit (π), and marginal profit (*M*π) appears as follows:

Electro-Optical, Inc., Spreadsheet Given Price, Quantity, and Total Cost

Quantity (Q)	Price (P)	Total Revenue (TR)	Marginal Revenue (MR)	Total Cost (TC)	Average Cost (AC)	Marginal Cost (MC)	Total Profit (π)	Marginal Profit (Mπ)
0	$31,800	$0	—	$1,000,000	—	—	−$1,000,000	—
5	31,550	157,750	31,300	1,046,600	209,320	9,640	−888,850	21,660
10	31,300	313,000	30,800	1,096,400	109,640	10,280	−783,400	20,520
15	31,050	465,750	30,300	1,149,400	76,627	10,920	−683,650	19,380
20	30,800	616,000	29,800	1,205,600	60,280	11,560	−589,600	18,240
25	30,550	763,750	29,300	1,265,000	50,600	12,200	−501,250	17,100
30	30,300	909,000	28,800	1,327,600	44,253	12,840	−418,600	15,960
35	30,050	1,051,750	28,300	1,393,400	39,811	13,480	−341,650	14,820
40	29,800	1,192,000	27,800	1,462,400	36,560	14,120	−270,400	13,680
45	29,550	1,329,750	27,300	1,534,600	34,102	14,760	−204,850	12,540
50	29,300	1,465,000	26,800	1,610,000	32,200	15,400	−145,000	11,400
55	29,050	1,597,750	26,300	1,688,600	30,702	16,040	−90,850	10,260
60	28,800	1,728,000	25,800	1,770,400	29,507	16,680	−42,400	9,120
65	28,550	1,855,750	25,300	1,855,400	28,545	17,320	350	7,980
70	28,300	1,981,000	24,800	1,943,600	27,766	17,960	37,400	6,840
75	28,050	2,103,750	24,300	2,035,000	27,133	18,600	68,750	5,700
80	27,800	2,224,000	23,800	2,129,600	26,620	19,240	94,400	4,560
85	27,550	2,341,750	23,300	2,227,400	26,205	19,880	114,350	3,420
90	27,300	2,457,000	22,800	2,328,400	25,871	20,520	128,600	2,280
95	27,050	2,569,750	22,300	2,432,600	25,606	21,160	137,150	1,140
100	26,800	2,680,000	21,800	2,540,000	25,400	21,800	140,000	0
105	26,550	2,787,750	21,300	2,650,600	25,244	22,440	137,150	−1,140
110	26,300	2,893,000	20,800	2,764,400	25,131	23,080	128,600	−2,280
115	26,050	2,995,750	20,300	2,881,400	25,056	23,720	114,350	−3,420
120	25,800	3,096,000	19,800	3,001,600	25,013	24,360	94,400	−4,560
125	25,550	3,193,750	19,300	3,125,000	25,000	25,000	68,750	−5,700
130	25,300	3,289,000	18,800	3,251,600	25,012	25,640	37,400	−6,840
135	25,050	3,381,750	18,300	3,381,400	25,047	26,280	350	−7,980
140	24,800	3,472,000	17,800	3,514,400	25,103	26,920	−42,400	−9,120
145	24,550	3,559,750	17,300	3,650,600	25,177	27,560	−90,850	−10,260
150	24,300	3,645,000	16,800	3,790,000	25,267	28,200	−145,000	−11,400

B. A graph with *TR*, *TC*, and π as dependent variables and units of Electro-Optical output (*Q*) as the independent variable appears as follows:

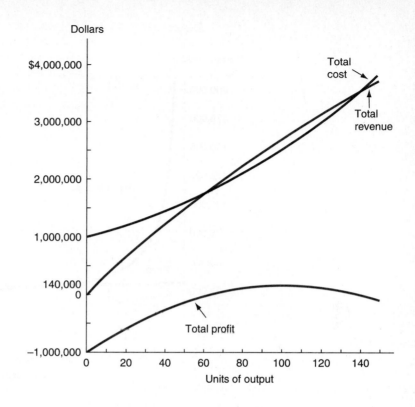

Total profit is maximized at the $Q = 100$ output level, where $MR = MC$ and $M\pi = 0$.

C. A graph with P, MR, AC, MC, and $M\pi$ as dependent variables and with units of Electro-Optical output (Q) as the independent variable appears at the top of page 62. Average cost is minimized at the $Q = 125$ output level, where $MC = AC$.

D. It is often true that the profit-maximizing output level differs from the average cost-minimizing activity level. In this instance, expansion to $Q = 125$, the average cost-minimizing activity level, cannot be justified because it would entail too great a price discount to move the last 25 units of sales. In other words, the revenue loss from increasing sales out to the average cost-minimizing activity level is too great to be compensated for by the resulting reduction in average costs. The profit maximizing activity level can be less than, greater than, or equal to the average cost-minimizing activity level, depending on the shape of relevant demand and cost relations.

Problems

P2.1 **Graph Analysis**

A. Given the output (Q) and price (P) data in the table on the following page, calculate the related total revenue (TR), marginal revenue (MR), and average revenue (AR) figures:

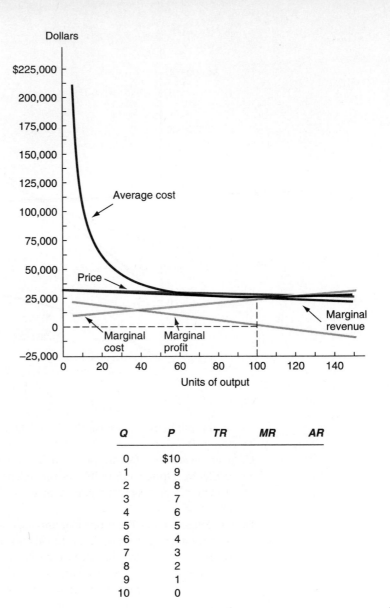

Q	P	TR	MR	AR
0	$10			
1	9			
2	8			
3	7			
4	6			
5	5			
6	4			
7	3			
8	2			
9	1			
10	0			

B. Graph these data using "dollars" on the vertical axis and "quantity" on the horizontal axis. At what output level is revenue maximized?

C. Why is marginal revenue less than average revenue at each price level?

P2.2 **The Marginal Concept**

A. Fill in the missing data for price (*P*), total revenue (*TR*), marginal revenue (*MR*), total cost (*TC*), marginal cost (*MC*), profit (*π*), and marginal profit (*Mπ*) in the following table:

Q	P	TR	MR	TC	MC	π	Mπ
0	$160	$ 0	$—	$ 0	$—	$ 0	$—
1	150	150	150	25	25	125	125
2	140			55	30		100
3		390			35	300	75
4			90	130		350	
5	110	550		175			
6		600	50		55	370	
7		630		290	60		-30
8	80	640		355		285	
9					75		-85
10		600		525			

    B. At what output level is profit maximized?

    C. At what output level is revenue maximized?

    D. Discuss any differences in your answers to Parts B and C.

P2.3 **Marginal Analysis.** Characterize each of the following statements as true or false, and explain your answers.

    A. If marginal revenue is less than average revenue, the demand curve is downward sloping.

    B. Profits are maximized when total revenue equals total cost.

    C. Given a downward-sloping demand curve and positive marginal costs, profit-maximizing firms always sell less output at higher prices than do revenue-maximizing firms.

    D. Marginal cost must be falling for average cost to decline as output expands.

    E. Marginal profit is the difference between marginal revenue and marginal cost and always equals zero at the profit-maximizing activity level.

P2.4 **Marginal Analysis: Tables.** Lucy Carmichael is a regional sales representative for Dental Laboratories, Inc. Carmichael sells alloy products created from gold, silver, platinum, and other precious metals to several dental laboratories in Maine, New Hampshire, and Vermont. Carmichael's goal is to maximize her total monthly commission income, which is figured at 7.5 percent of gross sales. In reviewing her monthly experience over the past year, Carmichael found the following relations between days spent in each state and monthly sales generated:

Maine		New Hampshire		Vermont	
Days	Gross Sales	Days	Gross Sales	Days	Gross Sales
0	$ 4,000	0	$ 0	0	$ 2,500
1	10,000	1	3,500	1	5,000
2	15,000	2	6,500	2	7,000
3	19,000	3	9,000	3	8,500
4	22,000	4	10,500	4	9,500
5	24,000	5	11,500	5	10,000
6	25,000	6	12,000	6	10,000
7	25,000	7	12,500	7	10,000

A. Construct a table showing Carmichael's marginal sales per day in each state.

B. If administrative duties limit Carmichael to only ten selling days per month, how should she spend them?

C. Calculate Carmichael's maximum monthly commission income.

P2.5   **Marginal Analysis: Tables.** William Riker, account supervisor for Control Enterprises, Inc., estimates that sales of defective thermostats cost the firm an average of $25 each for replacement or repair. An independent engineering consultant has recommended hiring quality control inspectors so that defective thermostats can be identified and corrected before shipping. The following schedule shows the expected relation between the number of quality control inspectors and the thermostat failure rate, defined in terms of the percentage of total shipments that prove to be defective:

Number of Quality Control Inspectors	Thermostat Failure Rate (%)
0	5.0
1	4.0
2	3.2
3	2.6
4	2.2
5	2.0

The firm expects to ship 250,000 thermostats during the coming year, and quality control inspectors each command a salary of $30,000 per year.

A. Construct a table showing the marginal failure reduction (in units) and the dollar value of these reductions for each inspector hired.

B. How many inspectors should the firm hire?

C. How many inspectors would be hired if additional indirect costs (lost customer goodwill and so on) were to average 30 percent of direct replacement or repair costs?

P2.6   **Profit Maximization: Equations.** Business Applications Software, Inc., develops and markets software packages for business computers. Although sales have grown rapidly during recent years, the company's management fears that a recent onslaught of new competitors may severely retard future growth opportunities. Therefore, the marketing director, Gloria Stivic, believes that the time has come to "get big or get out."

The marketing and accounting departments have provided management with the following monthly demand and cost information:

$$P = \$1,000 - \$1Q.$$
$$TC = \$50,000 + \$100Q.$$

A. Calculate monthly quantity, price, and profit at the short-run revenue-maximizing output level.

B. Calculate these same values for the short-run profit-maximizing level of output.

C. When would short-run revenue maximization lead to long-run profit maximization?

P2.7 **Order Cost Minimization.** Inventory management is an area in which the calculus of optimization is a valuable technique for decision making. Assume that usage of a specific inventory item is evenly distributed over time and that delivery of additional units is instantaneous once an order has been placed. Under these conditions, annual costs for acquisition and inventory of the item are as follows:

$$\text{Purchase Costs} = P \cdot X,$$

$$\text{Order Costs} = \Theta \cdot \frac{X}{Q},$$

and

$$\text{Carrying Costs} = C \cdot \frac{Q}{2},$$

where P is the purchase price per unit, X is the total quantity used per year, Θ is the cost of placing an order, Q is the quantity of the item ordered at any one point in time, and C is the per-unit inventory carrying cost (insurance, storage, investment cost, etc.). Thus, annual total costs associated with this inventory item are given by the expression

$$TC = PX + \Theta \frac{X}{Q} + C \frac{Q}{2}.$$

Inventory costs can be minimized by selecting an optimal order quantity, Q, sometimes called the economic order quantity, or EOQ. Develop an expression for determining the optimal EOQ by minimizing the preceding total cost function with respect to Q, the order quantity.

P2.8 **Average Cost Minimization.** Giant Screen TV, Inc., is a San Diego-based manufacturer and distributor of customized, 50-inch high-resolution television monitors for individual and commercial customers. Revenue and cost relations are

$$TR = \$5,100Q - \$0.25Q^2.$$

$$TC = \$7,200,000 + \$600Q + \$0.2Q^2.$$

A. Calculate output, marginal cost, average cost, price, and profit at the average cost-minimizing activity level.
B. Calculate these values at the profit-maximizing activity level.
C. Compare and discuss your answers to Parts A and B.

P2.9 **Lagrangian Multipliers.** Amos Jones and Andrew Brown own and operate Amos & Andy, Inc., a Minneapolis-based installer of conversion packages for vans manufactured by the major auto companies. Amos & Andy has fixed capital and labor expenses of $1.2 million per year, and variable materials expenses average $2,000 per van conversion. Recent operating experience suggests the following annual demand relation for Amos & Andy products:

$$Q = 1,000 - 0.1P,$$

where Q is the number of van conversions (output) and P is price.

A. Calculate Amos & Andy's profit-maximizing output, price, and profit levels.

B. Using the Lagrangian multiplier method, calculate profit-maximizing output, price, and profit levels in light of a parts shortage that limits Amos & Andy's output to 300 conversions during the coming year.

C. Calculate and interpret λ, the Lagrangian multiplier.

D. Calculate the value to Amos & Andy of having the parts shortage eliminated.

P2.10 **Not-for-Profit Analysis.** Bellview Health Center, Ltd., (BHC), is a non-profit foundation providing medical treatment to emotionally distressed children in the Seattle, Washington area. BHC has hired you as a business consultant to aid the foundation in the development of a hiring policy that would be consistent with its overall goal of providing the most patient service possible given scarce foundation resources. In your initial analysis, you have determined that service (Q) can be described as a function of medical (M) and social service (S) staff input as follows:

$$Q = M + 0.5S + 0.5MS - S^2.$$

BHC's staff budget for the coming year is $1.2 million. Annual employment costs are $30,000 for each social service staff member and $60,000 for each medical staff member.

A. Construct the Lagrangian function that you would use to determine the optimal or service-maximizing social service/medical staff employment combination.

B. Determine the optimal combination of social service and medical staff for BHC.

C. Solve for and interpret the Lagrangian multiplier in this problem.

D. Calculate the expected average cost per service unit during the coming period. Are average costs rising, falling, or constant?

CASE STUDY FOR CHAPTER 2

A Spreadsheet Approach to Finding the Economic Order Quantity

A spreadsheet is a table of data organized in a logical framework similar to an accounting income statement or balance sheet. At first this marriage of computers and accounting information might seem like a minor innovation. It is not. For example, with computerized spreadsheets it becomes possible to easily reflect the effects on revenue, cost, and profit of a slight change in demand conditions. Similarly, the effects on profit-maximizing or breakeven activity levels can be easily determined. Various "what if?" scenarios can also be tested to determine the optimal or profit-maximizing activity level under a wide variety of operating conditions. Thus, it becomes easy to quantify in dollar terms the pluses and minuses (revenues and costs) of alternate decisions. Each operating and planning decision can be easily evaluated in light of available alternatives. Through the use of spreadsheet formulas and so-called "macros," managers are able to locate maximum or minimum values for any objective function based on the relevant marginal relations. Therefore, spreadsheets are a very useful tool that can be used to analyze a variety of typical optimization problems.

To illustrate the use of spreadsheets in economic analysis, consider the case of the Neighborhood Pharmacy, Inc. (NPI), a small but rapidly growing operator of a number of large-scale discount pharmacies in the greater Boston, Massachusetts, metropolitan area. A key contributor to the overall success of the company is a system of tight controls over inventory acquisition and carrying costs. The company's total annual costs for acquisition and inventory of pharmaceutical items are composed of the purchase cost of individual products supplied by wholesalers (purchase costs); the clerical, transportation, and other costs associated with placing each individual order (order costs); and the interest, insurance, and other expenses involved with carrying inventory (carrying costs). The company's total inventory-related costs are given by the expression:

$$TC = P \cdot X + \Theta \cdot X/Q + C \cdot Q/2,$$

where TC is inventory-related total costs during the planning period, P is the purchase price of the inventory item, X is the total quantity of the inventory item that is to be ordered (used) during the planning period (use requirement), Θ is the cost of placing an individual order for the inventory item (order cost), C is inventory carrying costs expressed on a per unit of inventory basis (carrying cost), and Q is the quantity of inventory ordered at any one point in time (order quantity). Here Q is NPI's decision variable, whereas each other variable contained in the total cost function is beyond control of the firm (exogenous). In analyzing this total cost relation, NPI is concerned with picking the order quantity that will minimize total inventory-related costs. The optimal or total cost minimizing order quantity is typically referred to as the "economic order quantity."

During the relevant planning period, the per unit purchase cost for an important prescribed (ethical) drug is $P = \$4$, the total estimated use for the planning period is $X = 5,000$, the cost of placing an order is $\Theta = \$50$; and the per unit carrying cost is $C = \$0.50$, calculated as the current interest rate of 12.5 percent multiplied by the per unit purchase cost of the item.

A. Set up a table or spreadsheet for NPI's order quantity (Q), inventory-related total cost (TC), purchase price (P), use requirement (X), order cost (Θ), and carrying cost (C). Establish a range for Q from 0 to 2,000 in increments of 100 (i.e., 0, 100, 200, . . . , 2,000).

B. Based on the NPI table or spreadsheet, determine the order quantity that will minimize the company's inventory-related total costs during the planning period.

C. Placing inventory-related total costs, TC, on the vertical or y-axis and the order quantity, Q, on the horizontal or x-axis, plot the relation between inventory-related total costs and the order quantity.

D. Based on the same data as previously, set up a table or spreadsheet for NPI's order quantity (Q), inventory-related total cost (TC) and each component part of total costs, including inventory purchase (acquisition) costs, $P \cdot X$; total order costs, $\Theta \cdot X/Q$; and total carrying costs, $C \cdot Q/2$. Placing inventory-related total costs, TC, and each component cost category as dependent variables on the vertical or y-axis and the order quantity, Q, as the independent variable on the horizontal or x-axis, plot the relation between inventory-related cost categories and the order quantity.

Selected References

Alston, Richard M., J. R. Kearl, and Michael B. Vaugham. "Is There a Consensus among Economists in the 1990s?" *American Economic Review* 82 (May 1992): 203–209.

Bagchi, Prabir, and Ramesh P. Rao. "Decision Making in Mergers: An Application of the Analytic Hierarchy Process." *Managerial and Decision Economics* 13 (March–April 1992): 91–99.

Bar-Yosef, Sasson, and Pradyot K. Sen. "On Optimal Choice of Inventory Accounting Method." *Accounting Review* 67 (April 1992): 320–336.

Button, Kenneth J., and Thomas G. Weyman-Jones. "Ownership Structure, Institutional Organization, and Measured X-Efficiency." *American Economic Review* 82 (May 1992): 439–445.

Cappelli, Peter. "Examining Managerial Displacement." *Academy of Management Journal* 35 (March 1992): 203–217.

Conner, Patrick E. "Decision-Making Participation Patterns: The Role of Organizational Context." *Academy of Management Journal* 35 (March 1992): 218–231.

Debru, Gerard. "The Mathematization of Economic Theory." *American Economic Review* 81 (March 1991): 1–7.

Friedman, David. "Choosing Metarules for Legal Change." *American Economic Review* 82 (May 1992): 285–289.

Gander, James P. "Managerial Intensity, Firm Size and Growth." *Managerial and Decision Economics* 12 (June 1991): 261–266.

Hahn, Robert W., and Robert N. Stavins. "Economic Incentives for Environmental Protection: Integrating Theory and Practice." *American Economic Review* 82 (May 1992): 464–468.

Hunt, Shelby D. "For Reason and Realism in Marketing." *Journal of Marketing* 56 (April 1992): 89–102.

Kirman, Alan P. "Whom or What Does the Representative Individual Represent?" *Journal of Economic Perspectives* 6 (Spring 1992): 117–136.

Kumar, Nirmalya, Louis W. Stern, and Ravi S. Achral. "Assessing Reseller Performance from the Perspective of the Supplier." *Journal of Marketing Research* 29 (May 1992): 238–253.

Liebeskind, Julia, Margarethe Wiersema, and Gary Hansen. "LBOs, Corporate Restructuring, and the Incentive-Intensity Hypothesis." *Financial Management* 21 (Spring 1992): 73–88.

MATH ANALYSIS FOR MANAGERS

This appendix is designed to provide a brief, selective treatment of mathematical terms and methods commonly employed in managerial economics. The first section covers basic properties of real numbers that help us understand how to solve equations. It is followed by an explanation of the use of exponents and radicals. The next section describes the fundamentals of equations, their different forms, and the operations used to manipulate them. The following section explains the use of logarithms. The final section covers some basic rules for differentiating a function to find its marginal.

PROPERTIES OF REAL NUMBERS

This section reviews some important properties of real numbers. These properties are basic to the understanding of how to manipulate numerical values.

Transitive Property

If X, Y, and Z are real numbers, then

$$\text{if } X = Y \text{ and } Y = Z, X = Z.$$

If two numbers are both equal to a third number, they are equal to each other. For example, if $X = Y$ and $Y = 5$, then $X = 5$.

Commutative Properties

If X and Y are real numbers, then

$$X + Y = Y + X \text{ and } XY = YX.$$

This means that numbers can be added or multiplied in any order. For example, $2 + 3 = 3 + 2 = 5$ and $2(3) = 3(2) = 6$.

Associative Properties

If X, Y, and Z are real numbers, then

$$X + (Y + Z) = (X + Y) + Z \text{ and } X(YZ) = (XY)Z.$$

For purposes of addition or multiplication, numbers can be grouped in any convenient manner. For example, $3 + (4 + 5) = (3 + 4) + 5 = 12$ and $3(4 \times 5) = (3 \times 4)5 = 60$.

Distributive Properties

If X, Y, and Z are real numbers, then

$$X(Y + Z) = XY + XZ \text{ and } (X + Y)Z = XZ + YZ.$$

This means that within the context of an equation, the order of addition or multiplication is immaterial; that is, it is possible to first multiply and then add, or vice versa. For example, $3(4 + 5) = 3(4) + 3(5) = 27$ and $3(4 + 5) = 3(9) = 27$.

Inverse Properties

For each real number X, there is a number $-X$, called the *additive inverse* or *negative* of X, where

$$X + (-X) = 0.$$

For example, since $5 + (-5) = 0$, the additive inverse of 5 is -5. Similarly, the additive inverse of -5 is 5. For each real number X, there also is a unique number, X^{-1}, called the *multiplicative inverse* or *reciprocal* of X, where

$$X \cdot \frac{1}{X} = \frac{X}{X} = 1.$$

The expression $1/X$ can be written X^{-1}, so $X(1/X) = X \cdot X^{-1} = X/X = 1$. For example, $4(1/4) = 4 \cdot 4^{-1} = 4/4 = 1$. This property holds for all real numbers except 0, for which the reciprocal is undefined.

Exponents and Radicals

Exponents and radicals can be thought of as abbreviations in the language of mathematics. For example,

$$X \cdot X \cdot X = X^3.$$

In general, for a positive integer n, X^n is an abbreviation for the product of n Xs. In X^n, the letter X is called the *base* and the letter n the *exponent* (or *power*). If $Y = X^n$, X is called the nth root of Y. For example, $2 \cdot 2 \cdot 2 = 2^3 = 8$, and 2 is the third root of 8. Any number raised to the first power equals itself, $X^1 = X$ (for example, $7^1 = 7$), and any number raised to the zero power equals one—that is, $X^0 = 1$ for $X \neq 0$ (0^0 is not defined). Some numbers do not have an nth root that is a real number. For example, since the second power, or square, of any real number is nonnegative, there is no real number that is the second, or square, root of -9.

It is also common to write

$$\underbrace{\frac{1}{X \cdot X \cdot X \ldots \cdot X}}_{N \text{ factors}} = \frac{1}{X^N} = X^{-N}.$$

This implies that $1/X^{-N} = X^N$. In general, whenever a number raised to a power is moved from the numerator (top) to the denominator (bottom) of an expression, the sign of the exponent, or power, is multiplied by -1, and vice versa. For example, $1/(2 \cdot 2 \cdot 2) = 1/2^3 = 2^{-3} = 0.125$.

The symbol $\sqrt[n]{X}$ is called a *radical*. Here n is the *index*, $\sqrt{}$ is the *radical sign*, and X is the *radicand*. For convenience, the index is usually omitted in the case of principal square roots, $\sqrt{X}$ is written instead of $\sqrt[2]{X}$. Therefore, $\sqrt{16} = \sqrt[2]{16} = 4$. If X is positive and M and N are integers where N is also positive, then

$$\sqrt[N]{X^M} = X^{M/N}.$$

For example, $\sqrt{2^4} = 2^{4/2} = 2^2 = 4$. Similarly, $\sqrt{9} = 9^{1/2} = 3$.

The basic rule for multiplication is $X^M \cdot X^N = X^{M+N}$ and for division is $X^M/X^N = X^{M-N}$. For example, $3^3 \cdot 3^2 = 3^{3+2} = 3^5 = 243$, and $3^3/3^2 = 3^{3-2} = 3^1 = 3$.

EQUATIONS

A statement that two algebraic expressions are equal is called an *equation*. The two expressions that make up an equation are called its *members* or *sides*. They are separated by the symbol $=$, which is called an *equality sign* or *equal sign*. In solving an equation or finding its roots, it is often possible to manipulate the original equation to generate another equation that is somewhat easier to solve.

Equivalent Operations

There are three operations that can be performed on equations without changing their solution values; hence, the original and subsequent equations are called *equivalent*. These operations are:

Addition (Subtraction) Operation. Equivalence is maintained when adding (subtracting) the same variable to (from) both sides of an equation, where the variable is the same as that occurring in the original equation. For example, if $6X = 20 + 2X$, subtracting $2X$ from both sides gives the equivalent equation $4X = 20$.

Multiplication (Division) Operation. Equivalence is maintained when multiplying (dividing) both sides of an equation by the same nonzero constant. For example, if $4X = 20$, dividing both sides by 4 gives the equivalent equation $X = 5$.

Replacement Operation. Equivalence is maintained when replacing either side of an equation by an equivalent expression. For example, if $X(X - 4) = 3$, replacing the left side by the equivalent expression $X^2 - 4X$ gives an equivalent equation $X^2 - 4X = 3$.

It is worth emphasizing that each of these operations can be applied to any equation with the effect that the resulting equation is mathematically identical to the original.

Equations may take a wide variety of functional forms. Three of the more frequently encountered are described next.

Linear Equations

An equation *linear* in the variable X can be written

$$aX + b = 0,$$

where a and b are constants and a is called the slope *coefficient* and b the *intercept*.

A linear equation is sometimes referred to as a *first-degree equation* or an *equation of degree one*. To solve the linear equation $2X + 6 = 14$, it is necessary to apply the subtraction and division operations to find $2X = 8$ and $X = 4$.

Quadratic Equations   An equation *quadratic* in the variable X can be written

$$aX^2 + bX + c = 0,$$

where a, b, and c are constants and $a \neq 0$. Here a and b are slope coefficients and c is the intercept.

A quadratic equation is sometimes referred to as a *second-degree equation* or an *equation of degree two*. Whereas linear equations have only one root, quadratic equations sometimes have two different roots. The solutions to quadratic equations are easily found through application of the *quadratic* formula. If $aX^2 + bX + c = 0$ and a, b, and c are constants where $a \neq 0$, then

$$X = \frac{-b \pm \sqrt{b^2 - 4ac}}{2a}.$$

The solutions for the values of X are called the *roots* of the quadratic equation. For example, if $2X^2 - 15X + 18 = 0$, then $X = 15 \pm \sqrt{225 - 4(2)(18)}/2(2) = (15 \pm 9)/4 = 6$ and 1.5. In many instances, one of the solved values for a quadratic equation is negative (or both values are negative). If the quadratic equation is a profit function and X is output, for example, any root $X < 0$, implying negative output, is mathematically correct but meaningless from an economic standpoint. Therefore, when applying the quadratic formula to problems in managerial economics, one must use judgment to identify those solution values that are both mathematically correct and economically relevant.

Multiplicative Equations   An equation *multiplicative* in the variables X and Z can be written

$$Y = aX^{b_1}Z^{b_2},$$

where a is the constant and b_1 and b_2 are exponents.

For example, $Y = 5XZ^3$, where $X = 3$ and $Z = 4$, has the solution $Y = 5(3^2)(4^3) = 5(9)(64) = 2,880$. Multiplicative equations are often employed in managerial economics, particularly in demand, production, and cost analyses.

Exponential Functions   Certain multiplicative functions are referred to as *exponential functions*. The function $Y = b^x$, where $b > 0$, $b \neq 1$, and X is any real number, is referred to as an *exponential function to the base b*. Exponential functions often are constructed using e, the Naperian Constant ($= 2.71828 \ldots$) as a base. Thus, for example, the equation $Y = e^2$ means $Y = (2.71828 \ldots)^2$. While e may seem a curious number to adopt as the base in an exponential function, it is usefully employed in economic studies of compound growth or decline.

Logarithmic Functions   For the purposes of economic analysis, multiplicative or exponential relations often are transformed into a linear *logarithmic form,* where

$$Y = \log_b X \text{ if and only if } X = b^Y.$$

Here Y is a *logarithmic function to the base b*. $Y = \log_b X$ is the logarithmic form of the exponential $X = b^Y$. For example, $\log^{10} 1{,}000 = 3$ is the logarithmic equivalent of the exponential $10^3 = 1{,}000$. For much of the work in managerial economics, logarithms are written using either the base 10, called *common logarithms,* or the base e ($=$ Naperian Constant $= 2.71828 \ldots$), called *natural logarithms.* Natural logarithms typically are denoted by the notation "ln" rather than "$\log_e$."

Some important basic properties of logarithms are as follows:

Product Property.   The logarithm of a product is the sum of logarithms:

$$\ln XY = \ln X + \ln Y.$$

For example, $\ln 6 = \ln (3 \cdot 2) = \ln 3 + \ln 2 = 1.099 + 0.693 = 1.792$. It is important to note that the logarithm of a sum is *not* the sum of logarithms.

Quotient Property.   The logarithm of a quotient is the difference of logarithms:

$$\ln \frac{X}{Y} = \ln X - \ln Y.$$

For example, $\ln 1.5 = \ln 3/2 = \ln 3 - \ln 2 = 1.099 - 0.693 = 0.406$. Here, note that the logarithm of a quotient is *not* the quotient of logarithms.

Power Property.   The logarithm of a number X raised to the exponent n, X^n, is the exponent times the logarithm of X:

$$\ln X^n = n \ln X.$$

For example, $\ln 9 = \ln 3^2 = 2 \ln 3 = 2(1.099) = 2.198$.

Using the properties of logarithms, there is a simple logarithmic transformation for any multiplicative or exponential function. For example, the logarithm transformation of the multiplicative equation $Y = 5X^2Z^3$ can be written $\ln Y = \ln 5 + 2 \ln X + 3 \ln Z$. Here the natural logarithm of X is used, although the transformation would be the same using common logs or logs to any other base.

It is important to recognize the symmetry between the logarithmic and exponential functions. It is an important property of each that

$$\ln e^X = X \text{ and } e^{\ln X} = X.$$

In words, the logarithm to the base e of the number e raised to the power X equals X. Similarly, the number e raised to the power $\ln X$ equals X. For example, $\ln e^1 = 1$ and $e^{\ln 1} = 1$. This means that any number or equation transformed into logarithmic form through use of logarithms can be converted back into original form through exponential transformation. For example, recall from earlier discussion that the multiplicative equation $Y = 5X^2Z^3$ has the logarithmic equivalent $\ln Y = \ln 5 + 2 \ln X + 3 \ln Z$. It follows that if $X = 3$ and $Z = 4$, then $Y = 5(3^2)(4^3) = 5(9)(64) = 2{,}880$ and $\ln Y = \ln 5 + 2 \ln 3 + 3 \ln 4 = 1.609 + 2.197 + 4.159 = 7.965$. Equivalence requires that $\ln 2{,}880 = 7.965$ and $e^{7.965} = 2{,}880$, which is indeed the case.

The practical relevance of this symmetry between logarithms and exponential functions is that, for example, a multiplicative demand relation can be analyzed

FIGURE 2A.1   Graph of a Constant Function: $Y = $ **Constant;** $dY/dX = 0$

If the value of Y does not vary with changes in X, then $dY/dX = 0$.

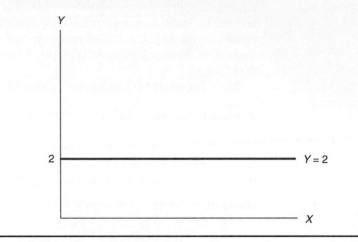

in linear logarithmic form using widely available computer software regression packages and converted back into original form through exponential transformation for purposes of numerical evaluation.

RULES FOR DIFFERENTIATING A FUNCTION

Determining the derivative of a function is not a particularly difficult task; it involves simply applying a basic formula to the function. This section presents the basic formulas or rules for differentiation. Proofs are omitted here but can be found in any introductory calculus textbook.

Constants

The derivative of a constant is always zero; that is, if Y is a constant, then

$$\frac{dY}{dX} = 0.$$

This situation is graphed in Figure 2A.1 for the example $Y = 2$. Since Y is defined as a constant, its value does not vary as X changes and, hence, dY/dX must be zero.

Powers

The derivative of a power function such as $Y = aX^b$, where a and b are constants, is equal to the exponent b multiplied by the coefficient a times the variable X raised to the $b - 1$ power:

$$Y = aX^b$$
$$\frac{dY}{dX} = b \cdot a \cdot X^{b-1}.$$

FIGURE 2A.2   **Graphs of Power Functions**

The derivative of the linear function $Y = 0.5X$ is constant. The derivative of the non-linear function $Y = X^3$ rises as X increases.

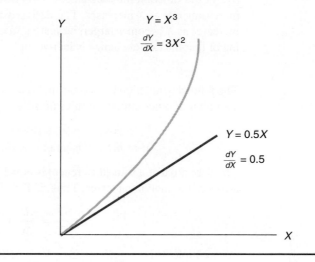

For example, given the function

$$Y = 2X^3,$$

then

$$\frac{dY}{dX} = 3 \cdot 2 \cdot X^{3-1}$$

$$= 6X^2.$$

Two further examples of power functions should clarify this rule. The derivative of the function $Y = X^3$ is given as

$$\frac{dY}{dX} = 3 \cdot X^2.$$

The exponent, 3, is multiplied by the implicit coefficient, 1, and in turn by the variable, X, raised to the second power.

Finally, the derivative of the function $Y = 0.5X$ is

$$\frac{dY}{dX} = 1 \cdot 0.5 \cdot X^0 = 0.5.$$

The implicit exponent, 1, is multiplied by the coefficient, 0.5, times the variable, X, raised to the zero power. Since any number raised to the zero power equals 1, the result is 0.5.

Again a graph may help clarify the power function concept. In Figure 2A.2, the last two power functions given above, $Y = X^3$ and $Y = 0.5X$, are graphed. Consider first $Y = 0.5X$. The derivative of this function, $dY/dX = 0.5$, is a constant, indicating that the slope of the function is a constant. This can be readily seen from the graph. The derivative measures the *rate of change*. If the rate of change is constant, as it must be if the basic function is linear, the derivative of the function must be constant. The second function, $Y = X^3$, rises at an increasing rate as X increases. The derivative of the function, $dY/dX = 3X^2$, also increases as X becomes larger, indicating that the slope of the function is increasing or that the rate of change is increasing.

Sums and Differences

The following notation is used throughout the remainder of this section to express a number of other important rules of differentiation:

$$U = g(X): U \text{ is an unspecified function, } g, \text{ of } X.$$
$$V = h(X): V \text{ is an unspecified function, } h, \text{ of } X.$$

The derivative of a sum (difference) is equal to the sum (difference) of the derivatives of the individual terms. Thus, if $Y = U + V$, then

$$\frac{dY}{dX} = \frac{dU}{dX} + \frac{dV}{dX}.$$

For example, if $U = g(X) = 2X^2$, $V = h(X) = -X^3$, and $Y = U + V = 2X^2 - X^3$, then

$$\frac{dY}{dX} = 4X - 3X^2.$$

Here the derivative of the first term, $2X^2$, is found to be $4X$ by the power rule; the derivative of the second term, $-X^3$, is found to be $-3X^2$ also by that rule; and the derivative of the total function is the sum of the derivatives of the parts.

Consider a second example of this rule. If $Y = 300 + 5X + 2X^2$, then

$$\frac{dY}{dX} = 0 + 5 + 4X.$$

The derivative of 300 is 0 by the constant rule; the derivative of $5X$ is 5 by the power rule; and the derivative of $2X^2$ is $4X$ by the power rule.

Products

The derivative of the product of two expressions is equal to the sum of the first term multiplied by the derivative of the second *plus* the second term times the derivative of the first. Thus, if $Y = U \cdot V$, then

$$\frac{dY}{dX} = U \cdot \frac{dV}{dX} + V \cdot \frac{dU}{dX}.$$

For example, if $Y = 3X^2(3 - X)$, then, letting $U = 3X^2$ and $V = (3 - X)$ gives

$$\frac{dY}{dX} = 3X^2\left(\frac{dV}{dX}\right) + (3 - X)\left(\frac{dU}{dX}\right)$$
$$= 3X^2(-1) + (3 - X)(6X)$$

$$= -3X^2 + 18X - 5X^2$$
$$= 18X - 9X^2.$$

The first factor, $3X^2$, is multiplied by the derivative of the second, -1, and added to the second factor, $3 - X$, times the derivative of the first, $6X$. Simplifying the expression results in the final expression shown above.

Quotients

The derivative of the quotient of two expressions is equal to the denominator multiplied by the derivative of the numerator *minus* the numerator times the derivative of the denominator, all divided by the square of the denominator. Thus, if $Y = U/V$, then

$$\frac{dY}{dX} = \frac{V \cdot \dfrac{dU}{dX} - U \cdot \dfrac{dV}{dX}}{V^2}.$$

For example, if $U = 2X - 3$ and $V = 6X^2$, then

$$Y = \frac{2X - 3}{6X^2}$$

and

$$\frac{dY}{dX} = \frac{6X^2 \cdot 2 - (2X - 3)12X}{36X^4}$$
$$= \frac{12X^2 - 24X^2 + 36X}{36X^4}$$
$$= \frac{36X - 12X^2}{36X^4}$$
$$= \frac{3 - X}{3X^3}.$$

The denominator, $6X^2$, is multiplied by the derivative of the numerator, 2. Subtracted from this is the numerator, $2X - 3$, times the derivative of the denominator, $12X$. The result is then divided by the square of the denominator, $36X^4$. Algebraic reduction results in the final expression of the derivative.

Logarithmic Functions

The derivative of a logarithmic function $Y = \ln X$ is given by the expression

$$\frac{dY}{dX} = \frac{d \ln X}{dX} = \frac{1}{X}.$$

This also implies that if $Y = \ln X$, then $dY = (1/X)dX = dX/X$. Since dX is the change in X by definition, dX/X is the percentage change in X. Derivatives of logarithmic functions have great practical relevance in managerial economics, given the prevalence of multiplicative (and hence linear in the logarithms) equations used to describe demand, production, and cost relations. For example, the expression $Y = aX^b$ has an equivalent logarithmic function $\ln Y = \ln a + b \ln X$, where $d \ln Y/d \ln X = dY/Y/dX/X = b$. Here b is called the *elasticity* of Y with respect to X, since it reflects the percentage effect on Y of a 1 percent change in X. The concept of elasticity is introduced and extensively examined in Chapter 5 and discussed throughout the remaining chapters.

Function of a Function (Chain Rule)

The derivative of a function of a function is found as follows: If $Y = f(U)$, where $U = g(X)$, then

$$\frac{dY}{dX} = \frac{dY}{dU} \cdot \frac{dU}{dX}.$$

For example, if $Y = 2U - U^2$ and $U = 2X^3$, then dY/dX is found as follows:
Step 1:

$$\frac{dY}{dU} = 2 - 2U.$$

Substituting for U creates the expression

$$\frac{dY}{dU} = 2 - 2(2X^3)$$
$$= 2 - 4X^3.$$

Step 2:

$$\frac{dU}{dX} = 6X^2.$$

Step 3:

$$\frac{dY}{dX} = \frac{dY}{dU} \cdot \frac{dU}{dX}$$
$$= (2 - 4X^3) \cdot 6X^2$$
$$= 12X^2 - 24X^5.$$

Further examples of this rule should indicate its usefulness in obtaining derivatives of many functions.
Example 1:

$$Y = \sqrt{X^2 - 1}$$

Let $U = X^2 - 1$. Then $Y = \sqrt{U} = U^{1/2}$.

$$\frac{dY}{dU} = \frac{1}{2} U^{-1/2}$$

$$= \frac{1}{2U^{1/2}}.$$

Substituting $X^2 - 1$ for U in the derivative results in

$$\frac{dY}{dU} = \frac{1}{2(X^2 - 1)^{1/2}}.$$

Since $U = X^2 - 1$,

$$\frac{dU}{dX} = 2X.$$

Using the function of a function rule, $dY/dX = dY/dU \cdot dU/dX$, so

$$\frac{dY}{dX} = \frac{1}{2(X^2 - 1)^{1/2}} \cdot 2X$$

$$= \frac{X}{\sqrt{X^2 - 1}}.$$

Example 2:

$$Y = \frac{1}{X^2 - 2}$$

Let $U = X^2 - 2$. Then $Y = 1/U$, and the quotient rule yields

$$\frac{dY}{dU} = \frac{U \cdot 0 - 1 \cdot 1}{U^2}$$

$$= -\frac{1}{U^2}.$$

Substituting $(X^2 - 2)$ for U obtains

$$\frac{dY}{dU} = -\frac{1}{(X^2 - 2)^2}.$$

Since $U = X^2 - 2$,

$$\frac{dU}{dX} = 2X.$$

Therefore,

$$\frac{dY}{dX} = \frac{dY}{dU} \cdot \frac{dU}{dX} = -\frac{1}{(X^2 - 2)^2} \cdot 2X$$

$$= -\frac{2X}{(X^2 - 2)^2}.$$

Example 3:

$$Y = (2X + 3)^2$$

Let $U = 2X + 3$. Then $Y = U^2$ and

$$\frac{dY}{dU} = 2U.$$

Since $U = 2X + 3$,

$$\frac{dY}{dU} = 2(2X + 3)$$
$$= 4X + 6$$

and

$$\frac{dU}{dX} = 2.$$

Thus,

$$\frac{dY}{dX} = \frac{dY}{dU} \cdot \frac{dU}{dX} = (4X + 6)2$$
$$= 8X + 12.$$

| # RISK ANALYSIS

Managers frequently know with certainty the outcomes that each possible course of action will produce. A firm with $100,000 in cash that can be invested in a 30-day Treasury bill yielding 6 percent ($493 interest for 30 days) or used to prepay a 10 percent bank loan ($822 interest for 30 days) can determine with certainty that prepayment of the bank loan provides a $329 higher one-month return. A retailer can just as easily predict the cost savings earned by placing a given order directly with the manufacturer versus through an independent wholesaler; manufacturers can often forecast the precise cost effect of meeting a rush order when overtime wages rather than standard labor rates are required. Order backlogs give a wide variety of consumer and producer goods manufacturers a clear indication of product demand conditions. Similarly, book, magazine, and trade journal publishers accurately judge product demand conditions on the basis of subscription revenues. Resort hotels can often foretell with a high degree of accuracy the amount of food, beverages, and linen service required to meet the daily needs of a 1,500-person convention, especially when such conventions are booked on a regular basis. Even when events cannot be predicted exactly, only a modest level of decision uncertainty is present in such situations.

Many other important managerial decisions are made under conditions of risk or uncertainty. **Economic risk** is the chance of loss because all possible outcomes and their probability of happening are unknown. Actions taken in such a decision environment are purely speculative, such as the buy and sell decisions made by traders and other speculators in commodity, futures, and options markets. In this type of risky decision environment, there is no such thing as an informed decision maker. All decision makers are equally likely to profit as well as to lose; luck is the sole determinant of success or failure. **Uncertainty** exists when the outcomes of managerial decisions cannot be predicted with absolute accuracy but all possibilities and their associated probabilities of occurrence are known. Under conditions of uncertainty, informed managerial decisions are possible. Experience, insight, and prudence allow managers to devise strategies for minimizing the chance of failing to meet business objectives. While luck still plays a role in determining ultimate success, managers can deal effectively with an uncertain decision environment by limiting the scope of individual projects and developing contingency plans for dealing with failure.

To assume that all future possibilities and their associated probabilities of happening are known with certainty involves an obvious abstraction from reality.

Economic risk

The chance of loss because all possible outcomes and their probability are unknown.

Uncertainty

A state that occurs when outcomes cannot be predicted with absolute accuracy but possibilities and probabilities are known.

81

Decision makers are seldom, if ever, able to precisely gauge future prospects and the chance that various end results will occur. However, practical experience is a powerful aide to decision making under uncertainty, and the range of probable outcomes can often be estimated with a high degree of reliability. General Mills, for example, is able to accurately predict demand for various lunch and dinner entrées at its Red Lobster restaurants on the basis of market demand data and store-specific information. Although the company's planning process cannot allow for all possible outcomes and future contingencies, it is able to minimize the chance of loss due to a shortage or surplus of inventory.

Successful companies incorporate risk analysis into their everyday decision making. When the level of risk and the attitudes toward risk taking are known, the effects of uncertainty can be directly reflected in the basic valuation model of the firm. The certainty equivalent method converts expected risky profit streams to their certain sum equivalents to eliminate value differences that result from different risk levels. For risk-averse decision makers, the value of a risky stream of payments is less than the value of a certain stream, and the application of certainty equivalent adjustment factors results in a downward adjustment in the value of expected returns. For risk-seeking decision makers, the value of a risky stream of payments is greater than that of a certain stream, and application of certainty equivalent adjustment factors results in an upward adjustment in the value of expected returns. In both cases, risky dollars are converted into certain-sum equivalents. Another method used to reflect uncertainty in the basic valuation model is the risk-adjusted discount rate approach. In this technique, the interest rate used in the denominator of the basic valuation model depends on the level of risk associated with a given cash flow. For highly risk-averse decision makers, higher discount rates are implemented; for less risk-averse decision makers, lower discount rates are employed. Using this technique, discounted expected profit streams reflect risk differences and become directly comparable.

This chapter begins by showing various means for assessing and measuring risk. The certainty equivalent and risk-adjusted discount rate approaches are then considered in detail. These are the two primary methods employed for adapting the basic valuation model to account for decisions made under conditions of uncertainty. Finally, decision trees, simulation, and game theory techniques are discussed as further aids to decision making under conditions of uncertainty.

PROBABILITY CONCEPTS

Business risk
The chance of loss.

Business risk is typically described as the chance of loss associated with a given managerial decision. Such losses are to be expected as a normal by-product of the unpredictable variation in product demand and cost conditions. Business risk must be dealt with effectively; it seldom can be eliminated. Risk is associated with the chance or probability of undesirable outcomes. The more likely an undesirable outcome, the riskier the decision. As such, a clear understanding of probability concepts provides a helpful background for discussing various methods for making effective managerial decisions under conditions of uncertainty.

The Probability Distribution

Probability
The chance of occurrence.

Probability distribution
A list of possible events and probabilities.

The **probability** of an event is the chance, or odds, that the incident will occur. If all possible events or outcomes are listed, and if a probability of occurrence is assigned to each event, the listing is called a **probability distribution.** For example, suppose a sales manager observes that there is a 70 percent chance that a given customer will place a specific order, versus a 30 percent chance that the customer will not. This situation is described by the following probability distribution:

Event (1)	Probability of Occurrence (2)
Receive order	0.7 = 70%
Do not receive order	0.3 = 30%
Total	1.0 = 100%

Both possible outcomes are listed in Column 1, and the probabilities of each outcome, expressed as decimals and percentages, appear in Column 2. Notice that the probabilities sum to 1.0, or 100 percent, as they must if the probability distribution is complete. In this very simple example, risk can be read from the probability distribution as the 30 percent chance of the firm not receiving the order. For most managerial decisions the relative desirability of alternative events or outcomes is not so absolute. A more general measure of the relation between risk and the probability distribution is typically required to adequately incorporate risk considerations into the decision-making process. The need for a more general measure of risk can be illustrated by the following example.

▶ Suppose that a firm is able to choose only one of two investment projects, each calling for an outlay of $10,000. Assume also that profits earned from the two projects are related to the general level of economic activity during the coming year, as shown in Table 3.1. This table is known as a **payoff matrix** since it illustrates the dollar outcome associated with each possible state of nature. Both projects provide a $5,000 profit in a normal economy, higher profits in an economic boom, and lower profits if a recession occurs. However, Project *B* profits vary far more according to the state of the economy than do profits from Project *A*. In a normal economy, both projects return $5,000 in profit. Should the economy be in a recession next year, Project *B* will produce nothing, whereas Project *A* still provides a $4,000 profit. If the economy is booming next year, Project *B*'s profit will increase to $12,000, but profit for Project *A* will increase only moderately, to $6,000.

Payoff matrix
A table that shows outcomes associated with each possible state of nature.

Project *A* is clearly more desirable if the economy is in recession, whereas Project *B* is superior in a boom. In a normal economy the projects offer the same profit potential, and both are equally desirable. To choose the best project, one needs to know the likelihood of a boom, a recession, or normal economic conditions. If such probabilities are available, the expected profits and variability of profits for each project can be determined. These measures make it possible to evaluate each project in terms of expected return and risk, where risk is measured by the deviation of profits from expected values.

TABLE 3.1   **Payoff Matrix for Projects** *A* **and** *B*

State of the Economy	Profits	
	Project *A*	Project *B*
Recession	$4,000	$ 0
Normal	5,000	5,000
Boom	6,000	12,000

TABLE 3.2   **Calculation of Expected Values**

	State of the Economy (1)	Probability of This State Occurring (2)	Profit Outcome if This State Occurs (3)	Expected Profit Outcome (4) = (2) × (3)
Project *A*	Recession	0.2	$ 4,000	$ 800
	Normal	0.6	5,000	3,000
	Boom	0.2	6,000	1,200
		1.0		Expected Profit *A* $5,000
Project *B*	Recession	0.2	$ 0	$ 0
	Normal	0.6	5,000	3,000
	Boom	0.2	12,000	2,400
		1.0		Expected Profit *B* $5,400

Expected Value

Expected value
Anticipated realization.

The **expected value** is the anticipated realization from a given payoff matrix and specified probability distribution. It is the *weighted average* payoff, where the weights are defined by the probability distribution.

To continue with the previous example, assume that forecasts based on the current trend in economic indicators suggest a two in ten chance of recession, a six in ten chance of a normal economy, and a two in ten chance of a boom. As probabilities, the probability of recession is 0.2, or 20 percent; the probability of normal economic activity is 0.6, or 60 percent; and the probability of a boom is 0.2, or 20 percent. These probabilities add up to 1.0 (0.2 + 0.6 + 0.2 = 1.0), or 100 percent, and thereby form a complete probability distribution, as shown in Table 3.2.

If each possible outcome is multiplied by its probability of happening and then summed, the weighted average outcomes are determined. In this calculation, the weights are the probabilities of occurrence, and the weighted average is called the expected outcome. Column 4 of Table 3.2 illustrates the calculation of expected profits for Projects *A* and *B*. Each possible profit level in Column 3 is multiplied by its probability of occurrence from Column 2 to obtain weighted values of the possible profits. Summing Column 4 of the table for each project gives a weighted average of profits under various states of the economy. This weighted average is the expected profit from the project.

The expected profit calculation is expressed by the equation

$$\text{Expected Profit} = E(\pi) = \sum_{i=1}^{N} \pi_i \times p_i. \qquad (3.1)$$

Here, π_i is the profit level associated with the ith outcome, p_i is the probability that outcome i will occur, and N is the number of possible outcomes or states of nature. Thus, $E(\pi)$ is a weighted average of possible outcomes (the π_i values), with each outcome's weight being equal to its probability of occurrence.

The expected profit for Project A is obtained as follows:

$$
\begin{aligned}
E(\pi_A) &= \sum_{i=1}^{3} \pi_i \times p_i \\
&= \pi_1 \times p_1 + \pi_2 \times p_2 + \pi_3 \times p_3 \\
&= \$4{,}000(0.2) + \$5{,}000(0.6) + \$6{,}000(0.2) \\
&= \$5{,}000.
\end{aligned}
$$

The results in Table 3.2 are shown as a bar chart in Figure 3.1. The height of each bar signifies the probability that a given outcome will occur. The range of probable outcomes for Project A is from \$4,000 to \$6,000, with an average, or expected, value of \$5,000. For Project B, the expected value is \$5,400 and the range of possible outcomes is from \$0 to \$12,000.

For simplicity, this example assumes that only three states of nature can exist in the economy: recession, normal, and boom. The actual state of the economy ranges from deep depression, as in the early 1930s, to tremendous booms, such as in the mid- to late 1980s, with an unlimited number of possibilities in between. Suppose sufficient information exists to assign a probability to each possible state of the economy and a monetary outcome in each circumstance for every project. A table similar to Table 3.2 could then be compiled that would include many more entries for Columns 1, 2, and 3. This table could be used to calculate expected values as shown, and the probabilities and outcomes could be approximated by the continuous curves in Figure 3.2.

Figure 3.2 is a graph of the probability distribution of returns for Projects A and B. In general, the tighter the probability distribution, the more likely it is that actual outcomes will be close to expected values. The more loose the probability distribution, the less likely it is that actual outcomes will be close to expected values. Because Project A has a relatively tight probability distribution, its actual profit is more likely to be close to its expected value than is that of Project B.

Absolute Risk Measurement

Absolute risk
Overall dispersion of possible payoffs.

Risk is a complex concept, and some controversy surrounds attempts to define and measure it. Common risk measures that are satisfactory for most purposes are based on the observation that tight probability distributions imply low risk because of the correspondingly small chance that actual outcomes will differ greatly from expected values. From this perspective, Project A is less risky than Project B.

Standard deviation, shown as σ (sigma), is a popular and useful risk measure of absolute risk. **Absolute risk** is the overall dispersion of possible payoffs. The

FIGURE 3.1   **Relation between State of the Economy and Project Returns**

Project *B* has a greater expected return and a higher dispersion in returns (risk) than Project *A*.

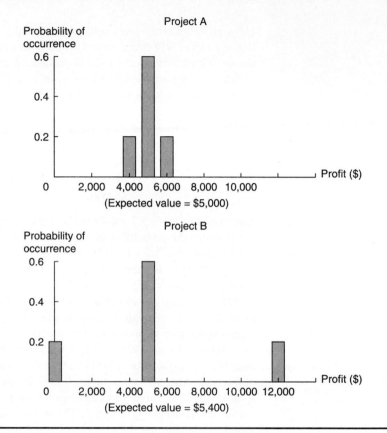

smaller the standard deviation, the tighter the probability distribution and the lower the risk in absolute terms. To calculate standard deviation using probability information, the expected value or mean of the return distribution must first be calculated as

$$\text{Expected Value} = E(\pi) = \sum_{i=1}^{N} (\pi_i p_i). \tag{3.2}$$

In this calculation, π_i is the profit or return associated with the ith outcome; p_i is the probability that the ith outcome will occur; and $E(\pi)$, the expected value, is a weighted average of the various possible outcomes, each weighted by the probability of its occurrence.

The deviation of possible outcomes from the expected value must then be derived:

$$\text{Deviation}_i = \pi_i - E(\pi).$$

FIGURE 3.2 **Probability Distributions Showing Relation between State of the Economy and Project Returns**

The actual return from Project *A* is likely to be close to the expected value. It is less likely that the actual return from Project *B* will be close to the expected value.

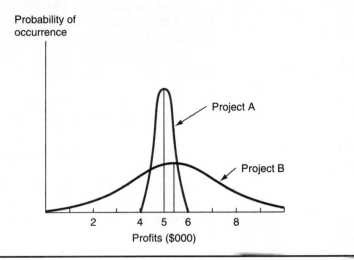

The squared value of each deviation is then multiplied by the relevant probability of occurrence and summed. This arithmetic mean of the squared deviations is the variance of the probability distribution:

$$\text{Variance} = \sigma^2 = \sum_{i=1}^{N} [\pi_i - E(\pi)]^2 p_i. \tag{3.3}$$

The standard deviation is found by obtaining the square root of the variance:

$$\text{Standard Deviation} = \sigma = \sqrt{\sum_{i=1}^{N} [\pi_i - E(\pi)]^2 p_i}. \tag{3.4}$$

The standard deviation of profit for Project *A* can be calculated to illustrate this procedure:

Deviation $[\pi_i - E(\pi)]$	Deviation² $[\pi_i - E(\pi)]^2$	Deviation² × Probability $[\pi_i - E(\pi)]^2 \times p_i$
$4,000 − $5,000 = − $1,000	$1,000,000	$1,000,000(0.2) = $200,000
$5,000 − $5,000 = $0	$0	$0(0.6) = $0
$6,000 − $5,000 = $1,000	$1,000,000	$1,000,000(0.2) = $200,000
		Variance = σ^2 = $400,000

$$\text{Standard Deviation} = \sigma = \sqrt{\sigma^2} = \sqrt{\$400,000} = \$632.46$$

Using the same procedure, the standard deviation of Project *B*'s profit is $3,826.23. Since Project *B* has a larger standard deviation of profit, it is the riskier project.

Relative Risk Measurement

Problems sometimes arise when the standard deviation is used as the measure of risk. If an investment project is relatively expensive and has large expected cash flows, it will have a large standard deviation of returns without being truly riskier than a smaller project. Suppose a project has an expected return of $1 million and a standard deviation of only $1,000. Some might reasonably argue that it is less risky than an alternative investment project with expected returns of $1,000 and a standard deviation of $900. The *absolute* risk of the first project is greater, and the risk of the second project is much larger relative to the expected payoff. **Relative risk** is the variation in possible returns compared with the expected payoff amount.

Relative risk
The variation in possible returns compared with the expected payoff amount.

A popular method for determining relative risk is to calculate the coefficient of variation. Using probability concepts, the coefficient of variation is as follows:

$$\text{Coefficient of Variation} = v = \frac{\sigma}{E(\pi)}. \tag{3.5}$$

In general, when comparing decision alternatives with costs and benefits that are not of approximately equal size, the coefficient of variation measures relative risk better than does the standard deviation.

Other Risk Measures

The standard deviation and coefficient of variation risk measures are based upon the *total* variability of returns. In some situations, however, a project's total variability overstates its risk. This is because projects with returns that are less than perfectly correlated can be combined, and the variability of the resulting portfolio of investment projects is less than the sum of individual project risks. Much recent work in finance is based on the idea that a project's risk should be measured in terms of its contribution to total return variability on the firm's asset portfolio. The contribution of a single investment project to the overall variation of the firm's asset portfolio is measured by a concept known as *beta*. **Beta** is a measure of the systematic variability or covariance of one asset's returns with returns on other assets.

Beta
A measure of the systematic variability of one asset's returns with returns on other assets.

The concept of beta is discussed fully in Chapter 16 and should be employed when the returns from potential investment projects are likely to greatly affect or be greatly affected by current projects. However, in most circumstances the standard deviation and coefficient of variation measures provide adequate assessments of risk.

THE STANDARD NORMAL CONCEPT

Managers often estimate the scope of investment project payoff possibilities to construct a range of optimistic and pessimistic scenarios. Once this has been done, the risk of a given course of action can be characterized in terms of the distribution of possible outcome values. The standard normal concept is an intuitive and practical means for assessing the dispersion of possible outcomes in terms of the expected value and standard deviation measures.

FIGURE 3.3   **Probability Ranges for a Normal Distribution**

When returns display a normal distribution, actual outcomes will lie within ± 1 standard deviation of the mean 68.26 percent of the time, within ± 2 standard deviations 95.46 percent of the time, and within ± 3 standard deviations 99.74 percent of the time.

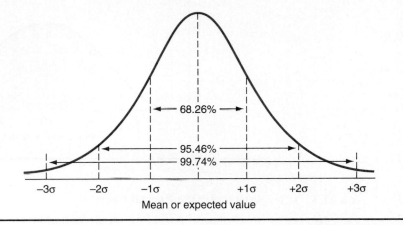

Notes:

a. The area under the normal curve equals 1.0, or 100 percent. Thus, the areas under any pair of normal curves drawn on the same scale, whether they are peaked or flat, must be equal.

b. Half of the area under a normal curve is to the left of the mean, indicating a 50 percent probability that the actual outcome will be less than the mean and a 50 percent probability that it will be greater than the mean.

c. Of the area under the curve, 68.26 percent is within ± 1σ of the mean, indicating that the odds are 68.26 percent that the actual outcome will be within the range (mean − 1σ) to (mean + 1σ).

d. For a normal distribution, the larger the value of σ, the greater the probability that the actual outcome will vary widely from, and hence perhaps be far below, the most likely outcome. Since "risk" is the odds of having the actual results turn out to be bad, and since σ measures these odds, σ is a measure of risk.

The Normal Distribution

Normal distribution
A symmetrical distribution about the mean or expected value.

The relation among risk, standard deviation, and the coefficient of variation can be clarified by examining the characteristics of a normal distribution, as shown in Figure 3.3. A **normal distribution** has a symmetrical distribution about the mean or expected value. If a probability distribution is normal, the actual outcome will lie within ± 1 standard deviation of the mean roughly 68 percent of the time; the probability that the actual outcome will be within ± 2 standard deviations of the expected outcome is approximately 95 percent; and there is a greater than 99 percent probability that the actual outcome will occur within ± 3 standard deviations of the mean. The smaller the standard deviation, the tighter the distribution about the expected value and the smaller the probability of an outcome that is very different from the expected value.

Probability distributions can be viewed as a series of *discrete values* represented by a bar chart, such as in Figure 3.1, or as a *continuous function* represented by a smooth curve, such as that in Figure 3.2. The probabilities associated with the outcomes in Figure 3.1 are given by the *heights* of the bars, whereas in Figure 3.2, the probabilities must be found by calculating the area under the curve

FIGURE 3.4 **Continuous Probability Distribution**

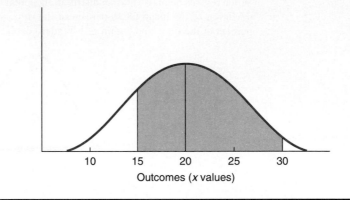

TABLE 3.3 **Area under the Normal Curve**

z^a	Area from the Mean to the Point of Interest	Ordinate
0.0	0.0000	0.3989
0.5	0.1915	0.3521
1.0	0.3413	0.2420
1.5	0.4332	0.1295
2.0	0.4773	0.0540
2.5	0.4938	0.0175
3.0	0.4987	0.0044

[a] z is the number of standard deviations from the mean. Some area tables are set up to indicate the area to the left or right of the point of interest; in this book, we indicate the area between the mean and the point of interest.

between points of interest. Consider, for example, the continuous probability distribution shown in Figure 3.4. This is a normal curve with a mean of 20 and a standard deviation of 5; x could be dollars of sales, profits, or costs; units of output; percentage rates of return; or any other units. To learn the probability that an outcome will fall between 15 and 30, one must calculate the area beneath the curve between these points, the shaded area in the diagram.

The area under the curve between 15 and 30 can be determined by painstaking graphic analysis or, since the distribution is normal, by reference to tables of the area under the normal curve, such as Table 3.3 or Appendix B to this book. To use these tables, it is necessary to know only the mean and standard deviation of the distribution.

Standardized Variables

Any distribution of costs or revenues to be investigated must first be transformed or standardized. A **standardized variable** has a mean of 0 and a standard deviation equal to 1. Any distribution of revenue, cost, or profit data can be standardized with the following formula:

$$z = \frac{x - \mu}{\sigma},\tag{3.6}$$

Standardized variable

A variable with a mean of 0 and a standard deviation equal to 1.

where z is the standardized variable, x is the outcome of interest, and μ and σ are the mean and standard deviation of the distribution, respectively. If the point of interest is 1σ away from the mean, then $x - \mu = \sigma$, so $z = \sigma/\sigma = 1.0$. When $z = 1.0$, the point of interest is 1σ away from the mean; when $z = 2$, the value is 2σ away from the mean; and so on.

In the present example, the probability that an outcome will fall between 15 and 30 can be easily calculated. Using Equation 3.6, these points of interest are normalized as follows:

$$z_1 = \frac{15 - 20}{5} = -1, \qquad z_2 = \frac{30 - 20}{5} = 2.$$

The negative sign on z_1 is ignored, since the normal curve is symmetrical around the mean; the minus sign merely indicates that the point of interest lies to the left of the mean. A plus sign (or no sign) indicates that a point of interest lies to the right of the mean. The areas under the normal curve associated with these z values are found in Table 3.3 to be 0.3413 and 0.4773. This means that the probability is 0.3413, or 34.13 percent, that the actual outcome will fall between 15 and 20, and 0.4773, or 47.73 percent, that it will fall between 20 and 30. Summing these probabilities shows that the probability of an outcome falling between 15 and 30 is 0.8186, or 81.86 percent.

Suppose that one is interested in determining the probability that an actual outcome would be greater than 15. Note that the probability is 0.3413, or 34.13 percent, that an outcome will be between 15 and 20, then observe that the probability is 0.5000, or 50 percent, of an outcome greater than the mean, 20. The probability is $0.3413 + 0.5000 = 0.8413$, or 84.13 percent, that a given outcome will exceed 15.

Some interesting properties of normal probability distributions can be seen by examining Table 3.3 and Figure 3.3, which is a graph of the normal curve. For any normal distribution, the probability of an outcome falling within ± 1 standard deviation from the mean is 0.6826, or 68.26 percent ($= 0.3413 \times 2.0$); the probability of an outcome falling within 2 standards of the mean is 95.46 percent; and 99.74 percent of all outcomes will fall within 3 standard deviations of the mean. Although the standard normal distribution theoretically runs from minus infinity to plus infinity, the probability of occurrences beyond 3 standard deviations is very near zero.

Use of the Standard Normal Concept: An Example

▶

An example illustrates use of the standard normal concept in managerial decision making. Suppose that the Harry Morton Realty is considering a boost in advertising in an attempt to reduce a large inventory of unsold homes. The firm's management plans to make its media decision using the data shown in Table 3.4 on the expected success of television versus newspaper promotions. For simplicity, assume that the returns from each promotion are normally distributed. If the television promotion costs $4,000 and the newspaper promotion costs $3,000, what is the probability that each will generate a profit?

TABLE 3.4   Return Distributions for Televison and Newspaper Promotions

	Market Response	Probability of Occurring (P_i)	Return (R_i) (Commission Revenues)
Television	Poor	0.25	$ 2,000
	Good	0.50	6,000
	Very Good	0.25	10,000
Newspaper	Poor	0.25	4,000
	Good	0.50	6,000
	Very Good	0.25	8,000

To calculate the probability that each promotion will generate a profit, it is necessary to calculate the portion of the total area under the normal curve that is to the right of (greater than) each breakeven point. Using methods described earlier, relevant expected values and standard deviations are $E(R_{TV}) = \$6,000$, $\sigma_{TV} = \$2,828.43$, $E(R_N) = \$6,000$, and $\sigma_N = \$1,414.21$. For the television promotion, the breakeven revenue level of $4,000 is 0.707 standard deviations to the left of the expected revenue level of $6,000 because

$$z = \frac{x_{TV} - E(R_{TV})}{\sigma_{TV}}$$

$$= \frac{\$4,000 - \$6,000}{\$2,828.43}$$

$$= -0.707.$$

The standard normal distribution function value for $z = -0.707$ is between that for $z = -0.70$ and $z = -0.71$:

z		Pr
−0.70		0.2580
	−0.707	0.2580 + *a*
−0.71		0.261

To find the precise probability value for $z = -0.707$, it is necessary to interpolate, where

$$\frac{a}{(0.261 - 0.2580)} = \frac{(-0.707 + 0.70)}{(-0.71 + 0.70)}$$

$$\frac{a}{0.0031} = \frac{0.007}{0.01}$$

$$a = 0.0022,$$

and the probability value for $z = -0.707$ is $0.2580 + 0.0022 = 0.2602$. This means that 0.2602, or 26.02 percent, of the total area under the normal curve lies between x_{TV} and $E(R_{TV})$, and it implies a profit probability for the television promotion of $0.2602 + 0.5 = 0.7602$, or 76.02 percent.

In calculating the newspaper promotion profit probability, z is calculated as follows:

$$z = \frac{x_N - E(R_N)}{\sigma_N}$$

$$= \frac{\$3,000 - \$6,000}{\$1,414.21}$$

$$= -2.121,$$

and the probability value for $z = -2.121$ is 0.4830. This means that 0.483, or 48.3 percent, of the total area under the normal curve lies between x_N and $E(R_N)$, and it implies a profit probability for the newspaper promotion of $0.483 + 0.5 = 0.983$, or 98.3 percent. In terms of profit probability, the newspaper advertisement is obviously the less risky promotion alternative.

UTILITY THEORY AND RISK ANALYSIS

The assumption of risk aversion is basic to many decision models in managerial economics. Because this assumption is so crucial, it is appropriate to examine attitudes toward risk and discuss why risk aversion holds in general.

Possible Risk Attitudes

Risk aversion
A desire to avoid or minimize uncertainty.

Risk neutrality
A focus on expected values, not return dispersion.

Risk seeking
A preference for speculation.

In theory, three possible attitudes toward risk are present: aversion to risk, indifference to risk, and preference for risk. **Risk aversion** characterizes individuals who seek to avoid or minimize risk. **Risk neutrality** characterizes decision makers who focus on expected returns and disregard the dispersion of returns (risk). **Risk seeking** characterizes decision makers who prefer risk. Given a choice between more risky and less risky investments with identical expected monetary returns, a risk averter selects the less risky investment and a risk seeker selects the riskier investment. Faced with the same choice, the risk-neutral investor is indifferent between the two investment projects. Some individuals prefer high-risk projects and the corresponding potential for substantial returns, especially when relatively small sums of money are involved. Entrepreneurs, innovators, inventors, speculators, and lottery ticket buyers are all examples of individuals who sometimes display risk-seeking behavior. Risk-neutral behavior is exhibited in some business decision making. However, both logic and observation suggest that business managers and investors are predominantly risk averters, especially when substantial dollar amounts are involved.

W hy should risk aversion generally hold? Given two alternatives, each with the same expected dollar returns, why do most decision makers prefer the less risky one? Several explanations have been proposed, but perhaps the most satisfying one involves utility theory.

Relation between Money and Its Utility

At the heart of risk aversion is the notion of **diminishing marginal utility** for money. If someone with no money receives $5,000, it can satisfy his or her most immediate needs. If such a person then receives a second $5,000, it will obviously

Diminishing marginal utility
When additional increments of money bring ever smaller increments of added benefit.

be useful, but the second $5,000 is not quite so necessary as the first $5,000. Thus, the value, or *utility,* of the second, or *marginal,* $5,000 is less than the utility of the first $5,000, and so on. Diminishing marginal utility of money implies that the marginal utility of money income or wealth diminishes for additional increments of money. Figure 3.5 graphs the relation between money and its utility, or value. In the figure, utility is measured in units of value or satisfaction, an index that is unique to each individual. While the concept of utility is very important for understanding economic behavior, the actual numerical values for utility have little interpretive value.

For risk averters, money has diminishing marginal utility. If such an individual's wealth were to double suddenly, he or she would experience an increase in happiness or satisfaction, but the new level of well-being would not be twice the previous level. In cases of diminishing marginal utility of money, a less than proportional relation holds between total utility and money. Accordingly, the utility of a doubled quantity of money is less than twice the utility of the original level. In contrast, those who are indifferent to risk perceive a strictly proportional relationship between total utility and money. Such a relation implies a constant marginal utility of money, and the utility of a doubled quantity of money is exactly twice the utility of the original level. Risk seekers perceive a more than proportional relation between total utility and money. In this case, the marginal utility of money increases. With increasing marginal utility of money, the utility of doubled wealth is more than twice the utility of the original amount. These relations are illustrated in Figure 3.5.

Even though total utility increases with increased money for risk averters, risk seekers, and those who are indifferent to risk, the relation between total utility and money is quite different for each group. These differences lead to dissimilar risk attitudes. Because individuals with a diminishing marginal utility for money suffer more pain from a dollar lost than the pleasure derived from a dollar gained, they seek to avoid risk. Risk averters require a very high return on any investment that is subject to much risk. In Figure 3.6, for example, a gain of $5,000 from a base of $10,000 brings two units of additional satisfaction, but a $5,000 loss causes a four-unit loss in satisfaction. A person with this utility function and $10,000 would be unwilling to make an investment with a 50/50 chance of winning or losing $5,000. The nine-unit expected utility of such a gamble [$E(u) =$ 0.5 times the utility of $5,000 + 0.5 times the utility of $15,000 = $0.5 \times 6 +$ $0.5 \times 12 = 9$] is less than the ten units of utility obtained by forgoing the gamble and keeping $10,000 in certain wealth.

Since an individual with a constant marginal utility for money values a dollar gained just as highly as a dollar lost, the expected utility from a fair gamble always exactly equals the utility of the expected outcome. An individual indifferent to risk makes decisions on the basis of expected monetary outcomes and is not concerned with possible variation in the distribution of outcomes.

An Example of Risk Aversion

▶

A second and more detailed example should clarify the relation between utility and risk aversion. Assume that government bonds are riskless securities that currently offer a 9 percent rate of return. If an individual buys a $10,000 U.S.

FIGURE 3.5 **Risk Attitudes and the Relation between Money and Its Utility**

(a) Doubling wealth from Y to $2Y$ brings a less than proportional increase in utility for a risk averter. (b) Under risk neutrality, doubling wealth proportionally increases (doubles) utility. (c) For a risk seeker, doubling wealth causes a more than proportional increase in utility.

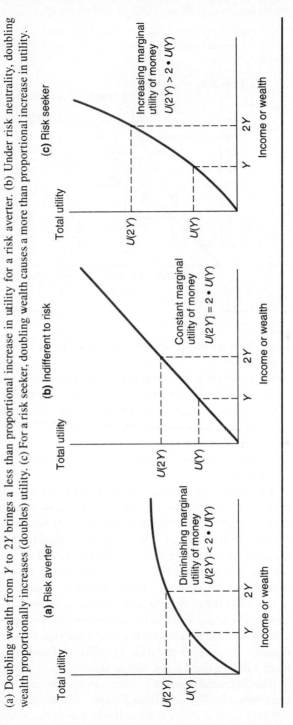

FIGURE 3.6   **An Example of a Money/Utility Relation**

A risk seeker's marginal utility of money increases. A risk-indifferent individual has a constant marginal utility of money. A risk averter displays a diminishing marginal utility of money.

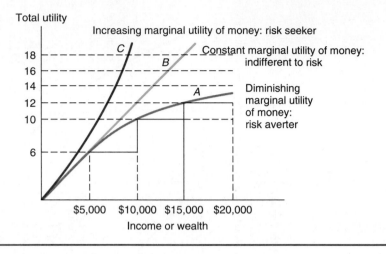

Treasury bond and holds it for one year, he or she will end up with $10,900, a gain of $900.

Suppose that in an alternative investment opportunity, the $10,000 would back a wildcat oil-drilling venture. If the drilling venture is successful, the investment will be worth $20,000 at the end of the year. If it is unsuccessful, investors can liquidate their holdings and recover $5,000. There is a 60 percent chance that oil will be discovered and a 40 percent chance of a dry hole. Should an investor with only $10,000 to invest choose the riskless government bond or the risky drilling operation?

To analyze this question, the expected monetary values of the two investments must be calculated, as in Table 3.5. The calculation in the table is not really necessary for the government bond; a $10,900 outcome occurs regardless of what happens in the oil field. The oil venture calculation shows that the $14,000 expected value of this venture is higher than that of the bond. However, this does not necessarily mean that the investor should invest in the wildcat well. That depends on the investor's utility function. If an investor's marginal utility for money diminishes sharply, thus indicating strong risk aversion, then the utility from a producing well might not compensate for the potential loss of utility from a dry hole. This is precisely the case if the risk averter's utility function shown in Figure 3.5 applies. Four units of utility will be lost if no oil is found, and only three will be gained if the well produces.

The expected monetary value calculation can be modified to reflect utility considerations. Reading from Figure 3.5, this particular risk-averse investor will enjoy 13 units of utility if he or she invests in the wildcat venture and oil is found, but only 6 units of utility will be experienced if no oil is found. This information is used in Table 3.6 to calculate the expected utility for the oil investment. No

MANAGERIAL APPLICATION 3.1

Unlikely Risk Insurance

The success of state-run lotteries provides convincing evidence that many people display risk-seeking behavior, especially when small sums of money are involved. The profitability of state-run lotteries stems from the fact that ticket buyers are willing to pay $1 for a bet that has an expected return of less than $1. When only 50 percent of lottery-ticket revenues are paid out in the form of prizes, for example, each $1 ticket has an expected return of only 50¢. The willingness to overpay for the unlikely chance at perhaps millions of dollars stems from the fact that such opportunities are rare and lottery-ticket buyers value them highly. Many have no opportunity for hitting the jackpot in their careers. The lottery is their only chance, however remote, at a substantial sum of money. The success of state-run lottery promotions is noteworthy because it is fairly unusual. Typically, consumers and investors display risk-averse behavior, especially when substantial sums of money are involved.

Evidence of the risk-averse behavior typical of individuals is provided by travelers who routinely spend relatively small amounts to overinsure the highly unlikely risk of extremely negative or catastrophic outcomes. For example, rather than run the risk of having a vacation ruined by the theft or loss of a large amount of cash, many heed the advice of TV commercials and buy traveler's checks. This risk is very slight, however, and American Express, among others, has found the business of selling traveler's checks to be highly profitable. Auto rental companies earn a large share of their total profit from selling accident insurance to motorists who are already covered on their personal auto insurance policies. One specialty insurance company, Replacement Lens, Inc., (RLI) got its start selling replacement contact lens insurance through eye-care professionals. Today, RLI sells a broad range of special-risk insurance products. One of its more unusual, and profitable, divisions in southern California insures celebrity homes against fire and commercial buildings against earthquakes. RLI average rate of return on stockholders' equity is roughly twice that of the cas-

ualty insurance industry in general. Flight insurance offered in the lobbies of major airports is also extremely profitable for insurers. A wag is said to have remarked that coin-operated flight insurance machines are two-armed bandits. Unlike slot machines ("one-armed bandits"), they never seem to make any payoffs.

Special-risk medical insurance is another area in which consumers are willing to overinsure the very small possibility of a catastrophic outcome. The probability that each of us will die is 100%; death from some natural or accidental cause is inevitable. However, the chance that any one of us will die from a specific disease is quite small. As a result, specific-illness medical insurance is typically a poor choice for the consumer and highly profitable for the insurance industry. The more terrible the illness, the more willing people are to buy insurance and the more profitable it becomes. For example, cancer insurance is one of the most popular and profitable forms of specific-illness insurance on the market today.

Of course no insurance company is more famous than Lloyd's of London for insuring customers against strange and unusual risks that other insurers are loathe to touch. Lloyd's still retains its reputation as a pioneer and an innovator, adept at developing insurance for satellites, computer fraud, war risk, and executive kidnapping. In the early 1990s, Lloyd's was staggered by losses from natural disasters such as Hurricane Hugo, and from man-made disasters such as the Exxon Valdez oil spill. Claims on directors' and officers' insurance resulting from failed savings and loans could cost billions more, according to observers. Nevertheless, losses from such claims are quite unusual. The biggest threat to Lloyd's comes from numerous well-heeled competitors that are stealing large chunks of market share. Ninety years ago, Lloyd's controlled 50 percent of the world's insurance business; now its share is under 2 percent. This massive new entry into the exotic risk market suggests that there is indeed money to be made in providing "unlikely risk" insurance.

Source: G. Bruce Knecht, "Beleaguered Lloyd's: Famed British Insurer Is Fighting For Survival," *Barron's,* June 1, 1992, 15–17.

T A B L E 3.5　**Expected Returns from Two Projects**

	Drilling Operation				Government Bond		
State of Nature	Probability (1)	Outcome (2)	(3) = (1) × (2)		Probability (1)	Outcome (2)	(3) = (1) × (2)
Oil	0.6	$20,000	$12,000		0.6	$10,900	$ 6,540
No oil	0.4	5,000	2,000		0.4	10,900	4,360
		Expected value	$14,000			Expected value	$10,900

T A B L E 3.6　**Expected Utility of the Oil-Drilling Project**

State of Nature	Probability (1)	Monetary Outcome (2)	Associated Utility (3)	Weighted Utility (4) = (1) × (3)
Oil	0.6	$20,000	13.0	7.8
No oil	0.4	5,000	6.0	2.4
			Expected utility	10.2

calculation is needed for the government bond; its utility is 10.7 units regardless of the outcome of the oil venture. The investor will have 10.7 units of utility with certainty by choosing the government bond.

Because the expected utility from the wildcat venture is only 10.2 units, versus 10.7 from the government bond, the government bond is the preferred investment. Even though the expected monetary value for the oil venture is higher, expected utility is greater for the bond investment. Risk considerations dictate that the investor should buy the government bond.

ADJUSTING THE VALUATION MODEL FOR RISK

Diminishing marginal utility leads directly to risk aversion, and risk aversion is reflected in the basic valuation model used to determine the worth of a firm. If a managerial decision affects the firm's risk level, the value of the firm is affected. Two primary methods are used to adjust the basic valuation model to account for decision making under conditions of uncertainty. These methods are considered in detail in the following section.

The Basic Valuation Model

The basic valuation model developed in Chapter 1 is

$$V = \sum_{t=1}^{N} \frac{\pi_t}{(1 + i)^t}. \tag{3.7}$$

This model states that the value of the firm is equal to the discounted present worth of future profits. Under conditions of certainty, the numerator of this expression is profit, and the denominator is a time-value adjustment using the risk-free rate of return *i*. After time-value adjustment, the profits to be earned from various projects are strictly and completely comparable.

Under conditions of uncertainty, the profits shown in the numerator of the valuation model as π equal the expected value of profits during each future period. This expected value is the best available estimate of the amount to be earned during any given period. However, since profits cannot be predicted with absolute precision, some variability is to be anticipated. If the firm must choose between two alternative methods of operation, one with high expected profits and high risk and another with smaller expected profits and lower risks, some technique must be available for making the alternative investments comparable. An appropriate ranking and selection of projects is possible only if each respective investment project can be adjusted for considerations of both time value of money and risk. At least two popular methods are employed to make such adjustments. In the first, the expected profits to be realized from various investment projects are adjusted to account for risk. In the second, the interest rate used in the denominator of the valuation model is increased to reflect risk considerations. Either method can be used to ensure that value-maximizing decisions are made under conditions of uncertainty.

Certainty Equivalent Adjustments

Certainty equivalent
The assured sum that equals an expected risky amount in utility terms.

The **certainty equivalent** method is an adjustment to the numerator of the basic valuation model to account for risk. Under the certainty equivalent approach, decision makers specify the certain sum that they regard comparable to the expected value of a risky investment alternative. The certainty equivalent of an expected risk amount typically differs in dollar terms but not in terms of the amount of utility provided. To illustrate, suppose that you face the following choices in an investment decision:

- Invest $100,000. From a successful project, you receive $1,000,000; if it fails, you receive nothing. If the probability of success is 0.5, or 50 percent, the investment's expected payoff is $500,000 ($= 0.5 \times \$1,000,000 + 0.5 \times \$0$).
- You do not make the investment; you keep the $100,000.

If you find yourself indifferent between the two alternatives, $100,000 is your certainty equivalent for the risky expected return of $500,000. In other words, a certain or riskless amount of $100,000 provides exactly the same utility as the 50/50 chance to earn $1,000,000 or $0. You are indifferent between these two alternatives.

In this example, any certainty equivalent of less than $500,000 indicates risk aversion. If the maximum amount that you are willing to invest in the project is less than $500,000, you are exhibiting very risk-averse behavior. Each certain dollar is "worth" five times as much as each risky dollar of expected return. Alternatively, each risky dollar of expected return is worth only 20¢ in terms of certain dollars. In general, any risky investment with a certainty equivalent less than the expected dollar value indicates risk aversion. A certainty equivalent greater than the expected value of a risky investment indicates risk preference.

Certainty equivalent adjustment factor, α
The ratio of a certain sum divided by an expected risky amount, where both dollar values provide the same level of utility.

Any expected risky amount can be converted to an equivalent certain sum using the **certainty equivalent adjustment factor, α,** calculated as the ratio of a certain sum divided by an expected risky amount, where both dollar values provide the same level of utility:

$$\begin{matrix} \text{Certainty} \\ \text{Equivalent} \\ \text{Adjustment} \\ \text{Factor} \end{matrix} = \alpha = \frac{\text{Equivalent Certain Sum}}{\text{Expected Risky Sum}}. \qquad (3.8)$$

The certain sum numerator and expected return denominator may vary in dollar terms, but they provide the exact same reward in terms of utility. In the previous investment problem, in which a certain sum of $100,000 provides the same utility as an expected risky return of $500,000, the certainty equivalent adjustment factor $\alpha = 0.2 = \$100,000/\$500,000$. This means that the "price" of one dollar in risky expected return is 20¢ in certain dollar terms.

The following general relations enable managers to use the certainty equivalent adjustment factor to analyze risk attitudes:

If	Then	Implies
Equivalent certain sum < Expected risky sum	$\alpha < 1$	Risk aversion
Equivalent certain sum = Expected risky sum	$\alpha = 1$	Risk indifference
Equivalent certain sum > Expected risky sum	$\alpha > 1$	Risk preference

The appropriate α value for a given managerial decision varies according to the level of risk and degree of the decision maker's risk aversion. Figure 3.7 shows a series of risk–return combinations among which the decision maker is indifferent. For example, Point A represents an investment with a perceived degree of risk v_A and expected dollar return of $3,000. The risk–return tradeoff function, or indifference curve, shows a person who is indifferent to a certain $1,000, an expected $2,000 with risk v_B, and an expected $3,000 with risk v_A.

The indifference curve shown in Figure 3.7 can be used to construct a risk-aversion function such as the one illustrated in Figure 3.8. This conversion is obtained by dividing each risky return into its certainty equivalent amount to obtain a certainty equivalent adjustment factor, α, for each level of risk, v. For example, the certainty equivalent adjustment factor for risk level v_B is

$$\alpha_A = \frac{\$1,000}{\$3,000} = 0.33.$$

For risk level v_B, the relevant calculation is

$$\alpha_B = \frac{\$1,000}{\$2,000} = 0.5.$$

Conceptually, α values could be developed for all possible levels of v (risk). Assuming risk aversion, the range for α is from $\alpha = 1$ for $v = 0$, to $\alpha \approx 0$ for extremely large values of v.

FIGURE 3.7 **Certainty Equivalent Returns**

An indifference curve shows risk–return tradeoffs that provide the same utility to a given individual.

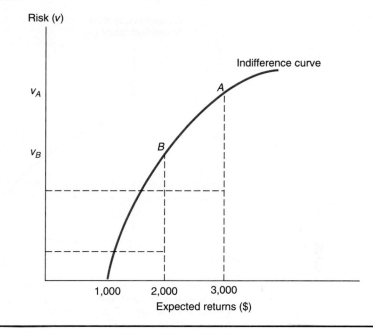

Given complete information from an appropriate risk-aversion function, and evidence on the degree of risk inherent in a given risky return, the certainty equivalent of the expected return is calculated as

$$\text{Certainty Equivalent of } E(\pi_t) = \alpha E(\pi_t).$$

Risk-adjusted valuation model

A valuation model that reflects time-value and risk considerations.

The basic valuation model (Equation 3.7) can then be converted into a **risk-adjusted valuation model,** one that explicitly accounts for risk:

$$V = \sum_{t=1}^{N} \frac{\alpha E(\pi_t)}{(1 + i)^t}. \tag{3.9}$$

In this risk-adjusted valuation model, expected future profits, $E(\pi_t)$, are converted to their certainty equivalents, $\alpha E(\pi_t)$, and are discounted at a risk-free rate, i, to obtain the risk-adjusted present value of a firm or project. With the valuation model in this form, one can appraise the effects of different courses of action with different risks and expected returns.

To use Equation 3.9 for real-world decision making, managers must estimate appropriate α's for various investment opportunities. Deriving such estimates can prove difficult, since α varies according to the size and riskiness of investment projects as well as according to the risk attitudes of managers and investors. In many instances, however, the record of past investment decisions offers a guide

FIGURE 3.8   **Hypothetical Risk-Aversion Function**

For a risk-averse individual, the acceptable certainty equivalent adjustment factor will decline as risk increases.

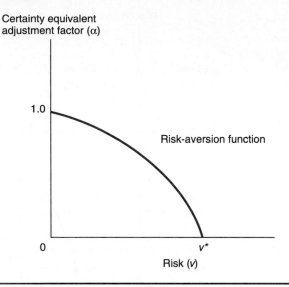

Note: As we have drawn it, the risk-aversion function assumes that $\alpha = 0$ when $v \geq v^*$. Theoretically, α would never actually reach zero; rather, it would approach zero as risk became quite high.

that can be used to determine appropriate certainty equivalent adjustment factors. The following example illustrates how managers use certainty equivalent adjustment factors in practical decision making.

A Certainty Equivalent Adjustment Example

▶

Assume that operations at Burns & Allen Industries have been seriously disrupted by problems with a faulty boiler at its main fabrication facility. In fact, state fire marshals shut the facility down for an extended period recently following repeated overheating and minor explosions. The boiler problem was solved when it was discovered that a design flaw had made the pilot light safety switch inoperable.

Burns & Allen retained the Denver law firm of Dewey, Cheetum & Howe to recover economic damages from the boiler manufacturer. The company has filed suit in state court for $250,000 in damages. Prior to filing suit, the attorney estimated legal, expert witness, and other litigation costs of $10,000 for a fully litigated case, for which Burns & Allen had a 10 percent chance of receiving a favorable judgment. For simplicity, assume that a favorable judgment will award Burns & Allen 100 percent of the damages sought, whereas an unfavorable judgment will result in the firm receiving zero damages. Also assume that $10,000 is the most Burns & Allen would be willing to pay to sue the boiler manufacturer.

In filing suit against the boiler manufacturer, Burns & Allen has made a risky investment decision. By its willingness to bear litigation costs of $10,000, the company has implicitly stated that it regards the value of these out-of-pocket costs to be equivalent to the value of the risky expectation of receiving a favorable judgment against the boiler manufacturer. In other words, Burns & Allen is willing to exchange $10,000 in certain litigation costs for the possibility of receiving a $250,000 judgment against the boiler manufacturer.

Burns & Allen's investment decision can be characterized using the certainty equivalent adjustment method. To do this, it is important to realize that the $10,000 in litigation costs is incurred irrespective of the outcome of a fully litigated case. This $10,000 represents a certain sum that the company must value as highly as the expected risky outcome to be willing to file suit. The expected risky outcome, or expected return from filing suit, is

$$
\begin{aligned}
\text{Expected Return} &= \text{Favorable Judgment Payoff} \times \text{Probability} \\
&\quad + \text{Unfavorable Judgment Payoff} \times \text{Probability} \\
&= \$250,000(0.1) + \$0(0.9) \\
&= \$25,000.
\end{aligned}
$$

To justify filing suit, Burns & Allen's certainty equivalent adjustment factor for investment projects of this risk class must be

$$
\begin{aligned}
\alpha &= \frac{\text{Certain Sum}}{\text{Expected Risky Sum}} \\
&= \frac{\text{Litigation Costs}}{\text{Expected Return}} \\
&= \frac{\$10,000}{\$25,000} \\
&= 0.4.
\end{aligned}
$$

Therefore, each risky dollar of expected return from the litigation effort is worth, in terms of utility, 40¢ in certain dollars. Alternatively, $10,000 is the certain sum equivalent of the risky expected return of $25,000.

Now assume that after Burns & Allen goes to court, incurring $5,000 in litigation costs, especially damaging testimony by an expert witness dramatically changes the outlook of the case in Burns & Allen's favor. In response, the boiler manufacturer's attorney offers an out-of-court settlement in the amount of $30,000. However, Burns & Allen's attorney recommends that the company reject this offer, estimating that it now has a 50/50 chance of obtaining a favorable judgment in the case. Should Burns & Allen follow the attorney's advice and reject the settlement offer?

In answering this question, one must keep in mind that having already spent ("sunk") $5,000 in litigation costs, Burns & Allen must consider as relevant litigation costs only the additional $5,000 necessary to complete litigation. These $5,000 litigation costs, plus the $30,000 out-of-court settlement offer, represent the relevant certain sum, since proceeding with the suit will require an "investment" of these additional litigation plus opportunity costs. Given the revised outlook for a favorable judgment, the expected return to full litigation is

$$\text{Expected Return} = (\$250,000)(0.5) + (\$0)(0.5)$$
$$= \$125,000.$$

In light of Burns & Allen's earlier decision to file suit on the basis that each dollar of expected risky return was "worth" 40¢ in certain dollars, this expected return would have a $50,000 certainty equivalent value ($125,000 × 0.4). Since this amount exceeds the settlement offer plus remaining litigation costs, the settlement offer seems deficient and should be rejected. On the basis of Burns & Allen's revealed risk attitude, an out-of-court settlement offer has to be at least $45,000 to receive favorable consideration. At that point the settlement plus saved litigation costs of $5,000 would equal the certainty equivalent value of the expected return from continuing litigation.

This simple example illustrates that historical investment decisions offer a useful guide to current risky investment decisions. If a potential project's required investment and risk levels are known, the α implied by a decision to accept the investment project can be calculated. This project-specific α can then be compared with αs for prior projects with similar risks. Risk-averse individuals should invest in projects if calculated αs are *less* than or equal to those for accepted historical projects in the same risk class. Furthermore, given an estimate of expected return and risk, the maximum amount that the firm should be willing to invest in a given project can also be determined from the certainty equivalent adjustment factor. Risk-averse management will accept new projects if the level of required investment per dollar of expected return is less than or equal to that for historical projects of similar risk.

Risk-Adjusted Discount Rates

Risk-adjusted discount rate
The risk-free rate of return plus the required risk premium.

Risk premium
The added expected return for a risky asset over that of a riskless asset.

Another way to incorporate risk in managerial decision making is to adjust the discount rate or denominator of the basic valuation model (Equation 3.7). Like certainty equivalent factors, **risk-adjusted discount rates** are based on the trade-off between risk and return for individual investors. Suppose risk-averse investors are willing to trade between risk and return, as shown in Figure 3.9. This curve is called a market indifference curve or a risk–return tradeoff function. The average investor is indifferent to a riskless asset with a sure 10 percent rate of return, a moderately risky asset with a 20 percent expected return, and a very risky asset with a 30 percent expected return. As risk increases, higher expected returns on investment are required to compensate investors for the additional risk.

The difference between the expected rate of return on a risky asset and the rate of return on a riskless asset is the **risk premium** on the risky asset. In the example shown in Figure 3.9, the riskless rate is assumed to be 10 percent. A 4 percent risk premium is required to compensate for the level of risk indicated by $\sigma = 0.5$; a 20 percent risk premium is required for an investment with a risk of $\sigma = 1.5$. Observe that the required risk premium is directly related to the level of risk associated with a particular investment.

The basic valuation model shown in Equation 3.7 can be adapted to account for risk through adjustment of the discount rate, i, where

FIGURE 3.9   **Relation between Risk and Rate of Return**

As risk rises, investors typically demand higher expected returns to compensate for the increased risk.

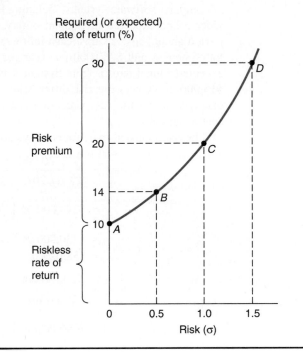

$$V = \sum_{t=1}^{N} \frac{E(\pi_t)}{(1 + k)^t}.$$ (3.10)

The risk-adjusted discount rate k is the sum of the risk-free rate of return, R_F, plus the required risk premium, R_p:

$$k = R_F + R_p.$$

In Equation 3.10, value is measured by the present worth of expected future income or profits, $E(\pi_t)$, discounted at a risk-adjusted rate. If the risk–return tradeoff illustrated in Figure 3.8 is appropriate, returns for a project with risk level $\sigma = 0.5$ should be adjusted using a 14 percent discount rate, comprised of the 10 percent risk-free rate plus a 4 percent risk premium. A riskier project with $\sigma = 1.5$ requires a risk premium of 20 percent and should be evaluated using a 30 percent discount rate or the 10 percent risk-free rate plus a 20 percent risk premium.

A Risk-Adjusted
Discount Rate
Example

The following example further illustrates the use of risk-adjusted discount rates in managerial decision making. Suppose the Property & Casualty Insurance Company is contemplating purchase of one of the two data base and file manage-

▶ ment computer software programs offered by Rockford Files, Inc. System *A* is specifically designed for P&C's current computer software system and cannot be used with those of other providers; System *B* is compatible with a broad variety of computer software systems, including P&C's and those of other software providers. The expected investment outlay is $600,000 for each alternative. Expected annual cost savings (cash inflows) over five years are $220,000 per year for System *A* and $260,000 per year for System *B*. The standard deviation of expected annual returns from System *A* is $10,000, whereas that of System *B* is $15,000. In view of this risk differential, P&C management has decided to evaluate System *A* with a 20 percent cost of capital and System *B* with a 30 percent cost of capital.

The risk-adjusted value for each system is as follows:[1]

$$\text{Value}_A = \sum_{t=1}^{5} \frac{\$220,000}{(1.20)^t} - \$600,000$$

$$= \$220,000 \times \left(\sum_{t=1}^{5} \frac{1}{(1.20)^t} \right) - \$600,000$$

$$= \$220,000 \times 2.991 - \$600,000$$

$$= \$58,020.$$

$$\text{Value}_B = \sum_{t=1}^{5} \frac{\$260,000}{(1.30)^t} - \$600,000$$

$$= \$260,000 \times \left(\sum_{t=1}^{5} \frac{1}{(1.30)^t} \right) - \$600,000$$

$$= \$260,000 \times 2.436 - \$600,000$$

$$= \$33,360.$$

Because the risk-adjusted value of System *A* is larger than that for System *B*, P&C should choose System *A*. This choice maximizes the value of the firm.

DECISION TREES AND COMPUTER SIMULATION

A variety of additional techniques for decision making under uncertainty are available to supplement the use of probability concepts, certainty equivalents, and risk-adjusted discount rate methods. Decision trees that follow the sequential

---

[1] The terms

$$\sum_{t=1}^{5} \frac{1}{(1.20)^t} = 2.991$$

and

$$\sum_{t=1}^{5} \frac{1}{(1.30)^t} = 2.436$$

are present-value-of-an-annuity interest factors. Tables of interest factors for various interest rates and years (*t* values) appear in Appendix A.

MANAGERIAL APPLICATION 3.2

Morton International's High-Stakes Payoff

How promising does this sound? Suppose a business you acquire includes a product that hasn't gone anywhere for 14 years. The product is a nightmare of potential legal liability because it's made of highly volatile explosives and is diabolically hard to build. Leading rivals have already given up on the business and to make a go of it would require huge additional investment. To make matters worse, assume that potential customers hate the product and will require new government regulations to force their purchases.

You might call that a clear product abandonment decision, but it wasn't to Morton International when the company acquired Thiokol in 1982. The product in question is the automotive air bag, a product that is now poised to become Morton's hottest source of profitability and growth. In 1991, Morton sold $225 million of air bags to automakers, a relatively small portion of the company's overall business, but sales could reach $1 billion by 1995 when a new U.S. law mandating air bags for all vehicles takes effect.

Morton acquired Thiokol largely for its specialty chemical, space, and defense businesses; air bags were a small part of the overall acquisition. Thiokol's rocket business was sold in 1989 after faulty O-rings contributed to the fatal explosion of the space shuttle *Challenger*. Morton kept only the specialty chemicals and air bag operations. "The big question for us was whether there was ever going to be a real market," says Morton CEO Charles Locke. At first, prospects for the air bag business looked dismal. Automakers in Detroit were bitterly fighting proposed air bag regulations, and Morton couldn't get a single insurance company to provide product liability coverage.

Then Mercedes-Benz knocked on Locke's door late in 1983 and asked Morton to supply air bags as a standard driver-side feature in all of its cars for the United States beginning in 1985. That deal solidified Morton's commitment to the air bag business, and the company entered what Locke refers to as a "highstakes poker game." Morton had only one air bag competitor, a small unit of Talley Industries (bought by TRW in 1989) and only one customer. But, says Locke, "I believed that as this new device became a standard feature on autos, the business would turn into a real dogfight. And I decided that the guy with the lowest cost and highest reliability would be the one to win."

During the 1980s, Morton invested more than $100 million in an air bag plant and equipment. It automated labor-intensive production lines and computerized inspection to ensure quality control. New devices were installed to x-ray every bag for defects and each one was coded to facilitate tracing in the event of recall. Morton even built two separate plants in case one was closed by an explosion—always a risk because of the volatile chemicals that trigger air bag inflation.

The payoff came into sight in 1987, when Chrysler decided to make Morton its sole supplier and put driver-side air bags in all 1990 cars. Almost overnight, air bags became a competitive advantage for automakers that discovered that safety sells. Meanwhile, insurance companies turned around and began courting Morton's product liability business because of the company's near-flawless safety record.

Morton clearly faces big challenges. It must double its $300 million investment and double employment to 4,000 during the mid-1990s. To invade European markets, Morton has teamed up with engineering giant Robert Bosch, which will provide the crash sensors and diagnostic systems that tell the air bag to go off. Before European markets can be fully developed, however, Morton must nearly triple output at home without losing control of costs and product quality. Rapidly growing worldwide demand, estimated at up to $3 billion a year, is also likely to attract more competition. Still, because Morton invested heavily in leading-edge technology long before air bags represented a viable business, the company is now in the driver's seat with 55 percent of the world market and a glowing reputation for product quality.

Source: Jessica Skelly von Brachel, "Morton International: A High-Stakes Bet That Paid Off," *Fortune,* June 15, 1992, 121–122.

nature of the decision-making process are often used to provide a logical framework for decision analysis under conditions of uncertainty. When a high degree of uncertainty exists and data are not readily available for analysis, computer simulation is often used to provide the basis for reasonable conjecture. Application of these methods was once arduous and time-consuming. Today, new spreadsheet software such as *@Risk,* available in both professional and low-cost student versions, fully automates the process of decision tree analysis and computer simulation. More than ever before, these techniques constitute useful and practical means for risk assessment and effective managerial decision making under conditions of uncertainty.

Decision Trees

Decision tree

A map of a sequential decision-making process.

A **decision tree** is a map of a sequential decision-making process. Decision trees are designed for analyzing decision problems that involve a series of choice alternatives that are constrained by previous decisions. They illustrate the complete range of future possibilities and their associated probabilities in terms of a logical progression from an initial decision point, through each subsequent constrained decision alternative, to an ultimate outcome.

Decision trees are widely employed because many important decisions are not made at one point in time but rather in stages. For example, a pharmaceutical company considering expansion into the generic prescription drug market might take the following steps:

- Spend $100,000 to survey supply and demand conditions in the generic drug industry.
- If survey results are favorable, spend $2 million on a pilot plant to investigate production methods.
- Depending on cost estimates and potential demand, either abandon the project, build a large plant, or build a small one.

These decisions are made in stages; subsequent determinations depend upon prior judgments. The sequence of events can be mapped out to visually resemble the branches of a tree—hence the term *decision tree.*

Figure 3.10 illustrates the decision-tree method for the pharmaceutical company decision problem. Assume that the company has completed its industry supply-and-demand analysis and has determined that it should develop a full-scale production facility. Either a large plant or a small plant can be built. The probability is 50 percent for high demand, 30 percent for medium demand, and 20 percent for low demand. Depending on actual demand, the present value of net cash flows, defined as sales revenue minus operating costs, ranges from $8.8 million to $1.4 million for a large plant and from $2.6 million to $1.4 million for a small plant.

Because demand probabilities are known, the expected value of cash flow can be determined, as in Column 5 of Figure 3.10. Investment outlays are deducted from expected net cash flow to obtain the expected net present value for each decision. The expected net present value is $730,000 for the large plant and $300,000 for the small one. Notice the wide range of possible outcomes for the large plant. Actual net present values for the large plant investment equal the present value of cash flows (Column 4) minus the large plant investment cost of

FIGURE 3.10   Illustrative Decision Tree

The expected net present value of each investment alternative (Column 5) is determined by linking possible outcomes (Column 2), probabilities (Column 3), and monetary values (Column 4).

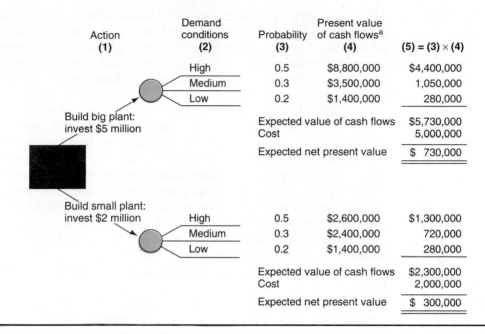

Action (1)	Demand conditions (2)	Probability (3)	Present value of cash flows[a] (4)	(5) = (3) × (4)
	High	0.5	$8,800,000	$4,400,000
	Medium	0.3	$3,500,000	1,050,000
	Low	0.2	$1,400,000	280,000
Build big plant: invest $5 million			Expected value of cash flows	$5,730,000
			Cost	5,000,000
			Expected net present value	$ 730,000
Build small plant: invest $2 million	High	0.5	$2,600,000	$1,300,000
	Medium	0.3	$2,400,000	720,000
	Low	0.2	$1,400,000	280,000
			Expected value of cash flows	$2,300,000
			Cost	2,000,000
			Expected net present value	$ 300,000

[a] The figures in Column 4 are the annual cash flows from operation—revenues minus cash operating costs—discounted at the firm's cost of capital.

$5 million. These values vary from $3.8 million to −$3.6 million. Actual net present values for the small plant investment range only from $600,000 to −$600,000. Clearly, the smaller plant appears less risky based on the width of the range of possible net present value outcomes. Because the investment requirement differs for each plant, the coefficient of variation for each plant's net present value can be examined to provide an alternate measure of relative risk. The coefficient of variation for the large plant's present value is 4.3, whereas that for the small plant is only 1.5.[2] Again, risk appears greater for the large plant alternative.

These risk and expected return differentials can be incorporated into the decision-making process in a variety of ways. Assigning utility values to the cash flows given in Column 4 of Figure 3.10 would state Column 5 in terms of expected utility. The company could then choose the plant size that provided the greatest expected utility. Alternatively, present values given in Column 4 could be

[2] Using Equation 3.4 and data on possible returns in Figure 3.10, the standard deviation for the big plant is $3.155 million and for the small plant is $458,260. Dividing these standard deviations by the appropriate expected return for each respective plant size, as in Equation 3.5, gives the coefficient of variation.

adjusted using the certainty equivalent or risk-adjusted discount rate method. The plant that offers the largest risk-adjusted net present value is the optimal choice.

A More Complex Decision Tree Example

Decision points
Instances when management must select among choice alternatives.

Chance events
Possible outcomes following each decision point.

The decision tree illustrated in Figure 3.10 is quite simple; actual decision trees are frequently complex and involve large numbers of sequential decision points. An example of a more complex tree is illustrated in Figure 3.11. Numbered boxes represent **decision points,** or instances when management must select among several choice alternatives. The circles represent **chance events,** or possible outcomes following each decision point. At Decision Point 1, the firm has three choices: invest $3 million in a large plant, invest $1.3 million in a small plant, or spend $100,000 on market research. If the large plant is built, the firm follows the upper branch, and its position is fixed; it can only hope that demand will be high. If it builds the small plant, it follows the lower branch. If demand is low, no further action is required. If demand is high, Decision Point 2 is reached, and the firm can either do nothing or expand the plant at a cost of an additional $2.2 million. Notice that if the company obtains a large plant through expansion the cost is $500,000 greater than if it had built a large plant in the first place.

If the decision at Point 1 is to pay $100,000 for more information, the firm moves to the center branch. This research modifies the firm's information about potential demand. Initially, the probabilities were 70 percent for high demand and 30 percent for low demand. The research survey will show either favorable or unfavorable demand prospects. If they are favorable, the probability for high final demand is 87 percent and for low demand is 13 percent. If demand prospects are unfavorable, the odds on high final demand are only 35 percent and on low demand are 65 percent.

If the firm builds a large plant and demand is high, sales and profits will be substantial. If it builds a large plant and demand is low, sales will be depressed and it will incur losses. If the company builds a small plant and demand is high, sales and profits will be lower than they could have been had a large plant been built, yet the chance of loss in the event of low demand can be eliminated. Building the large plant is obviously riskier than building the small plant. The cost of market research is, in effect, an expenditure serving to reduce the degree of uncertainty.

The decision tree in Figure 3.11 is incomplete because no dollar outcomes (or utility values) are assigned to each point on the decision tree. If such values were assigned, similar to the way values are shown in the last two columns of Figure 3.10, the expected value and risk of each decision alternative could be calculated to help arrive at an appropriate managerial decision.

Computer Simulation

Another technique designed to assist managers in making decisions under uncertainty is **computer simulation.** Computer simulation involves the use of computer software and workstations or sophisticated desktop computers to create a wide variety of decision outcome scenarios. These simulations illustrate a broad range of possible outcomes to help managers assess the possible and probable consequences of decision alternatives. Using the computer simulation technique, a variety of hypothetical "What if?" questions can be asked and answered on the

FIGURE 3.11 Decision Tree with Multiple Decision Points

The decision tree allows the decision maker to illustrate the return possibilities and probabilities at each decision point.

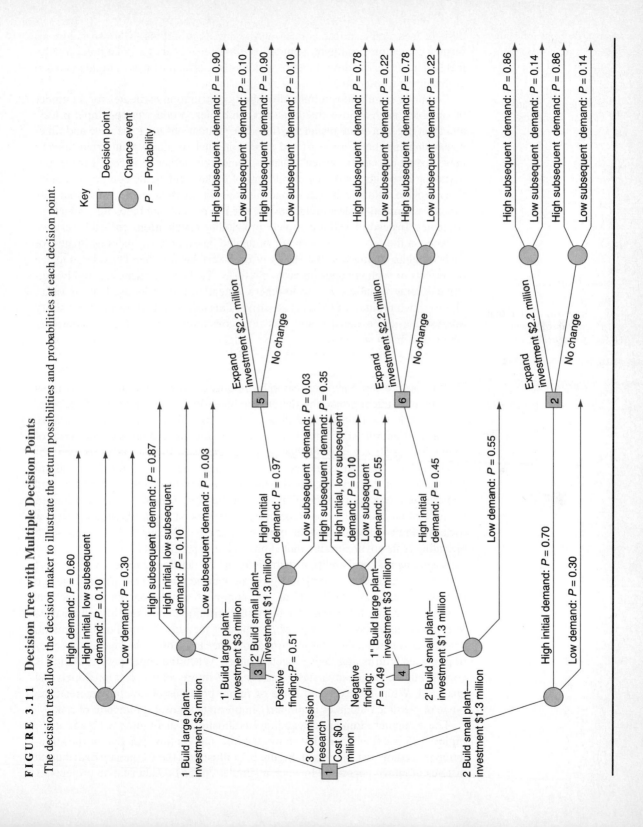

Computer simulation

The use of computer software and workstations or sophisticated desktop computers to create outcome scenarios.

basis of measurable differences in underlying assumptions. More than just informed conjecture, computer simulation allows managers to make precise judgments concerning the desirability of various choices on the basis of highly detailed probability information.

Computer simulations require probability distribution estimates for a number of variables, such as investment outlays, unit sales, product prices, input prices, and asset lives. In some instances, full-scale simulations are expensive and time-consuming and therefore restricted to projects such as major plant expansions or new-product decisions. When a firm is deciding whether to accept a major undertaking involving an outlay of millions of dollars, full-scale computer simulations provide valuable insights that are well worth their cost. Somewhat less expensive, limited-scale simulations are used to project outcomes for projects or strategies. Instead of using complete probability distributions for each variable included in the problem, results are simulated based on best-guess estimates for each variable. Changes in the values of each variable are then considered to see the effects of such changes on project returns. Typically, returns are highly sensitive to some variables, less so to others. Attention is then focused on the variables to which profitability is most sensitive. This technique, known as **sensitivity analysis,** is less expensive and less time-consuming than full-scale computer simulation, but it still provides valuable insight for decision-making purposes.

Sensitivity analysis

A limited form of computer simulation that focuses on important decision variables.

A Computer Simulation Example

▶

To illustrate the computer simulation technique, consider the evaluation of a new minimill investment project by Remington Steel, Inc. The exact cost of the plant is not known, but it is expected to be about $150 million. If no difficulties arise in construction, this cost can be as low as $125 million. An unfortunate series of events such as strikes, greater than projected increases in material costs, or technical problems could drive the required investment outlay as high as $225 million. Revenues from the new facility depend on the growth of regional income and construction, competition, developments in the field of metallurgy, steel import quotas and tariffs, and so on. Operating costs depend on production efficiency, the cost of raw materials, and the trend in wage rates. Because sales revenues and operating costs are uncertain, annual profits are unpredictable.

Assuming that probability distributions can be developed for each major cost and revenue category, a computer program can be constructed to simulate the pattern of future events. In effect, the computer simulation randomly selects revenue and cost levels from each relevant distribution and uses this information to estimate future profits, net present values, or the rate of return on investment. This process is repeated a large number of times to identify the central tendency of projected returns and their expected values. When the computer simulation is completed, the frequency pattern and range of future returns can be plotted and analyzed. While the expected value of future profits is of obvious interest, the range of possible outcomes is similarly important as a useful indicator of risk.

The computer simulation technique is illustrated in Figures 3.12 and 3.13. Figure 3.12 is a flow chart that shows the information flow pattern for the simulation procedure just described. Figure 3.13 illustrates the frequency distribution of rates of return generated by such a simulation for two alternative projects, *X*

FIGURE 3.12 **Simulation for Investment Planning**

Computer simulation allows detailed analysis of managerial problems involving complex cost and revenue relations.

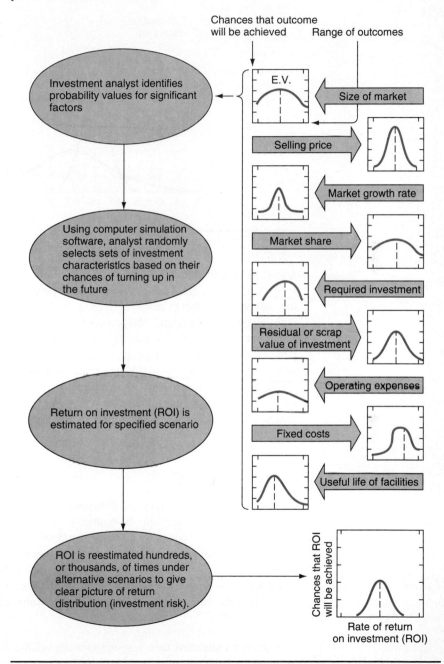

FIGURE 3.13   **Expected Rates of Return on Investments X and Y**

Investments X and Y both have continuous distributions of returns around their expected values.

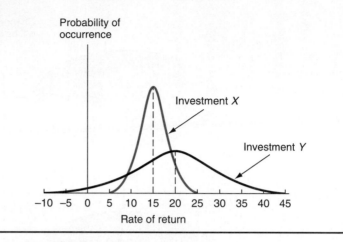

and Y, each with an expected cost of $20 million. The expected rate of return on Investment X is 15 percent and that on Investment Y is 20 percent. However, these are only average rates of return derived by the computer simulation. The range of simulated returns is from -10 percent to 45 percent for Investment Y and from 5 percent to 25 percent for Investment X. The standard deviation for X is only 4 percent; that for Y is 12 percent. Based on this information, the coefficient of variation is 0.267 for Project X and 0.60 for Project Y. Investment Y is clearly riskier than Investment X. A decision about which alternative to choose can be made on the basis of expected utility, or on the basis of a present value determination that incorporates either certainty equivalents or risk-adjusted discount rates.

GAME THEORY

Game theory

A decision framework for making choices in hostile environments and under extreme uncertainty.

The decision criterion stressed throughout managerial economics is value maximization. In an uncertain economic environment, value maximization is achieved using the risk-adjusted valuation models described in this chapter. Under certain circumstances, especially when the decision environment is hostile rather than neutral and when extreme uncertainty exists, other **game theory** decision criteria may be appropriate. Game theory is a useful decision framework employed to make choices in hostile environments and under extreme uncertainty.

Maximin Decision Rule

One decision standard that is sometimes applicable for decision making under uncertainty is the **maximin criterion.** This criterion states that the decision maker should select the alternative that provides the best of the worst possible outcomes. This is done by finding the worst possible (minimum) outcome for

●

MANAGERIAL APPLICATION 3.3

How Risk Takers Win . . . and Lose

Business Week's annual list of hot growth companies is compiled from a universe of more than 3,500 publicly traded corporations with sales of less than $150 million per year, as tracked by Standard & Poor's *Compustat* Services, Inc. *Business Week* chooses its top 100 based on the average rate of growth in sales, earnings, and return on invested capital over the prior three-year period. Average revenue growth for this list of dynamic growers averages over 50 percent per year, while the rate of growth in earnings often averages over 100 percent per year. Earnings expressed as a rate of return on capital typical average over 25 percent per year.

To appreciate the significance of such torrid rates of growth one need only recall what financial analysts refer to as the "Rule of 72." Just take any growth rate and divide that amount into 72 to determine the number of years required to double in size. For example, a firm that grows by 7.2 percent per year will double in roughly 10 years; a firm that grows by 14.4 percent per year will double in roughly 5 years, and so on. This means that any firm growing at say 35 to 40 percent per year will double in size in roughly two years. Stated differently, approximately one-half of the people that will be working for the firm in just two years have not been hired yet! Any company that is able to maintain such scorching rates of growth is running an educational institution as much as it is a typical business. The rookie sales trainee hired today will be a member of the company's veteran sales staff within a year and a marketing director before too long after that. The potential for employee growth and development is enormous in rapidly growing companies; so too is the potential for hiring mistakes and minor snafus that snowball into major disasters. The corporate landscape is littered with examples of once rapid growers that were highly profitable until they seemingly spun out of control, crashed, and burned.

Business Week's annual survey reflects a number of once-hot companies that have suffered flameouts. New accounting rules, for example, put a chill on revenue for software companies. Recent data also suggest that the number of new small public companies is shrinking. The universe of more than 3,500 companies from which *Business Week* culls its list has shrunk markedly; back in 1988, it was 4,500. To be sure, some companies have outgrown the $150 million sales cap. But the group of businesses that might normally step up and take their place has been shrinking. Data from Dun & Bradstreet show that the number of new business incorporations has declined noticeably since its peak in 1986. One reason might be that entrepreneurs were simply waiting in 1991 for better economic conditions to launch their firms. Starting a new business at the end of a long up cycle in the economy is difficult; many budding entrepreneurs rationally hold off launching a new enterprise until they see the economy start to improve. Money has also been scarce for those trying to get a new business off the ground. Besides the tightening of bank credit, other sources of financing are holding back. Venture capitalists say that the 1986 hike in capital-gains tax rates made venture-capital pools less attractive to investors. And the rising rate of business failures, up 31 percent over from the early- to mid-1980s, has made venture capitalists skittish.

The bottom line for new businesses is that one has to assume that the market is very selective; unless it is an outstanding project, it won't get financed. By their very nature, *Business Week*'s hot growth companies can be an ephemeral lot. Of the 100 companies that appeared on the hot growth list in any given year, only about one-third return for an encore the following year. A few companies, usually five or ten, outgrow the list. The rest just don't make the grade. Staying on the list gets even harder as the years go by; just 10 percent of the 1988 class appeared on the 1991 list. Therefore, even among this highly select list of successful risk takers, only the very strongest survive.

Source: Suzanne Woolley, "Will Today's Hot Stars Turn Cold Tomorrow?" *Business Week,* May 25, 1992, 96.

Maximin criterion

Decision choice method that provides the best of the worst possible outcomes.

each decision alternative and then choosing the option whose worst outcome provides the highest (maximum) payoff. This criterion instructs one to maximize the minimum possible outcome.

To illustrate, consider Table 3.7, which shows the weekly profit contribution payoffs from alternative gasoline-pricing strategies by the self-service U-Pump gas station in Jackson, Wyoming. Assume that U-Pump has just been notified of a 3¢ reduction in the wholesale price of gas. If U-Pump reduces its current self-service price by 3¢ per gallon, its weekly profit contribution will depend upon the reaction, if any, of its nearest competitor. If U-Pump's competitor matches the price reduction, a $2,500 profit contribution will result. Without any competitor reaction, U-Pump would earn $3,000. If U-Pump and its competitor both maintain current prices, U-Pump will earn $5,000, whereas if U-Pump did not match the competitor's price cut, U-Pump would earn only $1,000. The worst possible outcome following a price reduction by U-Pump is $2,500, but a $1,000 outcome is possible if U-Pump maintains its current price. The maximin criterion requires U-Pump to reduce its price, since the minimum possible outcome from this decision is greater than the minimum $1,000 payoff possible by maintaining the current price.

Although the maximin criterion suffers from the obvious shortcoming of focusing on the most pessimistic outcome for each decision alternative, it should not be dismissed as naive and unsophisticated. The maximin criterion implicitly assumes a very strong aversion to risk and is quite appropriate for decisions involving the possibility of catastrophic outcomes. When decision alternatives involve outcomes that endanger worker lives or the survival of the organization, for example, the maximin criterion can be an appropriate technique for decision making. Similarly, if the state of nature that prevails depends on the course of action taken by the decision maker, the maximin criterion might be appropriate. In the preceding example, one might expect that a decision by U-Pump to reduce prices would cause the competitor to follow suit, resulting in the worst possible outcome for that decision alternative.

Minimax Regret Decision Rule

Minimax regret criterion

Decision choice method that minimizes the maximum possible regret (opportunity loss) associated with a wrong decision *after the fact.*

A second useful decision criterion focuses on the opportunity loss associated with a decision rather than on its worst possible outcome. This decision rule, known as the **minimax regret criterion,** states that the decision maker should minimize the maximum possible regret (opportunity loss) associated with a wrong decision *after the fact.* This criterion instructs one to minimize the difference between possible outcomes and the best outcome for each state of nature.

To illustrate this decision technique, the concept of opportunity loss, or regret, must be examined in greater detail. In game theory, **opportunity loss** is defined as the difference between a given payoff and the highest possible payoff for the resulting state of nature. Opportunity losses result because returns actually received under conditions of uncertainty are frequently lower than the maximum return that would have been possible had perfect knowledge been available beforehand.

Table 3.8 shows the opportunity loss or regret matrix associated with U-Pump's gasoline-pricing problem. It was constructed by finding the maximum

TABLE 3.7   **Weekly Profit Contribution Payoff Matrix**

	States of Nature	
Decision Alternatives	**Competitor Reduces Prices**	**Competitor Maintains Current Price**
Reduce price	$2,500	$3,000
Maintain current price	$1,000	$5,000

TABLE 3.8   **Weekly Profit Contribution Opportunity Loss or Regret Matrix**

	States of Nature	
Decision Alternatives	**Competitor Reduces Price**	**Competitor Maintains Current Price**
Reduce price	$0 (= $2,500 − $2,500)	$2,000 (= $5,000 − $3,000)
Maintain current price	$1,500 (= $2,500 − $1,000)	$0 (= $5,000 − $5,000)

Opportunity loss

The difference between a given payoff and the highest possible payoff for the resulting state of nature.

payoff for a given state of nature in Table 3.7 and then subtracting from this amount the payoffs that would result from various decision alternatives. Opportunity loss is always a positive figure or zero, since each alternative payoff is subtracted from the largest payoff possible in a given state of nature. For example, if U-Pump's competitor reduced its price, the best possible decision for that state of nature would be for U-Pump to have also reduced prices. After the fact, U-Pump would have no regrets had it done so. Should U-Pump maintain its current price, the firm would experience a $1,500 opportunity loss, or regret. To calculate this amount, subtract the $1,000 payoff associated with U-Pump maintaining its current price despite a competitor price reduction from the $2,500 payoff that it would have received from matching the competitor's price reduction. Similarly, if U-Pump would reduce its price while its competitor maintains the current price, U-Pump would experience a $2,000 opportunity loss or regret after the fact.

The minimax regret criterion would cause U-Pump to maintain the current retail price of gasoline because this decision alternative minimizes the maximum regret, or opportunity loss. The maximum regret in this case is limited to the $1,500 loss that would result if the competitor reduced its current price. If U-Pump were to reduce its price while the competitor maintained its current price, U-Pump's opportunity loss would be $2,000 per week, $500 more than the maximum regret from U-Pump maintaining its current price.

The Cost of Uncertainty

An unavoidable opportunity loss is the cost associated with uncertainty. Therefore, the expected opportunity loss associated with a decision provides a measure of the expected monetary gain from the removal of all uncertainty about future events. From the opportunity loss or regret matrix, the **cost of uncertainty** is

TABLE 3.9 **Calculation of Expected Opportunity Loss**

From the Loss Matrix

State of Nature	Reduce Price			Maintain Current Price		
	Probability of This State of Nature (1)	Opportunity Loss of This Outcome (2)	Expected Opportunity Loss (3) = (1) × (2)	Probability of This State of Nature (1)	Opportunity Loss of This Outcome (2)	Expected Oppportunity Loss (3) = (1) × (2)
Competitor reduces price	0.5	$ 0	$ 0	0.5	$1,500	$750
Competitor maintains current price	0.5	$2,000	$1,000	0.5	$ 0	$ 0
			$1,000			$750

Cost of uncertainty = Minimum expected opportunity loss = $750.

From the Payoff Matrix

State of Nature	Reduce Price			Maintain Current Price		
	Probability (1)	Outcome (2)	(3) = (1) × (2)	Probability (1)	Outcome (2)	(3) = (1) × (2)
Competitor reduces price	0.5	$2,500	$1,250	0.5	$1,000	$ 500
Competitor maintains current price	0.5	$3,000	$1,500	0.5	$5,000	$2,500
			$2,750			$3,000

Expected value of a correct decision after the fact = $2,500(0.5) + $5,000(0.5) = $3,750.
Cost of uncertainty = Expected value of a correct decision − Expected value of best alternative
= $3,750 − $3,000 = $750.

Cost of uncertainty

The minimum expected opportunity loss.

measured by the minimum expected opportunity loss. From the payoff matrix, the cost of uncertainty is measured by the difference between the expected payoff associated with choosing the correct alternative under each state of nature (which will be known only after the fact) and the highest expected payoff available from among the decision alternatives. The cost of uncertainty is the unavoidable economic loss that is due to chance. Using this concept, it becomes possible to judge the value of gaining additional information before choosing among decision alternatives.

The previous gasoline-pricing problem can illustrate this use of opportunity loss. On the basis of the data in Table 3.8, the expected opportunity loss of each decision alternative can be calculated as shown in Table 3.9. Here it is assumed that U-Pump projects a 50/50, or 50 percent, chance of a competitor price reduction. The minimum expected opportunity cost in this case is $750 and represents U-Pump's loss from not knowing its competitor's pricing reaction with certainty. This cost of uncertainty represents the $750 value to U-Pump of resolving doubt about its competitor's pricing policy. U-Pump would be better off if it could eliminate this uncertainty by making an expenditure of less than $750 on information gathering.

Firms often engage in activities aimed at reducing the uncertainty of various alternatives before making an irrevocable decision. For example, a food-manufacturing company will employ extensive marketing tests in selected areas to gain better estimates of sales potential before going ahead with large-scale introduction of a new product. Manufacturers of consumer goods frequently install new equipment in a limited number of models to judge reliability and customer reaction before including the equipment in all models. Similarly, competitors often announce price changes well in advance of their effective date to elicit the reaction of rivals.

SUMMARY

Risk analysis plays an integral role in the decision process for most business problems. This chapter defines the concept of economic risk and illustrates how the concept can be employed in the managerial decision-making process.

• **Economic risk** is the chance of loss due to the fact that all possible outcomes and their probability of occurrence are unknown. **Uncertainty** exists when the outcomes of managerial decisions cannot be predicted with absolute accuracy but all possibilities and their associated probabilities of occurrence are known. **Business risk** is the chance of loss associated with a given managerial decision.

• The **probability** of an event is the chance, or odds, that the incident will occur. If all possible events or outcomes are listed, and if a probability of occurrence is assigned to each event, the listing is called a **probability distribution.** A **payoff matrix** illustrates the outcome associated with each possible state of nature. The **expected value** is the anticipated realization from a given payoff matrix.

• **Absolute risk** is the overall dispersion of possible payoffs. The smaller the standard deviation, the tighter the probability distribution and the lower the risk in absolute terms. **Relative risk** is the variation in possible returns compared with the expected payoff amount. **Beta** is a measure of the systematic variability or covariance of one asset's returns with returns on other assets.

• A **normal distribution** has a symmetrical distribution about the mean or expected value. If a probability distribution is normal, the actual outcome will lie within ± 1 standard deviation of the mean roughly 68 percent of the time; the probability that the actual outcome will be within ± 2 standard deviations of the expected outcome is approximately 95 percent; and there is a greater than 99 percent probability that the actual outcome will occur within ± 3 standard deviations of the mean. A **standardized variable** has a mean of 0 and a standard deviation equal to 1.

• **Risk aversion** characterizes individuals who seek to avoid or minimize risk. **Risk neutrality** characterizes decision makers who focus on expected returns and disregard the dispersion of returns (risk). **Risk seeking** characterizes decision makers who prefer risk. At the heart of risk aversion is the notion of **diminishing marginal utility,** where additional increments of money bring ever smaller increments of marginal utility.

• Under the **certainty equivalent** approach, decision makers specify the certain sum that they regard comparable to the expected value of a risky investment alternative. The certainty equivalent of an expected risk amount typically differs in dollar terms but not in terms of the amount of utility provided. Any expected risky amount can be converted to an equivalent certain sum using the **certainty equivalent adjustment factor, α,** calculated as the ratio of a certain sum divided by an expected risky amount, where both dollar values provide the same level of utility.

• The difference between the expected rate of return on a risky asset and the rate of return on a riskless asset is the **risk premium** on the risky asset. The **risk-adjusted discount rate** k is the sum of the risk-free rate of return, R_F, plus the required risk premium, R_p.

• A **decision tree** is a map of a sequential decision-making process. Decision trees are designed for analyzing decision problems that involve a series of choice alternatives that are constrained by previous decisions. **Decision points** represent instances when management must select among several choice alternatives. **Chance events** are possible outcomes following each decision point.

• **Computer simulation** involves the use of computer software and workstations or sophisticated desktop computers to create a wide variety of decision outcome scenarios. **Sensitivity analysis** focuses on those variables that most directly affect decision outcomes; it is less expensive and less time-consuming than full-scale computer simulation.

• **Game theory** is a useful decision framework employed to make choices in hostile environments and under extreme uncertainty. One decision standard that is sometimes applicable for decision making under uncertainty is the **maximin criterion,** which states that the decision maker should select the alternative that provides the best of the worst possible outcomes. The **minimax regret criterion** states that the decision maker should minimize the maximum possible regret (opportunity loss) associated with a wrong decision *after the fact.* In game theory, **opportunity loss** is defined as the difference between a given payoff and the highest possible payoff for the resulting state of nature. From the opportunity loss or regret matrix, **the cost of uncertainty** is measured by the minimum expected opportunity loss.

Decision making under conditions of uncertainty is greatly facilitated by use of the tools and techniques discussed in this chapter. While uncertainty can never be eliminated, it can be assessed and dealt with to minimize its harmful consequences.

Questions   Q3.1   Define the following terms:
A. Probability distribution
B. Expected value
C. Standard deviation
D. Coefficient of variation
E. Risk
F. Diminishing marginal utility of money
G. Certainty equivalent
H. Risk-adjusted discount rate

I. Decision tree

J. Simulation

Q3.2   What is the main difficulty associated with making decisions solely on the basis of comparisons of expected returns?

Q3.3   The standard deviation measure of risk implicitly gives equal weight to variations on both sides of the expected value. Can you see any potential limitations of this treatment?

Q3.4   "Utility is a theoretical concept that cannot be observed or measured in the real world. Hence, it has no practical value in decision analysis." Discuss this statement.

Q3.5   Graph the relation between money and its utility for an individual who buys both household fire insurance and state lottery tickets.

Q3.6   When the basic valuation model is adjusted using the risk-free rate, i, what economic factor is being explicitly accounted for?

Q3.7   If the expected net present value of returns from an investment project is $50,000, what is the maximum price that a risk-neutral investor would pay for it? Explain.

Q3.8   "Market estimates of investors' reactions to risk cannot be measured precisely, so it is impossible to set risk-adjusted discount rates for various classes of investment with a high degree of precision." Discuss this statement.

Q3.9   What is the value of decision trees in managerial decision making?

Q3.10 When is it most useful to use game theory in decision analysis?

Self-Test Problem   Quality Foods, Inc., is a leading grocery retailer in the greater Washington, D.C., metropolitan area. The company is currently engaged in an aggressive store-refurbishing program and is contemplating expansion of its in-store delicatessen department. A number of investment alternatives are being considered, including the construction of facilities for a new restaurant-quality carryout service for Chinese food. This investment project is to be evaluated using the certainty equivalent adjustment factor method and the risk-adjusted discount rate method. If the project has a positive value when *both* methods are employed, the project will be undertaken. The project will not be undertaken if either evaluation method suggests that the investment will fail to increase the value of the firm. Expected cash flow after tax (CFAT) values over the five-year life of the investment project and relevant certainty equivalent adjustment factor information pare as follows:

Time Period (Years)	Alpha	Project E(CFAT)
0	1.00	($75,000)
1	0.95	22,500
2	0.95	25,000
3	0.90	27,500
4	0.85	30,000
5	0.70	32,500
Total		$62,500

At the present time, an 8 percent annual rate of return can be obtained on short-term U.S. government securities; the company uses this rate as an estimate of the risk-free rate of return.

A. Use the 8 percent risk-free rate to calculate the present value of the investment project.

B. Using this present value as a basis, utilize the certainty equivalent adjustment factor information given previously to determine the risk-adjusted present value of the project.

C. Use an alternative risk-adjusted discount rate method of project valuation on the assumption that a 15 percent rate of return is appropriate in light of the level of risk undertaken.

D. Compare and contrast your answers to Parts B and C. Should the investment be made?

Solution to
Self-Test Problem

A. The present value of this investment project can be calculated easily using a hand-held calculator with typical financial function capabilities or by using the tables found in Appendix A. Using the appropriate discount factors corresponding to an 8 percent risk-free rate, the present value of the investment project is calculated as follows:

Time Period (Years)	Present Value of $1 at 8%	Project E(CFAT)	Present Value of E(CFAT) at 8%
0	1.0000	($75,000)	($75,000)
1	0.9259	22,500	20,833
2	0.8573	25,000	21,433
3	0.7938	27,500	21,830
4	0.7350	30,000	22,050
5	0.6806	32,500	22,120
Total		$62,500	$33,266

B. Using the present value given in Part A as a basis, the certainty equivalent adjustment factor information given previously can be employed to determine the risk-adjusted present value of the project:

Time Period (Years)	Present Value of $1 at 8%	Project E(CFAT)	Present Value of E(CFAT) at 8%	Alpha	Risk-Adjusted Value
0	1.0000	($75,000)	($75,000)	1.00	($75,000)
1	0.9259	22,500	20,833	.095	19,791
2	0.8573	25,000	21,433	.095	19,290
3	0.7938	27,500	21,830	.090	18,556
4	0.7350	30,000	22,050	0.85	16,538
5	0.6806	32,500	22,120	0.70	15,484
Total		$62,500	$33,266		$14,659

C. An alternative risk-adjusted discount rate method of project valuation based upon a 15 percent rate of return gives the following project valuation:

Time Period (Years)	Present Value of $1 at 15%	Project E(CFAT)	Present Value of E(CFAT) at 15%
0	1.0000	($75,000)	($75,000)
1	0.8696	22,500	19,566
2	0.7561	25,000	18,903
3	0.6575	27,500	18,081
4	0.5718	30,000	17,154
5	0.4972	32,500	16,159
Total		$62,500	$14,863

D. The answers to Parts B and C are fully compatible; both suggest a positive risk-adjusted present value for the project. In Part B, the certainty equivalent adjustment factor method reduces the present value of future receipts to account for risk differences. As is typical, the example assumes that money to be received in the more distant future has a greater risk and, hence, a lesser certainty equivalent value. In the risk-adjusted discount rate approach of Part C, the discount rate of 15 percent entails a time-factor adjustment of 8 percent plus a risk adjustment of 7 percent. Like the certainty equivalent adjustment factor approach, the risk-adjusted discount rate method gives a risk-adjusted present value for the project. Since the risk-adjusted present value of the project is positive under either approach, the investment should be made.

Problems

P3.1 **Risk Preferences.** Identify each of the following as being consistent with risk-averse, risk-neutral, or risk-seeking behavior in investment project selection. Explain your answers.
A. Larger risk premiums for riskier projects
B. Preference for smaller, as opposed to larger, coefficients of variation
C. Valuing certain sums and expected risky sums of equal dollar amounts equally
D. Having an increasing marginal utility of money
E. Ignoring the risk levels of investment alternatives

P3.2 **Certainty Equivalents.** The certainty equivalent concept can be widely employed in the analysis of personal and business decision making. Indicate whether each of the following statements is true or false and explain why:
A. The appropriate certainty equivalent adjustment factor, α, indicates the minimum price in certain dollars that an individual should be willing to pay per risky dollar of expected return.
B. An $\alpha \neq 1$ implies that a certain sum and a risky expected return of different dollar amounts provide equivalent utility to a given decision maker.

C. If previously accepted projects with similar risk have αs in a range from $\alpha = 0.4$ to $\alpha = 0.5$, an investment with an expected return of $150,000 is acceptable at a cost of $50,000.

D. A project for which NPV > 0 using an appropriate risk-adjusted discount rate has an implied α factor that is too large to allow project acceptance.

E. State lotteries that pay out 50 percent of the revenues that they generate require players who place at least a certain $2 value on each $1 of expected risky return.

P3.3   **Expected Value.** Duddy Kravitz, a broker with Caveat Emptor, Ltd., offers free investment seminars to local PTA groups. On average, Kravitz expects 1 percent of seminar participants to purchase $25,000 in tax-sheltered investments and 5 percent to purchase $5,000 in stocks and bonds. Kravitz earns a 4 percent net commission on tax shelters and a 1 percent commission on stocks and bonds. Calculate Kravitz's expected net commissions per seminar if attendance averages ten persons.

P3.4   **Probability Concepts.** Aquarius Products, Inc., has just completed development of a new line of skin-care products. Preliminary market research indicates two feasible marketing strategies: (1) creating general consumer acceptance through media advertising or (2) creating distributor acceptance through intensive personal selling by company representatives. The marketing manager has developed the following estimates for sales under each alternative:

Media Advertising Strategy		Personal Selling Strategy	
Probability	Sales	Probability	Sales
0.1	$ 500,000	0.3	$1,000,000
0.4	1,500,000	0.4	1,500,000
0.4	2,500,000	0.3	2,000,000
0.1	3,500,000		

A. Assume that the company has a 50 percent profit margin on sales (that is, profits equal one-half of sales revenue). Calculate expected profits for each plan.

B. Construct a simple bar graph of the possible profit outcomes for each plan. Which plan appears to be riskier?

C. Assume that management's utility function resembles the one illustrated in the figure at the top of the following page. Which strategy should the marketing manager recommend?

P3.5   **Probability Concepts.** Sam Malone, marketing director for Narcissism Records, Inc., has just completed an agreement to rerelease a recording of "The Boss's Greatest Hits." (The Boss had a number of hits on the rock and roll charts during the early 1980s.) Preliminary market research indicates two feasible marketing strategies: (1) concentration on developing general consumer acceptance by advertising on late-night television or (2) concentration on developing distributor acceptance through

The Relation Between Total Profit and Utility for Aquarius Products, Inc.

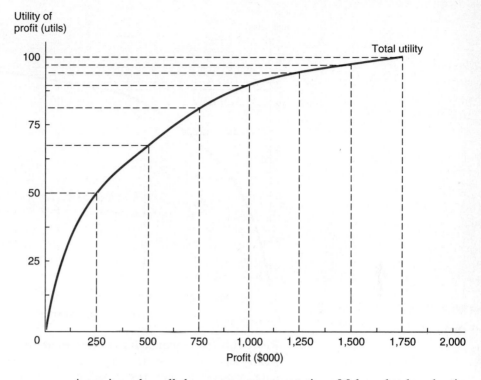

intensive sales calls by company representatives. Malone developed estimates for sales under each alternative plan and has constructed payoff
matrices according to his assessment of the likelihood of product acceptance under each plan. These data are as follows:

Strategy 1: Consumer Television Promotion		Strategy 2: Distributor-Oriented Promotion	
Probability	Outcome (Sales)	Probability	Outcome (Sales)
0.32	$ 250,000	0.125	$ 250,000
0.36	1,000,000	0.750	750,000
0.32	1,750,000	0.125	1,250,000

A. Assuming that the company has a 50 percent profit margin on sales,
   calculate the expected profits for each plan.
B. Construct a simple bar graph of the possible profit outcomes for each
   plan. Which plan appears to be riskier?
C. Calculate the standard deviation of the profit distribution associated
   with each plan.
D. Assume that the management of Narcissism has a utility function like
   the one illustrated in the following figure. Which marketing strategy
   should Malone recommend?

The Relation Between Total Utility and Profit for Narcissism Records, Inc.

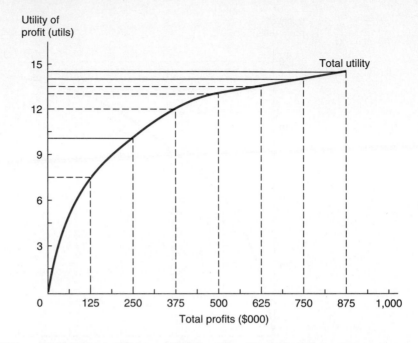

P3.6   **Risk-Adjusted Discount Rates.** One-Hour Dryclean, Inc., is contemplating replacing an obsolete dry cleaning machine with one of two innovative pieces of equipment. Alternative 1 requires a current investment outlay of $25,373, whereas Alternative 2 requires an outlay of $24,199. The following cash flows (cost savings) will be generated each year over the new machines' four-year lives:

	Probability	Cash Flow
Alternative 1	0.18	$ 5,000
	0.64	10,000
	0.18	15,000
Alternative 2	0.125	$ 8,000
	0.75	10,000
	0.125	12,000

A. Calculate the expected cash flow for each investment alternative.
B. Calculate the standard deviation of cash flows (risk) for each investment alternative.
C. The firm will use a discount rate of 12 percent for the cash flows with a higher degree of dispersion and a 10 percent rate for the less risky cash flows. Calculate the expected net present value for each investment. Which alternative should be chosen?

P3.7   **Certainty Equivalent Method.** Tex-Mex, Inc., is a rapidly growing chain of Mexican food restaurants. The company has a limited amount of capital for expansion and must carefully weigh available alternatives.

Currently, the company is considering opening restaurants in Santa Fe or Albuquerque, New Mexico. Projections for the two potential outlets are as follows:

City	Outcome	Annual Profit Contribution	Probability
Albuquerque	Failure	$100,000	0.5
	Success	200,000	0.5
Santa Fe	Failure	$ 60,000	0.5
	Success	340,000	0.5

Each restaurant would require a capital expenditure of $700,000, plus land acquisition costs of $500,000 for Albuquerque and $1 million for Santa Fe. The company uses the 10 percent yield on riskless U.S. Treasury bills to calculate the risk-free annual opportunity cost of investment capital.

A. Calculate the expected value, standard deviation, and coefficient of variation for each outlet's profit contribution.

B. Calculate the minimum certainty equivalent adjustment factor for each restaurant's cash flows that would justify investment in each outlet.

C. Assuming that the management of Tex-Mex is risk averse and uses the certainty equivalent method in decision making, which is the more attractive outlet? Why?

P3.8 **Decision Trees.** Keystone Manufacturing, Inc., is analyzing a new bid to supply the company with electronic control systems. Alpha Corporation has been supplying the systems and Keystone is satisfied with its performance. However, a bid has just been received from Beta Controls, Ltd., a firm that is aggressively marketing its products. Beta has offered to supply systems for a price of $120,000. The price for the Alpha system is $160,000. In addition to an attractive price, Beta offers a money-back guarantee. That is, if Beta's systems do not match Alpha's quality, Keystone can reject and return them for a full refund. However, if it must reject the machines and return them to Beta, Keystone will suffer a delay costing the firm $60,000.

A. Construct a decision tree for this problem and determine the maximum probability that Keystone could assign to rejection of the Beta system before it would reject that firm's offer, assuming that it decides on the basis of minimizing expected costs.

B. Assume that Keystone assigns a 50 percent probability of rejection to the Beta controls. Would Keystone be willing to pay $15,000 for an assurance bond that would pay $60,000 in the event that the Beta controls fail the quality check? (Use the same objective as in Part A.) Explain.

P3.9 **Standard Normal Concept.** Speedy Business Cards, Inc., supplies customized business cards to commercial and individual customers. The company is preparing a bid to supply cards to the Nationwide Realty Company, a large association of independent real estate agents. Since

paper, ink, and other costs cannot be determined precisely, Speedy anticipates that costs will be normally distributed around a mean of $20 per
unit (each 500-card order) with a standard deviation of $2 per unit.

A. What is the probability that Speedy will make a profit at a price of
$20 per unit?

B. Calculate the unit price necessary to give Speedy a 95 percent chance
of making a profit on the order.

C. If Speedy submits a successful bid of $23 per unit, what is the prob-
ability that it will make a profit?

P3.10 **Game Theory.** Sierra Mountain Bike, Inc., is a producer and wholesaler
of rugged bicycles designed for mountain touring. The company is considering an upgrade to its current line by making high-grade chrome alloy
frames standard. Of course, the market response to this upgrade in product quality depends on the competitor's reaction, if any. The company's
comptroller projects the following annual profits (payoffs) following resolution of the upgrade decision:

	States of Nature	
Sierra's Decision Alternatives	Competitor Upgrade	No Competitor Upgrade
Upgrade	$1,000,000	$1,500,000
Do not upgrade	800,000	2,000,000

A. Which decision alternative would Sierra choose given a maximin
criterion? Explain.

B. Calculate the opportunity loss or regret matrix.

C. Which decision alternative would Sierra choose given a minimax
regret criterion? Explain.

CASE STUDY FOR CHAPTER 3

Time Warner Is Playing Games with Stockholders

Time Warner, Inc., the world's largest media and entertainment company, was
created through the July 1989 merger of Time, Inc., and Warner Communications, Inc. The company is best known as the publisher of magazines such as
Fortune, Time, Life, People, and *Sports Illustrated* as well as owner of the highly
profitable Book-of-the Month Club. Perhaps less well known is the fact that Time
Warner also owns leading pay TV networks such as *Home Box Office* and *Cine-
max,* and it controls one of the nation's largest cable TV systems through its
American Television and Communications subsidiary. The company also has a
leading position in the recorded music business and enjoys major interests in both
movie making and TV entertainment program production. Time Warner has the

potential to profit whether people go to theaters, buy or rent videocassettes, watch cable or broadcast TV, or listen to records.

Just as impressive as Time Warner's commanding presence in the entertainment field is its potential for better capitalizing on its recognized strengths during coming years. Time Warner is a leader in terms of embracing new entertainment-field technology, as typified by its installation of the world's first fiber-optic 150-channel two-way cable TV system in Queens, New York. This revolutionary cable system allows subscribers to rent movies, purchase a wide array of goods and services, and participate in game shows and consumer surveys—all within the privacy of their own homes. Wide channel flexibility also gives the company the opportunity to expand pay-per-view TV offerings to meet demand from specialized market niches. In areas where cable systems have sufficient capacity, HBO subscribers are now offered a choice of programming on different channels. Time Warner also set up a TVKO network to offer boxing events on a regular pay-per-view basis following its success with the Holeyfield-Foreman fight during the spring of 1991. More examples of specialized programming are sure to follow during the mid-1990s.

Time Warner is an interesting case study in decision making under uncertainty given the company's controversial plan during 1991 to raise new equity capital through use of a complex "contingent" rights offering. After months of assuring Wall Street that it was close to raising new equity from other firms through strategic alliances, Time Warner instead asked its shareholders to ante up more cash. Under the plan, the company granted holders of its 57.8 million shares of common stock the rights to 34.5 million shares of new common, or 0.6 rights per share. Each right enabled a shareholder to pay Time Warner $105 for an *unspecified* number of new common shares. Since the number of new shares that might be purchased for $105 was unspecified, so too was the price per share. In an unusual twist, Time Warner's Wall Street advisers structured the offer so that the new stock would be offered at cheaper prices if fewer shareholders chose to exercise their rights.

In an unusual arrangement, the rights from all participating shareholders were to be placed in a pool to determine their *pro rata* share of the 34.45 million shares to be distributed. If 100 percent of Time Warner shareholders chose to exercise their rights, the price per share would be $105, the number of shares owned by each shareholder would increase by 60 percent, and each shareholder would retain his or her same proportionate ownership in the company. In the event that less than 100 percent of the shareholders chose to participate, participating shareholders would receive a discount price and increase their proportionate interest in the company. If only 80 percent of Time Warner shareholders chose to exercise their rights, the price per share would be $84; if 60 percent chose to exercise their rights, the price per share would be $63. These lower prices reflect the fact that if only 80 percent of Time Warner shareholders chose to exercise their rights, each $105 right would purchase 1.25 shares; if 60 percent chose to exercise their rights, each $105 right would purchase roughly 1.667 shares. Finally, to avoid the possibility of issuing equity at fire-sale prices, Time Warner reserved the privilege to cancel the equity offering entirely if less than 60 percent of holders chose to exercise their rights.

The terms of the offer were designed to make Time Warner shareholders feel compelled to exercise their rights in hopes of getting cheap stock and avoiding seeing their holdings diluted. Although such contingent rights offerings are a common capital-raising technique in Britain, prior to the Time Warner offering they had never been proposed on such a large scale in the United States. Wall Street traders and investment bankers lauded the Time Warner offer as a brilliant coercive device—a view that might have been colored by the huge fees they stood to make on the offering. Advisory fees for Merrill Lynch and Time Warner's seven other key advisers were projected at from $41.5 million to $145 million, depending on the number of participating shareholders. An additional $20.7 million to $34.5 million was set aside to pay other investment bankers for soliciting shareholders to exercise their rights. Time Warner's advisers argued that their huge fees totaling 5.22 percent of the proceeds to the company were justified because the offering entered uncharted ground in terms of Wall Street experience. Disgruntled shareholders noted that a similar contingent rights offering by Bass PLC of Britain involved a fee of only 2.125 percent of the proceeds to the company, despite the fact that the lead underwriter Schroders PLC agreed to buy and resell any new stock that wasn't claimed by rights holders. This led to charges that Time Warner's advisers were charging underwriters' fees without risking any of their own capital.

Proceeds from the offering were earmarked to help pay down the $11.3 billion debt Time Inc. took on to buy Warner Communications Inc. two years previously when Time Warner was formed. Time Warner maintained that it was in intensive talks with potential strategic partners and that the rights offering would strengthen its hand in those negotiations by improving the company's balance sheet. Time Warner said that the rights offering would enhance its ability to enter into strategic alliances or joint ventures with partners overseas. Such alliances would help the company penetrate markets in Japan, Europe, and elsewhere. Critics of the plan argued that the benefits from strategic alliances come in small increments and that Time Warner had failed to strike any such deals previously because it wants both management control and a premium price from potential partners. These critics also maintained that meaningful revenue from any such projects is probably years away.

Stockholder reaction to the Time Warner offering was immediate and overwhelmingly negative. On the day the offering was announced, Time Warner shares closed at $99.50, down $11.25, in New York Stock Exchange composite trading. This is in addition to a decline of $6 suffered the previous day on the basis of a report in *The Wall Street Journal* that some form of equity offering was being considered. After trading above $120 per share in the days prior to the first reports of a pending offer, Time Warner shares plummeted by more than 25 percent to $88 per share within a matter of days. This is yet one more disappointment for the company's long-suffering common stockholders. During the summer of 1989, Time cited a wide range of synergistic benefits to be gained from a merger with Warner Communications and spurned a $200 per share buyout offer from Paramount Communications, Inc. This despite the fact that the Paramount offer represented a fat 60 percent premium to the then prevailing market price of $125 for Time stock. During the succeeding two-year period, Time Warner stock failed to rise above this $125 level and traded as low as $66 per share during the fall of 1990. Meanwhile, the hoped-for Time Warner synergy has yet to emerge.

A. Was Paramount's above-market offer for Time, Inc. consistent with the notion that the prevailing market price for common stock is an accurate reflection of the discounted net present value of future cash flows? Was management's rejection of Paramount's above-market offer for Time, Inc. consistent with the value-maximization concept?

B. Assume that a Time Warner shareholder could buy additional shares at a market price of $90 or participate in the company's rights offering. Construct the payoff and regret matrices per share that correspond to a $90 per share purchase decision versus a decision to participate in the rights offering with subsequent 100 percent, 80 percent, and 60 percent participation by all Time Warner shareholders.

C. Describe the relevant maximin and minimax shareholder strategies.

D. Explain why the price of Time Warner common stock fell following the announcement of the company's controversial rights offering. Is such an offering in the best interests of current shareholders?

Selected References

Berry, S. Keith. "Ramsey Pricing in the Presence of Risk." *Managerial and Decision Economics* 13 (March–April 1992): 111–117.

Bromiley, Philip. "Testing a Causal Model of Corporate Risk Taking and Performance." *Academy of Management Journal* 34 (March 1991): 37–59.

Chew, W. Bruce, and Timothy B. Blodgett. "The Case of the High-Risk Safety Product." *Harvard Business Review* 70 (May–June 1992): 14–27.

Cropper, Maureen L., Sema K. Aydede, and Paul Portney. "Rates of Time Preference for Saving Lives." *American Economic Review* 82 (May 1992): 469–472.

Davidson, Paul. "Is Probability Theory Relevant for Uncertainty? A Post Keynesian Perspective." *Journal of Economic Perspectives* 5 (Winter 1991): 129–143.

Fornell, Claes. "A National Customer Satisfaction Barometer: The Swedish Experience." *Journal of Marketing* 56 (January 1992): 6–21.

Ingersoll, Jonathan E., and Stephen A. Ross. "Waiting to Invest: Investment and Uncertainty." *Journal of Business* 65 (January 1992): 1–29.

Logue, Dennis E., and James K. Seward. "The Time Warner Rights Offering: Strategy, Articulation and the Destruction of Shareholder Value." *Financial Analysts Journal* 49 (March–April 1992): 37–46.

Montgomery, Cynthia A., and Birger Wernerfelt. "Risk Reduction and Umbrella Branding." *Journal of Business* 65 (January 1992): 31–50.

Palma, André de. "A Game-Theoretic Approach to the Analysis of Simple Congested Networks." *American Economic Review* 82 (May 1992): 494–500.

Persky, Joseph. "Pareto's Law." *Journal of Economic Perspectives* 6 (Spring 1992): 181–192.

Power, Michael, and Elizabeth Jewkes. "Simulating Natural Gas Discoveries." *Interfaces* 22 (March–April 1992): 38–51.

Skaperdas, Stergios. "Conflicts and Attitudes toward Risk." *American Economic Review* 81 (May 1991): 116–120.

Thakor, Anjan V. "Game Theory in Finance." *Financial Management* 20 (Spring 1991): 71–94.

Vickrey, William. "An Updated Agenda for Progressive Taxation." *American Economic Review* 82 (May 1992): 257–262.

P A R T DEMAND ANALYSIS

CHAPTER 4

DEMAND AND SUPPLY

Nothing is more important to the economic survival of any organization than the need to effectively identify and respond to product demand and supply conditions. In economic terms, demand refers to the amount of a product that people are willing and able to buy under a given set of conditions. Need or desire is a necessary component but must be accompanied by financial capability before an economic demand is created. Thus, economic demand requires potential buyers with a desire to use or possess something and the financial ability to acquire it. With vibrant demand for its products, the firm is able to attract the necessary resources to expand and grow. Without demand for a firm's products, no revenues are generated to pay suppliers, workers, and stockholders. Without demand, no amount of efficiency in production can ensure the firm's long-term survival. Without demand, the firm simply ceases to exist.

Once demand for the firm's products has been identified or created, the firm must thoroughly understand supply conditions to efficiently meet customer needs. Supply is the amount of a good or service that firms make available for sale under a given set of economic conditions. Just as demand requires a desire to purchase combined with the economic resources to do so, supply requires a desire to sell along with the economic capability to bring a product to market. The amount of product supplied is determined by the profitability of doing so. Supply increases when additional profits are generated; supply decreases when production results in losses.

Combining the concepts of demand and supply provides a framework for analyzing the interaction of buyers and sellers. Using that framework, it is possible to examine the determination of price and activity levels in economic markets and the conditions required for market equilibrium—a state in which the quantities demanded and supplied of a good or service are in perfect balance. Comparative statics analysis is used extensively in the study of economic markets. This analysis involves comparisons of market equilibrium conditions before and after a change in one or more factors underlying demand or supply. Comparative statics analysis provides a useful framework for evaluating the consequences of changes in market demand and supply conditions.

The concepts of demand, supply, and equilibrium provide a basis for analyzing the interactions of buyers and sellers in the markets for all goods and services. The overview presented in this chapter provides a useful framework for the more detailed study of demand and supply concepts in Chapters 5 through 14. The study of demand and supply is also important because together they determine the market structure and level of competition in all industries. The importance of demand and supply as determinants of both business practice and public policy is investigated in Chapters 10 through 15.

THE BASIS FOR DEMAND

Demand

The total quantity of a good or service that customers are willing and able to purchase.

Demand is the quantity of a good or service that customers are willing and able to purchase during a specified period under a given set of economic conditions. The time frame might be an hour, a day, a year, or any other time period. The conditions that must be considered include the price of the good in question, prices and availability of related goods, expectations of price changes, consumer incomes, tastes and preferences, advertising expenditures, and so on. The amount of the product that consumers are prepared to purchase—its demand—depends on all these factors.

For managerial decision making, the primary focus is on market demand, which is merely the aggregate of individual or personal demand. Therefore, insight into market demand relations is gained by understanding the nature of individual demand. Individual demand is determined by the value associated with acquiring and using any good or service and by the ability to acquire such goods or services. Both are necessary for effective individual demand. Desire without purchasing power may lead to want but not to demand.

Direct Demand

Direct demand

Demand for consumption products.

Utility

Value or worth.

There are two basic models of individual demand. One, known as the theory of consumer behavior, relates to the **direct demand** for personal consumption products. This model is appropriate for analyzing individual demand for goods and services that directly satisfy consumer desires. The value or worth of a good or service, its **utility**, is the prime determinant of direct demand. Individuals are viewed as attempting to maximize the total utility or satisfaction provided by the goods and services they acquire and consume. This optimization process requires that consumers consider the marginal utility (gain in satisfaction) of acquiring additional units of a given product or of acquiring one product as opposed to another. Product characteristics, individual preferences (tastes), and the ability to pay are all important determinants of direct demand.

Derived Demand

Derived demand

Demand for all inputs used in production.

Some goods and services are acquired not for their direct consumption value but because they are important inputs in the manufacture and distribution of other products. The output of engineers, production workers, salespersons, managers, lawyers, consultants, office business machines, production facilities and equipment, natural resources, and commercial airplanes are all examples of goods and services demanded not for direct final personal consumption but for their use in providing other goods and services. Their demand is derived from the demand for the products they are used to provide. The demand for all inputs used by a firm is **derived demand.**

The demand for mortgage money is an example of derived demand. The quantity of mortgage credit demanded is not determined directly; rather, it is derived from the more fundamental demand for housing. Similarly, the demand for air transportation to major resort areas is not a direct demand but rather is derived from the demand for recreation. The demand for all producers' goods and services used in the manufacture of products for final consumption is derived. The aggregate demand for consumption goods and services determines demand for the capital equipment, materials, labor, and energy used to manufacture them. For example, the demands for steel, aluminum, and plastics are all derived demands, as are the demands for machine tools and labor. None of these producers' goods are demanded because of their direct value to consumers but because of the role they play in the production of final goods and services.

As one might expect, the demand for producers' goods and services is closely related to the demand for the final products they make. Therefore, an examination of final product demand is an important part of the demand analysis for intermediate, or producers', goods. For products whose demand is derived rather than direct, the theory of the firm provides the basis for analyzing individual demand. Demand for these goods stems from their value in the manufacture and sale of other products. They have value because their employment has the potential to generate profits. Key components in the determination of derived demand are the marginal benefits and marginal costs associated with employing a given input or factor of production. The amount of any good or service employed rises when its marginal benefit, measured in terms of the value of resulting output, is greater than the marginal costs of employing the input, measured in terms of wages, interest, raw material costs, or related expenses. Conversely, the amount of any input employed in production falls when the resulting marginal benefits are less than the marginal cost of employment. In short, derived demand is related to the profitability of employing a good or service.

Regardless of whether a good or service is demanded by individuals for final consumption (direct demand) or as an input factor used in providing other goods and services (derived demand), the fundamentals of economic analysis provide a basis for investigating the characteristics of demand. For final consumption products, utility maximization—as described by the theory of consumer behavior—explains the basis for direct demand. For inputs used in the production of other products, profit maximization provides the underlying rationale for derived demand. Since both demand models are based on optimization (they differ only in the nature of their objectives), it comes as no surprise that, while various characteristics that affect demand may differ, the fundamental relations are essentially the same. The principles of managerial economics, and particularly the principles of optimal resource use, provide a basis for understanding demand by both firms and consumers.

THE MARKET DEMAND FUNCTION

Demand function
The relation between demand and factors influencing its level.

The market **demand function** for a product is a statement of the relation between the aggregate quantity demanded and all factors that affect this quantity.

MANAGERIAL APPLICATION 4.1

A Market Economy Takes Root in Eastern Europe

Under the Polish communist regime, entrepreneurs had as much to fear from success as from failure. As owners of Poland's few private companies, they found it necessary to bribe the secret police and conceal growth to stay out of jail. During the 1990s as the Poles move toward a market economy, rapid economic and social change is clearly evident. Within a scant 15 months from when the communists lost power in 1989, thousands of entrepreneurs opened new shops and plants in the former East Bloc countries of Poland, Hungary, and Czechoslovakia. While the popular press has focused on the dramatic shrinkage of state economies in each of these countries, the astonishing growth of private economies has been largely overlooked. Both private and public sources of statistics report over 250,000 new companies in Hungary, 300,000 in Czechoslovakia, and over one-half million in Poland—all within this brief 15-month period.

While the region's fragile new state governments face daunting challenges, the grass-roots economy is clearly taking hold. Throughout the former East Bloc countries, the most important characteristic of a market-based economy is clearly evident: the decentralization of production and operating decisions. No centralized government agency or industry trade association makes decisions about what types of products should be produced or the quantity or quality of output. Instead, these decisions are made by individual firms based on their perceptions of consumer preferences and market opportunities. The price consumers are willing to pay for established goods and services is a signal to which firms respond through their production and operating decisions. Firms that are able to offer goods and services in a relatively attractive fashion in terms of price, quantity, and quality tend to grow and prosper. Similarly, firms that successfully anticipate changes in consumer preferences reap substantial economic rewards. Those that do not tend to fall by the wayside. In other words, a market-based economy relies only on the profit motive as a means for assuring the production of the types and quantities of goods and services that consumers want and need (demand). As economist Adam Smith said more than 200 years ago, by acting in their own self-interests, individuals are moved as if by an "invisible hand" to promote the common welfare.

At first, a market-based economy might appear to be a risky and costly means for organizing economic activity. Of course, the human disruption caused by bankruptcy, along with other economic costs, is often substantial. Economic losses associated with lost production because of work stoppages, retraining and relocation costs for managers and other workers, and expenses associated with factory retooling are obvious social costs incurred when bankruptcy takes place. What workers in former East Bloc countries have come to realize is that the economic costs of bankruptcy are less than the costs of production errors made when the forces of demand and supply are ignored. When compared to the costs of centralized economic planning, the virtues of the market system become readily apparent. In Budapest, activity in private restaurants and shops bustles until late evening, while managers at the state phone company quit work at 3:00 p.m. Since trade with the Soviet market collapsed during late 1990, industrial production from state-owned enterprise has disintegrated. In fact, private companies form something of a safety net in these countries. The private sector throughout former East Bloc countries is hiring thousands of workers deserting bankrupt state companies. In Poland alone, at least one-third of the 1.2 million workers laid off during 1990 were rehired by private enterprises.

Long ago, Budapest, Prague, and Warsaw were hubs of European culture and business. New ties to the West have helped rekindle a Central European intellectual, scientific, and cultural renaissance. With old laws no longer being enforced, and new ones yet to be written, what seems to work best is the oldest law of all: the law of demand and supply.

Source: Barry Newman, "As Capitalism Takes Root, Dreams Grow among Many Poles," *The Wall Street Journal,* May 18, 1992, A1.

*Determinants
of Demand*

Written in general functional form, the demand function may be expressed as

Quantity of
Product X $= Q_X =$ f(Price of X; Prices of Related
Goods; Expectations of Price
Changes; Consumer Incomes, Tastes   **(4.1)**
Demanded   and Preferences; Advertising
Expenditures; and so on).

The generalized demand function expressed in Equation 4.1 lists variables that influence demand. For use in managerial decision making, the demand function must be made explicit. The relation between quantity and each demand-determining variable must be clearly and explicitly specified. To illustrate what is involved, assume that the demand function for the automobile industry has been specified as follows:

$$Q = a_1 P + a_2 Y + a_3 Pop + a_4 i + a_5 A. \qquad (4.2)$$

This equation states that the number of automobiles demanded during a given year, Q, is a linear function of the average price of cars, P; per capita income, Y; population, Pop; the average interest rate on car loans (in percent), i; and advertising expenditures, A. The terms $a1, a2, \ldots, a5$ are called the parameters of the demand function. For purposes of illustration, assume that the parameters of this demand function are known with certainty as shown in the following equation:

$$Q = -1,000P + 100Y + 0.08Pop - 1,000,000i + 0.01A \qquad (4.3)$$

Equation 4.3 states that automobile demand falls by 1,000 units for each $1 increase in the average price charged; it increases by 100 units for each $1 increase in per capita income; it increases by 0.08 units for each additional person in the population; it decreases by 1 million units for every 1 percent rise in interest rates; and it increases by 0.01 units for each $1 spent on advertising.

To derive an estimate of industry demand in any given year, each parameter in Equation 4.3 is multiplied by the value of the related variable and then summed. Table 4.1 illustrates this process, showing that the estimated demand for autos is 10 million units, assuming the stated values of the independent variables.

*Industry Demand
versus Firm Demand*

Market demand functions can be specified for an entire industry or for an individual firm, though somewhat different variables would typically be used in each case. Most important, variables representing competitors' actions would be stressed in firm demand functions. For example, a firm's demand function would typically include competitors' prices and advertising expenditures. Demand for the firm's product line is negatively related to its own prices but positively related to the prices charged by competing firms. Similarly, demand for the firm's products would typically increase with its own advertising expenditures, but it could increase or decrease with additional advertising by other firms.

In most instances, the parameters for specific variables differ in industry demand functions and firm demand functions. To illustrate, consider the influence of population on the demand for Ford automobiles as opposed to automobiles in general. While a larger population would increase demand in each instance, the

TABLE 4.1 **Estimating an Industry Supply Function for the Automobile Industry**

Independent Variable (1)	Parameter (2)	Estimated Value of the Variable for the Coming Year (3)	Estimated Total Demand (4) = (2) × (3)
Average price (*P*)	−1,000	$18,000	−18,000,000
Disposable income (*Y*)	100	$30,000	3,000,000
Population (*Pop*)	0.08	250,000,000	20,000,000
Average interest rate (*i*) (in percent)	−1,000,000	10%	−10,000,000
Advertising expenditures (*A*)	0.01	$1,500,000,000	15,000,000
Total demand			10,000,000

parameter value in the Ford demand function would be smaller than that in the industry demand function. Only if Ford had 100 percent of the market—that is, if Ford were the industry—would the parameters for firm and industry demand be identical.

Because firm and industry demand functions differ, different models, or equations, must be estimated for analyzing these two levels of demand. However, it is important to recognize that the demand concepts developed in this chapter apply to both firm and industry demand functions.

THE DEMAND CURVE

Demand curve

The relation between price and the quantity demanded, holding all else constant.

The demand function specifies the relation between the quantity demanded and all variables that determine demand. The **demand curve** is the part of the demand function that expresses the relation between the price charged for a product and the quantity demanded, holding constant the effects of all other variables. Frequently, a demand curve is shown in the form of a graph, and all variables in the demand function except the price and quantity of the product itself are held fixed at specified levels. In the automobile demand function given in Equation 4.3, for example, one must hold income, population, interest rates, and advertising expenditures constant to identify the demand curve with which to examine the relation between automobile prices and the quantity demanded.

Demand Curve Determination

To illustrate this process, consider the relation depicted in Equation 4.3 and Table 4.1. Assuming that income, population, interest rates, and advertising expenditures are all held constant at their Table 4.1 values, the relation between the quantity demanded and price is expressed as

$$Q = -1,000P + 100(30,000) + 0.08(250,000,000) - 1,000,000(10)$$
$$+ 0.01(1,500,000,000)$$
$$= 28,000,000 - 1,000P. \tag{4.4}$$

Equation 4.4 represents the demand curve for automobiles given the specified values for all of the other variables in the demand function. It is shown graphically in Figure 4.1. As is typical, a reduction in price increases the quantity

FIGURE 4.1   **A Hypothetical Automobile Industry Demand Curve**

The slope coefficient of the demand curve reveals that a $1 increase in the price of automobiles reduces the quantity demanded by 1,000 units, holding constant the effects of all other variables.

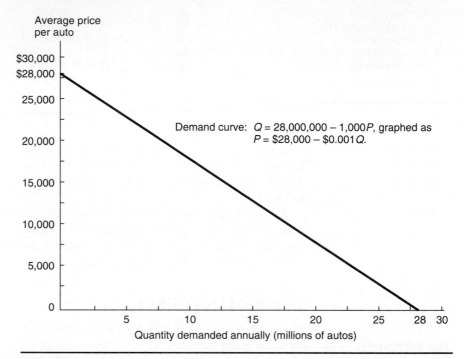

Note: The dependent variable (quantity demanded) is plotted on the horizontal axis and the independent variable (price) on the vertical axis. Ordinarily, one would expect to see the dependent variable on the vertical scale and the independent variable on the horizontal scale. This point can be confusing, because it is easy to write a demand equation as in Equation 4.4, then to incorrectly graph it by treating the 28,000,000 as the y-axis intercept instead of the x-axis intercept as, similarly, to misspecify the slope of the curve.

The practice of plotting price on the vertical axis and quantity on the horizontal axis originated many years ago with the theory of competitive markets. Here firms have no control over price but can control output, and output, in turn, determines market price. Hence, in the original model, price was the dependent variable and quantity (supplied, not demanded) was the independent variable. For that reason, price/quantity graphs appear as they do.

demanded and, conversely, an increase in price decreases the quantity demanded. The − 1,000 slope coefficient for the price variable in Equation 4.4 means that a $1 increase in the average price of automobiles would reduce the quantity demanded by 1,000 units. Similarly, a $1 decrease in the average price of automobiles would increase quantity demanded by 1,000 units.

Relation between Demand Curve and Demand Function

The relation between the demand curve and the demand function is important and worth considering in somewhat greater detail. Figure 4.2 shows three demand curves for automobiles. Each curve is constructed in the same manner as that

FIGURE 4.2 **Hypothetical Automobile Demand Curves**

A shift in the original demand curve from D_2 to D_1 reveals that a 5-percent increase in interest rate decreases demand by 5 million units, from D_2 to D_3.

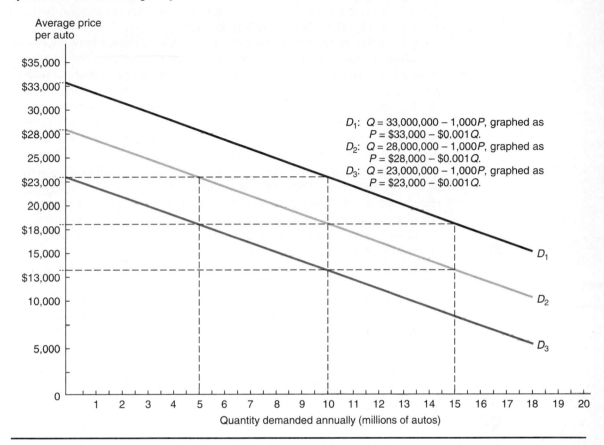

depicted in Equation 4.4 and then portrayed in Figure 4.1. In fact, D_2 is the same automobile demand curve characterized by Equation 4.4 and Figure 4.1. If D_2 is the appropriate demand curve, then 10 million automobiles can be sold at an average price of $18,000, 15 million automobiles can be sold at an average price of $13,000, but only 5 million automobiles can be sold at an average price of $23,000. This variation is described as a **change in the quantity demanded,** defined as movement along a single demand curve. As average price drops from $23,000 to $18,000 to $13,000 along D_2, the quantity demanded rises from 5 million to 10 million to 15 million automobiles. A change in the quantity demanded refers to the effect on sales of a change in price, holding constant the effects of all other demand-determining factors.

A **shift in demand,** or a switch from one demand curve to another, reflects a change in one or more of the nonprice variables in the product demand function. In the automobile demand-function example, a decrease in interest rates causes

Change in the quantity demanded
Movement along a given demand curve reflecting a change in price and quantity.

Shift in demand
Switch from one demand curve to another following a change in a nonprice determinant of demand.

an increase in automobile demand, because the interest rate parameter of $-1,000,000$ indicates that demand and interest rates are inversely related—that is, they change in opposite directions. When demand is inversely related to a factor such as interest rates, a reduction in the factor leads to rising demand and an increase in the factor leads to falling demand.

D_1 is another automobile demand curve. The sole difference between D_1 and D_2 is that D_1 assumes an interest rate of 5 percent rather than the 10 percent interest rate used to construct D_2. Since the interest rate parameter is negative, a decrease in interest rates causes an increase in automobile demand. Holding all else equal, a 5 percent reduction in interest rates leads to a 5-million-unit $[= -1,000,000 \times (-5)]$ increase in automobile demand. A 5 percent decrease in average interest rates leads to an upward or rightward shift in the original demand curve D_2 to the new demand curve D_1. This means that a 5 percent interest rate reduction will increase automobile demand by 5 million units at each price level. At a price of \$18,000, for example, a 5 percent reduction in interest rates increases automobile demand from 10 million to 15 million units per year. Alternatively, after a 5 percent decrease in interest rates, the original quantity of 10 million automobiles that could be sold at a price of \$18,000 on demand curve D_2 could be sold at the higher price of \$23,000. Notice that demand curve D_2 indicates that only 5 million units could be sold at an average industry price of \$23,000 when interest rates average 10 percent per year.

A 5 percent increase in interest rates, from 10 to 15 percent, causes an inward or leftward shift in the original demand curve D_2 to the new demand curve D_3. A 5 percent increase in interest rates reduces automobile demand by 5 million units at each price level. At a price of \$18,000, a 5 percent increase in interest rates reduces automobile demand from 10 million cars, the D_2 level, to only 5 million units. With interest rates at 15 percent, demand for 10 million cars would only occur at the lower average price of \$13,000, again holding all other demand-determining factors constant.

From the advertising parameter of 0.01, it is possible to infer that demand and advertising are positively related. Rising demand follows increases in advertising, and falling demand follows reductions in advertising. The shift from D_2 to D_1 in Figure 4.2, for example, could have resulted from a \$100,000,000 increase in industry advertising rather than from a 5 percent reduction in interest rates, or it could be the result of a \$50,000,000 increase in industry advertising coupled with a 2.5 percent reduction in interest rates. In each case, the resulting demand curve is given by the equation $Q = 33,000,000 - 1,000P$, or $P = \$33,000 - \$0.001Q$. On the other hand, the downward shift from D_2 to D_3 in Figure 4.2 could have resulted from a \$100,000,000 decrease in industry advertising rather than a 5 percent increase in interest rates, or it could be the result of a \$50,000,000 decrease in industry advertising coupled with a 2.5 percent increase in interest rates. In each case, the resulting demand curve is given by the equation $Q = 23,000,000 - 1,000P$, or $P = \$23,000 - \$0.001Q$.

The distinction between changes in the quantity demanded (which reflect movements along a given demand curve) and shifts in demand (which reflect switches from one demand curve to another) is extremely important. Failure to understand the causes of changes in demand for a company's products can lead

MANAGERIAL APPLICATION 4.2

The Import Supply Battle in the U.S. Auto Industry

The U.S. auto industry provides an interesting case study of the dynamics of changing demand and supply conditions. In contrast to just a few years ago, when the Big Three auto makers dominated the industry, today there are six major companies that have a substantial share of the U.S. market, and a handful of other companies able to profitably exploit important market niches.

On an overall basis, the "Big Three" U.S. manufacturers account for 60 to 65 percent of the U.S. market, Japanese name plates for roughly 30 percent, and European name plates are responsible for the remainder. Despite a continuing erosion in market share during the 1970s and 1980s, General Motors remains by far the largest company in the U.S. auto market. GM's current market share is in the 30- to 35-percent range, followed by the Ford Motor Company with roughly a 20-percent market share, Chrysler and Toyota both with 10 percent, Honda roughly 8 percent, Nissan roughly 5 percent; other companies such as Mazda, Mitsubishi, Subaru, and Volkswagen, account for the rest.

There is widespread concern in the industry that the economic downturn of the early 1990s will cause a sharp drop in the demand for automobiles and trucks. As a result, a continuing flood of new products is emerging as the companies fight for market share. Many of these new products are aimed at market segments that didn't even exist during the mid-1970s, when the industry suffered its last major downturn. Chrysler, for example, was able to return from the edge of bankruptcy to record profits largely on the basis of its astonishing success with minivans. By the mid-1990s, however, there will be at least a dozen new vehicles aimed at this market, some with highly popular four-wheel drive. To counter this attack on its most profitable market segment, Chrysler introduced a new generation of minivans in 1991—some with value pricing packages that cut prices to levels not seen since the mid-1980s. At the same time, Ford took aim at Chrysler's lucrative Jeep franchise with the Ford Explorer and outran both

Jeep and Chevrolet to take first place in the hot sport-utility truck market.

To gain entry into a large number of important market niches, some companies are entering into joint ventures. Mazda Motor Corporation and Ford, for example, work closely together in both automobile and truck segments of the industry. Ford has long been recognized as an innovative industry leader in trucks and has agreed to share its expertise with Mazda. Meanwhile, Mazda designs and builds cars for Ford. Ford will also begin to market minivans made with Nissan during the mid-1990s. Mitsubishi makes cars with Chrysler, and three Japanese companies and one Korean company make cars marketed by GM. Interestingly, each of the three largest U.S. manufacturers has taken important equity interests in a number of foreign producers. As a result, the distinction between foreign and domestic producers has begun to blur.

One important difference that remains between domestically produced and imported autos and trucks stems from the tariff and quota protection that domestic manufacturers have been able to obtain from Congress. Despite objections from consumers, the Big Three auto companies have been able to obtain significant protection from foreign competition. Not satisfied with voluntary quotas on Japanese auto imports, domestic manufacturers successfully fought during the late 1980s to extend a 25 percent import tariffs on hot-selling imported vans and sport-utility vehicles. Although vans and sport-utility vehicles account for only 15 percent of all vehicles sold in the United States, and imports enjoyed only a 10 percent share of this market segment, such vehicles are among the most profitable in the industry. Based upon its earlier success, the auto industry asked for and received Bush administration protection from minivan "dumping" in the U.S. market by Japanese manufacturers. Unfortunately for consumers, the administration failed to note that the last time import restrictions were tightened, the auto industry used the opportunity to raise both prices and profits—with the consumer an obvious loser.

Source: Larry Armstrong and Karen Lowrey Miller, "Japan's Sudden Deceleration," *Business Week,* June 8, 1991, 27.

to costly, even disastrous, mistakes in managerial decision making. The task of demand analysis is made especially difficult by the fact that under normal circumstances, not only prices but also income, population, interest rates, advertising, and most other demand-related factors vary from period to period. Sorting out the impact of each factor makes demand analysis one of the most challenging aspects of managerial economics. This important topic is investigated thoroughly in Chapter 5.

THE BASIS FOR SUPPLY

Supply
The total quantity offered for sale.

The term **supply** refers to the quantity of a good or service that producers are willing and able to sell during a certain period and under a given set of conditions. Conditions, or factors, that must be specified include the price of the good in question, prices of related goods, the current state of technology, levels of input prices, weather, and so on. The amount of product that producers bring to the market—the supply of the product—depends on all these factors.

Factors That Influence Supply

The supply of a product in the market is merely the aggregate of the amounts supplied by individual firms. The theory of the firm provides the basis for analyzing factors related to both individual firm and market supply. The supply of products arises from their ability to enhance the firm's value-maximization objective. Key components in this supply determination are the marginal benefits and marginal costs associated with expanding output. The amount of any good or service supplied will rise when the marginal benefit to producers, measured in terms of the value of output, is greater than the marginal costs of production. The amount of any good or service supplied will fall when the marginal benefit to producers is less than the marginal costs of production. Thus individual firms will expand or reduce supply based on the expected profits of each action.

Among the factors influencing the supply of a product, the price of the product itself is perhaps the most important. Higher prices increase the quantity of output producers want to bring to market. Holding marginal production costs constant, higher output prices increase the marginal benefits of added production and make expansion profitable. When marginal revenue exceeds marginal cost, firms increase supply to earn the greater profits associated with expanded levels of output. Higher prices allow firms to pay the higher production costs that are sometimes associated with expansions in output. Conversely, lower prices typically cause producers to supply a lower quantity of output. At the margin, lower prices can have the effect of making previous levels of production unprofitable.

The prices of related goods and services can also play an important role in determining supply of a product. If a firm employs limited resources that can be used to produce several different products, it can be expected to switch production from one product to another depending on market conditions. For example, the supply of gasoline typically declines in autumn when the price of heating oil rises. On the other hand, gasoline supply typically increases during the spring and summer months with the seasonal decline in heating oil prices. Whereas the substitution of one output for another can cause an inverse relation between the supply of one product and the price of a second, complementary production relationships result in a positive relation between supply and the price of a related product. For example, ore deposits containing lead often also contain silver. An increase in the price of lead can therefore lead to an expansion in both lead and silver production.

Technology is a key determinant of product supply. The current state of technology refers to the manner in which inputs are transformed into output. An improvement in the state of technology, including any product invention or process innovation that reduces production costs, increases the quantity and/or quality of products offered for sale at a given price.

Changes in input prices also affect supply in that an increase in input prices will raise costs and reduce the quantity that can be supplied profitably at a given market price. Alternatively, a decrease in input prices increases profitability and the quantity supplied at a given price.

For some products, especially agricultural products, weather can play an important role in determining supply. Temperature, rainfall, and wind all influence the quantity that can be supplied. Heavy rainfall in early spring, for example, can delay or prevent the planting of crops, significantly limiting supply. Abundant rain during the growing season, on the other hand, can greatly increase the available supply at harvest time. An early freeze that prevents full maturation or heavy rain or snow that limits harvesting activity reduces the supply of agricultural products.

Managerial decision making requires an understanding of both individual firm supply and market supply conditions. As already mentioned, market supply is the aggregate of individual firm supply, so it is ultimately determined by factors affecting firm supply. Firm supply is examined in detail in Chapters 7 and 8. For now, meaningful insight can be gained by understanding the nature of market supply.

THE MARKET SUPPLY FUNCTION

Supply function
The relation between supply and all factors influencing its level.

The market **supply function** for a product is a statement of the relation between the quantity supplied and all factors affecting that quantity.

Determinants of Supply

Written in general functional form, the supply function can be expressed as

$$\begin{array}{ll} \text{Quantity of} & f(\text{Price of } X; \text{ Prices of Related} \\ \text{Product } X = Q = & \text{Goods; Current State of Technology;} \quad \textbf{(4.5)} \\ \text{Supplied} & \text{Input Prices; Weather; and so on)}. \end{array}$$

The generalized supply function expressed in Equation 4.5 lists variables that influence supply. As is true with the demand function, the supply function must be made explicit to be useful for managerial decision making. To illustrate, consider the automobile industry example discussed previously and assume that the supply function has been specified as follows:

$$Q = b_1 P + b_2 P_T + b_3 P_L + b_4 i + b_5 T. \quad \textbf{(4.6)}$$

This equation states that the number of domestic plus foreign automobiles supplied during a given period, *Q*, is a linear function of the average price of cars, *P;* the average price of trucks, P_T; the average price of labor (wages), P_L; the average interest rate (price of capital), *i;* and government taxes (tariffs) on imports, *T*. The terms $b_1, b_2, \ldots, b_5$ are the parameters of the supply function. Note that no explicit term describes technology, or the method by which inputs are combined to produce output, in the industry supply function. The current state of technology is an underlying or implicit factor in the supply function.

Specifying a set of assumed parameter values into Equation 4.6 gives the following supply function for the automobile industry:

$$Q = 4{,}000P - 3{,}700P_T - 50{,}000P_L - 400{,}000i - 1{,}000T. \qquad \textbf{(4.7)}$$

Equation 4.7 states that automobile supply increases by 4,000 units for each $1 increase in the average price charged; it decreases by 3,700 units for each $1 increase in the price of trucks; it decreases by 50,000 units for each $1 increase in wage rates; it decreases by 400,000 units if interest rates rise 1 percent; and it decreases by 1,000 units with each $1 increase in the tax on imported cars. Thus, each parameter indicates the effect of the related factor on supply from domestic plus foreign manufacturers. For example, although a tax on imports will limit the supply of foreign cars, such a tax can increase supply from domestic manufacturers, as was the case during the mid-1980s in the United States. On balance, however, an import tax can be expected to have a negative overall effect on the total supply of automobiles since its direct impact on foreign manufacturers is ·greater than its indirect impact on domestic firms.

To estimate the supply of automobiles during the coming period, each parameter in Equation 4.7 is multiplied by the value of its respective variable and these products are then summed. Table 4.2 illustrates this process, showing that the supply of autos, assuming the stated values of the independent variables, is 10 million units.

Industry Supply versus Firm Supply

Just as in the case of demand, supply functions can be specified for either an entire industry or an individual firm. Even though factors affecting supply are highly similar in industry versus firm supply functions, the relative importance of such influences can differ dramatically. At one extreme, if all firms used identical production methods and identical equipment, had salaried and hourly employees who were equally capable and identically paid, and had equally skilled management, then individual firm and industry supply functions would have an obvious and close relation. Each firm is likely to be similarly affected by changes in the factors underlying supply. Each parameter in the individual firm supply functions would be smaller than in the industry supply function, however, and would reflect each firm's relative share of the market.

More typically, firms within a given industry adopt somewhat different production methods, use equipment of different vintages, and employ labor of varying skills and compensation levels. In such cases, individual firms' supply levels can be affected quite differently by various factors. Japanese and Korean automakers, for example, may be able to offer subcompacts profitably at average

TABLE 4.2 Estimating an Industry Supply Function for the Automobile Industry

Independent Variable (1)	Parameter (2)	Estimated Value of the Variable for the Coming Year (3)	Estimated Total Demand (4) = (2) × (3)
Average price (P)	4,000	$18,000	72,000,000
Average price of trucks (P_T)	−3,700	$15,000	−55,500,000
Average price of labor (P_L) (per hour)	−50,000	$30	−1,500,000
Average interest rate (i) (in percent)	−400,000	10%	−4,000,000
Tariff on imported cars (T)	−1,000	$1,000	−1,000,000
Total supply			10,000,000

industry prices as low as, say, $12,500 per automobile. On the other hand, U.S. auto manufacturers, who have historically operated with a labor cost disadvantage, may only be able to offer supply at average industry prices in excess of, say, $15,500. This means that at relatively high average prices for the industry above $15,500 per unit, both foreign and domestic auto manufacturers would be actively engaged in subcompact production. At relatively low average prices below $15,500, only foreign producers would offer subcompacts. This would be reflected by different parameters describing the relation between price and quantity supplied in the individual firm supply functions for Japanese, Korean, and U.S. automobile manufacturers.

It is worth emphasizing that individual firms supply output only when doing so is profitable. When industry prices are high enough to cover the marginal costs of increased production, individual firms expand output, thereby increasing total profits and the value of the firm. To the extent that the economic capabilities of industry participants vary, so too does the scale of output supplied by individual firms at various industry prices.

Similarly, supply is affected by the production technology of various firms. Firms operating with highly automated facilities incur large fixed costs and relatively small variable costs. The supply of product from such firms is likely to be relatively insensitive to price changes when compared with less automated firms, for which variable production costs are higher and thus more closely affected by production levels. Relatively low-cost producers can and do supply output at relatively low market prices. Of course, both relatively low-cost and high-cost producers are able to supply output profitably when market prices are high.

THE SUPPLY CURVE

Supply curve

The relation between price and the quantity supplied, holding all else constant.

The supply function specifies the relation between the quantity supplied and all variables that determine supply. The **supply curve** is the part of the supply function that expresses the relation between the price charged for a product and the quantity supplied, holding constant the effects of all other variables. As is true with demand curves, supply curves are often shown graphically, and all independent variables in the supply function except the price of the product itself are assumed to be fixed at specified levels. In the automobile supply function

FIGURE 4.3   **A Hypothetical Automobile Industry Supply Curve**

For industry average prices above $15,500, the slope coefficient of the supply curve reveals that a $1 increase in the average price of automobiles increases industry supply by 4,000 units.

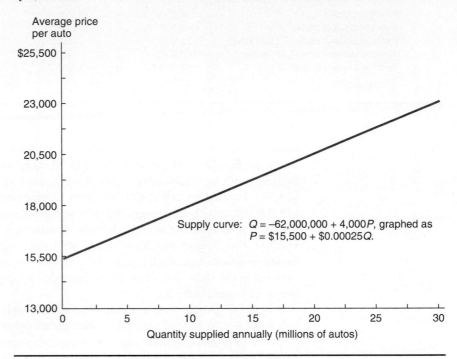

given in Equation 4.7, for example, it is necessary to hold constant the price of trucks, the price of labor, interest rates, and import taxes in order to examine the relation between automobile price and the quantity supplied.

Supply Curve Determination

To illustrate the supply determination process, consider the relation depicted in Equation 4.7. Assuming that the price of trucks, the price of labor, interest rates, and import taxes are all held constant at their Table 4.2 values, the relation between the quantity supplied and price is

$$Q = 4,000P - 3,700(15,000) - 50,000(30) - 400,000(10)$$
$$- 1,000(1,000)$$
$$= -62,000,000 + 4,000P. \tag{4.8}$$

Equation 4.8, representing the supply curve for automobiles given the specified values of all other variables in the supply function, is shown graphically in Figure 4.3. When the supply function is pictured with price as a function of quantity, or as $P = \$15,500 + \$0.00025Q$, the industry-average price must increase by $0.00025 to cause a one-unit increase in the supply of automobiles. Industry supply increases by 4,000 units for each $1 increase in the average price

FIGURE 4.4   Hypothetical Automobile Supply Curves

A shift in the original supply curve from S_2 to S_3 reveals that a 5 percent increase in the cost of capital reduces automobile supply by 2 million units at every price level. A 5 percent decrease in the cost of capital increases supply by 2 million units, from S_2 to S_1.

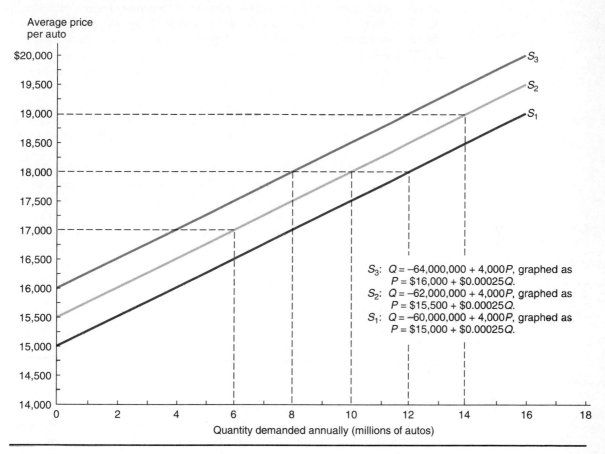

Within the figure:

S_3: $Q = -64{,}000{,}000 + 4{,}000P$, graphed as
       $P = \$16{,}000 + \$0.00025Q$.
S_2: $Q = -62{,}000{,}000 + 4{,}000P$, graphed as
       $P = \$15{,}500 + \$0.00025Q$.
S_1: $Q = -60{,}000{,}000 + 4{,}000P$, graphed as
       $P = \$15{,}000 + \$0.00025Q$.

Axis labels: Average price per auto ($20,000 down to $14,000); Quantity demanded annually (millions of autos), 0 to 18.

of automobiles above \$15,500 per unit. The \$15,500 intercept in this supply equation implies that the industry would not supply any cars at all if the industry average price fell below \$15,500.

Relation between Supply Curve and Supply Function

Like the relation between the demand curve and the demand function, the relation between the supply curve and the supply function is very important in managerial decision making. Figure 4.4 shows three supply curves for automobiles: S_1, S_2, and S_3. S_2 is the same automobile supply curve determined by Equation 4.8 and shown in Figure 4.3. If S_2 is the appropriate supply curve, then 10 million automobiles would be offered for sale at an industry average price of \$18,000. Only 6 million automobiles would be offered for sale at an average price of \$17,000; but industry supply would total 14 million automobiles at an average price of \$19,000. Such movements along a given supply curve reflect a

Change in the quantity supplied

Movement along a given supply curve reflecting a change in price and quantity.

change in the quantity supplied. As the average price rises from $17,000 to $18,000 to $19,000 along S_2, the quantity supplied increases from 6 million to 10 million to 14 million automobiles.

Supply curves S_1 and S_3 are similar to S_2. The differences are that S_1 is based on a 5 percent interest rate, whereas S_3 assumes a 15 percent interest rate. Recall that S_2 is based on an interest rate of 10 percent. Since the supply function interest rate parameter is $-400,000$, a 5 percent fall in interest rates leads to a 2-million-unit $[= -400,000 \times (-5)]$ increase in automobile supply at each automobile price level. This increase is described as a downward or rightward shift in the original supply curve S_2 to the new supply curve S_1. Conversely, a 5 percent rise in interest rates leads to a 2-million-unit $(= -400,000 \times 5)$ reduction in automobile supply at each automobile price level. This reduction is described as an upward or leftward shift in the original supply curve S_2 to the new supply curve S_3.

At a price of $18,000, for example, a 5 percent rise in interest rates reduces automobile supply from 10 million units, the S_2 level, to 8 million units, the S_3 level. This reduction in supply reflects the fact that previously profitable production no longer generates a profit because of the increase in capital costs. At a price of $18,000, a 5 percent reduction in interest rates increases automobile supply from 10 million units, the S_2 level, to 12 million units, the S_1 level. Supply rises following this decline in interest rates since, given a decline in capital costs, producers find that they can profitably expand output at the $18,000 price level from 10 million to 12 million units.

Shift in supply

Switch from one supply curve to another following a change in a nonprice determinant of supply.

A **shift in supply,** or a switch from one supply curve to another, indicates a change in one or more of the nonprice variables in the product supply function. In the automobile supply function example, an increase in truck prices leads to a decrease in automobile supply, since the truck price parameter of $-3,700$ indicates that automobile supply and truck prices are inversely related. This reflects the fact that as truck prices rise, holding all else constant, auto manufacturers have an incentive to shift from automobile to truck production. Similarly, given the tariff variable coefficient of $-1,000$, an increase in the tariff on imports leads to a 1,000-unit reduction in total industry supply. Obviously, the negative effect on supply is most dramatic for imports following such a change; the supply of domestically produced automobiles might be little affected, or even rise as consumers shift to now relatively less expensive domestic automobiles. When automobile supply is inversely related to a factor such as truck prices, rising truck prices lead to falling automobile supply and falling truck prices lead to rising automobile supply. From the negative parameters for the price of labor, interest rates, and taxes, it is also possible to infer that automobile supply is inversely related to each of these factors as well.

A change in interest rates is not the only factor that might be responsible for a change in the supply curve from S_2 to S_3 or S_1. From the labor cost parameter of $-500,000$, it is possible to infer that supply and labor costs are inversely related. Falling supply follows an increase in labor costs, and rising supply follows a decrease in labor costs. The shift from S_2 to S_1 in Figure 4.4, for example, could have resulted from a $4-per-hour decrease in industry-average labor costs rather than a 5 percent decrease in interest rates from 10 to 5 percent. Alternatively, this

MANAGERIAL APPLICATION 4.3

Demand and Supply Conditions for Economists

The forces of demand and supply exert a powerful influence on the market for goods and services, as well as on the markets for labor and other inputs. An interesting case in point is the economics industry itself.

The demand for economists originates in the private sector, where they are employed in business—usually in staff rather than line positions—as consultants and commentators; in government, where economic analysis often guides public policy; and in academia, where economists are employed in teaching capacities, primarily at the college and university levels.

During recent years, financial economists have made quite a splash on Wall Street, offering their services in the pricing and marketing of complex financial instruments. Although perhaps no more than 500 to 1,000 economists are actually employed in this capacity, the rapid growth of the industry and bonus-based compensation plans that run into the several hundred thousand dollars per year for a handful of stars have made this business highly visible. Many more economists, perhaps a few thousand, are employed in industry for their forecasting input concerning trends in macroeconomic conditions, as well as for their microeconomic advice concerning pricing, output, and other decisions. The National Association of Business Economists, for example, counts roughly 3,000 members in a wide variety of industries. However, employment in this sector of the industry can be quite cyclical. During the recession of 1991, for example, several brokerages, banks and other financial institutions trimmed their economics staff considerably. Consulting and speech making, while a fairly small segment, is the glamour end of the business. Stars such as Lester Thurow, dean of the Sloan School of Management at the Massachusetts Institute of Technology, have the capacity to earn hundreds of thousands of dollars per year in fees for consulting, speaking engagements, and publishing. The earnings of celebrity economists such as Milton Friedman, John Kenneth Galbraith, Robert Heilbroner, Arthur Laffer, Paul Samuelson, and Lester Thurow are high in large part because they are so rare. The supply of such "superstars" is severely limited.

In terms of sheer numbers of jobs, perhaps the best employment opportunities for economists are in academia, especially for those who hold a doctoral degree. According to *Job Openings for Economists,* a publication of the American Economic Association, roughly 80 to 90 percent of the total number of job opportunities in economics are in four-year colleges and universities. An overwhelming majority of the roughly 20,000 members of the AEA hold academic jobs.

Since the mid-1970s, the number of new Ph.D.s in economics has held steady at roughly 750 to 800 per year. This means that the supply of new academic economists is quite high when compared to the number of new Ph.D.s in related disciplines such as accounting, finance, management, and marketing. In fact, each year the number of new Ph.D.s in economics is roughly equivalent to the number of Ph.D.s granted in all of the functional areas of business administration combined. Thus, academic job-market candidates from leading programs in economics may count themselves lucky to receive two or three attractive job offers after graduation, whereas similar candidates from leading business programs often enjoy two or three times as many job opportunities and typically at substantially greater salaries.

New Ph.D.s in accounting, for example, total no more than 100 to 150 per year. At that pace, it will take 20 years to fill current vacancies in accounting. Therefore, it is perhaps not surprising that salaries for new academic Ph.D.s in economics are in the $40,000 per year range, but they are in excess of $60,000 per year in accounting. What is surprising is how slowly the supply of accounting Ph.D.s from high-quality doctoral programs has grown during recent years. Apparently, employment opportunities in the private sector are so attractive that talented accounting undergraduates do not find the Ph.D. sufficiently rewarding to encourage them to pursue advanced degrees. Although this might explain the failure of accounting students to pursue advanced degrees, why don't economics Ph.D. students switch to accounting?

Source: Dana Wechsler Linden, "Dreary Days in the Dismal Science," *Forbes,* January 21, 1991, 68–71; American Economic Association, *Job Openings for Economists,* December, 1992.

change could be the result of a $2 decrease in industry-average labor costs plus a 2.5 percent decrease in interest rates. In each case, the resulting supply curve is given by the equation $Q = -60,000,000 + 4,000P$, or $P = \$15,000 - \$0.00025Q$. Similarly, the shift from S_2 to S_3 in Figure 4.4 could have resulted from a $4-per-hour increase in industry-average labor costs rather than a 5 percent increase in interest rates from 10 to 15 percent. This change could also be the result of a $2 increase in industry-average labor costs plus a 2.5 percent increase in interest rates. In each case, the resulting supply curve is given by the equation $Q = -64,000,000 + 4,000P$, or $P = \$16,000 - \$0.00025Q$.

For some products, a positive relation between supply and other factors such as weather is often evident. This is especially true for agricultural products. If supply were positively related to weather, perhaps measured in terms of average temperature, then rising supply would follow rising average temperature and falling supply would accompany falling average temperature. Weather is not included in the automobile supply function described here, meaning that there is no close relation between automobile supply and weather.

The distinction between changes in the quantity supplied, which reflect movements along a given supply curve, and a shift in supply, which reflects movement from one supply curve to another, is important, as was the distinction between changes in the quantity demanded and a shift in demand. Since the prices of related products, input prices, taxes, weather, and other factors affecting supply can be expected to vary from one period to the next, assessing the individual importance of each factor becomes a challenging aspect of managerial economics. This topic is explored more fully in Chapters 7 and 8.

MARKET EQUILIBRIUM

Integrating the concepts of demand and supply establishes a framework for understanding how they interact to determine market prices and quantities for all goods and services. When the quantity demanded and the quantity supplied of a product are in perfect balance at a given price, the market for the product is said to be in **equilibrium.** An equilibrium is stable when the factors underlying demand and supply conditions remain unchanged in both the present and the foreseeable future. During those instances when the factors underlying demand and supply are dynamic rather than constant, a change in current market prices and quantities is likely. A temporary market equilibrium of this type is often referred to as an unstable equilibrium. To understand the forces that drive market prices and quantities either up or down to achieve equilibrium, the concepts of surplus and shortage must be introduced.

Equilibrium

Perfect balance in demand and supply.

Surplus and Shortage

Surplus

Excess supply.

A **surplus** is created when producers supply more of a product at a given price than buyers demand. Quite simply, surplus describes a condition of excess supply. Conversely, a **shortage** is created when buyers demand more of a product at a given price than producers are willing to supply. Shortage describes a condition of excess demand. Neither surplus nor shortage will occur when a market is in equilibrium, since equilibrium is defined as a condition in which the quantities

FIGURE 4.5   **Surplus, Shortage, and Market Equilibrium**

At an industry average market price of $19,000, the resulting surplus exerts downward pressure on both price and output levels. Similarly, excess demand at a price of $17,000 exerts upward pressure on both prices and output. Equilibrium is achieved when price equals $18,000 and quantity equals 10 million units.

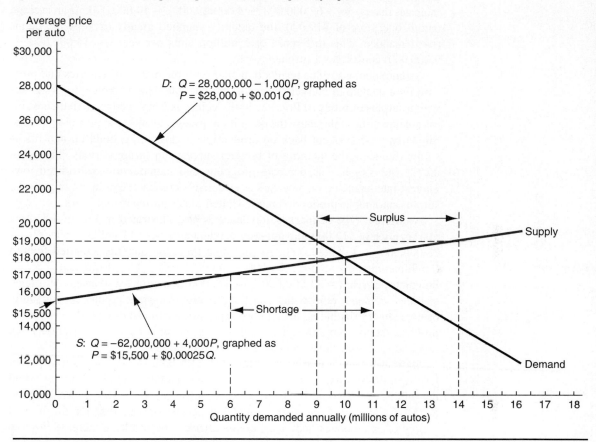

Shortage

Excess demand.

demanded and supplied are exactly in balance at the current market price. Surplus and shortage describe situations of market disequilibrium because either will result in powerful market forces being exerted to change the prices and quantities offered in the market.

To illustrate the concepts of surplus and shortage and, in the process, the concept of market equilibrium, consider the demand and supply curves for the automobile industry example depicted in Figure 4.5. Note that the demand curve is the same hypothetical demand curve shown in Figure 4.1, and it is also D_2 in Figure 4.2. The supply curve shown is the same one illustrated in Figure 4.3, and shown as S_2 in Figure 4.4. To clarify the concepts of surplus, shortage, and market equilibrium, it becomes useful to focus on the relation of the quantity supplied and the quantity demanded at each of three different hypothetical market prices.

At a market price of $19,000, the quantity demanded is 9 million units. This is easily derived from Equation 4.4, the market demand curve; $Q_D = 28,000,000 - 1,000(19,000) = 9,000,000$. The quantity supplied at an industry-average price of $19,000 is derived from the market supply curve, Equation 4.8, which indicates that $Q_S = -62,000,000 + 4,000(19,000) = 14,000,000$. At an average automobile price of $19,000, the quantity supplied greatly exceeds the quantity demanded. This difference of 5 million units per year ($= 14,000,000 - 9,000,000$) constitutes a surplus.

An automobile surplus results in a near-term buildup in inventories and pressure for a decline in market prices and production. This is typical for a market with a surplus of product. Prices tend to decline as firms recognize that consumers are unwilling to purchase the quantity of product available at prevailing prices. Similarly, producers cut back on production as inventories build up and prices soften, reducing the quantity of product supplied in future periods. The automobile industry has used rebate programs and manufacturer-subsidized low-interest-rate financing on new cars to effectively combat the problem of periodic surplus automobile production in the United States during recent years.

A different type of market imbalance is also illustrated in Figure 4.5. At a market price of $17,000, the quantity demanded rises to 11 million units, $Q_D = 28,000,000 - 1,000(17,000)$. At the same time, the quantity supplied falls to 6 million units, $Q_S = -62,000,000 + 4,000(17,000)$. This difference of 5 million units per year ($= 11,000,000 - 6,000,000$) constitutes a shortage. Shortage, or excess demand, reflects the fact that, given the current productive capability of the industry (including technology, input prices, and so on), producers cannot profitably supply more than 6 million units of output per year at an average price of $17,000, despite buyer demand for more output.

Shortages exert a powerful upward force on both market prices and output levels. In this example, with only 6 million automobiles supplied, buyers would be willing to pay an industry average price of $22,000 ($= $28,000 - $0.001(6,000,000)$). Consumers would bid against one another for the limited supply of automobiles and cause prices to rise. The resulting increase in price motivates manufacturers to increase production while reducing the number of buyers willing and able to purchase cars. The resulting increase in the quantity supplied and reduction in quantity demanded work together to eventually eliminate the shortage.

The market situation at a price of $18,000 and a quantity of 10 million automobiles per year is displayed graphically as a balance between the quantity demanded and the quantity supplied. This is a condition of market equilibrium. There is no tendency for change in either price or quantity at a price of $18,000 and a quantity of 10 million units. The graph shows that any price above $18,000 produces a surplus. Prices in this range create excess supply, a buildup in inventories, and pressure for an eventual decline in prices to the $18,000 equilibrium level. At prices below $18,000, shortages occur and create pressure for price increases. With prices moving up, producers are willing to supply more product and the quantity demanded declines, thus reducing the shortage.

Only a market price of $18,000 brings the quantity demanded and the quantity supplied into perfect balance. This price is referred to as the **market equilibrium**

Market equilibrium price

Market clearing price.

TABLE 4.3 **Surplus, Shortage, and Market Equilibrium in the Automobile Industry**

Average Price per Auto (1)	Quantity Supplied (Q_S) (2)	Quantity Demanded (Q_D) (3)	Surplus (+) or Shortage (−) (4) = (2) − (3)
$28,000	50,000,000	0	+50,000,000
25,500	40,000,000	2,500,000	+37,500,000
23,000	30,000,000	5,000,000	+25,000,000
20,500	20,000,000	7,500,000	+12,500,000
18,000	10,000,000	10,000,000	0
15,500	0	12,500,000	−12,500,000

price, or the market clearing price, since it just clears the market of all supplied product. Table 4.3 shows the surplus of quantity supplied at prices above the market equilibrium price and the shortage that results at prices below the market equilibrium price.

In short, surplus describes an excess in the quantity supplied over the quantity demanded at a given market price. A surplus results in downward pressure on both market prices and industry output. Shortage describes an excess in the quantity demanded over the quantity supplied at a given market price. A shortage results in upward pressure on both market prices and industry output. Market equilibrium describes a condition of perfect balance in the quantity demanded and the quantity supplied at a given price. In equilibrium, there is no tendency for change in either price or quantity.

Comparative Statics

Comparative statics analysis
The study of changing demand and supply conditions.

Managers typically control a number of the factors that affect product demand or supply. To make appropriate decisions concerning those variables, it is often useful to know how altering them changes market conditions. Similarly, the direction and magnitude of changes in demand and supply that are due to uncontrollable external factors, such as income or interest rate changes, need to be understood so that managers can develop strategies and make decisions that are consistent with the market conditions they face.

One relatively simple but quite useful analytical technique involves examining the effects on market equilibrium of changes in economic factors underlying product demand and supply. This is called **comparative statics analysis.** In comparative statics analysis, the role of factors influencing demand is often analyzed while holding supply conditions constant. Similarly, the role of factors influencing supply can be analyzed by studying changes in supply while holding demand conditions constant. Comparing market equilibrium price and output levels before and after various hypothetical changes in demand and supply conditions has the potential to yield useful predictions of expected changes.

Figures 4.6 and 4.7 illustrate the comparative statics of changing demand and supply conditions. Figure 4.6a combines the three automobile demand curves shown in Figure 4.2 with the automobile supply curve S_2 of Figure 4.4. The demand-related effects of changes in interest rates on the market price and quantity of automobiles are illustrated. Given the supply curve S_2, *and assuming for*

FIGURE 4.6   The Comparative Statics of (a) Changing Demand and (b) Changing Supply Conditions

(a) Holding supply conditions constant, demand will vary with changing interest rates.

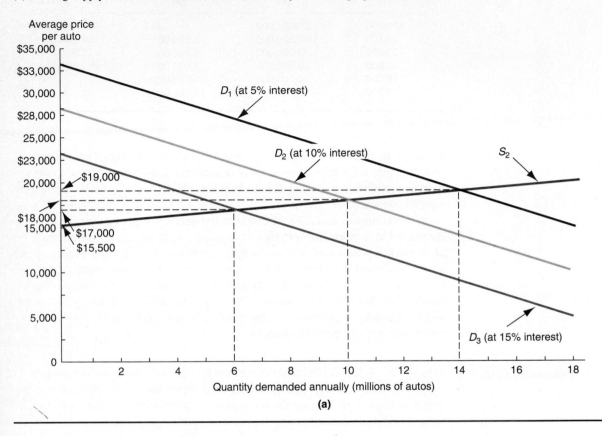

Quantity demanded annually (millions of autos)

(a)

the moment that supply does not change in response to changes in interest rates, the intersections of the three demand curves with the supply curve indicate the market price and quantity combinations expected at different interest rates.

At the intersection of D_1, which corresponds to a 5 percent interest rate, and S_2, supply and demand are equal at a price of \$19,000 and quantity of 14 million units. This result is obtained by simultaneously solving the equations for D_1 and S_2 to find the single price and quantity that satisfies both:

$$D_1: Q_S = 33,000,000 - 1,000P.$$
$$S_2: Q_S = -62,000,000 + 4,000P.$$

Demand and supply are equal at a price of \$19,000 because

$$Q_D = Q_S$$
$$33,000,000 - 1,000P = -62,000,000 + 4,000P$$
$$5,000P = 95,000,000$$
$$P = \$19,000.$$

(b) Holding demand conditions constant, supply will vary with changing interest rates.

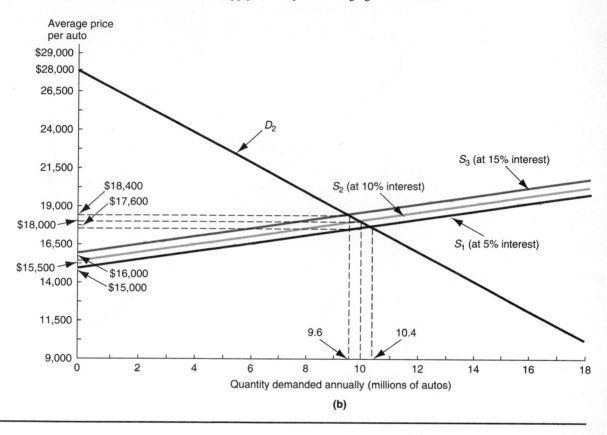

(b)

The related quantity is found by substituting this $19,000 price into either the demand curve D_1 or the supply curve S_2:

$$D_1: Q_D = 33,000,000 - 1,000P$$
$$= 33,000,000 - 1,000(\$19,000)$$
$$= 14,000,000 \text{ units.}$$
$$S_2: Q_S = -62,000,000 + 4,000P$$
$$= -62,000,000 + 4,000(\$19,000)$$
$$= 14,000,000 \text{ units.}$$

Using the same procedure to find the combination of market clearing price and quantity for the intersection of D_2 (the demand curve for a 10 percent interest rate) with S_2, a price of $18,000 and quantity of 10 million units is found. With interest rates at 15 percent (curve D_3), the market clearing price and quantity are $17,000 and 6 million units. Clearly, the level of interest rates plays an important role in the buyer's purchase decision. With higher interest rates, car buyers pur-

FIGURE 4.7   **The Comparative Statics of Changing Demand and Changing Supply Conditions**

The market equilibrium price/output combination reflects the combined effects of changing demand and supply conditions.

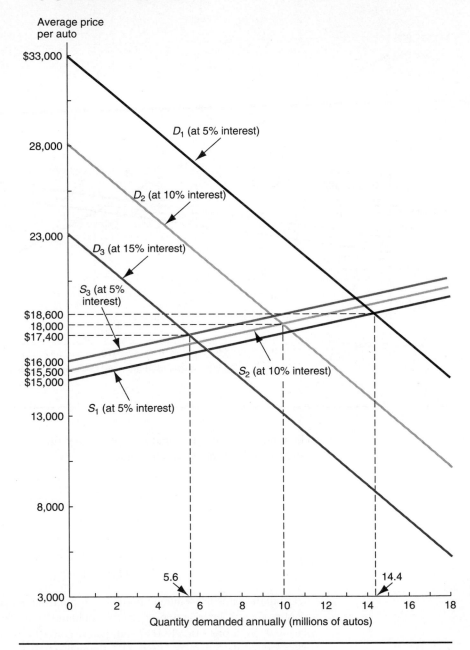

chase fewer automobiles and only at progressively lower prices. In part, this reflects the fact that most car purchases are financed, and at higher interest rates the cost of purchasing an automobile is greater.

Figure 4.6b combines the three automobile supply curves shown in Figure 4.4 with the automobile demand curve D_2 of Figure 4.2. The market equilibrium price and quantity effects of changing interest rates are illustrated, holding demand conditions constant *and, in particular, assuming that demand does not change in response to changes in interest rates.* Given the market demand curve D_2, a 5 percent fall in interest rates from 15 percent to 10 percent causes the equilibrium quantity supplied to rise from 9.6 million units on S_3 to 10 million units on S_2; a further 5 percent drop in interest rates from 10 percent to 5 percent causes the equilibrium quantity supplied to rise from 10 million units on S_2 to 10.4 million units on S_1. Similarly, in light of the market demand curve D_2, a 5 percent fall in interest rates from 15 percent to 10 percent causes the equilibrium price to fall from \$18,400 to \$18,000; a further 5 percent drop in interest rates from 10 percent to 5 percent causes the equilibrium price to fall from \$18,000 to \$17,600. As interest rates fall, producers find that they can profitably supply more output, even as average price falls, given the capital cost savings that would accompany lower interest rates. The effects of lower interest rates on supply are dramatic, and they reflect the highly capital-intensive nature of the automobile industry.

From this analysis of hypothetical automobile demand and supply relations it is clear that interest rates are an important factor influencing demand *and* supply. This is a typical circumstance: Factors related to overall economic activity often have important influences on both demand and supply. Figure 4.7 illustrates the comparative statics of changing demand *and* changing supply conditions by showing the net effects of changing interest rates. Here S_1 and D_1, both of which assume a 5 percent interest rate, yield an equilibrium price–output combination of \$18,600 and 14.4 million units; S_2 and D_2, which assume a 10 percent interest rate, yield an equilibrium price–output combination of \$18,000 and 10 million units; S_3 and D_3, which assume a 15 percent interest rate, result in a price–output equilibrium of \$17,400 and 5.6 million units. These price–output combinations reflect the combined effects of changing interest rates on demand and supply. The comparative statics of changes in any of the other factors that influence demand and supply can be analyzed in a similar fashion.

SUMMARY

This chapter illustrates how the forces of supply and demand combine to establish the prices and quantities observed in the markets for all goods and services.

• **Demand** is the quantity of a good or service that customers are willing and able to purchase during a specified period under a given set of economic conditions. **Direct demand** is the demand for personal consumption products that directly satisfy consumer desires. The value or worth of a good or service, its **utility,** is the prime determinant of direct demand. The demand for all inputs used by a firm is **derived demand,** and it is determined by the profitability of using various inputs to produce output.

• The market **demand function** for a product is a statement of the relation between the aggregate quantity demanded and all factors that affect this quantity. The **demand curve** is the part of the demand function that expresses the relation between the price charged for a product and the quantity demanded, holding constant the effects of all other variables.

• A **change in the quantity demanded** is a movement along a single given demand curve. A **shift in demand,** or a switch from one demand curve to another, reflects a change in one or more of the nonprice variables in the product demand function.

• The term *supply* refers to the quantity of a good or service that producers are willing and able to sell during a certain period and under a given set of conditions. The market **supply function** for a product is a statement of the relation between the quantity supplied and all factors affecting that quantity. A **supply curve** expresses the relation between the price charged for a product and the quantity supplied, holding constant the effects of all other variables.

• Movements along a given supply curve reflect a **change in the quantity supplied.** A **shift in supply,** or a switch from one supply curve to another, indicates a change in one or more of the nonprice variables in the product supply function.

• A market is in **equilibrium** when the quantity demanded and the quantity supplied of a product are in perfect balance at a given price. **Surplus** describes a condition of excess supply; **shortage** describes a condition of excess demand. The **market equilibrium price,** or market clearing price, just clears the market of all supplied product.

• In **comparative statics analysis,** the role of factors influencing demand or supply is analyzed by examining the effects of changing equilibrium conditions.

A fundamental understanding of demand and supply concepts is essential to the successful operation of any economic organization. The concepts introduced in this chapter provide the structure for the more detailed analysis of demand and supply in subsequent chapters and thereby make an important contribution to any discussion of managerial economics.

Questions

Q4.1   What key ingredients are necessary for the creation of economic demand?

Q4.2   Describe the difference between direct demand and derived demand.

Q4.3   Explain the rationale for each of the demand variables in Equation 4.1.

Q4.4   Distinguish between a demand function and a demand curve. What is the difference between a change in the quantity demanded and a shift in the demand curve?

Q4.5   What key ingredients are necessary for the creation of economic supply?

Q4.6   Explain the rationale for each of the supply variables in Equation 4.5.

Q4.7   Distinguish between a supply function and a supply curve. What is the difference between a change in the quantity supplied and a shift in the supply curve?

Q4.8 "Dynamic rather than static demand and supply conditions are typically observed in real-world markets. Therefore, comparative statics analysis has only limited value." Discuss this statement.

Q4.9 Contrast the supply and demand conditions for new Ph.D.s in economics and accounting. Why do such large differences in starting salaries seem to persist over time?

Q4.10 "A famous economist once argued, 'Supply creates its own demand'. It would have been more accurate to argue 'Demand creates its own supply'." Discuss this statement.

Self-Test Problem

The following relations describe demand and supply conditions in the lumber/forest products industry:

$$Q_D = 80,000 - 20,000P, \quad \text{(Demand)}$$
$$Q_S = -20,000 + 20,000P, \quad \text{(Supply)}$$

where Q is quantity measured in thousands of board feet (one square foot of lumber, one inch thick) and P is price in dollars.

A. Set up a table or spreadsheet to illustrate the effect of price (P) on the quantity supplied (Q_S), quantity demanded (Q_D), and the resulting surplus ($+$) or shortage ($-$) as represented by the difference between the quantity demanded and the quantity supplied at various price levels. Calculate the value for each respective variable based on a range for P from \$1.00 to \$3.50 in increments of 10¢ (i.e., \$1.00, \$1.10, \$1.20, . . ., \$3.50).

B. Using price (P) on the vertical axis (y-axis) and quantity (Q) on the horizontal axis (x-axis), plot the demand and supply curves for the lumber/forest products industry over the range of prices indicated previously.

Solution to Self-Test Problem

A. A table or spreadsheet that illustrates the effect of price (P) on the quantity supplied (Q_S), quantity demanded (Q_D), and the resulting surplus ($+$) or shortage ($-$) as represented by the difference between the quantity demanded and the quantity supplied at various price levels is as follows:

Price	Quantity Supplied	Quantity Demanded	Shortage/ Surplus
$1.00	0	60,000	−60,000
1.10	2,000	58,000	−56,000
1.20	4,000	56,000	−52,000
1.30	6,000	54,000	−48,000
1.40	8,000	52,000	−44,000
1.50	10,000	50,000	−40,000
1.60	12,000	48,000	−36,000
1.70	14,000	46,000	−32,000
1.80	16,000	44,000	−28,000
1.90	18,000	42,000	−24,000
2.00	20,000	40,000	−20,000
2.10	22,000	38,000	−16,000
2.20	24,000	36,000	−12,000

continued

Price	Quantity Supplied	Quantity Demanded	Shortage/ Surplus
2.30	26,000	34,000	−8,000
2.40	28,000	32,000	−4,000
2.50	30,000	30,000	0
2.60	32,000	28,000	4,000
2.70	34,000	26,000	8,000
2.80	36,000	24,000	12,000
2.90	38,000	22,000	16,000
3.00	40,000	20,000	20,000
3.10	42,000	18,000	24,000
3.20	44,000	16,000	28,000
3.30	46,000	14,000	32,000
3.40	48,000	12,000	36,000
3.50	50,000	10,000	40,000

B. Using price (*P*) on the y-axis and quantity (*Q*) on the x-axis, a plot of the demand and supply curves for the lumber/forest products industry is as follows:

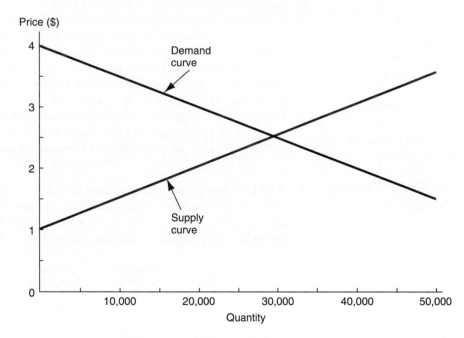

Problems

P4.1   **Demand and Supply Curves.** The following relations describe monthly demand and supply conditions in the metropolitan area for recyclable aluminum:

$$Q_D = 317,500 - 10,000P, \quad \text{(Demand)}$$

$$Q_S = 2,500 + 7,500P, \qquad \text{(Supply)}$$

where *Q* is quantity measured in pounds of scrap aluminum and *P* is price in cents.

Complete the following table:

Price (1)	Quantity Demanded (2)	Quantity Supplied (3)	Surplus (+) or Shortage (−) (4) = (2) − (3)
15¢			
16			
17			
18			
19			
20			

P4.2   **Demand and Supply Curves.** The following relations describe monthly demand and supply relations for dry cleaning services in the metropolitan area:

$$Q_D = 500,000 - 50,000P, \qquad \text{(Demand)}$$

$$Q_S = -100,000 + 100,000P, \qquad \text{(Supply)}$$

where Q is quantity measured by the number of items dry cleaned per month and P is average price in dollars.

A. At what average price level would demand equal zero?
B. At what average price level would supply equal zero?
C. Calculate the equilibrium price/output combination.

P4.3   **Demand Analysis.** The demand for housing is often described as being highly cyclical, and it is very sensitive to housing prices and interest rates. Given these characteristics, describe the effect of each of the following in terms of whether it would increase or decrease the quantity demanded or the demand for housing. Moreover, when price is expressed as a function of quantity, indicate whether the effect of each of the following is an upward or downward movement along a given demand curve or instead involves an outward or inward shift in the relevant demand curve for housing. Explain your answers.

A. An increase in housing prices
B. A fall in interest rates
C. A rise in interest rates
D. A severe economic recession
E. A robust economic expansion

P4.4   **Demand and Supply Curves.** Demand and supply conditions in the market for unskilled labor are important concerns to business and government decision makers. Consider the case of a federally mandated minimum wage set above the equilibrium, or market clearing, wage level. Some of the following factors have the potential to influence the demand or quantity demanded of unskilled labor. Influences on the supply or quantity supplied may also result. Holding all else equal, describe these influences as increasing or decreasing, and indicate the direction of the resulting movement along or shift in the relevant curve(s).

A. An increase in the quality of secondary education

B. A rise in welfare benefits

C. An increase in the popularity of self-service gas stations, car washes, and so on

D. A fall in interest rates

E. An increase in the minimum wage

P4.5   **Demand Function.** The Creative Publishing Company (CPC) is a coupon book publisher with markets in several southeastern states. CPC coupon books are either sold directly to the public, sold through religious and other charitable organizations, or given away as promotional items. Operating experience during the past year suggests the following demand function for CPC's coupon books:

$$Q = 5,000 - 4,000P + 0.02Pop + 0.5I + 1.5A,$$

where Q is quantity, P is price ($\$$), Pop is population, I is disposable income per household ($\$$), and A is advertising expenditures ($\$$).

A. Determine the demand faced by CPC in a typical market in which $P = \$10$, $Pop = 1,000,000$ persons, $I = \$30,000$, and $A = \$10,000$.

B. Calculate the level of demand if CPC increases annual advertising expenditures from $\$10,000$ to $\$15,000$.

C. Calculate the demand curves faced by CPC in Parts A and B.

P4.6   **Demand Curves.** The Eastern Shuttle, Inc., is a regional airline providing shuttle service between New York and Washington, D.C. An analysis of the monthly demand for service has revealed the following demand relation:

$$Q = 26,000 - 500P - 250P_{OG} + 200I_B - 5,000S,$$

where Q is quantity measured by the number of passengers per month, P is price ($\$$), P_{OG} is a regional price index for other consumer goods ($1967 = 1.00$), I_B is an index of business activity, and S, a binary or dummy variable, equals 1 in summer months and 0 otherwise.

A. Determine the demand curve facing the airline during the winter month of January if $P_{OG} = 4$ and $I_B = 250$.

B. Determine the demand curve facing the airline, quantity demanded, and total revenues during the summer month of July if $P = \$100$ and all other price-related and business activity variables are as specified previously.

P4.7   **Supply Function.** A review of industrywide data for the jelly and jam manufacturing industry suggests the following industry supply function:

$$Q = -59,000,000 + 500,000P - 250,000P_L$$
$$- 500,000P_K + 2,000,000W,$$

where Q is cases supplied per year, P is the wholesale price per case ($\$$), P_L is the average price paid for unskilled labor ($\$$), P_K is the average price of capital (in percent), and W is weather measured by the average seasonal rainfall in growing areas (in inches).

A. Determine the industry supply curve for a recent year when $P_L = \$4$, $P_K = 10$ percent, and $W = 20$ inches of rainfall. Show the industry supply curve with quantity expressed as a function of price and price expressed as a function of quantity.

B. Calculate the quantity supplied by the industry at prices of $50, $60, and $70 per case.

C. Calculate the prices necessary to generate a supply of 4 million, 6 million, and 8 million cases.

P4.8 **Supply Curve Determination.** Information Technology, Inc., is a supplier of math coprocessors (computer chips) used to speed the processing of data for analysis on personal computers. Based on an analysis of monthly cost and output data, the company has estimated the following relation between the marginal cost of production and monthly output:

$$MC = \$100 + \$0.004Q.$$

A. Calculate the marginal cost of production at 2,500, 5,000, and 7,500 units of output.

B. Express output as a function of marginal cost. Calculate the level of output when $MC = \$100, \$125$, and $\$150$.

C. Calculate the profit-maximizing level of output if wholesale prices are stable in the industry at $150 per chip and, therefore, $P = MR = \$150$.

D. Derive the company's supply curve for chips assuming $P = MR$. Express price as a function of quantity and quantity as a function of price.

P4.9 **Supply Curve Determination.** Cornell Pharmaceutical, Inc., and Penn Medical, Ltd., supply generic drugs to treat a wide variety of illnesses. A major product for each company is a generic equivalent of an antibiotic used to treat postoperative infections. Proprietary cost and output information for each company reveals the following relations between marginal cost and output:

$$MC_C = \$10 + \$0.004Q_C. \quad \text{(Cornell)}$$
$$MC_P = \$8 + \$0.008Q_P. \quad \text{(Penn)}$$

The wholesale market for generic drugs is vigorously price-competitive, and neither firm is able to charge a premium for its products. Thus, $P = MR$ in this market.

A. Determine the supply curve for each firm. Express price as a function of quantity and quantity as a function of price. (Hint: Set $P = MR = MC$ to find each firm's supply curve.)

B. Calculate the quantity supplied by each firm at prices of $8, $10, and $12. What is the minimum price necessary for each individual firm to supply output?

C. Assuming these two firms make up the entire industry, determine the industry supply curve when $P < \$10$.

D. Determine the industry supply curve when $P > \$10$. To check your answer, calculate quantity at an industry price of $12 and compare your answer with Part B.

P4.10   **Market Equilibrium.** Eye-de-ho Potatoes is a product of the Coeur d'Alene Growers' Association. Producers in the area are able to switch back and forth between potato and wheat production depending upon market conditions. Similarly, consumers tend to regard potatoes and wheat (bread and bakery products) as substitutes. As a result, the demand and supply of Eye-de-ho Potatoes are highly sensitive to changes in both potato and wheat prices.

Demand and supply functions for Eye-de-ho Potatoes are as follows:

$$Q_D = -1{,}450 - 25P + 12.5P_W + 0.2Y, \qquad \text{(Demand)}$$

$$Q_S = -100 + 75P - 25P_W - 12.5P_L + 10R, \qquad \text{(Supply)}$$

where P is the average wholesale price of Eye-de-ho Potatoes ($ per bushel), P_W is the average wholesale price of wheat ($ per bushel), Y is income (GNP in $ billions), P_L is the average price of unskilled labor ($ per hour), and R is the average annual rainfall (in inches). Both Q_D and Q_S are in millions of bushels of potatoes.

A. When quantity is expressed as a function of price, what are the Eye-de-ho Potatoes demand and supply curves if $P = \$2$, $P_W = \$4$, $Y = \$7{,}500$ billion, $P_L = \$8$, and $R = 20$ inches?

B. Calculate the surplus or shortage of Eye-de-ho Potatoes when $P = \$1.5$, $\$2$, and $\$2.50$.

C. Calculate the market equilibrium price/output combination.

CASE STUDY FOR CHAPTER 4

A Spreadsheet Analysis of Product Demand and Supply Conditions

Spreadsheet analysis is an appropriate means for studying the demand and supply effects of possible changes in various exogenous and endogenous variables. Endogenous variables include all important demand and supply-related factors that are within the control of the firm. Examples include product pricing, advertising, product design, and so on. Exogenous variables consist of all significant demand and supply-related influences that are beyond the control of the firm. Examples include competitor pricing, competitor advertising, the weather, general economic conditions, and related factors.

In comparative statics analysis, the marginal influence on demand and supply of a change in any one factor can be isolated and studied in depth. The advantage of this approach is that causal relationships can be identified and responded to, if appropriate. The disadvantage of this marginal approach is that it becomes rather tedious to investigate the marginal effects of a wide range of demand and supply influences. It is here that spreadsheet analysis of demand and supply conditions becomes useful. Using spreadsheet analysis, it is possible to learn the demand and supply implications of an almost limitless range of operating scenarios. Rather than calculating the effects of only a few possibilities, it is feasible to consider even rather unlikely outcomes. A complete picture can be drawn of the firm's operating environment, and strategies for responding to a host of operating conditions can be drawn up.

To illustrate this process, consider the case of Sunbest Orange Juice, a product of California's Orange County Growers' Association. Both demand and supply of the product are highly sensitive to changes in the weather. During hot summer months, demand for Sunbest and other beverages grows rapidly. On the other hand, hot, dry weather has an adverse effect on supply by reducing the size of the orange crop.

Demand and supply functions for Sunbest are as follows:

$$Q_D = 12{,}275{,}000 - 2{,}500{,}000P + 200{,}000P_S + 75Y + 5{,}000T \quad \text{(Demand)}$$

$$Q_S = -21{,}450 + 6{,}000{,}000P - 2{,}400{,}000P_L - 220{,}000P_K - 200{,}000T$$
$$\text{(Supply)}$$

where P is the average wholesale price of Sunbest ($ per case), P_S is the average wholesale price of canned soda ($ per case), Y is disposable income per household ($), T is the average daily high temperature (degrees), P_L is the average price of unskilled labor ($ per hour), and P_K is the risk-adjusted cost of capital (in percent).

During the coming planning period, a wide variety of operating conditions are possible. To gauge the sensitivity of demand and supply to changes in these operating conditions, a number of scenarios that employ a range from optimistic to relatively pessimistic assumptions have been drawn up:

Operating Environment for Demand		Price of Sunbest (P)	Price of Soda (P_s)	Disposable Income (I)	Temperature (T)
Optimistic					
Scenario	1	$5.00	$4.00	$39,500	78.75
	2	4.80	4.10	39,400	79.00
	3	4.60	4.20	39,300	79.25
	4	4.40	4.30	39,200	79.50
	5	4.20	4.40	39,100	79.75
	6	4.00	4.50	39,000	80.00
	7	3.80	4.60	38,900	80.25
	8	3.60	4.70	38,800	80.50
	9	3.40	4.80	38,700	80.75
Pessimistic					
Scenario	10	3.20	4.90	38,600	81.00

Operating Environment for Supply		Price of Sunbest (P)	Price of Labor (P_L)	Cost of Capital (P_K)	Temperature (T)
Optimistic					
Scenario	1	$5.00	$8.00	9.00%	78.00
	2	4.80	8.15	9.25	77.75
	3	4.60	8.30	9.50	77.50
	4	4.40	8.45	9.75	77.25
	5	4.20	8.60	10.00	77.00

continued

Operating Environment for Supply	Price of Sunbest (P)	Price of Labor (P_L)	Cost of Capital (P_K)	Temperature (T)
6	4.00	8.75	10.25	76.75
7	3.80	8.90	10.50	76.50
8	3.60	9.05	10.75	76.25
9	3.40	9.20	11.00	76.00
Pessimistic Scenario 10	3.20	9.35	11.25	75.75

Demand and supply functions for Sunbest orange juice can be combined with data on the operating environment to construct estimates of demand, supply, and the amount of surplus or shortage under each operating scenario.

   A. Set up a table or spreadsheet to illustrate the effects of changing economic assumptions on the demand for Sunbest orange juice. Use the demand function to calculate demand based upon three different underlying assumptions concerning changes in the operating environment. First, assume that all demand factors change in unison from levels indicated in the Optimistic Scenario #1 to the levels indicated in Pessimistic Scenario #10. Second, fix all demand factors except the price of Sunbest at Scenario #6 levels, and then calculate the quantity demanded at each scenario price level. Finally, fix all demand factors except temperature at Scenario #6 levels, and then calculate demand at each scenario temperature level.

   B. Set up a table or spreadsheet to illustrate the effects of changing economic assumptions on the supply of Sunbest orange juice. Use the supply function to calculate supply based upon three different underlying assumptions concerning changes in the operating environment. First, assume that all supply factors change in unison from levels indicated in the Optimistic Scenario #1 to the levels indicated in Pessimistic Scenario #10. Second, fix all supply factors except the price of Sunbest at Scenario #6 levels, and then calculate the quantity supplied at each scenario price level. Finally, fix all supply factors except temperature at Scenario #6 levels, and then calculate supply at each scenario temperature level.

   C. Set up a table or spreadsheet to illustrate the effect of changing economic assumptions on the surplus or shortage of Sunbest orange juice that results from each scenario detailed in Part A and Part B. Which operating scenario results in market equilibrium?

   D. Are demand and supply more sensitive to changes in the price of Sunbest or to changes in temperature?

Selected References   Alexeev, Michael, Clifford Gaddy, and Jim Leitzel. "Economics in the Former Soviet Union." *Journal of Economic Perspectives* 6 (Spring 1992): 137–148.

Battalio, Raymond C., John H. Kagel, and Carl A. Kogut. "Experimental Confirmation of the Existence of a Giffen Good." *American Economic Review* 81 (September 1991): 961–970.

Bayus, Barry L. "The Consumer Durable Replacement Buyer." *Journal of Marketing* 55 (January 1991): 42–51.

Clarida, Richard H., and Ronald Findlay. "Government, Trade and Comparative Advantage." *American Economic Review* 82 (May 1992): 122–127.

Durlauf, Steven N. "Multiple Equilibria and Persistence in Aggregate Fluctuations." *American Economic Review* 81 (May 1991): 70–74.

Irwin, Douglas A. "Strategic Trade Policy and Merchantilist Trade Rivalries." *American Economic Review* 82 (May 1992): 134–139.

Keller, Kevin Lane. "Cue Compatibility and Framing in Advertising." *Journal of Marketing Research* 28 (February 1991): 42–57.

Reichheld, Frederick F., and W. Earl Sasser, Jr. "Zero Defections: Quality Comes to Services." *Harvard Business Review* 68 (September–October 1990): 105–111.

Rentz, Joseph O., and Fred D. Reynolds. "Forecasting the Effects of an Aging Population on Product Consumption: An Age-Period-Cohort Framework." *Journal of Marketing Research* 28 (August 1991): 355–360.

Rivera-Batiz, Louis A., and Danyang Xie. "GATT, Trade and Growth." *American Economic Review* 82 (May 1992): 422–427.

Roth, Alvin E. "A Natural Experiment in the Organization of Entry-Level Labor Markets: Regional Markets for New Physicians and Surgeons in the United Kingdom." *American Economic Review* 81 (June 1991): 415–440.

Sachs, Jeffrey. "Privatization in Russia: Some Lessons from Eastern Europe." *American Economic Review* 82 (May 1992): 43–48.

Shackelford, Douglas A. "The Market for Tax Benefits: Evidence from Leveraged ESOPs." *Journal of Accounting & Economics* 14 (June 1991): 117–145.

Shiller, Robert J., Maxim Boycko, and Vladimir Korobov. "Popular Attitudes Toward Free Markets: The Soviet Union and the United States Compared." *American Economic Review* 81 (June 1991): 385–400.

Weitzman, Martin L. "Price Distortion and Shortage Deformation, or What Happened to the Soap?" *American Economic Review* 81 (June 1991): 401–414.

DEMAND ANALYSIS

Successful product design, development, and pricing all require a clear understanding of the breadth and depth of product demand. Effective execution of the firm's marketing function is necessary to ensure the firm's economic viability. No matter how efficient the firm's production process, and regardless of overall managerial skill, it is impossible to operate profitably unless product demand exists or can be created. A vital determinant of firm success is the extent to which management can identify and meet product demand.

Because of the role played by demand as a fundamental determinant of profitability, management must have accurate information about demand conditions to make effective short-run operating decisions and strategic long-run planning decisions. To price the firm's products effectively, managers must know how changing prices affect the quantity demanded. Similarly, they must understand how advertising and credit terms affect demand to appraise the attractiveness of current or proposed credit and promotional strategies. Dependable estimates of the sensitivity of demand to changes in both population and income are helpful in the analysis of the firm's growth potential and, therefore, in the long-range planning process.

Production decisions are profoundly influenced by the demand characteristics of the firm's products. Relatively stable demand allows long, continuous production runs. If demand fluctuates widely, either flexible production processes must be employed or sizable inventories must be carried to avoid stock outages. Demand conditions in the product market also affect the firm's labor and capital requirements. If product demand is strong and growing, financial managers must arrange to fund the firm's growing capital requirements; and the personnel department must recruit and train a work force sufficient to produce and sell the firm's expanded product line.

Product demand also plays an important role in determining the market structure in which a firm operates and, hence, the nature of competition. Demand characteristics such as the number of potential buyers and the willingness of consumers to accept substitute products are important in determining the level and form of competition in a market. This topic is developed in Chapters 12 through 15, in which market structure, pricing practices, and the role of government in the market economy are examined.

Demand analysis and estimation are complex subjects, but they must be thoroughly understood if managers are to reach their goals. This chapter examines the basics of consumer demand as a framework for the study of the elasticity concept, a useful means for quantifying the sensitivity or responsiveness of demand to changes in underlying conditions. Elasticity measures are developed to characterize the effects of changes in prices, income, advertising, and any other factors with an important influence on the demand for a company's products. These concepts are employed to formulate models that can be used to estimate demand functions and various demand elasticities.

Three primary methods used by successful managers to estimate demand relations are considered in some detail. First, the consumer interview or survey method is often used to estimate potential demand for new products or to test the potential reaction to prospective changes in prices or advertising for established products. Second, just as physical scientists conduct laboratory experiments, managers and market researchers use market experiments to evaluate customer reactions to new or improved products in a controlled setting. Like the consumer survey method, market experiments are well suited to demand estimation problems involving new or improved products. A third method for demand estimation involves the use of historical market data and the powerful analytical technique of regression analysis. Given the rapid rate of improvement in the capabilities of relatively inexpensive desktop computers and user-friendly software, popular regression-based techniques are bound to become even more widespread in the years ahead. As a result, the regression analysis method of demand estimation merits careful consideration.

THE BASIS FOR CONSUMER DEMAND

The ability of goods and services to satisfy consumer wants is the basis for consumer demand. Chapter 4 introduced the utility concept as a measure of satisfaction or well-being derived from consumption. This section explores the basis for consumer demand by developing the rationale for consumer purchases.

Utility Functions

Utility function

A descriptive statement that relates satisfaction or well-being to the consumption of goods and services.

A **utility function** is a descriptive statement that relates total utility (i.e., satisfaction or well-being) to the consumption of goods and services. Utility functions are shaped both by the tastes and preferences of consumers and by the quantity and quality of available products.

The concept of a utility function can be illustrated using a simple two-product example. These two products can be closely related, such as basketball and football tickets, or relatively unrelated, such as clothing and medical care. The only requirement is that each can satisfy consumer wants—that is, each provides utility. Such a utility function can be written in the following general form:

$$\text{Utility} = f(\text{Goods, Services}). \qquad \textbf{(5.1)}$$

Table 5.1 charts a two-product utility function. Each element in the table shows the amount of utility derived from the consumption of each respective combination of goods (Y) and services (X). For example, consumption of 3 units of X and 3 units of Y provides 68 utils (units of satisfaction), consumption of 1 X and 10 Y provides 80 utils, and so on. Each product is measured in terms of, for

TABLE 5.1 **Utility Derived from Consumption of Various Combinations of Goods and Services**

	Services (X)									
Goods (Y)	1	2	3	4	5	6	7	8	9	10
1	25	36	46	55	63	70	76	81	85	88
2	37	48	58	67	75	82	88	93	97	100
3	47	58	68	77	85	92	98	103	107	110
4	55	66	76	85	93	100	106	111	115	118
5	62	73	83	92	100	107	113	118	122	125
6	68	79	89	98	106	113	119	124	128	131
7	73	84	94	103	111	118	124	129	133	136
8	77	88	98	107	115	122	128	133	137	140
9	79	90	100	109	117	124	130	135	139	142
10	80	91	101	110	118	125	131	136	140	143

TABLE 5.2 **Total and Marginal Utility Derived from Hamburger Consumption**

Hamburgers per Meal, H	Total Utility, U	Marginal Utility $MU_H = \Delta U / \Delta H$	Maximum Acceptable Hamburger Price at 20¢ per MU_H
0	0	—	—
1	5	5	$1.00
2	9	4	0.80
3	12	3	0.60
4	14	2	0.40
5	15	1	0.20
6	15	0	0.00

instance, the *number* of dresses, *hours* of financial planning services, *days* of vacation, and so on.

The utility derived from consumption is intangible. However, consumers reveal their preferences through purchase decisions and thereby provide tangible evidence of the utility they derive from various products.

The utility function depicted in Table 5.1 can also be displayed graphically, as in Figure 5.1. The height of the bar associated with each combination of goods and services indicates the level of utility provided through the consumption of those items.

Marginal Utility

Whereas total utility measures the consumer's overall level of satisfaction derived from consumption activities, **marginal utility** measures the added satisfaction derived from a one-unit increase in consumption of a particular good or service, *holding consumption of all other goods and services constant.* Marginal utility tends to diminish as consumption of a product increases within a given time interval.

FIGURE 5.1   **Representative Utility Function for the Consumption of Goods and Services**

Total utility increases with a rise in the consumption of goods and services.

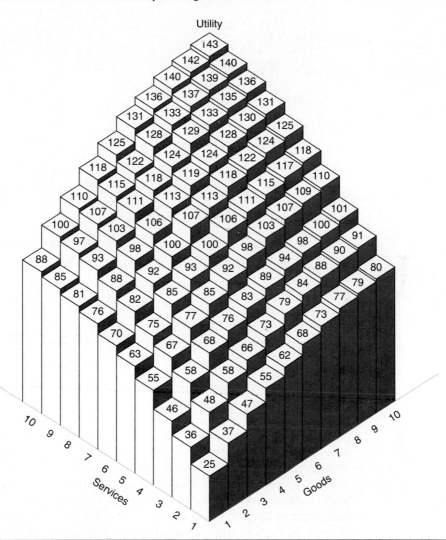

Marginal utility

The added utility derived from increasing consumption of a particular product by one unit.

For example, suppose Table 5.2 illustrates the utility that a typical college-age customer of the Hamburger Stand derives from hamburger consumption during a single meal. According to the table, the marginal utility from consuming an initial hamburger is 5 units ($MU_{H=1} = 5$). Marginal utility is 4 units for a second hamburger, 3 units for a third, and so on.

If each hamburger costs $1, the cost per unit (util) of satisfaction derived from consuming the first hamburger is 20¢ (= $1/5 utils). A second hamburger costing $1 produces 4 utils of additional satisfaction at a cost of 25¢ per unit. Note that a diminishing marginal utility for hamburgers increases the cost of each marginal

FIGURE 5.2   **Downward-Sloping Demand Curve for Hamburgers**

The demand curve for hamburgers is downward sloping.

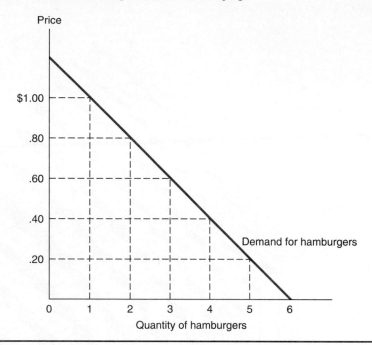

unit of satisfaction. Consequently, if the typical Hamburger Stand customer had alternative consumption opportunities providing one additional unit of utility for 20¢ each, she or he would be willing to increase the quantity of hamburgers purchased only if hamburger prices were to fall. If the required price/marginal utility trade-off for hamburgers is 20¢ per util because this is the cost per unit of utility derived from other products, then the typical Hamburger Stand customer would pay a price of $1 for a single hamburger. However, a hamburger price of 80¢ (= 20¢ × 4 utils) would be necessary to induce her or him to buy a second hamburger, 60¢ would be needed for a third, 40¢ for a fourth, and so on. This gives rise to the downward-sloping demand curve shown in Figure 5.2.[1]

The Law of Diminishing Marginal Utility

Law of diminishing marginal utility

As consumption of a given product increases, the added benefit derived diminishes.

In general, the **law of diminishing marginal utility** states that as an individual increases consumption of a given product, the marginal utility gained from consumption eventually declines. This law gives rise to a downward-sloping demand curve not only for hamburgers but also for all other goods and services. The law of diminishing marginal utility is illustrated in Table 5.3, which is derived from the data in Table 5.1. When service is held constant at 4 units, the marginal utility

[1] The demand curve in Figure 5.2 assumes that a consumer is free to purchase the quantity desired at each price. It does not represent the case in which a seller can force an all-or-nothing purchase decision at each price.

TABLE 5.3   **Total and Marginal Utility of Goods and Services**

Quantity	Goods (Y) Total Utility	Goods (Y) Marginal Utility ($MU_Y \mid X = 4$)	Services (X) Total Utility	Services (X) Marginal Utility ($MU_X \mid Y = 1$)
1	55	—	25	—
2	67	12	36	11
3	77	10	46	10
4	85	8	55	9
5	92	7	63	8
6	98	6	70	7
7	103	5	76	6
8	107	4	81	5
9	109	2	85	4
10	110	1	88	3

derived from consuming goods falls with each successive unit of consumption. Similarly, the consumption of services is subject to diminishing marginal utility. Holding goods consumption constant at 1 unit, the marginal utility derived from consuming services falls continuously. The added benefit derived through consumption of each product grows progressively smaller as consumption increases, holding the other constant.

CONSUMER CHOICE

The decision to consume an individual product is seldom made in isolation. Instead, products are consumed as parts of a "market basket" of goods and services. To a greater or lesser degree, goods and services can be substituted for one another. For example, an executive may own many suits and dry clean each suit only occasionally or instead may own only a few and dry clean each suit more frequently. In the first instance, the executive has bought a market basket with a high proportion of total expenditures devoted to suits (goods) and relatively little devoted to dry-cleaning services. In the latter case, a market basket weighted less toward goods and more toward services has been purchased.

Indifference Curves

Indifference curve

A curve that identifies all combinations of goods and services that provide the same utility.

With the wide variety of alternative combinations of goods and services that are typically available, a large number of market baskets can be created that provide the same level of utility to the consumer. An **indifference curve** represents all market baskets among which the consumer is indifferent about choosing.

To illustrate, Figure 5.3 shows two indifference curves based on the data contained in Table 5.1. Note that 100 units of satisfaction can be derived from the consumption of 3 X and 9 Y (Point A), 5 X and 5 Y (Point B), 6 X and 4 Y (Point C), and 10 X and 2 Y (Point D). Therefore, each of these points lies on the $U_1 = 100$ indifference curve. Similarly, 118 units of satisfaction are derived from consumption of 5 X and 10 Y (Point E), 6 X and 7 Y (Point F), 8 X and 5 Y (Point G),

FIGURE 5.3   Representative Indifference Curves Based on Table 5.1 Data

Indifference curves show market baskets of goods and services that provide the same utility.

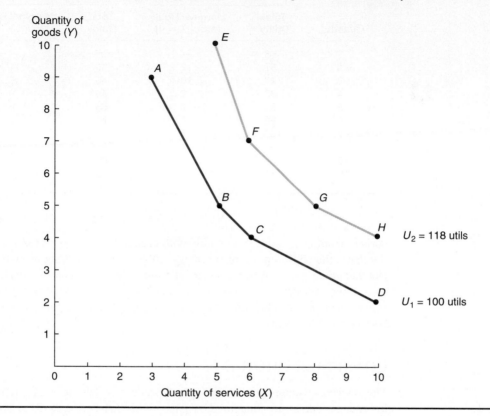

and 10 X and 4 Y (Point H). Therefore, all these points lie on the $U_2 = 118$ indifference curve.

An indifference curve is constructed by connecting all the points representing consumption baskets that provide the same level of utility. This construction assumes that consumption can be split between consumption baskets. For example, the line segment between Points A and B on the $U_1 = 100$ indifference curve represents a combination of market baskets A and B. The midpoint of this line segment represents consumption of one-half of market basket A plus one-half of market basket B. Similarly, the midpoint of the GH line segment represents a 50/50 combination of the G and H market baskets.

The discrete utility-function data used to derive the indifference curves shown in Figure 5.3 (see Table 5.1 and Figure 5.1) can be generalized by assuming that the consumption of goods and services can be varied continuously rather than in an incremental fashion, as was assumed in the previous example. With the resulting utility function, indifference curves will have the smooth shapes shown in Figure 5.4. The slope at each point along such indifference curves measures the consumer's rate of substitution among products.

FIGURE 5.4 **Indifference Curves with Continuous Substitution of** *X* **and** *Y*

Indifference curves have smooth U shapes when *X* and *Y* can be continuously substituted for each other.

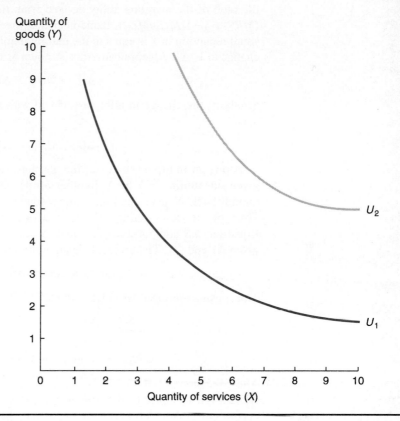

Marginal Rate of
Substitution

Marginal rate of
substitution
The amount of one
product that must be
substituted for another
if utility is to remain
unchanged.

In Figure 5.4 the slope of each indifference curve equals the change in goods (ΔY) divided by the change in services (ΔX). This relation, called the **marginal rate of substitution,** is simply the change in consumption of *Y* (goods) necessary to offset a given change in the consumption of *X* (services) if the consumer's overall level of utility is to remain constant. This can be stated algebraically:

$$MRS = \frac{\Delta Y}{\Delta X} = \text{Slope of an Indifference Curve.} \qquad (5.2)$$

The marginal rate of substitution (*MRS*) is usually not constant but diminishes as the amount of substitution increases. For example, in Figure 5.3, as more goods are substituted for services, the amount of services necessary to compensate for a given loss of goods will continue to fall. Alternatively, as more services are substituted for goods, the amount of goods necessary to compensate for a given loss of services will continue to fall. This means that the negative slope of each indifference curve tends to approach zero as one moves along from left to right.

The product substitution relation indicated by the slope of an indifference curve is directly related to the concept of diminishing marginal utility introduced earlier. This is because the marginal rate of substitution is equal to -1 times the ratio of the marginal utility derived from the consumption of each product ($MRS = -1(MU_X/MU_Y)$). Remember that the loss in utility associated with a small reduction in Y is equal to the marginal utility of Y, MU_Y, multiplied by the change in Y, ΔY. Algebraically, this is shown as follows:

$$\Delta U = MU_Y + \Delta Y. \tag{5.3}$$

Similarly, the change in utility associated with a change in the consumption of X is:

$$\Delta U = MU_X \times \Delta X. \tag{5.4}$$

Along an indifference curve, the absolute value of ΔU must be equal for a given substitution of Y for X. In other words, since utility is held constant along an indifference curve, the loss in utility following a reduction in Y must be fully offset by the gain in utility associated with an increase in X. Thus, ΔU in both Equations 5.3 and 5.4 must be equal in size and have an opposite sign from a given ΔY and ΔX. Therefore, along an indifference curve,

$$-(MU_X \times \Delta X) = MU_Y \times \Delta Y. \tag{5.5}$$

Transposing the variables in Equation 5.5 produces

$$-\frac{M_X}{M_Y} = \frac{\Delta Y}{\Delta X} \tag{5.6}$$

$$MRS_{XY} = \text{Slope of an Indifference Curve.}$$

Thus, the slope of an indifference curve, shown in Equation 5.2 to be equal to $\Delta Y/\Delta X$, is determined by the ratio of marginal utilities derived from each product. As one moves from left to right in Figure 5.4, the slope of each indifference curve goes from a large negative number toward zero. As seen in Equation 5.6, this implies that MU_X decreases relative to MU_Y as the relative consumption of X progressively increases.

Budget Lines

Budget line

All combinations of products that can be purchased for a fixed dollar amount.

To fully understand consumer decisions, the concept of a budget line must be introduced. A **budget line** represents all combinations of products that can be purchased for a fixed dollar amount. To derive a budget line, it is necessary only to add up the amount of spending on goods and services that is feasible with a given budget. The amount of spending on goods is equal to the product of P_Y, the price of goods, times Y, the quantity purchased. Similarly, total spending on services is $P_X \times X$. When these amounts are added together, the budget line formula is derived:

$$\text{Total Budget} = \text{Spending on Goods} + \text{Spending on Services}$$
$$B = P_Y Y + P_X X.$$

Solving this expression for Y so that it can be graphed as in Figure 5.5(a) results in

$$Y = \frac{B}{P_Y} - \frac{P_X}{P_Y}X. \qquad (5.7)$$

Note that the first term in Equation 5.7 is the y-axis intercept of the budget line. This y-axis intercept indicates the quantity of Product Y that can be purchased with a given budget, *assuming that zero units of Product X are purchased.* The slope of the budget line is equal to $-P_X/P_Y$ and, therefore, is a measure of the relative prices of the products being purchased. It follows that a change in the budget level B leads to a parallel shift in the budget line, whereas a change in the relative prices of items being purchased causes the slope of the budget line to rotate.

For example, if the price for goods is $250 per unit and for services is $100 per unit, the relevant budget line can be written as follows:

$$B = \$250Y + \$100X$$

or

$$Y = \frac{B}{\$250} - \frac{\$100}{\$250}X.$$

Given a $1,000 budget, a maximum of 4 units of goods ($Y = \$1,000/\$250$) could be purchased. This assumes, of course, that the entire $1,000 is spent on goods and none on services. If all $1,000 is devoted to the purchase of services, a maximum of 10 units of services ($X = \$1,000/\$100$) could be purchased. These market baskets ($0X$, $4Y$ and $10X$, $0Y$), represent the endpoints of the $B_1 = \$1,000$ budget line shown in Figure 5.5(a). This budget line identifies all combinations of goods and services that can be purchased for $1,000. Notice that $1,000 is insufficient to purchase any market basket lying on the $U_1 = 100$ or $U_2 = 118$ indifference curves. A minimum expenditure of $1,500 is necessary before the $U_1 = 100$ level of satisfaction can be achieved, and a minimum of $2,000 is necessary before the $U_2 = 118$ level can be reached.

Again, the effect of a budget increase is to shift a budget line outward and to the right. The effect of a budget decrease is to shift a budget line inward and to the left. So long as the relative prices of goods and services remain constant, budget lines will remain parallel, as is shown in Figure 5.5(a). This follows because so long as relative prices remain constant, the slope of the budget line also remains constant.

The effect of a change in relative prices is shown in Figure 5.5(b). Here the budget of $1,500 and the $100-per-unit price of services remain constant, while the price of goods falls progressively from $250 to $150 to $75 per unit. As the price of goods falls, a given budget will purchase more goods. Thus, a maximum of 6 units of goods can be purchased at a price of $250 per unit, 10 units can be purchased at a price of $150, and 20 units at a price of $75.

In general, a fall in the price of goods or services permits an increase in consumption and consumer welfare. If both prices fall by a given percentage, a parallel rightward shift in the budget line occurs that is identical to the effect of an increase in budget. For example, the increase in consumption made possible by an increase in budget from $B_2 = \$1,500$ to $B_3 = \$2,000$ as shown in Figure

FIGURE 5.5   Consumption Effects of Changes in Budget and Relative Prices

(a) An increase in budget results in a parallel outward shift in the budget line. (b) A price cut allows purchase of a greater quantity with a given budget.

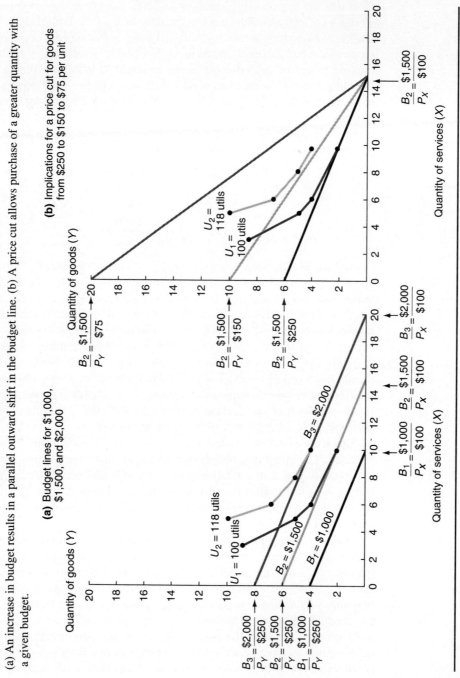

(a) Budget lines for $1,000, $1,500, and $2,000

(b) Implications for a price cut for goods from $250 to $150 to $75 per unit

FIGURE 5.6   **Income and Substitution Effects Following Reduction in the Price of Goods**

A price change will result in both income and substitution effects.

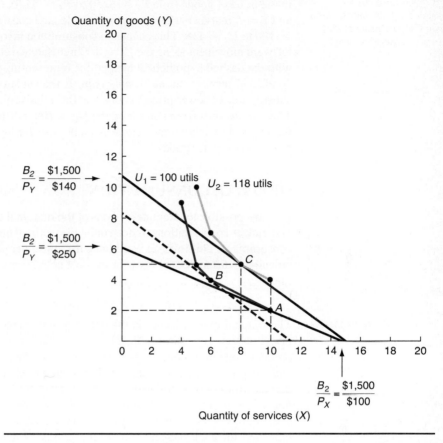

Quantity of services (X)

5.5(a) could also be realized following a decrease in the price of goods from $250 to $187.50 and of services from $100 to $75.

Income and Substitution Effects

Income effect

Shift to a new indifference curve following a change in aggregate consumption caused by a price change.

When product prices change, the consumer is affected in two ways. The **income effect** of a price change is the increase in overall consumption made possible by a price cut or the decrease in overall consumption that follows a price increase. The income effect results in a shift to a higher indifference curve following a price cut or a shift to a lower indifference curve following a price increase. The **substitution effect** of a price change describes the change in relative consumption that occurs as consumers substitute cheaper products for more expensive products. The substitution effect results in an upward or downward movement along a given indifference curve. The total effect of a price change on consumption is the sum of income and substitution effects.

Using the previous example, the total effect of a change in the price of goods is shown in Figure 5.6. When $P_Y = \$250$ and $P_X = \$100$, $U_1 = 100$ is the

Substitution effect

Movement along an indifference curve reflecting the substitution of cheaper products for more expensive ones.

highest level of satisfaction that can be achieved with a $1,500 budget. This involves consumption of 10 units of service and 2 units of goods. Following a cut in the price of goods from $P_Y = \$250$ to $P_Y = \$140$, consumption of the $X = 8$ and $Y = 5$ market basket becomes possible, and consumer welfare rises from $U_1 = 100$ to $U_2 = 118$. This change in consumption involves two components. The leftward movement along the $U_1 = 100$ indifference curve to Point B, a tangency with the dashed hypothetical budget line representing the new relative prices for goods and services but *no income gain,* is the substitution effect. It reflects the substitution of lower-priced goods for the relatively more expensive services. The upward shift from Point B on the $U_1 = 100$ indifference curve to Point C on the $U_2 = 118$ indifference curve is made possible by the income effect of the price reduction for goods.

OPTIMAL CONSUMPTION

It is now possible to integrate analysis of the marginal rate of substitution, prices, and budget considerations to determine the optimal combination of products for consumption. This involves combining the consumer preference information provided by indifference curves with the cost considerations incorporated in budget lines.

Utility Maximization

The optimal market basket is the one that maximizes a consumer's utility for a given budget expenditure. To allocate expenditures efficiently among various products, one must consider both the marginal utility derived from consumption and the prices for each product. Utility is maximized when the marginal utility derived from each individual product is proportional to the price paid. This is illustrated graphically in Figure 5.7, which shows multiple indifference curves and multiple budget lines. Optimal market baskets of goods and services are indicated for each budget level by the points of tangency between respective indifference curves and budget lines. To see why, assume that an individual has the funds indicated by budget line B_1. In this case, the optimal consumption combination occurs at Point A, the point of tangency between the budget line and indifference curve U_1. At that point, goods (Y) and services (X) are combined in proportions that maximize the utility attainable with budget expenditure B_1. No other combination of X and Y that can be purchased along budget line B_1 provides as much satisfaction, or utility. All other X,Y combinations along the budget line B_1 must intersect indifference curves representing lower levels of utility. Alternatively stated, the combination X_1Y_1 is the lowest-cost consumption market basket that provides the U_1 level of utility. All other X,Y combinations on the U_1 indifference curve lie on higher budget lines. Similarly, X_2Y_2 is the lowest-cost combination of goods and services that provides utility at the U_2 level, X_3Y_3 is the lowest-cost market basket that provides a U_3 level of utility, and so on. All other market baskets providing U_1, U_2, and U_3 levels of utility are intersected by higher budget lines and, therefore, require a higher level of expenditure.

That optimal consumption combinations occur at points of tangency between budget lines and indifference curves leads to a very important economic principle.

FIGURE 5.7 **Optimal Market Baskets for Consumption**

The optimal path for consumption is found when $P_X/P_Y = MU_X/MU_Y$.

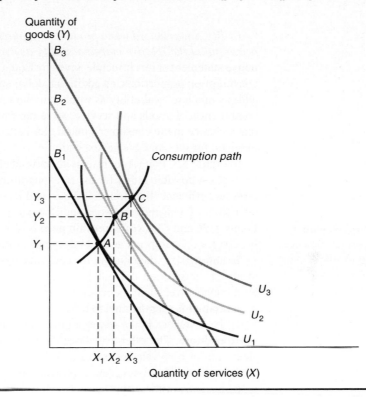

The slope of a budget line was shown to be -1 times the ratio of the product prices, or $-P_X/P_Y$. Recall also that the slope of an indifference curve was shown to be equal to the marginal rate of substitution of one consumption item for another when utility is held constant at a given level. The marginal rate of substitution is shown in Equation 5.6 as -1 times the ratio of the marginal utilities for each product. Thus, the slope of an indifference curve equals $-MU_X/MU_Y$.

At each point at which goods and services are combined optimally, there is a tangency between the budget line and the indifference curve; hence, their slopes are equal. For optimal consumption combinations, the ratio of the prices of the goods and services must be equal to the ratio of their marginal utilities:

$$\text{Slope of an Indifference Curve} = \text{Slope of a Budget Line}$$

$$-\frac{MU_X}{MU_Y} = -\frac{P_X}{P_Y}, \tag{5.8}$$

and

$$\frac{MU_X}{MU} = \frac{P_X}{P}.$$

Alternatively,

$$\frac{MU_X}{P_X} = \frac{MU_Y}{P_Y}.$$ **(5.8a)**

Utility is maximized when products are purchased at such levels that relative prices equal the relative marginal utility derived from consumption. The alternative statement of this principle, given by Equation 5.8a, shows that with optimal consumption proportions, an additional dollar spent on a given consumption item adds as much to total utility as would a dollar spent on any other such item. Any combination of goods and services violating this rule is suboptimal in the sense that a change in the consumer's market basket could result in greater utility being obtained for the same budget expenditure.

In Figure 5.7, Point *A* represents an optimal allocation, since X_1 and Y_1 provide the highest possible utility for the B_1 expenditure level. Similarly, Points *B* and *C* represent efficient allocations for the B_2 and B_3 expenditure levels. By connecting all points of tangency between indifference curves and budget lines (such as Points *A, B,* and *C*), a **consumption path** is identified that depicts optimal market baskets for consumption as the budget expenditure level grows.

Consumption path

Optimal combinations of products as consumption increases.

To summarize, the demand for consumer goods and services is based on the utility or satisfaction derived from consumption. This utility is maximized at each budget level when the relative marginal utility derived from consumption of each product is proportional to the price paid. Only then will each product be an attractive purchase in the sense of providing the same marginal utility per dollar of expenditure. The effective allocation of a consumer's budget requires a consideration of both relative prices and the relative marginal utility derived from consumption. This background provides the framework necessary for a detailed analysis of the important roles played by prices, advertising, income, and other factors in determining the level of demand for a firm's products. Such an analysis focuses on the sensitivity of demand to changes in important demand-determining factors.

DEMAND SENSITIVITY ANALYSIS: ELASTICITY

For constructive managerial decision making, the firm must know the sensitivity or responsiveness of demand to changes in factors that make up the underlying demand function.

The Elasticity Concept

One measure of responsiveness employed not only in demand analysis but throughout managerial decision making is **elasticity,** defined as the percentage change in a dependent variable, *Y,* resulting from a 1 percent change in the value of an independent variable, *X.* The equation for calculating elasticity is

$$\text{Elasticity} = \frac{\text{Percentage Change in } Y}{\text{Percentage Change in } X}.$$ **(5.9)**

MANAGERIAL APPLICATION 5.1

Bargain Hunting Catches On in Japan

Shopping for value is quite the rage in Japan these days. Consumers are checking prices on everything from shampoo to designer-brand clothes, specialized discount stores are sprouting up nationwide, and companies are rushing to offer "better-value" goods. Although such price-consciousness may be second nature to most shoppers, it is a startling change in behavior for Japanese consumers. During the spending boom of the 1980s, many Japanese consumers were willing to pay top-dollar prices for high-value products. Discount stores were regularly spurned by the Japanese consumer as sellers of low-quality, miscellaneous goods secured from dubious sources. Besides, discounters were limited to offering only a narrow range of products, such as electronic goods.

The early 1990s crash of the Tokyo stock market and subsequent downturn in economic activity intensified the Japanese trend toward value shopping. Although consumers in general weren't panicked by the market's downturn, slow economic growth made them much more cautious buyers. "The trend may be back to basics—back to the simple functions (and away from) a lot of unnecessary frills," says Susumu Taketomi, chief economist of the Industrial Bank of Japan. The emergence and rapid growth of large, specialized discount stores for general merchandise is the biggest change to hit Japanese retailing in the past 20 years. Discount stores still account for less than 1 percent of Japan's approximately 1.6 million retailers, but the number of discount liquor store outlets, for example, doubled in the 1990–1992 period. The rate of growth in sales for discount retailers in Japan is simply astounding. For example, suburban discount apparel stores sales are increasing by 25 percent per year compared with meager growth of 7 to 8 percent for traditional department stores, which are floundering.

In addition, the trend toward discount retailers is opening up Japan to foreign companies such as Helene Curtis Inc., a Chicago-based hair care concern that wants to sell their products at lower prices than Japanese competitors. A recent change in the nation's retail law has also relaxed some key barriers to entry. Many foreign companies, including Toys "R" Us, are now finding it easier to crack Japan's complicated distribution system. Even luxury goods makers, which have long assumed that Japanese consumers associate high prices with high quality, are reversing their strategies. In 1992, for example, Parfums Christian Dior Japan reduced prices on 21 fragrance items by 10 to 20 percent. Japanese department stores are also getting into the price-cutting act. Noting that midpriced suits were replacing more expensive suits in popularity, Isetan Co., a Tokyo-based department store, doubled the number of "Isetan Quality" middle-of-the-road product lines. "The real expensive things don't sell anymore," says Akinori Ohtake, an Isetan spokesperson. "You've got to have quality products at reasonable prices."

Japanese consumers never fought for large stores that offer cheaper prices but relentless pressure by U.S. trade officials nudged the Japanese government to deregulate the country's rigid large-scale retail law. Before recent changes, local mom-and-pop retail stores were able to prevent the opening of any large chain or store in a given area for as long as 10 years. Since 1992, however, local retailers must now approve or disapprove stores of more than 5,400 square feet within 12 months. As a result, stores like Toys "R" Us are opening at a quicker pace. The discount toy retailer, for example, opened its first Japanese store in December 1991 and plans to open 10 more by the end of 1993.

A growing number of large retail stores is causing havoc in a Japanese distribution system that has traditionally been more interested in keeping wholesalers and retailers happy than in lowering prices. Partly as a result, reaping profits from large discount stores remains much harder in Japan than in the United States. However, as Japanese merchants study and imitate the success of Wal-Mart, K-Mart, and others, the profitability of Japanese discount stores is sure to rise. Once Japanese customers realize the benefits of discount pricing, discount retailers are sure to flourish in Japan as they have in the United States and elsewhere.

Source: Yumiko Ono, "Bargain Hunting Catches On in Japan, Boosting Fortunes of Discount Stores," *The Wall Street Journal*, May 9, 1992, B1.

Elasticity

The percentage change in a dependent variable resulting from a 1 percent change in an independent variable.

The concept of elasticity is quite general. It simply involves the percentage change in one variable associated with a given percentage change in another variable. In addition to being used in demand analysis, the concept is used in finance, where the impact of changes in sales on earnings under different production levels (operating leverage) and different financial structures (financial leverage) is measured by an elasticity factor. Elasticities are also used in production and cost analysis to evaluate the effects of changes in input on output as well as the effects of output changes on costs.

Endogenous variables

Factors controlled by the firm.

Exogenous variables

Factors outside the control of the firm.

Factors such as price and advertising that are within the control of the firm are called **endogenous variables.** It is important for management to know the effects of altering these variables when making decisions. Other important factors outside the control of the firm, such as consumer incomes, competitor prices, and the weather, are called **exogenous variables.** The effects of changes in both types of influences must be understood if the firm is to respond effectively to changes in the economic environment. For example, a firm must understand the effects on demand of changes in both prices and consumer incomes to determine the price cut necessary to offset a decline in sales caused by a business recession (fall in income). Similarly, the sensitivity of demand to changes in advertising must be quantified if the firm is to respond appropriately with price or advertising changes to an increase in competitor advertising. Determining the effects of changes in both controllable and uncontrollable influences on demand is the focus of demand analysis.

Point Elasticity and Arc Elasticity

Elasticity can be measured in two different ways, point elasticity and arc elasticity. **Point elasticity** measures elasticity at a given point on a function. The point elasticity concept is used to measure the effect on a dependent variable Y of a very small or marginal change in an independent variable X. Although the point elasticity concept can often give accurate estimates of the effect on Y of very small (less than 5 percent) changes in X, it is not used to measure the effect on Y of large-scale changes, because elasticity typically varies at different points along a function. To assess the effects of large-scale changes in X, the arc elasticity concept is employed. **Arc elasticity** measures the average elasticity over a given range of a function.

Point elasticity

Elasticity at a given point on a function.

Arc elasticity

Average elasticity over a given range of a function.

Using the lowercase Greek letter ϵ (epsilon) as the symbol for point elasticity, the point elasticity formula is written

$$\text{Point Elasticity} = \epsilon_X = \frac{\text{Percentage Change in } Y}{\text{Percentage Change in } X},$$

$$= \frac{\Delta Y/Y}{\Delta X/X}, \qquad (5.10)$$

$$= \frac{\Delta Y}{\Delta X} \times \frac{X}{Y}.$$

The $\Delta Y/\Delta X$ term in the point elasticity formula is the marginal relation between Y and X, and it shows the effect on Y of a one-unit change in X. Point elasticity is determined by multiplying this marginal relation by the relative size of X to Y, or the X/Y ratio at the point being analyzed.

Point elasticity measures the percentage effect on Y of a percentage change in X at a given point on a function. If $\epsilon_X = 5$, a 1 percent increase in X will lead to a 5 percent increase in Y, and a 1 percent decrease in X will lead to a 5 percent decrease in Y. Thus, when $\epsilon_X > 0$, Y changes in the same positive or negative direction as X. Conversely, when $\epsilon_X < 0$, Y changes in the opposite direction of changes in X. For example, if $\epsilon_X = -3$, a 1 percent increase in X will lead to a 3 percent decrease in Y, and a 1 percent decrease in X will lead to a 3 percent increase in Y.

An example can be used to illustrate the calculation and use of a point elasticity estimate. Assume that management is interested in analyzing the responsiveness of movie-ticket demand to changes in advertising for the Empire State Cinema Corporation, a regional chain of movie theaters. Also assume that analysis of monthly data for six outlets covering the past year suggests the following demand function:

$$Q = 6{,}600 - 5{,}000P + 3{,}500P_V + 40I + 1{,}000A, \qquad (5.11)$$

where Q is the quantity of movie tickets, P is average ticket price (in dollars), P_V is the three-day movie rental price at video outlets in the area (in dollars), I is average disposable income per household (in thousands of dollars), and A is monthly advertising expenditures (in thousands of dollars). (Note that I and A are expressed in thousands of dollars in this demand function.) For a typical theater, $P = \$5$, $P_V = \$2$, and income and advertising are \$35,000 and \$20,000, respectively. The demand for movie tickets at a typical theater can be estimated as

$$
\begin{aligned}
Q &= 6{,}600 - 5{,}000(5) + 3{,}500(2) + 40(35) + 1{,}000(20) \\
&= 10{,}000.
\end{aligned}
$$

The numbers that appear before each variable in Equation 5.11 are called coefficients or parameter estimates. They indicate the expected change in movie-ticket sales associated with a one-unit change in each relevant variable. For example, the number 5,000 indicates that the quantity of movie tickets demanded falls by 5,000 units with every \$1 increase in the price of movie tickets, or $\Delta Q/\Delta P = -5{,}000$. Similarly, a \$1 increase in the price of videocassette rentals causes a 3,500-unit increase in movie-ticket demand, or $\Delta Q/\Delta P_V = 3{,}500$; a \$1,000 (one-unit) increase in disposable income per household leads to a 40-unit increase in demand. In terms of advertising, the expected change in demand following a one-unit (\$1,000) change in advertising, or $\Delta Q/\Delta A$, is 1,000. With advertising expenditures of \$20,000, the point advertising elasticity at the 10,000-unit demand level is

$$
\begin{aligned}
\epsilon_A &= \text{Point Advertising Elasticity} \\
&= \frac{\text{Percentage Change in Quantity } (Q)}{\text{Percentage Change in Advertising } (A)} \\
&= \frac{\Delta Q/Q}{\Delta A/A} \\
&= \frac{\Delta Q}{\Delta A} \times \frac{A}{Q} \qquad\qquad (5.12)
\end{aligned}
$$

$$= 1,000 \times \frac{\$20}{10,000}$$

$$= 2.$$

Thus, a 1 percent change in advertising expenditures results in a 2 percent change in movie-ticket demand. This elasticity is positive, indicating a direct relation between advertising outlays and movie-ticket demand. An increase in advertising expenditures leads to higher demand; a decrease in advertising leads to lower demand.

For many business decisions, managers are concerned with the impact of substantial changes in a demand-determining factor, such as advertising, rather than with the impact of very small (marginal) changes. In these instances the point elasticity concept suffers a conceptual shortcoming.

To see the nature of the problem, consider the calculation of the advertising elasticity of demand for movie tickets as advertising increases from $20,000 to $50,000. Assume for this example that all other demand-influencing variables retain their previous values. With advertising at $20,000, demand is 10,000 units. Changing advertising to $50,000 ($\Delta A = 30$) results in a 30,000-unit increase in movie-ticket demand, so total demand at that level is 40,000 tickets. Using Equation 5.10 to calculate the advertising point elasticity for the change in advertising from $20,000 to $50,000 indicates that

$$\text{Advertising Elasticity} = \frac{\Delta Q}{\Delta A} \times \frac{A}{Q} = \frac{30,000}{\$30} \times \frac{\$20}{10,000} = 2.$$

The advertising point elasticity is $\epsilon_A = 2$, just as that found previously. Consider, however, the indicated elasticity if one moves in the opposite direction—that is, if advertising is decreased from $50,000 to $20,000. The indicated elasticity point is

$$\text{Advertising Elasticity} = \frac{\Delta Q}{\Delta A} \times \frac{-30,000}{-\$30} \times \frac{\$50}{40,000} = 1.25.$$

The indicated elasticity $\epsilon_A = 1.25$ is now quite different. This problem occurs because elasticities are not typically constant but vary at different points along a given demand function. The advertising elasticity of 1.25 is the advertising point elasticity when advertising expenditures are $50,000 and the quantity demanded is 40,000 tickets.

To overcome the problem of changing elasticities along a demand function, the arc elasticity formula was developed to calculate an average elasticity for incremental as opposed to marginal changes. The arc elasticity formula is

$$E = \text{Arc Elasticity} = \frac{\dfrac{\text{Change in } Q}{\text{Average } Q}}{\dfrac{\text{Change in } X}{\text{Average } X}} = \frac{\dfrac{Q_2 - Q_1}{(Q_2 + Q_1)/2}}{\dfrac{X_2 - X_1}{(X_2 - X_1)/2}} \qquad \textbf{(5.13)}$$

$$= \frac{\dfrac{\Delta Q}{(Q_2 + Q_1)}}{\dfrac{\Delta X}{(X_2 + X_1)}} = \frac{\Delta Q}{\Delta X} \times \frac{X_2 + X_1}{Q_2 + Q_1}.$$

Again the percentage change in quantity demanded is divided by the percentage change in a demand-determining variable, but the bases used to calculate percentage changes are averages of the two data endpoints rather than the initially observed value. The arc elasticity equation eliminates the problem of the elasticity measure depending on which end of the range is viewed as the initial point. This yields a more accurate measure of the relative relation between the two variables over the *range* indicated by the data. The advertising arc elasticity over the $20,000–$50,000 range of advertising expenditures can be calculated as

$$\text{Advertising Arc Elasticity} = \frac{\text{Percentage Change in Quantity } (Q)}{\text{Percentage Change in Advertising } (A)}$$

$$= \frac{(Q_2 - Q_1)/(Q_2 + Q_1)}{(A_2 - A_1)/(A_2 + A_1)}$$

$$= \frac{\Delta Q}{\Delta A} \times \frac{A_2 + A_1}{Q_2 + Q_1}$$

$$= \frac{30,000}{\$30} \times \frac{\$50 + \$20}{40,000 + 10,000}$$

$$= 1.4.$$

Thus, a 1 percent change in the level of advertising expenditures in the range of $20,000 to $50,000 results, on average, in a 1.4 percent change in movie-ticket demand.

To summarize, it is important to remember that point elasticity is a marginal concept. It measures the elasticity at a specific point on a function. Proper use of point elasticity is limited to analysis of very small changes, say 0 to 5 percent, in the relevant independent variable. Arc elasticity is a better concept for measuring the average elasticity over an extended range when the change in a relevant independent variable is 5 percent or more. It is the appropriate tool for incremental analysis.

PRICE ELASTICITY OF DEMAND

Price elasticity of demand

Responsiveness of the quantity demanded to changes in the price of the product, holding constant the values of all other variables in the demand function.

The most widely used elasticity measure is the **price elasticity of demand,** which measures the responsiveness of the quantity demanded to changes in the price of the product, holding constant the values of all other variables in the demand function.

Using the formula for point elasticity, price elasticity of demand is found as

$$\epsilon_P = \text{Point Price Elasticity} = \frac{\text{Percentage Change in Quantity } (Q)}{\text{Percentage Change in Price } (P)}$$

$$= \frac{\delta Q/Q}{\delta P/P}$$

$$= \frac{\delta Q}{\delta P} \times \frac{P}{Q}, \tag{5.14}$$

where $\delta Q/\delta P$ is the marginal change in quantity following a one-unit change in price, and P and Q are price and quantity, respectively, at a given point on the demand curve.

The concept of point price elasticity can be illustrated by referring to Equation 5.11:

$$Q = 6{,}600 - 5{,}000P + 3{,}500P_V + 40I + 1{,}000A.$$

The coefficient for the price variable indicates the effect on quantity demanded of a one-unit change in price:

$$\frac{\delta Q}{\delta P} = -5{,}000, \text{ a constant.}$$

At the typical values of $P_V = \$2$, $I = \$35{,}000$, and $A = \$20{,}000$, the demand curve is calculated as

$$Q = 6{,}600 - 5{,}000(P) + 3{,}500(2) + 40(35) + 1{,}000(20)$$
$$= 35{,}000 - 5{,}000P.$$

This demand curve relation can be used to calculate ϵ_P at two points: (1) where $P_1 = \$5$ and $Q_1 = 10{,}000$ and (2) where $P_2 = \$6$ and $Q_2 = 5{,}000$:

$$(1) \ \epsilon_{P_1} = -5{,}000 \times \left(\frac{\$5}{10{,}000}\right) = -2.5.$$

$$(2) \ \epsilon_{P_2} = -5{,}000 \times \left(\frac{\$6}{5{,}000}\right) = -6.$$

Therefore, a 1 percent increase in price from the $5 movie-ticket price level results in a 2.5 percent reduction in the quantity demanded. At the $6 price level, a 1 percent increase results in a 6 percent reduction in the quantity demanded. This indicates that movie-ticket buyers, like most consumers, become increasingly price sensitive as average price increases. This example illustrates how price elasticity tends to vary along a linear demand curve, with ϵ_P increasing in absolute value at higher prices and lower quantities. Although price elasticity always varies along a linear demand curve, under certain conditions it can be constant along a curvilinear demand curve. This point will be illustrated in a later section.

When evaluating price elasticity estimates, it is important to recognize that price elasticities are uniformly negative. This follows because the quantity demanded for all goods and services is inversely related to price. In the previous example, at a $5 price, a 1 percent *increase* in price leads to a 2.5 percent *decrease* in the quantity of movie tickets demanded. Conversely, a 1 percent *decrease* in price leads to a 2.5 percent *increase* in the quantity demanded. For expository convenience, the equation for price elasticity is sometimes multiplied by -1 to change price elasticities to positive numbers. Therefore, when price elasticities are reported as positive numbers, or in absolute value terms, it is important to remember the underlying inverse relation between price and quantity.

Using the arc elasticity concept, the equation for price elasticity is

$$E_P = \text{Arc Price Elasticity} = \frac{\text{Percentage Change in Quantity } (Q)}{\text{Percentage Change in Price } (P)}$$

$$= \frac{(Q_2 - Q_1)/(Q_2 + Q_1)}{(P_2 - P_1)/(P_2 + P_1)}$$

$$= \frac{\Delta Q}{\Delta P} \times \frac{P_2 + P_1}{Q_2 + Q_1}. \qquad (5.15)$$

This form is especially useful for analyzing the average sensitivity of demand to price changes over an extended range of prices. For example, the average price elasticity over the price range from $5 to $6 is

$$E_P = \frac{\Delta Q}{\Delta P} \times \frac{P_2 + P_1}{Q_2 + Q_1}$$

$$= \frac{-5,000}{1} \times \frac{\$6 + \$5}{5,000 + 10,000}$$

$$= -3.67.$$

This means that, on average, a 1 percent change in price leads to a 3.67 percent change in quantity demanded when price is between $5 and $6 per ticket.

Price Elasticity and Total Revenue

One of the most important features of the price elasticity concept is that it provides a useful summary measure of the effect of a price change on revenues. Depending on the degree of price elasticity, a reduction in price can increase, decrease, or leave total revenue unchanged. A good estimate of price elasticity makes it possible to accurately estimate the effect of price changes on total revenue.

For decision-making purposes, three specific ranges of price elasticity have been identified. Using $|\epsilon_P|$ to denote the absolute value of the price elasticity, three ranges for price elasticity are

(1) $|\epsilon_P| > 1.0$, defined as elastic demand.
        Example: $\epsilon_P = -3.2$ and $|\epsilon_P| = 3.2$.

(2) $|\epsilon_P| = 1.0$, defined as unitary elasticity.
        Example: $\epsilon_P = -1.0$ and $|\epsilon_P| = 1.0$.

Elastic demand

A situation in which a price change leads to a more than proportionate change in quantity demanded.

(3) $|\epsilon_P| < 1.0$, defined as inelastic demand.
        Example: $\epsilon_P = -0.5$ and $|\epsilon_P| = 0.5$.

Unitary elasticity

A situation in which price and quantity changes exactly offset each other.

With **elastic demand,** $|\epsilon_P| > 1$ and the relative change in quantity is larger than the relative change in price. A given percentage increase in price causes quantity to decrease by a larger percentage. If demand is elastic, a price increase lowers total revenue and a decrease in price raises total revenue. **Unitary elasticity** describes a situation in which the percentage change in quantity divided by the percentage change in price equals -1. Since price and quantity are inversely related, a price elasticity of -1 means that the effect of a price change is *exactly* offset by the effect of a change in quantity demanded. The result is that total revenue, the product of price times quantity, remains constant. With **inelastic demand** a price increase produces less than a proportionate decline in the quantity demanded, so total revenues rise. Conversely, when demand is inelastic, a price decrease generates a less than proportionate increase in quantity demanded, so total revenues fall. These relations are summarized in the following table:

Inelastic demand

A situation in which a price change leads to a less than proportionate change in quantity demanded.

Elasticity	Implies	Following a Price Increase:	Following a Price Decrease:
Elastic demand, $|\epsilon_P| > 1$.	$\%\Delta Q > \%\Delta P$	Revenue decreases.	Revenue increases.
Unitary elasticity, $|\epsilon_P| = 1$.	$\%\Delta Q = \%\Delta P$	Revenue unchanged.	Revenue unchanged.
Inelastic demand, $|\epsilon_P| < 1$.	$\%\Delta Q < \%\Delta P$	Revenue increases.	Revenue decreases.

Price elasticity can range from completely inelastic, where $\epsilon_P = 0$, to perfectly elastic, where $\epsilon_P = -\infty$. To illustrate, consider first an extreme case in which the quantity demanded is independent of price so that some fixed amount, Q^*, is demanded regardless of price. When the quantity demanded of a product is completely insensitive to price, $\delta Q/\delta P = 0$, and price elasticity will equal zero, irrespective of the value of P/Q. The demand curve for such a good or service is perfectly vertical, as shown in Figure 5.8.

The other limiting case, that of infinite price elasticity, describes a product that is completely sensitive to price. The demand curve for such a good or service is perfectly horizontal, as shown in Figure 5.9. Here the ratio $\delta Q/\delta P = -\infty$ and $\epsilon_P = -\infty$, regardless of the value of P/Q.

The economic as well as mathematical properties of these limiting cases should be understood. A firm faced with a vertical or perfectly inelastic demand curve could charge any price and still sell Q^* units. Theoretically, such a firm could appropriate all of its customers' income or wealth. Conversely, a firm facing a horizontal or perfectly elastic demand curve could sell an unlimited quantity of output at the price P^* but would lose all sales if it raised prices by even a small amount. Such extreme cases are rare in the real world, but monopolies that sell necessities such as pharmaceuticals enjoy relatively inelastic demand, whereas firms in highly competitive industries such as grocery retailing face highly elastic demand curves.

Varying Elasticity at Different Points on a Demand Curve

All linear demand curves, except perfectly elastic or perfectly inelastic ones, are subject to varying elasticities at different points on the curve. In other words, any linear demand curve is price elastic at some output levels but inelastic at others. To see this, recall again the definition of point price elasticity expressed in Equation 5.14:

$$\epsilon_P = \frac{\delta Q}{\delta P} \times \frac{P}{Q}.$$

FIGURE 5.8 **Completely Inelastic Demand Curve: $\epsilon_P = 0$**

With perfectly inelastic demand, a fixed level of output is demanded irrespective of price.

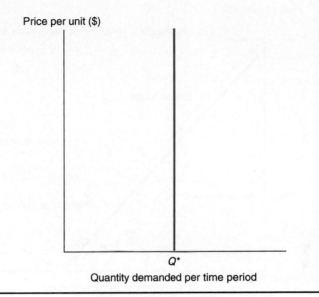

FIGURE 5.9 **Completely Elastic Demand Curve: $\epsilon_P = -\infty$**

With perfectly elastic demand, all output is sold at a fixed price.

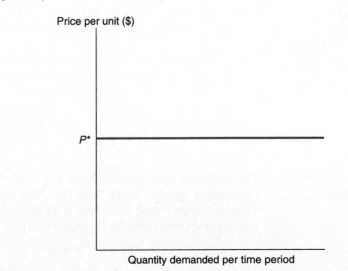

FIGURE 5.10   Elasticities along a Linear Demand Curve

The price elasticity of demand will vary from 0 to $-\infty$ along a linear demand curve.

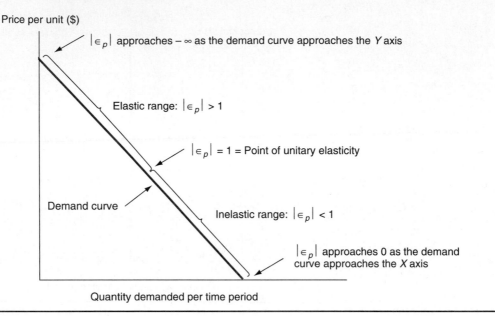

Quantity demanded per time period

The slope of a linear demand curve, $\delta P/\delta Q$, is constant; thus, so is its reciprocal, $1/(\delta P/\delta Q) = \delta Q/\delta P$. However, the ratio P/Q varies from 0 at the point where the demand curve intersects the horizontal axis and price $= 0$, to $+\infty$ at the vertical price axis intercept where quantity $= 0$. Since the price elasticity formula for a linear curve involves multiplying a negative constant by a ratio that varies between 0 and $+\infty$, the price elasticity of a linear curve must range from 0 to $-\infty$.

Figure 5.10 illustrates this relation. As the demand curve approaches the vertical axis, the ratio P/Q approaches infinity and ϵ_P approaches minus infinity. As the demand curve approaches the horizontal axis, the ratio P/Q approaches 0, causing ϵ_P also to approach 0. At the midpoint of the demand curve, $(\delta Q/\delta P) \times (P/Q) = -1$; this is the point of unitary elasticity.

Price Elasticity and Revenue Relations

The relation between price elasticity and total revenue can be further clarified by examining Figure 5.11 and Table 5.4. Figure 5.11(a) reproduces the demand curve shown in Figure 5.10 along with the associated marginal revenue curve. The demand curve shown in Figure 5.11(a) is of the general linear form

$$P = a - bQ, \qquad (5.16)$$

where a is the intercept and b is the slope coefficient. It follows that total revenue (TR) can be expressed as

FIGURE 5.11   **Relations among Price Elasticity and Marginal, Average, and Total Revenue: (a) Demand (Average Revenue) and Marginal Revenue Curves; (b) Total Revenue**

In the range in which demand is elastic with respect to price, marginal revenue is positive and total revenue increases with a reduction in price. In the inelastic range, marginal revenue is negative and total revenue decreases with price reductions.

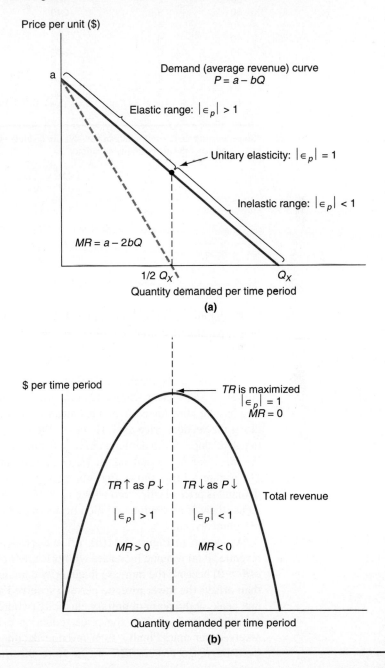

Price per unit ($)

a

Demand (average revenue) curve
$P = a - bQ$

Elastic range: $|\epsilon_p| > 1$

Unitary elasticity: $|\epsilon_p| = 1$

Inelastic range: $|\epsilon_p| < 1$

$MR = a - 2bQ$

$1/2\ Q_X$ Q_X

Quantity demanded per time period

(a)

$ per time period

TR is maximized
$|\epsilon_p| = 1$
$MR = 0$

$TR \uparrow$ as $P \downarrow$ $TR \downarrow$ as $P \downarrow$

$|\epsilon_p| > 1$ $|\epsilon_p| < 1$

Total revenue

$MR > 0$ $MR < 0$

Quantity demanded per time period

(b)

TABLE 5.4   **Price Elasticity and Revenue Relations: A Numerical Example**

Price, P	Quantity, Q	Total Revenue, TR = P × Q	Marginal Revenue, MR = ΔTR	Arc Elasticity[a], E_P
$100	1	$100	—	—
90	2	180	$80	−6.33
80	3	240	60	−3.40
70	4	280	40	−2.14
60	5	300	20	−1.44
50	6	300	0	−1.00
40	7	280	−20	−0.69
30	8	240	−40	−0.47
20	9	180	−60	−0.29
10	10	100	−80	−0.16

[a]Since the price and quantity data in the table are discrete numbers, the price elasticities have been calculated using the arc elasticity equation:

$$E_P = \frac{\Delta Q}{\Delta P} \times \frac{P_2 + P_1}{Q_2 + Q_1}.$$

$$TR = P \times Q$$
$$= (a - bQ) \times Q$$
$$= aQ - bQ^2.$$

By definition, marginal revenue (*MR*) is the change in revenue following a one-unit expansion in output, $\delta TR/\delta Q$, and can be written

$$MR = \delta TR/\delta Q = a - 2bQ. \qquad (5.17)$$

The relation between the demand (average revenue) and marginal revenue curves becomes clear when one compares Equations 5.16 and 5.17. Each equation has the same intercept *a*. This means that both curves begin at the same point along the vertical price axis. However, the marginal revenue curve has twice the negative slope of the demand curve. This means that the marginal revenue curve intersects the horizontal axis at $1/2\ Q_X$, given that the demand curve intersects at Q_X. Figure 5.11(a) shows that marginal revenue is positive in the range where demand is price elastic, zero where $\epsilon_P = -1$, and negative in the inelastic range. Thus, there is an obvious relation between price elasticity and both average and marginal revenue.

As shown in Figure 5.11(b), price elasticity is also closely related to total revenue. Total revenue increases with price reductions in the elastic range (where $MR > 0$) because the increase in quantity demanded at the new lower price more than offsets the lower revenue per unit received at that reduced price. Total revenue peaks at the point of unitary elasticity (where $MR = 0$), since the increase in quantity associated with the price reduction exactly offsets the lower revenue received per unit. Finally, total revenue declines when price is reduced in the inelastic range (where $MR < 0$). Here the quantity demanded continues to

MANAGERIAL APPLICATION 5.2

What's in a Name?

No one denies that the payoff from brand-name advertising can be huge. Companies that offer well-established brand-name products to immense consumer markets have enjoyed a stream of enormous profits over the years and continue to do so both in the United States and abroad. Owning strong brands has allowed them to price their products at a premium and to reap literally billions of dollars in above-normal profits. While the top-selling brands have undergone remarkably little change in ranking over decades, some marketing analysts charge that brand names may now be in trouble (see table). Several leading companies do not appear to be spending enough on advertising to support these valuable assets, and the products that carry them are losing their premium status.

Cost-conscious retailers have been forcing manufacturers to divert dollars from brand-name advertising into costly trade promotions, such as payments for space on store shelves, which dims the prominence of brand names. Advertising effectiveness has also faded because of a decline in mass media that has made it harder to hammer home a single, coherent message. For example, TV viewers no longer flock to the networks as they once did, and advertisers now find it necessary to address narrower and more specialized audiences on cable and through printed media. The net effect is that some important brands are being devalued. While brand products aren't disappearing, consumers seem more willing than ever before to switch to cheaper products.

Two recent studies show the seriousness of this trend. A survey by DDB Needham Worldwide Inc. found that 62 percent of consumers polled in 1990 say they buy only well-known brand names, compared with 77 percent in 1975. A 1991 study by Grey Advertising Inc. says that 61 percent of consumers regard brand names as an assurance of quality—a drop of six percentage points since July 1989. In the same study, 66 percent were trading down to lower-priced brands and almost half are buying more store or generic brands.

Launching a new brand name costs more and is riskier than ever before. Roughly nine out of ten new brands fail, according to marketing specialists, and a mistake can cost dearly. According to *Gorman's New Product News,* just 5 percent of the 6,125 new products

Shelf Lives of Some of the Most Durable Brand Names

Category	Leading Brand in 1923	Current Rank
Cameras	*Kodak*	1
Canned fruit	*Del Monte*	1
Chewing gum	*Wrigley's*	1
Crackers	*Nabisco*	1
Razors	*Gillette*	1
Soft drinks	*Coca-Cola*	1
Soap	*Ivory*	1
Soup	*Campbell*	1
Toothpaste	*Colgate*	2

placed on shelves in the first five months of 1991 bore new brand names. The rest are variations on existing brands such as Tropicana Twister Light fruit juices or Huggies baby wipes. During risky periods, companies depend heavily on product line extensions because of the giant investments involved with introducing a new product. However, today even normally safe product line extensions have fallen on rough times. Clorox Co. spent $225 million to develop a new line of laundry detergents but couldn't persuade enough shoppers to buy detergent from a company famous for bleach and abandoned that market in May 1991.

Not all marketing managers agree that the trend away from brand names is serious. Brands are more important than ever at Campbell Soup Co.'s North American operations, which is spending millions of dollars on ads to revive the Campbell Kids. Brand-name advertising is also important at Frito-Lay, Inc. Frito's parent, PepsiCo Inc., like Coca-Cola and other competitors, continues to advertise heavily, while other big marketers are retrenching.

The fortunes of companies with heavily entrenched brands wax and wane slowly. It took years for once-powerful monikers such as *Pepsodent* toothpaste and *Oxydol* laundry detergent to become marketing also rans, and it will take at least a decade to determine whether other leading brands today are really in trouble. Still, it's not too soon for marketers to start worrying about their good names.

Source: Mark Landler, "What's in a Name? Less and Less," *Business Week,* July 8, 1991, 66–67; and Laura Bird, "Ad Study Finds Dazzle Rarely Equals Dollars," *The Wall Street Journal,* May 19, 1992, B1.

increase with reductions in price, but the relative increase in quantity is less than the percentage decrease in price, and thus is not large enough to offset the reduction in revenue per unit sold.

The numerical example in Table 5.4 illustrates these relations. It shows that from 1 to 5 units of output, demand is elastic, $|\epsilon_P| > 1$, and a reduction in price increases total revenue. For example, decreasing price from $80 to $70 increases output from 3 to 4 units. Marginal revenue is positive over this range of output, and total revenue increases from $240 to $280. For output above 6 units and prices below $50, demand is inelastic, $|\epsilon_P| < 1$. Here price reductions result in lower total revenue, because the increase in quantity demanded is not large enough to offset the lower price per unit. With total revenue decreasing as output expands, marginal revenue must be negative. For example, reducing price from $30 to $20 results in revenue declining from $240 to $180 even though output increases from 8 to 9 units; marginal revenue in this case is $-\$60$.

Price Elasticity and Optimal Pricing Policy

Firms use price discounts, specials, coupons, and rebate programs to test the price sensitivity of demand for their products. As a practical matter, firms often maintain current and detailed information concerning the price elasticity of demand for their products, even when they may not be able to completely derive underlying demand functions. It is interesting that price elasticity estimates along with relevant cost data represent sufficient information for setting a pricing policy that is consistent with value maximization. This is because a relatively simple mathematical relation holds between marginal revenue, price, and the point price elasticity of demand. Given any point price elasticity estimate, relevant marginal revenues can be determined easily. When this marginal revenue information is combined with pertinent marginal cost data, the basis for an optimal pricing policy is created.

The relation between marginal revenue, price, and the point price elasticity of demand follows directly from the mathematical definition of a marginal relation. Marginal revenue is the derivative of the total revenue function. That is, $MR = dTR/dQ$. Since total revenue equals price times quantity ($TR = P \times Q$), marginal revenue is found by taking the derivative of the function $P \times Q$ with respect to Q:

$$MR = \frac{d(P \times Q)}{dQ}.$$

Because price and quantity are interdependent in the typical demand situation, the rule for differentiating a product must be employed in taking the preceding derivative:

$$MR = \frac{dTR}{dQ} = \frac{d(P \times Q)}{dQ} = P \times \frac{dQ}{dQ} + Q \times \frac{dP}{dQ}$$

$$= P \times 1 + Q \times \frac{dP}{dQ}$$

$$= P + Q \times \frac{dP}{dQ}.$$

This relation is a completely general specification of marginal revenue, which, if P is factored out from the right-hand side, can be rewritten as

$$MR = P\left(1 + \frac{Q}{P} \times \frac{dP}{dQ}\right).$$

Note that the term $Q/P \times dP/dQ$ in the preceding expression is the reciprocal of the definition for point price elasticity, $\epsilon_P = dQ/dP \times (P/Q)$:

$$\frac{Q}{P} \times \frac{dP}{dQ} = \frac{1}{\dfrac{dQ}{dP} \times \dfrac{P}{Q}} = \frac{1}{\epsilon_P}.$$

Thus, marginal revenue can be rewritten as

$$MR = P\left(1 + \frac{1}{\epsilon_P}\right). \tag{5.18}$$

This simple relation between marginal revenue, price, and the point price elasticity is very useful in the setting of pricing policy. To see the usefulness of Equation 5.18 in practical pricing policy, consider the pricing problem faced by a profit-maximizing firm. Recall from Chapter 2 that profit maximization requires operating at the activity level where marginal cost equals marginal revenue. Most firms have extensive cost information and can estimate marginal cost reasonably well. By equating marginal costs with marginal revenue as identified by Equation 5.18, the profit-maximizing price level can be easily determined. Using Equation 5.18, set marginal cost equal to marginal revenue, where

$$MC = MR$$
$$= P\left(1 + \frac{1}{\epsilon_P}\right),$$

which implies that the optimal or profit-maximizing price, P^*, equals

$$P^* = \frac{MC}{\left(1 + \dfrac{1}{\epsilon_P}\right)}. \tag{5.19}$$

This simple relation between price, marginal cost, and the point price elasticity of demand may well be one of the most useful pricing tools that managerial economics has to offer.

▶   To illustrate the usefulness of Equation 5.19, suppose that manager George Stevens notes a 2 percent increase in weekly sales following a 1 percent price discount on The Kingfish fishing reels. The point price elasticity of demand for The Kingfish fishing reels is

$$\epsilon_P = \frac{\text{Percentage Change in } Q}{\text{Percentage Change in } P}$$
$$= \frac{2}{-1}$$
$$= -2.$$

What is the optimal retail price for The Kingfish fishing reels if the company's wholesale cost per reel plus display and marketing expenses—or relevant marginal costs—total $25 per unit? With marginal costs of $25 and $\epsilon_P = -2$, the profit-maximizing price is

$$P = \frac{\$25}{\left(1 + \dfrac{1}{-2}\right)}$$

$$= \$50.$$

Therefore, the profit-maximizing price on The Kingfish fishing reels is $50.

To see how Equation 5.19 can be used for planning purposes, suppose Stevens can order reels through a different distributor at a wholesale price that reduces marginal costs by $1 to $24 per unit. Under these circumstances, the new optimal retail price is

$$P = \frac{\$24}{\left(1 + \dfrac{1}{-2}\right)}$$

$$= \$48.$$

Thus, the optimal retail price would fall by $2 following a $1 reduction in The Kingfish's relevant marginal costs.

Equation 5.19 can serve as the basis for calculating profit-maximizing prices under current cost and market-demand conditions, as well as under a variety of potential circumstances. Table 5.5 shows how profit-maximizing prices vary for a product with a $25 marginal cost as the point price elasticity of demand varies. Note that the less elastic the demand, the greater the difference between price and marginal cost. Conversely, as the absolute value of the price elasticity of demand increases (that is, as demand becomes more price elastic), the profit-maximizing price gets closer and closer to marginal cost. This important demand relation will be examined further in Chapter 14, where pricing practices are analyzed in some detail.

Determinants of Price Elasticity

Why is the price elasticity of demand high for some products and low for others? In general, there are three major causes of differential price elasticities: (1) the extent to which a good is considered to be a necessity, (2) the availability of substitute goods to satisfy a given need, and (3) the proportion of income spent on the product. A relatively constant quantity of a service such as electricity for residential lighting will be purchased almost irrespective of price, at least in the short run and within price ranges customarily encountered. There is no close substitute for electric service. Other goods—designer jeans, for example—while desirable, face considerably more competition, and their demand depends more on price.

Similarly, the demand for "big ticket" items such as automobiles, housing, and vacation travel account for a large share of consumer income and will be relatively sensitive to price. Demand for less expensive products, such as soft

TABLE 5.5   **Price Elasticity and Optimal Pricing Policy**

Point Price Elasticity	Marginal Cost	Profit-Maximizing Price
−1.25	$25	$125.00
−1.50	25	75.00
−2.50	25	41.67
−5.00	25	31.25
−10.00	25	27.78
−25.00	25	26.04

drinks, movies, and fast food, can be relatively insensitive to price. Given the low percentage of income spent on "small ticket" items, consumers often find that searching for the best deal available is not worth the time and effort required. Accordingly, the elasticity of demand is typically higher for major purchases than for small ones. The price elasticity of demand for compact disk players, for example, is higher than that for CDs.

Price elasticity for an individual firm is seldom the same as that for the entire industry. The reason for this is discussed in detail in Chapters 12 and 13, which deal with market structure, but an intuitive explanation can be given here. In pure monopoly, the firm demand curve is also the industry demand curve, so obviously the elasticity of demand faced by the firm at any output level is the same as that faced by the industry. Consider the other extreme—pure competition, as approximated by wheat farming. The industry demand curve for wheat is downward sloping: the lower its price, the greater the quantity of wheat that will be demanded. However, the demand curve facing any individual wheat farmer is essentially horizontal. A farmer can sell any amount of wheat at the going price, but if the farmer raises price by the smallest fraction of a cent, sales collapse to zero. The wheat farmer's demand curve—or that of any firm operating under pure competition—is perfectly elastic. Figure 5.9 illustrates such a demand curve.

As explained in Chapter 4, the demand for producer goods and services is indirect, or derived from their value in use. Because the demand for all inputs is derived from their usefulness in producing other products, their demand is derived from the demand for final products. In contrast to the terms *final product* or *consumer demand,* the term *derived demand* is used to describe the demand for all producer goods and services. Although the demand for producer goods and services is related to the demand for the final products that they are used to make, this relation is not always as close as one might suspect.

In some instances, the demand for intermediate goods is less price sensitive than demand for the resulting final product. This is because intermediate goods sometimes represent only a small portion of the cost of producing the final product. For example, suppose the total cost to build a small manufacturing plant is $1 million, and $25,000 of this cost represents the cost of electrical fixtures and wiring. Even a doubling in electrical costs from $25,000 to $50,000 would have only a modest effect on the overall costs of the plant—which would increase by only 2.5 percent from $1 million to $1,025,000. Rather than being highly price sensitive, the firm might select its electrical contractor based on timeliness and the quality of service provided. In such an instance, the firm's price elasticity of demand for electrical fixtures and wiring is quite low, even if its price elasticity of demand for the overall project is quite high.

In other situations the reverse might hold. Continuing with our previous example, suppose that steel costs represent $250,000 of the total $1 million cost of building the plant. Because of its relative importance, a substantial increase in steel costs has a significant influence on the total costs of the overall project. As a result, the price sensitivity of the demand for steel will be close to that for the overall plant. If the firm's demand for plant construction is highly price elastic, the demand for steel is also likely to be highly price elastic.

Although the derived demand for producer goods and services is obviously related to the demand for resulting final products, this relation is not always close. When intermediate goods or services represent only a small share of overall costs, the price elasticity of demand for such inputs can be much different than that for the resulting final product. The price elasticity of demand for a given input and the resulting final product must be similar in magnitude only when the costs of that input represent a significant share of overall costs.

Uses of Price Elasticity Information

Price elasticity information is useful for a number of purposes. Obviously, firms are required to be aware of the price elasticity of demand when they price their products. For example, a profit-maximizing firm would never choose to lower its prices in the inelastic range of the demand curve. Such a price decrease would decrease total revenue and at the same time increase costs, since the quantity demanded would rise. A dramatic decrease in profits would result. Even over the range in which demand is elastic, a firm will not necessarily find it profitable to cut price. The profitability of a price cut in the elastic range of the demand curve depends on whether the marginal revenues generated exceed the marginal cost of added production. Price elasticity information can be used to answer questions such as

- What is the expected impact on sales of a 5 percent price increase?
- How great a price reduction is necessary to increase sales by 10 percent?
- Given marginal cost and price elasticity data, what is the profit-maximizing price?

The worldwide energy crisis that developed following the OPEC oil embargo illustrates the importance of price elasticity information. Electric utilities were forced to raise prices dramatically because of a rapid increase in fuel costs. The question immediately arose: How much of a cutback in quantity demanded and, hence, how much of a reduction in future capacity needs would these price increases cause? In other words, what was the price elasticity of electricity? In view of the long lead times required to build electricity-generating capacity and the major economic dislocations that arise from power outages, this was a critical question for both consumers and producers of electricity.

Price elasticity information has also played a major role in the debate over national energy policy. Some industry and government economists argue that the price elasticity of demand for energy is sufficiently large that an equilibrium of demand and supply will occur following only modest price changes. Others argue that energy price elasticities are so low that only unconscionable price increases are necessary to reduce the quantity demanded to meet pending supply shortfalls. Meanwhile, the collapse of oil prices during the late 1980s and early 1990s raises fears among some that low oil prices might increase demand so much that they may increase the Western world's already heavy reliance on imported oil. These same issues have also become a focal point in controversies surrounding nuclear energy, natural gas price deregulation, and alternative renewable energy sources. In this debate on energy policy, the relation between price and quantity supplied—the price elasticity of supply—is also an important component. As with most economic issues, both demand and supply sides of the marketplace must be analyzed to arrive at a rational decision. Strongly interrelated energy issues continue to have important implications for all sectors of the economy, and price elasticity analysis is playing an increasingly important role in the search for solutions.

Another example of the importance of price elasticity information relates to the widespread discounts or reduced rates offered different customer groups. The *Wall Street Journal* offers students bargain rates; airlines, restaurants, and most hotel chains offer discounts to vacation travelers and senior citizens; large corporate customers get discounts or rebates on desktop computers, auto leases, and many other items. Many such discounts are substantial, sometimes in the range of 30 to 40 percent off standard list prices. The question of whether reduced prices attract sufficient additional customers to offset lower revenues per unit is directly related to the price elasticity of demand. All group-based customer discounts must be supported by detailed estimates of differences in the relevant price elasticity of demand.

Additional uses of price elasticity information are examined in later chapters. At this point, it becomes useful to consider some other important demand elasticities.

CROSS-PRICE ELASTICITY OF DEMAND

The demand for most products is influenced by prices of other products. For example, the demand for beef is related to the price of chicken. As the price of chicken increases, so does the demand for beef; consumers substitute beef for the now relatively more expensive chicken. On the other hand, a price decrease for chicken leads to a decrease in the demand for beef as consumers substitute chicken for the now relatively more expensive beef. In general, a direct relation between the price of one product and the demand for a second product holds for all **substitutes.** A price increase for a given product will increase demand for substitutes; a price decrease for a given product will decrease demand for substitutes.

Some goods and services—for example, cameras and film—exhibit a completely different relation. Here price increases in one product typically lead to a reduction in demand for the other. Goods that are inversely related in this manner are known as **complements;** they are used together rather than in place of each other.

Substitutes

Related products for which a price increase for one leads to an increase in demand for the other.

Complements

Related products for which a price increase for one leads to a reduction in demand for the other.

Cross-price elasticity
Responsiveness of demand for one product to changes in the price of another.

The concept of **cross-price elasticity** is used to examine the responsiveness of demand for one product to changes in the price of another. Point cross-price elasticity is given by the following equation:

$$\epsilon_{PX} = \frac{\text{Percentage Change in Quantity of } Y}{\text{Percentage Change in Price of } X}$$

$$= \frac{\delta Q_Y/Q_Y}{\delta P_X/P_X} \qquad (5.20)$$

$$= \frac{\delta Q_Y}{\delta P_X} \times \frac{P_X}{Q_Y},$$

where Y and X are two different products. The arc cross-price elasticity relationship is constructed in the same manner as was previously described for price elasticity:

$$E_{PX} = \frac{\text{Percentage Change in Quantity of } Y}{\text{Percentage Change in Price of } X}$$

$$= \frac{(Q_{Y2} - Q_{Y1})/(Q_{Y2} + Q_{Y1})}{(P_{X2} - P_{X1})/(P_{X2} + P_{X1})} \qquad (5.21)$$

$$= \frac{\Delta Q_Y}{\Delta P_X} \times \frac{P_{X2} + P_{X1}}{Q_{Y2} + Q_{Y1}}.$$

The cross-price elasticity for substitutes is always positive; the price of one good and the demand for the other always move in the same direction. Cross-price elasticity is negative for complements; price and quantity move in opposite directions for complementary goods and services. Finally, cross-price elasticity is zero, or nearly zero, for unrelated goods where variations in the price of one good have no effect on demand for the second.

The concept of cross-price elasticity can be illustrated by considering the demand function for monitored in-home healthcare services provided by Home Medical Support, Inc. (HMS):

$$Q_Y = f(P_Y, P_D, P_H, P_T, i, I).$$

Here, Q_Y is the number of patient days of service per year; P_Y is the average price of HMS service; P_D is an industry price index for prescription drugs; P_H is an index of the average price of hospital service, a primary competitor; P_T is a price index for the travel industry; i is the interest rate; and I is disposable income per capita. Assume that the parameters of the HMS demand function have been estimated as follows:

$$Q_Y = 25,000 - 5P_Y - 3P_D + 10P_H + 0.0001P_T - 0.02i + 2.5I.$$

The effects on Q_Y caused by a one-unit change in the prices of other goods are

$$\frac{\partial Q_Y}{\partial P_D} = -3.$$

$$\frac{\partial Q_Y}{\partial P_H} = +10.$$

$$\frac{\partial Q_Y}{\partial P_T} = 0.0001 \approx 0.$$

Since both prices and quantities are always positive, the ratios P_D/Q_Y, P_H/Q_Y, and P_T/Q_Y are also positive. Therefore, the signs of the three cross-price elasticities in this example are determined by the sign of each relevant parameter estimate in the HMS demand function:

$\epsilon_{PD} = (-3)(P_D/Q_Y) < 0.$

    HMS service and prescription drugs are complements.

$\epsilon_{PH} = (+10)(P_H/Q_Y) > 0.$

    HMS service and hospital service are substitutes.

$\epsilon_{PT} = (+0.0001)(P_T/Q_Y) \approx 0$, so long as the ratio P_T/Q_Y is not extremely large.

    Demand for travel and HMS service are independent.

    The concept of cross-price elasticity serves two main purposes. First, it is important for the firm to be aware of how demand for its products is likely to respond to changes in the prices of other goods. Such information is necessary for formulating the firm's own pricing strategy and for analyzing the risks associated with various products. This is particularly important for firms with a wide variety of products, where meaningful substitute or complementary relations exist within the firm's own product line. Second, cross-price elasticity information allows managers to measure the degree of competition in the marketplace. For example, a firm might appear to dominate a particular market or market segment, especially if it is the only supplier of a particular product. However, if the cross-price elasticity between a firm's output and products produced in related industries is large and positive, the firm is not a monopolist in the true sense and is not immune to the threat of competitor encroachment. In the banking industry, for example, individual banks clearly compete with money market mutual funds, savings and loan associations, credit unions, and commercial finance companies. The extent of competition can be measured only in terms of the cross-price elasticities of demand for various services offered by banks and all relevant potential competitors.

    The importance of the concept of cross-price elasticity of demand is explored further in Chapters 12 and 13, where market structure is examined, and in Chapter 14, where its role in multiple product pricing is analyzed.

INCOME ELASTICITY OF DEMAND

For many goods, income is another important determinant of demand. Income is frequently as important as price, advertising expenditures, credit terms, or any other variable in the demand function. This is particularly true of luxury items such as big-screen TVs, country club memberships, elegant homes, and the like. In contrast, the demand for such basic commodities as salt, bread, and milk is not very responsive to income changes. These goods are bought in fairly constant amounts regardless of changes in income. Of course, income can be measured in many ways—for example, on a per capita, per household, or aggregate basis.

Gross national product, national income, personal income, and disposable personal income have all served as income measures in demand studies.

Income elasticity

Responsiveness of demand to changes in income, holding constant the effect of all other variables.

The **income elasticity** of demand measures the responsiveness of demand to changes in income, holding constant the effect of all other variables that influence demand. Letting I represent income, income point elasticity is defined as

$$
\begin{aligned}
\epsilon_I &= \frac{\text{Percentage Change in Quantity } (Q)}{\text{Percentage Change in Income } (I)} \\
&= \frac{\delta Q/Q}{\delta I/I} \\
&= \frac{\delta Q}{\delta I} \times \frac{I}{Q}.
\end{aligned}
\tag{5.22}
$$

Inferior goods

Products for which consumer demand declines as income rises.

Normal goods or superior goods

Products for which demand is positively related to income.

Income and the quantity purchased typically move in the same direction; that is, income and sales are directly rather than inversely related. Therefore, $\Delta Q/\Delta I$ and hence ϵ_I are positive. For a limited number of products termed **inferior goods,** this does not hold. For products such as beans and potatoes, for example, individual consumer demand is sometimes thought to decline as income increases, because consumers replace them with more desirable alternatives. More typical products, whose individual and aggregate demand is positively related to income, are defined as **normal goods or superior goods.**

To examine income elasticity over a range of incomes rather than at a single level, the arc elasticity relation is employed:

$$
\begin{aligned}
E_I &= \frac{\text{Percentage Change in Quantity } (Q)}{\text{Percentage Change in Income } (I)} \\
&= \frac{(Q_2 - Q_1)/(Q_2 + Q_1)}{(I_2 - I_1)/(I_2 + I_1)} \\
&= \frac{\Delta Q}{\Delta I} \times \frac{I_2 + I_1}{Q_2 + Q_1}.
\end{aligned}
\tag{5.23}
$$

Arc income elasticity provides a measure of the average responsiveness of demand for a given product to a relative change in income over the range from I_1 to I_2.

Countercyclical goods

Inferior goods whose demand falls with rising income and rises with falling income.

In the case of inferior goods, individual demand actually rises during an economic downturn. As workers get laid off from their jobs, for example, they might tend to substitute potatoes for meat, hamburgers for steak, bus rides for automobile trips, and so on. As a result, demand for potatoes, hamburgers, bus rides and other inferior goods can actually rise during recessions. Their demand is **countercyclical.**

Types of Normal Goods

For most products, income elasticity is positive, indicating that demand rises as the economy expands and national income increases. The actual size of the income elasticity coefficient is very important. Suppose, for example, that ϵ_I for a particular product is 0.3. This means that a 1 percent increase in income causes demand for the product to increase by only .3 percent. Given growing national income over time, such a product would not maintain its relative importance in the economy. Another product might have an income elasticity of 2.5; its demand increases 2.5 times as fast as income. If, on the other hand, $\epsilon_I < 1.0$ for a particular good, its producers will not share proportionately in increases in national income. On the other hand, if $\epsilon_I > 1.0$, the industry will gain more than a proportionate share of increases in income.

Noncyclical normal goods

Products for which demand is relatively unaffected by changing income.

Goods for which $0 < \epsilon_I < 1$ are often referred to as **noncyclical normal goods,** since demand is relatively unaffected by changing income. Sales of most convenience goods, such as toothpaste, candy, soda, movie tickets, and so on, account for only a small share of the consumer's overall budget, and spending on such items tends to be relatively unaffected by changing economic conditions. For goods having $\epsilon_I > 1$, referred to as **cyclical normal goods,** demand is strongly affected by changing economic conditions. Purchases of "big ticket" items such as homes, automobiles, boats, and recreational vehicles can be postponed and tend to be put off by consumers during economic downturns. As a result, housing demand, for example, can collapse during recessions and skyrocket during economic expansions. These relations between income and product demand are summarized in the following table:

Cyclical normal goods

Products for which demand is strongly affected by changing income.

Goods Category	Income Elasticity	Examples
Inferior goods (countercyclical)	$\epsilon_I < 0$	Basic foodstuffs, generic products, bus rides
Noncyclical normal goods	$0 < \epsilon_I < 1$	Toiletries, movies, liquor, cigarettes
Cyclical normal goods	$\epsilon_I > 1$	Automobiles, housing, vacation travel, capital equipment

These relations have important policy implications for both firms and government agencies. Firms whose demand functions have high income elasticities enjoy good growth opportunities in expanding economies, so forecasts of aggregate economic activity figure importantly in their plans. Companies faced with low income elasticities, in contrast, are relatively unaffected by the level of overall business activity. This is relatively desirable from the standpoint that such a business is harmed relatively little by economic downturns. Nevertheless, since such a company cannot expect to share fully in a growing economy, it might seek to enter industries that provide better growth opportunities.

Income elasticity can also play an important role in the marketing activities of a firm. If per capita or household income is found to be an important determinant of demand, this can affect the location and type of sales outlets. It can also have an impact on advertising and other promotional activities. For example, firms that provide goods or services with high income elasticities often target promotional efforts at young professionals, given their potential for increased future business over time.

At the national level, the question of income elasticity has figured importantly in several key areas. Agriculture, for example, has had problems for many years, partly because of the low income elasticity for most food products. This has made it difficult for farmers' incomes to keep up with those of urban workers, a problem that, in turn, has caused concern in Washington and in national capitals throughout the world.

A somewhat similar problem arises in housing. Congress and every U.S. president since the end of World War II has stated that improving the housing stock is a primary national goal. If, on the one hand, the income elasticity for housing is high and $\epsilon_I > 1$, an improvement in the housing stock will be a natural by-product of a prosperous economy. On the other hand, if the housing income elasticity $\epsilon_I < 1$, a relatively small percentage of additional income will be spent on houses. As a result, housing stock would not improve much over time even despite a growing economy and increasing incomes. In the event that $\epsilon_I < 1$, direct government investment in public housing or rent and interest subsidies might be necessary to bring about a dramatic increase in the housing stock over time. Not only has the income elasticity of housing been an important issue in debates on national housing policy, but these very debates have created a stimulus for economic research into the theory and measurement of income elasticities.

ADDITIONAL DEMAND ELASTICITY CONCEPTS

Using the elasticity concept is a simple way of measuring the effect of change in an independent variable on a dependent variable in any functional relation. The dependent variable in this chapter is the demand for a product, and the demand elasticity for any variable in the firm's demand function can be calculated. The three most common demand elasticities—price elasticity, cross-price elasticity, and income elasticity—are emphasized in this chapter. Examples of other demand elasticities can be used to reinforce the generality of the concept.

Other Demand Elasticities

Advertising elasticity plays an important role in marketing activities for a broad range of goods and services. A low advertising elasticity means that a firm must spend substantial sums to shift demand for its products through advertising. In such cases, alternative marketing approaches are often more productive.

In the housing market, mortgage interest rates are an important determinant of demand. Accordingly, interest rate elasticities have been used in analyzing and forecasting the demand for housing construction. To be sure, this elasticity coefficient varies over time as other conditions in the economy change. Other things are held constant when measuring elasticity, but in the real world other things do not typically remain constant. Studies indicate that the interest rate elasticity of residential housing demand averages about -0.15. This means that a 10 percent rise in interest rates decreases the demand for housing by 1.5 percent, provided that all other variables remain unchanged. If Federal Reserve policy is expected to cause interest rates to rise from 10 to 12 percent (a 20 percent increase) a 3 percent decrease ($-0.15 \times 20 = -3$) in housing demand can be projected, on average.

Not surprisingly, public utilities calculate the weather elasticity of demand for their services. They measure weather using degree days as an indicator of average

MANAGERIAL APPLICATION 5.3

The French Standard in Database Marketing

Long before database marketing became popular, a French dermatologist named Jacques Courtin, founder of Clarins S.A., was practicing it. For 20 years the cosmetics company had been carefully recording the names, physical traits, and opinions of customers buying its skin-care products. Every Clarins product, every tiny sample, includes a card inviting the buyer to reply. The extensive database it developed as a result served Clarins well in 1991 when it decided to bring out its first makeup products. Clarins was able to draw on some 2,000 responses from women who had written in over the years to ask about Clarins makeup. The company was therefore able to carefully tailor its products to meet specific customer needs and to design its product promotion strategy accordingly.

Clarins emphasizes no-frills marketing. It advertises in the same women's magazines as its rivals but it doesn't offer the same sizzle. There are no suggestive models that appear in Clarins ads, just a solid emphasis on purported product benefits. In its early days, Clarins was too small to spend lavish sums to create a luxurious image. Hence the attractiveness of positioning itself as a no-nonsense, substance-over-style brand. Even today, advertising for most of the 75 products in the Clarins line stresses the products' natural ingredients. Clarins' packaging is artfully unflashy, with an emphasis on extensive technical characteristics described in extensive detail on enclosed leaflets. Clarins advertising is so tame that it led *Forbes* magazine to suggest that the reader is reminded more of a type-heavy ad for Volvo's cars than an ad for a beauty product.

The Clarins approach has worked well in Europe. Despite raging competition and frequent imitation, Clarins continues to grow at two or three times the overall industry pace and has for years. The company is also systematic in its approach to foreign markets and tends to open carefully nurtured subsidiaries or exclusive agents. As an important part of its marketing plan for the 1990s, Clarins has stepped up marketing of its skin lotions and cleansers to U.S. consumers. Sales to U.S. customers have grown at roughly 30 percent per year to about $34 million in 1990. Still a relative newcomer to the U.S. market, Clarins maintains only one-half the sales outlets of giant rivals such as L'Oréal (Lancôme), Estée Lauder (Clinique), and Unilever (Elizabeth Arden, Calvin Klein). However, many retailers have high hopes for Clarins' expansion into makeup this fall. At Dayton Hudson and Marshall Field's stores, Clarins was the fastest-growing brand name in its sector during 1990. This growth is despite the fact that Clarins' products are costly. Its Doux spray deodorant cells for $10, compared with $3 or less for your local supermarket brand. Clarins, says Caroline Neville, a London marketing consultant, "is sort of a Body Shop for rich people." For many of its customers, the Clarins image is similar to that of expensive European cars.

A few years ago, Clarins introduced the first "climate controlled" skin treatment, called Multi-Active Day Cream. True to its reputation for catering to customers who are more skin conscious than price conscious, Clarins charges a whopping $34 for 50 milliliters of the product. The molecular structure of the cream is designed to respond to changes in humidity, releasing different ingredients under different conditions. To meet the needs of demanding customers, Clarins spends lavishly on product testing and development. Multi-Active Day Cream, for example, was tested on airline crews that flew from Paris to equatorial Africa all in a day's work. Clarins also plows more than 5 percent of its revenues into training its sales force. That's because the company expects its representatives to carefully study a customer's skin and thoughtfully recommend an appropriate Clarins product.

Importantly, Clarins approach to marketing translates into solid operating performance. Despite the worldwide economic recession of the early 1990s, the company anticipates gains of 15 to 20 percent per year in both sales and profits throughout the decade. Apparently, the use of database marketing to get to know and better satisfy your customers is very effective!

Source: John Marcom, Jr., "Forget the Sizzle, Sell the Steak," *Forbes,* August 5, 1991, 86–87.

temperatures. This elasticity factor is used, in conjunction with weather forecasts, to anticipate service demand and peak-load conditions.

The Time Factor in Elasticity Analysis

Time itself is also an important factor in demand elasticity analysis, given the lack of instantaneous responses in the marketplace. Consumers often react slowly to changes in prices and other demand conditions. To illustrate this delayed or lagged effect, consider the demand for electric power. Suppose that an electric utility raises its rates by 30 percent. How will this affect the quantity of electric power demanded? In the very short run, any effects will be slight. Customers may be more careful to turn off unneeded lights, but total demand, which is highly dependent on the appliances owned by the residential customers and the equipment operated by their industrial and commercial customers, will probably not be greatly affected. Prices will go up and quantity demanded will not fall much, so total revenue will increase substantially. In other words, the short-run demand for electric power is relatively inelastic.

In the long run, however, an increase in power rates can have a substantial effect on electricity demand. Residential users will reduce their purchases of air conditioners, electric heating units, and other appliances, and appliances that are purchased will be more energy efficient. This will reduce the long-run demand for power. Industrial users will also tend to switch to other energy sources, employ less energy-intensive production methods, or relocate to areas where electric costs are lower. Thus, the ultimate effect of a price increase on electricity demand may be substantial, but it might take a number of years before its full impact is felt.

In general, opportunities to respond to price changes tend to increase with time as consumers obtain more information or better perceive the price effects and as more substitutes are made available. There is a similar phenomenon with respect to income changes. It takes time for consumers' purchasing habits to respond to changed income levels. For these reasons, long-run elasticities tend to be greater than short-run elasticities for most demand variables.

SUMMARY

Product demand is a critical determinant of profitability, and demand estimates are key considerations in virtually all managerial decisions. This chapter introduced a number of factors that underlie the demand for all goods and services, as well as methods for quantifying and interpreting demand relations.

• A **utility function** is a descriptive statement that relates total utility (i.e., satisfaction or well-being) to the consumption of goods and services. **Marginal utility** measures the added satisfaction derived from a one-unit increase in consumption of a particular good or service, holding consumption of all other goods and services constant. The **law of diminishing marginal utility** states that as an individual increases consumption of a given product, the marginal utility gained from consumption eventually declines.

• An **indifference curve** represents all market baskets among which the consumer is indifferent about choosing. The **marginal rate of substitution** is simply the change in consumption of Y necessary to offset a given change in the consumption of X if the consumer's overall level of utility is to remain constant.

- A **budget line** represents all combinations of products that can be purchased for a fixed dollar amount. The **income effect** of a price change is the increase in overall consumption made possible by a price cut or the decrease in overall consumption made necessary by a price increase. The income effect results in a shift to a higher indifference curve following a price cut or a shift to a lower indifference curve following a price increase. The **substitution effect** of a price change describes the change in relative consumption that occurs as consumers substitute cheaper products for more expensive products. A **consumption path** depicts optimal market baskets for consumption as the budget expenditure level grows.

- Factors such as price and advertising that are within the control of the firm are called **endogenous variables;** factors outside the control of the firm, such as consumer incomes, competitor prices, and the weather, are called **exogenous variables.**

- **Elasticity** is the percentage change in a dependent variable, Y, resulting from a 1 percent change in the value of an independent variable, X. **Point elasticity** measures elasticity at a given point on a function. **Arc elasticity** measures the average elasticity over a given range of a function.

- The **price elasticity of demand** measures the responsiveness of the quantity demanded to changes in the price of the product, holding constant the values of all other variables in the demand function. With **elastic demand,** a price increase will lower total revenue and a decrease in price will raise total revenue. **Unitary elasticity** describes a situation in which the effect of a price change is exactly offset by the effect of a change in quantity demanded; total revenue, the product of price times quantity, remains constant. With **inelastic demand,** a price increase (decrease) produces a less (more) than proportionate decline in the quantity demanded, so total revenues rise (fall).

- A direct relation between the price of one product and the demand for another holds for all **substitutes.** A price increase for a product will increase demand for substitutes; a price decrease for a product will decrease demand for substitutes. Goods that are inversely related in terms of price and quantity are known as **complements;** they are used together rather than in place of each other. The concept of **cross-price elasticity** is used to examine the responsiveness of demand for one product to changes in the price of another.

- The **income elasticity** of demand measures the responsiveness of demand to changes in income, holding constant the effect of all other variables that influence demand. For a limited number of **inferior goods,** individual consumer demand is thought to decline as income increases, because consumers replace them with more desirable alternatives. Demand for such products is **countercyclical,** actually rising during recessions and falling during economic booms. More typical products, whose individual and aggregate demand is positively related to income, are defined as **normal goods** or **superior goods.** Goods for which $0 < \epsilon_I < 1$ are often referred to as **noncyclical normal goods,** since demand is relatively unaffected by changing income. For goods having $\epsilon_I > 1$, referred to as **cyclical normal goods,** demand is strongly affected by changing economic conditions.

Demand analysis and estimation is one of the most interesting and challenging topics in managerial economics. This chapter provided a valuable, albeit brief, introduction to several key concepts that are useful in the practical analysis and estimation of demand functions. As such, this material offers constructive input that is useful for understanding the underlying economic causes of demand.

Questions	**Q5.1** Is the economic demand for a product determined solely by its usefulness?

Q5.1 Is the economic demand for a product determined solely by its usefulness?

Q5.2 "The utility derived from consumption is intangible and thus unobservable. Therefore, the utility concept has no practical value." Discuss this statement.

Q5.3 Is an increase in total utility or satisfaction following an increase in income inconsistent with the law of diminishing marginal utility?

Q5.4 What would an upward-sloping demand curve imply about the marginal utility derived from consuming a given product?

Q5.5 Describe the income, substitution, and total effects on consumption following a price increase.

Q5.6 Define each of the following terms, giving each a verbal explanation and an equation:
A. Point elasticity
B. Arc elasticity
C. Price elasticity
D. Cross-price elasticity
E. Income elasticity

Q5.7 When is use of the arc elasticity concept valid as compared with the use of the point elasticity concept?

Q5.8 When is the price elasticity of demand typically greater: if computed for an industry or for a single firm in the industry? Why?

Q5.9 Is the cross-price elasticity concept useful for identifying the boundaries of an industry or market?

Q5.10 Individual consumer demand declines for inferior goods as personal income increases because consumers replace them with more desirable alternatives. Is an inverse relation between demand and *national* income likely for such products?

Self-Test Problem

Distinctive Designs, Inc., imports and distributes dress and sports watches. At the end of the company's fiscal year, brand manager Karla Wallace has asked you to evaluate sales of the sports watch line using the following data:

Month	Number of Sports Watches Sold, Q	Sports Watch Advertising Expenditures, A	Sports Watch Price, P	Dress Watch Price, P_D
July	4,500	$10,000	$26	$50
August	5,500	10,000	24	50

continued

Month	Number of Sports Watches Sold, Q	Sports Watch Advertising Expenditures, A	Sports Watch Price, P	Dress Watch Price, P_D
September	4,500	9,200	24	50
October	3,500	9,200	24	46
November	5,000	9,750	25	50
December	15,000	9,750	20	50
January	5,000	8,350	25	50
February	4,000	7,850	25	50
March	5,500	9,500	25	55
April	6,000	8,500	24	51
May	4,000	8,500	26	51
June	5,000	8,500	26	57

In particular, Wallace has asked you to estimate relevant demand elasticities. Remember that to estimate the required elasticities, you should consider months only when the other important factors considered in the preceding table have not changed. Also note that by restricting your analysis to consecutive months, changes in any additional factors not explicitly included in the analysis are less likely to affect estimated elasticities. Finally, the average arc elasticity of demand for each factor is simply the average of monthly arc elasticities calculated during the past year.

A. Indicate whether there was or was not a change in each respective independent variable for each month pair during the past year.

Month Pair	Sports Watch Advertising Expenditures, A	Sports Watch Price, P	Dress Watch Price, P_D
July–August	————	————	————
August–September	————	————	————
September–October	————	————	————
October–November	————	————	————
November–December	————	————	————
December–January	————	————	————
January–February	————	————	————
February–March	————	————	————
March–April	————	————	————
April–May	————	————	————
May–June	————	————	————

B. Calculate and interpret the average advertising arc elasticity of demand for sports watches.

C. Calculate and interpret the average arc price elasticity of demand for sports watches.

D. Calculate and interpret the average arc cross-price elasticity of demand between sports and dress watches.

Solution to Self-Test Problem

A.

Month Pair	Sports Watch Advertising Expenditures, A	Sports Watch Price, P	Dress Watch Price, P_D
July–August	No change	Change	No change
August–September	Change	No change	No change
September–October	No change	No change	Change
October–November	Change	Change	Change
November–December	No change	Change	No change
December–January	Change	Change	No change
January–February	Change	No change	No change
February–March	Change	No change	Change
March–April	Change	Change	Change
April–May	No change	Change	No change
May–June	No change	No change	Change

B. In the calculation of the advertising arc elasticity of demand, consider only consecutive months when there was a change in advertising but no change in the prices of sports and dress watches:

August–September

$$E_A = \frac{\Delta Q}{\Delta A} \times \frac{A_2 + A_1}{Q_2 + Q_1}$$

$$= \frac{4,500 - 5,500}{\$9,200 - \$10,000} \times \frac{\$9,200 + \$10,000}{4,500 + 5,500}$$

$$= 2.4.$$

January–February

$$E_A = \frac{\Delta Q}{\Delta A} \times \frac{A_2 + A_1}{Q_2 + Q_1}$$

$$= \frac{4,000 - 5,000}{\$7,850 - \$8,350} \times \frac{\$7,850 + \$8,250}{4,000 + 5,000}$$

$$= 3.6.$$

On average, $E_A = (2.4 + 3.6)/2 = 3$ and demand will rise 3 percent, with a 1 percent increase in advertising. Thus, demand appears to be quite sensitive to advertising.

C. In the calculation of the arc price elasticity of demand, consider only consecutive months when there was a change in the price of sports watches but no change in advertising or the price of dress watches:

July–August

$$E_P = \frac{\Delta Q}{\Delta P} \times \frac{P_2 + P_1}{Q_2 + Q_1}$$

$$= \frac{5,500 - 4,500}{\$24 - \$26} \times \frac{\$24 + \$26}{5,500 + 4,500}$$

$$= -2.5.$$

November–December

$$E_P = \frac{\Delta Q}{\Delta P} \times \frac{P_2 + P_1}{Q_2 + Q_1}$$

$$= \frac{15,000 - 5,000}{\$20 - \$25} \times \frac{\$20 + \$25}{15,000 + 5,000}$$

$$= -4.5.$$

April–May

$$E_P = \frac{\Delta Q}{\Delta P} \times \frac{P_2 + P_1}{Q_2 + Q_1}$$

$$= \frac{4,000 - 6,000}{\$26 - \$24} \times \frac{\$26 + \$24}{4,000 + 6,000}$$

$$= -5.$$

On average, $E_P = [(-2.5) + (-4.5) + (-5)]/3 = -4$. A 1 percent increase (decrease) in price will lead to a 4 percent decrease (increase) in the quantity demanded. The demand for sports watches is, therefore, elastic with respect to price.

D. In the calculation of the arc cross-price elasticity of demand, consider only consecutive months when there was a change in the price of dress watches but no change in advertising or the price of sports watches:

September–October

$$E_{PX} = \frac{\Delta Q}{\Delta P_X} \times \frac{P_{X2} + P_{X1}}{Q_2 + Q_1}$$

$$= \frac{3,500 - 4,500}{\$46 - \$50} \times \frac{\$46 + \$50}{3,500 + 4,500}$$

$$= 3.$$

May–June

$$E_{PX} = \frac{\Delta Q}{\Delta P_X} \times \frac{P_{X2} + P_{X1}}{Q_2 + Q_1}$$

$$= \frac{5,000 - 4,000}{\$57 - \$51} \times \frac{\$57 + \$51}{5,000 + 4,000}$$

$$= 2.$$

On average, $E_{PX} = (3 + 2)/2 = 2.5$. Since $E_{PX} > 0$, sports and dress watches are substitutes.

Problems   P5.1   A. **Marginal Utility.** Complete the following table, which describes the demand for goods:

Price	Units	Total Utility	Marginal Utility	Price/Marginal Utility
$11	0	0	—	—
10	1	25		
9	2	45		
8	3	60		
7	4	70		
6	5	75		

B. How does an increase in consumption affect marginal utility and the price/marginal utility ratio?

C. What is the optimal level of goods consumption if the marginal utility derived from the consumption of services costs 50¢ per util?

P5.2   **Marginal Utility.** Consider the following data:

Goods (G)		Services (S)	
Units	Total Utility	Units	Total Utility
0	0	0	0
1	100	1	70
2	160	2	124
3	210	3	175
4	250	4	220
5	275	5	250

A. Construct a table showing the marginal utility derived from the consumption of goods and services. Also show the trend in marginal utility per dollar spent (the MU/P ratio) if $P_G = \$20$ and $P_S = \$15$.

B. If consumption of two units of goods is optimal, what level of services consumption could also be justified?

C. If consumption of five units of services is optimal, what level of goods consumption could also be justified?

D. What is the optimal allocation of a $100 budget? Explain.

P5.3   **Optimal Consumption.** Alex P. Keaton is an ardent baseball fan. The following table shows the relation between the number of games he attends per month and the total utility he derives from baseball game consumption:

Number of Baseball Games per Month	Total Utility
0	0
1	50
2	90
3	120
4	140
5	150

A. Construct a table showing Keaton's marginal utility derived from baseball game consumption.

B. At an average ticket price of $10, Keaton is able to justify attending only one game per month. Calculate his cost per unit of marginal utility derived from baseball game consumption at this activity level.

C. If the cost/marginal utility trade-off found in Part B represents the most Keaton is willing to pay for baseball game consumption, calculate the prices at which he would attend two, three, four, and five games per month.

D. Plot Keaton's baseball game demand curve.

P5.4 **Elasticity.** The demand for personal computers can be characterized by the following point elasticities: price elasticity $= -5$, cross-price elasticity with software $= -4$, and income elasticity $= 2.5$. Indicate whether each of the following statements is true or false, and explain your answers.

A. A price reduction for personal computers will increase both the number of units demanded and the total revenue of sellers.

B. The cross-price elasticity indicates that a 5 percent reduction in the price of personal computers will cause a 20 percent increase in software demand.

C. Demand for personal computers is price elastic and computers are cyclical normal goods.

D. Falling software prices will increase revenues received by sellers of both computers and software.

E. A 2 percent price reduction would be necessary to overcome the effects of a 1 percent decline in income.

P5.5 **Demand Curves.** KRMY-TV is contemplating a T-shirt advertising promotion. Monthly sales data from T-shirt shops marketing the "Eye Watch KRMY-TV" design indicate that:

$$Q = 1,500 - 200P,$$

where Q is T-shirt sales and P is price.

A. How many T-shirts could KRMY-TV sell at $4.50 each?

B. What price would KRMY-TV have to charge to sell 900 T-shirts?

C. At what price would T-shirt sales equal zero?

D. How many T-shirts could be given away?

E. Calculate the point price elasticity of demand at a price of $5.

P5.6 **Optimal Pricing.** In an effort to reduce excess end-of-the-model-year inventory, Harrison Ford offered a 2.5 percent discount off the average list price of Mustangs sold during the month of August. Customer response was enthusiastic, with unit sales rising by 10 percent over the previous month's level.

A. Calculate the point price elasticity of demand for Harrison Ford Mustangs.

B. Calculate the profit-maximizing price per unit if Harrison Ford has an average wholesale cost of $9,000 and incurs marginal selling costs of $375 per unit.

P5.7 **Cross-Price Elasticity.** The Kitty Russell's Longbranch Cafe in Sausalito recently reduced Nachos Supreme appetizer prices from $5 to $3 for afternoon "early bird" customers and enjoyed a resulting increase in sales from 60 to 180 orders per day. Beverage sales also increased from 30 to 150 units per day.

A. Calculate the arc price elasticity of demand for Nachos Supreme appetizers.

B. Calculate the arc cross-price elasticity of demand between beverage sales and appetizer prices.

C. Holding all else equal, would you expect an additional appetizer price decrease to $2.50 to cause both appetizer and beverage revenues to rise? Explain.

P5.8 **Income Elasticity.** Ironside Industries, Inc., is a leading manufacturer of tufted carpeting under the Ironside brand. Demand for Ironside's products is closely tied to the overall pace of building and remodeling activity and, therefore, is highly sensitive to changes in national income. The carpet manufacturing industry is highly competitive, so Ironside's demand is also very price sensitive.

During the past year, Ironside sold 15 million square yards (units) of carpeting at an average wholesale price of $7.75 per unit. This year, GNP per capita is expected to surge from $17,250 to $18,750 as the nation recovers from a steep recession. Without any price change, Ironside's marketing director expects current-year sales to rise to 25 million units.

A. Calculate the implied income arc elasticity of demand.

B. Given the projected rise in income, the marketing director believes that current volume of 15 million units could be maintained despite an increase in price of 50¢ per unit. On this basis, calculate the implied arc price elasticity of demand.

C. Holding all else equal, would a further increase in price result in higher or lower total revenue?

P5.9 **Cross-Price Elasticity.** B. B. Lean is a catalog retailer of a wide variety of sporting goods and recreational products. Although the market response to the company's spring catalog was generally good, sales of B. B. Lean's $140 deluxe garment bag declined from 10,000 to 4,800 units. During this period, a competitor offered a whopping $52 off their regular $137 price on deluxe garment bags.

A. Calculate the arc cross-price elasticity of demand for B. B. Lean's deluxe garment bag.

B. B. B. Lean's deluxe garment bag sales recovered from 4,800 units to 6,000 units following a price reduction to $130 per unit. Calculate B. B. Lean's arc price elasticity of demand for this product.

C. Calculate the further price reduction necessary for B. B. Lean to fully recover lost sales (i.e., to regain a volume of 10,000 units).

P5.10 **Advertising Elasticity.** Enchantment Cosmetics, Inc., offers a line of cosmetic and perfume products marketed through leading department stores. Product Manager Erica Kane recently raised the suggested retail price on a popular line of mascara products from $9 to $12 following increases in the costs of labor and materials. Unfortunately, sales dropped sharply from 16,200 to 9,000 units per month. In an effort to regain lost sales, Enchantment ran a coupon promotion featuring $5 off the new regular price. Coupon printing and distribution costs totaled $5,000 per month and represented a substantial increase over the typical advertising budget of $3,250 per month. Despite these added costs, the promotion was judged to be a success, as it proved to be highly popular with consumers. In the period prior to expiration, coupons were used on 40 percent of all purchases and monthly sales rose to 15,000 units.

A. Calculate the arc price elasticity implied by the initial response to the Enchantment price increase.

B. Calculate the effective price reduction resulting from the coupon promotion.

C. In light of the price reduction associated with the coupon promotion and assuming no change in the price elasticity of demand, calculate Enchantment's arc advertising elasticity.

D. Why might the true arc advertising elasticity differ from that calculated in Part C?

CASE STUDY FOR CHAPTER 5
The Optimal Level of Advertising

The concept of multivariate optimization is important in managerial economics because many demand and supply relations involve more than two variables. In demand analysis, the concept is particularly important in markets where firms face the difficult question of how to set both prices and advertising at profit-maximizing levels. In demand analysis, it is often typical to consider the quantity sold as a function of the price of the product itself, the price of other goods, advertising, income, and other factors. In cost analysis, cost is determined by output, input prices, the nature of technology, and so on. As a result, the process of multivariate optimization is often employed in the process of optimization.

To further explore the concepts of multivariate optimization and the optimal level of advertising, consider once again the multivariate product demand function for MacGyver, Inc., which was introduced in Chapter 2. In that previous demand function, the demand for a product Q is determined by the price charged, P, and the level of advertising, A:

$$Q = 5,000 - 10P + 40A + PA - 0.8A^2 - 0.5P^2.$$

When analyzing multivariate relations such as these, one is interested in the marginal effect of each independent variable on the quantity sold, the dependent variable. Optimization requires an analysis of how a change in each independent variable affects the dependent variable, holding constant the effect of all other independent variables. The partial derivative concept is employed in this type of marginal analysis.

In light of the fact that the MacGyver, Inc. demand function includes two independent variables, the price of the product itself and advertising, it is possible to examine two partial derivatives: the partial of Q with respect to price, or $\delta Q/\delta P$, and the partial of Q with respect to advertising expenditures, or $\delta Q/\delta A$.

In determining partial derivatives, all variables except the one with respect to which the derivative is being taken remain unchanged. In this instance, A is treated as a constant when the partial derivative of Q with respect to P is analyzed; P is treated as a constant when the partial derivative of Q with respect to A is evaluated. Therefore, the partial derivative of Q with respect to P is:

$$\frac{\delta Q}{\delta P} = 0 - 10P + 0 + A - 0 - P,$$

$$= -10 + A - P.$$

The partial with respect to A is:

$$\frac{\delta Q}{\delta A} = 0 - 0 + 40 + P - 1.6A - 0.$$

$$= 40 + P - 1.6A.$$

As described in Chapter 2, the maximization or minimization of multivariate functions is similar to that for single variable functions. All first-order partial derivatives must equal zero. Thus, maximization of the function $Q = f(P, A)$ requires:

$$\frac{\delta Q}{\delta P} = 0,$$

and

$$\frac{\delta Q}{\delta A} = 0.$$

To maximize the value of the MacGyver, Inc., demand function, each partial must equal zero:

$$\frac{\delta Q}{\delta P} = -10 + A - P = 0,$$

and

$$\frac{\delta Q}{\delta A} = 40 + P - 1.6A = 0.$$

Solving these two equations simultaneously yields the optimal price-output-advertising combination. Since $-10 + A - P = 0$, $P = A - 10$. Substituting this value for P into $40 + P - 1.6A = 0$, gives $40 + (A - 10) - 1.6A = 0$, which implies that $0.6A = 30$ and $A = 50(100)$ or $5,000. Given this value, $P = A - 10 = 50 - 10 = 40.

Inserting these numbers for P and A into the MacGyver demand function results in a value for Q of 5,800. Therefore, the maximum value of Q is 5,800, which reflects an optimal price of $40 and optimal advertising of $5,000.

The process of simultaneously determining optimal levels of price and advertising can be visualized by referring to Figure 2.9, a three-dimensional graph of the MacGyver demand function. For positive values of P and A, this demand function maps out a surface with a peak at point X^*. At the peak, the surface of the figure is level. Alternatively stated, a plane that is tangent to the surface at point X^* is parallel to the PA plane. This means that the slope of the figure with respect to either P or A is zero; as is required for locating the maximum of a multivariate function.

Unfortunately, on the basis of Figure 2.9 it is not possible to conclusively determine whether point X^* locates an optimal point for price and advertising that will result in maximum profits, or an *inflection* point that indicates only a local maximum for profits. On the basis of Figure 2.9, it does not appear that point X^* is a local or global point for *minimum* profits, but in the absence of further analysis, the process described above can lead to mistakes in identifying minimums versus maximums, and vice versa. Absent a check of second-order conditions, the possibility of misidentifying inflection points and points of maxima and minima is always present.

One attractive use of computer spreadsheet analysis is to create simple numerical examples that can be used to conclusively show the change in sales, profits and other variables that occurs as one moves beyond points such as point X^* identified for MacGyver, Inc.

A. Set up a table or spreadsheet for MacGyver, Inc., that illustrates the relationships among quantity (Q), price (P), the optimal level of advertising (A), the advertising-sales ratio (A/S) and sales revenue (S). In this spreadsheet, use the relations developed in the case study to define appropriate values for each of these items. Importantly,

$$Q = 5,000 - 10P + 40A + PA - 0.8A^2 - 0.5P^2,$$
$$A = \$25 + \$0.625P,$$
$$A/S = (1,000 \times A)/S,$$
$$S = P \times Q.$$

Establish a range for P from 0 to $125 in increments of $5 (i.e., $0, $5, $10, . . . , $125). To test the sensitivity of all other variables to extreme bounds for the price variable, also set price equal to $1,000, $2,500, and $10,000.

B. Based on the MacGyver table or spreadsheet, determine the price-advertising combination that will maximize the number of units sold.

C. Give an analytical explanation of the negative quantity and sales revenue levels observed at very high price-advertising combinations. Do these negative values have an economic interpretation as well?

Selected References

Becker, Gary S., Michael Grossman, and Kevin M. Murphy. "Rational Addiction and the Effect of Price on Consumption." *American Economic Review* 81 (May 1991): 237–241.

Blinder, Alan S. "Why Are Prices Sticky? Preliminary Results from an Interview Study." *American Economic Review* 81 (May 1991): 89–96.

Cohen, Dorothy. "Trademark Strategy Revisited." *Journal of Marketing* 55 (July 1991): 46–59.

Curren, Mary T., Valerie S. Folkes, and Joel H. Steckel. "Explanations for Successful and Unsuccessful Marketing Decisions: The Decision Maker's Perspective." *Journal of Marketing* 56 (April 1992): 18–31.

Herrnstein, R. J. "Experiments on Stable Suboptimality in Individual Behavior." *American Economic Review* 81 (May 1991): 360–364.

Holland, John H., and John H. Miller. "Artificial Adaptive Agents in Economic Theory." *American Economic Review* 81 (May 1991): 365–370.

Keller, Kevin Lane, and David A. Aaker. "The Effects of Sequential Introduction of Brand Extensions." *Journal of Marketing Research* 29 (February 1992): 35–50.

Krishna, Aradhna, Imran S. Currim, and Robert W. Shoemaker. "Consumer Perceptions of Promotional Activity." *Journal of Marketing* (April 1991): 4–16.

Loderer, Claudio, John W. Cooney, and Leonard D. Van Drunen. "The Price Elasticity of Demand for Common Stock." *Journal of Finance* 46 (June 1991): 621–652.

Meyers-Levey, Joan, and Brian Sternthal. "Gender Differences in the Use of Message Cues." *Journal of Marketing Research* 28 (February 1991): 84–96.

Nevett, Terence. "Historical Investigation and the Practice of Marketing." *Journal of Marketing* 55 (July 1991): 13–23.

Reed, G. V., M. R. Binks, and C. T. Ennew. "Matching the Characteristics of a Service to the Preferences of Customers." *Managerial and Decision Economics* 12 (June 1991): 231–240.

Samiee, Saeed, and Kendall Roth. "The Influence of Global Marketing Standardization on Performance." *Journal of Marketing* 56 (April 1992): 1–17.

Sethuraman, Raj, and Gerkard J. Tellis. "An Analysis of the Tradeoff Between Advertising and Price Discounting." *Journal of Marketing Research* 28 (May 1991): 160–174.

Yang, Xiaokai, and He-ling Shi. "Specialization and Product Diversity." *American Economic Review* 82 (May 1992): 392–398.

CHAPTER | # DEMAND ESTIMATION

Demand estimation is sometimes relatively simple, especially in the case of stable short-run demand relations. If a manufacturer has a substantial backlog of purchase orders, the pace of future sales can sometimes be estimated with a high degree of confidence. Aerospace manufacturers such as Boeing, McDonnell Douglas, and Lockheed sell options for the delivery of future airplanes to United Airlines, American Airlines, Delta, and a number of independent leasing companies. This allows manufacturers to predict the pace of future sales with a high degree of reliability and adjust production schedules accordingly. This results in significant cost savings, a portion of which can be passed on to customers. Still, demand estimation involves some error, even when a large and growing backlog of customer orders is evident. During the recession of 1992, for example, several large airlines canceled orders for hundreds of millions of dollars of aircraft following an unexpected downturn in passenger and freight traffic. With hundreds of idle aircraft parked in the California desert, the airline industry decided that newer, more energy-efficient aircraft were simply not necessary. Delivery options were canceled at a cost of millions of dollars for the airlines, and production schedules had to be reworked at a similar expense for the aircraft manufacturers.

In most real-world situations, accurate demand estimation is far from simple. The changing nature of demand relations makes it difficult to make accurate short-run estimates and still more difficult to determine the effect on demand of changes in specific variables such as price, advertising expenditures, credit terms, prices of competing products, and so on. The unpredictable nature of general economic conditions is another factor that makes demand estimation difficult for many products. When the income elasticity of demand is high, demand tends to vary more than the parallel change in economic activity. This is especially true for cyclical goods such as household appliances, machine tools, and raw materials, the demand for which tends to be highly variable and extremely sensitive to changes in aggregate economic conditions, which are always difficult to predict. The demand for most goods and services is also highly sensitive to changes in competitor prices, advertising, interest rates, and the weather. Unexpected changes in these important underlying variables constitute a considerable challenge to accurate short-run demand estimation.

The estimation of long-run demand relations involves all of the difficulties encountered in short-run demand estimation, but they tend to be magnified. In

●

MANAGERIAL APPLICATION 6.1
Micromarketing Is Getting Big

Consumer-product companies are concluding it isn't enough to focus on a region, state, or city. Increasingly the marketing target is narrowing to a market segment no bigger than an individual neighborhood or a single store. To help bring their customers into clear focus, consumer-products companies have come to rely more than ever before on detailed point-of-sale information in so-called micromarketing.

Market Metrics collects facts on customers at 30,000 supermarkets around the country. They know, for example, exactly how many people per week shop at the local A&P and how the local A&P's market share compares with that of its nearest rivals. Based on traffic patterns and roads, Market Metrics also identifies the easiest access to each location, and records the demographic repercussions. In a particular grocery store market, for example, Market Metrics recorded that 26 percent of the people are no older than 14, and many are under five. The locals are predominantly white, have

blue-collar jobs, own two cars, and live with three or four people in households that average $42,912 in incomes. Marrying the consumption patterns of hundreds of grocery items with these demographic characteristics, Market Metrics determines precisely what should sell. In this grocery store market example, the winners include baby food and grooming items, baking mixes, desserts, dry dinner mixes, flour shortening and oils, cigarettes, laundry supplies, first-aid products, and milk. The bottom of the list includes sugar and artificial sweeteners, tea, pet food and supplies, books, film, cosmetics, foil, breakfast food, fruit, juice, prepared food, yogurt, liquor, and wine.

With many children, a given store could also emphasize marketing directly to kids. With the current trend to micromarketing, that might be a market analyst appearing as Easter Bunny in front of your grocery store next Easter!

Hitting the Bull's-Eye

Micromarketers can now target a product's best customers and the stores where they're most likely to shop. Here's one company's analysis of three products' best targets in the New York area.

Brand	Heavy User Profile	Life-Style and Media Profile	Top 3 Stores
Peter Pan Peanut Butter	Households with kids headed by 18–54 year olds, in suburban and rural areas.	• Heavy video renters • Go to theme parks • Below average TV viewers • Above average radio listeners	Foodtown Super Market, 3350 Hempstead Turnpike Levittown, NY Pathmark Supermarket, 3635 Hempstead Turnpike Levittown, NY King Kullen Market, 598 Stewart Ave., Bethpage, NY
Stouffers Red Box Frozen Entrees	Households headed by people, 55 and older, and upscale suburban households headed by 35–54 year olds	• Go to gambling casinos • Give parties • Involved in public activities • Travel frequently • Heavy newspaper readers • Above average TV viewers	Dan's Supreme Super Market, 69–62 188th St., Flushing, NY Food Emporium, Madison Ave. & 74th St., NYC Waldbaum Super Market, 196–35 Horace Harding Blvd., Flushing, NY
Coors Light Beer	Head of household, 21–34, middle to upper income, suburban and urban	• Belong to a health club • Buy rock music • Travel by plane • Give parties, cookouts • Rent videos • Heavy TV sports viewers	Food Emporium, 1498 York Ave., NYC Food Emporium, First Ave. & 72nd St., NYC Gristedes Supermarket, 350 E. 86th St., NYC

Source: Michael J. McCarthy, "Marketers Zero in on Their Customers," *The Wall Street Journal*, March 18, 1991, B1; Mark Robichaux, "Cable Operators Refine 'Micro-Marketing'," *The Wall Street Journal*, April 16, 1992, B8.

the long run, it is especially difficult to predict changes in the nature and scope of competition from established competitors. When competitors have years instead of just weeks or months to develop effective pricing, promotion, and product-development strategies, the sensitivity of demand to changes in any of these factors is much more significant than during the short run. The effects of unanticipated changes in technology, foreign competition, and government regulation also influence demand, especially in the long run. As a result, demand estimation, particularly long-run demand estimation, is a compelling challenge to managers.

This chapter considers a variety of methods used to estimate product demand. The consumer interview or survey method is employed to estimate demand for new products or to test customer reaction to changes in the price or advertising for established products. Managers utilize market experiments to evaluate customer reaction to new or improved products in a controlled setting. Like the consumer survey method, market experiments are well suited to demand estimation problems involving new or improved products. Another method for demand estimation involves the use of historical market data and the powerful analytical technique of regression analysis. Given the amazing capability of relatively inexpensive desktop computers and user-friendly software, popular regression-based techniques are bound to become even more widespread in the years ahead. This tool is drawn on extensively in later chapters.

THE IDENTIFICATION PROBLEM

In algebra, groups of equations are often worked out to determine the value of unknown variables. To solve any such system of equations, the number of unknown variables to be solved for must not exceed the number of known equations. In other words, there must be at least as much known information (equations) as unknown variables. This is analogous to a significant problem faced in demand estimation: there must be sufficient known information to allow precise identification of all unknown variables.

The Interplay of Demand and Supply

It is sometimes difficult to obtain accurate estimates of demand relations because linkages exist among most economic variables. To see why this poses problems, consider the difficulty of estimating the demand curve for a given Product *X*. If data are available on the price charged and the quantity purchased at several points in time, a logical first step is to plot this information as in Figure 6.1. Can the line *AB* be interpreted as a demand curve and points 1, 2, and 3 as various combinations of price and quantity demanded on the demand curve? The curve connecting the points is negatively sloped, indicating the typical inverse relation between the price charged for a product and the quantity demanded. Moreover, each data point represents the quantity of *X* purchased at a particular price. Nevertheless, these data offer an insufficient basis to draw the conclusion that *AB* is in fact the demand curve for *X*.

While Figure 6.1 plots several observations on the price charged for *X* and the quantity purchased, this does not necessarily trace out a demand curve. A demand

FIGURE 6.1   A Price/Quantity Plot for Product *X*

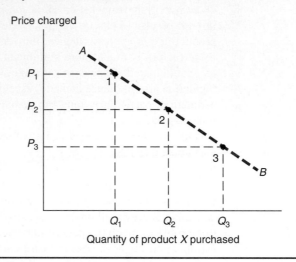

Price charged

curve shows the relation between the price charged for a product and the quantity demanded, *holding constant the effects of all other variables in the demand function*. To plot a demand curve, it is necessary to vary price to obtain data on the price/quantity relation, while keeping fixed the effects of all factors in the demand function.

The price/quantity data used to construct Figure 6.1 are insufficient to produce a demand curve because the effects of all other demand-related variables may or may not have changed. The line *AB* might be a demand curve, but then again, it might not be. Consider *Figure 6.2,* in which the price/quantity data are again plotted, along with hypothesized actual supply and demand curves for Product *X*. These data points indicate the synchronous solution of supply and demand relations at three points in time. These price/quantity data reflect the interplay between the quantity of *X* supplied by producers and the quantity demanded by consumers. The intersection of the supply curves and demand curves at each point in time results in the plotted price/quantity points, but the line *AB* is *not* a demand curve. In Figure 6.2, nonprice variables in the supply and demand functions have changed between each data point.

Shifts in Demand and Supply

Suppose, for example, that new and more efficient facilities for producing *X* are completed between observation dates. This would cause a shift of the supply curve from S_1 to S_2 to S_3. Similarly, the price of a complementary product may have fallen or consumer incomes may have risen, so at any given price, larger quantities of *X* are demanded in later periods. Such influences result in a shift of the demand curve from D_1 to D_2 to D_3. When supply and/or demand curves are shifting over time, as is often the case, the accurate estimation of demand/supply relations at any one point in time is made difficult.

In the present example, both the supply curve and the demand curve shift over time. This results in a declining price and an increasing quantity purchased. The

FIGURE 6.2 **Supply and Demand Curves**

Price/quantity data sometimes reflect the intersection of several different demand and supply curves.

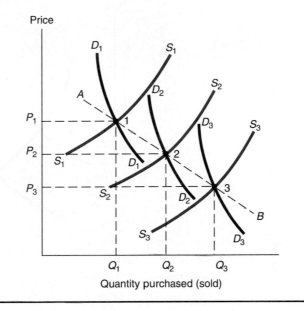

three intersection points of the supply curves and the demand curves shown in Figure 6.2—points 1, 2, and 3—are the same points plotted in Figure 6.1. But these are not three points on a single demand curve for Product X. Each point is on a *distinct* product demand curve that reflects different underlying economic conditions. The relevant demand curve is shifting over time, so connecting each data point does not trace out a single product demand curve for X.

Incorrectly interpreting the line *AB,* which connects points 1, 2, and 3, as a demand curve can lead to wrong managerial decisions. If a firm makes this mistake, it might infer a high price elasticity for the product and assume that a reduction in price from P_1 to P_2 would increase quantity demanded from Q_1 to Q_2. An expansion of this magnitude might well justify such a price reduction. However, such a price cut would actually result in a much smaller increase in the quantity demanded since the true demand curve, D_1, is much less elastic than the line *AB.* Thus, a price reduction is in fact much less desirable than implied by the line *AB.*

Given the close link between demand and supply curves, data on prices and quantities must be employed carefully in demand curve estimation. If the demand curve has not shifted but the supply curve *has* shifted, price/quantity data can be employed to estimate demand relations. Alternatively, if there exists sufficient information to determine how each curve has shifted between data observations, demand curve estimation is possible. For example, if a technical breakthrough occurs in the manufacture of a product so that industry costs fall while demand conditions are stable, the situation depicted in Figure 6.3 may arise. The demand

FIGURE 6.3   **Shifting Supply Curve Tracing Out Stable Demand Curve**

A demand curve is revealed *if* prices fall while demand conditions are held constant.

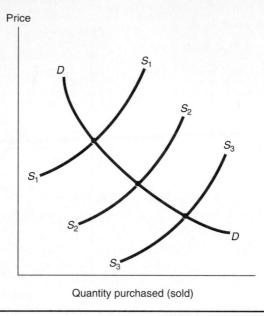

curve, which initially was unknown, is assumed to be stable. The supply curve shifts from S_1 to S_2 to S_3. Each price/quantity point represents the intersection of the supply curves and the demand curves. Because demand-determining factors other than price are assumed to be stable, points 1, 2, and 3 all lie on the same demand curve. The demand curve *DD* is estimated by connecting the three data points. Although relatively rare in some industries, such a situation occurs frequently in computers and electronics. Rapid innovation allows prices for watches, calculators, personal computers, and related products to fall markedly within a very short period of time.

Simultaneous Relations

Simultaneous relation
Concurrent association.

Identification problem
The difficulty of estimating an economic relation in the presence of simultaneous relations.

Since the market price/output equilibrium at any point in time is determined by the forces of demand and supply, a **simultaneous relation,** or concurrent association, exists between demand and supply. When demand and supply curves are closely related, the simultaneity problem can be overcome only if sufficient information exists to *identify* each interrelated function. Shifts in demand and supply curves must be distinguished from movements along individual supply and demand curves. The problem of estimating any given economic relation in the presence of important simultaneous relations is known as the **identification problem.** To separate shifts in demand or supply from changes or movements along a single curve, it is necessary to have more than just price/quantity data. Information about changes in demand and supply conditions is necessary to identify and estimate demand and supply relations. Sometimes, this information is not easily obtained. In such instances, standard statistical techniques, such as ordinary least squares (OLS) regression analysis, do not provide reliable estimates of demand or supply functions. More advanced statistical techniques, such as two-stage least squares (2SLS) or seemingly unrelated regression (SUR) analysis, are necessary. Fortunately, the identification problem is usually not so severe as to preclude the use of widely familiar regression analysis. Moreover, even when the identification problem is quite severe, consumer interviews and market experiments can sometimes be used to obtain relevant information. These techniques are also useful for generating the information necessary for more detailed statistical analyses.

INTERVIEW AND EXPERIMENTAL METHODS

Demand information is valuable. Knowledge about customer sensitivity to modifications in prices, advertising, packaging, and product innovations all play an important role in product-development strategy. Similarly, details about customer reactions to changes in competitor prices and the caliber of competing products play a significant part in the formation of competitive strategy. As a result, successful companies devote considerable resources toward answering the question: What do customers want? Not only are current customers asked this important question, potential customers are also solicited for their input.

Consumer Interviews

Consumer interview
Questioning customers to estimate demand relations.

The **consumer interview,** or survey, method requires questioning customers or potential customers in an attempt to estimate the relation between demand for a firm's products and a variety of factors thought to be important for marketing and profit-planning purposes. The technique can be applied in a naive fashion by simply stopping shoppers and asking questions about the quantity of the product they would purchase at different prices. In more sophisticated approaches, trained interviewers present detailed questions to a carefully selected sample to elicit desired information. Consumer surveys can provide excellent information on many important demand relations. A firm might question its customers about projected purchases under a variety of different conditions relating to price, advertising expenditures, prices of substitutes and complements, income, and any number of other variables in the demand function. By aggregating data, the firm could then forecast total demand by estimating important parameters in the product demand function.

Unfortunately, this procedure does not always work smoothly in practice. The quantity and quality of information obtainable through this technique are sometimes limited. Consumers are often unable or unwilling to provide accurate answers to hypothetical questions about how they would react to changes in key demand variables. Consider the problem of attempting to determine the effect of just two variables, price and advertising expenditures, on the demand for consumer goods. If an interviewer asked how you would react to a 1, 2, or 3 percent increase (or decrease) in the price of a specific brand of spaghetti sauce, could you respond accurately? Could you accurately predict the effect on your personal demand of shifting the emphasis of the firm's media advertising campaign from the product's natural ingredients to the fact that it is high in fiber or low in cholesterol? Because most consumers are unable to answer such questions—even for major expense categories such as apparel, food, and entertainment—it is obviously difficult to use such techniques to estimate demand relations.

This is not to imply that consumer surveys have little value in demand analysis. Using subtle inquiries, a trained interviewer can extract useful information from consumers. For example, an interviewer might ask questions about the relative prices of several competing goods and learn that most customers are unaware of existing price differentials. This is an indication that demand may not be highly responsive to price changes, so a producer would not attempt to increase demand by reducing prices. Consumers would probably not notice such price reductions. Similar questions can be used to determine whether consumers are aware of advertising programs, what their reaction is to the ads, and so on. Thus, certain useful information is obtainable by surveys, and the quality of the results is adequate for some decision purposes.

Also, for certain kinds of demand information there is no substitute for the consumer interview. For example, in short-term demand or sales forecasting, consumer attitudes and expectations about future business conditions frequently make the difference between an accurate estimate and one that misses by a wide margin. Subjective information is often best obtained through interview methods.

Market Experiments

Market experiments

Demand estimation in a controlled environment.

An alternative technique for obtaining useful information about product demand involves **market experiments.** One market experiment technique entails examining consumer behavior in actual markets. The firm locates one or more markets with specific characteristics, then varies prices, packaging, advertising, and other controllable variables in the demand function, with the variations occurring either over time or between markets. For example, Del Monte Corporation may have determined that uncontrollable consumer characteristics are quite similar in Denver and Salt Lake City. Del Monte could raise the price of sliced pineapple in Salt Lake City in relation to that in Denver, then compare pineapple sales in the two markets. Alternatively, Del Monte could make a series of weekly or monthly price changes in one market, then determine how these changes affect sales. With several markets, the firm might also be able to use census or survey data to determine how demographic characteristics such as income, family size, educational level, and ethnic background affect demand.

Market experiments, however, have several serious shortcomings. They are expensive and usually undertaken on a scale too small to allow high levels of confidence in the results. Related to this is the problem of short-run versus long-run effects. Market experiments are seldom run for sufficiently long periods to indicate the long-run effects of various price, advertising, or packaging strategies. The experiment analyst is thus forced to examine short-run data and to attempt to extend it to a longer period. Difficulties associated with uncontrolled parts of market experiments also hinder their use as an estimating tool. A change in economic conditions during the experiment is likely to invalidate the results, especially if the experiment includes the use of several separate markets. A local strike, layoffs by a major employer, or a severe snowstorm in one of the market areas might well ruin the experiment. Likewise, a change in a competing product's promotion, price, or packaging can distort the results. There is also the danger that customers lost during the experiment as a result of price manipulations may not be regained when the experiment ends.

A second method uses a controlled laboratory experiment wherein consumers are given funds with which to shop in a simulated store. By varying prices, product packaging, displays, and other factors, the experimenter can learn a great deal about consumer behavior. The laboratory experiment, while providing information similar to that of field experiments, has the advantages of lower cost and greater control of extraneous factors. However, the consumer clinic or laboratory experiment technique also has shortcomings. The primary difficulty is that the subjects invariably know that they are part of an experiment, and this knowledge may distort their shopping habits. They may, for example, exhibit considerably more price consciousness than is typical in their everyday shopping. Moreover, the high cost of such experiments necessarily limits the sample size, which makes inference from the sample to the general population tenuous at best. The drawback of high costs associated with maintaining a controlled setting tends to limit the use of experiments to those situations in which the information needed for statistical demand estimation cannot be obtained from historical records. In fact, market experiments are sometimes used to develop some of the data required for more detailed statistical analysis of demand relations.

The Demand for Oranges: An Illustrative Market Experiment

▶

In a classic example of the market experiment technique, researchers from the University of Florida studied the demand for oranges in the Grand Rapids, Michigan, market.[1] The purpose of this market experiment was to examine the nature of competition between California and Florida Valencia oranges. The experiment was designed to provide estimates of the price elasticities of demand for the various oranges included in the study as well as to measure the cross-price elasticities of demand among specific varieties of oranges.

The researchers chose Grand Rapids because its size, economic base, and demographic characteristics are representative of the Midwestern market for oranges. Nine supermarkets located throughout the city cooperated in the experiment, which consisted of varying the prices charged for Florida and California Valencia oranges on a daily basis for 31 days and recording the quantities of each variety sold. Price variations for each variety of orange covered a range of 32¢ per dozen, or ±16¢ around the price per dozen that existed in the market at the time the study began. More than 9,250 dozen oranges were sold during the experiment.

Price and quantity data obtained in the study enabled researchers to examine the relation between sales of each variety of orange and its price, as well as

[1] See Marshall B. Godwin, W. Fred Chapman, Jr., and William T. Hanley, *Competition between Florida and California Valencia Oranges in the Fruit Market*, Bulletin 704, December 1965, Agricultural Experiment Stations, Institute of Food and Agricultural Services, University of Florida, Gainesville, Florida, in cooperation with the U.S. Department of Agriculture, Florida Citrus Commission.

TABLE 6.1   Demand Elasticities for California and Florida Valencia Oranges

A 1 Percent Change in the Price of	Percentage Change in the Sales of		
	Florida Indian River	Florida Interior	California
Florida Indian River	−3.07	+1.56	+0.01
Florida Interior	+1.16	−3.01	+0.14
California	+0.18	+0.09	−2.76

relations between sales quantities and the price charged for competing varieties. The results of this study are summarized in Table 6.1, where the elasticities of each price variable are reported. Numbers along the diagonal represent the price elasticities of the three varieties of oranges; off-diagonal figures estimate the cross-price elasticities of demand.

The price elasticity of demand for all three varieties of oranges is quite high. The price elasticity $\epsilon_P = -3.07$ for Florida Indian River oranges means that a 1 percent decrease in their price results in a 3.07 percent increase in sales. Florida Interior oranges have a similar price elasticity of $\epsilon_P = -3.01$, meaning that a 1 percent decrease in their price results in a 3.01 percent increase in sales. It is interesting that the price elasticity of the California orange is somewhat lower, $\epsilon_P = -2.76$, indicating that demand for California oranges is somewhat less responsive to price changes than is demand for the two varieties of Florida oranges.

Cross-price elasticities of demand reveal some interesting insights concerning the demand for oranges. Note that cross-price elasticities of demand between the two varieties of Florida oranges are positive and relatively large. The $\epsilon_{PX} = 1.16$ means that a 1 percent increase in the price of Florida Interior oranges leads to a 1.16 percent rise in demand for Florida Indian River oranges. The $\epsilon_{PX} = 1.56$ means that a 1 percent increase in the price of Florida Indian River oranges leads to a 1.56 percent rise in demand for Florida Interior oranges. This indicates that consumers view the two varieties of Florida oranges as close substitutes for one another, and they are willing to switch readily between them when price differentials exist. The cross-price elasticities of demand between the Florida and California oranges, on the other hand, are quite small. These cross-price elasticities range from only $\epsilon_{PX} = 0.01$ to $\epsilon_{PX} = 0.18$. Apparently, consumers do not view Florida and California oranges as close substitutes. In Grand Rapids, the market for California oranges appears quite distinct from the market for Florida oranges.

This market experiment offers estimates of two important demand relations— the price elasticity of demand for Florida and California oranges and their cross-price elasticities of demand. Researchers were able to identify and measure these relations because the 31-day study period was brief enough to prevent changes in incomes, tastes, population, and other variables that influence the demand for oranges. At the same time, researchers were able to ensure that adequate quantities of oranges were available to consumers at each experimental price.

The market experiment technique for studying demand estimation clearly has the potential to offer valuable demand information, as is indicated by the example of estimating demand for Florida and California oranges. Unfortunately, the high cost of running controlled experiments limits their use to situations in which reliable market information is not available.

REGRESSION ANALYSIS

Regression analysis

A statistical technique that describes relations among dependent and independent variables.

Frequently, the most compelling challenge faced by management is the accurate estimation of demand, cost, and profit relations. Not only must the range of important factors that affect demand, costs, and profits be determined, but the relative magnitude of each influence must also be assessed. **Regression analysis** is a powerful and extremely useful statistical technique that describes the way in which one important economic variable is related to one or more other economic variables. While there are clear limitations to the technique, regression analysis is often used to provide successful managers with valuable insight concerning a variety of significant economic relations. Given the widespread success of regression analysis in real-world applications, it is well worth gaining a careful understanding of the technique.

What Is a Statistical Relation?

Deterministic relation

An association that is known with certainty.

To understand when the use of regression analysis is appropriate, one must appreciate a basic difference between two broad classes of economic relations.

A **deterministic relation** is a relation between variables that is known with certainty. For example, total revenue equals price times quantity, or $TR = P \times Q$. Once the levels of price and output are known with certainty, total revenue can be exactly determined. Thus, the total revenue relation is an example of a deterministic relation. Similarly, if total cost = \$5 $\times$ quantity, then total cost can be exactly determined once the level of quantity is known, just as quantity can be determined once the total cost level is known. If all economic relations were deterministic, then managers would never be surprised by higher- or lower-than-expected profits, because both total revenues and total costs could be exactly determined at the start of every planning period. However, few economic relations are deterministic in nature. It is far more common that economic variables are related to each other in ways that cannot be predicted with absolute accuracy. Almost all economic relations must be estimated.

Statistical relation

An imprecise link between two variables.

A **statistical relation** exists between two economic variables if the average of one is related to another, but it is impossible to predict with certainty the value of one based on the value of another. In the earlier example, if $TR = \$5Q$ *on average,* then a one-unit increase in quantity would tend to result in an average \$5 increase in total revenue. Sometimes the actual increase in total revenue would be more than \$5, sometimes it would be less. In such circumstances, a statistical relation is said to exist between total costs and output.

Time series

A daily, a weekly, a monthly, or an annual sequence of economic data.

When a statistical relation exists, the exact, or "true," relation between two economic variables is not known with certainty and must be estimated. Perhaps the most common means for doing so is to gather and analyze historical data on the economic variables of interest. A **time series** of data is a daily, a weekly, a

FIGURE 6.4   Scatter Diagrams of Various Unit Cost/Output Relations

A scatter plot of the data can suggest an underlying relation between X and Y.

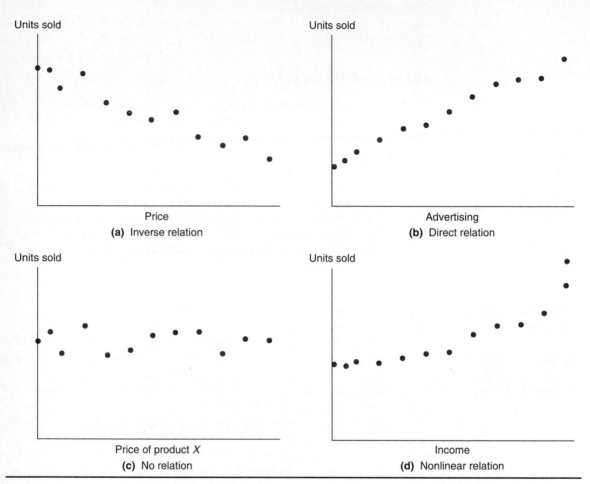

Cross section

A sample of firm, market, or product data taken at a given point in time.

monthly, or an annual sequence of data on an economic variable such as price, income, cost, or revenue. To judge the trend in profitability over time, a firm would analyze the time series of profit numbers. A **cross section** of data is a group of observations on an important economic variable at any given point in time. If a firm were interested in learning the relative importance of market share versus advertising as determinants of profitability, it might analyze a cross section of profit, advertising, and market share data for a variety of regional or local markets. To assess the effectiveness of a quality management program, the firm might consider both time series and cross section data.

Scatter diagram

A plot of XY data.

The simplest and most common means for analyzing a sample of historical data is to plot and visually study the data. A **scatter diagram** is a plot of data where the *dependent* variable is plotted on the vertical axis (y axis), and the *independent* variable is plotted on the horizontal axis (x axis). Figure 6.4 shows

MANAGERIAL APPLICATION 6.2

Statistical Demand Analysis in the 1990s

After you have received a specific number of collect calls, you will automatically be contacted by MCI Corporation to test your interest in a personal toll-free 800 number. Quaker Oats Co. tracks how your household redeems coupons and uses this information to refine future promotional advertising. Merrill Lynch & Co. compiles financial information on its customers and gives this detailed statistical profile to its brokers to help promote the company's mutual funds and other products. In each of these instances, the data gathering and analysis capabilities of high-speed mainframe computers and modern computer software are helping firms precisely identify the types of products with the greatest potential appeal for specific customers. Given the ever greater speed with which large new data bases are assembled and evaluated, marketers are increasingly able to identify the ultimate narrow market segment: the individual.

How computers have allowed firms to refine their marketing focus is truly amazing. In the 1950s, for example, a producer of laundry products might have targeted a customer defined as a suburban, middle-class housewife. By the 1980s, that focus had narrowed to neighborhoods of childless couples likely to play racquetball, for example, or to blocks of elderly consumers who like to travel. Using data on the habits and preferences of individual customers, advertisers can now pitch products with laser-beam precision. For a growing number of firms, the advantage of modern data management systems lies in their ability to focus on individuals rather than broader market niches. Not only does directly targeted advertising reduce the need for increasingly expensive media advertising, firms have also found that consumers respond better to personalized promotions.

For example, Stash Tea Co., based in Portland, Oregon, advertised a catalog for its products on the back of tea-bag wrappers in an effort to expand its market beyond the restaurant supply business. To measure the power of a personalized touch, Stash sent one group of customers the catalog along with a chatty letter based on some of the information customers had included with their letters. Another group of customers received just the catalog. The result: orders were placed by one-third of the customers that also received a letter, only 10 percent of those receiving just the catalog responded. Waldenbooks, a unit of Kmart Corp., has enrolled close to four million customers, at $5 each, in a program that rewards frequent book buyers with discounts and extra service. The program has increased store visits by club members by over 40 percent and allowed the company to promote specific titles based on individual club member shopping habits. To revive a lagging brand, consumer products giant Phillip Morris ran ads in *Time, Newsweek,* and other magazines offering samples to consumers willing to fill out a detailed questionnaire concerning their buying habits. Over two million consumers responded, more than half of whom used competitors' products. By analyzing the responses, Phillip Morris identified 500,000 hot prospects. The company then sent out individualized coupon and sample promotions to these targeted consumers in what the company calls "conquest marketing."

The future of personalized or "one-on-one" marketing appears very bright. Some experts predict that the full advantages of personalized promotion will be realized only when firms can electronically deliver their message directly to consumers. By the mid-1990s, technology already available will be widely used to help companies such as L. L. Bean offer specific customer discounts or promotions via electronic mail messages that appear on your home telephone answering machine or TV screen. Similarly, cable TV operators will soon be able to offer pay-per-view special events and other products at prices that reflect the buying habits and price sensitivity of individual households. In the not-too-distant future, TV advertising may even be sold on a household-by-household basis, much like individuals are now put on mailing lists. In short, advances in computer technology and statistical analysis software are sure to play an increasingly important role in determining not only what, but also how consumers purchase products during the 1990s.

Source: Kathleen Deveny, "Segments of One," *The Wall Street Journal,* March 22, 1991, B4.

scatter diagrams that plot the relation between the quantity sold and six different factors that have the potential to influence demand. In these examples, each potential determinant of demand represents a different independent variable, or X variable, because the levels of these demand-determining factors are determined separately from quantity. The quantity sold is the dependent variable, or Y variable, because the amount of demand is determined by the levels observed for each independent X variable. Figure 6.4a depicts an inverse relation between the quantity sold and price, the independent X variable. An increase in price leads to a decrease in the quantity demanded; a reduction in price leads to an increase in the quantity demanded. In Figure 6.4b, a direct relation is illustrated between the amount of advertising and demand. This means that an increase in advertising causes an increase in the level of product demand; conversely, a decrease in advertising causes a decrease in demand. No relation is evident between demand and the price of Product X, an independent good, as shown in Figure 6.4c. In panel 6.4d, a positive nonlinear relation between demand and income is illustrated. This implies that Product Y is a cyclical normal good.

The obvious reason for analyzing scatter plot diagrams is to gain an instinctive "feel" for the data. The approach benefits from being entirely inductive and intuitive. While the examination of scatter diagrams has this undeniable value as a starting point in the analysis of simple statistical relations, its inherent lack of structure can also limit its value. For example, the choice of which variable to call "dependent" or "independent" is often haphazard. The fact that an expansion in advertising causes an increase in product demand may seem obvious. However, in some circumstances, the directional nature of the link between economic variables is not apparent. Scatter diagrams can be helpful by illustrating the linkage or simple correlation between variables; by themselves they do not establish causality. To warrant the inference of cause and effect, the correlation between two series of data must be interpreted in light of previous experience or economic theory. In the study of regression analysis techniques, it is important to keep in mind that economic theory provides the underlying rationale for model specification.

Specifying the Regression Model

The first step in regression analysis is to specify the variables to be included in the regression equation or model. Product demand, measured in physical units, is the dependent variable when specifying a demand function. The list of independent variables, or those that influence demand, always includes the price of the product and generally includes such factors as the prices of complementary and competitive products, advertising expenditures, consumer incomes, and population of the consuming group. Demand functions for expensive durable goods, such as automobiles and houses, include interest rates and other credit terms; those for such items as ski equipment, beverages, or air conditioners include weather conditions. Determinants of demand for capital goods, such as industrial machinery, include corporate profitability, capacity utilization ratios, interest rates, trends in wages, and so on. Total or unit cost is the dependent variable; independent variables always include the level of output and typically include wage rates, interest rates, raw material prices, and so on.

The second step in regression analysis is to obtain reliable estimates of the variables. Data must be gathered on total output or demand, measures of price, credit terms, capacity utilization ratios, wage rates, and the like. Obtaining accurate estimates of these variables is not always easy, especially if the study involves time series data over a number of years. Moreover, some key variables may have to be estimated. Consumer attitudes toward product quality and expectations about future business conditions, both quite important in demand functions for many consumer goods, often have to be estimated. Survey questionnaire and interview techniques introduce an element of subjectivity into the data and the possibility of error or bias.

Once variables have been specified and the data have been gathered, the functional form of the regression equation must be determined. This form reflects the way in which independent variables are assumed to affect the dependent variable.

Linear model

A straight-line relation.

The most common specification is a **linear model,** such as the following demand function:

$$Q = b_0 + b_P P + b_A A + b_I I. \tag{6.1}$$

Here, Q represents the unit demand for a particular product, P is the price charged, A represents advertising expenditures, and I is per capita disposable income. Unit demand is assumed to change in a linear fashion with changes in each independent variable. For example, if $b_P = -1.5$, the quantity demanded will decline by one and one-half units with each one-unit increase in price. This implies a linear, or straight line, demand curve. Each coefficient measures the marginal change in Y following a one-unit change in each respective X variable. Note that the size of this influence does not depend on the size of the X variable. In a linear regression model, the marginal effect of each X variable on Y is constant. The broad appeal of linear functions stems from the fact that many demand and cost relations are in fact approximately linear. Furthermore, the most popular regression technique, the method of least squares, can be used to estimate the coefficients b_0, b_P, b_A, and b_I for linear equations.

Multiplicative model

A nonlinear relation that involves X variable interactions.

Another common regression model form is the **multiplicative model:**

$$Q = b_0 P^{b_P} A^{b_A} I^{b_I}. \tag{6.2}$$

A multiplicative model is used when the marginal effect of each independent variable is thought to depend on the value of all independent variables in the regression equation. For example, the effect on quantity demanded of a price increase often depends not just on the price level but also on the amount of advertising, competitor prices, and so on. Similarly, the effect on costs of a wage hike can depend on the output levels, raw material prices, R&D expenditures, and so on. Allowing for such changes in the marginal relation is sometimes more realistic than the implicit assumption of a constant marginal in the linear model.

The benefits of added realism for the multiplicative model have no offsetting costs in terms of added complexity or difficulty in estimation. As described in Appendix 2A, Equation 6.2 can be transformed into a linear relation using logarithms and then estimated by the least squares technique. Thus, Equation 6.2 is equivalent to

$$\log Q = \log b_0 + b_P \cdot \log P + b_A \cdot \log A + b_I \cdot \log I. \tag{6.3}$$

When written in this form, the coefficients log b_0, b_P, b_A, and b_I can be easily estimated. Given the multiplicative or log-linear form of the regression model, these coefficient estimates can also be interpreted as estimates of the constant *elasticity* of Y with respect to X, or the percentage change in Y due to a 1 percent change in X (see Appendix 2A). Much more will be said about elasticity later on in the book, but for now it is worth noting that multiplicative or log-linear models imply constant elasticity.

To summarize, multiplicative models imply a changing absolute effect on the Y variable due to changes in the various independent variables. This is sometimes attractive in demand analysis because the marginal effect of a dollar spent on advertising, for example, can vary according to overall levels of advertising, prices, income, and so on. Similarly, this is sometimes appealing in cost analysis since the effect on costs of a one-unit change in output can depend on the level of output, wages, raw material prices, and so on. The changing marginal effect implicit in the multiplicative or log-linear model contrasts with the constant marginal effect of independent variables in linear models. Multiplicative demand and cost functions are also based on the assumption of constant elasticities, whereas elasticity varies along linear demand functions. Of course, the specific form of any regression model—linear, multiplicative, or otherwise—should always be chosen to reflect the true relation among the economic variables being studied. Care must be taken to ensure that the model chosen is consistent with underlying economic theory.

The Least Squares Method

▶

Regression equations are typically estimated, or "fitted," by the method of least squares. This method can be illustrated by considering a simple demand estimation example. Assume that monthly data have been assembled by Maggie O'Connell, a consultant retained by Electronic Data Processing (EDP), Inc. EDP is a small but rapidly growing firm that provides electronic data processing services to companies, hospitals, and other organizations. EDP's main business is to maintain and monitor payroll records on a contractual basis and to issue payroll checks, W-2 forms, and so on to the employees of client customers. The company has aggressively expanded its personal selling efforts and experienced a rapid expansion in the number of units sold during the past year. Table 6.2 shows EDP monthly data on contract sales (Q) and personal selling expenses (PSE) over the past year (twelve observations).

If a linear regression model is used to describe the relation between the unit sales and personal selling expenditures, the general form of the EDP regression equation is

$$\text{Unit Sales} = Y = b_0 + b_X X, \qquad (6.4)$$

Simple regression model

The relation between one dependent Y variable and one independent X variable.

where unit sales is the dependent Y variable and personal selling expenditures is the independent X variable. Such a regression equation is called a **simple regression model** because it involves only one dependent Y variable and one independent X variable. A **multiple regression model** also entails one Y variable but includes two or more X variables. Other possibilities for independent X variables

Multiple regression model

The relation between one Y variable and two or more X variables.

TABLE 6.2 **Units Sold and Personal Selling Expenditures for Electronic Data Processing, Inc.**

Month	Units Sold	Personal Selling Expenditures	Fitted Value for Units Sold	Unexplained Residual
January	2,500	$43,000	2702.04	−202.04
February	2,250	39,000	2330.47	−80.47
March	1,750	35,000	1958.91	−208.91
April	1,500	34,000	1866.01	−366.01
May	1,000	26,000	1122.88	−122.88
June	2,500	41,000	2516.26	−16.26
July	2,750	40,000	2423.36	326.64
August	1,750	33,000	1773.12	−23.12
September	1,250	26,000	1122.88	127.12
October	3,000	45,000	2887.82	112.18
November	2,000	32,000	1680.23	319.77
December	2,000	34,000	1866.01	133.99
Average	2,020.83	$35,666.67	2,020.83	0.00

that might be included in a multiple regression analysis of demand include price, advertising expenditures, income, and so on.

The method of least squares estimates, or fits, the regression line that minimizes the sum of the squared deviations between the best-fitting line and the set of original data points. The technique is based upon the minimization of squared deviations to avoid the problem of having positive and negative deviations cancel one another out. Employing the least squares technique, it is possible to estimate the intercept a and slope coefficient b that correspond to the best-fitting regression line. To illustrate, a simple regression model that relates unit sales and personal selling expenditures for EDP is written

$$\text{Unit Sales}_t = Y_t = b_0 + b_X X_t + u_t, \tag{6.5}$$

where unit sales in month t is the dependent Y variable and the level of personal selling expenditures in month t is the independent output, or X variable; u_t is a residual or disturbance term that reflects the influences of stochastic or random elements and of any other determinants of unit sales levels that have been omitted from the regression equation. When time series data are examined, as they are in this example, the term t is used to signify a time-period-specific subscript. If cross section data are being examined—for example, unit sales in a number of regional markets during any given month—the various regional markets would be designated using an observation-specific subscript i.

Figure 6.5 shows a plot of actual EDP unit sales and personal selling expense data from Table 6.2 along with a plot of the best-fitting line for the relevant simple regression model. The a intercept marks the intersection of the regression line with the sales axis. The b slope coefficient is the slope of the regression line, and the u_t error term measures the vertical deviation of each tth data point from the fitted regression line. The least squares technique minimizes the total sum of squared u_t values by the choice of the a and b coefficients. When b_0 and b_X

FIGURE 6.5   **Regression Relation between Units Sold and Personal Selling Expenditures for Electronic Data Processing (EDP), Inc.**

The regression line minimizes the sum of squared deviations.

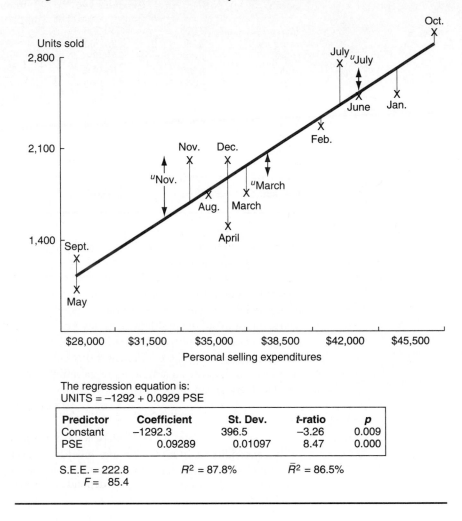

The regression equation is:
UNITS = −1292 + 0.0929 PSE

Predictor	Coefficient	St. Dev.	t-ratio	p
Constant	−1292.3	396.5	−3.26	0.009
PSE	0.09289	0.01097	8.47	0.000

S.E.E. = 222.8 R^2 = 87.8% $\bar{R}^2$ = 86.5%
F = 85.4

coefficient estimates are combined with actual data on the independent X variable (the level of personal selling expenditures) as shown in Equation 6.5, the estimated, or fitted, total unit sales values shown in Table 6.2 can be calculated. These fitted values are connected to form the fitted regression line drawn in Figure 6.5. Fitted values for the dependent Y variable are extremely valuable to management because they indicate the expected unit sales level associated with a given level of personal selling expenditures, or X variable. Regression analysis also provides management with a number of additional insights concerning the unit sales demand relation. In the next section, important insights offered by commonly reported regression statistics are investigated.

MEASURES OF REGRESSION
MODEL SIGNIFICANCE

Just a few years ago, the process of estimating demand relations was painstaking and costly. Only the largest and most advanced organizations could afford the necessary investment in sophisticated computers and highly trained staff. Today, powerful desktop personal computers with sophisticated, user-friendly statistical software make the estimation of even complex demand relations both quick and easy. As a result, the accurate estimation of demand relations has become a standard tool of the successful manager in organizations of all sizes. The two leading software programs used for this purpose are *Minitab* statistical software, published by Minitab, Inc., and *MicroTSP,* published by Quantitative Micro Software. Both are inexpensive and easy to learn, and they offer a wealth of powerful techniques for data analysis and regression model estimation. Less comprehensive statistical software that run along with *Lotus 1-2-3* and other spreadsheet programs can also be useful, especially when detailed statistical analysis is not necessary. This section focuses on the interpretation of least squares regression output.

Standard Error of the Estimate

Standard error of the estimate (S.E.E.)

The standard deviation of the dependent Y variable after controlling for the influence of all X variables.

A very useful measure for examining the accuracy of any regression model is the **standard error of the estimate (S.E.E.),** or the standard deviation of the dependent Y variable after controlling for the influence of all X variables. The standard error of the estimate increases with the amount of scatter about the sample regression line. If each data point were to lie exactly on the regression line, then the standard error of the estimate would equal zero since each $\hat{Y}_t$ would exactly equal Y_t. There is no scatter about the regression line when the standard error of the estimate equals zero. If there is a great deal of scatter about the regression line, then $\hat{Y}_t$ often differs greatly from each Y_t, and the standard error of the estimate will be large.

The standard error of the estimate provides a very useful means for estimating confidence intervals around any particular $\hat{Y}_t$ estimate, given values for the independent X variables. In other words, the standard error of the estimate is used to determine a range within which the dependent Y variable can be predicted with varying degrees of statistical confidence based on the regression coefficients and values for the X variables. Since the best estimate of the tth value for the dependent variable is $\hat{Y}_t$, as predicted by the regression equation, the standard error of the estimate is used to determine just how accurate a prediction $\hat{Y}_t$ is likely to be. If the u_t error terms are normally distributed about the regression equation, as would be true when large samples of more than 30 or so observations are analyzed, there is a 95 percent probability that observations of the dependent variable will lie within the range $\hat{Y}_t \pm (1.96 \times \text{S.E.E.})$, or within roughly 2 standard errors of the estimate. The probability is 99 percent that any given $\hat{Y}_t$ will lie within the range $\hat{Y}_t \pm (2.576 \times \text{S.E.E.})$, or within roughly 3 standard errors of its predicted value. When very small samples of data are analyzed, "critical" values slightly larger than 2 or 3 are multiplied by the S.E.E. to obtain the 95 and 99 percent confidence intervals. Precise values can be obtained from a t table

FIGURE 6.6   Illustration of the Use of the Standard Error of the Estimate to Define Confidence Intervals

The standard error of the estimate (S.E.E.) is used to construct a confidence interval.

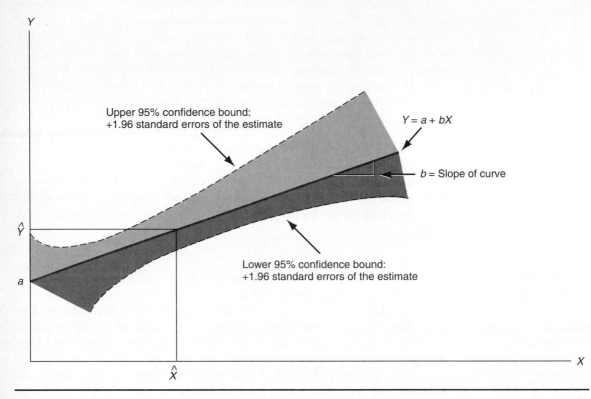

such as that found in Appendix B, as described in the following discussion of *t* statistics. For both small and large samples of data, greater predictive accuracy for the regression model is obviously associated with smaller standard errors of the estimate.

The standard error of the estimate concept is portrayed graphically in Figure 6.6. The least squares regression line is illustrated as a bold straight line; the upper and lower 95 percent confidence interval limits are shown as broken curved lines. On average, 95 percent of all actual data observations will lie within roughly 2 standard errors of the estimate. Given a value X_t, the interval between the upper and lower confidence bounds can be used to predict the corresponding Y_t value with a 95 percent probability that the actual outcome will lie within that confidence interval. Notice that this confidence interval widens for sample observations that are much higher or much lower than the sample mean. This is because the standard error of the estimate calculation is based on observations drawn from the sample rather than from the overall population, and it provides only an approximation to the true distribution of errors. Confidence bounds are closest to the regression line in the vicinity of mean values for X_t and Y_t, or at the center of the scatter diagram. Confidence bounds diverge from the regression line toward the extreme values of the sample observations. An obvious implication worth remembering is that *relatively little confidence can be placed in the predictive value of a regression equation extended beyond the range of sample observations.*

In the EDP demand estimation example, the standard error of the estimate is 222.8. This means that the standard deviation of actual Y_t values about the regression line is 222.8 sales units, since the standard error of the estimate is always in the same units as the dependent Y variable. There is a 95 percent probability that any given observation Y_t will lie within roughly 2 standard errors of the relevant $\hat{Y}_t$ estimate.[2] For example, unit sales during the month of July total 2,750 units, and the expected or fitted total cost level for unit sales is 2,453.68 [= −1,292.3 + 0.9289(40,000)]. The corresponding confidence bounds for the 95 percent confidence interval are 2,453.68 ± (2 × 222.8). This means that there is roughly a 95 percent chance that actual unit sales for a month in which $40,000 is spent on personal selling will fall in a range from 1,562.48 to 3,344.88. Similarly, there is a 99 percent probability that actual total costs will fall within roughly 3 standard errors of the predicted value, or in the range from 1,785.28 to 3,122.08. The wider the confidence interval, the higher the confidence level that actual values will be found within the predicted range. Greater predictive accuracy is obviously also associated with smaller standard errors of the estimate.

Goodness of Fit, r, and R^2

Correlation coefficient

A measure of the goodness of fit for a simple regression model.

Coefficient of determination

A goodness of fit measure for a multiple regression model; the square of the coefficient of multiple correlation.

In a simple regression model with only one independent variable, the **correlation coefficient,** r, measures goodness of fit. The correlation coefficient falls in the range between 1 and −1. If $r = 1$, there is a perfect direct linear relation between the dependent Y variable and the independent X variable. If $r = -1$, there is a perfect inverse linear relation between Y and X. In both instances, all actual values for Y_t fall exactly on the regression line. The regression equation explains all of the underlying variation in the dependent Y variable in terms of variation in the independent X variable. If $r = 0$, zero correlation exists between the dependent and independent variables; they are autonomous. When $r = 0$, there is no relation at all between actual Y_t observations and fitted $\hat{Y}_t$ values.

In multiple regression models where more than one independent X variable is considered, the squared value of the coefficient of multiple correlation is used in a similar manner. The square of the coefficient of multiple correlation, called the **coefficient of determination,** or R^2, shows how well a multiple regression model explains changes in the value of the dependent Y variable. R^2 is defined as the

---

[2] The precise "critical" number used in the multiplication of S.E.E. is found in a t-table such as that in Appendix B. This value is adjusted downward when sample size n is small relative to the number of coefficients k estimated in the regression model. To find the precise critical value, calculate the number of degrees of freedom, defined as $df = n - k$, and read the appropriate t-value from the table. In this example, $df = n - k = 12 - 2 = 10$, and there is a 95 percent probability that any given observation Y_t will lie within precisely 2.228 standard errors of the relevant $\hat{Y}_t$ estimate. There is a 99 percent probability that actual total costs will fall within precisely 3.169 standard errors of the predicted value. Therefore, even for the very small sample size analyzed in this example, 2 standard deviations for the 95 percent confidence bounds and 3 standard deviations for the 99 percent confidence bounds work quite well.

proportion of the total variation in the dependent variable that is explained by the full set of independent variables. In equation form, R^2 is written

$$R^2 = \frac{\text{Variation Explained by Regression}}{\text{Total Variation of } Y}. \tag{6.6}$$

Accordingly, R^2 can take on values ranging from 0, indicating that the model provides no explanation of the variation in the dependent variable, to 1.0, indicating that all the variation is explained by the independent variables. The coefficient of determination for the regression model illustrated in Figure 6.5 is 87.8, indicating that 87.8 percent of the total variation in EDP unit sales can be explained by the underlying variation in the level of personal selling expenditures. If R^2 is relatively high, deviations about the regression line are relatively small, as shown in Figure 6.7. In such instances, actual Y_t values are close to the regression line and values for u_t are small. As the size of the deviations about the regression line increases, the coefficient of determination falls. At the extreme, the sum of the squared error terms equals the total variation in the dependent variable, and $R^2 = 0$. In this case, the regression model is unable to explain *any* variation in the dependent Y variable.

A relatively low value for R^2 indicates that a given model is inadequate in terms of its overall explanatory power. The most general cause for this problem is the omission of some important explanatory variable or variables. In practice, the coefficient of determination seldom equals either 0 or 100 percent. In the EDP example, $R^2 = 87.8$ percent and a relatively high level of explanatory power is realized by the regression model. Fully 87.8 percent of unit sales variation is explained by the variation in the level of personal selling expenditures—a level of explanation that is often very useful for planning purposes. In empirical demand estimation, values for R^2 of 80.0, indicating that 80 percent of demand variation has been explained, are often quite acceptable. For goods with highly stable and predictable demand patterns, demand function R^2s as high as 90 to 95 percent are sometimes achieved. Similarly, very high levels of R^2 can be attained in cost function analysis of output produced under controlled conditions. Generally speaking, demand and cost analysis for a given firm or industry over time (time series analysis) will lead to higher levels for R^2 than would a similar analysis across firms or industries at a given point in time (cross section analysis). This is because most economic phenomena are closely related to the overall level of economic activity and thus have an important time or trend element. Such exogenous forces are held constant in cross section analyses and therefore cannot contribute to the overall explanatory power of the regression model. In judging whether a given R^2 is sufficiently high so as to be satisfactory, the type of analysis conducted and the anticipated use of statistical results must be considered.

The Corrected Coefficient of Determination, $\bar{R}^2$

As stated previously, an R^2 of 100 percent results when each data point lies exactly on the regression line. Although one might think that any regression model with an $R^2 = 100$ percent would prove highly reliable as a predictive device, this is not always the case. The coefficient of determination for any regression equation is artificially high when too small a sample is used to estimate the model's coef-

FIGURE 6.7   **Explained and Unexplained Variations of the Dependent Variable in a Regression Model**

R^2 is high when unexplained variation is low.

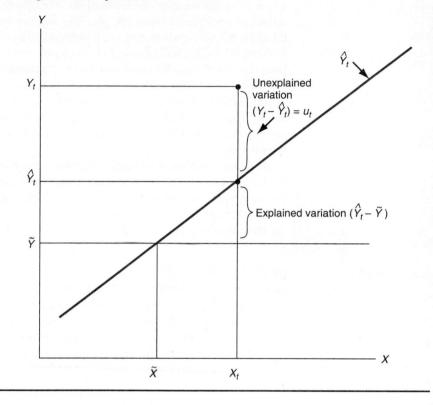

ficients. R^2 always equals 100 percent when the number of estimated coefficients equals or exceeds the number of observations because each data point can then be placed exactly on the regression line.

To conduct meaningful regression analysis, the sample used to estimate the regression equation must be sufficiently large so as to accurately reflect the important characteristics of the overall population. This typically means that 30 or more data observations are needed to adequately fit a regression model. More precisely, what is usually required is 30 or more degrees of freedom (df). **Degrees of freedom** is the number of observations beyond the absolute minimum needed to calculate a given regression statistic. For example, to calculate an intercept term, at least one observation is needed; to calculate an intercept term plus one slope coefficient, at least two observations are required; and so on. Since R^2 approaches 100 percent as degrees of freedom approach zero for any regression model, statisticians have developed a method for correcting or adjusting R^2 to account for the number of degrees of freedom. The **corrected coefficient of determination,** denoted by the symbol $\bar{R}^2$, is calculated using the expression

Degrees of freedom

The number of observations beyond the minimum needed to calculate a given regression statistic.

Corrected coefficient of determination

A downward adjustment to R^2 in light of the number of data points and estimated coefficients.

$$\bar{R}^2 = R^2 - \left(\frac{k-1}{N-k}\right)(1 - R^2),\qquad\textbf{(6.7)}$$

where N is the number of observations (data points) and k is the number of estimated coefficients (intercept plus the number of slope coefficients). From Equation 6.7 it is obvious that the downward adjustment to R^2 is large when N, the sample size, is small relative to k, the number of coefficients being estimated. Note that the $\bar{R}^2$ calculation always involves a downward adjustment to R^2. This downward adjustment to R^2 is small when N is large relative to k.

In the EDP example, $\bar{R}^2 = 86.5$ percent—a relatively modest downward adjustment to $R^2 = 87.8$ percent; it suggests that the high level of explanatory power achieved by the regression model cannot be attributed to an overly small sample size.

As with R^2, statistical software programs typically perform the $\bar{R}^2$ adjustment, so there is often no need to actually make such calculations in practice. Still, knowing what is involved makes the reasons for the practice obvious. Confidence in the reliability of a given regression model is clearly higher when both R^2 and the number of degrees of freedom are substantial.

The F Statistic

F statistic

A measure of statistical significance for the share of dependent variable variation explained by the regression model.

Both the coefficient of determination R^2 and corrected coefficient of determination $\bar{R}^2$ provide evidence on whether the proportion of explained variation is relatively high or low. However, neither tells if the independent variables as a group explain a *statistically significant* share of variation in the dependent Y variable. The **F statistic** provides evidence on whether a statistically significant proportion of total variation in the dependent variable has been explained. Like $\bar{R}^2$, the F statistic is adjusted for degrees of freedom and is defined as

$$F_{k-1,\,N-k} = \frac{\text{Explained Variation} / (k-1)}{\text{Unexplained Variation} / (N-k)}.\qquad\textbf{(6.8)}$$

Here, once again, N is the number of observations (data points) and k is the number of estimated coefficients (intercept plus the number of slope coefficients). Also like $\bar{R}^2$, the F statistic can be calculated in terms of the coefficient of determination, where

$$F_{k-1,\,N-k} = \frac{R^2 / (k-1)}{(1 - R^2) / (N-k)}.\qquad\textbf{(6.9)}$$

The F statistic is used to indicate whether a significant share of the variation in the dependent variable has been explained by the regression model. The hypothesis actually tested is that the dependent Y variable is statistically *unrelated* to all of the independent X variables included in the model. If this hypothesis cannot be rejected, the total explained variation in the regression is quite small. At the extreme, if $R^2 = 0$, then $F = 0$ and the regression equation provides absolutely no explanation of the variation in the dependent Y variable. As the F statistic increases from zero, the hypothesis that the dependent Y variable is not statistically related to one or more of the regression's independent X variables becomes easier to reject. At some point the F statistic becomes sufficiently large to reject the independence hypothesis and warrants the conclusion that at least some of the model's X variables are significant factors in explaining variation in the dependent Y variable.

The F test is used to determine whether a given F statistic is statistically significant. Performing F tests involves comparing F statistics with critical values from a table of the F distribution. If a given F statistic *exceeds* the critical value from the F distribution table, the hypothesis of no relation between the dependent Y variable and the set of independent X variables can be rejected. Taken as a whole, the regression equation can then be seen as explaining significant variation in the dependent Y variable. Critical values for the F distribution are provided at the 10 percent, 5 percent, and 1 percent significance levels in Appendix B. If the F statistic for a given regression equation exceeds the F value in the table, there can be 90 percent, 95 percent, or 99 percent confidence, respectively, that the regression model explains a significant share of variation in the dependent Y variable. The 90 percent, 95 percent, and 99 percent confidence levels are popular levels for hypothesis rejection, because they imply that a true hypothesis will be rejected only one out of 10, one out of 20, or one out of 100 items, respectively. Such error rates are quite small and typically quite acceptable.

Critical F values depend on degrees of freedom related to both the numerator and the denominator of Equation 6.9. In the numerator, the degrees of freedom equal one less than the number of coefficients estimated in the regression equation $(k - 1)$. The degrees of freedom for the denominator of the F statistic equal the number of data observations minus the number of estimated coefficients $(N - k)$. The critical value for F can be denoted as F_{f_1, f_2}, where f_1, the degrees of freedom for the numerator, equals $k - 1$, and f_2, the degrees of freedom for the denominator, equals $N - k$. For example, the F statistic for the EDP example involves $f_1 = k - 1 = 2 - 1 = 1$, and $f_2 = N - k = 12 - 2 = 10$ degrees of freedom. Also note that the calculated $F_{1, 10} = 71.73 > 10.04$, the critical F value for the $\alpha = 0.01$ or 99 percent confidence level. This means there is less than a 1 percent chance of observing such a high F statistic when there is in fact no variation in the dependent Y variable explained by the regression model. Alternatively, the hypothesis of no link between the dependent Y variable and the entire group of X variables can be rejected with 99 percent confidence. Given the ability to reject the hypothesis of no relation at the 99 percent confidence level, it will always be possible to reject this hypothesis at the lower, 95 percent and 90 percent, confidence levels. Since the significance with which the no-relation hypothesis can be rejected is an important indicator of overall model fit, rejection should always take place at the highest possible confidence level.

As a rough rule of thumb and assuming a typical regression model including four or five independent X variables plus an intercept term, a calculated F statistic greater than 3 permits rejection of the hypothesis that there is no relation between the dependent Y variable and the X variables at the $\alpha = 0.05$ significance level (with 95 percent confidence). As seen in Figure 6.8, a calculated F statistic greater than 5 typically permits rejection of the hypothesis that there is no relation between the dependent Y variable and the X variables at the $\alpha = 0.01$ significance level (with 99 percent confidence). However, as seen in the earlier discussion, critical F values are adjusted upward when sample size is small in relation to the

F I G U R E   6 . 8   **The *F* Distribution with 4 and 30 Degrees of Freedom (for a Regression Model with an Intercept plus Four *X* Variables Tested over 35 Observations)**

The *F* distribution is skewed to the right but tends toward normality as both numbers of degrees of freedom become very large.

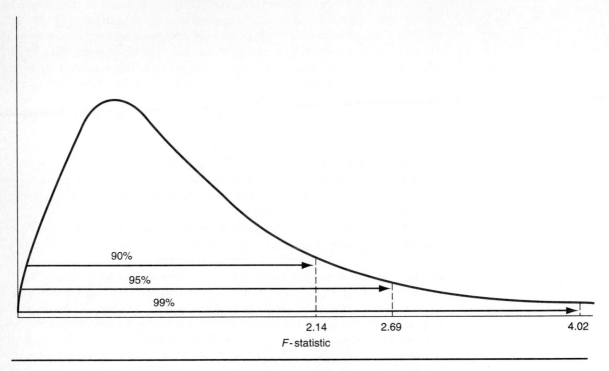

number of coefficients included in the regression model. In such instances, precise critical *F* values must be obtained from an *F* table, such as that found in Appendix B.

MEASURES OF INDIVIDUAL VARIABLE SIGNIFICANCE

The standard error of the estimate indicates the precision with which the regression model can be expected to predict the dependent *Y* variable. The standard deviation (or standard error) of each individual coefficient provides a similar measure of precision for the relation between the dependent *Y* variable and a given *X* variable. When the standard deviation of a given estimated coefficient is relatively small, a strong relation is suggested between *X* and *Y*. When the standard deviation of a coefficient estimate is relatively large, the underlying relation between *X* and *Y* is typically weak.

The t Statistic

A variety of interesting statistical tests can be conducted based on the size of an estimated coefficient and its standard deviation. These tests are based on alternate

FIGURE 6.9 The *t* Distribution

For large samples, the *t* statistic is normally distributed with a mean of zero and a standard deviation of 1.

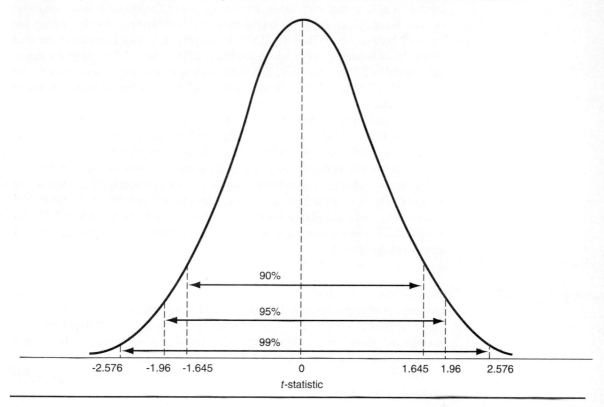

---

t statistic

An *approximately* normal test statistic with a mean of zero and a standard deviation of 1.

versions of the *t* **statistic,** or test statistic. The *t* statistic has an *approximately* normal distribution with a mean of zero and a standard deviation of 1. It describes the difference between an estimated coefficient and some hypothesized value in terms of "standardized units," or by the number of standard deviations of the coefficient estimate. The *t* statistic is normally distributed for large samples, as shown in Figure 6.9. When relatively small samples of data are considered, the *t* distribution does not display a perfectly symmetrical distribution around the mean of zero.

Notice that the bulk of the region under the bell-shaped curve in Figure 6.9 lies in the area around zero, the mean value of the *t* statistic. Fully 95 percent of the region under the bell-shaped curve lies within the territory between −1.96 and +1.96, or roughly ±2. For descriptive purposes, statisticians say that *t* statistics between −1.96 and +1.96 are "close" to the mean value of zero. This area is sometimes referred to as the 95 percent confidence interval, since one can be 95 percent certain that the *t* statistic is close to the mean of zero. Only 5 percent of the area under the bell-shaped curve lies in the "tails" of the distribution, or in the region below the value −1.96 or beyond the value +1.96. For descriptive purposes, statisticians say that *t* statistics outside the bounds of

−1.96 and +1.96 are "not close" to, or different from, the mean value of zero. This area is sometimes referred to as the rejection region, since one can be 95 percent confident that such values are *not* typical of *t* statistics with a true mean of zero. Since 99 percent of the region under the bell-shaped curve lies within the territory between −2.576 and +2.576, or roughly ±3, only 1 percent of the area under the bell-shaped curve lies in the lower tail below −2.576, or in the upper tail beyond +2.576. Therefore, it is even more apparent that *t* values outside the bounds of −2.576 and +2.576 are "not close" to, or different from, the mean value of zero.

Since *t* statistics describe the difference between an estimated coefficient and some hypothesized value in terms of "standardized units," the estimated coefficient is quite different than the hypothesized value whenever very small or large *t* statistics are encountered. Statistically speaking, it is very rare to find a calculated *t* statistic that falls outside the bounds ±1.96, or roughly ±2, when a true value of zero is encountered. This occurs less than 5 percent of the time. It is rarer still to find a calculated *t* statistic that falls outside the bounds ±2.576, or roughly ±3, when a true value of zero is encountered; this happens less than 1 percent of the time.

Two-Tail t Tests

In regression analysis, the most common *t* test is performed to learn if an individual slope coefficient estimate $b = 0$. If X and Y are indeed unrelated, then the b slope coefficient for a given X variable equals zero. If the $b = 0$ hypothesis can be rejected, then it is possible to infer that $b \neq 0$ and that a relation between Y and a given X variable does in fact exist.

The *t* statistic with $N - k$ degrees of freedom used to test the $b = 0$ hypothesis is given by the expression

$$t_{N-k} = \frac{\hat{b}}{\text{Standard Deviation of } \hat{b}}, \qquad \textbf{(6.10)}$$

where, once again, N is the number of observations (data points) and k is the number of estimated coefficients (intercept plus the number of slope coefficients). Notice that this *t* statistic measures the size of an individual coefficient estimate relative to the size of its underlying standard deviation.

The *t* statistic measures the size of the b coefficient relative to its standard deviation because both the size of b and its underlying stability are important in determining if, on average, $b \neq 0$. The *t* statistic measures the number of standard deviations between the estimated regression coefficient, $\hat{b}$, and zero. Since the *t* statistic is only approximately normal, 2 standard deviations for the 95 percent confidence interval and 3 standard deviations for the 99 percent confidence interval hold only for large samples. When $N - k$ is large, say in excess of 30, a calculated *t* statistic greater than 2 usually permits rejection of the hypothesis that there is no relation between the dependent Y variable and a given X variable at the $\alpha = 0.05$ significance level (with 95 percent confidence). A calculated *t* statistic greater than 3 typically permits rejection of the hypothesis that there is no relation between the dependent Y variable and a given X variable at the $\alpha = 0.01$ significance level (with 99 percent confidence). However, critical *t* values are adjusted upward when sample size is small in relation to the number of estimated coefficients. When $N - k < 30$, precise critical *t* values can be obtained from a *t* table, such as that found in Appendix B.

If the calculated *t* statistic is greater than the relevant critical *t* value, taken from a table of values such as that found in Appendix B, the $b = 0$ hypothesis can be rejected. Conversely, if the calculated *t* statistic is not greater than the critical *t* value, it is not possible to reject the $b = 0$ hypothesis. In that case, there is no evidence of a relation between *Y* and a given *X* variable. Tests of the hypothesis $b = 0$ are referred to as **two-tail *t* tests** because either very small negative *t* values or very large positive *t* values can lead to rejection. Hypothesis tests that simply relate to matters of effect or influence are called two-tail *t* tests.

Returning to the EDP example, the estimated coefficient for the personal selling expenditures *X* variable is 0.09289. Given a standard deviation of only 0.01097, the calculated *t* statistic = 8.47 > 3.169, the critical *t* value for a two-tail test with $N - k = 10$ degrees of freedom at the $\alpha = 0.01$ significance level. With 99 percent confidence, the hypothesis of no effect can be rejected. Alternatively, the probability of encountering such a large *t* statistic is less than 1 percent [hence the probability (*p*) value of 0.000 in Figure 6.5] when there is in fact no relation between the total units *Y* variable and the personal selling expenditures *X* variable.

Two-tail *t* tests

Tests of the $b = 0$ hypothesis.

One-Tail t Tests

Some managerial questions go beyond the simple matter of whether *X* influences *Y*. In these instances, it is interesting to determine whether a given variable, *X*, has a positive or a negative effect on *Y* or whether the effect of variable X_1 is greater or smaller than the effect of variable X_2. Tests of direction (positive or negative) or comparative magnitude are called **one-tail *t* tests.** Although one-tail *t* tests are less commonly employed than two-tail tests, the usefulness of regression-based demand analysis is greatly enhanced when both types of tests are understood.

To understand the difference between one-tail and two-tail *t* tests, it is necessary to appreciate the nature of the *t* distribution. As shown in Figure 6.9, 90 percent of the area under the bell-shaped curve is between $t = -1.645$ and $t = +1.645$, 95 percent is between $t = -1.96$ and $t = +1.96$, and 99 percent is between $t = -2.576$ and $t = +2.576$. At these values, both tails of the *t* statistic distribution contain 10 percent, 5 percent, and 1 percent of the total area, respectively. For example, if there is in fact no relation between *Y* and a given *X* variable, the probability of a calculated *t* value that falls outside the bounds ± 1.645 is only 10 percent. Under these circumstances, the chance of a calculated *t* value that is less than -1.645 is only 5 percent; the chance of a calculated *t* value greater than $+1.645$ is 5 percent. If $t = 1.645$, it is possible to reject the $b = 0$ hypothesis with 90 percent confidence; it is possible to reject the $b < 0$ or $b > 0$ hypotheses with 95 percent confidence. In a two-tail *t* test, rejection of the null hypothesis occurs with a finding that the *t* statistic is not in the region around zero. In one-tail *t* tests, rejection of the null hypothesis occurs when the *t* statistic is in one specific tail of the distribution.

One-tail *t* tests

Tests of direction or comparative magnitude.

▶   In the EDP example, the estimated coefficient for the personal selling expenditures X variable is 0.09289 with a standard deviation of 0.01097. The calculated t statistic $= 8.47 > 2.764$, the critical t value for a one-tail t test with $N - k = 10$ degrees of freedom at the $\alpha = 0.01$ significance level. With 99 percent confidence, the negative effect hypothesis can be rejected. The probability of encountering such a large positive t statistic is less than 1 percent [hence the probability (p) value of 0.000 in Figure 6.5] when there is in fact a negative relation between the total units Y variable and the personal selling expenditures X variable.

PRACTICAL SOLUTIONS TO REGRESSION PROBLEMS

A number of pitfalls can be encountered in regression analysis. Not the least of these is the problem that correlation by itself does not imply causality. Even if observed correlation reflects a causal relation, the direction of causality may run in the opposite direction from that implied by the regression. Does advertising cause (produce) sales? Do sales cause (fund) advertising? Or does causality run in *both* directions? In light of this and other difficulties encountered in using historical data to project future relations, some caveats are in order concerning the use of the regression technique. This section suggests some practical solutions to some of the problems typically encountered when using the regression analysis.

Choosing the Best Model

The specific form of a regression equation is typically based on a demand or cost model derived from economic theory. Nevertheless, some experimentation might sometimes prove appropriate. One of the most practical uses of the regression technique is to judiciously experiment in the attempt to discover the exact nature of the relation between important economic variables. As a first step, it is possible to experiment with various measures of the dependent and independent variables. Quite often it is worthwhile to try separate output measures based upon different product classifications. The costs of producing output can and do vary widely depending on the types of product characteristics required by customers. Similarly, demand conditions often depend upon unique product characteristics that are obscured when sales are aggregated into a product class that is too broad.

The specific functional form of the regression model is also often a worthy subject of some experimentation. After the data on relevant dependent and independent variables have been collected, managers may have little prior reason to suspect whether the linear or log-linear (multiplicative) form of the regression equation model is most appropriate. Trying both forms and then relying on the form that consistently provides the best fit seems quite reasonable. Similarly, some careful experimentation with the range of independent X variables incorporated in the regression model might be proper. Some managers use a regression method called **stepwise multiple regression,** which relies on the underlying correlation between X and Y variables to indicate the independent X variables to be included in the model. In this method, X variables are actually selected by the computer software according to their ability to reduce the overall level of unex-

Stepwise multiple regression

An experimental method of independent variable selection based upon XY correlation.

●

MANAGERIAL APPLICATION 6.3

Spreadsheet and Statistical Software for the PC

The personal computer revolution in business really got started with the publication of *Lotus 1-2-3* spreadsheet software. A spreadsheet is simply a tabular collection of business data in the style of an accounting worksheet that can be easily manipulated and analyzed. An instant hit that still dominates the market for basic spreadsheet software, *Lotus 1-2-3* makes income statement and balance sheet analysis quick and easy. Recent versions incorporate a broad range of tools for analysis, including net present value, internal rate of return, and regression. Users of *Lotus 1-2-3* are also able to take advantage of numerous "add-in" customized routines to solve specialized business problems.

For example, *@Risk* is a *Lotus 1-2-3* add-in software application that allows managers to employ proven risk analysis techniques in the evaluation of any uncertain business situation. To prepare for the possibility of lower than forecast sales, it is often not enough to test worst-case, most-likely, and best-case scenarios. *@Risk* can be used to run thousands of simulations to show the likelihood of each possible scenario and calculate the economic consequences. *What-If-Solver,* another *Lotus 1-2-3* add-in, provides linear, nonlinear, and mixed integer optimization with full sensitivity analysis—for up to 120 variables and 120 constraints. *ForeCalc* makes it possible to use a wide variety of broadly accepted exponential smoothing models to generate sales and cost forecasts without leaving the spreadsheet. *Ready-to-Run Accounting* incorporates powerful tools for financial analysis in a best-selling general ledger add-in software. In addition to regular business editions, each of these four *Lotus 1-2-3* add-ins is published in user-friendly student editions with excellent written documentation by Addison-Wesley Publishing Co.

Statistical software for the PC facilitates detailed analysis of business data. In business and in many leading business schools around the country, *Minitab Statistical Software,* published by Minitab, Inc., is an acknowledged leader in basic statistical software. *Minitab* is command-driven, meaning that users type in a command sequence to perform a given statistical analysis. However, the language of *Minitab* is intuitive and easy to learn. To run a regression of the data in column one on one predictor (*x*-variable) contained in column two, the command is simply: REGRESS C1 1 C2. The command for correlation is CORRELATE, for the arithmetic mean it is MEAN, and so on. For nonspecialized users who want to get up and running in a hurry, *Minitab* is a top choice. *MicroTSP,* published by Quantitative Micro Software, is another leading basic statistical package used in business and in several leading business schools. *MicroTSP* is designed to address problems encountered in the statistical analysis of economic relations, or econometric modeling, and is especially well suited to the study of managerial economics. *MicroTSP* began primarily as a time-series processor; today *MicroTSP* offers a wide range of capabilities for studying time-series and cross-sectional data sets. One of the strongest features of *MicroTSP* is its outstanding documentation and excellent tutorials on both the software itself, and on econometric modeling techniques in general. For many business applications, *MicroTSP* serves very well as a general purpose statistical package.

Advanced statistical software packages allow users to conduct a broad range of highly sophisticated statistical analyses on large data sets. Multivariate analysis, time-series analysis, factor analysis, and nonlinear regression are typical capabilities that distinguish advanced statistical packages from more basic offerings. Some advanced statistical software programs are derived from well known mainframe statistical programs. Although comprehensive, these software programs are often more difficult to learn than advanced statistical programs specifically written for desktop personal computers. An advanced statistical software program with an excellent combination of comprehensive statistical capability and excellent documentation with a user-friendly interface for users of desktop computers is *SPSS/PC+,* offered by SPSS, Inc. Using *SPSS/PC+,* it is possible to easily conduct a detailed analysis of problems facing the smallest firm or Fortune 500 company. Moreover, *SPSS/PC+* is available in a comprehensive package of statistical and graphics software to offer users a complete solution to their data modeling, analysis, and report preparation needs.

Source: David C. Churbuck, "Learning By Example," *Forbes,* June 8, 1992, 130–131.

plained variation. Using this technique, the regression analysis method has the potential to become wholly inductive in character, where the nature of the data, rather than the prior expectations of the manager, determine the specific form of the regression function.

The benefit of experimentation lies in its potential for improving regression model fit and thereby improving overall understanding concerning the economic relation of interest. The danger of experimentation is that the resulting regression model might bear little resemblance to a robust and durable economic relation. As was described in the degrees of freedom discussion, R^2 can typically be increased by the addition of further independent variables, even if no true relation exists between the dependent Y variable and the additional X variables. An approach where absolutely every variable is tried can lead to models that effectively pick up idiosyncratic aspects of unique samples of data but prove incapable of widespread explanation. Perhaps the safest approach to adopt when using an experimental method is to always retain a holdout, or test sample, of data where the experimental model can be verified. If an experimental model achieves a relatively high level of explanation over samples of data that were not used in its development, then chances are improved that it offers useful insight. If an experimental model fails to achieve relatively high levels of explanation over samples of data that were not used in its development, then chances are that it offers little useful insight.

Dealing with Multicollinearity

Multicollinearity
The situation in which two or more independent variables are very highly correlated.

Suppose that the coefficient of determination for a regression model is near 100 percent, thus indicating that the model as a whole explains much of the variation in the dependent variable. Assume further that standard errors for the individual coefficient estimates are also relatively large and that t statistics for many, if not all, independent variables are insignificant. This describes a situation where the regression model indicates a significant relation between the dependent Y variable and the group of independent X variables, but the technique is unable to identify the various X variables as uniquely important. This problem is due to **multicollinearity,** a situation in which two or more independent variables are very highly correlated. The independent variables are not really independent of one another but have values that are jointly or simultaneously determined. Home ownership and family income provide a good example. A firm might believe that whether a given family will buy its product depends on, among other things, the family's income and whether the family owns a home or rents. Because families who own their homes tend to have relatively high incomes, these two variables are highly correlated and it is difficult to determine the marginal influence of each in demand analysis.

In time series analysis, where the pervasive influence of economic growth is at work, multicollinearity problems can be equally pervasive. In cases of perfect or near perfect collinearity between two independent variables, it becomes impossible to estimate coefficients for both variables. Even when it is possible to estimate regression coefficients for each variable, high multicollinearity reduces the reliability of coefficient estimates—particularly in relation to each coefficient estimate's standard deviation. As the number of independent variables grows, so too does the potential for multicollinearity problems. Thus, it becomes important to check the correlation among independent variables, especially when several independent X variables are being considered. If the correlation between any two coefficients is near 1 or -1, multicollinearity is likely to be a problem.

One practical approach for dealing with multicollinearity is to deflate or otherwise transform the independent variables. For example, to discover the independent effects of rising price levels (inflation) and rising income levels on demand, it may be appropriate to convert nominal data into real (inflation-adjusted) terms. If both age and experience contribute to employee productivity, it may be attractive to combine the two variables by multiplying them together and creating an employee "age and experience" variable. Alternatively, it is sometimes suggested to remove all but one of the correlated independent variables from the regression model. Even then, the resulting coefficient estimate assigned to the remaining variable reflects its own influence and that of the other excluded variables. The regression model still has not identified the separate effects of the mutually correlated variables. However, so long as the relation between the correlated independent variables does not change, the resulting regression model can be used for predictive purposes. If the problem of multicollinearity cannot be avoided in these ways, at least the problem can be recognized and allowed for in the interpretation of regression statistics.

Residual Analysis

Residual
Error or unexplained variation.

Serial correlation
Time-related linkages in the residuals.

Durbin-Watson statistic
A measure of the extent of serial correlation.

The least squares regression technique makes four assumptions about the distribution of the error term, or **residual,** u_t. Residuals are assumed to have a normal distribution, a random distribution, an expected value of zero, and constant variance. A violation of any one of these assumptions impairs the validity of the technique. Using most standard statistical software, residuals can be calculated and plotted. Three basic graphs of the residuals can be used to indicate most of the common violations of the basic assumptions.

Plotting the residuals on a linear scale, as in Figure 6.10a, provides a frequency distribution. This distribution can be examined to determine whether the residuals appear to be normally distributed and have a mean equal to zero. In most cases, frequency plots do not form a perfect bell-shaped (normal) curve, but any serious deviation will be readily indicated. A plot of the residuals in their order of occurrence provides another useful means for detecting violations of basic assumptions. This plot is most beneficial for time series models, in which case the sequence of the data has an economic interpretation. For example, when plotting annual residuals in their order of occurrence, they should be randomly distributed about a mean of zero. Residuals plotted in sequence should display a horizontal band centered about the value zero, as is true of the dots in Figure 6.10b. Within that band there should also be no systematic pattern—unlike the pattern of Xs in Figure 6.10b. The repetitive sequence in the plot of Xs indicates that these residuals are not independent but are serially correlated.

The problem of **serial correlation** (or autocorrelation) occurs frequently and is not always easily detected using graphic methods. The **Durbin-Watson statistic,** or the sum of squared first differences of the residuals divided by the sum of squared residuals, is often calculated and used to measure the extent of

FIGURE 6.10   **Residual Analysis**

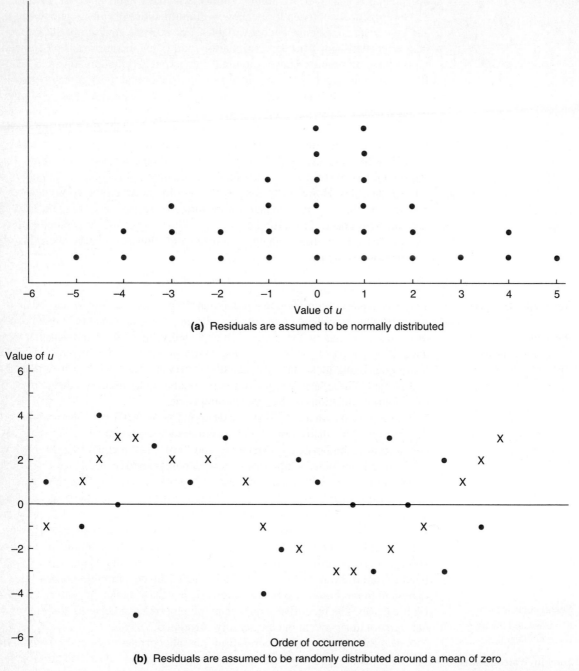

(a) Residuals are assumed to be normally distributed

(b) Residuals are assumed to be randomly distributed around a mean of zero

FIGURE 6.11 **Undesirable Residual Patterns**

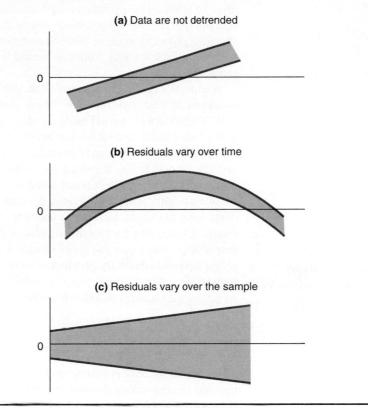

(a) Data are not detrended

(b) Residuals vary over time

(c) Residuals vary over the sample

serial correlation.[3] A value of approximately 2 for the Durbin-Watson statistic indicates the absence of serial correlation; deviations from this value indicate that

[3] The Durbin-Watson statistic, d, is calculated by the equation

$$d = \frac{\sum_{i=1}^{N} (u_i - u_{i-1})^2}{\sum_{i=1}^{N} u_i^2}.$$

Essentially, the sum of the squared first differences of the residuals, $(u_i - u_{i-1})^2$, is divided by the sum of the squared residuals. The above equation can also be rewritten as

$$d = \frac{2\sum_{i=1}^{N} u_i^2 - 2\sum_{i=1}^{N} u_i u_{i-1}}{\sum_{i=1}^{N} u_i^2} = 2(1 - \rho),$$

where ρ is the correlation coefficient between successive residuals. Thus, if $\rho = 0$, indicating that the residuals are serially independent, then $d = 2$. As ρ approaches $+1$, indicating positive serial correlation, d will fall toward 0; and if ρ is negative, indicating negative serial correlation, d will increase, with an upper limit of $+4$ being associated with perfect negative serial correlation ($\rho = -1$).

the residuals are not randomly distributed. When serial correlation exists, it can often be removed through data transformation, such as taking first differences. In demand analysis, serial correlation among the residuals is often caused by slowly changing prices, income, or taste. Specification of the demand model in terms of changes in each variable from one period to the next frequently overcomes this problem.

A sequence plot of the residuals can also be used to uncover three additional violations of basic assumptions. These three patterns are illustrated in Figure 6.11. The pattern shown in Figure 6.11(a) occurs frequently in time series regression where a trend variable has not been included in the model. Demand is slowly changing over time because of changing tastes, growing income, or other factors; and the model can be improved by explicitly accounting for this trend factor. Sometimes the trend effect is not constant over time, and a sequence plot of the residuals might appear as in Figure 6.11(b). Inclusion of a quadratic time factor (time squared) would correct this problem. The residual sequence plot shown in Figure 6.11(c), called a megaphone plot, indicates that the variance of the residuals is not constant over the entire sample. Common corrective action for this so-called **heteroskedasticity** problem is to transform the regression variables into logarithmic or ratio form prior to estimation or to use more sophisticated weighted least squares regression methods.

Heteroskedasticity

Nonconstant variance in the disturbance term.

SUMMARY

This chapter introduces various qualitative and quantitative methods for characterizing and estimating demand relations. An understanding of these techniques is necessary not only for the successful analysis of demand relations but also for understanding the nature of any statistical relation.

- Since the market price/output equilibrium at any point in time is determined by the forces of demand and supply, a **simultaneous relation,** or concurrent association, exists between demand and supply. The problem of estimating an economic relation in the presence of such simultaneity is the **identification problem.**

- The **consumer interview,** or survey, method involves questioning customers or potential customers to estimate demand relations. An alternative technique for obtaining useful information about product demand involves **market experiments.**

- **Regression analysis** is a powerful statistical technique that describes the way in which a dependent Y variable is related to one or more independent X variables.

- A **deterministic relation** is a relation between variables that is known with certainty. A **statistical relation** exists if the average of one variable is related to another, but it is impossible to predict with certainty the value of one based on the value of another. A **time series** is a daily, a weekly, a monthly, or an annual sequence of data on an economic variable such as price, income, cost, or revenue. A **cross section** of data is a group of observations on an important economic variable at any given point in time.

• The simplest and most common means for analyzing a sample is to plot and visually study the data. A **scatter diagram** is a data illustration where the *dependent* variable is plotted on the vertical axis and the *independent* variable is shown on the horizontal axis. The most common regression model specification is a **linear model** or straight-line relation. Another common regression model form is a **multiplicative model,** which involves interactions among all the X variables. A **simple regression model** involves one dependent Y variable and one independent X variable. A **multiple regression model** entails one Y variable but includes two or more X variables.

• A useful measure for examining the overall accuracy of regression models is the **standard error of the estimate (S.E.E.),** or the standard deviation of the dependent Y variable after controlling for the influence of all X variables. In a simple regression model with only one independent variable, the **correlation coefficient,** r, measures goodness of fit. The square of the coefficient of multiple correlation, called the **coefficient of determination,** or R^2, shows how well a multiple regression model explains changes in the value of the dependent Y variable. In statistical studies, the sample analyzed must be large enough to provide 30 or more **degrees of freedom,** or observations beyond the minimum needed to calculate a given regression statistic. The **corrected coefficient of determination,** denoted by the symbol $\bar{R}^2$, is a downward adjustment in R^2 in light of the number of data points and estimated coefficients. The F **statistic** offers evidence on the statistical significance of the proportion of dependent variable variation that has been explained.

• The t **statistic** is a test statistic that has an *approximately* normal distribution with a mean of zero and a standard deviation of 1. Hypothesis tests that simply relate to matters of effect or influence of the independent variables are called **two-tail** t **tests.** Tests of direction (positive or negative) or comparative magnitude are called **one-tail** t **tests.**

• A number of estimation problems are commonly encountered in regression analysis. The problem of **multicollinearity** arises when two or more independent variables are highly correlated and the regression technique is incapable of determining individual causal relations. The least squares regression technique makes four assumptions about the distribution of the error term, or **residual,** u_t. Residuals are assumed to have a normal distribution, a random distribution, an expected value of zero, and constant variance. A violation of any one of these assumptions impairs the validity of the technique. The problem of **serial correlation** (or autocorrelation) is best detected using the **Durbin-Watson statistic.** If the variance of the residuals is not constant over the entire sample, **heteroskedasticity** is said to exist. When residual term assumptions are violated, regression variables are sometimes transformed into logarithmic or ratio form prior to estimation, or more sophisticated weighted least squares regression methods are employed.

Methods examined in this chapter are commonly employed by large and small organizations in their ongoing analysis of statistical demand relations. Given the continuing rise in the diversity and complexity of the economic environment, the use of such tools is certain to grow in the years ahead.

Questions

Q6.1   What is the identification problem, and how does it make demand estimation difficult?

Q6.2   Why might customers be unwilling or unable to provide accurate demand information? When might this prove helpful?

Q6.3   How do linear and log-linear models differ in terms of their assumptions about the nature of demand elasticities?

Q6.4   If a regression model estimate of total profit is $50,000 with a standard error of the estimate of $25,000, what is the chance of an actual loss?

Q6.5   A simple regression $TR = a + bQ$ is not able to explain 19 percent of the variation in total revenue. What is the coefficient of correlation between TR and Q?

Q6.6   In a regression-based estimate of a demand function, the beta coefficient for advertising equals 3.75 with a standard deviation of 1.25 units. What is the range within which there can be 99 percent confidence that the actual parameter for advertising can be found?

Q6.7   Describe the benefits and risks involved in the experimental stepwise regression method of analysis.

Q6.8   Describe a circumstance in which multicollinearity is likely to be a problem, and discuss a possible remedy.

Q6.9   Is serial correlation apt to be a problem in a time series analysis of quarterly sales data over a ten-year period? Identify a possible remedy, if necessary.

Q6.10 Managers often study the profit margin–sales relation over the life cycle of individual products, rather than the more direct profit–sales relation. In addition to the economic reasons for doing so, are there statistical advantages as well? (Note: Profit margin equals profit divided by sales.)

Self-Test Problem

The use of regression analysis for demand estimation can be further illustrated by expanding the Electronic Data Processing (EDP), Inc., example described in the chapter. As you recall, EDP is a small but rapidly growing firm that provides electronic data processing services to companies, hospitals, and other organizations. EDP's main business is to maintain and monitor payroll records on a contractual basis and to issue payroll checks, W-2 forms, and so on to the employees of client customers. During the past year, EDP has aggressively expanded its personal selling efforts and experienced a rapid expansion in annual revenues. In a tough economic environment, year-end sales revenue grew to $5.2 million per month, a rate of $62.4 million per year. The link between units sold and personal selling expenditures described in the chapter gives only a partial view of the impact of important independent variables. Potential influences of other important independent variables can be studied in a multiple regression analysis of EDP data on contract sales (Q), personal selling expenses (PSE), advertising expenditures (AD), and average contract price (P). Because of a stagnant national economy, industry-wide growth was halted during the year, and the usually positive effect of income growth on demand was missing. Thus, the trend in national income was not relevant during this period. For simplicity, assume that relevant factors influencing EDP's monthly sales are as follows:

Month	Units Sold	Price	Advertising Expenditures	Personal Selling Expenditures
January	2,500	$3,800	$26,800	$43,000
February	2,250	3,700	23,500	39,000
March	1,750	3,600	17,400	35,000
April	1,500	3,500	15,300	34,000
May	1,000	3,200	10,400	26,000
June	2,500	3,200	18,400	41,000
July	2,750	3,200	28,200	40,000
August	1,750	3,000	17,400	33,000
September	1,250	2,900	12,300	26,000
October	3,000	2,700	29,800	45,000
November	2,000	2,700	20,300	32,000
December	2,000	2,600	19,800	34,000
Average	2,020.83	$3,175.00	$19,966.67	$35,666.67

If a linear relation between unit sales, contract price, advertising, and personal selling expenditures is hypothesized, the EDP regression equation takes the following form:

$$\text{Sales} = Y_t = b_0 + b_P P_t + b_{AD} AD_t + b_{PSE} PSE_t + u_t,$$

where Y is the number of contracts sold, P is the average contract price per month, AD is advertising expenditures, PSE is personal selling expenses, and u is a random disturbance term—all measured on a monthly basis over the past year.

When this linear regression model is estimated over the EDP data, the following regression equation is estimated (t-statistics in parentheses):

$$\text{Units}_t = -117.513 - 0.296P_t + 0.036AD_t + 0.066PSE_t,$$
$$(-0.35) \quad (-2.91) \quad (2.56) \quad (4.61)$$

where P_t is price, AD_t is advertising, PSE_t is selling expense, and t statistics are indicated within parentheses. The standard error of the estimate, or S.E.E., is 123.9 units, the coefficient of determination or $R^2 = 97.0$ percent, the adjusted coefficient of determination is $\bar{R}^2 = 95.8$ percent, and the relevant F statistic is 85.4.

A. What is the economic meaning of the $b_0 = -117.513$ intercept term? How would you interpret the value for each independent variable's coefficient estimate?

B. How is the standard error of the estimate (S.E.E.) employed in demand estimation?

C. Describe the meaning of the coefficient of determination, R^2, and the adjusted coefficient of determination, $\bar{R}^2$.

D. Use the EDP regression model to estimate fitted values for units sold and unexplained residuals for each month during the year.

Solution to Self-Test Problem

A. The intercept term $b_0 = -117.513$ has no clear economic meaning. Caution must always be exercised when interpreting points outside the range of observed data—this intercept, like most, lies far from typical values. This intercept cannot be interpreted as the expected level of unit sales at a zero price, assuming both advertising and personal selling expenses are completely eliminated. Similarly, it would be hazardous to use this regression model to predict sales at prices, selling expenses, or advertising levels well in excess of sample norms.

Slope coefficients provide estimates of the change in sales that might be expected following a one-unit increase in price, advertising, or personal selling expenditures. In this example, sales are measured in units, and each independent variable is measured in dollars. Therefore, a one-dollar increase in price can be expected to lead to a 0.296-unit reduction in sales volume per month. Similarly, a one-dollar increase in advertising can be expected to lead to a 0.036-unit increase in sales; a one-dollar increase in personal selling expenditures can be expected to lead to a 0.066-unit increase in units sold. In each instance, the effect of independent X variables appears quite consistent over the entire sample. The t statistics for price and advertising exceed the value of 2, meaning that there can be 95 percent confidence that price and advertising have an effect on sales. The chance of observing such high t statistics for these two variables when in fact price and advertising have no effect on sales is less than 5 percent. The t statistic for the personal selling expense variable exceeds the value of 3, the critical t value for the $\alpha = 0.01$ (99 percent confidence level). The probability of observing such a high t statistic when in fact no relation exists between sales and personal selling expenditures is less than 1 percent.[4] Again, caution must be used when interpreting these individual regression coefficients. It is important not to extend the analysis beyond the range of data used to estimate the regression coefficients.

B. The standard error of the estimate, or S.E.E., of 123.9 units can be used to construct a confidence interval within which actual values are likely to be found based on the size of individual regression coefficients and various values for the X variables. For example, given this regression model and the values $P_t = \$3,800$, $AD_t = \$26,800$, and $PSE_t = \$43,000$ for each respective independent X variable during the month of January; the fitted value $\hat{Y}_t = 2,566.88$ can be calculated (see Part D). Given these values for the independent X variables, 95 percent of the time actual observations for the month of January will lie within roughly 2 standard errors of the estimate; 99 percent of the time actual observations will lie within roughly 3 standard errors of the estimate. Thus, approximate bounds for the 95 percent confidence interval are given by the expression $2,566.88 \pm (2 \times 123.9)$, or from 2,319.08 to 2,814.68 sales units. Approximate bounds for the 99 percent confidence interval are given by the expression $2,566.88 \pm (3 \times 123.9)$, or from 2,195.18 to 2,938.58 sales units.

---

[4] The t statistic for personal selling expenses exceeds 3.355, the precise critical t value for the $\alpha = 0.01$ level and $N - k = 12 - 4 = 8$ degrees of freedom. The t statistic for price and advertising exceeds 2.306, the critical t value for the $\alpha = 0.05$ level and 8 degrees of freedom, meaning that there can be 95 percent confidence that price and advertising affect sales. Note also that $F_{3,8} = 85.40 > 7.58$, the precise critical F value for the $\alpha = 0.01$ significance level.

C. The coefficient of determination is $R^2 = 97.0$ percent; it indicates that 97 percent of the variation in EDP demand is explained by the regression model. Only 3 percent is left unexplained. Moreover, the adjusted coefficient of determination is $\bar{R}^2 = 95.8$ percent; this reflects only a modest downward adjustment to R^2 based upon the size of the sample analyzed relative to the number of estimated coefficients. This suggests that the regression model explains a significant share of demand variation—a suggestion that is supported by the F statistic. $F_{3,\,8} = 85.4$ and is far greater than 5, meaning that the hypothesis of no relation between sales and this group of independent X variables can be rejected with 99 percent confidence. There is less than a 1 percent chance of encountering such a large F statistic when in fact there is no relation between sales and these X variables as a group.

D. Fitted values and unexplained residuals per month are as follows:

Month	Units Sold	Price	Advertising Expenditures	Personal Selling Expenditures	Fitted Value for Units Sold	Unexplained Residuals
January	2,500	$3,800	$26,800	$43,000	2,566.88	−66.88
February	2,250	3,700	23,500	39,000	2,212.98	37.02
March	1,750	3,600	17,400	35,000	1,758.35	−8.35
April	1,500	3,500	15,300	34,000	1,646.24	−146.24
May	1,000	3,200	10,400	26,000	1,029.26	−29.26
June	2,500	3,200	18,400	41,000	2,310.16	189.84
July	2,750	3,200	28,200	40,000	2,596.51	153.49
August	1,750	3,000	17,400	33,000	1,803.83	−53.83
September	1,250	2,900	12,300	26,000	1,186.56	63.44
October	3,000	2,700	29,800	45,000	3,133.35	−133.35
November	2,000	2,700	20,300	32,000	1,930.90	69.10
December	2,000	2,600	19,800	34,000	2,074.97	−74.97
Average	2,020.83	$3,175.00	$19,966.67	$35,666.67	2,020.83	0.00

Problems

P6.1   **Demand Concepts.** Identify each of the following statements as true or false and explain why.
A. The effect of a $1 change in price is constant, but the elasticity of demand will vary along a linear demand curve.
B. In practice, price and quantity tend to be individually rather than simultaneously determined.
C. A demand curve is revealed if prices fall while supply conditions are held constant.
D. The effect of a $1 change in price will vary, but the elasticity of demand is constant along a log-linear demand curve.
E. Consumer interviews are a useful means for incorporating subjective information into demand estimation.

P6.2   **Regression Analysis.** Identify each of the following statements as true or false and explain why:
A. A parameter is a population characteristic that is estimated by a coefficient derived from a sample of data.
B. A one-tail t test is used to indicate whether the independent variables as a group explain a significant share of demand variation.

C. Given values for independent variables, the estimated demand relation can be used to derive a predicted value for demand.

D. A two-tail t test is an appropriate means for testing direction (positive or negative) of the influences of independent variables.

E. The coefficient of determination shows the share of total variation in demand that cannot be explained by the regression model.

P6.3   **Demand Curve Analysis.** Anathema Computers, Inc., is a leading supplier of high-quality IBM-compatible personal computers. Average price and annual unit sales data for the Model 486 high-speed laptop machine with a 120 Mb hard drive (data storage device) are as follows:

	1988	1989	1990	1991	1992
Price ($)	$9,000	$8,000	$6,000	$5,000	$3,000
Units sold	25,000	50,000	100,000	125,000	175,000

A. Complete the following table, and use these data to derive intercept and slope coefficients for the linear demand curve.

Year	Price	Quantity	ΔPrice	ΔQuantity	Slope = $\Delta P/\Delta Q$
1988	$9,000	25,000	—	—	—
1989	8,000	50,000			
1990	6,000	100,000			
1991	5,000	125,000			
1992	3,000	175,000			

B. Assuming that demand conditions are held constant, use the preceding data to plot a linear demand curve.

P6.4   **The Identification Problem.** Business is booming for Consulting Services, Inc. (CSI), a leading supplier of data processing consulting services. The company can profitably employ technicians as quickly as they can be trained. The average hourly rate billed by CSI for trained technician services and the number of billable hours (output) per quarter over the past six quarters are as follows:

	Q-1	Q-2	Q-3	Q-4	Q-5	Q-6
Hourly rate ($)	$20	$25	$30	$35	$40	$45
Billable hours	2,000	3,000	4,000	5,000	6,000	7,000

Quarterly demand and supply curves for CSI services are

$$Q_D = 4,000 - 200P + 2,000T \qquad \text{(Demand)},$$
$$Q_S = -2,000 + 200P \qquad \text{(Supply)},$$

where Q is output, P is price, T is a trend factor, and $T = 1$ during Q-1 and increases by one unit per quarter.

A. Express each demand and supply curve in terms of price as a function of output.

B. Plot the quarterly demand curves for the last six quarterly periods. (Hint: Let $T = 1$ to find the Y intercept for Q-1, $T = 2$ for Q-2, and so on.)

C. Plot the CSI supply curve on the same graph.

D. What is this problem's relation to the identification problem?

P6.5 **Demand Estimation.** Colorful Tile, Inc., is a rapidly growing chain of ceramic tile outlets that caters to the do-it-yourself home remodeling market. In 1992, 33 stores were operated in small to medium-size metropolitan markets. An in-house study of sales by these outlets revealed the following (standard errors in parentheses):

$$Q = 5 - 5P + 1.5A + 0.5I + 0.2HF$$
$$(3) \quad (1.8) \quad (0.7) \quad (0.2) \quad (0.1)$$
$$R^2 = 0.93, \text{ Standard Error of the Estimate } = 6.$$

Here, Q is tile sales (in thousands of cases), P is tile price (per case), A is advertising expenditures (in thousands of dollars), I is disposable income per household (in thousands of dollars), and HF is household formation (in hundreds).

A. Fully evaluate and interpret these empirical results on an overall basis.

B. Is quantity demanded sensitive to "own" price?

C. Austin, Texas, was a typical market covered by this analysis. During 1992 in the Austin market, price was $5, advertising was $40,000, income was an average $20,000 per household, and the number of household formations was 5,000. Calculate and interpret the relevant advertising point elasticity.

D. Assume that the preceding model and data are relevant for the coming period. Estimate the probability that the Austin store will make a profit during 1993 if total costs are projected to be $300,000.

P6.6 **Elasticity Estimation.** Getaway Tours, Inc., has estimated the following multiplicative demand function for packaged holiday tours in the East Lansing, Michigan, market using quarterly data covering the past four years (16 observations):

$$Q_y = 10P_y^{-1.10} P_x^{0.5} A_y^{3.8} A_x^{2.5} I^{1.85},$$
$$R^2 = 0.80, \quad \text{Standard Error of the Estimate} = 20.$$

Here, Q_y is the quantity of tours sold, P_y is average tour price, P_x is average price for some other good, A_y is tour advertising, A_x is advertising of some other good, and I is per capita disposable income. The standard errors of the exponents in the preceding multiplicative demand function are

$$b_{P_y} = 0.04, b_{P_x} = 0.35, b_{A_y} = 0.5, b_{A_x} = 0.9, \text{ and } b_I = 0.45.$$

A. Is tour demand elastic with respect to price?

B. Are tours a normal good?

C. Is X a complement good or a substitute good?

D. Given your answer to Part C, can you explain why the demand effects of A_y and A_x are both positive?

P6.7   **Correlation and Simple Regression.** Market Research, Inc., has conducted a survey to learn the car buying intentions of an $n = 15$ sample of service department customers. The survey asked each service department customer the age of the oldest automobile in their household and whether they intended to buy a new car during the next six months. Survey results were as follows:

Buy in Six Months (1 = Yes, 0 = No)	Age of Oldest Automobile in Household (in years)
0	1
1	5
0	3
0	1
0	2
1	3
1	2
1	6
1	4
0	2
0	3
1	5
0	1
0	3
1	5

A. Interpret the coefficient of correlation between the BUY and AGE variables of 0.727.

B. Interpret the following results for a simple regression over this sample where BUY is the dependent Y variable and AGE is the independent X variable:

The regression equation is

$$BUY = -0.242 + 0.231 \text{ AGE}.$$

Predictor	Coefficient	Standard Deviation	t Ratio	p
Constant	-0.2419	0.2087	-1.16	0.267
AGE	0.23105	0.06057	3.81	0.002

S.E.E. $= 0.3681$, $R^2 = 52.8\%$, $\bar{R}^2 = 49.2\%$, F statistic $= 14.55$ $(p = 0.002)$

P6.8   **Simple Regression.** Ninja Pizza, Inc., is a regional franchisor of home delivery pizza outlets. To better assess the effects of price, advertising, and income on pizza demand, the company recently compiled the following survey of monthly sales and operating data at 15 of the company's outlets in southern California:

Quantity Sold	Price	Advertising Expenditures per Month	Disposable Income per Household
42,100	$11.77	$46,100	$38,000
55,500	9.96	47,200	39,100
71,100	12.36	60,900	40,100
63,200	12.49	55,600	44,200
77,200	10.68	64,400	41,800
70,900	12.07	60,700	44,800
55,600	11.97	52,100	39,900
70,700	11.23	57,900	43,600
71,400	11.26	55,600	41,700
79,400	9.79	60,100	41,200
60,600	12.29	50,700	44,000
50,800	12.70	46,500	43,300
61,800	12.33	58,600	41,000
40,500	10.88	42,800	38,300
85,300	10.14	64,800	42,100

A. As a first step in their analysis, the company ran simple regressions of pizza demand on each of the three potentially important independent variables.

The first simple regression equation is

$$\text{QUANTITY} = 117763 - 4713 \text{ PRICE.}$$

Predictor	Coefficient	Standard Deviation	t Ratio	p
Constant	117763	40211	2.93	0.012
PRICE	−4713	3497	−1.35	0.201

S.E.E. = 12800, R^2 = 12.3%, $\bar{R}^2$ = 5.5%, F statistic = 1.82 (p = 0.201)

The second simple regression equation is

$$\text{QUANTITY} = -32655 + 1.75 \text{ ADVERTISING.}$$

Predictor	Coefficient	Standard Deviation	t Ratio	p
Constant	−32655	10305	−3.17	0.007
ADVERTISING	1.7548	0.1862	9.43	0.000

S.E.E. = 4883, R^2 = 87.2%, $\bar{R}^2$ = 86.3%, F statistic = 88.84 (p = 0.000)

The third simple regression equation is

$$\text{QUANTITY} = -58386 + 2.94 \text{ INCOME.}$$

Predictor	Coefficient	Standard Deviation	t Ratio	p
Constant	−58386	61403	−0.95	0.359
INCOME	2.940	1.476	1.99	0.068

S.E.E. = 11962, R^2 = 23.4%, $\bar{R}^2$ = 17.5%, F statistic = 3.97 (p = 0.068)

Based on these results, do any of the potentially important independent variables affect pizza demand?

B. What is the difference between each simple regression coefficient estimate and that which might be estimated using a multiple regression approach including all three independent variables?

P6.9   **Stepwise Regression.** As a second phase in the analysis of Ninja Pizza, Inc., survey data, the company wishes to study an experimental stepwise regression model of pizza demand. Stepwise regression model results for this sample of data are as follows (stepwise regression of quantity on three predictors, with $N = 15$):

STEP	1	2	3
CONSTANT	− 32655.0	817.6	− 33301.7
ADVERTISING	1.75	1.69	1.45
t RATIO	9.43	10.19	9.59
PRICE		− 2618	− 4042
t RATIO		− 2.20	− 3.88
INCOME			1.53
t RATIO			2.98
S.E.E.	4883	4290	3333
R^2	87.23	90.90	94.97

A. Provide a brief evaluation of estimation results for each step in the stepwise regression model.

B. Do the Step 3 estimation results differ from those obtained from a multiple regression of demand on all three independent variables?

P6.10 **Multiple Regression.** In the third phase of the Ninja Pizza, Inc., survey data analysis, the company wishes to study a multiple regression model of pizza demand. The company feels it is quite likely that the marginal influence of advertising depends upon the average price charged and income levels in the market area. Similarly, the effects of these two latter independent variables are thought to depend upon the level of advertising. Therefore, a multiplicative demand model has been estimated in log-linear form as follows.

The multiplicative regression model estimated in log-linear form is

$$\text{LOG}_e\, Q = - 13.6 - 0.670\, \text{LOG}_e\, P + 1.29\, \text{LOG}_e\, AD + 1.15\, \text{LOG}_e\, Y.$$

Predictor	Coefficient	Standard Deviation	t Ratio	p
Constant	− 13.637	3.230	− 4.22	0.001
$\text{LOG}_e\, P$	− 0.6702	0.2002	− 3.35	0.007
$\text{LOG}_e\, AD$	1.2944	0.1424	9.09	0.000
$\text{LOG}_e\, Y$	1.1467	0.3721	3.08	0.010

S.E.E. $= 0.05795$, $R^2 = 94.6\%$, $\bar{R}^2 = 93.1\%$, F statistic $= 63.86$ ($p = 0.000$)

A. Interpret the coefficient estimate for each respective independent variable.

B. Characterize the overall explanatory power of this log-linear regression model with that for the Step 3 multiple regression model described in P6.9.

CASE STUDY FOR CHAPTER 6
Demand Estimation for Branded Consumer Products

Demand estimation for brand-name consumer products is made difficult by the fact that managers must rely on proprietary data. There simply isn't any publicly available data that can be used to estimate demand elasticities for brand-name orange juice, frozen entrèes, pies, and the like—and with good reason. Competitors would be delighted to know profit margins across a broad array of competing products so that advertising, pricing policy, and product development strategy could all be targeted for maximum benefit. Product demand information is valuable, and jealously guarded.

To see the process that might be undertaken to develop a better understanding of product demand conditions, consider the example of Mrs. Smyth's Inc., a Chicago-based food company. In early 1993, Mrs. Smyth's initiated an empirical estimation of demand for its deluxe frozen fruit pies. The firm is formulating pricing and promotional plans for the coming year, and management is interested in learning how pricing and promotional decisions might affect sales. Mrs. Smyth's has been marketing frozen fruit pies for several years, and its market research department has collected quarterly data over two years for six important marketing areas, including sales quantity, the retail price charged for the pies, local advertising and promotional expenditures, and the price charged by a major competing brand of frozen pies. Statistical data published by *Sales Management* magazine on population and disposable income in each of the six market areas were also available for analysis. It was therefore possible to include a wide range of hypothesized demand determinants in an empirical estimation of fruit pie demand. These data appear in Table 6.3.

The following regression equation was fit to these data:

$$Q_{it} = b_0 + b_1 P_{it} + b_2 A_{it} + b_3 PX_{it} + b_4 Y_{it} + b_5 Pop_{it} + b_6 T_{it} + u_{it}.$$

Q is the quantity of pies sold during the tth quarter; P is the retail price in cents of Mrs. Smyth's frozen pies; A represents the dollars (in thousands) spent for advertising and promotional activities; PX is the price, measured in cents, charged for competing pies; Y is thousands of dollars of disposable income per household; Pop is the population of the market area (in thousands of persons); and T is the trend factor (1991–1 = 1, . . . , 1992–4 = 8). The subscript i indicates the regional market from which the observation was taken, whereas the subscript t represents the quarter during which the observation occurred. Least squares estimation of the regression equation on the basis of the 48 data observations (eight quarters of data for each of six areas) resulted in the estimated regression coefficients and other statistics given in Table 6.4.

T A B L E   6 . 3   **Mrs. Smyth's Frozen Fruit Pie Regional Market Demand Data, 1991–1 to 1992–4**

	Year-Quarter	Unit Sales (Q)	Price (cents)	Advertising Expenditure ($000)	Competitors' Price (cents)	Income (000)	Population (000)	Time Variable (T)
Atlanta, GA	1992–4	27,500	550	$10.0	375	$41.5	2,650	8
	1992–3	25,000	600	7.5	375	40.5	2,500	7
	1992–2	25,000	575	10.0	375	40.0	2,450	6
	1992–1	25,000	575	5.0	400	39.5	2,350	5
	1991–4	27,500	525	10.0	400	39.5	2,300	4
	1991–3	22,500	500	7.5	325	39.0	2,250	3
	1991–2	25,000	525	7.5	375	39.5	2,150	2
	1991–1	22,500	600	5.0	425	39.5	2,150	1
Baltimore, MD	1992–4	27,500	600	5.0	425	40.0	2,300	8
	1992–3	25,000	600	5.0	400	39.5	2,300	7
	1992–2	27,500	525	10.0	425	39.5	2,250	6
	1991–1	25,000	550	5.0	400	39.0	2,200	5
	1991–4	22,500	600	5.0	400	39.0	2,250	4
	1991–3	22,500	550	5.0	375	39.0	2,200	3
	1991–2	22,500	625	5.0	400	39.0	2,200	2
	1991–1	22,500	600	7.5	400	38.5	2,150	1
Chicago, IL	1992–4	32,500	600	5.0	400	46.0	6,200	8
	1992–3	32,500	550	15.0	375	45.5	6,150	7
	1992–2	27,500	600	5.0	375	45.0	6,100	6
	1992–1	22,500	600	10.0	350	44.5	6,150	5
	1991–4	30,000	550	5.0	375	45.0	6,200	4
	1991–3	30,000	575	15.0	350	44.5	6,250	3
	1991–2	25,000	600	5.0	450	44.5	6,100	2
	1991–1	27,500	575	5.0	375	44.0	6,050	1
Denver, CO	1992–4	35,000	500	15.0	400	47.5	1,600	8
	1992–3	32,500	575	10.0	400	47.0	1,650	7
	1992–2	32,500	550	7.5	425	47.0	1,600	6
	1992–1	30,000	600	12.5	400	46.5	1,550	5
	1991–4	27,500	550	5.0	350	46.0	1,550	4
	1991–3	25,000	600	5.0	325	46.5	1,500	3
	1991–2	27,500	575	10.0	350	47.0	1,450	2
	1991–1	30,000	550	10.0	425	46.5	1,450	1
Erie, PA	1992–4	17,500	600	2.5	375	35.5	300	8
	1992–3	17,500	625	2.5	375	35.0	290	7
	1992–2	15,000	600	5.0	375	34.5	285	6
	1992–1	17,500	575	2.5	350	34.5	270	5
	1991–4	15,000	625	2.5	325	34.0	265	4
	1991–3	17,500	575	2.5	375	34.0	270	3
	1991–2	15,000	575	5.0	350	34.0	275	2
	1991–1	17,500	575	2.5	400	34.0	280	1
Fort Lauderdale, FL	1992–4	27,500	625	5.0	400	46.0	1,500	8
	1992–3	27,500	625	12.5	350	46.0	1,450	7
	1992–2	27,500	625	5.0	450	45.0	1,300	6
	1992–1	25,000	625	5.0	375	44.5	1,450	5
	1991–4	30,000	550	7.5	425	44.5	1,350	4
	1991–3	30,000	575	12.5	425	44.0	1,100	3
	1991–2	27,500	600	12.5	400	43.5	1,050	2
	1991–1	25,000	575	10.0	400	43.5	1,025	1

TABLE 6.4 **Estimated Demand Function for Mrs. Smyth's Frozen Fruit Pies**

Variable (1)	Coefficient (2)	Standard Error of Coefficient (3)	t-Statistic (4) = (2) ÷ (3)
Intercept	−4,516.291	4,988.242	−0.91
Price (*P*)	−35.985	7.019	5.13
Advertising (*A*)	203.713	77.292	2.64
Competitor price (*PX*)	37.960	7.065	5.37
Income (*Y*)	777.051	66.423	11.70
Population (*Pop*)	0.256	0.125	2.04
Time (*T*)	356.047	92.288	3.86

Coefficient of determination $= R^2 = 0.93$
Standard error of estimate $= S.E.E. = 1,442$

The individual coefficients for the Mrs. Smyth's pie demand regression equation can be interpreted as follows. The intercept term, −4,516.291, has no economic meaning in this instance; it lies far outside the range of observed data and obviously cannot be interpreted as the demand for Mrs. Smyth's frozen fruit pies when all the independent variables take on zero values. The coefficient for each independent variable indicates the marginal relationship between that variable and sales of pies, holding constant the effect of all the other variables in the demand function. For example, the −35.985 coefficient for *P,* the price charged for Mrs. Smyth's pies, indicates that when the effects of all other demand variables are held constant, each 1¢ increase in price causes quarterly sales to decline by roughly 36 pies. Similarly, the 203.713 coefficient for *A,* the advertising and promotion variable, indicates that for each $1,000 (one-unit) increase in advertising during the quarter, roughly 204 additional pies are sold. The 37.960 coefficient for the competitor-price variable indicates that demand for Mrs. Smyth's pies rises by roughly 38 pies with every 1¢ increase in competitor prices. The 777.051 coefficient for the *Y* variable indicates that, on average, a $1,000 (one-unit) increase in the average disposable income per household for a given market leads to roughly a 777-unit increase in quarterly pie demand. Similarly, a 1,000 person (one-unit) increase in the population of a given market area leads to a small 0.256-unit increase in quarterly pie demand. Finally, the 356.047 coefficient for the trend variable indicates that pie demand is growing in a typical market by roughly 356 units per quarter. This means that Mrs. Smyth's is enjoying secular growth in pie demand, perhaps as a result of the growing popularity of Mrs. Smyth's products or of frozen foods in general.

Individual coefficients provide useful estimates of the expected marginal influence on demand following a one-unit change in each respective variable. However, they are only estimates. For example, it would be very unusual for a 1¢ increase in price to cause exactly a −35.985-unit change in the quantity demanded. The actual effect could be more or less. For decision-making purposes, it would be helpful to know if the marginal influences suggested by the regression model are stable or instead tend to vary widely over the sample analyzed.

In general, if it is known with certainty that $Y = a + bX$, then a one-unit change in X will always lead to a b-unit change in Y. If $b > 0$, X and Y will be directly related; if $b < 0$, X and Y will be inversely related. If no relation at all holds between X and Y, then $b = 0$. Although the true parameter b is unobservable, its value is estimated by the regression coefficient $\hat{b}$. If $\hat{b} = 10$, a 1-unit change in X will increase Y by 10 units. This effect may appear to be large but it will be statistically significant only if it is stable over the entire sample. To be statistically reliable, $\hat{b}$ must be large relative to its degree of variation over the sample.

In a regression equation, there is a 68-percent probability that b lies in the interval $\hat{b} \pm$ one standard error (or standard deviation) of the coefficient $\hat{b}$. There is a 95-percent probability that b lies in the interval $\hat{b} \pm$ two standard errors of the coefficient. There is a 99-percent probability that b is in the interval $\hat{b} \pm$ three standard errors of the coefficient. When a coefficient is at least twice as large as its standard error, one can reject at the 95-percent confidence level the hypothesis that the true parameter b equals zero. This leaves only a 5-percent chance of concluding incorrectly that $b \neq 0$ when in fact $b = 0$. When a coefficient is at least three times as large as its standard error (standard deviation), the confidence level rises to 99 percent and chance of error falls to 1 percent.

A significant relation between X and Y is typically indicated whenever a coefficient is at least twice as large as its standard error; significance is even more likely when a coefficient is at least three times as large as its standard error. The independent effect of each independent variable on sales is measured using a two-tail t-statistic where:

$$t\text{-statistic} = \frac{\hat{b}}{\text{Standard error of } \hat{b}}.$$

This t-statistic is a measure of the number of standard errors between $\hat{b}$ and a hypothesized value of zero. If the sample used to estimate the regression parameters is large (for example, $n > 30$), the t-statistic follows a normal distribution and properties of a normal distribution, can be used to make confidence statements concerning the statistical significance of $\hat{b}$. Hence $t = 1$ implies 68-percent confidence, $t = 2$ implies 95-percent confidence, $t = 3$ implies 99-percent confidence, and so on. For small sample sizes (for example, $d.f. = n - k < 30$), the t-distribution deviates from a normal distribution, and a t-table should be used for testing the significance of estimated regression parameters.

Another regression statistic, the standard error of the estimate *(S.E.E.)*, is used to predict values for the dependent variable given values for the various independent variables. Thus, it is helpful in determining a range within which one can predict values for the dependent variable with varying degrees of statistical confidence. Although the best estimate of the value for the dependent variable is $\hat{Y}$, the value predicted by the regression equation, the standard error of the estimate can be used to determine just how accurate this prediction $\hat{Y}$ is likely to be. Assuming that the standard errors are normally distributed about the regression equation, there is a 68-percent probability that actual observations of the dependent variable Y will lie within the range $\hat{Y} \pm$ one standard error of the estimate. The probability that an actual observation of Y will lie within two standard errors of its predicted value increases to 95 percent. There is a 99-percent chance that an actual observed value for Y will lie in the range $\hat{Y} \pm$ three standard errors. Obviously, greater predictive accuracy is associated with smaller standard errors of the estimate.

Mrs. Smyth's could forecast the total demand for its pies by forecasting sales in each of the six market areas, then summing these area forecasts to obtain an estimate of total pie demand. Using the results from the demand estimation model and data from each individual market, it would also be possible to construct a confidence interval for total pie demand based on the standard error of the estimate.

A. Describe the statistical significance of each individual independent variable included in the Mrs. Smyth's frozen fruit pie demand equation.
B. Interpret the coefficient of determination (R^2) for the Mrs. Smyth's frozen fruit pie demand equation.
C. What is the expected value of next quarter's unit sales in the Baltimore market?
D. To illustrate use of the standard error of the estimate statistic, derive the 95-percent confidence interval for next quarter's actual unit sales in the Baltimore market.

Selected References

Cole, Rosanne. "Reviving the Federal Statistical System: A View from Industry." *American Economic Review* 80 (May 1990): 333–336.

Corfman, Kim P. "Perceptions of Relative Influence: Formation and Measurement." *Journal of Marketing Research* 28 (May 1991): 125–136.

DeJong, Douglas V., and Robert Forsythe. "A Perspective on the Use of Laboratory Market Experimentation in Auditing Research." *Accounting Review* 67 (January 1992): 157–170.

Friedman, Milton, and Anna J. Schwartz. "Alternative Approaches to Analyzing Economic Data." *American Economic Review* 8 (March 1991): 39–49.

Heide, Jan B., and George John. "Do Norms Matter in Marketing Relationships?" *Journal of Marketing* 56 (April 1992): 32–44.

Herzel, Leo. "Corporate Governance Through Statistical Eyes." *Journal of Financial Economics* 27 (October 1990): 581–593.

Homburg, Christian. "Cross-Validation and Information Criteria in Causal Modeling." *Journal of Marketing Research* 28 (May 1991): 137–144.

Lastovicka, John L., and Kanachana Thamodaran. "Common Factor Score Estimates in Multiple Regression Problems." *Journal of Marketing Research* 28 (February 1991): 105–112.

Leftwich, Richard. "Aggregation of Test Statistics: Statistics vs. Economics." *Journal of Accounting & Economics* 12 (January 1990): 37–44.

Mason, Charlotte H., and William D. Perreault, Jr. "Collinearity, Power, and Interpretation of Multiple Regression Analysis." *Journal of Marketing Research* 28 (August 1991): 268–280.

Mazis, Michael B., Debra Jones Ringold, Elgin S. Perry, and Daniel W. Denman. "Perceived Age and Attractiveness of Models in Cigarette Advertisements." *Journal of Marketing* 56 (January 1992): 22–37.

Mirowski, Philip. "The When, the How and the Why of Mathematical Expression in the History of Economic Analysis." *Journal of Economic Perspectives* 5 (Winter 1991): 145–157.

Neuberger, Hugh, and Houston H. Stokes. "Testing the Appropriateness of Statistical Methods." *Financial Analysts Journal* 47 (July-August 1991): 83–88.

Norwood, Janet. "Data Quality and Public Policy." *Journal of Economic Perspectives* 4 (Spring 1990): 3–12.

O'Callaghan, Ramon, Patrick J. Kaufmann, and Benn R. Konsynski. "Adoption Correlates and Share Effects of Electronic Data Interchange Systems in Marketing Channels." *Journal of Marketing* 56 (April 1992): 45–56.

FORECASTING

Success in business depends on management's ability to develop and execute a long-range strategic plan that takes advantage of the organization's comparative strength. This planning process involves a number of important related activities. Management must decide the range of products that the firm will offer its customers. This involves a careful investigation of various alternatives to determine the product and geographic markets in which the firm can earn the highest returns. Management must then forecast the level of demand in these markets under assorted conditions. Typically, the effects of pricing policy, promotional activity, competition, and general economic conditions must all be considered. In addition to compiling a range of demand forecasts, management must also forecast costs of producing different levels of output in light of changing technology, wage rates, and raw materials prices. Once management has successfully integrated demand and cost forecasts, it becomes necessary to decide on the optimal operating plan. In other words, after all relevant data have been collected and analyzed, managers must pick and choose from among a range of reasonable decision scenarios to select the value-maximizing operating plan. Finally, management must acquire capital resources, hire and train workers, obtain raw materials, and so on to implement the value-maximizing operating plan.

Once the optimal operating plan has been determined, it must be carried out in the control phase. Planning and control are closely related. In practice, they are often inseparable. Operating procedures that are monitored during the control process must be carefully geared to the firm's plans. If forecasts about demand, the cost of inputs, technology, and other planning considerations are seriously in error, the plan will be of little practical use. In instances in which forecast errors have the potential to adversely affect the realization of planning objectives, the control phase of the planning process must be flexible enough to allow for necessary changes and modifications. At the same time, the planning and control process must be sufficiently structured to allow for a methodical realization of firm objectives.

The theory and practice of forecasting merits careful consideration in managerial economics because it makes an essential contribution to the planning and control function of management. This chapter describes and illustrates a number of important forecasting techniques that have proved to be successful in a wide variety of real-world applications.

FORECASTING METHODS

Several techniques are available for forecasting economic variables. They range from simple forecasting methods that are somewhat naive and relatively inexpensive to approaches that are quite complex and very expensive. Some forecasting techniques are basically quantitative; others are largely qualitative.

Common Forecasting Techniques

In general, the most commonly applied forecasting techniques can be divided into the following broad categories:

- Qualitative analyses
- Trend analysis and projection
- Econometric methods
- Input-output analysis

It is impossible to argue that any one of these forecasting approaches is inherently superior to the others. Each method has its strengths and weaknesses. The best forecast methodology for a particular task depends on the nature of a specific forecasting problem. When making a choice among forecast methodologies, a number of important factors must be considered. It is always worth considering the distance into the future that one must forecast, the lead time available for making decisions, the level of accuracy required, the quality of data available for analysis, the stochastic or deterministic nature of forecast relations, and the cost and benefits associated with the forecasting problem.

Techniques such as trend analysis, market experiments, consumer surveys, and the leading indicator approach to forecasting are well suited for short-term projections. Forecasting with complex econometric models and systems of simultaneous equations have proven somewhat more useful for long-run forecasting. Within each class of forecasting technique, the level of sophistication also varies. Typically, the greater the level of sophistication, the higher the cost. If the required level of accuracy is low, less sophisticated methods can provide adequate results at minimal cost.

Choice of Forecasting Method

The choice of an appropriate forecasting methodology depends on both the underlying characteristics of the forecasting problem and the level of accuracy required. In all instances, the most sophisticated forecast methodology to employ is that which provides sufficiently accurate results at minimum cost. No one flies a jet to the grocery store—similarly, no manager would find costly and difficult methods appropriate for solving trivial forecasting problems.

To determine a suitable level of forecast accuracy, one must compare the costs and benefits of increased accuracy. When forecast accuracy is low, the probability of significant forecasting error is high, as is the chance of making suboptimal managerial decisions. Conversely, when forecast accuracy is high, the probability of substantial forecasting error is reduced and the chance of making erroneous managerial decisions is low. It is reasonable to require a relatively high level of forecast accuracy when the costs of forecast error are high. When only minor costs result from forecast error, only inexpensive and typically less precise methods can be justified.

The material that follows examines the advantages and limitations of various forecasting techniques. By understanding the strengths and weaknesses of such methodologies, managers can select the appropriate method to generate required forecast values. In many instances, especially when difficult forecasting problems are being addressed, managers find it helpful to employ multiple forecasting approaches. When a variety of forecast techniques yields highly comparable results, managers can be confident of a high degree of forecast accuracy. When different methods yield widely divergent forecast results, managers must be cautious in their interpretation and use of forecast information.

QUALITATIVE ANALYSES

Qualitative analysis
An intuitive judgmental approach to forecasting based on opinion.

Qualitative analysis, an intuitive judgmental approach to forecasting, can be a highly useful technique if it allows for the systematic collection and organization of data derived from unbiased, informed opinion. However, qualitative methods can produce biased results when specific individuals dominate the forecasting process through reputation, force of personality, or strategic position within the organization.

Expert Opinion

Personal insight
Forecast method based on personal or organizational experience.

Panel consensus
Forecast method based on the informed opinion of several individuals.

Delphi method
Method that uses forecasts derived from an independent analysis of expert opinion.

The most basic form of qualitative analysis used in forecasting is **personal insight** in which an informed individual uses personal or organizational experience as a basis for developing future expectations. Although this approach is highly subjective, the reasoned judgment of informed individuals often provides valuable insight. When the informed opinion of several individuals is relied on, the approach is called forecasting through **panel consensus.** The panel consensus method assumes that several experts can arrive at forecasts that are superior to those that individuals generate. Direct interaction among experts is used in the panel consensus method with the hope that resulting forecasts embody all available objective and subjective information.

Although the panel consensus method often results in forecasts that embody the collective wisdom of consulted experts, it can sometimes be unfavorably affected by the forceful personality of one or a few key individuals. A related approach, the **delphi method,** has been developed to counter this disadvantage. In the delphi method, members of a panel of experts individually receive a series of questions relating to the underlying forecasting problem. Responses are analyzed by an independent party, who then tries to elicit a consensus opinion by providing feedback to panel members in a manner that prevents direct identification of individual positions. This method helps limit the steamroller or bandwagon problems of the basic panel consensus approach.

Survey Techniques

Survey techniques
An interview or mailed questionnaire approach to forecasting.

Survey techniques that skillfully employ interviews or mailed questionnaires constitute another important forecasting tool, especially for short-term projection. Designing surveys that provide unbiased and reliable information is a challenging task. When properly carried out, however, survey research can provide managers with valuable information that would otherwise be unobtainable.

Surveys generally use interviews or mailed questionnaires asking business firms, government agencies, and individuals about their future plans. Business firms plan and budget virtually all their expenditures in advance of actual purchases or production. Surveys asking about capital budgets, sales budgets, and operating budgets can thus provide much useful information for forecasting. Government departments also prepare formal budgets well before the actual spending is done, and surveys of budget material, congressional appropriations hearings, and the like can provide a wealth of information to the forecaster. Finally, even individual consumers routinely plan expenditures for such major items as automobiles, furniture, housing, vacations, and education well ahead of the purchase date, so surveys of consumer intentions often accurately predict future spending on consumer goods.

Survey information may be all that is obtainable in certain forecasting situations, as, for example, when a firm is attempting to project the demand for a new product. Although surveys sometimes serve as an alternative to quantitative forecasting techniques, they frequently supplement rather than replace quantitative analysis. Their value stems from two influences. First, a nonquantifiable psychological element is inherent in most economic behavior; surveys and other qualitative methods are especially well suited to picking up on this phenomenon. Second, quantitative models generally assume stable consumer tastes. If these tastes are actually changing, survey data can suggest the nature and direction of such changes.

Common Sources of Survey Information

Surveys useful for forecasting business activity in various sectors of the U.S. economy are published periodically by both private and government sources. Some of the most widely utilized are those employed to forecast plant and equipment expenditures. Surveys of business intentions to expand plant and equipment are conducted by the U.S. Department of Commerce, the Securities and Exchange Commission, the National Industrial Conference Board, and McGraw-Hill, Inc., among others. Several trade associations also publish expenditure surveys for specific industries. For example, the Edison Electric Institute and the American Gas Association publish information that is widely employed in forecasting capacity utilization and investment expenditure plans for the energy sector. Changes in inventories and sales revenue expectations are published by the U.S. Department of Commerce and private organizations such as McGraw-Hill, Dun and Bradstreet, and the National Association of Purchasing Agents. These surveys, although not nearly as accurate as those for long-term investment, provide a useful check on other forecasting methods. Consumer intentions surveys of the Census Bureau, the University of Michigan Research Center, and the Sindlinger-National Industrial Conference Board all provide information on planned purchases of specific products, such as automobiles, housing, and appliances. In addition, these surveys often indicate consumer confidence in the economy and, therefore, spending expectations in general.

Some of the most readily available survey information is that published regularly in leading business newspapers and magazines. For example, *Barron's* is a national business and financial weekly that offers a wide range of useful survey

MANAGERIAL APPLICATION 7.1
How Reliable Are Government Statistics?

"Excess confidence in government statistics can be damaging to the health of your business" is the warning sounded by some economists. Economists are especially critical of the consumer price index, or CPI, as it is known to the general public. One reason economists are so critical is that the CPI, compiled by the Labor Department's Bureau of Labor Statistics (BLS), didn't behave as expected during economic recession of the early 1990s. Economic theory suggests that the inflation rate should slow during a recession given the fall-off in consumer and industrial demand. Nevertheless, the "core" rate of inflation continued to rise during this period at a relatively high annual rate of 5.5 percent, confounding business economists in the process.

To better understand the strengths and weaknesses of the CPI it is important to recognize the daunting task presented by the need to accurately measure price changes. Collecting data for 95,000 items may seem overwhelming, and the myriad of details involved with discovering the rate of change in prices is indeed breathtaking. The BLS surveys consumers every year on what they buy and every four years on where they buy it. Based on this survey information, the BLS sends 350 data collectors to visit the nation's shopping malls, hospitals, and other suppliers of consumer goods and services to compare price changes from month to month. On any given day, a BLS worker can gather 30 to 70 different prices.

For example, a display of limes might say "3 for 99¢," the same price as charged in the previous month. Although this suggests an absence of inflation, this is not necessarily the case. The BLS always weighs products that are sold on a per unit basis to see if they're smaller or larger than comparable products sold in previous months. In the case of fruits, three limes might now weigh 5 ounces, compared with the previous month when they tipped the scales at 8 ounces. Instead of no price change, the cost of limes per ounce has skyrocketed by 60 percent.

This lime pricing example shows a major shortcoming of the CPI: it is a fixed-weight index. Each item carries the same importance from month to month, and none can be substituted for another cheaper product in the survey. Because items cannot be switched, the CPI misses an important way that consumers deal with inflation: They simply don't buy a product that becomes too expensive. While the BLS only checks the price of Macintosh apples, a consumer might buy the Golden Delicious variety if it's cheaper. The CPI's rigid product mix is one reason why the GDP price deflator used for consumer spending—which captures substitution— can differ markedly from the CPI.

Another criticism of the CPI is the use of list prices. By haggling or offering to pay cash instead of using a credit card, shoppers often get discounts from list prices, and detractors say that the CPI misses this. The BLS also fails to adjust the changes in prices that come from improvements in the quality of services, especially medical care, one of the fastest-growing components of the CPI. In the services sector, no part of the CPI has come under as much fire as the housing component. This is especially true of the segment called homeowners' equivalent rent, which accounts for roughly 20 percent of the total index. The BLS measures the change in homeowner's costs by estimating how much a homeowner would pay to lease a home. Field operators call renters to find out what this month's rent is. The reported rent from leased housing is then used to determine what rent an owner would pay for his or her home. However, because most leases are set once a year, only a small proportion of rents are adjusted in any given month. This means it sometimes takes several months for changes in the housing market to show up in BLS numbers.

Given the difficulties encountered in accurately measuring price changes, some economists argue that if government statistics don't match theoretical projections, perhaps the theory is right but the numbers themselves are wrong!

Source: Maggie Mahar, "Numbers Game: A Census Bureau Wage Report Takes Five Months to Surface," *Barron's,* May 18, 1992, 16–17.

information. *Barron's* weekly market survey of economic indicators shows rates of change in the overall level of economic activity as indicated by gross domestic product (GDP), durable and nondurable manufacturing, factory utilization, and other statistics. Also provided are more specific data on the level of production in a wide range of basic industries such as autos, electric power, paper, petroleum, and steel, among others. Data published weekly in *Barron's* include not only the level of production (what is made), but also distribution (what is sold), inventories (what is on hand), new orders received, unfilled orders, purchasing power, employment, and construction activity. *Forbes* magazine publishes its own biweekly index of economic activity using government data on consumer prices, manufacturer's new orders and inventories, industrial production, new housing starts, personal income, new unemployment claims, retail sales, and consumer installment credit. To measure these eight elements of the *Forbes Index,* ten series of U.S. government data are monitored over a 14-month period. *Fortune* and *Business Week* magazines also offer interesting regular coverage and analysis of data on current and projected levels of economic activity. For instance, the quarterly *Fortune Forecast* of economic activity is based on a proprietary econometric model developed by the company's own staff economists. At a minimum, the forecast data and analysis published in these leading business newspapers and magazines provides managers with a useful starting point in the development of their own future expectations. Managers of large and small organizations will find both the data and the analysis provided to be most helpful in developing the background of information necessary for successful forecasting.

TREND ANALYSIS AND PROJECTION

Trend analysis

Forecasting the future path of economic variables based on historical patterns.

Trend analysis is based on the assumption that economic performance follows an established pattern and, therefore, that historical data can be used to predict future business activity. Trend analysis techniques involve characterizing the historical pattern of an economic variable and then projecting or forecasting its future path based on past experience.

The many variations of forecasting by trend projection are all predicated on a continuation of the past relation between the variable being projected and the passage of time, so all of them employ time series data. As described in Chapter 6, an economic time series is a sequential array of data on the value of an economic variable. Weekly, monthly, or annual series of data on sales and costs, personal income, population, labor force participation rates, and GNP are all examples of economic time series.

Trends in Economic Data

Secular trend

Long-run pattern of increase or decrease.

All time series, regardless of the nature of the economic variable involved, can be described in terms of a few important underlying characteristics. A **secular trend** is the long-run pattern of increase or decrease in a series of economic data. **Cyclical fluctuation** describes the rhythmic variation in economic series that is due to a pattern of expansion or contraction in the overall economy. **Seasonal variation** is a rhythmic annual pattern in sales or profits caused by weather, habit, or social custom. **Irregular or random influences** are unpredictable shocks to

FIGURE 7.1 **Time Series Characteristics: (a) Secular Trend and Cyclical Variation in Women's Clothing Sales; (b) Seasonal Pattern and Random Fluctuations**

(a) The cyclical pattern in sales varies significantly from the normal secular trend. (b) Seasonal patterns, random fluctuations, and other influences cause deviations around the cyclical pattern of sales.

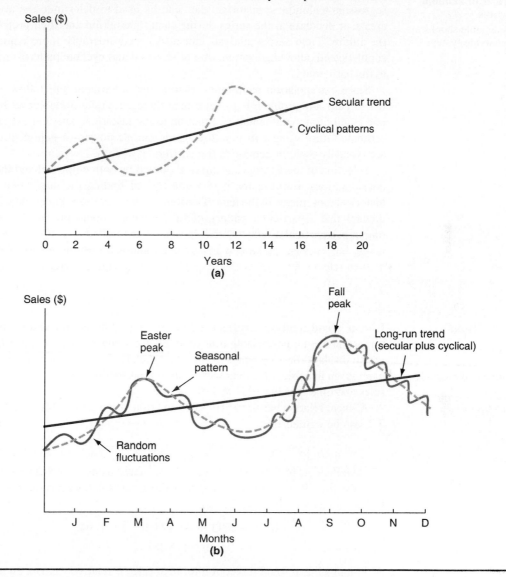

Cyclical fluctuation

Rhythmic fluctuation in an economic series due to expansion or contraction in the overall economy.

the economic system and the pace of economic activity caused by wars, strikes, natural catastrophes, and so on.

These four patterns are illustrated in Figure 7.1. Figure 7.1(a) shows secular and cyclical trends in sales of women's clothing. Figure 7.1(b) shows a seasonal pattern superimposed over the long-run trend (which, in this case, is a composite

Seasonal variation

Rhythmic annual patterns in sales or profits.

Irregular or random influences

Unpredictable shocks to the economic system.

of the secular and cyclical trends) and random fluctuations around the seasonal curve.

Time series analysis can be as simple as projecting or extrapolating the unadjusted trend. When one applies either simple graphic analysis or least squares regression techniques, historical data can be used to determine the average increase or decrease in the series during each time period and then projected into the future. Time series analysis can also be considerably more complex and sophisticated, allowing examination of seasonal and cyclical patterns in addition to the basic trend.

Since extrapolation techniques assume that a variable will follow an established path, the problem is to determine the appropriate trend curve. In theory, one could fit any mathematical function to the historical data and extrapolate to estimate future values. In practice, linear, simple power, or exponential curves are typically used for economic forecasting.

Selection of the appropriate curve is guided by both empirical and theoretical considerations. Empirically, it is a question of finding the curve that best fits historical movements in the data. Theoretical considerations intervene when logic dictates that a particular pattern of future events should prevail. For example, output in a particular industry may have been expanding at a constant rate historically, but because of known resource limitations, one might use a declining growth-rate model to reflect the expected slowdown in growth.

Linear Trend Analysis

Linear trend analysis

Assumes constant *unit* change over time.

Linear trend analysis assumes a constant period-by-period *unit* change in an important economic variable over time. Such a trend is illustrated in Figure 7.2, which displays the 15 years of actual sales data for The American Express Company given in Table 7.1, along with a curve representing a linear relation between sales and time over the 1977 to 1991 period.

A linear relation between firm sales and time, such as that illustrated in Figure 7.2, can be written as

$$S_t = a + b \times t. \tag{7.1}$$

The coefficients of this equation can be estimated using American Express sales data for the 1977 to 1991 period and the least squares regression method as follows (*t* statistics in parentheses):

$$S_t = -\$982 + \$1,773.4t \quad \bar{R}^2 = 94.5\% \tag{7.2}$$
$$(-0.94) \quad (15.48)$$

Although a linear trend projection for firm sales is relatively naive, an important trend element is obvious in American Express sales data. Using the linear trend equation estimated over the 1977 to 1991 period, it is possible to forecast firm sales for future time periods. To do so, it is important to realize that in this model, $t = 1$ for 1977, $t = 2$ for 1978, and so on. This means that $t = 0$ in the 1976 base period. To forecast sales in any future period, simply subtract 1976 from the year in question to determine a relevant value for t.

FIGURE 7.2 **The American Express Company Sales Revenue, 1977–91**

Sales data points lie in a pattern around the fitted regression line, indicating that the slope of the sales/time line may not be constant.

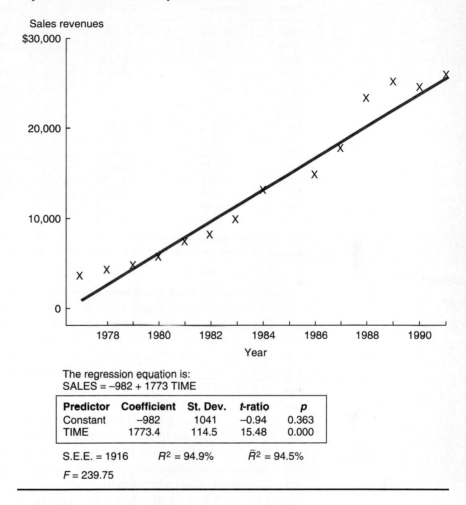

The regression equation is:
SALES = −982 + 1773 TIME

Predictor	Coefficient	St. Dev.	*t*-ratio	*p*
Constant	−982	1041	−0.94	0.363
TIME	1773.4	114.5	15.48	0.000

S.E.E. = 1916 R^2 = 94.9% $\bar{R}^2$ = 94.5%

F = 239.75

For example, a sales forecast for 1995 using Equation 7.2 is

$$t = 1995 - 1976 = 19$$
$$S_{1995} = -\$982 + \$1,773.4(19)$$
$$= \$32,712.6 \text{ million.}$$

Similarly, a sales forecast for American Express in the year 2000 is

$$t = 2000 - 1976 = 24$$
$$S_{2000} = -\$982 + \$1,773.4(24)$$
$$= \$41,579.6 \text{ million.}$$

TABLE 7.1   **The American Express Company Sales Revenue, 1977–91**

Year	Sales Revenue ($ millions)	Natural Logarithm of Sales Revenue (base *e*)	Common Logarithm of Sales Revenue (base 10)	Time Period (years)
1991	$25,763	10.1567	4.4110	15
1990	24,332	10.0995	4.3862	14
1989	25,047	10.1285	4.3988	13
1988	23,132	10.0490	4.3642	12
1987	17,626	9.7771	4.2462	11
1986	14,652	9.5923	4.1659	10
1985	11,850	9.3801	4.0737	9
1984	12,895	9.4646	4.1104	8
1983	9,770	9.1871	3.9899	7
1982	8,093	8.9988	3.9081	6
1981	7,210	8.8832	3.8579	5
1980	5,505	8.6134	3.7408	4
1979	4,666	8.4481	3.6689	3
1978	4,086	8.3153	3.6113	2
1977	3,447	8.1453	3.5374	1

Source: The Value Line Investment Survey, March 13, 1992, p. 2051.

Note that these sales projections are based on a linear trend line, which implies that sales increase by a constant dollar amount each year. In this example, American Express sales are projected to grow by $1,773.4 million per year. However, there are important reasons for believing that the true trend for American Express sales is nonlinear and that the forecasts generated by this constant change model will be relatively poor estimates of actual values. To see why a linear trend relation may not be accurate, consider the relation between actual sales data and the linear trend shown in Figure 7.2. Remember that the least squares regression line minimizes the sum of squared residuals between actual and fitted values over the sample data. As is typical, actual data points lie above and below the fitted regression line. Note, however, that the pattern of differences between actual and fitted values varies dramatically over the sample period. Differences between actual and fitted values are generally positive in both early (1977 to 1979) and later (1988 to 1990) periods, whereas they are generally negative in the intervening 1980 to 1988 period. These differences suggest that the slope of the sales/time relation may not be constant but rather may be generally increasing over the 1977 to 1991 time period. Under these circumstances it may be more appropriate to assume that sales are changing at a constant annual *rate* rather than a constant annual *amount.*

Growth Trend Analysis

Growth trend analysis

Assumes constant *percentage* change over time.

Growth trend analysis assumes a constant period-by-period *percentage* change in an important economic variable over time. Such a forecast model has the potential to better capture the increasing annual sales pattern described by the 1977 to 1991 American Express sales data. This model is appropriate for forecasting when sales appear to change over time by a constant proportional amount rather than by the constant absolute amount assumption implicit in a simple linear model. The constant annual rate of growth model, assuming *annual* compounding, is described as follows:

$$\text{Sales in } t \text{ Years} = \text{Current Sales} \times (1 + \text{Growth Rate})^t \qquad (7.3)$$

$$S_t = S_0(1 + g)^t.$$

In words, Equation 7.3 means that sales in t years in the future are equal to current-period sales, S_0, compounded at a constant annual growth rate, g, for a period of t years. Use of the constant annual rate of growth model involves determining the average historical rate of growth in a variable such as sales and then using that rate of growth in a forecast equation such as Equation 7.3 to project future values. This approach is identical to the compounding value model used in finance.

Just as it is possible to estimate the constant rate of unit change in an economic time series by fitting historical data to a linear regression model of the form $Y = a + bt$, a constant annual rate of growth can be estimated using that same technique. In this case, the relevant growth rate is estimated using a linear regression model that is fit to a logarithmic transformation of the historical data. Taking common logarithms (to the base 10) of both sides of Equation 7.3 results in the expression

$$\log S_t = \log S_0 + \log (1 + g) \times t. \qquad (7.4)$$

Notice that Equation 7.4 is an expression of the form

$$Y_t = a + bt,$$

where $Y_t = \log S_t$, $a = \log S_0$, $b = \log (1 + g)$, and t is an independent, or X, variable. The coefficients $\log S_0$ and $\log (1 + g)$ can be estimated using the least squares regression technique.

Applying this technique to the American Express sales data in Table 7.1 for the 1977 to 1991 period results in the linear constant annual rate of growth regression model (t statistics in parentheses):

$$\log S_t = \underset{(143.33)}{3.498} + \underset{(24.84)}{0.067t} \qquad \bar{R}^2 = 97.8\%. \qquad (7.5)$$

Sales revenue forecasts (in millions of dollars) can be determined by transforming this estimated equation back to its original form:

$$S_t = (\text{Antilog } 3.498) \times (\text{Antilog } 0.067)t,$$

or $\qquad\qquad\qquad\qquad\qquad\qquad\qquad\qquad\qquad\qquad\qquad\qquad (7.6)$

$$S_t = \$3{,}147.75(1.17^t).$$

In this model, \$3,147.75 million is the adjusted level of sales for $t = 0$, or 1976, because the first year of data used in the regression estimation, $t = 1$, was 1977. The number 1.17 equals 1 plus the average rate of growth using annual compounding, meaning that American Express sales increased at a 17 percent annual rate from 1977 to 1991.

To forecast sales in any future year using this model, subtract 1976 from the year being forecast to determine t. Thus, a constant annual rate of growth model forecast for sales in 1995 is

$$t = 1995 - 1976 = 19$$
$$S_{1995} = \$3,147.75(1.17^{19})$$
$$= \$62,163 \text{ million.}$$

Similarly, a constant growth model forecast of American Express sales in the year 2000 is

$$t = 2000 - 1976 = 24$$
$$S_{2000} = \$3,147.75(1.17^{24})$$
$$= \$136,289 \text{ million.}$$

Another frequently used form of the constant growth model is based on an underlying assumption of *continuous,* as opposed to annual, compounding. The continuous growth model is expressed by the exponential equation

$$Y_t = Y_0 e^{gt}. \tag{7.7}$$

Taking the natural logarithm (to the base e) of Equation 7.7 gives

$$\ln Y_t = \ln Y_0 + gt.$$

Under an exponential rate of growth assumption, the regression model estimate of the slope coefficient, g, is a direct estimate of the continuous rate of growth. For example, a continuous growth model estimate for American Express sales is (t statistics in parentheses)

$$\ln S_t = \underset{(143.33)}{8.054} + \underset{(24.84)}{0.154t} \qquad \bar{R}^2 = 97.8\%. \tag{7.8}$$

In this equation, the coefficient 0.154 ($= 15.4$ percent) is a direct estimate of the continuous compounding growth rate for American Express sales. Notice that t statistics for the intercept and slope coefficients are identical to those derived for the constant annual rate of growth regression model (Equation 7.5).

Again, sales revenue forecasts (in millions of dollars) can be derived by transforming this estimated equation back to its original form:

$$S_t = (\text{Exponentiate } 8.054) \times (\text{Exponentiate } 0.154)^t,$$

or $\tag{7.9}$

$$S_t = \$3,146.35(1.17^t).$$

The very small difference between the intercept estimates for Equations 7.6 and 7.9 can be attributed to rounding error; otherwise they are identical. Subject to rounding error, identical 1995 and 2000 sales forecasts result using either the constant annual rate of growth or the continuous compounding assumption. Either method can be relied on with an equal degree of confidence as a useful basis for a constant growth model approach to forecasting.

MANAGERIAL APPLICATION 7.2

Economic Forecasting: The Art and the Science

Accurate forecasts of future aggregate economic activity would be extremely valuable to firms making hiring, inventory, and other investment decisions. Similarly, consumers making purchase and career decisions would find accurate forecasts of short-term and long-term economic trends extremely useful. The fact that most firms and consumers base important decisions on their expectations about the pace of future economic activity creates a substantial demand for economic forecasts. So extensive is this demand that the supply of economic forecasting services has exploded during recent years. For example, a wide variety of newsletters offering economic forecasts are now available. Moreover, economic forecasts by academic, business, and government economists are prominently featured on television and radio and in the print media. This high level of business and consumer interest, and the resulting media coverage, give rise to an extraordinary level of visibility for the few hundred economists who provide forecasting services.

This high level of visibility has focused attention on both the strong points and the limitations of economic forecasting. In terms of limitations, the accuracy of economic forecasts is sometimes criticized. Very high levels of forecast accuracy are often sought. For example, will real economic growth next year be 2.0 percent or 2.5 percent? The difference, although rather small, can be very important for sectors such as capital equipment, for which business conditions are closely related to the level of aggregate economic activity. The demand for capital equipment might rebound vigorously with a 2.5 percent growth in GDP but remain sluggish with a 2.0 percent rise. Thus, a difference of only 0.5 percent in GDP growth might make a difference of millions of dollars for some companies. Sometimes it is easy to forget that the degree of forecast accuracy sought by consumers and businesses is demanding indeed.

Many also don't understand why disagreement among forecasting economists is common and why this disagreement sometimes produces widely divergent economic forecasts. Both are valid reasons for concern, yet these criticisms sometimes reflect too little appreciation of the nature and scope of economic forecasting.

Forecasting aggregate economic activity is an extraordinarily difficult problem. In the real world, "all else held equal" doesn't hold very often, if ever. To forecast the future course of GDP, for example, one must be able to accurately predict the future pattern of government spending, tax and monetary policy, consumer and business spending, dollar strength against foreign currencies, weather, and so on. Although typical patterns can be inferred on the basis of past trends, unexpected atypical departures often have important economic consequences that complicate economic forecasting. An unexpected drought, winter storm, or labor strike can disrupt economic activity, and upset the accuracy of economic forecasts in the process.

Given the uncertainties involved, it seems reasonable that different forecasting economists would accord differing importance to a wide variety of economic influences. Just as individual forecasters assess different probabilities to an increase in government spending, they might also interpret the likely consequences differently. Forecasters' judgment is reflected not only in the interpretation they give to the data generated by complex computer models but also in the models themselves. Computers may generate economic forecasts, but they do so on the basis of programs written by economists. Computer-generated economic forecasts are only as sophisticated as the data employed, model analyzed and the subsequent analysis.

It is not surprising that economic forecasts and the methodology of economic forecasting generate a great deal of controversy. In fact, the success of economic forecasting is responsible, at least in part, for some of its failures. Users have come to expect a nearly unattainable level of forecast accuracy. At the same time, users forget that forecasts can, by themselves, have important economic consequences. When consumers and businesses cut back on spending in reaction to the forecast of an impending mild recession, for example, they change the basis for the forecasters' initial prediction. By their behavior, they may also cause a steeper recession. This is the forecaster's dilemma: The future as we know it doesn't exist. In fact, it can't.

Source: Howard Banks, "What's Ahead For Business," *Forbes,* June 8, 1992, 38–39.

Linear and Growth Trend Comparison

The importance of selecting the correct structural form for a trending model can be demonstrated by comparing the sales projections that result from the two basic approaches that have been considered. Recall that with the constant change model, sales were projected to be $62.2 billion in 1995 and $136.3 billion in 2000. Compare these sales forecasts with the projections of $32.7 billion in 1995 and $41.6 billion in 2000 for the constant growth rate model. Notice that the difference in the near-term forecasts (1995) is smaller than the difference between longer-term (2000) projections. This shows that if an economic time series is growing at a constant rate rather than increasing by a constant dollar amount, forecasts based on a linear trend model will tend to be less accurate the further out into the future one forecasts.

Of course, the pattern of future sales for any company, and therefore the reasonableness of a linear trend projection using either a constant change model or a constant growth model, remains a matter for conjecture. Whether a firm is able to maintain a rapid pace of growth depends on a host of factors both within and beyond its own control. Successfully managing rapid growth over extended periods is extraordinarily difficult and is rarely observed in practice. In fact, the sales pattern shown in Figure 7.2 might describe a company experiencing phases of rapid growth (1970s), maturation (1980s), and then decline (1990s). Individual products often display such a sales pattern, as do some firms and industries. When applying trend projection methods, it is important to establish the degree of similarity in growth opportunities between the historical and forecast periods. Prudence also suggests that the forecast horizon be limited to a relatively short time frame (five or ten years, maximum).

Although trend projection methods provide adequate results for some forecasting purposes, a number of serious shortcomings limit their usefulness. One problem is that simple trend projection techniques lack the ability to predict cyclical turning points or other short-term fluctuations. Another is that trend projections implicitly assume that historical patterns will continue unabated into the future. This is not always the case. There are many examples of the disastrous effects of using this forecasting method just prior to economic recessions in 1975, 1982, and 1990. Finally, trend analysis doesn't reflect any underlying causal relations and hence offers no help in describing *why* a particular series moves as it does. As a result, the method is incapable of predicting the effects of policy decisions or exogenous shocks.

CYCLICAL AND SEASONAL VARIATION

Many important economic time series are regularly influenced by cyclical and seasonal variations. Figure 7.1 illustrated how such variations can influence demand patterns for a typical consumer product. It is worth considering these influences further, since the treatment of cyclical and seasonal variations plays an important role in time series analysis and projection.

The Business Cycle

One of the most fascinating topics in managerial economics is the **business cycle,** or rhythmic pattern of contraction and expansion observed in the overall economy. On any given business day, it is possible to find a wide variety of news

Business cycle
Rhythmic pattern of contraction and expansion in the overall economy.

reports, press releases, and analyst comments concerning the current state and future direction of the overall economy. The reason for such intense interest is obvious. The profit and sales performance of all companies depends to a greater or lesser extent on the vigor of the overall economy. On average, business activity in the United States expands at a rate of 2.5 to 3 percent per year when measured in terms of inflation-adjusted, or real-dollar, GNP. During robust expansions, the pace of growth in real GNP can increase to an annual rate of 5 percent or more for brief periods. During especially severe recessions, real GNP can actually decline for an extended period. In the case of firms that employ significant financial and operating leverage, a difference of a few percentage points in the pace of overall economic activity can make the difference between vigorous expansion and gut-wrenching contraction.

Table 7.2 shows the pattern of business cycle expansion and contraction that has been experienced in the United States from the mid-1800s to the 1990s. Between December 1854 and July 1990, there have been 30 complete business cycles. The average duration of each cyclical contraction is 18 months, when duration is measured from the previous cyclical peak to the low point, or trough, of the subsequent business contraction. The average duration of each cyclical expansion is 35 months, as measured by the length of time from the previous cyclical trough to the peak of the following business expansion. In the post–World War II period, there have been 8 complete business cycles, with the typical contraction lasting only 11 months, less than a year, and the typical expansion lasting 50 months, or roughly four years. Clearly, periods of economic expansion predominate, as is indicative of a healthy and growing economy.

Whether the current economy is in a state of boom, moderate expansion, moderate contraction, or outright recession, there is sure to be widespread disagreement among analysts concerning current or future business prospects. This reflects the fact that, despite intense interest and widespread news coverage, the causes of economic contractions and expansions remain something of a mystery. *Why* the economy shifts from boom to bust and how such shifts might be predicted and controlled are still largely beyond our knowledge. Hopefully, the ever-increasing quality of economic data from both private sources and the government and the amazing power of new computer hardware and software will allow analysts to unlock further mysteries of the business cycle during the 1990s. In the meantime, changes in the pattern and pace of economic activity remain a matter for intense debate and conjecture.

Economic Indicators

Whereas cyclical patterns in most economic time series are erratic and make simple projection a hazardous short-term forecasting technique, a relatively consistent relation often exists among various economic variables over time. Even though many series of economic data do not exhibit a consistent pattern over time, it is often possible to find a high degree of correlation *across* these series. Should the forecaster have the good fortune to discover an economic series that leads the one being forecast, the leading series can be used as a barometer for forecasting short-term change, just as a meteorologist uses changes in a mercury barometer to forecast changes in the weather.

TABLE 7.2 Business Cycle Expansions and Contractions

Business Cycle Reference Dates		Duration in Months			
		Contraction (trough from previous peak)	Expansion (trough to peak)	Cycle	
Trough	Peak			Trough from Previous Trough	Peak from Previous Peak
December 1854	June 1857	—	30	—	—
December 1858	October 1860	18	22	48	40
June 1861	April 1865	8	*46*	30	*54*
December 1867	June 1869	*32*	18	*78*	50
December 1870	October 1873	18	34	36	52
March 1879	March 1882	65	36	99	101
May 1885	March 1887	38	22	74	60
April 1888	July 1890	13	27	35	40
May 1891	January 1893	10	20	37	30
June 1894	December 1895	17	18	37	35
June 1897	June 1899	18	24	36	42
December 1900	September 1902	18	21	42	39
August 1904	May 1907	23	33	44	56
June 1908	January 1910	13	19	46	32
January 1912	January 1913	24	12	43	36
December 1914	August 1918	23	*44*	35	*67*
March 1919	January 1920	*7*	10	*51*	17
July 1921	May 1923	18	22	28	40
July 1924	October 1926	14	27	36	41
November 1927	August 1929	13	21	40	34
March 1933	May 1937	43	50	64	93
June 1938	February 1945	13	*80*	63	*93*
October 1945	November 1948	*8*	37	*88*	45
October 1949	July 1953	11	*45*	48	*56*
May 1954	August 1957	*10*	39	*55*	49
April 1958	April 1960	8	24	47	32
February 1961	December 1969	10	*106*	34	*116*
November 1970	November 1973	*11*	36	*117*	47
March 1975	January 1980	16	58	52	74
July 1980	July 1981	6	12	64	18
November 1982	July 1990	16	92	28	108
Average, all cycles:					
1854–1990 (30 cycles)		18	35[1]	51	53
1854–1919 (16 cycles)		22	27	48	49[2]
1919–1945 (6 cycles)		18	35	53	53
1945–1990 (8 cycles)		11	50[3]	56	61[3]
Average, peacetime cycles:					
1854–1990 (25 cycles)		19	29[4]	46	48
1854–1919 (14 cycles)		22	24	46	47[5]
1919–1945 (5 cycles)		20	26	46	45
1945–1990 (6 cycles)		11	43[6]	46	53[6]

[1] 31 cycles.   [2] 15 cycles.   [3] 9 cycles.   [4] 26 cycles.   [5] 13 cycles.   [6] 7 cycles.

Note: Figures printed in bold italic are the wartime expansions (Civil War, World Wars I and II, Korean War, and Vietnam War), the postwar contractions, and the full cycles that include the wartime expansions.

Source: U.S. Department of Commerce, *Survey of Current Business,* April 1992, C-25.

TABLE 7.3 **Leading, Coincident, and Lagging Economic Indicators of Business Cycle Peaks**

Eleven Leading Indicators	Average workweek for manufacturing workers
	Average weekly initial claims for state unemployment insurance
	New orders for consumer goods and materials
	Vendor performance measured by companies receiving slower deliveries
	Contracts and orders for plant and equipment
	Index of new building permits for private housing units
	Change in unfilled factory orders for durable goods
	Change in sensitive materials prices
	Index of stock prices for 500 common stocks
	Money supply
	Index of consumer expectations
Four Roughly Coincident Indicators	Employees on nonagricultural payrolls
	Personal income minus transfer payments
	Index of total industrial production
	Manufacturing and trade sales
Seven Lagging Indicators	Average duration of unemployment
	Ratio of constant-dollar inventories to sales for manufacturing and trade
	Labor cost per unit of manufacturing output
	Average prime rate charged by banks
	Commercial and industrial loans outstanding
	Ratio of consumer installment credit to personal income
	Change in prices for consumer services

Economic indicators

Data that describe projected, current, or past economic activity.

Composite index

A weighted average of leading, coincident, or lagging economic indicators.

The Survey of Current Business, a monthly publication of the Bureau of Economic Analysis of the Department of Commerce, provides extensive data on a wide variety of **economic indicators,** or data series that successfully describe the pattern of projected, current, or past economic activity. Table 7.3 lists 11 leading, 4 roughly coincident, and 7 lagging economic indicators of business cycle peaks that are described in that publication and broadly relied upon in business cycle forecasting. Figure 7.3 shows the pattern displayed by composite indexes of these leading, coincident, and lagging indicators from the mid-1950s through the early 1990s. A **composite index** is a weighted average of leading, coincident, or lagging economic indicators. Combining individual series into a composite index results in a forecasting series with less random fluctuation, or noise. These composite series are smoother than the underlying individual data series and have less tendency to produce false signals of change in economic conditions. Notice how the composite index of leading indicators consistently turns down just prior to the start of each recessionary period. Similarly, notice how this data series bottoms out and then starts to rise just prior to the start of each subsequent economic expansion. Just as leading indicators seem to earn that description based on their performance, coincident and lagging indicators perform as expected over this period.

FIGURE 7.3   Composite Indexes of 11 Leading, 4 Coincident, and 7 Lagging Indicators (Index: 1982 = 100)

P indicates a "peak" in an economic expansion; T indicates a "trough" in an economic recession. Therefore, PT shows the time frame of an economic recession.

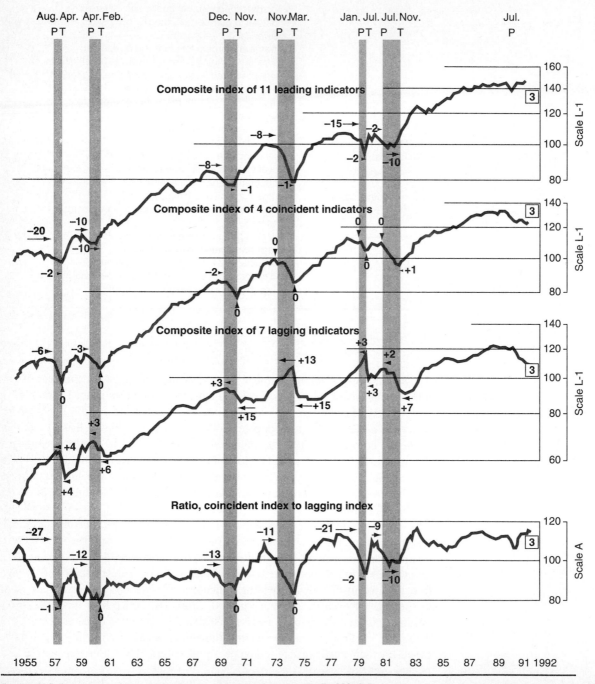

Source: U.S. Department of Commerce, *Survey of Current Business,* April 1992, C-7.

Barometric Forecasting

Barometric forecasting
Predictive method based on the observed relation among economic time series.

Barometric forecasting is a predictive method based on the observed relation among economic time series. Changes in some series appear to be consistently related to changes in one or more other series. The theoretical basis for some of these leads and lags is obvious. For example, building permits issued precede housing starts, and orders for plant and equipment lead production in durable goods industries. Each of these indicators directly reflects plans or commitments for the activity that follows. Other barometers are not so directly related to the economic variables they forecast. An index of common stock prices is a good leading indicator of general business activity. Although the causal linkage may not be readily apparent, stock prices reflect aggregate profit expectations by business managers and investors and thus describe future business conditions.

Barometric methods of forecasting require the identification of an economic time series that consistently leads the series being forecast. Once this relation is established, forecasting directional changes in the lagged series involves keeping track of movement in the leading indicator. In practice, several problems prevent such an easy solution to the forecasting problem. Few series always correctly indicate changes in another economic variable. Even the best leading indicators forecast directional changes in business conditions with no more than 80 to 90 percent accuracy. Also, even indicators that have good records of forecasting directional changes generally fail to lead by a consistent period. If a series is to be an adequate barometer, it must not only indicate directional changes but must also provide a relatively constant lead time. Few series meet the test of lead-time consistency. Finally, barometric forecasting suffers in that, even when leading indicators prove to consistently indicate directional changes with stable lead times, they provide very little information about the magnitude of change in the forecast variable.

Diffusion index
Percentage of leading, coincident, or lagging indicators that are rising at any point in time.

To partially overcome the difficulties of barometric forecasting, economists use both composite and diffusion indexes. Unlike a composite index, which combines a number of leading indicators into a single standardized index, a **diffusion index** indicates the percentage of leading, coincident, or lagging indicators that are rising at any point in time. Figure 7.4 shows the pattern displayed by diffusion indexes for the 11 leading indicator components, 4 coincident indicator components, and 7 lagging indicator components from the mid-1950s through the early 1990s. If all 11 leading indicators are relatively reliable advance indicators of heavy equipment sales, a diffusion, or pressure, index shows the percentage of those indicators that is increasing at the present time. If 7 are rising, the diffusion index of leading indicators is 7/11, or 64 percent. With only 3 rising, the diffusion index registers 27 percent. Forecasting with diffusion indexes typically involves projecting an increase in a given economic variable if the relevant diffusion index is above 50 percent and a decline when it is below 50 percent.

There is evidence that the leading indicator, or barometric, approach to business forecasting is nearly as old as business itself. More than 2,000 years ago, merchants used the arrival of trading ships as indicators of business activity. Over 100 years ago, Andrew Carnegie is reported to have used the number of smoking industrial chimneys to forecast business activity and hence the demand for steel. Today, the barometric approach to forecasting has been refined considerably,

F I G U R E 7 . 4   **Rates of Change and Diffusion Indexes for
Cyclical Indicator Composite Indexes**

P indicates a ''peak'' in an economic expansion; T indicates a ''trough'' in an economic recession. Therefore, PT
shows the time frame of an economic recession.

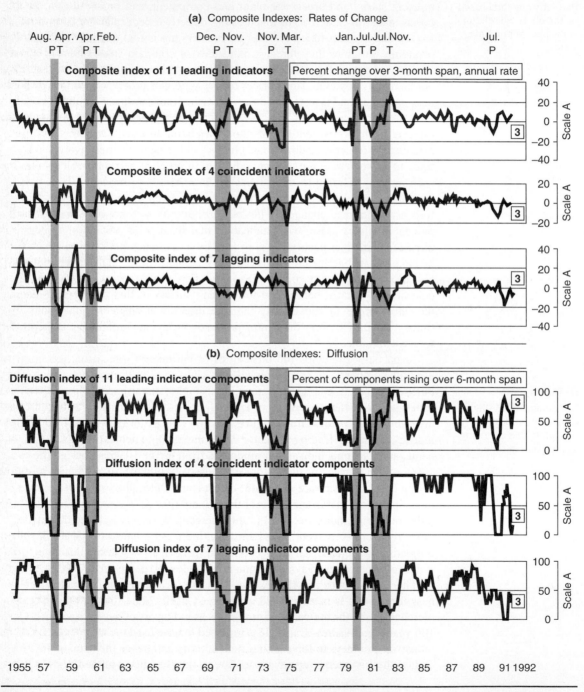

(a) Composite Indexes: Rates of Change

(b) Composite Indexes: Diffusion

Source: U.S. Department of Commerce, *Survey of Current Business,* April 1992, C-8.

primarily through the work of the National Bureau of Economic Research and the U.S. Department of Commerce. However, even with the use of composite and diffusion indexes, the barometric forecasting technique is a relatively poor tool for estimating the magnitude of change in an economic variable. Although barometric methods represent a considerable improvement over simple extrapolation techniques, the barometric forecasting methodology is not a fool-proof solution to the problem of calling turning points in economic conditions.

Seasonal Variation   Many important series of economic data are influenced not only by cyclical variation but also by seasonal patterns of business activity. For example, new housing starts constitute an important economic time series that is regularly influenced by both seasonal and cyclical variations. Understandably, housing starts tend to be high in the months of May, June, and July and relatively low in November, December, and January. The obvious reason for such variation is the weather. In many northern states, it is difficult, if not impossible, to maintain a high level of housing starts during colder winter months. After adjusting for the seasonal element in housing starts, a regular pattern of cyclical variation is typically observed. Seasonally adjusted annual data show that housing starts declined precipitously just prior to and during the economic downturns of 1975, 1982, and 1990 and illustrate why housing starts are considered a leading economic indicator.

Although housing starts are an obvious and classic example of economic data subject to seasonal and cyclical variation, they are by no means a unique case. For example, economic activity in the retailing, recreation, travel, automobile, and related industries are all affected by seasonal variation. Even in grocery retailing, an important seasonal element is reflected in the demand for meats. For example, turkey demand skyrockets at Thanksgiving and Christmas, whereas hamburger and hot dog demand surges on the Fourth of July. Similarly, summertime demand is especially strong for grocery products such as soda, charcoal, shampoo, deodorant soap, and so on. As a result, controlling for seasonal and cyclical variations is an important aspect of time series analysis and projection. For many economic projections, an analysis of seasonal and cyclical fluctuations can vastly improve forecasting results, especially for short-run forecasting.

There are several techniques for estimating seasonal variations. A simple one examines the ratio of actual monthly data to the trend projection. For example, if monthly sales for a product indicate that, on average, December volume is 20 percent above trend, a seasonal adjustment factor of 1.20 can be applied to the trend projection to forecast December sales. If February sales are typically 15 percent below trend, an adjustment factor of 0.85 can be used to project February sales. To illustrate, annual sales might be forecast at $1.2 million, or $100,000 a month. When the seasonal factor is introduced, however, December sales would be projected at $120,000 (= $100,000 × 1.20) and February sales at $85,000 (= $100,000 × 0.85). Production, inventory, and financing requirements could be scheduled accordingly.

The Box-Jenkins technique is one among a group of more complex methods for time series analysis that provide sophisticated means for analyzing the various components—trend, seasonal, cyclical, and random—that make up an economic time series. Such techniques enable one to analyze the wide variety of complex patterns that might exist in actual profit and sales data. For many forecasting applications, they provide a substantial improvement over simple extrapolation procedures.

ECONOMETRIC METHODS

Econometric methods

Use of economic theory and mathematical and statistical tools to forecast economic relations.

Econometric methods of forecasting combine economic theory with mathematical and statistical tools to analyze economic relations. Econometric forecasting techniques have several distinct advantages over alternative methods. For one, they force the forecaster to make explicit assumptions about the linkages among the variables in the economic system being examined. In other words, the forecaster must deal with causal relations. This process reduces the probability of logical inconsistencies in the forecast model and increases the reliability and acceptability of the results.

A second advantage of econometric methods lies in the consistency of the techniques from period to period. The forecaster can compare forecasts with actual results and use the insights gained to improve the forecast model. By feeding past forecasting errors back into the model, new parameter estimates can be generated that should improve future forecasting results.

The type of output provided by econometric forecasts is another major advantage of this technique. Since econometric models offer estimates of actual values for forecasted variables, these models indicate not only the direction of change but also the magnitude of change. This is a notable improvement over the barometric approach, which provides little information about the magnitude of expected changes.

Perhaps the most important advantage of econometric models relates to their basic characteristic of *explaining* economic phenomena. In the vast majority of business forecasting problems, management has a degree of control over some of the variables in the relationship being examined. For example, when forecasting sales of a product, the firm must take into account the price it will charge, the amount it has spent and will spend on advertising, and many other variables over which it may or may not have any influence. Only by thoroughly understanding the interrelations involved can management hope to forecast accurately and to make optimal decisions as it selects values for controllable variables.

Single-Equation Models

Many managerial forecasting problems can be adequately addressed with single-equation econometric models. The first step in developing an econometric model is to express relevant economic relations in the form of equations. When constructing a model for forecasting the regional demand for portable personal computers, one might hypothesize that computer demand (C) is determined by price (P), disposable income (I), population (Pop), interest rates (i), and advertising expenditures (A). A linear model expressing this relation is

$$C = a_0 + a_1P + a_2I + a_3Pop + a_4i + a_5A. \qquad (7.10)$$

The next step in econometric modeling is to estimate the parameters of the system, or values of the coefficients, as in Equation 7.10. The most frequently used technique for parameter estimation is the application of least squares regression analysis with either time series or cross section data.

Once the coefficients of the model have been estimated, forecasting with a single-equation model consists of evaluating the equation with specific values for the independent variables. This means that an econometric model used for forecasting purposes must contain independent or explanatory variables whose values for the forecast period can be readily obtained.

Multiple-Equation Systems

Although forecasting problems can often be analyzed with a single equation model, in some cases complex relations among economic variables require use of multiple-equation systems. Variables whose values are determined within such a model are referred to as *endogenous,* meaning originating from within, and those determined outside, or external to, the system are referred to as *exogenous.* The values of endogenous variables are determined by the model; the values of exogenous variables are given externally. Endogenous variables are equivalent to the dependent variable in a single-equation system; exogenous and predetermined variables are equivalent to the independent variables.

Multiple-equation econometric models are composed of two basic kinds of expressions—identities and behavioral equations. **Identities** express relations that are true by definition. The statement that profits (π) equal total revenue (TR) minus total cost (TC) is an example of an identity:

$$\pi = TR - TC. \tag{7.11}$$

Profits are *defined* by the relation expressed in Equation 7.11.

The second group of equations encountered in econometric models, **behavioral equations,** reflects hypotheses about how the variables in a system interact with one another. Behavioral equations may indicate how individuals and institutions are expected to react to various stimuli, or they may be technical, as, for example, a function that indicates production system relations.

Perhaps the easiest way to illustrate the use of multiple-equation systems is to examine a simple three-equation model of equipment and related software sales for a personal computer retailer. As you recall, Equation 7.10 expressed a single-equation model that might be used to forecast regional demand for portable personal computers. However, total revenues for a typical retailer usually include not only sales of personal computers but also sales of software programs (including computer games) and sales of peripheral equipment (video display terminals, printers, and so on). Although actual econometric models used to forecast total sales revenue from these items might include several equations and many important economic variables, the simple system described in this section should suffice to provide insight into the multiple-equation approach without being overly complex. The three equations are

$$S_t = b_0 + b_1 TR_t + u_1 \tag{7.12}$$

Identities
Economic relations that are true by definition.

Behavioral equations
Economic relations that are hypothesized to be true.

$$P_t = c_0 + c_1 C_{t-1} + u_2 \qquad \text{(7.13)}$$

$$TR_t = S_t + P_t + C_t, \qquad \text{(7.14)}$$

where S is software sales, TR is total revenue, P is peripheral sales, C is personal computer sales, t is the current time period, $t - 1$ is the previous time period, and u_1 and u_2 are error, or residual, terms.

Equations 7.12 and 7.13 are behavioral hypotheses. Equation 7.12 hypothesizes that current-period software sales are a function of the current level of total revenues; Equation 7.13 hypothesizes that peripheral sales depend on previous-period personal computer sales. The last equation in the system, Equation 7.14, is an identity. It defines total revenue as being equal to the sum of software, peripheral equipment, and personal computer sales.

The stochastic disturbance terms in the behavioral equations, u_1 and u_2, are included because the hypothesized relations are not exact. In other words, other factors that can affect software and peripheral sales are not accounted for in the system. So long as these stochastic elements are random and their expected values are zero, they do not present a barrier to empirical estimation of system parameters. However, if the error terms are not randomly distributed, parameter estimates will be biased and the reliability of model forecasts will be questionable. Large error terms, even if they are distributed randomly, reduce forecast accuracy.

Empirical estimation of the parameters for multiple equation systems (the bs and cs in Equations 7.12 and 7.13) often requires the use of statistical techniques that go beyond the scope of this text. However, the use of such a system for forecasting purposes can be illustrated.

To forecast next year's software and peripheral sales and total revenue for the firm represented by this illustrative model, it is necessary to express S, P, and TR in terms of variables whose values are known or can be estimated at the moment the forecast is generated. In other words, each endogenous variable (S_t, P_t, and TR_t) must be expressed in terms of the exogenous and predetermined variables (C_{t-1} and C_t). Such relations are called reduced-form equations because they reduce complex simultaneous relations to their most basic and simple form. Consider the manipulations of equations in the system necessary to solve for TR via its reduced-form equation.

Substituting Equation 7.12 into 7.14—that is, replacing S_t with Equation 7.12—results in[1]

$$TR_t = b_0 + b_1 TR_t + P_t + C_t. \qquad \text{(7.15)}$$

A similar substitution of Equation 7.13 for P_t produces

$$TR_t = b_0 + b_1 TR_t + c_0 + c_1 C_{t-1} + C_t. \qquad \text{(7.16)}$$

Collecting terms and isolating TR in Equation 7.16 gives

$$(1 - b_1)TR_t = b_0 + c_0 + c_1 C_{t-1} + C_t,$$

---

[1] The stochastic disturbance terms (us) have been dropped from the illustration because their expected values are zero. The final equation for TR, however, is stochastic in nature.

or, alternatively,

$$TR_t = \frac{b_0 + c_0 + c_1 C_{t-1} + C_t}{(1 - b_1)}$$

$$= \frac{b_0 + c_0}{(1 - b_1)} + \frac{c_1}{(1 - b_1)} C_{t-1} + \frac{1}{(1 - b_1)} C_t.$$

(7.17)

Equation 7.17 now relates current total revenues to previous-period and current-period personal computer sales. Assuming that data on previous-period personal computer sales can be obtained and that current-period personal computer sales can be estimated using Equation 7.9, Equation 7.17 provides a forecasting model that takes into account the simultaneous relations expressed in this simplified multiple-equation system. Of course, in real-world situations, it is possible, perhaps even likely, that personal computer sales depend on the price, quantity, and quality of available software and peripheral equipment. Then *S, P,* and *C,* along with other important factors, may all be endogenous, involving a large number of relations in a highly complex multiple-equation system. Disentangling the important but often subtle relations involved in such a system makes forecasting with multiple-equation systems both challenging and intriguing.

INPUT-OUTPUT ANALYSIS

Input-output analysis
Forecasting method that shows the interrelated nature of economic data.

A forecasting method known as **input-output analysis** provides perhaps the most complete examination of all the complex interrelations within an economic system. Input-output analysis shows how an increase or a decrease in the demand for one industry's output affects other industries. For example, an increase in the demand for trucks will lead to increased production of steel, plastics, tires, glass, and other materials. The increase in demand for these materials will also have secondary effects—the increase in demand for glass will lead to a further increase in the demand for steel, as well as for trucks used in the manufacture of glass and steel, and so on. Input-output analysis traces through all these interindustry relations to provide information about the total impact on all industries of the original increase in the demand for trucks.

Input-output forecasting is based on a set of tables that describes the linkages among all the component parts of the economy. The construction of input-output tables is a formidable task; fortunately, such tables are available for the United States from the Office of Business Economics, U.S. Department of Commerce. To use the tables effectively, one must understand their construction. The construction of these tables and their use are examined in this section.

Input-Output Tables

The starting point for constructing input-output tables is the set of accounts upon which gross domestic product (GDP) is based. GDP is a measure of aggregate business activity as described by the value at final point of sale of all goods and services produced in the domestic economy during a year by both domestic and

TABLE 7.4 List of National Income and Product Accounts Used to Construct GDP

National Income Accounts
1. Compensation of employees
2. Proprietors' income
3. Rental income of persons
4. Corporate profits and inventory valuation adjustment
5. Net interest
6. Business transfer payments
7. Indirect business tax and nontax liability
8. Less: Subsidies less current surplus of government enterprises
9. Capital consumption allowances

⎬ Gross Domestic Product

Final Product Accounts
10. Personal consumption expenditures
11. Gross private domestic investment
12. Net export of goods and services
13. Government purchases of goods and services

⎬ Gross Domestic Product

foreign-owned enterprises.[2] Basic GDP accounts are listed in Table 7.4. This table shows that GDP is equal to the sum of the national income accounts (items 1 through 9) or, alternatively, the sum of the final product flows to consuming sectors (items 10 through 13).

Input-output tables break down income and product account data and provide information about interindustry transactions. Table 7.5 is an example of a simplified input-output table. It is a matrix of the same GDP data contained in Table 7.4 but with the addition of a shaded section showing interindustry transactions as well. Although the illustrated input-output table has only eight industry classifications, actual U.S. input-output tables are far more complex, containing over 500 separate industry classifications. The industry-to-industry flows in the shaded area depict the input-output structure of the economy. For example, the manufacturing row, Row 4, shows sales by manufacturing firms to other manufacturing firms, to other industries, and to final users. Thus, Cell 4,2 shows sales from manufacturers to mining companies; Cell 4,4 from manufacturers to other manufacturers; and Cell 4,7 from manufacturers to service firms such as banks, entertainment companies, and the like. The manufacturing column, Column 4, shows the sources of goods and services purchased by manufacturers for production, as well as the value added in their production of output. For example, Cell 2,4 shows manufacturing firms' purchases from mining companies; Cell 6,4 shows manufacturing firms' purchases from the transportation industry.

Since interindustry sales are included in the value of products sold to various final consumers, they must be omitted from the measurement of GDP. To avoid double counting, producer-to-producer sales must be excluded from the determination of GDP. The same is true when calculating GNP using national income accounts; interindustry transactions must be eliminated to avoid redundancy. Accordingly, the entire shaded area of Table 7.5 is ignored in determining GDP.

[2] Gross national product (GNP) is the value at final point of sale of all goods and services produced by *domestic* firms. As such, GNP does not reflect domestic production by foreign-owned firms (e.g., Toyota Camrys produced in Kentucky).

T A B L E 7.5 Input-Output Flow Table

	Interindustry Transactions								Final Markets (National Product Accounts)			
	Agriculture (1)	Mining (2)	Construction (3)	Manufacturing (4)	Trade (5)	Transportation (6)	Services (7)	Other (8)	Persons (9)	Investors (10)	Foreigners (11)	Government (12)
Agriculture (1)									Personal consumption expenditures (Account 10)	Gross private domestic investment (Account 11)	Net exports of goods and services (Account 12)	Government purchases of goods and services (Account 13)
Mining (2)				2, 4								
Construction (3)												
Manufacturing (4)		4, 2		4, 4			4, 7					
Trade (5)												
Transportation (6)				6, 4								
Services (7)												
Other (8)												
Employees (9)	Compensation of employees (Account 1)											
Owners of business and capital (10)	Profit-type income and capital consumption allowances (Accounts 2, 3, 4, 5, 6, 9)											
Government (11)	Indirect business taxes, current surplus of government enterprises, and so forth (Accounts 7, 8)											

Interindustry Transactions

Value Added (National Income Accounts)

Gross domestic product

301

GDP is calculated either as the total of all the cells shown in the Final Markets columns or as the total of cells in the Value Added rows.

Use of Input-Output Analysis

Input-output analysis has a variety of applications, ranging from forecasting the sales of an individual firm to probing the implications of national economic policies. The major contribution of input-output analysis is that it facilitates measurement of the effects on all industrial sectors of changes in the activity of any one sector.

The usefulness of input-output analysis can be illustrated by considering the effect of an increase in consumer demand for passenger cars. The first effect of the change in demand is an increase in the output of the automobile industry; there are further effects, however. The increase in auto output requires more steel production, which in turn requires more chemicals, more iron ore, more limestone, and more coal. Auto production also requires other products for which demand will increase, including upholstery fabrics, synthetic fibers, plastics, and glass. There will still be further reactions; for example, the production of synthetic fibers and other chemicals will lead to increased demand for electricity, containers, and transportation services. Input-output analysis traces this intricate chain reaction through all industrial sectors and measures the effects, both direct and indirect, on the output of each of the affected industries.

The industry outputs derived in this way can be used for estimating related industry requirements. For example, with supplementary data, the estimated output of each industry can be translated into requirements for employment or for additional plants and equipment. Or, bolstered by information on the geographic distribution of industries, input-output analysis can also shed light on the regional implications of changes in national GDP.

Recognizing the unique ability of input-output analysis to account completely for the complex interaction among industries, many businesses have been guided in their decision making by this analysis. For example, input-output analysis has been used to evaluate market prospects for established products, identify potential markets for new products, spot prospective shortages in supplies, add new dimensions and greater depth to the analysis of the economic environment in which the firms can expect to operate, and evaluate investment prospects in various industries.

Input-output analysis has also been employed in the decision-making processes of government agencies at every level. A notable federal application has been in the study of long-term growth of the economy and its implications for labor force requirements. Input-output analysis has also been used to calculate the effect of U.S. exports and imports on employment in various industries and regions. A number of state and local governments have sponsored the construction of input-output tables for use in evaluating the effects of different types of economic development. Others have used input-output analysis to study the industrial impact of alternative tax programs. In some states, input-output analysis is a central element in large-scale systems for forecasting demographic and economic variables. It also serves as an aid in planning land use, expenditure and revenue programs, industrial development, and so on.

Many regions throughout the country have become increasingly concerned about the adequacy of water resources. Input-output analysis is being used as part of a total system to measure industrial requirements for water. The analysis is particularly helpful in identifying activities that generate important demands for water, not only as direct users but also because suppliers of materials, power, and other inputs also require water.

Forecasting with Input-Output Tables

It should be obvious that the data required to construct an input-output system are extensive, and the analytical task of tracing the intricate interrelations is immense. Because of the enormous costs of constructing and maintaining input-output tables, individual firms, even the largest ones, rely on U.S. Department of Commerce tables instead of constructing their own. However, firms can and do extend published tables in order to apply them to unique situations.

To use input-output tables, it is necessary to appreciate the nature of an input-output system. To facilitate such understanding, it is helpful to trace through a very simple hypothetical economy containing only three producing sectors. Table 7.6 provides the basic national accounting data for this hypothetical system. The upper section contains the detailed interindustry relationships necessary for construction of input-output tables; the lower section gives the national income and product accounts that make up GDP.

Table 7.7 shows all of this information reformulated in an input-output matrix for the system. The Producers rows contain information about the distribution of output. For example, Industry *A* produces and sells a total of $130 billion, with $10 billion going to other firms in Industry *A*, $2 billion to Industry *B*, $50 billion to Industry *C*, $40 billion to individuals for personal consumption, and $28 billion to the government. As is shown in the Producers columns, firms in Industry *A* buy $10 billion of goods and services from other *A* firms and $3 billion from *B* firms, pay $100 billion in wages, and have $17 billion left for depreciation and profits. GDP can be obtained from the input-output table by summing either the Value Added section or the Final Markets section. Cells in the producer-to-producer section of the matrix are eliminated in the calculation of GDP to avoid double counting.

For forecasting purposes, two additional types of matrices are constructed from the Producers section of Table 7.7. One is the percentage distribution of gross output matrix, which indicates where each industry sells its products and thus how dependent it is on various sectors of the system. Table 7.8 shows the percentage distribution matrix for this hypothetical economy. Each element in that table is found by dividing the corresponding element in Table 7.7 by its row total. For example, the 8 percent in Cell *A,A* was found by dividing the $10 billion of sales that Industry *A* makes for itself by the $130 billion total sales of that industry. The 4 percent in Cell *B,A* indicates that Industry *B* sells 4 percent of its output to Industry *A*.

Other input-output matrices derived from the producer-to-producer sector of Table 7.7, the *direct* and *total requirements* tables, are especially useful when individual firms are making demand forecasts. Table 7.9 is the direct requirements table for the hypothetical economy. The entries in each column show the

T A B L E   7.6   National Accounting Data for a Hypothetical Economy (in billions of dollars)

Industry Production Accounts

	Receipts			Expenses + Profits	
Industry A	Sales to Industry A	$ 10		Purchases from Industry A	$ 10
	Sales to Industry B	2		Purchases from Industry B	3
	Sales to Industry C	50		Wages (employee compensation)	100
	Sales to persons	40		Depreciation	10
	Sales to government	28		Profits	7
		$130			$130
Industry B	Sales to Industry A	$ 3		Purchases from Industry A	$ 2
	Sales to Industry C	15		Purchases from Industry C	25
	Sales to persons	30		Wages (employee compensation)	25
	Sales to government	20		Depreciation	8
	Sales to exports	2		Profits	10
		$ 70			$ 70
Industry C	Sales to Industry B	$ 25		Purchases from Industry A	$ 50
	Sales to persons	65		Purchases from Industry B	15
				Wages (employee compensation)	20
				Profits	5
		$ 90			$ 90

National Income and Product Accounts

	Wages	$145		Personal consumption expenditures	$135
	Profits	22		Government	48
	Depreciation	18		Exports	2
		$185			$185

T A B L E   7.7   Input-Output Matrix for a Hypothetical Economy (in billions of dollars)

		Producers			Final Markets			
		A	B	C	Personal Consumption	Government	Exports	Row Totals
Producers	A	10	2	50	40	28		130
	B	3		15	30	20	2	70
	C		25		65			90
Value Added	Wages	100	25	20				145 } GDP
	Profit plus depreciation	17	18	5	40			40 } = $185
	Column totals	130	70	90	135	48	2	

GDP = $185

TABLE 7.8 **Percentage Distribution of Gross Output**

Producing Industry	Industry A	Industry B	Industry C	Persons	Government	Export	Total
A	8	1	38	31	22	0	100
B	4	0	21	43	29	3	100
C	0	28	0	72	0	0	100

Percentage Sales to Each Consuming Sector

TABLE 7.9 **Direct Requirements per Dollar of Gross Output**

Supplying Industry	A	B	C
A	0.08	0.03	0.56
B	0.02	0.00	0.17
C	0.00	0.36	0.00

Producing Industry

dollar inputs required directly from each industry given in the rows to produce $1 of output. Industry *C,* for example, requires direct inputs costing $0.56 from Industry *A* and those costing $0.17 from Industry *B* to produce an additional $1 of output. These direct requirements figures are found by dividing each element in the industry columns in Table 7.7 by the column total. Thus, the 0.08 figure for Cell *A,A* in Table 7.9 is found by dividing the $10 billion of purchases among Industry *A* firms by the $130 billion total found in the first column of Table 7.7.

The direct requirements matrix in Table 7.9 permits systematic examination of all the interrelations among the various industries and final demand sectors. For example, assume that Industry *A* is expected to produce $1 million of output for sale to final consumers. The first column of Table 7.9 illustrates that Industry *A* will use $80,000 ($1,000,000 × 0.08) of its own production in the process of manufacturing the $1 million of output for final consumption. Thus, the industry must actually produce a minimum of $1.080 million of output. Production of $1.080 million of output by *A* also requires $21,600 ($1,080,000 × 0.02) of input from Industry *B*. As shown by the 0.00 element in the last row of the first column, Industry *A* requires no direct inputs from Industry *C*.

Calculating the total effect of the original $1 million final demand for *A*'s output requires further analysis. Note that Industry *A* requires $21,600 in inputs from Industry *B*. To meet this requirement, *B* needs inputs of $648 ($21,600 × 0.03) from Industry *A* and $7,776 ($21,600 × 0.36) from Industry *C*. These requirements, in turn, must be fed back into the system to determine the second-round effects, which in turn produce further reactions as the cycle continues. Each successive reaction is smaller than the preceding one, and the reactions converge on the final effects of the original demand.

Table 7.10 presents the *total requirements*—direct plus indirect—for the hypothetical economy. Total requirements tables provide the solution values, or the

TABLE 7.10   **Total Requirements (Direct plus Indirect) per Dollar of Output for Final Consumption**

Supplying Industry	Producing Industry		
	A	B	C
A	1.09	0.27	0.66
B	0.03	1.07	0.19
C	0.01	0.39	1.07

values on which the chain reaction converges. Each column in the table shows the inputs required, both direct and indirect, by the producing industry; each row shows the demand that supplying industries can expect per dollar of final consumption demand. To continue the example of a $1 million final consumer demand for the output of Industry *A,* it is clear that, in order to produce the $1 million to meet the final demand, Industry *A* production must total $1.09 million, Industry *B* must produce $0.03 million, and Industry *C* must produce $0.01 million. In total, production must amount to $1.13 million to supply $1 million of final output of Product *A,* with the $0.13 million being the input required to produce the $1 million final output.

This illustration of the construction and use of input-output tables indicates the versatility of the technique in a variety of forecasting situations. It should be apparent that a large part of that versatility depends on the detail contained in the basic input-output matrix. That is, the finer the industry distinctions in the input-output tables, the more valuable they are for forecasting purposes.

The most recent input-output table for the U.S. economy, completed by the Bureau of Economic Analysis of the Department of Commerce, segments the industrial sector of the system into over 500 industry categories. This compares with less specific classifications for earlier input-output tables. The greater detail provided by the latest tables increases their value to managerial decision makers and should lead to greater use of the techniques of input-output analysis for industry and firm forecasting purposes.

JUDGING FORECAST RELIABILITY

Forecast reliability
Predictive consistency.

One of the most challenging aspects of forecasting is judging the reliability of forecasts obtained from various models. How well do various methodologies deal with specific forecasting problems? In comparing forecast and actual values, how close is close enough? Is **forecast reliability,** or predictive consistency, over one sample or time period necessarily transferable to other samples and time periods? Each of these questions is fundamentally important and must be adequately addressed prior to the implementation of any successful forecasting program.

Tests of Predictive Capability

Ideally, to test predictive capability, a model generated from data of one sample or period is used to forecast data for some alternative sample or period. Thus, the reliability of a model for predicting firm sales, such as that shown in Equation

The Year 2000

In 1980, *Forbes* managing editor Malcolm S. Forbes challenged his readers, "If you're so smart, here's $10,000 for accurately forecasting economic conditions in the year 1990." Based on the results, the "smartest" of the 660 readers that responded to *Forbes* challenge was Jack Rankin of Round Hill, Virginia. The winner is a wise (and lucky) man who isn't taking it all too seriously. Said Rankin when entering the contest ten years ago, "I may be just a dumb farmer, but I sure know good odds when I see 'em." With no cost to enter, and a possible $10,000 first prize, the *Forbes* offer was one that Rankin just couldn't resist. When informed that he had won, Rankin wrote, "The only downside is remembering the promises I made last year when you reported that I was harmlessly tied for second place. Most notable was a promise to my son of a trip to Bayreuth to attend a Wagnerian Ring Cycle. Oh well, easy come, easy go!"

Most entrants in the *Forbes* contest simply extrapolated recent trends into the future (see table). Readers thought that the United States would encounter significantly higher inflation than that which was actually experienced. Many also badly underestimated the rapid increase in the stock market during the 1980s. There was some real money to be made by anyone who could have predicted the 1980s boom that saw the Dow Jones Industrial Average (DJIA) soar to over three times its 1979 level, especially surprising since the DJIA had failed to budge during the previous decade. There was also money to be made by anyone who could have predicted the PC revolution that caused a one hundred and seventy five-fold increase in the number of computers in the U.S.

Given the success of its initial contest, *Forbes* has offered its readers a chance to make some profitable prophecies for the year 2000. A $100,000 prize awaits the reader best able to forecast a wide range of economic/political projections. For example, can you accurately project the number of pro baseball teams, U.S. population, or number of countries to emerge from the old U.S.S.R.?

Category	1970	1979	1989	Winner
Value of $1	$1	$0.54	$0.29	$0.33
Dow Jones industrials	800	838	2753	1150
Average daily NYSE volume	11.6 mil	32 mil	165 mil	55 mil
Oil—price of Saudi crude	$1.80/bbl	$24.00/bbl	$18.40/bbl	$59.00/bbl
Hamburger—Big Mac	$0.49	$0.95	$1.79*	$1.60
New home	$35,000	$74,000	$148,800	$137,000
Home mortgage	8.25%	13%	9.76%	11.5%
Prime rate	8.5%	15%	10.5%	11.5%
Employed workers	81 mil	100 mil	119 mil	120 mil
Per capita income	$3,893	$8,800*	$15,186*	$14,080
GNP (actual)	$982 bil	$2.4 tril*	$5.2 tril	$4.2 tril
GNP (in 1970 dollars)	$982 bil	$1.3 tril*	$1.5 tril	$2.3 tril
Pro football teams	20	28	28	28
Operating steel mills	148	154	127	126
Shopping malls	12,170	19,201	34,683*	30,000
Federal budget	$197 bil	$547 bil*	$1.1 tril	$900 bil
National debt	$370 bil	$845 bil*	$3.0 tril	$1.2 tril
Computers (U.S.)	65,000	300,000	52.4 mil	900,000
Coast-to-coast call	$0.75	$0.21	$0.25	$0.49
First-class stamp	$0.06	$0.15	$0.25	$0.50
Credit cards	450 mil	579 mil	908 mil	775 mil
Lawyers	355,242	464,851	725,574	700,000
Stockbrokers	50,787	50,466	438,701	50,000
U.S. population	203 mil	222 mil	249 mil*	247 mil

*Estimate. Forbes is the final judge; no Forbes employees or their relatives are eligible. Figures for 1970 and 1979 are taken from the book, *Getting By on $100,000 a Year,* by Andrew Tobias; these figures were the basis for the $10,000 contest in Forbes. Because of space limitations, only 24 of 37 *Forbes* forecast categories are shown.

Source: Malcolm S. Forbes, Jr., "Profitable Prophecies," *Forbes,* June 11, 1990, 20.

Test group

Subsample of data used to generate a forecast model.

Forecast group

Subsample of data used to test a forecast model.

7.2, can be tested by examining the relation between forecast and actual data for years beyond 1991, given that the model was generated using data from the 1977 to 1991 period. However, it is often desirable to test a model without waiting for new data to become available. In such instances, one can divide available data into two subsamples, called a **test group** and a **forecast group.** The forecaster then estimates a forecasting model using data from the test group and uses the resulting model to forecast the data of interest in the forecast group. A comparison of forecast and actual values can then be conducted to test the stability of the underlying cost or demand relation.

Correlation Analysis

In analyzing a model's forecast capability, the correlation between forecast and actual values is of substantial interest. The formula for the simple correlation coefficient, r, for forecast and actual values, f and x, respectively, is

$$r = \frac{\sigma_{fx}}{\sigma_f \sigma_x},$$ **(7.18)**

where σ_{fx} is the covariance between the forecast and actual series, and σ_f and σ_x are the sample standard deviations of the forecast and actual series, respectively. Most basic statistical software programs and many hand-held calculators readily provide these data, making the calculation of r a relatively simple task. Generally speaking, correlations between forecast and actual values in excess of 0.99 (99 percent) are highly desirable and indicate that the forecast model being considered constitutes an effective tool for analysis. However, in cross section analysis, in which the important trend element in most economic data is held constant, a correlation of 99 percent between forecast and actual values is rare. When unusually difficult forecasting problems are being addressed, correlations between forecast and actual data of 90 or 95 percent may prove satisfactory. In contrast, in critical decision situations, forecast values may have to be estimated at very precise levels. In such instances, forecast and actual data may have to exhibit an extremely high level of correlation, 99.5 or 99.75 percent, to generate a high level of confidence in forecast reliability. The correlation between forecast and actual values necessary to reach a threshold reliability acceptance level depends in large part on the difficulty of the forecasting problem being analyzed and the cost of forecast error.

Sample Mean Forecast Error Analysis

Sample mean forecast error

Estimate of average forecast error.

Further evaluation of a model's predictive capability can be made through consideration of a measure called the **sample mean forecast error,** which provides a useful estimate of the average forecast error of the model. It is sometimes called the root mean squared forecast error and is denoted by the symbol U. The sample mean forecast error is calculated as

$$U = \sqrt{\frac{1}{N}\sum_{i=1}^{N}(f_i - x_i)^2},$$ **(7.19)**

where N is the number of sample observations, f_i is a forecast value, and x_i is the corresponding actual value. The deviations between forecast and actual values are squared in the calculation of the mean forecast error to prevent positive and negative deviations between forecast and actual values from canceling one another out. The smaller the sample mean forecast error, the greater the accuracy associated with the forecasting model.

SUMMARY

Managerial decision making is often based on forecasts of future events. This chapter examines several techniques for economic forecasting, including qualitative analysis, trend analysis and projection, econometric models, and input-output methods.

- **Qualitative analysis** is an intuitive judgmental approach to forecasting that is useful when it provides for the systematic analysis of data derived from unbiased, informed opinion. The **personal insight** method is one in which an informed individual uses personal or organizational experience as a basis for developing future expectations. The **panel consensus** method relies on the informed opinion of several individuals. In the **delphi method,** responses from a panel of experts are analyzed by an independent party to elicit a consensus opinion.

- **Survey techniques** that skillfully employ interviews or mailed questionnaires constitute another important forecasting tool, especially for short-term projections.

- **Trend analysis** involves characterizing the historical pattern of an economic variable and then projecting or forecasting its future path based on past experience. A **secular trend** is the long-run pattern of increase or decrease in a series of economic data. **Cyclical fluctuation** describes the rhythmic variation in economic series that is due to a pattern of expansion or contraction in the overall economy. **Seasonal variation** is a rhythmic annual pattern in sales or profits caused by weather, habit, or social custom. **Irregular or random influences** are unpredictable shocks to the economic system and the pace of economic activity caused by wars, strikes, natural catastrophes, and so on.

- A simple **linear trend analysis** assumes a constant period-by-period *unit* change in an important economic variable over time. **Growth trend analysis** assumes a constant period-by-period *percentage* change in an important economic variable over time.

- The **business cycle** is the rhythmic pattern of contraction and expansion observed in the overall economy. **Economic indicators** are series of data that successfully describe the pattern of projected, current, or past economic activity. A **composite index** is a weighted average of leading, coincident, or lagging economic indicators. **Barometric forecasting** is a predictive method based on the observed relation among economic time series. A **diffusion index** indicates the percentage of leading, coincident, or lagging indicators that are rising at any point in time.

- **Econometric methods** use economic theory and mathematical and statistical tools to forecast economic relations. **Identities** are economic relations that are true by definition. **Behavioral equations** are hypothesized economic relations that are estimated using econometric methods.

• **Input-output analysis** shows how an increase or decrease in the demand for one industry's output affects all other industries in the economy.

• **Forecast reliability,** or predictive consistency, must be accurately judged in order to assess the degree of confidence that should be placed in economic forecasts. No forecasting assignment is complete until reliability has been quantified and evaluated.

All forecasting methods have particular strengths and shortcomings. The appropriate technique to apply in a given forecasting situation depends on such factors as the distance into the future being forecast, the lead time available, the accuracy required, the quality of data available for analysis, and the nature of the economic relations involved in the forecasting problem. In many instances, comparing results from multiple forecasting techniques provides a useful basis for judging forecast reliability.

Questions

Q7.1 What is the delphi method? Describe its main advantages and limitations.

Q7.2 Describe the main advantages and limitations of survey data.

Q7.3 What is trend projection, and why is this method often employed in economic forecasting?

Q7.4 What is the basic shortcoming of trend projection that barometric approaches improve on?

Q7.5 What advantage do diffusion and composite indexes provide in the barometric approach to forecasting?

Q7.6 Explain how the econometric model approach to forecasting could be used to examine various "what if" questions about the future.

Q7.7 Describe the data requirements that must be met if regression analysis is to provide a useful basis for forecasting.

Q7.8 Would a linear regression model of the advertising/sales relation be appropriate for forecasting the advertising levels at which threshold or saturation effects become prevalent?

Q7.9 Cite some examples of forecasting problems that might be addressed using input-output analysis.

Q7.10 What are the main characteristics of accurate forecasts?

Self-Test Problem

Gross domestic product (GDP) is a measure of overall activity in the economy. It is defined as the value at the final point of sale of all goods and services produced during a given time period by both domestic and foreign-owned enterprises. GDP and changes in GDP are sometimes reported in current-year, or nominal, dollars. In 1993, for example, current-year GDP provides a useful measure of productive output valued at then-current prices. However, inflation that causes economywide changes in the price level can distort nominal GDP figures and create a picture of robust activity when the economy is actually sluggish. As a result, GDP and changes in GDP are also measured in inflation-adjusted, or real, terms. When GDP is evaluated using constant 1987 dollars, the effects of economywide inflation are controlled, and the pace of real economic activity is revealed. For this reason, inflation-adjusted GDP figures are often referred to as real GDP terms. The accompanying table shows current-year and real GDP figures for the U.S. economy for the 32-year period from 1959 to 1991.

Year	GDP in Current Dollars*	GDP in 1987 Dollars*	Time Period (in years)
1991	$5,671.8	$4,848.4	33
1990	5,513.8	4,884.9	32
1989	5,244.0	4,836.9	31
1988	4,900.4	4,718.6	30
1987	4,539.9	4,540.0	29
1986	4,268.6	4,405.5	28
1985	4,038.7	4,279.8	27
1984	3,777.2	4,148.5	26
1983	3,405.0	3,906.6	25
1982	3,149.6	3,760.3	24
1981	3,030.6	3,843.1	23
1980	2,708.0	3,776.3	22
1979	2,488.6	3,796.8	21
1978	2,232.7	3,703.5	20
1977	1,974.1	3,533.2	19
1976	1,768.4	3,380.8	18
1975	1,585.9	3,221.7	17
1974	1,458.6	3,248.1	16
1973	1,349.6	3,268.6	15
1972	1,207.0	3,107.1	14
1971	1,097.2	2,965.1	13
1970	1,010.7	2,875.8	12
1969	959.5	2,877.1	11
1968	889.3	2,801.0	10
1967	814.3	2,690.3	9
1966	769.8	2,622.3	8
1965	702.7	2,473.5	7
1964	648.0	2,343.3	6
1963	603.1	2,218.0	5
1962	571.6	2,129.8	4
1961	531.8	2,025.6	3
1960	513.4	1,973.2	2
1959	494.2	1,931.3	1

*Dollar figures are in billions of dollars.

Source: *Economic Report of the President* (Washington, D.C.: U.S. Government Printing Office, 1992), pp. 298, 300.

GDP data for the entire 1959–1991 period offer the basis to test the ability of a simple constant growth model to describe the trend in GDP over time. However, such a regression model cannot be used to forecast GDP over any subpart of that period. To do so would be to overstate the forecast capability of the regression model since, by definition, the regression line minimizes the sum of squared deviations over the estimation period. To test forecast reliability, it is necessary to test the predictive capability of a given model over data that was not used to generate the regression model. These data offer an interesting basis for evaluating the usefulness of the simple growth model approach to economic forecasting. In the absence of GDP data for the 1991–1995 period, the reliability of alternative forecast technique can be illustrated by arbitrarily dividing historical GDP data into two subsamples: a 1959–1983 test group and a 1984–1991 forecast group. A regression model estimated over the test group can be used to forecast actual GDP over the 1984–1991 period. Estimation results over the 1959–1983 subperiod provide a forecast model that can be used to evaluate the predictive reliability of a constant growth model over the 1984–1991 forecast period.

A. Set up a table or computer spreadsheet with GDP data for the 1959–1991 period as shown in the previous table. Transform these GDP data using natural logarithms so that it will become possible to analyze them using a constant growth model with continuous compounding.

B. Use the simple regression model approach to estimate, in turn, (1) the linear relation between the natural logarithm of nominal GDP and time and (2) real GDP (ln GDP) and time. Estimate each model over two time intervals: the entire 1959–1991 period and the 1959–1983 test subperiod, where

$$\ln Y_t = b_0 + b_1 T_t + u_t,$$

and where $\ln Y_t$ is the natural logarithm of each respective measure of GDP in year t; T is a time trend variable (where $T_1 = 1959$, $T_2 = 1960$, $T_3 = 1961, \ldots,$ and $T_{25} = 1983$); and u is a residual term that includes the effects of all factors that have been omitted from the regression models and the effects of random or stochastic elements. These are called constant growth models because they are based on the assumption of a constant percentage growth in economic activity per year. How well does each constant growth model fit actual GDP data?

C. Create a spreadsheet that shows actual and forecast GDP values for the 1984–1991 period. Each GDP forecast is derived using the coefficients estimates for each model in Part B along with values for each respective time trend variable over the 1984–1991 period. Remember that $T_{26} = 1984$, $T_{27} = 1986$, $T_{28} = 1987, \ldots,$ and $T_{33} = 1991$ and that each constant growth model provides predicted, or forecast, values for the relevant $\ln Y_t$ variable. To obtain values for Y_t, simply take the antilog (exponent) of each predicted $\ln Y_t$ variable. Place these forecast values in the spreadsheet alongside actual figures. Then, subtract actual figures from forecast values to obtain annual estimates of forecast error for each Y_t variable, plus an estimate of average forecast error for each Y_t variable over the 1984–1991 period.

D. Compute the correlation coefficient between actual and forecast values for each Y_t variable over the 1984–1991 period. Also compute the sample mean forecast error for each Y_t variable. Based upon these findings, how well do constant growth models generated using data over the 1959–1983 period forecast actual GDP data over the 1984–1991 period?

Solution to Self-Test Problem

A. A table with GDP data for the 1959–1991 period shown in natural logarithm form is as follows:

Year	ln GDP in Current Dollars	ln GDP in 1987 Dollars	Time Period (in years)
1991	$8.6433	$8.4864	33
1990	8.6150	8.4939	32
1989	8.5648	8.4840	31
1988	8.4971	8.4593	30
1987	8.4207	8.4207	29
1986	8.3590	8.3906	28
1985	8.3037	8.3617	27
1984	8.2367	8.3305	26
1983	8.1330	8.2704	25
1982	8.0550	8.2323	24
1981	8.0165	8.2540	23
1980	7.9040	8.2365	22
1979	7.8195	8.2419	21
1978	7.7110	8.2170	20
1977	7.5879	8.1700	19
1976	7.4778	8.1259	18
1975	7.3689	8.0777	17
1974	7.2852	8.0858	16
1973	7.2076	8.0921	15
1972	7.0959	8.0414	14
1971	7.0005	7.9947	13
1970	6.9184	7.9641	12
1969	6.8664	7.9645	11
1968	6.7904	7.9377	10
1967	6.7023	7.8974	9
1966	6.6461	7.8718	8
1965	6.5549	7.8134	7
1964	6.4739	7.7593	6
1963	6.4021	7.7044	5
1962	6.3484	7.6638	4
1961	6.2763	7.6136	3
1960	6.2411	7.5874	2
1959	6.2029	7.5659	1

Source: *Economic Report of the President* (Washington, D.C.: U.S. Government Printing Office, 1992), pp. 298, 300.

B. Simple regression models have the potential to illustrate the linear relation between the natural logarithm of nominal GDP and time and real GDP (ln GDP) and time.

Descriptive Regression Models, 1959–1991 (33 observations):

The nominal GDP descriptive regression equation is

$$\text{LOG}_e \text{ NOMINAL GDP} = 6.00 + 0.0834 \text{ TIME.}$$

Predictor	Coefficient	Standard Deviation	*t* Ratio	*p*
Constant	5.99783	0.02074	289.26	0.000
TIME	0.083419	0.001064	78.39	0.000

S.E.E. = 0.05821, R^2 = 99.5%, $\bar{R}^2$ = 99.5%, F = 6,144.81

The real GDP descriptive regression equation is

$$LOG_e \text{ REAL GDP} = 7.60 + 0.0287 \text{ TIME}.$$

Predictor	Coefficient	Standard Deviation	t Ratio	p
Constant	7.59732	0.01405	540.84	0.000
TIME	0.0286962	0.0007209	39.80	0.000

S.E.E. = 0.03943, R^2 = 98.1%, $\bar{R}^2$ = 98.0%, F = 1,584.41

Forecast Regression Models, 1959–1983 (25 observations):

The nominal GDP forecast regression equation is

$$LOG_e \text{ NOMINAL GDP} = 5.98 + 0.0845 \text{ TIME}.$$

Predictor	Coefficient	Standard Deviation	t Ratio	p
Constant	5.98462	0.02437	245.57	0.000
TIME	0.084525	0.001639	51.56	0.000

S.E.E. = 0.05911, R^2 = 99.1%, $\bar{R}^2$ = 99.1%, F = 2,658.56

The real GDP forecast regression equation is

$$LOG_e \text{ REAL GDP} = 7.58 + 0.0304 \text{ TIME}.$$

Predictor	Coefficient	Standard Deviation	t Ratio	p
Constant	7.58015	0.01709	443.41	0.000
TIME	0.030398	0.001150	26.43	0.000

S.E.E. = 0.04146, R^2 = 96.8%, $\bar{R}^2$ = 96.7%, F = 698.79

From these data it is clear that the simple constant growth model approach offers a very high level of description of nominal and real GDP data over both 1959–1991 and 1959–1983 time periods.

C. The following spreadsheet shows actual and forecast GDP values for the 1984–1991 forecast period:

Year	GDP in Current Dollars	Natural Logarithm of GDP in Current Dollars	Natural Logarithm of GDP Forecast in Current Dollars	GDP Forecast in Current Dollars	Forecast Error (Forecast-Actual)	Squared Forecast Error (Forecast-Actual)^2	Time Period (in years)
1991	$5,671.8	8.6433	8.7739	$6,463.6	791.8	627,011.6	33
1990	5,513.8	8.6150	8.6894	5,939.8	426.0	181,436.8	32
1989	5,244.0	8.5648	8.6049	5,458.3	214.3	45,937.0	31
1988	4,900.4	8.4971	8.5204	5,015.9	115.5	13,345.9	30
1987	4,539.9	8.4207	8.4358	4,609.4	69.5	4,827.1	29
1986	4,268.6	8.3590	8.3513	4,235.8	(32.8)	1,077.1	28
1985	4,038.7	8.3037	8.2668	3,892.5	(146.2)	21,384.6	27
1984	3,777.2	8.2367	8.1823	3,577.0	(200.2)	40,089.7	26
Average	$4,744.3	8.4550	8.4781	$4,899.0	$154.7	$116,888.7	29.5

Year	GDP in 1987 Dollars	Natural Logarithm of GDP in 1987 Dollars	Natural Logarithm of GDP Forecast in 1987 Dollars	GDP Forecast in 1987 Dollars	Forecast Error (Forecast-Actual)	Squared Forecast Error (Forecast-Actual)^2	Time Period (in years)
1991	$4,848.4	8.4864	8.5833	$5,341.6	493.2	243,259.3	33
1990	4,884.9	8.4939	8.5529	5,181.7	296.8	88,079.6	32
1989	4,836.9	8.4840	8.5225	5,026.5	189.6	35,963.0	31
1988	4,718.6	8.4593	8.4921	4,876.0	157.4	24,787.8	30
1987	4,540.0	8.4207	8.4617	4,730.0	190.0	36,118.9	29
1986	4,405.5	8.3906	8.4313	4,588.4	182.9	33,463.1	28
1985	4,279.8	8.3617	8.4009	4,451.0	171.2	29,326.1	27
1984	4,148.5	8.3305	8.3705	4,317.8	169.3	28,656.2	26
Average	$4,582.8	8.4284	8.4769	$4,814.1	$231.3	$64,956.8	29.5

Note: Dollar figures are in billions of dollars.

D. The correlation coefficient between actual and forecast nominal GDP is $r_{GDP, FGDP} = 0.993$; the correlation between actual and forecast real GDP is $r_{RGDP, FRGDP} = 0.964$. The sample mean forecast error is $341.9 billion ($= \$116,888.7$), or 7.2% of nominal GDP, and $254.9 billion ($= \$64,956.8$), or 5.6% of real GDP. Notice that despite higher correlation between actual and forecast values, forecast errors represent a greater share of average nominal GDP than of real GDP. In both instances, however, the correlation between actual and forecast values is high and forecast error appears low.

Problems

P7.1 **Sales Trend Analysis.** Rent-A-Car, Inc., provides daily auto rental service to individuals while their own cars are being repaired. Annual sales revenue has grown rapidly from $2.5 million to $10 million during the past five-year period.

A. Calculate the five-year growth rate in sales using the constant growth model with annual compounding.

B. Calculate the five-year growth rate in sales using the constant growth model with continuous compounding.

C. Compare your answers to Parts A and B, and discuss any differences.

P7.2 **Growth Rate Estimation.** Mr. Ed's BBQ is a small restaurant featuring Texas-style barbecue. Wilbur Post, owner of Mr. Ed's, is concerned about the restaurant's erratic revenue pattern during recent years.

A. Complete the following table showing annual sales data for Mr. Ed's during the 1987–1992 period.

Year (1)	Sales (2)	Current Sales ÷ Previous Period Sales (3)	Growth Rate (4) = [(3) − (1)] × 100
1987	$250,000	—	—
1988	200,000		
1989	400,000		
1990	500,000		*continued*

continued

Year (1)	Sales (2)	Current Sales ÷ Previous Period Sales (3)	Growth Rate (4) = [(3) − (1)] × 100
1991	500,000		
1992	250,000		

    B. Calculate the geometric average annual rate of growth for the 1987–1992 period. (Hint: Calculate this growth rate using sales from 1987 and 1992.)

    C. Calculate the arithmetic average annual rate of growth for the 1987–1992 period. (Hint: This is the average of Column 4 figures.)

    D. Discuss any differences in your answers to Parts B and C.

P7.3 **Sales Trend Analysis.** Environmental Designs, Inc., produces and installs energy-efficient window systems in commercial buildings. During the past ten years, sales revenue has increased from $25 million to $65 million.

    A. Calculate the company's growth rate in sales using the constant growth model with annual compounding.

    B. Derive a five-year and a ten-year sales forecast.

P7.4 **Cost Forecasting.** Bullwinkle J. Moose, a quality-control supervisor for Rocket Devices, Inc., is concerned about unit labor cost increases for the assembly of electrical snap-action switches. Costs have increased from $80 to $100 per unit over the previous three years. Moose thinks that importing switches from foreign suppliers at a cost of $115.90 per unit may soon be desirable.

    A. Calculate the company's unit labor cost growth rate using the constant rate of change model with continuous compounding.

    B. Forecast when unit labor costs will equal the current cost of importing.

P7.5 **Unit Sales Forecast Modeling.** Joyce Davenport has discovered that the change in Product A demand in any given week is inversely proportional to the change in sales of Product B in the previous week. That is, if sales of B rose by X percent last week, sales of A can be expected to fall by X percent this week.

    A. Write the equation for next week's sales of A, using the variables A = sales of Product A, B = sales of Product B, and t = time. Assume that there will be no shortages of either product.

    B. Last week, 100 units of A and 90 units of B were sold. Two weeks ago, 75 units of B were sold. What would you predict the sales of A to be this week?

P7.6 **Sales Forecast Modeling.** H. M. Murdock must convince the loan officer at a local bank of the viability of Mr. T's, a retail outlet for T-shirts, posters, and novelty items. In doing so, Murdock must generate a sales forecast. Murdock assumes that next-period sales are a function of current income, advertising, and advertising by a competing retailer.

    A. Write an equation for predicting sales if Murdock assumes that the percentage change in sales is twice as large as the percentage change in income and advertising but that it is only one-half as large as, and of the opposite sign of, the percentage change in competitor advertising. Use the variables S = sales, Y = income, A = advertising, and CA = competitor advertising.

B. During the current period, sales total $500,000, median family income is $35,700, advertising is $25,000, and competitor advertising is $66,000. Previous-period levels were $20,000 (income), $30,000 (advertising), and $60,000 (competitor advertising). Forecast next-period sales.

P7.7 **Cost Forecast Modeling.** Matty Walker, product safety manager at Volatile Products, Inc., is evaluating the cost-effectiveness of a preventive maintenance program. Walker believes that monthly downtime on the packaging line caused by equipment breakdown is related to the hours spent each month on preventive maintenance.

A. Write an equation to predict next month's downtime using the variables D = downtime, M = preventive maintenance, t = time, a_0 = constant term, a_1 = regression slope coefficient, and u = random disturbance. Assume that downtime in the forecast (next) month decreases by the same percentage as preventive maintenance increased during the month preceding the current one.

B. If 40 hours were spent last month on preventive maintenance and this month's downtime was 500 hours, what should downtime be next month if preventive maintenance this month is 50 hours? Use the equation developed in Part A.

P7.8 **Sales Forecast Modeling.** Toys Unlimited Ltd. must forecast sales for a popular adult computer game to avoid stockouts or excessive inventory charges during the coming Christmas season. In percentage terms, the company estimates that game sales fall at double the rate of price increases and that they grow at triple the rate of customer traffic increases. Furthermore, these effects seem to be independent.

A. Write an equation for estimating the Christmas season sales, using the variables S = sales, P = price, T = traffic, t = time, and u = a random disturbance term.

B. Forecast this season's sales if Toys Unlimited sold 10,000 games last season at $15 each, this season's price is anticipated to be $16.50, and customer traffic is expected to rise by 15 percent over previous levels.

P7.9 **Simultaneous Equations.** Mid-Atlantic Cinema, Inc., runs a chain of movie theaters in the east-central states and has enjoyed great success with a Tuesday Night at the Movies promotion. By offering half off its regular $6 admission price, average nightly attendance has risen from 500 to 1,500 persons. Popcorn and other concession revenues tied to attendance have also risen dramatically. Historically, Mid-Atlantic has found that 50 percent of all moviegoers buy a $2 cup of buttered popcorn. Eighty percent of these popcorn buyers, plus 40 percent of the moviegoers that do not buy popcorn, each spend an average of $1.25 on soda and other concessions.

A. Write an expression describing total revenue from tickets plus popcorn plus other concessions.

B. Forecast total revenues for both regular and special Tuesday night pricing.

C. Forecast the total profit contribution earned for the regular and special Tuesday night pricing strategies if the profit contribution is 25 percent on movie ticket revenues and 80 percent on popcorn and other concession revenues.

P7.10 **Simultaneous Equations.** Supersonic Industries, based in Seattle, Washington, manufactures a wide range of parts for aircraft manufacturers. The company is currently evaluating the merits of building a new plant to fulfill a new contract with the federal government. The alternatives to expansion are to use additional overtime, to reduce other production, or both. The company will add new capacity only if the economy appears to be expanding. Therefore, forecasting the general pace of economic activity for the United States is an important input to the decision-making process. The firm has collected data and estimated the following relations for the U.S. economy:

$$\text{Last year's total profits (all corporations)} \ P_{t-1} = \$500 \text{ billion.}$$
$$\text{This year's government expenditures} \ G = \$1,500 \text{ billion.}$$
$$\text{Annual consumption expenditures} \ C = \$300 \text{ billion} + 0.75Y + u.$$
$$\text{Annual investment expenditures} \ I = \$550 \text{ billion} + 0.9P_{t-1} + u.$$
$$\text{Annual tax receipts} \ T = 0.2GDP.$$
$$\text{National income} \ Y = GDP - T.$$
$$\text{Gross domestic product (GDP)} = C + I + G.$$

Forecast each of the preceding variables through the simultaneous relations expressed in the multiple equation system. Assume that all random disturbances average out to zero.

CASE STUDY FOR CHAPTER 7

Forecasting Global Operating Performance
for a Mickey Mouse Organization

The Walt Disney Company is one of the best known and best managed entertainment companies in the world. As the cornerstone of a carefully integrated entertainment marketing strategy, the company owns and operates the most acclaimed amusement parks and entertainment facilities in the world. Some of the best known and most successful among these are Disneyland, California, and Walt Disney World, Florida—an immense entertainment center that includes the Magic Kingdom, Epcot Center, and Disney-MGM Studios. During recent years the company has extended its amusement park business to foreign soil with Tokyo Disneyland and Euro Disneyland, located just outside of Paris, France. Disney's

TABLE 7.11 **Operating Performance During the 1980s for the Walt Disney Company**

Year	Revenues ($ Millions)	Net Profit ($ Millions)	Net Profit Margin (%)
1990	$5,844.0	$824.0	14.1
1989	4,594.0	703.3	15.3
1988	3,438.2	522.0	15.2
1987	2,876.8	392.3	13.6
1986	2,470.9	247.3	10.0
1985	2,015.4	173.5	8.6
1984	1,656.0	107.8	6.5
1983	1,307.4	93.2	7.1
1982	1,030.3	100.1	9.7
1981	1,005.0	121.5	12.1
1980	914.5	135.2	14.8

Source: The Value Line Investment Survey, June 5, 1992, 1758.

foreign operations provide an interesting example of the company's shrewd combination of marketing and financial skills. To conserve scarce capital resources, Disney was able to entice foreign investors to put up 100 percent of the financing required for both the Tokyo and Paris facilities. In turn, Disney is responsible for the design and operation of both operations, retains a 49 percent equity interest, and enjoys significant royalties on all gross revenues. Disney's innovative means for financing foreign operations has enabled the company to greatly expand its revenue and profit base without any commensurate increase in capital expenditures. As a result, the success of its foreign operations has allowed the company to increase its already enviable rate of return on stockholders' equity to more than 20 percent per year.

Disney is also a major force in the movie picture production business with Buena Vista, Touchstone, and Hollywood Pictures, in addition to the renowned Walt Disney Studios. The company is well known for hit movies such as *Beauty and the Beast, Dick Tracy, Three Men and a Little Lady,* and *The Little Mermaid.* It is also known for an aggressive and highly successful video marketing strategy for new films and re-releases from the company's extensive film library. Royalties from sales of movie tie-in merchandise, books, and recorded music also make a significant contribution to the bottom line, as do profits from the cable TV Disney Channel and KCAL-TV in Los Angeles. The company's overall marketing strategy to "lighten the load" and entertain is so successful that Disney characters such as Mickey Mouse, Donald Duck, and Goofy have become an integral part of Americana. Given its ability to turn whimsy into outstanding operating performance, the Walt Disney Company is one firm that wouldn't mind being described as a "Mickey Mouse Organization."

Table 7.11 shows revenues, net profits, and profit margin performance for the Walt Disney Corporation during the 1980s. During this period, revenues grew at an annual rate of 20.4 percent per year, net profits grew by 19.8 percent per year, and net profit margins held steady in the range of 14 percent of sales. All of these performance measures exceed industry and economy-wide norms by a

TABLE 7.12 **National Income and Interest Rate Series Used for Forecasting Purposes by the Value Line Investment Survey**

Year	GNP ($ Bill.)	Real GNP ($ Bill. 1982)	Cons. Spend. ($ Bill.)	Cap. Spend. ($ Bill.)	Ind. Prod. (1987 = 100)	Hous. Starts (Mill. Units)	Car Sales (Mill. Units)	Savings (%)
1994–96*	7211	4699	4845	674	122.6	1.4	9.9	4.0
1992*	5972	4296	3994	541	110.4	1.2	9.0	4.1
1991*	5658	4177	3790	518	106.6	1.1	8.6	4.1
1990	5464	4156	3659	524	109.2	1.2	9.5	4.5
1989	5201	4118	3450	512	108.1	1.4	9.9	4.6
1988	4874	4017	3238	488	105.4	1.5	10.6	4.2
1987	4516	3845	3009	445	100.0	1.6	10.2	2.9
1986	4232	3718	2797	435	95.3	1.8	11.4	4.2
1985	4015	3619	2629	443	94.4	1.7	11.0	4.4
1984	3772	3501	2430	416	92.8	1.8	10.4	6.2
1983	3406	3279	2235	357	84.9	1.7	9.2	5.4
1982	3166	3166	2051	367	81.9	1.1	8.0	6.8
1981	3053	3249	1915	369	85.7	1.1	8.5	7.5
1980	2732	3187	1733	323	84.1	1.3	9.0	7.1

Year	Unemp. (%)	AAA Rate (%)	T-Bond (%)	T-Bill (%)	Real GNP (%)	GNP Price Def. (%)	CPI (%)
1994–96*	5.9	9.4	9.0	7.1	3.1	3.7	4.4
1992*	6.5	9.2	8.6	6.3	2.9	2.6	3.5
1991*	6.6	9.0	8.3	6.0	0.5	3.0	4.6
1990	5.5	9.3	8.6	7.5	0.9	4.1	5.4
1989	5.3	9.3	8.4	8.1	2.5	4.1	4.8
1988	5.5	9.7	9.0	6.7	4.5	3.3	4.1
1987	6.2	9.4	8.6	5.8	3.4	3.1	3.7
1986	7.0	9.0	7.8	6.0	2.7	2.6	1.9
1985	7.2	11.4	10.8	7.5	3.4	3.0	3.5
1984	7.5	12.7	12.4	9.5	6.8	3.8	4.4
1983	9.6	12.0	11.2	8.6	3.6	3.8	3.2
1982	9.7	13.8	12.8	10.6	−2.5	6.4	6.2
1981	7.5	14.2	13.4	14.0	1.9	9.7	10.4
1980	7.1	11.9	11.3	11.4	−0.2	9.0	13.5

Source: Value Line Investment Survey, April 12, 1991, 550.

substantial margin. Disney employees, CEO Michael D. Eisner, and all stockholders are among those who profited greatly from the company's outstanding performance. At the start of the 1980s, Disney common stock traded in the range of $10 per share, after adjusting for a four-for-one stock split during 1986. By late 1989, Disney stock traded at a price in excess of $135 per share—thus representing more than a 30 percent annual rate of return and making Disney one of the truly outstanding stock market performers during the 1980s.

How will Disney perform during the 1990s? Will the company be able to continue its sizzling recent growth, or, like many companies, will Disney find it impossible to maintain such stellar performance? On the one hand, Tokyo Disneyland and Euro Disneyland promise significant future revenues and profits from previously untapped markets. Anyone with young children who has visited

TABLE 7.13 **Experimental Stepwise Regression Results Explaining Walt Disney Company Sales Revenue, Net Profits, and Net Profit Margin (15 Possible Predictors, $n = 11$ Annual Observations)**

Stepwise regression for sales revenue:

STEP	1	2	3	4	5
CONSTANT	-4368	-6169	1144	4121	2834
GNP	1.69	1.96	3.92	5.62	5.91
T-RATIO	9.84	13.58	7.18	9.86	22.53
CPI		126	210	367	369
T-RATIO		3.30	6.29	7.75	17.37
INDPROD			-165	-299	-310
T-RATIO			-3.63	-6.55	-15.07
HOUSING				1284	1610
T-RATIO				3.65	9.43
SAVINGS					141
T-RATIO					4.98
S	494	342	215	129	58.0
R^2	91.49	96.39	98.75	99.61	99.93

Stepwise regression for net profits:

STEP	1	2	3
CONSTANT	-2002.6	-1573.2	-577.3
INDPROD	24.4	30.0	25.4
T-RATIO	7.27	14.31	12.90
CARSALES		-97	-117
T-RATIO		-494	-8.10
T-BOND			-36
T-RATIO			-3.30
S	106	55.7	37.2
R^2	85.44	96.41	98.60

Stepwise regression for net profit margin:

STEP	1	2
CONSTANT	23.02	27.14
UNEMP	-1.62	-1.94
T-RATIO	-3.25	-5.57
RGNP%		-0.73
T-RATIO		-3.42
S	2.36	1.59
R^2	54.05	81.35

Disneyland or Disney World has seen their delight and fascination with Disney characters. It is also impossible not to notice how much foreign travelers to the United States seem to enjoy the Disney experience. Donald Duck and Mickey Mouse will do a lot of business abroad. Future expansion possibilities in Malaysia, China, or the Soviet Union also hold the potential for rapid company growth well into the next century. On the other hand, growth of 20 percent per year is exceedingly hard to maintain for any length of time. At that pace, the 52,000 workers employed by Disney would grow to 322,000 by the year 2000, and to 2 million by the year 2010. Maintaining control with such a rapidly growing workforce would be challenge enough; maintaining Disney's creative energy might not be possible.

Given the extreme uncertainties faced by Disney and any major corporation, long-term forecasts of operating performance by industry analysts are usually restricted to a fairly short time perspective. The *Value Line Investment Survey,* one of the most widely respected forecast services, focuses on a three to five year time horizon. To forecast performance for any individual company, *Value Line* starts with an underlying forecast of the economic environment three to five years hence. During mid-1991, *Value Line* forecast a 1994 to 1996 economic environment in which unemployment will average 5.9 percent of the workforce, a significant increase from 1990s 5.0 percent as shown in Table 7.12. Worker productivity will be expanding about 1.3 percent per year, and inflation will continue at 4.4 percent per year as measured by the Consumer Price Index. Long-term interest rates are projected in the 9 to 9.5 percent range, with real GNP growing at a rate near 3 percent per year, a level more than 30 percent greater than that experienced during 1990. As *Value Line* states, things may turn out differently, but these plausible assumptions offer a fruitful basis for measuring the relative growth potential of various firms.

As a first step in generating a useful forecast of Disney operating performance during the period 1994 to 1996, an experimental stepwise multiple regression analysis was run using Disney operating data and fifteen series of annual statistics used for forecasting purposes by *Value Line*. Table 7.13 shows forecast models for Disney revenues, net profits, and net profit margins based on a statistically significant link between various economic variables and Disney performance over the 1980 to 1990 period.

A. Do each of the three models shown above describe a sizeable share of the variation in Disney operating performance?

B. Do the limitations of small sample size affect your confidence in each of these regression results?

C. Use relevant *Value Line* estimates of 1994 to 1996 economic variables and each descriptive model to generate econometric forecasts of Disney operating performance. It might prove interesting to compare these forecasts with *Value Line* 1994 to 1996 forecasts for Disney of $9.7 billion in revenues, $1,390 million in net profits, and a net profit margin of 14.3 percent. Even more interesting would be to consult a recent edition of the *Value Line Investment Survey* so as to compare both sets of forecasts with recent Disney operating experience.

Selected References   Abarbanell, Jeffery S. "Do Analysts' Earnings Forecasts Incorporate Information in Prior Stock Price Changes?" *Journal of Accounting & Economics* 14 (June 1991): 147–165.

Ali, Ashig, April Klein, and James Rosenfeld. "Analysts' Use of Information about Permanent and Transitory Earnings Components in Forecasting EPS." *Accounting Review* 67 (January 1992): 183–198.

Allen, Steven G. "Changes in the Cyclical Sensitivity of Wages in the United States, 1981–1987." *American Economic Review* 82 (March 1992): 122–140.

Cheng, Leonard K., and Elias Dinopoulos. "Schumpeterian Growth and International Business Cycles." *American Economic Review* 82 (May 1992): 409–414.

Christiano, Lawrence J., and Martin Eichenbaum. "Current Real-Business-Cycle Theories and Aggregate Labor-Market Fluctuations." *American Economic Review* 82 (June 1992): 430–450.

Estrella, Arturo, and Gikas A. Hardouvelis. "The Term Structure as a Predictor of Real Economic Activity." *Journal of Finance* 46 (June 1991): 555–576.

Hafer, R. W., Scott E. Hein, and S. Scott MacDonald. "Market and Survey Forecasts of the Three-month Treasury Bill Rate." *Journal of Business* 65 (January 1992): 123–138.

Hamilton, James D. "Was the Deflation During the Great Depression Anticipated? Evidence from the Commodity Futures Market." *American Economic Review* 82 (March 1992): 157-178.

Hartzmark, Michael L. "Luck Versus Forecast Ability: Determinants of Trader Performance in Futures Markets." *Journal of Business* 64 (January 1991): 49–74.

Lahiri, Kajal, and Geoffrey H. Moore, eds. *Leading Economic Indicators: New Approaches and Forecasting Records.* (New York: Cambridge University Press, 1991).

Lawrence, David B. "Managerial Evaluation of Exogenous Forecast Sources." *Managerial and Decision Economics* 12 (June 1991): 249–259.

Leitch, Gordon, and J. Ernest Tanner. "Economic Forecast Evaluation: Profit versus the Conventional Error Measures." *American Economic Review* 81 (June 1991): 580–590.

Paxson, Christina H. "Using Weather Variability to Estimate the Response of Savings to Transitory Income in Thailand." *American Economic Review* 82 (March 1992): 15–33.

Pindyck, Robert, and Dan Rubinfeld. *Economic Models and Economic Forecasts.* Hightstown, NJ: McGraw-Hill, 1991.

Reichenstein, William. "Touters Trophies: Ranking Economists' Forecasts." *Financial Analysts' Journal* 47 (July–August 1991): 20–21.

PRODUCTION AND COST ANALYSIS

CHAPTER | # PRODUCTION ANALYSIS AND ESTIMATION

The production process is the manner in which resource inputs are transformed into valuable goods and services output. It is the essentially creative endeavor at the heart of every successful organization. To be successful, the production process must reflect an efficient use of human and capital resources in the creation of needed products. Not only must resources be used effectively, but products that are produced must meet customer specifications in terms of price, quality, and timely delivery. To successfully master the production process, organizations must focus on both what customers want and how to effectively meet those needs. To master one without the other is a recipe for failure. The corporate landscape is littered with examples of firms that once introduced innovative product and process improvements only to see their early lead and dominant position in the marketplace eroded by later and more efficient rivals. Similarly, a number of firms have fallen prey to the mistake of striving and succeeding at being the low-cost producer in a vanishing market. Productive efficiency is not simply about *what* or *how* to produce—it is about *both*.

For the production process to be successful, management must constructively address a number of important related questions. Given product demand conditions, how does a firm determine the optimal level of output during any given production period? When several alternative production methods are available, how does a firm choose the best one? How will investment in new manufacturing equipment affect worker productivity and the unit costs of production? If the firm undertakes an expansion program to increase productive capacity, will cost per unit be higher or lower after the expansion? Each of these questions can be critically important to firm success. Valuable insights and further questions that make ultimate answers obvious are provided by the study of production.

Production concepts have broad application and are equally relevant to the manufacture of physical goods and to the provision of services. In each instance, production analysis focuses on the efficient use of inputs to create outputs that meet the demonstrated demand of customers. Technical and economic characteristics of production methods used in the manufacture of both goods and services are studied to determine the low-cost means of meeting specific customer needs.

It is worth emphasizing that the study of production involves much more than the simple physical transformation of resources. Production involves all the activities associated with providing goods and services. The hiring of workers (from unskilled labor to top management), personnel training, and the organizational structure adopted to maximize efficiency are all part of the production process. The acquisition of capital resources and its efficient employment are also parts of production, as are the design and use of appropriate accounting control and management information systems.

In addition to providing a useful foundation for understanding the nature of demand/supply and cost/output and relations, production analysis enhances appreciation for the integrated nature of the firm. No other topic in managerial economics so clearly lays out the linkage between the market demand signals from customers and the supply response from firms. In this way, contributions made by the functional areas of accounting, finance, marketing, and management can be seen as key ingredients in the value-maximization process.

PRODUCTION FUNCTIONS

Production function

The maximum output that can be produced for a given amount of input.

A **production function** is a descriptive statement that relates inputs to outputs. It specifies the maximum possible output that can be produced for a given amount of input or, alternatively, the minimum quantity of input necessary to produce a given level of output. Production functions are determined by the technology available for employing plant, equipment, labor, materials, and so on. Any improvement in technology, such as better equipment or a training program that enhances worker productivity, results in a new production function.

Basic properties of production functions can be illustrated by examining a simple two-input, one-output system. Consider a production process in which various quantities of two inputs, X and Y, can be used to produce a product, Q. The inputs X and Y might represent resources such as labor and capital or energy and raw materials. The product Q could be physical goods such as television sets, baseball gloves, or breakfast cereal; Q could also represent services such as medical care, education, or banking.

The production function for such a system can be written

$$Q = f(X, Y). \tag{8.1}$$

Table 8.1 is a representation of a two-input, single-output production system. Each element in the table shows the maximum quantity of Q that can be produced with a specific combination of X and Y. Table 8.1 shows, for example, that 2 units of X and 3 units of Y can be combined to produce 49 units of output; 5 units of X coupled with 5 units of Y results in 92 units of output; 4 units of X and 10 units of Y produce 101 units of Q, and so on. The units of input could represent *hours* of labor, *dollars* of capital, *cubic feet* of natural gas, *tons* of raw materials, and so on. Units of Q could be *numbers* of television sets or baseball gloves, *cases* of cereal, *patient days* of hospital care, customer *transactions* at an ATM banking facility, and so on.

Discrete production function

A production function with distinct input patterns.

The **discrete production function** described in Table 8.1 involves distinct, or "lumpy," patterns for input combination that can be illustrated graphically, as in

TABLE 8.1   A Representative Production Table

Units of Y Employed	Output Quantity									
10	52	71	87	101	113	122	127	129	130	131
9	56	74	89	102	111	120	125	127	128	129
8	59	75	91	99	108	117	122	124	125	126
7	61	77	87	96	104	112	117	120	121	122
6	62	72	82	91	99	107	111	114	116	117
5	55	66	75	84	92	99	104	107	109	110
4	47	58	68	77	85	91	97	100	102	103
3	35	49	59	68	76	83	89	91	90	89
2	15	31	48	59	68	72	73	72	70	67
1	5	12	35	48	56	55	53	50	46	40
	1	2	3	4	5	6	7	8	9	10

Units of X Employed

Figure 8.1. The height of the bars associated with each input combination indicates the output produced. The tops of the output bars map the production surface for the system.

The discrete production data shown in Table 8.1 and Figure 8.1 can be generalized by assuming that the underlying production function is continuous. A **continuous production function** is one in which inputs can be varied in an unbroken marginal fashion rather than incrementally, as in the preceding example.

The three-dimensional diagram in Figure 8.2 is a graphic illustration of a continuous production function for a two-input, single-output system. Following the x axis outward indicates that increasing amounts of Input X are being used; going out the y axis represents an increasing usage of $Y;$ and moving up the Q axis means that larger amounts of output are being produced. The maximum amount of Q that can be produced with each combination of Inputs X and Y is represented by the height of the production surface above the input plane. Q^*, for example, is the maximum amount of output that can be produced using the input combination X^*, Y^*.

Continuous production function

A production function where inputs can be varied in an unbroken marginal fashion.

Returns to Scale and Returns to a Factor

Returns to scale

The output effect of a proportional increase in all inputs.

In studying production functions, two important relations between inputs and outputs are of interest in managerial decision making. One is the relation between output and the variation in *all inputs* taken together. This is known as the **returns to scale** characteristic of a production system. Returns to scale play an important role in managerial decisions. They affect the optimal scale, or size, of a firm and its production facilities. They also affect the nature of competition in an industry and thus are important in determining the profitability of investment in a particular economic sector.

A second important relation in any production system is that between output and variation in only *one of the inputs* employed. **Returns to a factor** denotes

FIGURE 8.1   **Representative Production Surface**

This discrete production function illustrates the output level resulting from each combination of inputs *X* and *Y*.

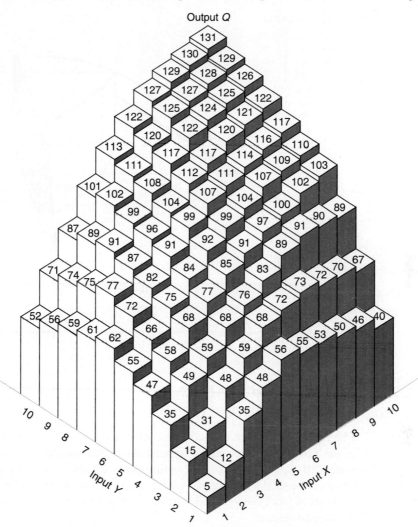

Returns to a factor

The relation between output and variation in only one input.

the relation between the quantity of an individual input (or factor of production) employed and the level of output produced. Factor productivity is the key to determining the optimal combination of inputs that should be used to manufacture a given product. Factor productivity analysis provides the basis for efficient resource employment in all production systems. Because an understanding of factor productivity aids in the study of returns to scale, it is worth considering factor productivity concepts first.

F I G U R E 8 . 2   **A Continuous Production Function for a Two-Input, Single-Output System**

In a continuous production function, inputs can be varied continuously.

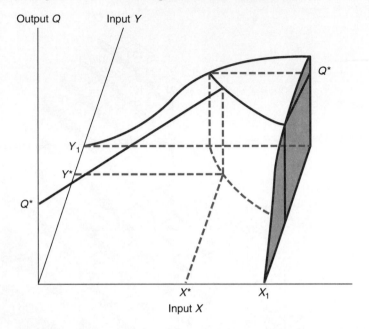

TOTAL, MARGINAL, AND AVERAGE PRODUCT

The economic concept of factor productivity or returns to a factor is important in the process of determining optimal input combinations for any production system. Because the process of optimization entails an analysis of the relation between the total and marginal values of a function, it is useful to introduce the concepts of total, average, and marginal products for the resources employed in a production system.

Total Product

Total product

The whole output from a production system.

Total product is the complete output from a production system. It is synonymous with Q in Equation 8.1. Total product is a measure of the total output or product that results from employing a specific quantity of resources in a given production system.

The total product concept is used to describe the relation between output and variation in only one input in a production function. For example, suppose that Table 8.1 represents a production system in which Y is a capital resource and X represents a labor input. If a firm is operating with a given level of capital (say, $Y = 2$), then the relevant production function for the firm in the short run is

TABLE 8.2 **Total Product, Marginal Product, and Average Product of Factor X, Holding $Y = 2$**

Input Quantity (X)	Total Product of the Input (Q)	Marginal Product of Input X $(MP_X = \Delta Q / \Delta X)$	Average Product of Input X $(AP_X = Q/X)$
1	15	+15	15.0
2	31	+16	15.5
3	48	+17	16.0
4	59	+11	14.8
5	68	+9	13.6
6	72	+4	12.0
7	73	+1	10.4
8	72	−1	9.0
9	70	−2	7.8
10	67	−3	6.7

represented by the row in Table 8.1 corresponding to that level of fixed capital.[1] Operating with two units of capital, output or total product depends on the quantity of labor (X) employed. This total product of X can be read from the $Y = 2$ row in Table 8.1. It is also shown in Column 2 of Table 8.2 and is illustrated graphically in Figure 8.3.

More generally, the total product of a production factor can be expressed as a function relating output to the quantity of the resource employed. Continuing the example, the total product of X is given by the production function

$$Q = f(X|Y = 2).$$

This equation relates the output quantity Q (the total product of X) to the quantity of Input X employed, fixing the quantity of Y at two units. One would, of course, obtain other total product functions for X if the factor Y were fixed at levels other than two units.

Figure 8.4 illustrates the more general concept of the total product of an input as the schedule of output obtained as that input increases, *holding constant the amounts of other inputs employed.* This figure depicts a continuous production function where inputs can be varied in a marginal unbroken fashion rather than discretely. Suppose the firm wishes to fix, or hold constant, the amount of Input Y at the level Y_1. The total product curve of Input X, holding Input Y constant at Y_1, originates at Y_1 and rises along the production surface as the use of Input X is increased. Four other total product curves are shown in the figure: another for X, holding Y constant at Y_2, and three for Input Y, holding X fixed at X_1, X_2, and X_3, respectively.

---

[1] In economic terminology the *short run* is a period of time during which at least one resource in a production system is fixed; that is, the quantity of that resource is constant regardless of the quantity of output produced. This concept is further developed in Chapter 9.

FIGURE 8.3   **Total, Average, and Marginal Product for Input X, Given $Y = 2$**

(a) Holding Y at two units, total production first rises but then falls as the amount of X employed grows. (b) Total product rises as long as marginal product is positive.

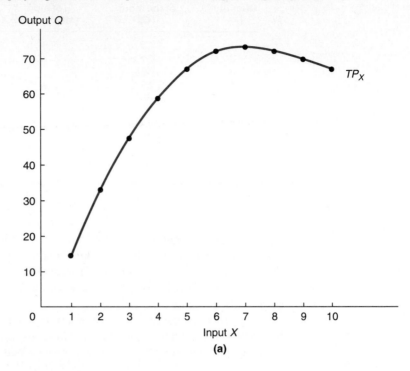

(a)

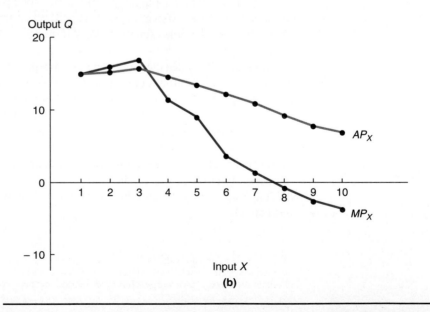

(b)

FIGURE 8.4   Total Product Curves for *X* and *Y*

Total product curves show the increase in output following an increase in input usage.

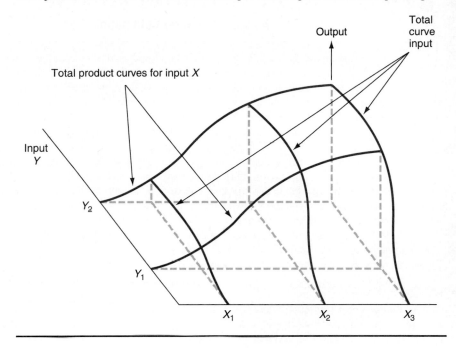

Marginal Product

Marginal product

Change in output associated with a one-unit change in a single input.

Given the total product function for an input, both marginal and average products can be easily derived. The **marginal product** of a factor, MP_X, is the change in output associated with a one-unit change in the factor input, holding all other inputs constant. For a total product function such as that shown in Table 8.2 and Figure 8.4(a), the marginal product is expressed as

$$MP_X = \frac{\delta Q}{\delta X},$$

where δQ is the change in output resulting from a one-unit change, δX, in the variable factor. This expression assumes that the quantity of the other input, Y, remains unchanged.

Average Product

Average product

Total product divided by units of input employed.

Average product is total product divided by the number of units of input employed:

$$AP_X = \frac{Q}{X}. \tag{8.2}$$

The average product for X given $Y = 2$ units is shown in Column 4 of Table 8.2 and in Figure 8.3(b).

For a continuous total product function, as illustrated in Figure 8.5(a), marginal product equals the slope of the total product curve, whereas the average

●

MANAGERIAL APPLICATION 8.1

Making Computer Automation Work

What has been automated over the past 20 to 30 years reflects how business was traditionally done, and not necessarily how to best serve a rapidly changing marketplace. In the 1950s, companies used the new "electronic brains" of computers to mechanize routine office and factory procedures. Sophisticated management information systems emerged during the 1960s and 1970s, allowing firms to collect and organize data for centralized analysis and control of the business. Systems integration became the goal during the 1980s, as computer users sought to connect various brands and sizes of computers to better share information.

In the 1990s, re-engineering is a main concern for computer users as they fundamentally rethink business processes with the aim of cutting time-to-market for new products and services and dramatically improving productivity. Major computer makers such as IBM, Digital Equipment, Unisys, and Wang Laboratories are all seizing on job re-engineering as a new marketing approach. Job re-engineering involves using computer technology to dramatically reshape the nature of work by redefining the task to be performed. Rather than just more quickly completing an already established task or routine, computer manufacturers are urging customers to use their equipment to offer dramatically new goods and services. A similar theme is being sounded by Electronic Data Systems and Andersen Consulting, the nation's largest systems integration consultants.

Re-engineering first surfaced in the 1980s in the manufacturing sector. Such concepts as concurrent engineering and just-in-time inventory stocking and product deliveries have produced profound changes in the ways manufacturers do business. These manufacturing processes, all but impossible without sophisticated computer systems, upended traditional ways of doing things. Rather than isolate tasks into discrete departments defined along functional lines, manufacturers began tearing down artificial barriers between engineering, manufacturing, sales, and support operations. Customer feedback to marketing personnel can now be passed along to design departments, who in turn work with production staff to better meet customer needs. Similarly, design personnel are able to adjust product design characteristics to meet reliability and cost objectives set by financial staff. What makes this whole re-engineering process work with both speed and precision is that improved feedback from the marketplace has enabled more activities to take place in parallel, not sequential, order. Information flows in a continuous fashion among marketing, design, production, and financial departments. Products get to market faster and with lower cost and higher quality.

With the documented success of computer re-engineering at the shop, plant, and divisional level, entire businesses are now being re-engineered from the ground up. That inevitably means now a broad range of new computers and software and a significant investment in worker and management training. When you change the basic nature of work, it changes the way information and resources are moved around within the organization. As a result, the entire management information system needs an overhaul.

An interesting example of a manufacturing company that successfully embraces the use of computers to fundamentally reshape its business is provided by Hallmark Cards Inc., located in Kansas City. Hallmark is re-engineering its business to get new greeting cards, wrapping papers, and gift items to market sooner to meet customers' fast-changing tastes. That process now takes up to two years, but the goal is to get the job done in less than 12 months. Hallmark is setting up small teams of workers from its art, design, and sales departments to more quickly move products from the concept stage to market. It also is bringing suppliers such as lithographers onto projects earlier so that their feedback can be used to coordinate product development. To improve feedback from the marketplace, Hallmark equips its 1,700 retailers with computer-based cash registers, at no charge to the stores.

Using computer technology, businesses are steadily shortening the time between the design and manufacture of goods and delivery to the ultimate consumer. With significant productivity gains already evident, and dramatic cost-cutting in distribution, leading companies clearly rely upon computer automation to fundamentally improve their way of doing business.

Source: Peter Coy, "The New Realism in Office Systems," *Business Week,* June 15, 1992, 128–132.

FIGURE 8.5 **Total, Marginal, and Average Product Curves: (a) Total Product Curve for X, Holding $Y = Y_1$; (b) Marginal Product Curve for X, Holding $Y = Y_1$**

MP_X reaches a maximum at point A', where the slope of the TP_X curve is greatest. AP_X is at a maximum where $MP_X = AP_X$. At point C, TP_X is at a maximum and $MP_X = 0$.

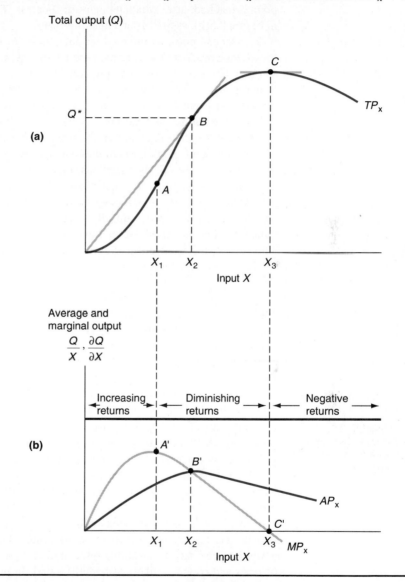

product equals the slope of a line drawn from the origin to a point on the total product curve. The average and marginal products for Input X can be determined in this manner, and these points are plotted to form the average and marginal product curves shown in Figure 8.5(b).

Three points of interest, *A, B,* and *C,* can be identified on the total product curve in Figure 8.5(a). Each has a corresponding location on the average or marginal curves. Point *A* is the inflection point of the total product curve. The marginal product of *X* (the slope of the total product curve) increases until this point is reached, after which it begins to decrease. This phenomenon can be seen in Figure 8.5(b), as MP_X is at a maximum at *A'*.

The second point on the total product curve, *B,* indicates the output at which the average product and marginal product are equal. The slope of a line from the origin to any point on the total product curve measures the average product of *X* at that point, whereas the slope of the total product curve equals the marginal product. At Point *B,* where X_2 units of Input *X* are employed, a line from the origin is tangent to the total product curve, so $MP_X = AP_X$. Note also that the slopes of successive lines drawn from the origin to the total product curve increase until Point *B,* after which their slopes decline. The average product curve rises until it reaches *B,* then declines; this feature is also shown in Figure 8.5(b) as Point *B'*. Here again $MP_X = AP_X$ and AP_X is at a maximum.

The third point, *C,* indicates where the slope of the total product curve is zero and the curve is at a maximum. Beyond *C* the marginal product of *X* is negative, indicating that increased use of Input *X* results in a *reduction* of total product. The corresponding point in Figure 8.5(b) is *C'*, the point where the marginal product curve intersects the *x* axis.

The Law of Diminishing Returns to a Factor

Law of diminishing returns

As the quantity of a variable input increases, the resulting rate of output increase eventually diminishes.

The total and the marginal product curves in Figure 8.5 demonstrate the property known as the **law of diminishing returns.** This law states that as the quantity of a variable input increases, with the quantities of all other factors being held constant, the resulting rate of increase in output eventually diminishes. Alternatively, the law of diminishing returns states that the marginal product of a variable factor must eventually decline as increasingly more of the variable factor is combined with other fixed resources. The law of diminishing returns is sometimes called the law of diminishing marginal returns to emphasize the fact that it deals specifically with the diminishing marginal product of a variable input factor. The law of diminishing returns cannot be derived deductively. It is a generalization of an empirical regularity associated with every known production system. The basis for this relation is easily demonstrated for the labor input in a production process in which a fixed amount of capital is employed.

Consider a factory with an assembly line for the production of refrigerators. If only one employee is put to work, that individual must perform each of the activities necessary to assemble refrigerators. Output from such a combination of labor and capital is likely to be quite small. In fact, it may be less than could be achieved with a smaller amount of capital given the inefficiency of having one employee accompany a refrigerator down an assembly line rather than building it at a single station. As additional units of labor are added to this production system—holding capital input constant—output is likely to expand rapidly. The intensity with which the capital resource is used increases with additional labor, and increasingly efficient input combinations result. The improved use of capital resulting from the increase in labor could cause the marginal product or rise in output associated with each successive employee to actually increase over some range of additional labor. This increasing marginal productivity might result from each unit of labor using a more manageable quantity of capital than is possible with less total labor input. Worker specialization that often accompanies increased employment is another factor that might lead to increasing returns to labor as successive workers are employed.

An illustration of a production situation in which the marginal product of an input increases over some range is presented in Table 8.2. The first unit of labor (Input X) results in 15 units of production. With 2 units of labor, 31 units can be produced. The marginal product of the second unit of labor $MP_{X=2} = 16$ exceeds that of the $MP_{X=1} = 15$. Similarly, the addition of another unit of labor results in output increasing to 48 units, indicating a marginal product of $MP_{X=3} = 17$ for the third unit of labor.

Eventually, sufficient labor is combined with the fixed capital input so that the benefits of further labor additions will not be as large as the benefits achieved earlier. When this occurs, the rate of increase in output per additional unit of labor, the marginal product of labor, will drop. Although the marginal product of labor is positive and total output increases as more units of labor are employed, the rate of increase in output eventually declines. In other words, the marginal product of labor remains positive but eventually decreases. This diminishing marginal productivity of labor is exhibited by the fourth, fifth, sixth, and seventh units of Input X in Table 8.2.

Finally, a point might be reached where the quantity of the variable input factor is so large that total output actually begins to decline with additional employment of that factor. In the refrigerator assembly example, this might occur when the labor force became so large that additional employees actually got in each other's way and hindered the manufacturing process. This happens in Table 8.2 when more than 7 units of Input X are combined with 2 units of Input Y. The eighth unit of X results in a one-unit reduction in total output, $MP_{X=8} = -1$; units 9 and 10 cause output to fall by 2 and 3 units, respectively. In Figure 8.5(b), regions where the variable input factor X exhibits increasing, diminishing, and negative returns have been labeled. The concepts of total and marginal product and the law of diminishing returns to a factor are important in identifying efficient as opposed to inefficient input combinations. This can be illustrated with yet another example.

▶ Suppose Tax Advisors, Inc., has an office for processing tax returns in Scranton, Pennsylvania. Table 8.3 provides information on the production function for processing tax returns in that office. If the office employs one certified public accountant (CPA), it can process 0.2 tax returns per hour. Adding a second CPA increases production to 1 return per hour, and with a third, output jumps to 2.1 returns processed per hour. Note that in this production system, the marginal product for the second CPA is 0.8 returns per hour as compared with 0.2 for the first CPA employed. The marginal product for the third CPA is 1.4 returns per hour.

It is instructive to examine the source of this relative burst in productivity for the second and third CPAs. After all, $MP_{CPA=2} = 0.8$ seems to indicate that the second CPA is four times as productive as the first, and $MP_{CPA=3} = 1.4$ says that

TABLE 8.3   Production Function for Tax-Return Processing

Units of Labor Input Employed (CPAs)	Total Product of CPAs— Tax Returns Processed/Hour ($TP_{CPA} = Q$)	Marginal Product of CPAs ($MP_{CPA} = \Delta Q$)	Average Product of CPAs ($AP_{CPA} = Q/X$)
1	0.2	0.2	0.20
2	1.0	0.8	0.50
3	2.1	1.4	0.70
4	2.5	0.4	0.63
5	2.7	0.2	0.52
6	2.4	−0.3	0.40

the third CPA is more productive still. In production analysis, however, it is assumed that each unit of an input factor is like all other units of that same factor, meaning that each CPA is equally competent and efficient. If individual differences in the CPA inputs do not account for this increasing productivity, what does?

Typically, it is advantages from increased specialization and better utilization of other factors in the production process that allow factor productivity to grow. As the number of CPAs increases, each can specialize, for example, in processing personal returns, partnership returns, corporate returns, and so on. Also, additional CPAs may be better able to fully utilize computer, clerical, and other resources employed by the firm. Advantages from specialization and increased coordination among all resources cause output to rise at an increasing rate, from 0.2 to 1 return processed per hour as the second CPA is employed, and from 1 to 2.1 returns per hour as the third CPA is added.

In practice it is very rare to see input combinations that exhibit increasing returns for any factor. With increasing returns to a factor, every industry would come to be dominated by one very large producer—and this is seldom the case. Input combinations in the range of diminishing returns are commonly observed. If, for example, four CPAs could process 2.5 returns per hour, then the marginal product of the fourth CPA ($MP_{CPA=4} = 0.4$) would be less than the marginal product of the third CPA ($MP_{CPA=3} = 1.4$) and diminishing returns to the CPA labor input would be encountered.

The irrationality of employing inputs in the negative returns range, beyond X_3 in Figure 8.5(b), can be illustrated by noting that adding a sixth CPA would cause total output to fall from 2.7 to 2.4 returns per hour. The marginal product of the sixth CPA is −0.3 ($MP_{CPA=6} = -0.3$), perhaps because of problems with coordinating work among greater numbers of employees or limitations in other important inputs. Would the firm pay an additional employee's salary when employing that person reduces the level of salable output? Obviously not, which demonstrates the irrationality of employing inputs in the range of negative returns.

INPUT COMBINATION CHOICE

The concept of factor productivity can be more fully explored using isoquant analysis, which explicitly recognizes the potential variability of both factors in a two-input, one-output production system. This technique is introduced in the following section to examine the role of input substitutability in determining efficient input combinations.

Production Isoquants

Isoquant

Different input combinations used to efficiently produce a specified output.

Technical efficiency

Least-cost production of a target level of output.

Although one can examine the properties of production functions graphically using three-dimensional production surfaces, a two-dimensional representation using isoquants is simpler to use and equally instructive. The term *isoquant*—derived from *iso,* meaning equal, and *quant,* from quantity—denotes a curve that represents the different combinations of inputs that can be efficiently used to produce a specified quantity of output. Efficiency in this case refers to **technical efficiency,** meaning the least-cost production of a target level of output. If 2 units of X and 3 units of Y can be combined to produce 49 units of output, but they can also be combined less efficiently to produce only 45 units of output, the $X = 2$, $Y = 3$ input combination will lie only on the $Q = 49$ isoquant. The $X = 2$, $Y = 3$ combination resulting in $Q = 45$ is not technologically efficient, because this same input combination can produce a larger output quantity. Such a combination would not appear in the production function nor on the $Q = 45$ isoquant. Production theory assumes that only the most efficient techniques are used in converting resource inputs into products. For example, from Table 8.1 it is clear that 91 units of output can be produced efficiently using the input combinations $X = 3$, $Y = 8$; $X = 4$, $Y = 6$; $X = 6$, $Y = 4$; or $X = 8$, $Y = 3$. These four input combinations all lie on the $Q = 91$ isoquant. Similarly, the combinations $X = 6$, $Y = 10$; $X = 7$, $Y = 8$; $X = 10$, $Y = 7$ all result in 122 units of production and, hence, lie on the $Q = 122$ isoquant.

These two isoquants are illustrated in Figure 8.6. Each point on the $Q = 91$ isoquant indicates a different combination of X and Y that can produce 91 units of output. For example, 91 units can be produced with 3 units of X and 8 units of Y, with 4 units of X and 6 units of Y, or with any other combination of X and Y on the isoquant $Q = 91$. A similar interpretation can be given the isoquant for $Q = 122$ units of output.

Isoquants for the continuous production function displayed in Figure 8.2 are located by passing a series of planes through the production surface, horizontal to the XY plane, at various heights. Each plane represents a different level of output. Two such planes are passed through the production surface shown in Figure 8.7 at heights Q_1 and Q_2. Every point on the production surface with a height of Q_1 above the input plane—that is, all points along curve Q_1—represent an equal quantity, or isoquant, of Q_1 units of output. The curve Q_2 maps out the locus of all input combinations that result in Q_2 units of production.

These isoquant curves can be transferred to the input surface, as indicated by the dashed curves Q'_1 and Q'_2 in Figure 8.7, then further transferred to the two-dimensional graph shown in Figure 8.8. These latter curves represent the standard form of an isoquant.

FIGURE 8.6 **Representative Isoquants from Table 8.1**

Each point on an isoquant represents a different combination of Inputs X and Y that can be used to produce the same level of output.

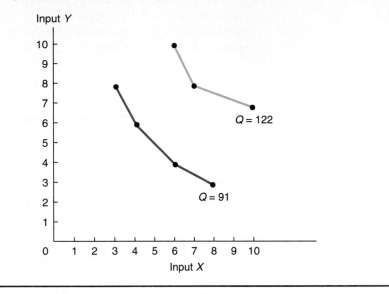

FIGURE 8.7 **Isoquant Determination for a Continuous Production Function**

Each plane in a continuous production surface identifies an isoquant.

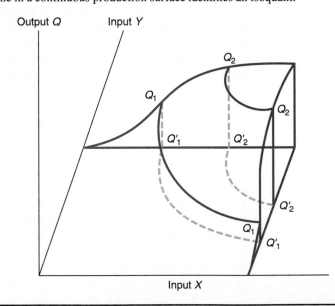

FIGURE 8.8 **Production Isoquants for a Continuous Production Function**

Isoquants are typically C-shaped and concave to the origin.

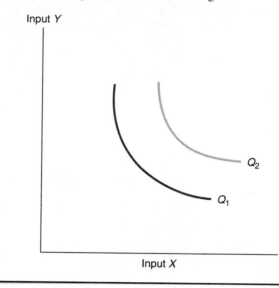

Input Factor Substitution

Input substitution
The systematic replacement of productive factors.

The shapes of isoquants reveal a great deal about the substitutability of input factors—that is, the ability to replace one input for another in the production process. This point is illustrated in Figure 8.9(a), (b), and (c).

In some production systems, **input substitution** or replacement is readily accomplished. In the production of electricity, for example, fuels used to power generators often represent readily substitutable inputs. Figure 8.9(a) shows isoquants for such an electric power generation system. The technology, a power plant with boilers equipped to burn either oil or gas, is given. Various amounts of electric power can be produced by burning gas only, oil only, or varying amounts of each. In this instance, gas and oil are perfect substitutes, and the electricity isoquants are straight lines. Other examples of readily substitutable inputs include fish meal and soybeans to provide protein in a feed mix, energy and time in a drying process, and United Parcel Service and the U.S. Postal Service for package delivery. In each case, production isoquants are linear.

At the other extreme of input substitutability lie production systems in which inputs are perfect complements for each other. In these situations, exact amounts of each input are required to produce a given quantity of output. Figure 8.9(b) illustrates isoquants for bicycles and completely fixed input combinations. Exactly two wheels and one frame are required to produce a bicycle, and in no way can wheels be substituted for frames, or vice versa. Pants and coats for suits, engines and bodies for trucks, barbers and shears for haircuts, and chemicals in compounds for prescription drugs are further examples of complementary inputs. Production isoquants for complementary inputs take the shape of right angles, as indicated in Figure 8.9(b).

FIGURE 8.9 **Isoquants for Inputs with Varying Degrees of Substitutability: (a) Electric Power Generation; (b) Bicycle Production; (c) Dress Production**

(a) Straight-line isoquants indicate perfect substitution. (b) A right-angle shape for isoquants reflects inputs that are perfect complements. (c) C-shaped isoquants indicate imperfect substitutability among inputs.

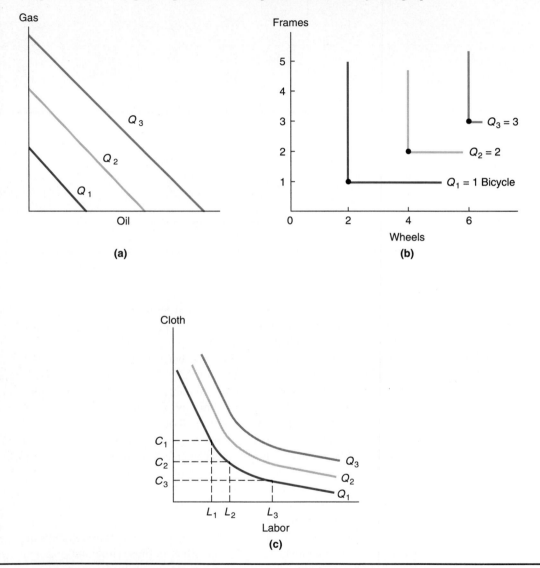

(a)

(b)

(c)

Figure 8.9(c) shows a production process in which inputs can be substituted for each other within limits. A dress can be made with a relatively small amount of labor (L_1) and a large amount of cloth (C_1). The same dress can also be made with less cloth (C_2) if more labor (L_2) is used because the dressmaker can cut the material more carefully and reduce waste. Finally, the dress can be made with still less cloth (C_3), but workers must be so extremely painstaking that the labor input requirement increases to L_3. Note that although a relatively small addition of labor, from L_1 to L_2, reduces the input of cloth from C_1 to C_2, a very large increase in labor, from L_2 to L_3, is required to obtain a similar reduction in cloth from C_2 to C_3. The substitutability of labor for cloth diminishes from L_1 to L_2 to L_3. The substitutability of cloth for labor in the manufacture of dresses also diminishes, as can be seen by considering the quantity of cloth that must be added to replace each unit of reduced labor in moving from L_3 to L_1.

Most labor–capital substitutions in production systems exhibit this diminishing substitutability. Energy and insulation used to provide home heating exhibit diminishing substitutability, as do doctors and medical technicians in providing healthcare services.

Marginal Rate of Technical Substitution	Isoquant slope provides the key input substitutability. In Figure 8.9(c), the slope of the isoquant is simply the change in Input Y (cloth) divided by the change in Input X (labor). The **marginal rate of technical substitution**[2] (**MRTS**) is the amount of one input factor that must be substituted for one unit of another input factor to maintain a constant level of output. Algebraically,

Marginal rate of technical substitution
The amount of one input that must be substituted for another to maintain constant output.

$$MRTS = \frac{\Delta Y}{\Delta X} = \text{Slope of an Isoquant.} \qquad \textbf{(8.3)}$$

The marginal rate of technical substitution usually diminishes as the amount of substitution increases. In Figure 8.9(c), for example, as more and more labor is substituted for cloth, the increment of labor necessary to replace cloth increases. At the extremes, isoquants may even become positively sloped, indicating that the range over which input factors can be substituted for each other is limited. A classic example is the use of land and labor to produce a given output of wheat. At some point, as labor is substituted for land, the farmers will trample the wheat. As more labor is added, more land eventually must be added if wheat output is to be maintained. The farmers must have some place to stand.

The input substitution relation indicated by the slope of a production isoquant is directly related to the concept of diminishing marginal productivity introduced earlier. This is because the marginal rate of technical substitution is equal to -1 times the ratio of the marginal products of the input factors [$MRTS = -1(MP_X/MP_Y)$]. To see this, note that the loss in output resulting from a small reduction in Y equals the marginal product of Y, MP_Y, multiplied by the change in Y, δY. That is,

$$\delta Q = MP_Y \times \delta Y. \qquad \textbf{(8.4)}$$

Similarly, the change in Q associated with the increased use of Input X is given by the expression

$$\delta Q = MP_X \times \delta X. \qquad \textbf{(8.5)}$$

---

[2] The term *marginal rate of technical substitution* is often shortened to *marginal rate of substitution*.

With substitution of X for Y along an isoquant, the absolute value of δQ in Equations 8.3 and 8.4 must be the same. That is, the change in output associated with the reduction in Input Y must be exactly offset by the change in output resulting from the increase in Input X for output to remain constant—as it must along an isoquant. Thus, the δQs in Equations 8.4 and 8.5 must be of equal size and opposite sign. Therefore, along an isoquant,

$$-(MP_X \times \delta X) = (MP_Y \times \delta Y). \tag{8.6}$$

Transposing the variables in Equation 8.6 produces

$$-\frac{MP_X}{MP_Y} = \frac{\Delta Y}{\Delta X}. \tag{8.7}$$

In words, this means that the marginal rate of technical substitution is equal to the slope of a production isoquant:

$$MRTS_{XY} = \text{Slope of an Isoquant.}^3$$

The slope of a production isoquant such as in Equation 8.3 is equal to $\delta Y/\delta X$ and is determined by the ratio of the marginal products of both inputs. In Figure 8.9(c) the isoquant Q_1 has a very steep negative slope at the point $L_1 C_1$. When cloth is relatively abundant, the marginal product of labor is relatively high as compared with the marginal product of cloth. When labor is relatively abundant at, say, point $L_3 C_3$, the marginal product of labor is low relative to the marginal product of cloth.

Equation 8.7 provides a basis for examining the concept of irrational input combinations. It is irrational for a firm to combine resources in such a way that the marginal product of any input is negative, since this implies that output could be increased by using less of that resource.[4] Note from Equation 8.6 that if the inputs X and Y are combined in proportions such that the marginal product of either factor is negative, then the slope of the production isoquant will be positive. For a production isoquant to be positively sloped, one of the input factors must have a negative marginal product. From this it follows that input combinations

---

[3] This result can also be demonstrated by noting that along any isoquant the total differential of the production function must be zero (output is fixed along an isoquant). Thus, for the production function given by Equation 8.1, setting the total differential equal to zero gives

$$\frac{\delta Q}{\delta X} dX + \frac{\delta Q}{\delta Y} dY = 0,$$

and, rearranging terms,

$$(-)\frac{\delta Q/\delta X}{\delta Q/\delta Y} = \frac{dY}{dX}.$$

Or, since $\delta Q/\delta X = MP_X$ and $\delta Q/\delta Y = MP_Y$,

$$(-)\frac{MP_X}{MP_Y} = \frac{dY}{dX} = \text{Slope of the Isoquant.}$$

[4] This is technically correct only if the resource has a positive cost. Thus, for example, a firm might employ additional workers even though the marginal product of labor was negative if it received a government subsidy for that employment that more than offset the cost of the output reduction.

FIGURE 8.10 **Maximum Variable Proportions for Inputs X and Y**

The rational limits of substitution between Y and X occur where the isoquants become positively sloped.

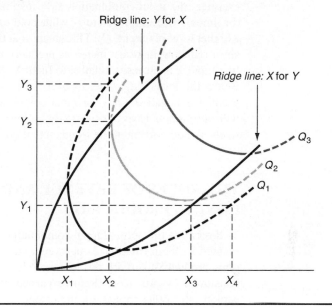

lying along a positively sloped portion of a production isoquant are irrational and would be avoided by the firm.

In Figure 8.10, the rational limits of input substitution are where the isoquants become positively sloped. Limits to the range of substitutability of X for Y are indicated by the points of tangency between the isoquants and a set of lines drawn perpendicular to the y axis. Limits of economic substitutability of Y for X are shown by the tangents of lines perpendicular to the x axis. Maximum and minimum proportions of Y and X that would be combined to produce each level of output are determined by points of tangency between these lines and the production isoquants.

Ridge lines

Graphic bounds for positive marginal products.

It is irrational to use any input combination outside these tangents, or **ridge lines,** as they are called. Such combinations are irrational because the marginal product of the relatively more abundant input is negative outside the ridge lines. Addition of the last unit of the excessive input factor actually reduces output. Obviously, it would be irrational for a firm to buy and employ additional units that cause production to decrease. To illustrate, suppose a firm is currently operating with a fixed quantity of Input Y equal to Y_1 units, as shown in Figure 8.10. In such a situation the firm would never employ more than X_3 units of Input X, because employment of additional units of X results in production of successively lower output quantities. For example, if the firm combines Y_1 and X_4, output is equal to Q_1 units. By reducing usage of X from X_4 to X_3, output can be increased from Q_1 to Q_2.

A similar relation is shown for Input *Y*. In the area above the upper ridge line, the relative amount of *Y* is excessive. In this area it is possible to increase production and move to a higher isoquant by reducing the amount of *Y* employed. For example, the input combination X_2Y_3 results in Q_1 units of output. By reducing the amount of *Y* employed to Y_2 while holding *X* constant at X_2, the firm produces a higher level of output, Q_2. This means that the marginal product of *Y* is negative, since reducing its usage increases production. In the area above the upper ridge line Input *Y* is excessive relative to Input *X*, and *Y*'s marginal product is negative. Below the lower ridge line, Input *X* is excessive relative to *Y*, and *X*'s marginal product is negative. Only for input combinations lying between the ridge lines will *both* inputs have positive marginal products. It is here and along the negatively sloped portion of the isoquant that optimal input combinations are found.

THE ROLES OF REVENUE AND COST IN PRODUCTION

To determine the optimal input combination, technical relations must be supplemented with information about revenues and costs. In an advanced market economy, productive activity results in goods and services that are sold rather than consumed by producers. Returns earned by the providers of labor, materials, capital, and other inputs are important. To gain an understanding of how the factors of production should be combined for maximum efficiency, it is necessary to shift from the analysis of the *physical* productivity of inputs to an examination of their *economic* productivity, or net revenue-generating capability.

Marginal Revenue Product

Marginal revenue product

The amount of revenue generated by employing the last input unit.

The economic productivity of an input is its **marginal revenue product,** or the additional net revenue generated by the last unit employed. In equation form, the marginal revenue product of input *X*, MRP_X, equals the input marginal product multiplied by the marginal revenue of output:

$$MRP_X = \frac{\delta TR}{\delta Q}$$
$$= \frac{\delta Q}{\delta X} \times \frac{\delta TR}{\delta Q} \qquad (8.8)$$
$$= MP_X \times MR_Q .$$

Marginal revenue product is the economic value of a marginal unit of an input factor. For example, if the addition of one more worker generates two incremental units of a product that can be sold for $5 each, the marginal product of labor is 2, and its marginal revenue product is $10 (= 2 \times \$5$). Table 8.4 illustrates marginal revenue product for a simple one-factor production system. The marginal revenue product values shown in Column 4 assume that each unit of output can be sold for $5. The marginal revenue product of the first unit of *X* employed equals the 3 units of output produced times the $5 revenue received per unit, or $MRP_{X=1} = \$15$. The second unit of *X* adds 4 units of production, so $MRP_{X=2} = 4$. For the

TABLE 8.4   **Marginal Revenue Product for a Single Input**

Units of Input (X)	Total Product of X (Q)	Marginal Product of X ($MP_x = \Delta Q$)	Marginal Revenue Product of X ($MP_x \times \$5$)
1	3	3	$15
2	7	4	20
3	10	3	15
4	12	2	10
5	13	1	5

second unit of input, $MRP_{X=2} = \$20$. Marginal revenue products for each additional unit of X are all determined in this manner.

Optimal Level of a Single Input

To illustrate how the economic productivity of an input, as defined by its marginal revenue product, is related to factor use, consider the following question: If the price of input X in the production system depicted in Table 8.4 is $12, how many units of X will a firm use? Clearly, the firm will employ 3 units of X because the value of adding each of these units as measured by their marginal revenue products exceeds their marginal cost. When 3 units of X are employed, the third and marginal unit causes total revenues to rise by $15 while costing only $12. At the margin, employing the third unit of X increases total profit by $3 ($= \$15 - \$12$). A fourth unit of X would not be employed because the value of its marginal product ($10) is less than the cost of employment ($12); profit would decline by $2.

The relation between resource productivity, as measured by marginal revenue product, and optimal employment or factor use can be generalized by referring to the basic marginal principles of profit maximization developed in Chapter 2. Recall that so long as marginal revenue exceeds marginal cost, profits must increase. In the context of production decisions, this means that profit will increase so long as the marginal revenue generated by an input, or its marginal revenue product, exceeds the marginal cost of employment. Conversely, when marginal revenue product is less than the cost of employing the factor, marginal profit is negative, and the firm would reduce employment.

The concept of optimal resource use can be clarified by examining a simple production system in which a single variable labor input, L, is used to produce a single product, Q. Profit maximization requires production at a level such that marginal revenue equals marginal cost. Because the only variable factor in the system is Input L, the marginal cost of production is

$$MC_Q = \frac{\delta \text{Total Cost}}{\delta \text{Output}}$$

$$= \frac{P_L}{MP_L}.$$

(8.9)

●

Pay for Performance Is Spreading

One of the most striking changes taking place in business today is the dramatic reshaping of compensation plans. More than ever before, employee pay is contingent on firm profitability and stock price performance. Incentive pay plans set the compensation of workers and top management according to how well the company achieves a number of preset objectives. In addition to salary, it is now possible for top executives to earn thousands, if not millions, of dollars of incentive pay in the form of bonuses, deferred compensation, and stock options. Many boards of directors want to avoid the problems involved with measuring corporate performance using accounting data, and therefore they set incentive pay almost solely on the basis of the company's stock price performance. The underlying logic is that by tying top executive pay to stock price performance, a direct incentive to maximize the value of the firm is created. Given the booming stock market of the 1980s, such incentive pay plans resulted in an astonishing boost in pay for some top executives. Until the mid-1980s, total compensation in excess of $1 million for chief executive officers (CEOs) of Fortune 500 firms was uncommon. Today, several top executives earn tens of millions of dollars per year in total compensation, and hundreds earn in excess of $1 million annually.

Proponents of this new trend in top executive pay contend that several companies have been revitalized when management has focused on bottom-line performance. Opponents argue that such plans reflect CEOs taking unfair advantage of their positions. They cite examples of millions of dollars in compensation being earned by top executives in the auto, steel, and other industries following wage cuts for blue-collar workers, mass layoffs, and plant closures. Although proponents admit the need for close public scrutiny, they argue that corporate restructuring is an important requirement of a vital economy and a key task facing top executives. Proponents also note that running a large modern corporation is an exceedingly complex task and requires an individual with rare management skills. They point out that top-executive pay represents a very small share of the sales and profits being earned by large companies. Moreover, stock-based rewards often accumulate over a number of years, but because they are exercised all at once, they tend to overstate a single year's compensation.

The clearest indication that incentive pay plans are here to stay comes from the fact that they are rapidly spreading from the executive suite to the shop floor. The most widely employed form of such plans is profit sharing, whereby employees receive annual bonuses based on corporate profit performance. More than 30 percent of U.S. companies employ some form of profit sharing, with most companies putting at least some of these bonuses into employee retirement plans. Companies with 500 or fewer employees sometimes use an alternate form of profit sharing called gain sharing. Under gain sharing, all workers receive a set bonus when a specific performance target has been met. Some companies have found gain sharing to be an effective means for achieving improvements in product quality and customer service. Two newer forms of incentive pay for broad groups of employees are lump-sum bonuses and pay-for-knowledge plans. Lump-sum bonuses are one-time cash payments tied to performance that do not become a part of the employee's subsequent base pay. Pay-for-knowledge plans result in higher employee salaries following an increase in the number of tasks the employee is able to perform and are an effective means for enhancing worker skills.

The design of an effective and fair incentive pay plan is a daunting challenge. Pay must be closely linked to performance measures that managers and other affected employees can directly influence. Moreover, the *marginal* impact of each employee's effort must be separated from the influence of others and more general companywide or economywide influences. Never easy, pay plan design is especially demanding for service businesses that rely upon employee cooperation. While difficult to devise, many companies have discovered that the rewards of incentive pay plans far outweigh the risks.

Source: Shawn Tully, "What CEOs Really Make," *Fortune,* June 15, 1992, 94–101.

Dividing P_L, the price of a marginal unit of L, by MP_L, the number of units of output gained by the employment of an added unit of L, provides a measure of the marginal cost of producing each additional unit of output.

Marginal revenue must equal marginal cost at the profit-maximizing output level. Therefore, MR_Q can be substituted for MC_Q in Equation 8.9, resulting in the expression

$$MR_Q = \frac{P_L}{MP_L}. \tag{8.10}$$

Equation 8.10 must hold for profit maximization because its right-hand side is just another expression for marginal cost. Solving Equation 8.10 for P_L results in

$$P_L = MR_Q \times MP_L,$$

or, since $MR_Q \times MP_L$ is defined as the marginal revenue product of L,

$$P_L = MRP_L. \tag{8.11}$$

Equation 8.11 states the rule that *a profit-maximizing firm will always set marginal revenue product equal to marginal cost (price) for every input*. If marginal revenue product exceeds the cost of an input, profits could be increased by employing additional units of that input factor. Conversely, when the marginal cost of an input factor is greater than its marginal revenue product, profit would increase by reducing employment. Only when $MRP = P$ is profit maximized for individual firms. Optimal employment and **economic efficiency** are achieved in the overall economy when all firms employ resources so as to equate each input's marginal revenue product and marginal cost.

Economic efficiency

Achieved when all firms equate input marginal revenue product and marginal cost (maximize profits).

Determination of the optimal input level can be clarified by reconsidering the Tax Advisors, Inc., example, illustrated in Table 8.3. If three CPAs can process 2.1 returns per hour and employing a fourth CPA increases average output per hour to 2.5, then employing a fourth CPA reduces marginal product from $MP_{CPA=3} = 1.4$ to $MP_{CPA=4} = 0.4$. This describes a situation in which employment is in a range of diminishing returns to the labor factor. For optimal resource employment, the question must be answered: Should a fourth CPA be hired? The answer depends on whether expanding employment will increase or decrease total profits. A fourth CPA should be hired if doing so will increase profits; otherwise, a fourth CPA should not be hired.

For simplicity, assume that CPA time is the only input required to process additional tax returns and that CPAs earn \$35 per hour, or roughly \$70,000 per year including fringe benefits. If Tax Advisors, Inc., receives \$100 in revenue for each tax return prepared by the fourth CPA, a comparison of the price of labor and marginal revenue product for the fourth CPA reveals

$$P_{CPA} < MRP_{CPA=4} = MR_Q \times MP_{CPA=4}$$

because

$$\$35 < \$40 = \$100 \times 0.4.$$

This implies that if a fourth CPA is hired, total profits will rise by \$5 per hour ($= \$40 - \$35$). The additional CPA should be employed.

Since the marginal product for the fifth CPA equals 0.2, $MP_{CPA=5} = 0.2$, and the marginal revenue product falls to only $20 per hour, or less than the $35-per-hour cost of hiring that person. The firm would incur a $10-per-hour loss by expanding hiring to that level and would, therefore, stop at an employment level of four CPAs.

For simplicity, this example assumes that CPA time is the only variable input involved in tax-return preparation. In reality, for this product, like most, other inputs are likely to be necessary to increase output. Additional computer time, office supplies, and clerical support may also be required to increase output. If such were the case, determining the independent contribution or value of CPA input would be more complex. If *variable* overhead for CPA support staff and

Net marginal revenue

Marginal revenue after all variable costs.

supplies equals 50 percent of sales revenue, then the **net marginal revenue,** or marginal revenue after all variable costs, for CPA time would be only $50 per unit ($= 0.5 \times MR_Q$). In this instance, Tax Advisors, Inc., would find that the $20 [$= 0.4 \times (0.5)(\$100)$] net marginal revenue product generated by the fourth CPA would not offset the necessary $35 per hour cost (wage rate). It would, therefore, employ no more than three CPAs, a level at which $MRP = 1.4 \times (0.5)(\$100) = \$70 > \$35 = P_{CPA}$. The firm will employ additional CPAs only so long as their net marginal revenue product equals or exceeds their marginal cost (price of labor).

This explains why, for example, a law firm might hire new associates at annual salaries of $80,000 when it expects them to generate $150,000 per year in gross billings, or 1,500 billable hours at a rate of $100 per hour. If variable costs are $70,000 per associate, only $80,000 is available to cover associate salary expenses. When customers pay $100 per hour for legal services, they are in fact paying for attorney time and expertise plus the support of legal secretaries, law clerks, office staff, supplies, facilities, and so on. By itself, new associate time is worth much less than $100 per hour, or $150,000 per year. The net marginal revenue of new associate attorney time, or CPA time in the preceding Tax Advisors, Inc., example, is the *marginal* value created after allowing for the variable costs of all other inputs that must be increased to provide service.

The simple concept that inputs will be employed so long as their value in production as measured by their net marginal revenue product exceeds their cost is the foundation of production analysis. The section that follows shows that it is the basis for determining optimal input combinations and the profit-maximizing level of output. As is illustrated in Figure 8.7, it also underlies the demand for input factors.

The Input Demand Function

Data on the marginal revenue product of labor and wage rates present firms with clear incentives regarding the level of employment. When $MRP_L > P_L$ it will pay to expand labor usage; when $MRP_L < P_L$ it will pay to cut back. When $MRP_L = P_L$, the level of employment is optimal. When an unlimited supply of labor can be employed at a given wage rate, determining the optimal level of employment involves a simple comparison of MRP_L and P_L. However, when higher wages are necessary to expand the level of employment, this fact must be taken into account in the determination of an optimal level of employment.

To illustrate, consider the case of Micromachines, Inc., in Chapel Hill, North Carolina. Micromachines is a high-tech company that assembles and markets Lilliputian-size machines: tiny gears and cranks the size of large specks of dust. The firm plans to introduce a new microscopic motor with the following demand conditions:

$$Q = 187{,}500 - 2{,}500P,$$

or

$$P = \$75 - \$0.0004Q.$$

Motor parts are purchased from a number of independent subcontractors and then put together at Micromachines' assembly plant. Each unit of output is expected to require two hours of labor. Total costs for parts acquisition *before* assembly labor costs are as follows:

$$TC = \$250{,}000 + \$15Q.$$

Business is booming for Micromachines' established products, and the company has no excess assembly staff. To assemble this additional product, the firm will need to hire and train a new staff of technical assistants. Given tight labor market conditions, Micromachines expects that an increase in employment will be possible only at higher wage rates. Based on data compiled by its director of human resource management, the firm projects the following labor supply curve in the highly competitive local labor market:

$$L_S = 10{,}000P_L.$$

Based on the above information, it is possible to derive Micromachines' demand curve for labor. To do so, simply note that because two hours of labor are required for each unit of output, the company's profit function can be written as

$$
\begin{aligned}
\pi &= TR - TC_{PARTS} - TC_{ASSEMBLY} \\
&= (\$75 - \$0.0004A)Q - \$250{,}000 - \$15Q - 2P_LQ \\
&= -\$0.0004Q^2 + 60Q - 2P_LQ - \$250{,}000.
\end{aligned}
$$

To find Micromachines' labor demand curve, it is necessary to determine the firm's optimal level of output. The profit-maximizing level of output is found by setting marginal profit equal to zero ($M\pi = \delta\pi/\delta Q = 0$), where

$$\delta\pi/\delta Q = -\$0.0008Q + \$60 - 2P_L = 0.$$

This implies a direct relation between the price of labor, P_L, and the firm's optimal level of output:

$$2P_L = \$60 - \$0.0008Q.$$
$$P_L = \$30 - \$0.0004Q.$$

This expression can be used to indicate a profit-maximizing level of output and the optimal employment level. In setting $M\pi = MR - MC = 0$ the firm has also implicitly set $MR = MC$. In terms of employment, this means that $MRP_L = P_L$ for each and every input at the profit-maximizing activity level. Therefore, Micromachines' marginal revenue product of labor is given by the expression $MRP_L = \$30 - \$0.0004Q$.

To identify Micromachines' optimal level of employment at any given price of labor, simply determine the amount of labor required to produce the relevant profit-maximizing level of output. Because each unit of output requires *two* units of labor, $L = 2Q$ and $Q = 0.5L$. By substitution, the firm's demand curve for labor is

$$P_L = MRP_L$$
$$= \$30 - \$0.0004(0.5L)$$
$$= \$30 - \$0.0002L$$

or

$$L_D = 150,000 - 5,000P_L.$$

At any given wage rate, this expression indicates Micromachines' optimal level of employment. At any given employment level, this expression also indicates Micromachines' optimal wage rate. As can be expected, a higher wage results in a lower level of labor demand, and the amount of labor demanded rises as the wage rate falls.

The equilibrium wage rate and employment level in the local labor market can be determined by setting the demand for labor equal to the supply of labor:

$$\text{Labor Demand} = \text{Labor Supply}$$
$$150,000 - 5,000P_L = 10,000P_L$$
$$15,000P_L = 150,000$$
$$P_L = \$10 \text{ (wage rate)}.$$

To determine the equilibrium employment level, set labor demand equal to labor supply at a wage rate of $10:

$$\text{Labor Demand} = \text{Labor Supply}$$
$$150,000 - 5,000(\$10) = 10,000(\$10)$$
$$100,000 = 100,000 \text{ (worker hours)}.$$

This implies that Micromachines has a profit-maximizing activity level of 50,000 micromotors (units of output) because $Q = 0.5L = 0.5(100,000) = 50,000$ units.

Using the firm's demand curve for micromotors and total profit function, it is now possible to calculate the optimal output price and profit levels:

$$P = \$75 - \$0.0004(50,000)$$
$$= \$55.$$
$$\pi = \$0.0004(50,000^2) + \$60(50,000) - 2(\$10)(50,000) - \$250,000$$
$$= \$750,000.$$

From this example it becomes clear that the input demand function and the optimal level of employment can be derived by calculating the profit-maximizing level of output and then determining the amount of labor necessary to produce that output level. In the earlier Tax Advisors, Inc., example, the point where

FIGURE 8.11   **The *MRP* Curve Is an Input Demand Curve**

Profits are maximized at L^*, where $P_L^* = MRP_L$.

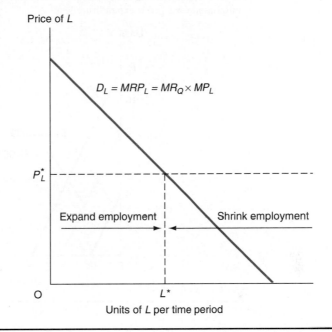

$MRP_L = P_L$ indicates the optimal employment level. This is similar to setting $MR = MC$ for each input. In the Micromachines, Inc., example, labor costs are directly incorporated into the profit function and the point where $M\pi = 0$ is found. Both approaches yield the same profit-maximizing result because if $M\pi = MR - MC = 0$, then $MR = MC$ and $P_L = MRP_L$. Either method can be used to determine an optimal employment level.

Figure 8.11 shows the marginal revenue product for an input, L, along with its market price, P_L^*. Over the range OL^*, expanding L usage increases total profits, since the marginal revenue product gained from employing each unit of L exceeds its price. Beyond L^*, increased usage of L reduces profits, because the benefits gained (MRP_L) are less than the costs incurred (P_L). Only at L^*, where $P_L^* = MRP_L$, is total profit maximized. Of course, if P_L^* were higher, the quantity of L demanded would be reduced. Similarly, if P_L^* were lower, the quantity of L purchased would be greater.

Optimal Combination of Multiple Inputs

The results of preceding sections can be extended to determine the optimal input proportions in production systems employing several input factors. Among the several possible approaches to this task, one of the simplest involves combining technical and market relations through the use of isoquant and isocost curves. Optimal input proportions can be found graphically for a two-input, single-output system by adding an **isocost curve,** a line of constant costs, to the diagram of production isoquants. Each point on the isocost curve represents a combination

Isocost curve
Line of constant costs.

FIGURE 8.12 **Isocost Curves**

Each point on an isocost line represents a different combination of inputs that can be purchased for a given expenditure level.

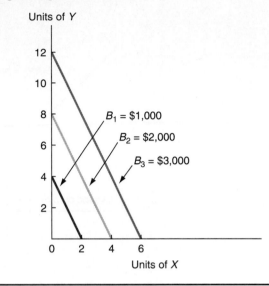

of inputs, say X and Y, whose cost equals a constant expenditure. The budget lines illustrated in Figure 8.12 are constructed in the following manner: Let $P_X =$ $500 and $P_Y =$ $250, the prices of X and Y. For a given budget, say $B_1 =$ $1,000, the firm can purchase 4 units of Y ($=$ $1,000/$250) and no units of X, or 2 units of X ($=$ $1,000/$500) and none of Y. These two quantities represent the X and Y intercepts of a budget line, and a straight line connecting them identifies all combinations of X and Y that $1,000 can purchase.

The equation for a budget line is merely a statement of the various combinations of inputs that can be purchased for a given dollar amount. For example, the various combinations of X and Y that can be purchased for a fixed budget, B, are given by the expression

$$B = B_X \times X + P_Y \times Y.$$

Solving this expression for Y so that it can be graphed, as in Figure 8.12, results in

$$Y = \frac{B}{P_Y} - \frac{P_X}{P_Y} \times X.$$ (8.12)

Note that the first term in Equation 8.12 is the y-axis intercept of the isocost curve. It indicates the quantity of Input Y that can be purchased with a given budget or expenditure limit, *assuming zero units of Input X are bought.* The slope of a budget line $\delta Y/\delta X$ equals $-P_X/P_Y$ and measures relative input prices. A change in the budget level, B, leads to a parallel shift in the budget line; changes in input prices alter the slope of the budget line.

FIGURE 8.13 **Optimal Input Combinations**

The points of tangency between the isoquant and isocost curves depict optimal input combinations at different activity levels.

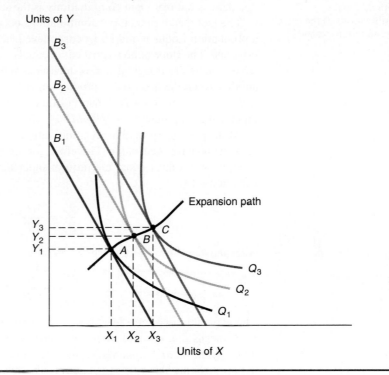

These relations can be clarified by considering further the example illustrated in Figure 8.12. With a $1,000 budget, the y-axis intercept of the budget line has already been shown to be 4 units. Relative prices determine the slope of the budget line. Thus, in Figure 8.12 the slope of the isocost curves is given by the expression

$$\text{Slope} = \frac{P_X}{P_Y} = -\frac{\$500}{\$250} = -2.$$

Suppose that a firm has only $1,000 to spend on inputs for the production of Q. Combining a set of production isoquants with the budget lines of Figure 8.12 to form Figure 8.13 indicates that the optimal input combination occurs at Point A, the point of tangency between the budget line and a production isoquant. At that point, X and Y are combined in proportions that maximize the output attainable for an expenditure B_1. No other combination of X and Y that can be purchased for $1,000 will produce as much output. All other X, Y combinations along the budget line through X_1, Y_1 must intersect isoquants representing lower output quantities. Alternatively, the combination X_1, Y_1 is the least-cost input combination that can produce output Q_1. All other X, Y combinations on the Q_1 isoquant lie on higher budget lines. Similarly, X_2Y_2 is the least-cost input combination for producing Q_2, and so on. All other possible combinations for producing Q_1, Q_2, and Q_3 are intersected by higher budget lines. By connecting points of tangency between isoquants and budget lines (Points *A, B,* and *C*), an **expansion path** is identified that depicts optimal input combinations as the scale of production expands.

Expansion path

Optimal input combinations as the scale of production expands.

The fact that optimal input combinations occur at points of tangency between a production isoquant and an isocost curve leads to a very important economic principle. The slope of an isocost curve equals $-P_X/P_Y$. The slope of an isoquant curve equals the marginal rate of technical substitution of one input factor for another when the quantity of production is held constant. The marginal rate of technical substitution was shown in Equation 8.6 to equal -1 times the ratio of input marginal products, $-MP_X/MP_Y$.

At the point of optimal input combination, the isocost and isoquant curves are tangent and have equal slope. Therefore, for optimal input combinations, the ratio of input prices must equal the ratio of input marginal products, as is shown in Equation 8.13:

$$\frac{P_X}{P_Y} = \frac{MP_X}{MP_Y}. \tag{8.13}$$

Alternatively, the ratios of marginal product to price must be equal for each input:

$$\frac{MP_X}{P_X} = \frac{MP_Y}{P_Y}. \tag{8.14}$$

The economic rule for a least-cost combination of inputs, as given in Equation 8.12, means that *optimal input proportions are employed when an additional dollar spent on any input yields the same increase in output.* Any input combination violating this rule is suboptimal because a change in input proportions could result in the same quantity of output at lower cost.

▶ The Tax Advisors, Inc., example can further illustrate these relations. Assume that in addition to three CPAs, four bookkeepers are employed at a wage (including fringes) of $15 per hour and that $MP_{B=4} = 0.3$. This compares with a CPA wage of $35 per hour and $MP_{CPA=3} = 1.4$. Based on these assumptions, the marginal product per dollar spent on each input is

$$\frac{MP_{B=4}}{P_B} = \frac{0.3}{\$15} = 0.02 \text{ Units per Dollar (for bookkeepers)}$$

and

$$\frac{MP_{CPA=3}}{P_{CPA}} = \frac{1.4}{\$35} = 0.04 \text{ Units per Dollar (for CPAs).}$$

Such an input combination violates the optimal proportions since the ratios of marginal products to input prices are not equal. The last dollar spent on the bookkeeper labor input produces ("buys") 0.02 units of output (tax-return preparations), whereas the last dollar spent on CPA time produces twice as much, 0.04 units. By transferring $1 of cost from bookkeeper time to CPA time, the firm could increase total output by 0.02 tax-return preparations per hour without increasing total cost. Expenditures on the CPA input represent a better use of firm resources, and the company should reallocate resources to employ relatively more CPAs and relatively fewer bookkeepers.

In Equation 8.9 it was shown that the marginal product to price ratio indicates the marginal cost of output from a marginal unit of input X or Y. In terms of this example, this implies that

$$MC_Q = \frac{P_B}{MP_{B=4}} = \frac{\$15}{0.3} = \$50 \text{ per Unit (using bookkeepers)}$$

and

$$MC_Q = \frac{P_{CPA}}{MP_{CPA=3}} = \frac{\$35}{1.4} = \$25 \text{ per Unit (using CPAs)}.$$

Again, the superior economic productivity of CPAs is indicated; they are able to produce output at one-half the marginal cost of output produced by bookkeepers.

It is important to recognize that the preceding analysis for determining optimal proportions of multiple inputs considers input price and input marginal product (productivity) relations only. Since the economic value of output is not considered, these data are insufficient to allow calculation of optimal employment *levels*. Notice in the Tax Advisors, Inc., example that the marginal cost of output using either input is much less than the $100 marginal revenue per tax return. It is quite possible that more CPAs *and* more bookkeepers should be hired. The next section introduces output value to determine the optimal level of resource employment in production systems with multiple inputs.

Optimal Levels of Multiple Inputs

Combining inputs in proportions that satisfy Equations 8.13 and 8.14 ensures that any output quantity is produced at minimum cost. Cost minimization requires only that the ratios of marginal product to price be equal for all inputs. Alternatively, cost minimization dictates that inputs be combined in optimal proportions for a given or target level of output. Profit maximization, however, requires that a firm employ optimal input proportions *and* produce an optimal quantity of output. Therefore, *cost minimization and optimal input proportions are necessary but not sufficient conditions for profit maximization.*

Profit maximization requires that the firm employ inputs up to the point where $MC_Q = MR_Q$. As a result, profit maximization requires for each and every input that

$$\frac{P_X}{MP_X} = MR_Q \qquad\qquad (8.15)$$

and

$$\frac{P_Y}{MP_Y} = MR_Q. \qquad\qquad (8.16)$$

Rearranging produces

$$P_X = MP_X \times MR_Q = MRP_X \qquad\qquad (8.17)$$

and

$$P_Y = MP_Y \times MR_Q = MRP_Y. \qquad (8.18)$$

Profits are maximized when inputs are employed so that price equals marginal revenue product for each input. The difference between cost minimization and profit maximization is quite simple. Cost minimization and the employment of optimal input proportions requires considering only the supply-related factors of input prices and marginal productivity. Profit maximization requires consideration of these supply related factors *and* the demand-related marginal revenue of output. When a firm employs each input in a production system so that input MRP = Price, the firm ensures that inputs are being combined in optimal proportions *and* that the total level of resource employment is optimal.

▶   A final look at the Tax Advisors, Inc., example illustrates these relations. Recall that for a production system with three CPAs and four bookkeepers the ratio of marginal products to price for each input indicates a need to employ more CPAs relative to the number of bookkeepers. Assume that hiring one more bookkeeper leaves unchanged their marginal product of 0.3 tax returns processed per hour ($MP_{B=5} = 0.3$). In addition, assume that with this increased employment of bookkeepers the marginal product of the fourth CPA increases from 0.4 to 0.7 tax returns processed per hour. This assumption reflects the fact that the marginal productivity of an input factor (CPAs) is typically enhanced when used in conjunction with more of a complementary input, bookkeepers in this case. Now $MP_{B=5} = 0.3$ and $MP_{CPA=4} = 0.7$. With the costs of each input remaining constant at P_B = \$15 and P_{CPA} = \$35, the marginal product-to-price ratios are now equal:

$$\frac{MP_{B=5}}{P_B} = \frac{0.3}{\$15} = 0.02 \text{ Units per Dollar (for bookkeepers)}$$

and

$$\frac{MP_{CPA=4}}{P_{CPA}} = \frac{0.7}{\$35} = 0.02 \text{ Units per Dollar (for CPAs).}$$

The combination of four CPAs and five bookkeepers is now optimal from a cost-minimizing standpoint, and input *proportions* are optimal. However, it is still unclear whether an optimal *level* of inputs has been employed. In other words, does the resulting output level maximize profit? To answer this question it becomes necessary to determine if marginal revenue product equals the marginal cost of each input. If net marginal revenue (*NMR*) per return remains at \$50 = (\$100 × 0.5), then

$$MRP_B = MP_B \times NMR_Q$$
$$= 0.3 \times \$50 = \$15$$
$$MRP_B = \$15 = P_B$$

and

$$MRP_{CPA} = MP_{CPA} \times NMR_Q$$
$$= 0.7 \times \$50 = \$35$$
$$MRP_{CPA} = \$35 = P_{CPA}.$$

MANAGERIAL APPLICATION 8.3

World-Class Quality

Fortune regularly features a dazzling variety of goods and services made in America that merit the superlative "the world's best" (see table). The *Fortune* list is arbitrarily limited to 100 nonmilitary products and is therefore by no means exhaustive. To be considered, an item had to be made by a company headquartered in the United States, with at least half its value added coming from design or manufacture within American borders. In compiling the list, *Fortune* consulted scores of industry associations, trade publications, security analysts, management consultants, quality experts, and customers who buy the products. To make the final cut, a good or service had to incorporate the best technology, design, and reliability, and offer the greatest value for its price. In narrowing the number of products to be considered, *Fortune* gave priority to those that have blazed new technical frontiers or have demonstrated sustained market leadership.

In considering this list it is important to keep in mind that such product-quality success often translates to higher profits and superior stock-price performance. As suggested by Andrew Grove, CEO of Intel Corp., whose advanced microprocessors have long been the computer industry standard: "When your products are and remain the best, you define, on your terms, the game your competitors have to play and cannot win."

Product (Manufacturers)	Product (Manufacturers)	Product (Manufacturers)
Communications Satellites (General Electric, Hughes Aircraft)	Workstation Systems (Santa Cruz, Unix System Labs)	Ultra-Precision Grinders (Moore Special Tool)
Computer Network Connectors (Cisco Systems)	Bulldozers (Caterpillar)	Amusement Parks (Walt Disney)
Facsimile Modems (Rockwell International)	Large Tractors, Combines (J.I. Case, Deere)	Backpacks (Gregory, Osprey)
Fiber Optics (Corning)	Off-Highway Trucks (Caterpillar)	Chessboards & Tables (Drueke)
Satellite Navigation Devices (Trimble Navigation)	Row-Crop Planting Equipment (J.I. Case, Deere, White New Idea)	Cruising Sailboats (Alden Yachts, Pacific Seacraft)
Small Satellite Earth Stations (GTE, Hughes, Scientific-Atlantic)	Skid-Steer Loaders (Melroe)	Instant Film (Polaroid)
CISC Microprocessors (Intel, Motorola)	Small Trenchers (Charles Machine Works)	Powerboats (Brunswick, Cigarette, Outboard Marine)
Desktop Computers (Apple, Compaq, IBM)	Tractor Loader Backhoes (J.I. Case)	Racing Sailboats (J. Boats)
Digital Plotters (Hewlett-Packard)	All-Purpose Lubricants (WD-40)	Fine Stationery (Crane, Neenah Paper)
Massively Parallel Supercomputers (Intel, Thinking Machines)	Artificial Sweeteners (Nutrasweet [Equal])	Handbags (Judith Leiber)
Minicomputers, Small Mainframes (Digital Equipment, HP, IBM)	Cigarettes (Philip Morris [Marlboro])	Mechanical Writing Instruments (A.T. Cross)
Minisupercomputers (Convex Computer)	Fast Food (Burger King, McDonald's, Pizza Hut)	Pianos (Steinway & Sons)
Office Furniture (Herman Miller)	Faucets (Chicago Faucet, Kohler, Moen)	Artificial Heart Valves (St. Jude Medical)
RISC Microprocessor Design (MIPS, Sun)	Jeans (Levi Strauss)	Artificial Hips, Knees (Osteonics)
Supercomputers (Cray Research)	Razors (Gillette [Sensor])	Car Rental (Avis, Hertz)
Technical Workstations (Digital, HP, IBM, Silicon Graphics, Sun)	Roach-Bait Trays (Combat)	Hazardous-Waste Treatment Services (Chemical Waste Management)
Applications: Mainframes, Minis (Consilium, D&B Software)	Rugged Outdoor Shoes (L.L. Bean, Timberland)	Management Consulting (BCG, Booz Allen, McKinsey)
Desktop Publishing, Word Processing (Adobe, Aldus, Microsoft, Wordperfect)	Soft Drinks (Coca-Cola, PepsiCo)	Television News (Cable News Network)
	Underwear for Men (Hanes, Jockey Int'l)	Temporary Services (Manpower)
Desktop Spreadsheet (Borland, Lotus, Microsoft)	Washers, Dryers, Dishwashers (Maytag, Whirlpool)	Solid-Waste Disposal (Waste Management)
Desktop Systems (Apple, Microsoft)	Building Temperature Controls (Honeywell)	Commercial Avionics Systems (Honeywell)
Engineering and Design (Autodesk, Cadence, Mentor Graphics)	Ceramic Matrix Composites (Lanxide)	Compact, Full-Size Pickup Trucks (Chrysler, Ford, Chevrolet)
Local Area Networks (Novell)	CNC Tool and Cutter Grinders (S.E. Huffman)	Large Aircraft (Boeing)
Systems: Mainframes, Minis (Digital, IBM, Unix System Labs)	Industrial Controls (Honeywell)	Medium-Wt. Corporate Helicopters (Sikorsky)
	Manufacturing Process Chemicals (Betz Laboratories, Nalco Chemical)	Minivans (Chrysler)
	Pressure Transmitters (Rosemount)	Sport Utility Vehicles (Ford)
	Programmable Controllers (Rockwell International)	Ultralight Utility Helicopters (Robinson Helicopter)
	Rapid Prototyping Systems (3-D Systems)	

Source: Louis S. Richman, "What America Makes Best," *Fortune,* Spring/Summer 1991, 78–88.

Marginal revenue product equals cost for each input. The combination of four CPAs and five bookkeepers is an optimal *level* of employment because the resulting output quantity maximizes profit.

RETURNS TO SCALE

Constant returns to scale

When a given percentage increase in all inputs leads to an identical percentage increase in output.

Closely related to the productivity of individual inputs is the question of how a proportionate increase in all inputs will affect total production. This is the question of returns to scale, and there are three possible situations. First, **constant returns to scale** exist when a given percentage increase in all inputs leads to that same percentage increase in output. For example, if a simultaneous doubling of all inputs leads to a doubling of output, then returns to scale are constant. **Increasing returns to scale** are prevalent if the proportional increase in output is larger than the underlying proportional increase in inputs. If output increases at a rate less than the proportionate increase in inputs, **decreasing returns to scale** are present.

Evaluating Returns to Scale

Increasing returns to scale

When the proportional increase in output is larger than an underlying proportional increase in input.

Decreasing returns to scale

When output increases at a rate less than the proportionate increase in inputs.

The returns-to-scale concept can be clarified by reexamining the production data in Table 8.1. Assume that the production system represented by those data is currently operating with 1 unit of Input X and 3 units of Input Y. Production from such an input combination would be 35 units. Doubling X and Y results in an input combination of $X = 2$ and $Y = 6$. Output from this input combination would be 72 units. A 100 percent increase in both X and Y increases output by 37 units ($= 72 - 35$), a 106 percent increase ($= 37/35 = 1.06$). Over this range, output increases more than proportionately to the increase in the productive factors. The production system exhibits increasing returns to scale over this range of input use.

The returns to scale of a production system can vary over different levels of input usage. Consider, for example, the effect of a 50 percent increase in X and Y from the input combination $X = 2$, $Y = 6$. Increasing X by 50 percent results in employment of 3 units of that factor ($= 2 \times 1.5$), whereas a 50 percent increase in Y leads to 9 units ($= 6 \times 1.5$) of that input being used. The new input combination results in 89 units of production. Therefore, a 50 percent increase in input employment generates only a 24 percent [$= (89 - 72)/72$] increase in output. Since the increase in output is less than proportionate to the underlying increase in input, the production system exhibits decreasing returns to scale over this range.

Isoquant analysis can be used to examine returns to scale for a two-input, single-output production system. Consider the production of Q_1 units of output using the input combination of X_1Y_1 as shown in Figure 8.14. Doubling both inputs shifts production to Q_2. If Q_2 is precisely twice as large as Q_1, the system is said to exhibit constant returns to scale over the range X_1Y_1 to X_2Y_2. If Q_2 is greater than twice Q_1, returns to scale are increasing, and if Q_2 is less than double Q_1, the system exhibits decreasing returns to scale.

The returns to scale implicit in a given production function can also be examined in terms of two- and three-dimensional graphs, such as those drawn in

FIGURE 8.14 **Returns to Scale**

Returns to scale are measured by comparing the percentage change in output with the percentage change in all inputs.

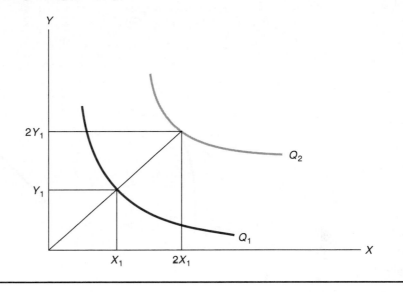

Figures 8.15 through 8.18. In these graphs, the slope of a curve drawn from the origin up the production surface indicates whether returns to scale are constant, increasing, or decreasing.[5] In the production system illustrated in Figure 8.15(a), for example, a curve drawn from the origin will have a constant slope, indicating that returns to scale are constant. Accordingly, the outputs for optimal combinations of *X* and *Y* shown in Figure 8.15(b) are increasing exactly proportionally to increases in *X* and *Y*. In Figure 8.16, the backbone curve from the origin exhibits a constantly increasing slope, indicating increasing returns to scale. The situation is reversed in Figure 8.17, where the production surface increases at a decreasing rate, indicating decreasing returns to scale.

A more general condition is a production function with first increasing, then decreasing returns to scale, as shown in Figure 8.18. The region of increasing returns is attributable to specialization. As output increases, specialized labor can be used and efficient, large-scale machinery can be employed in the production process. Beyond some scale of operation, however, not only are further gains from specialization limited, but problems of coordination may also begin to increase costs substantially. When coordination expenses more than offset additional benefits of specialization, decreasing returns to scale set in.

---

[5] Both inputs *X* and *Y* can be plotted on the horizontal axis of the (b) portions of Figures 8.15 through 8.18 because they bear constant proportions to one another. What is actually being plotted on the horizontal axis is the number of units of some fixed input combination.

FIGURE 8.15 **Constant Returns to Scale**

A production function that can be represented by a straight line from the origin indicates constant returns to scale. A given percentage change in all inputs will cause the same percentage change in output.

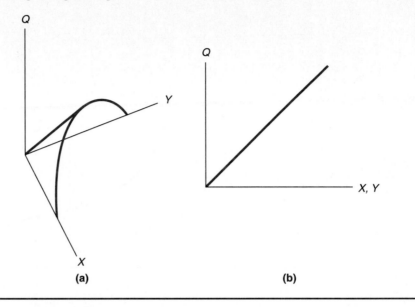

(a)　　　　　　　　　　　　　(b)

FIGURE 8.16 **Increasing Returns to Scale**

A curve drawn from the origin with constantly increasing slope depicts increasing returns to scale. A given percentage change in all inputs will lead to a larger percentage change in output.

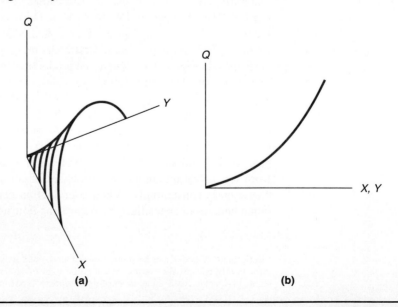

(a)　　　　　　　　　　　　　(b)

FIGURE 8.17 **Decreasing Returns to Scale**

When the slope of a line drawn from the origin is constantly falling, decreasing returns to scale are indicated. A given percentage change in all inputs will lead to a smaller percentage change in output.

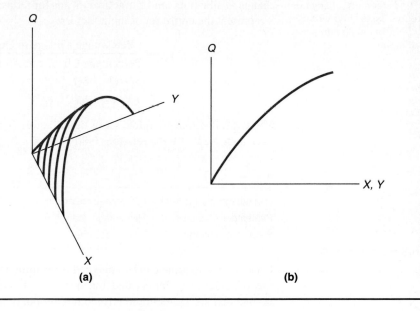

(a)　　　　　　　　　　　　　　(b)

FIGURE 8.18 **Variable Returns to Scale**

When the slope of a line drawn from the origin varies, varying returns to scale are indicated.

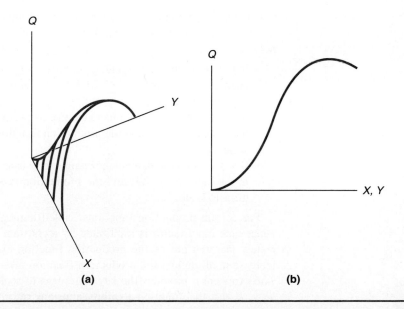

(a)　　　　　　　　　　　　　　(b)

Output Elasticity and Returns to Scale

Output elasticity
The percentage change in output associated with a 1 percent change in all inputs.

Even though graphic representations of returns to scale like Figures 8.15 through 8.18 are intuitively appealing, returns to scale can be more accurately determined for production functions through analysis of output elasticities. **Output elasticity, ϵ_Q,** is the percentage change in output associated with a 1 percent change in all inputs, and a practical means for returns to scale estimation. Letting $\underline{X}$ represent the entire set of input factors,

$$\epsilon_Q = \frac{\text{Percentage Change in Output } (Q)}{\text{Percentage Change in All Inputs } (\underline{X})} \qquad (8.19)$$

$$= \frac{\delta Q / Q}{\delta \underline{X} / \underline{X}} = \frac{\delta Q}{\delta \underline{X}} \times \frac{\underline{X}}{Q},$$

where $\underline{X}$ refers to a complete set of input factors (i.e., $\underline{X}$ = capital, labor, energy, etc.), then the following relations hold:

If	Then	Returns to Scale Are:
Percentage change in $Q >$ Percentage change in $\underline{X}$,	$\epsilon_Q > 1$.	Increasing.
Percentage change in $Q =$ Percentage change in $\underline{X}$,	$\epsilon_Q = 1$.	Constant.
Percentage change in $Q <$ Percentage change in $\underline{X}$,	$\epsilon_Q < 1$.	Diminishing.

Thus, returns to scale can be analyzed by examining the relationship between the rate of increase in inputs and the quantity of output produced. For example, assume that all inputs in the unspecified production function $Q = f(X, Y, Z)$ are increased using the constant factor k, where $k = 1.01$ for a 1 percent increase, $k = 1.02$ for a 2 percent increase, and so on. Then the production function can be rewritten as

$$hQ = f(kX, kY, kZ), \qquad (8.20)$$

where h is the proportional increase in Q resulting from a k-fold increase in each input factor. From Equation 8.20, it is evident that the following relationships hold:

- If $h > k$, then the percentage change in Q is greater than the percentage change in the inputs, $\epsilon_Q > 1$, and the production function exhibits increasing returns to scale.
- If $h = k$, then the percentage change in Q equals the percentage change in the inputs, $\epsilon_Q = 1$, and the production function exhibits constant returns to scale.
- If $h < k$, then the percentage change in Q is less than the percentage change in the inputs, $\epsilon_Q < 1$, and the production function exhibits decreasing returns to scale.

For certain production functions, called homogenous production functions, when each input factor is multiplied by a constant k, the constant can be completely factored out of the production function expression. Following a k-fold increase in all inputs, the production function takes the form $hQ = k^n f(X, Y, Z)$. The exponent n provides the key to returns-to-scale estimation. If $n = 1$, then $h = k$ and the function exhibits constant returns to scale. If $n > 1$, then

$h > k$, indicating increasing returns to scale, whereas $n < 1$ indicates $h < k$ and decreasing returns to scale. In all other instances, the easiest means for determining the nature of returns to scale can be easily determined through numerical example.

To illustrate, consider the production function $Q = 2X + 3Y + 1.5Z$. Returns to scale can be determined by learning how an arbitrary, say 2 percent, increase in all inputs affects output. If, initially, $X = 100$, $Y = 200$, and $Z = 200$, output is found to be

$$Q_1 = 2(100) + 3(200) + 1.5(200)$$
$$= 200 + 600 + 300 = 1,100 \text{ units.}$$

Increasing all inputs by 2 percent (letting $k = 1.02$) leads to the input quantities $X = 102$, $Y = 204$, and $Z = 204$, and

$$Q_2 = 2(102) + 3(204) + 1.5(204)$$
$$= 204 + 612 + 306 = 1,122 \text{ units.}$$

Because a 2 percent increase in all inputs has led to a 2 percent increase in output ($1.02 = 1,122/1,100$), this production system exhibits constant returns to scale.

PRODUCTION FUNCTION ESTIMATION

From a theoretical standpoint, the most appealing functional form for production function estimation might be cubic, such as the equation

$$Q = a + bXY + cX^2Y + dXY^2 - eX^3Y - fXY^3. \quad (8.21)$$

This form, graphed in Figure 8.18, is general in that it exhibits stages of first increasing and then decreasing returns to scale. The marginal products of the input factors exhibit a pattern of first increasing and then decreasing returns, as was illustrated in Figure 8.3.

Given enough input/output observations, either over time for a single firm or at a single point in time for a number of firms in an industry, regression techniques can be used to estimate the parameters of the production function. Frequently, however, the data observations do not exhibit enough dispersion to indicate the full range of increasing and then decreasing returns. In these cases, simpler functional specifications can be used to estimate the production function within the range of available data. In other words, the full generality of a cubic function may be unnecessary, and an alternative linear or log-linear model specification can be usefully applied in empirical estimation. The multiplicative production function described in the next section is one such approximation that has proven extremely useful in empirical studies of production relationships.

Power Production Functions

One function commonly employed in production studies is the **power production function,** a multiplicative relation between output and input that takes the form

$$Q = b_0 X^{b_1} Y^{b_2}. \quad (8.22)$$

Power production function

A multiplicative relation between input and output.

Power functions have properties that are useful in empirical research. Most important, power functions allow the marginal productivity of a given input to depend on the levels of *all* inputs employed, a condition that often holds in actual production systems. Power functions are also easy to estimate in log-linear form using least squares regression analysis (see Chapter 6). That is, Equation 8.22 is equivalent to

$$\log Q = \log b_0 + b_1 \log X + b_2 \log Y. \tag{8.23}$$

The least squares technique can be used to easily estimate the coefficients of Equation 8.23 and thus the parameters of Equation 8.22. Returns to scale are also easily calculated by summing the exponents of the power function or, alternatively, by summing the log-linear model coefficient estimates. If the sum of power function exponents is less than 1, diminishing returns are indicated. A sum greater than 1 indicates increasing returns. If the sum of exponents is exactly 1, returns to scale are constant, and the powerful tool of linear programming, described in Chapter 11, can be used to determine optimal input-output relations for the firm.

Power functions have been successfully employed in a large number of empirical production studies since Charles W. Cobb and Paul H. Douglas's pioneering work in the late 1920s. The impact of their work is so great that power production functions are now frequently referred to as Cobb-Douglas production functions.

Functional Form Selection for Empirical Studies

Many functional forms are available for empirical production study. As with empirical demand estimation, the primary determinant of the functional form used to estimate any model of production depends on the relation hypothesized by the researcher. In many instances, a simple linear approach will be adequate. In others a power function or log-linear approach can be justified. When specification uncertainty is high, a number of plausible alternative model specifications can be fitted to the data to determine which form seems most representative of actual conditions.

SUMMARY

This chapter introduces and analyzes the creative process of production. Several important properties of production systems are examined in some detail.

• A **production function** specifies the maximum output that can be produced for a given amount of inputs. A **discrete production function** involves distinct, or "lumpy," patterns for input combinations. In a **continuous production function,** inputs can be varied in an unbroken marginal fashion.

• The **returns to scale** characteristic of a production system describes the output effect of a proportional increase in all inputs. The relation between output and variation in only one of the inputs employed is described as the **returns to a factor.**

• The **total product** indicates the total output from a production system. The **marginal product** of a factor, MP_X, is the change in output associated with a one-unit change in the factor input, holding all other inputs constant. A factor's

average product is the total product divided by the number of units of that input employed.

• The **law of diminishing returns** states that as the quantity of a variable input increases, with the quantities of all other factors being held constant, the resulting rate of increase in output eventually diminishes.

• An **isoquant** represents the different combinations of inputs that can be used efficiently to produce a specified quantity of output. Efficiency in this case refers to **technical efficiency,** meaning the least-cost production of a target level of output.

• **Input substitution,** or the systematic replacement of productive factors, is an important consideration when judging the efficiency of any production system. The **marginal rate of technical substitution** measures the amount of one input that must be substituted for another to maintain a constant level of output. It is irrational for a firm to use any input combination outside the **ridge lines** that indicate the bounds of positive marginal products.

• The **marginal revenue product** of an input is found by multiplying the marginal product of the input by the marginal revenue resulting from the sale of goods or services produced. This is the amount of revenue generated by employing the last input unit. Profit maximization requires that marginal revenue product and marginal cost be set equal for each input. **Economic efficiency** is achieved in the overall economy when all firms employ resources so as to equate each input's marginal revenue product and marginal cost. In all instances, it is important to consider the **net marginal revenue** of each input, or marginal revenue after all variable costs. Similarly important is the firm's **isocost curve,** or line of constant costs. An **expansion path** depicts optimal input combinations as the scale of production expands.

• **Constant returns to scale** exist when a given percentage increase in all inputs leads to that same percentage increase in output. **Increasing returns to scale** are prevalent if the proportional increase in output is larger than the underlying proportional increase in inputs. If output increases at a rate less than the proportionate increase in inputs, **decreasing returns to scale** are present.

• **Output elasticity,** ϵ_Q, is the percentage change in output associated with a 1 percent change in all inputs, and it is a practical means for returns-to-scale estimation. **Power production function** indicates a multiplicative relation between input and output and is often used in production function estimation.

The successful analysis and estimation of production relations is fundamental to the ongoing success of any organization. Concepts developed in this chapter can be used to understand, refine, and improve the policies of successful companies.

Questions

Q8.1   Use the total product curve illustrated in the figure at the top of page 368 to answer the following questions.

   A. Describe both geometrically and verbally the marginal product and the average product associated with Output Q_1.

   B. At what points along the curve will the marginal and the average products be maximized?

A Total Product Curve

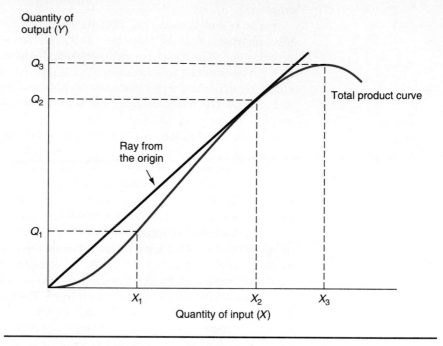

The Optimal Production of Output

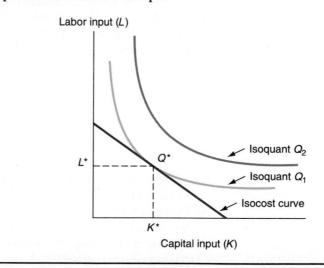

C. How could you use the related marginal product curve to identify the maximum rational quantity of input for Factor *X,* holding constant the amounts of all other inputs?

Q8.2 Review the bottom figure on page 368 (in which *L** and *K** indicate the optimal combination for producing Output *Q** as determined by the point of tangency between an isocost curve and an isoquant curve):

A. What would be the effect in this production system on the isocost and isoquant curves and on the optimal input combination of an increase in the relative productivity of labor, *L?*

B. What would be the effect on the curves and on the input combination referred to in Part A of a technological change that increased the productivity of capital, *K?*

C. What would be the effect of a change that proportionally increased the effectiveness of both labor and capital simultaneously?

Q8.3 Using a diagram of isoquant and isocost curves like those shown in Question 8.2, demonstrate that both relative input prices and factor productivity play roles in determining optimal input combinations.

Q8.4 Is the use of least-cost input combinations a necessary condition for profit maximization? Is it a sufficient condition? Explain.

Q8.5 "Output per worker is expected to increase by 10 percent during the next year. Therefore, wages can also increase by 10 percent with no harmful effects on employment, output prices, or employer profits." Discuss this statement.

Q8.6 Commission-based and piece-rate-based compensation plans are commonly employed by businesses. Use the concepts developed in the chapter to explain these phenomena.

Q8.7 "Hourly wage rates are an anachronism. Efficiency requires incentive-based pay tied to performance." Discuss this statement.

Q8.8 Explain why the *MP/P* relation is deficient as the sole mechanism for determining the optimal level of resource employment.

Q8.9 Develop the appropriate relations for determining the optimal quantities of all inputs to employ in a production system, and explain the underlying rationale.

Q8.10 Suppose that labor, capital, and energy inputs must be combined in fixed proportions. Does this mean that returns to scale will be constant?

Self-Test Problem

Medical Testing Labs, Inc., provides routine testing services for blood banks in the Los Angeles area. Tests are supervised by skilled technicians using equipment produced by two leading competitors in the medical equipment industry. Records for the current year show an average of 27 tests per hour being performed on the Testlogic-1 and 48 tests per hour on a new machine, the Accutest-3. The Testlogic-1 is leased for $18,000 per month, and the Accutest-3 is leased at $32,000 per month. On average, each machine is operated 25 eight-hour days per month.

A. Describe the logic of the rule used to determine an optimal *mix* of input usage.

B. Does Medical Testing Lab usage reflect an optimal mix of testing equipment?

C. Describe the logic of the rule used to determine an optimal *level* of input usage.

D. If tests are conducted at a price of $6 each while labor and all other costs are fixed, should the company lease more machines?

Solution to Self-Test Problem

A. The rule for an optimal combination of Testlogic-1 (T) and Accutest-3 (A) equipment is

$$\frac{MP_T}{P_T} = \frac{MP_A}{PA}.$$

This rule means that an identical amount of additional output would be produced with an additional dollar expenditure on each input. Alternatively, an equal marginal cost of output is incurred irrespective of which input is used to expand output. Of course, marginal products and equipment prices must both reflect the same relevant time frame, either hours or months.

B. On a per hour basis, the relevant question is

$$\frac{27}{\$18,000/(25 \times 8)} \overset{?}{=} \frac{48}{\$32,000/(25 \times 8)}$$

$$0.3 \overset{\checkmark}{=} 0.3$$

On a per month basis, the relevant question is

$$\frac{27 \times (25 \times 8)}{\$18,000} \overset{?}{=} \frac{48 \times (25 \times 8)}{\$32,000}$$

$$0.3 \overset{\checkmark}{=} 0.3$$

In both instances, the last dollar spent on each machine increased output by the same 0.3 units, indicating an *optimal mix* of testing machines.

C. The rule for optimal input employment is

$$MRP = MP \times MR_Q = \text{Input Price.}$$

This means that the level of input employment is optimal when the marginal sales revenue derived from added input usage is just equal to input price, or the marginal cost of employment.

D. For each machine hour, the relevant question is

Testlogic-1

$$MRP_T = MP_T \times MR_Q \overset{?}{=} P_T$$

$$27 \times \$6 \overset{?}{=} \$18,000/(25 \times 8)$$

$$\$162 > \$90.$$

Accutest-3

$$MRP_A = MP_A \times MR_Q \overset{?}{=} P_A$$

$$48 \times \$6 \overset{?}{=} \$32,000/(25 \times 8)$$

$$\$288 > \$160.$$

Or, in per month terms:

Testlogic-1

$$MRP_T = MP_T \times MR_Q \overset{?}{=} P_T$$

$$27 \times (25 \times 8) \times \$6 \overset{?}{=} \$18,000$$

$$\$32,400 > \$18,000.$$

Accutest-3

$$MRP_A = MP_A \times MR_Q \overset{?}{=} P_A$$

$$48 \times (25 \times 8) \times \$6 \overset{?}{=} \$32,000$$

$$\$57,600 > \$32,000.$$

In both cases, each machine returns more than its marginal cost (price) of employment, and expansion would be profitable.

Problems

P8.1   Marginal Rate of Technical Substitution. The following production table provides estimates of the maximum amounts of output possible with different combinations of two input factors, X and Y. (Assume that these are just illustrative points on a spectrum of continuous input combinations.)

Units of Y Used	Estimated Output per Day				
5	210	305	360	421	470
4	188	272	324	376	421
3	162	234	282	324	360
2	130	188	234	272	305
1	94	130	162	188	210
	1	2	3	4	5
	Units of X used				

A. Do the two inputs exhibit the characteristics of constant, increasing, or decreasing marginal rates of technical substitution? How do you know?

B. Assuming that output sells for $3 per unit, complete the following tables:

		X Fixed at 2 Units		
Units of Y Used	**Total Product of Y**	**Marginal Product of Y**	**Average Product of Y**	**Marginal Revenue Product of Y**
1				
2				
3				
4				
5				

		Y Fixed at 3 Units		
Units of X Used	**Total Product of X**	**Marginal Product of X**	**Average Product of X**	**Marginal Revenue Product of X**
1				
2				
3				
4				
5				

C. Assume that the quantity of X is fixed at 2 units. If output sells for $3 and the cost of Y is $120 per unit, how many units of Y will be employed?

D. Assume that the company is currently producing 162 units of output per day using 1 unit of X and 3 units of Y. The daily cost per unit of X is $120 and that of Y is also $120. Would you recommend a change in the present input combination? Why or why not?

E. What is the nature of the returns to scale for this production system if the optimal input combination requires that $X = Y$?

P8.2   **Production Function Concepts.** Indicate whether each of the following statements is true or false. Explain your answer.

A. Decreasing returns to scale and increasing average costs are indicated when $\epsilon_Q < 1$.

B. If the marginal product of capital falls as capital usage grows, the returns to capital are decreasing.

C. L-shaped isoquants describe production systems in which inputs are perfect substitutes.

D. Marginal revenue product measures the profit earned through expanding input usage.

E. The marginal rate of technical substitution will be affected by a given percentage increase in the marginal productivity of all inputs.

P8.3   **Factor Productivity.** During recent years, computer-aided design (CAD) and computer-aided manufacturing (CAM) have become prevalent in many U.S. industries. Holding all else equal, indicate whether each of the following factors would be responsible for increasing or decreasing this prevalence. Explain your answers.

A. Rising worker pension costs

B. Technical advances in computer mainframe design

C. An increase in the import share of the market

D. Falling prices for industry output

E. Computer software that is increasingly user-friendly

P8.4 **Returns to Scale.** Determine whether the following production functions exhibit constant, increasing, or decreasing returns to scale.

A. $Q = 0.5X + 2Y + 40Z$

B. $Q = 3L + 10K + 500$

C. $Q = 4A + 6B + 8AB$

D. $Q = 7L^2 + 5LK + 2K^2$

E. $Q = 10L^{0.5}K^{0.3}$.

P8.5 **Optimal Input Mix.** World Wide Sports, Inc., based in St. Paul, Minnesota, distributes a complete line of sporting equipment. President Frank Furillo is reviewing the company's sales force compensation plan. Currently, the company pays its three experienced sales staff members a salary based on years of service, past contributions to the company, and so on. New sales trainee Phil Esterhaus is paid a more modest salary. Monthly sales and salary data for each employee are as follows:

Sales Staff	Average Monthly Sales	Monthly Salary
Lucy Bates	$160,000	$6,000
Mick Belker	199,000	4,500
Joe Coffey	90,000	3,600
Phil Esterhaus	75,000	2,500

Esterhaus has shown great promise during the past year, and Furillo believes that a substantial raise is clearly justified. At the same time, some adjustment to the compensation paid to other sales personnel also seems appropriate. Furillo is considering changing from the current compensation plan to one based on a 5 percent commission. He sees such a plan as being fairer to the parties involved and believes it would also provide strong incentives for needed market expansion.

A. Calculate World Wide's salary expense for each employee expressed as a percentage of the monthly sales generated by that individual.

B. Calculate monthly income for each employee under a 5 percent of monthly sales commission-based system.

C. Will a commission-based plan result in efficient relative salaries, efficient salary levels, or both?

P8.6 **Optimal Input Mix.** The First National Bank received 3,000 inquiries following the latest advertisement describing its 30-month IRA accounts in the *Boston World,* a local newspaper. The most recent ad in a similar advertising campaign in *Massachusetts Business,* a regional business magazine, generated 1,000 inquiries. The newspaper ads cost $500, whereas each magazine ad cost $125.

A. Assuming that additional ads would generate similar response rates, is the bank running an optimal mix of newspaper and magazine ads? Why or why not?

B. Holding all else equal, how many inquiries must a newspaper ad attract for the current advertising mix to be optimal?

P8.7 **Optimal Input Level.** The I-70 Truck Stop, Inc. sells gasoline to both self-service and full-service customers. Those who pump their own gas benefit from the lower self-service price of $1.25 per gallon. Full-service customers enjoy the service of an attendant, but they pay a higher price of $1.30 per gallon. The company has observed the following relation between the number of attendants employed per day and full-service output:

Number of Attendants per Day	Full-Service Output (gallons)
0	0
1	2,000
2	3,800
3	5,400
4	6,800
5	8,000

A. Construct a table showing the net marginal revenue product derived from attendant employment.

B. How many attendants would I-70 employ at a daily wage rate of $64?

C. What is the highest daily wage rate I-70 would pay to hire three attendants per day?

P8.8 **Optimal Input Level.** Ticket Services, Inc., offers ticket promotion and handling services for concerts and sporting events. The Chicago branch office makes heavy use of spot radio advertising on WNDY-AM, with each 30-second ad costing $100. During the past year, the following relation between advertising and ticket sales per event has been observed:

$$\text{Sales (units)} = 5,000 + 100A - 0.5A^2.$$

Here, A represents a 30-second radio spot ad, and sales are measured in numbers of tickets.

Harry Stone, manager for the Chicago office, has been asked to recommend an appropriate level of advertising. In thinking about this problem, Stone noted its resemblance to the optimal resource employment problem he had studied in a managerial economics course that was part of his M.B.A. program. The advertising/sales relation could be thought of as a production function, with advertising as an input and sales as the output. The problem is to determine the profit-maximizing level of employment for the input, advertising, in this "production" system. Stone recognized that to solve the problem, he needed a measure of output value. After reflection, he determined that the value of output is $2 per ticket, the net marginal revenue earned by Ticket Services (price minus all marginal costs except advertising).

A. Continuing with Stone's production analogy, what is the "marginal product" of advertising?

B. What is the rule for determining the optimal amount of a resource to employ in a production system? Explain the logic underlying this rule.

C. Using the rule for optimal resource employment, determine the profit-maximizing number of radio ads.

P8.9   **Net Marginal Revenue.** Robert Hartley & Associates is a large human resource management consulting firm with offices located throughout the United States. Output at the firm is measured in billable hours, which vary between partners and associates.

Partner time is billed to clients at a rate of $100 per hour, whereas associate time is billed at a rate of $50 per hour. On average, each partner generates 25 billable hours per 40-hour workweek, with 15 hours spent on promotion, administrative, and supervisory responsibilities. Associates generate an average of 35 billable hours per 40-hour workweek and spend 5 hours per week in administrative and training meetings. Variable overhead costs average 50 percent of revenues generated by partners and, given supervisory requirements, 60 percent of revenues generated by associates.

A. Calculate the annual (50 workweeks) net marginal revenue product of partners and associates.

B. Assuming that partners earn $65,000 and associates earn $30,000 per year, does the company have an optimal combination of partners and associates? If not, why not? Make your answer explicit and support any recommendations for change.

P8.10   **Production Function Estimation.** Consider the following Cobb-Douglas production function for bus service in a typical metropolitan area:

$$Q = b_0 L^{b_1} k^{b_2} F^{b_3},$$

where

$$Q = \text{output in millions of passenger miles,}$$
$$L = \text{labor input in worker hours,}$$
$$k = \text{capital input in bus transit hours, and}$$
$$F = \text{fuel input in gallons.}$$

Each of the parameters of this model was estimated by regression analysis using monthly data over a recent three-year period. Results obtained were as follows (standard errors in parentheses):

$$\hat{b}_0 = 1.2; \quad \hat{b}_1 = 0.28; \quad \hat{b}_2 = 0.63; \quad \text{and } \hat{b}_3 = 0.12.$$
$$(0.4) \qquad (0.15) \qquad (0.12) \qquad \qquad (0.07)$$

A. Estimate the effect on output of a 4 percent decline in worker hours (holding *k* and *F* constant).

B. Estimate the effect on output of a 3 percent reduction in fuel availability accompanied by a 4 percent decline in bus transit hours (holding *L* constant).

C. Estimate the returns to scale for this production system.

CASE STUDY FOR CHAPTER 8
Productivity Measurement and Enhancement in the Services Sector

The measurement and enhancement of worker productivity is an important challenge facing all managers. Productivity enhancement is vital given the role of labor as a key input in the production of goods and services and in light of the generally increasing vigor of domestic and import competition. Of course, before incentives to enhance worker productivity can be introduced, the multiple dimensions of worker productivity must be made explicit and accurately measured. Management must be able to clearly articulate the many important dimensions of worker output and communicate this information effectively to workers.

The business and popular press is replete with examples of firms and industries that have foundered because of problems tied to the inaccurate measurement of "blue-collar" worker productivity. When worker incentives are carelessly tied to piece-rate production, mass quantities of low-quality output sometimes result. Similarly, worker incentive pay plans that emphasize high-quality output can fail to provide necessary incentives for timely delivery. What is often overlooked in discussion of workers' efficiency and labor productivity is that the definition and measurement of productivity are perhaps even more difficult in the case of managers and other "white-collar" workers. Problems encountered in the definition and measurement of white-collar-worker productivity can be illustrated by considering the productivity of college and university professors.

For most two-year and four-year college and university professors, teaching is a primary component of their work assignment. Faculty members have a standard teaching load, defined by the number of class hours per term, number of students taught, or a multiple of the two called "student contact hours." However, not all student contact hours are alike. For example, it is possible to generate large numbers of student contact hours per faculty member simply by offering courses in a mass lecture setting with hundreds of students per class. In other cases, a faculty member might work with a very small number of students in an advanced seminar or laboratory course, generating relatively few student credit hours. The teaching "product" in each of these course settings is fundamentally similar, and few would argue that the number of students taught is an irrelevant basis for comparing the productivity of professors teaching these different types of classes.

On the other hand, few would suggest defining teaching productivity solely in terms of the sheer quantity of students taught. Student course evaluations are typically required to provide evidence from student "customers" concerning the quality of instruction. Many schools rely on such data as an exclusive measure of teaching quality. At other schools, student course-evaluation data are supplemented by peer review of teaching methods and materials, interviews of former students, and so on. Measures of both the quantity and quality of instruction must be employed in the measurement of teaching productivity.

In addition to their important teaching role, faculty members are expected to play an active role in the ongoing administration of their academic institution. At a minimum, they participate in the peer review of faculty, in student and faculty recruiting, and in curriculum and program development. Faculty often play an active role on committees that conduct the everyday management of the institution. This faculty governance system is an important organizational difference between most academic and nonacademic institutions. Faculty members are both workers *and* management. Measuring "output" as related to these activities, and hence productivity, is very difficult.

At many schools, faculty members also play an important liaison role with external constituents. Alumni provide important financial resources to colleges and universities and appreciate programs designed for their benefit. Nondegree "short courses" are often offered on topical subjects at nominal charge for the benefit of alumni and the community at large. Similarly, faculty are asked to give lectures to local groups, interviews for local media, and informal consulting services to local firms and organizations. Often these services are provided for free or at nominal charge as part of the faculty member's "service" function. Similarly, faculty are sometimes called on to provide service to external academic and professional organizations. Participation at national and regional academic conventions, editing academic journals, and helping design and write professional exams are typical examples of expected but unpaid services.

The preceding duties are supplemented by faculty research requirements at most four-year colleges and universities and at all graduate institutions. This requirement is fundamental to the growth and development of colleges and universities but is often misunderstood by those outside of academia. To be granted the doctoral degree, doctoral candidates must complete a rigorous series of courses and exams and meet a dissertation requirement. A doctoral dissertation is a book-length independent study that makes an important contribution to knowledge in a scholarly discipline. In fulfilling this requirement, doctoral students demonstrate their capacity to participate in the discovery of new knowledge. A key difference between the role of university professors and that of other teachers is that professors must be intimately involved with the creation *and* dissemination of new knowledge. Thus, the research component is a key ingredient of professorial output.

Research output is extremely varied. In the physical sciences, new compounds or other physical products may result. Similarly, such research may lead to new process techniques. In most academic fields, the primary research product is new knowledge communicated in the form of research reports or other scholarly publications. As with teaching, measuring the quantity and quality of research output proves to be most challenging. Judging the value of a research product is often quite subjective, and its worth may not be recognized for years.

Given the difficulties involved with evaluating highly specialized and detailed research, many institutions consider the dollar amount of research funds awarded to an individual to be a useful indicator of the quantity and quality of research output. It is anomalous that a school's best researchers and highest-paid faculty members may be the least expensive in terms of their net costs to the institution. When established researchers are able to consistently obtain external funding in excess of incremental costs, their net employment costs can be nil. In such instances, the disadvantages to an institution of losing a star researcher are obvious.

Of course, just as in the case of measuring teaching quality, difficulties are encountered in measuring the quality of published research output. In most instances, the quality of published articles and books is judged in terms of the reputation of the publisher or editor, the level of readership enjoyed, and so on. Over time, the number of new research outlets has grown to keep pace with the growing level of specialization in the various disciplines. In economics, for example, there are as many as 200 possible research outlets. However, only a relative handful are widely read in any given subdiscipline. Competition for scarce journal space in such outlets is fierce. Acceptance rates at leading journals often average no more than 5 to 10 percent of these articles submitted. When one considers that a productive scholar is typically able to complete no more than one or two substantial research projects per year, the odds are very much against achieving publication of one or two first-rate journal articles per year. Thus, research productivity is usually measured in terms of both the quantity and quality of published research.

In sum, defining the role of professors at colleges and universities provides an interesting example of the difficulties involved in measuring worker productivity. Each individual academic institution must define on an ongoing basis the relative importance of the teaching, research, and service components of faculty output. Once this has been determined, the difficult task of defining and measuring faculty-member productivity on each dimension must begin.

Based on the preceding information and in light of the focus of your academic institution, answer the following questions:

A. How would you define faculty-member productivity?
B. Do you agree with the view that many elements of professorial output don't easily lend themselves to quantitative evaluation? How might you measure such productivity?
C. Would productivity clauses for professors' contracts make sense economically? What problems do you see in implementing such clauses in actual practice?
D. Reconsider your answers to Parts A through C for other service-industry occupations (for example, doctors, lawyers, and legislators). Are the issues discussed unique to academia?

Selected References   Allen, Beth. "Choosing R&D Projects: An Informational Approach." *American Economic Review* 81 (May 1991): 257–261.

Baysinger, Barry D., Rita D. Kosnik, and Thomas A. Tork. "Effects of Board and Ownership Structure on Corporate R&D Strategy." *Academy of Management Journal* 34 (March 1991): 205–214.

Bound, John, and George Johnson. "Changes in the Structure of Wages in the 1980s: An Evaluation of Alternative Explanations." *American Economic Review* 82 (June 1992): 371–392.

Brownstein, Andrew R., and Morris J. Panner. "Who Should Set CEO Pay? The Press? Congress? Shareholders?" *Harvard Business Review* 70 (May–June 1992): 28–38.

Coughlan, Anne T., and Chakravarthi. "An Empirical Analysis of Sales-Force Compensation Plans." *Journal of Business* 65 (January 1992): 93–121.

Crystal, Graef S. *In Search of Excess: The Overcompensation of American Executives.* (New York: W. W. Norton, 1991).

Ehrenfeld, Tom. "The Case of the Unpopular Pay Plan." *Harvard Business Review* 70 (January–February 1992): 14–23.

Hoerr, John. "What Should Unions Do?" *Harvard Business Review* 69 (May–June 1991): 30–45.

Johnston, William B. "Global Workforce 2000: The New World Labor Market." *Harvard Business Review* 69 (March–April 1991): 115–127.

Lane, Sarah. "The Determinants of Investment in New Technology." *American Economic Review* 81 (May 1991): 262–265.

MaCurdy, Thomas. "Work Disincentive Effects of Taxes: A Reexamination of Some Evidence." *American Economic Review* 82 (May 1992): 243–249.

Maskel, Brian H. *Performance Measurement for World Class Manufacturing: A Model for American Companies.* (Cambridge, MA: Productivity Press, Inc., 1991).

Mayers, David, and Clifford W. Smith, Jr. "Executive Compensation in the Life Insurance Industry." *Journal of Business* 65 (January 1992): 51–74.

Sinha, Rajiv K., and Murali Chandrashekaran. "A Split Hazard Model for Analyzing the Diffusion of Innovations." *Journal of Marketing Research* 29 (February 1992): 116–127.

Zuboff, Shoshana. "Can Research Reinvent the Corporation?" *Harvard Business Review* 69 (March–April 1991): 164–175.

A CONSTRAINED OPTIMIZATION APPROACH TO DEVELOPING THE OPTIMAL INPUT COMBINATION RELATIONSHIPS

It was noted in Chapter 8 that the determination of optimal input proportions could be viewed either as a problem of maximizing output for a given expenditure level or, alternatively, as a problem of minimizing the cost of producing a specified level of output. This appendix shows how the Lagrangian technique for constrained optimization can be used to develop the optimal input proportion rule.

CONSTRAINED PRODUCTION MAXIMIZATION

Consider the problem of maximizing output from a production system described by the general equation:

$$Q = f(X, Y) \tag{8A.1}$$

subject to a budget constraint. The expenditure limitation can be expressed as:

$$E^* = P_X \cdot X + P_Y \cdot Y, \tag{8A.2}$$

which states that the total expenditure on inputs, E^*, is equal to the price of Input X, P_X, times the quantity of X employed, plus the price of Y, P_Y, times the quantity of that resource used in the production system. Equation 8A.2 can be written in the form of a Lagrangian constraint, as developed in Chapter 2, as:

$$O = E^* - P_X \cdot X - P_Y \cdot Y. \tag{8A.3}$$

The Lagrangian function for the maximization of the production function, Equation 8A.1, subject to the budget constraint expressed by Equation 8A.3, can then be written as:

$$Max\ L_Q = f(X, Y) + \lambda(E^* - P_X \cdot X - P_Y \cdot Y). \tag{8A.4}$$

Maximization of the constrained production function is accomplished by setting the partial derivatives of the Lagrangian expression taken with respect to X, Y, and λ equal to zero, and then solving the resultant system of equations. The partials of Equation 8A.4 are:

$$\frac{\delta L_Q}{\delta X} = \frac{\delta f(X, Y)}{\delta X} - \lambda P_X = 0. \tag{8A.5}$$

$$\frac{\delta L_Q}{\delta Y} = \frac{\delta f(X, Y)}{\delta Y} - \lambda P_Y = 0, \tag{8A.6}$$

and

$$\frac{\delta L_Q}{\delta \lambda} = E^* - P_X \cdot X - P_Y \cdot Y = 0. \tag{8A.7}$$

Equating these three partial derivatives to zero results in a set of conditions that must be met for output maximization subject to the budget limit.

Note that the first terms in Equations 8A.5 and 8A.6 are the marginal products of X and Y, respectively. In other words, $\delta f(X, Y)/\delta X$ equals $\delta Q/\delta X$, which by definition is the marginal product of X; and the same is true for $\delta f(X, Y)/\delta Y$. Thus, those two expressions can be rewritten as:

$$MP_X - \lambda P_X = 0$$

and

$$MP_Y - \lambda P_Y = 0,$$

or, alternatively, as:

$$MP_X = \lambda P_X \tag{8A.8}$$

and

$$MP_Y = \lambda P_Y \tag{8A.9}$$

The conditions required for constrained output maximization, expressed by Equations 8A.8 and 8A.9, can also be expressed by the ratio of equations. Thus:

$$\frac{MP_X}{MP_Y} = \frac{\lambda P_X}{\lambda P_Y}. \tag{8A.10}$$

Canceling the lambdas in Equation 8A.10 results in the condition required for optimal input use developed in the chapter:

$$\frac{MP_X}{MP_Y} = \frac{P_X}{P_Y}. \tag{8A.11}$$

For maximum production, given a fixed expenditure level, the input factors must be combined in such a way that the ratio of their marginal products is equal to the ratio of their prices. Alternatively, transposing Equation 8A.11 derives the expression:

$$\frac{MP_X}{P_X} = \frac{MP_Y}{P_Y}.$$

Optimal input proportions require that the ratio of marginal product to price must be equal for all input factors.

CONSTRAINED COST MINIMIZATION

The relationship developed above can also be derived from the problem of minimizing the cost of producing a given quantity of output. In this case, the constraint states that some level of output, Q^*, must be produced from the production system described by the function $Q = f(X, Y)$. Written in the standard Lagrangian format, the constraint is $0 = Q^* - f(X, Y)$. The cost, or expenditure, function is given as $E = P_X \cdot X + P_Y \cdot Y$. The Lagrangian function for the constrained cost minimization problem, then, is:

$$L_E = P_X \cdot X + P_Y \cdot Y + \lambda[Q^* - f(X, Y)] \qquad \textbf{(8A.12)}$$

As shown above, the conditions for constrained cost minimization are provided by the partial derivatives of Equation 8A.12:

$$\frac{\delta L_E}{\delta X} = P_X - \lambda \frac{\delta(fX, Y)}{\delta X} = 0 \qquad \textbf{(8A.13)}$$

$$\frac{\delta L_E}{\delta Y} = P_Y - \lambda \frac{\delta(fX, Y)}{\delta Y} = 0 \qquad \textbf{(8A.14)}$$

and

$$\frac{\delta L_E}{\delta \lambda} = Q^* - f(X, Y) = 0. \qquad \textbf{(8A.15)}$$

Notice that the terms on the left-hand side in Equations 8A.13 and 8A.14 are the marginal products of X and Y, respectively, so each of these expressions can be rewritten as:

$$P_X - \lambda MP_X = 0$$

and

$$P_Y - \lambda MP_Y = 0,$$

or, alternatively, as:

$$P_X = \lambda MP_X \qquad \textbf{(8A.16)}$$

and

$$P_Y = \lambda MP_Y. \qquad \textbf{(8A.17)}$$

Taking the ratio of Equation 8A.16 to Equation 8A.17 and canceling the lambdas again produces the basic input optimality relation:

$$\frac{P_X}{P_Y} = \frac{MP_X}{MP_Y}.$$

Problem

8A.1   Assume that a firm produces its product in a system described in the following production function and price data:

$$Q = 3X + 5Y + XY$$
$$P_X = \$3$$
$$P_Y = \$6.$$

Here, X and Y are two variable input factors employed in the production of Q.

A. What are the optimal input proportions for X and Y in this production system? Is this combination rate constant regardless of the output level?

B. It is possible to express the cost function associated with the use of X and Y in the production of Q as Cost $= P_X X + P_Y Y$, or Cost $= \$3X + \$6Y$. Use the Lagrangian technique to determine the maximum output that the firm can produce operating under a $1,000 budget constraint for X and Y. Show that the inputs used to produce that level of output meet the optimality conditions derived in Part A.

C. What is the additional output that could be obtained from a marginal increase in the budget?

D. Assume that the firm is interested in minimizing the cost of producing 14,777 units of output. Use the Lagrangian method to determine what optimal quantities of X and Y to employ. What will be the cost of producing that output level? How would you interpret λ, the Lagrangian multiplier, in this problem?

COST ANALYSIS

Cost analysis is made difficult by the effects of unforeseen inflation, unpredictable changes in technology, and the dynamic nature of input and output markets. Wide divergences between economic costs and accounting valuations are common. For example, corporate restructuring during the late 1980s and early 1990s often involved the disposal of nonstrategic operations in order to redeploy assets and strengthen core lines of business. When nonessential assets are disposed of in a depressed market, there is often no relation between low "fire sale" proceeds and book value, historical cost, or replacement cost. Conversely, when assets are sold to others who can more effectively utilize such resources, sale proceeds can approximate replacement valuations and greatly exceed historical costs and book values. Even under normal circumstances, the link between economic and accounting values can be tenuous. Economic worth as determined by profit-generating capability, rather than accounting value, is always the most relevant consideration when determining the cost and use of specific assets.

Accurate cost analysis involves careful consideration of all relevant decision alternatives. In many instances, the total costs of making a given decision are clear only when viewed in light of what is actually done *and* what is not done. For example, suppose that a company is contemplating closing satellite distribution facilities in Houston and St. Louis and opening a major regional distribution center in Dallas. Careful decision analysis includes a comparison of the relative costs and benefits of each decision alternative. Neither option can be viewed in isolation; each choice plays an important role in shaping the relevant costs and benefits of *both* decision alternatives. The process of cost analysis is one of measuring and weighing the relative costs of decision alternatives.

Cost analysis plays an essential role in managerial economics because virtually every managerial decision requires a careful comparison between costs and benefits. Evaluation of a proposal to expand output requires that the increased revenues gained from added sales be compared with the higher production costs incurred. In weighing a recommendation to expand capital resources, managers must compare the revenues derived from investment and the cost of needed funds. The expected benefits of advertising promotion must be measured in relation to the costs of personal selling, media promotion, and direct marketing. Even a decision to pave the employees' parking lot or refurbish the company lunchroom involves a comparison between projected costs and the expected benefits derived from improved morale and worker productivity. In every case, the decision-making process involves a comparison between the costs and the benefits resulting from various decision alternatives.

A number of fundamental cost concepts are analyzed in this chapter. Central to all of these concepts is the notion that relevant cost determination depends on a careful consideration of all applicable decision alternatives. The cost implications of production function relations are also investigated to develop long-run and short-run cost functions suitable for empirical measurement. Materials developed in this chapter are not only useful for managerial decision making, but they also help to explain how industry structure evolves and develops. A useful backdrop is also provided for characterizing the implications of regulation and antitrust policy that alter the structure of industry, a subject studied in some detail in Chapter 15.

HISTORICAL VERSUS CURRENT COSTS

The term *cost* can be defined in a number of ways, and the correct definition varies from situation to situation. In popular terminology, cost generally refers to the price that must be paid for an item. If a firm buys an input for cash and uses it immediately, few problems arise in defining and measuring its cost. However, if an input is purchased, stored for a time, and then used, complications can arise. The problem is even more acute if the item is a long-lived asset like a machine tool or a building that will be used at varying rates for an indeterminate period.

Why Do Historical and Current Costs Differ?

Historical cost
Actual cash outlay.

Current cost
Amount paid under prevailing market conditions.

When costs are calculated for a firm's income tax returns, the law requires use of the actual dollar amount spent to purchase the labor, raw materials, and capital equipment used in production. For tax purposes, **historical cost,** or actual cash outlay, is the relevant cost. This is also generally true for annual 10-K reports to the Securities and Exchange Commission and for reports to stockholders.

Historical costs are not appropriate for many managerial decisions. Current costs or projected future costs are typically much more relevant. **Current cost** is the amount that must be paid for an item under prevailing market conditions. Current cost is influenced by market conditions measured by the number of buyers and sellers, the current state of technology, inflation, and so on. For assets purchased recently, historical cost and current cost are typically the same. For assets purchased several years ago, historical cost and current cost are often quite different. During the post–World War II period throughout most of the world, inflation has been an obvious source of large differences between current and historical costs. With the current inflation rate of roughly 5 percent per year, prices double in less than 15 years and triple in roughly 22 years. Land purchased for $50,000 in 1970 often has a current cost in excess of $150,000. In California, Florida, Texas, and other rapidly growing areas, current costs can and do run much higher. Just as no homeowner would sell his or her home for a lower price based on lower historical costs, no manager can afford to sell assets or products for less than current costs.

A firm also cannot assume that the accounting historical cost is the same as the relevant economic cost of using a given piece of equipment. For example, it is not always appropriate to assume that use costs equal zero just because a machine has been fully depreciated using Accelerated Cost Recovery System (ACRS) accounting methods. If a machine could be sold for $10,000 now, but its market value is expected to be only $2,000 one year from now, the relevant cost of using the machine for one additional year is $8,000.[1] Again, there is little relation between the $8,000 relevant cost of using the machine and the zero cost that would be reported on the firm's income statement.

Historical costs provide a measure of the market value of an asset at the time of purchase. Current costs are a measure of the market value of an asset at the present time. Traditional accounting methods and the IRS rely heavily on the historical cost concept because it can be applied consistently across firms and is easily verifiable. However, when historical and current costs differ markedly, reliance on historical costs can sometimes lead to operating decisions with disastrous consequences. The recent savings and loan (S&L) industry debacle provides a clear case in point. On a historical cost basis, almost all thrifts appeared to have solid loan assets to back up deposit liabilities. On a current cost basis, however, many S&Ls proved insolvent because loan assets had a current market value below the current market value of liabilities. The present move by federal and state bank regulators toward market-value-based accounting methods is motivated by a desire to avoid S&L-type disasters in the future.

Replacement Cost

Replacement cost

The cost of duplicating productive capability using current technology.

While it is typical for current costs to exceed historical costs, this is not always the case. Computers and many types of electronic equipment cost much less today than they did just a few years ago. In these high-tech industries, the rapid pace of advancement in technology has been so fast that it has overcome the general rate of inflation. As a result, current costs are falling. Current costs for used computers and electronic equipment are determined by what is referred to as **replacement cost,** or the cost of duplicating productive capability using current technology. Business computers and workstations purchased in 1990 are much cheaper today. In many instances, costs have fallen by 25 to 40 percent or more. In valuing such assets, the appropriate measure is the much lower replacement cost—not the historical cost. Similarly, if a company holds electronic components in inventory, the relevant cost consideration for pricing purposes is replacement costs.

In a more typical example, consider a construction company that has an inventory of 1,000,000 board feet of lumber, purchased at a historical cost of $200,000, or $200 per 1,000 board feet (a board foot of lumber is one square foot of lumber, one inch thick). Assume that lumber prices rise by 50 percent, and the company is asked to bid on a new construction project that would require use of the lumber. What cost should the construction company assign to the lumber—the $200,000

---

[1] This statement involves a slight oversimplification. The economic cost of using a machine for one year is its current market value minus the discounted present value of its worth one year from now. This adjustment is necessary to account for the fact that future dollars have a lower *present* value than dollars received today.

historical cost or the $300,000 replacement cost? The answer is the current or replacement cost of $300,000. The company will have to pay $300,000 to replace the lumber it uses on the new construction project. In fact, should it choose to do so, the construction company could sell its current inventory of lumber to others for the prevailing market price of $300,000. Under current market conditions, the lumber has a value, worth, and cost of $300,000. The amount of $300,000 is the relevant economic cost for purposes of bidding on the new construction project. For income tax purposes, however, the appropriate cost basis for the lumber inventory is still the $200,000 historical cost.

OPPORTUNITY COSTS

The preceding replacement cost discussion is based on an alternative-use concept. Economic resources like lumber have value because they can be used to produce products that consumers desire. When a firm uses such a resource for producing a particular product, it bids against alternative users. Thus, the firm must offer a price at least as great as the resource's value in alternative use. The role played by choice alternatives in cost analysis is formalized by the opportunity cost concept.

The Opportunity Cost Concept

Opportunity cost
Foregone value associated with current rather than next-best use of an asset.

Opportunity cost is the foregone value associated with the current rather than next-best use of a given asset. In other words, the cost of a given asset is determined by the highest-valued *opportunity* that must be foregone to allow current use. The cost of aluminum used in the manufacture of soft drink containers, for example, is determined by its value in alternative uses. Soft drink bottlers must pay an aluminum price equal to this value or the aluminum will be used in the production of alternative goods, such as airplanes, building materials, cookware, and so on. Similarly, if a firm owns capital equipment that can be used to produce either Product *A* or Product *B,* the relevant cost of producing *A* includes the profit of the alternative Product *B* that cannot be produced because the equipment is tied up manufacturing Product *A.*

The opportunity cost concept explains asset use in a wide variety of circumstances. Gold and silver are pliable yet strong precious metals. As such, they make excellent material for dental fillings. However, when precious metals speculation drove prices skyrocketing during the 1970s, plastic and ceramic materials became a common substitute for dental gold and silver. More recently, lower market prices have again allowed widespread dental use of both metals. Still, dental customers must be willing to pay a price for dental gold and silver that is competitive with the price of jewelry and industrial demand.

Explicit and Implicit Costs

Explicit costs
Out-of-pocket expenditures.

Typically, the costs of using resources in production involve both out-of-pocket costs, or **explicit costs,** and other noncash costs, called **implicit costs.** Wages paid, utility expenses, payment for raw materials, interest paid to the holders of the firm's bonds, and rent on a building are all examples of explicit expenses. The implicit costs associated with any decision are much more difficult to compute. These costs do not involve cash expenditures and are therefore often overlooked

Implicit costs
Noncash costs.

in decision analysis. Since cash payments are not made for implicit costs, the opportunity cost concept must be used to measure them. The rent that a shop owner could receive on buildings and equipment if they were not used in the business is an implicit cost of the owner's own retailing activity, as is the salary that an individual could receive by working for someone else instead of operating his or her own retail establishment.

▶   An example should clarify these cost distinctions. Consider the costs associated with the purchase and operation of a law practice. Assume that an established practice and office space can be bought for $225,000, with an additional $25,000 needed for initial working capital. Grace Van Owen has personal savings of $250,000 to invest in such an enterprise; Michael Kuzak, another possible buyer, must borrow the entire $250,000 at a cost of 15 percent, or $37,500 per year. Assume that operating costs are the same no matter who owns the practice, and that Van Owen and Kuzak are equally capable of completing the purchase. Does the $37,500 in annual interest expenses make Kuzak's potential operating cost greater than that of Van Owen? For managerial decision purposes, the answer is no. Even though Kuzak has higher explicit interest costs, true financing costs may well be the same for both individuals. Van Owen has an implicit interest cost equal to the amount that could be earned on an alternative $250,000 investment. If a 15 percent return can be earned by investing in other assets of equal risk, then Van Owen's implicit investment opportunity cost is $37,500 per year. In this case, Van Owen and Kuzak each have a financing cost of $37,500 per year. Van Owen's cost is implicit and Kuzak's is explicit.

Will total operating costs be identical for both individuals? Not necessarily. Just as the implicit cost of Van Owen's capital must be included in the analysis, so too must implicit labor costs be included for each individual. If Van Owen is a senior partner in a major Los Angeles law firm earning $150,000 a year and Kuzak is a junior partner earning $100,000 annually, implicit labor costs will not be equal for the two. The implicit labor expense for each potential buyer is the amount of income foregone by quitting his or her present job. Thus, implicit labor costs are $150,000 for Van Owen and $100,000 for Kuzak. On an annual basis, Van Owen's total capital plus labor costs are $187,500, all of which are implicit. Kuzak's total annual costs are $137,500, including explicit capital costs of $37,500 plus implicit labor costs of $100,000.

INCREMENTAL AND SUNK COSTS IN DECISION ANALYSIS

Value maximization requires that every managerial decision be justified on the basis of its contributing more in added benefits than in added costs. Relevant costs and benefits for any decision are limited to those that are affected by it. Factors that are relevant to a managerial decision can be obscured by the introduction of extraneous cost information. To limit the confounding influence of irrelevant cost information, it is helpful to focus on the causal relation between costs and a given managerial decision, as well as on the reversible or nonreversible nature of some cost categories.

MANAGERIAL APPLICATION 9.1

What in Heck Is a FASB?

The Financial Standards Board (FASB) is a nongovernmental body empowered by the Securities and Exchange Commission with responsibility for determining the nature and scope of accounting information. Started in 1973 as the logical successor to the accounting profession's Accounting Principles Board, the FASB develops new accounting standards in an elaborate process that reflects the views of accountants, business executives, security analysts, and the public. As a result, the FASB plays a key role in defining the specific information that must be incorporated in published corporate financial statements.

The FASB also plays an important role in the resolution of a broad range of important and controversial accounting issues. For example, the FASB plays a key role in the debate over accounting policy issues, including the controversy on whether to require firms to use current market values rather than historical cost book values for accounts receivables, bonds, and loan portfolios—including loans to troubled Latin American countries. This is a highly controversial issue, because the market-value approach would lead to a much different picture of corporate assets and liabilities for many companies. In some instances, money center banks would show a substantial negative net worth with a market-value treatment of debts owed by Third World countries. Similarly, some large corporations would see a dramatic decline in reported profits and a big jump in debt equity ratios, if they were required to fully reflect the magnitude of unfunded pension liabilities.

Corporate executives typically resist the FASB's efforts to install new accounting rules, citing the higher operating expenses sometimes required to meet new guidelines. Most new standards require the capture of new data or the reworking of existing accounting information. At times, however, more subtle unspoken interests may be responsible for corporate opposition to new FASB standards. During inflationary periods, as has been the case in the United States since World War II, the use of historical book values tends to overstate net income numbers, and to understate the value of tangible plant and equipment. As a result, reported profit rates, such as the key return-on-stockholders'-equity measure, can be inflated when book-value data are used.

Because of the effects of inflation, a market-value standard provides a more economically meaningful picture of "true" corporate profitability, but it typically results in lower profit rates. The fact that a market-value standard lowers reported profits is an important concern to many executives, especially those with compensation plans tied to reported profits.

One of the most important accounting innovations promoted by the FASB during recent years involves the new cash-flow statements that all companies are now required to provide. By minimizing distortions that are sometimes introduced by imperfect accrual accounting methods, cash-flow data are intended to provide a clearer picture of current corporate performance. Needless to say, many corporations oppose new cash-flow reporting requirements, especially when meeting them causes perceived (reported) performance to falter.

On Wall Street, some observers view ongoing disputes between the FASB and the corporate community as being based on a rather myopic view of the information-processing capability of both professional and institutional investors. Clearly, the takeover and corporate restructuring boom of the late 1980s was based on a sophisticated awareness of corporate cash flows, an awareness that preceded new FASB cash-flow reporting requirements. Nevertheless, new cash-flow statements will help individual investors by providing them with another low-cost basis for evaluating corporate performance.

Given the wide range of important accounting issues being addressed, the role played by the FASB has grown steadily. At times, the public perception of the FASB has failed to match this pace. Slowly but surely, this is changing as the FASB's public visibility increases. New guidelines took effect in 1991 for the roughly 23,000 U.S. companies per year that file for Chapter 11 bankruptcy and thousands more working through reorganization. These FASB-inspired guidelines allow companies to reemerge from bankruptcy protection with reported assets closer to their real economic value. For investors, there is a more detailed disclosure of liabilities, and for the first time, standardized accounting rules.

Source: Ford S. Worthy, "The Battle of the Bean Counters," *Fortune,* June 1, 1992, 117–126.

Incremental Cost

Incremental cost

Change in cost caused by a given managerial decision.

Incremental cost is the change in cost caused by a given managerial decision. Like marginal cost, the incremental cost concept plays an important role in the optimization process. The difference between the two concepts is that marginal cost is defined as the change in cost following a one-unit change in output, whereas incremental costs typically involve multiple units of output. For example, incremental costs are the relevant consideration when an air carrier considers the cost of adding an additional departure from New York's La Guardia Airport to upstate New York. When all current departures are full, it simply is not practical for the carrier to consider adding a single additional passenger-mile unit of output. Similarly, the incremental cost concept comes into play when judging the costs of adding a new product line, advertising campaign, production shift, or organization structure.

Inappropriate managerial decisions can result when the incremental concept is ignored or applied incorrectly. Consider, for example, a commercial real estate firm that refuses to rent excess office space for $750 per month because it figures cost as $1,000 per month—or incremental operating costs of $150 plus interest and overhead charges of $850. If the relevant incremental cost is indeed only $150 per month, turning away the prospective renter causes a $600 (= $750 − $150) per month loss in **profit contribution,** or profit before fixed charges. Interest and overhead charges will be incurred irrespective of whether or not the excess space is rented. By adding the prospective renter, the landlord has the same interest and overhead expenses as before, *plus* $600 in added revenues after incremental operating expenses. The net effect of rejecting such a renter would be to reduce profit contribution and net profits by $600.

Profit contribution

Profit before fixed charges.

Care must be also exercised to ensure against incorrectly assigning a lower than appropriate incremental cost. If excess capacity results from a temporary reduction in demand, this must be taken into account. Accepting the $750 per month renter in the previous example might well be a mistake if doing so causes full-price and more profitable renters to be turned away. When excess capacity is caused by an unpredictable temporary drop in demand, only short-term or month-to-month leases should be offered at the bargain price of $750 per month. In this way, pricing flexibility can be maintained while the net cost of temporary excess capacity is minimized. In any event, all incremental costs, including those that might be incurred in the future, must be considered.

Sunk Costs

Inherent in the incremental cost concept is the principle that any cost not affected by a decision is irrelevant to that decision. A cost that does not vary across decision alternatives is called a **sunk cost;** such costs do not play a role in determining the optimal course of action.

Sunk cost

Cost that does not vary across decision alternatives.

For example, suppose a firm has spent $5,000 on an option to purchase land for a new factory at a price of $100,000. Also assume that it is later offered an equally attractive site for $90,000. What should the firm do? The first thing to recognize is that the $5,000 spent on the purchase option is a sunk cost that must be ignored. To understand this, consider the firm's current decision alternatives. If the firm proceeds to purchase the first property, it must pay a price of $100,000. The newly offered property requires an expenditure of $90,000 and results in a

$10,000 savings. In retrospect, purchase of the $5,000 option was a mistake. It would be a compounding of this initial error to follow through with purchase of the first property and lose an additional $10,000.

In managerial decision making, care must be taken to ensure that only those costs actually affected by a decision are considered. These incremental costs can include both implicit and explicit costs. If long-term commitments are involved, both current and future incremental costs must also be accounted for. Any costs not affected by available decision alternatives are sunk and irrelevant.

SHORT-RUN AND LONG-RUN COSTS

Cost function
The cost–output relation.

Short-run cost functions
Basis for day-to-day operating decisions.

Long-run cost functions
Basis for long-range planning.

Proper use of relevant cost concepts requires an understanding of the relation between cost and output, or the **cost function.** Cost functions depend on the underlying production function and input prices. Production functions specify the technical relation between inputs and output and, when combined with input prices, determine cost functions. Two basic cost functions are used in managerial decision making: **short-run cost functions,** used for day-to-day operating decisions, and **long-run cost functions,** used for long-range planning.

How Is the Operating Period Defined?

Short run
Operating period during which at least one input is fixed.

Long run
Planning period with complete input flexibility.

The **short run** is the operating period during which the availability of at least one input is fixed. In the **long run,** the firm has complete flexibility with respect to input use. In the short run, operating decisions are typically constrained by prior capital expenditures. In the long run, no such restrictions exist. For example, a management consulting firm operating out of rented office space might have a short-run period as brief as several weeks, the time remaining on the office lease. In contrast, a firm in the hazardous waste disposal business with 25- to 30-year leases on disposal sites has significant long-lived assets and faces a lengthy period of operating constraints.

The economic life of an asset and the degree of specialization affect the time length of operating period constraints. Consider, for example, a health maintenance organization's (HMO's) automobile purchase for making prescription deliveries. If the car is a standard model without modification, it represents an unspecialized input factor with a resale market based on the used car market in general. However, if the car has been modified by adding refrigeration equipment for transporting perishable medicines, it becomes a more specialized input with full value only for those who need a vehicle with refrigeration equipment. In this case, the market price of the car might not equal its value in use to the HMO; hence, the short run is extended. To the extent that specialized input factors are employed, the short run is lengthened. When only unspecialized factors are utilized, the short run becomes a very condensed time period.

The length of time required to order, receive, and install new assets also influences the duration of the short run. Many manufacturers face delays of several months when ordering new plant and equipment. Air carriers must place their equipment orders five or more *years* in advance with Boeing, McDonnell Douglas, and other airplane manufacturers. Electric utilities frequently require eight or more *years* to bring new generating plants on line. For all such firms, the short-run operating period involves an extended period of time.

In summary, the long run is a period of sufficient length to permit a complete change in productive facilities. The short run is a period during which at least some productive inputs cannot be altered. Long-run cost curves are called *planning curves;* short-run cost curves are called *operating curves.* In the long run, plant and equipment are variable, so management can plan the most efficient physical plant, given an estimate of the firm's demand function. Once the optimal plant has been determined and the resulting investment in equipment has been made, operating decisions will be constrained by these prior decisions.

Fixed and Variable Costs

Fixed cost
Expense that does not vary with output.

Variable cost
Expense that fluctuates with output.

Fixed costs do not vary with output. Included are interest expenses, rent on leased plant and equipment, depreciation charges associated with the passage of time, property taxes, and salaries for employees not laid off during periods of reduced activity. Since all costs are variable in the long run, long-run fixed costs always equal zero. The concept of fixed costs is applicable only in the short run. **Variable costs** fluctuate with output. Expenses for raw materials, depreciation associated with the use of equipment, the variable portion of utility charges, some labor costs, and sales commissions are all examples of variable expenses. In the short run, both variable and fixed costs are often incurred. In the long run, all costs are variable.

A sharp distinction between fixed and variable costs is not always possible nor realistic. For example, CEO and staff salaries may be largely fixed, but during severe business downturns, even CEOs take a pay cut. Similarly, salaries for line managers and supervisors are fixed only within certain output ranges. Below a lower limit, supervisors and managers would be laid off. Above an upper limit, additional supervisors and managers would be hired. The longer the duration of abnormal demand, the greater the likelihood that some fixed costs will actually vary. In recognition of this, such costs are sometimes referred to as *semivariable.*

SHORT-RUN COST CURVES

Short-run cost curve
Cost–output relation for a specific plant and operating environment.

A **short-run cost curve** shows the minimum cost impact of output changes for a specific plant size and in a given operating environment. Such curves reflect the optimal or least-cost input combination for producing output under fixed circumstances. Wage rates, interest rates, plant configuration, and all other operating conditions are held constant.

Any change in the operating environment leads to a *shift* in short-run cost curves. For example, a general rise in wage rates leads to an upward shift; a fall in wage rates leads to a downward shift. Such changes must not be confused with *movements along* a given short-run cost curve caused by a change in production levels. For an existing plant, the short-run cost curve illustrates the minimum cost of production at various output levels under current operating conditions. Short-run cost curves are a useful guide to operating decisions.

TABLE 9.1 **Short-Run Cost Relations**

Q	TC	TFC	TVC	ATC	AFC	AVC	MC
1	$120	$100	$ 20	$120.0	$100.0	$20.0	$20
2	138	100	38	69.0	50.0	19.0	18
3	151	100	51	50.3	33.3	17.0	13
4	162	100	62	40.5	25.0	15.5	11
5	175	100	75	35.0	20.0	15.0	13
6	190	100	90	31.7	16.7	15.0	15
7	210	100	110	30.0	14.3	15.7	20
8	234	100	134	29.3	12.5	16.8	24
9	263	100	163	29.2	11.1	18.1	29
10	300	100	200	30.0	10.0	20.0	37

Short-Run Cost Categories

Both fixed and variable costs affect short-run costs. Total cost at each output level is the sum of total fixed costs (a constant) and total variable costs. Using *TC* to represent total cost, *TFC* for total fixed cost, *TVC* for total variable cost, and *Q* for the quantity of output produced, various unit costs are calculated as follows:

$$\text{Total Cost} = TC = TFC + TVC. \tag{9.1}$$

$$\text{Average Fixed Cost} = AFC = \frac{TFC}{Q}. \tag{9.2}$$

$$\text{Average Variable Cost} = AVC = \frac{TVC}{Q}. \tag{9.3}$$

$$\text{Average Total Cost} = ATC = \frac{TC}{Q} = AFC + AVC. \tag{9.4}$$

$$\text{Marginal Cost} = MC = \frac{\delta TC}{\delta Q}. \tag{9.5}$$

These cost categories are portrayed in Table 9.1. Using these data, it is possible to identify the various cost relations as well as to examine cost behavior. Table 9.1 shows that *AFC* declines continuously with increases in output. *ATC* and *AVC* also decline as long as they exceed *MC*, but they increase when they are less than *MC*. Alternatively, as long as *MC* is less than *ATC* and *AVC*, both average cost categories will decline. When *MC* is greater than *ATC* and *AVC*, both average cost categories will rise. Also note that *TFC* is invariant with increases in output and that *TVC* at each level of output equals the sum of *MC* up to that output.

Marginal cost is the change in cost associated with a one-unit change in output. Because fixed costs do not vary with output, fixed costs do not affect marginal costs. Only variable costs affect marginal costs. Therefore, marginal costs equal the change in total costs *or* the change in total variable costs following a one-unit change in output:

$$MC = \frac{\delta TC}{\delta Q} = \frac{\delta TVC}{\delta Q}.$$

Short-Run Cost Relations

The relations among short-run cost categories are shown in Figure 9.1. Figure 9.1(a) illustrates total cost and total variable cost curves. The shape of the total cost curve is determined entirely by the total variable cost curve. The slope of the total cost curve at each output level is identical to the slope of the total variable cost curve. Fixed costs merely shift the total cost curve to a higher level. This means that marginal costs are totally independent of fixed cost.

The shape of the total variable cost curve, and hence the shape of the total cost curve, is determined by the productivity of the variable input factors employed. The variable cost curve in Figure 9.1 increases at a decreasing rate up to output level Q_1, then at an increasing rate. Assuming constant input prices, this implies that the marginal productivity of variable inputs first increases, then decreases. Variable input factors exhibit increasing returns in the range from 0 to Q_1 units and show diminishing returns thereafter. This is a typical finding. Fixed plant and equipment are usually designed to operate at a target production level. Operating below the target output level results in some excess capacity. In the below-target output range, production can be increased more than proportionately to increases in variable inputs. At above-target output levels, fixed factors are intensively utilized, and the law of diminishing returns takes over. There, a given percentage increase in variable inputs results in a smaller relative increase in output.

The relation between short-run costs and the productivity of variable input factors is also reflected by short-run unit cost curves, as shown in Figure 9.1(b). Marginal cost declines over the range of increasing productivity and rises thereafter. This imparts the familiar U-shape to average variable cost and average total cost curves. At first, marginal cost curves also typically decline rapidly in relation to the average variable cost curve and the average total cost curve. Near the target output level, the marginal cost curve turns up and intersects each of the *AVC* and *ATC* short-run curves at their respective minimum points.[2]

LONG-RUN COST CURVES

Long-run cost curve
Cost–output relation for the optimal plant in the present operating environment.

In the long run, the firm has complete input flexibility. Therefore, all long-run costs are variable. A **long-run cost curve** shows the minimum cost impact of output changes for the optimal plant size in the present operating environment. Such curves reflect the optimal or least-cost input combination for producing output assuming an *ideal* input selection. As in the case of short-run cost curves, wage rates, interest rates, plant configuration, and all other operating conditions are held constant. Any change in the operating environment leads to a shift in long-run cost curves. For example, product inventions and process improvements that occur over time cause a downward *shift* in long-run cost curves. Such changes must not be confused with *movements along* a given long-run cost curve caused by changes in the output level. Long-run cost curves reveal the nature of returns to scale and optimal plant sizes. They are a helpful guide to planning decisions.

---

[2] Relations among total, average, and marginal curves are discussed in greater detail in Chapter 2.

FIGURE 9.1   Short-Run Cost Curves

(a) The productivity of variable input factors determines the slope of both the total and variable cost curves. An increase (decrease) in fixed costs shifts the total cost curve upward (downward), but it has no effect on variable cost curves. (b) Marginal cost declines to Q_1. Both average total cost and average variable costs fall (rise) when marginal cost is lower (higher).

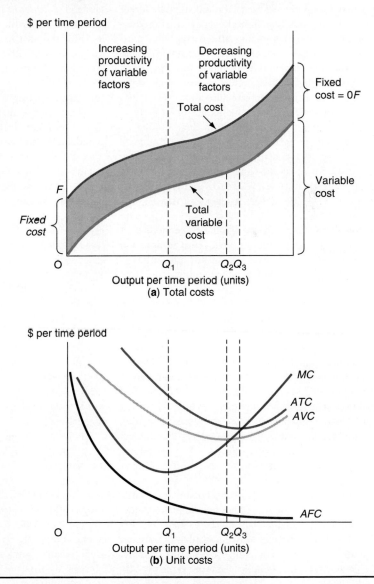

MANAGERIAL APPLICATION 9.2
Is Big Always Better?

When economies of scale are substantial, larger firms are able to achieve lower costs of production or distribution than their smaller rivals. These cost advantages translate into higher and more stable profits, and a permanent competitive advantage for larger firms in some industries. Diseconomies of large-scale organizations work in the opposite direction. When diseconomies of scale are operative, larger firms suffer a cost disadvantage when compared to their smaller rivals. Smaller firms are then able to translate the benefits of small size into a distinct competitive advantage. Rather than losing profits and sales opportunities to their larger rivals, these smaller firms can enjoy higher profit rates and a gain in market share over time.

In general, industries dominated by large firms tend to be those in which there are significant economies of scale, important advantages to vertical integration, and a prevalence of mass marketing. As a result, large organizations with sprawling plants emphasize large quantities of output at low production costs. Use of national media, especially TV advertising, is common. In contrast, industries in which "small is beautiful" tend to be those characterized by diseconomies of scale, considerable advantages to subcontracting for "just in time" assembly and manufacturing, and niche marketing that emphasizes the use of highly skilled individuals adept at personal selling. Small factories with flexible production schedules are common. Rather than mass quantity, many smaller companies emphasize quality. Instead of the sometimes slow-to-respond hierarchical organizations of large companies, smaller companies feature "flat" organizations with decentralized decision making and authority.

Even though the concept of diseconomies of large size is well known, it is sometimes not appreciated how common the phenomenon is in actual practice. In many sectors, smaller companies have emerged as a dominant competitive force. In many industries offering business and consumer services, smaller firms are typically better able to quickly meet the specialized needs of their customers and have successfully met competition from large companies. Many sectors of industrial manufacturing have also found that the highly flexible and customer-sensitive nature of many smaller companies can lead to distinct competitive advantages. For example,

although early advances in large mainframe computers were historically the domain of larger companies such as IBM, the vast majority of innovations in the computer industry during the 1980s—the personal computer, minicomputer, supercomputer, and user-friendly software—have been started or commercialized by venture-backed entrepreneurial companies.

The villain sometimes encountered by large-scale firms is not any diseconomy of scale in the production process itself but rather the burden that size places on effective management. Big often means complex, and complexity results in inefficiencies and bureaucratic snarls that can strangle effective communication. In the former Soviet Union, a huge, highly centralized, run-from-the-top system came crashing down of its own gigantic weight. Hoping to avoid a similar fate, many large organizations are now splitting assets into smaller independent operating units that can react quickly to customer needs without the long delays typical of large organizations. IBM, for example, has split into independent operating units that compete directly with one another in providing customers with the latest in computer equipment and software. GM, seeking to become more like lean and agile Japanese competitors, established Saturn as an independent operating unit. These examples suggest that the Fortune 500 is going through a metamorphism that will favor large organizations that are especially adept at reallocating capital among nimble, entrepreneurial operating units.

In the past, when foreign visitors wanted to experience firsthand the latest innovations in U.S. business and administrative practice, they found it mandatory to stop and visit major corporations in Chicago, Detroit, New York, and Pittsburgh. Today, it is more likely that they would make stops at Boston's Route 128, California's Silicon Valley, or North Carolina's Research Triangle. From electronics instruments to specialized steel, smaller companies have replaced larger companies in positions of industry leadership. The trend towards a higher level of efficiency for smaller companies has become widespread. Larger companies are finding that meeting the needs of the customer sometimes requires a dramatic downsizing of the large-scale organization.

Source: Brian Dumaine, "Is Big Still Good?" *Fortune,* April 20, 1992, 50–60.

*Long-Run
Total Costs*

If input prices are not affected by the amount purchased, a *direct* relation exists between cost and production functions. Consider a production function that exhibits constant returns to scale. Such a production function is linear, and doubling inputs leads to doubled output. With constant input prices, doubling inputs doubles total cost and results in a linear total cost function, as illustrated in Figure 9.2.

If production is subject to decreasing returns to scale, inputs must more than double to cause a twofold increase in output. Assuming constant input prices, the cost function associated with such a production system rises at an increasing rate with output, as shown in Figure 9.3.

A production function exhibiting first increasing and then decreasing returns to scale is illustrated, along with its implied cubic cost function, in Figure 9.4. Here, costs increase less than proportionately with output over the range in which returns to scale are increasing but at more than a proportionate rate after decreasing returns set in.

The direct relations between production and cost functions illustrated to this point are based on constant input prices. If input prices are a function of output, cost functions will reflect this. Large-volume discounts can lower unit costs as output rises, just as costs rise with the need to pay higher wages to attract additional workers at high output levels. The cost function for a firm facing constant returns to scale but rising input prices as output expands takes the shape shown in Figure 9.3. Costs rise more than proportionately as output increases. Quantity discounts, however, produce a cost function that increases at a decreasing rate, as in the increasing returns section of Figure 9.4.

Although cost and production are clearly related, the nature of input prices must be examined before any cost function can be related to the underlying production function. Input prices and productivity jointly determine cost functions.

Returns to Scale

Economies of scale
Decreasing long-run average costs.

Many factors combine to produce the frequently encountered pattern of first increasing, then constant, then decreasing returns to scale. Increasing returns, or **economies of scale,** which originate from production and market-related sources, cause long-run average costs to decline. Labor specialization often gives rise to economies of scale. In small firms workers generally do several jobs, and proficiency sometimes suffers from a lack of specialization. Labor productivity can be higher in large firms where individuals are hired to perform specific tasks. This can reduce unit costs for large-scale operations.

Technical factors can also lead to economies of scale. Large-scale operation permits the use of highly specialized equipment, as opposed to the more versatile but less efficient machines used in smaller firms. Also, the productivity of equipment frequently increases with size much faster than its cost. A 500,000-kilowatt electricity generator costs considerably less than two 250,000-kilowatt generators, and it also requires less fuel and labor when operated at capacity.

Quantity discounts give rise to money-related pecuniary economies through large-scale purchasing of raw materials, supplies, and other inputs. These economies extend to the cost of capital when large firms have greater access to capital

FIGURE 9.2   **Total Cost Function for a Production System Exhibiting Constant Returns to Scale**

With constant returns to scale and constant input prices, an increase in all inputs will lead to a proportionate increase in total costs and output.

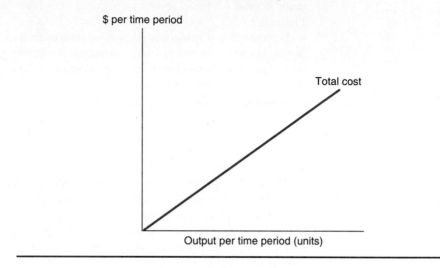

FIGURE 9.3   **Total Cost Function for a Production System Exhibiting Decreasing Returns to Scale**

With decreasing returns to scale and constant input prices, input usage and total costs rise faster than a given increase in output.

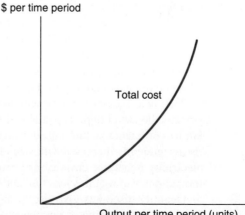

FIGURE 9.4   **Total Cost Function for a Production System Exhibiting
Increasing, then Decreasing Returns to Scale**

Total cost functions often display an S-shape, reflecting varying returns to scale at
various activity levels.

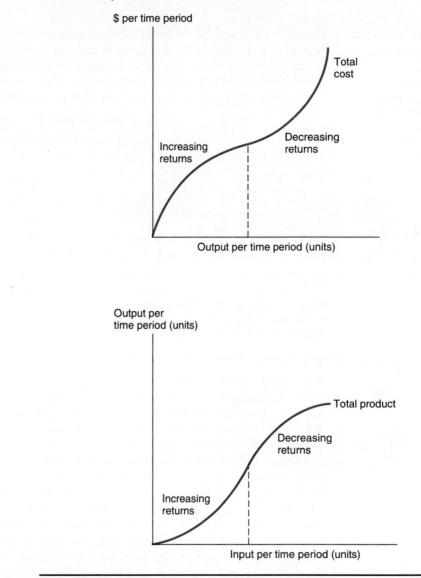

markets and can acquire funds at lower rates. These factors and many more lead
to increasing returns to scale and decreasing average costs.

At some output level, economies of scale are typically exhausted, and average
costs level out or begin to rise. Increasing average costs at high output levels are
often attributed to limitations in the ability of management to coordinate large-

scale organizations. Staff overhead also tends to grow more than proportionately with output, again raising unit costs. The trend toward small to medium-sized businesses during the 1980s and 1990s indicates that diseconomies do indeed limit firm sizes in many industries.

Cost Elasticities and Returns to Scale

Cost elasticity
Percentage change in total cost associated with a 1 percent change in output.

Figures 9.2, 9.3, and 9.4 are useful for illustrating the total cost/output relation to returns to scale. Still, it is often easier to calculate scale economies for a given production system by considering cost elasticities. **Cost elasticity, ϵ_C,** measures the percentage change in total cost associated with a 1 percent change in output.

Algebraically, the elasticity of cost with respect to output is

$$\epsilon_C = \frac{\text{Percentage Change in Total Cost } (TC)}{\text{Percentage Change in Output } (Q)}$$

$$= \frac{\delta TC/C}{\delta Q/Q}$$

$$= \frac{\delta TC}{\delta Q} \times \frac{Q}{TC}.$$

Cost elasticity is related to economies of scale as follows:

If	Then	Returns to Scale Are:
Percentage change in TC < Percentage change in Q,	$\epsilon_C < 1$.	Increasing.
Percentage change in TC = Percentage change in Q,	$\epsilon_C = 1$.	Constant.
Percentage change in TC > Percentage change in Q,	$\epsilon_C > 1$.	Decreasing.

With a cost elasticity of less than one ($\epsilon_C < 1$), costs increase at a slower rate than output. Given constant input prices, this implies a higher output-to-input ratio and increasing returns to scale. If $\epsilon_C = 1$, output and costs increase proportionately, implying constant returns to scale. And finally, if $\epsilon_C > 1$, for any increase in output, costs increase by a greater relative amount, implying decreasing returns to scale. To prevent confusion concerning cost elasticity and returns to scale, remember that an inverse relation holds between costs and scale economies and a direct relation holds between resource usage and scale economies. Thus, although $\epsilon_C < 1$ implies increasing returns to scale, because costs are increasing more slowly than output, recall from Chapter 7 that an output elasticity greater than 1 ($\epsilon_Q > 1$) implies increasing returns to scale, because output is increasing faster than input usage. Similarly, decreasing returns to scale are implied by $\epsilon_C > 1$ and by $\epsilon_Q < 1$. These relations are the result of the correspondence between cost functions and underlying production functions.

Long-Run Average Costs

Additional insight into scale economies and the relation between long-run and short-run costs is obtained by examining long-run average cost (*LRAC*) curves. Short-run cost curves relate costs and output for a specific scale of plant, whereas long-run cost curves identify optimal scales of plant for each production level. *LRAC* curves can be thought of as an envelope of short-run average cost (*SRAC*)

FIGURE 9.5   **Short-Run Cost Curves for Four Scales of Plant**

Short-run cost curves represent the most efficient range of output for a given plant size. The solid portion of each *SRAC* curve indicates the minimum long-run average cost for each level of output.

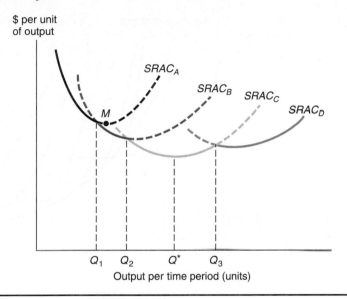

curves. This concept is illustrated in Figure 9.5, which shows four short-run average cost curves representing four different scales of plant. Each of the four plants has a range of output over which it is most efficient. Plant *A,* for example, provides the least-cost production system for output in the range 0 to Q_1 units; Plant *B* provides the least-cost system for output in the range Q_1 to Q_2; Plant *C* is most efficient for output quantities Q_2 to Q_3; and Plant *D* provides the least-cost production process for output above Q_3.

The solid portion of each curve in Figure 9.5 indicates the minimum long-run average cost for producing each level of output, assuming only four possible scales of plant. This can be generalized by assuming that plants of many sizes are possible, each only slightly larger than the preceding one. As shown in Figure 9.6, the long-run average cost curve is then constructed tangent to each short-run average cost curve. At each point of tangency, the related scale of plant is optimal; no other plant can produce that particular level of output at so low a total cost. Cost systems illustrated in Figures 9.5 and 9.6 display first increasing, then decreasing returns to scale. Over the range of output produced by Plants *A, B,* and *C* in Figure 9.5, average costs are declining; these declining costs mean that total costs are increasing less than proportionately with output. Since Plant *D*'s minimum cost is greater than that for Plant *C,* the system exhibits decreasing returns to scale at this higher output level.

Production systems that reflect first increasing, then constant, then diminishing returns to scale result in U-shaped long-run average cost curves such as the one illustrated in Figure 9.6. With a U-shaped long-run average cost curve, the

FIGURE 9.6   Long-Run Average Cost Curve as the Envelope of Short-Run Average Cost Curves

The long-run average cost curve is the envelope of short-run average cost curves. The optimal scale for a plant is found at the point of minimum long-run average costs.

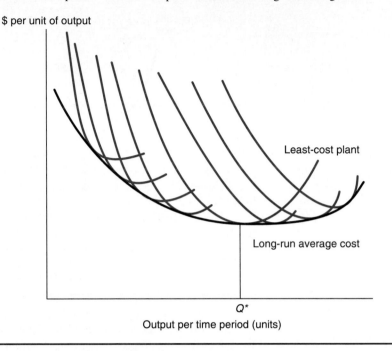

most efficient plant for each output level is typically not operating at the point where short-run average costs are minimized, as can be seen in Figure 9.5. Plant A's short-run average cost curve is minimized at Point M, but at that output level, Plant B is more efficient; B's short-run average costs are lower. In general, when returns to scale are increasing, the least-cost plant will operate at less than full capacity. Here, **capacity** refers not to a physical limitation on output but rather to the point at which short-run average costs are minimized. Only for that single output level at which long-run average cost is minimized (output Q^* in Figures 9.5 and 9.6) is the optimal plant operating at the minimum point on its short-run average cost curve. At any output level greater than Q^*, decreasing returns to scale prevail, and the most efficient plant is operating at an output level slightly greater than capacity.

Capacity

Output level at which short-run average costs are minimized.

MINIMUM EFFICIENT SCALE

The shape of long-run average cost curves is important not only because of implications for plant scale decisions but also because of effects on the potential level of competition. Even though U-shaped cost relations are quite common, they are not universal. In some industries, firms encounter first increasing, then constant returns to scale. In such instances, an L-shaped long-run average cost curve emerges, and very large plants are at no relative cost disadvantage compared with smaller plants. The number of competitors and ease of entry is typically greater in industries with U-shaped long-run average cost curves than in those with L-shaped or continuously downward-sloping long-run average cost curves. Insight on the competitive implications of cost/output relations can be gained by considering the minimum efficient scale concept.

Competitive Implications of Minimum Efficient Scale

Minimum efficient scale
Output level at which long-run average costs are minimized.

Minimum efficient scale (*MES*) is the output level at which long-run average costs are minimized. Thus, *MES* is at the minimum point on a U-shaped long-run average cost curve (output Q^* in Figures 9.5 and 9.6) and at the corner of an L-shaped long-run average cost curve.

Generally speaking, the number of competitors is large and competition is vigorous when *MES* is low relative to total industry demand. This follows from the correspondingly low barriers to entry from capital investment and skilled labor requirements. Competition can be less vigorous when *MES* is large relative to total industry output, because barriers to entry tend to be correspondingly high and can limit the number of potential competitors. When considering the competitive impact of *MES,* industry size must always be considered. Some industries are large enough to accommodate substantial numbers of very large competitors. In such instances, even though *MES* is large in an absolute sense, it can be quite small in a relative sense and can allow vigorous competition.

When the cost disadvantage of operating plants that are of less than *MES* size is relatively small, there will seldom be serious anticompetitive consequences. The somewhat higher production costs of small producers can be overcome by superior customer service and regional location to cut transport costs and delivery lags. In such instances, statistically significant advantages to large-scale operation have little economic relevance. Therefore, the barrier-to-entry effects of *MES* depend on the size of *MES* relative to total industry demand *and* the slope of the long-run average cost curve at points of less-than-*MES*-size operations. Both must be considered.

Transportation Costs and MES

Transportation costs play an important role in determining the efficient scale of operation. Transportation costs include terminal, line-haul, and inventory charges associated with moving output from production facilities to customers. Terminal charges consist of handling expenses necessary for loading and unloading shipped materials. Since terminal charges do not vary with the distance of shipment, they are as high for short hauls as for long hauls.

Line-haul expenses include equipment, labor, and fuel costs associated with moving a given commodity a specified distance. They vary directly with the distance shipped. Although line-haul expenses are relatively constant on a per mile basis, they vary widely from one commodity to another. It costs more to ship a ton of fresh fruit 500 miles than to ship a ton of coal a similar distance. Fresh fruit comes in odd shapes and sizes and requires more container space than a product like coal, which can be compactly loaded. Any product that is perishable, fragile, or particularly susceptible to theft (e.g., consumer electronics,

FIGURE 9.7   **Effect of Transportation Costs on Optimal Plant Size**

High transportation costs reduce the *MES* plant size from Q_A^* to Q_B^*. As transportation costs rise relative to production costs, *MES* plant size will fall.

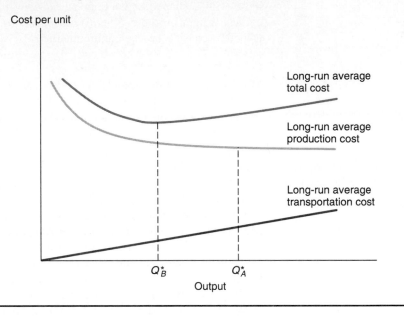

cigarettes, liquor) has high line-haul expenses because of greater equipment, insurance, and labor costs.

Finally, there is an inventory cost component to transportation costs related to the time element involved in shipping goods. The time required for transit is extremely important because slower modes such as railroads and barges delay the receipt of sale proceeds from customers. Even though out-of-pocket expenses are greater, air cargo or motor carrier shipment can reduce the total economic costs of transportation because of their greater speed in delivery.

Transportation costs play an important role in determining optimal plant sizes. As more output is produced at a given plant, it becomes necessary to reach out to more distant customers. This can lead to increased transportation costs per unit sold. Figure 9.7 illustrates an L-shaped long-run average cost curve reflecting average production costs that first decline and then become nearly constant. Assuming relatively modest terminal and inventory costs, greater line-haul expenses cause transportation costs per unit to increase at a relatively constant rate. Before transportation costs, Q_A^* represents the *MES* plant size. Including transportation expenses, the *MES* plant size falls to Q_B^*. In general, as transportation costs become increasingly important, *MES* will fall. In the extreme, when transportation costs are large in relation to production costs, as is the case with milk, bottled soft drinks, gravel, cement, and many other products with high weight-to-value (or bulk-to-value) ratios, even small, relatively inefficient production facilities can be profitable when located near important markets. In contrast, when transportation costs are relatively insignificant—as is the case for relatively low-weight, compact, high-value products such as writing pens, electronic components, and medical instruments—markets are national or international in scope, and increasing returns to scale cause output to be produced at only a few large plants.

FIRM SIZE AND PLANT SIZE

Production and cost functions exist at the level of the individual plant and, for multiplant firms, at the level of the entire firm. The cost function for a multiplant firm can be the sum of the cost functions for individual plants. It can also be greater or less than this figure. For this reason, it becomes important to examine the relative importance of economies of scale that arise within production facilities; intraplant economies; and economies of scale that arise between and among plants, or multiplant economies of scale.

Multiplant Economies and Diseconomies of Scale ▶

Multiplant economies of scale

Cost advantages from operating multiple facilities in the same line of business or industry.

Multiplant diseconomies of scale

Cost disadvantages from managing multiple facilities in the same line of business or industry.

Multiplant economies of scale are cost advantages that arise from operating multiple facilities in the same line of business or industry. Conversely, **multiplant diseconomies of scale** are cost disadvantages that arise from managing multiple facilities in the same line of business or industry.

To illustrate, assume a U-shaped long-run average cost curve for a given plant, as shown in Figure 9.6. If demand is sufficiently large, the firm will employ N plants, each of optimal size and producing Q^* units of output. In this case, what is the shape of the firm's long-run average cost curve? Figure 9.8 shows three possibilities. Each possible long-run average cost curve has important implications for the minimum efficient firm size, Q_F^*. First, the long-run average cost curve can be L-shaped, as in Figure 9.8(a), if no economies or diseconomies result from combining plants. Second, costs could decline throughout the entire range of output, as in (b), if multiplant firms are more efficient than single-plant firms. Such cases, when they exist, are caused by economies of multiplant operation. For example, all plants may use a central billing service, a common purchasing or distribution network, centralized management, and so on. The third possibility, shown in (c), is that costs first decline beyond Q^*, the output of the most efficient plant, and then begin to rise. In this case, multiplant economies of scale dominate initially, but they are later overwhelmed by the higher costs of coordinating many operating units.

All three shapes of cost curves shown in Figure 9.8 are found in the U.S. economy. Since optimal plant and firm sizes are identical only when multiplant economies are negligible, the magnitude of both influences must be carefully considered in evaluating the effect of scale economies. Both intraplant and multiplant economies can have an important impact on minimum efficient firm size.

The Economics of Multiplant Operation: An Example

An example can help clarify the relation between firm size and plant size as well as the important minimum efficient scale concept. Consider Plainfield Electronics, a New Jersey-based company that manufactures a line of large industrial control panels for a national market. Currently, the firm's production is consolidated at a single eastern-seaboard facility. Because of growth in demand for the

FIGURE 9.8   **Three Possible Long-Run Average Cost Curves for a Multiplant Firm**

(a) Constant costs characterize a multiplant facility that has neither economies nor diseconomies of scale. (b) Average costs decline if a multiplant firm is more efficient than a single-plant firm. (c) The average costs of operating several plants can eventually rise when coordinating costs overcome multiplant economies.

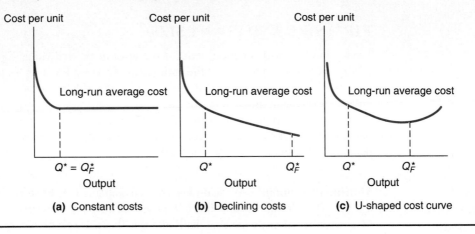

firm's products, a multiplant alternative to centralized production is being considered. Estimated demand, marginal revenue, and *single-plant* production plus transportation cost curves for the firm are as follows:

$$P = \$940 - \$0.02Q.$$

$$MR = \frac{\delta TR}{\delta Q} = \$940 - \$0.04Q.$$

$$TC = \$250,000 + \$40Q + \$0.01Q^2.$$

$$MC = \frac{\delta TC}{\delta Q} = \$40 + \$0.02Q.$$

Plainfield's total profit function is

$$\begin{aligned}
\pi &= TR - TC \\
&= P \times Q - TC \\
&= (\$940 - \$0.02Q)Q - \$250,000 - \$40Q - \$0.01Q^2 \\
&= -\$0.03Q^2 + \$900Q - \$250,000.
\end{aligned}$$

The profit-maximizing activity level with centralized production is identified by locating the output level at which $\delta\pi = MR - MC = 0$ and, therefore, $MR = MC$.

Setting marginal revenue equal to marginal cost and solving for the related output quantity gives

$$\begin{aligned}
MR &= MC \\
\$940 - \$0.04Q &= \$40Q + \$0.02Q \\
\$0.06Q &= \$900 \\
Q &= 15,000.
\end{aligned}$$

At $Q = 15,000$,

$$P = \$940 - \$0.02Q$$
$$= \$940 - \$0.02(15,000)$$
$$= \$640,$$

and

$$\pi = -\$0.03(15,000)^2 + \$900(15,000) - \$250,000$$
$$= \$6,500,000.$$

Therefore, profits are maximized at the $Q = 15,000$ output level under the assumption of centralized production. At that activity level, $MC = MR = \$340$, and $M\pi = 0$.

To gain insight into the possible advantages of operating multiple smaller plants as opposed to one large centralized production facility, the average cost function for a single plant must be examined. To simplify matters, assume that multiplant production is possible under the same cost conditions described previously. That is, over the range of reasonable plant-size options, the firm's individual plant cost functions are the same with either single or multiplant operations. Also assume that there are no other multiplant economies or diseconomies of scale with which to contend.

The activity level at which average cost is minimized is found by setting marginal cost equal to average cost and solving for Q:

$$AC = TC/Q$$
$$= (\$250,000 + \$40Q + \$0.01Q^2)/Q$$
$$= \$250,000Q^{-1} + \$40 + \$0.01Q$$

and

$$MC = AC$$
$$\$40 + \$0.02Q = \$250,000Q^{-1} + \$40 + \$0.01Q$$
$$250,000Q^{-1} = 0.01Q$$
$$Q^{-2} = \frac{0.01}{250,000}$$
$$Q^2 = \frac{250,000}{0.01}$$
$$Q = \sqrt{25,000,000}$$
$$= 5,000.$$

Average cost is minimized at an output level of 5,000. This output level is the minimum efficient plant scale. Since the average cost-minimizing output level of 5,000 is far less than the single-plant profit-maximizing activity level of 15,000 units, the profit-maximizing level of total output occurs at a point of rising average costs. Assuming centralized production, Plainfield would maximize profits at an activity level of $Q = 15,000$ rather than $Q = 5,000$ because market-demand conditions are such that, despite the higher costs experienced at $Q = 15,000$, the firm can profitably supply output up to that level. Profit maximization requires consideration of both revenue and cost conditions.

Since centralized production maximized profits at an activity level well beyond that at which average cost is minimized, Plainfield has an opportunity to reduce costs and increase profits by adopting the multiplant alternative. Although the single-plant $Q = 15,000$ profit-maximizing activity level and the $Q = 5,000$ average cost-minimizing activity level might suggest that multiplant production at three facilities is optimal, this is incorrect. Profits were maximized at $Q = 15,000$ under the assumption of centralized production because at that activity level, both marginal revenue and marginal cost equal \$340. However, with multiplant production and each plant operating at the $Q = 5,000$ activity level, marginal cost will be lowered and multiplant production will entail a new, higher profit-maximizing activity level. At $Q = 5,000$,

$$MC = \$40 + \$0.02Q$$
$$= \$40 + \$0.02(5,000)$$
$$= \$140.$$

With multiple plants all operating at 5,000 units per year, $MC = \$140$. Therefore, it is profitable to expand production as long as the marginal revenue obtained exceeds this minimum $MC = \$140$. This assumes, of course, that each production facility is operating at the optimal activity level of $Q = 5,000$ per plant.

The optimal multiplant activity level for the firm, assuming optimal production levels of $Q = 5,000$ at multiple plants, can be calculated by equating MR to the multiplant $MC = \$140$:

$$MR = \$140 = MC$$
$$\$940 - \$0.04Q = \$140$$
$$\$0.04Q = \$800$$
$$Q = 20,000.$$

Given optimal multiplant production of 20,000 units and average cost-minimizing activity levels of 5,000 units for each plant, multiplant production at four facilities is suggested:

$$\frac{\text{Optimal Number of}}{\text{Plants}} = \frac{\text{Optimal Multiplant Activity Level}}{\text{Optimal Production per Plant}}$$
$$= \frac{20,000}{5,000}$$
$$= 4.$$

At $Q = 20,000$,

$$P = \$940 - \$0.02(20,000)$$
$$= \$540,$$

and

$$\pi = TR - TC$$
$$= P \times Q - 4 \times TC \text{ per plant}$$
$$= \$540(20,000) - 4[\$250,000 + \$40(5,000) + \$0.01(5,000^2)]$$
$$= \$8,000,000.$$

FIGURE 9.9 **Plainfield Electronics: Single versus Multiplant Operation**

In this example, profit is maximized at a production level well beyond that at which average cost is minimized for a single plant. Profits are greater with four plants because output can then be produced at minimum cost.

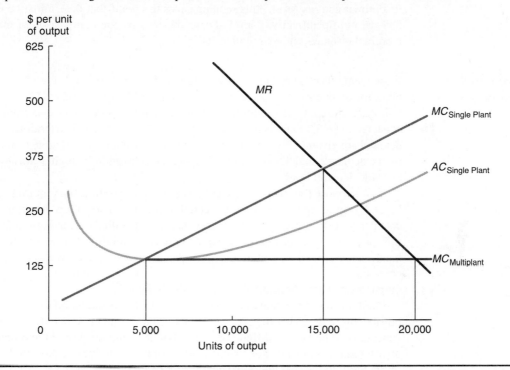

Note: The horizontal portion of the multiplant marginal cost curve shown here is only an approximation of the actual relation. The true multiplant marginal cost curve cycles up somewhat between the 5,000-, 10,000-, 15,000-, and 20,000-unit output levels as each individual plant operates at an output level above or below 5,000 units. As can be seen from the shape of the single-plant marginal cost curve around 5,000 units, the effect would not be large.

Given these cost relations, multiplant production is much preferable to the centralized production alternative because it results in maximum profits that are $1.5 million larger. As shown in Figure 9.9, this follows from the firm's ability to concentrate production at the minimum point on the single-plant U-shaped average cost curve.

The multiplant cost advantages indicated in this example could stem from a variety of factors. One possibility, given that Plainfield's product is a large, heavy industrial control panel, is transportation cost savings from regional rather than centralized production. The role of distribution costs can be significant for industries in which final-product transport costs are large relative to production costs.

Finally, it is important to recognize that the optimal multiplant activity level of 20,000 units described in this example is based on the assumption that each production facility produces exactly 5,000 units of output and, therefore, $MC = \$140$. Marginal cost will equal $140 only when $Q = 5,000$ or some round multiple thereof (e.g., $Q = 10,000$ from two plants, $Q = 15,000$ from three plants, and so on). The optimal multiplant activity-level calculation is somewhat more complicated when this assumption is not met. Plainfield could not produce $Q = 21,000$ at $MC = \$140$. For an output level in the 20,000 to 25,000 range, it is necessary to equate marginal revenue with the marginal cost of each plant at its optimal activity level. This reemphasizes the point that determination of the optimal multiplant activity level always depends on the comparison of relevant marginal revenues and marginal costs.

Plant Size and Flexibility

Is the plant that can produce a given output at the lowest possible cost the optimal plant for producing that expected level of output? Not necessarily. Consider the following situation. Although actual demand for a product is uncertain, it is expected to be 5,000 units per year. Two possible probability distributions for this demand are given in Figure 9.10. Distribution *L* exhibits a low degree of variability in demand, and Distribution *H* indicates substantially higher variation in possible demand levels.

Now suppose that two plants can be employed to produce the required output. Plant *A* is quite specialized and is geared to produce a specified output at a low cost per unit. If, however, more or less than the specified output is produced (in this case 5,000 units), unit production costs rise rapidly. Plant *B*, on the other hand, is more flexible. Output can be expanded or contracted without excessive cost penalties, but unit costs are not as low as those of Plant *A* at the optimal output level. These two cases are shown in Figure 9.11.

Plant *A* is more efficient than Plant *B* between 4,500 and 5,500 units of output; outside this range, *B* has lower costs. Which plant should be selected? The answer depends on relative cost differentials at different output levels and the probability distribution for demand. The firm should make its plant-size decision on the basis of the level and variability of expected average total costs. If the demand probability distribution with low variation, Distribution *L*, is correct, the more specialized facility is optimal. If probability Distribution *H* more correctly describes the demand situation, the lower minimum cost of more specialized facilities is more than offset by the possibility of very high costs of producing outside the 4,500- to 5,500-unit range. Plant *B* could then have lower expected costs or a more attractive combination of expected costs and potential variation.

LEARNING CURVES

For many manufacturing processes, average costs decline substantially as *cumulative* total output increases. This results as both management and labor become more knowledgeable about production techniques and their experience levels increase. Improvements in the use of production equipment and procedures are important in this process, as are reduced waste from defects and reduced labor requirements as workers become more proficient in their jobs.

The Learning Curve Concept

When knowledge gained from manufacturing experience is used to improve production methods so that output is produced with increasing efficiency, the resulting decline in average costs is said to reflect the effects of the firm's **learning curve.** The learning curve or experience curve phenomenon affects average costs

FIGURE 9.10   **Probability Distributions of Demand**

Distribution *L* has a low degree of variability from the expected demand level. Distribution *H* varies substantially from the expected demand level.

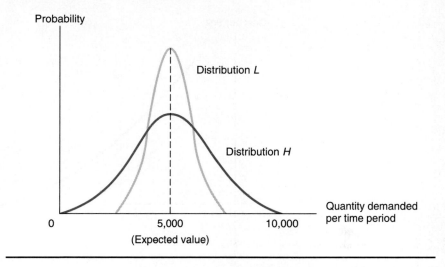

FIGURE 9.11   **Alternative Plants for Production of Expected 5,000 Units of Output**

Unit costs are lower for Plant *A* than for Plant *B* between 4,500 and 5,500 units of output. Outside this range, Plant *B* has lower unit costs.

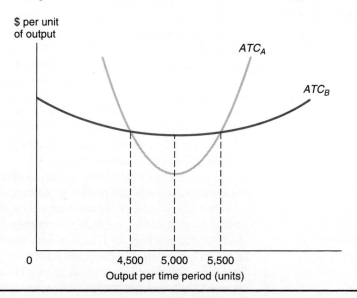

FIGURE 9.12   Long-Run Average Cost Curve Effects of Learning

Learning will cause a downward shift from $LRAC_t$ to $LRAC_{t+1}$. An average cost decline from C to A reflects the effects of both learning and economies of scale.

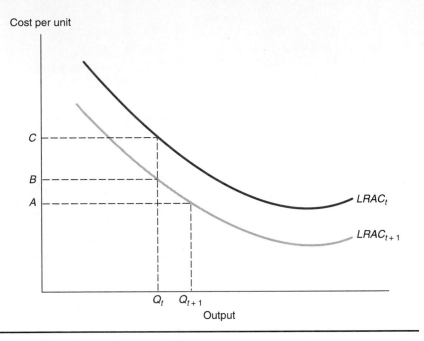

Learning curve

Average cost reduction over time due to production experience.

in a way similar to that for any technical advance that improves productive efficiency. Both involve a downward shift in the long-run average cost curve at all levels of output. Learning through production experience permits the firm to produce output more efficiently at each and every output level.

To illustrate, consider Figure 9.12, which shows hypothetical long-run average cost curves for periods t and $t + 1$. With increased knowledge about production methods gained through the experience of producing Q_t units in period t, long-run average costs have declined for every output level in period $t + 1$. This means that Q_t units could be produced during period $t + 1$ at an average cost of B rather than the earlier cost of C. The learning curve cost savings is BC. If output were expanded from Q_t to Q_{t+1} between these periods, average costs would fall from C to A. This decline in average costs reflects both the learning curve effect, BC, and the effect of economies of scale, AB.

To isolate the effect of learning or experience on average cost, it is necessary to identify carefully that portion of average-cost changes over time which is due to other factors. One of the most important of these is the effect of economies of scale. As seen before, the change in average costs experienced between periods t and $t + 1$ can reflect the effects of both learning and economies of scale. This is a typical situation. Similarly, the effects of important technical breakthroughs, causing a downward shift in $LRAC$ curves, and input-cost inflation, causing an upward shift in $LRAC$ curves, must be constrained to examine learning curve

FIGURE 9.13   **Learning Curve of an Arithmetic Scale**

The learning curve reflects the percentage decline in average cost as total cumulative output doubles from Q_t to $2Q_t$.

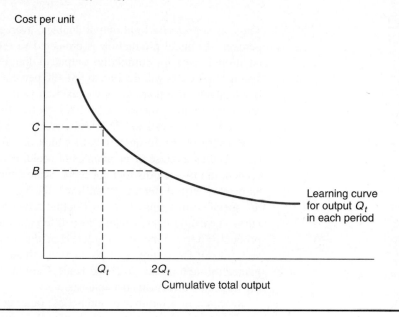

characteristics. Only when output scale, technology, and input prices are all held constant can the learning curve relation be accurately represented.

Figure 9.13 depicts the learning curve relation suggested by Figure 9.12. Note that learning results in dramatic average cost reductions at low total production levels, but it generates increasingly modest savings at higher cumulative production levels. This reflects that many improvements in production methods become quickly obvious and are readily adopted. Later gains often come more slowly and are less substantial.

A Learning Curve Example

Given this typical shape of the learning curve relation, the learning curve, or experience curve, phenomenon is often characterized as a constant percentage decline in average costs as cumulative output increases. This percentage represents the proportion by which unit costs decline as the cumulative quantity of total output doubles. Suppose, for example, that average costs per unit for a new product were $100 during 1991 but fell to $90 during 1992. Furthermore, assume that average costs are in constant dollars, reflecting an accurate adjustment for input-price inflation and an identical basic technology being used in production. Given equal output in each period to ensure that the effects of economies of scale are not incorporated in the data, the learning or experience rate, defined as the percentage by which average cost falls as output doubles, is the following:

$$\text{Learning Rate} = \left(1 - \frac{AC_2}{AC_1}\right) \times 100$$

$$= \left(1 - \frac{\$90}{\$100} \right) \times 100$$
$$= 10\%.$$

Thus, as *cumulative* total output doubles, average cost is expected to fall by 10 percent. If annual production is projected to remain constant, it will take two additional years for cumulative output to double again. One would project that average unit costs will decline to $81 (90 percent of $90) in 1994. Since cumulative total output at that time will equal four years' production, at a constant annual rate, output will again double by 1998. At that time, the learning curve will have reduced average costs to $72.90 (90 percent of $81).

Because of the frequency with which one finds the learning curve concept described as a cause of economies of scale, it is worth repeating that although related, the two are distinct concepts. Scale economies relate to cost differences associated with different output levels during a single production period. They are specified in terms of the cost/output relation measured *along* a single *LRAC* curve. Learning curves relate cost differences to total cumulative output for a product. They are measured in terms of *shifts* in *LRAC* curves over time. These shifts result from improved production efficiencies stemming from knowledge gained through production experience. Care must be exercised to separate learning and scale effects in cost analysis.

Research in a number of industries, ranging from aircraft manufacturing to semiconductor memory-chip production, has shown that a constant percentage of savings in average costs as a result of learning or experience can be very important in some production systems. Learning or experience rates of 20 to 30 percent are sometimes reported. These high learning rates imply rapidly declining manufacturing costs as cumulative total output increases. It should be noted, however, that many learning curve studies fail to account adequately for the expansion of annual production levels, and, therefore, reported learning or experience rates include the effects of both learning and economies of scale. Nevertheless, actual learning rates can sometimes be quite significant.

The learning curve concept is useful for a variety of managerial purposes. Managers have found that use of the learning curve concept substantially improves their ability to forecast production costs based on projected cumulative output. This in turn improves pricing decisions and production strategies. Managers in electronics industries have used their knowledge of the learning curve to price new products from emergent technologies. These pricing strategies explicitly account for the cost reductions expected to accompany rapid increases in total production. Indeed, managers in a wide variety of industries have found that the learning curve concept has considerable strategic implications.

Strategic Implications of the Learning Curve Concept

The learning curve can play a central role in determining long-run success or failure and, thereby, assumes an important role in competitive strategy. What makes the learning curve phenomenon important for competitive strategy is its possible contribution to achieving and maintaining a dominant position in a given market. By virtue of their large relative volume, dominant firms have greater opportunity for learning than do smaller, nonleading firms. In some instances, the market share leader is able to drive down its average cost curve faster than its competitors, underprice them, and permanently maintain a leadership position. Nonleading firms face an important and perhaps insurmountable barrier to relative improvement in performance. Where the learning curve advantages of leading firms are important, it may be prudent to relinquish nonleading positions and redeploy assets to markets in which a dominant position can be achieved or maintained.

▶   A classic example illustrating the successful use of the learning curve concept is provided by Texas Instruments (TI). TI is a large and highly profitable growth company headquartered in Dallas, Texas. Despite some well-publicized problems in its consumer products division (personal computers, calculators, and video games), TI has long enjoyed a dominant position as a supplier in the electronics industry. TI's main business is producing semiconductor chips, key components used to store information in computers and a wide array of electronic products. With growing applications for computers and "intelligent" electronics during recent years, the demand for semiconductors is growing rapidly. Some years ago, TI was one among a number of leading semiconductor manufacturers. At this early stage in the development of the industry, TI made the decision to price its semiconductors well below then-current production costs, given expected learning curve advantages in the 20 percent range. TI's learning curve strategy proved spectacularly successful. With low prices, volume increased dramatically. Soon TI was making so many chips that average costs were even lower than anticipated, it could price below the competition, and dozens of competitors were knocked out of the world market. Given a relative cost advantage and strict quality controls, TI rapidly achieved a position of dominant leadership in a market that became a source of large and rapidly growing profits.

Generally speaking, in order for learning to play an important role in an effective competitive strategy, a number of conditions must be satisfied. Learning must be significant, resulting in average cost savings of 20 to 30 percent as cumulative output doubles. If only modest effects of learning are present, relative product quality or customer service is likely to play a greater role in determining firm success than is a modest average cost advantage. Learning is also likely to be much more important in industries with an abundance of new products or new production techniques than in mature industries with stable and well-known production methods. Similarly, learning tends to be important in industries producing standardized products in which competition is based on price rather than product variety or service. It is important that the learning curve phenomenon be managed. It is definitely not automatic. The beneficial effects of learning are realized only under management systems that tightly control costs and monitor potential sources of increased production efficiency. Continuous feedback of information between production and management personnel is essential. To ensure the flow of useful information and a cooperative attitude among all employees, incentive pay programs that reward increased productivity are often established. This allows employees and employers to jointly benefit through learning.

Finally, although the learning curve phenomenon is important in new industries producing undifferentiated products, many sectors of the economy do not fit this pattern. As a result, learning curve advantages that influence both cost conditions and competitive strategy are an industry-specific rather than an economy-wide influence.

ECONOMIES OF SCOPE

For many firms, cost analysis focuses not just on the question of how much to produce but also on the question of what combination of products to offer. By virtue of their efficiency in the production of a given product, firms often enjoy cost advantages in the production of related products. Identifying and taking advantage of such efficiencies is often crucial to long-run success.

The Economies of Scope Concept

▶

Economies of scope
Cost reduction from producing complementary products.

Economies of scope exist for multiple outputs when the cost of joint production is less than the cost of producing each output separately. In other words, a firm will produce products that are complementary in the sense that producing them together costs less than producing them individually. Suppose that a regional airline offers regularly scheduled passenger service between midsize city pairs and that it expects some excess capacity. Also assume that there is a modest local demand for air parcel and small-package delivery service. Given current airplane sizes, configuration, and so on, it is often less costly for a single carrier to provide both passenger and cargo services in small regional markets than to specialize in one or the other. Thus, regional air carriers often provide both services. This can be seen as an example of economies of scope. Other examples of scope economies abound in the provision of both goods and services. In fact, the economies of scope concept seems to explain best why firms produce multiple rather than single products.

Studying economies of scope forces management to consider both the direct and indirect benefits associated with individual lines of business. For example, on a product line basis, some firms that offer financial services regard checking accounts and money market mutual funds as "loss leaders." When one considers just the revenues and costs associated with marketing and offering checking services or running a money market mutual fund, they may just break even or yield only a marginal profit. However, successful firms like Dreyfus, Fidelity, and Merrill Lynch correctly evaluate the profitability of their money market mutual funds within the context of overall operations. These funds are a valuable delivery vehicle for the vast array of financial products and services that they offer. By offering money market funds on an attractive basis, each of these financial services companies establishes a working relation with an ideal group of prospective customers for stocks, bonds, tax shelters, and so on. When viewed as a delivery vehicle or marketing device, money market mutual funds may be one of the industry's most profitable financial product lines.

Exploiting Scope Economies

Economies of scope are important because they permit a firm to translate superior skill or productive capability in a given product line into unique advantages in the production of complementary products. An effective competitive strategy emphasizes the development or extension of product lines related to a firm's

▶ current stars, or areas of recognized strength. For example, PepsiCo, Inc., has long been a leader in the soft drink market. Over time, the company has gradually broadened its product line to include various brands of regular and diet soft drinks, Fritos and Doritos corn chips, Grandma's Cookies, and other snack foods. PepsiCo can no longer be considered just a soft drink manufacturer. It is a widely diversified snack foods company for whom well over one-half of total current profits come from non–soft drink lines. PepsiCo's snack foods product line extension strategy was effective because it capitalized on the product development capabilities, distribution network, and marketing developed in the firm's soft drink business. In the case of PepsiCo, snack foods and soft drinks are a natural fit and a good example of how a firm has been able to take the skills gained in developing one star (soft drinks) and use them to develop a second (snack foods).

The economies of scope concept plays an important role in managerial decision making because it offers a useful means for evaluating the potential of current and prospective lines of business. It naturally leads to definition of those areas in which the firm has a comparative advantage and thus its greatest profit potential.

COST-VOLUME-PROFIT ANALYSIS

Cost-volume-profit analysis

Analytical technique used to study relations among costs, revenues, and profits.

Cost-volume-profit analysis, sometimes called breakeven analysis, is an important analytical technique used to study relations among costs, revenues, and profits. Both graphic and algebraic methods are employed. The approach that should be used in any given situation depends on the complexity of the cost problem being analyzed. For simple problems, simple graphic methods work best. In more complex situations, analytic methods, possibly involving the use of *Lotus 1-2-3* or other spreadsheet software programs, are preferable.

Cost-Volume-Profit Charts

The nature of cost-volume-profit analysis is depicted in Figure 9.14, a basic cost-volume-profit chart composed of a firm's total cost and total revenue curves. Volume of output is measured on the horizontal axis; revenue and cost are shown on the vertical axis. Since fixed costs are constant regardless of the output produced, they are indicated by a horizontal line. Variable costs at each output level are measured by the distance between the total cost curve and the constant fixed costs. The total revenue curve indicates the price/demand relation for the firm's product; profits or losses at each output are shown by the distance between total revenue and total cost curves.

In the example depicted in Figure 9.14, fixed costs of $60,000 are represented by a horizontal line. Variable costs are assumed to be $1.80 per unit, so total costs rise by that amount for each additional unit of output produced. The product is assumed to be sold for $3 per unit. Total revenue is a straight line through the origin. The slope of the total revenue line is steeper than that of the total cost line because the firm receives $3 per unit in revenue but spends only $1.80 on labor, materials, and other variable inputs.

Below the breakeven point, found at the intersection of the total revenue line and the total cost line, the firm suffers losses. Beyond that point, it begins to

MANAGERIAL APPLICATION 9.3
The Japanese Cost-Management System

Like its famed quality philosophy, Japan's cost-management system stands Western practice on its head. For example, American companies developing a new product typically design it first and then calculate its cost. If the expected unit cost is too high, the product goes back to the drawing board or the company settles for a smaller profit. In a reversal of this typical American process of product development, the Japanese first start with a target cost based on a market price that is likely to appeal to consumers. All else follows from this crucial judgment.

After deducting the desired profit margin from the expected selling price, product managers develop cost estimates for each of the elements that make up total costs: design and engineering, manufacturing, sales and marketing. Each of these cost categories is further subdivided to identify the minimum cost of each component that goes into the finished product. As a result, all parties involved with the product development process have a precise estimate of the cost implications of each individual product characteristic. Then, designers, engineers, and marketing staff are directed to meet these stringent cost and pricing targets.

Every manufacturing part or function thereby becomes the focus of an intense bargaining process among departments of the manufacturing company, as well as between the company and its outside suppliers. While initial estimates may exceed cost targets by 20 percent or more, the final result of intense bargaining between product designers, process engineers, and marketing specialists often results in final cost projections that are well within the original target. This is in sharp contrast to U.S. companies where roughly 85 percent of product costs are determined by design specifications. There is often too little feedback between design and engineering personnel on how slight modifications to product design could cut costs without any resulting penalty in terms of product reliability.

Japanese manufacturers also use cost-targeting techniques to improve existing products. In what is known as "tear-down" analysis, such manufacturers often methodically take apart and analyze different products manufactured by actual or potential competitors. Companies analyze the raw material utilized and the way the product is assembled or molded to estimate the probable cost of manufacturing. From this tear-down method of analysis, the company is able to adopt the probable lowest cost as its own cost target. Thus, the cost target for an automobile manufacturer might derive the target cost for a steering mechanism from a Toyota, the brake pedal from Ford, and so on. Engineers also use this type of reverse engineering to better understand and imitate their competitors' most successful products. What results is better quality products at the absolute minimum cost. The Japanese cost management system also encourages managers to make cost-based judgments for each individual product in terms of the long-run cost and revenue implications for related products. Sony, for example, believed that even a smaller version of its so-called *Pixy* personal stereo component system would be a hit with consumers. Despite uninspiring market forecasts, the company went ahead with the product as a means of heading off potential competition to its existing line. To Sony's surprise, the smaller version was an instant hit and soon became the industry standard.

The Japanese have taught Western managers that pricing precision can sometimes be an impediment to rational costing. Obsessive attention to allocating expenses from labor to overhead against each product consumes effort that could better be spent on systematic efforts to drive costs down. It also limits the ability of managers to strengthen a product line by enhancing it with low-margin products that themselves may have large untapped potential. Direct performance indicators that employees can readily grasp and influence, such as the set-up time for a manufacturing line, also have the potential to prove more effective than goals based on complex, financially oriented yardsticks that are incomprehensible to workers. Effective cost management requires that all employees clearly understand how their work directly affects company performance.

Source: Ford S. Worthy, "Japan's Smart Secret Weapon," *Fortune,* August 12, 1991, 72–75; and Emily Thornton, "How Japan Got Burned in the USA," *Fortune,* June 15, 1992, 114–116.

FIGURE 9.14 **Linear Cost-Volume-Profit Chart**

Output levels below the breakeven point produce losses. As output grows beyond the breakeven point, increasingly higher profits result.

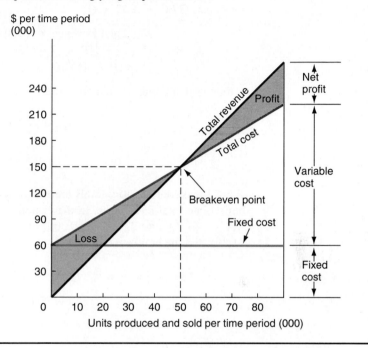

make profits. Figure 9.14 indicates a breakeven point at a sales and cost level of $150,000, which occurs at a production level of 50,000 units.

Algebraic Cost-Volume-Profit

Analysis

Although cost-volume-profit charts are often used to portray profit/output relations, algebraic techniques are typically more efficient for analyzing decision problems. The algebra of cost-volume-profit analysis can be illustrated as follows. Let

$$P = \text{Price per unit sold;}$$
$$Q = \text{Quantity produced and sold;}$$
$$TFC = \text{Total fixed costs;}$$
$$AVC = \text{Average variable cost;}$$
$$\pi_C = \text{Profit contribution.}$$

As described previously, profit contribution, π_C, is the difference between revenues and variable cost. On a per unit basis, profit contribution equals price minus average variable cost ($\pi_C = P - AVC$). Profit contribution can be applied to cover fixed costs and then to provide profits. It is the foundation of cost-volume-profit analysis.

Breakeven quantity

A zero profit activity level.

One useful application of cost-volume-profit analysis lies in the determination of breakeven activity levels for a product. A **breakeven quantity** is a zero profit activity level. At breakeven quantity levels, total revenue ($P \times Q$) exactly equals total costs ($TFC + AVC \times Q$):

$$\text{Total Revenue} = \text{Total Cost}$$
$$P \times Q = TFC + AVC \times Q$$
$$(P - AVC)Q = TFC.$$

It follows that breakeven quantity levels occur where

$$Q_{BE} = \frac{TFC}{P - AVC}$$

$$= \frac{TFC}{\pi_C}.$$

(9.6)

Thus, breakeven quantity levels are found by dividing the per unit profit contribution into total fixed costs. In the example illustrated in Figure 9.14, $P = \$3$, $AVC = \$1.80$, and $TFC = \$60,000$. Profit contribution is $\$1.20$ ($= \$3.00 - \$1.80$), and the breakeven quantity is

$$Q = \frac{\$60,000}{\$1.20}$$
$$= 50,000 \text{ units.}$$

Textbook Publishing: A Further Cost-Volume-Profit Example

A more extensive example of cost-volume-profit analysis is helpful in illustrating additional uses of the concept in managerial decision making. The textbook publishing business provides a good illustration of the effective use of cost-volume-profit analysis for new product decisions.

Consider the hypothetical cost-volume-profit analysis data shown in Table 9.2. Fixed costs can be estimated quite accurately. Variable costs are linear and set by contract. List prices are variable, but competition keeps prices within a sufficiently narrow range to make a linear total revenue curve reasonable. Variable costs for the proposed book are $\$52$ a copy, and the price is $\$60$. This means that each copy sold provides $\$8$ in profit contribution. Applying the breakeven formula from Equation 9.6, the breakeven sales volume is 12,500 units, calculated as

$$Q = \frac{\$100,000}{\$8}$$
$$= 12,500 \text{ units.}$$

Publishers can evaluate the size of the total market for a given book, competition, and other factors. With these data in mind, they estimate the probability that a given book will reach or exceed the breakeven point. If the publisher estimates that the book will neither meet nor exceed the breakeven point, they may consider cutting production costs by reducing the number of illustrations, doing only light copy editing, using a lower grade of paper, negotiating with the author to reduce the royalty rate, and so on.

TABLE 9.2   Cost-Volume-Profit Analysis for Textbook Publishing

Cost Category	Dollar Amount
Fixed Costs	
Copy editing and other editorial costs	$ 15,750
Illustrations	32,750
Typesetting	51,500
Total fixed costs	$100,000
Variable Costs per Copy	
Printing, binding, and paper	$16.85
Bookstore discounts	12.50
Sales staff commissions	5.25
Author's royalties	4.80
General and administrative costs	12.60
Total variable costs per copy	$52.00
List price per copy	$60.00

Assume now that the publisher is interested in determining how many copies must sell to earn a $20,000 profit on the text. Because profit contribution is the amount available to cover fixed costs and provide profit, the answer is found by adding the profit requirement to the book's fixed costs and then dividing by the per unit profit contribution. The sales volume required in this case is 15,000 books, found as follows:

$$Q = \frac{\text{Fixed Costs } + \text{ Profit Requirement}}{\text{Profit Contribution}}$$
$$= \frac{\$100,000 + \$20,000}{\$8}$$
$$= 15,000 \text{ units.}$$

Consider yet another decision problem that might confront the publisher. Assume that a book club has indicated an interest in purchasing copies of the textbook for its members and has offered to buy 3,000 copies at a price of $45 per copy. Cost-volume-profit analysis can be used to determine the incremental effect of such a sale on the publisher's profits.

Since fixed costs do not vary with respect to changes in the number of textbooks sold, they should be ignored in the analysis. Variable costs per copy are $52, but note that $12.50 of this cost represents bookstore discounts. Since the 3,000 copies are being sold directly to the club, this cost will not be incurred and, hence, the relevant variable cost is $39.50. Profit contribution per book sold to the book club then is $5.50 (= $45 - $39.50), and $5.50 times the 3,000 copies sold indicates that the order will result in a total profit contribution of $16,500. Assuming that these 3,000 copies would not have been sold through normal sales channels, the $16,500 profit contribution indicates the increase in profits to the publisher from accepting this order.

The Degree of Operating Leverage

Cost-volume-profit analysis is also a useful tool for analyzing the financial characteristics of alternative production systems. This analysis focuses on how total costs and profits vary with output as the firm operates in a more mechanized manner and substitutes fixed costs for variable costs. Operating leverage reflects the extent to which fixed production facilities, as opposed to variable production facilities, are used in the firm's operation.

The relation between operating leverage and profit variation is shown in Figure 9.15, which contrasts the experience of three firms, *A, B,* and *C,* with differing degrees of leverage. The fixed costs of Firm *B* are typical. Firm *A* uses relatively less capital equipment and has lower fixed costs, but it has a steeper rate of increase in variable costs. Firm *A* breaks even at a lower activity level than does Firm *B.* For example, at a production level of 40,000 units, *B* is losing $8,000, but *A* breaks even. Firm *C* is highly automated and has the highest fixed costs, but its variable costs rise slowly. Firm *C* has a higher breakeven point than either *A* or *B,* but once *C* passes the breakeven point, profits rise faster than those of the other two firms.

Degree of operating leverage

Percentage change in profit from a 1 percent change in output.

The **degree of operating leverage** is the percentage change in profit that results from a 1 percent change in units sold:

$$\text{Degree of Operating Leverage} = \frac{\text{Percentage Change in Profit}}{\text{Percentage Change in Sales}}$$

$$= \frac{\delta\pi/\pi}{\delta Q/Q}$$

$$= \frac{\delta\pi}{\delta Q} \times \frac{Q}{\pi}. \tag{9.7}$$

The degree of operating leverage is an elasticity concept, and it can be understood as the elasticity of profits with respect to output. When based on linear cost and revenue curves, this elasticity varies depending on the point of the breakeven graph being considered. The degree of operating leverage is always greatest close to the breakeven point. There a small change in volume produces a large percentage increase in profits, because base profits are near zero.

For Firm *B* in Figure 9.15, the degree of operating leverage at 100,000 units of output is 2.0, calculated as follows:[3]

$$DOL_B = \frac{\delta\pi/\pi}{\delta Q/Q}$$

$$= \frac{(\$41,600 - \$40,000)/\$40,000}{(102,000 - 100,000)/100,000} = \frac{\$1,600/\$40,000}{2,000/100,000}$$

$$= \frac{4\%}{2\%} = 2.$$

Here, π is profit and Q is the quantity of output in units.

---

[3] This calculation arbitrarily assumes that $\delta Q = 2,000$. If $\delta Q = 1,000$ or $\delta Q = 4,000$, the degree of operating leverage still equals 2, because these calculations are based on linear cost and revenue curves. However, if a base other than 100,000 units is chosen, the degree of operating leverage will vary.

FIGURE 9.15 **Breakeven and Operating Leverage**

The breakeven point for Firm *C* occurs at the highest output level. Once this level is reached, profits rise at a faster rate than for Firm *A* or *B*.

Firm *A*

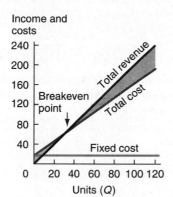

Selling price = $2.00
Fixed cost = $20,000
Variable cost = 1.50Q$

Units sold (Q)	Sales	Cost	Profit
20,000	$ 40,000	$ 50,000	− $10,000
40,000	80,000	80,000	0
60,000	120,000	110,000	10,000
80,000	160,000	140,000	20,000
100,000	200,000	170,000	30,000
120,000	240,000	200,000	40,000

Firm *B*

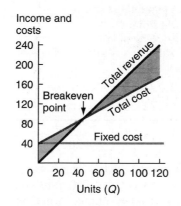

Selling price = $2.00
Fixed cost = $40,000
Variable cost = 1.20Q$

Units sold (Q)	Sales	Cost	Profit
20,000	$ 40,000	$ 64,000	− $24,000
40,000	80,000	88,000	− 8,000
60,000	120,000	112,000	8,000
80,000	160,000	136,000	24,000
100,000	200,000	160,000	40,000
120,000	240,000	184,000	56,000

Firm *C*

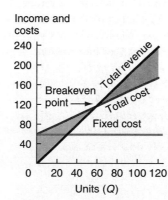

Selling price = $2.00
Fixed cost = $60,000
Variable cost = 1.00Q$

Units sold (Q)	Sales	Cost	Profit
20,000	$ 40,000	$ 80,000	− $40,000
40,000	80,000	100,000	− 20,000
60,000	120,000	120,000	0
80,000	160,000	140,000	20,000
100,000	200,000	160,000	40,000
120,000	240,000	180,000	60,000

For linear revenue and cost relations, the degree of operating leverage can be calculated at any level of output. The change in output is ΔQ. Fixed costs are constant, so the change in profit is $\delta Q(P - AVC)$, where P is price per unit and AVC is average variable cost.

Any initial profit level is $Q(P - AVC) - TFC$, so the percentage change in profit is

$$\frac{\delta \pi}{\pi} = \frac{\delta Q(P - AVC)}{Q(P - AVC) - TFC}.$$

The percentage change in output is $\Delta Q/Q$, so the ratio of the percentage change in profits to the percentage change in output, or profit elasticity, is

$$\frac{\delta \pi / \pi}{\delta Q / Q} = \frac{\delta Q(P - AVC)/[Q(P - AVC) - TFC]}{\delta Q / Q}$$

$$= \frac{\delta Q(P - AVC)}{Q(P - AVC) - TFC} \times \frac{Q}{\delta Q}.$$

After simplifying, the degree of operating leverage formula at any given level of output is[4]

$$\frac{\text{Degree of Operating Leverage}}{\text{at Point } Q} = \frac{Q(P - AVC)}{Q(P - AVC) - TFC}. \qquad \textbf{(9.8)}$$

Using Equation 9.8, Firm B's degree of operating leverage at 100,000 units of output is calculated as

$$DOL_B \text{ at } 100,000 \text{ units} = \frac{100,000(\$2.00 - \$1.20)}{100,000(\$2.00 - \$1.20) - \$40,000}$$

$$= \frac{\$80,000}{\$40,000} = 2.$$

Equation 9.8 can also be applied to Firms A and C. When this is done, Firm A's degree of operating leverage at 100,000 units equals 1.67 and Firm C's equals 2.5. With a 2 percent increase in volume, Firm C, the firm with the most operating leverage, will experience a profit increase of 5 percent. For the same 2 percent gain in volume, the firm with the least leverage, Firm A, will have only a 3.3 percent profit gain. As seen in Figure 9.15, the profits of Firm C are most sensitive to changes in sales volume, whereas Firm A's profits are relatively insensitive to volume changes. Firm B, with an intermediate degree of leverage, lies between these two extremes.

---

[4] Since $TFC = Q(AFC)$ and $AC = AVC + AFC$, where AFC is average fixed cost, Equation 9.8 can be reduced further to a form that is useful in some situations:

$$DOL = \frac{Q(P - AVC)}{Q(P - AVC) - Q(AFC)}$$

$$= \frac{P - AVC}{P - AC}.$$

Limitations of Linear Cost-Volume-Profit Analysis

Cost-volume-profit analysis helps explain relations among volume, prices, and costs. It is also useful for pricing, cost control, and other financial decisions. However, linear cost-volume-profit analysis has its limitations.

Linear cost-volume-profit analysis has a weakness in what it implies about sales possibilities for the firm. Linear cost-volume-profit charts are based on constant selling prices. To study profit possibilities with different prices, a whole series of charts is necessary, with one chart for each price. However, using sophisticated spreadsheet software such as *Lotus 1-2-3,* the creation of a wide variety of cost-volume-profit charts is relatively easy. Using such software, profit possibilities for different pricing strategies can be quickly determined. Alternatively, nonlinear cost-volume-profit analysis can be used to show the effects of changing prices.

Linear cost-volume-profit analysis is also somewhat limited by the underlying assumption of constant average costs. The linear cost relations assumed in cost-volume-profit charts cannot be expected to hold at all output levels. As unit sales increase, existing plant and equipment can be worked beyond capacity, thus reducing their efficiency. The need for additional workers, longer work periods, and, especially, overtime wages can also cause variable costs to rise sharply. If additional plant and equipment is required, fixed costs will also rise. Finally, over time the products sold by the firm change in quality and quantity. Such changes in product mix influence both the level and the slope of cost functions.

Although linear cost-volume-profit analysis has proved to be useful as a tool for managerial decision making, care must be taken to ensure that it is not applied in situations in which underlying assumptions are violated. Like any decision tool, cost-volume-profit analysis must be used with discretion.

SUMMARY

Cost analysis plays a key role in most managerial decisions. This chapter introduces a number of cost concepts, shows the relation between cost functions and production functions, and examines several cost analysis issues.

- For tax purposes, actual **historical cost,** or historical cash outlay, is the relevant cost. This is also generally true for annual 10-K reports to the Securities and Exchange Commission and for reports to stockholders. **Current cost,** the amount that must be paid under prevailing market conditions, is typically much more relevant for decision-making purposes.

- Current costs are often determined by **replacement costs,** or the cost of duplicating productive capability using present technology. Another prime determinant of current cost is **opportunity cost,** or the foregone value associated with the current rather than the next-best use of a given asset. Both of these cost categories typically involve out-of-pocket costs, or **explicit costs,** and other noncash costs, called **implicit costs.**

- **Incremental cost** is the change in cost caused by a given managerial decision. Whereas marginal cost is the change in cost following a one-unit change in output, incremental costs often involve multiple units of output. Incremental costs are a prime determinant of the **profit contribution,** or profit before fixed charges, associated with a given managerial decision. Neither are affected by **sunk costs,** which do not vary across decision alternatives.

- Proper use of relevant cost concepts requires an understanding of the cost/output relation, or **cost function. Short-run cost functions** are used for day-to-day operating decisions; **long-run cost functions** are employed in the long-range planning process. The **short run** is the operating period during which the availability of at least one input is fixed. In the **long run,** the firm has complete flexibility with respect to input use. **Fixed costs** that do not vary with output are incurred only in the short run. **Variable costs** fluctuate with output in both the short and the long run.

- A **short-run cost curve** shows the minimum cost impact of output changes for a specific plant size and in a given operating environment. A **long-run cost curve** shows the minimum cost impact of output changes for the optimal plant size using current technology in the present operating environment.

- Increasing returns, or **economies of scale,** which originate from production and market-related sources, cause long-run average costs to decline. **Cost elasticity,** ϵ_C, measures the percentage change in total cost associated with a 1 percent change in output.

- **Capacity** refers to the output level at which short-run average costs are minimized. **Minimum efficient scale** (*MES*) is the output level at which long-run average costs are minimized.

- **Multiplant economies of scale** are cost advantages that arise from operating multiple facilities in the same line of business or industry. Conversely, **multiplant diseconomies of scale** are cost disadvantages that arise from managing multiple facilities in the same line of business or industry.

- When knowledge gained from manufacturing experience is used to improve production methods so that output is produced with increasing efficiency, the resulting decline in average cost is said to reflect the effects of the firm's **learning curve. Economies of scope** exist for multiple outputs when the cost of joint production is less than the cost of producing each output separately.

- **Cost-volume-profit analysis,** sometimes called breakeven analysis, is an important analytical technique used to study relations among costs, revenues, and profits. A **breakeven quantity** is a zero profit activity level. The **degree of operating leverage** is the percentage change in profit that results from a 1 percent change in units sold; it can be understood as the elasticity of profits with respect to output.

Cost analysis poses a continuing challenge to management in all types of organizations. Using the concepts and tools discussed in this chapter, successful managers are able to manage costs effectively.

Questions   Q9.1   The relevant cost for most managerial decisions is the current cost of an input. The relevant cost for computing income for taxes and stockholder reporting is the historical cost. What advantages or disadvantages do you see in using current costs for tax and stockholder reporting purposes?

Q9.2 What are the relations among historical costs, current costs, and opportunity costs?

Q9.3 What is the difference between marginal and incremental cost?

Q9.4 What is a sunk cost, and how is it related to a decision problem?

Q9.5 What is the relation between production functions and cost functions? Be sure to include in your discussion the effect of conditions in input factor markets.

Q9.6 Explain why $\epsilon_Q > 1$ and $\epsilon_C < 1$ both indicate increasing returns to scale. (See Chapter 8 for the definition of output elasticity.)

Q9.7 The president of a small firm has been complaining to his controller about rising labor and materials costs. However, the controller notes that average costs have not increased during the past year. Is this possible?

Q9.8 Given the short-run total cost curve in Figure 9.1, explain why (a) Q_1 is the minimum of the *MC* curve, (b) Q_2 is the minimum of the *AVC* curve, (c) Q_3 is the minimum of the *ATC* curve, and (d) the *MC* curve cuts the *AVC* and *ATC* curves at their minimum points.

Q9.9 Will firms in industries in which high levels of output are necessary for minimum efficient scale tend to have substantial degrees of operating leverage?

Q9.10 Do operating strategies of average cost minimization and profit maximization always lead to identical levels of output?

Self-Test Problem

An engineering cost analysis indicates total production costs of $TC = \$500,000 + \$200Q - \$0.1Q^2$. Indicate whether each of the following statements is true or false and why.

A. Fixed costs equal $500,000.

B. Cost elasticities will vary with output.

C. This production system illustrates first decreasing, then increasing returns to scale.

D. If output per period doubles from 1,000 to 2,000 units, average costs will fall from $600 to $250 per unit.

E. The decline in average costs from $600 to $250 described in Part D indicates a learning curve advantage of roughly 58 percent.

Solution to Self-Test Problem

A. True. By definition, fixed costs do not vary with output and, therefore, are costs that will be incurred at the zero output level. Here, Total Fixed Costs = $500,000 + \$200(0) - \$0.1(0^2) = \$500,000$.

B. True. By definition, the cost elasticity formula is $\epsilon_C = \Delta C / \Delta Q \times Q/C$. Here, $\epsilon_C = (200 - 0.2Q) \times Q/C$ and will vary with the level of output.

C. False. $AC = TC/Q = (\$500,000 + \$200Q - 0.1Q^2)/Q = \$500,000/Q + \$200 - \$0.1Q$. Therefore, average costs will fall continuously as output expands, and this production system illustrates increasing returns throughout (natural monopoly).

D. True. At $Q = 1,000$, $AC = [\$500,000 + \$200(1,000) - \$0.1(1,000^2)]/1,000 = \$600$. Similarly, at $Q = 2,000$, $AC = [\$500,000 + \$200(2,000) -$

$0.1(2,000^2)]/2,000 = 250. Therefore, as output doubles from 1,000 to 2,000 units, average costs will fall from $600 to $250 per unit.

E. False. The decline in average costs from $600 to $250 as output doubles from $Q = 1,000$ to $Q = 2,000$ is an economy of scale rather than a learning curve effect.

Problems

P9.1 **Cost and Production Functions.** The total product curve shown below describes a production system in which X is the only variable input. Answer the following questions relating production to costs:

A Production System in Which X Is the Only Variable Input

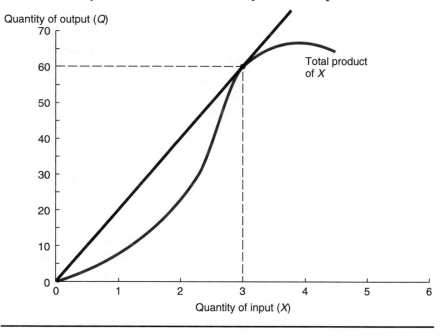

A. Over approximately what range of Input X will marginal costs be falling if P_X is not affected by the amount purchased?

B. At approximately what level of employment of Input X will average variable costs be minimized?

C. If $P_X = 25, what is the minimum average variable cost in this production system?

D. What is the marginal cost of production at 60 units of output?

E. If the price of output is $2 per unit, is employment of 3 units of X optimal for a profit-maximizing firm (assuming again that X costs $25 per unit)? Explain.

P9.2 **Cost Relations.** Determine whether each of the following is true or false. Explain why.

A. Average cost equals marginal cost at the minimum efficient scale of plant.

B. When total fixed cost and price are held constant, an increase in average variable cost will typically cause a reduction in the breakeven activity level.

C. If $\epsilon_C > 1$, diminishing returns to scale and increasing average costs are indicated.

D. When long-run average cost is decreasing, it can pay to operate larger plants with some excess capacity rather than smaller plants at their peak efficiency.

E. An increase in average variable cost always increases the degree of operating leverage for firms making a positive net profit.

P9.3   **Cost Curves.** Indicate whether each of the following involves an upward or downward shift in the long-run average cost curve or, instead, involves a leftward or rightward movement along a given curve. Also indicate whether each will have an increasing, decreasing, or uncertain effect on the level of average cost.

A. A rise in wage rates
B. A decline in output
C. An energy-saving technical change
D. A fall in interest rates
E. An increase in learning or experience

P9.4   **Incremental Cost.** Paladin Instruments, Inc., produces precision measuring instruments that it sells to other manufacturers, who then customize and distribute the products to research laboratories. The yearly volume of output is 15,000 units. The selling price and costs per unit are as follows:

Selling price		$250
Costs:		
Direct material	$40	
Direct labor	60	
Variable overhead	30	
Variable selling expenses	25	
Fixed selling expenses	20	$175
Unit profit before tax		$ 75

Management is evaluating the alternative of performing the necessary customizing to allow Paladin to sell its output directly to laboratories for $300 per unit. Although no added investment is required in productive facilities, additional processing costs are estimated as follows:

Direct labor	$30 per unit
Variable overhead	$5 per unit
Variable selling expenses	$2 per unit
Fixed selling expenses	$20,000 per year

Calculate the incremental profit that Paladin would earn by customizing its instruments and marketing them directly to end users.

P9.5   **Accounting and Economic Costs.** Three graduate business students are considering operating a frozen yogurt stand in the Harbor Springs, Michigan, resort area during their summer break. This is an alternative to summer employment with a local firm, where they would each earn $6,000 over the three-month summer period. A fully equipped facility can be leased at a cost of $8,000 for the summer. Additional projected costs are $1,000 for insurance and 40¢ per unit for materials and supplies. Their frozen yogurt would be priced at $1 per unit.

A. What is the accounting cost function for this business?

B. What is the economic cost function for this business?

C. What is the economic breakeven number of units for this operation? (Assume a $1 price and ignore interest costs associated with the timing of the lease payments.)

P9.6   **Profit Contribution.** Diane Chambers is manager of a Quick Copy franchise in White Plains, New York. Chambers projects that by reducing copy charges from 5¢ to 4¢ each, Quick Copy's $600-per-week profit contribution will increase by one-third.

A. If average variable costs are 2¢ per copy, calculate Quick Copy's projected increase in volume.

B. What is Chambers's estimate of the arc price elasticity of demand for copies?

P9.7   **Cost Elasticity.** Power Brokers, Inc. (PBI), a discount brokerage firm, is contemplating opening a new regional office in Providence, Rhode Island. An accounting cost analysis of monthly operating costs at a dozen of its regional outlets reveals average fixed costs of $4,500 per month and average variable costs of

$$AVC = \$59 - \$0.006Q,$$

where AVC is average variable costs (in dollars) and Q is output measured by number of stock and bond trades.

A typical stock or bond trade results in $100 gross commission income, with PBI paying 35 percent of this amount to its sales representatives.

A. Estimate the trade volume necessary for PBI to reach a target return of $7,500 per month for a typical office.

B. Estimate and interpret the elasticity of cost with respect to output at the trade volume found in Part A.

P9.8   **Multiplant Operation.** Appalachia Beverage Company, Inc., a regional soft drink bottler operating in southeastern states, is considering two alternative proposals for expansion into the Midwest. Alternative 1: Construct a single plant in Indianapolis, Indiana, with a monthly production capacity of 300,000 cases, a monthly fixed cost of $262,500, and a variable cost of $3.25 per case. Alternative 2: Construct three plants, one each in Muncie, Indiana; Normal, Illinois; and Dayton, Ohio, with capacities of 120,000, 100,000, and 80,000, respectively, and monthly fixed costs of $120,000, $110,000, and $95,000 each. Variable costs would be only $3 per case because of lower distribution costs. To achieve these cost savings, sales from each smaller plant would be limited to demand within its home state. The total estimated monthly sales volume of 200,000 cases in these three midwestern states is distributed as follows: 80,000 cases in Indiana, 70,000 cases in Illinois, and 50,000 cases in Ohio.

A. Assuming a wholesale price of $5 per case, calculate the breakeven output quantities for each alternative.

B. At a wholesale price of $5 per case in all states, and assuming sales at the projected levels, which alternative expansion scheme provides Appalachia with the highest profit per month?

C. If sales increase to production capacities, which alternative would prove to be more profitable?

P9.9 **Learning Curves.** The St. Thomas Winery plans to open a new production facility in the Napa Valley of California. Based on information provided by the accounting department, the company estimates fixed costs of $250,000 per year and average variable costs of

$$AVC = \$10 + \$0.01Q,$$

where AVC is average variable cost (in dollars) and Q is output measured in cases of output per year.

A. Estimate total cost and average total cost for the coming year at a projected volume of 4,000 cases.

B. An increase in worker productivity because of greater experience or learning during the course of the year resulted in a substantial cost saving for the company. Estimate the effect of learning on average total cost if actual total cost was $522,500 at an actual volume of 5,000 cases.

P9.10 **Cost-Volume-Profit Analysis.** Untouchable Package Service (UPS) offers overnight package delivery to Canadian business customers. UPS has recently decided to expand its facilities to better satisfy current and projected demand. Current volume totals two million packages per week at a price of $12 each, and average variable costs are constant at all output levels. Fixed costs are $3 million per week, and profit contribution averages one-third of revenues on each delivery. After completion of the expansion project, fixed costs will double, but variable costs will decline by 25 percent.

A. Calculate the change in UPS's weekly breakeven output level that is due to expansion.

B. Assuming that volume remains at two million packages per week, calculate the change in the degree of operating leverage that is due to expansion.

C. Again assuming that volume remains at two million packages per week, what is the effect of expansion on monthly profit?

CASE STUDY FOR CHAPTER 9

The Economics of Multiplant Operation

The analysis of potential economies and diseconomies of multiplant operation is fascinating subject in managerial economics. Consider the case of a company that seeks to better serve current and new customers using a multiplant alternative to centralized production. It is necessary for any such firm to analyze various production alternatives and make a plant-size decision on the basis of expected costs and benefits. To gain insight on the types of issues faced, consider the following demand and production cost relations as descriptive for the upcoming year:

$$P = \$200 - \$0.00003Q,$$
$$TC = \$7,812,500 + \$100Q + \$0.00002Q^2.$$

As a first step in the analysis, it is necessary to calculate output, price, and profits at the profit-maximizing activity level based on the assumption of centralized production at one production facility. To find the profit-maximizing output level, set $d\pi/dQ = 0$ and solve for Q. Thus,

$$\begin{aligned}
\pi &= PQ - TC \\
&= (\$200 - \$0.00003Q)Q - \$7,812,500 - \$100Q \\
&\quad - \$0.00002Q^2 \\
&= -\$0.00005Q^2 + \$100Q - \$7,812,500 \\
d\pi/dQ &= -0.0001Q + 100 = 0 \\
&\quad\quad 0.0001Q = 100 \\
&\quad\quad\quad\quad Q = 1,000,000 \\
P &= \$200 - \$0.00003Q \\
&= \$200 - \$0.00003(1,000,000) \\
&= \$170 \\
\pi &= -\$0.00005(1,000,000^2) + \$100(1,000,000) \\
&\quad - \$7,812,500 \\
&= \$42,187,500
\end{aligned}$$

Since $d^2\pi/dQ^2 = -0.0001 < 0$, and $Q = 1,000,000$ is a profit maximum.

The second step is to find the average-cost minimizing level of output. To find this output level, set $dAC/dQ = 0$ and solve for Q. Thus,

$$\begin{aligned}
AC &= TC/Q \\
&= \$7,812,500Q^{-1} + \$100 + \$0.00002Q \\
dAC/dQ &= -7,812,500Q^{-2} + 0.00002 = 0 \\
&\quad\quad 7,812,500/Q^2 = 0.00002 \\
&\quad\quad\quad\quad Q^2 = 7,812,500/0.00002 \\
&\quad\quad\quad\quad Q = \sqrt{390,625,000,000} \\
&\quad\quad\quad\quad\quad = 625,000
\end{aligned}$$

Since $d^2AC/dQ^2 = 15,625,000Q^{-3} > 0$, and $Q = 625,000$ is an AC minimum.

Observe that the average-cost minimizing output level of 625,000 is far less than the profit-maximizing output level of 1,000,000. This means that, given market conditions, the profit-maximizing level of output falls at a point of steeply rising average costs. To determine the optimal number of plants with multiplant production, make the relevant *MC* and *MR* comparison at the levels suggested by multiplant production.

$$\text{At } Q = 625{,}000,$$
$$MC = dTC/dQ$$
$$= \$100 + \$0.00004Q$$
$$= \$100 + \$0.00004(625{,}000)$$
$$= \$125$$

An optimal multiplant production level is found by equating MR to this multiplant MC level. Thus,

$$MR = dTR/dQ = \$125 = MC$$
$$\$200 - \$0.00006Q = \$125$$
$$0.00006Q = 75$$
$$Q = 1{,}250{,}000$$

Given optimal multiplant production of 1,250,000 and average-cost minimizing activity levels of 625,000 for each plant, optimal multiplant production at 2 facilities is suggested.

$$\text{At } Q = 1{,}250{,}000,$$
$$P = \$200 - \$0.00003(1{,}250{,}000)$$
$$= \$162.50$$
$$\pi = TR - TC$$
$$= \$162.50(1{,}250{,}000) - 2[\$7{,}812{,}500$$
$$+ \$100(625{,}000) + \$0.00002(625{,}000^2)]$$
$$= \$46{,}875{,}000$$

As far as it goes, this type of traditional analysis is correct and provides management with significant useful information. However, it leaves unanswered a number of important questions. In particular, management might be interested in the following issues:

- Assuming centralized production at one plant, what is the sensitivity of average cost and marginal cost to output changes over the relevant range?
- What does the optimal pattern of production look like as output expands if more than one production facility is employed?
- At what activity level does it make sense to add a second production facility?
- What is the source of the cost savings made possible through multiplant operation?

To shed light on these issues,

A. Illustrate the sensitivity of average cost and marginal cost to output changes over the relevant range based on the assumption of centralized production at one facility. To do so, set up a table or spreadsheet that illustrates the relationships among quantity (Q), price (P), marginal revenue (MR), total revenue (TR), average cost (AC), marginal cost (MC), total cost (TC), marginal profit ($M\pi$) and total profits (π). Establish a range for Q from 0 to 2.5 million in increments of 125,000 (i.e., 0, 125,000, 250,000, . . . , 2,500,000).

B. Portray the sensitivity of operating data to output changes over this same range of output for multiple plants, based on the assumption that no more than one plant will be employed at less than full capacity.

C. Identify the output level at which the company would commence operation of a second production facility.

D. Describe the cost savings possible through multiplant operation as an example of economies of scale or learning curve advantages. Explain your answer.

Selected References

Atkinson, John Hawley, Jr., Gregory Hohner, Barry Mundt, Richard B. Troxel, and William Winchell. *Current Trends in Cost of Quality: Linking the Cost of Quality and Continuous Improvement.* (Montvale, New Jersey: National Association of Accountants, 1991).

Bailey, Charles D., and Edward V. McIntyre. "Some Evidence on the Nature of Relearning Curves." *Accounting Review* 67 (April 1992): 368–378.

Brief, Richard P., and Raef A. Lawson. "The Role of the Accounting Rate of Return in Financial Statement Analysis." *Accounting Review* 67 (April 1992): 411–426.

Cummins, J. David, and Sharon Tennyson. "Controlling Automobile Insurance Costs." *Journal of Economic Perspectives* 6 (Spring 1992): 95–115.

Flory, Steven M., Thomas J. Phillips, Jr., R. Eric Reidenbach, and Donald P. Robin. "A Multidimensional Analysis of Selected Ethical Issues in Accounting." *Accounting Review* 67 (April 1992): 284–302.

Gray, Wayne B., and Carol Adaire Jones. "Are OSHA Health Inspections Effective? A Longitudinal Study in the Manufacturing Sector." *Review of Economics and Statistics* 73 (August 1991): 504–507.

Jaditz, Ted. "Monitoring Costs as a Basis for the Dispersion of Firm Ownership." *Managerial and Decision Economics* 13 (January–February 1992): 23–30.

Kaplan, Robert S., and David P. Norton. "The Balanced Scorecard—Measures That Drive Performance." *Harvard Business Review* 70 (January–February 1992): 71–79.

Kaserman, David L., and John W. Mayo. "The Measurement of Vertical Economies and the Efficient Structure of the Electric Utility Industry." *Journal of Industrial Economics* 39 (September 1991): 483–502.

Kester, W. Carl, and Timothy A. Luehrman. "The Myth of Japan's Low-Cost Capital." *Harvard Business Review* 70 (May–June 1992): 130–138.

Lieberman, Marvin B. "Determinants of Vertical Integration: An Empirical Test." *Journal of Industrial Economics* 39 (September 1991): 451–466.

McGrath, Michael E., and Richard W. Hoole. "Manufacturing's New Economies of Scale." *Harvard Business Review* 70 (May–June 1992): 94–102.

Ronen, Joshua, Anthony Saunders, and Ashwin Paul C. Sondhi, ed. *Off-Balance Sheet Activities.* (Westport, CT: Quorum Books, 1990).

Schaffer, Robert H., and Harvey A. Thomson. "Successful Orange Programs Begin with Results." *Harvard Business Review* 70 (January–February 1992): 80–89.

Shaftel, Timothy L. "Accounting Methods and Managerial Discretion: The Case of Dollar-Value LIFO." *Managerial and Decision Economics* 13 (March–April 1992): 119–133.

CHAPTER | # COST ESTIMATION

Detailed knowledge of short-run and long-run cost relations plays an important role in the managerial decision-making process. Short-run cost curves provide information that is useful for making operating decisions. When the marginal revenue derived from sales exceeds the marginal cost of production, an expansion in the level of output is profitable. Conversely, when the marginal revenue derived from sales is less than the marginal cost of output, an expansion in the level of output would be unwise and would lead to lower profits.

Long-run cost curves provide information that is useful in the long-range planning process. When economies of scale and relatively low distribution costs are prevalent, an expansion in demand can often be met efficiently through an expansion in the level of output at only one or a few large production facilities. When a product involves only low or moderate economies of scale combined with high distribution costs, efficient production often calls for smaller plants located closer to regional markets.

To properly incorporate cost considerations in managerial decisions, precise cost estimates must be available to show how short-run and long-run cost curves are related to a number of important factors both within and outside the control of the firm. This chapter considers various cost estimation techniques useful for obtaining such information. The strengths and weaknesses of statistical cost estimation techniques that rely primarily on accounting data are explored. Also examined is accounting information that provides a logical, historical perspective that is very useful but has limitations when used for estimating future costs. Imperfections in accrual accounting methods, as well as the failure to reflect current market values and opportunity costs associated with the use of various inputs, can lead to errors when costs are estimated using unadjusted accounting data. A powerful approach to statistical cost estimation involves the regression-based analysis of accounting data developed from sophisticated management information systems. Computer-generated data on product quantity, quality, and cost characteristics, combined with familiar least squares regression methods of data analysis, constitute a powerful low-cost tool for cost estimation. Engineering cost estimation techniques that rely on the physical relations expressed in the production function for a particular product or firm offer an alternative to statistical cost analysis based on historical data. A change in relative input prices, for example, can cause firms to change their input requirements and thereby undermine the accuracy of engineering cost estimates. As will become clear in following sections, each of the various cost estimation techniques has its own strengths and weaknesses. Successful managers often find that accurate cost estimation requires reliance on a combination of methods.

SHORT-RUN COST ESTIMATION PROBLEMS

If it can be assumed that the firm is operating efficiently, or if inefficiencies can be isolated and accounted for, it is possible to estimate cost functions through statistical analysis. Time series and cross section regression techniques are the most popular methods of cost function estimation. Such studies regress cost on output, typically in a model that includes a number of other variables—including input prices, operating conditions, and related factors—whose cost effects managers wish to analyze.

Cost Allocation Problems

Relevant cost categories
Appropriate divisions of costs among fixed and variable components.

Future costs
Prospective costs.

In the estimation of short-run cost relations, the total variable cost function rather than the total cost function is estimated to avoid the difficulty of properly allocating fixed costs. Since fixed costs do not vary with respect to output, they do not affect average variable costs, nor do they influence marginal costs used for short-run operating decisions. They can safely be eliminated from the short-run cost estimation process. Many difficulties encountered in statistical cost analysis arise from errors in the specification of **relevant cost categories**, or appropriate divisions of costs among fixed and variable components. Problems also arise in the collection and modification of cost data. Before examining the types of regression models actually used to estimate short-run cost functions, it is worth mentioning several caveats concerning the specification, collection, and modification of cost data.

Since managerial decision making relates largely to future activities and events, relevant costs for managerial decisions are **future costs**, or prospective costs, as opposed to current or historical costs. Cost estimates based on historical accounting data that record current or past costs must be considered only as first approximations to relevant costs. Historical costs must be modified before they can be used for decision making. Typical adjustments involve setting input prices at projected levels, for labor, raw materials, and energy.

A significant conceptual problem frequently occurs given the failure of many management information systems to reflect opportunity costs. Opportunity costs are usually the largest and most important costs in a short-run decision problem. For example, if a line at a bottling plant is used to bottle diet cola rather than caffeine-free diet cola, the cost of current rather than alternative employment is the revenue lost from the alternative soda product. To overlook such costs would be foolish. What manager would choose to bottle diet cola when projected sales are higher for the caffeine-free variety? Similarly, what manager would choose to bottle the caffeine-free variety when higher sales could be obtained for the diet cola product? To ignore decision alternatives is to disregard important costs and benefits associated with any operating or planning decision.

Cost/Output Matching Problems

Economic depreciation
Rate of market-value decline for productive assets.

Obstacles often arise in the attempt to directly relate specific costs or cost categories to output. In short-run cost analysis, only costs that vary with output should be included. In many instances, it is difficult to distinguish between costs that are related and costs that are not related to changes in output. For example, calculating the rate of **economic depreciation** for capital equipment is seldom easy. Economic depreciation is the rate of market-value decline for productive assets. For most depreciable assets, both time and usage determine the rate of decline in value, but only the cost component related to actual usage should be included in the estimation of the short-run cost/output relation. Typically, however, these costs are combined in accounting data on depreciation costs, and it is often impossible to separate use costs from obsolescence or time-related costs.

Semivariable costs
Expenses that rise or fall in a less than strictly proportional basis with changes in output.

Semivariable costs also present a problem in cost/output matching. Semivariable costs are expenses that rise or fall on a less than strictly proportional basis with changes in output. Cost categories such as administrative overhead, personnel expenses, and insurance costs are constant when output changes over limited ranges, but they will change once a threshold level of activity has been breached for a sustained period. Accurate estimation of short-run cost/output relations requires that the full range of variable and semivariable cost categories be considered.

Time Period Specification Problems

Cost observation period
Time frame for cost analysis.

Difficulties also arise from the use of accounting data in relating relevant costs to the corresponding output. Care must be taken to adjust the data for leads and lags between cost reporting and output production. Maintenance expense provides a typical example of this problem. Production in one period often leads to higher maintenance expenses in subsequent periods. During a period of high production, recorded maintenance expenses will be unusually low because the firm's equipment is being used at full capacity, and maintenance is postponed if possible. Repairs are usually temporary in nature, aimed at getting the equipment back into production rapidly until some slack enters the production system. Without careful adjustment, this problem can cause significant errors in statistically estimated cost functions.

Short-run and long-run cost curves are, by definition, cost/output relations for a plant of a specific scale and technology. If such curves are to be accurately estimated, the period of examination must be one during which the product remains essentially unchanged and plant facilities remain fixed. It should be noted that even though a firm's book value of assets remains relatively constant during the **cost observation period,** or time frame for cost analysis, the plant may have actually changed a great deal. Consider a firm that replaces a number of obsolete, manually operated machines that have been fully depreciated with a single automated machine that it leases. The firm's production function, and hence its total cost function, undoubtedly change considerably even though the book value of assets remains constant. The problem of changing plant and output characteristics can be minimized by limiting the length of time over which data are analyzed. For satisfactory statistical estimation, however, the cost analyst needs an adequate sample size with a fairly broad range of outputs. This requirement tends to lengthen the necessary period of data observations and, in turn, necessitates a careful examination of a firm's total activities during the cost study period to achieve accurate results.

Given the need for statistical reliability, frequent data observations covering short production periods are desirable from the standpoint of allowing wide variability in the cost/output relation. Although the best time span for the observation period will vary from one situation to another, monthly data are often employed in empirical cost analysis. In such studies, monthly changes in output are compared with corresponding monthly changes in various cost categories. A total time frame of perhaps two to three years provides enough data for reliable statistical analysis yet is still short enough that measurement problems due to changing variable characteristics can be avoided. Still, it is not possible to generalize about the best time frame for all empirical cost studies. Data availability and measurement considerations will vary from one instance to another.

Price Level Adjustment Problems

Inflation
Rising prices.

Deflation
Falling prices.

In time series analysis, historical data are used for statistical cost studies. **Inflation,** or rising prices, and **deflation,** or falling prices, have the potential to create a serious challenge to accurate cost estimation. During inflationary periods, the costs of labor, raw materials, and other items increase; during deflationary periods, the costs of labor, raw materials, and other items decrease. A generally expanding economy causes the output of most firms to rise; a generally contracting economy causes the output of most firms to fall. During periods of economic growth, current output is typically larger than in previous periods. During inflationary periods, recent production has a relatively higher cost in nominal, or current-dollar, terms. Since both economic growth and inflation are typical during the post–World War II period, unsophisticated cost analysis might incorrectly suggest that costs rise rapidly with increases in output. To eliminate this bias, cost data must be adjusted for price-level changes. Because input prices increase at variable rates, composite price indexes used to adjust for input price changes often do not provide satisfactory results. It is better to use an index for each input category. The problem of adjusting for price changes is compounded because input-price changes caused by a lasting change in input demand and supply conditions must not be removed. Only price changes that are independent of the production system under examination should be eliminated; otherwise, the statistically estimated cost function will misstate the true cost of production. If an increase in production causes the price of a scarce input to rise, the resulting increase in input costs is a direct result of output expansion. Such costs must be considered as a predictable consequence of output level decisions and part of the cost estimation process.

The cost implications of changing input prices are sometimes hard to estimate because firms alter input usage in light of relative prices for available substitutes. For example, as the price of fuel oil increases, natural gas becomes a more attractive source of energy for heating. Firms can be expected to switch from one energy source to another as changes in relative input prices increase or decrease relative attractiveness. Therefore, it is inappropriate to assume that a 20 percent rise in fuel oil costs will necessarily lead to a 20 percent rise in heating expenses; the actual rise may be less if cheaper alternatives are available. Economywide inflation rarely leads to proportional changes in the prices of all goods and services. Changes in optimal input combinations that result from differences in the price-level changes of various inputs have a significant impact on the cost projections that are relevant for managerial decision making.

This brief examination of some of the problems encountered in cost analysis illustrates the importance of proper data collection within the firm. The value of cost analysis depends greatly on the quality of the firm's cost accounting records. With this in mind, many firms have developed advanced management information systems to allow sophisticated analysis of cost/output relations. It must be emphasized that, to benefit managerial decision making, these management information systems must go beyond collecting and reporting the types of data found in traditional accounting systems. Careful planning and a clear understanding of relevant cost concepts are required to establish a cost reporting system that provides the necessary input for proper decision analysis.

EMPIRICAL COST FUNCTIONS

Once data problems have been solved, cost analysts are faced with the problem of determining the proper functional form of the cost curve. A variety of linear and nonlinear models suitable for least squares regression analysis are available. If there are good theoretical reasons for using a particular approach, that model will be selected. Often, however, there is no a priori reason for choosing one model over another. In such instances, a typical procedure involves fitting several models to the cost/output data under consideration and then using the model that seems to fit best in terms of R^2, the coefficient of determination. If one model has an R^2 of 0.90, indicating that the model explains 90 percent of the variation in total variable costs, and another model has an R^2 of 0.95, the second model will be relied upon for decision making. This assumes that the independent variables in each model are the same; only the model structure is different. Without this proviso it would be possible to artificially inflate the R^2 for one model merely by adding additional explanatory variables. For this reason, the adjusted coefficient of determination, $\bar{R}^2$, and the F test described in Chapter 6 are typically used with the coefficient of determination in evaluating the goodness of fit for empirical cost functions.

Linear Cost Functions

Linear cost function
A straight-line cost/output relation.

For a great many production systems, a **linear cost function** of the following form provides an adequate fit of cost/output data:

$$C = b_0 + b_1 Q + \sum_{i=2}^{N} b_i X_i. \tag{10.1}$$

C refers to relevant costs during a typical observation period; Q is the quantity of output produced during that period; X_i designates all other independent variables whose cost effects the analyst wants to account for; and b_0, b_1, and b_i are the coefficients of the model as estimated by the least squares regression technique. Other independent variables to be accounted for include such items as wage rates, fuel and materials costs, weather, input quality, production lot size, the product

MANAGERIAL APPLICATION 10.1

The Push for Global Accounting Standards

The London-based International Accounting Standards Committee (IASC) is rolling out universal accounting standards, and some U.S. companies are getting worried. U.S. companies are concerned that standards set in London may one day replace those currently used in the United States and have dramatic consequences for reported earnings. Especially worrisome are IASC's proposals in the accounting for mergers and acquisitions, goodwill amortization, inventory accounting, and accounting for research and development (R&D) expenditures.

When U.S. firms acquire other companies for stock, acquired assets are typically accounted for on a "pooling of interest" basis. Acquired assets are entered into the balance sheet without marking up (or down) asset values, thus avoiding any charge off against current or future reported earnings. Under the IASC proposal, the pooling of interests method of accounting would be discontinued. This could make a huge difference to reported earnings in some instances. Consider AT&T's $7.5 billion stock merger with NCR during 1991. Using the pooling of interests method, AT&T was able to combine NCR assets with AT&T assets at book values. If IASC's proposed rules had been effective during 1991, AT&T would have been forced to use the "purchase" method of accounting for business combinations. Under the purchase method, when an amount in excess of book value is paid for a company in a merger or acquisition, the difference is recognized as "goodwill" that must be charged off against reported earnings. Under the purchase method, the AT&T–NCR merger would have resulted in recognition of as much as $5.7 billion in goodwill to be written off against AT&T earnings. Current U.S. accounting rules allow companies to write off goodwill over as long as 40 years. Using a straight-line approach and the maximum 40-year amortization period, a purchase method of accounting for the NCR merger would have depressed AT&T's reported earnings by a whopping $142.5 million per year. Fearing a negative reaction from shareholders who focus on reported earnings per share, AT&T may not have gone ahead with the NCR merger if the purchase method had been required.

Proposed IASC standards would also cut the goodwill amortization period to a maximum of 20 years, with 5 years used in all but the most unusual situations. If AT&T were forced to write off NCR goodwill over 5 years, reported earnings would be reduced by more than $1 billion per year. Although shorter goodwill amortization periods would depress the earnings reported by U.S. companies, effects on foreign firms would be even greater. Currently, regulators in Britain, Germany, and Japan allow companies to write off goodwill immediately against the book value of stockholders' equity, with no charge to earnings. Any global accounting standard that requires income statement recognition of goodwill charges will thus benefit reported earnings for U.S. companies on a relative basis.

Inventory accounting is another area of IASC concern. U.S. companies typically adopt LIFO (last in, first out) or FIFO (first in, first out) inventory accounting methods. LIFO is preferred in an inflationary environment because it reduces inventory profits and minimizes tax liabilities. Proposed IASC standards would forbid LIFO inventory accounting and force all companies to use FIFO. Critics contend that while standard use of FIFO inventory accounting would result in more realistic inventory valuations, huge swings in reported earnings and increases in the tax liability of many companies would result.

R&D accounting policy is the final major area of focus for the IASC. In the United States, all R&D costs must be recorded as expenses against reported earnings in the year they are incurred. Proposed IASC rules would allow some development costs to be capitalized and recorded on the balance sheet as assets. Such a change would boost bottom lines of many U.S. drug and high-tech companies, but might also give many foreign companies better access to U.S. capital markets.

With support from the Securities & Exchange Commission, new IASC rules should be finalized by the end of 1993. The immediate result will be confusion, but global comparisons of operating performance should eventually become easier.

Source: Roula Khalaf, "Esperanto for Accountants." *Forbes,* March 2, 1992, 50–51.

mix, and changes in product design. Including such factors in the cost estimation model enables the analyst to better estimate the relation between cost and output. A linear statistical cost function implies a straight-line relation between costs, output, and other important cost-determining variables.

The intercept coefficient b_0 in this model is typically irrelevant. In short-run cost analysis, the intercept term cannot be interpreted as the firm's fixed costs because such costs are not included within variable cost categories. Even if total costs, as opposed to total variable costs, are used as the dependent variable, the intercept coefficient b_0 usually does not reflect the firm's fixed costs. This coefficient is simply the intercept of the estimated cost curve with the vertical axis. This intersection occurs at the point where output is zero and usually lies far outside the typical range of cost/output data. As in demand estimation, extending any regression equation very far beyond the range of data observations is a hazardous procedure likely to result in significant estimation error. In those limited instances in which firms or plants with very small levels of output are being considered and measured costs include fixed expenses, the b_0 coefficient can be taken as an estimate, albeit an imperfect one, of fixed costs. In all instances, the interpretation of individual coefficient estimates must be restricted to the relevant range of data observations.

Although a linear form for the cost/output relation may be accurate for the range of available data, extrapolation far outside this range can lead to serious misstatement. Since the short run is the period during which the law of diminishing returns is operative, varying economies of scale can distort cost/output relations at very low and very high output levels. A linear relation is typically only

Curvilinear cost function

A cost/output relation that deviates from a straight line in a smooth, continuous fashion.

an approximation valid over limited output ranges to an underlying **curvilinear cost function.** A curvilinear cost/output relation is one that deviates from a straight line in a smooth, continuous fashion. The problem of extrapolation outside the observation range is illustrated in Figure 10.1. Within the observed output range, Q_1 to Q_2, a linear function closely approximates the true cost/output relation. Extrapolation beyond these limits leads to inaccurate estimates of the firm's variable costs.

Coefficient b_1 is perhaps the most important one estimated in a linear cost/output model. As shown in Figures 10.1 and 10.2, b_1 is an estimate of average variable costs per unit within the relevant output range. Since marginal costs represent the cost effect of a one-unit increase in output, b_1 is also an estimate of marginal costs within the relevant output range. Therefore, the coefficient estimate b_1 has important implications for operating purposes. When marginal revenue exceeds marginal cost, output should be expanded; when marginal revenue falls short of marginal cost, output should be reduced.

Quadratic Cost Functions

Perhaps the most prevalent nonlinear model for cost estimation is the **quadratic cost function.** A quadratic cost function involves both first-order and second-order (squared) terms for the output variable. A quadratic cost function is written as follows:

$$C = b_0 + b_1 Q + b_2 Q^2 + \sum_{i=3}^{N} b_i X_i + \epsilon.\qquad\textbf{(10.2)}$$

FIGURE 10.1 **Linear Approximation of the Cost/Output Function**

Within the range of data observations, a linear function will often closely approximate true cost/output relations.

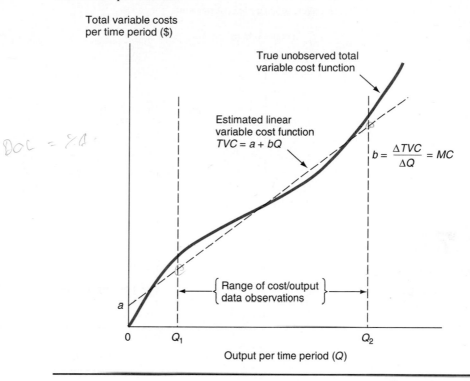

Quadratic cost function

A cost function that involves first-order and second-order (squared) output terms.

Again, *C* refers to relevant costs during a typical observation period; *Q* is the quantity of output produced during that period; and X_i designates all other independent variables whose cost effects the analyst wants to account for. The coefficients b_0, b_1, b_2, and b_i are estimated using the least squares regression technique. Since marginal costs represent the cost effect of a one-unit increase in output, marginal cost is given by the expression

$$\text{Marginal Cost} = \delta C / \delta Q = b_1 + 2b_2 Q. \qquad (10.3)$$

It is commonly found that the estimated coefficients $b_1 > 0$ and $b_2 > 0$ and, therefore, that marginal costs per unit are positive and rise with an increase in the level of production. Figure 10.3 illustrates the typical average variable cost and marginal cost curves associated with a quadratic cost function. Notice that in a quadratic total cost relation, the average variable cost curve is U-shaped, but the marginal cost relation is linear with a positive slope.

Quadratic cost functions are estimated easily using ordinary least squares (OLS) regression techniques. To apply that method, output values are simply squared to create a second independent variable in a multiple regression model. The one dependent variable is cost, and the two independent variables are output

FIGURE 10.2   **Average Variable Cost and Marginal Cost for a Linear Cost Function: $TVC = a + bQ$**

For a linear total cost function, the slope coefficient b estimates a constant marginal cost and average variable cost per unit.

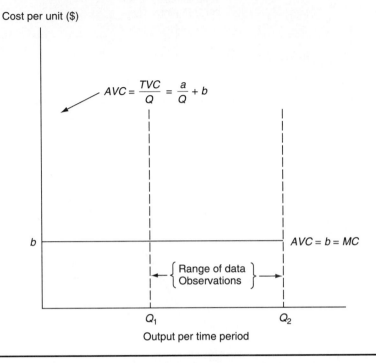

Note: If $a = 0$, $AVC = b$, a constant. However, if $a > 0$, AVC declines continuously but at a decreasing rate as output increases, because as Q becomes larger, a/Q becomes smaller and smaller.

(Q) and output squared (Q^2). Although Q and Q^2 are obviously related, coefficient estimates for each variable can be statistically significant when important non-linearities in the cost/output relation are operative.

Cubic Cost Functions

Cubic cost function

A cost function that involves first-order, second-order (squared), and third-order (cubed) output terms.

Another commonly employed nonlinear model for cost estimation is the **cubic cost function.** A cubic cost function involves first-order, second-order (squared), and third-order (cubed) terms for the output variable. A cubic cost function is expressed as

$$C = b_0 + b_1 Q + b_2 Q^2 + b_3 Q^3 + \sum_{i=4}^{N} b_i X_i + \epsilon. \qquad \textbf{(10.4)}$$

Again, C refers to relevant costs during a typical observation period; Q is the quantity of output produced during that period; and X_i designates all other independent variables whose cost effects the analyst wants to account for. The coefficients b_0, b_1, b_2, b_3, and b_i are estimated using the least squares regression

FIGURE 10.3 **Average Variable Cost and Marginal Cost Curves for a Quadratic Total Variable Cost Function:** $TVC = a + bQ = cQ^2$

A quadratic total cost function assumes a linear marginal cost function and a U-shaped average variable cost function.

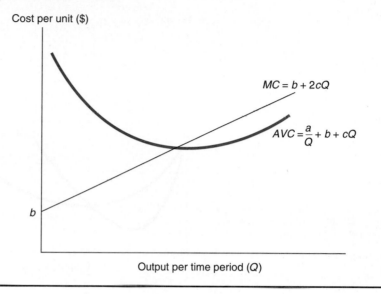

technique. Marginal cost per unit derived from a cubic total cost function is given by the expression

$$\text{Marginal Cost} = \delta C/\delta Q = b_1 + 2b_2 Q + 3b_3 Q^2. \tag{10.5}$$

Observe that the marginal cost relation derived from a cubic cost function is itself a quadratic cost function. This means that the cubic model allows for both total and marginal costs per unit to vary widely over the span of observed values. It is commonly found that the estimated coefficient for the first-order output variable is positive; therefore, $b_1 > 0$. On the other hand, the estimated coefficient for the second-order output variable is typically negative, $b_2 < 0$; whereas the estimated coefficient for the third-order output variable is again positive, $b_3 > 0$. This gives rise to average variable cost and marginal cost curves that first fall, then bottom out at minimum values, and then ascend at very high levels of output. Figure 10.4 illustrates the typical average variable cost and marginal cost curves associated with a cubic cost function. Note that in a cubic total cost relation, both the average variable cost curve and the marginal cost curve are U-shaped in nature.

Cubic cost functions are also estimated easily using OLS regression techniques. Output values are merely cubed to create a third independent variable in a multiple regression model. The one dependent variable is again cost, and the three independent variables are output (Q), output squared (Q^2), and output cubed (Q^3). While Q, Q^2, and Q^3 are typically closely related, coefficient estimates for each variable are statistically significant when important nonlinearities exist in the cost/output relation.

FIGURE 10.4   **Average Variable Cost and Marginal Cost Curves for a Cubic Variable Cost Function:** $TVC = a + bQ - cQ^2 + dQ^3$

A cubic total cost function assumes that both marginal cost and average variable cost functions have U shapes.

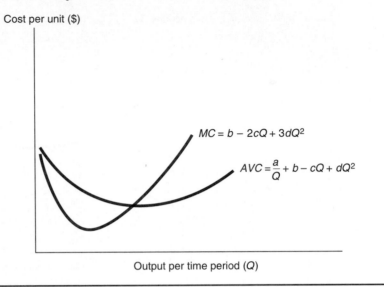

In a cubic total cost relation, the average variable cost curve and the marginal cost relation are both U-shaped. Both functional forms are flexible in the sense that they allow a nonlinear linkage, if present, to emerge between cost and output.

Multiplicative Cost Functions

Multiplicative cost function

A model where cost is determined by the product of output and all other X variables.

Another common nonlinear regression model used in cost estimation is the **multiplicative cost function:**

$$C = b_0 Q^{b_1} X_i^{b_i} . \tag{10.6}$$

C again refers to relevant costs during a typical observation period; Q is the quantity of output produced during that period; and X_i designates all other independent variables whose cost effects the analyst wants to account for. A multiplicative model is used when the marginal effect of each independent variable is thought to depend on the value of all independent variables in the regression equation. For example, the effect on cost of an increase in output often depends on the level of wage rates, the vintage of technology employed, weather, and so on. Similarly, the effect on costs of a wage hike can depend on the output level, raw material prices, R&D expenditures, and other factors. Allowing for such changes in the marginal relation is sometimes more realistic than an implicit assumption of constant marginal costs, as in the linear cost model, or linear marginal costs, as in the quadratic cost model.

The benefits of added realism for the multiplicative cost model have no offsetting costs in terms of added complexity or difficulty in estimation. As described

●

MANAGERIAL APPLICATION 10.2
Workstations Work for Cost Estimation

Business cost analysts are finding that computer workstations can provide detailed cost estimates for a fraction of the amount necessary as recently as the late 1980s. Workstations are built around reduced instruction-set computing (RISC) chips or Intel's i486 or i586 microprocessors—both are capable of lightning-fast calculations. Virtually all workstations employ Unix operating system software that allows them to perform several tasks on screen at once, portray dazzling graphics, and collect data from many different sources. Unix also permits workstations to easily communicate on a network, even with machines from different manufacturers. Just as important as their amazing capabilities is how the rapid pace of technology has reduced workstation prices. The popularity of workstations has been fueled by the fact that many models now cost only $5,000 to $10,000 per unit, or little more than top-of-the-line personal computers (PCs). Today, cost analysts are catching onto what many engineers and programmers already know: networks of souped-up personal computers, or workstations, can often do more at far lower cost than can be accomplished using giant mainframe computers.

The speed and capability of workstations are perhaps best illustrated by the fact that they are largely used to replace much more expensive minicomputers and mainframes. Prudential Securities reports that more than 50 percent of workstation purchases displace minicomputers, roughly one-quarter replace mainframes, and the rest represent an upgrade from PCs. Though relatively small with roughly $20 billion per year in annual sales, the workstation industry is growing very rapidly. Annual workstation sales grew at a scorching 38 percent pace during the late 1980s; growth in the 20 to 25 percent per year range is predicted throughout the mid-1990s. The fastest growing part of the workstation market is for customers outside engineering, programming, and technical departments. Sales to manufacturing and retail buyers are growing at an astounding 50 percent per year pace.

Workstations are surfacing in business applications on Wall Street, in the airlines, retailing, and many other industries. Big Wall Street brokerages were the first nontechnical users of workstations. Brokers use workstations to handle back-office recordkeeping chores and to analyze trends in market data and the complex pricing models used to spot bargains. More recent converts to the workstation market include Northwest Airlines (NWA), who acquired a major scheduling and ticket pricing headache when it purchased Republic Airlines in 1986. NWA found it had to track revenues from nearly twice as many tickets but couldn't afford new mainframe computers to automate the process. Instead, the company opted to purchase a network of 600 Sun workstations. NWA now automatically analyzes every ticket purchase for proper pricing rather than just a 10 percent sample, as had been done previously. The millions of dollars in cost savings helped NWA pay for its new Sun system in just a few months. American Airlines, Inc. recently moved its crew-scheduling task off its old IBM mainframe to a new workstation network produced by MIPS Computer Systems Inc. The MIPS system allows American to schedule 25,000 crew members in only six hours, a job that used to take 24 hours—and at a savings in excess of $1.5 million per year. In light of this success, American also added a large workstation network for flight scheduling. Workstations are also surfacing at retailing giant Wal-Mart stores and at the City of Chicago's Bureau of Parking, where a Sun workstation streamlined collection procedures and hiked 1990 parking-ticket revenues by $40 million.

The overall market for workstations is expected to double by the mid-1990s as new producers scramble to meet the demand of both scientific and nonscientific customers. Sun, Digital Equipment, Hewlett-Packard, and NeXT have all introduced workstations that retail for less than $5,000 and provide stiff competition for high-powered PCs marketed by Compaq, IBM, and others. Some i486-based workstations can be purchased for as little as $2,500. Perhaps the greatest benefit of such firepower is that it makes power-hungry user-friendly software available to line managers. Those directly responsible for cost estimation and management are thus given the means for faster and more accurate cost estimates than ever before—with business the beneficiary.

Source: Robert D. Hof, "Battle Stations for Workstation Makers," *Business Week*, January 20, 1992, 30.

in Appendix 2A, Equation 10.6 can be transformed into a linear cost relation using logarithms and then estimated using the OLS technique. Thus, Equation 10.6 is equivalent to

$$\log C = \log b_0 + b_1 \log Q + \sum_{i=2}^{N} b_i \log X_i + \epsilon. \qquad \textbf{(10.7)}$$

When written in this form, the coefficients $\log b_0$, b_1, and b_i can be easily estimated using the OLS technique. Given the multiplicative or log-linear form of the regression model, these coefficient estimates can also be interpreted as estimates of the constant *elasticity* of cost with respect to output, and the cost elasticity for each other important independent X_i variable included in the model. Each coefficient estimate indicates the percentage change in C due to a 1 percent change in Q or some other X variable (see Appendix 2A). As mentioned in Chapter 6, it is worth remembering that multiplicative or log-linear models imply constant elasticity.

Multiplicative cost models also imply a changing absolute effect on the dependent Y variable (cost) due to changes in output and other various independent X variables. This is sometimes attractive in cost analysis because the effect on costs of a one-unit change in output can depend on the level of output, wages, raw material prices, and so on. The changing marginal effect implicit in the multiplicative or log-linear cost model contrasts with the constant marginal effect of independent variables in linear cost models. Multiplicative cost functions are based on the assumption of constant elasticities, whereas the elasticity of cost with respect to output varies along linear cost functions. Of course, the specific form of any regression model used to estimate cost/output relations—linear, quadratic, cubic, multiplicative, or otherwise—should always be chosen to reflect the true cost/output relation. Care must be taken to ensure that the model chosen is consistent with underlying economic theory.

AN EXAMPLE OF SHORT-RUN COST ESTIMATION

Accounting cost analysis
Cost estimation based on historical cash outlays and estimates of noncash expenses, as defined in accounting standards.

Statistical cost analysis
Empirically derived estimates of cost/output relations.

Short-run cost/output relations are estimated using accounting, engineering, and statistical methods. **Accounting cost analysis** estimates the cost of production on the basis of the historical record of cash outlays and estimates of noncash expenses tied to production, as defined in professional accounting standards. **Statistical cost analysis** measures the cost of production on the basis of empirically derived estimates of cost/output relations. Accounting techniques typically rely on an underlying assumption of linearity in cost/output relations; statistical methods leave open the possibility of nonlinearity. As such, statistical methods are most appropriate for estimating the fundamental nature of cost/output relations.

Statistical Short-Run Cost Analysis

To illustrate the regression method of statistical short-run cost analysis, consider the example of the Tric-E Razor Company. Weekly razor output in thousands of units and *TVC* in dollars per week are shown for the most recent six-month period

**TABLE 10.1   Total Variable Cost and Average Variable Cost
Data for the Tric-E Razor Company**

Week	Output (thousands)	Total Variable Cost (dollars)	Average Variable Cost ($ per unit)
1	27.5	$4,750	$172.73
2	30.0	5,000	166.67
3	32.5	5,750	176.92
4	40.0	8,500	212.50
5	10.0	4,250	425.00
6	27.5	5,500	200.00
7	30.0	6,000	200.00
8	32.5	5,750	176.92
9	35.0	6,000	171.43
10	37.5	7,000	186.67
11	40.0	9,250	231.25
12	10.0	4,000	400.00
13	12.5	4,250	340.00
14	15.0	4,500	300.00
15	22.5	4,250	188.89
16	25.0	4,750	190.00
17	12.5	4,250	340.00
18	15.0	4,250	283.33
19	17.5	4,500	257.14
20	20.0	4,750	237.50
21	22.5	4,500	200.00
22	25.0	4,500	180.00
23	35.0	6,750	192.86
24	37.5	7,750	206.67
25	17.5	4,250	242.86
26	20.0	4,250	212.50

(26 observations) in Table 10.1. These data suggest the familiar S-shaped total variable cost/output relationship illustrated in Figure 10.5(a). As a result, *AVC* and output display a U-shaped relationship, as shown in Figure 10.5(b). Based on a simple visual scan of the data, a cubic (or third-order polynomial) regression model seems appropriate for estimating both the *TVC* and the *AVC* models. Nevertheless, it is instructive to compare the descriptive capability of these cubic models with the simpler linear and quadratic (second-order polynomial) regression model approaches.

Table 10.2 shows least squares cost-estimation results for linear, quadratic, and cubic models for both *TVC* and *AVC* functions. The underlying S-shaped relationship between true *TVC* and output, and the U-shaped relationship between true *AVC* and output, are readily apparent in these estimation results. Notice the relatively greater descriptive capability displayed by the nonlinear quadratic and cubic cost models. Each of these cost/output relations displays significant nonlinearity.

Observe that the linear model is unable to describe a high proportion of the underlying variation in variable costs. The roughly one-half ($R^2 = 0.58$) to three-

FIGURE 10.5 **Cubic Total Variable Cost and Average Variable Cost Curves for the Tric-E Razor Company**

A cubic cost function provides a good description of the variation in costs experienced by the Tric-E Razor Company.

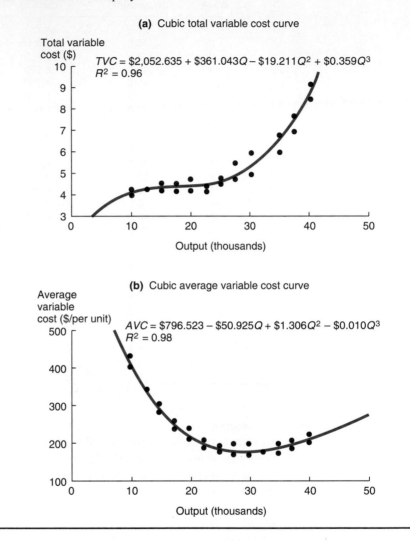

(a) Cubic total variable cost curve

$$TVC = \$2{,}052.635 + \$361.043Q - \$19.211Q^2 + \$0.359Q^3$$
$$R^2 = 0.96$$

Total variable cost (\$)

Output (thousands)

(b) Cubic average variable cost curve

$$AVC = \$796.523 - \$50.925Q + \$1.306Q^2 - \$0.010Q^3$$
$$R^2 = 0.98$$

Average variable cost (\$/per unit)

Output (thousands)

quarters ($R^2 = 0.75$) of variation in variable costs explained by the linear model may not form a reasonable basis for managerial decision making. On the other hand, it is quite possible that the roughly 95 percent of the variation in variable costs explained by the alternative quadratic and cubic cost models forms a reasonable basis for both production-related and marketing-related decisions. At a minimum, the cubic model approach seems to offer a useful starting point for a further and more detailed analysis of the variable cost/output relation.

TABLE 10.2 **Tric-E Razor Company Cost Estimation (*t* statistics in parentheses)**

Total Variable Cost Models

Linear	$TVC = \$2,114.011 + \$129.670Q$ (5.15) (8.44)	$R^2 = 0.75$ S.E.E. = \$732.97
Quadratic	$TVC = \$6,259.366 - \$255.944Q + \$7.712Q^2$ (10.78) (−5.05) (7.72)	$R^2 = 0.93$ S.E.E. = \$395.13
Cubic	$TVC = \$2,052.635 + \$361.043Q - \$19.211Q^2 + \$0.359Q^3$ (1.60) (2.01) (−2.50) (3.52)	$R^2 = 0.96$ S.E.E. = \$323.00

Average Variable Cost Models

Linear	$AVC = \$377.662 - \$5.734Q$ (14.25) (−5.78)	$R^2 = 0.58$ S.E.E. = \$47.35
Quadratic	$AVC = \$680.455 - \$33.901Q + \$0.563Q^2$ (34.41) (−19.66) (16.56)	$R^2 = 0.97$ S.E.E. = \$13.46
Cubic	$AVC = \$796.523 - \$50.925Q + \$1.306Q^2 - \$0.010Q^3$ (16.66) (−7.61) (4.57) (−2.61)	$R^2 = 0.98$ S.E.E. = \$12.02

Notes: TVC = Total Variable Cost (\$)

          Q = Output (thousands)

       AVC = Average Variable Cost (\$)

      S.E.E. = Standard Error of the Estimate

LONG-RUN COST ESTIMATION PROBLEMS

Statistical estimation of long-run cost curves is often somewhat more complex than short-run cost estimation, although similar in many respects. In the long run, all costs are variable, and the problem is to determine the shape of the least-cost production curve for plants of different sizes. Total cost curves must be estimated, and this introduces a number of additional difficulties.

The Problem of Changing Economic Conditions over Time

As with short-run cost analysis, one can analyze long-run cost/output relations by examining a single firm over a significant period of time. In long-run cost analysis, the relevant time frame might encompass monthly data over 10 to 15 years (120 to 180 observations). The dependent variable is total cost; independent variables include output and any other important exogenous or endogenous influences that the cost analyst wants to account for in the cost function. If technology, wage rates, weather, and all other important exogenous and endogenous factors are held constant, then the long-run cost/output relation can be estimated efficiently. If factors such as technology and wage rates are changing, such changes must be meticulously reflected in the cost function to accurately isolate the cost effects of a change in output. If changes in technology, wage rates, and other factors are not accurately reflected in the cost function, then the true cost/output relation is likely to be only crudely estimated.

Unfortunately, it is almost impossible to find situations in which the scale of the organization has been variable enough to allow statistical estimation of a long-run cost curve while general economic conditions have remained constant. The most serious problem that must be confronted in long-run cost analysis is that absolute and relative wage rates, raw material costs, equipment expenses, technology, and so on, are *always* changing over time. For example, the rapid pace of technical advance in many industries makes production methods obsolete in as few as five to ten years, if not sooner. When technology is rapidly changing, estimated long-run cost functions bear little resemblance to the relevant long-run cost function necessary for planning purposes. Similarly, when wage rates, raw material prices, or machinery expenses change dramatically over time, it becomes difficult to rely on historical cost/output relations as a guide to future cost expectations.

The Problem of Differing Economic Conditions at One Point in Time

Because of the difficulties posed by changing economic conditions over time, cross section regression analysis is frequently relied upon in the study of long-run cost/output relations. Cross section cost analysis entails the study of cost/output relations for various plants, firms, or industries at a given point in time. In contrast, time series cost analysis involves the examination of cost/output relations for a given plant, firm, or industry over a significant period of time.

The cross section cost analysis technique compares different-size firms (or plants) at a point in time by regressing total costs against a set of independent variables. The key independent variable is again a measure of output, and other independent variables—such as regional wage rates, fuel costs, and the like—are included to account for the effect on cost of factors other than the level of output.

The use of cross section information as opposed to time series data for estimating long-run cost functions reduces some estimation problems while others might be magnified. For example, since cross section data incorporates input prices at a given point in time, the problem of economywide changes in prices is removed. A different problem can arise, however, because factor input prices have a tendency to vary due to different supply/demand conditions in regional markets. Unless all sample observations are located in the same region, interregional price variations have the potential to distort the analysis.

Another difficulty in cross section studies can be traced to firm-by-firm variations in accounting procedures. Different depreciation, amortization, or cost accrual methods among firms can greatly distort empirically estimated cost/output relations unless the data are adjusted for accounting policy differences. A similar distortion in statistical cost analysis can arise if various firms or plants use differing compensation schemes. One firm might pay relatively high salaries and hourly wages but have no profit-sharing arrangement with its employees. Another firm might pay relatively low salaries and hourly wages but might have a considerable profit-sharing program. If labor costs are to be comparable across firms, differences that are difficult to estimate in compensation packages must be allowed for to facilitate meaningful cost comparisons.

FIGURE 10.6 **Estimating Long-Run Average Cost Curves with Cross Section Data**

Cross section data can be used to estimate the long-run average cost curve for an industry at a given point in time.

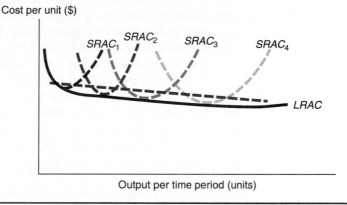

The Problem of Variable Economic Efficiency

A basic assumption in cost/output analysis is that all firms are producing output efficiently given the scale of their operation. Differences in unit costs are presumed to reflect size-associated advantages in production due to economies of scale or size-associated disadvantages due to diseconomies of scale. All firms are believed to be operating in an efficient manner and are using the most efficient plant available for providing whatever level of output they are producing. If this assumption holds true, the empirically estimated cost/output relation traces a long-run cost curve, such as that shown as *LRAC* in Figure 10.6. If this basic assumption is violated, and some firms are operating at less than peak efficiency, then the least squares regression line will lie above the true *LRAC* curve. In this instance, estimated costs will overstate true costs.

Even more serious than the prospect of a uniform overstatement of average costs is the possibility that the curvature of the long-run average cost curve might be distorted by variable rates of economic efficiency among large versus small firms. For example, suppose that larger firms are more likely than smaller firms to employ an optimal plant size. If the smaller firms in Figure 10.6 are operating well to the right of their optimal output levels, the estimated *LRAC* curve will have a downward slope that is much steeper than the true *LRAC* curve. This small-firm bias will cause empirically estimated cost/output relations to overstate the magnitude of economies of scale in the industry. If larger firms tend to be less conscientious than smaller firms in terms of their scale of plant selection, the estimated *LRAC* curve could have a downward slope that is less steep than the true *LRAC* curve. Such a large-firm bias will cause empirically estimated cost/output relations to understate the magnitude of scale economies. Similarly, scale economies may be underestimated because of a selection bias that results if small, high-cost firms fail to compete successfully, go bankrupt, and thus fail to get included in the cost study.

EMPIRICAL ESTIMATES OF
COST/OUTPUT RELATIONS

Several empirical studies have been undertaken to establish the character of cost/output relations, particularly short-run cost/output relations. Investigations covering industries as diverse as electric power generation, textile and steel production, and retailing have found, by and large, that both industry and firm average cost functions tend to be linear. This implies constant marginal costs, whereas the law of diminishing marginal productivity described in Chapter 8 leads one to expect that most real-world short-run marginal cost functions would be increasing. The reasons why most empirically estimated short-run marginal cost functions are linear are obvious when one considers the dynamics of the changing economy, employment practices, and the effects of transportation costs.

Cost/Output Relations for Goods and Services

U-shaped average cost functions

Average cost functions that first fall, then rise.

L-shaped average cost functions

Average cost functions that first fall, then become horizontal.

When marginal costs per unit are constant, average costs are also constant, and constant returns to scale predominate. Size leads to neither significant disadvantages nor significant advantages in production. Increasing marginal costs impart the traditional U shape to the average variable cost curve. Such **U-shaped average cost functions** are descriptive of firms and industries that display first decreasing, then constant, then increasing average costs. **L-shaped average cost functions** are descriptive of firms and industries that display first decreasing, then constant average costs. While theory predicts U-shaped or L-shaped average cost functions in competitive industries, most empirically estimated cost functions display constant marginal costs. Several reasons exist to explain why empirically estimated short-run costs are constant.

Perhaps the most obvious explanation as to why constant marginal costs are commonly observed is that the changing nature of the modern economy favors constant-cost industries. The most conspicuous characteristic of the post–World War II explosion in economic growth is that it tends to greatly favor the production of constant-cost service industries rather than goods-producing sectors that might display increasing returns to scale in production.

Table 10.3 illustrates the breakdown of current-dollar GDP among goods, services, and structures over the 1959–1991 period. At the beginning of this period, GDP totaled $494.2 billion, with $249.3 represented by goods production, $180.7 billion by services, $61.7 billion by structures. The 1959 shares of overall GDP were 50.4 percent for goods production, 36.6 percent for services, and 12.5 percent for structures. By 1991, GDP totaled $5,671.8 billion, reflecting an annual growth rate of 7.9 percent per year. Over this same period, goods production rose by only 7 percent per year to $2,192.8 billion, whereas growth in the provision of services averaged 9.2 percent per year to $3,012.7 billion. In the U.S. economy today, the provision of services far outstrips goods production—the value of services is more than 137 percent of the value of goods produced.

The rapid growth of services has direct implications for empirically estimated cost/output relations. Service industries are typically labor intensive rather than capital intensive; constant marginal costs and constant returns to scale predominate. Barber shops, dry cleaners, grocery stores, movie theaters, real estate agen-

TABLE 10.3   Shares of Current-Year GDP Represented by Goods, Services, and Structures, 1950–1991

Year	GDP in Current Dollars	Goods Current Dollars	(%)	Services Current Dollars	(%)	Structures Current Dollars	(%)
1991	5,671.8	2,192.8	38.7	3,012.7	53.1	466.4	8.2
1990	5,513.8	2,167.6	39.3	2,834.0	51.4	512.2	9.3
1989	5,244.0	2,098.1	40.0	2,634.7	50.2	511.3	9.8
1988	4,900.4	1,942.0	39.6	2,460.9	50.2	497.5	10.2
1987	4,539.9	1,794.5	39.5	2,267.2	49.9	478.2	10.5
1986	4,268.6	1,705.3	39.9	2,097.3	49.1	466.0	10.9
1985	4,038.7	1,652.6	40.9	1,939.0	48.0	447.1	11.1
1984	3,777.2	1,591.9	42.1	1,770.7	46.9	414.7	11.0
1983	3,405.0	1,407.3	41.3	1,636.3	48.1	361.5	10.6
1982	3,149.6	1,315.0	41.8	1,494.2	47.4	340.4	10.8
1981	3,030.6	1,324.6	43.7	1,357.4	44.8	348.6	11.5
1980	2,708.0	1,176.2	43.4	1,215.4	44.9	316.4	11.7
1979	2,488.6	1,100.2	44.2	1,079.6	43.4	308.8	12.4
1978	2,232.7	989.1	44.3	975.5	43.7	268.1	12.0
1977	1,974.1	880.4	44.6	870.4	44.1	223.3	11.3
1976	1,768.4	798.8	45.2	782.2	44.2	187.5	10.6
1975	1,585.9	715.1	45.1	706.9	44.6	163.8	10.3
1974	1,458.6	662.8	45.4	631.3	43.3	164.5	11.3
1973	1,349.6	616.6	45.7	571.0	42.3	161.9	12.0
1972	1,207.0	537.4	44.5	523.6	43.4	145.9	12.1
1971	1,097.2	493.3	45.0	476.6	43.4	127.2	11.6
1970	1,010.7	467.0	46.2	433.8	42.9	108.6	10.7
1969	959.5	456.5	47.6	395.4	41.2	107.1	11.2
1968	889.3	428.7	48.2	362.8	40.8	98.9	11.1
1967	814.3	395.4	48.6	330.4	40.6	88.5	10.9
1966	769.8	379.7	49.3	302.3	39.3	86.9	11.3
1965	702.7	342.7	48.8	275.4	39.2	83.8	11.9
1964	648.0	313.1	48.3	256.2	39.5	77.6	12.0
1963	603.1	293.0	48.6	237.5	39.4	71.9	11.9
1962	571.6	281.5	49.2	222.3	38.9	67.0	11.7
1961	531.8	260.9	49.1	207.7	39.1	62.8	11.8
1960	513.4	257.3	50.1	194.2	37.8	61.1	11.9
1959	494.2	249.3	50.4	180.7	36.6	61.7	12.5

Note: Dollar figures are in billions of dollars; percentages may not add to 100% due to rounding.

Source: *Economic Report of the President* (Washington, D.C.: U.S. Government Printing Office, 1992); pp. 298, 300.

cies, restaurants, retail boutiques, styling salons, and a host of other service establishments exhaust all available economies of scale at very low employment and output levels. As a result, empirically estimated cost curves in these and most other service industries tend to display constant marginal and average costs.

Even in manufacturing, the traditional bastion of large-scale enterprise, the extent of economies of scale is much less than commonly perceived. Table 10.4 shows the size distribution of manufacturing establishments according to two-digit Standard Industrial Classification codes. (As will be described in Chapter 12, two-digit SIC codes identify major groups of industries; numbers between 20

TABLE 10.4 Major Manufacturing Group Statistics by Employment Size of Establishment

Major Group	Total Number of Establishments	Establishments with an Average Number of Employees of:									
		1–4	5–9	10–19	20–49	50–99	100–249	250–499	500–999	1,000–2,499	>2,500
Food and Kindred Products (20)	22,130	5,091	2,974	3,384	4,383	2,609	2,310	925	345	98	11
Tobacco Products (21)	163	46	13	10	21	15	39	18	14	6	4
Textile Mill Products (22)	6,630	1,378	725	864	1,197	774	894	487	240	64	7
Apparel and Other Textile Products (23)	24,391	6,468	3,251	3,765	5,057	2,784	2,109	738	188	28	3
Lumber and Wood Products (24)	32,984	15,752	6,230	4,689	3,643	1,529	910	197	28	6	0
Furniture and Fixtures (25)	10,003	3,109	1,638	1,627	1,735	897	649	23	92	22	2
Paper and Allied Products (26)	6,381	754	580	957	1,449	1,031	1,103	29 4	146	65	2
Printing and Publishing (27)	53,406	23,174	11,015	8,346	6,145	2,525	1,493	422	176	88	22
Chemicals and Allied Products (28)	11,901	3,119	1,977	2,026	2,170	1,095	822	347	205	105	35
Petroleum and Coal Products (29)	2,322	692	440	342	368	197	153	63	43	22	2
Rubber and Miscellaneous Plastic Products (30)	13,449	3,193	2,043	2,235	2,806	1,579	1,143	301	91	53	5
Leather and Leather Products (31)	2,735	711	341	370	457	304	298	206	42	5	1
Stone, Clay, and Glass Products (32)	16,545	5,352	3,261	3,179	2,720	950	711	233	111	26	2
Primary Metal Industries (33)	7,061	1,152	880	1,125	1,452	905	910	341	174	73	49
Fabricated Metal Products (34)	35,560	8,799	6,086	7,033	7,369	3,228	2,123	630	199	69	24
Machinery (except electrical) (35)	52,912	17,847	10,855	9,946	7,642	2,984	2,088	840	437	215	58
Electric and Electronic Equipment (36)	16,453	4,201	2,176	2,242	2,893	1,694	1,672	806	440	227	102
Transportation Equipment (37)	9,443	2,806	1,393	1,444	1,476	806	740	332	186	122	138
Instruments and Related Products (38)	8,045	2,443	1,328	1,259	1,255	661	589	298	125	72	15
Miscellaneous Manufacturing Products (39)	15,871	7,046	2,867	2,390	2,003	803	525	164	51	22	0
All Manufacturing Industries	**348,385**	**113,133**	**60,073**	**57,233**	**56,241**	**27,370**	**21,281**	**7,874**	**3,333**	**1,388**	**482**

Source: 1982 *Census of Manufacturers: General Summary*, Part 2, *Industry Statistics by Employment Size of Establishment* (Washington D.C., U.S. Government Printing Office, 1985.)

and 40 identify groups of manufacturing industries.) Notice that 113,120 out of the 348,385 manufacturing establishments, or 32.5%, have as few as 1 to 4 employees. Fully 230,426, or 66.1%, of all manufacturing establishments have less than 20 employees. Only 1,876, or 0.5%, of all manufacturing establishments are giant factories with 1,000 or more employees. More than ever before, customers demand a very high level of product quality that often entails a specialized combination of goods *and* services that favor shorter production runs. The traditional assembly line is ideally suited for mass production; it is less well suited for production of the high-quality niche products increasingly demanded by consumers.

Employment Practices and Cost/ Output Relations

Because the dynamics of the modern economy tend to favor the growth of constant-cost service industries, the prevalence of empirically estimated U-shaped and L-shaped average cost curves has lessened. However, such cost curves are seldom observed even in goods-producing manufacturing industries that display increasing-cost or decreasing-cost characteristics.

In theory, the quantity of a fixed factor employed in the production process is held constant in the short run as changeable quantities of variable factors are utilized. Theory states that once a certain minimum level of production is reached, variable inputs exhibit diminishing marginal productivity because of limitations imposed by the fixed factor. In real-world production systems, however, fixed factors are frequently set with respect to cost but are quite changeable with respect to actual usage. A firm producing electronic devices may vary output by changing the number of assembly stations it operates, keeping the ratio of capital (fixed factor) to labor (variable factor) actually employed constant over short-run production periods. Textile mills, where the number of spindles in operation varies with output, and electricity generation plants, where the number of generators in actual use varies to increase or decrease output, provide other examples of variable employment of "fixed" factors. Given the current state of technology, it is simply uneconomic to vary capital/labor ratios in many industries.

Negotiated work rules can also add to the fixity of capital and labor input ratios. Many labor contracts specify within a narrow range the combination of labor and capital equipment that can be utilized. In situations such as these, the rate of short-run capacity utilization is nearly constant regardless of the production level. Since fixed and variable inputs are being used in constant proportions over wide ranges of output, the law of diminishing marginal productivity is not observed, and constant marginal costs emerge in empirical cost analyses.

Of course, increasing average costs will never be observed in actual business practice, so long as manufacturers have the opportunity to produce output at smaller, and therefore more efficient, plants. This means that the upward portions of U-shaped and average cost curves are seldom, if ever, seen in actual practice. Output levels that are too low or too high to be economic are simply not possible. Similarly, the higher average costs indicated by the upward portion of an L-shaped average cost function are seldom economic and, therefore, rarely observed. This is always true in competitive industries but especially so in competitive industries with significant transportation costs.

Transportation Costs and Cost/Output Relations

As described in Chapter 9, transportation costs play an important role in determining the minimum efficient scale of operation. Terminal, line-haul, and inventory charges associated with moving output from production facilities to customers represent a substantial share of the overall cost of many products.

Line-haul expenses for labor and fuel are typically larger than the sum of terminal charges for loading and unloading plus inventory costs related to the length of transit time. Since line-haul costs are typically constant on a per mile basis, an increase in transportation costs per unit usually means a constant per unit increase in average costs. As shown in Chapter 9, as more output is produced at a given production facility it becomes necessary to reach out to more distant customers. This typically leads to a commensurate increase in transportation costs per unit sold by firms that feature large centralized production facilities. Transport costs are an important concern, even for firms that enjoy steeply sloped long-run average cost curves that reflect a rapid decline in average production costs as output expands. Such firms often find that average total costs are constant or even rising when the transportation costs associated with serving distant customers are considered. As a result, regional production at small plants close to major markets is favored over production at large centralized facilities. The size of production facilities therefore tends to be limited by the size of the regional market that can be efficiently served. This gives rise to a number of regional production facilities with fairly constant plant sizes and constant average costs per unit.

The tendency toward regional production and constant average costs is most obvious when transportation costs are large in relation to production costs, as is the case with milk, bottled soft drinks, gravel, cement, and many other products with high weight-to-value (or bulk-to-value) ratios. When transportation costs are relatively insignificant—as is the case for relatively low-weight, compact, high-value products such as writing pens, electronic components, and medical instruments—markets are national or international in scope, and declining average costs can give rise to production at only a few large plants (see Table 10.4). However, low transportation costs do not necessarily lead to centralized production when only modest advantages of large-scale production are present.

ALTERNATIVE COST ESTIMATION TECHNIQUES

Because of the difficulties involved with obtaining satisfactory estimates of long-run cost/output relations, alternative cost estimation methods have been developed. Some of these techniques have proven useful for circumstances in which statistical cost estimation is made difficult by a lack of sufficient reliable data. In other instances, alternative cost estimation techniques offer a useful check to the reliability of statistical methods.

MANAGERIAL APPLICATION 10.3

Estimating U.S.–Japan Labor Cost Differentials

Executives of Caterpillar, Inc., made an eye-opening claim during their bitter 1991–1992 labor dispute with the United Auto Workers (UAW) union. Hourly labor costs at the construction equipment company, they contend, are 25 to 30 percent higher than those at its chief rival, Komatsu Ltd. of Japan. Unfortunately, substantiating such claims is very difficult. "We don't know exactly what Komatsu's costs are," Caterpillar spokesman William Lane acknowledges. During the 5½-month-long strike that ended in April 1992, Lane echoed the labor-cost statements made by Chairman Donald Fites, Group President Glen Barton, and others. Caterpillar officials explain they based their analysis not on Komatsu figures but on labor-cost data from two Japanese facilities of Caterpillar's own joint venture with Mitsubishi Heavy Industries Ltd., Shin Caterpillar Mitsubishi Ltd.

Scrutiny of the labor-cost claims made by both Peoria, Illinois-based Caterpillar and the UAW illustrates just how difficult, and deceptive, such comparisons can sometimes be. Take away health care expenses, for example, and actual wages appear to be about the same. Add in labor cost differences due to dissimilar perks, living costs, and currency exchange rates, and even labor cost experts throw up their hands in confusion. Sam Bernstein of Hewitt Associates tries to steer clients away from direct comparisons of labor costs between U.S. and Japanese firms. The employee-benefits consultant says it is possible to come up with five or six ways to do it. Each would show very different results, yet each would be technically correct.

Caterpillar is confident that its own labor-cost figures are accurate, although company officials refuse to provide details on the similarity between its joint-venture labor costs and those of Komatsu. This is despite the fact that Caterpillar's labor-cost claims were a crucial part of its argument that any contract with the UAW shouldn't follow the pattern set at Deere & Co., Caterpillar's largest domestic rival. The UAW isn't any more forthcoming than Caterpillar in substantiating its December 1991 claim that Komatsu workers in Japan earn 94 percent of the $20.91 hourly compensation of UAW-Caterpillar workers in the U.S. The UAW refers to the International Metalworkers' Federation as the source of Komatsu data but refuses to elaborate or make the statistics publicly available. The UAW contends that useful comparisons must take productivity differences into account to adjust for what the union believes is the higher productivity of Caterpillar workers.

It is interesting to look at the numbers behind the Caterpillar-UAW dispute. Even Caterpillar concedes that when the cost of benefits is eliminated, wages at Caterpillar and Komatsu are very close. Caterpillar figures that cash compensation for Shin Caterpillar workers in Japan is about $2 per hour less than the $22.26 an hour paid to its UAW workers in the United States. However, benefits as health care, pensions and time off add another $10 per hour to Caterpillar's U.S. labor costs. Differences in health care expenses explains much of this gap. Komatsu workers are covered under Japan's national health insurance program, and the premium for each worker is 8.7 percent of annual salary before bonus, or an indicated average of about 310,000 yen (roughly $2,430). Komatsu is responsible for 59.8 percent, and the workers pay the rest. In contrast, Caterpillar's health-care expenses in 1990 averaged about $6,500 for each U.S. worker, and more in 1991. Caterpillar pays the full cost for UAW members but now requires that workers use specified doctors and hospitals.

As global competition intensifies, disputes over labor-cost differences are bound to escalate. Based upon this comparison of U.S. and Japanese labor cost differentials, the conflict over national health insurance in the United States is likely to be a major battleground. Large unionized companies like Caterpillar are pushing hard for national health insurance as a means of shifting some of their production costs onto taxpayers. However, whether or not Caterpillar and others can reduce health care costs more effectively at the ballot box than they have at the bargaining table remains to be seen.

Source: Robert L. Rose and Masayoshi Kanabayashi, "Comparing U.S.-Japan Labor-Cost Data Can be Murky: Claims in Caterpillar-UAW Dispute Are Easier to Voice than Verify." *The Wall Street Journal,* June 4, 1992, B3.

Survivor Analysis

Survivor principle

Postulates that efficient firms with relatively lower average costs survive and prosper through time.

Survivor analysis

The systematic study of firm or plant size classes that are relatively efficient in the sense of maintaining or growing their share of industry output over time.

The **survivor principle** was developed by Nobel laureate George Stigler. According to Stigler, efficient firms with relatively lower average costs will survive and prosper through time. Inefficient firms with relatively higher average costs will succumb to competitive pressures and die. Therefore, by examining changes in the size of an industry over time, one can determine the nature of industry cost/output relations.

Survivor analysis is the systematic study of industry output patterns to determine firm or plant size classes that are relatively efficient in the sense of maintaining or growing their share of industry output over time. Specifically, one must classify the firms in an industry by size and calculate the share of industry output or capacity accounted for by each size class over time. If the market share of one class declines over time, that size of firm or production facility is assumed to be relatively inefficient. If market share increases, firms or plants of that size are presumed to be relatively efficient and to have lower average costs.

Survivor analysis has been used to examine the returns to scale characteristic of several industries. In a pioneering study, Stigler examined the distribution of steel production among firms of varying sizes.[1] For the period 1930–1951, Stigler found that the percentage of industry output accounted for by the smallest and largest classes declined, while the output share of medium-size firms increased. Stigler also applied the survivor technique to the automobile industry and found that the smallest firms showed a continual decline in their share of total industry output. Stigler concluded from this that average costs decline with increasing size. Moreover, market-share losses by smaller firms were distributed equally among medium-size and larger firms, indicating first increasing, then constant returns to scale. In the absence of any indication of diseconomies of scale at very high output levels, Stigler concluded that the automobile industry's long-run average cost curve is L-shaped. Other economists have used the survivor technique to study economies of scale in banking, cement, and many other industries. Today it is considered an especially useful approach in industry studies when individual firms are reluctant to release proprietary cost information for competitive reasons.

Although the survivor technique is a valuable tool for examining cost/output relations, it does have limitations. It presumes that survival is directly related to minimization of long-run average costs. As is demonstrated in more detail in Chapter 12, this premise implicitly assumes that the firms examined are operating in a highly competitive market structure. If markets are protected by regulation or barriers to entry, even inefficient smaller firms can survive for extended periods. High transportation costs also make survival possible for strategically located firms despite operating inefficiencies. In some industries, smaller firms with relatively high average costs also survive by emphasizing personalized service or customized production. Successful product differentiation often makes it possible for smaller firms not only to survive but to flourish in the face of competition from larger, more cost-efficient rivals.

Finally, because of the very long-run nature of the analysis, the survivor technique is particularly susceptible to the problem of distorted results arising from

---

[1] George J. Stigler, "The Economies of Scale," *Journal of Law and Economics* 1 (October 1958): 54–71.

changing technology. In many instances, inventions or innovations over time favor firms in specific size classes. Resulting changes in the distribution of industry output may reveal less about movements along industry long-run average cost curves (i.e., economies of scale) than they do about downward shifts in cost/output relations.

Engineering Cost Analysis

Engineering cost analysis

Calculation of expected cost on the basis of physical production relationships and the expected cost of necessary inputs.

When new production methods are contemplated, historical cost/output relations are unreliable predictors of expected cost relations. When new product introductions are considered, historical cost/output data are simply unavailable. In both instances, some alternative to statistical and survivor cost estimation techniques is required. Such situations are ideally suited for **engineering cost analysis.**

Engineering cost analysis involves calculation of the expected cost of production on the basis of physical production relationships and the expected cost of necessary inputs. The engineering method of cost analysis is based on the physical relations expressed in the production function for a particular product or firm. The optimal input combination for producing any given output quantity is determined on the basis of knowledge concerning the production technology to be employed. Expected cost curves are formulated by multiplying each input level derived from the least-cost input combination by each input price and then summing to develop the relevant cost function.

Engineering cost analysis comes closer than any other estimation method to reflecting the timeless nature of theoretical cost functions. It is based on currently available technology, and it alleviates the possibility of confounding results through improper data observations. Whereas the data used for statistical cost estimation may be contaminated by any number of extraneous factors, engineering cost estimation avoids such complications by coupling current price quotations from suppliers with estimates of required input quantities.

The engineering method of cost estimation has proven especially useful for examining cost/output relations in such areas as oil refining and exploration, chemical production, and nuclear power generation. Engineering techniques have pitfalls, however, and care must be exercised to develop accurate cost functions using this method. The difficulty often comes in trying to extend engineering production functions beyond the range of existing systems or in going from pilot-plant operations to full-scale production facilities. Unexpected production delays, strikes, and changes in the cost and availability of raw material inputs can all result in significant engineering cost estimation error. While the engineering method can provide a useful alternative to statistical cost estimation, it too must be applied with great care if costs are to be estimated accurately.

SUMMARY

Managerial economics focuses on the change in benefits and costs associated with management decisions. As a result, cost considerations play an important role in all managerial decisions. This chapter considers a variety of cost estimation techniques useful for obtaining reliable cost information.

• Most difficulties encountered in statistical cost analysis arise from errors in the specification of **relevant cost categories,** or appropriate divisions of costs among fixed and variable components. Managerial decisions relate largely to future activities and events. Relevant costs are **future costs** as opposed to being current or historical costs.

• Economic cost categories are often difficult to identify with precision. For example, calculating the rate of **economic depreciation** for capital equipment is seldom easy. Economic depreciation is the rate of market-value decline for productive assets. The calculation of **semivariable costs,** or expenses that rise or fall in a less than strictly proportional basis with changes in output, is likewise troublesome. Correspondingly difficult is accounting for changes in plant and equipment during the **cost observation period,** or time frame for cost analysis. **Inflation,** or rising prices, and **deflation,** or falling prices, often give rise to serious cost estimation problems.

• For a great many production systems, **linear cost functions,** or straight-line relations, provide an adequate fit of cost/output data. However, a linear relation is usually only an approximation that is valid over limited output ranges to an underlying **curvilinear cost function.** A curvilinear cost/output relation is one that deviates from a straight line in a smooth, continuous fashion.

• One of the most prevalent nonlinear models for cost estimation is the **quadratic cost function.** A quadratic cost function involves both first-order and second-order (squared) terms for the output variable. A **cubic cost function** involves first-order, second-order (squared), and third-order (cubed) terms for the output variable.

• Another familiar nonlinear regression model used in cost estimation is the **multiplicative cost function.** The multiplicative model is used when the marginal effect of each independent variable is thought to depend on the value of all independent variables in the regression equation.

• **Accounting cost analysis** estimates the cost of production on the basis of the historical record of cash outlays and estimates of noncash expenses tied to production, as defined in professional accounting standards. **Statistical cost analysis** measures the cost of production on the basis of empirically derived estimates of cost/output relations.

• **U-shaped average cost functions** are descriptive of firms and industries that display first decreasing, then constant, then increasing average costs. **L-shaped average cost functions** are descriptive of firms and industries that display first decreasing, then constant average costs.

• The **survivor principle** posits that efficient firms with relatively lower average costs will survive and prosper through time. Inefficient firms with relatively higher average costs will succumb to competitive pressures and die. **Survivor analysis** is the systematic study of industry output patterns to determine firm or plant size classes that are relatively efficient in the sense of maintaining or growing their share of industry output over time.

• **Engineering cost analysis** involves calculation of the expected cost of production on the basis of physical production relationships and the expected cost of necessary inputs. The engineering method of cost analysis is based on the physical relations expressed in the production function for a particular product or firm.

It is particularly appropriate in the case of new product introductions and when new production methods are contemplated.

This chapter seeks to identify some of the most important strengths and weaknesses of commonly employed cost estimation techniques. Each of the methods examined has its own virtues and problems. Successful managers are aware of both and seek to employ that method or combination of methods that holds the best potential for discovering the true nature of cost/output relations.

Questions

Q10.1   For purposes of cost estimation, how long is the short-run time period?

Q10.2   Name and briefly elaborate upon three common problems encountered in short-run cost analysis.

Q10.3   Short-run statistical cost studies have been reported for a wide variety of industries. Long-run cost studies, on the other hand, have been restricted to a few industries. Why do you suppose so many more short-run studies than long-run studies have been conducted?

Q10.4   The law of diminishing productivity leads one to expect that short-run marginal (and average variable) cost curves will be U-shaped. Nevertheless, most empirical studies find constant marginal costs for many firms. Why?

Q10.5   What requirements must be met before a long-run cost function can be estimated?

Q10.6   Is a linear model appropriate for estimating the point of minimum efficient scale in an industry?

Q10.7   For long-run statistical cost estimation, cross section analysis rather than time series analysis is used, partly to overcome the problem of changing technology. Does the use of cross section data eliminate this problem? Why or why not?

Q10.8   If the total cost/output relation is analyzed using regression analysis, can the intercept term be interpreted as an unbiased estimate of fixed costs?

Q10.9   Does the survivor technique for estimating long-run cost/output relations overcome the problem of changing technology?

Q10.10   Discuss the similarities between the engineering technique of cost estimation and the market experiment approach to demand estimation.

Self-Test Problem

Environmental & Engineering Controls (EEC) is a multinational manufacturer of materials handling, accessory, and control equipment. During the past year, EEC has had the following cost experience following introduction of a new fluid control device:

Output	Cost 1	Cost 2	Cost 3
0	$17,000	$11,000	$ 0
100	10,000	7,000	1,000
200	8,000	13,000	2,000
500	20,000	10,000	6,000
900	14,000	12,000	10,000

continued

Output	Cost 1	Cost 2	Cost 3
1,000	8,000	19,000	11,000
1,200	15,000	16,000	13,000
1,300	14,000	15,000	15,000
1,400	6,000	16,000	18,000
1,500	18,000	23,000	19,000
1,700	8,000	21,000	22,000
1,900	16,000	25,000	24,000

A. Calculate the mean (average observation), median (middle observation), range, and standard deviation for output and each cost category variable.

B. Describe each cost category as fixed or variable based upon the following simple linear cost function regression results where COST is the dependent Y variable and OUTPUT is the independent X variable.

The first simple regression equation is

$$\text{COST } 1 = \$13{,}123 - \$0.30 \text{ OUTPUT.}$$

Predictor	Coefficient	Standard Deviation	t Ratio	p
Constant	13123	2635	4.98	0.000
OUTPUT	−0.297	2.285	−0.13	0.899

S.E.E. = $4,871, R^2 = 0.2%, $\bar{R}^2$ = 0.0%, F statistic = 0.02 (p = 0.899)

The second simple regression equation is

$$\text{COST } 2 = \$8{,}455 + \$7.40 \text{ OUTPUT.}$$

Predictor	Coefficient	Standard Deviation	t Ratio	p
Constant	8455	1550	5.45	0.000
OUTPUT	7.397	1.345	5.50	0.000

S.E.E. = $2,866, R^2 = 75.2%, $\bar{R}^2$ = 72.7%, F statistic = 30.26 (p = 0.000)

The third simple regression equation is

$$\text{COST } 3 = -\$662 + \$12.7 \text{ OUTPUT}$$

Predictor	Coefficient	Standard Deviation	t Ratio	p
Constant	−661.5	488.4	−1.35	0.205
OUTPUT	12.7298	0.4236	30.05	0.000

S.E.E. = $902.8, R^2 = 98.9%, $\bar{R}^2$ = 98.8%, F statistic = 903.1 (p = 0.000)

C. Are the quadratic and cubic cost functions likely to improve upon the level of fit provided by the linear cost function? Is it likely that such models would *reduce* the overall level of cost explanation?

D. What other independent *X* variables might the analyst like to include in such a cost analysis?

Solution to Self-Test Problem

A. Variable descriptive statistics for the level of output and each cost category over the past year are as follows:

N	Mean	Median	Standard Deviation	Minimum	Maximum	Output
12	975	1,100	643	0	1,900
COST 1	12	12,833	14,000	4,648	6,000	20,000
COST 2	12	15,667	15,500	5,483	7,000	25,000
COST 3	12	11,750	12,000	8,226	0	24,000

B. There is no apparent relation at all between COST 1 and OUTPUT. As a result, this cost category appears to be fixed in nature. On the other hand, there seems to be a very close linear relation between cost categories COST 2 and COST 3 and OUTPUT. Each of these cost categories can be described as variable in nature.

C. Yes, the quadratic and cubic cost function techniques hold some promise for improving upon the level of fit provided by the linear cost function. Particularly in the case of COST 1 and COST 2, the simple linear cost function offers a very modest level of explanation. In both instances, the possibility of important nonlinear influences may be worth investigating. In the case of COST 3, the linear model is able to explain a very high level of cost variation. This cost category appears to vary on a constant per unit basis, and quadratic or cubic approaches may offer little in the way of additional explanation. In any event, cost functions that employ quadratic (second-order) and cubic (third-order) approaches cannot reduce the level of variation explained by the linear regression model because they add to the number of potential explanatory variables. The coefficient of variation, R^2, cannot fall with a rise in the number of explanatory variables; at worst, the addition of extraneous explanatory variables leads to no increase in R^2. However, when extraneous independent variables are added to a cost model, the *adjusted R^2*, or $\bar{R}^2$ is reduced. Of course, economic theory must be relied upon to determine the variables that should be either introduced or deleted from any given model used for cost estimation.

D. Other independent *X* variables that the cost analyst might like to incorporate in such an analysis include any exogenous and endogenous factors that influence the level of cost. Exogenous factors outside the control of the firm might include changes in raw materials prices, changes in the cost of energy, weather patterns, and so on. Endogenous factors that are within the control of the firm that might be included are the mix of skilled and unskilled labor employed, the vintage of machinery used, changes in the speed of assembly, and so on.

Problems

P10.1 **Cost Estimation Issues.** Explain whether each of the following statements is true or false, and explain why.

A. Fixed costs do not vary with output and can safely be eliminated from the short-run cost estimation process.

B. Mistakes occur in the specification of relevant cost categories because of the difficulty of differentiating fixed costs from variable costs.

C. Statistical analysis of accounting cost information avoids the measurement error problems typical of accounting cost relations.

D. For most depreciable assets, both time and usage costs should be included in short-run cost estimation.

E. All input price changes must be eliminated to provide a reasonable basis for time series cost function analysis.

P10.2   **Empirical Cost Functions.** Answer whether each of the following statements is true or false, and explain why.

A. If a given empirical cost function has an R^2 of 0.90, the model fails to explain 10 percent of the cost variation.

B. A linear statistical cost function implies a constant effect on average costs per unit following a rise in wage rates.

C. The problem of extrapolation outside the observation range is more serious for linear as opposed to curvilinear cost functions.

D. The cost effect of an increase in energy process depends on the level of output in a multiplicative cost model.

E. The marginal cost relation derived from a cubic cost function is itself a linear function of output.

P10.3   **Linear Cost Functions.** Assume that a linear statistical cost curve of the following form provides an adequate explanation of short-run total variable costs for a firm during a given observation period:

$$C = b_0 + b_1 Q + \sum_{i=2}^{N} b_i X_i .$$

Indicate whether each of the following statements is true or false, and explain why.

A. X_i designates a variety of independent variables whose nonoutput-related cost effects the analyst wants to account for.

B. A cost elasticity estimate greater than 1 suggests increasing returns to scale.

C. The coefficient b_1 provides an estimate of marginal costs and average variable costs per unit.

D. The coefficient b_0 can be interpreted as the firm's fixed costs.

E. In a cost function of this type, the effects of a rise in energy prices are independent of a change in labor costs.

P10.4   **Cost/Output Analysis.** Manhattan Couriers, Inc. (MCI), provides same-day package delivery service to New York publishers at a price of $5 for each package delivered. Of this amount, the accounting-based estimate of profit contribution per unit is $1.25. MCI is considering an attempt to differentiate its service from several other competitors by providing insurance against loss caused by fire, theft, and so on. If offered, insured delivery would increase MCI's unit cost by 25 cents per package delivery. Current monthly profits are $5,000 on 12,000 package deliveries per month.

A. Assuming that average variable costs are constant at all output levels, what is MCI's total cost function before the proposed change?

B. What will be the total cost function if insured package delivery is offered?

C. Assuming that delivery prices remain stable at $5, estimate the percentage increase in deliveries necessary to maintain current profit levels.

P10.5 **Relevant Cost Categories.** Arnold Jackson, chief operating officer for TransAllied, Inc., is evaluating a senior management proposal calling for the company to build and test new custom machinery for a valued customer. TransAllied would receive $1.4 million for the work, and management believes the machinery can be built and tested using existing facilities. However, one piece of test equipment would have to be rented at a cost of $45,000. Labor requirements are estimated at 8,000 hours, and TransAllied calculates labor costs at $110 per hour. This labor cost is derived by adding a 20 percent fixed overhead charge to actual direct labor costs, plus a 100 percent charge for the firm's required profit margin. This profit margin charge is the amount that management believes can be earned under normal conditions. Materials and supplies costing $250,000 will be purchased for the project, and 1,000 pounds of a specialty steel currently in inventory will be used. This steel cost $20,000 when purchased, and TransAllied estimates inventory carrying costs at 20 percent of initial cost. The steel has a current market value of $18,000. Finally, management has determined that resources are currently fully employed, and acceptance of this job will require turning away other available business.

TransAllied's cost projection for the test job is as follows:

Direct labor cost (8,000 hours at $50 per hour)		$400,000
Direct materials:		
Purchased materials	$250,000	
Inventoried steel	24,000	274,000
Total direct labor and materials		674,000
Equipment rental		45,000
Overhead (20 percent of direct labor)		80,000
Required profit margin (100 percent of direct labor)		400,000
Total project cost		$1,199,000

A. For each of the five cost categories in the cost estimate, determine (1) whether the cost is relevant for the decision to accept or reject the contract, (2) whether the cost is an implicit or an explicit cost, and (3) whether the cost has been properly calculated, given the information in the problem.

B. Determine TransAllied's relevant cost (including all implicit as well as explicit costs) of accepting the contract.

C. How would an assumption that the economy was in a recession and that TransAllied didn't have enough business to keep its resources fully employed affect the relevant costs for this problem? Be specific and reestimate the costs of the job.

P10.6 **Quadratic Cost Functions.** Schneider Electric, Inc., sells a range of industrial drive products, including electric motors, servo products, and invertor and vector drives. Product manager Barbara Royer has just completed a cost study of its Indianapolis-based operations. By regressing total variable costs on unit output, the following cost equation was estimated:

$$\text{Total Variable Cost} = \$10,500 + \$0.89Q - \$0.005Q^2.$$
$$(6,000) \quad (0.18) \quad (0.002)$$

Here Q is unit output for a replacement part product, and the numbers in parentheses are the standard errors of the coefficients. The R^2 for the equation is 0.87, and the standard error of the estimate is 22. Monthly observations over a two-year period were used in the study.

A. Characterize the descriptive power of this estimated total variable cost function on an overall basis.

B. Interpret each individual coefficient estimate in the cost function.

C. Based on these estimation results, does Schneider Electric enjoy economies of scale in production?

P10.7 **Cubic Cost Functions.** Management analyst Laura Wilder has been asked to estimate total and variable costs for a new seafood dinner entrée addition to the Eating Light line of low-calorie frozen dinners. Since this is a new product, there is no historical data for Wilder to rely upon. Instead, she estimates the following total variable cost function based on detailed information provided by production, marketing, and accounting department personnel:

$$TVC = \$50,000 + \$5Q - \$0.01Q^2 + \$0.00001Q^3,$$

where TVC is total variable cost and Q is cases of output, when both are expressed on a weekly basis.

A. Calculate the estimated average variable cost and marginal cost per unit relations.

B. Set up a table or spreadsheet to calculate estimates of total variable cost, average variable cost, and marginal cost per unit. Provide these estimates for output levels between 0 and 2,500 units, in 250-unit increments (e.g., 0, 250, 500, . . . , 2,500).

C. Identify the range within which minimum average variable costs per unit are found.

P10.8 **Economic Cost Estimation.** Rowan & Martin, Inc., assembles custom configurations of modular freezers for sale to restaurants and other institutional buyers. Each freezer unit is self-contained and can be used individually or in tandem with additional modules of different shapes and sizes. During the current period, Rowan & Martin's controller estimates the following cost and demand relations for its line of modular freezers:

$$TC = \$150Q + \$0.02Q^2,$$
$$P = \$900 - \$0.03Q,$$

where TC is an accounting estimate of total costs, Q is output, and P is average price. In addition, an economic opportunity cost is incurred because production involves a commitment of $16 million in capital that would otherwise generate a 12.5 percent rate of return on investments of similar risk characteristics.

A. Derive Rowan & Martin's total economic cost function for this product.

B. Estimate the output level at which average economic cost will be minimized. $m\overline{E}$

C. Estimate the economic profit-maximizing output level.

D. Compare and discuss your answers to Parts B and C.

P10.9 **Minimum Efficient Scale Estimation.** Hammer & Sickle, Inc., is a leading producer and distributor of sodium bicarbonate. Consumer products include Hammer & Sickle baking soda, powder and liquid laundry detergent, and carpet and room deodorizers. Industrial products include bicarbonate and potassium carbonate for animal feed, chemicals, and pharmaceuticals. Barry Yeltzen, president of Hammer & Sickle, is considering further expansion in the household consumer products industry and has asked you to make an analysis of such a move's profit potential. In particular, the marketing department has suggested building a $10 million plant capable of producing two units of a new highly concentrated dry laundry detergent per year.

To facilitate your analysis, you consult a recent trade association study of plants in the industry, which found the following (t statistics in parentheses):

$$C = \$4,000 + \$18Q + \$0.001Q^2,$$
$$(12.5) \quad (6.8) \quad\quad (5.2)$$

where C = Total Costs (in thousands of dollars); Q = Output (in thousands of units); $R^2 = 0.96$; $N = 39$; $F = 132$; and S.E.E. = 2,000.

A. Define minimum efficient scale from a theoretical point of view, and discuss three aspects that determine its competitive consequences.

B. Estimate minimum efficient scale in this industry.

P10.10 **Expand or Liquidate Decision.** Ewing Oil Products, Inc., currently enjoys a 40 percent market share with its Digger Barnes line of high-stress drill bits. However, entry by new and highly sophisticated competitors is likely unless a substantial expansion program is undertaken. The time has come to expand rapidly or exit the industry. Engulf & Devour (E&D) has made the exit alternative more palatable with an offer to purchase privately held Ewing for $2 million (near current book value).

Ewing has retained you to advise it in its decision about whether to accept the E&D offer. You have conducted an engineering cost analysis of recent Ewing plant data and found the following:

$$TC = \$20 + \$5Q + \$0.25Q^2,$$

where TC is total cost (in millions of dollars) and Q is output (in thousands of drill bits).

Furthermore, you learn that in an average year, Ewing sells 9,000 drill bits at $9,500 each. Future growth is expected to expand the market for drill bits to 96,000 units within the decade.

A. Calculate and fully interpret the current break-even level of production.

B. Determine the output level of the minimum efficient scale (*MES*) plant size.

C. In light of the expected future size of the market for drill bits, how would you evaluate the future potential for competition in the industry?

D. If the current cost of capital for firms in Ewing's risk class is 15 percent, should Ewing expand or accept E&D's buyout offer?

CASE STUDY FOR CHAPTER 10
Estimating the Costs of Nursing Care

Cost estimation and cost containment are an important concern for a wide range of for-profit and not-for-profit organizations offering health care services. For such organizations, the accurate measurement of nursing costs per patient day (a measure of output) is necessary for effective management. Similarly, such cost estimates are of significant interest to public officials at the federal, state, and local government levels. For example, many state Medicaid reimbursement programs base their payment rates on historical accounting measures of average costs per unit of service. However, these historical average costs may or may not be relevant for hospital management decisions. During periods of substantial excess capacity, the overhead component of average costs may become irrelevant. When the facilities of providers are fully utilized and facility expansion becomes necessary to increase services, then all costs, including overhead, are relevant. As a result, historical average costs provide a useful basis for planning purposes only if appropriate assumptions can be made about the relative length of periods of peak versus off-peak facility usage. From a public policy perspective, a further potential problem arises when hospital expense reimbursement programs are based on historical average costs per day because the care needs and nursing costs of various patient groups can vary widely. For example, if the care received by the average publicly supported Medicaid patient actually costs more than that received by non-Medicaid patients, Medicaid reimbursement based on average costs for the entire facility would be inequitable to providers and could create access barriers for some Medicaid patients.

As an alternative to traditional cost estimation methods, one might consider using the engineering technique to estimate nursing costs. For example, the labor cost of each type of service could be estimated as the product of an estimate of the time required to perform each service times the estimated wage rate per unit of time. Multiplying this figure by an estimate of the frequency of service provides an estimate of the aggregate cost of the service. A possible limitation to the accuracy of this engineering cost-estimation method is that treatment of a variety of illnesses often requires a combination of nursing services. To the extent that multiple services can be provided simultaneously, the engineering technique will tend to overstate actual costs unless the effect on costs of service "packaging" is allowed for.

Nursing cost estimation is also possible by means of a carefully designed regression-based approach using variable cost and service data collected at the ward, unit, or facility level. Weekly labor costs for registered nurses (RNs), licensed practical nurses (LPNs), and nursing aides might be related to a variety of patient services performed during a given measurement period. With sufficient variability in cost and service levels over time, useful estimates of variable labor costs become possible for each type of service and for each patient category (Medicaid, non-Medicaid, etc.). An important advantage of a regression-based approach is that it explicitly allows for the effect of service packaging on variable costs. For example, if shots and wound-dressing services are typically provided together, this will be reflected in the regression-based estimates of variable costs per unit.

Long-run costs per nursing facility can be estimated using either cross-section or time-series methods. By relating total facility costs to the service levels provided by a number of hospitals, nursing homes, or outpatient care facilities during a specific period of time, useful cross-section estimates of total service costs are possible. If case mixes were to vary dramatically according to type of facility, then the type of facility would have to be explicitly accounted for in the regression model analyzed. Similarly, if patient mix or service-provider efficiency is expected to depend, at least in part, on the for-profit or not-for-profit organization status of the care facility, the regression model must also recognize this factor. These factors plus price-level adjustments for inflation would be accounted for in a time-series approach to nursing cost estimation.

To illustrate a regression-based approach to nursing cost estimation, consider the following cross-section analysis of variable nursing costs conducted by the Southeast Association of Hospital Administrators (SAHA). Using confidential data provided by 40 regional hospitals, SAHA studied the relation between nursing costs per patient day and four typical categories of nursing services. These annual data appear in Table 10.5. The four categories of nursing services studied include shots, intravenous (IV) therapy, pulse taking and monitoring, and wound dressing. Each service is measured in terms of frequency per patient day. An output of 1.50 in the shots service category means that, on average, patients received one and one-half shots per day. Similarly, an output of 0.75 in the IV service category means that IV services were provided daily to 75 percent of a given hospital's patients, and so on. In addition to four categories of nursing services, the not-for-profit or for-profit status of each hospital is also indicated.

TABLE 10.5   Nursing Costs per Patient Day, Nursing Services, and Profit Status for 40 Hospitals in Southeastern States

Hospital	Nursing Costs per Patient Day	Shots	IV Therapy	Pulse Taking	Wound Dressing	Profit Status (1 = for-profit, 0 = Not-for-profit)
1	125.00	1.50	0.75	2.25	0.75	0
2	125.00	1.50	0.75	2.25	0.75	0
3	115.00	1.50	0.50	2.00	0.50	1
4	125.00	2.00	0.75	2.25	0.75	0
5	122.50	1.50	0.50	2.25	0.75	0
6	120.00	1.50	0.75	2.25	0.75	1
7	125.00	1.75	0.75	2.00	0.50	0
8	130.00	1.75	0.75	2.25	0.75	0
9	117.50	1.50	0.50	2.25	0.50	0
10	130.00	1.75	0.75	3.25	0.75	0
11	125.00	1.50	0.75	3.00	0.50	0
12	127.50	1.50	0.75	2.50	0.75	0
13	125.00	1.75	0.75	2.50	0.50	0
14	125.00	1.50	0.50	2.50	0.75	0
15	120.00	1.50	0.75	2.25	0.50	0
16	125.00	1.50	0.50	2.25	0.75	0
17	130.00	1.75	0.75	2.50	0.75	0
18	120.00	1.50	0.50	2.25	0.50	0
19	125.00	1.50	0.75	2.25	0.75	0
20	122.50	1.50	0.50	2.50	0.75	0
21	117.50	1.75	0.50	2.00	0.50	1
22	120.00	1.50	0.50	2.50	0.50	0
23	122.50	1.50	0.75	2.50	0.75	1
24	117.50	1.50	0.50	2.50	0.50	0
25	132.50	1.75	0.75	2.50	0.75	0
26	120.00	1.75	0.50	2.25	0.50	1
27	122.50	1.75	0.50	2.50	0.50	0
28	125.00	1.50	0.75	2.50	0.75	0
29	125.00	1.50	0.50	2.00	0.75	0
30	130.00	1.75	0.75	2.25	0.75	0
31	115.00	1.50	0.50	2.00	0.50	0
32	115.00	1.50	0.50	2.25	0.50	0
33	130.00	1.75	0.75	2.50	0.75	0
34	132.50	1.75	0.75	3.00	0.75	0
35	117.50	1.50	0.50	2.00	0.50	1
36	122.50	1.50	0.50	2.50	0.75	0
37	112.50	1.50	0.50	2.00	0.50	0
38	130.00	1.50	0.75	3.25	0.75	0
39	130.00	1.50	0.75	3.25	0.75	1
40	125.00	1.50	0.75	3.00	0.75	1

Using a "dummy" (or binary) variable approach, the profit status variable equals one for the 8 for-profit hospitals included in the study and zero for the remaining 32 not-for-profit hospitals.

Cost estimation results for nursing costs per patient day derived using a regression-based approach are shown in Table 10.6.

TABLE 10.6   **Nursing Costs per Patient Day: Cost Estimation Results**

Variable Name	Coefficient (1)	Standard Error of Coefficient (2)	t-Statistic (1) + (2) = (3)
Intercept	76.1812	5.086	14.98
Shots	11.418	2.851	4.00
IV	10.052	3.646	2.76
Pulse	4.532	1.153	3.93
Wound dressing	18.933	3.370	5.62
For-profit status	−2.105	0.883	−2.38

Coefficient of determination = R^2 = 0.84
Standard error of estimate = S.E.E. = $2.21

A. Interpret the coefficient of determination (R^2) estimated for the nursing cost function.

B. Describe the economic and statistical significance of each estimated coefficient in the nursing cost function.

C. Average nursing costs for the 8 for-profit hospitals in the sample are only $120.94 per patient day or $3.28 per patient day less than the $124.22 average cost experienced by the 32 not-for-profit hospitals. How can this fact be reconciled with the estimated coefficient of −2.105 for the for-profit status variable?

D. Would such an approach for nursing cost estimation have practical relevance for publicly funded nursing cost reimbursement systems?

Selected References

Anderson, Evan E., and Yu-Min Chen. "Implicit Prices and Economies of Scale in Secondary Memory: The Case of Disk Drives." *Managerial and Decision Economics* 12 (June 1991): 241–248.

Blacconiere, Walter G. "Market Reactions to Accounting Regulations in the Savings and Loan Industry." *Journal of Accounting & Economics* 14 (June 1991): 91–113.

Boatsman, James B., Lawrence P. Grasso, Michael B. Ormiston, and J. Hal Reneau. "A Perspective on the Use of Laboratory Market Experimentation in Auditing Research." *Accounting Review* 67 (January 1992): 148–156.

Cooper, Robin, and Robert S. Kaplan. "Profit Priorities from Activity-Based Costing." *Harvard Business Review* 69 (May–June 1991): 130–135.

Copeland, Thomas E., and Daniel Friedman. "The Market Value of Information: Some Experimental Results." *Journal of Business* 65 (April 1992): 241–266.

DeBondt, Werner F. M., and Howard E. Thompson. "Is Economic Efficiency the Driving Force behind Mergers?" *Managerial and Decision Economics* 13 (January–February 1992): 31–44.

Feenstra, Robert C., James R. Markusen, and William Zeile. "Accounting for Growth with New Inputs: Theory and Evidence." *American Economic Review* 82 (May 1992): 415–421.

Frantz, Roger. "X-Efficiency and Allocative Efficiency: What Have We Learned?" *American Economic Review* 82 (May 1992): 434–439.

Hammer, Michael. "Reengineering Work: Don't Automate, Obliterate." *Harvard Business Review* 68 (July–August 1990): 104–112.

Holthausen, Robert W. "Accounting Method Choice: Opportunistic Behavior, Efficient Contracting, and Information Perspectives." *Journal of Accounting & Economics* 12 (January 1990): 207–218.

Krugman, Paul. "History and Industry Location: The Case of the Manufacturing Belt." *American Economic Review* 81 (May 1991): 80–83.

Livnat, Joshua, and Paul Zarowin. "The Incremental Information Content of Cash-flow Components." *Journal of Accounting & Economics* 13 (May 1990): 25–46.

Mann, Catherine L. "Industry Restructuring in East-Central Europe: The Challenge and Role for Foreign Investment." *American Economic Review* 81 (May 1991): 181–184.

Mian, Shehzad L., and Clifford W. Smith, Jr. "Accounts Receivable Management Policy: Theory and Evidence." *Journal of Finance* 47 (March 1992): 169–200.

Palmer, Karen. "Diversification by Regulated Monopolies and Incentives for Cost-Reducing R&D." *American Economic Review* 81 (May 1991): 266–270.

CHAPTER | # LINEAR PROGRAMMING

What if a company introduces a new stripped-down and bargain-priced version of its most popular product? What if customers are granted a one-year warranty against failures due to product defects? What if advertisers insist on audience guarantees that include a wide variety of exposure requirements? Answers to all of these questions typify the types of information necessary for effective managerial decision making during the 1990s. In fact, "What if?" is the question that launched the computer spreadsheet revolution of the 1980s. A computer spreadsheet consists of electronically stored data arrayed in the form of an accounting income statement or balance sheet. Using sophisticated but easy-to-learn spreadsheet software such as *Lotus 1-2-3* and powerful desktop computers, managers are able to investigate a wide variety of solutions to complex decision problems. However, traditional trial-and-error approaches led to hours and sometimes days of computer simulation analysis to find workable but suboptimal solutions.

Today, managers analyze spreadsheet information using a proven optimization tool called **linear programming** (LP) to isolate the best solution, or **optimal solution,** to decision problems. Linear programming is ideally suited to solving problems that involve an objective function to be maximized or minimized, where the relevant objective function is subject to a variety of underlying constraints. For example, the linear programming technique is able to answer important questions such as, "What product mix will produce the maximum profit?" or "What is the least amount of overtime that will meet minimum staffing requirements?" Just as important as the amazing power of linear programming techniques is the ease with which the method can be applied. Even complex linear programming problems can be set up and solved easily using popular LP software for the personal computer, such as *What's Best* and *What-if-Solver.* Before these software programs came along, a mainframe computer and an extensive background in mathematics were required to solve highly complex optimization problems. Now all that is needed is a desktop computer, a spreadsheet model, and a decision problem with plenty of variables.

Linear programming is a popular method for finding the optimal solution to decision problems because managers typically face constraints that restrict their course of action. Product design and product mix decisions are often constrained by the availability of essential raw materials, production equipment, or key personnel. Plant location and delivery routing decisions must be made in light of

Linear programming
A solution method for maximization or minimization decision problems subject to underlying constraints.

Optimal solution
Best answer.

production schedules, customer service requirements, and delivery costs. Inventory and cash management in accounting, capital budget decisions in finance, work scheduling and organization design in management, and media choice decisions in marketing all involve constraints on the allocation of scarce resources to achieve specific managerial goals. All are typical of the types of decision problems addressed using linear programming methods.

Constrained optimization problems that arise in the real world seldom have a simple rule-of-thumb solution. Relations between the objective function and the constraint conditions are often complex, as are relations among the constraint conditions themselves. Finding the optimal solution is further complicated because careful analysis of all decision alternatives is required. This chapter illustrates how the linear programming technique can be used to successfully analyze such complex decision problems. Emphasis is placed on the setup and interpretation of linear programming problems and their solutions. Simple examples are used to illustrate this process and the practical value of linear programming as a tool for managerial decisions.

BASIC ASSUMPTIONS

Many of the production or resource constraints faced by managers are inequalities. Constraints often limit resource use by specifying that the quantity employed must be less than or equal to ($\leq$) some fixed amount available. In other instances, constraints specify that the quantity or quality of output must be greater than or equal to ($\geq$) some minimum requirement. Linear programming handles constraint inequalities easily, making it a useful technique with several applications in managerial economics.

A typical linear programming problem might be to maximize output subject to the constraint that no more than 40 hours of skilled labor time per week be used. This labor constraint is expressed as an inequality where skilled labor ≤ 40 hours per week. Such an operating constraint means that although no more than 40 hours of skilled labor can be used, some excess capacity is permissible, at least in the short run. If 36 hours of skilled labor were fruitfully employed during a given week, the 4 hours per week of unused labor is called excess capacity. This is the type of production constraint that the linear programming approach is designed for.

As its name implies, linear programming can be applied only in situations in which the relevant objective function and constraint conditions are linear. Typical managerial decision problems that can be solved using the linear programming method involve revenue and cost functions and their composite, the profit function. Each of these must be linear; as output increases, revenues, costs, and profits must increase in a linear fashion. For revenues to be a linear function of output, product prices must be constant. For costs to be a linear function of output, both returns to scale and input prices must be constant. Constant input prices, when combined with constant returns to scale, result in a linear total cost function. If both output prices and unit costs are constant, then profit contribution and profits also rise in a linear fashion with output.

Product and input prices are said to be constant when a typical firm can buy unlimited quantities of input and sell unlimited amount of output without changing prices. This occurs under conditions of pure competition. Therefore, linear programming methods are clearly applicable for firms in purely competitive industries in which constant returns to scale are operative. However, the linear programming method is also applicable in many instances when these conditions are not met over extensive ranges of output. Because linear programming is used for marginal analysis, it focuses on the effects of fairly modest output, price, and input changes. For moderate changes in current operating conditions, a constant-returns-to-scale assumption is often valid. Similarly, input and output prices are typically unaffected by modest changes from current levels. As a result, sales revenue, cost, and profit functions are often linear when only moderate changes in operations are contemplated and use of linear programming methods is entirely valid.

▶ To illustrate, suppose that an oil company must choose the optimal output mix for a refinery with a capacity of 150,000 barrels of oil per day. The oil company may be perfectly valid in basing its analysis on the $20 per barrel prevailing market price for crude oil, regardless of how much is purchased or sold. This assumption might not be valid if the company were to quickly expand refinery output by a factor of 10, but within the 150,000 barrels per day range of feasible output, prices will be approximately constant. Up to capacity limits, it is also reasonable to expect that a doubling of crude oil input would lead to a doubling of refined output, and, therefore, returns to scale are constant. These same conditions hold for most services, as well as both producer products and consumer goods.

In many instances, the underlying assumption of linearity is entirely valid, and the linear programming technique can be used to solve a wide variety of managerial decision problems. In other instances in which the objective function and constraint conditions can be usefully approximated by linear relations, the linear programming technique can also be fruitfully applied. Only when objective functions and constraint conditions are inherently nonlinear must more complicated *mathematical programming* techniques be applied. In most managerial applications, even when the assumption of linearity does not hold precisely, linear approximations seldom distort the analysis.

PRODUCTION PLANNING FOR A SINGLE PRODUCT

Although linear programming has been widely applied in managerial decision making, it has been developed most fully and used most frequently in production decisions. Often the decision problem is to determine the least-cost combination of inputs needed to produce a particular product. In other cases, the problem may be to obtain the maximum possible output from a fixed quantity of resources. Both problems can be readily solved using linear programming techniques. To illustrate the method, a simple two-input/one-output problem is examined. Later sections consider more realistic and complex problems.

Production Processes   Assume that a firm produces a single product, Q, using two inputs, L and K, which might represent labor and capital. Instead of assuming continuous substitution between L and K, as in Chapter 8, assume that Q can be produced using only four input combinations. In other words, four different production processes are available for making Q, each of which uses a different fixed combination of inputs L and K. In most industries, this is an entirely reasonable assumption, much more reasonable than the possibility of continuous input substitution. The production processes might represent four different plants, each with its own fixed asset configuration and labor requirements. Alternatively, they could be four different assembly stations or assembly lines, each using a different combination of capital equipment and labor.

The four production processes are illustrated as rays in Figure 11.1. Process A requires the combination of 15 units of L and 1 unit of K for each unit of Q produced. Process B uses 10 units of L and 2 units of K for each unit of output. Processes C and D use 7.5 units of L and 3 units of K, and 5 units of L with 5 units of K, respectively, for each unit of Q produced. Each point along the production ray for Process A combines L and K in the ratio 15 to 1; Process rays B, C, and D are developed in the same way. Each point along a single production ray combines the two inputs in a fixed ratio, with the ratios differing from one production process to another. If L and K represent labor and capital inputs, the four production processes might be different plants employing different production techniques. Process A is very labor intensive in comparison with the other production systems, whereas B, C, and D are based on increasingly capital-intensive technologies.

Point A_1 indicates the combination of L and K required to produce one unit of output using the A process. Doubling both L and K doubles the quantity of Q produced; this is indicated by the distance moved along ray A from A_1 to A_2. Line segment $0A_2$ is exactly twice the length of line segment $0A_1$ and thus represents twice as much output. Along production process ray A, the distance $0A_1 = A_1A_2 = A_2A_3 = A_3A_4 = A_4A_5$. Each of these line segments indicates the addition of one unit of output using increased quantities of L and K in the fixed ratio of 15 to 1.

Output along the ray increases proportionately with increases in the input factors. If each input is doubled, output is doubled; if inputs increase by a factor of 10 percent, output increases by 10 percent. This follows from the linearity assumption noted previously: Each production process must exhibit constant returns to scale.

Output is measured in the same way along the three other production process rays in Figure 11.1. Point C_1 indicates the combination of L and K required to produce one unit of Q using Process C. The production of two units of Q using that process requires the combination of L and K indicated at point C_2; the same is true for points C_3, C_4, and C_5. Although production of additional units using Process C is indicated by line segments of equal length, just as for Process A, these line segments are of different lengths between the various production systems. Whereas each production process exhibits constant returns to scale, equal distances along *different* process rays do not ordinarily indicate equal output quantities.

FIGURE 11.1   Production Process Rays in Linear Programming

Points along each process ray represent combinations of inputs L and K required for that production process to produce output.

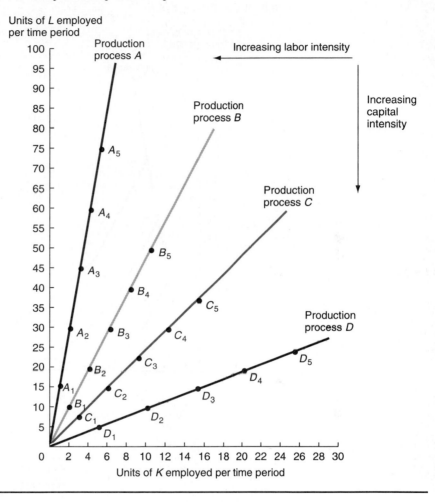

Production Isoquants

Joining points of equal output on the four production process rays creates a set of isoquant curves. Figure 11.2 illustrates isoquants for $Q = 1, 2, 3, 4,$ and 5. These isoquants have the same interpretation as those developed in Chapter 7. Each isoquant represents combinations of input factors L and K that can be used to produce a given quantity of output. Production isoquants in linear programming are composed of linear segments connecting the various production process rays. Each of these isoquant segments is parallel to one another. For example, line segment A_1B_1 is parallel to segment A_2B_2; isoquant segment B_3C_3 is parallel to B_2C_2.

Points along each segment of an isoquant between two process rays represent a combination of output from each of the two adjoining production processes.

FIGURE 11.2 **Production Isoquants in Linear Programming**

Each point along an isoquant represents the output level resulting from a given combination of inputs. For example, Point X depicts the production of 4 units of Q using 25 units of L and 16 units of K.

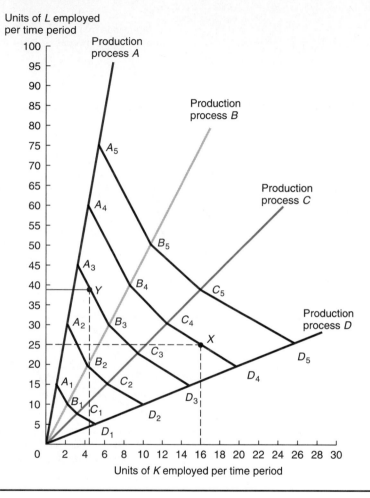

Consider Point X in Figure 11.2, which represents production of 4 units of Q using 25 units of L and 16 units of K. None of the available production processes can manufacture Q using L and K in the ratio of 25 to 16, but that combination is possible by producing part of the output with Process C and part with Process D. In this case, 2 units of Q can be produced using Process C and 2 units using Process D. Production of 2 units of Q with Process C utilizes 15 units of L and 6 units of K. For the production of 2 units of Q with Process D, 10 units each of L and K are necessary. Although no single production system is available that can produce 4 units of Q using 25 units of L and 16 units of K, Processes C and D together can produce that combination.

All points lying along production isoquant segments can be interpreted in a similar manner. Each point represents a linear combination of output using the production process systems that bound the particular segment. Point Y in Figure 11.2 provides another illustration. At Y, 3 units of Q are produced, using a total of 38.5 units of L and 4.3 units of K.[1] That input-output combination is possible through a combination of Processes A and B. This can be analyzed algebraically. To produce 1 unit of Q by Process A requires 15 units of L and 1 unit of K. Therefore, to produce 1.7 units of Q requires 25.5 (1.7×15) units of L and 1.7 (1.7×1) units of K. To produce a single unit of Q by Process B requires 10 units of L and 2 units of K, so 1.3 units of Q requires 13 (10×1.3) units of L and 2.6 (2×1.3) units of K. Thus, Point Y calls for the production of 3 units of Q in total, 1.7 units by Process A and 1.3 units by Process B, using a total of 38.5 units of L and 4.3 units of K.

One method of determining the quantity to be produced by each production process at varying points along the isoquant is called the relative distance method.

Relative distance method

Graphic technique used to solve linear programming problems.

The **relative distance method** is based on the fact that the location of a point along an isoquant determines the relative shares of production for the adjacent processes. If Point X in Figure 11.2 were on process ray C, all output would be produced using Process C. Similarly, if X were on process ray D, all output would be produced using Process D. Since Point X lies between process rays C and D, both Processes C and D will be used to produce this output. Process C will be used relatively more than Process D if X is closer to process ray C than to process ray D. Conversely, Process D will be used relatively more than Process C if X is closer to process ray D than to process ray C. Because Point X in Figure 11.2 lies at the midpoint of the $Q = 4$ isoquant segment between C_4 and D_4, it implies production using Processes C and D in equal proportions. Thus, at Point X, $Q = 4$, and $Q_C = 2$, and $Q_D = 2$.

The relative proportions of Process A and Process B used to produce $Q = 3$ at Point Y can be determined in a similar manner. Because Y lies closer to process ray A than to process ray B, Point Y entails relatively more output from process A than from process B. The share of total output produced using Process A is calculated by considering the distance B_3Y relative to B_3A_3. The share of total output produced using Process B is calculated by considering the distance A_3Y relative to A_3B_3. Starting from Point B_3, the segment B_3Y covers 56.6 percent of the total distance B_3A_3. This means that at Point Y, about 56.6 percent of total output is produced using Process A ($Q_A = 0.566 \times 3 = 1.7$) and 43.4 percent ($= 1.0 - 0.566$) using Process B ($Q_B = 0.434 \times 3 = 1.3$). Alternatively, starting from Point A_3, note that the segment A_3Y covers 43.4 percent of the total distance A_3B_3. At Point Y, 43.4 percent of total output is produced using Process

---

[1] Another assumption of linear programming is that fractional variables are permissible. In many applications, this assumption is not important. For example, in the present illustration we might be talking about labor hours and machine hours for the inputs. The solution value calling for $L = 38.5$ merely means that 38.5 hours of labor are required.

In some cases, however, inputs are large (whole plants, for example), and the fact that linear programming assumes divisible variables is important. In such cases, linear programming as described here may be inappropriate, and a more complex technique, integer programming, may be required.

FIGURE 11.3 **Determination of the Least-Cost Production Process**

The tangency between the isoquant and isocost lines at Point B_3 reveals the least-cost combination of inputs.

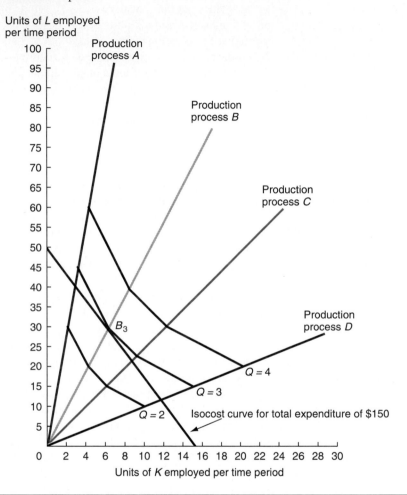

B and 56.6 percent using Process *A*. Extreme accuracy would require painstaking graphic detail, but in many instances the relative distance method can adequately approximate production intensities along isoquants.

Least-Cost Input Combinations

Adding isocost curves to a set of isoquants permits one to determine least-cost input combinations for the production of Product *Q*. This is shown in Figure 11.3 under the assumption that each unit of *L* costs $3 and each unit of *K* costs $10. The isocost curve illustrated indicates a total expenditure of $150.

The tangency between the isocost curve and the isoquant curve for *Q* = 3 at Point B_3 indicates that Process *B*, which combines Inputs *L* and *K* in the ratio 5 to 1, is the least-cost method of producing *Q*. For any expenditure level, production is maximized by using Process *B*. Alternatively, Process *B* is the least-cost method for producing any quantity of *Q*, given the assumed prices for *L* and *K*.

Optimal Input Combinations with Limited Resources

Frequently, firms faced with limited inputs during a production period find it optimal to use inputs in proportions other than the least-cost combination. To illustrate, consider the effect of limits on the quantities of *L* and *K* available in our example. Assume that only 20 units of *L* and 11 units of *K* are available during the current production period and that the firm seeks to maximize output of *Q*. These constraints are shown in Figure 11.4. The horizontal line drawn at *L* = 20 indicates the upper limit on the quantity of *L* that can be employed during the production period; the vertical line at *K* = 11 indicates a similar limit on the quantity of *K*.

Production possibilities for this problem are determined by noting that, in addition to limitations on Inputs *L* and *K*, the firm must operate within the area bounded by production process rays *A* and *D*. Combining production possibilities with input constraints restricts the firm to operation within the shaded area on 0*PRS* in Figure 11.4. This area is known as the **feasible space** in the programming problem. Any point within this space combines *L* and *K* in a technically feasible ratio without exceeding availability limits on *L* and *K*. Because the firm is trying to maximize production of *Q* subject to constraints on the use of *L* and *K*, it should operate at the feasible space point that touches the highest possible isoquant. This is Point *R* in Figure 11.4, where *Q* = 3.

Feasible space

Graphical region that is both technically and economically feasible and includes the optimal solution.

Although it is possible to solve problems like the foregoing example by using carefully drawn graphs, it is typically more useful to combine graphic analysis with analytical techniques to obtain accurate solutions efficiently. For example, consider Figure 11.4 again. Even if the isoquant for *Q* = 3 were not drawn, it would be apparent from the slopes of the isoquants for 2 or 4 units of output that the optimal solution to the problem must be at Point *R*. It is obvious from the graph that maximum production is obtained by operating at the point where both inputs are fully employed. Because *R* lies between processes *C* and *D*, the output-maximizing input combination uses only those two production processes. All 20 units of *L* and 11 units of *K* will be employed, since Point *R* lies at the intersection of these two input constraints.

Using this information from the graph, it is possible to quickly and easily solve for the optimal quantities to be produced using Processes *C* and *D*. Recall that each unit of output produced using Process *C* requires 7.5 units of *L*. Thus, the total *L* required in Process *C* equals $7.5 \times Q_C$. Similarly, each unit produced using Process *D* requires 5 units of *L*, so the total *L* used in Process *D* equals $5 \times Q_D$. At Point *R*, 20 units of *L* are being used in Processes *C* and *D* together, and the following must hold:

$$7.5Q_C + 5Q_D = 20. \qquad \textbf{(11.1)}$$

A similar relation can be developed for the use of *K*. Each unit of output produced from Process *C* requires 3 units of *K*, whereas Process *D* uses 5 units of *K* to produce each unit of output. The total use of *K* in Processes *C* and *D* equals 11 units at Point *R*, so

$$3Q_C + 5Q_D = 11. \qquad \textbf{(11.2)}$$

FIGURE 11.4   **Optimal Input Combination with Limited Resources**

Given limited resources, output is maximized at Point *R* because this point lies on the highest isoquant that intersects the feasible space.

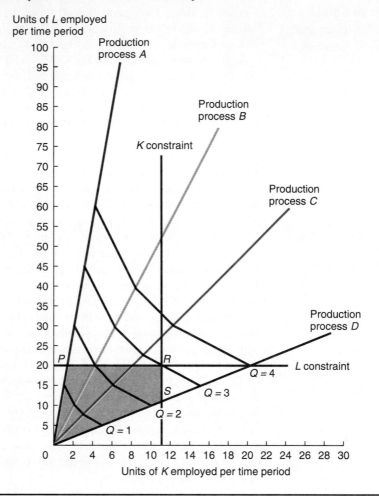

Equations 11.1 and 11.2 both must hold at Point *R*. Output quantities from Processes *C* and *D* at that location are determined by solving these equations simultaneously. Subtracting Equation 11.2 from Equation 11.1 to eliminate the variable Q_D isolates the solution for Q_C:

$$7.5Q_C + 5Q_D = 20$$
$$\text{minus } \underline{3.0Q_C + 5Q_D = 11}$$
$$4.5Q_C = 9$$
$$Q_C = 2.$$

●

MANAGERIAL APPLICATION 11.1
Karmarkar's LP Breakthrough

On a typical day, thousands of U.S. Air Force planes ferry cargo and military passengers around the globe. To keep those jets flying, the Military Airlift Command (MAC) must juggle schedules for pilots and other flight personnel. In addition, the MAC has to make literally millions of calculations to determine the most efficient flight route, cargo weight, fuel loading, and so on. After all of these details have been carefully accounted for, unexpected bad weather or emergency changes in priorities can force a complete recalculation of the entire flight plan.

Getting all of the pieces to fit together has been a classic linear programming (LP) dilemma. On one hand, if an LP computer program could help increase fuel efficiency by just 2 percent, it would be worth millions of dollars per year. On the other hand, the underlying complexity of the Air Force's transportation problem is so great that, until recently, it defied the capabilities of even the most sophisticated supercomputers.

In 1984, Narendra K. Karmarkar, a young scientist for AT&T Bell Laboratories, discovered an algorithm, or mathematical formula, that greatly speeds the process of solving even the most complex LP problems. In the traditional approach to solving LP problems, one corner of the feasible solution space is solved and compared with the solutions for adjacent points. If a better solution is found, the computer is instructed to move off in that direction. This iterative process continues until the program finds itself boxed in by inferior solutions. Karmarkar's algorithm employs a radically different geometric approach that finds an optimal solution more efficiently. Working from within the interior of the feasible space, the Karmarkar method avoids the tedious surface route and uses projective geometry to reconfigure the solution structure. By studying this structure, the program determines the direction in which the optimal solution is likely to lie. Then the problem structure is allowed to return to its original shape, and the program moves toward the solution, pausing at intervals to repeat the process until it finds the optimal solution.

Despite early skepticism, there is a great deal of excitement today in both the scientific and business communities concerning the potential of Karmarkar's method for solving complex LP problems. For example, AT&T is using Karmarkar's formula to forecast the most cost-effective method for meeting future demands on the telephone network linking countries with shores on the Pacific Ocean. AT&T must estimate current and future telephone demand between every pair of switching points within the network. With a ten-year horizon, the AT&T planning model includes over 42,000 variables. Considering that many variables, using the traditional LP solution method requires four to seven hours of mainframe computer time to answer each what-if question. Karmarkar's method finds answers in just a few minutes.

The cost savings possible using the Karmarkar method make the LP approach practical in a host of new applications. AT&T is now assessing its entire long-distance telephone network in an LP problem involving 800,000 variables. A multiprocessor supercomputer from Alliant Computer Systems Corporation and a software version of Karmarkar's algorithm have been optimized for high-speed parallel processing and are expected to be installed at St. Louis's Scott Air Force Base to help solve the MAC logistics problem cited previously.

So fast have been recent developments in the area that many new and unanticipated applications are sure to emerge as software for the Karmarkar algorithm becomes available. The possibilities include a broad range of applications, from assessing risk factors in stock and bond portfolios to setting up production schedules in industrial factories. The accuracy of economic forecasting may also increase if Karmarkar's method allows economists to study the effects of economic factors on highly detailed input/output tables that include both firm-specific and economy-wide influences. When combined with the capabilities of amazingly powerful supercomputers, the Karmarkar breakthrough promises to rapidly extend the application of LP techniques during the 1990s.

Source: William G. Wild and Otis Port, "The Startling Discovery Bell Labs Kept in the Shadows," *Business Week,* September 21, 1987, 69–76; and Jerry E. Bishop, "Mathematicians Find Solution to Old Puzzle," *The Wall Street Journal,* February 15, 1991, B1, B2.

Substituting 2 for Q_C in Equation 11.2 determines output from Process D:

$$3(2) + 5Q_D = 11,$$
$$5Q_D = 5,$$
$$Q_D = 1.$$

Total output at Point R is 3 units, composed of 2 units from Process C and 1 unit from Process D.

The combination of graphic and analytic techniques allows one to obtain precise linear programming solutions with relative ease.

PRODUCTION PLANNING FOR MULTIPLE PRODUCTS

Many production decisions are more complex than the preceding example. Consider the problem of finding the optimal output mix for a multiproduct firm facing restrictions on productive facilities and other inputs. This problem, faced by a host of companies producing consumer and producer goods alike, is readily solved with linear programming techniques.

Objective Function Specification

Consider a firm that produces Products X and Y and uses Inputs A, B, and C. To maximize total profit, the firm must determine optimal quantities of each product subject to constraints imposed on input availability. It is often useful to structure such a linear programming problem in terms of the maximization of profit contribution, or total revenue minus variable costs, rather than to explicitly maximize profits. Of course, fixed costs must be subtracted from profit contribution to determine net profits. However, because fixed costs are constant, maximizing profit contribution is tantamount to maximizing profit. The output mix that maximizes profit contribution also maximizes net profit.

An equation that expresses the goal of a linear programming problem is called the **objective function.** In the present example, assume that the firm wishes to maximize total profits from the two products, X and Y, during each time period. If per-unit profit contribution (the excess of price over average variable costs) is $12 for Product X and $9 for Product Y, the objective function is

Objective function

Equation that expresses the goal of a linear programming problem.

Maximize
$$\pi = \$12Q_X + \$9Q_Y. \tag{11.3}$$

Q_X and Q_Y represent the quantities of each product produced. The total profit contribution, π, earned by the firm equals the per-unit profit contribution of X times the units of X produced and sold, plus the profit contribution of Y times Q_Y.

Constraint Equation Specification

Table 11.1 specifies the available quantities of each input and their usage in the production of X and Y. This is all the information needed to form the constraint equations.

The table shows that 32 units of Input A are available in each period. Four units of A are required in the production of each unit of X, whereas 2 units of A

TABLE 11.1 **Inputs Available for Production of *X* and *Y***

Input	Quantity Available per Time Period	Quantity Required per Unit of Output	
		X	*Y*
A	32	4	2
B	10	1	1
C	21	0	3

are necessary to produce 1 unit of *Y*. Since 4 units of *A* are required for the production of a single unit of *X*, the total amount of *A* used to manufacture *X* can be written as $4Q_X$. Similarly, 2 units of *A* are required to produce each unit of *Y*, so $2Q_Y$ represents the total quantity of *A* used in the production of Product *Y*. Summing the quantities of *A* used in the production of *X* and *Y* provides an expression for the total usage of *A*. Because this total cannot exceed the 32 units available, the constraint condition for Input *A* is

$$4Q_X + 2Q_Y \leq 32. \qquad (11.4)$$

The constraint for Input *B* is determined in a similar manner. One unit of Input *B* is necessary for the production of each unit of either *X* or *Y*, so the total amount of *B* employed is $1Q_X + 1Q_Y$. The maximum quantity of *B* available in each time period is 10 units; thus, the constraint requirement associated with Input *B* is

$$1Q_X + 1Q_Y \leq 10. \qquad (11.5)$$

Finally, the constraint relation for Input *C* affects only the production of *Y*. Each unit of *Y* requires an input of 3 units of *C*, and 21 units of Input *C* are available. Usage of *C* is given by the expression $3Q_Y$, and the relevant constraint equation is

$$3Q_Y \leq 21. \qquad (11.6)$$

Constraint equations play a major role in solving linear programming problems. One further concept must be introduced, however, before the linear programming problem is completely specified and ready for solution.

Nonnegativity Requirement

Because linear programming is merely a mathematical tool for solving constrained optimization problems, nothing in the technique itself ensures that an answer makes economic sense. In a production problem for a relatively unprofitable product, the mathematically optimal output level might be a *negative* quantity, clearly an impossible solution. In a distribution problem, an optimal solution might indicate negative shipments from one point to another, which again is impossible.

To prevent economically meaningless results, a nonnegativity requirement must be introduced. This is merely a statement that all variables in the problem must be equal to or greater than zero. For the present production problem, the following expressions must be added:

$$Q_X \geq 0,$$

and

$$Q_Y \geq 0.$$

GRAPHIC SPECIFICATION AND SOLUTION

Having specified all the component parts of the firm's linear programming problem, the problem can now be illustrated graphically and analyzed algebraically.

Analytic Expression

The decision problem is to maximize total profit contribution, π, subject to resource constraints. This is expressed as

Maximize $\qquad\qquad\qquad \pi = \$12Q_X + \$9Q_Y$ $\qquad\qquad$ **(11.3)**

subject to the following constraints:

$$\text{Input } A: \qquad 4Q_X + 2Q_Y \leq 32, \qquad\qquad \textbf{(11.4)}$$

$$\text{Input } B: \qquad 1Q_X + 1Q_Y \leq 10, \qquad\qquad \textbf{(11.5)}$$

$$\text{Input } C: \qquad\qquad 3Q_Y \leq 21, \qquad\qquad \textbf{(11.6)}$$

where

$$Q_X \geq 0 \text{ and } Q_Y \geq 0.$$

Each variable and coefficient is exactly as specified previously.

Graphing the Feasible Space

In Figure 11.5, the graph of the constraint equation for Input A, $4Q_X + 2Q_Y = 32$, indicates the maximum quantities of X and Y that can be produced given the limitation on the availability of Input A. A maximum of 16 units of Y can be produced if no X is manufactured; 8 units of X can be produced if the output of Y is zero. Any point along the line connecting these two outputs represents the maximum combination of X and Y that can be produced with no more than 32 units of A.

This constraint equation divides the XY plane into two half spaces. Every point lying on the line or to the left of the line satisfies the constraint expressed by the equation $4Q_X + 2Q_Y \leq 32$; every point to the right of the line violates that expression. Only points on the constraint line or to the left of it are in the feasible space. The shaded area of Figure 11.5 represents the feasible area limited by the constraint on Input A.

In Figure 11.6 the feasible space is limited further by adding constraints for Inputs B and C. The constraint on Input B is expressed as $Q_X + Q_Y = 10$. If no Y is produced, a maximum of 10 units of X can be produced; if output of X is zero, 10 units of Y can be manufactured. All combinations of X and Y lying on or

FIGURE 11.5   Constraint Imposed by Limitations on Input *A*

The constraint equation for Input *A* represents the maximum combination of *X* and *Y* that can be produced with 32 units of *A*.

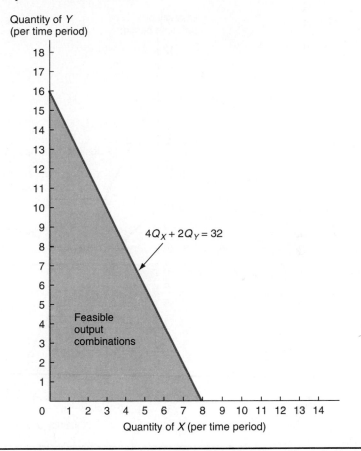

to the left of the line connecting these two points are feasible with respect to utilization of Input *B*.

The horizontal line at $Q_Y = 7$ in Figure 11.6 represents the constraint imposed by Input *C*. Since *C* is used only in the production of *Y*, it does not constrain the production of *X*. Seven units are the maximum quantity of *Y* that can be produced with 21 units of *C* available.

These three input constraints, together with the nonnegativity requirement, completely define the feasible space shown as the shaded area of Figure 11.6. Only points within this area meet all constraints.

Graphing the Objective Function

The objective function, $\pi = \$12Q_X + \$9Q_Y$, can be graphed in Q_XQ_Y space as a series of isoprofit curves. This is illustrated in Figure 11.7, where isoprofit curves for $36, $72, $108, and $144 are shown. Each isoprofit curve illustrates all possible combinations of *X* and *Y* that result in a constant total profit. For

FIGURE 11.6 **Feasible Space**

The feasible space is reduced further by the addition of constraints on Inputs B and C.
Only points within the shaded region meet all constraints.

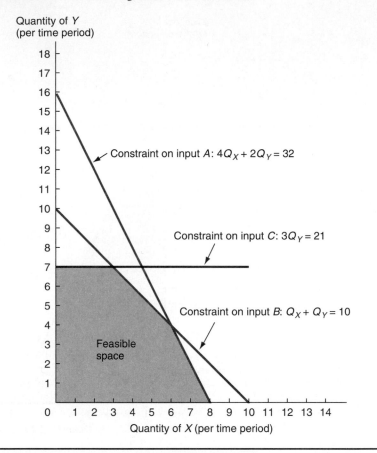

example, the isoprofit curve labeled $\pi = \$36$ identifies each combination of X
and Y that results in a total profit of $36; all output combinations along the $\pi = \$72$ curve provide a total profit contribution of $72; and so on. It is clear from
Figure 11.7 that isoprofit curves are a series of parallel lines that take on higher
values as one moves upward and to the right.

The general formula for isoprofit curves can be developed by considering the
profit function $\pi = aQ_X + bQ_Y$, where a and b are the profit contributions of
Products X and Y, respectively. Solving the isoprofit function for Q_Y creates an
equation of the following form:

$$Q_Y = \frac{\pi}{b} - \frac{a}{b} Q_X.$$

Given the individual profit contributions, a and b, the Q_Y intercept equals the
profit level of the isoprofit curve divided by the profit per unit earned on Q_Y, π/b.

FIGURE 11.7   Isoprofit Contribution Curves

Points along the isoprofit line represent all possible combinations of X and Y that result in the same profit level.

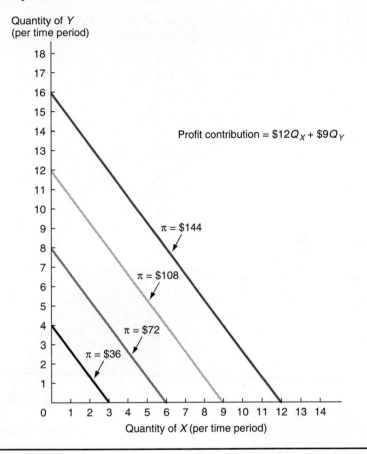

Slope of the objective function is given by the relative profitability of the two products, $-a/b$. Since the relative profitability of the products is not affected by the output level, the isoprofit curves consist of a series of parallel lines. In this example, all isoprofit curves have a slope of $-12/9$, or -1.33.

Graphic Solution

Because the firm's objective is to maximize total profit, it should operate on the highest isoprofit curve obtainable. Combining the feasible space limitations shown in Figure 11.6 with the family of isoprofit curves from Figure 11.7 illustrates a graphic solution to this linear programming problem. This combined graph is illustrated in Figure 11.8.

Point M in the figure indicates the solution to the problem. Here, the firm produces 6 units of X and 4 units of Y, and the total profit is $108 [= ($12 × 6) + ($9 × 4)], which is the maximum available under the conditions stated in the

FIGURE 11.8 **Graphic Solution of the Linear Programming Problem**

Point *M* is on the highest isoprofit curve that intersects the feasible space. Thus, it represents the output combination that will maximize total profit given input constraints.

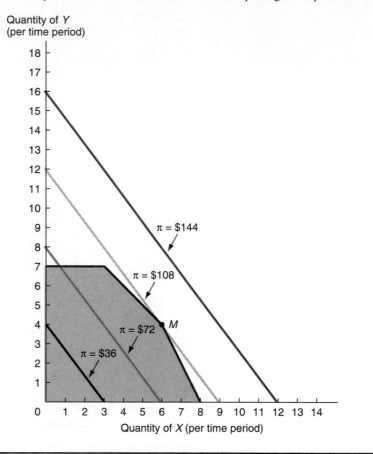

problem. No other point within the feasible spaces touches as high an isoprofit curve.

Using the combined graphic and analytical method introduced in the preceding section, Point *M* can be identified as the point where $Q_X = 6$ and $Q_Y = 4$. At *M*, constraints on Inputs *A* and *B* are binding. At *M*, 32 units of Input *A* and 10 units of Input *B* are being completely utilized in the production of *X* and *Y*. Thus, Equations 11.4 and 11.5 can be written as equalities and solved simultaneously for Q_X and Q_Y. Subtracting two times Equation 11.5 from Equation 11.4 gives

$$4Q_X + 2Q_Y = 32$$
$$\text{minus } \underline{2Q_X + 2Q_Y = 20}$$
$$2Q_X = 12$$
$$Q_X = 6.$$

FIGURE 11.9   **Graphic Solution of a Linear Programming Problem When the Objective Function Coincides with a Boundary of the Feasible Space**

When the objective function coincides with the boundary of the feasible space, several different output combinations will produce maximum profits.

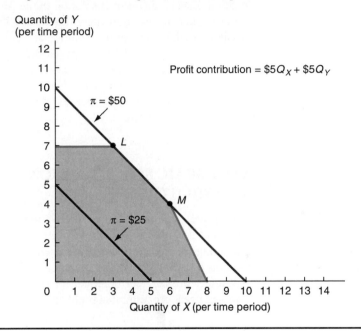

Substituting 6 for Q_X in Equation 11.5 results in

$$6 + Q_Y = 10,$$
$$Q_Y = 4.$$

Corner point

Spot in the feasible space where the x-axis, y-axis, or constraint conditions intersect.

Notice that the optimal solution to the linear programming problem occurs at a **corner point** of the feasible space. A corner point is a spot in the feasible space where the x-axis, y-axis, or constraint conditions intersect. When the objective function and all constraints are specified in linear form, as is always true in linear programming problems, the firm will always optimize at a point of capacity limitation on the feasible space boundary.

A final step is necessary to show that the optimal solution to any linear programming problem always lies at a corner of the feasible space. Because all of the relations in a linear programming problem must be linear by definition, every boundary of the feasible space is linear. Furthermore, the objective function is linear. Thus, the constrained optimization of the objective function takes place either at a corner of the feasible space, as in Figure 11.8, or at one boundary face, as is illustrated by Figure 11.9.

In Figure 11.9 the linear programming example has been modified by assuming that each unit of either X or Y yields a profit of $5. In this case, the optimal solution to the problem includes any of the combinations of X and Y found along

Line *LM*. All of these combinations are feasible and result in a total profit of $50. If all points along Line *LM* provide optimal combinations of output, the combinations found at Corners *L* and *M* are also optimal. Since the firm is indifferent about producing at Point *L* or at Point *M*, or at any point in between, any such location provides an optimal solution to the production problem. Even when the highest obtainable isoprofit curve lies along a boundary of the feasible space, it is possible to achieve an optimal solution at a corner of the feasible space.

As a result, the search for an optimal solution can be limited to just the corners of each linear programming problem's feasible space. In other words, the infinite number of points lying within the feasible space can be ignored and efforts can be concentrated solely on corner solutions. This greatly reduces the number of necessary computations.

ALGEBRAIC SPECIFICATION AND SOLUTION

The graphic technique just described illustrates the nature of linear programming, but it can be applied only in the two-output case. Since most linear programming problems contain far too many variables and constraints to allow solution by graphic analysis, algebraic methods must be employed. Algebraic techniques are of great practical relevance because they can be used to solve complex linear programming problems using modern computer software.

Slack Variables

Slack variables

Factors that indicate the amount by which constraint conditions are exceeded.

To solve linear programming problems algebraically, the concept of **slack variables** must be introduced. In the case of less-than-or-equal-to constraints, slack variables are used to *increase* the left side to equal the right side limits of the constraint conditions. In the illustrative problem, one slack variable is added to each constraint to account for excess capacity. The firm is faced with capacity constraints on Input Factors *A, B,* and *C,* so the algebraic specification of the problem contains three slack variables: S_A, indicating the units of *A* that are not used in any given solution; S_B, representing unused units of *B;* and S_C, which measures the unused units of *C.*

With slack variables, each constraint equation becomes an equality rather than an inequality. After adding the relevant slack variable, the constraint on Input *A,* $4Q_X + 2Q_Y \leq 32$, is

$$4Q_X + 2Q_Y + S_A = 32. \qquad \textbf{(11.7)}$$

$S_A = 32 - 4Q_X - 2Q_Y$ is the amount of Input *A* not used in the production of *X* or *Y.* Similar equality constraints can be specified for Inputs *B* and *C.* The equality form of the constraint on Input *B* is

$$1Q_X + 1Q_Y + S_B = 10. \qquad \textbf{(11.8)}$$

The constraint equation for Input *C* is

$$3Q_Y + S_C = 21. \qquad \textbf{(11.9)}$$

The introduction of slack variables not only simplifies algebraic analysis, but slack variables' solution values also provide useful information. In a production problem, for example, slack variables with *zero* values at the optimal solution indicate inputs that are limiting factors and cause bottlenecks. Slack variables with positive values at the optimal solution indicate excess capacity in the related input factor. Slack variables cannot take on negative values, since this would imply that the amount of resource use exceeds available supply. The information provided by slack variable solution values is important in long-range planning and is a key benefit derived from algebraic solution methods.

Algebraic Solution

The complete specification of the illustrative programming problem is as follows:

Maximize

$$\pi = \$12Q_X + \$9Q_Y, \qquad (11.3)$$

subject to these constraints:

$$4Q_X + 2Q_Y + S_A = 32, \qquad (11.7)$$

$$1Q_X + 1Q_Y + S_B = 10, \qquad (11.8)$$

$$3Q_Y + S_C = 21, \qquad (11.9)$$

where

$$Q_X \geq 0, Q_Y \geq 0, S_A \geq 0, S_B \geq 0, S_C \geq 0.$$

The problem is to find the set of values for Variables Q_X, Q_Y, S_A, S_B, and S_C that maximizes Equation 11.3 and at the same time satisfies the constraints imposed by Equations 11.7, 11.8, and 11.9.

As shown previously, a single exact solution to this linear programming problem cannot be determined. A simultaneous solution to the constraint equations must be found, but there are more unknowns (five) than constraint equations (three). In such circumstances, a unique solution does not exist; multiple solutions are possible. However, because the solution to any linear programming problem occurs at a corner of the feasible space, values can be determined for some of the unknown variables in Equations 11.7, 11.8, and 11.9. At each corner of the feasible space, the number of nonzero variables exactly equals the number of constraint equations. At each corner point, the number of known constraint conditions is exactly equal to the number of unknown variables. In such circumstances, a single unique solution can be found for each variable at each corner point of the feasible space. The optimal solution is that corner point solution with the most desirable value for the objective function.[2]

Consider Figure 11.10, in which the feasible space for the illustrative problem has been graphed once again. At the origin, where neither X nor Y is produced,

[2] In almost all linear programming problems, the number of nonzero-valued variables in all corner solutions exactly equals the number of constraints in the problem. Only under a particular condition known as *degeneracy,* when more than two constraints coincide at a single corner of the feasible space, are there fewer nonzero-valued variables. This condition does not hinder the technique of solution considered in this chapter.

FIGURE 11.10   **Determination of Zero-Valued Variables at Corners of the Feasible Space**

At all corner points of the feasible space, the number of nonzero-valued variables equals the number of constraint equations.

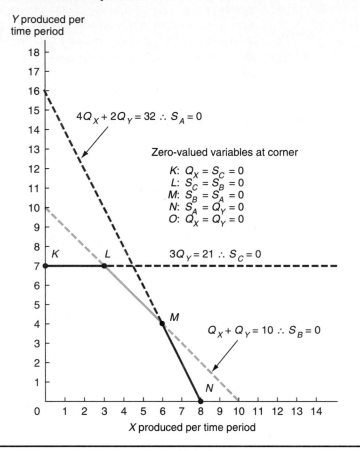

Q_X and Q_Y both equal zero. Slack exists in all inputs, however, so S_A, S_B, and S_C are all greater than zero. Now move up the vertical axis to Point K. Here Q_X and S_C both equal zero, because no X is being produced and Input C is being used to the fullest extent possible. However, Q_Y, S_A, and S_B all exceed zero. At Point L, Q_X, Q_Y, and S_A are all positive, but S_B and S_C equal zero. The remaining corners, M and N, can be examined similarly, and at each of them the number of nonzero-valued variables exactly equals the number of constraints. At each corner point, the constraints can be expressed as a system with three equations and three unknowns that can be solved algebraically.

Solving the constraint equations at each corner point provides values for Q_X and Q_Y, as well as for S_A, S_B, and S_C. The profit contribution at each corner is likewise determined by inserting relevant values for Q_X and Q_Y into the objective function (Equation 11.3). The corner solution that produces the maximum profit is the optimal solution to the linear programming problem.

Simplex solution method

Iterative technique used to provide algebraic-solution linear programming problems.

This iterative process is followed in what is called the **simplex solution method.** Computer programs find solution values for all variables at each corner point, then isolate that corner point with the optimal solution to the objective function. Long and tedious when done by hand, solving even highly complex linear programming problems takes only a few seconds when using the simplex method and high-speed desktop computers. While it is perhaps not worth delving into the simplex procedure in great detail, the method can be illustrated for the present example.

Although a unique solution for this problem is obtained when any two variables are set equal to zero, it is convenient to begin by setting Q_X and Q_Y equal to zero and examining the origin solution. Substituting zero values for Q_X and Q_Y into the constraint Equations 11.7, 11.8, and 11.9 results in a value for each slack variable that equals the total units available: $S_A = 32$, $S_B = 10$, and $S_C = 21$. At the origin, neither X nor Y is produced and no input is used in production. Total profit contribution at the origin corner of the feasible space is zero.

Similarly, it is possible to examine the solution at a second corner point, N in Figure 11.10, where Q_Y and S_A equal zero. After making the appropriate substitution into constraint Equation 11.7, the value for Q_X is

$$4Q_X + 2Q_Y + S_A = 32, \qquad (11.7)$$
$$(4 \times Q_Y) + (2 \times 0) = 32,$$
$$4Q_X = 32,$$
$$Q_X = 8.$$

With the value of Q_X determined, it is possible to substitute into Equations 11.8 and 11.9 and determine values for S_B and S_C:

$$Q_X + Q_Y + S_B = 10, \qquad (11.8)$$
$$8 + 0 + S_B = 10,$$
$$S_B = 2,$$

and

$$3Q_Y + S_C = 21, \qquad (11.9)$$
$$(3 \times 0) + S_C = 21,$$
$$S_C = 21.$$

Total profit contribution at this point is

$$\pi = \$12Q_X + \$9Q_Y$$
$$= (\$12 \times 8) + (\$9 \times 0)$$
$$= \$96. \qquad (11.3)$$

Next, assign zero values to S_B and S_A to reach solution values for Point M. Substituting zero values for S_A and S_B in Equations 11.7 and 11.8 results in two equations with two unknowns:

$$4Q_X + 2Q_Y + 0 = 32. \qquad (11.7)$$

$$Q_X + Q_Y + 0 = 10. \qquad (11.8)$$

498 **PART III** *Production and Cost Analysis*

TABLE 11.2 **Algebraic Solution to a Linear Programming Problem**

Solution at Corner	Value of Variable					Total Profit Contribution
	Q_X	Q_Y	S_A	S_B	S_C	
0	0	0	32	10	21	$ 0
N	8	0	0	2	21	96
M	6	4	0	0	9	108
L	3	7	6	0	0	99
K	0	7	18	3	0	63

Multiplying Equation 11.8 by two and subtracting this result from Equation 11.7 provides the solution value for Q_X:

$$4Q_X + 2Q_Y = 32 \tag{11.7}$$
$$\text{minus } 2Q_X + 2Q_Y = 20$$
$$2Q_X = 12$$
$$Q_X = 6.$$

Then, substituting 6 for Q_X in Equation 11.8 finds $Q_Y = 4$. Total profit contribution in this case is $108 [= (\$12 \times 6) + (\$9 \times 4)]$.

Similar algebraic analysis provides the solution for each remaining corner of the feasible space. However, rather than work through those corner solutions, the results are shown in Table 11.2. It is apparent, just as illustrated in the earlier graphic analysis, that the optimal solution occurs at Point *M,* where 6 units of *X* and 4 units of *Y* are produced. Total profit is $108, which exceeds the profit at any other corner of the feasible space.

Slack Variables at the Solution Point

At each corner point solution, values for each slack variable are also determined. For example, at the optimal solution (Corner *M*) reached in the preceding section, S_A and S_B both equal zero, meaning that Inputs *A* and *B* are used to the fullest extent possible. S_C is not equal to zero and must be solved for. To find the solution for S_C, $Q_Y = 4$ is substituted into constraint Equation 11.9:

$$3 \times Q_Y + S_C = 21, \tag{11.9}$$
$$3 \times 4 + S_C = 21,$$
$$S_C = 9.$$

The optimal combination of *X* and *Y* completely exhausts available quantities of Inputs *A* and *B,* but 9 units of Input *C* remain unused. Because Inputs *A* and *B* impose effective constraints on the firm's profits, more of each must be acquired to expand output. Input *C* is in excess supply, so the firm would certainly not want more capacity of *C;* it might even attempt to reduce its purchases of *C* during future periods. If *C* is a fixed facility, such as a machine tool, the firm might offer some of that excess capacity to other companies.

●

MANAGERIAL APPLICATION 11.2

LP on the PC!

Until recently, the complexity of real-world decision problems often made it impractical for the nonspecialist to use linear programming (LP) methods. As a result, the application of LP techniques had been largely restricted to managers of the relatively few firms that employ computer programmers and have expensive mainframe computers. Instead of using more appropriate LP methods, managers of many small-to-medium sized companies still plug hypothetical financial and operating data into spreadsheet software programs, and then recalculate profit figures to see how various changes might affect the bottom line. A major problem with this popular "What if?" approach to decision analysis is the haphazard way in which various alternatives are considered. Dozens of time-consuming recalculations are often necessary before suggestions emerge that lead to a considerable improvement in operating efficiency. Even then, managers have no assurance that superior decision alternatives are not available.

The frustrations and limitations of the "What if?" approach to decision analysis are sure to become a thing of the past following the recent publication of *What-if Solver* by Frontline Systems, Inc., a powerful userfriendly LP software program for the personal computer (PC) environment. *What-if Solver* is a powerful *Lotus 1-2-3* add-in that enables users to solve a wide range of optimization problems without leaving the spreadsheet environment. It uses the simplex method for linear constrained optimization and the generalized reduced gradient method for nonlinear constrained optimization. A professional version of *What-if Solver* is available to easily solve highly complex business and government problems at a cost of only a few hundred dollars. Better still, a student edition of *What-if Solver* is available at very modest cost that will solve most of the optimization problems that are typically encountered, including linear programming problems that involve up to 120 variables and 120 constraints. The student edition of *What-if Solver* also provides a complete sensitivity analysis for linear programming problems that will indicate, for example, objective function coefficient ranges, the potential for cost reduction, shadow prices, and so on. For users of the *Microsoft Windows* operating environment, LP software programs are often included as a basic feature of spreadsheet software. *Lotus 1-2-3 for Windows,* for example, incorporates a *Solver* LP tool that is capable of solving all but the toughest LP problems. *Solver* is extremely user-friendly for those with little LP training, and like most *Windows* programs, it requires little computer experience.

Of course, the practical value of any new tool for managerial decision making is measured in terms of how well it actually works. Early returns on this basis are very encouraging. Easy to follow linear programming applications in the student edition of *What-if Solver* illustrate how LP techniques can be used to solve problems in transportation routing, staff scheduling, and financial planning. Whenever a company needs to move a quantity of goods from and to multiple locations, such as plants, regional warehouses, or retail stores, it faces a practical LP problem. By minimizing route mileage, operating costs can also be minimized and outlays for capital investment can often be avoided. Many companies routinely save thousands of dollars per year on shipping costs by solving linear programming problems of this type. Similarly, many types of businesses and government agencies use LP methods to solve the problem of scheduling employees' working hours to meet customer service demands, which might vary by the hour or the day, in light of employee availability and preferences. Other examples of practical applications include the use of LP techniques to help banks decide on the best use of loanable funds, and models to help investors decide on the optimal allocation of a stock and bond portfolio.

What makes this advance in PC software so impressive is that it makes feasible the application of LP methods on a scale that previously was simply not possible. As new generations of user-friendly LP software emerge, appreciation of the value of the LP technique as a practical tool for decision analysis will continue to grow.

Source: Daniel H. Fylstra, *The Student Edition of What-if Solver* (Addison-Wesley Publishing Company, Reading, MA, 1991); *Lotus 1-2-3 for Windows* (Lotus Development Corporation, Cambridge, MA, 1992).

Computer-Based Solution Methods

The linear programming problem illustrated thus far is simple by design. It can be solved graphically and algebraically to illustrate the linear programming technique using both methods. However, linear programming problems encountered in the real world are often quite complex and frequently involve a large number of constraints and output variables. Such problems are too complicated to solve graphically. The geometry is messy for three outputs and impossible for four or more. In real-world applications, computer software programs use algebraic techniques to handle large numbers of variables and constraints. Although it is not necessary to extend this discussion to the use of computer-based solution methods, this approach has powerful problem-solving capability that merits the careful consideration of any user.

THE DUAL IN LINEAR PROGRAMMING

Primal

Original problem statement (symmetrical to dual).

Dual

Secondary problem statement (symmetrical to primal).

For every maximization problem in linear programming there exists a symmetrical minimization problem; for every minimization problem there exists a symmetrical maximization problem. These pairs of related maximization and minimization problems are known as the **primal** and **dual** linear programming problems. The symmetry or duality between constrained maximization and constrained minimization problems is a key concept in managerial economics. While the concept of duality has been implied earlier, an explicit examination of duality is helpful in showing the equivalence of alternative approaches to constrained optimization.

The Duality Concept

The concept of duality demonstrates the symmetry between the value of a firm's products and the value of resources used in production. With the duality concept it is possible to show that value maximization can be attained by focusing on either resource requirements and the revenue-generating capability of a firm's products or on the cost of resources and their productivity.

In addition to providing valuable insight into the economics of optimal resource employment, duality provides the key to solving difficult constrained optimization problems. Because of the symmetry between primal and dual problem specifications, either one can be constructed from the other and the solution to either problem can be used to solve both. This is helpful because it is sometimes easier to obtain the solution to the dual problem than to the original or primal problem.

Primal solution

Input for short-run operating decisions.

Dual solution

Input for long-range planning.

Finally, the duality concept also allows one to evaluate the solution to a constrained decision problem in terms of the activity required for optimization and in terms of the economic impact of constraint conditions. Analysis of the constraint conditions and slack variable solutions frequently provides important information for long-range planning. In fact, the **primal solution** is often described as a tool for short-run operating decisions, whereas the **dual solution** is often seen as a tool for long-range planning. The duality concept demonstrates the need to recognize that operating decisions and long-range planning are related.

Shadow Prices

Shadow prices

Implicit values associated with linear-programming-problem decision variables.

To examine the duality concept, the idea of implicit values or **shadow prices** must be introduced. In the primal linear programming problem discussed previously, the values Q_X and Q_Y maximize the firm's profit subject to constraints imposed by limitations of Input Factors *A, B,* and *C.* Duality theory indicates that an identical operating decision would result if one had instead chosen to minimize the costs of resources employed in producing Q_X and Q_Y, subject to an output constraint.

The key to this duality is that relevant costs are not the acquisition costs of inputs but, rather, the economic costs of using them. For a resource that is available in a fixed amount, this cost is not acquisition cost but opportunity cost. Consider, for example, a skilled labor force employed by a firm. If workers are fully utilized producing valuable products, a reduction in skilled labor will reduce valuable output, and an increase in skilled labor will increase the production of valuable output. If some labor is shifted from the production of one product to another, the cost of using skilled labor in this new activity is the value of the original product that can no longer be produced. The marginal cost of a constrained resource that is fully utilized is its opportunity cost as measured by the value of foregone production. If a limited resource such as skilled labor is not fully utilized, then at least the last unit of that resource is not productive and its marginal value is zero. Acquiring additional excess resources does not increase valuable output. The firm would incur a zero opportunity cost if it applied currently unused resources in some different activity.

The economic value, or opportunity cost, of a constrained resource depends on the extent to which it is utilized. When a limited resource is fully utilized, its marginal value in use is positive. When a constrained resource is not fully utilized, its marginal value in use is zero. Minimizing the value of limited resources used to produce valuable output is nothing more than minimizing the opportunity cost of employing those resources. Minimization of opportunity costs is equivalent to maximizing the value of output produced with those resources.

Since the economic value of constrained resources is determined by their value in use rather than by historical acquisition costs, such amounts are called implicit values or shadow prices. The term *shadow price* is used because it represents the price that a manager would be willing to pay for additional units of a constrained resource. Comparing the shadow price of a resource with its acquisition price indicates whether the firm has an incentive to increase or decrease the amount acquired during future production periods. If shadow prices exceed acquisition prices, the resource's marginal value exceeds marginal cost and the firm has an incentive to expand employment. If acquisition cost exceeds the shadow price, there is an incentive to reduce employment. These relations and the importance of duality can be clarified by relating the dual to the linear programming problem discussed previously.

The Dual Objective Function

In the original or primal problem statement, the goal is to maximize profits, and the (primal) objective function is

Maximize

$$\pi = \$12Q_X + \$9Q_Y. \tag{11.3}$$

The dual problem goal is to minimize implicit values or shadow prices for the firm's resources.[3] Defining V_A, V_B, and V_C as the shadow prices for Inputs A, B, and C, respectively, and π^* as the total implicit value of the firm's fixed resources, the dual objective function (the dual) is

Minimize

$$\pi^* = 32V_A + 10V_B + 21V_C. \qquad (11.10)$$

Since the firm has 32 units of A, the total implicit value of Input A is 32 times A's shadow price, or $32V_A$. If V_A, or Input A's shadow price, is found to be \$1.50 when the dual equations are solved, the implicit value of A is \$48 ($= 32 \times \$1.50$). Inputs B and C are handled in the same way.

The Dual Constraints

In the primal problem, the constraints stated that the total units of each input used in the production of X and Y must be equal to or less than the available quantity of input. In the dual, the constraints state that the total value of inputs used in the production of one unit of X or one unit of Y must not be less than the profit contribution provided by a unit of these products. In other words, the shadow prices of A, B, and C times the amount of each of the inputs needed to produce a unit of X or Y must be equal to or greater than the unit profit contribution of X or of Y. Because resources have value only when used to produce output, they can never have an implicit value, or opportunity cost, that is less than the value of output.

In the example, unit profit is defined as the excess of price over variable cost, price and variable cost are both constant, and profit per unit for X is \$12 and for Y is \$9. As shown in Table 11.1, each unit of X requires 4 units of A, 1 unit of B, and 0 units of C. The total implicit value of resources used to produce X is $4V_A + 1V_B$. The constraint requiring that the implicit cost of producing X be equal to or greater than the profit contribution of X is

$$4V_A + 1V_B \geq 12. \qquad (11.11)$$

Because 2 units of A, 1 unit of B, and 3 units of C are required to produce each unit of Y, the second dual constraint is

$$2V_A + 1V_B + 3V_C \geq 9. \qquad (11.12)$$

Since the firm produces only two products, the dual problem has only two constraint equations.

Dual Slack Variables

Dual slack variables can be incorporated into the problem, thus allowing the constraint conditions to be expressed as equalities. Letting L_X and L_Y represent the two slack variables, constraint Equations 11.11 and 11.12 become

$$4V_A + 1V_B - L_X = 12, \qquad (11.13)$$

[3]Note: Rules for constructing the dual linear programming problem from its related primal are provided in Appendix 11A at the end of this chapter.

and

$$2V_A + 1V_B + 3V_C - L_Y = 9. \qquad (11.14)$$

These slack variables are *subtracted* from the constraint equations, since greater-than-or-equal-to inequalities are involved. Using slack variables, the left side of the constraint conditions are thus *decreased* to equal the right side profit contributions. Dual slack variables measure the *excess* of input value over output value for each product. Alternatively, dual slack variables measure the opportunity cost associated with production of X and Y. This can be seen by examining the two constraint equations. Solving constraint Equation 11.13 for L_X, for example, provides

$$L_X = 4V_A + 1V_B - 12.$$

This expression states that L_X is equal to the implicit cost of producing 1 unit of X minus the profit contribution provided by that product. The dual slack variable L_X is a measure of the opportunity cost of producing Product X. It compares the profit contribution of Product X, $12, with the value to the firm of the resources necessary to produce it.

A zero value for L_X indicates that the marginal value of resources required to produce one unit of X is exactly equal to the profit contribution received. This is similar to marginal cost being equal to marginal revenue at the profit-maximizing output level. A positive value for L_X indicates that the resources used in the production of X are more valuable, in terms of the profit contribution they can generate, when used to produce the other product Y. A nonzero value of L_X measures the firm's opportunity cost (profit loss) associated with production of Product X. The slack variable L_Y is the opportunity cost of producing Product Y. It will have a value of zero if the implicit value of resources used to produce 1 unit of Y exactly equals the $9 profit contribution provided by that product. A positive value for L_Y measures the opportunity loss in terms of the foregone profit contribution associated with the production of Y.

A firm would not choose to produce if the value of resources required were greater than the value of resulting output. It follows that a product with a positive slack variable (opportunity cost) is included in the optimal production combination.

Solving the Dual Problem

The dual programming problem can be solved with the same algebraic technique that was employed to obtain the primal solution. In this case, the dual problem is

Minimize

$$\pi^* = 34V_A + 10V_B + 21V_C, \qquad (11.10)$$

subject to

$$4V_A + 1V_B - L_X = 12, \qquad (11.13)$$

and

$$2V_A + 1V_B + 3V_C - L_Y = 9, \qquad (11.14)$$

TABLE 11.3   Solutions for the Dual Programming Problem

Solution Number	Value of the Variable					Total Value Imputed to the Firm's Resources
	V_A	V_B	V_C	L_X	L_Y	
1	0	0	0	−12	−9	[a]
2	0	0	3	−12	0	[a]
3	0	0	[b]	0	[b]	[a]
4	0	9	0	−3	0	[a]
5	0	12	0	0	3	$120
6	0	12	−1	0	0	[a]
7	4.5	0	0	6	0	$144
8	3	0	0	0	−3	[a]
9	3	0	1	0	0	$117
10	1.5	6	0	0	0	$108

[a] Outside the feasible space.
[b] No real-number solution.

where

$$V_A, V_B, V_C, L_X, \text{ and } L_Y \text{ all} \geq 0.$$

Because there are only two constraints in this programming problem, the maximum number of nonzero-valued variables at any corner solution is two. One can proceed with the solution by setting three of the variables equal to zero and solving the constraint equations for the values of the remaining two. By comparing the value of the objective function at each feasible solution, the point at which the function is minimized can be determined. This is the dual solution.

To illustrate the process, first set $V_A = V_B = V_C = 0$, and solve for L_X and L_Y:

$$(4 \times 0) + (1 \times 0) - L_X = 12, \tag{11.13}$$
$$L_X = -12.$$

$$(2 \times 0) + (1 \times 0) + 0 + (3 \times 0) - L_Y = 9, \tag{11.14}$$
$$L_Y = -9.$$

Since L_X and L_Y cannot be negative, this solution is outside the feasible set.

The values just obtained are inserted into Table 11.3 as Solution 1. All other solution values can be calculated in a similar manner and used to complete Table 11.3. It is apparent from the table that not all solutions lie within the feasible space. Only Solutions 5, 7, 9, and 10 meet the nonnegativity requirement while also providing a number of nonzero-valued variables that are exactly equal to the number of constraints. These four solutions coincide with the corners of the dual problem's feasible space.

At Solution 10, the total implicit value of Inputs *A, B,* and *C* is minimized. Solution 10 is the optimum solution, where the total implicit value of employed resources exactly equals the $108 maximum profit primal solution. Thus, optimal solutions to primal and dual objective functions are identical.

At the optimal solution, the shadow price for Input *C* is zero, $V_C = 0$. Because shadow price measures the marginal value of an input, a zero shadow price implies that the resource in question has a zero marginal value to the firm. Adding another unit of this input adds nothing to the firm's maximum obtainable profit. A zero shadow price for Input C is consistent with the primal solution that Input C is not a binding constraint. Excess capacity exists in C, so additional units of C would not result in increased production of either X or Y. The shadow price for Input A of \$1.50 implies that this fixed resource imposes a binding constraint. If an additional unit of A is added, the firm can increase total profit by \$1.50. It would increase profits to buy additional units of Input A at any price less than \$1.50 per unit, at least up until the point at which A is no longer a binding constraint. This assumes that the cost of Input A is currently fixed. If those costs are variable, the firm would be willing to pay \$1.50 *above* the current price of Input A to eliminate this constraint. Since availability of B also imposes an effective constraint, the firm can also afford to pay up to \$6 for a marginal unit of B.

Finally, both dual slack variables equal zero at the optimal solution. This means that the implicit value of resources required to produce a single unit of X or Y is exactly equal to the profit contribution provided. The opportunity cost of producing X and Y is zero, meaning that the resources required for their production are not more valuable in some alternative use. This is consistent with the primal solution, since both X and Y are produced at the optimal solution. Any product with a positive opportunity cost is suboptimal and would not be produced.

Using the Dual Solution to Solve the Primal

The dual solution does not indicate optimal amounts of X and Y. It does, however, provide all the information necessary to determine the optimum output mix. The dual solution shows that Input C does not impose a binding constraint on output of X and Y. Further, it demonstrates that $\pi = \pi^* = \$108$ at the optimum output of X and Y. The dual solution also offers evidence on the value of primal constraint slack variables. To see this, recall the three constraints in the primal problem:

$$\text{Constraint on } A: \quad 4Q_X + 2Q_Y + S_A = 32,$$
$$\text{Constraint on } B: \quad 1Q_X + 1Q_Y + S_B = 10,$$
$$\text{Constraint on } C: \quad 3Q_Y + S_C = 21.$$

The dual solution indicates that the constraints on A and B are binding, because both inputs have positive shadow prices, and only resources that are fully utilized have a nonzero marginal value. Accordingly, the slack variables S_A and S_B equal zero, and the binding primal constraints can be rewritten as

$$4Q_X + 2Q_Y = 32,$$

and

$$1Q_X + 1Q_Y = 10.$$

With two equations and only two unknowns, this system can be solved for Q_X and Q_Y. Multiplying the second constraint by two and subtracting from the first provides

●

MANAGERIAL APPLICATION 11.3
A New LP Solution for an Old Puzzle

Using high-speed electronic computers and innovative computer software, researchers at the Du Pont Co. and Purdue University have found a solution to a classic and previously unsolved puzzle: the traveling salesperson problem, or TSP for short. The TSP is one of those riddles that have confounded mathematicians and business logistics personnel for centuries. The problem is to determine the shortest, least costly route for a salesperson to travel to visit a given set of cities. The salesperson must travel to each city once, never retrace steps, and return to the original location. Though a simple problem when only a few customer locations are involved, the difficulty of the problem quickly multiplies as the number of customers and customer locations grows. For more than a few stops, the complexity of the problem mushrooms.

Though simply stated, the TSP has many practical implications and is symptomatic of a large class of scientific and engineering problems that are frequently encountered in business and scientific applications. Until now, mathematicians have used algorithms, or computer-based solution routines, to map out routes that are longer or more costly than the optimal course but nevertheless provide the best information available. These so-called heuristic algorithms begin at a given location, cast about for the shortest path to the next nearest location, go there, and restart the process until a complete travel map has been developed. Heuristic algorithms are often used to solve realistic problems involving travel among 100,000 cities or so in a timely fashion on high-speed computer workstations. Of course, although such solutions might be helpful in scheduling travel for large multinational corporations, their more practical application is in the electronics industry where more than a million locations are often involved in the manufacture of circuit boards. Similarly, these routines are widely employed in scheduling manufacturing processes that involve several different machines or multiple sequential processes.

Exact algorithms have been limited to TSPs where the distances between cities or other locations are sym-

metric, meaning that it takes as long to go from point X to point Y as it does from point Y to point X. These algorithms can't deal with the complexity of asymmetric problems where, for example, one city might be in a costly and difficult to reach location such as a mountain top, while another might be in an easy to reach valley. Then it is more costly to go from Y to X than it is from X to Y. Such asymmetric problems are often encountered in scheduling manufacturing processes where, for example, it takes longer and is more costly to paint a black car white than a white car black. Asymmetric costs are also typical in the scheduling of chemical processes. Achieving the ideal of a "no-wait flow shop," in which processing moves smoothly from one machine to the next without waiting, is made difficult by the fact that processing times at each machine differ markedly.

The new method or algorithm for solving the TSP problem was reported in 1991 by Donald L. Miller of Du Pont's central research and development department in Wilmington, Delaware, and Joseph F. Penky of Purdue's chemical engineering school in West Lafayette, Indiana. They discovered a new set of procedures or computer instructions for exactly solving both symmetric and asymmetric TSPs at modest cost and in a reasonable amount of time. Previously available exact algorithms took from 25 to 30 hours to solve on a supercomputer, even for relatively modest symmetric problems involving roughly two thousand locations. Miller and Penky's algorithm is capable of providing exact solutions to complex asymmetric TSPs—such as a no-wait flow shop problem involving 100 jobs that have to be performed in exact sequence at four different locations. Using a Sun Microsoft 4/330 workstation, the new algorithm provides an exact solution to such problems in only 20 seconds.

Although Miller and Penky's new algorithm doesn't solve all types of TSPs, their work has generated a lot of business interest by demonstrating that exact practical solutions to TSPs are indeed possible.

Source: Jerry E. Bishop, "Mathematicians Find Solution to Old Puzzle," *The Wall Street Journal,* February 15, 1991, B1, B2.

$$4Q_X + 2Q_Y = 32,$$
$$\text{minus } \underline{2Q_X + 2Q_Y = 20,}$$
$$2Q_X = 12,$$
$$Q_X = 6,$$

and

$$6 + Q_Y = 10,$$
$$Q_Y = 4.$$

These values of Q_X and Q_Y, found after learning from the dual which constraints were binding, are identical to the values found by solving the primal problem directly. Having obtained the value for Q_Y, it is possible to substitute Constraint C and solve for the amount of slack in that resource:

$$3Q_Y + S_C = 21,$$
$$S_C = 21 - 3 \times 4 = 9.$$

These relations, which allow one to solve either the primal or the dual specification of a linear programming problem and then quickly obtain the solution to the other, can be generalized by the two following expressions:

$$\text{Primal Objective Variable}_i \times \text{Dual Slack Variable}_i \equiv 0 \qquad \textbf{(11.15)}$$

$$\text{Primal Slack Variable}_j \times \text{Dual Objective Variable}_j \equiv 0 \qquad \textbf{(11.16)}$$

Equation 11.15 states that if an ordinary variable in the primal problem takes on a nonzero value in the optimal solution to that problem, its related dual slack variable must be zero. Only if a particular Q_i is zero-valued in the solution to the primal can its related dual slack variable, L_i, take on a nonzero value. A similar relation holds between the slack variables in the primal problem and their related ordinary variables in the dual, as indicated by Equation 11.16. If the primal slack variable is nonzero valued, then the related dual variable will be zero valued, and vice versa.

CONSTRAINED COST MINIMIZATION: ANOTHER LINEAR PROGRAMMING EXAMPLE

▶ Constrained cost-minimization problems are frequently encountered in managerial decision making. One such example is the marketing problem of minimizing advertising expenditures subject to meeting certain audience exposure requirements. For example, consider a firm that is planning an advertising campaign for a new product. Goals set for the campaign include exposure to at least 100,000 individuals, no fewer than 80,000 of whom have an annual income of at least $50,000 and no fewer than 40,000 of whom are single. For simplicity, assume that the firm has only radio and television media available for this campaign. One television ad costs $10,000 and is expected to reach an average audience of 20,000 persons. Ten thousand of these individuals will have an income of $50,000 or

TABLE 11.4   **Advertising Media Relations**

	Radio	Television
Cost per ad	$ 6,000	$10,000
Total audience per ad	10,000	20,000
Audience per ad with income $\geq$ $50,000	10,000	10,000
Unmarried audience per ad	8,000	4,000

more, and 4,000 will be single. A radio ad costs $6,000 and reaches a total audience of 10,000, all of whom have at least $50,000 in income. Eight thousand of those exposed to a radio ad are single. Table 11.4 summarizes these data.

The Primal Problem   The objective is to minimize the cost of the advertising campaign. Since total cost is merely the sum of the amounts spent on radio and television ads, the objective function is

Minimize

$$\text{Cost} = \$6,000R + \$10,000TV,$$

where R and TV represent the number of radio and television ads, respectively, that are employed in the advertising campaign.

This linear programming problem has three constraint equations, including the minimum audience exposure requirement, the audience income requirement, and the marital status requirement. The minimum audience exposure requirement states that the number of persons exposed to radio ads plus the number exposed to television ads must be equal to or greater than 100,000 persons. Algebraically, 10,000 times the number of radio ads plus 20,000 times the number of television ads must be equal to or greater than 100,000:

$$10,000R + 20,000TV \geq 100,000.$$

The two remaining constraints can be constructed in a similar fashion from the data in Table 11.4. The audience income constraint is written

$$10,000R + 10,000TV \geq 80,000,$$

and the marital status constraint is given by

$$8,000R + 4,000TV \geq 40,000.$$

Combining the cost-minimization objective function with these three constraint conditions written in equality form using slack variables gives the complete linear programming problem:

Minimize

$$\text{Cost} = \$6,000R + \$10,000TV,$$

subject to

$$10{,}000R + 20{,}000TV - S_A = 100{,}000,$$
$$10{,}000R + 10{,}000TV - S_I = 80{,}000,$$
$$8{,}000R + 4{,}000TV - S_S = 40{,}000,$$

and

$$R, TV, S_A, S_I, \text{ and } S_S \geq 0.$$

S_A, S_I, and S_S are slack variables indicating the extent to which minimums on total audience exposure, exposure to individuals with incomes of at least $50,000, and exposure to single individuals, respectively, have been exceeded. Note that each slack variable is *subtracted* from the relevant constraint equation because greater-than-or-equal-to inequalities are involved. Excess capacity or nonzero slack variables for any of the constraints means that audience exposure minimums have been exceeded.

The solution to this linear programming problem is easily obtained using a combination of graphic and analytical methods. Figure 11.11 illustrates that solution. The feasible space problem is bordered by the three constraint equations and the nonnegativity requirements. An isocost curve shows that costs are minimized at Point *M,* where the total audience exposure and income constraints are binding. With these constraints binding, slack variables $S_A = S_I = 0$. Thus,

$$10{,}000R + 20{,}000TV = 100{,}000,$$
$$\text{minus } \underline{10{,}000R + 10{,}000TV = 80{,}000,}$$
$$10{,}000TV = 20{,}000,$$
$$TV = 2,$$

and

$$10{,}000R + 20{,}000(2) = 100{,}000,$$
$$10{,}000R = 60{,}000,$$
$$R = 6.$$

The firm should employ 6 radio ads and 2 television ads to minimize costs while still meeting audience exposure requirements. Total cost for such a campaign is $56,000.

The Dual Problem

The dual to the advertising-mix linear programming problem offers interesting and valuable information to management. The dual is a constrained-maximization problem, since the primal problem is a minimization problem. The objective function of the dual is expressed in terms of shadow prices or implicit values for the primal problem constraint conditions. Thus, the dual objective function includes an implicit value, or shadow price, for the minimum audience exposure requirement, the audience income requirement, and the marital status requirement. Since constraint limits in the primal problem become the dual objective function coefficients, the dual objective function is

FIGURE 11.11   **Advertising Cost-Minimization Linear Programming Problem**

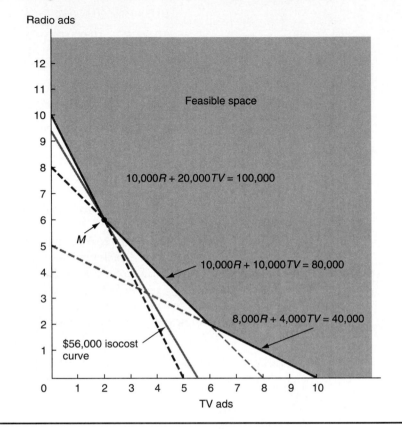

Maximize

$$C^* = 100{,}000V_A + 80{,}000V_I + 40{,}000V_S,$$

where V_A, V_I, and V_S are shadow prices for the minimum audience exposure, audience income, and marital status requirements.

Dual constraints are based on the two variables from the primal objective function. Thus, there are two constraint conditions in the dual, the first associated with radio ads and the second with television ads. Both constraints are of the less-than-or-equal-to type, since primal constraints are of the greater-than-or-equal-to type.

The radio advertising constraint limit is the $6,000 radio ads coefficient from the primal objective function. Coefficients for each shadow price in this constraint equation are given by the advertising effectiveness measures for a single radio ad. The coefficient for the audience exposure shadow price, V_A, is 10,000, the number of individuals reached by a single radio ad. Similarly, the coefficient for V_I is 10,000 and that for V_S is 8,000. Thus, the dual radio ads constraint is

$$10{,}000V_A + 10{,}000V_I + 8{,}000V_S \leq \$6{,}000.$$

The dual television advertising constraint is developed in the same fashion. Since each TV ad reaches a total audience of 20,000, this is the coefficient for the V_A variable in the second dual constraint equation. Coefficients for V_I and V_S are 10,000 and 4,000, respectively, because these are the numbers of high-income and single persons reached by one TV ad. The $10,000 cost of a television ad is the limit to the second dual constraint, which can be written

$$20{,}000V_A + 10{,}000V_I + 4{,}000V_S \leq \$10{,}000.$$

Following the introduction of constraint slack variables, the dual programming problem is

Maximize

$$C^* = 100{,}000V_A + 80{,}000V_I + 40{,}000V_S,$$

subject to

$$10{,}000V_A + 10{,}000V_I + 8{,}000V_S + L_R = \$\ 6{,}000,$$
$$20{,}000V_A + 10{,}000V_I + 4{,}000V_S + L_{TV} = \$10{,}000,$$

and

$$V_A, V_I, V_S, L_R, \text{ and } L_{TV} \geq 0.$$

Solving the Dual

It is possible but difficult to solve this dual problem using a three-dimensional graph or the simplex method. However, because the primal problem has been solved already, information from this solution can be used to easily solve the dual. Remember that the solution to the primal and dual of a single linear programming problem are complementary, and the following must hold:

$$\text{Primal Objective Variable}_i \times \text{Dual Slack Variable}_i \equiv 0.$$
$$\text{Primal Slack Variable}_j \times \text{Dual Objective Variable}_j \equiv 0.$$

In this linear programming problem,

$$R \times L_R = 0 \text{ and } TV \times L_{TV} = 0,$$

and

$$S_A \times V_A = 0, S_I \times V_I = 0, \text{ and } S_S \times V_S = 0.$$

Because both R and TV have nonzero solutions in the primal, the dual slack variables L_R and L_{TV} must equal zero at the optimal solution. Furthermore, since there is excess audience exposure to the single marital status category in the primal solution, $S_S \neq 0$, the related dual shadow price variable V_S must also equal zero in the optimal solution. This leaves only V_A and V_I as two unknowns in the two-equation system of dual constraints:

$$10{,}000V_A + 10{,}000V_I = \$\ 6{,}000,$$
$$20{,}000V_A + 10{,}000V_I = \$10{,}000.$$

Subtracting the second constraint equation from the first gives

$$-10,000V_A = -\$4,000,$$

$$V_A = \$0.40.$$

Substituting the value \$0.40 for V_A in either constraint equation produces a value of \$0.20 for V_I. Finally, substituting the appropriate values for V_A, V_I, and V_S into the dual objective function gives a value of $C^* = \$56,000\,(=[\$0.40 \times 100,000]+[\$0.20 \times 80,000]+[\$0 \times 40,000])$. This is the same figure as the \$56,000 minimum cost solution to the primal.

Interpreting the Dual Solution

The primal solution tells management the minimum-cost advertising mix. The dual problem results are equally valuable. Each dual shadow price indicates the change in cost that would accompany a one-unit change in the various audience exposure requirements. These prices show the marginal costs of increasing each audience exposure requirement by one unit. For example, V_A is the marginal cost of reaching the last individual in the overall audience. If there were a one-person reduction in the total audience exposure requirement, a cost saving of $V_A = \$0.40$ would be realized. The marginal cost of increasing total audience exposure from 100,000 to 100,001 individuals would also be 40¢.

Shadow prices for the remaining constraint conditions are interpreted in a similar manner. The shadow price for reaching individuals with incomes of at least \$50,000 is $V_I = \$0.20$, or 20¢. It would cost an extra 20¢ per person to reach more high-income individuals. A zero value for V_S, the marital status shadow price, means that the proposed advertising campaign already reaches more than the 40,000 minimum required number of single persons. Thus, a small change in the marital status constraint has no effect on total costs.

By comparing these marginal costs with the benefits derived from additional exposure, management is able to judge the effectiveness of its media advertising campaign. If the expected profit per exposure exceeds 40¢, it would prove profitable to design an advertising campaign for a larger audience. Likewise, if the expected return per exposure to high-income individuals is greater than 20¢, promotion to this category of potential customers should be increased. Conversely, if marginal profitability is less than marginal cost, audience size and/or income requirements should be reduced.

Dual slack variables also have an interesting interpretation. They represent opportunity costs of using each advertising medium. L_R measures the excess of cost over benefit associated with using radio, whereas L_{TV} indicates the excess of cost over benefit for television. Since $L_R = L_{TV} = 0$, the marginal benefit derived just equals the marginal cost incurred for both media. Both radio and TV are included in the optimal media mix, as was indicated in the primal solution.

This example again demonstrates the symmetry of the primal and dual specifications of linear programming problems. Either specification can be used to describe and solve the same basic problem. Both primal and dual problem statements and solutions offer valuable insight for decision making.

SUMMARY

Linear programming is a valuable technique for solving maximization or minimization problems in which inequality constraints are imposed on the decision maker. This chapter introduces graphic and analytic approaches for setting up, solving, and interpreting the solutions to such problems.

- **Linear programming** is a proven optimization tool used to isolate the best solution, or **optimal solution,** to decision problems. The technique is ideally suited to solving decision problems that involve an objective function to be maximized or minimized, where the relevant objective function is subject to underlying constraints.

- Simple linear programming problems can be solved graphically using the **relative distance method.** The **feasible space** is the graphical region showing the linear programming problem solution space that is both technically and economically feasible.

- An equation that expresses the goal of a linear programming problem is called the **objective function.**

- The optimal solution to a linear programming problem occurs at the intersection of the objective function and a **corner point** of the feasible space. A corner point is a spot in the feasible space where the x-axis, y-axis, or constraint conditions intersect.

- **Slack variables** indicate the amount by which constraint conditions are exceeded. In the case of less-than-or-equal-to constraints, slack variables are used to *increase* the left-side to equal the right-side limits of the constraint conditions. In the case of greater-than-or-equal-to constraints, slack variables are used to *decrease* the left-side to equal the right-side limits of the constraint conditions.

- The **simplex solution method** is an iterative method used to solve linear programming problems. In this procedure, computer programs find solution values for all variables at each corner point, then isolate that corner point with the optimal solution to the objective function.

- For every maximization problem in linear programming there exists a symmetrical minimization problem; for every minimization problem there exists a symmetrical maximization problem. These pairs of related maximization and minimization problems are known as the **primal** and **dual** linear programming problems.

- The **primal solution** is often described as a tool for short-run operating decisions, whereas the **dual solution** is often seen as a tool for long-range planning. Both provide management with valuable insight for the decision-making process.

- **Shadow prices** are implicit values or opportunity costs associated with linear-programming-problem decision variables. In the case of output, shadow prices indicate the marginal cost of a one-unit increase in output. In the case of the constraints, shadow prices indicate the marginal cost of a one-unit relaxation in the constraint condition.

During recent years, rapid advances in user-friendly computer software have allowed the widespread application of linear programming techniques to a broad range of complex managerial decision problems. With the background provided in this chapter, it is possible to apply this powerful technique to a wide array of problems in business, government, and the not-for-profit sector.

Questions

Q11.1   Give some illustrations of managerial decision situations in which you think the linear programming technique would be useful.

Q11.2   Why can't linear programming be used in each of the following situations?
A. Strong economies of scale exist.
B. As the firm expands output, the prices of variable factors of production increase.
C. As output increases, product prices decline.

Q11.3   Do equal distances along a given production process ray in a linear programming problem always represent an identical level of output?

Q11.4   Assume that output can be produced only using Processes A and B. Process A requires Inputs L and K to be combined in the fixed ratio $2L:4K$, and Process B requires $4L:2K$. Is it possible to produce output efficiently using $3L$ and $3K$? Why or why not?

Q11.5   Describe the relative distance method used in graphic linear programming analysis.

Q11.6   Is the number of isocost, isorevenue, or isoprofit lines in a typical two-input bounded feasible space limited?

Q11.7   In linear programming, why is it so critical that the number of nonzero-valued variables exactly equals the number of constraints at corners of the feasible space?

Q11.8   Will maximizing a profit contribution objective function always result in also maximizing total net profits?

Q11.9   The primal problem calls for determining the set of outputs that will maximize profit, subject to input constraints.
A. What is the dual objective function?
B. What interpretation can be given to the dual variables called the shadow prices or implicit values?
C. What does it mean if a dual variable or shadow price equals zero?

Q11.10   How are the solution values for primal and dual linear programming problems actually employed in practice?

Self-Test Problem

Idaho Natural Resources (INR) has two mines with different production capabilities for producing the same type of ore. After mining and crushing, the ore is graded into three classes: high, medium, and low. The company has contracted to provide local smelters with 24 tons of high-grade ore, 16 tons of medium-grade ore, and 48 tons of low-grade ore each week. It costs INR $10,000 per day to operate Mine A and $5,000 per day to run Mine B. In a day's time, Mine A produces 6 tons of high-grade ore, 2 tons of medium-grade ore, and 4 tons of low-grade ore. Mine B produces 2, 2, and 12 tons per day of each grade, respectively. Management's short-run problem is to determine how many days per week to operate each mine under current conditions. In the long run, management wishes to know how sensitive these decisions will be to changing economic conditions.

A report prepared for the company by an independent management consultant addressed the company's short-run operating concerns. The consultant claimed that the operating problem could be solved using linear programming techniques by which the firm would seek to minimize the total cost of meeting contractual requirements. Specifically, the consultant recommended that INR do the following:

Minimize

$$\text{Total Cost} = \$10,000A + \$5,000B,$$

subject to

$$6A + 2B \geq 24 \quad \text{(high-grade ore constraint)},$$
$$2A + 2B \geq 16 \quad \text{(medium-grade ore constraint)},$$
$$4A + 12B \geq 48 \quad \text{(low-grade ore constraint)},$$
$$A \leq 7 \quad \text{(Mine } A \text{ operating days in a week constraint)},$$
$$B \leq 7 \quad \text{(Mine } B \text{ operating days in a week constraint)},$$

or, in their equality form:

$$6A + 2B - S_H = 24,$$
$$2A + 2B - S_M = 16,$$
$$4A + 12B - S_L = 48,$$
$$A + S_A = 7,$$
$$B + S_B = 7,$$

where

$$A, B, S_H, S_M, S_L, S_A, \text{ and } S_B \geq 0.$$

Here, A and B represent the days of operation per week for each mine; S_H, S_M, and S_L represent excess production of high-, medium-, and low-grade ore, respectively; and S_A and S_B are days per week that each mine is not operated.

A graphic representation of the linear programming problem was also provided. The graph suggests an optimal solution at Point X, where Constraints 1 and 2 are binding. Thus, $S_H = S_M = 0$, and

$$6A + 2B - 0 = 24,$$
$$\text{minus } \underline{2A + 2B - 0 = 16,}$$
$$4A = 8,$$
$$A = 2 \text{ days per week.}$$

Substitute $A = 2$ into the high-grade ore constraint:

$$6(2) + 2B = 24,$$
$$12 + 2B = 24,$$
$$2B = 12$$
$$B = 6 \text{ days per week.}$$

A minimum total operating cost per week of $50,000 is suggested, since

$$\begin{aligned} \text{Total Cost} &= \$10{,}000A + \$5{,}000B \\ &= \$10{,}000(2) + \$5{,}000(6) \\ &= \$50{,}000. \end{aligned}$$

Idaho Natural Resources, Ltd., (INR) LP Graph

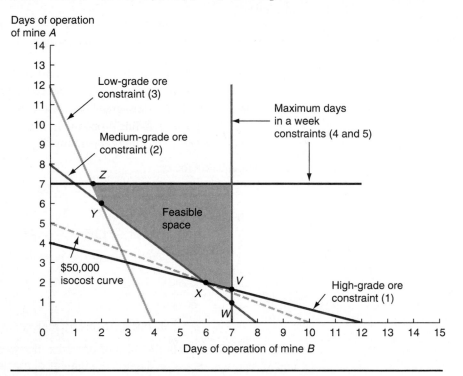

The consultant's report did not discuss a variety of important long-run planning issues. Specifically, INR wishes to know the following, holding all else equal:

A. How much, if any, excess production would result if the consultant's operating recommendation were followed?

B. What would be the cost effect of increasing low-grade ore sales by 50 percent?

C. What is INR's minimum acceptable price per ton if it is to renew a current contract to provide one of its customers with 6 tons of high-grade ore per week?

D. With current output requirements, how much would the cost of operating Mine *A* have to rise before INR would change its operating decision?

E. What increase in the cost of operating Mine *B* would cause INR to change its current operating decision?

Solution to
Self-Test Problem

A. If the consultant's operating recommendation of $A = 2$ and $B = 6$ were followed, 32 tons of excess low-grade ore production would result. No excess production of high- or medium-grade ore would occur. This can be shown by solving for S_H, S_M, and S_L at the recommended activity level.

From the constraint equations, we find the following:

$$(1) \qquad 6(2) + 2(6) - S_H = 24,$$
$$S_H = 0.$$

$$(2) \qquad 2(2) + 2(6) - S_M = 16,$$
$$S_M = 0.$$

$$(3) \qquad 4(2) + 12(6) - S_L = 48,$$
$$S_L = 32.$$

B. There would be a *zero cost impact* of an increase in low-grade ore sales from 48 to 72 tons ($= 1.5 \times 48$). With $A = 2$ and $B = 6$, 80 tons of low-grade ore are produced. A 50 percent increase in low-grade ore sales would simply reduce excess production from $S_L = 32$ to $S_L = 8$, since

$$(3') \qquad 4(2) + 12(6) - S_L = 72,$$
$$S_L = 8.$$

Graphically, the effect of a 50 percent increase in low-grade ore sales would be to cause a rightward shift in the low-grade ore constraint to a new constraint line with endpoints $(0B, 18A)$ and $(6B, 0A)$. While such a shift would reduce the feasible space, it would not affect the optimal operating decision of $A = 1$ and $B = 6$ (at Point X).

C. If INR didn't renew a contract to provide one of its current customers with 6 tons of high-grade ore per week, the high-grade ore constraint would fall from 24 to 18 tons per week. The new high-grade ore constraint, reflecting a parallel leftward shift, is written

$$(1') \qquad 6A + 2B - S_H = 18$$

and has endpoints $(0B, 3A)$ and $(9B, 0A)$. With such a reduction in required high-grade ore sales, the high-grade ore constraint would no longer be binding and the optimal production point would shift to Point W and $A = 1$ and $B = 7$ (since $S_M = S_B = 0$). At this point, high-grade ore production would equal 20 tons, or 2 tons more than the new high-grade ore requirement:

$$6(1) + 2(7) - S_H = 18,$$
$$S_H = 2,$$

with operating costs of

$$\text{Total Cost} = \$10,000A + \$5,000B$$
$$= \$10,000(1) + \$5,000(7)$$
$$= \$45,000.$$

Therefore, renewing a contract to provide one of its current customers with 6 tons of high-grade ore per week would result in our earlier operating decision of $A = 2$ and $B = 6$ and total costs of \$50,000, rather than the $A = 1$ and $B = 7$ and total costs of \$45,000 that would otherwise be possible. The marginal cost of renewing the 6-ton contract is \$5,000, or \$833 per ton.

$$\text{Marginal Cost} = \frac{\text{Change in Operating Costs}}{\text{Number of Tons}}$$

$$= \frac{\$50,000 - \$45,000}{6}$$

$$= \$833 \text{ per ton.}$$

D. In general, the isocost relation for this problem is

$$C_0 = C_A A + C_B B,$$

where C_0 is any weekly cost level, and C_A and C_B are the daily operating costs for Mines A and B, respectively. In terms of the graph, A is on the vertical axis and B is on the horizontal axis. From the isocost formula we find the following:

$$A = C_0/C_A - (C_B/C_A)B,$$

with an intercept of C_0/C_A and a slope equal to $-(C_B/C_A)$. The isocost line will become steeper as C_B increases relative to C_A. The isocost line will become flatter (slope will approach zero) as C_B falls relative to C_A.

   If C_A increases to slightly more than \$15,000, the optimal feasible point will shift from Point X (6B, 2A) to Point V (7B, 1.67A), since the isocost line slope will then be less than $-\frac{1}{3}$, the slope of the high-grade ore constraint [$A = 4 - (\frac{1}{3})B$]. Thus, an increase in C_A from \$10,000 to at least \$15,000, or an increase of *at least \$5,000*, is necessary before the optimal operating decision will change.

E. An increase in C_B of *at least \$5,000* to slightly more than \$10,000 will shift the optimal point from Point X to Point Y (2B, 6A), since the isocost line slope will then be steeper than -1, the slope of the medium-grade ore constraint ($A = 8 - B$).

   An increase in C_B to slightly more than \$30,000 will be necessary before Point Z (1.67B, 7A) becomes optimal. With $C_B \geq \$30,000$ and $C_A = \$10,000$, the isocost line slope will be steeper than -3, the slope of the low-grade ore constraint, $A = 12 - 3B$.

   As seems reasonable, the greater C_B is relative to C_A, the more Mine A will tend to be employed. The greater C_A is relative to C_B, the more Mine B will tend to be employed.

Problems

P11.1   **LP Basics.** Indicate whether each of the following statements is true or false and explain why.

A. Constant returns to scale and constant input prices are the only requirements for a total cost function to be linear.

B. Changing input prices will always alter the slope of a given isocost line.

C. In profit-maximization linear programming problems, negative values for slack variables imply that the amount of an input resource employed exceeds the amount available.

D. Equal distances along a given process ray indicate equal output quantities.

E. Nonbinding constraints are constraints that intersect at the optimum solution.

P11.2 **Fixed Input Combinations.** Cherry Devices, Inc., assembles connectors and terminals for electronic products at a plant in New Haven, Connecticut. The plant uses labor (L) and capital (K) in an assembly line process to produce output (Q), where

$$Q = 0.025L^{0.5}K^{0.5}.$$

A. Calculate how many units of output can be produced with 4 units of labor and 400 units of capital and with 16 units of labor and 1,600 units of capital. Are returns to scale increasing, constant, or diminishing?

B. Calculate the change in the marginal product of labor as labor grows from 4 to 16 units, holding capital constant at 400 units. Similarly, calculate the change in the marginal product of capital as capital grows from 400 to 1,600 units, holding labor constant at 4 units. Are returns to each factor increasing, constant, or diminishing?

C. Assume now and throughout the remainder of the problem that labor and capital must be combined in the ratio $4L{:}400K$. How much output could be produced if Cherry has a constraint of $L = 4,000$ and $K = 480,000$ during the coming production period?

D. What are the marginal products of each factor under the conditions described in Part C?

P11.3 **LP Setup and Interpretation.** The Syflansyd Nut Company has enjoyed booming sales following the success of its "Sometimes You Feel Like a Nut, Sometimes You Don't" advertising campaign. Syflansyd packages and sells four types of nuts in four different types of mixed-nut packages. These products include bulk (B), economy (E), fancy (F), and regular (R) mixed-nut packages. Each of these packages contains a different mixture of almonds (A), cashews (C), filberts (F), and peanuts (P). Based on its contracts with current suppliers, the company has the following daily inventory of each of the following nuts: almonds, 8,000 ounces; cashews, 7,000 ounces; filberts, 7,500 ounces; and peanuts, 10,000 ounces.

Given available inventory, it is management's goal to maximize profits by offering the optimum mix of the four package types. Profit earned per package type is as follows:

Bulk	$0.50
Economy	$0.25
Fancy	$1.25
Regular	$0.75

The composition of each of the four package types can be summarized as follows:

	Ounces per Package			
	Bulk	Economy	Fancy	Regular
Almonds	35	2	3	2
Cashews	35	1	4	2
Filberts	35	1	3	2
Peanuts	35	8	2	6
Total	140	12	12	12

Solution values for the optimal number of packages to produce (decision variables) and excess capacity (slack variables) are the following:

$$B = 0$$
$$E = 0$$
$$F = 1,100$$
$$R = 1,300$$
$$S_A = 2,100$$
$$S_C = 0$$
$$S_F = 1,600$$
$$S_P = 0$$

A. Identify and interpret the appropriate Syflansyd objective function.
B. Using both inequality and equality forms, set up and interpret the resource constraints facing the Syflansyd Company.
C. Calculate optimal daily profit, and provide a complete interpretation of the full solution to this linear programming problem.

P11.4   **Cost Minimization.** Delmar Custom Homes (DCH) uses two different types of crews on home construction projects. Type *A* crews consist of master carpenters and skilled carpenters, whereas *B* crews include skilled carpenters and unskilled labor. Each home involves framing (*F*), roofing (*R*), and finish carpentry (*FC*). During recent months, *A* crews have demonstrated a capability of framing one home, roofing two, and doing finish carpentry for no more than four homes per month. Capabilities for *B* crews are framing three homes, roofing two, and completing finish carpentry for one during a month. DCH has agreed to build ten homes during the month of July but has subcontracted 10 percent of framing and 20 percent of finish carpentry requirements. Labor costs are $60,000 per month for *A* crews and $45,000 per month for *B* crews.
A. Formulate the linear programming problem that DCH would use to minimize its total labor costs per month, showing both the inequality and equality forms of the constraint conditions.
B. Solve the linear programming problem and interpret your solution values.

C. Assuming that DCH can both buy and sell subcontracting services at prevailing prices of $8,000 per unit for framing and $14,000 per unit for finish carpentry, would you recommend that the company alter its subcontracting policy? If so, how much could the company save through such a change?

D. Calculate the minimum increase in *A*-crew costs necessary to cause DCH to change its optimal employment combination for July.

P11.5 **Optimal Credit Policy.** Shirley Feeney is a senior loan officer with Citybank in Milwaukee, Wisconsin. Feeney has both corporate and personal lending customers. On average, the profit contribution margin or interest rate spread is 1.5 percent on corporate loans and 2 percent on personal loans. This return difference reflects the fact that personal loans tend to be riskier than corporate loans. Feeney seeks to maximize the total dollar profit contribution earned, subject to a variety of restrictions on her lending practices. To limit default risk, Feeney must restrict personal loans to no more than 50 percent of the total loans outstanding. Similarly, to ensure adequate diversification against business-cycle risk, corporate lending cannot exceed 75 percent of loaned funds. To maintain good customer relations by serving the basic needs of the local business community, Feeney has decided to extend at least 25 percent of her total credit authorization to corporate customers on an ongoing basis. Finally, Feeney cannot exceed her current total credit authorization of $100 million.

A. Using the inequality form of the constraint conditions, set up and interpret the linear programming problem that Feeney would use to determine the optimal dollar amount of credit to extend to corporate (C) and personal (P) lending customers. Also formulate the LP problem using the equality form of the constraint conditions.

B. Use a graph to determine the optimal solution, and check your solution algebraically. Fully interpret solution values.

P11.6 **Optimal Portfolio Decisions.** The James Bond Fund is a mutual fund (open-end investment company) with an objective of maximizing income from a widely diversified corporate bond portfolio. The fund has a policy of remaining invested largely in a diversified portfolio of investment-grade bonds. Investment-grade bonds have high investment quality and receive a rating of Baa or better by Moody's, a bond rating service. The fund's investment policy states that investment-grade bonds are to be emphasized, representing at least three times the amount of junk bond holdings. Junk bonds pay high nominal returns but have low investment quality, and they receive a rating of less than Baa from Moody's. To maintain the potential for high investor income, at least 20 percent of the fund's total portfolio must be invested in junk bonds. Like many funds, the James Bond Fund cannot use leverage (or borrowing) to enhance investor returns. As a result, total bond investments cannot total more than 100 percent of the portfolio. Finally, the current expected return for investment-grade (I) bonds is 9 percent, and it is 12 percent for junk (J) bonds.

A. Using the inequality form of the constraint conditions, set up and interpret the linear programming problem that the James Bond Fund would use to determine the optimal portfolio percentage holdings of investment-grade (I) and junk (J) bonds. Also formulate the problem using the equality form of the constraint conditions. (Assume that the fund managers have decided to remain fully invested and therefore hold no cash at this time.)

B. Use a graph to determine the optimal solution, and check your solution algebraically. Fully interpret solution values.

C. Holding all else equal, how much would the expected return on junk bonds have to fall to alter the optimal investment policy determined in Part B? Alternatively, how much would the return on investment-grade bonds have to rise before a change in investment policy would be warranted?

D. In anticipation of a rapid increase in interest rates and a subsequent economic downturn, the investment committee has decided to minimize the fund's exposure to bond price fluctuations. In adopting a defensive position, what is the maximum share of the portfolio that can be held in cash given the investment policies stated in the problem?

P11.7   **Cost Minimization.** Carolina Power and Light (CP&L) is a small electric utility located in the Southeast. CP&L currently uses coal-fired capacity to satisfy its base load electricity demand, which is the minimum level of electricity demanded 24 hours per day, 365 days per year.

CP&L currently burns both high-sulfur eastern coal and low-sulfur western coal. Each type of coal has its advantages. Eastern coal is more expensive ($50 per ton) but has higher heat-generating capabilities. Although western coal doesn't generate as much heat as eastern coal, western coal is less expensive ($25 per ton) and doesn't cause as much sulfur dioxide pollution. CP&L's base load requirements are such that at least 2,400 million Btus must be generated per hour. Each ton of eastern coal burned generates 40 million Btus, and each ton of western coal burned generates 30 million Btus. To limit sulfur dioxide emissions, the state's Environmental Protection Agency (EPA) requires CP&L to limit its total burning of sulfur to no more than 1.5 tons per hour. This affects CP&L's coal usage, because eastern coal contains 2.5 percent sulfur and western coal contains 1.5 percent sulfur. The EPA also limits CP&L particulate emissions to no more than 900 pounds per hour. CP&L emits 10 pounds of particulates per ton of eastern coal burned and 15 pounds of particulates per ton of western coal burned.

A. Set up and interpret the linear program that CP&L would use to minimize hourly coal usage costs in light of its constraints.

B. Calculate and interpret all relevant solution values.

C. Holding all else equal, how much would the price of western coal have to rise before only eastern coal would be used? Explain.

P11.8   **Profit Maximization.** Creative Accountants, Ltd., is a small San Francisco-based accounting partnership specializing in the preparation of individual (*I*) and corporate (*C*) income tax returns. Prevailing prices in the local market are $125 for individual tax return preparation and $250 for corporate tax return preparation.

Five accountants run the firm and are assisted by four bookkeepers and four secretaries, all of whom work a typical 40-hour workweek. The firm must decide how to target its promotional efforts to best use its resources during the coming tax preparation season. Based on previous experience, the firm expects that an average of one hour of accountant time will be required for each individual return prepared. Corporate return preparation will require an average of two accountant hours and two bookkeeper hours. One hour of secretarial time will also be required for typing each individual or corporate return. In addition, variable computer and other processing costs are expected to average $25 per individual return and $100 per corporate return.

A. Set up the linear programming problem that the firm would use to determine the profit-maximizing output levels for preparing individual and corporate returns. Show both the inequality and equality forms of the constraint conditions.

B. Completely solve and interpret the solution values for the linear programming problem.

C. Calculate maximum possible net profits per week for the firm, assuming that the accountants earn $1,500 per week, bookkeepers earn $500 per week, secretaries earn $10 per hour, and fixed overhead (including promotion and other expenses) averages $5,000 per week.

D. After considering the preceding data, one senior accountant recommended letting two bookkeepers go while retaining the rest of the current staff. Another accountant suggested that if any bookkeepers were let go, an increase in secretarial staff would be warranted. Which is the more profitable suggestion? Why?

E. Using the equality form of the constraint conditions, set up, solve, and interpret solution values for the dual linear programming problem.

F. Does the dual solution provide information useful for planning purposes? Explain.

P11.9 **Revenue Maximization.** Architect Nick Yemana is managing partner of Designed for Sales (DFS), Inc., an Evanston, Illinois-based designer of single-family and multifamily housing units for real estate developers, building contractors, and so on. Yemana's challenge is to determine an optimal mix of output during the current planning period. DFS offers custom designs for single-family units, Q_1, for $3,000 and custom designs for multifamily units (duplexes, fourplexes, etc.), Q_2, for $2,000 each. Both types of output make use of scarce drafting, artwork, and architectural resources. Each custom design for single-family units requires 12 hours of drafting, 2 hours of artwork, and 6 hours of architectural input. Each custom design for multifamily units requires 4 hours of drafting, 5 hours of artwork, and 6 hours of architectural input.

Currently, DFS has 72 hours of drafting, 30 hours of artwork, and 48 hours of architectural services available on a weekly basis.

A. Using the equality form of the constraint conditions, set up the primal linear program that Yemana would use to determine the sales revenue maximizing product mix. Also set up the dual.

B. Solve for and interpret all solution values.

C. Would DFS's optimal product mix be different with a profit-maximization goal rather than a sales-revenue-maximization goal? Why or why not?

P11.10   **Optimal Output.** Omaha Meat Products (OMP) produces and markets Cornhusker Plumpers, an extra-large frankfurter product being introduced on a test market basis into the St. Louis, Missouri, area. This product is similar to several others offered by OMP, and it can be produced with currently available equipment and personnel using any of three alternative production methods. Method A requires 1 hour of labor and 4 processing-facility hours to produce 100 packages of plumpers, one unit of Q_A. Method B requires 2 labor hours and 2 processing-facility hours for each unit of Q_B, and Method C requires 5 labor hours and 1 processing-facility hour for each unit of Q_C. Because of slack demand for other products, OMP currently has 14 labor hours and 6 processing-facility hours available per week for producing Cornhusker Plumpers. Cornhusker Plumpers are currently being marketed to grocery retailers at a wholesale price of $1.50 per package, and demand exceeds current supply.

A. Using the equality form of the constraint conditions, set up the primal and dual linear programs that OMP would use to maximize production of Cornhusker Plumpers given currently available resources.

B. Calculate and interpret all solution values.

C. Should OMP expand its processing-facility capacity if it can do so at a cost of $40 per hour?

D. Discuss the implications of a new union scale calling for a wage rate of $20 per hour.

CASE STUDY FOR CHAPTER 11
An LP Pension Funding Model

Several companies have learned that a well-funded and comprehensive employee benefits package constitutes an important part of the compensation plan needed to attract and retain key personnel. An employee stock ownership plan, profit-sharing arrangements, and deferred compensation to fund employee retirement are all used to allow productive employees to share in the firm's growth and development. Among the fringe benefits offered under the cafeteria-style benefits plans is comprehensive medical and dental care furnished through local health maintenance organizations, on-site daycare centers for employee children, and "eldercare" support for the aging parents and other dependents of workers.

Many companies also provide their employees with so-called "defined benefit" pension plans. Under defined benefit plans, employers usually offer workers a fixed percentage of their final salary as a retirement annuity. In a typical arrangement, a company might offer employees a retirement annuity of 1.5% of their final salary for each year employed. A 10-year veteran would earn a retirement annuity of 15% of final salary, a 20-year veteran would earn a retirement annuity of 30% of final salary, and so on. Since each employee's retirement benefits are defined by the company, the company itself is obligated to pay for promised benefits.

Over time, numerous firms have found it increasingly difficult to forecast the future rate of return on invested assets; the future rate of inflation; and the morbidity (death rate) of young, healthy, and active retirees. As a result, numerous organizations have discontinued traditional defined benefit pension plans and instead begun to offer new "defined contribution" plans. A defined contribution plan features a matching of company plus employee retirement contributions, with no prescribed set of retirement income benefits defined beforehand. Each employee is typically eligible to contribute up to 10% of pre-tax income into the plan, with the company matching the first 5% or so of such contributions. Both company and employee contributions compound on a tax-deferred basis until the point of retirement. At that time, employees can use their pension funds to purchase an annuity or draw a pension income from earned interest, plus dividends and capital gains.

Defined contribution plans have some obvious advantages over traditional defined benefit pension plans. From the company's perspective, defined benefit pension plans became much less attractive when accounting rule changes during the late 1980s required them to record as a liability any earned but not funded pension obligations. Unfunded pension liabilities caused gigantic one-time charges against operating income during the early 1990s for AT&T, General Motors, IBM, and a host of other large corporations. Faced with enormous one-time charges during an initial catch-up phase, plus the prospect of massive and rapidly growing retirement expenses over time, many large and small firms have simply elected to discontinue their defined contribution plan altogether. From the employee's perspective, defined contribution plans are attractive because they are portable from one employer to another. Rather than face the prospect of losing pension benefits after changing from one employer to another, employees appreciate the advantage of being able to take their pension plans with them as they switch jobs. Defined contribution plans are also attractive because they allow employees to tailor retirement funding contributions to fit individual needs. Younger employees faced with the necessity of buying a home or paying for children's educational expenses can limit pension contributions to minimal levels; older workers with greater discretionary income and a more imminent retirement can provide the maximum pension contribution allowed by law. An added benefit of defined contribution compensation plans is that individual workers can allocate pension investments according to individual risk preferences. Older workers who are extremely risk averse can focus their investments on short-term government securities; younger and more venturesome employees can devote a larger share of their retirement investment portfolio to common stocks.

Workers appreciate companies that offer flexible defined contribution pension plans and closely related profit-sharing and deferred compensation arrangements. To maximize plan benefits, firms must make modest efforts to educate and inform employees about retirement income needs and objectives. Until recently, compensation consultants suggested that employees could retire comfortably on a retirement income that totaled 80 percent of their final salary. However, concerns about the underfunding of federal Social Security and Medicaid programs and apprehension about the rapid escalation of medical care costs make retirement with sufficient assets to fund a pension income equal to 100 percent of final salary a worthy goal. To fund such a nest egg requires substantial regular savings and an impressive rate of return on pension plan assets. Workers who save 10 percent of income for an extended period, say 30 years, have historically been able to fund a retirement income equal to 100% of final salary. This assumes, of course, that the pension plan portfolio is able to earn significant returns over time. Investing in a broadly diversified portfolio of common stocks has historically provided the best returns. Since 1926, the real (after-inflation) rate of return on NYSE stocks is 6.4 percent per year; the real return on bonds is only 0.5 percent per year. Indeed, over every 30-year investment horizon during that time interval, stocks have beat short-term bonds (money market instruments) and long-term bonds. The added return from common stocks is the predictable reward for assuming the greater risks of stock-market investing. However, to be sure of earning the market risk premium on stocks, one must invest in several different companies (at least 30) for several years (at least 30). For most pension plans, investments in no-load low-expense common stock index funds works best in the long run. However, bond market funds have a place in some pension portfolios, especially for those at or near the retirement age.

To illustrate the type of retirement income funding model that a company might make available to employees, consider the following scenario. Suppose that an individual employee has accumulated a pension portfolio worth $250,000 and hopes to receive initial post-retirement income of $500 per month, or $6,000 per year. To provide a total return from current income (yield) plus growth (capital gains) of at least 7 percent, a minimum of 25 percent of the portfolio should be invested in common stocks. To limit risk, stocks should total no more than 50 percent of the overall portfolio, and a minimum of 5 percent should be invested in long-term taxable bonds, 5 percent in medium-term tax-exempt bonds, and 5 percent in a short-term money-market mutual fund. Moreover, not over 75 percent of the overall portfolio should be invested in stocks plus long-term taxable bonds, and at least $30,000 should be available in money markets plus medium-term tax-exempt bonds to provide sufficient liquidity to fund emergencies. Assume that common stocks have a before-tax dividend yield of 3.5 percent, with expected growth from capital appreciation of 6.5 percent per year. Similar figures for long-term taxable bonds are 6 percent plus 1.5 percent, 4 percent plus 1 percent for medium-term tax-exempt bonds, and 4.5 percent plus 0 percent for money market instruments.

A. Set up the linear-programming problem that a benefits officer might use to determine the total-return maximizing allocation of the employee's pension portfolio. Use the inequality forms of the constraint conditions.
B. Solve this linear programming problem and interpret all solution values. Also determine the employee's expected before-tax and after-tax income levels.
C. Calculate the amount of unrealized capital gain earned per year on this investment portfolio.
D. What is the total return opportunity cost of the $6,000 after-tax income constraint?

Selected References

Anbil, Ranga, Eric Gelman, Bruce Patty, and Rajan Tanya. "Recent Advances in Crew-Pairing Optimization at American Airlines." *Interfaces* 21 (January–February 1991): 62–74.

Aubin, Jean. "Scheduling Ambulances." *Interfaces* 22 (March–April 1992): 1–10.

Berman, Lawrence. "Optimal Partitioning of Data Bases across Multiple Servers in a LAN." *Interfaces* 22 (March–April 1992): 18–27.

Buchanan, John, and John Scott. "Vehicle Utilization at Bay of Plenty Electricity." *Interfaces* 22 (March–April 1992): 28–35.

Erenguc, S. Selcuk, and Gary J. Koehler. "Survey of Mathematical Programming Models and Experimental Results for Linear Discriminant Analysis." *Managerial and Decision Economics* 11 (October 1990): 215–225.

Farley, A. A. "Planning the Cutting of Photographic Color Paper Rolls for Kodak (Australasia) Pty. Ltd." *Interfaces* 21 (January–February 1991): 92–106.

Lapin, Lawrence L. *Quantitative Methods for Business Decisions with Cases.* Chicago, IL: Harcourt Brace Jovanovich, 1991.

Levasseur, Robert E. "People Skills: What Every Professional Should Know about Designing and Managing Meetings." *Interfaces* 22 (March–April 1992): 11–14.

Markowski, Carol A. "On the Balancing of Error Rates for LP Discriminant Methods." *Managerial and Decision Economics* 12 (October 1990): 235–241.

Parker, Charles S. *Computers and Their Applications.* (Hinsdale, IL: The Dryden Press, 1991).

Quinn, Phil, Bruce Andrews, and Henry Parsons. "Allocating Telecommunications Resources at L. L. Bean, Inc." *Interfaces* 21 (January–February 1991): 75–91.

Rubin, Paul A. "Heuristic Solution Procedures for a Mixed-Integer Programming Discriminant Model." *Managerial and Decision Economics* 11 (October 1990): 255–266.

Small, Kenneth A. "Trip Scheduling in Urban Transportation Analysis." *American Economic Review* 82 (May 1992): 482–486.

Stam, Antonie, and Dennis G. Jones. "Classification Performance of Mathematical Programming Techniques in Discriminant Analysis: Results for Small and Medium Sample Sizes." *Managerial and Decision Economics* 11 (October 1990): 243–253.

Vasquez-Marquez, Alberto. "American Airlines Arrival Slot Allocation System (ASAS)." *Interfaces* 21 (January–February 1991): 42–61.

RULES FOR FORMING THE DUAL LINEAR PROGRAMMING PROBLEM

Given the importance of duality, a list of simple rules that can be used to form the dual program to any given primal program would be useful. Four such rules exist. They are as follows:

1. Change a maximize objective to minimize, and vice versa.
2. Reverse primal constraint inequality signs in dual constraints (i.e., change $\geq$ to $\leq$, and $\leq$ to $\geq$).
3. Transpose primal constraint coefficients to get dual constraint coefficients.
4. Transpose objective function coefficients to get limits in dual constraints, and vice versa.

(The word *transpose* is a matrix algebra term that simply means that each row of coefficients is rearranged into columns so that Row 1 becomes Column 1, Row 2 becomes Column 2, and so on.)

To illustrate the rules for transformation from primal and dual, consider the following simple example.

Primal Program

Maximize

$$\pi = \pi_1 Q_1 + \pi_2 Q_2,$$

subject to

$$a_{11}Q_1 + a_{12}Q_2 \leq r_1,$$
$$a_{21}Q_1 + a_{22}Q_2 \leq r_2,$$
$$Q_1, Q_2 \geq 0,$$

where π is profits and Q is output. Thus, π_1 and π_2 are unit profits for Q_1 and Q_2, respectively. The resource constraints are given by r_1 and r_2. The constants in the primal constraints reflect the input requirements for each type of output. For example, a_{11} is the amount of resource r_1 in one unit of output Q_1. Similarly, a_{12} is the amount of resource r_1 in one unit of output Q_2. Thus, $a_{11}Q_1 + a_{12}Q_2$ is the total amount of resource r_1 used in production. The remaining input requirements, a_{21} and a_{22}, have a similar interpretation. For convenience, this primal problem statement can be rewritten in matrix notation as follows:

Primal Program

Maximize

$$\pi + \pi_1 Q_1 + \pi_2 Q_2,$$

subject to

$$\begin{bmatrix} a_{11} & a_{12} \\ a_{21} & a_{22} \end{bmatrix} \times \begin{bmatrix} Q_1 \\ Q_2 \end{bmatrix} \leq \begin{bmatrix} r_1 \\ r_2 \end{bmatrix}$$
$$Q_1, Q_2 \geq 0.$$

Matrix notation is just a convenient means for writing large systems of equations. In going from matrix form back to equation form, one just multiplies each row element by each column element. Thus, the left side of the first constraint equation is $a_{11} \times Q_1$ plus $a_{12} \times Q_2$, or $a_{11}Q_1 + a_{12}Q_2$, and this sum must be less than or equal to r_1.

Given the expression of the primal program in matrix notation, the four rules for transformation given previously can be used to convert from the primal to the dual. Following these rules, the dual is written as follows:

Dual Program

Minimize

$$\pi^* = r_1V_1 + r_2V_2,$$

subject to

$$\begin{bmatrix} a_{11} \ a_{21} \\ a_{12} \ a_{22} \end{bmatrix} \times \begin{bmatrix} V_1 \\ V_2 \end{bmatrix} \geq \begin{bmatrix} \pi_1 \\ \pi_2 \end{bmatrix}$$

$$V_1, V_2 \geq 0.$$

Then, converting from matrix back to equation form gives the following:

Dual Program

Minimize

$$\pi^* = r_1V_1 + r_2V_2,$$

subject to

$$a_{11}V_1 + a_{21}V_2 \geq \pi_1,$$
$$a_{12}V_1 + a_{22}V_2 \geq \pi_2,$$
$$V_1, V_2 \geq 0.$$

Here, V_1 and V_2 are the shadow prices for resources r_1 and r_2, respectively. Since r_1 and r_2 represent the quantities of the two resources available, the objective function measures the total implicit value of the resources available. Recalling the interpretation of a_{11} and a_{21} from the primal, it is obvious that $a_{11}V_1 + a_{21}V_2$ is the total value of inputs used in production of one unit of output Q_1. Similarly, $a_{12}V_1 + a_{22}V_2$ is the total value of inputs used in production of a unit of output Q_2.

Finally, the primal and dual linear programming problems can be fully specified through the introduction of slack variables. Remember that with less-than-or-equal-to constraints, the left side of the constraint equation must be brought up to equal the right side. Thus, slack variables must be added to the left side of such constraint equations. With greater-than-or-equal-to constraints, the left side of the constraint equation must be brought down to equal the right side. Thus, slack variables must be *subtracted from* the left side of such constraint equations. With this, the full specification of the preceding primal and dual linear programs can be written as follows:

Primal Program   *Dual Program*

Maximize   Minimize

$$\pi = \pi_1 Q_1 + \pi_2 Q_2,$$ $$\pi^* = r_1 V_1 + r_2 V_2,$$

subject to   subject to

$$a_{11}Q_1 + a_{12}Q_2 + S_1 = r_1,$$ $$a_{11}V_1 + a_{21}V_2 - L_1 = \pi_1,$$

$$a_{21}Q_1 + a_{22}Q_2 + S_2 = r_2,$$ $$a_{12}V_1 + a_{22}V_2 - L_2 = \pi_2,$$

$$Q_1, Q_2, S_1, S_2 \geq 0,$$ $$V_1, V_2, L_1, L_2 \geq 0,$$

where S_1 and S_2 are slack variables representing excess capacity of resources r_1 and r_2, respectively. L_1 and L_2 are also slack variables; they represent the amount by which the value of resources used in the production of Q_1 and Q_2 exceeds the value of output as measured by π_1 and π_2, respectively. Thus, L_1 and L_2 measure the opportunity cost, or foregone profit, as a result of producing the last unit of Q_1 and Q_2.

Understanding these basic rules simplifies construction of the dual, given a primal program, and facilitates understanding and interpretation of the constraints and coefficients found in both primal and dual linear programming problems.

PART

MARKET STRUCTURE ANALYSIS AND ESTIMATION

CHAPTER | # PERFECT COMPETITION AND MONOPOLY

Market structure is the complete array of industry characteristics that directly affect the price/output decisions made by firms. One of the most important elements of market structure is the number and size distribution of sellers and buyers. Generally speaking, the greater the number of market participants, the more vigorous the competition. Similarly, the more even the balance of power between sellers and buyers, the more likely it is that the competitive process will yield maximum benefits. However, a link between the numbers of market participants and the vigor of competition does not always hold true. For example, there are literally thousands of producers active in most major milk markets. Despite this large number of competitors, price competition is nonexistent given an industry cartel that is sustained by a federal program of milk price supports. In contrast, real-world experience shows that competition can be spirited in newspaper, cable television, long-distance telephone service, and other markets with as few as two competitors. This is particularly true in instances in which the actions of market participants are constrained by the viable threat of potential entrants. The mere threat of entry by potential entrants is sometimes enough to keep industry prices and profits in check and to maintain a high level of productive efficiency.

In addition to the number and size distribution of actual and potential competitors, market structure is also described by the degree of product differentiation. Product differentiation includes any real or perceived differences in the quality of goods and services offered to consumers. Sources of product differentiation include all of the various forms of advertising promotion, plus new product and process developments made possible by effective programs of research and development. The availability and cost of information about prices and output quality is a similarly important determinant of market structure. Competition is always most vigorous when buyers and sellers have ready access to detailed price/performance information. Finally, market structure is broadly determined by entry and exit conditions. Low regulatory barriers, modest capital requirements, and nominal standards for skilled labor and other inputs all increase the likelihood that competition will be vigorous. Because all of these elements of market structure have important consequences for the price/output decisions made by firms, the study of market structure is an important ingredient of managerial economics.

Market structure analysis is so important that two full chapters are devoted to this topic. This chapter considers perfect (or pure) competition and monopoly. These market structure models can be viewed as the endpoints along a continuum of decreasing competition, moving from the models of perfect competition to monopolistic competition to oligopoly to monopoly. The perfect competition model describes the most vigorously competitive sectors of the economy, in which widespread price competition drives firms' profits to levels just sufficient to maintain required investment. At the opposite end of the market structure spectrum, monopoly describes price/output decision making in an economic environment in which lax competitive pressures can allow even inefficient firms to survive, if not prosper. In a monopoly environment, the firm can earn above-normal (economic) profits even in the long run. Since these economic profits are sometimes derived from market power rather than innovation, superior efficiency, or other socially valued activities, monopolies are often subject to state and federal regulation, the topic of Chapter 15. When direct government regulation is not desirable, market mechanisms such as countervailing power sometimes arise to combat the abuse of monopoly.

The study of perfect competition and monopoly is valuable not only as a necessary backdrop for understanding managerial decision making in each of these market settings but also as a framework for understanding monopolistic competition and oligopoly. These market structure models are the subject of Chapter 13.

THE CONTRAST BETWEEN PERFECT COMPETITION AND MONOPOLY

Stark differences between the perfect competition and monopoly models of buyer and seller behavior are evident along every important dimension of market structure. These differences are characterized briefly in this section and then are developed more fully in the rest of the chapter.

What Is Market Structure?

Market structure

The competitive environment in the market for a good or service.

Market

Firms and individuals willing and able to buy or sell a particular product.

Market structure describes the competitive environment in the market for any good or service. A **market** consists of all firms and individuals willing and able to buy or sell a particular product. This includes firms and individuals currently engaged in buying and selling a particular product, as well as potential entrants.

Market structure is typically characterized on the basis of four important industry characteristics: the number and size distribution of active buyers and sellers and potential entrants, the degree of product differentiation, the amount and cost of information about product price and quality, and conditions of entry and exit. The effects of market structure are measured in terms of the prices paid by consumers, availability and quality of output, employment and career advancement opportunities, and the pace of product innovation, among other factors.

A **potential entrant** is an individual or firm posing a sufficiently credible threat of market entry to affect the price/output decisions of incumbent firms.

Potential entrants

Firms and individuals with the economic resources to enter a particular market, given sufficient economic incentives.

Potential entrants play extremely important roles in many industries. Some industries with only a few active participants might at first appear to hold the potential for substantial economic profits. However, a number of potential entrants can have a substantial effect on the price/output decisions of incumbent firms. For example, IBM, Compaq, Apple, Digital Equipment, and other leading computer manufacturers are viable potential entrants into the computer component manufacturing industry. These companies use their threat of potential entry to obtain favorable prices from suppliers of microprocessors, video display terminals, and peripheral equipment. Despite having only a relative handful of active foreign and domestic participants, computer components manufacturing is both highly innovative and vigorously price competitive. Therefore, when characterizing market structure, it is important to consider the effects of both current rivals and potential entrants.

Perfect Competition

Perfect (pure) competition

A market structure characterized by a large number of buyers and sellers of an identical product.

Perfect (pure) competition is a market structure characterized by a large number of buyers and sellers of essentially the same product, where each market participant's transactions are so small that they have no influence on the market price of the product. Individual buyers and sellers are **price takers.** This means that firms take market prices as given and devise their production strategies accordingly. Free and complete demand and supply information is available in a perfectly competitive market, and there are no meaningful barriers to entry and exit. As a result, vigorous price competition prevails, and only a normal rate of return on investment is possible in the long run. Economic profits are possible only during periods of short-run disequilibrium before rivals mount an effective competitive response.

Monopoly

Price takers

Buyers and sellers whose individual transactions are so small that they do not affect market prices.

Monopoly

A market structure characterized by a single seller of a highly differentiated product.

Price makers

Buyers and sellers whose large transactions affect market prices.

Monopoly is a market structure characterized by a single seller of a highly differentiated product. Because a monopolist is the sole provider of a desired commodity, the monopolist *is* the industry. Producers must compete for a share of the consumer's overall market basket of goods, but monopolists face no effective competition for specific product sales from either established or potential rivals. As such, monopolists are **price makers** that exercise significant control over market prices. This allows the monopolist to determine simultaneously price and output for the firm (and the industry). Substantial barriers to entry or exit often deter potential entrants and offer both efficient and inefficient monopolists the opportunity for economic profits, even in the long run.

FACTORS THAT DETERMINE THE LEVEL OF COMPETITION

Two key conditions determine the level of competition in a given market: the number and relative size of buyers and sellers in the market and the extent to which the product is standardized. These factors, in turn, are influenced by the nature of the product and production systems, the scope of potential entry, and buyer characteristics.

Effect of Product Characteristics on Market Structure

Good substitutes for a product increase the degree of competition in the market for that product. To illustrate, rail service between two points is typically supplied by only one railroad. Transportation service is available from several sources, however, and railroads compete with bus lines, truck companies, barges, airlines, and private autos. The substitutability of these other modes of transportation for rail service increases the degree of competition in the transportation service market.

It is important to realize that market structures are not static. In the 1800s and early 1900s—before the introduction of trucks, buses, autos, and airplanes—railroads faced very little competition. Railroads could charge excessive prices and earn monopoly profits. Because of this exploitation, laws were passed giving public authorities permission to regulate railroad prices. Over the years, this regulation has become superfluous given intermodal competition. Other firms were enticed by railroad profits to develop competing transportation service systems, which led ultimately to a much more competitive market structure. Today, few would argue that railroads retain significant monopoly power, and public regulation of the railroads is being reduced in recognition of this.

The physical characteristics of a product can also influence the competitive structure of its market. A low ratio of distribution cost to total cost, for example, tends to increase competition by widening the geographic area over which any particular producer can compete. Rapid perishability of a product produces the opposite effect. Thus, in considering the level of competition for a product, the national, regional, or local nature of the market must be considered.

Effect of Production Characteristics on Competition

When minimum efficient scale is large in relation to overall industry output, only a few firms are able to attain the output size necessary for productive efficiency. In such instances, competitive pressures allow only a few firms to survive in an industry. On the other hand, when minimum efficient scale is small in relation to overall industry output, many firms are able to attain the size necessary for efficient operation. Holding all else equal, competition tends to be most vigorous when many efficient competitors are present in the market. This is especially true when firms of smaller than minimum efficient scale face considerably higher production costs, as well as when the construction of minimum-efficient-scale plants involves the commitment of substantial capital, skilled labor, and material resources. When construction of minimum-efficient-scale plants requires the commitment of only modest resources or when smaller firms face no important production cost disadvantages, economies of scale have little or no effect on the competitive potential of new or entrant firms.

Effect of Entry and Exit Conditions on Competition

Maintaining the above-normal profits or productive inefficiency of a monopolist over the long run requires substantial barriers to entry, mobility, or exit. A **barrier to entry** is any factor or industry characteristic that creates an advantage for incumbents over new arrivals. Legal rights such as patents and local, state, or federal licenses can present formidable barriers to new entry in pharmaceutical, cable television, television and radio broadcasting, and other industries. A **barrier to mobility** is any factor or industry characteristic that creates an advantage

Barrier to entry

Any advantage for industry incumbents over new arrivals.

Barrier to mobility

Any advantage for large leading firms over small nonleading rivals.

Barrier to exit

Any limit on asset redeployment from one line of business or industry to another.

Effect of Buyers on Competition

Monopsony

A market with one buyer.

for large leading firms over smaller nonleading rivals. Factors that sometimes create barriers to entry and/or mobility include substantial economies of scale, scope economies, large capital or skilled-labor requirements, and ties of customer loyalty created through advertising and other means.

It is important to recognize that barriers to entry and mobility can sometimes result in compensating advantages for consumers. Even though patents can lead to monopoly profits for inventing firms, they also spur valuable new product and process development. Although extremely efficient or innovative leading firms make new entry and nonleading firm growth difficult, they can have the favorable effect of lowering industry prices and increasing product quality. Therefore, a complete evaluation of the economic effects of entry barriers involves a consideration of both costs and benefits realized by suppliers and customers.

Whereas barriers to entry have the potential to impede competition by making entry or nonleading firm growth difficult, competitive forces can also be diminished through barriers to exit. A **barrier to exit** is any restriction on the ability of incumbents to redeploy assets from one industry or line of business to another. During the late 1980s, for example, several state governments initiated legal proceedings to impede plant closures by large employers in the steel, glass, automobile, and other industries. By imposing large fines or severance taxes or requiring substantial expenditures for worker retraining, they created significant barriers to exit.

By impeding the asset redeployment that is typical of any vigorous competitive environment, barriers to exit can dramatically increase both the costs and risks of doing business. Even though one can certainly sympathize with the difficult adjustments faced by both individuals and firms affected by plant closures, government actions that create barriers to exit can have the unintended effect of impeding industrial development and market competition.

The degree of market competition is affected by buyers as well as sellers. Generally speaking, if there are only a few buyers in a given market, there will be less competition than if there are many buyers. **Monopsony** exists when a single firm is the sole buyer of a desired product or input. Monopsony characterizes local labor markets with a single major employer, as well as many local agricultural markets with a single feed mill or livestock buyer. Similarly, the federal government is a monopsony buyer of military weapons and equipment. Major retailers such as Wal-Mart, Sears, and Kmart all enjoy monopsony power in the purchase of apparel, appliances, auto parts, and other consumer products. Such buyer power is especially strong in the purchase of "house brand" goods, where suppliers might sell much if not all of their production to a single retailer.

Monopsony is perhaps more common in factor input markets than in markets for final demand. In terms of economic efficiency, monopsony is least harmful, and can sometimes even be beneficial, in those markets in which a monopsony buyer faces a monopoly or just a few sellers. For example, consider the case of the town in which one mill is the sole employer of unskilled labor. The mill is a monopsony since it is a single buyer of labor, and it may be able to use its power to reduce wage rates below competitive levels. If workers organize a union to

●

MANAGERIAL APPLICATION 12.1

Intel Fights to Remain on Top

Intel is the fastest-growing and the most profitable maker of integrated circuits, the microscopic pieces of silicon chips used to power electronic computers, calculators, video games, and a burgeoning array of other products. *intel inside*™ is a valued trademark that identifies products produced by a company whose microprocessors are the brains of more than 100 million IBM-compatible personal computers, five times that of its nearest rival. So complete has been Intel's grip on the PC market that its sales skyrocketed nearly fourfold between 1986 and 1991, while profits doubled.

Despite obvious strengths, Intel's core business is facing its biggest challenge in a decade. Led by Advanced Micro Devices, Inc., and Texas Instruments, Inc., a number of companies are rushing to produce clones of Intel chips. High-quality clones can quickly erode the profits of early innovators like Intel, a company that has come to count on giant-sized operating margins of 18 percent to 25 percent since 1987. In mid-1992, investors were clearly worried as Intel's common stock tumbled by more than 25 percent. Is Intel's dominance of the integrated circuits market coming to an end?

Not without a fight, it won't. Intel is striking back at competitors on multiple fronts, dragging competitors into court for patent infringement, slashing prices, and for the first time, advertising its products on national television. Intel's strategic vision has also been revamped to focus more on computer microprocessor products, the core of its business. The company is establishing a close working relationship with manufacturers of end-user products, like personal computers, to ensure compatibility and maximize the benefits of new microprocessor innovations. Perhaps most importantly, Intel has launched a campaign to speed product development.

Intel is no longer satisfied to introduce one or two new generations of chips annually and new microprocessor families every three or four years. In 1992, for example, it marketed roughly 30 variants of its cutting-edge 486 chip. In the summer of 1992, several months ahead of schedule, it unveiled its next generation product, a veritable one-chip mainframe. For the rest of the 1990s, Intel expects to bring out new chip families at a two-year pace, a blistering tempo that the company hopes will keep competitors in a perpetual catch-up mode.

Intel's speedup of microprocessor technology will affect everyone who uses computers and other electronic products. The ever-increasing power of microprocessors has already catapulted the spread of office automation, computer networks, and "user-friendly" software that makes high-power computing available to even the novice. In the banking, retailing, and fast food industries, nearly every competitor already relies on microprocessors in cash register or personal computers to track revenues, measure product demand, and control costs. Each new generation of technology has produced new products, services, and productivity in these and many sectors. It is therefore reasonable to expect that any speedup in microprocessor technology will produce widespread benefits as worldwide competition grows more feverish and intense in a wide variety of industries.

Staying ahead of the competition is more than a matter of pride for Intel. Microprocessors provide about more than one-half of Intel's sales and the bulk of its profits. Those earnings enable Intel to spend more than any competitor on new product development and manufacturing innovations. In future years, the company hopes to become a force in supercomputers, interactive digital video and flash memory, a semiconductor alternative to storing data on magnetic disks. But none of these new products will have the support needed to bring them to market unless Intel can first protect its main turf from increasingly aggressive rivals.

To keep ahead, Intel has raised its research and development spending to more than $800 million per year and capital spending to more than $1 billion per year, both tops in the industry. Joint ventures with Japan's NMB Semiconductor Co., which is making Intel's flash-memory chips, also contribute to the companies' expertise in new product development. Thus, despite daunting challenges from competitors, Intel hasn't slipped—at least not yet. It will remain king of the integrated circuits industry so long as it maintains its sharp competitive edge.

Source: Robert D. Hoff, "Inside Intel: It's Moving Double-time to Head Off Competitors," *Business Week,* June 1, 1992, 86–94.

bargain collectively with their employer, a single monopoly seller of labor is created that could offset the employer's monopsony power and increase wages toward competitive market norms. Not only is monopsony accepted in such situations, it is sometimes encouraged by public policy.

PURE COMPETITION

Market characteristics described in the preceding section determine the level of competition in the market for any good or service. This section focuses on the special features of perfectly competitive markets and illustrates why pure competition is desirable from a social perspective. Monopoly is discussed in the subsequent section and is shown to be much less attractive than the perfectly competitive ideal.

Characteristics of Perfectly Competitive Markets

Pure competition exists when the individual producers have no influence on market prices; they are price takers as opposed to price makers. This lack of influence on price typically requires that each of the following conditions be met.

- *Large numbers of buyers and sellers.* Each firm in the industry produces a small portion of industry output, and each customer buys only a small part of the total.
- *Product homogeneity.* The output of each firm is perceived by customers to be essentially the same as the output of any other firm in the industry.
- *Free entry and exit.* Firms are not restricted from entering or leaving the industry.
- *Perfect dissemination of information.* Cost, price, and product quality information is known by all buyers and all sellers in the market.

These basic conditions are too restrictive for pure competition to be commonplace in actual markets. Although security and commodity exchanges approach the perfectly competitive ideal, imperfections occur even there. For example, the acquisition or sale of large blocks of securities by institutional investors clearly affects stock market prices, at least in the short run. Nevertheless, because up to 1,000 shares of any listed stock can be bought or sold at the current market price, the stock market approaches the ideal of a perfectly competitive market. Similarly, many firms must make output decisions without any control over price, and examination of a purely competitive market structure provides insights into these operating decisions. A clear understanding of pure competition also provides a reference point from which to analyze the more typically encountered market structures of monopolistic competition and oligopoly described in Chapter 13.

Market Price Determination

Market price in a competitive industry is determined by aggregate supply and demand; individual firms have no control over price. The total industry demand curve for a product reflects an aggregation of the quantities that individual purchasers will buy at each price. An industry supply curve reflects a summation of the quantities that individual firms are willing to supply at different prices. The intersection of industry demand and supply curves determines market price.

TABLE 12.1 **Market Supply Schedule Determination**

Price ($)	Quantity Supplied by Firm 1	+ 2	+ 3	+ 4	+ 5	= Partial Market Supply	× 1,000 = Total Market Supply
1	5	0	5	10	30	50	50,000
2	15	0	5	25	45	90	90,000
3	20	20	10	30	50	130	130,000
4	25	35	20	35	55	170	170,000
5	30	55	25	40	60	210	210,000
6	35	75	30	45	65	250	250,000
7	40	95	35	50	70	290	290,000
8	45	115	40	55	75	330	330,000
9	50	130	45	65	80	370	370,000
10	55	145	50	75	85	410	410,000

Data in Table 12.1 illustrate the process by which an industry supply curve is constructed. First, suppose that each of five firms in an industry is willing to supply varying quantities of the product at different prices. Summing the individual supply quantities of these five firms at each price determines their combined supply schedule, shown in the Partial Market Supply column. For example, at a price of $2, the output quantities supplied by the five firms are 15, 0, 5, 25, and 45 units, respectively, resulting in a combined supply of 90 units at that price. With a product price of $8, the supply quantities become 45, 115, 40, 55, and 75, for a total supply by the five firms of 330 units.

Now assume that the five firms, although representative of firms in the industry, account for only a small portion of the industry's total output. Assume that there are actually 5,000 firms in the industry, each with an individual supply schedule identical to one of the five firms illustrated in the table. There are 1,000 firms just like each one illustrated in Table 12.1; the total quantity supplied at each price is 1,000 times that shown under the Partial Market Supply schedule. This supply schedule is illustrated in Figure 12.1. Adding the market demand curve to the industry supply curve, as in Figure 12.2, allows one to determine the equilibrium market price.

Market price is found by equating market supply and market demand to find the equilibrium output level and then using either the demand or supply curve to find the market clearing price at that activity level. From the curves in Figure 12.2, the equilibrium output level is:

$$\text{Demand} = \text{Supply}$$
$$\$40 - \$0.0001Q = -\$0.254 + \$0.000025Q$$
$$\$0.000125Q = \$40.254$$
$$Q = 322{,}032$$
$$P = \$40 - \$0.0001(322{,}032)$$
$$= \$40 - \$32.20$$
$$= \$7.80.$$

FIGURE 12.1   **Hypothetical Industry Supply Curve**

Industry supply is the sum of the quantities that individual firms supply at each price.

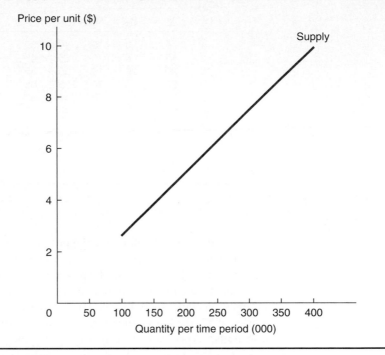

Although it is apparent from Figure 12.2 that both the quantity demanded and the quantity supplied depend on price, a simple example demonstrates the inability of an individual firm to affect price. The total demand function in Figure 12.2, which represents the summation at each price of the quantities demanded by individual purchasers, is described by the equation

$$\text{Quantity Demanded} = Q = 400{,}000 - 10{,}000P, \qquad \textbf{(12.1)}$$

or, solving for price,

$$\$10{,}000P = \$400{,}000 - Q,$$
$$P = \$40 - \$0.0001Q. \qquad \textbf{(12.1a)}$$

According to Equation 12.1a, a 100-unit change in output would cause only a $0.0001 change in price. A $0.0001 price increase would lead to a one-unit decrease in total market demand; a $0.0001 price reduction would lead to a one-unit increase in total market demand.

The demand curve shown in Figure 12.2 is redrawn for an individual firm in Figure 12.3. The slope of the curve is −0.0001, the same as in Figure 12.2, only the scales have been changed. The intercept $7.80 is the going market price as determined by the intersection of the market supply and demand curves in Figure 12.2.

FIGURE 12.2   **Market Price Determination in Perfect Competition**

The perfectly competitive market-equilibrium price/output combination can be determined by equating the market demand and supply curves.

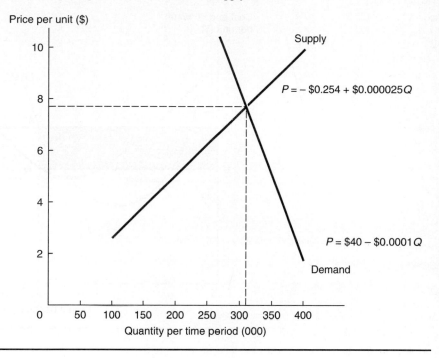

FIGURE 12.3   **Demand Curve for a Single Firm in Perfect Competition**

Firms face horizontal demand curves in perfectly competitive markets.

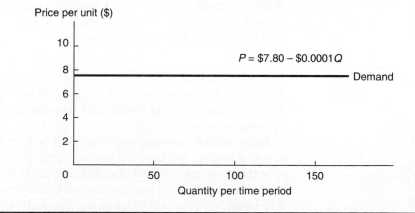

Note: With price constant at, say, P^*, $TR = P^* \times Q$, $AR = (P^* \times Q)/Q = P^*$, and $MR = dTR/dQ = P^*$.

FIGURE 12.4   **Competitive Firm's Optimal Price/Output Combination**

Given a horizontal demand curve, $P = MR$. Thus, short-run equilibrium occurs when $P = MR = MC$.

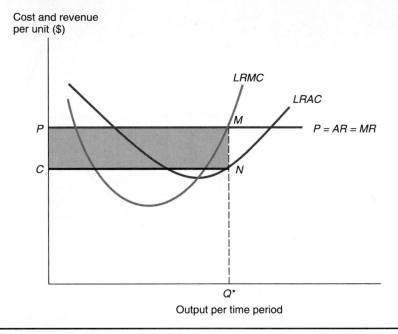

At the scale shown in Figure 12.3, the firm's demand curve is seen to be, for all practical purposes, a horizontal line. An output change of even 100 units by the individual firm results in only a $0.01 change in market price, and the data in Table 12.1 indicate that the typical firm would not vary output by this amount unless the market price changed by more than $10 a unit. Thus, it is clear that under pure competition, the individual firm's output decisions do not affect price in any meaningful way, and for pricing decisions, the demand curve is taken to be perfectly horizontal. Price is assumed to be constant irrespective of the output level at which the firm chooses to operate.

The Firm's Price/
Output Decision

Figure 12.4 illustrates the firm's price/output decision in a competitive market. Assume for simplicity that the curves graphed are those of a representative firm. Thus, the cost curves in Figure 12.4 represent an average firm in a perfectly competitive industry.

Profit maximization requires that a firm operate at the output level at which marginal revenue and marginal cost are equal. With price constant, average revenue (or price) and marginal revenue must always be equal. To maximize profits, market price must equal marginal cost for a firm operating in a perfectly competitive industry. In the example shown in Figure 12.4, the firm chooses to operate at output level Q^*, where price (and hence marginal revenue) equals marginal cost, and profits are maximized.

FIGURE 12.5 **Long-Run Equilibrium in a Competitive Market**

Long-run equilibrium is reached when Q^* units of output are produced at minimum
LRAC. Thus, $P = MR = MC = AC$, and economic (excess) profits equal zero.

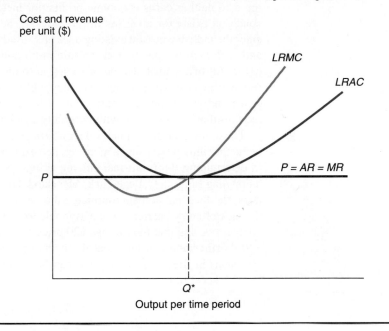

Notice from this illustration that above-normal or economic profits can exist
in the short run even under conditions of pure competition. A normal profit,
defined as the rate of return just sufficient to attract the capital investment necessary to operate and develop a firm (see Chapter 1) is included as a part of economic costs. Therefore, any profit shown in a graph such as Figure 12.4 (or 12.5)
is defined as economic profit and represents an above-normal rate of return. The
firm incurs economic losses whenever it fails to earn a normal profit. A firm
might show a small accounting profit but be suffering economic losses because
these profits are insufficient to provide an adequate return to the firm's stockholders. In such instances, firms are not able to replace plant and equipment and will
exit the industry in the long run.

In Figure 12.4 the firm produces and sells Q^* units of output at an average
cost of C dollars; with a market price P, the firm earns economic profits of
$P - C$ dollars per unit. Total economic profit, $(P - C)Q^*$, is shown by the
shaded rectangle *PMNC.*

Over the long run, positive economic profits attract additional firms into the
industry, lead to increased output by existing firms, or both. Expanding industry
supply puts downward pressure on market prices for the industry as a whole,
since industry output can expand only by offering the product at a lower price.
Expanded supply simultaneously pushes cost upward because of increased demand for factors of production. Long-run equilibrium is reached when all economic profits and losses have been eliminated and each firm in the industry is

operating at an output that minimizes long-run average cost (*LRAC*). The long-run equilibrium for a firm under pure competition is graphed in Figure 12.5. At the profit-maximizing output, price (or average revenue) equals average cost, so the firm neither earns economic profits nor incurs economic losses. When this condition exists for all firms in the industry, new firms are not encouraged to enter the industry nor are existing ones pressured into leaving it. Prices are stable, and each firm is operating at the minimum point on its short-run average cost curve. All firms must also be operating at the minimum-cost point on the long-run average cost curve; otherwise, they will make production changes, decrease costs, and affect industry output and prices. Accordingly, a stable equilibrium requires that firms operate with optimally sized plants.

▶   The optimal price/output level for a firm in a perfectly competitive market can be further illustrated using a more detailed example. Assume that one is interested in determining the profit-maximizing activity level for the Hair Stylist, Ltd., a hairstyling salon in College Park, Maryland. Given the large number of competitors, the fact that stylists routinely tailor services to meet customer needs, and the lack of entry barriers, it is reasonable to assume that the market is perfectly competitive and that the average $20 price equals marginal revenue, $P = MR = \$20$. Furthermore, assume that the firm's operating expenses are typical of the 100 firms in the local market and can be expressed by the following total and marginal cost functions:

$$TC = \$5,625 + \$5Q + \$0.01Q^2,$$
$$MC = \$5 + \$0.02Q,$$

where *TC* is total cost per month including capital costs and *Q* is the number of hairstylings provided.

The optimal price/output combination can be determined by setting marginal revenue equal to marginal cost and solving for *Q*:

$$MR = MC$$
$$\$20 = \$5 + \$0.02Q$$
$$\$0.02Q = \$15$$
$$Q = 750 \text{ hairstylings per month.}$$

At this output level, maximum economic profits are

$$\pi = TR - TC$$
$$= \$20Q - \$5,625 - \$5Q - \$0.01Q^2$$
$$= \$20(750) - \$5,625 - \$5(750) - \$0.01(750^2)$$
$$= \$0.$$

The $Q = 750$ activity level results in zero economic profits. This means that the Hair Stylist is just able to obtain a normal or risk-adjusted rate of return on investment since capital costs are already included in the cost function. The $Q = 750$ output level is also the point of minimum average production costs ($AC = MC = \$20$). Finally, with 100 identical firms in the industry, industry output totals 75,000 hairstylings per month.

FIGURE 12.6   **Competitive Firm's Short-Run Supply Curve**

The perfectly competitive firm's short-run supply curve is that portion of the *MC* curve lying above the *AVC* curve.

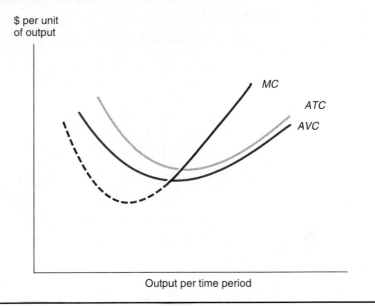

The Firm Supply Curve

Market supply curves are the summation of supply quantities for individual firms at various prices. To illustrate how supply is determined for individual firms, Figure 12.6 adds the firm's average variable cost curve to the average total cost and marginal cost curves of Figure 12.4. The perfectly competitive firm's short-run supply curve corresponds to that portion of the marginal cost curve that lies above the average variable cost curve. This is the solid portion of the marginal cost curve in Figure 12.6. Since $P = MR$ under perfect competition, the quantity supplied by the perfectly competitive firm is found at the point where $P = MC$, as long as price exceeds average variable cost.

To clarify this point, consider the options available to the firm. Profit maximization under pure competition requires that the firm operate at the output level at which marginal revenue equals marginal cost, if it produces any output at all. That is, the firm will either produce nothing and incur a loss equal to its fixed costs, or it will produce an output determined by the intersection of the horizontal demand curve and the marginal cost curve. It will choose the alternative that maximizes profits or minimizes losses, if losses must be incurred. If price is less than average variable costs, the firm should produce nothing and incur a loss equal to total fixed cost. Losses will increase if any output at all is produced and sold when $P < AVC$. If price exceeds average variable cost, then each unit of output provides at least some profit contribution to help cover fixed costs and provide profit. The firm should produce and sell its product under such conditions, because such production reduces losses or leads to profits. The minimum

FIGURE 12.7   **Price, Cost, and Optimal Supply Decisions for a Firm under Pure Competition**

The minimum point of $1.25 on the *AVC* curve is the lowest price level at which the firm will supply output.

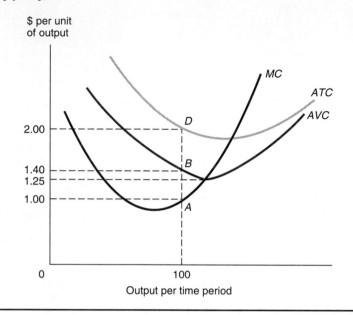

point on the firm's average variable cost curve determines the lower limit, or cutoff point, of its supply schedule.

This is illustrated in Figure 12.7. At a very low price such as $1, *MR = MC* at 100 units of output. The firm has a total cost per unit of $2 and a price of only $1, so it is incurring a loss of $1 per unit. Since the difference between the *ATC* and the *AVC* curves represents the fixed cost per unit of output, the total loss consists of a fixed cost component ($2.00 − $1.40 = $0.60) and a variable cost component ($1.40 − $1.00 = $0.40). Thus, the total loss is

$$\text{Total Loss} = (100 \text{ Units}) \times (\$0.60 \text{ Fixed Cost Loss} \\ + \$0.40 \text{ Variable Cost Loss}) \\ = \$100.$$

If the firm simply shut down and terminated production, it would cease to incur variable costs, and its loss would be reduced to the level of fixed costs, or 100($0.60) = $60.

Variable cost losses occur at any price less than $1.25, the minimum point on the *AVC* curve, so this is the lowest price at which the firm will operate. Above $1.25, price more than covers variable costs. Even though total costs are not covered at prices less than $2, it is preferable to operate when $1.25 < P < $2 and earn at least some profit contribution to cover a portion of fixed costs rather than to shut down and incur losses equal to total fixed costs.

●

MANAGERIAL APPLICATION 12.2

Is Ticketmaster a Monopoly?

Closely held Ticketmaster Corporation is responsible for one of the most impressive transformations of any major market during the 1980s. In less than a decade, Ticketmaster has transformed the computerized ticketing service industry. From a relatively minor $1 million per year in billings for sports and entertainment ticketing, the industry has grown into a huge and profitable business that generates in excess of $1 billion per year in fees. In the process, Ticketmaster has reshaped the industry by getting the public to pay added millions of dollars per year in extra ticket-buying charges.

Ticketmaster recognized that customers would pay a lot more for ticket-buying services than the market was demanding. As recently as the early 1980s, service charges were approximately $1 a ticket. Today, Ticketmaster charges average about $2.50 a ticket and in some cases such charges go much higher. For a recent rock concert by the Grateful Dead in Los Angeles, a $25 ticket carried a $6.50 service charge when ordered by phone (see table). Ticketmaster officials argue that the convenience and service offered by the company don't come cheap. Revenue from rising service charges gave Ticketmaster the money to compete with Ticketron, a major early competitor. Arenas used to pay Ticketron for its ticket-selling services, but Ticketmaster started paying millions of dollars to arenas for the right to sell their tickets. Ticketmaster also helped arenas develop marketing strategies based on who was buying tickets through their computer service. Thanks to Ticketmaster, selling tickets went from being a costly headache to suddenly putting a lot of money into the hands of facility operators. At the same time, arenas helped Ticketmaster by making it harder to buy tickets without using their services. Ticketmaster often has the initial hours of ticket sales all to itself for major rock concerts. Arena box offices only open later if any tickets are still left. Ticketmaster now accounts for 85 percent to 90 percent of ticket sales for its more than 1,600 clients.

In mid-1991, the transformation of the ticket buying services industry took an important turn when Ticketmaster bought out major rival Ticketron. While Ticketmaster argues that its market dominance is a natural result of the company's aggressive and innovative culture, others express considerable uneasiness about this market transformation. The market is going to look like a monopoly where charges are free to zoom and service to fall, says Robert D'Angelo, director of the Madison Civic Center in Madison, Wisconsin.

The Wall Street Journal reports that Ticketmaster wants to extend its control over former Ticketron clients and has a big bargaining chip with which to do so.

The Cost of Being a Fan: Selected Prices for Tickets Sold through Ticketmaster

Event	Ticket Price	Service Charge		Telephone Handling Fee[3]
		Outlet[1]	Telephone[2]	
Grateful Dead Concert	$25.00	$4.50	$6.50	$2.25
Pittsburgh Pirates	8.00	1.35	1.85	1.55
L.A. Dodgers	7.00	1.50	1.75	1.15
Minnesota North Stars	15.00	1.25	1.50	1.50
Doobie Brothers Concert	24.50	3.25	5.00	1.55
Alvin Ailey Dance	25.00	2.25	2.75	1.50
L.A. Lakers	11.50	2.75	3.75	2.05
Julio Iglesias Concert	35.00	3.50	5.00	1.50

[1]Per ticket; Ticketmaster outlets require cash.
[2]Per ticket; Ticketmaster phone service requires a credit card.
[3]Per order, regardless of number of tickets ordered, if tickets are mailed.

Source: John R. Emswiller, "Ticketmaster's Dominance Sparks Fears," *The Wall Street Journal,* June 19, 1991, B1.

To summarize, the perfectly competitive firm short-run supply curve is that portion of the marginal cost curve lying above the *AVC* curve. When marginal cost is below average cost but above average variable cost, losses can be reduced if the firm expands production. Despite losses, firms continue to produce when price exceeds average variable cost. Positive economic profits occur over that part of the supply function for which price (and marginal cost) exceeds average total cost. The firm's long-run supply function is similarly determined. Since all costs are variable in the long run, firms shut down unless total costs are completely covered. The portion of the firm's long-run marginal cost curve that lies above its long-run average cost curve represents its long-run supply schedule.

MONOPOLY

Pure monopoly lies at the opposite extreme from pure competition on the market structure continuum. Monopoly exists when a single firm is the sole producer of a good that has no close substitutes; in other words, there is a single firm in the industry. Pure monopoly, like pure competition, is seldom observed.

Characteristics of Monopoly Markets

Monopoly exists when an individual producer has the ability to substantially dictate market price. Monopoly firms are price makers as opposed to price takers. Their control over price typically requires that each of the following conditions be met.

- *A single seller.* A single firm produces all industry output. The monopoly is the industry.
- *Unique product.* Monopoly output is perceived by customers to be distinctive and preferable to its imperfect substitutes.
- *Blockaded entry and exit.* Firms are heavily restricted from entering or leaving the industry.
- *Imperfect dissemination of information.* Cost, price, and product quality information is withheld from uninformed buyers.

As in the case of pure competition, these basic conditions are too restrictive for monopoly to be commonplace in actual markets. Few goods are produced by single producers, and fewer still are free from competition of close substitutes. Even public utilities are imperfect monopolies in most of their markets. Electric companies, for example, typically approach a pure monopoly in their residential lighting market, but they face strong competition from gas and oil suppliers in the heating market. In all industrial and commercial power markets, electric utilities face competition from gas- and oil-powered private generators. Even though pure monopoly rarely exists, it is still worthy of careful examination. Many of the economic relations found under monopoly can be used to estimate optimal firm behavior in the less precise, but more prevalent, partly competitive and partly monopolistic market structures that dominate the real world. An understanding of monopoly also provides the background necessary to examine the economics of regulation, covered in Chapter 15, a topic of prime importance to business managers.

FIGURE 12.8 **Firm's Demand Curve under Monopoly**

The demand curve for a monopolist is the industry demand curve.

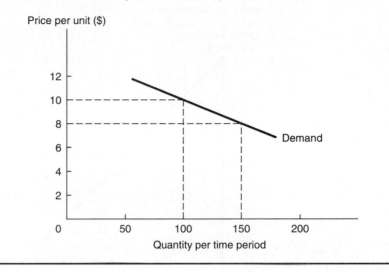

Price/Output Decision under Monopoly

Under monopoly, the industry demand curve is identical to the firm demand curve. Because industry demand curves slope downward, monopolists also face a downward-sloping demand curve. In Figure 12.8, for example, 100 units can be sold at a price of $10 a unit. At an $8 price, quantity demanded rises to 150 units. If the firm decides to sell 100 units, it will receive $10 a unit; if it wishes to sell 150 units, it must accept an $8 price. The monopolist can set either price or quantity, but not both. Given one, the value of the other is determined by the demand curve.

A monopoly uses the same profit-maximization rule as does any other firm: it operates at the output level at which marginal revenue equals marginal cost. The monopoly demand curve is not horizontal, however, so marginal revenue does not coincide with price at any but the first unit of output. Marginal revenue is always less than price for output quantities greater than one because of the negatively sloped demand curve. Since the demand (average revenue) curve is negatively sloped and hence declining, the marginal revenue curve must lie below it.

When a monopoly equates marginal revenue and marginal cost, it simultaneously determines the output level and the market price for its product. This decision is illustrated in Figure 12.9. The firm produces Q units of output at a cost of C per unit and sells this output at price P. Profits, which equal $(P - C) \times Q$, are represented by the area $PP'C'C$ and are at a maximum. Q is optimal short-run output only if average revenue, or price, is greater than average variable cost, as shown in Figure 12.9. If price is below average variable cost, losses are minimized by shutting down.

To further illustrate price/output decisions under monopoly, the previous Hair Stylist, Ltd., example can be modified to reflect an assumption that the firm has a monopoly in the College Park market, perhaps because of restrictive licensing

FIGURE 12.9   Price/Output Decision under Monopoly

Monopoly equilibrium occurs where *MR* = *MC*. However, *P* > *ATC,* and the firm earns economic (excess) profits.

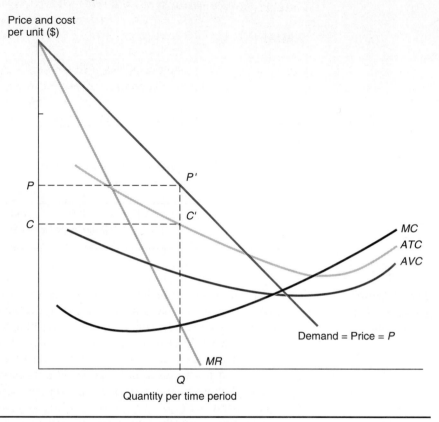

requirements. In the earlier example, each of 100 perfectly competitive firms had a profit-maximizing activity level of 750 hairstylings per month, for a total industry output of 75,000 hairstylings per month.

As a monopoly, the Hair Stylist provides all industry output. For simplicity, assume that the Hair Stylist operates a chain of salons and that the cost function for each shop is the same as in the previous example. By operating each shop at its average cost-minimizing activity level of 750 hairstylings per month, the Hair Stylist can operate with Marginal Cost = Average Cost = $20.

Assume that industry demand and marginal revenue curves for hairstylings in the College Park market are

$$P = \$80 - \$0.0008Q,$$
$$MR = \$80 - \$0.0016Q.$$

The monopoly profit-maximizing activity level is obtained by setting marginal revenue equal to marginal cost, or marginal profit equal to zero ($M\pi = 0$), and solving for *Q:*

$$MR = MC$$
$$\$80 - \$0.0016Q = \$20$$
$$\$0.0016Q = \$60$$
$$Q = 37,500 \text{ hairstylings per month.}$$

The optimal market price is

$$P = \$80 - \$0.0008(37,500)$$
$$= \$50.$$

At the $Q = 37,500$ activity level, the Hair Stylist will operate a chain of 50 salons ($= 37,500/750$). Although each outlet produces $Q = 750$ hair stylings per month, a point of optimum efficiency, the benefits of this efficiency accrue to the company in the form of economic profits rather than to consumers in the form of lower prices. Economic profits from each shop are

$$\pi = TR - TC$$
$$= P \times A - AC \times Q$$
$$= \$50(750) - \$20(750)$$
$$= \$22,500 \text{ per month.}$$

With 50 shops, the Hair Stylist earns total economic profits of $1,125,000 per month. As a monopoly, the industry provides only 37,500 units of output, down from the 75,000 units provided in the case of a perfectly competitive industry. The new price of $50 per hairstyling is up substantially from the perfectly competitive price of $20. The effects of monopoly power are reflected in terms of higher consumer prices, reduced levels of output, and substantial economic profits for the Hair Stylist, Inc.

In general, any industry characterized by monopoly *sells less* output at *higher prices* than would the same industry if it were perfectly competitive. From the perspective of the firm and its stockholders, the benefits of monopoly are measured in terms of the economic profits that are possible when competition is reduced or eliminated. From a broader social perspective, however, these private benefits must be weighed against the costs borne by consumers in the forms of higher prices and reduced availability of desired products. Employees and suppliers also suffer from the reduced employment opportunities associated with the lower production of monopoly market structures.

▶ Nevertheless, it is important to recognize that monopoly is not always as socially harmful as indicated in the previous example. In the case of Cray Research, Inc., for example, the genius of Seymore Cray and a handful of research associates created a dynamic early monopoly in supercomputers. The tremendous stockholder value created through their efforts, including millions of dollars in personal wealth for Cray and his associates, can be viewed only as a partial index of their contribution to society in general. Other similar examples include the DeKalb Corporation (hybrid seeds), Kellogg Company (ready-to-eat cereal), Lotus Corporation (spreadsheet software), and the Reserve Fund (money market mutual funds), among others. In instances such as these, monopoly profits are the just rewards flowing from truly important contributions of unique firms and individuals.

It is also important to recognize that monopoly profits are often fleeting. Early profits earned by each of the firms mentioned previously attracted a host of competitors. For example, note the tremendous growth in the money market mutual fund business since the November 1971 birth of the Reserve Fund. Today the Reserve Fund is only one of roughly 500 money market mutual funds available, and it accounts for only a small fraction of the roughly $1 trillion in industry assets. The tremendous social value of invention and innovation often remains long after early monopoly profits have dissipated.

Long-Run Equilibrium under Monopoly

In the long run, a monopoly continues to operate only if price at least equals long-run average cost. Because all costs are variable in the long run, the firm will not operate unless all costs are covered. No monopoly or perfectly competitive firm will operate in the long run if it suffers continual losses.

As shown earlier, in equilibrium, purely competitive firms must operate at the minimum point on the *LRAC* curve. This requirement does not hold under monopoly. For example, again consider Figure 12.9 and assume that the *ATC* curve represents the long-run average cost curve for the firm. The firm will produce *Q* units of output at an average cost of *C* per unit, somewhat above the minimum point on the *ATC* curve. Such a firm is a **natural monopoly,** since the market-clearing price, where $P = MC$, occurs at a point at which *long-run* average costs are still declining. In other words, market demand is insufficient to justify full utilization of even one minimum-efficient-scale plant. A single firm can produce the total market supply at a lower total cost than could any number of smaller firms, and competition naturally reduces the number of competitors until only a single supplier remains. Electric and local telephone utilities are classic examples of natural monopoly, since any duplication in production and distribution facilities would increase consumer costs.

Natural monopoly

An industry in which the market-clearing price occurs at a point at which the monopolist's long-run average costs are still declining.

Monopoly Regulation

Natural monopoly presents something of a dilemma. On the one hand, economic efficiency could be enhanced by restricting the number of producers to a single firm. On the other hand, monopolies have an incentive to underproduce and can earn economic profits. **Underproduction** results when a monopoly curtails output to a level at which the value of resources employed, as measured by the marginal cost of production, is less than the social benefit derived, where social benefit is measured by the price that customers are willing to pay for additional output. Under monopoly, marginal cost is less than price at the profit-maximizing output level. Although resulting economic profits serve the useful functions of providing incentives and helping allocate resources, it is difficult to justify above-normal profits that result from market power rather than from exceptional performance.

Underproduction

A situation that occurs when a monopolist curtails production to a level at which marginal cost is less than price.

How is it possible to escape the dilemma that monopoly can be efficient but can also lead to economic profits and underproduction? The answer sometimes lies in permitting monopolies to exist but regulating their prices and output quantity. The important topic of public regulation of natural monopolies is discussed in detail in Chapter 15. In other instances, market forces often emerge that effectively limit the profit potential of monopoly.

COUNTERVAILING POWER: THE MONOPOLY/MONOPSONY CONFRONTATION

Unregulated monopoly sellers facing perfectly competitive market demand will typically limit production and offer their products to consumers at high prices. The private and social costs of this behavior are often measured by above-normal profits, inefficient production methods, and lagging rates of innovation. How is this inefficiency reduced, if not eliminated, in unregulated markets? Sometimes the answer lies in the development of countervailing forces within markets.

Seller versus Buyer Power

Countervailing power

Buyer market power that offsets seller market power, and vice versa.

Countervailing power is an economic influence that creates a closer balance between previously unequal sellers and buyers. The classic example is a single employer in a small town that might take advantage of the local labor force by offering less-than-competitive wages. As the single employer, the company has a monopsony in the local labor market. Workers might decide to band together and form a union, a monopoly seller in the local labor market, to offset the monopsony power of the employer.

To illustrate this classic confrontation, consider Figure 12.10, which shows demand and supply relations in a local labor market. The downward-sloping demand for labor is simply the marginal revenue product of labor curve as discussed in Chapter 8. The marginal revenue product of labor (MRP_L) is simply the amount of net revenue generated through employment of an additional unit of labor ($\delta TR/\delta L$). It is the product of the marginal product of labor (MP_L) and the marginal revenue of output (MR_Q). Thus, $MRP_L = \delta TR/\delta L = MP_L \times MR_Q$. MRP_L tends to fall as employment expands because of the labor factor's diminishing returns. An upward-sloping supply curve reflects the fact that higher wages are typically necessary to expand the amount of labor offered. Perfectly competitive demand and supply conditions create an exact balance between demand and supply, and the competitive equilibrium wage, W_C, and employment level, E_C, are observed.

A monopsony employer facing a perfectly competitive supply of labor sets its marginal cost of labor, MC_L, equal to the marginal benefit derived from employment. Because the employer's marginal benefit is measured in terms of the marginal revenue product of labor, an unchecked monopsonist sets $MC_L = MRP_L$. Notice that the MC_L curve exceeds the labor supply curve at each point, based on the assumption that wages must be increased for all workers in order to hire additional employees. This is analogous to cutting prices for all customers in order to expand sales, causing the MR curve to lie below the demand curve. Since workers need to be paid only the wage rate indicated along the labor supply curve for a given level of employment, the monopsonist employer offers employees a wage of W_M and a less than competitive level of employment opportunities, E_M.

An unchecked union, or monopoly seller of labor, could command a wage of W_U if demand for labor were competitive. This solution is found by setting the marginal revenue of labor (MR_L) equal to the labor supply curve, which represents the marginal cost of labor to the union. Like any monopoly seller, the union can obtain higher wages (prices) only by restricting employment opportunities (out-

Monopoly Union and Monopsony Employer Confrontation in the Labor Market

In a perfectly competitive labor market, the equilibrium wage is at W_C. A monopoly union facing competitive labor demand will seek a higher wage of W_U. A monopsony employer facing a competitive labor supply will offer a lower wage of W_M.

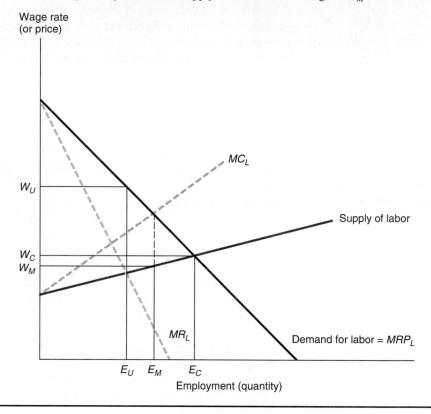

put) for union members. A union is able to offer its members only the less than competitive employment opportunities, E_U, if it attempts to maximize labor income.

The Compromise Solution

What is likely to occur in the case of the monopoly union/monopsony employer confrontation? Typically, wage/employment bargaining produces a compromise wage/employment outcome. Compromise achieved through countervailing power has the beneficial effect of moving the labor market away from the inefficient unchecked monopoly or monopsony solutions toward a more efficient labor market equilibrium. However, only in the unlikely event of perfectly matched monopoly/monopsony protagonists will the perfectly competitive outcome occur. Depending on the relative power of the union and the employer, either an above-market or a below-market wage outcome typically results, and employment opportunities are often somewhat below those under competitive conditions.

●

MANAGERIAL APPLICATION 12.3
Is This Why They Call It Hardball?

The only employer of baseball players in the United States is Major League Baseball. This association of 26 major league franchises and their owners operates in much the same way as does a large corporation with 26 different regional offices. Even though individual clubs compete with one another on the playing field, their financial competition is much different than that between true competitors. In a competitive market, the gain of one competitor comes at the expense of others. In baseball, the success of one franchise brings increased prosperity for all. Through revenue sharing, all clubs prospered when Hank Aaron chased and broke Babe Ruth's lifetime home run mark, as well as when Pete Rose chased and broke Ty Cobb's lifetime record for hits. Conversely, ineptitude and poor gate sales at one franchise weaken the profit picture for everyone. Tight pennant races make for prosperity; blowouts result in lost profits.

Baseball players are covered by a single basic labor contract negotiated through collective bargaining between the Major League Players Association (the sole union representative of the baseball players) and the owners. The players' association is a monopoly seller of baseball player talent, and the owners are a monopsony employer. During recent years, economic power in this labor market has clearly shifted from the owners toward the players. A key element of this shift has been the advent of free agency. Any baseball player with six years of major league service is eligible to become a free agent and sign with any team, with only modest compensation in the form of draft choices due to the player's former club. While not eligible for free agency, any player with three to six years' service is eligible for impartial salary arbitration. Since free agency was developed, baseball players' salaries have exploded.

In the early 1980s, baseball teams' front offices were often outwitted by sharp player agents. Occasional efforts to turn back player salaries fizzled since most owners still cared more about winning pennants than losing money, and the sport's leadership was too weak

to put up a fight. By the late 1980s, the average salary in baseball had risen to over $450,000 per year, not including substantial pensions and other fringe benefits. Baseball also piled up a $277 million operating loss from 1980 to 1984.

During Peter Ueberroth's reign as baseball commissioner the owners decided to strike back. The commissioner urged teams not to offer contracts longer than three years for regulars, two years for pitchers, and none longer than one year for marginal players. The commissioner even suggested rote responses to inquiries from free-agent players that eliminated any chance of clubs starting out too high. He also helped teams simply say no. Fully 29 of the 33 free agents during the 1985–86 period returned to their old teams after not having received any other offers. As a group, these free agents averaged only a 5 percent salary increase, and two-thirds got only a one-year contract. During this period, player salaries in general also stagnated despite a jump in industry revenues from roughly $750 million to $1 billion per year. Predictably, owner profits skyrocketed from breakeven levels to over $200 million per year.

Suspecting that the owners had indeed violated their collective bargaining agreement, the players' union filed its first grievance in February 1986. In over 200 days of hearings, spread over three years, the union took the collusion case through arbitration proceedings—the only remedy for alleged contract violations. In September 1990, arbitrator Thomas Roberts issued a ruling in the unions case on behalf of the 1985–86 crop of free agents: the owners were guilty as charged. A later ruling on the 1986–87 free agents also went against the owners. Total bill to the owners: $10.3 million per team to fund payments to free-agent players that were harmed by their collusion. Without owner collusion, player salaries jumped to an average over $1 million per year by 1992—powerful evidence that monopsony in the labor market can indeed harm salaries.

Source: John Helyar, "How Peter Ueberroth Led the Major Leagues in the 'Collusion Era,'" *The Wall Street Journal,* May 20, 1991, Al and David, "#&?!%* in Sports," *Business Week,* June 8, 1992.

Nevertheless, the countervailing power of monopoly/monopsony confrontation can have the beneficial effect of improving economic efficiency from that experienced under unchecked monopoly or monopsony.

MARKET STRUCTURE AND COMPETITIVE STRATEGY

Identifying the market structure and profit potential of any given industry can be difficult. In actual business practice, markets typically do not fall neatly within the definition of perfect competition or monopoly. Market structures usually embody elements of each of these models of economic behavior.

Strategic Considerations

As suggested earlier, product characteristics, the local or regional limits of the market, the time necessary for reactions by established or new competitors, the pace of innovation, unanticipated changes in government regulation and tax policy, and a host of additional considerations all play important roles in defining the method and scope of competition. Among other factors, it is always helpful to consider the number of competitors, degree of product differentiation, level of information available in the marketplace, and conditions of entry when attempting to define market structure.

Table 12.2 summarizes major characteristics typical of perfectly competitive and monopolistic market structures. To develop an effective competitive strategy, it is necessary to assess the degree to which the characteristics of an individual market more or less embody elements of each. As one might expect, the probability of successful entry is greater in perfectly competitive industries. Although entry into monopoly markets is more difficult, these markets hold the potential for substantial economic profits in the long run. The decision to enter any industry requires careful balancing of expected costs and benefits. The search for above-normal profits is likely to succeed only when the firm can create a distinctive and valuable characteristic in the goods and services it provides.

In equilibrium, a perfectly competitive market offers the potential for only a normal rate of return on investment. If many equally capable competitors offer identical products, vigorous price competition tends to eliminate above-normal profits. The only exception to this rule is that superior cost efficiency can sometimes lead to superior profits, even in perfectly competitive markets. For example, a grain producer located along a river or on exceptionally fertile soil would enjoy lower-than-average irrigation and fertilizer costs, and higher profits could result. However, potential buyers would have to pay a price premium for such productive land, and subsequent investors would earn only a normal rate of return on their investment.

Market Niche

Purchase of a business that enjoys recognized monopoly power is not likely to lead to economic profits because the anticipated abnormal returns on plant and equipment investment will be reflected in the purchase price. Much like fertile land brings a price premium in the real estate market, monopoly franchises bring

TABLE 12.2   **Summary of Perfect Competition and Monopoly (Monopsony) Market-Structure Characteristics**

	Perfect Competition	Monopoly (Monopsony)
Number of actual or potential competitors	Many small buyers and sellers	A single seller (buyer) of a valued product
Product differentiation	None—each buyer and seller deals in an identical product	Very high—no close substitutes available
Information	Complete and free information on price and product quality	Highly restricted access to price and product-quality information
Conditions of entry and exit	Complete freedom of entry and exit	Very high barriers caused by economies of scale (natural monopoly), patents, copyrights, government franchises, or other factors
Profit potential	Normal profit in long run; economic profits (losses) in short run only	Potential for economic profits in both short and long run
Examples	Some agricultural markets (grain); commodity, stock, and bond markets; some nonspecialized input markets (unskilled labor)	Monopoly (sellers): Local telephone service (basic hook-up); municipal bus companies; gas, water, and electric utilities. Monopsony (buyers): state and local governments (roads), U.S. government (defense electronics)

a premium purchase price in the stock market. As a result, purchase of a recognized monopoly leads to only a risk-adjusted normal rate of return for investors. However, new and unique products or services can create monopoly profits, which may be protected by patents, copyrights, or other means. In many instances, these above-normal profits reflect the successful exploitation of a market niche. A **market niche** is a segment of a market that can be successfully exploited through the special capabilities of a given firm or individual. To be durable, the above-normal profits derived from a niche in the market for goods and services must not be vulnerable to imitation by competitors.

Market niche
A specialized market segment.

For example, Avon Products, Inc., is rightly famous for its veritable army of door-to-door sales representatives. "Avon Calling!" is a greeting that has long generated huge cash returns for the company in the United States and abroad. In Japan, for example, Avon's profit rate and popularity appears to exceed even that enjoyed by the company in the U.S. market. Avon has succeeded where others have failed because it has developed and nurtured the market for in-home cosmetic sales. Better than anyone else, Avon knows the cosmetics, toiletries, costume jewelry, and other products that many women want and how much they are willing to pay for them. Despite numerous assaults from would-be competitors, and regular predictions that its primary market is a sure-fire casualty of dual-income households, Avon keeps on growing. Indeed, its domestic and foreign business is so profitable that Avon has been the subject of repeated takeover speculation. To thwart such advances, the company has initiated a dramatic program to streamline operations in an effort to enhance already high profits. In the meantime, Avon keeps on dominating its market niche.

Another interesting example of a firm that successfully exploits a profitable market niche is Templeton, Galbraith, and Hansberger, Ltd., mutual fund manager and distributor for the Templeton Group of mutual funds. Templeton, Galbraith, and Hansberger has a dominant and extraordinarily profitable market niche in the worldwide mutual fund business. Founder John Templeton is a pioneer of the global diversification concept for mutual fund investors. Not only has the idea proved popular to U.S. investors, but Japanese and European investors have jumped on the Templeton bandwagon as well. As a result, Templeton, Galbraith, and Hansberger enjoys double-digit growth, profit margins that average in excess of 35 percent of sales, and a rate of return on assets in excess of 50 percent per year.

Avon Products and Templeton, Galbraith, and Hansberger are only two examples of the many firms that enjoy tremendous success through market niche dominance. To attain similar success, a firm must first recognize the attractiveness of the market niche and then successfully apply the concept to its own business. Few firms achieve any great measure of success in trying to be all things to all customers. Success lies in exploiting those segments of the overall market that can be best served using the special capabilities of a given firm or individual.

Information Barriers to Competitive Strategy

Any use of market structure information as a guide to competitive strategy must address the considerable challenge posed by measurement problems encountered in defining both the magnitude and origin of above-normal rates of return. Accounting profit data derived from a historical perspective give much useful information for operating decisions and tax purposes. However, these data sometimes measure economic profits imperfectly. For example, advertising and research and development expenditures are expensed for both reporting and tax purposes, even though each can give rise to long-term economic benefits. An "expense as incurred" treatment of advertising and research and development expenditures can lead to errors in profit measurement. Similarly, imperfections in accrual accounting methods lead to imperfectly matched revenues and costs and, therefore, to some profit misstatement over time.

In addition to these and other obvious limitations of accounting data, business practices are often expressly intended to limit the loss of valuable trade secrets. Combined with the informational limitations of publicly available data on profitability, business practices create an information barrier that makes defining the costs and benefits of monopoly difficult for both private and public decision makers.

SUMMARY

Market structure analysis begins with the study of perfect competition and monopoly. Competition is said to be perfect when producers offer what buyers want at prices just sufficient to cover the marginal cost of output. No profits above the minimum required to maintain investment are possible. Monopoly is socially less desirable given its tendency for underproduction, high prices, and excess profits.

- **Market structure** describes the competitive environment in the market for any good or service. A **market** consists of all firms and individuals willing and able to buy or sell a particular product. This includes firms and individuals currently engaged in buying and selling a particular product, as well as potential entrants. A **potential entrant** is an individual or firm posing a sufficiently credible threat of market entry to affect the price/output decisions of incumbent firms.

- **Perfect (pure) competition** is a market structure characterized by a large number of buyers and sellers of essentially the same product, where each market participant's transactions are so small that they have no influence on the market price of the product. Individual buyers and sellers are **price takers.** Such firms take market prices as given and devise their production strategies accordingly.

- **Monopoly** is a market structure characterized by a single seller of a highly differentiated product. Monopoly firms are **price makers** that exercise significant control over market prices.

- A **barrier to entry** is any factor or industry characteristic that creates an advantage for incumbents over new arrivals. A **barrier to mobility** is any factor or industry characteristic that creates an advantage for large leading firms over smaller nonleading rivals. A **barrier to exit** is any restriction on the ability of incumbents to redeploy assets from one industry or line of business to another.

- **Monopsony** exists when a single firm is the sole buyer of a desired product or input.

- A **natural monopoly** occurs when the market-clearing price, where $P = MC,$ occurs at a point at which *long-run* average costs are still declining.

- **Underproduction** results when a monopoly curtails output to a level at which the value of resources employed, as measured by the marginal cost of production, is less than the social benefit derived, where social benefit is measured by the price customers are willing to pay for additional output.

- **Countervailing power** is an economic influence that creates a closer balance between previously unequal sellers and buyers.

- A **market niche** is a segment of a market that can be successfully exploited through the special capabilities of a given firm or individual. To be durable, the above-normal profits derived from a niche in the market must not be vulnerable to imitation by competitors.

Although the requirements for perfect competition and monopoly are quite restrictive and are seldom met exactly, these market structure concepts provide a crucial basis for understanding competition in all markets. Moreover, many real-world markets do in fact closely approximate the perfectly competitive ideal, and elements of monopoly are often encountered. As a result, these market structure concepts often provide a valuable guide to managerial decision making.

Questions

Q12.1   What are the primary elements of market structure?

Q12.2   Describe the perfectly competitive market structure, and provide some examples.

Q12.3   Describe the monopoly market structure, and provide some examples.

Q12.4   How are barriers to entry and exit similar? How are they different?

Q12.5   Why is the firm demand curve horizontal in perfectly competitive markets? Does this mean that the perfectly competitive industry demand curve is also horizontal?

Q12.6   Why are the perfectly competitive firm and the perfectly competitive industry supply curves upward sloping?

Q12.7   From a social standpoint, what is the problem with monopoly?

Q12.8   Why are both industry and firm demand curves downward sloping in monopoly market structure?

Q12.9   Give an example of monopoly in the labor market. Discuss such a monopoly's effect on wage rates and on inflation.

Q12.10   Describe the economic effects of countervailing power, and cite examples of markets in which countervailing power is observed.

Self-Test Problem

The City of Columbus, Ohio, is considering two proposals to privatize municipal garbage collection. First, a leading waste disposal firm has offered to purchase the city's plant and equipment at an attractive price in return for an exclusive franchise on residential service. A second proposal would allow several individual workers and small companies to enter the business without any exclusive franchise agreement or competitive restrictions. Under this plan, individual companies would bid for the right to provide service in a given residential area. The city would then allocate business to the lowest bidder.

The city has conducted a survey of Columbus residents to estimate the amount that they would be willing to pay for various frequencies of service. The city has also estimated the total cost of service per resident. Service costs are expected to be the same whether or not an exclusive franchise is granted.

A. Complete the following table.

Trash Pickups per Month	Price per Pickup	Total Revenue	Marginal Revenue	Total Cost	Marginal Cost
0	$5.00			$ 0.00	
1	4.80			3.75	
2	4.60			7.45	
3	4.40			11.10	
4	4.20			14.70	
5	4.00			18.00	
6	3.80			20.90	
7	3.60			23.80	
8	3.40			27.20	
9	3.20			30.60	
10	3.00			35.00	

B. Determine price and the level of service if competitive bidding results in a perfectly competitive price/output combination.

C. Determine price and the level of service if the city grants a monopoly franchise.

Solution to
Self-Test Problem

A.

Trash Pickups per Month	Price per Pickup	Total Revenue	Marginal Revenue	Total Cost	Marginal Cost
0	$5.00	$ 0.00	—	$ 0.00	—
1	4.80	4.80	$4.80	3.75	$3.75
2	4.60	9.20	4.40	7.45	3.70
3	4.40	13.20	4.00	11.10	3.65
4	4.20	16.80	3.60	14.70	3.60
5	4.00	20.00	3.20	18.00	3.30
6	3.80	22.80	2.80	20.90	2.90
7	3.60	25.20	2.40	23.80	2.90
8	3.40	27.20	2.00	27.20	3.40
9	3.20	28.80	1.60	30.60	3.50
10	3.00	30.00	1.20	35.00	4.40

B. In a perfectly competitive industry, $P = MR$, so the optimal activity level occurs where $P = MC$. Here, $P = MC = \$3.40$ at $Q = 8$ pickups per month.
C. A monopoly maximizes profits by setting $MR = MC$. Here, $MR = MC = \$3.60$ at $Q = 4$ pickups per month and $P = \$4.20$ per pickup.

Problems

P12.1   **Market Structure Concepts.** Indicate whether each of the following statements is true or false, and explain why.
  A. In long-run equilibrium, every firm in a perfectly competitive industry earns zero profit. Thus, if price falls, none of these firms will be able to survive.
  B. Pure competition exists in a market when all firms are price takers as opposed to price makers.
  C. A natural monopoly results when the profit-maximizing output level occurs at a point where long-run average costs are declining.
  D. Downward-sloping industry demand curves characterize both perfectly competitive and monopoly markets.
  E. A decrease in the price elasticity of demand would follow an increase in monopoly power.

P12.2   **Perfectly Competitive Firm Supply.** Mankato Paper, Inc., produces uncoated paper used in a wide variety of industrial applications. Newsprint, a major product, is sold in a perfectly competitive market. The following relation exists between the firm's newsprint output and total production costs:

Total Output (tons)	Total Cost (per ton)
0	$ 25
1	75
2	135
3	205

continued

Total Output (tons)	Total Cost (per ton)
4	285
5	375
6	475
7	600

A. Construct a table showing Mankato's marginal cost of newsprint production.

B. What is the minimum price necessary for Mankato to supply one ton of newsprint?

C. How much newsprint would Mankato supply at industry prices of $75 and $100 per ton?

P12.3   **Perfectly Competitive Equilibrium.** Demand and supply conditions in the perfectly competitive market for unskilled labor are as follows:

$$Q_D = 120 - 20P, \qquad \text{(Demand)}$$

$$Q_S = 10P, \qquad \text{(Supply)}$$

where Q is millions of hours of unskilled labor and P is the wage rate per hour.

A. Graph the industry demand and supply curves.

B. Determine the industry equilibrium price/output combination both graphically and algebraically.

C. Calculate the level of excess supply (unemployment) if the minimum wage is set at $4.50 per hour.

P12.4   **Perfectly Competitive Industry Supply.** Farm Fresh, Inc., supplies sweet peas to canners located throughout the Mississippi River Valley. Like some grain and commodity markets, the market for sweet peas is perfectly competitive. The company's total and marginal costs per ton are given by the following relations:

$$TC = \$250,000 + \$200Q + \$0.02Q^2,$$
$$MC = \$200 + \$0.04Q.$$

A. Calculate the industry price necessary for the firm to supply 5,000, 10,000, and 15,000 tons of sweet peas.

B. Calculate the quantity supplied by Farm Fresh at industry prices of $200, $500, and $1,000 per ton.

P12.5   **Perfectly Competitive Firm and Industry Supply.** New England Textiles, Inc., is a medium-size manufacturer of blue denim, the market for which is perfectly competitive. The total cost function for this product is described by the following relation:

$$TC = \$25,000 + \$1Q + \$0.000008Q^2,$$
$$MC = \$1 + \$0.000016Q,$$

where Q is square yards of blue denim produced per month.

A. Derive the firm's supply curve, expressing quantity as a function of price.

B. Derive the industry's supply curve if New England Textiles is one of 500 competitors.

C. Calculate industry supply per month at a market price of $2 per square yard.

P12.6 **Perfectly Competitive Equilibrium.** Yakuza, Ltd., supplies standard 256K-RAM chips to the U.S. computer and electronics industry. Like the output of its competitors, Yakuza's chips must meet strict size, shape, and speed specifications. As a result, the chip-supply industry can be regarded as perfectly competitive. The total cost and marginal cost functions for Yakuza are

$$TC = \$100,000 + \$2Q + \$0.00001Q^2,$$
$$MC = \$2Q + \$0.00002Q,$$

where Q is the number of chips produced.

A. Calculate Yakuza's optimal output and profits if chip prices are stable at $3 each.

B. Calculate Yakuza's optimal output and profits if chip prices rise to $6 each.

C. If Yakuza is typical of firms in the industry, calculate the firm's equilibrium output, price, and profit levels.

P12.7 **Monopoly Equilibrium.** Fluid Controls, Inc., is a major supplier of reverse osmosis and ultrafiltration equipment, which helps industrial and commercial customers achieve improved production processes and a cleaner work environment. The company has recently introduced a new line of ceramic filters that enjoy patent protection. Relevant cost and revenue relations for this product are as follows:

$$TR = \$300Q - \$0.001Q^2,$$
$$MR = \$300 - \$0.002Q,$$
$$TC = \$9,000,000 + \$20Q + \$0.0004Q^2,$$
$$MC = \$20 + \$0.0008Q,$$

where TR is total revenue, Q is output, MR is marginal revenue, TC is total cost, including a risk-adjusted normal rate of return on investment, and MC is marginal cost.

A. As a monopoly, calculate Fluid Controls' optimal price/output combination.

B. Calculate monopoly profits and the optimal profit margin at this profit-maximizing activity level.

P12.8 **Monopoly versus Perfectly Competitive Equilibrium.** Big Apple Music, Inc., enjoys an exclusive copyright on music written and produced by the Fab Four, a legendary British rock group. Total and marginal revenues for the group's records are given by the following relations:

$$TR = \$15Q - \$0.000005Q^2,$$
$$MR = \$15 - \$0.00001Q.$$

Marginal costs for production and distribution are stable at $5 per unit. All other costs have been fully amortized.

A. Calculate Big Apple's output, price, and profits at the profit-maximizing activity level.

B. What record price and profit levels would prevail following expiration of copyright protection based on the assumption that perfectly competitive pricing would result?

P12.9   **Monopoly versus Perfectly Competitive Equilibrium.** During recent years, the Big Blue Computer Company has enjoyed substantial economic profits derived from patents covering a wide range of inventions and innovations in the personal computer field. A recent introduction, the SP/2, has proved to be especially profitable. Market demand and marginal revenue relations for the SP/2 are as follows:

$$P = \$5,500 - \$0.005Q,$$
$$MR = \$5,500 - \$0.01Q.$$

Fixed costs are nil because research and development expenses have been fully amortized during previous periods. Average variable costs are constant at $4,500 per unit.

A. Calculate the profit-maximizing price/output combination and economic profits if Big Blue enjoys an effective monopoly on the SP/2 because of its patent protection.

B. Calculate the price/output combination and total economic profits that would result if competitors offer clones that make the SP/2 market perfectly competitive.

P12.10   **Monopoly/Monopsony Confrontation.** Safeguard Corporation offers a unique service. The company notifies credit card issuers after being informed that a subscriber's credit card has been lost or stolen. The Safeguard service is sold to card issuers on a one-year subscription basis. Relevant revenue and cost relations for the service are as follows:

$$TR = \$5Q - \$0.00001Q^2,$$
$$MR = \$5Q - \$0.00002Q,$$
$$TC = \$50,000 + \$0.5Q + \$0.000005Q^2,$$
$$MC = \$0.5 + \$0.00001Q,$$

where TR is total revenue; Q is output measured in terms of the number of subscriptions in force; MR is marginal revenue; TC is total cost, including a risk-adjusted normal rate of return on investment; and MC is marginal cost.

A. If Safeguard has a monopoly in this market, calculate the profit-maximizing price/output combination and optimal total profit.

B. Calculate Safeguard's optimal price, output, and profits if credit card issuers effectively exert monopsony power and force a perfectly competitive equilibrium in this market.

CASE STUDY FOR CHAPTER 12

Firm Size and Profitability within the Fortune 500

Does large firm size, pure and simple, give rise to monopoly profits? This question has been a source of great interest in both business and government, as well as the basis for lively debate over the years. Monopoly theory states that large *relative* firm size within a given economic market gives rise to the potential for above-normal profits. Monopoly theory makes no prediction at all about a link between large *absolute* firm size and the potential for above-normal profits. By itself, it is not clear what economic advantages are gained from large firm size. Pecuniary or money-related economies of large size in the purchase of labor, raw materials, or other inputs are sometimes suggested. For example, some argue that large firms enjoy a comparative advantage in the acquisition of investment funds given their ready access to organized capital markets. Others contend that capital markets are themselves very efficient in the allocation of scarce capital resources and that all firms, both large and small, must offer investors a competitive rate of return.

Still, without a doubt, firm size is a matter of significant business and public interest. Membership in the Fortune 500 roster of the largest industrial corporations in the United States is a matter of significant corporate pride for included companies and their top executives. Sales and profit levels achieved by such firms are widely reported and commented on in the business and popular press. At times, congressional leaders have called for legislation that would bar mergers among Fortune 500 companies on the premise that such combinations create monolithic giants that impair competitive forces. Movements up and down the Fortune 500 list are similarly chronicled, studied, and commented on. It is perhaps a little known fact that, given the dynamic nature of change in the overall economy, few companies are able to maintain, let alone enhance, their position in the Fortune 500 over a five- to ten-year period. As many as 30 to 50 companies are displaced from the Fortune 500 in a typical year. With an annual attrition rate of 6 to 10 percent, it indeed appears to be "slippery" at the top.

To evaluate the link, if any, between profitability and firm size, it is interesting to consider the data contained in Table 12.3. These data are taken from the 1992 Fortune 500 listing of the largest industrial corporations of the United States. All companies on this list derive at least 50 percent of their sales from manufacturing and/or mining and have published financial data. The sample of $N = 51$ firms is shown, including the top and every tenth Fortune 500 company. The simplest means for studying the link between profitability and firm size is to regress profits on firm size. Of course, size can be measured along a variety of different dimensions, including assets, employment, market value, sales, and stockholders' equity, to name but a few of the most popular accounting measures of firm size. *Fortune* uses sales as an index of size, so the relation between profits and sales is of obvious interest. Nonlinearities can be investigated through the use of second-order (quadratic or squared) and third-order (cubic) terms for the size variable. For example, a positive and statistically significant coefficient for the sales

TABLE 12.3   **Sales, Profits, Assets, and Stockholders' Equity for a Sample of Fortune 500 Firms**

Rank 1991	1990	Company	Sales ($ millions)	Profits ($ millions)	Assets ($ millions)	Stockholders' Equity ($ millions)
1	1	General Motors, Detroit, MI	$123,780.1	−$4,452.8	$184,325.5	$27,327.6
10	10	Chevron, San Francisco, CA	36,795.0	1,293.0	34,636.0	14,739.0
20	18	Dow Chemical, Midland, MI	19,305.0	942.0	24,727.0	9,441.0
30	33	Westinghouse Electric, Pittsburgh, PA	12,794.0	−1,086.0	20,159.0	3,746.0
40	46	Bristol-Myers Squibb, New York, NY	11,298.0	2,056.0	9,416.0	5,795.0
50	48	General Dynamics, Falls Church, VA	9,548.0	505.0	6,207.0	1,980.0
60	61	Archer-Daniels-Midland, Decatur, IL	8,567.7	466.7	6,260.6	3,922.3
70	75	Hanson Industries NA, New York, NY	7,103.7	660.2	13,222.5	4,179.6
80	68	Amerada Hess, New York, NY	6,416.3	84.3	8,841.4	3,132.0
90	94	Colgate-Palmolive, New York, NY	6,093.7	124.9	4,510.7	1,866.3
100	110	Warner-Lambert, Morris Plains, NJ	5,166.6	34.8	3,602.0	1,170.7
110	114	Chiquita Brands International, Cincinnati, OH	4,627.4	128.5	3,142.5	967.9
120	127	Tyson Foods, Springdale, AK	3,922.1	145.5	2,645.8	822.5
130	135	Times Mirror, Los Angeles, CA	3,624.1	82.0	4,052.2	1,844.0
140	141	Gannett, Arlington, VA	3,382.0	301.6	3,684.1	1,539.5
150	152	AMP, Harrisburg, PA	3,095.0	259.7	3,006.9	1,913.0
160	164	Hershey Foods, Hershey, PA	2,901.6	219.5	2,341.8	1,355.3
170	165	MAPCO, Tulsa, OK	2,646.4	125.9	1,702.3	412.7
180	168	Phelps Dodge, Phoenix, AZ	2,461.0	272.9	3,051.1	1,859.3
190	193	McDermott, New Orleans, LA	2,299.5	−10.7	2,647.4	673.1
200	294	Loral, New York	2,136.0	90.4	2,532.2	672.0
210	229	E-Systems, Dallas, TX	1,997.8	109.5	1,075.4	750.1
220	225	Adolph Coors, Golden, CO	1,918.4	25.5	1,986.3	1,099.4
230	246	Sundstrand, Rockford, IL	1,708.5	108.8	1,719.5	692.4
240	268	York International, York, PA	1,652.7	−4.3	1,205.6	253.8
250	230	Harnischfeger Industries, Brookfield, WI	1,623.9	64.6	1,506.9	594.4
260	287	Duracell International, Bethel, CT	1,524.1	−34.2	2,054.1	716.1
270	256	Fleetwood Enterprises, Riverside, CA	1,415.2	30.4	764.6	428.1

squared variable indicates that profits increase at a pace faster than the rate of change in sales. A positive and statistically significant coefficient for the sales cubed variable indicates a growing rate of increase.

It is also possible to consider the effect of firm size on profit *margins,* where profit margin is typically defined as profit divided by sales. Alternatively, the effects of firm size on relative profitability can be measured using assets or stockholders' equity as the relevant measure of firm size. When firm size is measured using the book value of total assets, it is interesting to see if the return on assets (ROA) is affected by size (asset level). Similarly, when firm size is measured using stockholders' equity, or the difference between total assets and total liabilities, it is worthwhile to consider the effect of stockholders' equity on relative profits measured by the return on stockholders' equity (ROE). A significant link between profitability and firm size is suggested to the extent that profit margins, ROA, and/or ROE tend to be higher among larger Fortune 500 firms.

In any given year, individual Fortune 500 firms report extraordinary losses or fail to make operating data available to the public. Both factors make it diffi-

| Rank | | | Sales | Profits | Assets | Stockholders' Equity |
1991	1990	Company	($ millions)	($ millions)	($ millions)	($ millions)
280	186	Great American Mgmt. & Invest., Chicago, IL	1,330.3	37.7	1,488.7	299.3
290	315	Federal-Mogul, Southfield, MI	1,251.7	−4.9	884.2	256.2
300	340	Intergraph, Huntsville, AL	1,204.7	71.1	996.6	755.0
310	318	Bemis, Minneapolis, MN	1,141.6	53.0	714.9	329.2
320	330	Leggett & Platt, Carthage, MO	1,081.8	39.4	656.1	332.6
330	304	Weirton Steel, Weirton, WV	1,039.5	−74.7	1,038.0	288.4
340	352	Pittway, Chicago, IL	983.9	25.5	758.6	399.6
350	337	Nortek, Providence, RI	925.8	−27.1	NA	NA
360	349	Consolidated Papers, Wisconsin Rapids, WI	882.4	91.4	1,410.7	960.1
370	389	Cray Research, Eagan, MN	862.5	113.0	1,079.0	758.7
380	384	Danaher, Washington, DC	837.4	13.3	735.0	319.3
390	437	Thorn Apple Valley, Southfield, MI	818.0	19.6	121.4	42.1
400		Du Pont Merck Pharmaceutical, Wilmington, DE	795.4	NA	1,059.2	NA
410	391	JPS Textile Group, Greenville, SC	761.0	−8.6	567.2	−73.1
420	392	Interlake, Lisle, IL	714.7	−13.7	478.1	−239.5
430	476	Safety-Kleen, Elgin, IL	696.9	51.6	903.8	463.6
440	467	Betz Laboratories, Trevose, PA	670.6	75.5	475.8	258.9
450	448	Riceland Foods, Stuttgart, AK	640.6	NA	241.4	139.0
460	477	Kennametal, Latrobe, PA	619.5	21.1	476.2	243.5
470	472	Bandag, Muscatine, IA	593.9	79.6	442.2	297.1
480	496	Westmoreland Coal, Philadelphia, PA	570.3	−13.4	320.7	144.3
490		Dell Computer, Austin, TX	546.2	27.2	246.2	112.0
500	500	Guilford Mills, Greensboro, NC	528.8	15.9	375.3	178.1
Sample Average			$6,064.7	$61.5	$7,264.6	$1,963.9
Sample Standard Deviation			$17,846.0	$761.2	$26,104.4	$4,426.4

Source: "The Fortune 500 Largest U.S. Industrial Corporations," *Fortune,* April 20, 1992, 212–239.

cult to investigate the link, if any, between size and profitability. For example, in 1991 GM reported huge losses following the downturn in sales brought about by a weak economy and growing competition in the auto industry. The fact that such a large company reported losses for the period makes it less likely that any significant link between firm size and profitability would be found over a sample of $N = 51$ firms from the 1992 Fortune 500. If such a link exists it would emerge during this period if GM were dropped from the sample, but eliminating the largest Fortune 500 firm from consideration introduces the risk of failing to include all relevant data in the analysis. Missing or incomplete observations create additional problems since they represent valuable lost information. However, there is usually no simple remedy for missing data, and affected observations typically must be dropped from consideration.

With these caveats in mind, the following table shows regression model estimation results for the link between firm size and profitability for a sample drawn

TABLE 12.4 **Estimation Results for the Profitability Effects of Firm Size within the Fortune 500 (*t*-statistics in parentheses)**

Dependent Variable (SIZE MEASURE)	Independent Variables					
	Constant	Size	Size²	Size³	R^2	*F*-Statistic
Profits (SALES)	−12.440	0.049	−0.025–05*	0.000–05	79.8%	63.30
	(−0.16)	(1.96)	(−0.25)	(−0.00)		
Profits (ASSETS)	32.870	0.038	−0.038–05	0.000–05	76.1%	50.80
	(0.40)	(1.33)	(−0.34)	(0.04)		
Profits (STK. EQ.)	−1.630	0.085	1.147–05	−0.000–05	83.6%	80.59
	(−0.02)	(1.34)	(1.46)	(−3.57)		
Margin (SALES)	0.032	2.52–05	−0.000–05	000.05	5.1%	0.84
	(2.94)	(−0.70)	(−0.61)	(0.54)		
ROA (ASSETS)	0.047	0.106–05	−0.000–05	0.000–05	3.9%	0.63
	(3.91)	(0.24)	(−0.41)	(0.42)		
ROE (STK. EQ.)	0.107	−0.484–05	0.000–05	−0.000–05	8.2%	1.27
	(3.47)	(−0.17)	(0.28)	(−0.45)		

Note: *In scientific notation, $-0.025-05$ is read as -0.025×10^{-5}, or -0.00000025.

from the 1992 Fortune 500. As shown in Table 12.4, a few sample firms had incomplete or missing information and had to be dropped from consideration in the various regressions.

A. On the basis of the coefficient of determination (R^2) criterion, does the link between profitability and size depend upon which measure of firm size is adopted?
B. Do profits, profit rates, or both increase with firm size?
C. What other important determinants of profitability might be included in a more detailed study of the profitability/firm size relation?

Selected References

Ambrose, Brent W., and Drew B. Winters. "Does an Industry Effect Exist for Leveraged Buyouts?" *Financial Management* 21 (Spring 1992): 89–101.
Bolton, Ruth N., and James H. Drew. "A Longitudinal Analysis of the Impact of Service Changes on Customer Attitudes." *Journal of Marketing* 55 (January 1991): 1–9.
Bower, Joseph L. "Business and Battles: Lessons from Defeat." *Harvard Business Review* 68 (July–August 1990): 48–53.
Chandler, Alfred D. "The Enduring Logic of Industrial Success." *Harvard Business Review* 68 (March–April 1990): 130–140.
Chatterjee, Rabikar, and Yoshi Sugita. "New Product Introduction under Demand Uncertainty in Competitive Industries." *Managerial and Decision Economics* 11 (February 1990): 1–12.
Crawford, Vincent P. "Explicit Communication and Bargaining Outcomes." *American Economic Review* 80 (May 1990): 213–219.
Erzan, Refik, and Alexander J. Yeats. "Implications of Current Factor Proportions Indices for the Competitive Position of the U.S. Manufacturing and Service Industries in the Year 2000." *Journal of Business* 64 (April 1991): 229–254.

Hirsch, Barry T. "Union Coverage and Profitability Among U.S. Firms." *Review of Economics and Statistics* 73 (February 1991): 69–77.

Leibenstein, Harvey, and Shlomo Maital. "Empirical Estimation and Partitioning of X-Inefficiency: A Data Envelopment Approach." *American Economic Review* 82 (May 1992): 428–433.

Maher, Michael W., Peter Tiessen, Robert Colson, and Amy J. Broman. "Competition and Audit Fees." *Accounting Review* 67 (January 1992): 199–211.

Palmer, Karen. "Diversification by Regulated Monopolies and Incentives for Cost-Reducing R&D." *American Economic Review* 81 (May 1991): 266–270.

Pearson, Andrall E. "Corporate Redemption and the Seven Deadly Sins." *Harvard Business Review* 70 (May–June 1992): 65–75.

Porter, Michael E. "The Competitive Advantage of Nations." *Harvard Business Review* 68 (March–April 1990): 73–93.

Shipley, David, and Elizabeth Bourdon. "Distributor Pricing in Very Competitive Markets." *Industrial Marketing Management* 19 (August 1990): 215–224.

Stegeman, Mark. "Advertising in Competitive Markets." *American Economic Review* 81 (March 1991): 210–223.

MONOPOLISTIC COMPETITION AND OLIGOPOLY

The economic environment faced by a majority of firms in the economy cannot be described as purely competitive. Likewise, few firms have a clear monopoly in terms of the goods and services they provide. Market structures encountered in the real world often embody elements of both perfect competition and monopoly. Firms often introduce valuable new products or process innovations that give rise to substantial economic profits or above-normal rates of return in the short run. In the long run, however, entry and imitation by new rivals erode the dominant market share enjoyed by early innovators, and profits eventually return to normal levels. Still, in sharp contrast to perfectly competitive markets, the unique product characteristics of individual firms often remain valued by consumers. Consumers often continue to prefer *Campbell's Soup, Dockers, Oil of Olay, Rubbermaid, Tide,* and other favorite brands long after comparable products have been introduced by rivals. The part-competitive, part-monopoly market structure encountered by firms in the apparel, food, hotel, retailing, and consumer products industries is called monopolistic competition. Given the lack of perfect substitutes, monopolistically competitive firms exercise some discretion in setting prices—they are not price takers. However, given vigorous competition from imitators offering close but not identical substitutes, such firms enjoy only a normal risk-adjusted rate of return on investment in long-run equilibrium.

Other imperfectly competitive markets are characterized by competition among few rather than many competitors, as is true of perfectly competitive and monopolistically competitive markets. Oligopoly is the market structure model that describes competition among a handful of competitors sheltered by significant barriers to entry. Oligopolists might produce a homogeneous product, such as aluminum, steel, or semiconductors; or differentiated products such as *Cheerios, Coca-Cola, Marlboro, MTV,* and *Nintendo.* Firms in the ready-to-eat cereal, beverage, cigarette, and computer games software industries, among others, have the potential for economic profits even in the long run. With few competitors, economic incentives also exist for such firms to devise illegal agreements to limit competition, fix prices, or otherwise divide markets. The history of antitrust enforcement in the United States provides numerous examples of "competitors" who illegally entered into such agreements. Yet, there are also examples of markets in which vigorous competition among a small number of firms generates obvious long-term benefits for consumers. It is therefore erroneous to draw a simple link between the number of competitors and the vigor of competition.

In characterizing the descriptive relevance of the monopolistic competition and oligopoly models of seller behavior, it is important to recognize the dynamic nature of real-world markets. For example, as late as the mid-1980s it seemed quite appropriate to regard the automobile and personal computer manufacturing markets as oligopolistic in nature. Today, it seems fairer to regard each industry as monopolistically competitive. So-called clones of IBM and Apple computers have dramatically reduced the relative attractiveness of PS/2 and Macintosh computers. Similarly, a veritable onslaught of competition from Honda, Hyundai, Mazda, Nissan, and Toyota, among others, has dramatically reduced the prices, market share, and profits of the "Big Three" U.S. automakers. In many formerly oligopolistic markets, the market discipline provided by a competitive fringe of smaller domestic and foreign rivals has become sufficient to limit the potential abuse of a few large competitors.

THE CONTRAST BETWEEN MONOPOLISTIC COMPETITION AND OLIGOPOLY

Monopolistic competition and oligopoly provide differing perspectives on the nature of competition in imperfectly competitive markets. Each entail important unique characteristics. Major attributes of the monopolistic competition and oligopoly market models are outlined in this section and then elaborated on in the rest of the chapter.

Monopolistic Competition

Monopolistic competition
A market structure characterized by a large number of sellers of differentiated products.

Monopolistic competition is similar to perfect competition and entails vigorous price competition among a large number of firms and individuals. The major difference between these two market structure models is that consumers perceive important differences among the products offered by monopolistically competitive firms, whereas the output of perfectly competitive firms is homogeneous. This gives monopolistically competitive firms at least some discretion in setting prices. However, the presence of many close substitutes limits this price-setting ability and drives profits down to a normal risk-adjusted rate of return in the long run. As in the case of perfect competition, above-normal profits are possible only in the short-run, before the monopolistically competitive firm's rivals can take effective countermeasures.

Oligopoly

In an industry characterized by **oligopoly,** only a few large rivals are responsible for the bulk of industry output. As in the case of monopoly, high to very high barriers to entry are typical. Under oligopoly, the price/output decisions of firms are interrelated in the sense that direct reactions among rivals can be expected.

●

MANAGERIAL APPLICATION 13.1

What Are the Characteristics of a Wonderful Business?

Since 1900, the rate of return on common stocks has averaged roughly 10 percent per year. Through depressions and economic booms, during world wars and periods of peaceful prosperity, and following countless federal, state, and local elections, common stocks have allowed patient investors to double their money roughly every seven years. After accounting for inflation of roughly 4 percent per year, common stocks have returned investors about 6 percent per year in inflation-adjusted, or "real," dollars. In real terms, common stocks have allowed patient investors to double their money every 12 years. These 10 percent nominal or 6 percent real rates of return reflect the yield that can be expected in the broad cross section of common stock investments. Of course, the challenge to professional managers and investors alike is to identify and invest in superior business opportunities. An interesting perspective on the characteristics of "wonderful businesses" is given in the writings of legendary Wall Street investors T. Rowe Price and Warren E. Buffett.

The late T. Rowe Price was the founder of Baltimore-based T. Rowe Price and Associates, Inc., one of the largest no-load mutual fund organizations, and the father of the "growth stock" theory of investing. According to Price, attractive growth stocks have low labor costs, superior research to develop products and markets, a high return on stockholders' equity (ROE) and profit margins, and rapid earnings per share (EPS) growth. These stocks also lack cutthroat competition and are comparatively immune from regulation. Omaha's Warren E. Buffett, the billionaire head of Berkshire Hathaway, Inc., also looks for companies that have strong franchises and enjoy pricing flexibility, high ROE and cash flow, owner-oriented management, and predictable earnings that are not natural targets of regulation.

To apply these investment criteria successfully, business managers and investors must be sensitive to the fundamental economic and demographic trends of the 1990s. Perhaps the most obvious of these is the aging of the population. Healthcare demands will continue to soar, and investors have bid up the shares of companies offering prescription drugs, healthcare, and healthcare cost containment (e.g., home health agencies). Perhaps less obvious is that an aging and increasingly wealthy population will save growing amounts for their children's education and retirement. This bodes well for mutual fund operators, insurance companies, and other firms that offer financial services.

As the overall population continues to enjoy growing income, spending on leisure activities is apt to grow and companies that offer distinctive goods and services in this area will do well. Helping well-heeled customers have fun has always been a good business. Productivity enhancement to combat economic stagnation is also likely to be a major thrust of the 1990s. In this area, it is perhaps easier to pick likely beneficiaries of emerging technologies than it is to chart the future course of technical advance. For example, catalog retailers, long-distance and cellular phone companies, and credit card providers are all major beneficiaries of the rapid pace of advance in computer and information technology and are likely to do well. Similarly, the major broadcasters, cable TV companies, moviemakers, and software providers are all prone to benefit from increasingly user-friendly technology for leisure-time activities.

Berkshire's investment portfolio names specific companies that meet these criteria. Berkshire holds a large stake in The American Express Company, a premier travel and financial services firm that is strategically positioned to benefit from aging baby boomers. Large positions are also held in Capital Cities/ABC, Inc.; The Washington Post Company; Federal Home Loan Mortgage Corporation; GEICO Corporation; The Gillette Company; Salomon, Inc.; and Wells Fargo & Company. The Coca-Cola Company, one of Berkshire's biggest and most successful holdings, typifies the concept of a wonderful business. Coca-Cola enjoys perhaps the world's strongest franchise, owner-oriented management, and a predictable and growing return of more than 35 percent on ROE; also the company is not subject to price or profit regulation. From the standpoint of being a wonderful business, Coca-Cola is clearly the "real thing." Given Price's and Buffett's well-documented successes as investors in wonderful businesses, shouldn't managers look for business investment opportunities that share similar characteristics?

Source: Walecia Konrad and Igor Reichlin, "The Real Thing Is Thundering Eastward," *Business Week,* April 13, 1992, 96–98.

Oligopoly
A market structure characterized by few sellers and interdependent price/output decisions.

As a result, decisions of individual firms are based in part on the likely responses of competitors. This competition among the few involves a wide variety of price and nonprice methods of rivalry, as determined by the institutional characteristics of each particular market. Even though limited numbers of competitors give rise to a potential for economic profits, above-normal rates of return are far from guaranteed. Competition among the few is sometimes vigorous.

MONOPOLISTIC COMPETITION

Pure competition and pure monopoly rarely exist in actual markets. Most firms are subject to competition, though perhaps not as vigorous as would exist under pure competition. Even though most firms compete with a large number of other firms producing highly substitutable products, many still have some control over the price of their product. They cannot sell all that they want at a fixed price, nor would they lose all their sales if they raised prices slightly. In other words, most firms face downward-sloping demand curves, signifying less-than-perfect competition.

Characteristics of Monopolistically Competitive Markets

Monopolistic competition exists in a market when individual producers have moderate influence over product prices, where each such product enjoys a degree of uniqueness in the perception of customers. This market structure has some important similarities and dissimilarities with perfectly competitive markets. Monopolistic competition is characterized by the following:

- *Large numbers of buyers and sellers.* Each firm in the industry produces a small portion of industry output, and each customer buys only a small part of the total.
- *Product heterogeneity.* The output of each firm is perceived by customers to be essentially different from, though comparable with, the output of other firms in the industry.
- *Free entry and exit.* Firms are not restricted from entering or leaving the industry.
- *Perfect dissemination of information.* Cost, price, and product quality information is known by all buyers and all sellers in the market.

These basic conditions are not as restrictive as those for pure competition and are fairly commonplace in actual markets. Vigorous monopolistic competition is evident in the banking, container and packaging, discount and fashion retail, electronics, food manufacturing, office equipment, paper and forest products, and most personal and professional service industries. Although individual firms are able to maintain some control over pricing policy, their pricing discretion is severely limited by competition from firms offering close but not identical substitutes.

Monopolistic competition is a realistic description of the competition encountered by firms in a wide variety of industries. As in perfectly competitive markets, a large number of competitors make independent decisions in monopolistically competitive markets. A price change by any one firm does not cause other firms to change prices. If price reactions did occur, then an oligopoly market structure would be present. The most distinctive characteristic of monopolistic competition is that each competitor offers a unique product that is only an imperfect substitute for those offered by competitors. Each firm is able to differentiate its product, at least to some degree, from those of rival firms. Nevertheless, each firm's demand function is significantly affected by the presence of numerous competitors producing goods that consumers view as reasonably close substitutes. Exogenous changes in demand and cost conditions also tend to have a similar effect on all firms and frequently lead to comparable pricing influences.

Product differentiation takes many forms. Quality differentials, packaging, credit terms, or superior maintenance service can all differentiate products, as can advertising that leads to brand-name identification. Not only is a tube of Crest toothpaste different from Colgate toothpaste, a tube of Crest at a nearby convenience store is different from an identical tube available at a distant discount retailer. Since consumers evaluate products on the basis of their ability to satisfy specific wants, as well as when and where they have them, products involve not only quantity, quality, and price characteristics but time and place attributes as well. The important factor in all of these forms of product differentiation is that some consumers prefer the product of one seller to those of others.

The effect of product differentiation is to create downward-sloping firm demand curves in monopolistically competitive markets. Unlike a price taker facing a perfectly horizontal demand curve, the firm is able to independently determine an optimal price/output combination. The degree of price flexibility enjoyed depends on the strength of product differentiation. The more differentiated a firm's product, the lower the substitutability of other products for it. Strong differentiation results in greater consumer loyalty and greater control over price. This is illustrated in Figure 13.1, which shows the demand curves of Firms *A* and *B*. Consumers view Firm *A*'s product as being only slightly differentiated from the bulk of industry output. Because many other firms offer acceptable substitutes, Firm *A* is close to being a price taker. Conversely, Firm *B* has successfully differentiated its product, and consumers are therefore less willing to accept substitutes for *B*'s output. Firm *B*'s demand is relatively less sensitive to price changes.

Price/Output Decisions under Monopolistic Competition

As its name suggests, monopolistic competition embodies elements of both monopoly and perfect competition. The monopoly aspect of monopolistic competition is most forcefully observed in the short run. Consider Figure 13.2. With the demand curve, D_1, and its related marginal revenue curve, MR_1, the optimum output, Q_1, is found at the point where $MR_1 = MC$. Short-run monopoly profits equal to the area P_1LMATC_1 are earned. Such profits can be derived from new product introductions, product and process improvements, creative packaging and marketing, or other factors such as an unexpected rise in demand.

Over time, short-run monopoly profits attract competition, and other firms enter the industry. This competitive aspect of monopolistic competition is seen most forcefully in the long run. As competitors emerge to offer close but imperfect substitutes, the market share and profits of the initial innovating firm diminish. Firm demand and marginal revenue curves shift to the left, as for example, from D_1 to D_2 and from MR_1 to MR_2 in Figure 13.2. Optimal long-run output

FIGURE 13.1   **Relation between Product Differentiation and Elasticity of Demand**

Firm *B*'s steeper demand curve relative to Firm *A*'s reflects stronger product differentiation and hence less sensitivity to price changes.

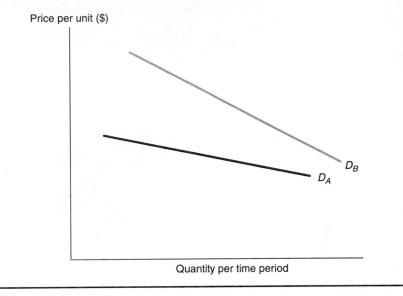

occurs at Q_2, the point where $MR_2 = MC$. Since the optimal price P_2 equals ATC_2, where cost includes a normal profit just sufficient to maintain capital investment, economic profits are zero.

The price/output combination P_2Q_2 describes a monopolistically competitive market equilibrium characterized by a high degree of product differentiation. If new entrants offered perfect rather than close substitutes, each firm's long-run demand curve would become more nearly horizontal, and the perfectly competitive equilibrium, D_3 with P_3 and Q_3, would be approached. Like the P_2Q_2 high-differentiation equilibrium, the P_3Q_3 no-differentiation equilibrium is something of an extreme case. In most instances, competitor entry reduces but does not eliminate product differentiation. An intermediate price/output solution, one between P_2Q_2 and P_3Q_3, is often achieved in long-run equilibrium. Indeed, it is the retention of at least some degree of product differentiation that distinguishes the monopolistically competitive equilibrium from that achieved in perfectly competitive markets.

Also important is that a firm will never operate at the minimum point on its average cost curve in monopolistically competitive equilibrium. Each firm's demand curve is downward sloping, so it is tangent to the *ATC* curve only at a point above the minimum of the *ATC* curve. However, this does not mean that a monopolistically competitive industry is inefficient, except in a superficial sense. The very existence of a downward-sloping demand curve implies that consumers value an individual firm's products more highly than they do products of other producers. If the number of producers were somehow reduced so that all the remaining firms could operate at their minimum cost point, some consumers

FIGURE 13.2   Price/Output Combinations under Monopolistic Competition

Long-run equilibrium under monopolistic competition occurs when $MR = MC$ and $P = AC$. This typically occurs between P_2Q_2 (the high-price/low-output equilibrium) and P_3Q_3 (the low-price/high-output equilibrium).

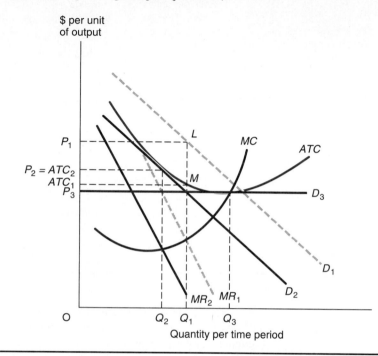

would clearly suffer a loss in welfare, *because the product variety they desire would no longer be available.* The higher prices and costs of monopolistically competitive industries, as opposed to perfectly competitive industries, reflect the economic cost of product variety. If consumers are willing to bear such costs, and often they are, then these costs must not be excessive. The success of many branded products in the face of generic competition is powerful testimony in support of this presumption.

Although the perfectly competitive and pure monopoly settings are comparatively rare in real-world markets, monopolistic competition is frequently observed. It often develops from the competitive forces that continually shape markets. For example, in 1960 a small ($37 million in sales) office-machine company, Haloid Xerox, Inc., revolutionized the copy industry with the introduction of the Xerox 914 copier. Xerography was a tremendous improvement over electro-fax and other coated-paper copiers. It permitted the use of untreated paper, which produced not only a more desirable copy but one that was less expensive on a cost-per-copy basis as well. Invention of the dry copier established what is now Xerox Corporation at the forefront of a rapidly growing office-copier industry and propelled the firm to a position of virtual monopoly by 1970. Between 1970 and 1980, the industry's market structure changed dramatically because of an influx of both domestic and foreign competition as many of Xerox's original patents expired. IBM entered the copier market in April 1970 with its Copier I model and expanded its participation in November 1972 with Copier II. Eastman Kodak made its entry into the market in 1975 with its Ektaprint model. Of course, Minnesota Mining and Manufacturing (3M) has long been a factor in the electro-fax copier segment of the market. A more complete list of Xerox's recent domestic and international competitors would include at least 30 firms. The effect of this entry on Xerox's market share and profitability was dramatic. Between 1970 and 1978, for example, Xerox's share of the domestic copier market fell from 98 to 56 percent, and its return on stockholders' equity fell from 23.6 to 18.2 percent.

The monopolistic dry-copier market of 1970 has evolved into a much more competitive industry in the 1990s. Because Canon, Kodak, 3M, Panasonic, and Sharp copiers are only close rather than perfect substitutes for Xerox machines, each company retains some price discretion, and today the industry can be described as monopolistically competitive.

▶ The process of price/output adjustment and the concept of equilibrium in monopolistically competitive markets can be further illustrated by the following example. Assume that the Skyhawk Trailer Company, located in Toronto, Ontario, owns patents covering important design features of its Tomahawk II, an ultralight camping trailer that can safely be towed by high-mileage subcompact cars. Skyhawk's patent protection has made it very difficult for competitors to offer similar ultralight trailers. The Tomahawk II is a highly successful product, and a veritable flood of similar products can be expected within five years as Skyhawk's patent protection expires.

Skyhawk has asked its financial planning committee to identify both short- and long-run pricing and production strategies for the Tomahawk II. To facilitate the decision-making process, the committee has received the following revenue and cost data from Skyhawk's marketing and production departments:

$$TR = \$20,000 - \$15.6Q,$$
$$MR = dTR/dQ = \$20,000 - \$31.2Q,$$
$$TC = \$400,000 + \$4,640Q + \$10Q^2,$$
$$MC = dTC/dQ = \$4,640 + \$20Q,$$

where *TR* is revenue (in dollars), *Q* is quantity (in units), *MR* is marginal revenue (in dollars), *TC* is total cost, including a risk-adjusted normal rate of return on investment (in dollars), and *MC* is marginal cost (in dollars).

As a first step in the analysis, one might determine the optimal price/output combination if the committee were to decide that Skyhawk should take full advantage of its current monopoly position and maximize short-run profits. To find the short-run profit-maximizing price/output combination, set Skyhawk's marginal revenue equal to marginal cost and solve for *Q:*

$$MR = MC,$$
$$\$20,000 - \$31.2Q = \$4,640Q - \$10Q^2,$$
$$\$51.2Q = \$15,360,$$
$$Q = 300 \text{ units},$$

and

$$P = \$20{,}000 - \$15.6(300)$$
$$= \$15{,}320.$$
$$\pi = TR - TC$$
$$= -\$25.6(300^2) + \$15{,}360(300) - \$400{,}000$$
$$= \$1{,}904{,}000.$$

Therefore, the financial planning committee should recommend a $15,320 price and 300-unit output level to Skyhawk management if the firm's objective is to maximize short-run profit. Such a planning decision results in roughly $1.9 million in profit during those years when Skyhawk's patent protection effectively deters competitors.

Now assume that Skyhawk can maintain a high level of brand loyalty and product differentiation in the long run, despite competitor offerings of similar trailers but that such competition eliminates any potential for economic profits. This is consistent with a market in monopolistically competitive equilibrium, where $P = AC$ at a point above minimum long-run average costs. Skyhawk's declining market share is reflected by a leftward shift in its demand curve to a point of tangency with its average cost curve. Although precise identification of the long-run price/output combination is very difficult, the planning committee can identify the bounds within which this price/output combination can be expected to occur.

The high-price/low-output combination is identified by the point of tangency between the firm's average cost curve and a new demand curve reflecting a *parallel leftward* shift in demand (D_2 in Figure 13.2). This parallel leftward shift assumes that the firm can maintain a high degree of product differentiation in the long run. The low-price/high-output equilibrium combination assumes no residual product differentiation in the long run, and it is identified by the point of tangency between the average cost curve and a new horizontal firm demand curve (D_3 in Figure 13.2). This is, of course, also the perfectly competitive market equilibrium price/output combination.

The equilibrium high-price/low-output combination that follows a parallel leftward shift in Skyhawk's demand curve can be determined by equating the slopes of the firm's original demand curve and its long-run average cost curve. Since a parallel leftward shift in firm demand results in a new demand curve with an identical slope, equating the slopes of the firm's initial demand and average cost curves identifies the monopolistically competitive high-price/low-output equilibrium.

For simplicity, assume that the previous total cost curve for Skyhawk also holds in the long run. To determine the slope of this average cost curve, one must find out how average costs vary with respect to output.

$$AC = TC/Q = (\$400{,}000 + \$4{,}640Q + \$10Q^2)/Q$$
$$= \frac{\$400{,}000}{Q} + \$4{,}640 + \$10Q$$
$$= \$400{,}000Q^{-1} + \$4{,}640 + \$10Q.$$

The slope of this average cost curve is given by the expression

$$\delta AC/\delta Q = -400,000Q^{-2} + 10.$$

The slope of the new demand curve is given by

$$dP/dQ = -15.6 \text{ (same as the original demand curve)}.$$

In equilibrium,

$$\text{Slope of } AC \text{ Curve} = \text{Slope of Demand Curve,}$$
$$-400,000Q^{-2} + 10 = -15.6,$$
$$Q^{-2} = 25.6/400,000,$$
$$Q^2 = 400,000/25.6,$$
$$Q = 125 \text{ Units,}$$
$$P = AC$$
$$= \frac{\$400,000}{125} + \$4,640 + \$10(125)$$
$$= \$9,090,$$

and

$$\pi = P \times Q - TC$$
$$= \$9,090(125) - \$400,000 - \$4,640(125) - \$10(125^2)$$
$$= \$0.$$

This high-price/low-output monopolistically competitive equilibrium results in a decrease in price from $15,320 to $9,090 and a fall in output from 300 to 125 units per year. Only a risk-adjusted normal rate of return will be earned, eliminating Skyhawk's economic profits. This long-run equilibrium assumes that Skyhawk would enjoy the same low price elasticity of demand that it experienced as a monopolist. This assumption may or may not be appropriate. New entrants often have the effect of both cutting a monopolist's market share and increasing the price elasticity of demand. It is often reasonable to expect entry to cause both a leftward shift of and some flattening in Skyhawk's demand curve. To see the extreme limit of the demand-curve flattening process, the case of a perfectly horizontal demand curve can be considered.

The low-price/high-output (perfectly competitive) equilibrium combination occurs at the point where $P = MR = MC = AC$. This reflects that the firm's demand curve is perfectly horizontal, and average costs are minimized. To find the output level of minimum average costs, set $MC = AC$ and solve for Q:

$$\$4,640 + \$20Q = \$400,000Q^{-1} + \$4,640 + \$10Q,$$
$$\$10Q = \$400,000Q^{-1},$$
$$Q^2 = 40,000,$$
$$Q = \sqrt{40,000}$$
$$= 200 \text{ units.}$$

$$P = AC$$
$$= \frac{\$400,000}{200} + \$4,640 + \$10(200)$$
$$= \$8,640,$$

and

$$\pi = PQ - TC$$
$$= \$8,640(200) - \$400,000 - \$4,640(200) - \$10(200^2)$$
$$= \$0.$$

Under this low-price equilibrium scenario, Skyhawk's monopoly price falls in the long-run from an original \$15,320 to \$8,640, and output falls from the monopoly level of 300 units to the competitive equilibrium level of 200 units per year. The company would earn only a risk-adjusted normal rate of return, and economic profits would equal zero.

Following expiration of its patent protection, management can expect that competitor entry will reduce Skyhawk's volume from 300 units per year to a level between $Q = 125$ and $Q = 200$ units per year. The short-run profit-maximizing price of \$15,320 will fall to a monopolistically competitive equilibrium price between $P = \$9,090$, the high-price/low-output equilibrium, and $P = \$8,640$, the low-price/high-output equilibrium. In deciding on an optimal short-run price/output strategy, Skyhawk must weigh the benefits of high near-term profitability against the long-run cost of lost market share resulting from competitor entry. Such a decision involves consideration of current interest rates, the speed of competitor imitation, and the future pace of innovation in the industry, among other factors.

OLIGOPOLY

The theory of monopolistic competition recognizes that firms often have some control over price but that their price flexibility is limited by a large number of close substitutes for their products. The theory assumes, however, that in making decisions, firms do not consider competitor reactions. Such a behavioral assumption is appropriate for some industries but inappropriate for others. When individual firm actions cause competitors to react, oligopoly exists.

Characteristics of Oligopoly Markets

Oligopoly exists when a handful of competitors dominate the market for a good or service, and each firm makes pricing and marketing decisions in light of the expected response by rivals. Individual firms have the ability to set pricing and production strategy, and they enjoy the potential for economic profits in both the short run and the long run. Oligopoly describes markets that can be characterized as follows:

- *Few sellers.* A handful of firms produces the bulk of industry output.
- *Homogeneous or unique product.* Oligopoly output can be perceived as homogeneous (e.g., aluminum) or distinctive (e.g., ready-to-eat cereal).

- *Blockaded entry and exit.* Firms are heavily restricted from entering or leaving the industry.
- *Imperfect dissemination of information.* Cost, price, and product quality information is withheld from uninformed buyers.

In the United States, aluminum, cigarettes, electrical equipment, filmed entertainment production and distribution, glass, long-distance telecommunications, and ready-to-eat cereals are all produced and sold under conditions of oligopoly. In each of these industries, a small number of firms produces a dominant percentage of all industry output. In the ready-to-eat breakfast cereal industry, for example, Kellogg, General Mills, General Foods (Phillip Morris), RJR Nabisco, Quaker Oats, and Ralston Purina are responsible for almost all domestic production in the United States. Durable customer loyalty gives rise to fat profit margins and rates of return on assets that are two to three times food industry norms. Corn Flakes, Sugar Frosted Flakes, Cheerios, Raisin Bran, Wheaties, and a handful of other brands continue to dominate the industry year after year and make successful entry extremely difficult. Even multinational food giant Nestlé sought and obtained a joint venture agreement with General Mills rather than entering the potentially lucrative European breakfast cereal market by itself. Long-distance telephone service is also highly concentrated, with AT&T, MCI, and Sprint providing almost all domestic service.

Oligopoly also is present in a number of local markets. In many retail markets for gasoline and food, for example, only a few service stations and grocery stores compete within a small geographic area. Drycleaning services are also sometimes provided by a relative handful of firms in small to medium-size cities and towns.

A limited number of sellers creates price/output decision interdependence under oligopoly. Consider the case of *duopoly,* a special form of oligopoly, under which only two firms provide a particular product. For simplicity, assume that a homogeneous product is offered and that customers choose between the firms solely on the basis of price. Assume also that both firms charge the same price and that each has an equal share of the market. Now suppose that Firm *A* attempts to increase its sales by lowering its price. All buyers will attempt to switch to Firm *A,* and Firm *B* will lose a substantial share of its market. To retain customers, *B* will react by lowering its price. Neither firm is free to act independently; actions taken by one lead to reactions by the other.

Price/Output Decisions under Oligopoly

Demand curves relate quantity demanded to price, *holding constant the effect of all other variables.* One variable that is typically assumed to remain fixed is the price charged by competing firms. In an oligopolistic market structure, however, if one firm changes its price, other firms react by changing their prices. The demand curve for the initial firm shifts position so that instead of moving along a single demand curve as it changes price, the firm moves to an entirely new demand curve.

The phenomenon of shifting demand curves is illustrated in Figure 13.3(a). Firm *A* is initially producing Q_1 units of output and selling them at a price of P_1. Demand curve D_1 applies here, assuming that prices charged by other firms remain fixed. Under this assumption, a price cut from P_1 to P_2 would increase

FIGURE 13.3 **Shifting Demand under Oligopoly**

(a) A price reduction to P_2 by Firm A temporarily increases output to Q_2. As other firms reduce prices, demand shifts back from D_1 to D_2 and Firm A's output drops to Q_3. (b) In contrast to D_1 and D_2, the demand curve D_3 reflects Firm A's projections of the price reactions of competitors.

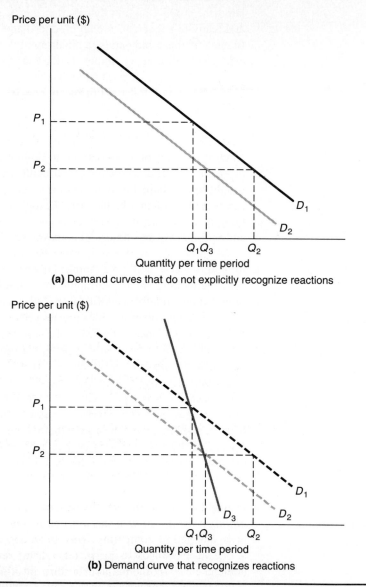

(a) Demand curves that do not explicitly recognize reactions

(b) Demand curve that recognizes reactions

demand to Q_2. Assume, however, that only a few firms operate in the market and that each has a fairly large share of total sales. If one firm cuts its price and obtains a substantial increase in volume, other firms lose a large part of their business. Furthermore, they know exactly why their sales have fallen and react by cutting their own prices. This action shifts Firm *A* down to the second demand curve, D_2, reducing its demand at P_2 from Q_2 to Q_3 units. The new curve is just as unstable as the old one, so knowledge of its shape is useless to Firm *A;* if it tries to move along D_2, competitors will react, forcing the company to yet another demand curve.

Shifting demand curves present no real difficulty in making price/output decisions *if each firm knows how rivals will react to price changes.* The reactions would just be built into the price/demand relation, and a new demand curve could be constructed to include interactions among firms. Curve D_3 in Figure 13.3(b) represents such a reaction-based demand curve; it shows how price reductions affect quantity demanded after competitive reactions have been taken into account. The problem with this approach is that different interfirm behavior leads to different pricing decision rules.

Cartel Arrangements

Cartel

Firms operating with a formal agreement to fix prices and output.

Collusion

A covert, informal agreement among firms in an industry to fix prices and output levels.

All firms in an oligopoly market benefit if they get together and set prices to maximize industry profits. In so doing, the firms set a monopoly price and extract the maximum amount of profit from consumers. A group of competitors operating under such a formal overt agreement is called a **cartel.** If an informal covert agreement is reached, the firms are said to be operating in **collusion.** Both practices are generally illegal in the United States. However, cartels are legal in many parts of the world, and multinational corporations often become involved with them in foreign markets. Several important domestic markets are also dominated by producer associations that operate like cartels and appear to flourish without interference from the government. Agricultural commodities such as milk are prime examples of products marketed under cartel-like arrangements.

A cartel that has absolute control over all firms in an industry can operate as a monopoly. To illustrate, consider the situation shown in Figure 13.4. The marginal cost curves of each firm are summed horizontally to arrive at an industry marginal cost curve. Equating the cartel's total marginal cost with the industry marginal revenue curve determines the profit-maximizing output and, simultaneously, the price, P^*, to be charged. Once this profit-maximizing price/output level has been determined, each individual firm finds its optimal output by equating its own marginal cost curve to the previously determined profit-maximizing marginal cost level for the industry.

Profits are often divided among firms on the basis of their individual level of production, but other allocation techniques can be employed. Market share, production capacity, and a bargained solution based on economic power have all been used in the past. For a number of reasons, cartels are typically rather short-lived. In addition to the long-run problems of changing products and of entry into the market by new producers, cartels are subject to disagreements among members. Although firms usually agree that maximizing joint profits is mutually

FIGURE 13.4   Price/Output Determination for a Cartel

Horizontal summation of the *MC* curves for each firm gives the cartel's *MC* curve. Output for each firm is found by equating its own *MC* to the industry profit-maximizing *MC* level.

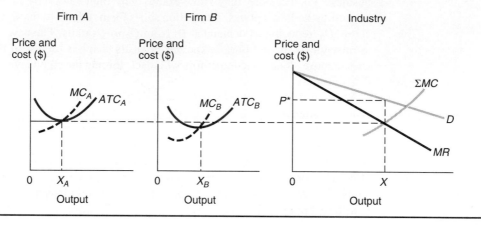

beneficial, they seldom agree on the equity of various profit-allocation schemes. This problem can lead to attempts to subvert the cartel agreement.

Cartel subversion can be extremely profitable to individual firms. With an industry operating at the monopoly price/output level, undetected secret price cutting can lead to a dramatic increase in profits for individual cartel members. The costs and benefits of such subversion are directly related to the number of firms included in the cartel. Consider a two-firm cartel in which each member serves 50 percent of the market. Cheating by either firm is very difficult, because any loss in market share is readily detected. The offending party can easily be identified and punished. Moreover, the potential profit and market share gain to successful cheating is exactly balanced by the potential profit and market share cost of detection and retribution. Conversely, a 20-member cartel promises substantial profits and market share gains to successful cheaters. At the same time, detecting the source of secret price concessions can be extremely difficult. History shows that cartels including more than a very few members have difficulty policing and maintaining member compliance. With respect to cartels, there appears to be little honor among thieves.

The OPEC cartel's loss of oil market control in the late 1980s is a classic example of a cartel that failed primarily because members could not agree on a profit- and market-sharing scheme. Unwieldy large size and pressure from new entrants attracted by relatively high oil prices added to the cartel's problems and caused it to become ineffectual.

Price Leadership   A less formal but still effective means of reducing oligopolistic uncertainty is through **price leadership.** Price leadership results when one firm establishes itself as the industry leader and all other firms accept its pricing policy. This leadership may result from the size and strength of the leading firm, from cost efficiency, or as a result of the recognized ability of the leader to forecast market

FIGURE 13.5   **Oligopoly Pricing with Dominant-Firm Price Leadership**

When the price leader has set an industry price of P_2, the price leader will maximize profits at Q_1 units of output. Price followers will supply a combined output of $Q_4 - Q_1$.

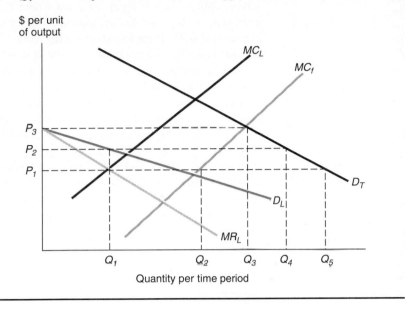

Price leadership

A situation in which one firm establishes itself as the industry leader and all other firms in the industry accept its pricing policy.

conditions accurately and to establish prices that produce satisfactory profits for all firms in the industry.

A typical case is price leadership by a dominant firm, usually the largest firm in the industry. The leader faces a price/output problem similar to monopoly, while other firms are price takers and face a competitive price/output problem. This is illustrated in Figure 13.5, where the total market demand curve is D_T, the marginal cost curve of the leader is MC_L, and the horizontal summation of the marginal cost curves for all of the price followers is labeled MC_f. Because price followers take prices as given, they choose to operate at the output level at which their individual marginal costs equal price, just as they would in a purely competitive market. Accordingly, the MC_f curve represents the supply curve for following firms. At price P_3, followers would supply the entire market, leaving nothing for the dominant firm. At all prices below P_3, the horizontal distance between the summed MC_f curve and the market demand curve represents the price leader's demand. At a price of P_1, for example, price followers provide Q_2 units of output, leaving demand of $Q_5 - Q_2$ for the price leader. Plotting all of the residual demand quantities for prices below P_3 produces the demand curve for the price leader, D_L in Figure 13.5, and the related marginal revenue curve, MR_L. More generally, the leader faces a demand curve of the following form:

$$D_L = D_T - S_f, \tag{13.1}$$

where D_L is the leader's demand, D_T is total demand, and S_f is the followers' supply curve found by setting price $= MC_f$ and solving for Q_f, the quantity that will be supplied by the price followers. Since D_T and S_f are both functions of price, D_L is likewise determined by price.

Because the price leader faces the demand curve D_L as a monopolist, it maximizes profit by operating at the point where marginal revenue equals marginal cost, $MR_L = MC_L$. At this optimal output level for the leader, Q_1, market price is established at P_2. Price followers supply a combined output of $Q_4 - Q_1$ units. If no one challenges the price leader, a stable short-run equilibrium is reached.

A second type of price leadership is **barometric price leadership.** In this case, one firm announces a price change in response to what it perceives as a change in industry supply and demand conditions. This change could stem from cost increases that result from a new industry labor agreement, higher energy or material prices, higher taxes, or a substantial shift in industry demand. With barometric price leadership, the price leader is not necessarily the largest or the dominant firm in the industry. The price-leader role might even pass from one firm to another over time. To be effective, the price leader must only be accurate in reading the prevailing industry view of the need for price adjustment. If the price leader makes a mistake, other firms may not follow its price move, and the price leader may have to rescind or modify the announced price change to retain its leadership position.

Barometric price leadership

A situation in which one firm in an industry announces a price change in response to what it perceives as a change in industry supply and demand conditions and other firms respond by following the price change.

Kinked Demand Curve

Kinked demand curve

A theory assuming that rival firms follow any decrease in price in order to maintain their respective market shares but refrain from following increases, allowing their market share to increase at the expense of the firm making the initial price increase.

An often-noted characteristic of oligopoly markets is "sticky" prices. Once a general price level has been established, whether through cartel agreement or some less formal arrangement, it tends to remain fixed for an extended period. Such rigid prices are often explained by what is referred to as the **kinked demand curve** theory of oligopoly prices. A kinked demand curve is a firm demand curve that has different slopes for price increases as compared with price decreases. The kinked demand curve describes a behavior pattern in which rival firms follow any decrease in price to maintain their respective market shares but refrain from following price increases, allowing their market shares to grow at the expense of the competitor increasing its price. The demand curve facing individual firms is kinked at the current price/output combination, as illustrated in Figure 13.6. The firm is producing Q units of output and selling them at a price of P per unit. If the firm lowers its price, competitors retaliate by lowering their prices. The result of a price cut is a relatively small increase in sales. Price increases, on the other hand, result in significant reductions in the quantity demanded and in total revenue, because customers shift to competing firms that do not follow the price increase.

Associated with the kink in the demand curve is a point of discontinuity in the marginal revenue curve. As a result, the firm's marginal revenue curve has a gap at the current price/output level, which results in price rigidity. To see why, recall that profit-maximizing firms always choose to operate at the point where marginal cost equals marginal revenue. Typically, any change in marginal cost leads to a new point of equality between marginal costs and marginal revenues and to a new optimal price. However, with a gap in the marginal revenue curve, the price/output combination at the kink can remain optimal despite fluctuations in marginal costs. As illustrated in Figure 13.6, the firm's marginal cost curve

MANAGERIAL APPLICATION 13.2

A Web of Cartels Ensnarls Europe

"Europe 1992" will be a borderless single market designed to unleash new competitive forces on the continent. Newly energized companies were supposed to emerge as tariff and other trade barriers went the way of the Berlin Wall. With trade barriers removed, mergers, combinations, and rapid internal growth were thought to be the means by which European companies would be able to enjoy the economies of scale enjoyed by larger Japanese and U.S. competitors. Firms in individual countries could also focus on their own comparative advantages, thus freeing resources for their best economic use. New economies of scope would also become available to European companies as they expanded product lines to take advantage of complementary advantages in the production and/or distribution of various goods and services. Unfortunately, what all of this wonderful theory failed to take account of was the willingness of various sovereign European governments to permit, if not encourage, widespread anticompetitive practices. Through mutual stakeholding, joint production and R&D agreements, and strategic alliances, Europe is ensnarled in a web of cartels as the 1992 "revolution" takes place.

At the start of Europe 1992, Europe's top companies are swapping shareholdings, merging subsidiaries, and pooling R&D and production; they are cooperating, not competing. At the center of the European web of cartels are the continent's two largest industrial groups, Germany's Daimler-Benz and Italy's Fiat. Daimler-Benz makes Mercedes-Benz automobiles, and Fiat produces cars under its own name and that of Lancia, Alfa-Romeo, and Ferrari. However, both Daimler-Benz and Fiat are diversifying rapidly. Daimler-Benz is expanding into electronics, software, and aerospace. Fiat and its controlling shareholders, the Agnelli family, are growing major businesses in food processing, telecommunications, and aerospace. Much of this expansion is by way of merger and acquisition rather than through internal growth.

Daimler-Benz is now affiliated with 3 of Europe's 11 other major automakers and has links to General Motors through GM's stake in Saab. Daimler-Benz has ties to Volvo and Renault through Daimler-Benz's strategic partnership with the Mitsubishi Group of Japan.

In 1992, Daimler-Benz was also expected to have its electronics and household appliances subsidiary join the existing collaboration between two of Germany's other largest industrial firms, Siemens and Bosch. Such a coalition would further solidify existing ties between Daimler-Benz and Fiat, through Britain's GEC and France's Aérospatiale.

European "trustbusters" tolerate such deals in the interest of creating world-size European competitors. With potential economies of scale as justification, Brussels bureaucrats looked the other way when Germany's Siemens and Britain's GEC linked together to carve up British electronics firm Plessey. Similarly, Fiat was allowed to get together with Europe's leading telecommunications company, Alcatel of France, ostensibly to fight off European encroachments made by AT&T from the United States. Among Europe's biggest defense contractors, Aérospatiale, British Aerospace, and Daimler-Benz's Deutsche Aerospace are all being allowed to pool R&D and production to ease the pain of defense spending cuts; the three are already partners in Europe's aerospace manufacturer Airbus Industrie. Such alliances are backed by trade barriers and political clout that will make life difficult for more efficient U.S. defense companies. Making matters more difficult for U.S. competitors is that Daimler-Benz has also planned to collaborate with the Netherlands' civilian plane maker, Fokker.

Companies from the United States are also getting into the act. For example, IBM has thrown itself into the European coupling frenzy by taking on joint projects with no fewer than five major European companies. As part of its plan to take a stake in French computer group Bull, IBM purchases chips and shares technology with the Franco-Italian partnership SGS. IBM has also agreed to pursue joint R&D and chip production with Siemens.

With almost every major European company related to everyone else, there is an obvious danger that the new Europe, like the old, will settle down to cozily divided and protected markets. Instead of fostering heightened competition, Europe 1992 may result in European giants joining hands to keep out unwelcome U.S. and Japanese rivals.

Source: Peter Fuhrman, "Getting in Bed Together." *Forbes,* May 11, 1992, 86–87.

FIGURE 13.6   **Kinked Demand Curve**

When price cuts are followed but price increases are not, a kink develops in the firm's demand curve. At the kink, the optimal price remains stable despite moderate changes in marginal costs.

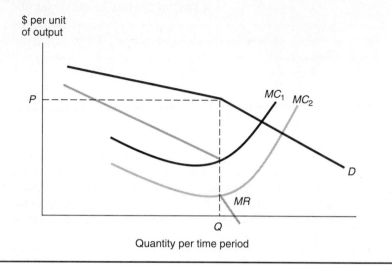

can vacillate between MC_1 and MC_2 without causing any change in the profit-maximizing price/output combination. Small changes in marginal costs have no effect; only large changes in marginal cost lead to price changes. In perfectly competitive grain markets, prices change every day. In the oligopolistic ready-to-eat cereals market, prices change only infrequently.

NONPRICE COMPETITION

New entrants to a market that hope to establish a position by merely cutting prices are often frustrated. Nonleading firms that hope to grow market share through price concessions alone are frequently thwarted. The problem in both instances is that price cuts are obvious and easily detected by competitors. "Meet it or beat it" is a pricing challenge that often results in quick competitor price reductions, and price wars favor the deep pockets of established incumbents. As a result, many successful firms find nonprice methods of competition an effective means for growing market share and profitability in the face of entrenched rivals.

Advantages of Nonprice Competition

Because rival firms are likely to retaliate against price cuts, oligopolists often emphasize nonprice competition to boost demand. To illustrate, assume that a firm demand function is given by Equation 13.2:

$$Q_A = f(P_A, P_X, Ad_A, Ad_X, SQ_A, SQ_X, I, POP, \ldots)$$
$$= a - bP_A + cP_X + dAd_A - eAd_X + fSQ_A \qquad \textbf{(13.2)}$$
$$- gSQ_X + hI + iPop + \ldots,$$

where Q_A is the quantity of output demanded from Firm A, P_A is A's price, P_X is the average price charged by other firms in the industry, Ad is advertising expenditures, SQ denotes an index of styling and quality, I represents income, and Pop is population. The firm can control three variables in Equation 13.2: P_A, Ad_A, and SQ_A. If it reduces P_A in an effort to stimulate demand, it will probably cause a reduction in P_X, offsetting the hoped-for effects of the initial price cut. Rather than boosting sales, Firm A may have simply started a price war.

Now consider the effects of changing Ad_A and SQ_A. Effective advertising shifts the firm's demand curve to the right, thus enabling the firm to increase sales at a given price or to sell the same quantity at a higher price. Any improvement in styling or quality would have a comparable effect, as would easier credit terms, better service, and more convenient retail locations. While competitors react to nonprice competition, their reaction is often slower and less direct than that for price changes. Nonprice changes are generally less obvious to rivals, and the design of an effective response is often time-consuming and difficult. Advertising campaigns have to be designed; media time and space must be purchased. Styling and quality changes frequently require long lead times, as do fundamental improvements in customer service. Furthermore, nonprice competition can alter customer buying habits, and regaining lost customers can prove to be difficult. Although it may take longer to establish a reputation through nonprice competition, its advantageous effects are likely to be more persistent than the fleeting benefits of a price cut.

The optimal level of nonprice competition is defined by resulting marginal benefits and marginal costs. Any form of nonprice competition should be pursued as long as marginal benefits exceed marginal costs. For example, suppose that a product has a market price of $10 per unit and a variable cost per unit of $8. If sales can be increased at an additional cost of less than $2 per unit, these additional expenditures will increase profits and should be made.

The Optimal Level of Advertising

Advertising is but one of the many different methods of nonprice competition employed in imperfectly competitive markets. However, promotional and selling expenses constitute a considerable share of costs in many industries and therefore merit special consideration. In addition to helping determine an appropriate level of promotional and selling expenses, the method for determining an optimal level of advertising illustrates the technique for determining profit-maximizing levels of expenditures for other forms of nonprice competition, such as improvements in product quality, expansions in customer service, research and development expenditures, and so on.

The rule that must be followed to determine a profit-maximizing level of expenditures for nonprice methods of competition is to set the marginal cost of the activity involved just equal to the marginal revenue or marginal benefit derived from it. This follows because if the marginal cost of any activity equals the marginal revenue derived, the total net profit generated will be maximized. The optimal level of advertising occurs at that point where the additional net revenues derived from advertising just offset the marginal cost of advertising expenditures.

Additional or net marginal revenues per unit of output derived from advertising are measured by the marginal profit contribution generated. This is the difference between marginal revenues, *MR,* and the marginal costs of production and distribution, MC_Q, *before* advertising costs:

$$\frac{\text{Net Marginal Revenue}}{\text{Derived from Advertising}} = \frac{\text{Marginal}}{\text{Revenue}} - \frac{\text{Marginal Cost}}{\text{of Output}}, \qquad \textbf{(13.3)}$$

$$NMR_A = MR - MC_Q.$$

The marginal cost of advertising, again expressed in terms of the marginal cost of selling one additional unit of output, can be written

$$\frac{\text{Marginal Cost}}{\text{of Advertising}} = \frac{\text{Change in Advertising Expenditures}}{\text{One Unit Change in Demand}}, \qquad \textbf{(13.4)}$$

$$MC_A = \frac{\delta\text{Advertising Expenditures}}{\delta\text{Demand}}.$$

The optimal level of advertising is found where

$$\frac{\text{Net Marginal Revenue}}{\text{Derived from Advertising}} = \text{Marginal Cost of Advertising},$$

$$MR - MC_Q = \frac{\delta\text{Advertising Expenditures}}{\delta\text{Demand}},$$

$$NMR_A = MC_A.$$

To illustrate, suppose that output in an individual line of business provides a profit contribution before advertising expenses of $2,500 per unit. The net marginal revenue derived from advertising that expands demand by one unit is $2,500. Marginal advertising and promotional expenditures up to this $2,500 level could then be justified. If one more unit of demand could be generated with an additional $1,000 in advertising expenditures, this additional advertising would be warranted because it generates an additional profit contribution of $1,500. In contrast, if an additional advertising expenditure of $3,000 were necessary to expand demand by one unit, the additional advertising expenditure would reduce firm profits and would not be justified.

In general, it will pay to expand advertising expenditures as long as $NMR_A > MC_A$. Since the marginal profit derived from advertising is

$$M\pi_A = NMR_A - MC_A, \qquad \textbf{(13.5)}$$

the optimal level of advertising occurs at the point where

$$M\pi_A = 0.$$

This relation is illustrated in Figure 13.7. As long as $NMR_A > MC_A$, $M\pi_A > 0$, and it will pay to expand the level of advertising. Conversely, if $NMR_A < MC_A$, then $M\pi_A < 0$, and it will pay to reduce the level of advertising expenditures. The optimal level of advertising is achieved when $NMR_A = MC_A$, and $M\pi_A = 0$.

FIGURE 13.7   **Optimal Level of Advertising**

A firm will expand the level of advertising up to the point where the net marginal revenue generated just equals the marginal cost of advertising.

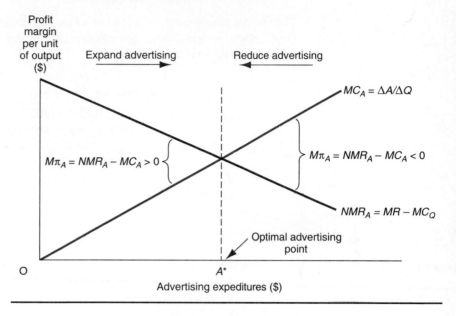

An Example of Optimal Advertising

▶

The effect of advertising on the optimal price/output combination can be further illustrated with a more detailed example. Suppose that Consumer Products, Inc., has a new prescription ointment called *Regain* that can be used to restore hair loss due to male pattern baldness in some patients. Currently, *Regain* is marketed through doctors without any consumer advertising. Given the newness of the product, demand for *Regain* is expected to increase rapidly following the initiation of consumer advertising. Samantha Stevens, an ad executive with the Mc-Mann & Tate Advertising Agency, projects that demand would double following the start of a $500,000 per month media advertising campaign developed by the agency. To illustrate the profit impact of the proposed television advertising campaign, it is necessary to identify the projected effect on demand and revenue relations.

Current monthly demand for the product is described by the following expressions:

$$Q = 25,000 - 100P,$$

or

$$P = \$250 - \$0.01Q.$$

This market demand implies total and marginal revenue functions of

$$TR = \$250Q - \$0.01Q^2,$$
$$MR = dTR/dQ = \$250 - \$0.02Q.$$

Assume total and marginal costs are given by the expressions

$$TC = \$250,000 + \$50Q,$$
$$MC = dTC/dQ = \$50.$$

The optimal price/output combination is found by setting $MR = MC$ and solving for Q. Since marginal costs are constant at $50 per unit, the pre-advertising optimal activity level for *Regain* is

$$MR = MC$$
$$\$250 - \$0.02Q = \$50,$$
$$0.02Q = 200,$$
$$Q = 10,000,$$

and

$$\begin{aligned}
P &= TR/Q, \\
&= (\$250Q - \$0.01Q^2)/Q \\
&= \$250 - \$0.01Q \\
&= \$250 - \$0.01(10,000) \\
&= \$150. \\
\pi &= TR - TC \\
&= \$250(10,000) - \$0.01(10,000^2) - \$250,000 - \$50(10,000) \\
&= \$750,000 \text{ per month.}
\end{aligned}$$

Following a 100 percent advertising-inspired increase in demand, the new monthly demand relations for *Regain* are

$$\begin{aligned}
Q &= 2(25,000 - 100P) \\
&= 50,000 - 200P
\end{aligned}$$

or

$$P = \$250 - \$0.005Q.$$

This new advertising-induced market demand implies new total and marginal revenue functions of

$$TR = \$250Q - \$0.005Q^2,$$
$$MR = \$250 - \$0.01Q.$$

The new optimal price/output combination is found by setting the new $MR = MC$ and solving for Q. Since marginal costs remain constant at $50 per unit, the new optimal activity level for *Regain* is

$$MR = MC$$
$$\$250 - \$0.01Q = \$50,$$
$$0.01Q = 200,$$
$$Q = 20,000,$$

and

$$P = \$250 - \$0.005Q,$$

$$= \$250 - \$0.005(20{,}000),$$
$$= \$150.$$
$$\pi = TR - TC,$$
$$= \$250(20{,}000) - \$0.005(20{,}000^2) - \$250{,}000$$
$$- \$50(20{,}000) - \$500{,}000,$$
$$= \$1{,}250{,}000 \text{ per month.}$$

Notice that sales have doubled from 10,000 to 20,000 at the $150 price. The effect on profits is dramatic, rising from $750,000 to $1.25 million, even after accounting for the additional $500,000 in media expenditures. Therefore, the new advertising campaign appears fully warranted. In fact, given the $1 million in profits that are generated by a doubling in unit sales at a price of $150, Consumer Products would be willing to pay up to that full amount to double sales. From this perspective, the $500,000 price charge by the advertising consultant represents a relative bargain. The profit implications of other forms of advertising, or other types of nonprice competition, can be measured in a similar fashion.

MARKET STRUCTURE MEASUREMENT

To formulate an effective competitive strategy, managers must accurately assess the current competitive environment for actual and potential products. Data gathered by the federal government, private market research firms, and trade associations are often useful for this purpose. This section shows the types of market structure data available from public sources and explains why they are important for decision-making purposes.

How Are Economic Markets Measured?

An economic market consists of all individuals and firms willing and able to buy or sell competing products during a given time period. In identifying competing products the key criterion is similarity in use. Precise determination of whether a specific good is a distinct economic product involves an evaluation of cross-price elasticities for broad classes of goods. When cross-price elasticities are large and positive, goods are substitutes for one another and can be thought of as competing products in a single market. Conversely, large negative cross-price elasticities indicate complementary products. Complementary products produced by a single firm must be evaluated as a single product line serving the same market. If complementary products are produced by other companies, evaluating the potential of a given product line involves incorporating exogenous influences beyond the firm's control. When cross-price elasticities are near zero, goods are in separate economic markets and can be separately analyzed as serving distinct consumer needs. Therefore, using cross-price elasticity criteria to desegregate the firm's overall product line into its distinct economic markets is an important task confronting managers.

To identify relevant economic markets and define their characteristics, firms in the United States make extensive use of economic data collected by the Bureau of the Census of the U.S. Department of Commerce. Because these data provide valuable information on economic activity across the broad spectrum of U.S.

industry, it is worthwhile to briefly consider the method and scope of the economic censuses.

The Economic Censuses

Economic censuses
Data collected by the U.S. Department of Commerce that provide a comprehensive statistical profile of large segments of the U.S. economy.

Economic censuses provide a comprehensive statistical profile of large segments of the national economy. They are taken at five-year intervals during years ending with the digits 2 and 7—for example, 1982, 1987, 1992, 1997, and so on. Included are censuses of manufacturing, retail and wholesale trade, services, minerals, and construction. In 1982, for example, sectors covered by the economic censuses accounted for nearly 70 percent of total economic activity originating in the private sector. Principal industry groups not covered are finance, insurance, real estate, agriculture, forestry, communications, public utilities, and transportation. However, limited transportation-related information is collected, including the distance that commodities are shipped and the type of transport employed.

Economic censuses are the primary source of data concerning changes in the number and size distribution of competitors, output, and employment in the economy. They are used extensively by the government in compiling national income accounts and as a basis for current surveys of industrial production, productivity, and prices. Census data are also used extensively by government agencies in setting public policy and monitoring economic programs. Manufacturers and distributors rely on census data to analyze current and potential markets. The censuses provide data for demand and cost forecasting; market penetration analysis; layout of sales territories; allocation of advertising budgets; and locations of plants, warehouses, and retail outlets. Trade and professional associations rely on census information to learn about changes in the number, size, and geographic dispersion of firms in their industry. State and local governments and chambers of commerce use census data to assess the business climate, as well as to gauge the success of programs designed to increase business investment and employment opportunities in local areas.

A further important characteristic of the economic censuses is their coverage of geographic trends. Recent *Census of Manufacturers* surveys measure industrial activity for legally constituted geographic units such as states, counties, and cities. Manufacturing activity levels are also provided on hundreds of SMSAs (Standard Metropolitan Statistical Areas). SMSAs are integrated economic and social units with a large volume of daily travel and communication between the central city (having 50,000 or more population) and outlying areas. Each SMSA consists of one whole county or more and may include both industrialized counties and adjoining counties that are largely residential in character. Detail for various industries is shown at the SMSA level if data for individual companies would not be disclosed and if the industry has at least 250 employees.

In addition to being a comprehensive source of information on economic activity, census data have the compelling virtues of easy access and widespread availability. Census reports can be purchased directly from the Government Printing Office at modest cost or can be consulted free of charge at most major public and college libraries. In addition, census data and reports are often republished and distributed by trade associations, business magazines, and newspapers.

TABLE 13.1   **Standard Industrial Classifications of Economic Activity**

Sector	Two-Digit SIC Codes
Agriculture, Forestry, and Fisheries	01–09
Mining	10–14
Contract Construction	15–17
Manufacturing	20–39
Transportation; Communication; Electric, Gas, and Sanitary Services	40–49
Wholesale and Retail Trade	50–59
Finance, Insurance, and Real Estate	60–67
Services	70–89
Public Administration	91–97
Nonclassifiable Establishments	99

TABLE 13.2   **Census Classification Example**

Digit Level	Number of Classifications	Example SIC Code	Description
Two	20	20	Food and Kindred Products
Three	144	202	Dairy Products
Four	452	2023	Condensed and Evaporated Milk Industry
Five	1,500	20232	Canned Milk
Six			(Not currently utilized)
Seven	13,000	2023212	Canned Evaporated Milk

The Census Classification System

Census data are collected at the establishment level—that is, at a single physical location engaged in a specific line of business. The establishment level is best suited for obtaining direct measures of output and inputs such as labor, materials, capital, and so on. It is also a useful level of aggregation for providing detailed industry and geographic tabulations. In contrast, statistics measuring overall income and balance sheet data are best collected at the company or enterprise level. Enterprise statistics on income and balance sheet data are made available to the public by the Internal Revenue Service in its *Statistics of Income* and by the Federal Trade Commission in its *Quarterly Financial Report for Manufacturing, Mining and Trade.*

The census classification of individual establishments by sector, industry group, industry, and products is called the Standard Industrial Classification (SIC) system. Table 13.1 shows the first step in this process and illustrates how the entire scope of economic activity is subdivided into sectors described by two-digit classifications. Below the two-digit major group or sector level, the SIC system proceeds to desegregated levels of increasingly narrowly defined activity. Currently, the SIC system proceeds from very general two-digit industry groups to very specific seven-digit product classifications. To illustrate, Table 13.2 shows the breakdown that occurs as one moves from the two-digit "food and kindred products" major group to the seven-digit "canned evaporated milk" product category. Economists generally agree that four-digit-level classifications correspond quite closely with the economic definition of a market. Establishments grouped at the four-digit level produce products that are ready substitutes for one another and thus function as competitors. Managers who analyze census data to learn about the number and size distribution of actual and potential competitors focus their attention primarily on data provided at the four-digit level. For this reason, attention is focused on four-digit-level concentration data in discussions of market structure.

CENSUS MEASURES OF MARKET CONCENTRATION

Market structure falls along the continuum from perfect competition to monopoly. Where an industry falls along this continuum is important for firms currently in the industry and for those contemplating entry. Price/output strategies vary markedly depending on the market structure encountered. Profit rates are also affected by the level of competitive pressures. Among the attributes describing market structure, perhaps the number and size distribution of competitors are most important. These data must be carefully considered in managerial decision making.

Concentration Ratios

In addition to those directly engaged in business, both government and the public share an interest in the size distribution of firms. A small number of competitors can sometimes have direct implications for regulation and antitrust policy. Thus, considerable public resources are devoted to monitoring both the size distribution and economic performance of firms in several important sectors of the economy. Data that describe these characteristics of the U.S. economy are regularly compiled and published in economic census reports published by the Department of Commerce. Among those sectors covered by the economic censuses, manufacturing is clearly the largest, accounting for approximately 20 percent of aggregate economic activity in the United States. Firm sizes in manufacturing are also much larger than in other major sectors such as retail and wholesale trade, construction, legal and medical services, and so on. Among the more than 16 million business enterprises in the United States, manufacturing is the domain of the large corporation. Thus, the manufacturing sector provides an interesting basis for considering data that are available on the size distribution of firms.

Table 13.3 shows numbers of competitors, industry sales, and leading-firm market share data for a small sample of four-digit industries taken from the 1982 *Census of Manufacturers*. As is generally the case, leading-firm market shares are calculated from sales data for the top four or eight firms in an industry. These market share data are called **concentration ratios** because they measure the percentage market share held by (concentrated in) an industry's top four (CR_4) or eight (CR_8) firms. When concentration ratios are low, industries tend to be made up of many firms and competition tends to be vigorous. Industries in which the four leading firms are responsible for less than 20 percent of total industry sales (i.e., $CR_4 < 20$) are highly competitive and approximate the pure competition

Concentration ratios
Data in the *Census of Manufacturers* that show the percentage market share held by an industry's leading firms.

TABLE 13.3   A Representative Sample of Four-Digit Census Industries

Standard Industrial Classification (SIC) Code	Description	Number of Firms	Industry Sales (millions of dollars)	Market Share (%)	
				Top Four Firms (CR_4)	Top Eight Firms (CR_8)
2011	Meat Packing Plants	1,658	$ 5,824.6	29	43
2043	Cereal Breakfast Foods	32	4,131.9	86	a
2047	Dog, Cat, and Other Pet Food	222	4,402.2	52	71
2067	Chewing Gum	9	915.3	95	a
2095	Roasted Coffee	118	5,826.9	65	76
2371	Fur Goods	503	419.3	12	19
2387	Apparel Belts	317	556.5	19	30
2621	Paper Mills	135	20,994.6	22	40
2711	Newspapers	7,520	21,276.3	22	34
3425	Handsaws and Saw Blades	119	487.3	47	65
3711	Motor Vehicles and Car Bodies	284	70,739.7	92	97
3721	Aircraft	139	28,024.3	64	81
3732	Boat Building and Repairing	1,834	2,369.2	14	22
3995	Burial Caskets	270	682.1	52	60

[a]Indicates an industry with so few competitors that the Census Bureau withholds data to avoid disclosing individual company information.

Source: U.S. Dept. of Commerce, Bureau of the Census, 1982 Census of Manufacturers: *Concentration Ratios in Manufacturing* (Washington, D.C.: U.S. Government Printing Office, 1986).

model. On the other hand, when concentration ratios are high, leading firms dominate following firms in terms of size, and leading firms may have more potential for pricing flexibility and economic profits. Industries in which the four leading firms control more than 80 percent of total industry sales (i.e., $CR_4 > 80$) are highly concentrated, and market structure can tend toward monopoly. However, industries with a $CR_4 < 20$ or $CR_4 > 80$ are quite rare. Three-quarters of all manufacturing activity takes place in industries with concentration ratios falling in the range $20 \leq CR_4 \leq 80$. In terms of relative importance, market structures that can be described as monopolistically competitive are much more common than pure competition or monopoly.

Limitations of Census Concentration Ratios

Despite the obvious attraction of census concentration ratio data as a useful source of information on the number and size distribution of current competitors, it is prudent to remain cautious in their use and interpretation. Various limitations of concentration ratio data are important in terms of both business and public policy considerations. By not recognizing these limitations, one might make incorrect judgments concerning market structure when relying on concentration ratio information.

A major drawback of concentration ratio data relates to the timing of their availability. It typically takes more than *five years* for detailed concentration ratio data to become widely available. Data for 1987 were not available until mid-1992, data for 1992 will not become available until mid-1997. In many fast-moving markets, these data are obsolete before they are published. Even in less dynamic markets, they provide only an imperfect guide to managerial decision making. As a result, most managers supplement census information with more current data available from market research firms.

A further important weakness of census concentration ratio data pertains to their coverage. Concentration data ignore domestic sales by foreign competitors (imports) as well as exports by domestic firms. Only data on domestic sales from *domestic production,* not total domestic sales, are reported. This means, for example, that if foreign imports have a market share of 25 percent, the four leading domestic automobile manufacturers account for 69 percent ($=$ 92 percent of 75 percent) of total U.S. foreign plus domestic car sales, rather than the 92 percent as Table 13.3 suggests. For industries in which import competition is important, concentration ratios significantly overstate the relative importance of leading domestic firms. Concentration ratios also overstate market power for several industries in which increasing foreign competition has been responsible for the liquidation or merger of many smaller domestic firms with older, less efficient production facilities. Despite reduced numbers of domestic firms and the consequent rise in concentration, an increase in foreign competition often makes affected industries more efficient and more competitive rather than less so. The impact of foreign competition is important in many industries, but it is particularly so in manufacturing industries such as apparel, steel, automobiles, cameras, copiers, motorcycles, and television sets.

Another limitation of concentration ratio data is that they are *national totals,* whereas a relevant economic market may be national, regional, or local in scope. If high transportation costs or other product characteristics keep markets regional or local rather than national in scope, concentration ratios can significantly understate the relative importance of leading firms. For example, the leading firm in many metropolitan newspaper markets often accounts for 90 percent or more of total market advertising and subscription revenues. Thus, a national CR_4 level for newspapers of 22 percent in 1982 significantly understates local market power in that industry. Whereas national concentration ratios in the 20 percent range usually suggest a highly competitive market structure, the local or regional character of some markets can make national concentration figures meaningless. Other examples of products with local or regional rather than national markets include milk, bread and bakery products, commercial printing, and ready-mix concrete.

Additional problems occur because concentration ratios provide an imperfect view of market structure by including only firms that are *currently active* in a particular industry. Recall that an economic market includes all firms willing and able to sell an identifiable product. Besides firms currently active in an industry, this includes those that can be regarded as likely potential entrants. Often the mere presence of one or more potential entrants constitutes a sufficient threat to force competitive market behavior in industries with only a handful of established competitors. Major retailers such as Wal-Mart, Kmart, and Sears, for example, use their positions as potential entrants into manufacturing to obtain attractive

●

MANAGERIAL APPLICATION 13.3
Government-Guaranteed Oligopoly

The Federal National Mortgage Association and the Federal Home Loan Mortgage Corp., or Fannie Mae and Freddie Mac, as they are affectionately called, enjoy the benefits of being government-sponsored entities and also for-profit, publicly traded stockholder-owned corporations. Both firms are huge and highly profitable. In 1991, for example, Fannie and Freddie purchased over half of the $400 billion in home mortgages written in the United States that they were eligible to purchase, up from about 25 percent of $125 billion in the early 1980s. Most of these loans are packaged and sold to investors as mortgage-backed securities, thus enabling home buyers to tap pension funds and other institutional money. Thanks to this added liquidity, the early 1990 credit squeeze for businesses and commercial borrowers did not translate into a credit crunch for U.S. home buyers. Provided they can qualify, U.S. home buyers can get all the financing they need in the most liquid and efficient home-finance market in the world. Largely as a result, Americans easily are the best-housed people in the world.

Even as Fannie and Freddie have done well for homeowners, they have done even better for their public shareholders. Fannie earned $1.4 billion during 1991, or $4.98 on each of its 274 million shares. This represented a 28 percent return on equity. At the same time, Freddie earned $555 million, $9.25 on each of its 600 million shares, and a 24 percent return on equity. Their stock-price performance has been nothing short of sensational. In 1991, Fannie's NYSE shares more than doubled and Freddie's tripled. Most Wall Street analysts remain bullish on both companies based on expected earnings growth of up to 15 percent per year during the 1990s.

Fannie and Freddie are potent competitors for banks, savings and loans, and other lenders. Both are considering expansion into such markets as home equity lending and housing for the elderly, and Fannie has test-marketed construction lending programs for home builders. Fannie has also lent over $100 million in home equity conversion loans, or "reverse mortgages," to people over 62 who have paid off most of their original mortgages. Fannie has also begun financing developers in the construction of single family and multifamily homes.

It is no surprise that competing financial institutions are unhappy about continued Fannie and Freddie expansion. They claim that the firms compete unfairly because they get a subsidy from the U.S. government. Indeed, according to the Treasury Department, Fannie and Freddie, as government-sponsored enterprises, get noncash subsidies that are worth between $2 billion and $4 billion per year. Both Fannie and Freddie have implied U.S. government guarantees on all of their liabilities. This earns them the highest possible credit ratings on their debt securities and allows them to attract institutional investors at the lowest possible interest rate. While the U.S. government charges nothing for its implied credit guarantee, Fannie and Freddie together reap *billions* of dollars in profits from having lower interest costs than their competitors.

By congressional charter, Fannie and Freddie are supposed to provide liquidity to the mortgage market and help low- and moderate-income families purchase adequate housing. To ensure a rapidly growing market for their services, Congress has allowed Fannie and Freddie to underwrite single-family home mortgages as high as $202,000, up from $133,000 in 1986. "Where do you draw the line? Today taxpayers are subsidizing a person who makes $100,000 a year and can afford a $250,000 home," says former Salomon Brothers mortgage finance pioneer Lewis Ranieri, who both competes with the federal entities as the head of United Savings Association of Texas and is a client of theirs as a mortgage banker.

The administration, encouraged by thrifts and banks, is pushing Congress to strengthen capital requirements for Freddie and Fannie and to require them to earmark 30 percent of their loans for low- and moderate-income families. Despite such limits, Fannie and Freddie are likely to survive what is left of the zeal for privatization in Washington and continue their prosperity. Clearly, there are tangible rewards to government-guaranteed oligopoly!

Source: Howard Rudnitsky and Matthew Schifrin, "Nice Work If You Can Get It," *Forbes,* May 11, 1992, 138–139.

prices on a wide range of private-label merchandise such as clothing, lawn mowers, washing machines, and so on.

Finally, considering concentration ratio data in isolation can result in misleading conclusions regarding the vigor of competition in an industry because the degree of competitiveness appears in more than one dimension. Concentration ratios measure only one element of market structure; other elements include the market shares of individual firms, barriers to entry or exit, vertical integration, and so on. Under certain circumstances, even a very few large competitors can compete vigorously. Although concentration ratios are helpful indicators of the relative importance of leading firms and perhaps the potential for market power, it must be remembered that a high level of concentration does not necessarily imply a lack of competition. In some instances, *competition among the few can be vigorous.* In addition to considering the number and size distribution of competitors as measured by concentration, firms must judge the competitive environment in light of foreign competition, transportation costs, regional product differences, likely potential entrants, advertising, customer loyalty, research and development, demand growth, and economies of scale in production, among other factors, to make accurate pricing and output decisions. All of these features of markets constitute important elements of market structure.

COMPETITIVE STRATEGY IN IMPERFECTLY COMPETITIVE MARKETS

Identifying the market structure and profit potential of any given industry is difficult. Product characteristics, the local or regional nature of the market, the time necessary for reactions by established or new competitors, the pace of innovation, unanticipated changes in government regulation and tax policy, and a host of additional considerations can all play important roles in defining the method and scope of competition.

Strategic Considerations

It is always helpful to consider the number of competitors, degree of product differentiation, level of information available in the marketplace, and conditions of entry when attempting to define market structure, but these data are seldom definitive. Conditions of entry and exit are both subtle and dynamic, as is the role of unseen potential entrants, and this contributes to the difficulty of correctly assessing the profit potential of a current or prospective line of business.

Table 13.4 summarizes major characteristics typical of the imperfectly competitive monopolistic competition and oligopoly market structures. To develop an effective competitive strategy, it is necessary to assess the degree to which the characteristics of an individual market embody elements of each of these market structures. Although the probability of successful entry is higher in monopolistically competitive markets, only difficult-to-enter oligopolistic markets (like monopolistic markets) hold the potential for meaningful above-normal returns in the long run.

Firms in imperfectly competitive markets can earn economic profits only to the extent that they impart a valuable degree of uniqueness to their goods or

TABLE 13.4 **Summary of Monopolistic Competition and Oligopoly (Oligopsony) Market-Structure Characteristics**

	Monopolistic Competition	Oligopoly
Number of actual or potential competitors	Many sellers	Few sellers whose decisions are directly related to those of competitors
Product differentiation	Consumers perceive differences among the products of various competitors	High or low, depending on entry and exit conditions
Information	Low-cost information on price and product quality	Restricted access to price and product-quality information; cost and other data are often proprietary
Conditions of entry and exit	Easy entry and exit	High entry or exit barriers because of economies of scale, capital requirements, advertising, research and development costs, or other factors
Profit potential	Economic (above-normal) profits in short run only; normal profit in long run	Potential for economic (above-normal) profits in both short and long run
Examples	Clothing, consumer financial services, professional services, restaurants	Automobiles, bottled and canned soft drinks, investment banking, long-distance telephone service, pharmaceuticals

services. Success, measured in terms of above-normal rates of return, requires a comparative advantage in production, distribution, or marketing that cannot easily be copied by others. Such success is difficult to achieve and is often rather fleeting.

Wendy's "Where's the Beef?" advertising campaign during the early 1980s is an interesting case in point. Like other highly successful and innovative advertising campaigns, the Wendy's promotion both captured the imagination of consumers and caught competitors by surprise. Sales surged as consumers became more aware of the larger amount of meat in Wendy's hamburgers. However, this success was short-lived, as a subsequent lottery-based promotion by industry leader McDonald's caught consumers' interest. The risks of advertising as an effective form of nonprice competition in the fast-food industry became even more readily apparent following the well-documented failure of Burger King's "Herb" (only a nerd wouldn't eat at Burger King) promotion. Burger King not only lost the millions of dollars it spent on an obviously ineffective advertising campaign, but it also lost valuable market share to rivals with more effective advertising. Only time will tell if Pepsi's "Uh-huh" advertising campaign of the 1990s proves successful in displacing Coca-Cola as the most popular soft drink.

This is not to suggest that advertising and other nonprice methods of competition have not been used to great advantage by many successful firms in imperfectly competitive markets. In fact, these techniques are often the primary factor in developing a strong basis for product differentiation in the minds of consumers.

***The Threat
of Potential
Competition***

It is important to recognize that the potential for above-normal rates of return is a powerful inducement to the entry of new competitors and to the rapid growth of nonleading firms. Imitation may be the sincerest form of flattery, but it is also the most effective enemy of above-normal rates of return. "Regression to the mean" is the rule rather than the exception for trends in corporate profit rates over time. During recent years, after-tax rates of return on corporate capital investment have usually been in the range of 10 to 12 percent per year. Very rarely have individual companies regularly earned in excess of 15 to 20 percent for more than a decade, and returns this high are unheard of for an entire industry with several competitors. Therefore, it seems reasonable to conclude that both price and non-price methods of competition are often vigorous, even in imperfectly competitive industries.

SUMMARY

This chapter extends the study of market structure to monopolistic competition and oligopoly. These models describe the behavior of competitors in imperfectly competitive markets across a broad spectrum of our economy in which both price competition and a wide variety of methods of nonprice competition are observed.

- **Monopolistic competition** is similar to perfect competition in that it entails vigorous price competition among a large number of firms and individuals. The major difference is that consumers perceive important differences among the products offered by monopolistically competitive firms, whereas the output of perfectly competitive firms is homogeneous.

- In an industry characterized by **oligopoly,** only a few large rivals are responsible for the bulk of industry output. High to very high barriers to entry are typical, and the price/output decisions of firms are interrelated in the sense that direct reactions from rivals can be expected. This "competition among the few" involves a wide variety of price and nonprice methods of rivalry.

- A group of competitors operating under a formal overt agreement is called a **cartel.** If an informal covert agreement is reached, the firms are said to be operating in **collusion.** Both practices are generally illegal in the United States. However, cartels are legal in many parts of the world, and multinational corporations often become involved with them in foreign markets.

- **Price leadership** results when one firm establishes itself as the industry leader and all other firms accept its pricing policy. This leadership may result from the size and strength of the leading firm, from cost efficiency, or as a result of the recognized ability of the leader to forecast market conditions accurately and to establish prices that produce satisfactory profits for all firms in the industry. Under a second type of price leadership, **barometric price leadership,** the price leader is not necessarily the largest or dominant firm in the industry. The price leader must only be accurate in reading the prevailing industry view of the need for price adjustment.

- An often-noted characteristic of oligopoly markets is "sticky" prices. Once a general price level has been established, whether through cartel agreement or some less formal arrangement, it tends to remain fixed for an extended period.

Such rigid prices are often explained by what is referred to as the **kinked demand curve** theory of oligopoly prices. A kinked demand curve is a firm demand curve that has different slopes for price increases versus price decreases.

- **Economic censuses** provide a comprehensive statistical profile of large segments of the national economy. They are taken at five-year intervals during years ending with the digits 2 and 7—for example, 1982, 1987, 1992, 1997, and so on. Included are censuses of manufacturing, retail and wholesale trade, services, minerals, and construction.

- **Concentration ratios** measure the percentage market share held by (concentrated in) an industry's top four (CR_4) or eight (CR_8) firms. When concentration ratios are low, industries tend to be made up of many firms and competition tends to be vigorous. Industries in which the four leading firms are responsible for less than 20 percent of total industry sales (i.e., $CR_4 < 20$) are highly competitive and approximate the pure competition model. On the other hand, when concentration ratios are high, leading firms dominate and sometimes have the potential for pricing flexibility and economic profits.

Public and private sources offer valuable service through their regular collection and publication of market structure data on the number and size distribution of competitors, market size, growth, capital intensity, investment, and so on. All of this information is useful to the process of managerial decision making and provides a useful starting point for the development of successful competitive strategy.

Questions

Q13.1 Describe the monopolistically competitive market structure, and provide some examples.

Q13.2 Describe the oligopolistic market structure, and provide some examples.

Q13.3 Explain the process through which economic profits are eliminated in a monopolistically competitive industry as compared with a perfectly competitive industry.

Q13.4 Would you expect the demand curve for a firm in a monopolistically competitive industry to be more or less elastic after economic profits have been eliminated?

Q13.5 "One might expect firms in a monopolistically competitive industry to experience greater swings in the price of their products over the business cycle than those in an oligopolistic industry. However, fluctuations in profits do not necessarily follow the same pattern." Discuss this statement.

Q13.6 Will revenue-maximizing firms have short-run profits as large as or larger than profit-maximizing firms? If so, when? If not, why not?

Q13.7 Is short-run revenue maximization necessarily inconsistent with the more traditional long-run profit-maximizing model of firm behavior? Why or why not?

Q13.8 Why is the four-firm concentration ratio only an imperfect measure of market power?

Q13.9   The statement "You get what you pay for" reflects the common perception that high prices indicate high product quality and low prices indicate low quality. Irrespective of market structure considerations, is this statement always correct?

Q13.10   "Economic profits result whenever only a few large competitors are active in a given market." Discuss this statement.

Self-Test Problem

Columbia Drugstores, Inc., based in Seattle, Washington, operates a chain of 30 drugstores in the Pacific Northwest. During recent years, the company has become increasingly concerned with the long-run implications of competition from a new type of competitor, the so-called superstore.

Based on the French concept of the hypermarket, the superstore is a relatively new marketing concept in the United States. Often covering more than 125,000 square feet of display space, superstores allow shoppers to buy everything from groceries to prescription drugs to oil changes and haircuts. Relying on huge volume spurred by deeply discounted prices, superstores have proved to be very popular with cost-conscious consumers. Even if high levels of consumer acceptance prove to be relatively short-lived, a costly loss in walk-in traffic for area drug and grocery stores can occur. Because Columbia, like many regional drug chains, depends on such traffic for its highly profitable impulse-buying business, a serious decline in profitability can immediately follow the opening of a superstore. Moreover, once shoppers change their regular buying habits, drugstores need to run expensive advertising campaigns to reestablish lost customer loyalty.

Columbia is especially vulnerable to superstore competition since all of its stores are currently located in major metropolitan areas. In fact, the effects of superstore competition are already being felt in eight regional markets, where superstores have located within five miles of company outlets. Given the high level of success enjoyed by superstores in other parts of the country, Columbia believes that in only a short time it will face a direct challenge in many, if not all, of its current markets. To devise an effective competitive strategy, Columbia must first assess the profit implications of superstore competition and then consider whether or not a shift in marketing strategy seems in order. For example, Columbia might shift its mix of products away from those on which it has a distinct pricing disadvantage, or it might shift its plans for expansion to smaller markets, where the superstore concept is not feasible.

To measure the effects of superstore competition on current profitability, Columbia asked management consultant Mindy McConnell to conduct a statistical analysis of the company's profitability in its various markets. To net out size-related influences, profitability was measured by Columbia's gross profit margin, or earnings before interest and taxes divided by sales. Columbia provided proprietary company profit, advertising, and sales data covering the last year for all 30 outlets, along with public trade association and Census Bureau data concerning the number and relative size distribution of competitors in each market, among other market characteristics.

As a first step in the study, McConnell decided to conduct a regression-based analysis of the various factors thought to affect Columbia's profitability. First among these is the relative size of leading competitors in the relevant market, measured at the Standard Metropolitan Statistical Area (SMSA) level. Columbia's market share, *MS,* in each market area is expected to have a positive effect on profitability given the pricing, marketing, and average-cost advantages that accompany large relative size. The market concentration ratio, *CR,* measured as the combined market share of the four largest competitors in any given market, is expected to have a negative effect on Columbia's profitability given the stiff competition from large, well-financed rivals. Of course, the expected negative effect of high concentration on Columbia profitability contrasts with the positive influence of high concentration on industry profits that is sometimes observed.

Both capital intensity, *K/S,* measured by the ratio of the book value of assets to sales, and advertising intensity, *A/S,* measured by the advertising-to-sales ratio, are expected to exert positive influences on profitability. Given that profitability is measured by Columbia's gross profit margin, the coefficient on capital intensity measured Columbia's return on tangible investment. Similarly, the coefficient on the advertising variable measures the profit effects of advertising. Growth, *GR,* measured by the geometric mean rate of change in total disposable income in each market, is expected to have a positive influence on Columbia's profitability, since some disequilibrium in industry demand and supply conditions is often observed in rapidly growing areas.

Store No.	Profit Margin	Market Share	Concentration	Capital Intensity	Advertising	Growth	Hypermarket (*H* = 1 if hypermarket present)
1	15.0	25.0	75.0	10.0	10.0	7.5	0
2	10.0	20.0	60.0	7.5	10.0	2.5	1
3	15.0	40.0	70.0	7.5	10.0	5.0	0
4	15.0	30.0	75.0	15.0	12.5	5.0	0
5	15.0	50.0	75.0	10.0	12.5	0.0	0
6	20.0	50.0	70.0	10.0	12.5	7.5	1
7	15.0	50.0	70.0	7.5	10.0	0.0	1
8	25.0	40.0	60.0	12.5	15.0	5.0	0
9	20.0	10.0	40.0	10.0	12.5	5.0	0
10	10.0	30.0	60.0	10.0	12.5	0.0	0
11	15.0	20.0	60.0	12.5	12.5	7.5	1
12	10.0	30.0	75.0	12.5	10.0	2.5	0
13	15.0	50.0	75.0	7.5	10.0	5.0	0
14	10.0	20.0	75.0	7.5	12.5	2.5	0
15	10.0	10.0	50.0	7.5	10.0	2.5	0
16	20.0	30.0	60.0	15.0	12.5	2.5	0
17	15.0	30.0	50.0	7.5	12.5	5.0	1
18	20.0	40.0	70.0	7.5	12.5	5.0	0
19	10.0	10.0	60.0	12.5	10.0	2.5	0
20	15.0	20.0	70.0	5.0	12.5	7.5	0
21	20.0	20.0	40.0	7.5	10.0	7.5	0
22	15.0	10.0	50.0	15.0	10.0	5.0	1
23	15.0	40.0	40.0	7.5	12.5	5.0	1
24	10.0	30.0	50.0	5.0	7.5	0.0	0

continued

Store No.	Profit Margin	Market Share	Concentration	Capital Intensity	Advertising	Growth	Hypermarket ($H = 1$ if hypermarket present)
25	20.0	40.0	70.0	15.0	12.5	5.0	0
26	15.0	40.0	70.0	12.5	10.0	5.0	1
27	10.0	20.0	75.0	7.5	10.5	2.5	0
28	15.0	10.0	60.0	12.5	12.5	5.0	0
29	10.0	30.0	75.0	5.0	7.5	2.5	0
30	10.0	20.0	75.0	12.5	12.5	0.0	0

Finally, to gauge the profit implications of superstore competition, McConnell used a "dummy" (or binary) variable where $H = 1$ in each market in which Columbia faced superstore competition and $H = 0$ otherwise. The coefficient on this variable measures the average profit rate effect of superstore competition. Given the vigorous nature of superstore price competition, McConnell expects the superstore coefficient to be both negative and statistically significant, indicating a profit-limiting influence. The Columbia profit-margin data and related information used in McConnell's statistical analysis are given in the preceding table. Regression model estimates for the determinants of Columbia's profitability are as follows:

Variable Name	Coefficient (1)	Standard Error of Coefficient (2)	t Statistic (3) = (1) ÷ (2)
Intercept	7.846	3.154	2.49
Market share	0.214	0.033	6.50
Concentration	−0.203	0.038	−5.30
Capital intensity	0.289	0.123	2.35
Advertising	0.722	0.233	3.09
Growth	0.842	0.152	5.56
Hypermarket	−2.102	0.828	−2.54

Coefficient of determination = R^2 = 0.84.
Standard error of the estimate = S.E.E. = 1.872 percent.

A. Describe the overall explanatory power of this regression model, as well as the relative importance of each continuous variable.

B. Based on the importance of the binary or dummy variable that indicates superstore competition, do superstores pose a serious threat to Columbia's profitability?

C. What factors might Columbia consider in the development of an effective competitive strategy to combat the superstore influence?

Solution to Self-Test Problem

A. The coefficient of determination (R^2) of 0.84 means that 84 percent of the total variation in Columbia's profit-rate variability is explained by the regression model. This is a relatively high level of explanation for a cross section study such as this, suggesting that the model provides useful insight concerning the determinants of profitability. The intercept coefficient of 7.846 has no economic meaning since it lies far outside the relevant range of observed data.

The 0.214 coefficient for the market-share variable means that, on average, a 1 percent (unit) rise in Columbia's market share leads to a 0.214 percent (unit) rise in Columbia's profit margin. Similarly, as expected, Columbia's profit margin is positively related to capital intensity, advertising intensity, and the rate of growth in the market area. Conversely, high concentration has the expected limiting influence. Because of the effects of leading-firm rivalry, a 1 percent rise in industry concentration will lead to a 0.203 percent decrease in Columbia's profit margin. This means that relatively large firms compete effectively with Columbia.

B. Yes, the regression model indicates that superstore competition in one of Columbia's market areas reduces Columbia's profit margin on average by 2.102 percent. Given that Columbia's rate of return on sales routinely falls in the 10 to 15 percent range, the profit-limiting effect of superstore competition is substantial. Looking more closely at the data, it appears that Columbia faces superstore competition in only one of the seven lucrative markets in which the company earns a 20 to 25 percent rate of return on sales. Both observations suggest that current and potential superstore competition constitutes a considerable threat to the company and one that must be addressed in an effective competitive strategy.

C. Development of an effective competitive strategy to combat the influence of superstores involves the careful consideration of a wide range of factors related to Columbia's business. It might prove fruitful to begin this analysis by more carefully considering market characteristics for Store No. 6, the one Columbia outlet able to earn a substantial 20 percent profit margin despite superstore competition. For example, this analysis might suggest that Columbia, like Store No. 6, should specialize in service (e.g., prescription drug delivery) or in a slightly different mix of merchandise. On the other hand, perhaps Columbia should follow the example set by Wal-Mart in its early development and focus its plans for expansion on small to medium-size markets. In the meantime, Columbia's still-profitable stores in major metropolitan areas could help fund future growth.

Although obviously only a first step, a regression-based study of market structure such as that described here can provide a very useful beginning to the development of an effective competitive strategy.

Problems   P13.1   **Market Structure Concepts.** Indicate whether each of the following statements is true or false and explain why.

A. Equilibrium in monopolistically competitive markets requires that firms be operating at the minimum point on the long-run average cost curve.

B. A high ratio of distribution cost to total cost tends to increase competition by widening the geographic area over which any individual producer can compete.

C. The price elasticity of demand tends to fall as new competitors introduce substitute products.

> D. An efficiently functioning cartel achieves a monopoly price/output combination.
>
> E. An increase in product differentiation tends to increase the slope of firm demand curves.

P13.2   **Monopolistically Competitive Demand.** Would the following factors increase or decrease the ability of domestic auto manufacturers to raise prices and profit margins? Why?

A. Decreased import quotas

B. Elimination of uniform emission standards

C. Increased automobile price advertising

D. Increased import tariffs (taxes)

E. A rising value of the dollar, which has the effect of lowering import car prices

P13.3   **Monopolistically Competitive Equilibrium.** Soft Lens, Inc., has enjoyed rapid growth in sales and high operating profits on its innovative extended-wear soft contact lenses. However, the company faces potentially fierce competition from a host of new competitors as some important basic patents expire during the coming year. Unless the company is able to thwart such competition, severe downward pressure on prices and profit margins is anticipated.

A. Use Soft Lens's current price, output, and total cost data to complete the following table:

Price ($)	Monthly Output (million)	Total Revenue ($million)	Marginal Revenue ($million)	Total Cost ($million)	Marginal Cost ($million)	Average Cost ($million)	Total Profit ($million)
$20	0			$ 0			
19	1			12			
18	2			27			
17	3			42			
16	4			58			
15	5			75			
14	6			84			
13	7			92			
12	8			96			
11	9			99			
10	10			105			

(Note: Total costs include a risk-adjusted normal rate of return.)

B. If cost conditions remain constant, what is the monopolistically competitive high-price/low-output long-run equilibrium in this industry? What are industry profits?

C. Under these same cost conditions, what is the monopolistically competitive low-price/high-output equilibrium in this industry? What are industry profits?

D. Now assume that Soft Lens is able to enter into restrictive licensing agreements with potential competitors and create an effective cartel in the industry. If demand and cost conditions remain constant, what is the cartel price/output and profit equilibrium?

P13.4 **Competitive Strategy.** Gray Computer, Inc., located in Colorado Springs, Colorado, is a privately held producer of high-speed electronic computers with immense storage capacity and computing capability. Although Gray's market is restricted to industrial users and a few large government agencies (e.g., Department of Health, NASA, National Weather Service, etc.), the company has profitably exploited its market niche.

Glen Gray, founder and research director, has recently announced his retirement, the timing of which will unfortunately coincide with the expiration of several patents covering key aspects of the Gray computer. Your company, a potential entrant into the market for supercomputers, has asked you to evaluate the short-run and long-run potential of this market. Based on data gathered from your company's engineering department, user surveys, trade associations, and other sources, the following market demand and cost information has been developed:

$$P = \$54 - \$1.5Q,$$
$$MR = \$54 - \$3Q,$$
$$TC = \$200 + \$6Q + \$0.5Q^2,$$
$$MC = \$6 + \$1Q,$$

where P is price, Q is units measured by the number of supercomputers, MR is marginal revenue, TC is total costs including a normal rate of return, MC is marginal cost, and all figures are in millions of dollars.

A. Assume that these demand and cost data are descriptive of Gray's historical experience. Calculate output, price, and economic profits earned by the Gray Company as a monopolist. What is the point price elasticity of demand at this output level?

B. Calculate the range within which a long-run equilibrium price/output combination would be found for individual firms if entry eliminated Gray's economic profits. (Note: Assume that the cost function is unchanged and that the high-price/low-output solution results from a parallel shift in the demand curve while the low-price/high-output solution results from a competitive equilibrium.)

C. Assume that the point price elasticity of demand calculated in Part A is a good estimate of the relevant arc price elasticity. What is the potential overall market size for supercomputers?

D. If no other near-term entrants are anticipated, should your company enter the market for supercomputers? Why or why not?

P13.5 **Cartel Behavior.** An oil cartel has been formed by the three leading oil producers. Total production costs at various levels of oil production per day are as follows:

Barrels per Day (millions)	Total Cost ($ millions)		
	Arabco (A)	Britannia (B)	Cinco (C)
0	$ 35	$ 50	$ 5
1	40	75	25
2	50	105	40
3	65	140	65
4	90	180	95
5	125	225	130

A. Construct a table showing the marginal cost of production per firm.
B. From the data in Part A, determine an optimal allocation of output and maximum profits if the cartel sets $Q = 8$ and $P = \$35$.
C. Is there an incentive for individual members to cheat by expanding output when the cartel sets $Q = 8$ and $P = \$35$?

P13.6 **Cartel Equilibrium.** The Hand Tool Manufacturing Industry Trade Association recently published the following estimates of demand and supply relations for hammers:

$$Q_D = 60{,}000 - 10{,}000P, \quad \text{(Demand)}$$
$$Q_S = 20{,}000P. \quad \text{(Supply)}$$

A. Calculate the perfectly competitive industry equilibrium price/output combination.
B. Now assume that the industry output is organized into a cartel. Calculate the industry price/output combination that will maximize profits for cartel members. (Hint: As a cartel, industry $MR = \$6 - \$0.0002Q$.)
C. Compare your answers to Parts A and B. Calculate the price/output effects of the cartel.

P13.7 **Kinked Demand Curves.** Safety Service Products (SSP) faces the following segmented demand and marginal revenue curves for its new infant safety seat:

1. Over the range from 0 to 10,000 units of output,

$$P_1 = \$60 - Q,$$
$$MR_1 = \$60 - \$2Q.$$

2. When output exceeds 10,000 units,

$$P_2 = \$80 - \$3Q,$$
$$MR_2 = \$80 - \$6Q.$$

The company's total and marginal cost functions are as follows:

$$TC = \$100 + \$20Q + \$0.5Q^2,$$
$$MC = \$20 + \$1Q,$$

where P is price (in dollars); Q is output (in thousands); MR is marginal revenue; *TC* is total cost; and *MC* is marginal cost, all in thousands of dollars.

A. Graph the demand, marginal revenue, and marginal cost curves.

B. How would you describe the market structure of the industry in which SSP operates? Explain why the demand curve takes the shape indicated previously.

C. Calculate price, output, and profits at the profit-maximizing activity level.

D. How much could marginal costs rise before the optimal price would increase? How much could they fall before the optimal price would decrease?

P13.8   **Supply Reactions.** Anaheim Industries, Inc., and Binghampton Electronics, Ltd., are the only suppliers to the U.S. Weather Service of an important electronic instrument. The Weather Service has established a fixed-price procurement policy, however, so $P = MR$ in this market. Total and marginal cost relations for each firm are as follows:

$$TC_A = \$7,000 + \$250Q_A + \$0.5Q_A^2, \quad \text{(Anaheim)}$$

$$MC_A = \frac{dTC_A}{dQ_A} = \$250 + \$1Q_A^2,$$

$$TC_B = \$8,000 + \$200Q_B + \$1Q_B^2, \quad \text{(Binghampton)}$$

$$MC_B = \frac{dTC_B}{dQ_B} = \$200 + \$2Q_B^2,$$

where *Q* is output in units, and $MC > AVC$ for each firm.

A. What is the minimum price necessary for each firm to supply output?

B. Determine the supply curve for each firm.

C. Based on the assumption that $P = P_A = P_B$, determine industry supply curves when $P < \$200$, $\$200 < P < \$250$, and $P > \$250$.

P13.9   **Nonprice Competition.** General Cereals, Inc., (GCI) produces and markets Sweeties!, a popular ready-to-eat breakfast cereal. In an effort to expand sales in the Secaucus, New Jersey, market, the company is considering a one-month promotion whereby GCI would distribute a coupon for a free daily pass to a local amusement park in exchange for three box tops, as sent in by retail customers. A 25 percent boost in demand is anticipated, even though only 15 percent of all eligible customers are expected to redeem their coupons. Each redeemed coupon costs GCI \$6, so the expected cost of this promotion is 30¢ (= 0.15 × \$6 ÷ 3) per unit sold. Other marginal costs for cereal production and distribution are constant at \$1 per unit. Current demand and marginal revenue relations for Sweeties! are:

$$Q = 16,000 - 2,000P,$$
$$MR = \$8 - \$0.001Q.$$

Demand and marginal revenue relations that reflect the expected 25 percent boost in demand for Sweeties! are the following:

$$Q = 20,000 - 2,500P,$$
$$MR = \$8 - \$0.0008Q.$$

A. Calculate the profit-maximizing price/output and profit levels for Sweeties! prior to the coupon promotion.

B. Calculate these same values subsequent to the Sweeties! coupon promotion and following the expected 25 percent boost in demand.

P13.10 **Price Leadership.** Louisville Communications, Inc., offers 24-hour telephone answering service for individuals and small businesses in southeastern states. Louisville is a dominant, price-leading firm in many of its markets. Recently, Memphis Answering Service, Inc., and Nashville Recording, Ltd., have begun to offer services with the same essential characteristics as Louisville's service. Total and marginal cost functions for Memphis (M) and Nashville (N) services are as follows:

$$TC_M = \$75,000 - \$7Q_M + \$0.0025Q_M^2,$$
$$MC_M = -\$7 + \$0.05Q_M,$$
$$TC_N = \$50,000 + \$3Q_N + \$0.0025Q_N^2,$$
$$MC_N = \$3 + \$0.05Q_N.$$

Louisville's total and marginal cost relations are as follows:

$$TC_L = \$300,000 + \$5Q_L + \$0.0002Q_L^2,$$
$$MC_L = \$5 + \$0.0004Q_L.$$

The industry demand curve for telephone answering service is

$$Q = 500,800 - 19,600P.$$

Assume throughout this problem that the Memphis and Nashville services are perfect substitutes for Louisville's service.

A. Determine the supply curves for the Memphis and Nashville services, assuming that the firms operate as price takers.

B. What is the demand curve faced by Louisville?

C. Calculate Louisville's profit-maximizing price and output levels. (Hint: Louisville's total and marginal revenue relations are $TR_L = \$25Q_L - \$0.00005Q_L^2$, and $MR_L = \$25 - \$0.0001Q_L$.)

D. Calculate profit-maximizing output levels for the Memphis and Nashville services.

E. Is the market for service from these three firms in short-run equilibrium?

CASE STUDY FOR CHAPTER 13
Firm Size and Profitability in Global Telecommunications Services

Sales revenue, net profits, and profit margin data are provided in Table 13.5 for a sample of firms from the global telecommunications services industry covered by *The Value Line Investment Survey*. Each row of information shows relevant 1992 data for one firm, with sample observations ranked from largest to smallest in terms of sales revenue. Average net profit per firm is $647.1 million; the average profit margin is 10.66 percent, and average sales revenue is $7,719.3 million. In each instance, the sample average reflects a simple sum of each respective value over the entire sample of $N = 34$ firms, all divided by 34, the total number of sample observations. In this particular sample, no individual observation has exactly the sample average level of net profit, profit margin, or sales revenue. With a net profit of $666 million, MCI Communications Corp. comes closest to the sample average net profit. Similarly, Bell Atlantic Corp., with a profit margin of 10.67 percent, and MCI Communications Corp., with sales revenue of $7,680 million, are relatively close to the sample average net profit margin and sales revenue levels, respectively. Based on the sample mean criterion, these observations can be described as typical of sample values. It is important to note, however, that there is substantial variation around the sample averages and the chance of atypical sample values appears to be correspondingly high.

With an overall sample size of $N = 34$, or any other even-numbered sample size, there is no single sample observation that falls exactly in the middle of the distribution for the global telecommunications services industry sample. In such instances, the median is calculated as the midway point between the two sample observations that straddle the middle of the sample distribution. For example, the median sales revenue observation occurs midway between the seventeenth and eighteenth sample observations, given exactly 17 larger and 17 smaller observations. Thus, the median sales revenue level is $3,232.7 million, or the midpoint between the $3,823.2 million reported by Telefonos de Mexico, S.A., and the $2,642.2 million reported by Reuters Holdings, PLC. Since profit and profit margin data are not rank ordered in Table 13.5, a rank ordering of these data is necessary before median levels can be easily calculated. By doing so, it is possible to verify that the median profit level is $451.4 million, or midway between the $522 million earned by AT&T and the $380.8 million earned by Reuters Holdings, PLC. Similarly, the median profit margin is 11.355 percent, or midway between the 11.37 percent earned by BellSouth Corp. and the 11.34 percent earned by Pacific Telesis Group. Based on the sample median criterion, each of these observations is typical of sample values.

Sample averages for both net profit and sales revenue appear to be skewed upward in that sample median values are far below average levels. This reflects that a few very large firms in the industry cause sample average values to be far greater than the typically observed levels. Differences between sample means and medians are to be expected for much economic data given the long upward "tail" provided by the giants of industry. However, there is no necessary reason to suspect any relation between profit margins and firm size. Profit margins are

TABLE 13.5   Firm Size, Net Profits, and Profit Margins in
Global Telecommunications Services

Company Name	Industry Name	Industry Code	Sales Revenue ($ millions)	Net Profit ($ millions)	Profit Margin (%)	Domicile (U.S. = 0, Other = 1)
AT&T	Telecomm Svc.	4810	$63,089.0	$ 522.0	0.83	0
British Telecommunications, PLC	Foreign Telecom	4812	23,019.5	3,193.8	13.87	1
GTE Corp.	Telecomm Svc.	4810	21,393.0	1,715.0	8.02	0
BCE, Inc.	Foreign Telecom	4812	18,373.0	1,227.0	6.68	1
BellSouth Corp.	Telecomm Svc.	4810	14,345.4	1,631.5	11.37	0
NYNEX Corp.	Telecomm Svc.	4810	13,585.3	1,208.1	8.89	0
Bell Atlantic Corp.	Telecomm Svc.	4810	12,298.0	1,312.5	10.67	0
Ameritech	Telecomm Svc.	4810	10,662.5	1,253.8	11.76	0
U S WEST, Inc.	Telecomm Svc.	4810	9,957.3	1,198.9	12.04	0
Pacific Telesis Group	Telecomm Svc.	4810	9,716.0	1,102.0	11.34	0
Southwestern Bell Corp.	Telecomm Svc.	4810	9,112.9	1,101.4	12.09	0
Telefonica de Espana, S.A.	Foreign Telecom	4812	8,903.8	1,700.7	19.10	1
Sprint, Inc.	Telecomm Svc.	4810	8,345.1	345.7	4.14	0
L.M. Ericsson Telephone, AB	Foreign Telecom	4812	8,029.2	606.1	7.55	1
MCI Communications Corp.	Telecomm Svc.	4810	7,680.0	666.0	8.67	0
Cable & Wireless, PLC	Foreign Telecom	4812	4,537.6	577.7	12.73	1
Telefonos de Mexico, S.A.	Foreign Telecom	4812	3,823.2	929.6	24.31	1
Reuters Holdings, PLC	Foreign Telecom	4812	2,642.2	380.8	14.41	1
Hong Kong Telecommunications, Ltd.	Foreign Telecom	4812	2,085.4	678.1	32.52	1
S. New England Telecom. Corp.	Telecomm Svc.	4810	1,619.3	153.6	9.49	0
ALLTEL Corp.	Telecomm Svc.	4810	1,573.8	192.8	12.25	0
Centel Corp.	Telecomm Svc.	4810	1,149.3	47.1	4.10	0
Cincinnati Bell, Inc.	Telecomm Svc.	4810	1,088.0	42.7	3.92	0
McCaw Cellular Corp.	Telecomm Svc.	4810	1,037.5	−594.0	−57.25	0
Vodafone Group, PLC	Foreign Telecom	4812	939.5	269.8	28.72	1
Rochester Telephone Corp.	Telecomm Svc.	4810	600.0	49.7	8.28	0
Citizens Utilities Co.	Telecomm Svc.	4810	547.6	112.4	20.53	0
Communications Satellite Corp.	Telecomm Svc.	4810	456.8	56.3	12.32	0
LIN Broadcasting Corp.	Telecomm Svc.	4810	378.1	136.5	36.10	0
Compania de Telefonos de Chile, S.A.	Foreign Telecom	4812	373.0	107.8	28.90	1
Advanced Telecommunications Corp.	Telecomm Svc.	4810	350.7	28.3	8.07	0
Telephone & Data Systems, Inc.	Telecomm Svc.	4810	294.6	27.2	9.23	0
Century Telephone Enterp.	Telecomm Svc.	4810	248.8	28.5	11.45	0
C-TEC Corp.	Telecomm Svc.	4810	200.4	−9.6	−4.79	0
Sample Average			$7,719.3	$647.1	10.66%	0.29
Sample Standard Deviation			$11,730.8	$741.3	14.89%	0.46

Source: *Value Line Value*/Screen Data Base, April 1, 1992.

defined as net profit as a percentage of sales revenue. Since sales revenue is a commonly used measure of firm size, profit margin data are "normalized," or size-adjusted, by virtue of being divided by sales. The sample average profit margin of 10.66 percent is relatively close to the sample median of 11.355 percent. This indicates that the distribution of profit margin data is fairly centered around the sample mean observation, as is often the case when "normalized" data are considered. It is important to note, however, that there is substantial variation around the sample averages for net profit, profit margin, and sales revenues, and the chance of atypical sample values appears correspondingly high. In this global telecommunications sample, no two firms have exactly the same profit, profit margin, or sales revenue levels.

In analyzing the profitability of firms in this sample it is important to recognize that important differences exist among various subsectors of the global telecommunications services industry. Individual firms in the industry have important underlying differences in their businesses. Cellular companies tend to be highly leveraged and risky given the relatively new nature of the industry and potential competition from new technology, like wireless systems and personal communications networks. Long-distance carriers benefit greatly from the growth of international communications and from the growing use of phone lines for transmitting data. As a result, both cellular companies and long-distance carriers have fundamental differences from the independent phone companies and regional operators, such as Ameritech, Southwestern Bell, and U S West, that emphasize the distribution of local phone services. In most countries, "local hookup" to long-distance networks is provided by monopoly firms that are regulated by local authorities.

In the United States, the profitability of local telephone service is lower and growing much more slowly than profits derived from long-distance services. In foreign markets, the already high profits of long-distance carriers are often sheltered from new competition by government barriers to entry and restrictive tariff policies. As a result, the profits of foreign telecommunications giants are especially high and rapidly growing. To analyze possible differences in the profitability of U.S. versus non-U.S. firms, each firm in the sample has been assigned a new dummy, or binary, variable called "Domicile," where $D = 1$ for companies domiciled outside the United States, and $D = 0$ if the company is based in the United States. By considering the effect of dummy variables in a regression model, it becomes possible to learn if country of origin has an influence on profit levels or profit rates.

A. Set up a table or spreadsheet that displays the rank in order of net profit of these global telecommunications industry data. What differences emerge when sample firms are ranked by profits versus sales (size)?

B. Set up a table or spreadsheet that displays the rank in order of profit margin of these global telecommunications industry data. What differences exist when sample firms are ranked by profit margin versus profits or sales (size)? Which measure of profitability is best for gauging firm performance?

C. A regression model estimate of the relation between net profits and sales revenue for this sample of $N = 34$ global telecommunications services companies is as follows:

$$\text{Profits} = 275.0 + 0.030 \text{ Sales} + 472.561 \text{ Domicile.}$$
$$(3.20) \quad (1.97)$$
$$\text{S.E.E.} = 636.11, R^2 = 30.8\%, F = 13.80.$$

How would you interpret these results?

D. Restructuring charges related to AT&T's acquisition of NCR led to a 1991 profit of only $522 million and profit margins of only 0.83 percent for AT&T. In light of its huge size, such minuscule profits make AT&T a significant "outlier," or atypical observation during this period. After excluding AT&T, a regression model estimate of the net profits and sales revenue relation for a reduced sample of $N = 33$ companies is as follows:

$$\text{Profits} = -39.2 + 0.100\,\text{Sales} + 276.553\,\text{Domicile}.$$
$$(11.75) \quad (2.30)$$
$$\text{S.E.E.} = 315.13, R^2 = 83.6\%, F = 152.93.$$

Is this model or that estimated over all $N = 34$ firms a better descriptor of the profit-sales relation for the overall sample?

E. A regression model estimate of the relation between net profit margin and sales revenue for the overall sample (including AT&T) is as follows:

$$\text{Profit Margin} = 0.082 + -0.0000012\,\text{Sales} + 0.116\,\text{Domicile}.$$
$$(-0.57) \quad (2.15)$$
$$\text{S.E.E.} = 0.14, R^2 = 14.0\%, F = 5.04.$$

Why is the R^2 from this regression model so much lower than that found for the net profit–sales relation?

Selected References   Aoki, Reiko. "R&D Competition for Product Innovation: An Endless Race." *American Economic Review* 81 (May 1991): 252–256.

Borenstein, Severin. "The Evolution of U.S. Airline Competition." *Journal of Economic Perspectives* 6 (Spring 1992): 45–73.

Chatterjee, Sayan. "Gains in Vertical Acquisitions and Market Power." *Academy of Management Journal* 34 (June 1991): 436–448.

Feinberg, Fred M., Barbara E. Kahn, and Leig McAlister. "Market Share Response When Consumers Seek Variety." *Journal of Marketing Research* 29 (May 1992): 227–237.

Hirsch, Barry T. "Union Coverage and Profitability Among U.S. Firms." *Review of Economics and Statistics* 73 (February 1991): 69–77.

Kanter, Rosabeth Moss. "Transcending Business Boundaries: 12,000 World Managers View Change." *Harvard Business Review* 69 (May–June 1991): 151–164.

Leibenstein, Harvey, and Shlomo Maital. "Empirical Estimation and Partitioning of X-Inefficiency: A Data Envelopment Approach." *American Economic Review* 82 (May 1992): 428–433.

Maher, Michael W., Peter Tiessen, Robert Colson, and Amy J. Broman. "Competition and Audit Fees." *Accounting Review* 67 (January 1992): 199–211.

Moore, Michael J., William Bounding, and Ronald C. Goodstein. "Pioneering and Market Share: Is Entry Time Endogenous and Does It Matter?" *Journal of Marketing Research* 28 (February 1991): 97–104.

Morck, Randall, and Bernard Yeung. "Why Investors Value Multinationality." *Journal of Business* 64 (April 1991): 165–187.

Morita, Akio. "Partnering for Competitiveness: The Role of Japanese Business." *Harvard Business Review* 70 (May–June 1992): 76–83.

N'Guyen, Godefroy Dang, and Robert F. Owen. "High-Tech Competition and Industrial Restructuring in Light of the Single Market." *American Economic Review* 82 (May 1992): 93–97.

Novak, Thomas P., Jan de Leeuw, and Bruce MacEvoy. "Richness Curves for Evaluating Market Segmentation." *Journal of Marketing Research* 29 (May 1992): 254–267.

Palmer, Karen. "Diversification by Regulated Monopolies and Incentives for Cost-Reducing R&D." *American Economic Review* 81 (May 1991): 266–270.

Pearson, Andrall E. "Corporate Redemption and the Seven Deadly Sins." *Harvard Business Review* 70 (May–June 1992): 65–75.

Porter, Michael E. "The Competitive Advantage of Nations." *Harvard Business Review* 68 (March–April 1990): 73–93.

Rappaport, Alfred. "CFOs and Strategists: Forging a Common Framework." *Harvard Business Review* 70 (May–June 1992): 84–91.

Schumacher, Ute. "Buyer Structure and Seller Performance in U.S. Manufacturing Industries." *Review of Economics and Statistics* 73 (May 1991): 277–284.

Shipley, David, and Elizabeth Bourdon. "Distributor Pricing in Very Competitive Markets." *Industrial Marketing Management* 19 (August 1990): 215–224.

Stalk, George, Philip Evans, and Lawrence E. Schulman. "Competing on Capabilities: The New Rules of Corporate Strategy." *Harvard Business Review* 70 (March–April 1992): 57–69.

Stegeman, Mark. "Advertising in Competitive Markets." *American Economic Review* 81 (March 1991): 210–223.

Tang, Ming-Je, and Zenon S. Zannetus. "Competition under Continuous Technological Change." *Managerial and Decision Economics* 13 (March–April 1992): 135–148.

Wiersema, Margarethe F., and Karen A. Bantel. "Top Management Team Demography and Corporate Strategic Change." *Academy of Management Journal* 35 (March 1992): 91–121.

PRICING PRACTICES

The pricing practices of successful firms sometimes seem to entail a bewildering array of different charges for assorted customers. For example, hotel-chain pricing practices might seem a bit peculiar. At a time when first-class hotel rooms in London, Tokyo, or Paris go for $300 to $500 per night, Holiday Inns offers summertime "Great Rates" from as low as $39 per room per night to families of weekend vacationers—more than 50 percent off regular prices. Not to be outdone, Howard Johnson's says vacations are more fun when "Kids Go HoJo" and offers summertime family rates as low as $29 per night. Meanwhile, Marriott offers low 21-day nonrefundable advance purchase summer rates for $79 per night in downtown Chicago or $114 at San Francisco's Fisherman's Wharf and $69 weekday, $39 weekend rates at the Raleigh Research Triangle Park. What is going on here? Have these successful U.S. companies gone mad?

Rather than representing a mad scramble to build market share at any cost, these hotel-chain rates represent a shrewd use of computers and information technology to maximize the revenue yield on hotel properties. Any night that hotel rooms stand empty represents lost revenue, and since hotel costs are largely fixed, revenue losses translate directly into lost profits. A room rate of $39 per night doesn't begin to cover fixed construction, maintenance, and interest costs, but it makes a nice profit contribution when the alternative is weekend vacancy. By segmenting their markets, hotels are able to charge the maximum amount the market will bear on weekdays and on weekends. Similarly, hotel marketing gets fierce for convention business, especially when conventions meet at traditionally slack periods. Is it any wonder why the American Economic Association traditionally holds its annual meeting around New Year's Day and typically in cold-weather cities?

The development of pricing practices to profitably segment markets has reached a fine art with the advent and use of high-speed computer technology. Why do *Business Week, Forbes, Fortune,* and the *Wall Street Journal* offer bargain rates to students, but not to business executives? It is surely not because it costs less to deliver the *Journal* to students, and it's not out of benevolence; it's because students aren't willing or able to pay the standard rate. Even at 50 percent off regular prices, student bargain rates more than cover marginal costs and make a significant profit contribution. Similarly, senior citizens who eat at Holiday Inns enjoy a 10 to 15 percent discount and make a meaningful contribution to profits.

Conversely, relatively high prices for popcorn at movie theaters, peanuts at the ball park, and clothing at the height of the season reflect that customers are relatively insensitive to prices at different places and at different times of the year. Regular prices, discounts, rebates, and coupon promotions all represent different pricing mechanisms used to maximize profitability.

Interestingly, all of these pricing practices can be effectively employed with little direct reference to marginal analysis. While profit maximization requires that prices be set so that marginal revenues equal marginal cost, it is not necessary to calculate both in order to set optimal prices. Just using information on marginal costs and the point price elasticity of demand, the calculation of profit-maximizing prices is quick and easy. Many firms derive an optimal pricing policy using a technique called **markup pricing,** whereby prices are set to cover all direct costs plus a percentage markup for profit contribution. Flexible markup pricing practices that reflect differences in marginal costs and demand elasticities constitute an efficient method for ensuring that $MR = MC$ for each line of products sold. Similarly, peak and off-peak pricing, price discrimination, and joint product pricing practices are efficient means for operating so that $MR = MC$ for each customer or customer group and product class.

Markup pricing
Setting prices to cover direct costs plus a percentage profit contribution.

This chapter examines a number of common pricing practices and illustrates their value in managerial decision making. When the underlying rationale for each of these pricing methods is fully understood, they can be seen as the practical means for achieving optimal prices under a wide variety of demand and cost conditions.

MARKUP PRICING

Surveys of business practice indicate that markup pricing is the most commonly employed pricing method. In a conventional approach, firms estimate the average variable costs of producing and marketing a given product, add a charge for overhead, and then add a percentage markup, or profit margin. The charge for overhead costs is usually determined by allocating these expenses among all products on the basis of their average variable costs. For example, if total overhead costs are projected at $1.3 million per year and variable costs for planned production total $1 million, then overhead is allocated to individual products at the rate of 130 percent of variable cost. If the average variable cost of a product is estimated to be $1, the firm adds a charge of 130 percent of variable costs, or $1.30, for overhead, obtaining a fully allocated cost of $2.30. To this figure the firm might add a 30 percent markup for profits, or 69¢, to obtain a price of $2.99 per unit.

Markup on Cost

Markup on cost is the profit margin for an individual product or product line expressed as a percentage of unit cost. The markup-on-cost, or *cost-plus,* formula is given by the expression

$$\text{Markup on Cost} = \frac{\text{Price} - \text{Cost}}{\text{Cost}}. \tag{14.1}$$

Markup on cost

The difference between price and cost, measured relative to cost, expressed as a percentage.

Profit margin

The difference between the price and cost of a product.

The numerator of this expression, called the **profit margin,** is measured by the difference between price and cost. In the example cited previously, the 30 percent markup on cost is calculated as

$$\text{Markup on Cost} = \frac{\text{Price} - \text{Cost}}{\text{Cost}}$$

$$= \frac{\$2.99 - \$2.30}{\$2.30}$$

$$= 0.30, \text{ or 30 percent.}$$

Solving Equation 14.1 for price provides the expression that determines price in a cost-plus pricing system:

$$\text{Price} = \text{Cost} (1 + \text{Markup on Cost}). \tag{14.2}$$

Continuing with the previous example, the product selling price is found as

$$\text{Price} = \text{Cost} (1 + \text{Markup on Cost})$$

$$= \$2.30(1.30)$$

$$= \$2.99.$$

Markup on Price

Markup on price

The difference between price and cost, measured relative to price, expressed as a percentage.

Profit margins, or markups, are sometimes calculated as a percentage of price instead of cost. **Markup on price** is the profit margin for an individual product or product line expressed as a percentage of price, rather than unit cost as in the markup-on-cost formula. This alternative means of expressing profit margins can be illustrated by the markup-on-price formula:

$$\text{Markup on Price} = \frac{\text{Price} - \text{Cost}}{\text{Price}}. \tag{14.3}$$

Profit margin is the numerator of the markup-on-price formula, as in the markup-on-cost formula. However, unit cost has been replaced by price in the denominator.

The markup-on-cost and markup-on-price formulas are simply alternative means for expressing the relative size of profit margins. To convert from one markup formula to the other, just use the following expressions:

$$\text{Markup on Cost} = \frac{\text{Markup on Price}}{1 - \text{Markup on Price}}. \tag{14.4}$$

$$\text{Markup on Price} = \frac{\text{Markup on Cost}}{1 + \text{Markup on Cost}}. \tag{14.5}$$

Therefore, the 30 percent markup on cost described in the previous example is equivalent to a 23 percent markup on price:

$$\text{Markup on Price} = \frac{0.3}{1 + 0.3} = 0.23.$$

An item with a cost of $2.30, a 69¢ markup, and a price of $2.99 has a 30 percent markup on cost and a 23 percent markup on price. This illustrates the importance of being consistent in the choice of a cost or price basis when comparing markups among products or sellers.

Markup pricing is sometimes criticized as a naive pricing method based solely on cost considerations—and the wrong costs at that. Some that employ the technique may ignore demand conditions, emphasize fully allocated accounting costs rather than marginal costs, and arrive at suboptimal price decisions. However, a categorical rejection of such a popular and successful pricing practice is clearly wrong. Although inappropriate use of markup pricing formulas will lead to suboptimal managerial decisions, successful firms typically employ the method in a way that is entirely consistent with profit maximization. In fact, markup pricing can be viewed as an efficient rule-of-thumb approach to setting optimal prices. It is important to be aware of both the value and limitations of the markup pricing technique to avoid potential pitfalls in its application.

The Role of Cost in Markup Pricing

Although a variety of cost concepts are employed in markup pricing, most firms use a standard, or fully allocated, cost concept. Fully allocated costs are determined by first estimating direct costs per unit, then allocating the firm's expected indirect expenses, or overhead, assuming a standard or normal output level. Price is then determined from the resulting standard cost per unit, irrespective of short-term variations in actual unit costs.

The standard cost concept is sometimes based on historical accounting costs, and this can give rise to several problems. First, firms may fail to properly adjust historical costs to reflect recent or expected price changes for key input factors. Unadjusted historical accounting costs may have little relevance for current decisions. The firm should estimate future costs that will be incurred during the period for which it is setting prices. Also, accounting costs may not reflect true economic costs. The concept of opportunity cost must be employed for optimal decision making.

The use of fully allocated costs as opposed to incremental costs can also cause errors in some pricing decisions. Fully allocated costs can be appropriate when a firm is operating at full capacity. During **peak** periods, when facilities are fully utilized, expansion is required to further increase production. Under these conditions, an increase in production requires an increase in all plant, equipment, labor, materials, and other expenditures. Fully allocated costs are relevant for pricing purposes in such a situation. If a firm has excess capacity, as during **off-peak** periods, only those costs that actually rise with production—the incremental costs per unit—should form a basis for setting prices. Successful firms that employ markup pricing typically base prices on fully allocated costs under normal conditions but then offer price discounts or accept lower margins during off-peak periods when substantial excess capacity is available. In this way, prices can accurately reflect the effects of capacity utilization.

In some instances, output produced during off-peak periods can cost dramatically less than output produced during peak periods. When fixed costs represent a substantial share of total production costs, discounts of 30 to 50 percent for output produced during off-peak periods can often be justified on the basis of lower costs.

Peak
Period of full capacity usage.

Off-peak
Period of excess capacity.

"Early Bird" or afternoon matinee discounts at movie theaters provide an interesting example. Except for cleaning expenses, which vary according to the number of customers, most of the operating expenses incurred at a typical movie theater are fixed. As a result, the revenue generated by adding customers during off-peak periods can significantly increase the theater's profit contribution. When these off-peak customers buy regularly priced candy, popcorn, and soda, it is an added bonus that can justify even lower afternoon ticket prices. Conversely, on Friday and Saturday nights when movie theaters operate at peak capacity, even a small increase in the number of customers would require a costly expansion of facilities. Ticket prices during these peak periods reflect fully allocated costs. Similarly, McDonald's, Burger King, Arby's, and many other fast-food outlets have increased their profitability substantially by introducing breakfast menus. If fixed restaurant expenses are covered by lunch and dinner business, even promotionally priced breakfast items can make a notable contribution to profits.

The Role of Demand in Markup Pricing

Firms differentiate the markup charged on different products or product lines on the basis of competitive pressure as reflected in varying demand elasticities. Even though companies have always been willing to adjust prices or profit margins on specific products as market conditions varied, a high level of flexibility is now commonplace and often is a key element of competitive strategy. For example, both foreign and domestic automobile companies regularly offer rebates or special equipment packages for slow-selling models. Similarly, airlines promote different pricing schedules for business and vacation travelers. The airline and automobile industries are examples of sectors in which vigorous competition requires a careful reflection of demand and supply factors in pricing practice. However, efforts to assess cost and revenue relations among products are by no means limited to these industries. In the production and distribution of both goods and services, successful firms demonstrate the ability to quickly adjust prices to different market conditions.

Examining the margins set by a successful regional grocery store chain provides interesting evidence that demand conditions play an important role in cost-plus pricing. Table 14.1 shows the firm's typical markup on cost and markup on price for a variety of products sold in its stores.

A field manager with over 20 years' experience in the grocery business provided the authors with useful insight into the firm's pricing practices. He stated that the "price sensitivity" of an item is the primary consideration in setting margins. Staple products like bread, coffee, ground beef, milk, and soup are highly price sensitive and carry relatively low margins. Products with high margins tend to be those for which demand is less price sensitive.

Note the wide range of margins applied to different items. The 0 to 10 percent markup on cost for ground beef, for example, is substantially lower than the 15 to 35 percent margin on steak. Hamburger is a relatively low-priced meat with wide appeal to families, college students, and low-income groups whose price sensitivity is high. In contrast, relatively expensive sirloin, T-bone, and porterhouse steaks appeal to higher-income groups with lower price sensitivity.

TABLE 14.1   **Markups Charged on a Variety of Grocery Items**

Item	Markup on Cost (%)	Markup on Price (%)
Bread—private label	0–5	0–5
Bread—brand name	30–40	23–29
Breakfast cereals (dry)	5–15	5–13
Cake mixes	15–20	13–17
Coffee	0–10	0–9
Cold cuts (processed meats)	20–45	17–31
Cookies	20–30	17–23
Delicatessen items	35–45	26–31
Fresh fruit—in season	40–50	29–33
Fresh fruit—out of season	15–20	13–17
Fresh vegetables—in season	40–50	29–33
Fresh vegetables—out of season	15–20	13–17
Ground beef	0–10	0–9
Ice cream	15–20	13–17
Laundry detergent	5–10	5–9
Milk	0–5	0–5
Nonprescription drugs	35–55	26–35
Pastries (cakes, pies, etc.)	20–30	17–23
Pet foods	15–20	13–17
Snack foods	20–25	17–20
Soft drinks	0–10	0–9
Spices	30–60	23–38
Soup	0–15	0–13
Steak	15–35	13–26
Toilet tissue	10–15	9–13
Toothpaste	15–20	13–17

It is also interesting to see how seasonal factors affect the demand for grocery items like fruits and vegetables. When a fruit or vegetable is in season, spoilage and transportation costs are at their lowest levels, and high product quality translates into enthusiastic consumer demand that leads to high margins. Consumer demand tends to shift away from high-cost/low-quality fresh fruits and vegetables when they are out of season, thereby reducing margins on these items.

In addition to seasonal factors that affect margins over the course of a year, some market forces affect margins within a given product class. In breakfast cereals, for example, the markup on cost for highly popular corn flakes averages only 5 to 6 percent, with brands offered by Post (General Foods Corporation) and Kellogg's competing with a variety of local store brands. Cheerios and Wheaties, both offered only by General Mills, Inc., enjoy a markup on cost of 15 to 20 percent. Thus, availability of substitutes directly affects the markups on various cereals. Finally, it is interesting to note that among the wide variety of items sold in a typical grocery store, the product class with the highest margin is spices. Apparently, consumer demand for nutmeg, cloves, thyme, bay leaves, and other spices is quite insensitive to price. The manager interviewed said that in more than 20 years in the grocery business, he could not recall a single store coupon or special offered on spices.

●

MANAGERIAL APPLICATION 14.1
Simple Air Fares Get Complicated

With its 1992 announcement of an overhaul in air fares, American Airlines, a unit of AMR Corp., kicked off a raging controversy and airline price war. According to Robert L. Crandall, chairman of the nation's largest airline, American's new four-tier fare structure was designed to simplify the industry's complicated domestic fare structure. The new plan was good for consumers, American said, because it cut top fares by 38 percent. It was even better for the airlines, because average fares would rise, and steep discounts would be eliminated. As a result, almost all the major carriers went along with the plan.

Unfortunately for American and its domestic competitors, the new simplified air fares left behind someone the airlines badly needed on board: passengers. Simplified but higher air fares simply failed to generate the hoped-for additional business. Airlines have lured travelers with special discounts and other promotions for years, and consumers balked when American eliminated them. The result was a brutal price war when Northwest Airlines, Inc. (NWA), teetering on the brink of bankruptcy under mountains of leveraged buyout debt, tried to boost traffic by offering a free ticket to any adult traveling with a child. Seeking to discipline NWA for tinkering with its fragile new fare structure, American countered NWA's special discount by offering travelers 50 percent off its own lowest fares. Other major carriers knew they had to follow NWA's and American's pricing lead as the busy summer travel season began, and the most ruthless industrywide fare war in airline history was on.

NWA quickly followed American's lead. So did everyone else, except Trans World Airlines, Inc. (TWA). Operating under bankruptcy court protection, TWA had carved a niche for itself by offering fares 20 percent below its healthier rivals and had been gaining a small amount of market share. After pondering American's move for three days, TWA introduced fares 10 to 20 percent below American's. "If the reason for [American] doing this fare is to try to get rid of a low-cost competitor, it's not going to work," said Carl Icahn, CEO of TWA. Indeed, American's new fares seemed designed not just to stimulate traffic but also to drive weak carriers out of business.

What is the long-term prognosis for airline pricing practices? Are recurrent fare wars possible or even likely? And why did the airline industry rush to sell discounted tickets? For answers to these and related questions, it is necessary to consider the basic economics of the airline industry.

Air travel is a capital-intensive business where cash flow is king. Given Federal Aviation Administration regulation of airline safety, customers are apt to travel on whichever carrier offers the lowest prices and most convenient departure schedule. With uniformly high safety standards, airline passenger service becomes an essentially commoditylike business. To attract passengers and build market share with "hub and spoke" travel networks, the carriers must order and pay for millions of dollars in new planes and other equipment, sometimes years in advance. This gives rise to huge fixed costs that must be met regardless of passenger traffic, so *any* revenue growth has the potential to make an important contribution toward covering fixed expenses and making a profit contribution.

The need for high cash flow makes for fierce pricing and recurrent operating losses in the airline industry on an ongoing basis. Taking the industry's gigantic 1991 losses into account, the airlines as a whole have actually *lost* money in accounting terms since the industry began. Despite continuing growth in both traffic and revenues, stockholders reap only meager dividends, if any, and little in the way of capital gains. In real terms, stockholders have lost money by investing in the airlines. This makes the outlook for the industry very bleak indeed. As long as excess capacity and at least a few competitors exist in important markets, recurrent fare wars and dismal operating profits are probable. This is definitely an industry where competitive conditions closely dictate pricing practices.

Source: Bridget O'Brian and James S. Hirsch, "Simplifying Their Fares Proves More Difficult than Airlines Expected," *Wall Street Journal,* June 4, 1992, A1, A6.

This retail grocery store pricing example provides valuable insight into how markup pricing rules can be used in setting an efficient pricing policy. Although the words "price elasticity" were never used in the discussion, it is clear that this concept plays a key role in the firm's markup pricing decisions. To examine those decisions further, it is necessary to develop a method for determining optimal markups in practical pricing policy.

MARKUP PRICING AND PROFIT MAXIMIZATION

Demand analysis plays an important role in the markup pricing practices of successful firms. In fact, there is a simple inverse relation between the optimal markup and the price sensitivity of demand. The optimal markup is large when the underlying price elasticity of demand is low; the optimal markup is small when the underlying price elasticity of demand is high. To identify the precise relation between the price elasticity of demand and the optimal markups on cost and price, two relations developed previously must be reconsidered.

*The Optimal
Markup on Cost*

Recall from Chapter 5 that there is a direct relation among marginal revenue, price elasticity of demand, and the profit-maximizing price for a product. This relation was expressed in Equation 5.18 as

$$MR = P\left(1 + \frac{1}{\epsilon_P}\right). \qquad \textbf{(14.6)}$$

To maximize profit, a firm must operate at the activity level at which marginal revenue equals marginal cost. Since marginal revenue always equals the right side of Equation 14.6, at the profit-maximizing output level, it follows that

$$P\left(1 + \frac{1}{\epsilon_P}\right) = MC, \qquad \textbf{(14.7)}$$

or

$$P = MC\left(\frac{1}{1 + \frac{1}{\epsilon_P}}\right). \qquad \textbf{(14.8)}$$

Equation 14.8 provides a formula for the profit-maximizing price for any product in terms of its price elasticity of demand. The equation states that the profit-maximizing price is found by multiplying marginal cost by the term

$$\left(\frac{1}{1 + \frac{1}{\epsilon_P}}\right).$$

To derive the optimal markup-on-cost formula, recall from Equation 14.2 that the price established by a cost-plus method equals cost multiplied by the expression (1 + Markup on Cost). Equation 14.8 implies that marginal cost is the appropriate cost basis for cost-plus pricing and that

$$MC(1 + \text{Markup on Cost}) = MC\left(\frac{1}{1 + \dfrac{1}{\epsilon_P}}\right).$$

By dividing each side of this expression by MC and subtracting 1 yields the expression

$$\text{Markup on Cost} = \left(\frac{1}{1 + \dfrac{1}{\epsilon_P}}\right) - 1.$$

Optimal markup on cost

The profit-maximizing cost markup, equal to minus one divided by the quantity one plus the price elasticity of demand.

After simplifying, the **optimal markup on cost,** or profit-maximizing markup-on-cost, formula can be written

$$\begin{matrix}\text{Optimal Markup} \\ \text{on Cost}\end{matrix} = OMC^* = \frac{-1}{\epsilon_P + 1}. \qquad \textbf{(14.9)}$$

The Optimal Markup on Price

Optimal markup on price

The profit-maximizing price markup, equal to minus one times the inverse of the price elasticity of demand.

Just as there is a simple inverse relation between a product's price sensitivity and the optimal markup on cost, so too is there a simple inverse relation between price sensitivity and the **optimal markup on price.** The profit-maximizing markup on price is easily determined using relations derived previously. Dividing each side of Equation 14.7 by P yields the expression

$$\frac{MC}{P} = \left(1 + \frac{1}{\epsilon_P}\right).$$

Subtracting 1 from each side of this equation and simplifying gives

$$\frac{MC - P}{P} = \frac{1}{\epsilon_P}.$$

Then, multiplying each side of this expression by -1 yields:

$$\frac{P - MC}{P} = \frac{-1}{\epsilon_P}. \qquad \textbf{(14.10)}$$

Notice that the left side of Equation 14.10 is an expression for markup on price. Thus, the optimal markup-on-price formula is

$$\begin{matrix}\text{Optimal Markup} \\ \text{on Price}\end{matrix} = OMP^* = \frac{-1}{\epsilon_P}. \qquad \textbf{(14.11)}$$

Table 14.2 shows the optimal markup on marginal cost and on price for products with varying price elasticities of demand. As the table indicates, the more elastic the demand for a product, the more price sensitive it is and the smaller the optimal margin. Products with relatively less elastic demand have higher optimal markups. In the retail grocery example, a very low markup is consistent with a

TABLE 14.2 **Optimal Markup on Marginal Cost and Price at Various Price Elasticity Levels**

Price Elasticity of Demand ϵ_P	Optimal Markup on Marginal Cost (%), $\dfrac{-1}{\epsilon_P + 1}$	Optimal Markup on Price (%), $\dfrac{-1}{\epsilon_P}$
−1.5	200.0	66.7
−2.0	100.0	50.0
−2.5	66.7	40.0
−5.0	25.0	20.0
−10.0	11.1	10.0
−25.0	4.2	4.0

high price elasticity of demand for milk. Demand for fruits and vegetables during their peak seasons is considerably less price sensitive, and correspondingly higher markups reflect this lower price elasticity of demand.

Far from being a naive rule of thumb, markup pricing practices allow firms to arrive at optimal prices in an efficient manner. Markup pricing seems to be one of the best methods for implementing marginal analysis in pricing practice, especially when one considers the high cost of market demand information for many individual products. The process of generating marginal revenue and marginal cost information will itself increase costs. The marginal concept requires that firms weigh any added expense against the added gain and act accordingly. In its pricing policy, the firm must determine whether the added expense associated with obtaining more complete estimates of marginal relations is more than offset by the expected gain in revenues from increased pricing precision. In many instances, markup pricing practices represent an efficient method for setting optimal prices over broad categories of products when one considers the expense involved with obtaining detailed marginal revenue and marginal cost information.

An Optimal Markup Example

▶

The use of the optimal markup formulas can be further illustrated by considering the case of Betty's Boutique, a small specialty retailer located in a suburban shopping mall. In setting its initial price for a new spring line of blouses, Betty's added a 100 percent markup on cost. Costs were estimated at the $12 purchase price of each blouse plus a 50 percent allocated fixed overhead charge. Customer response was so enthusiastic that Betty's raised prices by $3 per blouse, reducing sales from 80 to 70 blouses per week. Was Betty's initial price optimal? If not, what is the optimal price?

To determine whether Betty's initial price on blouses was profit maximizing, one must calculate Betty's initial price level, the price elasticity of demand, and the markup on relevant marginal cost, then apply the optimal markup formula. From the preceding data, it is clear that Betty's calculated cost per blouse is $18—the $12 purchase cost plus a 50 percent allocated fixed overhead charge. With a

100 percent markup on cost, Betty's initial price can be calculated from the markup-on-cost formula:

$$\text{Markup on Cost} = \frac{\text{Price} - \text{Cost}}{\text{Cost}},$$

$$1 = \frac{\text{Price} - \$18}{\$18},$$

$$\text{Price} = \$36.$$

Therefore, the point price elasticity of demand for blouses is

$$\epsilon_P = \delta Q/\delta P \times P/Q,$$
$$= [(70 - 80)/(\$39 - \$36)] \times \$36/80$$
$$= -1.5.$$

Before applying the optimal markup-on-cost formula, it is important to recognize that the relevant marginal cost per blouse is only \$12, the purchase price. The allocated fixed overhead charge of \$6 is irrelevant for pricing purposes since fixed overhead costs are unaffected by blouse sales. Betty's actual markup on relevant marginal costs per blouse is 200 percent, because

$$\text{Markup on Cost} = \frac{\$36 - \$12}{\$12}$$
$$= 2 \text{ (or 200 percent).}$$

This is indeed a profit-maximizing markup on cost, as can be verified from the optimal markup-on-cost formula:

$$\text{Optimal Markup on Cost} = \frac{-1}{\epsilon_P + 1}$$
$$= \frac{-1}{-1.5 + 1}$$
$$= 2 \text{ (or 200 percent).}$$

Similarly, Betty's markup on price is

$$\text{Markup on Price} = \frac{\$36 - \$12}{\$36}$$
$$= 0.67 \text{ (or 67 percent).}$$

This is also an optimal markup from the perspective of the optimal markup-on-price formula:

$$\text{Optimal Markup on Price} = \frac{-1}{\epsilon_P}$$
$$= \frac{-1}{-1.5}$$
$$= 0.67 \text{ (or 67 percent).}$$

Therefore, Betty's initial $36 price on blouses is optimal, and the subsequent $3 price increase should be rescinded.

This example teaches a simple lesson. Despite consideration of inappropriate fixed overhead costs and a markup that might at first appear inappropriate, Betty's pricing policy is entirely consistent with profit-maximizing behavior. As is often the case, the end result of Betty's practice is an efficient pricing policy. Given the prevalence of markup pricing in everyday business practice, and the wide variety of markup rules-of-thumb and cost allocations typically employed, it is important that these pricing practices be carefully analyzed before they are judged suboptimal. The widespread use of markup pricing methods among highly successful firms suggests that the method is commonly employed in ways that are entirely consistent with profit maximization.

PRICE DISCRIMINATION

Pricing and markup decisions are sometimes more complex when the firm sells products in a variety of markets. With multiple markets or customer groups, the potential can exist to enhance profits by charging different prices and different price markups to each relevant market segment. Such market segmentation is an important fact of life in a broad range of the services sector, including firms in the airline, entertainment, hotel, medical, legal, and consulting services industries. Firms that offer goods also often segment their market between wholesale and retail buyers and between business, educational, not-for-profit, and government customers. A careful understanding of the motivation, method, and results of these pricing practices is an important aspect of managerial economics.

Requirements for Profitable Price Discrimination

Price discrimination

A pricing practice that sets prices in different markets that are not related to differences in costs.

Price discrimination occurs whenever different classes of customers are charged different price markups for the same product. Price discrimination is evident whenever identical customers are charged different prices or when price differences are not proportional to cost differences. Thus, price discrimination can occur when different customers are charged the same price despite underlying cost differences or when price differentials fail to accurately reflect cost discrepancies.

A first requirement that must be met for profitable price discrimination is that different price elasticities of demand must exist in the various submarkets for a given product. Unless price elasticities differ among submarkets, there is no point in segmenting the market. With identical price elasticities and identical marginal costs, profit-maximizing pricing policy calls for the same price and markup to be charged in all market segments. A **market segment** is a division or fragment of the overall market with essentially different or unique demand or cost characteristics. For example, wholesale customers tend to buy in large quantities, are highly familiar with product costs and characteristics, and are well informed about available alternatives. Wholesale buyers are highly price sensitive. Conversely, retail customers tend to buy in small quantities, are sometimes poorly informed about product costs and characteristics, and are often ignorant about available alternatives. As a group, retail customers are often less price sensitive

Market segment

A division or fragment of the overall market with essentially unique characteristics.

than wholesale buyers. Markups charged to retail customers usually exceed those charged to wholesale buyers.

For price discrimination to be profitable, the firm must also be able to efficiently identify relevant submarkets and prevent transfers among affected customers. Detailed information must be obtained and monitored concerning customer buying habits, product preferences, and price sensitivity. Just as important, the price-discriminating firm must be able to monitor customer buying patterns in order to prevent reselling among customer subgroups. A highly profitable market segmentation between wholesale and retail customers can be effectively undermined if retail buyers are themselves able to obtain discounts through willing wholesalers. Similarly, price discrimination among buyers in different parts of the country can be undermined if customers are able to resell in high-margin territories those products obtained in bargain locales.

The Role Played by Consumers' Surplus

Consumers' surplus
The value to customers of goods and services above and beyond the amount they pay sellers.

The underlying motive for price discrimination can be better understood by introducing the concept of **consumers' surplus.** Consumers' surplus (or customers' surplus) is the value of purchased goods and services above and beyond the amount paid to sellers. To illustrate, consider Figure 14.1, in which a market equilibrium price/output combination of $P*$ and $Q*$ is shown. The total value of output to customers is given by the area under the demand curve, or area $0ABQ*$. Since the total revenue paid to producers is price times quantity, equal to area $0P*BQ*$, the area $P*AB$ represents the value of output above the amount paid to producers—that is, the consumers' surplus. For example, if a given customer is willing to pay $200 for a certain overcoat but is able to obtain a bargain price of $150, the buyer enjoys $50 worth of consumers' surplus. If another customer places a value of only $150 on the overcoat, he or she would enjoy no consumers' surplus following a purchase transaction.

Consumers' surplus arises because individual consumers place different values on goods and services. Customers that place a relatively high value on a given product are willing to pay high prices; customers that place a relatively low value on a product are only willing to pay low prices. As one proceeds from Point A downward along the market marginal curve in Figure 14.1, customers that place a progressively lower marginal value (utility) on the product enter the market. At low prices, both high-value and low-value customers are buyers; at high prices, only customers that place a relatively high value on a given product are buyers.

When product value differs greatly among various groups of customers, a motive for price discrimination is created. By charging higher prices to customers with a high marginal value of consumption, revenues will increase without affecting costs. Sellers with the ability to vary prices according to the value placed on their products by buyers are able to capture the value represented by consumers' surplus. Such price discrimination will always increase profits, because it allows the firm to increase total revenue without affecting costs. A firm that is precise in its price discrimination practices always charges the maximum each market segment is willing to pay. In most basic terms, price discrimination is charging what the market will bear.

FIGURE 14.1 **An Illustration of Consumers' Surplus**

Consumers' surplus is shown by the area *P*AB* and represents the value of output to consumers above and beyond the amount they pay to producers.

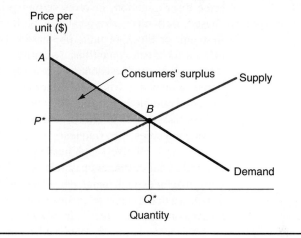

Finally, it is important to recognize that price discrimination does not carry any evil connotation in a moral sense. It is merely a pricing practice that must be judged good or bad on the merits of each specific situation. In some circumstances, price discrimination leads to lower prices for some customer groups and to a wider availability of goods and services. For example, a municipal bus company might charge lower prices for easily identifiable consumer groups, such as the elderly and the handicapped. In such circumstances, the bus company is price discriminating in favor of elderly and handicapped riders and against other customers. This type of price discrimination provides elderly and handicapped customers, who may be unable to afford the usual fare, an opportunity to ride the bus. Because of incremental revenues provided by elderly and handicapped riders, the bus company may be able to offer routes that could not be supported by revenues from full-fare customers alone, or it may be able to operate with a lower subsidy from taxpayers.

Degrees of Price Discrimination

First-degree price discrimination
Charging different prices to each customer.

The extent to which a firm can engage in price discrimination is classified into three major categories. Under **first-degree price discrimination,** the firm extracts the maximum amount each customer is willing to pay for its products. Each unit is priced separately at the price indicated along each product demand curve. Such pricing precision is rare because it requires that sellers know the maximum price each buyer is willing to pay for each unit of output. Purchase decisions must also be monitored closely to prevent reselling among customers. Although first-degree price discrimination is uncommon, it has the potential to emerge in any market where discounts from posted prices are standard and effective prices are individually negotiated between buyers and sellers. When sellers possess a significant amount of market power, consumer purchases of big-ticket items such as appliances, automobiles, homes, and both personal and professional services all have the potential to involve first-degree price discrimination.

Second-degree price discrimination, a more frequently employed type of price discrimination, involves setting prices on the basis of the quantity purchased. Bulk rates are typically set with high prices and markups charged for the first unit or block of units purchased, but progressively greater discounts are offered for greater quantities. Quantity discounts that lead to lower markups for large versus small customers are a common means of discriminating in price between retail and wholesale customers. Book publishers often charge full price for small purchases but offer 40 to 50 percent off list price when 20 or more units are purchased. Public utilities, such as electric companies, gas companies, and water companies, also frequently charge block rates that are discriminatory. Consumers pay a relatively high markup for residential service, whereas commercial and industrial customers pay relatively low markups. Office equipment such as copy machines and mainframe computers are other examples of products for which second-degree price discrimination is practiced, especially when time sharing among customers is involved.

The most commonly observed form of price discrimination, **third-degree price discrimination,** results when a firm separates its customers into several classes and sets a different price for each customer class. These customer classifications can be based on for-profit or not-for-profit status, regional location, or customer age, for example. IBM, Apple, Compaq, Zenith, and other major computer manufacturers routinely offer steep educational discounts that can be in excess of 30 to 40 percent off list prices. These manufacturers are eager to penetrate the classroom on the assumption that student users will become loyal future customers. Auto companies, magazine and newspaper publishers, and others also prominently feature educational discounts as part of their marketing strategy. Many hospitals also offer price discounts to various patient groups. If unemployed and uninsured patients are routinely charged only what they can easily afford to pay for medical service, whereas employed and insured medical patients are charged maximum allowable rates, the hospital is price discriminating in favor of the unemployed and against the employed. Widespread price discounts for senior citizens represent a form of price discrimination in favor of older customers and against younger customers.

Second-degree price discrimination
Charging different prices based on rates of quantities purchased.

Third-degree price discrimination
Charging different prices to each customer class.

A PRICE DISCRIMINATION EXAMPLE

Price discrimination is profitable because it allows the firm to enhance revenues without increasing costs. It is an effective means for increasing profits because it allows the firm to more closely match marginal revenues and marginal costs. A firm that can segment its market maximizes profits by operating at the point where marginal revenue equals marginal cost in each market segment. A detailed example is a helpful means for illustrating the process of price/output determination under price discrimination.

●

MANAGERIAL APPLICATION 14.2

Do Colleges Price Discriminate?

A number of economists have become vocal critics charging that the financial aid policies of major colleges and universities have changed the whole character of tuition pricing practices. Most of the students attending elite colleges receive so-called financial aid. At Harvard, for example, the average financial aid recipient comes from a family with an annual income of $45,000—and dozens came from families with incomes exceeding $100,000. Harvard is not unique in this respect. Similar patterns can be found at other private colleges across the country. As a result, some economists charge that college financial aid is not about "needy students" but is instead a means of price discrimination designed to extract all that the traffic will bear, both from students, their families, and from the government.

As with some commercial sellers of products and services, economists argue that colleges levy a list price (tuition), set far above what most people can or will pay, and then offer varying discounts (financial aid), so that each customer is charged what the traffic will bear. That is why financial aid recipients enjoy incomes far above what most Americans consider "needy," and often fall into a range that many might regard as wealthy. Unlike ordinary businesses who risk prosecution under the Robinson-Patman Act for price discrimination practices, academic institutions appear to engage in price discrimination as an accepted norm. Moreover, while a commercial enterprise may be able to separate its customers into only a few categories, to be charged different prices, the 23 elite Ivy League and related colleges recently investigated by the Justice Department were able to charge every single student a different price. Although there were thousands of students who applied to more than one college in this group, any given student would be charged the same net price (tuition minus financial aid), whether she or he went to Harvard or Yale, MIT or Amherst. Classmates might be charged different net prices, but each price would be the same from any college in the group. One student who considered the financial aid packages offered by Yale and

Brown to be inadequate discovered that each could consider altering its financial aid package only after consulting with the other. Economists say that such practices amount to carrying collusion and price discrimination right down to the individual customer level.

In addition to the kind of financial aid that is simply a paper discount, some financial aid involves money actually changing hands. Much of the latter is provided in the form of federal government grants and student loans. Unfortunately, the system virtually guarantees that tuition will rise to unaffordable levels. At the heart of government aid formulas is an "expected family contribution" based on family income, assets, the number of children, and so on. Government aid is available when the cost of college exceeds this "expected family contribution." Thus, even a small college could lose millions of dollars annually in federal aid if it kept tuition affordable. According to critics, federal subsidies and virtual exemption from antitrust laws have produced skyrocketing tuition, collusion, and price discrimination. Economist Milton Friedman estimates that colleges could operate at a profit by charging half what the Ivy League schools charge. But why should they, as long as parents and taxpayers are willing to pay more?

In defense of current financial aid practices, school administrators point out that many would be unable to afford college without some cross-subsidization among students. Private schools use endowment income to supplement student tuition and fees whereas public colleges and universities enjoy substantial tax-revenue income. Even the premiums paid by out-of-state students at leading state universities fail to cover fully allocated costs per student.

However, average costs may not be relevant for pricing purposes. The marginal cost per student is often nearly zero, and even very low net tuition-plus-fee income can often make a significant contribution to overhead. From an economic perspective, the pricing practices of colleges and universities may in fact be quite consistent with the theory of price discrimination.

Source: Gary Putka, "Ivy League Discussions on Finances Extended to Tuition and Salaries," *Wall Street Journal*, May 8, 1992, A1, A4.

Price/Output
Determination

▶

Suppose that Midwest State University (MSU) wants to reduce the athletic department's operating deficit and increase student attendance at home football games. To achieve these objectives, a new two-tier pricing structure for season football tickets is being considered.

A market survey conducted by the school suggests the following market demand and marginal revenue relations:

Public Demand	Student Demand
$P_P = \$225 - \$0.005Q_P$	$P_S = \$125 - \$0.00125Q_S$
$MR_P = dTR_P/dQ_P = \$225 - \$0.01Q_P$	$MR_S = dTR_S/dQ_S = \$125 - \$0.0025Q_S$

From these market demand curves it is obvious that the general public is willing to pay higher prices than are students. The general public is willing to purchase tickets up to a market price of $225, above which point market demand equals zero. Students are willing to enter the market only at ticket prices below $125.

During recent years, the football program has run on an operating budget of $1.5 million per year. This budget covers fixed salary, recruiting, insurance, and facility-maintenance expenses. In addition to these fixed expenses, the university incurs variable ticket-handling, facility-cleaning, insurance, and security costs of $25 per season ticketholder. The resulting total cost and marginal cost functions are

$$TC = \$1,500,000 + \$25Q,$$
$$MC = dTC/dQ = \$25.$$

What is the optimal football ticket prices and quantities for each market, assuming that MSU adopts a new season ticket pricing policy featuring student discounts? To answer this question, one must realize that since $MC = \$25$, the athletic department's operating deficit is minimized by setting $MR = MC = \$25$ in each market segment and solving for Q. This is also the profit-maximizing strategy for the football program. Therefore,

Public Demand

$$MR_P = MC$$
$$\$225 - \$0.01Q_P = \$25$$
$$\$0.01Q_P = \$200$$
$$Q_P = 20,000,$$

and

$$P_P = \$225 - \$0.005(20,000)$$
$$= \$125.$$

Student Demand

$$MR_S = MC$$
$$\$125 - \$0.0025Q_S = \$25$$
$$\$0.0025Q_S = \$100$$
$$Q_S = 40,000,$$

and

$$P_S = \$125 - \$0.00125(40,000)$$
$$= \$75.$$

The football program's resulting total operating surplus (profit) is

$$\text{Operating Surplus (Profit)} = TR_P + TR_S - TC$$
$$= \$125(20,000) + \$75(40,000)$$
$$- \$1,500,000 - \$25(60,000)$$
$$= \$2.5 \text{ million.}$$

To summarize, the optimal price/output combination with price discrimination is 20,000 in unit sales to the general public at a price of \$125 and 40,000 in unit sales to students at a price of \$75. This two-tier pricing practice results in an optimal operating surplus (profit) of \$2.5 million.

Comparison with the One-Price Alternative

To gauge the implications of this new two-tier ticket-pricing practice, it is interesting to contrast the resulting price/output and surplus levels with those that would result if MSU maintained its current one-price ticket policy.

▶ If tickets are offered to students and the general public at the same price, the total amount of ticket demand equals the sum of student plus general public demand. The student and general public market demand curves are

$$Q_P = 45,000 - 200P_P \quad \text{and} \quad Q_S = 100,000 - 800P_S.$$

Under the assumption $P_P = P_S$, total demand (Q_T) equals

$$Q_T = Q_P + Q_S$$
$$= 145,000 - 1,000P,$$

and

$$P = \$145 - \$0.001Q,$$

which implies that

$$MR = \$145 - \$0.002Q.$$

These aggregate student-plus-general-public market demand and marginal revenue curves hold only for prices below \$125, a level at which both the general public and students purchase tickets. For prices above \$125, only nonstudent purchasers buy tickets, and the public demand curve $P_P = \$225 - \$0.005Q_P$ represents total market demand as well. This causes the actual total demand curve to be kinked at a price of \$125, as shown in Figure 14.2.

The uniform season ticket price that maximizes operating surplus (or profits) is found by setting $MR = MC$ for the total market and solving for Q:

$$MR = MC$$
$$\$145 - \$0.002Q = \$25$$
$$\$0.002Q = \$120$$
$$Q = 60,000,$$
$$P = \$145 - \$0.001(60,000)$$
$$= \$85,$$

FIGURE 14.2 **Price Discrimination for an Identical Product Sold in Two Markets**

Price discrimination results in higher prices for market segments with low price elasticity (public) and lower prices for market segments with high price elasticity (students).

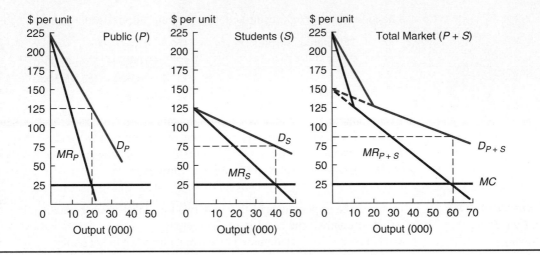

and

$$Q_P = 45,000 - 200(\$85) \qquad Q_S = 100,000 - 800(\$85)$$
$$= 28,000 \qquad\qquad\qquad = 32,000$$

$$\text{Operating surplus (profit)} = TR - TC$$
$$= \$85(60,000) - \$1,500,000 - \$25(60,000)$$
$$= \$2.1 \text{ million.}$$

Observe that the total number of tickets sold equals 60,000 under both the two-tier and the single-price policies. This results because the marginal cost of a ticket is the same under each scenario. Ticket-pricing policies featuring student discounts increase student attendance from 32,000 to 40,000 and maximize the football program's operating surplus at $2.5 million (rather than $2.1 million). It is the preferred pricing policy when viewed from MSU's perspective. However, such price discrimination creates both "winners" and "losers." Winners following adoption of student discounts include students and MSU. Losers include members of the general public, who wind up paying higher football ticket prices or find themselves priced out of the market.

Graphic Illustration   The MSU pricing problem and the concept of price discrimination can be illustrated graphically. Figure 14.2 shows demand curves for the general public in part (a) and for students in part (b). The aggregate demand curve in part (c) represents the horizontal sum of the quantities demanded at each price in the public and student markets. The associated marginal revenue curve, MR_{P+S}, has a similar interpretation. For example, marginal revenue equals $25 at an attendance level of 20,000 in the public market and $25 at an attendance level of

40,000 in the student market. Accordingly, one point on the total marginal revenue curve represents output of 60,000 units and marginal revenue of $25. From a cost standpoint, it does not matter whether tickets are sold to the public or to students. The single marginal cost curve $MC = \$25$ applies to each market.

Graphically solving this pricing problem involves a two-part process. The profit-maximizing total output level must first be determined, and then this output must be allocated between submarkets. Profit maximization occurs at the aggregate output level at which marginal revenue and marginal cost are equal. Figure 14.2(c) shows a profit-maximizing output of 60,000 tickets, where marginal cost and marginal revenue both equal $25. Proper allocation of total output between the two submarkets is determined graphically by drawing a horizontal line to indicate that $25 is the marginal cost in each market at the indicated aggregate output level. The intersection of this horizontal line with the marginal revenue curve in each submarket indicates the optimal distribution of sales and pricing structure. In this example, profits are maximized at an attendance (output) level of 60,000, selling 20,000 tickets to the public at a price of $125 and 40,000 tickets to students at a price of $75.

Price Discrimination Example Summary

The price charged in the less elastic public market is two-thirds higher than the price charged to students, whose demand is relatively elastic. This price differential adds substantially to MSU's profits. In the case of a uniform pricing policy, the school acts as though it faced only the single total market demand curve shown in Figure 14.2(c). Profit maximization requires operation at the output level where $MR = MC$—that is, at 60,000 tickets. The single price that would prevail is $85, the price determined by the intersection of a vertical line at 60,000 tickets with the total market demand curve, D_{P+S}.

Optimal price discrimination requires that marginal revenue equal marginal cost in each market. When an identical product is sold in two markets, as in this example, marginal revenue in each market is also equal, $MR_P = MR_S = MC$. This results because the products sold are indistinguishable from a production standpoint. If marginal costs of production and distribution are different in each market, profit maximization requires equating marginal revenues to marginal costs in each separate market.

MULTIPLE-PRODUCT PRICING

It is difficult to think of even a single firm that does not produce a variety of products. Almost all companies produce multiple models, styles, or sizes of output, and each of these variations can represent a separate product for pricing purposes. Although multiple-product pricing requires the same basic analysis as for a single product, the analysis is complicated by demand and production interrelations.

Demand Interrelations

Demand interrelations arise because of competition or complementarity among various products or product lines. If products are interrelated, either as substitutes or complements, a change in the price of one affects demand for the other.

Multiple-product pricing decisions must reflect such influences. In the case of a two-product firm, the marginal revenue functions for each product can be written as

$$MR_A = \frac{\delta TR}{\delta Q_A} = \frac{\delta TR_A}{\delta Q_A} + \frac{\delta TR_B}{\delta Q_A}, \qquad \textbf{(14.12)}$$

$$MR_B = \frac{\delta TR}{\delta Q_B} = \frac{\delta TR_B}{\delta Q_B} + \frac{\delta TR_A}{\delta Q_B}. \qquad \textbf{(14.13)}$$

Equations 14.12 and 14.13 are general statements describing the marginal revenue/output relations for the two products. The first term on the right side of each equation represents the marginal revenue directly associated with each product. The second term depicts the indirect marginal revenue associated with each product and indicates the change in revenues due to a change in sales of the alternative product. For example, $\delta TR_B/\delta Q_A$ in Equation 14.12 shows the effect on Product B revenues of an additional unit sold of Product A. Likewise, $\delta TR_A/\delta Q_B$ in Equation 14.13 represents the change in revenues received from Product A when an additional unit of Product B is sold.

Cross-marginal revenue terms that reflect demand interrelations can be positive or negative. For complementary products, the net effect is positive in that increased sales of one product lead to increased revenues from another. For substitute products, increased sales of one product reduce demand for another, and the cross-marginal revenue term is negative. Accurate price determination in the case of multiple products requires a complete analysis of pricing decision effects. This often means that optimal pricing requires an application of incremental analysis to ensure that the total implications of pricing decisions are reflected.

Production Interrelations

By-product

Output that is customarily produced as a direct result of an increase in the production of some other output.

Whereas many products are related to one another through demand relationships, others are related in terms of the production process. A **by-product** is any output that is customarily produced as a direct result of an increase in the production of some other output. While it is common to think of by-products as resulting only from physical production processes, they are also generated in the process of providing services. One of the primary reasons why top accounting firms have become such a leading force in the management information systems (MIS) consulting business is that information generated in the auditing process has natural MIS implications, and vice versa. In this way, auditing and consulting services are joint products produced in variable proportions. The cost of providing each service depends greatly on the extent to which the other is also provided. Given the efficiencies of joint production, it is common for an accounting firm's auditing clients to also become MIS consulting clients.

Multiple products are produced in variable proportions for a wide range of goods and services. In the refining process for crude oil, gasoline, diesel fuel, heating oil, and other products are produced in variable proportions. The cost and availability of any single by-product depends on the demand for others. By-products are also sometimes the unintended or unavoidable consequence of producing certain goods. Whenever lumber is produced, scrap bark and sawdust are also created and used in gardening and paper production. Whenever paper is produced, residual chemicals and polluted water are created that must be treated and recycled. Indeed, pollution can be thought of as the necessary by-product of many production processes. Since pollution is, by definition, a "bad" with harmful social consequences rather than a "good" with socially redeeming value, production processes must often be altered to minimize this type of negative joint product.

Production interrelations are sometimes so strong that the degree of jointness in production is relatively constant and unchanging. For example, many agricultural products are jointly produced in a fixed ratio. Wheat and straw, beef and hides, milk and butter are all produced in fixed proportions. In mining, gold and copper, silver and lead, and other precious metals and minerals are often produced jointly in fixed proportions. Appropriate pricing and production decisions are possible only when all such interrelations are accurately reflected.

Pricing practice differs in the case of joint products produced in variable proportions versus joint products produced in fixed proportions. It therefore pays to consider these relations in somewhat greater detail.

Joint Products Produced in Variable Proportions

Firms can often vary the proportions in which joint products are created. Even the classic example of fixed proportions in the joint production of beef and hides holds only over short periods: leaner or heavier cattle can be bred to provide differing proportions of these two products. When the proportions of joint output can be varied, it is possible to construct separate marginal cost relations for each product. This is illustrated in Table 14.3, a schedule of cost/output relations for two joint products, *A* and *B*. Since the marginal cost of either product is defined as the increase in total costs associated with a unit increase in that product, *holding constant the quantity of the other product produced,* the marginal costs of producing *A* can be determined by examining the data in each row of the table, and the marginal costs of *B* are obtained from each column. For example, the marginal cost of the fourth unit of *A,* holding the production of *B* at 2 units, is $5 (= $23 − $18); the marginal cost of the fifth unit of *B* when output of *A* is 3 units is $25 (= $78 − $53).

Optimal price/output determination for joint products in this case requires a simultaneous solution of cost and revenue relations. This process can be illustrated graphically through the construction of isorevenue and isocost curves, as in Figure 14.3. The isocost curves map out the locus of all production combinations that can be produced for a given total cost. The isorevenue curves indicate all combinations of the products that, when sold, result in a given revenue. The isorevenue relations in Figure 14.3 have been drawn as straight lines for simplicity. This reflects an underlying assumption that each product is sold in a competitive market. Only with a horizontal demand curve do prices not vary with respect to changing output. If pure competition does not exist and prices vary as output changes, isorevenue lines will be curved rather than straight, but the optimal output combination is still indicated by tangencies between isocost and isorevenue curves.

TABLE 14.3 **Cost/Output Schedule for Two Joint Products**

Output of B	Output of A				
	1	2	3	4	5
1	$ 5	$ 7	$10	$15	$ 22
2	10	13	18	23	31
3	20	25	33	40	50
4	35	43	53	63	75
5	55	67	78	90	105

FIGURE 14.3 **Optimal Price/Output Combinations for Joint Products Produced in Variable Proportions**

If joint products can be produced in variable proportions, profits are maximized where $MR = MC$ for each by-product. (All values are in dollars.)

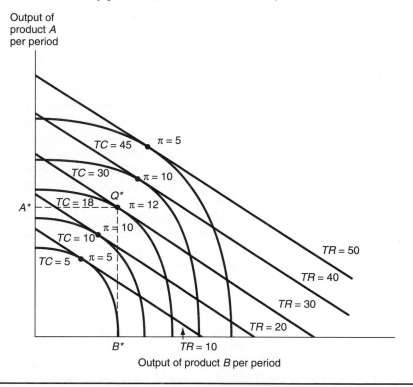

At points of tangency between isocost and isorevenue curves, the marginal costs of producing each product are proportionate to marginal revenues. Therefore, these tangencies indicate optimal proportions in which to produce the products. Because profit equals revenue minus cost, the firm maximizes profit by operating at the tangency between the isorevenue and isocost curves whose positive difference is greatest. At that tangency, the marginal cost of producing each product just equals the marginal revenue it generates. Point Q^* in Figure 14.3 indicates the profit-maximizing combination of Products A and B in the illustrated example. Production and sale of A^* units of A and B^* units of B result in a profit of 12, the maximum possible under the conditions shown.

While the preceding discussion demonstrates the possibility of determining the separate marginal costs of goods produced in variable proportions, it is impossible to determine their individual average costs. This is because of **common costs,** or expenses that are necessary for manufacture of a joint product. Common costs of production—raw material and equipment costs, management expenses, and other overhead—cannot be allocated to each individual by-product on any economically sound basis. Only costs that can be separately identified as associated with a specific by-product can and should be allocated. For example, tanning costs for hides and refrigeration costs for beef are separate identifiable costs of each by-product. Feed costs are common and cannot be allocated between hide and beef production. Any allocation of such common costs is wrong and arbitrary.

Common costs
Expenses that are necessary for manufacture of a joint product.

Joint Products Produced in Fixed Proportions

An interesting case of joint production is that of by-products produced in fixed proportions. In this situation, it makes no sense to attempt to separate the products from a production or cost standpoint. Products that must be produced in fixed proportions are not really multiple products from a production standpoint and should be considered as a package or bundle of output. This is because it is impossible to determine the costs of each individual by-product. When by-products are jointly produced in fixed proportions, all costs are common, and there is no economically sound method of allocation. Optimal price/output determination for output produced in fixed proportions requires analysis of the relation between marginal revenue and marginal cost for the combined output package. As long as the sum of marginal revenues obtained from each by-product is greater than the marginal cost of production, the firm gains by expanding output.

Figure 14.4 illustrates the pricing problem for two products produced in fixed proportions. Demand and marginal revenue curves for each by-product and the single marginal cost curve for production of the combined output package are shown. *Vertical* summation of the two marginal revenue curves indicates the total marginal revenue generated by both by-products. Marginal revenue curves are summed vertically because each unit of output provides revenues from the sale of both by-products. The intersection of the total marginal revenue curve MR_T with the marginal cost curve identifies the profit-maximizing output level.

The optimal price for each by-product is determined by the intersection of a vertical line at the profit-maximizing output level with each by-product's demand curve. Q_1 represents the optimal quantity of the output package to be produced, and P_A and P_B are the prices to be charged for each by-product. To illustrate, if this graph dealt with cattle, the joint package would consist of one hide and two sides of beef. Q_1 for the firm in question might be 3,000 steers, resulting in 6,000 sides of beef sold at a price of P_A and 3,000 hides sold at P_B per unit.

FIGURE 14.4   **Optimal Pricing for Joint Products Produced in Fixed Proportions**

For joint products produced in fixed proportions, the optimal activity level occurs at the point where the marginal revenues derived from both products (MR_T) equal the marginal cost of production.

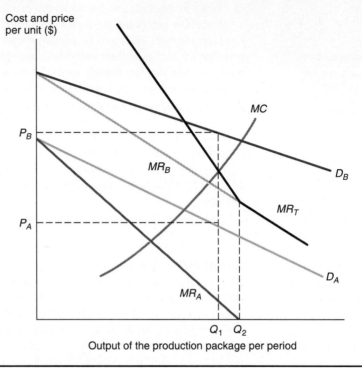

Output of the production package per period

Notice that the MR_T curve in Figure 14.4 coincides with the marginal revenue curve for Product B at all output quantities greater than Q_2. This is because MR_A becomes negative at that point, and the firm would not sell more than the quantity of Product A represented by Output Package Q_2. The total revenue generated by Product A is maximized at output Q_2; sales of any larger quantity of Product A would reduce revenues and profits.

If the marginal cost curve for the output package intersects the total marginal revenue curve to the right of Q_2, profit maximization requires that the firm raise output up to this point of intersection. At that point, Product B must be priced as indicated by its demand and marginal revenue curves. Since Product B sales offer the sole motivation for production beyond the Q_2 level, the marginal revenue generated from Product B sales must be sufficient to cover the marginal costs of producing the entire output package. In this instance, profit maximization requires that $MR_B = MC$. Beyond the Q_2 level, the marginal cost of Product A is zero; Product A is the unavoidable by-product of Product B production. Beyond the Q_2 level, the price of Product A is set in order to maximize profits in that $MR_A = MC_A = 0$. This pricing situation is illustrated in Figure 14.5, which shows the same demand and marginal revenue curves presented in Figure 14.4,

FIGURE 14.5 **Optimal Pricing for Joint Products Produced in Fixed Proportions with Excess Production of One Product**

When all of by-product A cannot be sold at a price that generates positive marginal revenue, its sales will be limited to the point where $MR_A = 0$. Excess production, shown as $Q_3 - Q_2$, will be destroyed or otherwise held off the market.

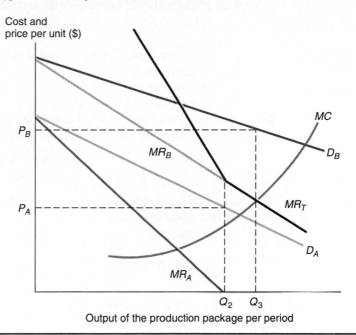

Cost and price per unit ($)

P_B

MR_B

MC

D_B

P_A

MR_T

D_A

MR_A

Q_2 Q_3

Output of the production package per period

along with a new marginal cost curve. The optimal output quantity is Q_3, determined by the intersection of the marginal cost curve and the total marginal revenue curve. Product B is sold in the amount indicated by Output Package Q_3 and is priced at P_B. The sales quantity of Product A is limited to the amount in output Q_2 and is priced at P_A. The excess quantity of Product A produced, shown as $Q_3 - Q_2$, must be destroyed or otherwise kept out of the market so that its price and total revenue are not lowered below those indicated at Q_2.

An example of joint output that is sometimes destroyed or otherwise held off the market is provided by sliced pineapple and pineapple juice, the juice being produced as a by-product as pineapples are peeled and sliced. Some years ago, an excessive amount of pineapple juice was produced, and rather than put it on the market and depress prices, the excess was destroyed. Seeing a profit-making opportunity, Dole, Del Monte, and other producers advertised heavily to shift the demand curve for juice outward. New products were also created, such as pineapple-grapefruit juice, to create a demand for the waste by-product. Canning machinery was also improved to reduce the percentage of product going into juice. Today, little if any excess juice by-product is produced in this industry. Similarly, firms in many other industries have discovered new and valuable uses for previously discarded by-products.

AN EXAMPLE OF JOINT PRODUCT PRICING

A graphic approach offers a useful introduction to the solution of joint product pricing problems, but many real-world problems require a more detailed analytic treatment. An example of a price/output decision for two products produced in fixed proportions will help clarify the technique.

Joint Products
without Excess
By-product

▶

The Vancouver Paper Company, located in Vancouver, B.C., produces newsprint and packaging materials in a fixed 1:1 ratio, or one ton of packaging materials per one ton of newsprint. These two products, A (newsprint) and B (packaging materials), are produced in equal quantities because newsprint production leaves scrap by-product that is useful only in the production of lower-grade packaging materials. The total and marginal cost functions for Vancouver can be written

$$TC = \$2,000,000 + \$50Q + \$0.01Q^2,$$
$$MC = dTC/dQ = \$50 + \$0.02Q,$$

where Q is a composite package or bundle of output consisting of one ton of Product A and one ton of Product B. Given current market conditions, demand and marginal revenue curves for each product are as follows:

Newsprint	Packaging Materials
$P_A = \$400 - \$0.01Q_A$	$P_B = \$350 - \$0.015Q_B$
$MR_A = dTR_A/dQ_A = \$400 - \$0.02Q_A$	$MR_B = dTR_B/dQ_B = \$350 - \$0.03Q_B$

For each unit of Q produced, the firm obtains one unit of Product A and one unit of Product B for sale to customers. The revenue derived from the production and sale of one unit of Q is composed of revenues from the sales of one unit of Product A plus one unit of Product B. Therefore, the total revenue function is merely a sum of the revenue functions for Products A and B:

$$TR = TR_A + TR_B$$
$$= P_AQ_A + P_BQ_B.$$

Substituting for P_A and P_B results in the total revenue function:

$$TR = (\$400 - \$0.01Q_A)Q_A + (\$350 - \$0.015Q_B)Q_B$$
$$= \$400Q_A - \$0.01Q_A^2 + \$350Q_B - \$0.015Q_B^2 .$$

Because one unit of Product A and one unit of Product B are contained in each unit of Q, $Q_A = Q_B = Q$. This allows substitution of Q for Q_A and Q_B to develop a total revenue function in terms of Q, the unit of production:

$$TR = \$400Q - \$0.01Q^2 + \$350Q - \$0.015Q^2$$
$$= \$750Q - \$0.025Q^2.$$

This total revenue function assumes that all quantities of Product A and B produced are also sold. It assumes no dumping or withholding from the market for either product. It is the appropriate total revenue function if, as in Figure 14.4, the marginal revenues of both products are positive at the profit-maximizing output level. When this occurs, revenues from each product contribute toward covering marginal costs.

The profit-maximizing output level is found by setting $MR = MC$ and solving for Q:

$$MR = MC$$
$$\$750 - \$0.05Q = \$50 + \$0.02Q$$
$$0.07Q = 700$$
$$Q = 10,000 \text{ units.}$$

At the activity level $Q = 10,000$ units, marginal revenues for each product are positive:

$$MR_A = \$400 - \$0.02Q_A \qquad\qquad MR_B = \$350 - \$0.03Q_B$$
$$= \$400 - \$0.02(10,000) \qquad\qquad = \$350 - \$0.03(10,000)$$
$$= \$200 \text{ (at 10,000 Units).} \qquad\qquad = \$50 \text{ (at 10,000 Units).}$$

Each product makes a positive contribution toward covering the marginal cost of production, where

$$MC = \$50 + \$0.02Q$$
$$= \$50 + \$0.02(10,000)$$
$$= \$250.$$

There is no reason to expand or reduce production because $MR = MR_A + MR_B = MC = \$250$, and each product generates positive marginal revenues.

Prices for each product and total profits for Vancouver can be calculated from the demand and total profit functions:

$$P_A = \$400 - \$0.01Q_A \qquad\qquad P_B = \$350 - \$0.015Q_B$$
$$= \$400 - \$0.01(10,000) \qquad\qquad = \$350 - \$0.015(10,000)$$
$$= \$300, \qquad\qquad = \$200,$$

and

$$\pi = P_A Q_A + P_B Q_B - TC$$
$$= \$300(10,000) + \$200(10,000) - \$2,000,000 - \$50(10,000)$$
$$\quad - \$0.01(10,000^2)$$
$$= \$1,500,000.$$

Vancouver should produce 10,000 units of output and sell the resulting 10,000 units of Product A at a price of $300 per ton and 10,000 units of Product B at a price of $200 per ton. An optimum total profit of $1.5 million is earned at this activity level.

Joint Production with Excess By-product (Dumping)

The determination of a profit-maximizing activity level is only slightly more complex if a downturn in demand for either Product A or B causes marginal revenue for one product to be negative when all output produced is sold to the marketplace.

Suppose that an economic recession causes the demand for Product B (packaging materials) to fall dramatically, while the demand for Product A (newsprint) and marginal cost conditions hold steady. Assume new demand and marginal revenue relations for Product B of

$$P'_B = \$290 - \$0.02Q_B,$$
$$MR'_B = \$290 - \$0.04Q_B.$$

A dramatically lower price of $90 per ton [= $290 − $0.02(10,000)] is now required to sell 10,000 units of Product B. However, this price and activity level are suboptimal.

To see why, the profit-maximizing activity level must again be calculated, assuming that all output is sold. The new marginal revenue curve for Q is

$$MR = MR_A + MR'_B$$
$$= \$400 - \$0.02Q_A + \$290 - \$0.04Q_B$$
$$= \$690 - \$0.06Q.$$

If all production is sold, the profit-maximizing level for output is found by setting $MR = MC$ and solving for Q:

$$MR = MC$$
$$\$690 - \$0.06Q = \$50 + \$0.02Q$$
$$0.08Q = 640$$
$$Q = 8,000.$$

At $Q = 8,000$, the sum of marginal revenues derived from both by-products and the marginal cost of producing the combined output package each equal $210, since

$$
\begin{array}{ll}
MR = \$690 - \$0.06Q & MC = \$50 + \$0.02Q \\
\quad = \$690 - \$0.06(8,000) & \quad = \$50 + \$0.02(8,000) \\
\quad = \$210. & \quad = \$210.
\end{array}
$$

However, the marginal revenue of Product B is no longer positive:

$$
\begin{array}{ll}
MR_A = \$400 - \$0.02Q_A & MR'_B = \$290 - \$0.04Q_B \\
\quad = \$400 - \$0.02(8,000) & \quad = \$290 - \$0.04(8,000) \\
\quad = \$240. & \quad = -\$30.
\end{array}
$$

Even though $MR = MC = \$210$, the marginal revenue of Product B is negative at the $Q = 8,000$ activity level. This means that the price reduction necessary to sell the last unit of Product B caused Vancouver's total revenue to decline by $30. Rather than sell Product B at such unfavorable terms, Vancouver would prefer to withhold some from the marketplace. In contrast, Vancouver would like to produce and sell more than 8,000 units of Product A since $MR_A > MC$ at the 8,000 unit activity level. It would be profitable for the company to expand production of Q just to increase sales of Product A, even if it had to destroy or otherwise withhold from the market the unavoidable added production of Product B.

Under these circumstances, set the marginal revenue of Product A, the only product sold at the margin, equal to the marginal cost of production to find the profit-maximizing activity level:

$$MR_A = MC$$
$$\$400 - \$0.02Q = \$50 + \$0.02Q$$
$$\$0.04Q = \$350$$
$$Q = 8,750 \text{ units.}$$

Under these circumstances, Vancouver should produce 8,750 units of $Q = Q_A = Q_B$. Since this activity level is based on the assumption that only Product A is sold at the margin and that the marginal revenue of Product A covers all marginal production costs, *the effective marginal cost of Product B is zero.* As long as production is sufficient to provide 8,750 units of Product A, 8,750 units of Product B are also produced without any additional cost.

With an effective marginal cost of zero for Product B, its contribution to firm profits is maximized by setting the marginal revenue of Product B equal to zero (its effective marginal cost):

$$MR'_B = MC_B$$
$$\$290 - \$0.04Q_B = \$0$$
$$\$0.04Q_B = \$290$$
$$Q_B = 7,250.$$

Whereas a total of 8,750 units of Q should be produced, only 7,250 units of Product B will be sold. The remaining 1,500 units of Q_B must be destroyed or otherwise withheld from the market.

Optimal prices and the maximum total profit for Vancouver are as follows:

$$P_A = \$400 - \$0.01Q_A \qquad\qquad P'_B = \$290 - \$0.02Q_B$$
$$= \$400 - \$0.01(8,750) \qquad\quad\; = \$290 - \$0.02(7,250)$$
$$= \$312.50, \qquad\qquad\qquad\quad\; = \$145,$$

$$\pi = P_A Q_A + P'_B Q_B - TC$$
$$= \$312.50(8,750) + \$145(7,250) - \$2,000,000$$
$$- \$50(8,750) - \$0.01(8,750^2)$$
$$= \$582,500.$$

No other price/output combination has the potential to generate as large a profit for Vancouver.

TRANSFER PRICING

Expanding markets brought about by improvements in communication and transportation, as well as falling trade barriers, have led to the development of large, multidivisional firms. To combat the problems of coordinating large-scale enterprises, separate profit centers are typically established for each important product or product line. Despite obvious advantages, this decentralization has

MANAGERIAL APPLICATION 14.3

How High Fixed Costs Cause Price Wars

Suppose a competitor lowers prices and then vows not to raise them for *five years*. Unlikely, you say? Tell that to Taco Bell President John Martin, who has done just that. Taco Bell, a unit of PepsiCo, Inc., sells Mexican fast food, but Martin thinks his cut-and-then-hold-the-lower-line pricing strategy can work elsewhere as well: "As we figure this thing out, I sure as hell am not going to be constrained to selling Mexican food. There are other consumers in other places." That's enough to get the attention of any fast-food executive.

Price wars, once a tool of limited strategic value in mature businesses, are becoming a disheartening fact of life in industries ranging from autos to credit cards to steel to computers. A growing number of companies trapped into protecting investments that are too big to write off are forced to pursue market share at all costs. Worse yet, using price wars to bump off competitors is less possible these days since weak competitors are often acquired by firms with deeper pockets, or they can file for bankruptcy court protection and keep operating. The only clear winners are consumers, who come to expect ever lower prices.

In supermarkets, permanent price wars rage for items such as coffee, cola, pet foods, paper products, and frozen foods. Top-of-the-line frozen food entrée prices dropped from $4.50 to about $2.99 during 1991–1992 as H.J. Heinz, Nestlé, ConAgra, Campbell's Soup, and Kraft General Foods battled for overcrowded freezer space. In the salty snacks business, PepsiCo and Borden, entering a third year of warfare, crumbled the margins of a once highly profitable business. In consumer electronics, Toshiba's definition of a price war is when prices drop every day, as is happening to laptop computers. By comparison, price slashing in television sets seems mild; television prices just drop steadily on a year-to-year basis.

Stiff price competition may be more than a simple by-product of the early 1990s recession. Research by the consulting firm Bain & Co. shows that the price of almost everything, except health care and education, follows a declining curve in real dollars over time. For instance, the price of crushed limestone, a basic construction material, is riding a 65-year downtrend. Borden's price and profit crunch in the snack food wars offers an interesting illustration. In the 1980s, Borden made a full-scale commitment to the salty snack business. With only one big national player, PepsiCo's Frito-Lay, Borden felt that there was plenty of room for another. Now Borden has too much money in fixed assets to get out. Borden has poured more than $500 million into the business and Anheuser-Busch has committed $250 million to $300 million. With such commitments, who is going to write those assets off? This is a classic case of high fixed costs giving rise to fierce price competition. The higher the market share, the more intent is the industry leader on preserving it, and the greater is the belief that somebody else will give in.

The slow process of rationalizing excess capacity is especially acute in industries that produce commodity-like products. The airline industry is a classic example, but the problem is also severe in the steel industry. The root cause of steel's problem is a combination of bankruptcies and continuing unfunded pension obligations. Any company that wants to get out of the steel business has to fund its pension obligations, which make it harder to exit than to enter. Says Richard Simmons, chairman of stainless-steel maker Allegheny Ludlum: "Rationalization would take place a lot faster in many industries if it weren't for that 800-pound gorilla called unfunded pension liability." In the stainless-steel industry, some mills have been shut down and mothballed, but not enough to let survivors boost prices.

The lesson to be learned from pricing practices in the airline, food, electronics, and steel industries is that businesses with high fixed costs are likely to display savage price competition. While companies feel significant pain in the process, consumers wouldn't have it otherwise.

Source: Bill Saporito, "Why the Price Wars Never End," *Fortune*, March 23, 1992, 68–78.

Transfer pricing

The pricing of products transferred among divisions of a firm.

Transfer Pricing for Products without External Markets

the potential to create problems of its own. Perhaps the most critical of these is the problem of **transfer pricing,** or the pricing of intermediate products transferred among divisions.

An effective transfer pricing system leads to activity levels in each division of the firm that are consistent with profit maximization for the overall enterprise. *When transferred products cannot be sold in external markets, the marginal cost of the transferring division is the optimal transfer price.*

To illustrate, consider Figure 14.6, which shows the demand, marginal revenue, and marginal cost curves for the entire operation of a multidivisional firm. Profit maximization requires that the firm expand as long as the marginal revenue of additional output exceeds marginal cost. In terms of Figure 14.6, this means that profits are maximized at output Q^* and price P^*.

Now consider the situation if the firm is composed of manufacturing and distribution divisions. The demand curve facing the distribution division is precisely the same as the firm's output demand curve. While the total cost function of the firm is unchanged, it can be broken down into the costs of manufacturing and distribution. When no external market exists for the intermediate product, the manufacturing division is not able to sell its product externally. Intrafirm transfers should take place at prices equal to the marginal costs of the transferring division, the manufacturing division in this case.

This relation is shown in Figure 14.7, which adds the net marginal revenue curve for the distribution division ($MR - MC_{Distr}$) and the marginal cost curve for the manufacturing division ($MC_{Mfg} = MC - MC_{Distr}$) to the overall firm revenue and cost curves illustrated in Figure 14.6. The net marginal revenue curve for the distribution division is found by subtracting the marginal costs of that division from the marginal revenues generated by its marketing activities. It is a net marginal profit curve for that division prior to taking into account the cost of the product transferred to it from the manufacturing division.

In Figure 14.7, the net marginal revenue curve for the distribution division intersects the marginal cost curve for the manufacturing division at Q^*, the firm's profit-maximizing activity level. This is not mere happenstance but must always occur. Recall that the distribution division's net marginal revenue curve is just the firm's marginal revenue curve minus the marginal cost of distribution. The manufacturing division's marginal cost curve is merely the firm's marginal cost curve minus the marginal cost of distribution. If the firm's marginal revenues and marginal costs are equal at Q^*, then

$$MR = MC,$$

and

$$MR - MC_{Distr} = MC - MC_{Distr} = MC_{Mfg}.$$

The correct transfer price for intermediate products for which there is no external market is the marginal cost of the transferring division, MC_{Mfg}. In Figure 14.7, this transfer price is P_T. This marginal cost transfer pricing rule can be implemented in one of two ways. The distribution division could be told that the

FIGURE 14.6 **Profit-Maximizing Price/Output Combination**

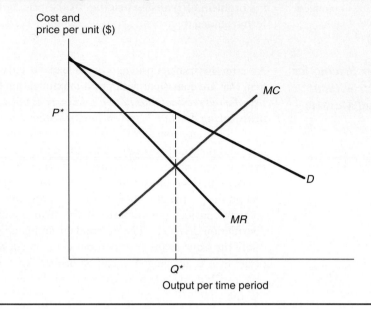

FIGURE 14.7 **Transfer Pricing with No External Market for the Intermediate Product**

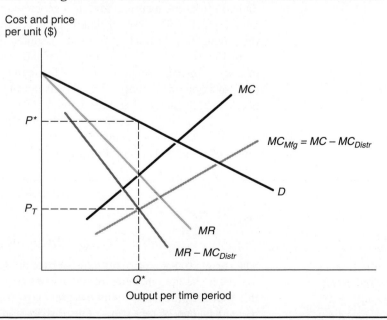

manufacturing division's marginal cost curve is the supply function to use in determining the quantity purchased internally. Alternatively, the manufacturing division could be supplied with data on the net marginal revenue curve for the distribution division and told to use this curve in determining the quantity supplied. In either instance, the divisions will voluntarily choose to operate at Q^*, and a transfer price of $P_T = MC_{Mfg}$ will prevail.

Transfer Pricing for Products with Perfectly Competitive External Markets

A different transfer pricing problem exists when competitive external markets are involved. *When transferred products can be sold in perfectly competitive external markets, the external market price is the optimal transfer price.*

To illustrate, again assume that the firm is composed of manufacturing and distribution divisions. Figure 14.8 shows demand, *D*, marginal revenue, *MR*, and marginal cost, *MC*, curves for the final product, *F*, as faced by the firm and the distribution division. Also shown are the demand, D_{Mfg}, marginal revenue, MR_{Mfg}, and marginal cost, MC_{Mfg}, curves for *T*, the intermediate or transferred product from the manufacturing division. Profit maximization requires intermediate product and final product output levels at which divisional marginal revenue equals divisional marginal cost. Given a perfectly competitive market for the transferred product, marginal revenue equals price in the external market, so $P_T = MR_{Mfg}$. The manufacturing division should supply Q_T units of the transferred product, the quantity at which $MR_{Mfg} = P_T = MC_{Mfg}$. The curve $MR - MC_{Distr}$ represents the final product net marginal contribution to overhead and profits *before* the transfer price is deducted. The distribution division should purchase Q_F units of the intermediate good and pay the market price P_T. At that activity level, the net marginal revenue of output from the distribution division, $MR - MC_{Distr}$, equals P_T, the marginal cost of the distribution division's input. Overall firm profits are maximized at Q_F since $MC = MR$.

This transfer pricing problem solution results in the distribution division demanding more units than the manufacturing division is willing to supply at price P_T. As a result, the distribution division will purchase Q_T units of the intermediate product internally from the manufacturing division and $Q_F - Q_T$ units in the external marketplace. The use of market prices for transferring intermediate products is also optimal if the quantity supplied is greater than internal demand. In that event, the manufacturing division merely transfers the quantity demanded internally at P_T and sells the remainder in the external market at that same price. As long as the intermediate product transferred within the firm can be sold in a competitive external market, the market price remains the proper transfer price. Only by transferring at that price can management ensure that the level of activity in both the supplying and using divisions will be optimal for the firm's profit maximization.

Transfer Pricing for Products with Imperfectly Competitive External Markets

When an imperfect external market exists for intermediate products, transfer pricing is only slightly more complex than discussed previously. *When transferred products can be sold in imperfectly competitive external markets, the optimal transfer price equates the marginal cost of the transferring division to the marginal revenue derived from the combined internal and external markets.*

FIGURE 14.8 **Transfer Price Determination with the Intermediate Product Sold Externally in a Competitive Market**

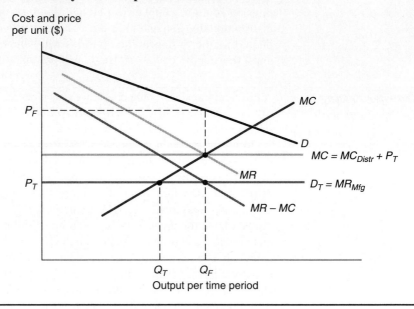

FIGURE 14.9 **Transfer Pricing with an Imperfect Market for the Intermediate Product**

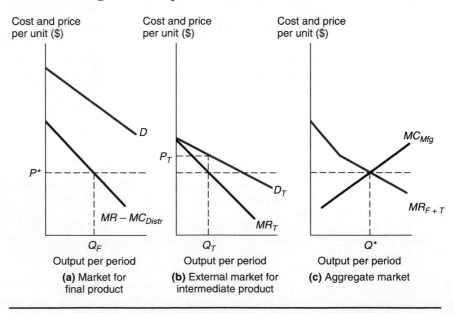

This case is illustrated in Figure 14.9(a), which shows demand and net marginal revenue curves for the final product, *F;* and Figure 14.9(b), which depicts imperfectly competitive external demand and marginal revenue curves for the intermediate product, *T.* In Figure 14.9(c), the net marginal revenue curve for the final product and the external marginal revenue curve for the intermediate product are summed horizontally to derive an aggregate marginal revenue curve, MR_{F+T}, for the intermediate product. The profit-maximizing output of the transferred product occurs at Q^*, where MR_{F+T} is set equal to MC_T, the marginal cost of production for the transferred product. Optimal output Q^* is divided between internal transfers and external sales. The amount of intermediate product that is transferred internally, Q_F, is determined by equating the marginal cost of the transferred product, shown as MC_{Mfg} in Figure 14.9(c), to the net marginal revenue derived from final product sales, shown as $MR_F - MC_{Distr}$ in Figure 14.9(a). The amount of the intermediate product that is sold in the external market, Q_T, is determined by equating this same marginal cost of the transferred product to the marginal revenue derived from external market sales, shown as MR_T in Figure 14.9(b). By setting the appropriate internal transfer price $P^* = MC_{Mfg}$ and external market price P_T, a profit-maximizing level of intermediate product output Q^* is ensured, where $Q^* = Q_F + Q_T$.

A GLOBAL TRANSFER PRICING EXAMPLE

The transfer pricing concept can be introduced conceptually through the use of graphic analysis. However, most real-world applications are too complex to be solved using this method. Algebraic techniques typically must be applied. For this reason, examination of a more detailed example can be fruitful.

Profit Maximization for an Integrated Firm

Hope Steadman & Sons, Inc., is a small integrated domestic manufacturer of material handling equipment. Demand and marginal revenue curves for the firm are the following:

$$P = \$100 - \$0.001Q,$$
$$MR = \$100 - \$0.002Q.$$

Relevant total cost, marginal cost, and profit functions are as follows:

$$TC = \$312,500 + \$25Q + \$0.0015Q^2,$$
$$MC = \$25 + \$0.003Q.$$
$$\pi = TR - TC$$
$$= \$100Q - \$0.001Q^2 - \$312,500 - \$25Q - \$0.0015Q^2$$
$$= -\$0.0025Q^2 + \$75Q - \$312,500.$$

Profit maximization occurs at the point where $MR = MC$, so the optimal output level is

$$MR = MC,$$
$$\$100 - \$0.002Q = \$25 + \$0.003Q,$$
$$75 = 0.005Q,$$
$$Q = 15,000.$$

This implies that

$$P = \$100 - \$0.001(15{,}000)$$
$$= \$85.$$
$$\pi = TR - TC$$
$$= -\$0.0025(15{,}000^2) + \$75(15{,}000) - \$312{,}500$$
$$= \$250{,}000.$$

Therefore, the optimal price/output combination is \$85 and 15,000 units for this integrated firm, and profits total \$250,000. To be optimal, transfer prices must ensure operation at these same levels.

Transfer Pricing with No External Market

Now consider how the situation changes if the firm is reorganized into separate manufacturing and distribution division profit centers, and no external market exists for the transferred product. The demand curve facing the distribution division is precisely the same as the firm's output demand curve. While the total cost function of the firm is unchanged, it can be broken down into the costs of manufacturing and distribution.

Assume that such a breakdown results in the following divisional cost functions:

$$TC_{Mfg} = \$250{,}000 + \$20Q + \$0.001Q^2,$$
$$MC_{Mfg} = \$20 + \$0.002Q,$$

and

$$TC_{Distr} = \$62{,}500 + \$5Q + \$0.0005Q^2,$$
$$MC_{Distr} = \$5 + \$0.001Q.$$

With divisional operation, the total and marginal cost functions for the firm are

$$TC = TC_{Mfg} + TC_{Distr},$$
$$MC = MC_{Mfg} + MC_{Distr},$$

and precisely the same as before. No substantive change has occurred.

To demonstrate the derivation of an appropriate transfer price, the net marginal revenue for the distribution division is set equal to the marginal cost of the manufacturing division to identify the firm's profit-maximizing activity level:

$$MR - MC_{Distr} = MC_{Mfg},$$
$$\$100 - \$0.002Q - \$5 - \$0.001Q = \$20 + \$0.002Q,$$
$$75 = 0.005Q,$$
$$Q = 15{,}000.$$

The 15,000-unit output level remains optimal for profit maximization, as must be the case. If the distribution division determines the quantity it will purchase by movement along its marginal revenue curve, and the manufacturing division supplies output along its marginal cost curve, then the market-clearing transfer price is the price that results when $MR - MC_{Distr} = MC_{Mfg}$. At 15,000 units of output, the optimal transfer price is

$$P_T = MC_{Mfg}$$
$$= \$20 + \$0.002(15,000)$$
$$= \$50.$$

At a transfer price of $P_T = \$50$, the quantity supplied by the manufacturing division equals 15,000. This is the same quantity demanded by the distribution division at a $P_T = \$50$, since

$$MR - MC_{Distr} = P_T,$$
$$\$100 - \$0.002Q - \$5 - \$0.001Q = \$50,$$
$$45 = 0.003Q,$$
$$Q = 15,000.$$

At a transfer price of $P_T > \$50$, the distribution division will accept fewer units of output than the manufacturing division wants to supply. If $P_T < \$50$, the distribution division will seek to purchase more units than the manufacturing division desires to produce. Only at a $50 transfer price are supply and demand in balance in the firm's internal market.

A Competitive External Market with Excess Internal Demand

To consider the effects of an external market for the transferred product, assume that the company is able to *buy* an unlimited quantity of a comparable product from a foreign supplier at a price of $35. The product supplied by the foreign manufacturer meets the exact same specifications as that produced by Hope Steadman & Sons. Since an unlimited quantity can be purchased for $35, a perfectly competitive external market exists for the transferred product, and the optimal transfer price equals the external market price. For $P_T = \$35$, the quantity demanded by the distribution division is

$$MR - MC_{Distr} = P_T,$$
$$\$100 - \$0.002Q - \$5 - \$0.001Q = \$35,$$
$$60 = 0.003Q,$$
$$Q = 20,000,$$

whereas the quantity supplied by the manufacturing division is

$$P_T = MC_{Mfg},$$
$$\$35 = \$20 + \$0.002Q,$$
$$15 = 0.002Q,$$
$$Q = 7,500.$$

In this case of excess internal demand, the distribution division will purchase all 7,500 units produced internally plus an additional 12,500 units from the foreign supplier. The price impact for customers and the profit impact for Hope Steadman & Sons is dramatic. Domestic customer prices and total profits are now calculated as

$$P = \$100 - \$0.001(20,000)$$
$$= \$80,$$

and

$$\begin{aligned}
\pi &= TR - TC_{Mfg} - TC_{For} - TC_{Distr} \\
&= \$100(20{,}000) - \$0.001(20{,}000^2) - \$250{,}000 - \$20(7{,}500) \\
&\quad - \$0.001(7{,}500^2) - \$35(12{,}500) - \$62{,}500 \\
&\quad - \$5(20{,}000) - \$0.0005(20{,}000^2) \\
&= \$343{,}750.
\end{aligned}$$

Hope Steadman & Sons' domestic customers benefit from the increased availability of goods, 20,000 versus 15,000 units, and lower prices, $80 versus $85 per unit. The opportunity to purchase goods at a price of $35 from a foreign supplier has also benefited Hope Steadman & Sons, since profits grow from $250,000 to $343,750. The company now manufactures only 7,500 of the units sold to customers and has become much more of a distributor than an integrated manufacturer and distributor. Hope Steadman & Sons has been able to make its business and profits grow by focusing efforts on distribution, where it enjoys a comparative advantage.

A Competitive External Market with Excess Internal Supply

It is interesting to contrast these results with those achieved under somewhat different circumstances. For example, assume that Hope Steadman & Sons is able to *sell* an unlimited quantity of its goods to a foreign distributor at a price of $80. For simplicity, also assume that sales to this new market have no impact on the firm's ability to sell to current domestic customers and that this market can be supplied under the same cost conditions as previously. If $P_T = \$80$, the quantity demanded by the distribution division is

$$\begin{aligned}
MR - MC_{Distr} &= P_T, \\
\$100 - \$0.002Q - \$5 - \$0.001Q &= \$80, \\
15 &= 0.003Q, \\
Q &= 5{,}000,
\end{aligned}$$

whereas the quantity supplied by the manufacturing division is

$$\begin{aligned}
P_T &= MC_{Mfg}, \\
\$80 &= \$20 + \$0.002Q, \\
60 &= 0.002Q, \\
Q &= 30{,}000.
\end{aligned}$$

In this instance of excess internal supply, the distribution division will purchase all 5,000 units desired internally, while the manufacturing division will offer an additional 25,000 units to the new foreign distributor. Again, the price impact for customers and the profit impact for Hope Steadman & Sons is dramatic. Domestic customer prices and total profits are now as follows:

$$\begin{aligned}
P &= \$100 - \$0.001(5{,}000) \\
&= \$95,
\end{aligned}$$

and

$$\pi = TR_{Dom} + TR_{For} - TC_{Mfg} - TC_{Distr}$$
$$= \$100(5{,}000) - \$0.001(5{,}000^2) + \$80(25{,}000) - \$250{,}000$$
$$\quad - \$20(30{,}000) - \$0.001(30{,}000^2) - \$62{,}500$$
$$\quad - \$5(5{,}000) - \$0.0005(5{,}000^2)$$
$$= \$625{,}000.$$

Under this scenario, Hope Steadman & Sons' domestic market shrinks from an initial 10,000 to 5,000 units, and prices rise somewhat from $85 to $95 per unit. At the same time, foreign customers benefit from the increased availability of goods, 25,000 versus none previously, and the attractive purchase price of $80 per unit. The opportunity to sell at a price of $80 to a foreign distributor has also benefited the company, since profits grow from $250,000 to $625,000. The company now distributes only 5,000 of 30,000 units sold to customers and has become much more of a manufacturer than a distributor. By emphasizing manufacturing, Hope Steadman & Sons makes its business and profits grow by focusing efforts on what it does best.

SUMMARY

This chapter examines a number of popular pricing practices. It becomes apparent that, when studied in detail, the methods commonly employed by successful firms reflect a careful appreciation of the use of marginal analysis to derive profit-maximizing prices.

* Many firms derive an optimal pricing policy using a technique called **markup pricing,** whereby prices are set to cover all direct costs plus a percentage markup for profit contribution. Flexible markup pricing practices that reflect differences in marginal costs and demand elasticities constitute an efficient method for ensuring that $MR = MC$ for each line of products sold.
* **Markup on cost** is the profit margin for an individual product or product line expressed as a percentage of unit cost. The numerator of this expression, called the **profit margin,** is the difference between price and cost. **Markup on price** is the profit margin for an individual product or product line expressed as a percentage of price, rather than unit cost.
* During **peak** periods, facilities are fully utilized. A firm has excess capacity during **off-peak** periods. Successful firms that employ markup pricing typically base prices on fully allocated costs under normal conditions but offer price discounts or accept lower margins during off-peak periods when substantial excess capacity is available.
* The **optimal markup on cost** formula is $OMC^* = -1/(\epsilon_P + 1)$. The **optimal markup-on-price** formula is $OMP^* = -1/\epsilon_P$. Either formula can be used to derive profit-maximizing prices solely on the basis of marginal cost and price elasticity of demand information.
* **Price discrimination** occurs whenever different market segments are charged different price markups for the same product. A **market segment** is a division or fragment of the overall market with essentially different or unique

demand or cost characteristics. Price discrimination is evident whenever identical customers are charged different prices, or when price differences are not proportional to cost differences. Through price discrimination, sellers are able to increase profits by appropriating the **consumers' surplus.** Consumers' surplus (or customers' surplus) is the value of purchased goods and services above and beyond the amount paid to sellers.

• The extent to which a firm can engage in price discrimination is classified into three major categories. Under **first-degree price discrimination,** the firm extracts the maximum amount each customer is willing to pay for its products. Each unit is priced separately at the price indicated along each product demand curve. **Second-degree price discrimination** involves setting prices on the basis of the quantity purchased. Quantity discounts that lead to lower markups for large versus small customers are a common means for second-degree price discrimination. The most commonly observed form of price discrimination, **third-degree price discrimination,** results when a firm separates its customers into several classes and sets a different price for each customer class. These customer classifications can be based on, for example, for-profit or not-for-profit status, regional location, or customer age.

• A **by-product** is any output that is customarily produced as a direct result of an increase in the production of some other output. Profit maximization requires that marginal revenue be set equal to marginal cost for each by-product. While the marginal costs of by-products produced in variable proportions can be determined, it is impossible to do so for by-products produced in fixed proportions. **Common costs,** or expenses that are necessary for manufacture of a joint product, cannot be allocated on any economically sound basis.

• **Transfer pricing** deals with the problem of pricing intermediate products transferred among divisions. When transferred products cannot be sold in competitive external markets, the marginal cost of the transferring division is the optimal transfer price. When transferred products can be sold in perfectly competitive external markets, the external market price is the optimal transfer price. When transferred products can be sold in imperfectly competitive external markets, the optimal transfer price equates the marginal cost of the transferring division to the marginal revenue derived from the combined internal and external markets.

Throughout the chapter, it has been shown that efficient pricing practices require a careful analysis of marginal revenues and marginal costs for each relevant product or product line. Among the most relevant marginal costs that must be considered are those costs involved with generating useful information on product demand and cost conditions. Rule-of-thumb pricing practices employed by successful firms can be reconciled with profit-maximizing behavior when the costs and benefits of pricing information are properly understood. These practices add tremendous value to the managerial decision-making process.

Questions

Q14.1   What is markup pricing?

Q14.2   Develop and explain the relation between the markup-on-cost and the markup-on-price formulas.

Q14.3 Identify and interpret the relation between the optimal markup on cost and the point price elasticity of demand.

Q14.4 Illustrate the relation between the optimal markup on price and the point price elasticity of demand.

Q14.5 "One of the least practical suggestions that economists have offered to managers is that they set marginal revenues equal to marginal costs." Discuss this statement.

Q14.6 "Marginal cost pricing, as well as the use of incremental analysis, is looked upon with favor by economists, especially those on the staffs of regulatory agencies. With this encouragement, regulated industries do indeed employ these "rational" techniques quite frequently. Unregulated firms, on the other hand, use marginal or incremental cost pricing much less frequently, sticking to cost-plus, or full-cost, pricing except under unusual circumstances. In my opinion, this goes a long way toward explaining the problems of the regulated firms vis-à-vis unregulated industry." Discuss this statement.

Q14.7 What is price discrimination?

Q14.8 What conditions are necessary before price discrimination is both possible and profitable? Why does price discrimination result in higher profits?

Q14.9 Discuss the role of common costs in pricing practice.

Q14.10 Why is it possible to determine the marginal costs of joint products produced in variable proportions but not those of joint products produced in fixed proportions?

Self-Test Problem

Cliff Claven is a project coordinator at Norm Peterson & Associates, Ltd., a large Boston-based painting contractor. Claven has asked you to complete an analysis of profit margins earned on a number of recent projects. Unfortunately, your predecessor on this project was abruptly transferred, leaving you with only sketchy information on the firm's pricing practices.

A. Use the available data to complete the following table:

Price	Marginal Cost	Markup on Cost (%)	Markup on Price (%)
$ 100	$ 25	300.0	75.0
240	72		
680	272	150.0	60.0
750		100.0	
2,800			40.0
	2,700	33.3	
	3,360		20.0
5,800			10.0
6,250		5.3	
	10,000		0.0

B. Calculate the missing data for each of the following proposed projects, based on the available estimates of the point price elasticity of demand, optimal markup on cost, and optimal markup on price:

Project	Price Elasticity	Optimal Markup on Cost (%)	Optimal Markup on Price (%)
1	−1.5	200.0	66.7
2	−2.0		
3		66.7	
4			25.0
5	−5.0	25.0	
6		11.1	10.0
7	−15.0		
8	−20.0		5.0
9			4.0
10	−50.0	2.0	

Solution to Self-Test Problem

A.

Price	Marginal Cost	Markup on Cost (%)	Markup on Price (%)
$ 100	$ 25	300.0	75.0
240	72	233.3	70.0
680	272	150.0	60.0
750	375	100.0	50.0
2,800	1,680	66.7	40.0
3,600	2,700	33.3	25.0
4,200	3,360	25.0	20.0
5,800	5,220	11.1	10.0
6,250	5,938	5.3	5.0
10,000	10,000	0.0	0.0

B.

Project	Price Elasticity	Optimal Markup on Cost (%)	Optimal Markup on Price (%)
1	−1.5	200.0	66.7
2	−2.0	100.0	50.0
3	−2.5	66.7	40.0
4	−4.0	33.3	25.0
5	−5.0	25.0	20.0
6	−10.0	11.1	10.0
7	−15.0	7.1	6.7
8	−20.0	5.3	5.0
9	−25.0	4.2	4.0
10	−50.0	2.0	2.0

Problems

P14.1 **Markup Calculation.** Controller Bailey Porter has asked you to review the pricing practices of Cincinnati Novelty Products, Inc., an importer and regional distributor of low-priced trinkets and curios. Use the following data to calculate the relevant markup on cost and markup on price for the following five items:

Product	Price	Marginal Cost	Markup on Cost (%)	Markup on Price (%)
A	10¢	1¢	900	90
B	29¢	6¢	383.33	79.31
C	59¢	18¢	227.78	69.5
D	89¢	31¢	187.00	65.17
E	99¢	40¢	147.5	59.6

P14.2 **Optimal Markup.** Management consultant David Addison has been retained to assess the pricing practices of Maddie Hayes's Moonlight Cafe. As Addison's assistant, use the following demand elasticity estimates to calculate the profit-maximizing markup on cost and markup on price for a variety of luncheon and dinner entrées.

Entrée	Price Elasticity	Optimal Markup on Cost (%)	Optimal Markup on Price (%)
A	−1	0	
B	−2	100%	
C	−3	50	
D	−4	33.3	
E	−5	25%	

P14.3 **Optimal Price.** Payless Shoe Stores, Inc., cut prices on women's dress shoes by 2 percent during the first quarter and enjoyed a 4 percent increase in unit sales over the period compared with a year earlier.

A. Calculate the point price elasticity of demand for Payless shoes.

B. Calculate the company's optimal shoe price if marginal cost is $10 per unit.

P14.4 **Markup on Cost.** Brake-Checkup, Inc., offers automobile brake analysis and repair at a number of outlets in the Philadelphia area. The company recently initiated a policy of matching the lowest advertised competitor price. As a result, Brake-Checkup has been forced to reduce the average price for brake jobs by 3 percent, but it has enjoyed a 15 percent increase in customer traffic. Meanwhile, marginal costs have held steady at $120 per brake job.

A. Calculate the point price elasticity of demand for brake jobs.

B. Calculate Brake-Checkup's optimal price and markup on cost.

P14.5 **Optimal Markup on Price.** TLC Lawncare, Inc., provides fertilizer and weed control lawn services to residential customers. Its seasonal service package, regularly priced at $250, includes several chemical spray treatments. As part of an effort to expand its customer base, TLC offered $50 off its regular price to customers in the Dallas area. Response was enthusiastic, with sales rising to 5,750 units (packages) from the 3,250 units sold in the same period last year.

A. Calculate the arc price elasticity of demand for TLC service.

B. Assume that the arc price elasticity (from Part A) is the best available estimate of the point price elasticity of demand. If marginal cost is $135 per unit for labor and materials, calculate TLC's optimal markup on price and its optimal price.

P14.6   **Peak/Off-Peak Pricing.** Simon & Simon Construction Company is a building contractor serving the Gulf Coast region. The company recently bid on a new office building construction project in Mobile, Alabama. Simon & Simon has incurred bid development and job cost-out expenses of $25,000 prior to submission of the bid. The bid was based on the following projected costs:

Cost Category	Amount
Bid development and job cost-out expenses	$ 25,000
Materials	881,000
Labor (50,000 hours @ $26)	1,300,000
Variable overhead (40 percent of direct labor)	520,000
Allocated fixed overhead (6 percent of total costs)	174,000
Total costs	$2,900,000

A. What is Simon & Simon's minimum acceptable (breakeven) contract price, assuming that the company is operating at peak capacity?

B. What is the Simon & Simon's minimum acceptable contract price if an economic downturn has left the company with substantial excess capacity?

P14.7   **Incremental Pricing Analysis.** The General Eclectic Company manufactures an electric toaster. Sales of the toaster have increased steadily during the previous five years, and, because of a recently completed expansion program, annual capacity is now 500,000 units. Production and sales during the coming year are forecast to be 400,000 units, and standard production costs are estimated as follows:

Materials	$ 6.00
Direct labor	4.00
Variable indirect labor	2.00
Fixed overhead	3.00
Allocated cost per unit	$15.00

In addition to production costs, General incurs fixed selling expenses of $1.50 per unit and variable warranty repair expenses of $1.20 per unit. General currently receives $20 per unit from its customers (primarily retail department stores), and it expects this price to hold during the coming year.

After making the preceding projections, General received an inquiry about the purchase of a large number of toasters by a discount department store. The inquiry contained two purchase offers:

- *Offer 1:* The department store would purchase 80,000 units at $14.60 per unit. These units would bear the General label and be covered by the General warranty.
- *Offer 2:* The department store would purchase 120,000 units at $14.00 per unit. These units would be sold under the buyer's private label, and General would not provide warranty service.

A. Evaluate the incremental net income potential of each offer.
B. What other factors should General consider when deciding which offer to accept?
C. Which offer (if either) should General accept? Why?

P14.8 **Price Discrimination.** Coach Industries, Inc., is a leading manufacturer of recreational vehicle products. Products include travel trailers, fifth-wheel trailers (towed behind pick-up trucks), and van campers, as well as parts and accessories. Coach offers its fifth-wheel trailers to both dealers (wholesale) and retail customers. Ernie Pantusso, Coach's controller, estimates that each fifth-wheel trailer costs the company $10,000 in variable labor and material expenses. Demand and marginal revenue relations for fifth-wheel trailers are

$$P_W = \$15,000 - \$5Q_W, \qquad \text{(Wholesale)}$$
$$MR_W = dTR_W/dQ_W = \$15,000 - \$10Q_W.$$
$$P_R = \$50,000 - \$20Q_R, \qquad \text{(Retail)}$$
$$MR_R = dTR_R/dQ_R = \$50,000 - \$40Q_R.$$

A. Assuming that the company can price discriminate between its two types of customers, calculate the profit-maximizing price, output, and profit contribution levels.
B. Calculate point price elasticities for each customer type at the activity levels identified in Part A. Are the differences in these elasticities consistent with your recommended price differences in Part A? Why or why not?

P14.9 **Joint Product Pricing.** Each ton of ore mined from the Baby Doe Mine in Leadville, Colorado, produces one ounce of silver and one pound of lead in a fixed 1:1 ratio. Marginal costs are $10 per ton of ore mined.

The demand and marginal revenue curves for silver are

$$P_S = \$11 - \$0.00003Q_S,$$
$$MR_S = dTR/dQ_S = \$11 - \$0.00006Q_S,$$

and the demand and marginal revenue curves for lead are

$$P_L = \$0.4 - \$0.000005Q_L,$$
$$MR_L = dTR/dQ_L = \$0.4 - \$0.00001Q_L,$$

where Q_S is ounces of silver and Q_L is pounds of lead.

A. Calculate profit-maximizing sales quantities and prices for silver and lead.

B. Now assume that wild speculation in the silver market has created a fivefold (or 500 percent) increase in silver demand. Calculate optimal sales quantities and prices for both silver and lead under these conditions.

P14.10 **Transfer Pricing.** Simpson Flanders, Inc., is a Motor City-based manufacturer and distributor of valves used in nuclear power plants. Currently, all output is sold to North American customers. Demand and marginal revenue curves for the firm are as follows:

$$P = \$1,000 - \$0.015Q,$$
$$MR = dTR/dQ = \$1,000 - \$0.03Q.$$

Relevant total cost, marginal cost, and profit functions are

$$TC = \$1,500,000 + \$600Q + \$0.005Q^2,$$
$$MC = dTC/dQ = \$600 + \$0.01Q,$$
$$\pi = TR - TC$$
$$= -\$0.02Q^2 + \$400Q - \$1,500,000.$$

A. Calculate the profit-maximizing activity level for Simpson Flanders when the firm is operated as an integrated unit.

B. Assume that the company is reorganized into two independent profit centers with the following cost conditions:

$$TC_{Mfg} = \$1,250,000 + \$500Q + \$0.005Q^2,$$
$$MC_{Mfg} = \$500 + \$0.01Q,$$

and,

$$TC_{Distr} = \$250,000 + \$100Q,$$
$$MC_{Distr} = \$100.$$

Calculate the transfer price that ensures a profit-maximizing level of profit for the firm, with divisional operation based on the assumption that all output produced is to be transferred internally.

C. Now assume that a major distributor in the European market offers to buy as many valves as Simpson Flanders wishes to offer at a price of $645. No impact on demand from the company's North American customers is expected, and current facilities can be used to supply both markets. Calculate the company's optimal price(s), output(s), and profits in this situation.

CASE STUDY FOR CHAPTER 14

Pricing Practices in the Madison, Wisconsin, and Denver, Colorado, Local Newspaper Markets

Why do you read the newspaper? Studies show that significant numbers of newspaper purchases from vending machines are motivated by the headline appearing on the front page. During the recent presidential election, for example, newspaper sales grew rapidly as readers sought the information on their favorite candidate. Others read the paper to get the latest sports information, business news, or weather report. Perhaps the *Wall Street Journal* is best known for providing timely and comprehensive business news, whereas *USA Today* is known for providing broad coverage of general news, sports, and entertainment. Both compete against the *New York Times,* the *Washington Post,* and other leading newspapers, as well as against *Business Week, Forbes, Fortune, Newsweek, Time,* and a host of specialized magazines. It is quite surprising that national newspapers compete to a much lesser degree with local newspapers. Local newspapers have a formidable niche in the provision of local news. If you want to read up on the latest Wall Street rumor, you can read the *Journal.* If you want to read up on the latest high school basketball scores, you must read the local newspaper. Similarly, the local newspaper is the only place to go for local want ads.

An interesting illustration of price discrimination can be found in the want-ad pricing policies of local newspapers. The value of want-ad advertising varies according to the value of the item advertised. Real estate advertising has a much greater value to customers than advertising of lower-priced household items, boats, pets, and so on. Given these differences, customers are willing to pay much more to advertise a personal residence, for example, than to seek new homes for Spotty and her kittens. Local newspapers satisfy the requirements necessary for profitable price discrimination, since they can easily identify the value of the item advertised and often enjoy a monopoly position in the sale of local advertising. Indeed, it is rare to find more than one newspaper company serving a local market, given the significant economies of scale in the industry.

Table 14.4 shows pricing policies during the early 1990s for local newspapers in the Madison, Wisconsin, and Denver, Colorado, markets. This comparison yields insight because of the difference in market structure. The Madison market, as is typical of local newspaper markets in the United States, is served by a single newspaper company, Madison Newspapers, Inc., with the *Wisconsin State Journal* (morning and Sunday) and the *Capital Times* (evening) editions. The Denver market, however, is served by two independent newspaper companies, the *Denver Post* and the *Rocky Mountain News.*

It is interesting that the monopoly position of Madison Newspapers is reflected in higher single-copy and subscription prices than either the *Post* or *News.* The 100 percent price premium on both daily and Sunday single-copy sales in the Madison market is dramatic, as is the more than 50 percent premium on daily plus Sunday subscription sales. These price differentials suggest that, by virtue of its monopoly position, Madison Newspapers enjoys a substantial pricing ad-

TABLE 14.4 **Pricing Practices and Market Shares in the Madison, Wisconsin, and Denver, Colorado, Local Newspaper Markets**

	Madison Newspapers	Denver Post	Rocky Mountain News
Newspaper Prices			
Single copy—Daily	$0.50	$0.25	$0.25
Single copy—Sunday	1.50	0.75	0.75
Subscription—Daily	7.20 (mo.)	6.00 (mo.)	6.00 (mo.)
Subscription—Daily + Sunday	12.00 (mo.)	7.60 (mo.)	7.25 (mo.)
Want-Ad Prices (Three-line ad)			
Real estate	25.20 (3 days)	27.00 (3 days)	27.90 (3 days)
	51.45 (7 days)	38.40 (10 days)	45.00 (10 days)
	92.40 (14 days)	76.80 (20 days)	90.00 (20 days)
	189.00 (30 days)	115.20 (30 days)	135.00 (30 days)
Merchandise	24.95 (10 days, < $15,000 value)	15.00 (10 days)	15.00 (10 days)
	16.95 (10 days, < $1,500 value)		
	11.50 (7 days, < $150 value)		
Circulation			
Daily (market share)	110,000 (100%)	278,000 (43%)	372,000 (57%)
Sunday (market share)	180,000 (100%)	450,000 (51%)	432,000 (49%)

vantage in its market when compared with the pricing discretion of either the *Post* or *News* in the Denver market.

The advantages of Madison Newspapers' monopoly position are even more apparent when want-ad pricing practices are considered. Madison Newspapers' real estate want-ad prices are quite comparable with those charged by the *Post* and *News,* despite that its overall market size is only 30 to 40 percent as large. This means that on a cost-per-exposure basis, Madison Newspapers' real estate want-ad prices are roughly two and one-half to three times higher than those charged by the *Post* and *News.* Although all three papers engage in price discrimination for want ads, Madison Newspapers' non-real estate merchandise (autos, etc.) want-ad pricing structure is much more closely tied to the value of the item advertised than that of either the *Post* or *News.*

A. What is the motivation for local newspaper price discrimination in want-ad advertising?

B. Widely differing fares for business and vacation travelers on the same flight have led some to accuse the airlines of price discrimination. Do airline fare differences or local newspaper want-ad rate differences provide stronger evidence of price discrimination?

C. Is price discrimination by local newspapers as likely in the case of locally placed national ads for Nike shoes as it is in the case of local want-ad advertising?

Selected References

Ashenfelter, Orley, and David Genesove. "Testing for Price Anomalies in Real-Estate Auctions." *American Economic Review* 82 (May 1992): 501–505.

Bagwell, Kyle, and Michael H. Riordan. "High and Declining Prices Signal Product Quality." *American Economic Review* 81 (March 1991): 224–239.

Blinder, Alan S. "Why Are Prices Sticky? Preliminary Results from an Interview Study." *American Economic Review* 81 (May 1991): 89–96.

Bryant, Peter G., and E. Woodrow Eckard. "Price Fixing: The Probability of Getting Caught." *Review of Economics and Statistics* 73 (August 1991): 531–536.

Cecchetti, Stephen G. "Prices During the Great Depression: Was the Deflation of 1930–1932 Really Unanticipated?" *American Economic Review* 82 (March 1992): 157–178.

Feinberg, Robert M., and Seth Kaplan. "The Response of Domestic Prices to Expected Exchange Rates." *Journal of Business* 65 (April 1992): 267–281.

Feinstein, Jonathan S. "Public-Good Provision and Political Stability in Europe." *American Economic Review* 82 (May 1992): 323–329.

Hannan, Timothy H., and Allen N. Berger. "The Rigidity of Prices: Evidence from the Banking Industry." *American Economic Review* 81 (September 1991): 938–945.

Hanson, Ward. "The Dynamics of Cost-Plus Pricing." *Managerial and Decision Economics* 13 (March–April 1992): 149–161.

Hendricks, Kenneth, and Robert H. Porter. "Joint Bidding in Federal OCS Auctions." *American Economic Review* 82 (May 1992): 506–511.

Hess, James D., and Eitan Gerstner. "Price-Matching Policies: An Empirical Case." *Managerial and Decision Economics* 12 (August 1991): 305–315.

Hubbard, R. Glen, and Robert J. Weiner. "Long-Term Contracting and Multiple-Price Systems." *Journal of Business* 65 (April 1992): 177–198.

Kalwani, Manohar V., and Chi Kin Yim. "Consumer Price Expectations: An Experimental Study." *Journal of Marketing Research* 29 (February 1992): 90–100.

McAfee, R. Preston, and Daniel Vincent. "Updating the Reserve Price in Common-Value Auctions." *American Economic Review* 82 (May 1992): 512–518.

Sethuraman, Raj, and Gerard J. Tellis. "An Analysis of the Tradeoff between Advertising and Price Discounting." *Journal of Marketing Research* 28 (May 1991): 160–174.

LONG-TERM INVESTMENT DECISION MAKING

GOVERNMENT REGULATION OF THE MARKET ECONOMY

When considering the role of government, it has been traditional to focus on how government influences economic activity through tax policies, law enforcement, and infrastructure investments in highways, water treatment facilities, and the like. More recently, interest has shifted to how and why the government regulates private market activity. Government regulation of the market economy consists of rules that constrain the way private companies operate and the types of products that they produce. The subject is interesting because tax policies, rules, and regulations fundamentally shape the competitive environment. Government affects what and how firms produce, influences conditions of entry and exit, dictates marketing practices, prescribes hiring and personnel policies, and imposes a host of other requirements on private enterprise. Government regulation of the market economy is a controversial topic because the power to tax or compel has direct and obvious economic consequences.

For example, local telephone service monopolies are protected by a web of local and federal regulation that gives rise to above-normal rates of return while providing access to below-market financing. Franchises that confer the right to offer cellular telephone service in a major metropolitan area are literally worth millions of dollars and can be awarded in the United States only by the Federal Communications Commission (FCC). The federal government also spends hundreds of millions of dollars per year to maintain artificially high price supports for selected agricultural products such as milk and grain but not for chicken and pork. At the same time, natural gas prices in the United States are held far below market prices. Careful study of the motivation and methods of such regulation is essential to the study of managerial economics because of regulation's key role in shaping the managerial decision-making process.

The pervasive and expanding influence of government in the market economy can be illustrated by considering the growing role played by the FCC, a once obscure agency known only for regulation of the broadcast industry and AT&T. The FCC currently holds the keys to success for a number of emerging communications technologies. In the immediate future, the FCC will determine the fate of digital audio broadcasting, which does away with static on car radio channels; personal communication networks that make users reachable anywhere with a pocket phone; and interactive television, which lets customers order goods and communicate with others through a television set. Rapid advances in communications technology will be obvious if you soon find yourself talking to your TV, if your car stereo sounds like a CD player, and if you can phone home from the top of Glacier National Park. If not, the FCC and overly restrictive regulation of the airwaves will be to blame.

Although all sectors of the U.S. economy are regulated to some degree, the method and scope of regulation vary widely. Most companies escape price and profit restraint, except during periods of general wage-price control, but they are subject to operating regulations governing pollution emissions, product packaging and labeling, worker safety and health, and so on. Other firms, particularly in the financial and the public utility sectors, must comply with financial regulation in addition to such operating controls. Banks and savings and loan institutions, for example, are subject to state and federal regulation of interest rates, fees, lending policies, and capital requirements. Unlike firms in the electric power and telecommunications industries, banks and savings and loans face no explicit limit on profitability. For this reason, regulation of depository institutions, insurance companies, and the securities business encompasses more than regulation in the nonfinancial sector but is less comprehensive than the regulation of public utilities.

This chapter begins its analysis of government regulation of the market economy by considering the economic and social rationale for regulation. Government regulation directly influences both productive efficiency and the distribution of income. Because public policy often makes some trade-off between these efficiency and equity considerations, both the process and the results of regulation are controversial issues. Property right grants and subsidies that provide firms with positive incentives for "desirable" activity, and tax policy, which constrains "undesirable activity," are also discussed in terms of their effects on production and marketing methods for a wide range of goods and services. Antitrust policy is considered as a useful means for helping maintain a workable level of competition in the overall economy. Finally, monopoly regulation and the trend toward deregulation and regulatory reform are investigated as ways of shedding light on the costs and benefits of government involvement in the market economy. Through this analysis it becomes clear that while the intentions of many regulations may be laudable, they can have an adverse impact on the general public. Appropriate government regulation is based on a balancing of costs and benefits to society in general, taking into account both obvious administrative costs and hidden costs borne by the private sector.

COMPETITION AND THE ROLE OF GOVERNMENT

Both economic and social considerations enter into decisions of what and how to regulate. Economic considerations relate to the cost and efficiency implications

Efficiency
Production of what consumers demand in a least-cost fashion.

Regulation
Government control of the market economy.

of regulatory methods. From an economic **efficiency** standpoint, a given mode of **regulation** or government control is desirable to the extent that benefits exceed costs. In terms of efficiency, the question is whether market competition by itself is sufficient, or if it needs to be supplemented with government regulation. **Equity,** or fairness, criteria must also be carefully weighed when social considerations bear on the regulatory decision-making process. Therefore, the *incidence,* or placement, of costs and benefits of regulatory decisions is important. If a given change in regulatory policy provides significant benefits to the poor, society may willingly bear substantial costs in terms of lost efficiency.

Economic Considerations

Equity
Just distribution of wealth.

Competitive markets have several compelling advantages. Perhaps most important, the discipline of competition encourages economic efficiency. In the short run, efficient firms gain market share from higher-cost competitors and earn above-normal profits. Ultimately, competition forces inefficient firms from the marketplace. Competition also ensures that the types of products preferred by customers are provided. In competitive markets, firms must react to customer preferences rather than dictate the quantity and quality of goods and services provided. A further advantage of competition is that profits and wage rates reflect the productive capability of firms and workers. Companies that earn higher profits tend to be those that best serve customer needs; high-wage workers tend to be those that are most productive. As a result, competition is desirable from both efficiency and equity perspectives.

Economic regulation began and continues in part because of the public's perception of market imperfections. It is sometimes believed that unregulated market activity can lead to inefficiency and waste or to market failure. **Market failure** is the inability of a system of market institutions to sustain socially desirable activities or to eliminate undesirable ones.

Market failure
The inability of market institutions to sustain desirable activity or eliminate undesirable activity.

Failure by market structure
Insufficient market participants for active competition.

A first cause of market failure is **failure by market structure.** For a market to realize the beneficial effects of competition, it must have many producers (sellers) and consumers (buyers), or at least the ready potential for many to enter. Some markets do not meet this condition. Consider, for example, water, power, and some telecommunications markets. If customer service in a given market area can be most efficiently provided by a single firm (a natural monopoly situation), such providers would enjoy market power and could earn economic profits by limiting output and charging high prices. As a result, utility prices and profits were placed under regulatory control, which has continued with the goal of preserving the efficiency of large-scale production while preventing the higher prices and economic profits of monopoly. When the efficiency advantages of large size are not thought to be compelling, antitrust policy limits the market power of large firms.

Failure by incentive
Breakdown of the pricing mechanism as a reflection of all costs and benefits of production and consumption.

Externalities
Differences between private and social costs or benefits.

A second kind of market failure is **failure by incentive.** In the production and consumption of goods and services, social values and costs often differ considerably from the private costs and values of producers and consumers. Differences between private and social costs or benefits are called **externalities.** A negative externality is a cost of producing, marketing, or consuming a product that is not borne by the product's producers or consumers. A positive externality is a benefit of production, marketing, or consumption that is not reflected in the product pricing structure and, hence, does not accrue to the product's producers or consumers.

Environmental pollution is one well-known negative externality. Negative externalities also arise when employees are exposed to hazardous working conditions for which they are not fully compensated. Similarly, a firm that dams a river or builds a solar collector to produce energy and thereby limits the access of others to hydropower or solar power creates a negative externality. Positive externalities can result if an increase in a firm's activity reduces costs for its suppliers, who pass these cost savings on to their other customers. The rapid growth of the computer industry has, for example, reduced input costs for both the computer and electronics industries. Economies of scale in semiconductor production made possible by increased computer demand lowered input costs for all users of semiconductors. As a result, prices have fallen for computers as well as a wide variety of "intelligent" electronic appliances, calculators, toys, and so on. Positive externalities in production can result when a firm trains employees who later apply their knowledge in work for other firms. Positive externalities also arise when an improvement in production methods is transferred from one firm to another without compensation. The dam cited previously for its potential negative externalities might also provide positive externalities by offering flood control or recreational benefits.

In short, externalities lead to a difference between the private and social costs and benefits of a given product or activity. These differences often have a notable effect on the economy. Firms that provide substantial positive externalities without compensation are unlikely to produce at the socially optimal level. Similarly, consumption activities that confer positive externalities may not reach the socially optimal level. In contrast, negative externalities can channel too many resources to a particular activity. Producers or consumers that generate negative externalities do not pay the full costs of production or consumption and tend to overutilize social resources. Instances in which market prices do not fully reflect costs or benefits provide an impetus for government intervention.

Social Considerations

Competition promotes efficiency by giving firms incentives to produce the types and quantities of products that consumers want. Competitive pressures force each firm to use resources wisely to earn at least a normal profit. The market-based resource allocation system is efficient when it responds quickly and accurately to consumer preferences. Not only are these features of competitive markets attractive on an economic basis, but they are also consistent with basic democratic principles. *Preservation of consumer choice or consumer sovereignty* is an important feature of competitive markets. By encouraging and rewarding individual initiative, competition greatly enhances personal freedom. For this reason, less vigorous competitive pressure indicates diminishing consumer sovereignty. Firms with market power can limit output and raise prices to earn economic profits, whereas firms in competitive markets refer to market prices to determine optimal output quantities. Monopolies have far more discretion than firms in competitive markets. Regulatory policy can be a valuable tool with which to control monopolies, restoring control over price and quantity decisions to the public.

A second social purpose of regulatory intervention is to *limit concentration of economic and political power.* It has long been recognized that economic and social relations become intertwined and that concentrated economic power is generally inconsistent with the democratic process. The laws of incorporation, first passed during the 1850s, play an important role in the U.S. economic system. These laws have allowed owners of capital (stockholders) to pool economic resources without also pooling political resources, thereby allowing big business and democracy to coexist. Of course, the large scale of modern corporations has sometimes diminished the controlling influence of individual stockholders. In these instances, regulatory and antitrust policies have limited the growth of large firms to avoid undue concentration of political power.

Important social considerations often constitute compelling justification for government intervention in the marketplace. Deciding whether a particular regulatory reform is warranted is complicated because social considerations can run counter to efficiency considerations. This is not to say that policies should never be pursued when the expected benefits are exceeded by expected costs. Costs in the form of lost efficiency may sometimes be borne to achieve more equitable economic solutions.

REGULATORY RESPONSE TO INCENTIVE FAILURES

One of the roles of government is to help preserve the competitive environment and, when markets are not performing well, to introduce regulation that accomplishes the goal of achieving approximately competitive outcomes. To reach this objective, government regulation responds to problems created by both positive and negative externalities in production, marketing, and consumption. In the effort to limit the frequency of market failure that is due to incentive problems, government frequently grants property rights and employs a variety of tax policies. In granting patents and operating subsidies, government provides compensation to reward activity that provides positive externalities. Local, state, and federal governments levy taxes (a form of negative subsidy) and set operating requirements or controls to limit the creation of negative externalities. Although property rights grants, taxes, and operating control policies are by no means the only government responses to incentive failures, they are among the most widely employed and provide a good introduction to this area of government/business interaction.

Property Rights Regulation

Property rights
The license to limit use by others.

Property rights give firms the prerogative to limit use by others of specific land, plant and equipment, and other assets. The deed to a piece of land, for example, explicitly defines a property right and gives the owner access to the courts if someone tries to use the property without the owner's permission. The establishment and maintenance of private property rights is essential to the workings of a competitive market. Property rights are so fundamental to the free market economy and democratic form of government that they are protected in the United States by the Fifth Amendment to the Constitution. While local zoning laws limit property rights by restricting the types of buildings allowed in a particular neighborhood, these laws cannot be so burdensome as to deprive owners from the rightful use of their property. Although the public interest might be served by regulations designed to preserve wetlands or endangered species, owners are entitled to compensation for any loss they might suffer as a result.

Regulation of property rights is a common, though seldom discussed, method of giving firms an incentive to promote service in the public interest. Common examples are FCC control of local television and radio broadcasting rights; federal and state regulatory bodies that govern national or state chartering of banks and savings and loan institutions; and insurance commissions that oversee insurance company licensing at the state level. In each of these instances, firms must be able to demonstrate fiscal responsibility and to provide evidence that they are meeting the needs of their service areas. Should firms fail to meet these established criteria, public franchises in the form of broadcasting rights, charters, or licenses can be withdrawn, or new franchises can be offered to potential competitors. Even though such drastic action is rare, the mere threat of such sanctions is often sufficient to compel compliance with prescribed regulations.

Although control of property rights can be an effective form of regulation, it often falls short of its full potential because of imprecise operating criteria. For example, is a television station that broadcasts poorly rated local programming 20 hours per week responding better to the needs of its service area than a station that airs highly popular reruns of hit shows? How progressive an attitude should a local bank take toward electronic funds transfer services? Without clear, consistent, and workable standards of performance, operating grant regulation will be hampered by inefficiency and waste. The cost of this inefficiency is measured by the low quality and limited quantity of desired goods and services and by the excessive profits and/or high costs of firms sheltered from competition by regulatory policies.

Patents and the Tort System

Patents
Exclusive property rights to produce, use, or sell an invention or innovation for a limited period of time.

With **patents,** the government grants an exclusive property right to produce, use, or sell an invention or innovation for a limited period of time (17 years in the United States). These valuable grants of legal monopoly power are intended to stimulate research and development. Without patents, competitors would quickly exploit and develop close, if not identical, substitutes for new products or processes, and inventing firms would fail to reap the full benefit of their technological breakthroughs. Patent policy is a regulatory attempt to achieve the benefits of both monopoly and competition in the field of research and development. In granting the patent, the public confers a limited opportunity for monopoly profits to stimulate research activity and the economic growth that it creates. By limiting the patent monopoly, competition is encouraged to extend and develop the common body of knowledge.

The patent monopoly is subject to other restrictions besides the time limit. Firms cannot use patents to unfairly monopolize or otherwise limit competition. For example, in 1973 the Federal Trade Commission (FTC) charged Xerox with

●

Growth and the Environment

Back in 1973, Donella and Dennis Meadows set off a furor in business with their book *Limits to Growth,* in which they argued that natural resources and the earth's ability to absorb pollution are strictly limited. The book sold nine million copies, but the authors were criticized in academic circles for underestimating the ability of the pricing mechanism to conserve resources and regulate environmental degradation. Now, the Meadowses have written a sequel titled *Beyond the Limits,* in which they argue that human activity has already overshot earth's ecological limits.

Both books are valuable because they raise important issues that demand the serious attention of business and public policy decision makers, even though the Meadows's central tenet may in fact be false. Simplistic extrapolations of past trends into the future are not likely to offer meaningful insight concerning future resource use and the potential burdens to be placed upon the environment. Freely competitive markets ration precious natural resources by placing even higher prices on them as expanding use makes them increasingly scarce and valuable. Similarly, the pricing mechanism is able to restrict environmental degradation when fines and penalties are used to limit air, noise, and water pollution. Thus, there is no logic to the argument that past rates of scarce resource use and environmental degradation will persist to the point of global catastrophe.

Nevertheless, to ensure a healthy and prosperous economic and physical environment, it is necessary to carefully consider the environmental impacts of both private and public decisions. From a global perspective, many people are worried about the continuing population explosion, a problem that is particularly acute in developing countries where people seem unwilling to voluntarily limit population growth. Since 1970, global population has leaped by an astounding 66 percent, to 5.3 billion, while world economic output has nearly doubled. In many areas, the cost to the environment is disturbingly evident. The Baltic Sea is dying from sewage and other pollution; millions breathe toxic air in Mexico City and Eastern Europe; China soon will have cut all its harvestable forests; millions of tons of topsoil are lost because of poor farming practices. The ozone layer appears to be thinning, the globe may be warming,

and untold economic and social repercussions may be in store.

The historical conflict between growth and the environment has caused many leaders to support the concept of "sustainable development." This emotionally charged proposal calls for preservation of the earth's "natural capital," including the air, water, and other ecological treasures. At the same time, proponents of sustainable development recognize that growth is necessary to eliminate poverty and raise the quality of life in developing nations.

To achieve sustainable development, proponents suggest furthering a number of essential social initiatives. Primary among these are the following:

- *Boost efficiency.* Adopt innovations that slash resource use and pollution. These include clean technologies and products such as electric cars; energy efficiency; recycling; "closed loop" production; less destructive agriculture; and products with less packaging, fewer materials, and longer lives.
- *Build a framework for change.* Account for environmental costs and benefits in economic transactions and GDP calculations. Forge international compacts to protect common resources and address global problems. Enact taxes and other incentives to curtail global destruction.
- *Stabilize population.* Encourage family planning to help lower birth rates, improve living standards, and enhance the status of women in developing nations.
- *Restrain consumption.* Foster life-styles that lower the burden on the environment, especially in industrial nations. Encourage "green consumerism."
- *Unleash bacterial power.* Encourage the growth of biotechnology that promises to create nonpolluting pesticides, crops that need less water, and pollution-fighting microbes. Less wasteful, less energy-intensive biological processes could increasingly replace chemical-based systems.

To be sure, the fate of the forest will reflect to a great extent the willingness of business and world governments to sacrifice narrow short-term goals in favor of the long-term benefits of sustainable development.

Source: Emily T. Smith, "Growth vs. the Environment," *Business Week,* May 11, 1992, 66–75.

dominating the office-copier industry through unfair marketing and patent practices. In its complaint, the FTC alleged that Xerox, in association with Battelle Memorial Institute, a private research corporation, had created an artificial "patent barrier to competition." A final consent order in 1975 resolved the FTC's monopolization suit against Xerox. The consent order required Xerox to license competitors to use its more than 1,700 copier patents with little or no royalty charges and restricted Xerox's freedom to acquire such rights from its competitors. Partially because of this action, entry into the copier industry grew rapidly during the late 1970s.

The rules of contract law provide for the enforcement of patents and other legal agreements among firms. Because it is impossible to specify all possible outcomes in writing a legal contract, the court system provides an open forum for dispute resolution. Even if all possible outcomes could be specified beforehand, legal enforcement would still be necessary to ensure that all parties honor their agreements. If a manufacturer fails to deliver goods to a wholesaler as promised, the wholesaler can go to the courts to enforce its agreement with the manufacturer. Without such enforcement, firms would have no recourse but to depend exclusively upon the goodwill of others. The legal system also includes a body of law designed to provide a mechanism for victims of accidents and injury to receive just compensation for their loss. Called the **tort system,** these laws create an incentive for firms and other parties to act responsibly in commerce. Because of the threat of being sued for their transgressions, firms are encouraged to prevent accidents and resulting economic damages.

Tort system
A body of law that provides a means for victims of accidents and injury to receive just compensation for their loss.

Like patents that are difficult and costly to enforce in the courts, the tort system can itself result in significant costs. For example, both sides to a legal dispute have almost unlimited ability to take sworn depositions from witnesses and seek documents in the pretrial "discovery" process. Since discovery must be provided without payment from the requesting party, there is no incentive to limit the size of any request. Requesting parties can and have used the discovery process to impose significant litigation costs on the other side, even in lawsuits that later prove frivolous. As a result, proposals have been made to place limits on the amount of free discovery that can be requested, set caps on the amount of punitive damages, foster proper use of expert testimony, and encourage other means of dispute resolution.

Subsidy Policy

Subsidy policy
Government grants that benefit firms and individuals.

Government also responds to positive externalities by providing subsidies to private business firms. **Subsidy policy** can be indirect, like government construction and highway maintenance grants that benefit the trucking industry. They can also take the form of direct payments, such as agricultural payment-in-kind (PIK) programs, special tax treatments, and government-provided low-cost financing.

Tax credits on business investment and depletion allowances on natural resource development are examples of tax subsidies that government sometimes gives in recognition of social benefits such as job creation, energy independence, and so on. Positive externalities associated with industrial parks induce government to provide local tax incremental or industrial revenue bond financing for

Pollution emission allowances

A controversial form of government subsidy that gives firms the property right to pollute and then sell that right to others.

Tax Policy

Tax policy

Fines and penalties that limit undesirable performance.

such facilities. This low-cost financing is thought to provide some compensation for the external benefits of economic development.

Pollution emission allowances are a new and controversial form of government subsidy; they are pollution licenses granted by the government to firms and other individuals. When firms and consumers pollute the environment, some of the costs of production or consumption are shifted onto third parties. Rather than spend millions of dollars on new equipment, raw materials, or production methods to meet pollution abatement regulations, firms sometimes purchase emission allowances from other companies. Therefore, pollution emission allowances are a valuable commodity that can be worth millions of dollars. Opponents of the pollution emission allowance system argue that they infringe on the public's right to a clean and safe environment. Proponents contend that the costs of pollution abatement become prohibitive as emissions are reduced toward zero, thus making some trade-offs inevitable. Moreover, they argue that an allowance trading system does not confer new licenses to pollute; it merely transfers licenses from one polluter to another. Nevertheless, by awarding pollution emission allowances worth millions of dollars to the worst offenders of a clean environment, environmentally sensitive firms and consumers have been hurt, at least on a relative basis.

Whereas subsidy policy gives firms positive incentives for desirable performance, **tax policy** contains penalties, or negative subsidies, designed to limit undesirable performance. Tax policy includes both regular tax payments and fines or penalties that may be assessed intermittently.

Local, state, or federal fines for exceeding specified weight limits on trucks, pollution taxes, and effluent charges are common examples of tax policies intended to limit negative externalities by shifting external costs of production back to firms and their customers. Determining an appropriate tax level is extremely difficult because of problems associated with estimating the magnitude of negative externalities. For example, calculating some of the social costs of air pollution, such as more frequent house painting, is relatively straightforward. Calculating the costs of increased discomfort—even death—for, say, emphysema patients is less so. Nevertheless, regulators must consider the full range of consequences of negative externalities to create appropriate and effective incentives for pollution control.

Although tax policy may appear simply to mirror subsidy and property rights grant policies, an important distinction should not be overlooked. If society wants to limit the harmful consequences of air pollution, either subsidies for pollution reduction or taxes on pollution can provide effective incentives. Implied property rights are, however, considerably different under the two approaches. The subsidy mechanism implies a firm's right to pollute, because society pays to reduce pollution. In contrast, a system of pollution tax penalties asserts society's right to a clean environment. Firms must reimburse society for the damage caused by their pollution. The difference is a distinction about who owns the environment. Many prefer tax policy as a method for pollution reduction on the grounds that it explicitly recognizes the public's right to a clean and safe environment.

Operating Controls

Operating controls
Regulation by
government directive.

Operating control regulation, or control by government directive, is an important and growing form of regulation. **Operating controls** are standards that limit undesirable behavior by prohibiting certain actions while compelling others. Operating control regulation that achieves 100 percent compliance creates a situation similar to that reached under a prohibitive tax policy. In each instance, the undesirable activity in question is completely eliminated, and no tax revenues are collected. When operating controls result in less than full compliance, operating control regulation becomes much like tax policy because fines and levies increase the costs to violators.

What kinds of operating controls are imposed on business firms? Controls over environmental pollution immediately come to mind, but businesses are also subject to many other kinds of constraints. Federal legislation limits automobile emissions and sets fuel efficiency and safety standards; firms handling foods, drugs, and other controlled substances are constrained under the Pure Food and Drug Act. Working conditions are governed under labor laws and health regulations, including provisions related to noise levels, noxious gases and chemicals, and safety standards. Antidiscrimination laws designed to protect minority groups and women can cause firms to modify their hiring and promotion policies. Wage and price controls, imposed during times of rapid inflation, restrict pricing practices and production decisions.

Like property rights regulation, the effectiveness of operating control regulations is often limited by vague or imprecise statutory specifications. If sanctions against violators are poorly defined or overly lenient, incentives for compliance can be weak. Beyond the difficulties created by poorly defined regulations and sanctions, problems can also result if conflicting operating controls are imposed. For example, mandatory safety standards and pollution controls have increased passenger car costs by several hundred dollars per unit. Such expenses are an obvious direct cost of meeting auto safety and pollution regulations, but other less obvious indirect costs are also incurred. Auto safety and pollution standards have the effect of reducing fuel efficiency and thus make more serious the U.S. dependence on imported oil.

Perhaps the clearest difference between operating control regulation and regulation via tax or subsidy policies is the reliance on nonmonetary incentives for compliance. There are no easy alternatives to operating control regulation in instances in which social costs are prohibitively great (e.g., nuclear disaster, groundwater contamination, and so on) or difficult, if not impossible, to measure (e.g., public health, worker death, or serious injury). In some instances, however, operating control regulations can cause firms to direct their efforts toward being exempted from regulation rather than toward reducing the negative externalities of concern to society. It is not clear that operating controls are more or less effective than tax and subsidy policies in ensuring that the results of regulatory efforts are both effective and equitable. Each approach has its place.

WHO PAYS THE COSTS OF REGULATION?

Among its many benefits, the legal system provides a mechanism for resolving disputes and establishes the ground rules for market transactions. This process is not without its expense, however. The regulatory system can retard economic growth if dispute resolution is slow, costs of litigation are high, and the outcomes of legal proceedings are risky. Socially beneficial regulatory reform, and reform of the legal system in particular, involves creating a set of rules that provides the basis for a fair and efficient settlement of disputes.

The question of who pays the costs of regulation designed to mitigate incentive failures is an important one. Although the point of tax collection, or the **tax incidence,** of pollution charges may be a heavily polluting foundry, the economic cost of pollution taxes, or the **tax burden,** may be passed on to customers or suppliers. The question of who pays for specific regulations can seldom be determined merely by identifying the fined, taxed, or otherwise regulated party.

Tax incidence
Point of tax collection.

Tax burden
Economic cost of tax.

Demand and Supply Effects

In general, who pays for operating control regulation depends on the elasticity of demand for the final products of affected firms. Figure 15.1 illustrates this issue by considering the theoretically polar extremes of perfectly elastic demand for final products, Figure 15.1(a), and perfectly inelastic demand for final products, Figure 15.1(b). Identically upward-sloping *MC* curves are assumed in each instance. Here, as is often the case, regulation is assumed to increase marginal costs by a fixed amount per unit. This amount, *t,* can reflect pollution taxes per unit of output or regulation-induced cost increases.

Figure 15.1(a) shows that good substitutes for a firm's product and highly elastic demand prevent producers from passing taxes or regulation-induced cost increases on to customers. As a result, producers (including investors, employees, and suppliers) are forced to bear the burden of regulatory costs, at least in the short run. In these instances, falling industry rates of return on invested capital and high rates of industry unemployment are symptomatic of regulatory influences.

Figure 15.1(b) shows the effect of regulation-induced cost or tax increases in the case of perfectly inelastic final-product demand. Without effective substitute products, producers can pass the burden of regulation on to customers. In contrast to the case of perfectly elastic demand, producers may encounter relatively few disadvantages because of regulation-induced cost increases.

Although the preceding analysis is greatly simplified, it points out that taxes or regulation-induced cost increases have widely differing effects on industries if demand relationships vary. Similarly, the effect of regulation on industries with similar product-demand elasticities varies to the extent that supply characteristics differ. For example, in industries in which marginal costs per unit are constant, per-unit taxes will increase output prices by an amount greater than in the case of rising marginal costs but by less than in the instance of falling marginal costs.

A Regulation Cost Sharing Example

▶

To illustrate the effects of regulation-induced cost or tax increases, consider the possible effects on consumers and producers of a new regulation prohibiting herbicide usage in corn production, perhaps because of fears about groundwater contamination. Assume that the industry is perfectly competitive, so the market price of $3 represents both average and marginal revenue per bushel

FIGURE 15.1   **Regulatory Burden Allocation under Elastic and Inelastic Demand**

(a) Highly elastic product demand places the burden of regulation-induced cost increases on producers, who must cut production from Q_1 to Q_2. (b) Low elasticity of product demand allows producers to raise prices from P_1 to P_2, and consumers bear the burden of regulation-induced cost increases.

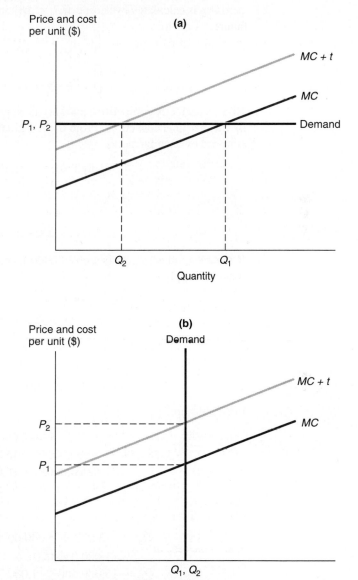

($P = MR = \$3$). The marginal cost relation for each farmer, before any new regulations are imposed, is

$$MC = dTC/dQ = \$0.6 + \$0.04Q,$$

where Q is bushels of corn (in thousands). The optimal level of corn production per farm is calculated by setting $MR = MC$ and solving for Q:

$$MR = MC$$
$$\$3 = \$0.6 + \$0.04Q$$
$$\$0.04Q = \$2.4$$
$$Q = 60(000) \text{ or } 60,000 \text{ bushels.}$$

Given a perfectly competitive market, the supply curve for each producer is given by the marginal cost curve. From the marginal cost relation, the quantity of corn supplied by each farmer is

$$\text{Supply Price} = \text{Marginal Cost}$$
$$P = \$0.6 + \$0.04Q,$$

or

$$Q = -15 + 25P.$$

If the corn industry consists of 200,000 farmers with farms of equal size, total industry supply is

$$Q_S = 200,000(-15 + 25P)$$
$$= -3,000,000 + 5,000,000P. \qquad \text{(Supply)}$$

To complete the industry profile prior to the new regulation on herbicides, assume that industry demand is given by the relation

$$Q_D = 15,000,000 - 1,000,000P. \qquad \text{(Demand)}$$

In equilibrium,

$$Q_S = Q_D$$
$$-3,000,000 + 5,000,000P = 15,000,000 - 1,000,000P$$
$$6,000,000P = 18,000,000$$
$$P = \$3 \text{ per bushel,}$$

and

$$Q_S = -3,000 + 5,000,000(3)$$
$$= 12,000,000(000), \text{ or } 12 \text{ billion bushels.}$$
$$Q_D = 15,000,000 - 1,000,000(3)$$
$$= 12,000,000(000), \text{ or } 12 \text{ billion bushels.}$$

Now assume that reducing herbicide usage increases the amount of tillage needed to keep weed growth controlled and causes the yield per acre to drop, resulting in a 25 percent increase in the marginal costs of corn production. For individual farmers, the effect on marginal costs is reflected as

$$MC' = 1.25(\$0.6 + \$0.04Q)$$
$$= \$0.75 + \$0.05Q.$$

If only a few farmers in a narrow region of the country are subject to the new regulation, as would be true in the case of state or local pollution regulations, then market prices would remain stable at \$3, and affected farmers would curtail production dramatically to 45,000 bushels each, because

$$MR = MC'$$
$$\$3 = \$0.75 + \$0.05Q$$
$$\$0.05Q = \$2.25$$
$$Q = 45(000), \text{ or } 45,000 \text{ bushels.}$$

Given a perfectly competitive industry and, therefore, a perfectly elastic demand for corn, local pollution regulations will force producers to bear the entire burden of regulation-induced cost increases.

A different situation arises when all producers are subject to the new herbicide regulation. In this instance, the revised individual-firm supply curve is

$$\text{Supply Price} = \text{Marginal Cost}$$
$$P = \$0.75 + \$0.05Q,$$

or

$$Q = -15 + 20P.$$

Total industry supply, assuming that all 200,000 farmers remain in business (something that may not happen if the resulting changes in profit levels are substantial), equals

$$Q'_S = 200,000(-15 + 20P)$$
$$= -3,000,000 + 4,000,000P. \qquad \text{(New Supply)}$$

The equilibrium industry price/output combination is found where

$$Q'_S = Q_D$$
$$-3,000,000 + 4,000,000P = 15,000,000 - 1,000,000P$$
$$5,000,000P = 18,000,000$$
$$P = \$3.60 \text{ per bushel,}$$

and

$$Q'_S = -3,000,000 + 4,000,000(3.60)$$
$$= 11,400,000(000), \text{ or } 11.4 \text{ billion bushels.}$$
$$Q_D = 15,000,000 - 1,000,000(3.60)$$
$$= 11,400,000(000), \text{ or } 11.4 \text{ billion bushels.}$$

At the new market price, each individual farm produces 57,000 bushels of corn:

$$Q = -15 + 20(3.60)$$
$$= 57(000), \text{ or } 57,000 \text{ bushels.}$$

●

MANAGERIAL APPLICATION 15.2
The FTC and FDA Carry Big Sticks

At the corner of Sixth Street and Pennsylvania Avenue in Washington, D.C., on the building that houses the Federal Trade Commission (FTC), stand a pair of statues entitled "Man Controlling Trade." Completed in 1941 by WPA instructor Michael Lantz, these pieces of government art depict a muscled fellow trying to break a wild horse. He has a rope around the beast's neck, and both sides have straining muscles, but it's clear that before long the horse's energy will be spent. The half-clothed hero of this statuary is a federal bureaucrat, while the dangerous steed represents the unbridled forces of the free market. (Wags have noted that the horse is standing on the bureaucrat's foot.)

Several federal agencies were nearly tamed during the Reagan administration, but "Man Controlling Trade" aptly describes the spirit pervading the FTC under the leadership of Chairwoman Janet Steiger, who was appointed by President Bush in 1989. FTC officials make clear they have no plans to return to the go-go activism of the late 1970s. But a surge in antitrust and consumer-protection enforcement actions under Steiger is sending a message to business that the no-go stance of the past decade is over. Steiger vows to "keep moving along, bringing more cases." Future targets for charges of deceptive advertising, according to FTC officials, include some healthcare ads, such as those for diets and cosmetic surgery; telemarketing fraud; ads aimed at children; and ads about nutritional value. The FTC also plans to hold hearings on whether there should be federal rules on environmental claims in advertising. The agency and several state attorneys general are investigating claims made by some plastics manufacturers that their products are degradable and therefore better for the environment. Targets for possible antitrust actions include manufacturers that force retailers to participate in "cooperative advertising" programs. Such programs, common among auto manufacturers, typically include a minimum price set by the supplier.

Equally active at the federal Food and Drug Administration (FDA) is Commissioner David A. Kessler. To restore public confidence in the agency, the FDA commissioner has prescribed a regimen of regulatory activity that is already getting the food industry's attention. In 1991, the FDA exercised power it hadn't used since 1978, taking major food company Procter & Gamble to court for making misleading freshness claims for its processed orange juice. The agency also took action against the no-cholesterol claims of vegetable oil manufacturers for products that, though lacking cholesterol, are loaded with fat. In the offing are more Kessler-inspired no-cholesterol cases against manufacturers of margarine, salad dressing, snack food, mayonnaise, and peanut butter. Says a spokesman for the Grocery Manufacturers Association: "He has our attention."

Kessler is a Harvard-trained pediatrician and University of Chicago law graduate who promises to jolt the prescription drug industry with a series of enforcement actions. An American Medical Association journal article he coauthored in 1990 was very critical of drug advertising and promotional practices. One likely upshot is that major pharmaceutical companies will be challenged for promoting unapproved uses for cancer-fighting drugs.

Some argue that both the FTC and the FDA, to fully regain credibility, need more money, more staff, and more enforcement powers. Critics contend that these agencies are charged with maintaining rules of commercial competition that are notoriously vague and encourage bureaucrats to claim broad authority to pry into already competitive markets. They argue that while it is far from clear that President Bush means to reregulate, absent strong directives to the contrary from the White House, both the FTC and the FDA tend to embrace the notion that the more controls and restraints, the better.

As always, the great unanswered question about FTC and FDA activity remains: How much good and how much harm do the agencies do? Measuring the latter must include the higher costs that businesses tend to pass along to consumers to comply with FTC and FDA edicts.

Source: Paul M. Barrett and Jeanne Saddler, "Under Steiger, FTC has Ended 'No-Go' Stance," *Wall Street Journal,* May 16, 1991, B1, B7; and Maggie Mahar, "Under a Microscope but FDA Chief David Kessler Keeps His Cool," *Barron's,* March 2, 1992, 12–15.

Thus, industrywide regulation of herbicides has a relatively smaller effect on producers because the effects of regulation are partially borne by consumers through the price increase from $3 to $3.60 per bushel. This example illustrates why state and local authorities find it difficult to regulate firms, such as farms, that operate in highly competitive national or worldwide markets. Such regulations usually are initiated at the national level.

Efficient Regulation

Regulations that affect the marginal costs of production typically have some combination of adverse price and output effects for producers and consumers. Realizing this, some policymakers have promoted taxes or regulations with fixed or "lump sum" charges for producers. Any tax that increases fixed costs affects neither price nor output levels for profit-maximizing firms in the short run. The idea is to promote a form of taxation that cannot be shifted forward onto consumers or backward onto employees or suppliers. Even this approach to regulation is far from painless, however, since heavily regulated producers may be compelled to leave the industry in the long run, should profitability be forced below the cost of capital.

As a result, both per unit and lump sum taxes used to pay the costs of economic regulation tend to have important economic consequences. This is not to suggest that even costly regulation cannot sometimes be justified. It simply means that all forms of regulation have costs that must be paid. To be efficient, these costs must be weighed carefully and justified by the benefits of regulation.

Efficient regulation of the market economy depends upon a balancing of all regulatory costs with the resulting benefits to society in general. While the intentions of many regulations are admirable, they can have unintended adverse impacts on firms and the general public. Obvious administrative costs plus hidden costs to consumers and industry must both be justified by the benefits provided. Deregulation is appropriate in markets that are or can be vigorously competitive; regulatory changes are fitting when they allow markets to function more efficiently and better serve consumers. From an efficiency perspective, regulation is only desirable when there can be a strong presumption that the net benefits to society are positive.

REGULATORY RESPONSE TO STRUCTURAL FAILURES

Chapters 12 and 13 illustrate that monopoly or oligopoly in an industry can result in too little output and in economic profits. Regulation intended to reduce or eliminate the socially harmful consequences of such structural failures can seek to control preexisting monopoly power or to prevent its emergence. Public utility regulation, which controls the prices and profits of established monopolies, is an important example of the effort to enjoy the benefits of low-cost production by large firms while avoiding the social costs of unregulated monopoly. Tax and antitrust policies also address the problem of structural failures by limiting not only the abuse of monopoly but also its growth.

FIGURE 15.2   **Price/Output Decision under Monopoly**

Without regulation, monopolies would charge excessively high prices and produce too little output.

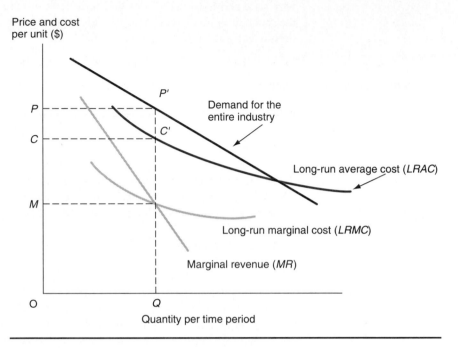

The Dilemma of Natural Monopoly

In some industries, the average costs of production continue to decline as output expands. A single large firm can produce total industry output more efficiently than any group of smaller producers. Demand equals supply at a point where the long-run average cost curve for a single firm is still declining. The term *natural monopoly* describes this situation, because monopoly naturally results from the superior efficiency of a single large producer.

For example, consider Figure 15.2. Here the firm will produce Q units of output at an average cost of C per unit. Note that this cost level is above the minimum point on the long-run average cost curve, and average costs are still declining. As a monopolist, the firm can earn an economic profit equal to the rectangle $PP'C'C$, or $Q(P - C)$. Local electric, gas, and water companies are classic examples of natural monopolies, since the duplication of production and distribution facilities would greatly increase costs if more than one firm served a given area.

This situation presents something of a dilemma. Economic efficiency could be enhanced by restricting the number of producers to a single firm. However, this entails certain risks, since monopolists tend to earn economic profits or incur unnecessary costs and also tend to underproduce. Recall that economic profits are profits so large that the firm earns an above-normal risk-adjusted rate of return on invested capital. Such profits are useful both for allocating resources and as an incentive for efficiency, but it is difficult to justify above-normal profits derived from market power rather than from exceptional performance.

Underproduction occurs when the firm curtails production to a level at which the marginal value of resources needed to produce an additional unit of output (marginal cost) is less than the benefit derived from the additional unit, as measured by the price that consumers are willing to pay for it. In other words, at output levels just greater than Q in Figure 15.2, consumers are willing to pay approximately P dollars per unit, so the value of additional units is P. However, the marginal cost of producing an additional unit is slightly less than M dollars and well below P, so cost does not equal value. Accordingly, society finds an expansion of output desirable.

Besides earning economic profits and withholding production, an unregulated natural monopolist could be susceptible to operating inefficiency. In competitive markets, firms must operate efficiently to remain in business. A natural monopoly feels no pressure for cost efficiency from established competitors. This means that the market power of the natural monopolist permits some inefficiency and waste. Even though excessive amounts of operating inefficiency attract new competitors, substantial losses in economic efficiency can persist for extended periods in the case of natural monopoly.

A real dilemma is posed because monopoly has the potential for greatest efficiency but unregulated monopoly can lead to economic profits, underproduction, and resource waste. One possible solution is to allow natural monopoly to persist but to impose price and profit regulations.

Utility Price and Profit Regulations

The most common method of monopoly regulation is price and profit controls. Such regulations typically result in larger output quantities than would be the case with unrestricted monopoly, reduced dollar profit, and a lower rate of return on investment. This situation is illustrated in Figure 15.3. A monopolist operating without regulation would produce Q_1 units of output and charge a price of P_1. If regulators set a ceiling on prices at P_2, the firm's effective demand curve becomes the kinked curve P_2AD. Since price is a constant from 0 to Q_2 units of output, marginal revenue equals price in this range; that is, P_2A is the marginal revenue curve over the output range $0Q_2$. For output beyond Q_2, marginal revenue is given by the original marginal revenue function. The marginal revenue curve is now discontinuous at Output Q_2, with a gap between Points A and L. This regulated firm maximizes profits by operating at Output Q_2 and charging the ceiling price, P_2. Marginal revenue is greater than marginal cost up to that output but is less than marginal cost beyond it.

Profits are also reduced by this regulatory action. Without price regulation, price P_1 is charged, a cost of C_1 per unit is incurred, and Output Q_1 is produced. Profit is $(P_1 - C_1) \times (Q_1)$, which equals the area P_1BFC_1. With price regulation, the price is P_2, the cost is C_2, Q_2 units are sold, and profits are represented by the smaller area P_2AEC_2.

To determine a fair price, the regulatory commission must estimate a fair or normal rate of return, given the risk inherent in the enterprise. The commission then approves prices that produce the target rate of return on the required level of investment. In the case illustrated by Figure 15.3, if the profit at Price P_2, when divided by the investment required to produce Q_2, were to produce more than the

FIGURE 15.3   **Monopoly Price Regulation: Optimal Price/Output Decision Making**

Monopoly regulation imposes a price ceiling at P_2 just sufficient to provide a fair return (area P_2AEC_2) on investment. Under regulation, price falls from P_1 to P_2 and output expands from Q_1 to Q_2.

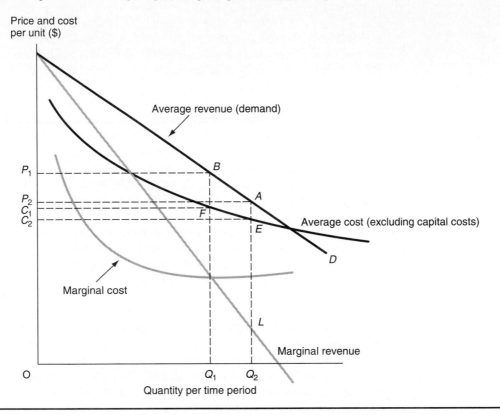

target rate of return, price would be reduced until actual and target rates of return became equal. This assumes, of course, that cost curves in Figure 15.3 do not include equity capital costs. The profit that the regulator allows is business profit, not economic profit.

A Utility Price and Profit Regulation Example

To further illustrate the concept of public utility regulation, consider the case of the Malibu Beach Telephone Company, a small telephone utility serving urban customers in southern California. At issue is the monthly rate for local telephone service, or basic hookup. The monthly demand for service is given by the relation

$$P = \$22.50 - \$0.00004Q,$$

where P is service price in dollars and Q is the number of customers served. Annual total cost and marginal cost curves, excluding a normal rate of return, are given by the following expressions:

$$TC = \$3,750,000 + \$70Q + 0.00002Q^2,$$
$$MC = dTC/dQ = \$70 + \$0.00004Q,$$

where cost is expressed in dollars.

To find the profit-maximizing level of output, demand and marginal revenue curves for annual service must be derived. This will give all revenue and cost relations a common annual basis. The demand curve for annual service is 12 times monthly demand:

$$P = 12(\$22.5 - \$0.00004Q)$$
$$= \$270 - \$0.00048Q.$$

Total and marginal revenue curves for this annual demand curve are

$$TR = \$270Q - \$0.00048Q^2,$$
$$MR = dTR/dQ = \$270 - \$0.00096Q.$$

The profit-maximizing level of output is found by setting $MC = MR$ (where $M\pi = 0$) and solving for Q:

$$MC = MR,$$
$$\$70 + \$0.00004Q = \$270 - \$0.00096Q,$$
$$\$0.001Q = \$200,$$
$$Q = 200,000.$$

The monthly service price is

$$P = \$22.50 - \$0.00004(200,000)$$
$$= \$14.50 \text{ per month (or } \$174 \text{ per year).}$$

This price/output combination generates annual total profits of

$$\pi = \$270Q - \$0.00048Q^2 - \$3,750,000 - \$70Q - \$0.00002Q^2$$
$$= -\$0.0005Q^2 + \$200Q - \$3,750,000$$
$$= -\$0.0005(200,000^2) + \$200(200,000) - \$3,750,000$$
$$= \$16,250,000.$$

If the company has \$125 million invested in plant and equipment, the annual rate of return on investment is

$$\text{Return on Investment} = \frac{\$16,250,000}{\$125,000,000} = 0.13, \text{ or } 13 \text{ percent.}$$

Now assume that the State Public Utility Commission decides that a 12 percent return is fair given the level of risk taken and conditions in the financial markets. With a 12 percent return on total assets, Malibu Beach would earn business profits of

$$\pi = \text{Allowed Return} \times \text{Total Assets}$$
$$= 0.12 \times \$125,000,000$$
$$= \$15,000,000.$$

To determine the level of output that would generate this level of total profits, total profit must be set equal to $15 million:

$$\pi = TR - TC$$
$$\$15,000,000 = -\$0.0005Q^2 + \$200Q - \$3,750,000.$$

This implies that

$$-\$0.0005^2 + \$200Q - \$18,750,000 = 0,$$

which is a function of the form $aQ^2 + bQ - c = 0$. Solving for the roots of this equation provides the target output level. We use the quadratic equation as follows:

$$
\begin{aligned}
Q &= \frac{-b \pm \sqrt{b^2 - 4ac}}{2a} \\
&= \frac{-200 \pm \sqrt{200^2 - 4(-0.0005)(18,750,000)}}{2(-0.0005)} \\
&= \frac{-200 \pm \sqrt{2,500}}{-0.001} \\
&= 150,000 \text{ or } 250,000.
\end{aligned}
$$

Because public utility commissions generally want utilities to provide service to the greatest possible number of customers at the lowest possible price, the upper figure $Q = 250,000$ is the appropriate output level. To induce Malibu Beach Telephone to operate at this output level, regulatory authorities would determine the maximum allowable price for monthly service as

$$P = \$22.50 - \$0.00004(250,000)$$
$$= \$12.50.$$

This $12.50-per-month price provides service to the broadest customer base possible, given the need to provide Malibu Beach with the opportunity to earn a 12 percent rate of return on investment.

Problems with Utility Price and Profit Regulation

Although the concept of utility price and profit regulation is simple, several practical problems arise in the regulation of public utilities. In practice it is impossible to exactly determine cost and demand schedules, or the minimum investment required to support a given level of output. Moreover, since utilities serve several classes of customers, many different rate schedules could produce the desired profit level. If profits for the local electric power company are too low, should rates be raised for summer (peak) or for winter (off-peak) users? Should industrial, commercial, or residential customers bear the burden of higher rates equally or unequally? These questions have no easy economic answer.

Further problems with utility regulation are involved because regulators make mistakes with regard to the optimal level and growth of service. For example, if a local telephone utility is permitted to charge excessive rates, system expansion will grow at a faster-than-optimal rate. Similarly, when the allowed rate of return exceeds the cost of capital, electric, gas, and water utilities have an incentive to

FIGURE 15.4 **Efficient and Inefficient Utility Companies**

Inefficient utilities harm consumers through higher prices, P_2 versus P_1, and lower output, Q_2 versus Q_1. (Here, AC_1 and AC_2 do not include equity capital costs.)

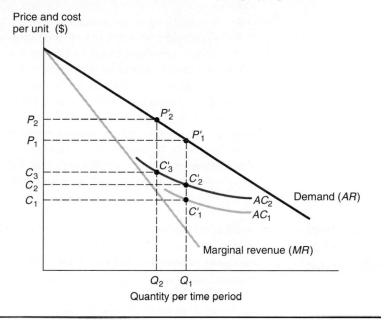

overexpand fixed assets and shift to overly capital-intensive methods of production. In contrast, if prices allowed to natural gas producers are too low, consumers will be encouraged to deplete scarce gas supplies, producers will limit exploration and development, and gas shortages can occur. If gas prices are too low and offer only a below-market rate of return on capital, necessary expansion will be thwarted.

Regulatory lag

The delay between when a change in regulation is appropriate and the date it becomes effective.

A related problem is that of **regulatory lag,** or the delay between when a change in regulation is appropriate and the date it becomes effective. During the 1970s and 1980s, inflation exerted constant upward pressure on costs. At the same time, consumers and voters were able to reduce, delay, or even deny reasonable rate increases. This caused severe financial hardship for a number of utilities and their stockholders.

Traditional forms of regulation can also lead to inefficiency. If a utility is guaranteed a minimum return on investment, operating inefficiencies can be offset by higher prices. Consider the situation portrayed in Figure 15.4. A regulated utility faces the demand curve *AR* and the marginal revenue curve *MR*. If the utility operates at peak efficiency, the average cost curve AC_1 applies. At a regulated price, P_1, the quantity demanded is Q_1, cost per unit is C_1, and profits equal the rectangle $P_1P_1'C_1'C_1$. Assume that these profits are just sufficient to provide a reasonable return on invested capital.

Now suppose that another utility with less capable managers is operating under similar conditions. Because management is less efficient, the firm's cost curve is represented by AC_2. If price is set at P_1, the firm will still sell Q_1 units, but average cost equals C_2; profits equal only $P_1P_1'C_2'C_2$; and the company earns less than the required rate of return. Under regulation, the inefficient utility can request—and probably will receive—a rate increase to P_2. Here it can sell Q_2 units of output, incur an average cost of C_3 per unit, and earn profits of $P_2P_2'C_3'C_3$, resulting in a rate of return on investment approximately equal to that of the efficient company. Utility regulation sometimes has the unfortunate effect of reducing the free market profit incentive for efficiency.

Finally, the process of utility regulation itself is costly. Detailed demand and cost analyses are necessary to provide a reasonable basis for rate decisions. It is expensive to pay regulatory officials, full-time utility commission staffs, record-keeping costs, and the expense of processing rate cases. All of these expenses are ultimately borne by consumers. Although many economists can see no reasonable alternative to utility regulation for electric, gas, local telephone, and private water companies, the costs and inefficiency of such regulation is troubling to all.

Nonutility Price Controls and Windfall Profits Taxes

Price controls
Short-term limits on prices charged by nonutilities.

Windfall profits
Economic profits due to unwarranted good fortune.

Another method of monopoly regulation is through the use of short-term **price controls** and **windfall profits** taxes on nonutilities to limit perceived abuses of monopoly power. Windfall profits are above-normal returns that result from unexpected and unwarranted good fortune, as opposed to economic profits that result from superior operating efficiency, innovation, economies of scale, and so on. Windfall profit taxes have frequently been imposed during wartime to eliminate the excess profits earned by providers of critical goods and services. More recently, the federal government imposed price controls and windfall profits taxes on U.S. oil companies.

The intent of oil price controls and windfall profits taxes on the oil companies was to reduce the harm to consumers from the rapid increase in crude oil prices that took place during the 1970s. Unfortunately, oil price controls, begun in 1971 and abandoned during 1981, had the unintended effect of aggravating the effects of the two oil crises experienced during the 1970s. Spot shortages of gasoline erupted and long gasoline lines resulted. In contrast, during the 1990–1991 Persian Gulf crisis, a short-term spike in oil prices reflected the potential scarcity of oil created by Iraq's invasion of Kuwait. Higher prices encouraged consumers to conserve, thus avoiding the need for government allocation. Once the crisis passed, it became apparent that future supply disruptions were unlikely, and prices receded.

The most serious challenge to a successful windfall profits tax policy is the problem of correctly determining the magnitude of unwarranted profits. Prices, operating expenses, and investment policies of affected firms must be carefully scrutinized. Industry expertise is necessary to avoid potential abuses of a windfall profits tax policy. If firms perceive that a windfall profits tax is only temporary, they may incur unnecessary operating expenses or undertake unwarranted investments in anticipation of future benefits. For example, the railroad industry substantially rebuilt or replaced its right-of-way (track and related) investments during World War II. Although some reinvestment in plant and equipment was undoubtedly necessary to meet wartime demands for freight and passenger service, one can only speculate about how much investment was undertaken simply to avoid wartime windfall profits taxes. Railroad executives obviously preferred newer plant and equipment over increased tax payments. Quite different problems may result from the windfall taxes on oil company profits.

Beyond the obvious problem of defining the magnitude of windfall profits to be taxed, windfall profits taxes can increase the level of risk or uncertainty in doing business. If oil company executives perceive that profits from successful exploration activities will be taxed severely, the risk of obtaining a satisfactory return from the firm's entire drilling program could rise. Higher required profits and industry prices would naturally result. Following the collapse of worldwide oil prices in the late 1980s, it was interesting that many domestic oil companies, especially smaller operators, reported large after-tax losses, or even filed bankruptcy, while paying substantial windfall profits taxes. Legislative determination of economic profits can lag behind economic reality.

Small Company Tax Preferences

During recent years, the U.S. corporate income tax system has become relatively more favorable to small business. The stated rationale is quite broad. Growth in small business is seen as being consistent with democratic principles of self-determination and individual decision making. Small firms also form an important competitive fringe in many industries, exerting downward pressure on the prices and profits of leading firms. In addition, small firms are an important source of invention and innovation. To some extent, progressive taxes are considered to partially offset the relatively high costs that regulation and government reporting requirements impose on small business.

Whatever the rationale, it is clear that small business plays an important role in the U.S. economy. The extent to which tax and other regulatory preferences enhance the competitive positions of small firms is not fully known, but use of these preferences to ensure continued success of small business seems likely.

New Forms of Incentive Regulation

Incentive regulation

Rules that benefit firms and customers through enhanced efficiency.

State and federal regulators have begun to address the high cost and other problems of price and profit regulations through new methods of **incentive regulation,** or rules whereby both utilities and their customers benefit through enhanced efficiency. For example, a particular commission might believe that 12 percent is a reasonable rate of return on stockholders' equity, but it might allow efficient companies to earn up to 12.5 percent and penalize inefficient companies by holding them to returns of less than 12 percent. The problem with this approach is that each utility operates in a unique setting, so it is extremely difficult to make valid comparisons. One electric company might have a cost of 2¢ per kilowatt hour, and another in the same state might have a cost of 2.5¢. It is often very difficult to determine if the first company is more efficient than the second or if it merely benefits from cost advantages that result from differences in fuel type, plant size, labor costs, customer mix, and so on. Until recently, such difficulties have limited the explicit use of efficiency differentials in setting profit rates for local electric utilities.

However, federal regulators have begun incentive-based regulation for long-distance telephone service. Since January 1991, the FCC has adopted a "price cap" for the seven regional Baby Bells and other local telephone companies. By limiting prices rather than the rate of return that monopoly local phone companies can earn on long-distance calls, the FCC hopes to accelerate the Bell companies' efforts to reduce their work forces and streamline operations. Such price caps have worked well in the case of regulating industry-leader AT&T. Since 1990, long-distance price increases for AT&T have been regulated to the general rate of inflation as measured by the gross domestic product price index *minus* 3 percent per year. That adjustment represents an expected 2.5 percent annual productivity gain based on AT&T's past experience, plus a 0.5 percent "consumer dividend." This is an exciting innovation in regulation and holds great promise for benefiting both consumers and the stockholders of regulated companies.

ANTITRUST POLICY

In the late nineteenth century, a movement toward industrial consolidation developed in the United States. Industrial growth was rapid, and, because of economies of scale or unfair competitive practices, oligopolistic structures emerged in several important industries. In some instances, pricing decisions were made by industry leaders who recognized that they could attain higher profits through cooperation rather than competition. They formed voting trusts in which voting rights to the stocks of various firms in an industry were consolidated to achieve monopoly price/output solutions. The oil and tobacco trusts of the 1880s are well-known examples.

Although profitable, the trusts were socially unacceptable. Public indignation resulted in the 1890 passage of the Sherman Act, the first important U.S. antitrust statute. Other notable antitrust legislation includes the Clayton Act (1914), the Federal Trade Commission Act (1914), the Robinson-Patman Act (1936), and the Celler-Kefauver Act (1950). Each of these acts is designed to prevent anticompetitive actions, the effects of which are more likely to reduce competition than to lower costs by increasing operating efficiency. This section presents an overview of antitrust law and a brief chronology of major antitrust legislation.

Overview of Antitrust Law

Antitrust laws
Laws that promote competition and prevent monopoly.

Antitrust laws are legal statutes designed to promote competition and prevent unwarranted monopoly. These laws seek to improve economic efficiency by enhancing consumer sovereignty and the impartiality of resource allocation while limiting concentrations in both economic and political power.

There is no single antitrust statute in the United States. Rather, federal antitrust law is based on two important statutes, the Sherman Act and the Clayton Act, and their amendments. An important characteristic of these laws is that they broadly and somewhat vaguely ban, but never define, "restraints of trade," "monopolization," "unfair competition," and so on. By never precisely defining such key terms, the statutes left the courts to decide the specific legality or illegality of various business practices. Because of this, many principles in antitrust law rest on judicial interpretation. Individual court decisions, called case law, and statutory standards, called statutory law, must be consulted to assess the legality of business behavior.

Sherman Act

The Sherman Act of 1890 was the first federal antitrust legislation. It is brief and to the point. Section 1 forbade contracts, combinations, or conspiracies in restraint of trade, which were then offenses under common law. Section 2 forbade monopolies. Both sections could be enforced through civil court actions or by criminal proceedings, with the guilty liable to pay fines or serve jail sentences. In 1974, an amendment to the Sherman Act made violations felonies rather than misdemeanors. The act now provides for $1 million maximum fines against corporations and up to $100,000 in fines and three years' imprisonment for individuals. In addition to fines and prison sentences, firms and individuals violating the Sherman Act face the possibility of paying triple damages to injured parties who bring civil suits.

However, the Sherman Act is often characterized as being too vague. Even with landmark decisions against the tobacco, powder, and oil trusts, enforcement has been sporadic. On the one hand, businesspeople claim not to know what is legal; on the other, the Justice Department is sometimes criticized as being ignorant of monopoly-creating practices and failing to act in a timely fashion.

Despite its shortcomings, the Sherman Act remains one of the government's main weapons against anticompetitive behavior. In 1978 a federal judge imposed some of the stiffest penalties in U.S. antitrust history on eight firms and eleven of their officers when they were convicted of violating the Sherman Act. These convictions for price fixing in the electrical wiring devices industry resulted in fines totaling nearly $900,000 and jail terms for nine of the eleven officers charged.

Clayton Act

Congress passed two measures in 1914 to overcome weaknesses in the Sherman Act. The more important of these, the Clayton Act, addressed problems of mergers, interlocking directorates, price discrimination, and tying contracts. The other was the Federal Trade Commission Act, which outlawed unfair methods of competition in commerce and established the FTC, an agency intended to enforce the Clayton Act.

Section 2 of the Clayton Act prohibited sellers from discriminating in price among business customers, unless cost differentials in serving various customers justified the price differentials or lower prices were offered to meet the competition. As a primary goal, the act sought to prevent a strong regional or national firm from employing selective price cuts to drive weak local firms out of business. Once competitors in one market were eliminated, the national firm could then charge monopoly prices and use resulting excess profits to subsidize cutthroat competition in other areas. The Robinson-Patman Act, passed in 1936, amended the section of the Clayton Act dealing with price discrimination. It declared specific forms of price discrimination illegal, especially those related to chainstore purchasing practices.

Section 3 of the Clayton Act forbade tying contracts that reduce competition. A firm, particularly one with a patent on a vital process or a monopoly on a natural resource, could use licensing or other arrangements to restrict competition. One such method was the tying contract, whereby a firm tied the acquisition of one item to the purchase of another. For example, IBM once refused to sell its business machines. It only rented machines to customers and then required them to buy IBM punch cards, materials, and maintenance service. This had the effect of reducing competition in these related industries. The IBM lease agreement was declared illegal under the Clayton Act, and the company was forced to offer machines for sale and to separate leasing arrangements from agreements to purchase other IBM products.

Finally, although the Sherman Act prohibited voting trusts that lessened competition, interpretation of the act did not always prevent one corporation from acquiring the stock of competing firms and then merging these firms into itself. Section 7 of the Clayton Act prohibited such mergers if they were found to reduce competition. Either the antitrust division of the Justice Department or the FTC can bring suit under Section 7 to prevent mergers. If mergers have been consummated prior to the suit, divestiture can be ordered. The Clayton Act also prevents individuals from serving on the boards of directors of two competing companies. So-called competitors having common directors would obviously not compete very hard. Although the Clayton Act made it illegal for firms to merge through stock transactions when the effect is to lessen competition, the law left a loophole. A firm could purchase the assets of a competing firm, integrate the operations into its own, and thus reduce competition. The Celler-Kefauver Act closed this loophole, making asset acquisitions illegal when the effect of such purchases is to reduce competition. By a slight change in wording, it made clear Congress's intent to attack all mergers that threatened competition, whether vertical mergers between buyers and sellers, horizontal and market extension mergers between actual or potential competitors, or purely conglomerate mergers between entirely unrelated firms.

Antitrust Enforcement

Public enforcement of the antitrust laws is the dual responsibility of the antitrust division of the Department of Justice and the FTC. Generally speaking, the Justice Department concerns itself with significant or flagrant offenses under the Sherman Act, as well as with mergers for monopoly covered by Section 7 of the Clayton Act. In most instances, the Justice Department brings charges under the Clayton Act only when broader Sherman Act violations are also involved. In addition to policing law violations, the Sherman Act also assigns the Justice Department the duty of restraining possible future violations. Firms found to be in violation of the law often receive detailed federal court injunctions that regulate future business activity. Injunctive relief in the form of dissolution or divestiture decrees is a much more typical outcome of Justice Department suits than are criminal penalties.

Although the Justice Department can institute civil proceedings in addition to the criminal proceedings discussed previously, civil proceedings are typically the responsibility of the FTC. The FTC is an administrative agency of the executive branch that has quasi-judicial powers with which it enforces compliance with the Clayton Act. Because the substantive provisions of the Clayton Act do not create criminal offenses, the FTC has no criminal jurisdiction. The FTC holds hearings about suspected violations of the law and issues cease and desist orders if violations are found. Cease and desist orders under the Clayton Act are subject to review by appellate courts.

Economic Analysis
in Antitrust Actions

▶

Antitrust policy is applied if a specific business practice is thought to substantially lessen competition. Mergers are not illegal if they do not affect the vigor of competition. However, it is very difficult to accurately predict the competitive implications of a given merger. If two firms, each with 1 percent of a market served by 100 competitors, merge, few would argue that the merger reduces competition. After the merger, 99 firms remain, and the 1 percent market share advantage of the merged firm is not likely to be significant. However, merger of two firms that each had a substantial share of the market, leaving only a few firms after the merger, might affect competition. The problem lies in defining a "substantial" share of the market and quantifying a "few" remaining firms. Where should these lines be drawn? Furthermore, if a particular merger would not itself reduce competition but a series of similar mergers would do so, should the original merger be permitted? Assume that 20 firms, each with a 5 percent share of the market, are in competition. Suppose that two of these firms merge, and a judgment is made that competition suffers no harm. Approval of the merger might induce other firms to seek to merge, with the ultimate result being reduced competition. At what point should the trend toward concentration be stopped?

Market concentration is a key element in making judgments about the effect of a merger on competition, but drawing industry boundaries is often difficult. Suppose that two banks in lower Manhattan seek to merge. Over 10,000 banks operate in the United States, and the national banking concentration ratio is low. However, the entire United States is not a relevant market for most banking services; a local area is the relevant market. But what local area? Should metropolitan New York be deemed the market? The City of New York? The Borough of Manhattan? Lower Manhattan only? For certain classes of services, especially loans to major national corporations, the nation as a whole constitutes the appropriate market. For personal checking account and loan services, the local market area is much more relevant.

The problem is even more complex when competing products or industries are considered. A particular bank might, for example, be the only one serving a given neighborhood, but the bank might still face intense competition from savings and loan associations, credit unions, and money market mutual funds that offer service by mail and toll-free telephone numbers. Similar problems are found in other aspects of antitrust policy. Given the difficulties in estimating costs for multiproduct firms, determining the presence and magnitude of price discrimination becomes difficult. A comprehensive economic cost analysis is often required to detect price discrimination, and even then the issue is often less than clear-cut.

As these examples illustrate, antitrust policy is complex, and generalizations are difficult. Nevertheless, because antitrust policy constitutes a serious constraint to many business decisions, antitrust considerations are an important, if nebulous, aspect of managerial economics.

MANAGERIAL APPLICATION 15.3

The Tort Tax

How much does litigation cost the U.S. economy? *Forbes* estimated the tort system's direct costs at $80 billion a year in 1984. That figure includes lawyers' fees, payouts to claimants, and insurers' administrative costs. In October 1991, Joan Claybrook, president of Ralph Nader's Public Citizen group, told *Adam Smith's Money World* that the annual cost of torts is only $30 billion. Claybrook attributed this lower estimate to figures provided by Rand Corporation's respected Institute for Civil Justice and asserted that the *Forbes* figure had no statistical basis.

If anything, *Forbes*'s estimate of the true cost of the tort system may be understated. In a recent study, Hartford-based actuarial consulting firm Tillinghast, Inc., estimated that tort claims cost the country $117 billion during 1987, the most recent year for which figures are available. While the Rand study set out to measure only the costs directly related with state and federal lawsuits, the Tillinghast study took into account the costs of resolving potential lawsuits and the costs to insurers of processing claims and defending suits. It is ironic that James Kakalik, coauthor of the Rand study cited by Claybrook, says it is Tillinghast's $117 billion number, not Rand's $30 billion to $36 billion range, that represents the direct "tort tax" consumers end up paying.

Robert Sturgis, who wrote the latest Tillinghast study, notes that U.S. tort costs grew in line with the overall economy from 1933 until 1950. Since 1950, however, they have grown at a compound rate of 12 percent a year, much faster than the overall economy. Assuming that tort costs kept growing at 12 percent, the 1990 cost came to roughly $165 billion; by the end of the decade, they will total over $500 billion per year. With a U.S. population of roughly 250 million persons, the tort tax in 2000 will total over $2,000 per capita if present trends continue.

Where does the money go? One-quarter compensates the economic losses of plaintiffs; another quarter pays for plaintiffs' "pain and suffering." The other half goes to cover insurance administration costs, lawyer fees, and expenses for discovery and expert witnesses. Beyond these direct costs are the harder-to-measure in-

direct expenses that are involved. For example, a 1989 American Medical Association study estimated that for every $1 doctors spend on insurance premiums, they spend $2.70 performing unnecessary tests and beefing up record keeping to avoid litigation. By excluding premium costs of about $5 billion to $6 billion per year, the indirect tort tax related to medical malpractice liability alone may cost the economy $15 billion per year. How much of the nation's $738-billion-a-year healthcare bill can be blamed on the tort system? Hard numbers are difficult to come by, but a 1991 study of auto injury claims in Hawaii by the Insurance Research Council gives some indication. That study reports that medical treatment of a typical neck sprain from whiplash comes to about $1,300 if handled without a lawyer, on a no-fault basis. The cost to treat the same injury if part of a tort claim is roughly $8,000.

Safeguarding the right to sue for damages helps protect everyone from incompetent professionals, negligent manufacturers, and careless consumers. Unfortunately, the tort industry has grown so large that it is reducing the quality and availability of many goods and services. For example, toxic leak detectors, useful for handling poisonous substances, were designed in the mid-1970s but were kept off the market out of fear of potential liability. Very few technologically advanced single-engine and twin-engine planes are manufactured today because of potential liability to the manufacturer. Older and more dangerous aircraft stay in use longer than they otherwise would. Even the IRS is afraid to answer taxpayer questions in writing; they *believe* that the oral advice they give is accurate but are unwilling to back it up in writing.

To help reform the tort system and curb abuse, such areas as frivolous lawsuits, arbitrary punitive damages, and "junk science" in the courtroom have all been targeted. Among proposals being considered are a ban on contingency fees for expert witnesses, limits on punitive damages, and a requirement that losers pay the winners' court costs (as is the case in England). While there is plenty of room for cutting the tort tax, do taxpayers have the will?

Source: Leslie Spencer, "The Tort Tax," *Forbes*, February 17, 1992, 40–42.

PROBLEMS WITH REGULATION

For effective decision making, managers must be aware of both the causes and effects of regulatory processes. This chapter has briefly addressed this need by considering economic and social factors that stimulate regulatory responses to market failures caused by incentive or structural problems. Both positive and negative aspects of various regulatory methods are evident. At this point, it is useful to look closely at both the problems and the unfilled promise of economic regulation.

Costs of Regulation

Many economists like to quote the phrase, "There is no such thing as a free lunch." With respect to regulation, this means that every government program and policy has economic costs. The economic costs of regulatory policies are measured in terms of administrative burdens for regulatory agencies, deviations from optimal methods of production, and the misallocation of economic resources.

An obvious cost of regulation is the cost to local, state, and federal governments for supervisory agencies. Estimates for federal expenditures on business regulation have grown from roughly $3.5 billion per year in 1970 to more than $9.5 billion per year in the early 1990s (see Figure 15.5). Billions more are spent annually by local and state agencies. It is interesting that the largest regulatory budgets at the federal level are not those of traditional regulatory agencies, such as the Securities and Exchange Commission (SEC) or Interstate Commerce Commission (ICC), but are those devoted to the broader regulatory activities of the Department of Labor for employment and job safety standards and the Department of Agriculture for food inspection.

Although the direct costs of regulation are substantial, they may be far less than hidden or indirect costs. For example, the extensive reporting requirements of the Occupational Safety and Health Administration (OSHA) drive up administrative costs and product prices. Consumers also bear the cost of auto emission standards mandated by the Environmental Protection Agency (EPA). In the case of auto emissions, the National Academy of Sciences and the National Academy of Engineering estimate the annual benefits of the catalytic converter at only one-half the billions of dollars in annual costs. One might ask if the noneconomic, social advantages of this method of pollution control are sufficient to offset what appear to be significant economic disadvantages. Similarly, the economic and noneconomic benefits of regulation must be sufficient to offset considerable private costs for pollution control, OSHA-mandated noise reductions, health and safety equipment, FTC-mandated business reports, and so on.

Neither business nor the public can regard the economic costs of regulation as insignificant. For example, the EPA estimates that U.S. expenditures to reduce pollution alone totaled at least $115 billion in 1990. Estimates of the total direct and indirect costs of regulation run in excess of $150 billion per year, or more than $600 per year for each man, woman, and child in the United States. Given this magnitude, consideration of the total costs of regulation must play a prominent role in decisions about what and how to regulate. Where important concerns

FIGURE 15.5   **Administrative Costs of Federal Regulation**

The administrative costs of federal regulation have increased greatly since 1970.

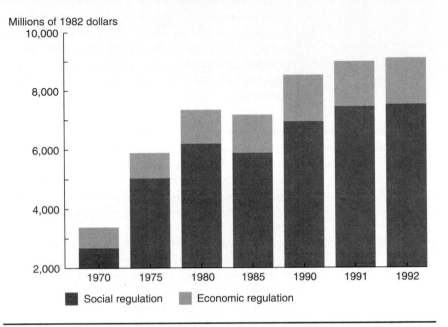

Note: 1991 and 1992 figures are projected.
Source: *Economic Report of the President* (Washington, D.C.: U.S. Government Printing Office, 1992), p. 172.

for the public's health and safety are apparent, business and government can accomplish much through cooperative effort. The public must also participate by supervising the regulatory process to ensure that government/business interactions yield policies in the public interest.

The Size-Efficiency Problem

Natural monopoly creates a dilemma because a single seller can achieve superior cost efficiency but may also restrict output, raise prices, and earn economic profits. This conflict between the superior efficiency of large firms and the harmful consequences of limited numbers of competitors is one of the oldest controversies in antitrust and regulation. Federal legislation proposed during recent years would limit mergers between firms of a certain size, say $100 million or more in annual sales. These proposals reflect the belief that such mergers increase monopoly power and have no offsetting advantages in terms of economic efficiency. However, research on the economic causes and consequences of mergers and other corporate restructuring indicates that underutilized resources are transferred by these means to more efficient uses. Unfriendly takeovers are especially unfriendly to inefficient management, which is subsequently replaced. Perhaps one of the greatest dangers to a blanket prohibition of all mergers involving large firms is that it could protect inefficient management, or management that is insensitive to stockholder interests.

Antitrust policy concerning the breakup of long-established firms is especially complex, as illustrated by the classic Justice Department case against IBM. Although it did not invent the electronic computer, IBM was one of the first companies to realize the enormous opportunities it presented. IBM's involvement with the computer transformed what was once a modestly successful business machines company into the dominant firm in a rapidly expanding industry. During the 1950s and 1960s, IBM became the leader in the mainframe equipment sector of the industry while playing a lesser role in peripherals and terminal equipment, software services, and other areas. Concerned with the potentially anticompetitive effects of IBM's market position, the antitrust divisions of the Justice Department filed suit in 1969 to break up the firm. The case foundered. No one could doubt that IBM was a large and highly profitable company, but the sources of its success were a matter of substantial dispute. Was IBM highly profitable merely because of its leadership position (monopoly power), or was IBM a highly profitable industry leader by virtue of its ability to offer innovative products at attractive prices (efficiency)? In the first case, breaking up IBM could lead to lower prices, eliminate monopoly profits, and increase consumer welfare. In the second case, breaking up IBM would penalize the type of efficiency that competitive markets are meant to encourage. Innovation and efficiency in the industry could be blunted. Determining the source of IBM's success and the costs and benefits from a possible breakup became a problem with no obvious answer. In 1982, after more than a decade of litigation costing both sides tens of millions of dollars, the Justice Department dismissed its suit. Free from antitrust concerns, IBM clearly became more aggressive in terms of pricing and new-product development during the 1980s, with obvious benefits for users of business and personal computers.

A second interesting example of antitrust policy in this area is the 1974 Justice Department suit to break up AT&T. The Department argued that breaking up AT&T would stimulate competition in the telephone equipment and long-distance sectors of the industry and provide consumers with improved goods and services at lower prices. To avoid the expense and uncertainty of a prolonged antitrust case, AT&T agreed to divest itself of its local phone companies. As of January 1, 1984, a "new" AT&T was created, consisting largely of AT&T communications (long-distance phone service), AT&T information systems (computer systems), AT&T international (foreign operations), Bell Labs (research and development), and Western Electric (telephone equipment). The seven local companies created were Ameritech, Bell Atlantic, Bell South, Nynex, Pacific Telesis, Southwestern Bell, and U S West. Whether this reorganization of the telecommunications industry, and AT&T's subsequent merger with computer-maker NCR, will lead to benefits for consumers remains to be seen. In the meantime, the enormous costs and risks involved make clear why such "experiments" are so rare.

The "Capture" Problem

It is a widely held belief that regulation is in the public interest and influences firm behavior toward socially desirable ends. However, this view is not held universally. In the early 1970s, Nobel laureate George Stigler introduced the

Capture theory
Economic hypothesis suggesting that regulation is sometimes sought to limit competition and obtain government subsidies.

capture theory of economic regulation. According to Stigler, the machinery and power of the state are a potential resource to every industry. With its power to prohibit or compel, to take or give money, the state can and does selectively help or hurt a vast number of industries. Because of this, regulation may be actively sought by industry. Stigler contends that regulation is typically *acquired* by industry and is designed and operated primarily for industry's benefit. Although some regulations are undeniably onerous, these are thought to be the exception rather than the rule.

Stigler asserts that the types of state favors commonly sought by regulated industries include direct money subsidies, control over entry by new rivals, control over substitutes and complements, and price fixing. Domestic "air-mail" subsidies, Federal Deposit Insurance Corporation (FDIC) regulation that reduces the rate of entry into commercial banking, suppression of margarine sales by butter producers, price fixing in motor carrier (trucking) regulation, and American Medical Association control of medical training and licensing can be interpreted as historical examples of regulatory process control by regulated industries.

In summarizing his views on regulation, Stigler suggests that the Interstate Commerce Commission should be criticized for its pro-industry policies no more than should the Great Atlantic and Pacific Tea Company (A&P) for selling groceries or politicians for seeking popular support. Current methods of enacting and carrying out regulations only make the pro-industry stance of regulatory bodies more likely. Stigler contends that the only way to get different results from regulation is to change the political process of regulator selection and to provide economic rewards to regulators who serve the public interest effectively.

Public interest theory
A view of regulation as a government-imposed means of private-market control.

Capture theory is in stark contrast to more traditional **public interest theory,** which sees regulation as a government-imposed means of private-market control. Rather than viewing regulation as a "good" to be obtained, controlled, and manipulated, public interest theory views regulation as a method for improving economic performance by limiting the harmful effects of market failure. Public interest theory is silent on the need to provide regulators with economic incentives to improve regulatory performance. Unlike capture theory, a traditional view has been that the public can trust regulators to make a good-faith effort to establish regulatory policy in the public interest.

To be sure, suggestions of a capture problem with economic regulation are debatable. The need to provide regulators with positive economic incentives to ensure regulation in the public interest is also highly controversial. Nevertheless, growing dissatisfaction with the costs and results of traditional approaches to government regulation led to the birth of a deregulation movement that continues in the 1990s.

THE DEREGULATION MOVEMENT

Deregulation
The reduction of government control of the free market.

Growing concern with the costs and problems of government regulation gave birth in the early 1970s to a **deregulation** movement that has grown to impressive dimensions. Although it is difficult to pinpoint a single catalyst for the movement, it is hard to overlook the role played by Stigler and other economists (notably,

Alfred E. Kahn) who illustrated that the regulatory process can sometimes harm rather than help consumer interests.

Major Steps toward Deregulation

Table 15.1 highlights some of the major steps taken toward deregulation since 1970. Although many industries have felt the effects of changing state and local regulation, changing federal regulation has been most pronounced in the financial, telecommunications, and transportation sectors. Since 1975, for example, it has been illegal for securities dealers to fix commission rates. This broke a 182-year tradition under which the New York Stock Exchange (NYSE) set minimum rates for each 100-share ("round lot") purchase. Until 1975, everyone charged the minimum rate approved by the NYSE. Purchase of 1,000 shares cost a commission of ten times the minimum, even though the overhead and work involved are roughly the same for small and large stock transactions. This system not only generated large profits for NYSE members, but it also covered the higher costs of inefficient firms. Following deregulation, commission rates tumbled, and, predictably, some of the least efficient brokerage firms merged or otherwise went out of business. Today, more than a decade later, commission rates (prices) have fallen by 50 percent or more, and the industry is noteworthy for its increasing productivity and variety of new product introductions. It is also worth mentioning that during the 1975–1982 period, the number of sales offices in the industry increased by 80 percent, total employment rose by two-thirds, and profits increased to $1.5 billion per year, more than ten times the 1974 level. All of this may lead observers to conclude that deregulation can benefit consumers without causing any lasting damage to industry. In fact, a leaner, more efficient industry may be one of the greatest benefits of deregulation.

Despite obvious successes following deregulation, the movement has its critics. When airline ticket prices reflect the cost of service, as they must without regulation, bargain fares are available on heavily traveled routes between major cities (e.g., New York to Los Angeles, Chicago to Miami), but relatively high fares result for lightly traveled routes (e.g., Pittsburgh to Buffalo, New York; Kansas City to Omaha). Similarly, deregulation in the telecommunications industry caused rates for long-distance telephone calls to fall but monthly charges for local service to rise. Deregulation in the intercity bus market brought many travelers lower prices but forced the Greyhound bus company to suffer a costly strike to convince workers that wage levels would have to be reduced. Inefficient firms, consumers who buy goods and services whose cost is partly subsidized by other customers, and workers who take home inflated wages all oppose the process of deregulation. Still, the net gains from deregulation are significant.

Is Deregulation Working?

Consumers benefit from deregulation as newly competitive and cost-conscious firms dramatically cut prices and increase product quality. Inevitably, some inefficient competitors are forced out of business. Although such losses are often viewed as the typical result of heightened competition, some concern has emerged that a loss of competitors in some previously regulated industries has the potential to stifle competition and lead to monopoly profits.

TABLE 15.1 **Recent Major Steps toward Deregulation**

1970	Federal Reserve Board frees interest rates on large bank deposits with short maturities ($100,000 or more for six months or less).
1971	Federal Communications Commission (FCC) allows companies to set up long-distance telephone networks and compete with AT&T by offering private-line services.
1975	Securities and Exchange Commission prohibits fixed commissions on stock and bond sales.
1978	Congress deregulates prices for airline passenger service.
1979	FCC allows AT&T to sell a limited range of unregulated services (e.g., data processing).
1980	Congress allows banks to pay interest on checking, increases competition for commercial loans.
1981	FCC allots airwave space for two cellular phone franchises in every city—one for the local telephone company and one for a competing provider.
1982	Congress allows savings and loans to make commercial loans and related investments.
1982	Congress deregulates prices for intercity passenger bus service.
1982	Department of Justice and Federal Trade Commission relax merger guidelines.
1984	Department of Justice order splitting off AT&T's seven operating subsidiaries becomes effective. Judge Harold Greene retains indefinite control of the "Baby Bells."
1986	Congress deregulates interest rates for passbook and statement savings accounts.
1990	FCC caps AT&T's long-distance rates and institutes limited profit-rate deregulation.
1991	FCC caps long-distance rates and institutes limited profit-rate deregulation for the Baby Bells.
1992	FCC eases caps on radio and TV station ownership.

In trucking, previously regulated shippers of less-than-truckload quantities of freight operate national networks of consolidation centers surrounded by satellite terminals that offer door-to-door delivery. These networks feature sophisticated computer dispatch systems that permit the companies to utilize available truck capacity efficiently. By eliminating empty backhauls, for example, the firms can dramatically cut fuel, labor, and equipment costs. Part of these cost savings pass on to customers; major companies use the rest to build their markets. Today, major trucking companies are raising their market share at the expense of smaller firms, which often find themselves unable to afford the investment necessary for efficient networking.

Similarly, major airlines have come to dominate traffic at several major airports by forming efficient "hub-and-spoke" networks. Northwest Airlines, for example, dominates the Minneapolis-St. Paul (MSP) International Airport "hub." Northwest fills its departures from the MSP airport with traffic generated by its own "spoke," or feeder, flights from smaller cities across the Midwest, along with traffic fed into the company's system by commuter airlines that have operating agreements with Northwest. This captive traffic enables Northwest to increase its load factor (capacity utilization rate) and profits while making successful entry into the MSP market difficult. Changes in the FCC's regulation of long-distance telephone service rates appear to have created a significant competitive advantage for AT&T. No longer able to get bargain rates on rental of AT&T's long-distance facilities, MCI and U.S. Sprint (AT&T's main competitors) have been forced to seek alternative means of offsetting the AT&T networking edge.

Distinguished economists such as Cornell's Alfred E. Kahn, former head of the Civil Aeronautics Board and an early proponent of deregulation, have voiced their concern. Kahn believes that recent mergers in previously regulated industries have raised concentration to the point where anticompetitive effects can be expected in some markets. Even the pro-merger Justice Department of the Reagan administration opposed the Department of Transportation's approval of Northwest Airlines' takeover of Republic Airlines. Others have been quick to point out that competition in transportation and communication markets can be vigorous even among only a few actual and potential competitors. In the Minneapolis-St. Paul market, for example, Continental and United Airlines have proved to be formidable competitors for Northwest in the long-distance flights to large cities. Similarly, intermodal competition from passenger automobiles and intercity bus systems limits Northwest's pricing discretion on local routes, for which it may be the only scheduled airline.

In evaluating the effects of deregulation, and in gauging the competitive implications of market exit by previously viable firms, it is important to remember that protecting competition is definitely not the same thing as protecting competitors. Without regulation, it is inevitable that some competitors will fall by the wayside and that concentration will rise in some markets. Although such trends must be watched closely for anticompetitive effects, they are sometimes the necessary characteristics of a vigorously competitive environment.

The Regulation versus Deregulation Controversy

Although some think that there is simply a question of regulation versus deregulation, this is seldom the case. On grounds of economic and political feasibility, it is often most fruitful to consider approaches to improving existing methods of regulation.

As suggested previously, an important problem with regulation is that regulators seldom have the information or expertise to specify, for example, the correct level of utility investment, the minimum transportation costs, or the optimum method of pollution control. Because technology changes rapidly in most regulated industries, only industry personnel working at the frontier of current technology have such specialized knowledge. One method for dealing with this technical expertise problem is to have regulators focus on the preferred outcomes of regulatory processes, rather than on the technical means that industry adopts to achieve those ends. The FCC's decision to adopt downward-adjusting price caps for long-distance rates is an example of this developing trend. If providers of long-distance telephone service are able to reduce costs faster than the FCC-mandated decline in prices, they will enjoy an increase in profitability. By setting price caps that fall over time, the FCC ensures that consumers share in expected cost savings while companies enjoy a positive incentive to innovate. This approach to regulation focuses on the *objectives* of regulation while allowing industry to meet those objectives in new and unique ways. Tying regulator rewards and regulated industry profits to objective, output-oriented performance criteria has the potential to create a desirable win/win situation for regulators, utilities, and the general public. For example, the public has a real interest in safe, reliable, and low-cost electric power. State and federal regulators who oversee the operations of utilities could develop objective standards for measuring utility safety, reliability, and cost efficiency. Tying firm profit rates to such performance-oriented criteria could stimulate real improvements in utility and regulator performance.

In sum, competitive forces provide a persistent and socially desirable constraining influence on firm behavior. When vigorous competition is absent, government regulation can be justified through both efficiency and equity criteria. When regulation is warranted, business, government, and the public must work together to ensure that regulatory processes represent not only large or special interests but also those with individually small but collectively large stakes in regulatory decisions.

REGULATORY REFORM FOR THE 1990s

Regulatory reform
Improvement in government control to enhance efficiency and fairness.

Although natural gas is a relatively clean-burning fuel with abundant domestic supply, total U.S. consumption of natural gas declined precipitously from the mid-1970s to the early 1990s. One important barrier to increased gas use is the restrictive process employed to grant permits for new natural gas pipelines. Given the resultant significant environmental costs entailed, some ongoing reform of natural gas regulation is inevitable. Similarly, the unnecessary costs of other forms of regulation dictate that **regulatory reform** is likely to remain a significant social concern throughout the 1990s.

Promoting Competition in Electric Power Generation

The electric power industry comprises three different components: the generation of electric power, the transmission of electric power from generators to local utilities, and the distribution of electricity by local utilities to commercial and residential customers. All three segments of the industry are currently subject to some state and federal regulation. Competition has generally been regarded as unlikely in the transmission and local distribution of electricity given their natural monopoly characteristics. However, competition has emerged in the wholesale generation of electric power, and regulators now face the question of how to foster and encourage such competition.

The ability to buy and sell electric power permits utilities to efficiently employ existing capacity. By buying power from other sources, utilities can meet peak-load demands on hot days or during winter storms and avoid the need to invest in additional production facilities. When utilities purchase power from others, the Federal Power Act of 1935 requires the Federal Energy Regulatory Commission (FERC) to ensure that prices charged on interstate sales are "just and reasonable" in light of necessary costs. With the emergence of competition in the electric power generation market, however, the need for FERC regulation of all interstate sales on a cost-of-service basis has diminished.

When purchasers of electric power have a number of alternative sources, a competitive market can develop and market prices can take the place of prices based upon cost-of-service regulation. Indeed, by the early 1990s, the availability of alternative power sources had encouraged more than a dozen states to use competitive procurement policies for intrastate acquisition of electric power, rather than cost-of-service regulation. Competition in the electric power generation industry can be promoted by allowing local utilities access to transmission facilities that link them with alternative energy sources, provided that the owners of transmission facilities are compensated for their use. In addition, federal legislation may be required to repeal sections of the Public Utility Holding Company Act of 1935 that create barriers to entry and obstacles to the development of new wholesale power sources.

Fostering Competition in the Cable Television Industry

Cable television is available to more than 90 percent of U.S. households, and more than 60 percent of all such households subscribe to cable service. Services historically provided include improved reception for television programs broadcast over the air on advertiser-supported networks such as CBS, NBC, ABC, and the FOX network; and specialized programming from cable networks such as CNN, MTV, and the Disney Channel. In the 1990s, much of the growth in cable TV revenues will come from the provision of new shopping and data transmission services. The problem is that consumers in most communities receive these services from a single monopoly provider; using current technology, it is simply uneconomic to encourage multiple providers to serve a single community. Regulators must decide how to encourage continued innovation in programming and in the development of new cable services, while at the same time restraining industry prices.

The Cable Communications Policy Act of 1984 barred cable regulation in communities with "effective competition," defined by the FCC as those communities that receive at least three over-the-air broadcast networks. By the end of 1989, only 3 percent of all cable franchises in the United States remained under local or state regulation. Between the end of 1986, when the Cable Act took effect, and the end of 1990, the average price for the lowest-price basic service increased by roughly one-third in constant dollars. While cable operators explain the rise in prices as necessary to pay for greater program variety, critics contend that competition from over-the-air broadcasters and from videotape rentals is insufficient to constrain monopoly pricing in the cable industry.

One possible competitor for existing cable companies is the local telephone company, although they might have to install new fiber-optic cable to provide competitive services. Standing in the way of such competition, however, is the Cable Act and FCC regulations that prohibit competition from telephone companies. Rules that would allow telephone companies to carry television programming and other video services would clearly enhance competition in the industry. Similarly, requiring local cable companies to transmit programming provided by others would free up access to local markets. Rules would have to be put in place to guarantee open access to local cable markets and reasonable fees to the local cable companies for program transmission.

Another potential competitor for existing cable companies is provided by "sky cable" and new emerging technologies for over-the-air transmission of specialized programming and data. Such technologies hold great potential as an effective competitor for local cable companies, especially in large cities and residential areas with dense population. If such forms of competition meet their advertised potential, the local cable monopoly problem may become moot before the turn of the century.

Improving Regulation of Health and Safety

Decisions to smoke cigarettes, go scuba diving in Baja California, or ride a roller coaster at an amusement park involve balancing concerns about risk against the benefits derived from consumption. Similarly, decisions to take a job as a management consultant, as an ironworker in the construction trades, or as a commodities broker involve a trade-off between the risks and perceived benefits of employment. In the United States, government seeks to control these risks by offering consumers and employees redress for wrongful injury through the tort system and by an extensive and growing policy of health and safety regulation.

Proponents of expanded government health and safety regulation assert that consumers and employees either do not have sufficient information or are incapable of making appropriate decisions in these areas. If certain risks are extremely high or prohibitively expensive, society sometimes assumes the burden of paying for them out of equity considerations. For example, health and safety costs for burn and trauma centers are usually paid for out of public funds. The growth of government health and safety regulation has been fueled in part by the public's perception that risk is increasing over time. In truth, because life expectancy is growing steadily argues that life is becoming less risky rather than more risky. Public concern over risk has sometimes given rise to legislation that requires all risk to be eliminated. For example, the Delaney Clause of the Food, Drug, and Cosmetics Act prohibits the use in food of any "substance shown to cause cancer in animals or humans." The courts have interpreted this clause to prohibit any dose no matter how small, even if animals show carcinogenicity only after having been fed unrealistically large doses.

Just as firms and individuals must balance risk and benefits when making any decision, so too must regulators. While regulators often target catastrophic risks that have a small probability of occurring, they often overlook more modest risks that occur frequently. It may be good politics to target products with a very small chance of leading to cancer, but it may be more economic to focus on methods for increasing consumer awareness on the dangers of obesity. In regulating health and safety, as in other areas, government should focus on those regulations that feature benefits that outweigh their unavoidable costs.

Reforming Environmental Regulation

Government regulation of industrial use of the environment expanded greatly during the 1970s and 1980s. By requiring firms and consumers to account for the costs forced upon others through pollution, the Clean Air Act, the Clean Water Act, and the Resource Conservation and Recovery Act have all limited environmental waste. At the same time, each of these environmental regulations imposes significant costs on the private economy. Between 1972 and 1990, pollution control costs in the United States tripled in constant dollars, rising from 0.9 percent to 2.1 percent of GDP. The Environmental Protection Agency expects this total to rise to 2.6 percent by the year 2000. While the U.S. already spends more on pollution abatement than any industrialized nation, this total is sure to rise sharply in the years ahead. Economists estimate that the Clean Air Amendments of 1990 will by themselves cost between $25 billion and $30 billion per year when fully implemented in 2005.

Significant uncertainties surround many environmental issues, and the costs and benefits of various means of environmental regulation. For example, the $550 million National Acid Precipitation Assessment Program, conducted between 1980 and 1990, found that soil and other conditions had a far greater influence on the acidity of lakes and rivers than did acid rain derived from industrial pollution. Scientific consensus has also shifted concerning the costs and risks associated with dioxin, asbestos, and radon. These examples illustrate the importance of gaining complete information before proposing expensive new means of environmental regulation that may or may not prove effective.

In the case of acid rain, studies show that simple mitigation strategies can be much more cost-effective than the types of regulatory controls favored by Congress. Similarly, there may exist more efficient alternatives for correcting externalities associated with gasoline consumption. A rise in gasoline consumption increases the nation's vulnerability to oil price shocks and pollution. The most direct way of dealing with such problems would be to impose a user fee per gallon on gasoline consumption that was commensurate with resulting externalities. Proponents of the current corporate average fuel economy (CAFE) standards tend to overlook the advantages of direct user fees and the indirect costs imposed by CAFE standards. To comply with CAFE standards, manufacturers have been forced to favor the production of smaller cars that are less safe, thereby leading to an increase in deaths and injuries on the nation's highways.

More demanding than the environmental issues facing any one nation are the global concerns confronting us all. For example, global warming is an issue of increasing concern. "Greenhouse gases" such as carbon dioxide, methane, and water vapor in the atmosphere have helped maintain surface temperatures at historic levels during recent years. These gases retain and reflect some of the heat given off by the earth back to the surface, thereby causing a type of greenhouse effect. Industrial and consumption activities that result in an emission of greenhouse gases may be responsible for some global warming and possible effects on the earth's climate. However, too little is known at this point to establish conclusively whether the earth's climate is indeed warmer today than usual, whether greenhouse gas emissions from human activity are significant, or whether such externalities are positive (longer growing seasons in Canada), negative (a rise in sea level), or some mix of both.

The scope and importance of environmental concerns will become clearer as better information becomes available and more effective methods of regulation begin to yield fruit. At this point, it seems clear that economic incentives decrease compliance costs by allowing firms the flexibility to meet environmental regulations in the most efficient manner possible. With economic incentives tied to environmental objectives, rather than to the means used to achieve them, firms and society in general benefit through a practical approach to protecting the environment.

SUMMARY

Government rules, regulations, and tax policy play a key role in shaping competitive forces. By understanding the rationale for government involvement in the market economy, a better appreciation of the part played by business is gained. For this reason, study of the role of government in the market economy is an important component of managerial economics.

• From an economic **efficiency** standpoint, a given mode of **regulation** or government control is desirable to the extent that benefits exceed costs. In terms of efficiency, the question is whether market competition by itself is adequate, or if government regulation is desirable. **Equity,** or fairness, criteria must also be carefully weighed when social considerations bear on the regulatory decision-making process.

• **Market failure** is the failure of market institutions to sustain socially desirable activities or to eliminate undesirable ones. **Failure by market structure** occurs in markets with too few buyers and sellers for effective competition. **Failure by incentive** occurs when some important benefits or costs of production and consumption are not reflected in industry prices. Differences between private and social costs or benefits are called **externalities.** For example, air pollution is a type of negative externality.

• **Property rights** give firms the prerogative to limit use by others of specific land, plant and equipment, and other assets. The establishment and maintenance of private property rights is essential to the workings of a competitive market. With **patents,** government grants an exclusive property right to produce, use, or sell an invention or innovation for a limited period of time (17 years in the United States). These valuable grants of legal monopoly power are intended to stimulate research and development. The **tort system** includes a body of law designed to provide a mechanism for victims of accidents and injury to receive just compensation for their loss. These laws create an incentive for firms and other parties to act responsibly in commerce.

• Government also responds to positive externalities by providing subsidies to private business firms. **Subsidy policy** can be direct or indirect, like government construction and highway maintenance grants that benefit the trucking industry. **Pollution emission allowances** are a new and controversial form of government subsidy that gives firms the property right to pollute and to sell that right to others if they wish. Whereas subsidy policy gives firms positive incentives for desirable performance, **tax policy** contains penalties, or negative subsidies, designed to limit undesirable performance. Tax policy includes both regular tax payments and fines or penalties that may be assessed intermittently.

• **Operating controls** are regulations or standards that limit undesirable behavior by compelling certain actions while prohibiting others. The question of who pays for such regulation is seldom answered by simply referring to the point of tax collection, or point of **tax incidence.** The economic cost of regulation, or the **tax burden,** is often passed on to customers or suppliers.

• The process of regulation is expensive in terms of administrative costs, lost operating efficiency, and the misallocation of scarce resources. Contributing to these costs is the problem of **regulatory lag,** or delay between the time a change in regulation is appropriate and the date it becomes effective. Another method of monopoly regulation is through the use of short-term **price controls** and **windfall profits** taxes on nonutilities to limit perceived abuses of monopoly power. Like other forms of regulation, such rules are often imposed or maintained long after they are economically appropriate.

• State and federal regulators have begun to address the high cost and other problems of utility price regulation through new methods of **incentive regulation,** whereby both utilities and their customers benefit through enhanced efficiency.

• **Antitrust laws** are designed to promote competition and prevent unwarranted monopoly. These laws seek to improve economic efficiency by enhancing consumer sovereignty and the impartiality of resource allocation while limiting concentrations in both economic and political power.

• The **capture theory** of economic regulation says that the power of the state to prohibit or compel and to take or give money is often manipulated to selectively help or hurt a vast number of industries. Because of this, regulation may be actively *sought* by an industry. Capture theory contrasts sharply with the more traditional **public interest theory** view of regulation as a government-imposed means of private-market control.

• In recognition that the regulatory process can sometimes harm rather than help consumer interests, a **deregulation** movement has sprung up and has grown to impressive dimensions. Similarly, the unnecessary costs of other forms of regulation dictate that **regulatory reform** is likely to remain a significant social concern throughout the 1990s.

Government regulation of the market economy is a natural by-product of public concern that unrestricted market competition has the potential to harm economic performance. As the benefits and costs of government/business interaction become better understood, the potential grows for a more constructive approach to government regulation.

Questions

Q15.1   Define the term *market failure* and cite some causes. Also, cite some examples of market failure.

Q15.2   What role does the price elasticity of demand play in determining the short-run effects of regulations that increase fixed costs? What if they lead to increased variable costs?

Q15.3   Given the difficulties encountered with utility regulation, it has been suggested that nationalization might lead to a more socially optimal allocation of resources. Do you agree? Why or why not?

Q15.4   Antitrust statutes in the United States have been used to attack monopolization by big business. Does labor monopolization by giant unions have the same potential for the misallocation of economic resources?

Q15.5   When will an increase in the minimum wage increase employment income for unskilled laborers? When will it cause this income to fall? Based on your experience, which is more likely?

Q15.6   Explain why state tax rates on personal income vary more on a state-by-state basis than do corresponding tax rates on corporate income.

Q15.7   Do the U.S. antitrust statutes protect competition or competitors? What is the distinction between the two?

Q15.8   Define price discrimination. When is it legal? When is it illegal? Cite some common examples of price discrimination.

Q15.9   Is the deregulation movement of the 1970s and 1980s consistent or inconsistent with the capture theory of economic regulation?

Q15.10   "Regulation is often proposed on the basis of equity considerations and opposed on the basis of efficiency considerations. As a result, the regulation versus deregulation controversy is not easily resolved." Discuss this statement.

Self-Test Problem

During each 24-hour period, coal-fired electricity-generating plants emit substantial amounts of sulfur dioxide and particulate pollution into the atmosphere. Concerned citizens are appalled at the aesthetic and environmental implications of such pollution, as well as the potential health hazard to the local population.

In analyzing remedies to the current situation, three general methods used to control pollution are generally considered:

- *Regulations*—licenses, permits, compulsory standards, and so on.
- *Payments*—various types of government aid to help companies install pollution-control equipment. Aid can take the form of forgiven local property taxes, income tax credits, special accelerated depreciation allowances for pollution-control equipment, low-cost government loans, and so on.
- *Charges*—excise taxes on polluting fuels (coal, oil, and so forth), pollution discharge taxes, and other taxes.

Answer the following questions in light of these alternative methods of pollution control.

A. Pollution is a negative production externality and an example of market failure. Why do markets fail?

B. What is the incentive provided to polluters under each method of pollution control?

C. Who pays for a clean environment under each form of control?

D. On the basis of both efficiency and equity considerations, which form of pollution control is most attractive?

Solution to Self-Test Problem

A. Market failure sometimes occurs because the number of buyers and sellers is too small to ensure vigorous competition. Small numbers of sellers are sometimes caused by economies of scale in production, distribution, or marketing; barriers to entry caused by high capital, skilled labor, or other input requirements; or government-imposed barriers due to franchise grants, rules, or regulations.

Market failure can also occur if some of the costs or benefits of production or consumption are not reflected in market prices. Air, water, and noise pollution that emits from an industrial facility represent a cost of production that is imposed on society in general. Without appropriate charges for such pollution, producers, suppliers, and customers receive an implicit subsidy from the public at large. By failing to pay such environmental costs, they avoid paying the full cost of production and consumption. In general, if some product benefit (cost) is not reflected in firm revenues (costs), then suboptimal production quantities and output prices will result and provide both firms and their customers improper economic incentives.

B. Each alternative method of pollution control provides producers with a different set of incentives. With rules and regulations, producers often have an incentive to litigate or otherwise petition to be made a "special case" and thereby avoid regulatory costs. Rules and regulations are also sometimes difficult to monitor and enforce given the problems of determining legislative intent and regulated firm compliance. With a scheme of payments to reduce the flow of pollution, polluters have positive incentives to reduce and improve economic performance. A benefit of this approach is that firms often respond better to the "carrot" of promised rewards than to the "stick" of threatened penalties. Under a pollution control method of fines or dollar penalties for noncompliance, firms have an economic incentive to reduce pollution in order to avoid charges. However, this method of forcing compliance is sometimes regarded as coercive and met with resistance.

C. When polluters are forced to respond to rules and regulations, the company, customers, employees, and stockholders are all faced with the prospect of paying the costs of pollution reduction. The incidence of pollution cleanup costs depends upon the elasticity of demand for the firm's products and upon the elasticity of supply. When product demand is highly inelastic, customers have no good substitutes for the products of the polluting firm and therefore must ultimately pay the costs of cleanup. When product demand is highly elastic, customers are able to avoid the costs of pollution reduction by transferring their business to other providers who needn't charge for such expenses. In such circumstances, the firm, suppliers, employees, and stockholders bear the costs of pollution reduction. This situation is very similar to that faced by firms subject to pollution charges. In both instances, society's right to a clean environment is implied.

A system of payments to encourage pollution reduction contrasts in fundamental ways with rules and regulations and pollution charges and taxes. This method of pollution reduction is obviously attractive to polluters in that it is free and voluntary, rather than compulsory. It even provides a profit-making opportunity in pollution reduction that increases according to the scope of pollution. Moreover, when society pays a firm to reduce the level of its own pollution, the company's right to pollute is implicitly recognized.

D. Efficiency considerations typically favor payments and charges over rules and regulations as the more efficient methods of pollution control. From an efficiency standpoint, pollution charges are especially attractive in that they recognize pollution as a sometimes necessary cost of doing business, and they force cleanup costs to be borne by those who benefit most directly.

However, equity considerations make the choice among pollution control methods less certain. The regulatory process is attractive from an equity standpoint in that it ensures due process (a day in court) for the polluter. All parties are also treated equitably in the sense that all polluters are equal before the law. Payments for pollution reduction are sometimes favored on an equity basis in that it avoids penalizing polluters with "sunk" investment costs, and employees that work in older production facilities that face new domestic and foreign competitors. Pollution charges are often favored on an equity basis in that it forces a close link between prices and full economic costs. Pollution charges, like payments for pollution reduction, are sometimes criticized as favoring large companies versus their smaller competitors.

Therefore, there is no single "best" method of pollution regulation. All are employed because each has the ability to meet efficiency and equity criteria in specific circumstances.

Problems

P15.1 **Costs of Regulation.** People of many different age groups and circumstances take advantage of part-time employment opportunities provided by the fast-food industry. Given the wide variety of different fast-food vendors, the industry is fiercely competitive, as is the so-called unskilled labor market. In each of the following circumstances, indicate whether the proposed changes in government policy are likely to have an *increasing,* a *decreasing,* or an *uncertain* effect on employment opportunities in this industry.

A. Elimination of minimum wage law coverage for those working less than 20 hours per week.

B. An increase in spending for education that raises basic worker skills.

C. An increase in the employer portion of federally mandated FICA insurance costs.

D. A requirement that employers install expensive new worker-safety equipment.

E. A state requirement that employers pay 8 percent of wages to fund a new national healthcare program.

P15.2 **Advertising Regulation.** The Tobacco Products Control Act, which took effect January 1, 1989, bans all print and broadcast advertising of tobacco products in Canada. The act also orders the phase-out of all existing billboard and in-store tobacco advertising and requires stronger health warnings on tobacco packaging. Explain why this legislation is likely to *increase, decrease,* or *have no effect* on the following:

A. Consumption of tobacco products

B. Industry advertising costs

C. Short-run industry profits

D. Nonadvertising methods of competition

E. Barriers to entry.

P15.3   **Price Fixing.** On May 8, 1992, the *Wall Street Journal* (p. A1) carried an article titled "Ivy League Discussions on Finances Extended to Tuition and Salaries." The article described a May 1991 consent decree between the Justice Department and the Ivy League—Brown, Columbia, Cornell, Harvard, Princeton, and Yale Universities; Dartmouth College; and the University of Pennsylvania. The schools admitted no wrongdoing in the settlement but agreed not to collude on tuitions, salaries, or financial aid in the future. The following is an excerpt from that article:

> *When Ivy League presidents gathered at the Harvard Club in New York on Dec. 3, 1986, each had special concerns. . . .*
>
> *Ostensibly competitors, the eight private schools divulged to each other sensitive information: their plans for increasing tuition and faculty salaries—their industry's prices.*
>
> *Months before telling students or the public, Harvard told other Ivy League schools that its tuition would rise 5.8% to 5.9% in 1987–88. Princeton said 6.25%. With one exception, each school was planning tuition increases in a tight range between 5.8% and 7.5% and salary increases of 5% to 6.5%. The exception was Dartmouth.*
>
> *"When I told them that we were considering salary [increases] of 8% to 8.5% and tuition increases not far off that number, there was an audible gasp," Mr. McLaughlin said in a Dec. 5, 1986, memo to his staff. "In view of [this] information, we will need to rethink our proposed salary and tuition scheduled increases and to do so rather promptly."*
>
> *And Dartmouth did; it brought its tuition increase into line with the others. Meanwhile, Princeton and Yale moved up, according to figures published later. The net result: Final 1987–88 charges, including room, board and fees, were bunched closely between $16,841 and $17,100 at seven of the eight schools, leaving students and their families no financial reason to shop around. Cornell, an exception at $16,320, receives subsidies from New York state.*

A. How would you determine whether the outcome of the presidents' meeting is an example of price fixing?

B. If price fixing did indeed occur at these meetings, which laws in particular might be violated?

P15.4   **Price Discrimination.** During recent years, U.S. car manufacturers have charged lower car prices in western states in an effort to head off competition by popular Japanese imports. Subcompacts produced by GM, Ford, and others have cost consumers $100 to $150 less in western states than in other parts of the country. This two-tier pricing scheme has raised the ire of eastern dealers, who view it as discriminatory and a violation of antitrust laws.

A. Is this pricing scheme discriminatory in the economic sense? What conditions would be necessary for it to be profitable to the automakers?

B. Carefully describe how price discrimination could violate U.S. antitrust laws, and be sure to mention which laws in particular might be violated.

P15.5   **Benefits of Regulation.** Three leading concrete suppliers have entered into a secret cartel to fix prices and allocate repair business for the Garden State Parkway. The marginal costs per unit for supplying concrete are as follows:

Cubic Yards of Concrete (thousands)	Atlantic City Supply, Inc. (A)	Brunswick Contractors, Ltd. (B)	Camden Construction, Inc. (C)
1	$10	$20	$20
2	15	20	15
3	20	30	10
4	25	40	25
5	30	50	35

A. Determine the cartel's optimal allocation of output and maximum profits if it sets $Q = 8$ and $P = \$25$.
B. Calculate the perfectly competitive industry price for $Q = 8$.
C. How much output would a perfectly competitive industry supply at $P = \$25$?
D. Describe the value to society of breaking up the cartel.

P15.6   **Costs of Regulation.** Kildare Gillespie Instruments, Inc., manufactures an innovative piece of diagnostic equipment used in medical laboratories and hospitals. OSHA has determined that additional safety precautions are necessary to bring radioactive leakage occurring during use of this equipment down to acceptable levels. Total and marginal production costs, including a normal rate of return on investment but *before* additional safeguards are installed, are as follows:

$$TC = \$5,000,000 + \$5,000Q,$$
$$MC = dTC/dQ = \$5,000.$$

Market demand and marginal revenue relations are the following:

$$P_L = \$15,000 - \$12.5Q_L, \qquad \text{(Medical Laboratory Demand)}$$
$$MR_L = dTR/dQ_L = \$15,000 - \$25Q_L,$$
$$P_H = \$10,000 - \$1Q_H, \qquad \text{(Hospital Demand)}$$
$$MR_H = dTR/dQ_H = \$10,000 - \$2Q_H.$$

A. Assuming that the company faces two distinct markets, calculate the profit-maximizing price/output combination in each market and Kildare Gillespie's level of economic profits.
B. Describe the short- and long-run implications of meeting OSHA standards if doing so raises Kildare Gillespie's marginal cost by $1,000 per machine.

C. Calculate the point price elasticity at the initial (Part A) profit-maximizing activity level in each market. Are the differential effects on sales in each market that were seen in Part B typical or atypical?

P15.7 **Incidence of Regulation Costs.** The Smokey Mountain Coal Company sells coal to electric utilities in the southeast. Unfortunately, Smokey's coal has a high particulate content, and, therefore, the company is adversely affected by state and local regulations governing smoke and dust emissions at its customers' electricity-generating plants. Smokey's total and marginal cost relations are

$$TC = \$1,000,000 + \$5Q + \$0.0001Q^2,$$
$$MC = \$5 + \$0.0002Q,$$

where Q is tons of coal produced per month and TC includes a risk-adjusted normal rate of return on investment.

A. Calculate Smokey's profit at the profit-maximizing activity level if prices in the industry are stable at $25 per ton and therefore $P = MR = \$25$.

B. Calculate Smokey's optimal price, output, and profit levels if a new state regulation results in a $5-per-ton cost increase that can be fully passed on to customers.

C. Determine the effect on output and profit if Smokey must fully absorb the $5-per-ton cost increase.

P15.8 **Cost of Import Tariffs.** Topo Gigo Imports, Ltd., located in San Francisco, California, is an importer and distributor of a leading Japanese-made desktop dry copier. The U.S. Commerce Department recently informed the company that it will be subject to a new 5.75 percent tariff on the import cost of copiers. Topo Gigo is concerned that the tariff will slow its sales, given the highly competitive nature of the copier market. Relevant market demand and marginal revenue relations are as follows:

$$P = \$13,800 - \$0.23Q,$$
$$MR = \$13,800 - \$0.46Q.$$

Topo Gigo's marginal cost per copier equals the import cost of $8,000 per unit, plus 15 percent to cover transportation, insurance, and related selling expenses. In addition to these costs, Topo Gigo's fixed costs, including a normal rate of return, come to $15 million per year.

A. Calculate Topo Gigo's optimal price/output combination and economic profits before imposition of the tariff.

B. Calculate Topo Gigo's optimal price/output combination and economic profits after imposition of the tariff.

C. Compare your answers to Parts A and B. Who pays the economic burden of the import tariff?

P15.9 **Utility Regulation.** The Woebegone Water Company, a small water utility serving rural customers in Minnesota, is currently engaged in a rate case with the regulatory commission under whose jurisdiction it operates. At issue is the monthly rate that the company will charge for unmetered sewer and water service. The demand curve for monthly service is $P = \$40 - \$0.01Q$. This implies annual demand and marginal revenue curves of

$$P = \$480 - \$0.12Q,$$
$$MR = \$480 - \$0.24Q,$$

where P is service price in dollars and Q is the number of customers served. Total and marginal costs per year (before investment return) are described by the following function:

$$TC = \$70,000 + \$80Q + \$0.005Q^2,$$
$$MC = \$80 + \$0.01Q.$$

The company has assets of $2 million and the utility commission has authorized an 11.5 percent return on investment.

A. Calculate Woebegone's profit-maximizing price (monthly and annually), output, and rate-of-return levels.

B. Woebegone has requested a monthly price of $22. Calculate Woebegone's output and total return on investment if the request were to be granted. Why are these values different from those calculated in Part A?

C. What monthly price should the commission grant to limit Woebegone to an 11.5 percent rate of return?

P15.10 **Pollution Control Costs.** Fred Ziffel, Inc., processes hogs at a large facility in Hooterville, Iowa. Each hog processed yields both pork and a render by-product in a fixed 1:1 ratio. Although the by-product is unfit for human consumption, some can be sold to a local pet food company for further processing. Relevant annual demand and cost relations are as follows:

$$P_P = \$110 - \$0.00005Q_P,$$
(Demand for pork)
$$MR_P = \$110 - \$0.0001Q_P,$$
(Marginal revenue from pork)
$$P_B = \$10 - \$0.0001Q_B,$$
(Demand for render by-product)
$$MR_B = \$10 - \$0.0002Q_B,$$
(Marginal revenue from render by-product)
$$TC = \$10,000,000 + \$60Q,$$
(Total cost)
$$MC = \$60.$$
(Marginal cost)

Here P is price in dollars, Q is the number of hogs processed (with an average weight of 100 pounds), and Q_P and Q_B are pork and render by-product per hog, respectively; both total and marginal costs are in dollars. Total costs include a risk-adjusted normal return of 15 percent on a $50 million investment in plant and equipment.

Currently, the city allows the company to dump excess by-product into its sewage treatment facility at no charge, viewing the service as an attractive means of keeping a valued employer in the area. However, the sewage treatment facility is quickly approaching peak capacity and must be expanded at an expected operating cost of $3 million per year. This is an impossible burden on an already strained city budget.

A. Calculate the profit-maximizing price/output combination and optimal total profit level for Fred Ziffel.

B. How much by-product will the company dump into the Des Moines sewage treatment facility at the profit-maximizing activity level?

C. Calculate output and total profits if the city imposes a $35 per unit charge on the amount of by-product Fred Ziffel dumps.

D. Calculate output and total profits if the city imposes a fixed $3-million-per-year tax on Fred Ziffel to pay for the sewage treatment facility expansion.

E. Will either tax alternative permit Fred Ziffel to survive in the long run? In your opinion, what should the city of Des Moines do about its sewage treatment problem?

CASE STUDY FOR CHAPTER 15
The Network Television Regulation versus Deregulation Controversy

When viewers think of Federal Communication Commission (FCC) regulation of network television, they might think of censorship or the FCC controlling the renewal of local broadcast licenses. While TV censors are the butt of frequent jokes by Jay Leno on NBC's "The Tonight Show," TV censorship in the United States is very mild when compared with that in many foreign countries, and it has little economic or political impact. Although more important, FCC control over the renewal of local broadcast licenses has little direct effect on the network broadcasting business. To be sure, local affiliates must be careful to merit license renewal by serving the special community interests of local viewing areas. Since the networks are able to own up to 12 local stations serving up to 25 percent of the U.S. market, they too are affected in their company-owned affiliates but not in their broadcasting operations.

It might come as a big surprise to many viewers that network television is subject to heavy economic regulation in terms of what are referred to as financial interest and network syndication rules. These so-called fin/syn rules were adopted in the early 1970s to prevent ABC, CBS, and NBC from collectively dominating the broadcast industry. The financial interest rule prohibits networks from having an ownership interest in shows produced for them by others. The network syndication rule prohibits networks from selling internally produced programs into the domestic syndication or rerun market. Limits on network access to the rerun market are an important disincentive to network production of new television shows. A single half-hour episode of prime-time programming can sometimes cost up to $1 million. Given these tremendous costs, few television programs, even popular hit shows like "Cheers," "The Cosby Show," or "The Simpsons" make money on their initial runs. The big profits come from subsequent syndication sales of reruns to network affiliates or independent stations in the late afternoon or early evening hours.

Fin/syn rules have effectively brought about a separation between the production of television entertainment programming and broadcasting. This is especially true ever since a 1980 consent decree that limited the amount of prime-time programming that networks could produce internally. With the exception of prime-time sports and news coverage, which they can offer without restriction, the networks serve as distributors of entertainment programs produced by independent Hollywood producers and others. The networks pay fees for the rights to distribute specific shows and they hope to make enough money from selling advertising time on their initial run to more than offset fees and earn a profit.

Back in the 1970s and early 1980s, this method of regulation made much more sense than it does today. Without it, Hollywood producers would have been at a big disadvantage in negotiating terms with the networks, since there were only three major networks that could buy their shows. But in the 1990s, things are much different. Not only has the number of independent stations proliferated, but cable TV has become a major power. CNN offers stiff competition for network news programming, while ESPN gives the networks a run for their money in sports programming. Of most direct relevance to fin/syn regulation is the 1980s proliferation of entertainment programming outlets such as A&E, the Disney Channel, Lifetime, Nickelodeon, TNT, and the USA network, among others. The new Fox network is also becoming a bigger factor in the industry, with surging ratings and hit shows.

Consistent with the Bush Administration's push for deregulation, FCC chairman Alfred C. Sikes argued in early 1991 that the fin/syn rules were antiquated and unwarranted and should be repealed. However, in a startling rebuke of the chairman, the FCC voted 3–2 in April 1991 to retain the fin/syn rules with only modest changes. Effective June 15, 1991, the networks gained the opportunity to acquire foreign-syndication rights for network programs, but only after giving independent producers the opportunity to make other distribution deals. The networks were also allowed into the domestic-syndication market for entertainment programming, but only for programs produced in-house and for no more than 40 percent of the networks' prime-time schedule. By failing to abolish fin/syn rules, the FCC ruling represented a major victory for Jack Valenti, head of the Motion Picture Association of America, and a stunning defeat for the networks.

Briefly explain the following:

A. The causes and consequences of regulation according to the public interest theory of regulation

B. The causes and consequences of regulation according to the capture theory of regulation

C. How the network television regulation versus deregulation controversy supports or contradicts each theory

---

Selected References

Ballentine, J. Gregory. "The Structure of the Tax System Versus the Level of Taxation: An Evaluation of the 1986 Act." *Journal of Economic Perspectives* 6 (Winter 1992): 59–68.

Bosch, Jean-Claude, and E. Woodward Eckard, Jr. "The Profitability of Price Fixing: Evidence From Stock Market Reaction to Federal Indictments," *Review of Economics and Statistics* 73 (May 1991): 309–317.

Cahan, Steven F. "The Effect of Antitrust Investigations on Discretionary Accruals: A Refined Test of the Political Cost Hypothesis." *Accounting Review* 67 (January 1992): 77–96.

Crandall, Robert W. "Corporate Average Fuel Economy Standards." *Journal of Economic Perspectives* 6 (Spring 1992): 171–180.

Ellingsen, Tore. "Strategic Buyers and the Social Cost of Monopoly." *American Economic Review* 81 (June 1991): 648–657.

Friedman, David D., William M. Landes, and Richard A. Posner. "Some Economics of Trade Secret Law." *Journal of Economic Perspectives* 5 (Winter 1991): 61–72.

Helfand, Gloria E. "Standards versus Standards: The Effects of Different Pollution Restrictions." *American Economic Review* 81 (June 1991): 622–634.

Litan, Robert E. "The Safety and Innovation Effects of U.S. Liability Law." *American Economic Review* 81 (May 1991): 59–64.

Minarik, Joseph J. "Federal Tax Policy for the 1990s: The Prospect from the Hill." *American Economic Review* 82 (May 1992): 268–273.

Noguchi, Yukio. "The Changing Japanese Economy and the Need for a Fundamental Shift in the Tax System." *American Economic Review* 82 (May 1992): 226–230.

Schelling, Thomas. "Some Economics of Global Warming." *American Economic Review* 82 (March 1992): 1–14.

Schultze, Charles. "Is there a Bias Toward Excess in U.S. Government Budgets or Deficits?" *Journal of Economic Perspectives* 6 (Spring 1992): 25–43.

Terpstra, David E., and Douglas D. Baker. "Outcomes of Federal Court Decisions on Sexual Harassment." *Academy of Management Journal* 35 (March 1992): 181–190.

Wallin, David E. "Legal Recourse and the Demand for Auditing." *Accounting Review* 67 (January 1992): 121–147.

Werner, Ray O., ed. "Legal Developments in Marketing." *Journal of Marketing* 56 (April 1992): 103–109.

CAPITAL BUDGETING

Management invests hundreds of billions of dollars per year in fixed assets. By their very nature, these investment decisions have the potential to affect a firm's fortunes over several years. A good decision can boost earnings sharply and dramatically increase the value of the firm. A bad decision can lead to bankruptcy. Effective planning and control are essential if the health and long-run viability of the firm is to be assured.

The term *capital* refers to the funds employed to finance fixed assets used in production, while a budget is a detailed plan of projected inflows and outflows over future periods.

Capital budgeting
Long-term investment planning process.

Capital budgeting is the process of planning expenditures that generate cash flows expected to extend beyond one year. The choice of one year is arbitrary, of course, but it is a convenient cutoff for distinguishing between classes of expenditures. Examples of capital outlays are expenditures for land, buildings, and equipment and for additions to working capital (e.g., inventories and receivables) made necessary by expansion. New advertising campaigns or research and development programs are also likely to have impacts beyond one year and come within the classification of capital budgeting expenditures.

Capital budgeting integrates the various elements of the firm. Although the financial manager generally has administrative control of the capital budgeting process, the effectiveness of a firm's capital investments depends on input from all major departments. The marketing department makes a key contribution by providing sales forecasts. Because operating costs must be estimated, the accounting, production, engineering, and purchasing departments are also involved. The initial outlay, or investment cost, must be estimated; again engineering and purchasing typically provide input. Obtaining funds and estimating their cost are major tasks of the financial manager. Finally, these various estimates must be drawn together in the form of a project evaluation. Although the finance department generally writes up the evaluation report, top management ultimately sets standards of acceptability.

This chapter describes the mechanics of capital budgeting as an application of marginal analysis. In capital budgeting, marginal revenue is measured in terms of the incremental cash flows generated by investment projects; marginal cost is measured by the marginal cost of new investment capital. The chapter begins with an overview of the process that managers use to generate new investment ideas. Techniques for estimating project cash flows, the marginal cost of capital determination, and the relative attractiveness of alternative investment projects are then considered.

THE CAPITAL BUDGETING PROCESS

A firm's growth and development, even its ability to remain competitive and to survive, depend on a constant flow of ideas for new products and ways to make existing products better and at a lower cost. A well-managed firm goes to great lengths to develop good capital budgeting proposals. For example, a sales representative may report that customers are asking for a particular product that the company does not now produce. The sales manager then will discuss the idea with the marketing research group to determine the size of the market for the proposed product. If it appears likely that a substantial market does exist, cost accountants and engineers will be asked to estimate production costs. If it appears that the product can be produced and sold to yield a sufficient profit, the project will be undertaken.

If a firm has capable and imaginative managers and other employees, and if its incentive system is working properly, several ideas for capital investment will be advanced. Since some ideas will be good ones while others will not, procedures must be established for screening projects.

Project Classification

Analyzing capital expenditure proposals is not a costless operation; benefits can be gained from careful analysis, but such investigations are costly. For certain types of projects, a relatively detailed analysis may be warranted; for others, cost/benefit studies suggest that simpler procedures should be used. Firms generally classify projects into a number of categories and analyze those projects in each category somewhat differently.

Replacement projects
Maintenance of business investments.

Replacement projects, or maintenance of business projects, consist of expenditures necessary to replace worn-out or damaged equipment used to produce profitable products. These projects are necessary if the firm is to continue in its current businesses. The relevant issues are (a) Should the company continue to offer current products and services? and (b) Should existing plant and equipment be employed for this purpose? Usually, the answers to both questions are yes, so maintenance decisions are typically routine and made without going through an elaborate decision process.

Cost reduction projects
Expenditures to replace obsolete plant and equipment.

Cost reduction projects include expenditures to replace serviceable but obsolete plant and equipment. The purpose of these investment projects is to lower production costs by lowering expenses for labor, raw materials, heat, or electricity. These decisions are often discretionary, so a more detailed analysis is generally required to support the expenditure. Decision-making authority usually rests at the manager or higher level in the organization.

Safety and environmental projects
Mandatory nonrevenue-producing investments.

Capital expenditures made necessary by government regulation, collective bargaining agreements, or insurance policy requirements fall into a further **safety and environmental projects** category. Such capital expenditures are sometimes called "mandatory" investments because they often are nonrevenue-producing in nature. How they are handled depends on their size and complexity; most often they are quite routine and their treatment is similar to replacement and cost reduction projects.

Expansion projects
Expenditures to increase availability of existing products.

Expansion projects involve expenditures to increase the availability of existing products and services. For example, investment projects to expand the number of service outlets or distribution facilities are included in this category. These investment decisions are relatively complex because they require an explicit forecast of the firm's future supply and demand conditions. Mistakes are quite possible, so detailed analysis is required and the final decision is made at a high level within the firm, perhaps at the level of the controller or chief financial officer.

Expansion into new products or markets requires expenditures necessary to produce new products and services or to expand into new geographic areas. Strategic decisions that could change the fundamental nature of the firm's business are involved. Expenditures of large sums over extended investment horizons are often necessary. Detailed analysis is invariably required, and final decisions are often made by the chief executive officer or board of directors.

To summarize, relatively simple calculations and only a few supporting documents are required for replacement decisions, especially maintenance-type investments in profitable plants. More complete analysis is required for cost reduction projects, for expansion of existing product lines, and especially for investments in new product lines or geographic areas. Within each capital investment project category, projects are treated differently, depending on the level of expenditure required. The larger the required investment, the more detailed the analysis and the higher the level of decision-making authority required. A plant manager may be authorized to approve maintenance expenditures costing less than $10,000 to $25,000 on the basis of a relatively cursory analysis. At the other extreme, the entire board of directors may review decisions that involve more than $1 million or that entail a major strategic shift in the firm's focus. Highly detailed and thorough analysis is typically required in such instances.

STEPS IN CAPITAL BUDGETING

If an individual investor identifies and invests in a stock or bond whose expected return is greater than the cost of funds, the investor's portfolio will increase in value. Similarly, if a firm identifies or creates an investment opportunity with a present value greater than its cost, the value of the firm will increase. This increase in the firm's value as a result of successful capital budgeting will be reflected in the firm's future growth. The more effective the firm's capital budgeting process, the higher its growth rate and the greater its future value. In theory, the capital budgeting process involves six logical steps.

First, the cost of the project must be determined. This is similar to finding the price that must be paid for a stock or bond. Next, management must estimate the expected cash flows from the project, including the value of the asset at a specified terminal date. This is similar to estimating the future dividend or interest payment stream on a stock or bond. Third, the riskiness of projected cash flows must be estimated. To do this, management needs information about the probability distributions of future cash flows. Fourth, given the riskiness of projected

●

MANAGERIAL APPLICATION 16.1
Does the United States Need an Industrial Policy?

The United States economy has turned in a dismal productivity performance for two decades. Since 1973, output per worker has risen at a 0.8 percent annual rate, less than one-third of the 2.5 percent rate typical of the previous 25 years. Had productivity kept pace with the rest of the post–World War II period, today's median family income would exceed $47,000 instead of its current $35,000. At the same time, other industrial nations are enjoying rapidly improving living standards. And these countries, especially Japan, have been planning for even better economic performance by investing heavily in future productivity growth.

Stagnant incomes and low productivity growth have hampered the United States economy for years. What may be new is that the ending of the Cold War offers a historic opportunity to get the economy back on a fast-growth path. That is why one of the most controversial questions in recent political history is being raised: Should the United States have a new industrial policy?

Proponents argue that government can become a key player in the "knowledge economy." They advocate a boost in government research spending across a wide range of technologies and in financial support to the next generation of scientists and engineers. Supporters also contend that the United States needs tax laws that make it a lot cheaper for the private sector to invest in research and development (R&D) and new plant and equipment. They advocate giving smaller companies technical assistance to learn the latest manufacturing techniques. Government spending to enhance productivity by building up the infrastructure, especially by encouraging the development of high-speed communications networks, is also proposed. A new trade policy that focuses on opening up foreign markets while resisting protectionism at home is also favored.

Advocates of a knowledge-based industrial policy recommend that the federal government:

- *Boost industrial R&D support.* Increase federal spending on civilian R&D; cut defense R&D. Support a wide range of projects, from basic research to new manufacturing technologies.
- *Provide technical assistance to industry.* Increase funding for programs to help smaller manufacturers adopt up-to-date technologies and production

methods. Provide training grants and low-cost equipment loans.
- *Improve data collection.* Spread information on the successful R&D and manufacturing practices of foreign competitors. Identify emerging technologies that merit support.
- *Rebuild infrastructure.* Rebuild roads and bridges, and increase funding for high-speed data networks, to encourage new high-tech industries.
- *Expand exports.* Make export financing easier to obtain for creditworthy small and midsize exporters. Boost export promotion for nonagricultural products.
- *Fund education.* Raise funding for all levels of science, mathematics, and engineering education.
- *Cut taxes.* Institute permanent R&D and investment tax credits, so companies can do long-range planning.

Adversaries argue that adopting an industrial policy for the United States would be a colossal mistake. "We don't have any confidence in government policy that reallocates resources from one sector to another," says David M. McIntosh, executive director of the Council on Competitiveness. However, pro-growth policies have deep roots in the United States. In the nineteenth century, the federal government backed railroad development by granting enormous tracts of land to get the job done. The government also sponsored a network of universities, extension services, and research to help United States farmers successfully develop and promote agriculture. More recently, government funds nurtured such infant industries as airlines and electronics. Even the Reagan administration pursued a form of industrial policy by offering tax breaks for real estate development and basic research.

A knowledge-based growth policy doesn't call on government to pick winning and losing industries. Nor does it create massive bureaucracies or shelter stumbling companies from tough foreign competition. It asks government to provide venture capital and it asks the private sector to risk its own money to develop commercially viable ideas. In an enlightened industrial policy, it is the market, not government, that picks the winners and losers.

Source: Christopher Farrell and Michael J. Mandel, "Industrial Policy," *Business Week,* April 6, 1992, 70–75.

cash flows and the cost of funds under prevailing economic conditions as reflected by the riskless rate, k_{RF}, the firm must determine the appropriate discount rate, or cost of capital, at which the project's cash flows are to be discounted. This is equivalent to finding the required rate of return on a stock or bond investment. Fifth, expected cash flows are converted to a present value to obtain a clear estimate of the investment project's value to the firm. This is equivalent to finding the present value of expected future dividends or interest plus principal payment. Finally, the present value of expected cash inflows is compared with the required outlay, or cost, of the project. If the present value of cash flows derived from a project exceeds the cost of the investment, the project should be accepted. Otherwise, the project should be rejected.

CASH FLOW ESTIMATION

The most important and most difficult step in the analysis of a capital budgeting project is estimating its cash flows—the investment outlays and the annual net cash inflows after the project goes into operation. Many variables are involved in cash flow forecasting, and several individuals and departments participate in the process. For example, forecasts of unit sales and sales prices are normally made by the marketing department, based on its knowledge of price elasticity, advertising effects, the state of the economy, competitors' reactions, and trends in consumers' tastes. The size of necessary capital outlays associated with a new product is generally obtained from the engineering and product development staffs, while operating costs are estimated by cost accountants, production experts, personnel specialists, purchasing agents, and so forth.

It is difficult to make accurate forecasts of the costs and revenues associated with a large, complex project, so forecast errors can be large. For example, when several major oil companies decided to build the Alaska pipeline, the original cost forecasts were in the neighborhood of $700 million, but the final cost was closer to $7 billion. Similar, perhaps even worse, miscalculations are common in forecasts of product design costs, such as the costs to develop a new personal computer. As difficult as plant and equipment costs are to estimate, sales revenues and operating costs over the life of the project are generally even more uncertain. For example, when AT&T originally developed the Videophone, it envisaged large sales in both the residential and business markets. As of the early 1990s, such sales have yet to materialize. Because of its financial strength, AT&T has been able to absorb losses on the project, but the Videophone venture would have forced a weaker firm into bankruptcy.

The financial staff's role in the forecasting process involves coordinating the efforts of the other departments, such as engineering and marketing, ensuring that everyone involved with the forecast uses a consistent set of economic assumptions, and making sure that no biases are inherent in the forecasts. This last point is extremely important, because division managers often become emotionally involved with pet projects or develop empire-building complexes, leading to cash flow forecasting biases that make bad projects look good—on paper. The AT&T Videophone project is an example of this problem. For the capital budgeting process to be successful, the pattern of expected cash inflows and outflows must be established within a consistent and unbiased framework.

Incremental Cash Flows

Accounting income statements reflect a mix of cash and noncash expenses and revenues. Accountants deduct labor costs, which are cash outflows, from revenues, which may or may not be entirely in cash because sales are often made on credit. At the same time, accountants do not deduct capital outlays, which are cash outflows, but they do deduct depreciation expenses, which are not cash outflows. In capital budgeting, it is critical that decisions are based strictly on cash flows, the actual dollars that flow into and out of the company during each time period.

The relevant cash flows for capital budgeting purposes are the incremental cash flows attributable to a project. **Incremental cash flows** are the period-by-period changes in net cash flows that are due to an investment project:

Incremental cash flows

Change in net cash flows due to an investment project.

$$\text{Project } CF_t = \begin{array}{c} CF_t \text{ for Corporation} \\ \text{with Project} \end{array} - \begin{array}{c} CF_t \text{ for Corporation} \\ \text{without Project.} \end{array} \quad \textbf{(16.1)}$$

It is possible to construct a firm's pro forma cash flow statements with and without a project for each year of the project's life and then measure annual project cash flows as the differences in cash flows between the two sets of statements. In practice, a number of problems must be addressed successfully if the incremental cash flows from a given investment project are to be estimated successfully.

▶ As described in Chapter 9, a sunk cost is any expenditure outlay that has already occurred or has been agreed to on a contractual basis. Sunk costs are not incremental costs, they are not relevant to subsequent investment decisions, and they should not be included in the analysis of such decisions. Suppose, for example, that Gourmet Foods, Ltd., is evaluating the possibility of opening a retail store in a newly developed section of Albuquerque. A year ago, Gourmet Foods hired a consulting firm to perform an on-site analysis at a cost of $100,000, and this $100,000 has already been paid and expensed for tax purposes. Is this expenditure a relevant cost with respect to Gourmet's still-pending capital budgeting decision? The answer is no. The $100,000 represents a sunk cost. Gourmet Foods cannot recover this amount regardless of whether the new facility is opened. This money is gone. Whether the pending investment project should be accepted or rejected depends on the incremental costs and revenues associated with the project from this point *forward*. Whether the earlier commitment of $100,000 looks good or bad in hindsight is irrelevant. It is essential that irrelevant sunk costs not confound investment decisions. It sometimes turns out that a project looks unprofitable when all costs, including sunk costs, are considered. On an incremental basis, however, many of these same projects have the potential to generate a significant profit contribution when only incremental cash flows are included. An investment project should be undertaken only when incremental cash flows exceed the cost of investment on a present-value basis. It is essential that irrelevant sunk costs be deleted from the analysis so that correct forward-looking investment decisions can be made.

A second potential problem relates to the improper treatment of opportunity costs. All relevant opportunity costs must be included in the capital budgeting process. For example, suppose Gourmet Foods already owns a piece of land that is suitable for the new store. When evaluating the new retail facility, should the cost of the land be disregarded because no additional cash outlay would be required? Certainly not, because there is an opportunity cost inherent in the use of the property. Suppose that the land could be sold to net $150,000 after commissions and taxes. Use of the site for the new store would require foregoing this inflow, so the $150,000 must be charged as an opportunity cost against the project. The proper land cost is the $150,000 market-determined value, irrespective of historical acquisition costs.

A further potential problem involves the effects of the project on other parts of the firm. For example, suppose that some of the new outlet's customers are already customers at Gourmet Foods' downtown store. Revenues and profits generated by these customers would not be new to the firm but would represent transfers from one outlet to another. Cash flows produced by such customers should not be treated as incremental in the capital budgeting analysis. On the other hand, having a new suburban store might actually increase customer awareness in the local market and thereby attract additional customers to the downtown outlet. In this case, additional revenues projected to flow to the downtown store should be attributed to the new suburban facility. Although they are often difficult to identify and quantify, externalities such as these are important and must be considered.

A fourth problem relates to the timing of cash flows. Year-end accounting income statements seldom reflect exactly when revenues or expenses occur. Because of the time value of money, capital budgeting cash flows should be analyzed according to when they occur. A time line of daily cash flows would in theory be most accurate but is sometimes costly to construct and unwieldy to use. In the case of Gourmet Foods, it may be appropriate to measure incremental cash flows on a quarterly or monthly basis using an electronic spreadsheet such as *Lotus 1-2-3* or *Microsoft Excel*. In other cases, it may be appropriate simply to assume that all cash flows occur at the end or midpoint of every year.

Finally, tax considerations are often important because they can have a major impact on cash flows. In some cases, tax effects can make or break a project. It is critical that taxes be dealt with correctly in capital budgeting decisions. This is difficult because the tax laws are extremely complex and are subject to interpretation and change. For example, salvage value has no effect on the depreciable basis and hence on the annual depreciation expense that can be taken. Still, when performing a cash flow analysis, the market value of an asset at the end of the project represents a relevant expected cash inflow. Any difference between salvage value and depreciated book value at the end of a project is currently treated as ordinary income and is taxed at the firm's marginal tax rate. The staff in charge of evaluating capital investment projects must rely heavily on the firm's accountants and tax lawyers and also must develop a working knowledge of current tax law.

Accounting income statements provide a crucial basis for estimating the relevant cash flows from investment projects. This information must be adjusted, however, to carefully reflect the economic pattern of inflows and outflows so that value-maximizing investment decisions can be made. Though a formidable task, firms can and do overcome problems posed by sunk costs, opportunity costs, spillovers, and tax considerations. To illustrate, the following section offers a simplified example of cash flow estimation.

A Cash Flow Estimation Example

▶

To illustrate several important aspects of cash flow analysis and see how they relate to one another, consider a capital budgeting decision that faces Silicon Valley Controls Corp. (SVCC), a California-based high-tech firm. SVCC's research and development department has been applying its expertise in microprocessor technology to develop a small computer specifically designed to control home appliances. Once programmed, the computer system automatically controls the heating and air-conditioning systems, security system, hot water heater, and even small appliances such as a coffee maker. By increasing the energy efficiency of a home, the appliance control computer can save on energy costs and hence pay for itself. The project evaluation effort has reached the stage at which a decision about whether to go forward with production must be made.

SVCC's marketing department plans to target sales of the appliance control computer to the owners of larger homes; the computer is cost-effective only for homes with 2,000 or more square feet of heated/air-conditioned space. The marketing vice-president believes that annual sales would be 25,000 units if the appliance control computers were priced at $2,200 each. The engineering department has estimated that the firm would need a new manufacturing facility. Such a plant could be built and made ready for production in two years, once the "go ahead" decision is made. The plant would require a 25-acre site, and SVCC currently has an option to purchase a suitable tract of land for $1.2 million. If the decision is made to go ahead with the project, building construction could begin immediately and would continue for two years. Since the project has an estimated economic life of six years, the overall planning period is eight years: two years for plant construction (Years 1 and 2) plus six years for operation (Years 3 through 8). The building would cost $8 million and have a 31.5-year life for tax purposes. A $4 million payment would be due the building contractor at the end of each year of construction. Manufacturing equipment, with a cost of $10 million and a seven-year life for tax purposes, is to be installed and paid for at the end of the second year of construction, just prior to the beginning of operations.

The project also requires a working capital investment equal to 12 percent of estimated sales during the coming year. The initial working capital investment is to be made at the end of Year 2 and is increased at the end of each subsequent period by 12 percent of the expected increase in the following year's sales. After completion of the project's six-year operating period, the land is expected to have a market value of $1.7 million; the building, a value of $1 million; and the equipment, a value of $2 million. The production department has estimated that variable manufacturing costs would total 65 percent of dollar sales and that fixed overhead costs, excluding depreciation, would be $8 million for the first year of operations. Sales prices and fixed overhead costs, other than depreciation, are

TABLE 16.1   **Investment Outlay Analysis for New Plant Investment Project**

Fixed Assets	Year 0	Year 1	Year 2	Total Costs	Depreciable Basis
Land	$1,200,000	$ 0	$ 0	$ 1,200,000	$ 0
Building	0	4,000,000	4,000,000	8,000,000	8,000,000
Equipment	0	0	10,000,000	10,000,000	10,000,000
Total fixed assets	$1,200,000	$4,000,000	$14,000,000	$19,200,000	
Net working capital[a]	0	0	6,600,000	6,600,000	
Total investment	$1,200,000	$4,000,000	$20,600,000	$25,800,000	

[a]Twelve percent of first year's sales, or 0.12 ($55,000,000) = $6,600,000.

projected to increase with inflation, which is expected to average 6 percent per year over the six-year production period.

SVCC's marginal federal-plus-state tax rate is 40 percent, and its weighted average cost of capital is 15 percent. For capital budgeting purposes, the company's policy is to assume that cash flows occur at the end of each year. Since the plant would begin operations at the start of Year 3, the first operating cash flows would be realized at the end of Year 3. As one of the company's financial analysts, you have been assigned the task of supervising the capital budgeting analysis. For now, you may assume that the project has the same risk as the firm's current average project, and hence you may use the corporate 15 percent cost of capital for this project.

Cash Flow Analysis

The first step in the analysis is to summarize the investment outlays required for the project; this is done in Table 16.1. Note that the land cannot be depreciated, and hence its depreciable basis is $0. Because the project will require an increase in net working capital during Year 2, this is shown as an investment outlay for that year.

Having estimated capital requirements, operating cash flows that will occur once production begins must be estimated; these are set forth in Table 16.2. The operating cash flow estimates are based on information provided by SVCC's various departments. Note that the sales price and fixed costs are projected to increase each year by the 6 percent inflation rate, and since variable costs are 65 percent of sales, they too will rise by 6 percent each year. The changes in net working capital (*NWC*) represent the additional investments required to support sales increases (12 percent of the next year's sales increase, which in this case results only from inflation) during Year 3 through Year 7, as well as the recovery of the cumulative net working capital investment in Year 8. Amounts for depreciation were obtained by multiplying the depreciable basis by the Accelerated Cost Recovery System (*ACRS*) depreciation allowance rates set forth in footnote c to Table 16.2.

The analysis also requires an estimation of the cash flows generated by salvage values. Table 16.3 summarizes this analysis. First is a comparison between projected market and book values for salvageable assets. Land cannot be depreciated and has an estimated salvage value greater than the initial purchase price. Thus,

TABLE 16.2   **Net Cash Flows from Operations for New Plant Investment Project**

	Year					
	3	**4**	**5**	**6**	**7**	**8**
Unit sales	25,000	25,000	25,000	25,000	25,000	25,000
Sale price[a]	$ 2,200	$ 2,332	$ 2,472	$ 2,620	$ 2,777	$ 2,944
Net sales[a]	$55,000,000	$58,300,000	$61,800,000	$65,500,000	$69,425,000	$73,600,000
Variable costs[b]	35,750,000	37,895,000	40,170,000	42,575,000	45,126,250	47,840,000
Fixed costs (overhead)[a]	8,000,000	8,480,000	8,988,800	9,528,128	10,099,816	10,705,805
Depreciation (building)[c]	120,000	240,000	240,000	240,000	240,000	240,000
Depreciation (equipment)[c]	2,000,000	3,200,000	1,900,000	1,200,000	1,100,000	600,000
Earnings before taxes	$ 9,130,000	$ 8,485,000	$10,501,200	$11,956,872	$12,858,934	$14,214,195
Taxes (40%)	3,652,000	3,394,000	4,200,480	4,782,749	5,143,574	5,685,678
Projected net operating income	$ 5,478,000	$ 5,091,000	$ 6,300,720	$ 7,174,123	$ 7,715,360	$ 8,528,517
Add back noncash expenses[d]	2,120,000	3,440,000	2,140,000	1,440,000	1,340,000	840,000
Cash flow from operations[e]	$ 7,598,000	$ 8,531,000	$ 8,440,720	$ 8,614,123	$ 9,055,360	$ 9,368,517
Investment in net working capital (NWC)[f]	(396,000)	(420,000)	(444,000)	(471,000)	(501,000)	8,832,000
Net salvage value[g]						5,972,000
Total projected cash flows	$ 7,202,000	$ 8,111,000	$ 7,996,720	$ 8,143,123	$ 8,554,360	$ 24,172,517

[a]Year 3 estimate increased by the assumed 6 percent inflation rate.

[b]Sixty-five percent of net sales.

[c]*ACRS* depreciation rates were estimated as follows:

	Year					
	3	**4**	**5**	**6**	**7**	**8**
Building	1.5%	3%	3%	3%	3%	3%
Equipment	20	32	19	12	11	6

These percentages are multiplied by the depreciable basis to get the depreciation expense for each year. Note that the allowances have been rounded for ease of computation.

[d]In this case, depreciation on building and equipment.

[e]Net operating income plus noncash expenses.

[f]Twelve percent of next year's increase in sales. For example, Year 4 sales are $3.3 million over Year 3 sales, so the addition to NWC in Year 3 required to support Year 4 sales is $(0.12)(\$3,300,000) = \$396,000$. The cumulative working capital investment is recovered when the project ends.

[g]See Table 16.3 for the net salvage value calculation.

SVCC would have to pay taxes on the profit. The building has an estimated salvage value less than the book value; it will be sold at a loss for tax purposes. This loss will reduce taxable income and thus will generate a tax savings; in effect, the company has been depreciating the building too slowly, so it will write off the loss against ordinary income. Equipment, however, will be sold for more than book value, so the company will have to pay ordinary taxes on the $2 million profit. In all cases, the book value is the depreciable basis minus accumulated

TABLE 16.3   **Net Salvage Value Calculation for New Plant Investment Project**

	Land	Building	Equipment
Salvage (ending market) value	$1,700,000	$ 1,000,000	$ 2,000,000
Initial cost	1,200,000	8,000,000	10,000,000
Depreciable basis (Year 2)	0	8,000,000	10,000,000
Book value (Year 8)[a]	1,200,000	6,680,000	0
Capital gains income	$ 500,000	$ 0	$ 0
Ordinary income (loss)[b]	0	(5,680,000)	2,000,000
Taxes[c]	$ 200,000	($2,272,000)	$ 800,000
Net salvage value (Salvage Value − Taxes)	$1,500,000	$ 3,272,000	$ 1,200,000

Total Cash Flow from Salvage Value = $1,500,000 + $3,272,000 + $1,200,000 = $5,972,000.

[a]Book value for the building in Year 8 equals depreciable basis minus accumulated ACRS depreciation of $1,320,000. The accumulated depreciation on the equipment is $10,000,000. See Table 16.2.

[b]Building: $1,000,000 market value − $6,680,000 book value = $5,680,000 depreciation shortfall, which is treated as an operating expense in Year 8.

Equipment: $2,000,000 market value − $0 book value = $2,000,000 depreciation recapture, which is treated as ordinary income in Year 8.

[c]Since capital gains are now taxed at the ordinary income rate, all taxes are based on SVCC's 40 percent marginal federal-plus-state rate. The table is set up to differentiate ordinary income from capital gains because Congress may reinstate differential tax rates on those two income sources.

depreciation, and the total cash flow from salvage is merely the sum of the land, building, and equipment components.

As illustrated by this SVCC example, cash flow estimation involves a detailed analysis of demand, cost, and tax considerations. Even for fairly simple projects, such as that described here, the analysis can become complicated. Innovative and powerful spreadsheet software such as *Lotus 1-2-3* and *Microsoft Excel* make possible the accurate estimation of cash flows under a variety of operating assumptions, for even the most complex projects. More than just allowing managers to enter and manipulate data in several useful ways, these spreadsheet programs also incorporate various effective techniques for project evaluation. Among these techniques are a number of valuable capital budgeting decision rules.

CAPITAL BUDGETING DECISION RULES

An economically sound capital budgeting decision rule must consistently lead to the acceptance of projects that will increase the value of the firm. When the discounted present value of expected future cash flows exceeds the cost of investment, a project represents a worthy use of scarce resources and should be accepted for investment. When the discounted present value of expected future cash flows is less than the cost of investment, a project represents an inappropriate use of scarce resources and should be rejected. An effective capital budgeting decision rule must also lead to a consistent ranking of projects from most to least desirable and should be easy to apply. Net present value (NPV) analysis meets all of these criteria. As a result, it is the most commonly employed capital budgeting decision rule. However, the NPV method is only one of four capital budgeting decision rules that might be encountered in practice. Other techniques that are sometimes used to rank capital investment projects include the profitability index or benefit/cost ratio method, the internal rate of return approach, and the payback period. Each of these alternative capital budgeting decision rules, with the possible exception of the payback period, incorporates the essential features of NPV analysis and can be used to provide useful information on the desirability of individual projects. A comparison across methods is useful.

Net Present Value Analysis

Net present value

Current-dollar difference between marginal revenues and marginal costs.

Net present value (*NPV*) is the difference between the marginal revenues and marginal costs for individual investment projects, when both revenues and costs are expressed in present value terms. *NPV* analysis is typically based on the timing and magnitude of cash inflows and outflows, since traditional accounting data can be obscured by differences between cash and noncash expenses and revenues, tax considerations, and so on. *NPV* analysis is commonly used by managers to correctly employ marginal analysis in the capital budgeting process. To see *NPV* analysis as a reflection of marginal analysis and the value maximization theory of the firm, recall from Chapter 2 the basic valuation model:

$$
\begin{aligned}
\text{Value} &= \sum_{t=1}^{N} \frac{\pi_t}{(1 + k)^t} \\
&= \sum_{t=1}^{N} \frac{\text{Total Revenue}_t - \text{Total Cost}_t}{(1 + k)^t} \\
&= \sum_{t=1}^{N} \frac{\text{Net Cash Flow}_t}{(1 + k)^t} .
\end{aligned}
\qquad \textbf{(16.2)}
$$

In this equation, Net Cash Flow$_t$ represents the firm's total after-tax profit plus noncash expenses such as depreciation; k, which is based on an appraisal of the firm's overall riskiness, represents the average cost of capital to the firm. The value of the firm is simply the discounted present value of the difference between total cash inflows and total cash outflows. Any investment project is desirable if it increases the firm's net present value, and it is undesirable if accepting it causes the firm's net present value to decrease.

The use of net present value analysis in capital budgeting involves the application of the present value model described in Equation 16.2 to individual projects rather than to the firm as a whole. The procedure starts with an estimation of the expected net cash flows. Depending on the nature of the project, these estimates will have a greater or lesser degree of risk. For example, the benefits from replacing a piece of equipment used to produce a stable, established product can be estimated more accurately than those from an investment in equipment to produce a new and untried product. Next, the expected cost or investment outlay of the project must be estimated. This cost estimate will be quite accurate for purchased equipment, since cost equals the invoice price plus delivery and installation charges. Cost estimates for other kinds of projects may be highly uncertain or speculative. The next step involves the determination of an appropriate dis-

Cost of capital

Discount rate.

count rate, or **cost of capital,** for the project. A high discount rate is used for high-risk projects, and a low discount rate is used for low-risk projects. The cost of capital is considered in detail later in this chapter, but for now it may be thought of as being determined by the riskiness of the project—that is, by the uncertainty of the expected cash flows and the investment outlay. Finally, the present value of expected cash outflows must be subtracted from the present value of expected cash inflows to determine the net present value of the project. If $NPV > 0$, the project should be accepted. If $NPV < 0$, the project should be rejected. In equation form, the net present value of an individual project can be written as follows:

$$NPV_i = \sum_{t=1}^{N} \frac{E(CF_{it})}{(1 + k_i)^t} - \sum_{t=1}^{N} \frac{C_{it}}{(1 + k_i)^t}, \qquad (16.3)$$

where NPV_i is the *NPV* of the *i*th project, $E(CF_{it})$ represents the expected cash inflows of the *i*th project in the *t*th year, k_i is the risk-adjusted discount rate applicable to the *i*th project, and C_i is the project's investment cost or cash outflow.

▶ To illustrate the *NPV* method, consider the SVCC capital investment project discussed earlier. Table 16.4 shows net cash flows per year over the entire eight-year planning period in nominal dollars, as well as in dollars discounted using the firm's 15 percent cost of capital. Overall, the net cash flow earned on the project expressed in nominal dollars is $38,379,720. This amount is the sum of Column 2 and is equal to the last entry in Column 3, which shows the culmination of net cash flows over the life of the project. Net nominal cash flow is a misleading measure of the attractiveness of the project, however, since cash outlays necessary to fund the project must be made substantially before cash inflows are realized. A much more relevant measure of the attractiveness of this project is net cash flow expressed in present-value terms, where each dollar of cash outflow and inflow is converted on a common current-dollar basis. In Column 3, net nominal cash flows from Column 2 are multiplied by present-value interest factors from Column 4 that reflect a 15 percent cost of capital assumption. These present value interest factors are used to convert the nominal dollar outlays and returns from various periods on a common present-value basis.

The *NPV* for this investment project is given by the cumulative net discounted cash flow of $7,732,321 earned over the entire life of the project. This amount is given at the base of Column 5 and is the sum of net discounted cash flows over the life of the project. Note also that this amount is given as the last entry in Column 8, because it reflects the cumulative net discounted cash flow earned by the end of the project, Year 8. Alternatively, NPV is simply the difference between the $27,987,141 present value of cash inflows from Column 5, Year 3 through Year 8, minus the $20,254,820 present value of cash outflows from Column 5, Year 0 through 2. In equation form, the *NPV* for this project is calculated as follows:

$$NPV = PV \text{ of Cash Inflows} - PV \text{ of Cash Outflows} \qquad (16.4)$$
$$= \$27,987,141 - \$20,254,820$$
$$= \$7,732,321.$$

TABLE 16.4 Consolidated End-of-Year Net Cash Flow Analysis for New Plant Investment Project Example

Year (1)	Net Nominal Cash Flows (2)	Cumulative Net Nominal Cash Flows (3)	Present Value Interest Factor (*PVIF*) at 15% (4)	Net Discounted Cash Flows (5) = (3) × (4)	Cumulative Net Discounted Cash Flows (6)
0	($ 1,200,000)	($ 1,200,000)	1.0000	($ 1,200,000)	($ 1,200,000)
1	(4,000,000)	(5,200,000)	0.8696	(3,478,261)	(4,678,261)
2	(20,600,000)	(25,800,000)	0.7561	(15,576,560)	(20,254,820)
3	7,202,000	(18,598,000)	0.6575	4,735,432	(15,519,389)
4	8,111,000	(10,487,000)	0.5718	4,637,491	(10,881,898)
5	7,996,720	(2,490,280)	0.4972	3,975,783	(6,906,115)
6	8,143,123	5,652,843	0.4323	3,520,497	(3,385,618)
7	8,554,360	14,207,203	0.3759	3,215,901	(169,717)
8	24,172,517	38,379,720	0.3269	7,902,039	7,732,321
Sum	$38,379,720			$ 7,732,321	

Note: Negative net cash flows represent net cash outlays and are shown within parentheses.

Because dollar inflows received in the future are worth less than necessary dollar outlays at the beginning of the project, the *NPV* for the project is much less than the $38,379,720 received in net nominal cash flows (see Columns 2 and 3). This divergence between nominal and discounted cash flow figures reflects the time value of money. In present-value terms, the difference between the marginal costs and marginal revenues derived from this project is $7,732,321. This is a desirable project that if undertaken would increase the value of the firm by this amount.

Firms typically make investments in projects showing positive net present values, reject those with negative net present values, and choose between mutually exclusive investments on the basis of higher net present values. For many capital budgeting problems, the use of the *NPV* method is far more complex than the preceding description suggests. The capital budgeting problem may require analysis of mutually exclusive projects with different expected lives or with substantially different initial costs. A complication also arises when the size of the firm's capital budget is limited. Under these conditions, a variant of the simple NPV is used to select projects that maximize the value of the firm.

Profitability Index or Benefit/Cost Ratio

Although individual projects might promise relatively attractive yields, combining them can create unforeseen difficulties. Undertaking a large number of projects simultaneously can require a very fast rate of expansion. Additional personnel requirements and organizational problems can arise that diminish overall rates of return. At some point in the capital budgeting process, management must decide what total volume of favorable projects the firm can successfully undertake without significantly reducing projected returns. Another reason for limiting the capital budget at some firms is the reluctance or inability to obtain external financing by issuing debt or selling stock. For example, considering the plight of firms with substantial amounts of debt during economic recession, management may simply refuse to use high levels of debt financing. Such capital rationing complicates the capital budgeting process and requires more complex tools of analysis.

A variant of *NPV* analysis that is often used in complex capital budgeting situations is called the **profitability index** (*PI*), or the benefit/cost ratio method. The profitability index is calculated as follows:

Profitability index
Benefit/cost ratio.

$$PI = \frac{PV \text{ of Cash Inflows}}{PV \text{ of Cash Outflows}} = \frac{\sum_{t=1}^{N} [E(CF_{it})/(1 + k_i)^t]}{\sum_{t=1}^{N} [C_{it}/(1 + k_i)^t]}. \tag{16.5}$$

The *PI* shows the *relative* profitability of any project, or the present value of benefits per dollar of cost.

In the SVCC example described in Table 16.4, *NPV* > 0 implies a desirable investment project and *PI* > 1. To see that this is indeed the case, we can use the profitability index formula, given in Equation 16.5, and the present value of cash inflows and outflows from the project, given in Equation 16.4. The profitability index for the SVCC project is

$$
\begin{aligned}
PI &= \frac{PV \text{ of Cash Inflows}}{PV \text{ of Outflows}} \\
&= \frac{\$27,987,141}{\$20,254,820}, \\
&= 1.38
\end{aligned}
$$

This means that the SVCC capital investment project returns $1.38 in cash inflows for each dollar of cash outflow, when both figures are expressed in present-value terms.

In *PI* analysis, a project with *PI* > 1 should be accepted and a project with *PI* < 1 should be rejected. Projects will be accepted provided that they return more than a dollar of discounted benefits for each dollar of cost. Thus, the *PI* and *NPV* methods always indicate the same accept/reject decisions for independent projects, since *PI* > 1 implies *NPV* > 0 and *PI* < 1 implies *NPV* < 0. However, for alternative projects of unequal size, *PI* and *NPV* criteria can give different project rankings. This can sometimes cause problems when mutually exclusive projects are being evaluated. Before investigating the source of such conflicts, however, it is worthwhile to introduce two additional capital budgeting decision rules.

Internal Rate
of Return

The **internal rate of return** (*IRR*) is the interest or discount rate that equates the present value of the future receipts of a project to the initial cost or outlay. The equation for calculating the internal rate of return is simply the *NPV* formula set equal to zero:

Internal rate of return
Discount rate that equates
present value of cash
inflows and outflows.

$$NPV_i = 0 = \frac{\sum_{t=1}^{N} E(CF_{it})}{(1 + k_i^*)^t} - \frac{\sum_{t=1}^{N} C_{it}}{(1 + k_i^*)^t}. \tag{16.6}$$

Here the equation is solved for the discount rate, k_i^*, that produces a zero net present value or causes the sum of the discounted future receipts to equal the initial cost. That discount rate is the internal rate of return earned by the project.

Because the net present value equation is complex, it is difficult to solve for the actual internal rate of return on an investment without a computer or sophisticated calculator. For this reason, trial and error is sometimes employed. One begins by arbitrarily selecting a discount rate. If it yields a positive *NPV*, the internal rate of return must be greater than the interest or discount rate used, and another higher rate is tried. If the chosen rate yields a negative *NPV*, the internal rate of return on the project is lower than the discount rate, and the *NPV* calculation must be repeated using a lower discount rate. This process of changing the discount rate and recalculating the net present value continues until the discounted present value of the future cash flows equals the initial cost. The interest rate that brings about this equality is the yield, or internal rate of return on the project.

Using trial and error, an electronic calculator, or a spreadsheet software program such as *Lotus 1-2-3* or *Microsoft Excel,* the internal rate of return for the SVCC investment project is IRR $= 25.1\%$. Since this *IRR* exceeds the 15 percent cost of capital, the project is attractive and should be undertaken. In general, internal rate of return analysis suggests that projects should be accepted when the *IRR* $> k$ and rejected when the *IRR* $< k$. When the *IRR* $> k$, the marginal rate of return earned on the project exceeds the marginal cost of capital. As in the case of projects with an *NPV* > 0 and *PI* > 1, the acceptance of all investment projects with *IRR* $> k$ will lead management to maximize the value of the firm. In instances in which capital is scarce and only a limited number of desirable projects can be undertaken at one point in time, the IRR can be used to derive a rank ordering of projects from most desirable to least desirable. Like a rank ordering of all *NPV* > 0 projects from highest to lowest PIs, a rank ordering of potential investment projects from highest to lowest IRRs allows managers to effectively employ scarce funds.

Payback Period

Payback period

Number of years required to recover initial investment.

The **payback period** is the expected number of years of operation required to recover an initial investment. When project cash flows are discounted using an appropriate cost of capital, the discounted payback period is the expected number of years required to recover the initial investment from discounted net cash flows. Using actual or discounted net cash flows, calculation of the payback period is quick and easy. In equation form, the payback period is

$$\text{Payback Period} = \text{Number of Years to Recover Investment.} \quad \textbf{(16.7)}$$

The payback period can be thought of as a breakeven time period. The shorter the payback period, the more desirable the investment project. The longer the payback period, the less desirable the investment project.

▶ To illustrate, consider the SVCC capital investment project discussed earlier. Table 16.4 shows net cash flows per year over the entire eight-year planning period in nominal dollars, as well as in dollars discounted using the firm's 15 percent cost of capital. In nominal dollars, the total amount of investment is $25.8

million, which is the sum of the dollar outlays given in the first three rows of Column 2. As shown in the third row of Column 3, a negative $25.8 million is also the cumulative value of the nominal net cash flow as of the end of Year 2, just prior to the beginning of plant operations. When the nominal cash outlay of $25.8 million is discounted using the firm's 15 percent cost of capital, the present value of the investment cash outlay is $20,254,820, the sum of discounted cash outlays given in the first three rows of Column 5. As shown in the third row of Column 6, a negative $20,254,820 is also the cumulative value of net discounted cash flow as of the end of Year 2, just prior to the beginning of plant operations.

Based on nominal dollar cash outflows and inflows, the payback period is completed between the end of Year 5, when the cumulative net nominal cash flow is a negative $2,490,280, and the end of Year 6, when the cumulative net nominal cash flow is a positive $5,652,843. Using nominal dollars, the payback period of years is calculated as

$$\text{Nominal Payback Period} = 5.00 + \$2,490,280/\$8,143,123$$
$$= 5.30 \text{ years.}$$

Based on cash outflows and inflows discounted using the firm's 15 percent cost of capital, the payback period is completed between the end of Year 7, when the cumulative net discounted cash flow is a negative $169,717, and the end of Year 8, when the cumulative net discounted cash flow is a positive $7,732,321. Using discounted net cash flows, the payback period of years is calculated as

$$\text{Discounted Payback Period} = 7.00 + \$169,717/\$7,902,039$$
$$= 7.02 \text{ years.}$$

Of course, these payback period calculations are based on the typical assumption that cash inflows are received continuously throughout the operating period. If cash inflows are received only at the end of the operating period, then the nominal payback period in this example would be six years and the discounted payback period would be eight years. The exact length of the payback period depends on underlying assumptions concerning the pattern of cash inflows.

Note that the payback period is a breakeven calculation in that if cash flows come in at the expected rate until the payback year, the project will break even in an accounting sense. However, the nominal payback period does not take into account the cost of capital; the cost of the debt and equity used to undertake the project is not reflected in the cash flow calculation. The discounted payback period does take account of capital costs—it shows the breakeven year after covering debt and equity costs. Both payback methods have the serious deficiency of not taking into account any cash flows beyond the payback year. Other capital budgeting decision rules are more likely to lead to better project rankings and selections. The discounted payback period, however, does provide useful information about how long funds will be tied up in a project. The shorter the discounted payback period, the greater the project's liquidity. Also, cash flows expected in the distant future are generally regarded as riskier than near-term cash flows. Therefore, the discounted payback period is a useful but rough measure of liquidity and project risk.

●

MANAGERIAL APPLICATION 16.2
Effective Capital Budgeting for the 1990s

Management today faces the serious challenge of adding value to the businesses they manage. Historically, when management thought about competition, it considered the effects of actual and potential competitors in current or future product markets. Today, management must be concerned with yet another type of competition—the competition to manage resources in the market for corporate control.

Stock market prices reflect the discounted net present value of a company's expected future cash flows. To the extent that management gets full value out of the assets under its control, the firm's stock price will maintain its maximum potential value. If management gets less than full value out of its assets, the stock price will be lower than its full potential value. In the rapidly changing economic environment of the 1980s, a number of companies could not achieve the synergistic and other benefits of conglomerate businesses. Similarly, the weakened span of control that sometimes resulted when management tried to oversee a large portfolio of companies led to underutilization of corporate resources. As a result, many such firms were bought out by competitors and other outside "raiders" at high stock-price premiums. Radically restructured, they emerged as leaner, more focused, and more profitable companies. Increased stock market values made possible by higher profitability allowed both selling stockholders and buying firms or individuals to benefit from this restructuring—win-win situations for investors but not for displaced managements.

To meet the need for efficient resource utilization, managements have increasingly incorporated modern financial theory in a "value-based planning" approach to capital budgeting. Value-based planning presumes that the purpose of managerial decision making is to increase the value of the firm as measured by the current market price of the company's common stock. Given the typically close relation between stock prices and cash flow data, corporate management has increasingly evaluated the profitability of investment proposals on the basis of their ability to generate net or "free" cash flows (cash flows minus investment requirements). This

contrasts with more traditional approaches that focus on accounting earnings. Attention has shifted from accounting earnings to cash flows and stock prices because accounting data sometimes obscure the true economic performance of the firm. To increase the value of the firm, value-based capital budgeting simply emphasizes projects with the potential to generate maximum cash flows. These flows can then either be profitably reinvested or paid out to shareholders as dividends or in stock repurchase programs. Of course, discounted cash flow analysis and cost-of-capital calculations have long been a standard tool for capital budgeting. What is different with value-based planning in the current corporate environment is that NPV techniques are being increasingly applied to each separate line of business, investments, and products.

The 1992 European market retrenchment strategy adopted by Federal Express Corp. provides a good case in point. The air-express giant tried and failed to build a package-delivery franchise in Europe from the ground up, and instead decided to cut its losses by relying on local partners to deliver many of its European parcels. While Federal Express still expects to deliver almost one-half of its European parcels itself, the company stopped delivering between European cities. Local operations will remain, but Federal Express plans to keep employees there primarily to ensure that its local partners are meeting Federal Express delivery standards.

A prime factor behind this change in Federal Express policy is that the company could no longer justify the corporate commitment to Europe in light of increasingly vigorous competition in the U.S. market. United Parcel Service of America, Inc., and Airborne Freight Corp. are strong rivals that have been gaining market share during recent years. By stemming European losses, Federal Express is poised to further consolidate its market-leading position in the United States. Apparently, Wall Street approves. On the day Federal Express announced its European decision, the company's common stock finished at $55.25 per share, up $1.25 in heavy volume.

Source: Daniel Pearl, "Federal Express Pins Hopes on New Strategy in Europe," *The Wall Street Journal,* March 18, 1992, B4.

CHOOSING AMONG
ALTERNATIVE PROJECTS

The preceding section shows how application of the net present value method in the capital budgeting process permits a rank ordering of investment projects from most attractive to least attractive. An investment project is attractive and should be pursued as long as the discounted net present value of cash inflows is greater than the discounted net present value of the investment requirement, or net cash outlay. Because the attractiveness of individual projects increases with the magnitude of this difference, high *NPV* projects are inherently more appealing and are preferred to low *NPV* projects. Any investment project that is incapable of generating sufficient cash inflows to cover necessary cash outlays, when both are expressed on a present-value basis, should not be undertaken. In the case of a project with $NPV = 0$, project acceptance would neither increase nor decrease the value of the firm. Management would be indifferent to pursuing such a project. *NPV* analysis represents a practical application of the marginal concept, in which the marginal revenues and marginal costs of investment projects are considered on a present-value basis. Use of the *NPV* technique in the evaluation of alternative investment projects allows managers to apply the principles of marginal analysis in a simple and clear manner. The widespread practical use of the *NPV* technique also lends support to the view of value maximization as the prime objective pursued by managers in the capital budgeting process.

Just as acceptance of $NPV > 0$ projects will enhance the value of the firm, so too will acceptance of projects for which the $PI > 1$ and the $IRR > k$. Acceptance of projects for which $NPV < 0$, $PI < 1$, or $IRR < k$ would be unwise and would reduce the value of the firm. Because each of these project evaluation techniques shares a common focus on the present value of net cash inflows and outflows, they display a high degree of consistency in terms of the project accept/reject decision. This high degree of consistency might even lead one to question the usefulness of having these alternative ways of project evaluation when only one, the *NPV* method, seems sufficient for decision-making purposes. However, even though these alternative capital budgeting decision rules will consistently lead to the same project accept/reject decision, they involve important differences in terms of project ranking. Projects ranked most favorably using the *NPV* method may appear less so when analyzed using the *PI* or *IRR* methods. Projects ranked most favorably using the *PI* or *IRR* methods may appear less so when analyzed using the *NPV* technique. The purpose of this section is to explain the reasons for these differences in project rankings and to illustrate how such differences can be dealt with.

Reasons for Decision
Rule Conflict

If the application of a capital budgeting decision rule is to consistently lead to correct investment decisions, it must consider the time value of money in the evaluation of all cash flows and must rank projects according to their ultimate impact on the value of the firm. *NPV, PI,* and *IRR* methods satisfy both criteria, and each can be used to value and rank capital budgeting projects. The payback method does not meet both of the preceding criteria and should be used only as a complement to the other techniques. However, each of the *NPV, PI,* and *IRR* methods incorporates certain assumptions that can and do affect project rankings. Understanding the sources of these differences and learning how to deal with them is an important part of knowing how to correctly evaluate alternative investment projects.

As discussed earlier, *NPV* is the difference between the marginal revenues and marginal costs of an individual investment project, when both revenues and costs are expressed in present-value terms. *NPV* measures the relative attractiveness of alternative investment projects by the discounted dollar difference between revenues and costs. *NPV* is an *absolute* measure of the attractiveness of a given investment project. Conversely, the *PI* reflects the difference between the marginal revenues and marginal costs of an individual project in ratio form. The *PI* is the ratio of the discounted present value of cash inflows divided by the discounted present value of cash outflows. *PI* is a *relative* measure of project attractiveness. It follows that application of the *NPV* method leads to the highest ranking for large profitable projects. Use of the *PI* method leads to the highest ranking for projects that return the greatest amount of cash inflow per dollar of outflow, regardless of project size. At times, application of the *NPV* method can create a bias for larger as opposed to smaller projects—a problem when all favorable *NPV* > 0 projects cannot be pursued. When capital is scarce, application of the *PI* method has the potential to create a better project mix for the firm's overall investment portfolio.

Both *NPV* and *PI* methods differ from the *IRR* technique in terms of their underlying assumptions regarding the reinvestment of cash flows during the life of the project. In the *NPV* and *PI* methods, excess cash flows generated over the life of the project are "reinvested" at the firm's cost of capital. In the *IRR* method, excess cash flows are reinvested at the *IRR*. For especially attractive investment projects that generate an exceptionally high rate of return, the *IRR* can actually overstate project attractiveness because reinvestment of excess cash flows at a similarly high *IRR* is not possible. When reinvestment at the project-specific *IRR* is not possible, the *IRR* method must be adapted to take into account the lower rate of return that can actually be earned on excess cash flows generated over the life of individual projects. Otherwise, use of the *NPV* or *PI* methods is preferable.

The Ranking Reversal Problem

A further and more serious conflict can arise between *NPV* and *IRR* methods when projects differ significantly in terms of the magnitude and timing of cash flows. When the size or pattern of alternative project cash flows differs greatly, each project's *NPV* can react quite differently to changes in the discount rate. As a result, changes in the appropriate discount rate can sometimes lead to reversals in project rankings.

To illustrate the potential for conflict between *NPV* and *IRR* rankings and the possibility of ranking reversals, Table 16.5 shows a further development of the SVCC plant investment project example. Assume that the company is considering the original new plant investment project in light of an alternative proposal to buy and remodel an existing plant. Old plant and equipment can be purchased for an

T A B L E 1 6 . 5　**A Comparison of the "Build New Plant" versus "Remodel Old Plant" Investment Project Example Using Alternative Capital Budgeting Decision Rules**

A. Investment Project Cash Flow Projections

Year	Build New Plant Project Net Nominal Cash Flows	Remodel Old Plant Project Net Nominal Cash Flows
0	($ 1,200,000)	($11,500,000)
1	(4,000,000)	(2,000,000)
2	(20,600,000)	(8,600,000)
3	7,202,000	7,202,000
4	8,111,000	8,111,000
5	7,996,720	7,996,720
6	8,143,123	8,143,123
7	8,554,360	8,554,360
8	24,172,517	24,172,517
Sum	$38,379,720	$42,079,720
IRR	25.06%	23.57%

Note: Negative net cash flows represent net cash outlays and are shown within parentheses.

B. Evaluation Using Alternative Capital Budgeting Decision Rules

	Build New	Remodel Old
0% Discount Rate:		
PV of cash inflows	$64,179,720	$64,179,720
PV of cash outflows	($25,800,000)	($22,100,000)
NPV	$38,379,720	$42,079,720
PI	2.49	2.90
Discounted payback period	5.30	4.85
15% Discount Rate:		
PV of cash inflows	$27,987,142	$27,987,142
PV of cash outflows	($20,254,820)	($19,741,966)
NPV	$ 7,732,321	$ 8,245,176
PI	1.38	1.42
Discounted payback period	7.02	6.89
25% Discount Rate:		
PV of cash inflows	$17,614,180	$17,614,180
PV of cash outflows	($17,584,000)	($18,604,000)
NPV	$ 30,180	($ 989,820)
PI	1.00	0.95
Discounted payback period	7.99	—

initial cash outlay of $11.5 million and can be remodeled at a cost of $2 million per year over the next two years. As before, a net working capital investment of $6.6 million will be required just prior to opening the remodeled production facility. For simplicity, assume that after Year 2, all cash inflows and outflows are the same for the remodeled and new plant facilities.

Note that the new plant proposal involves an initial nominal cash outlay of $25.8 million, whereas the remodeled plant alternative involves a nominal cash outlay of $22.1 million. In addition to this difference in project size, the two investment alternatives differ in terms of the timing of cash flows. The new plant alternative involves a larger but later commitment of funds. To see the implications of these differences, notice how the "remodel old plant" alternative is preferred at and below the firm's 15 percent cost of capital using *NPV* and *PI* methods, even though the *IRR* of 25.06 percent for the new plant project exceeds the *IRR* of 23.57 percent for the "remodel old plant" alternative. Also troubling is that the relative ranking of these projects according to *NPV* and *PI* methods is reversed at higher discount rates. Notice how the "build new plant" alternative is preferred using *NPV* and *PI* techniques when a 25 percent discount rate is employed.

Net present value profile
Graph relating *NPV* to the discount rate.

Figure 16.1 displays the potential conflict between *NPV, PI,* and *IRR* project rankings at various interest rates by showing the effect of discount rate changes on the *NPV* of each alternative investment project. This **net present value profile**

FIGURE 16.1   *NPV* **Profiles for the "Build New Plant" versus "Remodel Old Plant" Investment Project Alternatives**

Each profile relates project *NPV* to the discount rate used in the *NPV* calculation.

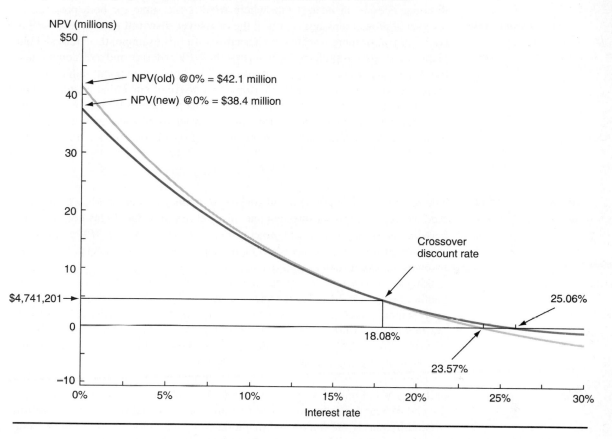

relates the *NPV* for each project to the discount rate used in the *NPV* calculation. Using a $k = 0$ percent discount rate, the *NPV* for the "build new plant" investment project is $38.4 million, and it is $42.1 million for the "remodel old plant" alternative. These *NPV* values correspond to the difference between nominal dollar cash inflows and outflows for each project and also coincide with *NPV* line y-axis intercepts of $38.4 million for the "build new plant" project and $42.1 million for the "remodel old plant" alternative. The x-axis intercept for each curve occurs at the discount rate where *NPV* = 0 for each project. Since *NPV* = 0 when the discount rate is set equal to the *IRR*, or when *IRR* = k, the x-axis intercept for the "build new plant" alternative is at the *IRR* = 25.06 percent level, and it is at the *IRR* = 23.57 percent level for the "remodel old plant" alternative.

Figure 16.1 illustrates how ranking reversals can occur at various *NPV* discount rates. Given higher nominal dollar returns and, therefore, a higher y-axis intercept, the "remodel old plant" alternative is preferred when very low discount rates are used in the *NPV* calculation. Given a higher *IRR* and, therefore, a higher x-axis intercept, the "build new plant" alternative is preferred when very high discount rates are used in the calculation of *NPV*. Between very high and low discount rates is an interest rate where *NPV* is the same for both projects. A reversal of project rankings occurs at the **crossover discount rate,** where *NPV* is equal for two or more investment alternatives. In this example, the "remodel old plant" alternative is preferred when using the *NPV* criterion and a discount rate *k* that is less than the crossover discount rate. The "build new plant" alternative is preferred when using the *NPV* criterion and a discount rate *k* that is greater than the crossover discount rate. This ranking reversal problem is typical of situations in which investment projects differ greatly in terms of their underlying *NPV* profiles. Hence, a potentially troubling conflict exists between *NPV, PI,* and *IRR* methods.

Crossover discount rate

Interest factor that equates *NPV* for two or more investments.

Making the Correct Investment Decision

The ranking reversal problem and suggested conflict between *NPV, PI,* and *IRR* methods is much less serious than one might at first imagine. Many comparisons between alternative investment projects involve neither crossing *NPV* profiles nor crossover discount rates as shown in Figure 16.1. Some other project comparisons involve crossover discount rates that are either too low or too high to affect project rankings at the current cost of capital. As a result, there is often no meaningful conflict between *NPV* and *IRR* project rankings.

When crossover discount rates are relevant, they can be easily calculated as the *IRR* of the cash-flow *difference* between two investment alternatives. To see that this is indeed the case, consider how cash flows differ between each of the two plant investment alternatives considered previously. The "build new plant" alternative involves a smaller initial cash outflow of $1.2 million versus $11.5 million, a $10.3 million saving, but it requires additional outlays of $2 million at the end of Year 1 plus an additional $12 million at the end of Year 2. Except for these differences, the timing and magnitude of cash inflows and outflows from the two projects are identical. The *IRR* for the cash flow difference between two investment alternatives exactly balances the present-value cost of higher cash outflows with the present-value benefit of higher cash inflows. At this *IRR,* the cash flow difference between the two investment alternatives has an *NPV* equal to zero. When *k* is less than this crossover *IRR,* the investment project with the greater nominal dollar return will have a larger *NPV* and will tend to be favored. In the present example, this is the "remodel old plant" alternative. When *k* is greater than the crossover *IRR,* the project with an earlier cash flow pattern will have the larger *NPV* and be favored. In the current example, this is the "build new plant" alternative. When *k* equals the crossover *IRR,* the cash flow difference between projects has an *NPV* = 0, and each project has exactly the same *NPV*.

Once an economically relevant crossover discount rate has been determined, management must decide whether to rely on *NPV* or *IRR* decision rules in the resolution of the ranking reversal problem. Logic suggests that the *NPV* ranking should dominate because that method will result in a value-maximizing selection of projects. In most situations, it is also more realistic to assume reinvestment of excess cash flows during the life of a project at the current cost of capital *k*. This again favors *NPV* over *IRR* rankings. As a result, conflicts between *NPV* and *IRR* project rankings are usually resolved in favor of the *NPV* rank order.

Finally, given the size-based conflict between the *NPV* and *PI* methods, which one should be relied on in the ranking of potential investment projects? Alternatively stated: Is it better to use the net present value approach on an absolute basis (*NPV*) or on a relative basis (*PI*)? For a firm with substantial investment resources and a goal of maximizing shareholder wealth, the *NPV* method is better. For a firm with limited resources, the *PI* approach allocates scarce resources to the projects with the greatest relative effect on value. Using the *PI* method, projects are evaluated on the basis of their *NPV* per dollar of investment, avoiding a possible bias toward larger projects. In some cases, this leads to a better combination of investment projects and higher firm value. The *PI,* or benefit/cost ratio, approach has also proved to be a useful tool in public-sector decision making, where allocating scarce public resources among competing projects is a typical problem.

As seen in the evaluation of alternative capital budgeting decision rules, the attractiveness of investment projects varies significantly depending on the interest rate used to discount future cash flows. Determination of the correct discount rate is a vitally important aspect of the capital budgeting process. This important issue is the subject of the next section.

THE COST OF CAPITAL

If firms typically considered projects one by one and raised investment funds for each project separately, calculation of a suitable discount rate would be easy. The correct discount rate to employ for each investment project would simply be the marginal cost of capital for that project. However, determination of the correct discount rate for individual projects is seldom that straightforward. Firms rarely consider individual projects in isolation but instead tend to evaluate *portfolios* of potential investment projects to be funded from an ongoing stream of new capital funds generated by retained earnings and new capital raising efforts. New projects are funded by a mix of debt and equity financing, and each debt and equity component of new capital can be expected to have different costs. Calculation of the correct discount rate for any given potential investment project typically involves weighing the relative importance of each component cost of new financing.

The Component Cost of Debt Financing

Component cost of debt

Interest rate investors require on debt, adjusted for taxes.

The **component cost of debt** is the interest rate that investors require on debt, adjusted for taxes. If a firm borrows $100,000 for one year at 10 percent interest, the before-tax cost is $10,000 and the before-tax interest rate is 10 percent. However, interest payments on debt are deductible for income tax purposes. It is necessary to account for this tax deductibility by adjusting the cost of debt to an after-tax basis. The deductibility of interest payments means, in effect, that the government pays part of a firm's interest charges. This reduces the firm's cost of debt financing. The after-tax component cost of debt is given by the following expression:

$$k_d = (\text{Interest Rate}) \times (1.0 - \text{Tax Rate}). \qquad (16.8)$$

Assuming that the firm's marginal federal-plus-state tax rate is 40 percent, the after-tax cost of debt will be 60 percent ($= 1.0 - 0.4$) of the nominal interest rate.

The relevant component cost of debt applies only to *new* debt, not to the interest on old or previously outstanding debt. In other words, the cost of new debt financing is what is relevant in terms of the *marginal cost of debt.* It is irrelevant that the firm borrowed at higher or lower rates in the past.

The Component Cost of Equity Financing

Component cost of equity

Rate of return stockholders require on common stock.

Risk-free rate of return

Investor reward for postponing consumption.

Risk premium

Investor reward for risk taking.

Beta coefficient

A measure of relative stock-price variability.

The **component cost of equity** is the rate of return stockholders require on common stock. This return includes a compensation to investors for postponing their consumption, plus a return to compensate for risk taking. Therefore, the component cost of equity consists of a **risk-free rate of return,** R_F, plus a **risk premium,** R_P:

$$k_e = R_F + R_P. \tag{16.9}$$

The risk-free return is typically estimated by the interest rate on short-term U.S. government securities. On a daily basis, these rates of return can be obtained from the *Wall Street Journal* and other sources. Various methods can be used to estimate R_P for different securities. Because dividends paid to stockholders are not deductible for income tax purposes, dividend payments must be made with after-tax dollars. There is no tax adjustment for the component cost of equity capital.

A first method for estimating k_e and R_P is based on the capital asset pricing model, or *CAPM.* This method assumes that the risk of a stock depends on the sensitivity of its return to changes in the return on all securities. A stock that is twice as risky as the overall market would entail twice the market risk premium; a security that is one-half as risky as the overall market would earn one-half the market risk premium, and so on. In the *CAPM* approach, the riskiness of a given stock is measured in terms of the variability of its return relative to the variability of returns on all stocks, perhaps as represented by the volatility in the Standard and Poor's 500 Index. A firm's **beta coefficient,** β, is a measure of this variability. In a simple regression model, the beta coefficient for an individual firm, β_i, is estimated as

$$R_i = \alpha_i + \beta_i R_M + e, \tag{16.10}$$

where R_i is the weekly or monthly return on a given stock and R_M is a similar return on the market as a whole (e.g., Standard and Poor's 500 Index). A stock with average risk has a beta of 1.0. Low-risk stocks have betas less than 1.0; high-risk stocks have betas greater than 1.0. Although beta estimation is a relatively simple task, managers seldom need to actually run such regressions. Analysts at Merrill Lynch and other leading brokerage houses, as well as investment advisory services such as *The Value Line Investment Survey,* provide beta estimates that can be used for equity capital cost estimation.

In addition to data on the R_F rate and β_i for a given company, the *CAPM* approach requires an estimate of the expected rate of return on the market as a whole. This return, k_M, is a relative benchmark for measuring the risk premium on the market. With these three inputs, R_F, β_i, and k_M, the *CAPM* estimate of the required rate of return on any given stock is

$$k_e = R_F + \beta(k_M - R_F), \tag{16.11}$$

where the value $(k_M - R_F)$ is the market risk premium, or risk premium on an average stock. Multiplying this market risk premium by the index of risk for a particular stock, β, gives the risk premium for that stock.

To illustrate, assume that $R_F = 8\%$, $k_M = 14\%$, and $\beta_i = 0.5$ for a given stock. Remember, $\beta_i = 0.5$ means that a given stock is only one-half as risky as the overall market. Under such circumstances, the stock's required return is

$$k_e = 8 + 0.5(14 - 8) = 8 + 3 = 11\%.$$

If $\beta = 1.5$, indicating that a stock is 50 percent riskier than the average security, then k_e is

$$k_e = 8 + 1.5(14 - 8) = 8 + 9 = 17\%.$$

A second common technique adds a premium of 4 or 5 percent onto the risk premium paid on a firm's long-term bonds. Using this approach, the total risk premium on equity equals the difference between the yield on the firm's debt and that on risk-free government bonds, *plus* 4 to 5 percent. For example, if risk-free government bonds yield 8 percent, and a firm's bonds are priced to yield 10 percent, the cost of equity, k_e, is

$$k_e = \text{Firm Bond Rate} + 4\% \text{ to } 5\% \text{ Risk Premium}$$

$$= 10\% + 4\% \text{ to } 5\% = 14\% \text{ to } 15\%.$$

Given an 8 percent return on risk-free government bonds, this implies a total risk premium for equity of 6 percent to 7 percent, since

$$14\% \text{ to } 15\% = 8\% + R_P$$

$$R_P = 6\% \text{ to } 7\%.$$

Managers who rely on this method often cite historical studies suggesting that the long-term 1930–1990 annual risk premium on investments in common stocks is generally 6 to 7 percent over that earned on government bonds. The primary difficulty with estimating risk premiums from historical returns is that historical returns differ depending on the beginning and ending dates of the estimation period, and past differences in stock and bond returns may not precisely indicate future required risk premiums.

Yet another method for determining the cost of equity is to use a constant growth model. If earnings, dividends, and the stock price all grow at the same rate, then

$$\text{Required Return} \atop \text{on Equity} = \text{Dividend Yield} + \text{Capital Gains}$$

$$= \frac{\text{Expected Dividend}}{\text{Current Stock Price}} + \frac{\text{Expected}}{\text{Growth Rate}} \quad \textbf{(16.12)}$$

$$= \frac{\text{Dividend}}{\text{Price}} + \frac{\text{Expected}}{\text{Growth Rate}},$$

$$k_e = \frac{D_1}{P_0} + g .$$

The rationale for this equation is that stockholder returns are derived from dividends and capital gains. If past growth rates in earnings and dividends have been relatively stable, and if investors expect a continuation of past trends, then g may be based on the firm's historic growth rate. However, if the company's growth has been abnormally high or low, either because of its own unique situation or because of general economic conditions, investors will not project historical growth rate into the future. Security analyst estimates of g must then be relied on. These earnings forecasts are regularly published by *Business Week, Forbes, Value Line,* and other sources and offer a useful proxy for the growth expectations of investors in general. When security analyst growth projections are combined with the dividend yield expected during the coming period, k_e can be estimated as

$$k_e = \frac{D_1}{P_0} + \frac{\text{Growth Rate Projected}}{\text{by Security Analysts}} . \quad \textbf{(16.13)}$$

In practice, it is often best to use all of these methods and try to arrive at a consensus estimate.

The Weighted Average Cost of Capital

Suppose that the interest rate on new debt is 10 percent and the firm's marginal federal-plus-state income tax rate is 40 percent. This implies a 6 percent after-tax component cost of debt. Also assume that the firm has decided to finance next year's projects by selling debt. Does this mean that next year's investment projects have a 6 percent cost of capital? The answer is no, at least not usually. In financing a particular set of projects with debt, the firm typically uses up some of its potential for obtaining further low-cost debt financing. As expansion takes place, the firm typically finds it necessary to raise additional high-cost equity to avoid unacceptably high leverage. As a result, the current component cost of debt seldom measures the true long-term opportunity cost of debt financing. To illustrate, suppose that the firm has a current 6 percent cost of debt and a 15 percent cost of equity. In the first year it borrows heavily, using up its debt capacity in the process, to finance projects yielding 7 percent. In the second year it has projects available that yield 13 percent, almost twice the return on first-year projects, but it cannot accept them because they would have to be financed with 15 percent equity. To avoid this problem, the firm should be viewed as an ongoing concern, and the cost of capital should be calculated as a weighted average of the various types of funds it uses.

Weighted average cost of capital

The marginal cost of a composite dollar of debt and equity financing.

The **weighted average cost of capital** is the interest rate necessary to attract additional funds for new capital investment projects. It is the marginal cost of a

FIGURE 16.2 **Hypothetical Cost-of-Capital Schedules for an Industry**

A U-shaped weighted average cost of capital curve reflects, first, lower capital costs because of the tax benefits of debt financing and, second, increasing capital costs as bankruptcy risk increases for highly leveraged firms.

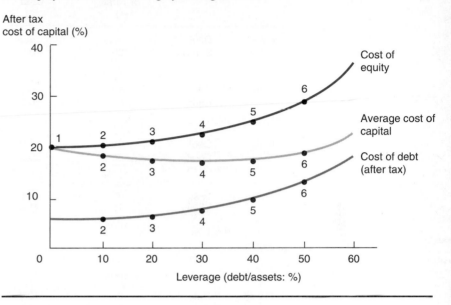

Optimal capital structure

Combination of debt and equity that minimizes the firm's weighted average cost of capital.

composite dollar of debt and equity financing. The proper set of weights to employ in computing the weighted average cost of capital is determined by the firm's optimal capital structure. The **optimal capital structure** is the combination of debt and equity financing that minimizes the firm's overall weighted average cost of capital.

In general, the risk to investors is lower on debt and higher on common stock. Risk aversion among investors makes debt the lowest component-cost source of funds and equity the highest component-cost source. However, the firm's risk increases as debt financing grows, because the higher the debt level, the greater the probability that under adverse conditions the firm will not make interest and principal payments. Because interest rates on debt are lower than the expected rate of return (dividends plus capital gains) on common stock, this can cause the weighted average cost of capital to decline with modest amounts of debt financing. More debt means higher financial risk, which offsets this effect to some extent. As a result, the weighted average cost of capital first declines as a firm moves from zero debt to some positive amount of debt, hits a minimum (perhaps over a range rather than at some specific amount of debt), and then rises as an increasing level of debt drives the firm's risk position beyond acceptable levels. Thus, each firm has an optimal amount of debt that minimizes its cost of capital and maximizes its value.

Figure 16.2 shows, for a hypothetical industry, how the cost of capital changes as the debt ratio increases. The average cost of capital figures in the graph are calculated in Table 16.6. In the figure, each dot represents one of the firms in the

TABLE 16.6   **Calculation of Average Cost of Capital for Hypothetical Firms with Different Debt Ratios**

		Percentage of Total (1)	Component Cost (2)	Weighted Cost $\frac{(1) \times (2)}{100}$ (3)
Firm 1	Debt	0	6.0	0.00
	Equity	100	20.0	20.00
		100%		Average cost 20.00%
Firm 2	Debt	10	6.0	0.60
	Equity	90	20.0	18.00
		100%		Average cost 18.60%
Firm 3	Debt	20	6.0	1.20
	Equity	80	20.0	16.00
		100%		Average cost 17.20%
Firm 4	Debt	30	7.0	2.10
	Equity	70	21.0	14.70
		100%		Average cost 16.80%
Firm 5	Debt	40	9.0	3.60
	Equity	60	22.5	13.50
		100%		Average cost 17.10%
Firm 6	Debt	50	12.0	6.00
	Equity	50	24.0	12.00
		100%		Average cost 18.00%
Firm 7	Debt	60	17.0	10.20
	Equity	40	27.5	11.00
		100%		Average cost 21.20%

industry. For example, the dot labeled "1" represents Firm 1, a company with no debt. Because its projects are financed entirely with 20 percent equity money, Firm 1's average cost of capital is 20 percent. Firm 2 raises 10 percent of its capital as debt, and it has a 6 percent after-tax cost of debt and a 20 percent cost of equity. Firm 3 also has a 6 percent cost of debt and 20 percent cost of equity, even though it uses 20 percent debt. Firm 4 has a 21 percent cost of equity and a 7 percent cost of debt; it uses 30 percent debt, and a risk premium of 1 percent has been added to the required return on equity to account for the additional risk of financial leverage. Providers of debt capital also believe that because of the added risk of financial leverage at this debt level, they should obtain higher yields on the firm's securities. In this particular industry, the threshold debt ratio that begins to worry creditors is about 20 percent. Below 20 percent debt, creditors are unconcerned about any risk induced by debt; above 20 percent, they are aware of the higher risk and require compensation in the form of higher rates of return.

In Table 16.6, the debt and equity costs of the various firms are averaged on the basis of their respective proportions of the firm's total capital. Firm 1 has a

MANAGERIAL APPLICATION 16.3

Capital Allocation at Berkshire Hathaway, Inc.

Warren E. Buffett, then 34 years old, gained control of textile manufacturer Berkshire Hathaway in 1965. Buffett gradually built Berkshire into a conglomerate with a string of property casualty insurance companies, See's Candies, the *Buffalo News, World Book Encyclopedia,* and so on. During more than 25 years of Buffett's stewardship, Berkshire's net worth per share has compounded at 24 percent per year. In an era when median *Fortune* 500 companies count themselves lucky to earn half that much, Buffett's accomplishment can only be viewed as amazing—especially for a debt-free company.

In addition to being uniquely capable as an investor and manager, Buffett has the uncommon ability to communicate his insights on management in a disarmingly modest and interesting fashion. In a recent annual report to shareholders, Buffett describes his "Mistakes of the First Twenty-five Years," a witty primer for new and experienced managers alike. Among the most important dos and don'ts learned by Buffett are the following ten lessons.

- *It is far better to buy a wonderful company at a fair price than a fair company at a wonderful price.* In a difficult business, no sooner is one problem solved than another surfaces. "There is never just one cockroach in the kitchen."
- *When a management with a reputation for brilliance tackles a business with a reputation for bad economics, it is the reputation of the business that remains intact.* According to Buffett, attractive economics include a 20 percent plus rate of return on capital without leverage or accounting gimmicks, high margins, high cash flow, low capital investment requirements, a lack of government regulation, and strong prospects for continuing growth. "Good jockeys do well on good horses," Buffett says, "but not on broken down old nags."
- *Management does better by avoiding dragons, not slaying them.* Buffett attributes his success to avoiding, rather than solving, tough business problems. As Buffett says, "We have been successful because we concentrated on identifying one-foot hurdles that we could step over rather than because we acquired any ability to clear seven-footers."
- *As if governed by Newton's first law of motion, an institution will resist any change in its current direction.* Too often, the call for necessary change is blithely ignored.
- *Just as work expands to fill available time, corporate projects or acquisitions will materialize to soak up available funds.* Even when plainly called for, dividends or share buybacks are seldom seen as the best use of funds.
- *Any business craving of the leader, however foolish, will be quickly supported by detailed rate-of-return and strategic studies prepared by the troops.* Rationality frequently wilts when the institutional imperative comes into play.
- *The behavior of peer companies, whether they are expanding, acquiring, setting compensation, or whatever, will be mindlessly imitated.* Institutional dynamics often set management on a misguided course.
- *It is not a sin to miss a business opportunity outside one's area of expertise.* By inference, it is a sin to miss opportunities that you are fully capable of understanding.
- *If your actions are sensible, you are certain to get good results.* Leverage moves things along faster, but at the unavoidable risk of anguish or default.
- *Do not join with managers that lack admirable qualities, no matter how attractive the prospects of their business.* When searching for businesses to buy, Buffett looks for first-class businesses accompanied by first-class management.

How well do these capital allocation rules work in practice? Consider that when Buffett gained control of Berkshire Hathaway in 1965 the company had a stock price of $12 per share. By mid-1992, Berkshire's stock price had risen to over $9,000 per share, making Buffett's 44.7 percent stake worth in excess of $5 billion. All in all, not too shabby!

Source: R. Hutchings Vernon, "The Warren and Charlie Show," *Barron's,* May 11, 1992, 14, 19.

weighted average cost of capital equal to 20 percent, Firm 2 has a weighted average cost of 18.6 percent, Firm 3 has a weighted average cost of 17.2 percent, and Firm 4 has a weighted average cost of 16.8 percent. These weighted costs, together with those of the other firms in the industry, are also plotted in Figure 16.2. Firms with approximately 30 percent debt in their capital structure have the lowest weighted average cost of capital. Accordingly, proper calculation of the cost of capital requires that the cost of equity for a firm in the industry be given a weight of 0.70 and the cost of debt be given a weight of 0.30—the firm's optimal capital structure.

THE OPTIMAL CAPITAL BUDGET

A profit-maximizing firm operates at the point where marginal revenue equals marginal cost. In terms of the capital budgeting process, this implies that projects will be accepted as long as they return a cash inflow that is at least equal to the required cash outflow, when both are expressed in present-value terms. At the margin, the present value of inflows is exactly equal to the present value of cash outflows. Alternatively, the marginal rate of return earned on the last acceptable investment project is just equal to the firm's relevant marginal cost of capital. The **optimal capital budget** is the funding level required to underwrite a value-maximizing level of new investment. In a complete analysis of the capital budgeting process, it is necessary to show how investment project returns and costs can be integrated to help define the optimal capital budget.

Optimal capital budget
Funding required to underwrite a value-maximizing level of new investment.

Investment Opportunity Schedule

Investment opportunity schedule
Pattern of returns for all potential investment projects.

The **investment opportunity schedule** (*IOS*) shows the pattern of returns for all of the firm's potential investment projects. Figure 16.3(a) shows an investment opportunity schedule for a hypothetical firm. The horizontal axis measures the dollar amount of investment commitments made during a given year. The vertical axis shows both the rate of return earned on each project and the percentage cost of capital. Each box denotes a given project. Project *A,* for example, calls for an outlay of $3 million and promises a 17 percent rate of return; Project *B* requires an outlay of $1 million and promises a 16 percent yield, and so on. The last investment, Project *E,* simply involves buying 9 percent government bonds. By displaying this stepwise pattern of potential returns on a single graph, the firm's *IOS* is depicted. Figure 16.3(b) generalizes the *IOS* concept to show a smooth pattern of potential returns. The curve labeled *IRR* shows the internal rate of return potential for each project in the portfolio of investment projects available to the firm. It is important to remember that these projects are arrayed from left to right in terms of declining attractiveness as measured by the *IRR* criterion. Therefore, Project *A* is more attractive than Project *E,* and the *IRR* schedule is downward sloping from left to right.

Although the *IOS* provides important input into the capital budget decision-making process, by itself it is insufficient for determining the optimal capital budget. Both the returns *and* costs of potential projects must be considered. To define the optimal capital budget, a means for evaluating the marginal cost of funds must be incorporated into the process.

FIGURE 16.3 **Illustrative Capital Budgeting Decision Process**

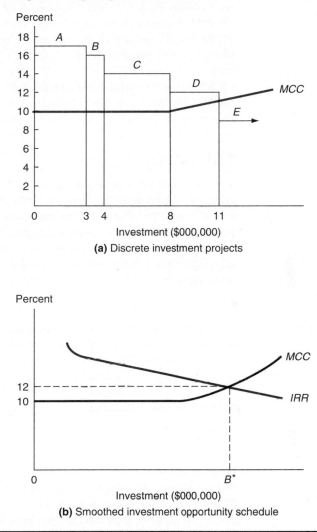

(a) Discrete investment projects

(b) Smoothed investment opportunity schedule

(a) The rates of return of Projects *A* through *D* exceed the marginal cost of capital, and they should be accepted. However, Project *E* should be rejected because its marginal cost of capital is greater than its internal rate of return. (b) Point *B** is the optimal investment level at which the marginal cost of capital equals the marginal return on the last project accepted.

Marginal Cost of Capital

Marginal cost of capital
Financing cost of an additional investment project, expressed on a percentage basis.

The **marginal cost of capital** (*MCC*) is the extra financing cost necessary to fund an additional investment project, expressed on a percentage basis. When the firm is considering an entire portfolio of potential investment projects, the marginal cost of capital is the incremental financing cost of a relevant mix of debt and equity financing. Therefore, the *MCC* is typically given by the firm's weighted average cost of capital. As drawn in Figure 16.3(b), the marginal cost of capital is constant at 10 percent up until the point where the firm has raised an additional $8 million. After this point, capital costs begin to rise. Given these *IOS* and *MCC* schedules, the firm should accept Projects *A* through *D,* obtaining and investing $11 million. Project *E,* the government bond investment alternative, should be rejected. The smooth curves in Figure 16.3(b) indicate that the firm should invest *B** dollars, the optimal capital budget. At this investment level, the marginal cost of capital is 12 percent, exactly the same as the *IRR* on the marginal investment project.

Whenever the optimal capital budget *B** is determined, the *IOS* always equals the *MCC* for the last project undertaken. The condition that must be met for any budget to be optimal is that *IOS* = *MCC*. This means that the final project accepted for investment is a breakeven project, in that it provides an *IRR* that is just equal to the discount rate. For this project, *NPV* = 0, *PI* = 1, and *IRR* = *k*. By accepting all earlier and more attractive projects, value maximization is assured because the firm has accepted all projects where *NPV* > 0, *PI* > 1, and *IRR* > *k*. This means that the area above the *MCC* schedule but below the *IOS* (or *IRR*) schedule represents the net profit earned on the firm's new investment projects. The *IOS* = *MCC* optimal capital budget condition is completely analogous to the *MR* = *MC* requirement for profit maximization. When *MR* = *MC,* all profitable units have been produced and sold. When *IOS* = *MCC,* all profitable investment projects have likewise been accepted.

The Postaudit

Postaudit

Careful reconciliation of actual and predicted results.

To assure that an optimal capital budget has indeed been determined, the methods and data employed must often be carefully reexamined at the end of the capital budgeting process. The **postaudit** is a careful examination of actual and predicted results, coupled with a detailed reconciliation of any differences.

One of the most important advantages of the postaudit is that managerial forecasts of revenues and costs tend to improve when decision makers systematically compare projections to actual outcomes. Conscious or subconscious biases can be observed and eliminated, and new forecasting methods can be sought as their need becomes apparent. People simply tend to work better if they know that their actions are being monitored. It is important to remember that businesses are run by people, and people can perform at higher or lower levels of efficiency. When a divisional team has made a forecast in a capital budgeting proposal, it is putting its reputation on the line. Because of the postaudit, these managers have every incentive to make good on their projections. If costs rise above predicted levels or sales fall below expectations, managers in production, sales, and related areas have incentives to strive to bring results into line with earlier forecasts.

Of course, it must be recognized that each element of the cash flow forecast is subject to uncertainty, so a percentage of all projects undertaken by a reasonably aggressive firm will prove to be unsuccessful. This must be considered when appraising the performances of managers who submit capital expenditure requests. Projects also sometimes fail to meet expectations for reasons that no one could realistically have anticipated. For example, wild fluctuations in both oil prices and interest rates during recent years have made long-term forecasts of any sort very difficult. It is also sometimes hard to separate the operating results of one investment from those of contemporaneous projects. If the postaudit process is not used carefully, managers may be reluctant to suggest potentially profitable but risky projects. Because of these difficulties, some firms tend to play down the importance of the postaudit. However, the best-run and most successful organizations in business and government are those that put the greatest emphasis on postaudits. Accordingly, the postaudit process is one of the most important elements in an effective capital budgeting system.

SUMMARY

Long-term investment decisions are among the most important and difficult of those faced by managers in all types of organizations. They are important because substantial amounts of funds are often committed for extended periods. They are difficult because they entail forecasts of uncertain future events that must be relied on heavily. To minimize obvious risks, the process of planning long-term investment decisions must itself become an important concern of management.

- **Capital budgeting** is the process of planning expenditures that generate cash flows expected to extend beyond one year. Several different types of investment projects may be involved, including **replacement projects,** or maintenance of business projects; **cost reduction projects** to replace obsolete plant and equipment; mandatory nonrevenue-producing **safety and environmental projects;** and **expansion projects** to increase the availability of existing products and services.

- In all cases, the focus is on **incremental cash flows,** or the period-by-period changes in net cash flows that are due to the investment project. The most common tool for project valuation is **net present value** (*NPV*) analysis, where *NPV* is the difference between project marginal revenues and marginal costs, when both are expressed in present-value terms. The conversion to present value terms involves use of an appropriate discount rate, or **cost of capital.**

- Alternative decision rules include the **profitability index** (*PI*), or benefit/cost ratio; **internal rate of return** (*IRR*), or discount rate that equates the present value of receipts and outlays; and the **payback period,** or number of years required to recover the initial investment.

- Managers must be aware of the **net present value profile** for individual projects, a graph that relates the *NPV* for each project to the discount rate used in the *NPV* calculation. A reversal of project rankings occurs at the **crossover discount rate,** where *NPV* is equal for two or more investment alternatives.

- To properly value cash flows over the life of a project, the cost of capital funds must be determined. The **component cost of debt** is the interest rate that investors require on debt, adjusted for taxes. The **component cost of equity** is the rate of return stockholders require on common stock. This includes a **risk-free rate of return** to compensate investors for postponing their consumption, plus a **risk premium** to compensate them for risk taking. The riskiness of a given stock is measured in terms of the firm's **beta coefficient,** a measure of return variability.

- The **weighted average cost of capital** is the marginal cost of a composite dollar of debt and equity financing. The proper set of weights to employ in computing the weighted average cost of capital is determined by the firm's **opti-mal capital structure,** or combination of debt and equity financing that mini-mizes the firm's overall weighted average cost of capital.

• The **optimal capital budget** is the funding level required to underwrite a value-maximizing level of new investment. Graphically, the optimal capital budget is determined by the intersection of the **investment opportunity sched-ule** (*IOS*), or pattern of returns for all of the firm's potential investment projects, and the **marginal cost of capital** (*MCC*), or *IRR* schedule.

• The **postaudit** is the final step in the capital budgeting process and consists of a careful examination of actual and predicted results, coupled with a detailed reconciliation of any differences.

Taken as a whole, the capital budgeting process is one in which the principles of marginal analysis are applied in a systematic way to long-term investment decision making. As such, the process provides further evidence of managers actually going through the process of value maximization.

Questions

Q16.1   What is capital budgeting?

Q16.2   What major steps are involved in the capital budgeting process?

Q16.3   Why do accounting income statements provide only an imperfect basis for investment decisions, and what steps must be taken to adjust these data?

Q16.4   Explain the underlying rationale for using the *NPV* approach to invest-ment project selection.

Q16.5   Why do the *NPV, PI,* and *IRR* capital budgeting decision rules sometimes provide conflicting rank orderings of investment project alternatives?

Q16.6   How is a crossover discount rate calculated, and how does it affect capital budgeting decisions?

Q16.7   In an earlier chapter, it was argued that factors should be used in such proportions that the marginal product/price ratios for all inputs are equal. In terms of capital budgeting, this implies that the marginal net cost of debt should equal the marginal net cost of equity in the optimal capital structure. Yet firms often issue debt at interest rates substantially below the yield that investors require on the firm's equity shares. Does this mean that such firms are not operating with optimal capital struc-tures? Explain.

Q16.8   Explain why the intersection of the *IOS* and *MCC* curves defines an economically optimal capital budget.

Q16.9   Recent academic studies in financial economics conclude that stock-holders of target firms in takeover bids "win" (earn abnormal returns) and that stockholders of successful bidders do not lose subsequent to takeovers, even though takeovers usually occur at substantial premiums over pre-bid market prices. Is this observation consistent with capital market efficiency?

Q16.10 What important purposes are served by the postaudit?

Self-Test Problem

Assume that you have been retained by the *Los Angeles Tribune* to analyze two proposed capital investments, Projects X and Y. Each project has a cost of $10,000, and the cost of capital for both projects is 12 percent. The projects' expected net cash flows are as follows:

	Expected Net Cash Flow	
Year	Project X	Project Y
0	($10,000)	($10,000)
1	6,500	3,500
2	3,000	3,500
3	3,000	3,500
4	1,000	3,500

A. Calculate each project's nominal payback period, net present value (NPV), internal rate of return (IRR), and profitability index (PI).
B. Which projects should be accepted if they are independent?
C. Which projects should be accepted if they are mutually exclusive?
D. How might a change in the cost of capital produce a conflict between the NPV and IRR rankings of these two projects? At what values of k would this conflict exist? (Hint: Plot the NPV profiles for each project to find the cross-over discount rate k.)
E. Why does a conflict exist between NPV and IRR rankings?

Solution to Self-Test Problem

A. *Payback:*

To determine the nominal payback period, construct the cumulative cash flows for each project:

	Cumulative Cash Flow	
Year	Project X	Project Y
0	($10,000)	($10,000)
1	(3,500)	(6,500)
2	(500)	(3,000)
3	2,500	500
4	3,500	4,000

$$\text{Payback}_X = 2 + \frac{\$500}{\$3,000} = 2.17 \text{ years.}$$

$$\text{Payback}_Y = 2 + \frac{\$3,000}{\$3,500} = 2.86 \text{ years.}$$

Net Present Value (NPV):

$$NPV_X = -\$10,000 + \frac{\$6,500}{(1.12)^1} + \frac{\$3,000}{(1.12)^2} + \frac{\$3,000}{(1.12)^3} + \frac{\$1,000}{(1.12)^4}$$

$$= \$966.01.$$

$$NPV_Y = -\$10,000 + \frac{\$3,500}{(1.12)^1} + \frac{\$3,500}{(1.12)^2} + \frac{\$3,500}{(1.12)^3} + \frac{\$3,500}{(1.12)^4}$$

$$= \$630.72.$$

Internal Rate of Return (IRR):
To solve for each project's *IRR*, find the discount rates that set *NPV* to zero:

$$IRR_X = 18.0\%.$$
$$IRR_Y = 15.0\%.$$

Profitability Index (PI):

$$PI_X = \frac{PV\,\text{Benefits}}{PV\,\text{Costs}} = \frac{\$10,966.01}{\$10,000} = 1.10.$$

$$PI_Y = \frac{\$10,630.72}{\$10,000} = 1.06.$$

B. Using all methods, Project *X* is preferred over Project *Y.* In addition, both projects are acceptable under the *NPV, IRR,* and *PI* criteria. Thus, both projects should be accepted if they are independent.
C. Choose the project with the higher *NPV* at $k = 12\%$, or Project *X.*
D. To determine the effects of changing the cost of capital, plot the *NPV* profiles of each project. The crossover rate occurs at about 6 to 7 percent. To find this rate exactly, create a Project Δ, which is the difference in cash flows between Projects *X* and *Y:*

Year	Project X − Project Y = Project Δ Net Cash Flow
0	$ 0
1	3,000
2	(500)
3	(500)
4	(2,500)

Then find the *IRR* of Project Δ:

$$IRR_\Delta = \text{Crossover Rate} = 6.2\%.$$

Thus, if the firm's cost of capital is less than 6.2 percent, a conflict exists, since $NPV_Y > NPV_X$ but $IRR_X > IRR_Y.$ Graphically, the crossover discount rate is illustrated in the figure on the following page.
E. The basic cause of conflict is the differing reinvestment rate assumptions between *NPV* and *IRR.* The conflict occurs in this situation because the projects differ in their cash flow timing.

Problems   P16.1   **Cost of Capital.** Identify each of the following statements as true or false, and explain your answers.
A. Information costs both increase the marginal cost of capital and reduce the internal rate of return on investment projects.

NPV **Profiles for Project** *X* **and Project** *Y*

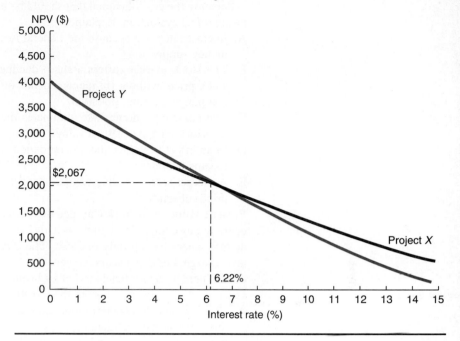

B. Depreciation expenses involve no direct cash outlay and can be safely ignored in investment project evaluation.

C. The marginal cost of capital will be less elastic for larger firms than for smaller firms.

D. In practice, the component costs of debt and equity are jointly rather than independently determined.

E. Investments necessary to replace worn-out or damaged equipment tend to have low levels of risk.

P16.2 **Decision Rule Criteria.** The net present value (*NPV*), profitability index (*PI*), and internal rate of return (*IRR*) methods are often employed in project valuation. Identify each of the following statements as true or false, and explain your answers.

A. The *IRR* method can tend to understate the relative attractiveness of superior investment projects when the opportunity cost of cash flows is below the *IRR*.

B. A *PI* = 1 describes a project with an *NPV* = 0.

C. Selection solely according to the *NPV* criterion will tend to favor larger rather than smaller investment projects.

D. When *NPV* = 0, the *IRR* exceeds the cost of capital.

E. Use of the *PI* criterion is especially appropriate for larger firms with easy access to capital markets.

P16.3   **Cost of Capital.** Indicate whether each of the following would increase or decrease the cost of capital that should be used by the firm in investment project evaluation. Explain.

A. Interest rates rise because the Federal Reserve System tightens the money supply.

B. The stock market suffers a sharp decline, as does the company's stock price, without (in management's opinion) any decline in the company's earnings potential.

C. The company's home state eliminates the corporate income tax in an effort to keep or attract valued employers.

D. In an effort to reduce the federal deficit, Congress raises corporate income tax rates.

E. A merger with a leading competitor increases the company's stock price substantially.

P16.4   **Present Value.** New York City licenses taxicabs in two classes: (1) for operation by companies with fleets and (2) for operation by independent driver-owners having only one cab. The city also fixes the rates that taxis charge. For many years, no new licenses have been issued in either class. There is an unofficial market for licenses (medallions), the market value of which is currently more than $100,000.

A. Discuss the factors determining the value of a license. To make your answer concrete, estimate numerical values for the various components that together can be summarized in a price of $100,000.

B. What factors would determine whether a change in the fare fixed by the city would raise or lower the value of a license?

C. Cab drivers, whether hired by companies or as owners of their own cabs, seem unanimous in opposing any increase in the number of cabs licensed. They argue that an increase in the number of cabs would increase competition for customers and drive down what they regard as an already unduly low return to drivers. Is their economic analysis correct? Who would benefit and who would lose from an expansion in the number of licenses issued at a nominal fee?

P16.5   *NPV and PI.* The Pacific Princess luxury cruise line is contemplating leasing an additional cruise ship to expand service from the Hawaiian Islands to Long Beach or San Diego. A financial analysis by staff personnel resulted in the following projections for a five-year planning horizon:

	Long Beach	San Diego
Cost	$2,000,000	$3,000,000
PV of expected cash flow @ $k = 15\%$	2,500,000	3,600,000

A. Calculate the net present value for each service. Which is more desirable according to the *NPV* criterion?

B. Calculate the profitability index for each service. Which is more desirable according to the *PI* criterion?

C. Under what conditions would either or both of the services be undertaken?

P16.6 *NPV and PI.* Louisiana Drilling and Exploration, Inc. (LD&E), has the funds necessary to complete one of two risky oil and gas drilling projects. The first, Permian Basin 1, involves the recovery of a well that was plugged and abandoned five years ago but that may now be profitable given improved recovery techniques. The second, Permian Basin 2, is a new onshore exploratory well that appears to be especially promising. Based on a detailed analysis by its technical staff, LD&E projects a ten-year life for each well with annual net cash flows as follows:

Project	Probability	Annual Cash Flow
Permian Basin 1	0.08	$ 50,000
	0.84	1,000,000
	0.08	1,500,000
Permian Basin 2	0.18	300,000
	0.64	900,000
	0.18	1,500,000

In the recovery-project valuation, LD&E uses an 8 percent riskless rate and a standard 12 percent risk premium. For exploratory drilling projects, the company uses larger risk premiums proportionate to project risks as measured by the project coefficient of variation. For example, an exploratory project with a coefficient of variation one and one-half times that for recovery projects would require a risk premium of 18 percent (= 1.5 × 12 percent). Both projects involve land acquisition, as well as surface preparation and subsurface drilling costs of $3 million each.

A. Calculate the expected value, standard deviation, and coefficient of variation for annual net operating revenues from each well.

B. Calculate and evaluate the NPV for each project using the risk-adjusted discount rate method.

C. Calculate and evaluate the PI for each project.

P16.7 **Investment Project Choice.** The Shady Rest Hotel is considering investment in two alternative capital budgeting projects. Project *A* is an investment of $75,000 to replace working but obsolete refrigeration equipment. Project *B* is an investment of $150,000 to expand dining room facilities. Relevant cash-flow data for the two projects over their expected two-year lives are as follows:

Project A

Year 1		Year 2	
Probability	Cash Flow	Probability	Cash Flow
0.18	$ 0	0.08	$ 0
0.64	50,000	0.84	50,000
0.18	100,000	0.08	100,000

continued

Project B

Year 1		Year 2	
Probability	Cash Flow	Probability	Cash Flow
0.50	$ 0	0.125	$ 0
0.50	200,000	0.75	100,000
		0.125	200,000

A. Calculate the expected value, standard deviation, and coefficient of variation of cash flows for each project.

B. Calculate the risk-adjusted *NPV* for each project using a 15 percent cost of capital for the riskier project and a 12 percent cost of capital for the less risky one. Which project is preferred using the *NPV* criterion?

C. Calculate the *PI* for each project, and rank the projects according to the *PI* criterion.

D. Calculate the *IRR* for each project, and rank the projects according to the *IRR* criterion.

E. Compare your answers to Parts B, C, and D, and discuss any differences.

P16.8   **Cash Flow Estimation.** Cunningham's Drug Store, a medium-size drug store located in Milwaukee, Wisconsin, is owned and operated by Richard Cunningham. Cunningham's sells pharmaceuticals, cosmetics, toiletries, magazines, and various novelties. Cunningham's most recent annual net income statement is as follows:

Sales revenue	$1,800,000
Total costs	
Cost of goods sold	$1,260,000
Wages and salaries	200,000
Rent	120,000
Depreciation	60,000
Utilities	40,000
Miscellaneous	30,000
Total	1,710,000
Net profit before tax	$ 90,000

Cunningham's sales and expenses have remained relatively constant over the past few years and are expected to continue unchanged in the near future. To increase sales, Cunningham is considering using some floor space for a small soda fountain. Cunningham would operate the soda fountain for an initial three-year period and then would reevaluate its profitability. The soda fountain would require an incremental investment of $20,000 to lease furniture, equipment, utensils, and so on. This is the only capital investment required during the three-year period. At the end of that time, additional capital would be required to continue operating the soda fountain, and no capital would be recovered if it were shut down. The soda fountain is expected to have annual sales of

$100,000 and food and materials expenses of $20,000 per year. The soda fountain is also expected to increase wage and salary expenses by 8 percent and utility expenses by 5 percent. Because the soda fountain will reduce the floor space available for display of other merchandise, sales of non-soda fountain items are expected to decline by 10 percent.

A. Calculate net incremental cash flows for the soda fountain.

B. Assume that Cunningham has the capital necessary to install the soda fountain and that he places a 12 percent opportunity cost on those funds. Should the soda fountain be installed? Why or why not?

P16.9 **Cash Flow Analysis.** The Patriotic Press, Inc. (PPI), is analyzing the potential profitability of three printing jobs put up for bid by the State Department of Revenue:

	Job A	Job B	Job C
Projected winning bid (per unit)	$5.00	$8.00	$7.50
Direct cost per unit	$2.00	$4.30	$3.00
Annual unit sales volume	800,000	650,000	450,000
Annual distribution costs	$90,000	$75,000	$55,000
Investment required to produce annual volume	$5,000,000	$5,200,000	$4,000,000

Assume that: (1) the company's marginal city-plus-state-plus-federal tax rate is 50 percent; (2) each job is expected to have a six-year life; (3) the firm uses straight-line depreciation; (4) the average cost of capital is 14 percent; (5) the jobs have the same risk as the firm's other business; and (6) the company has already spent $60,000 on developing the preceding data. This $60,000 has been capitalized and will be amortized over the life of the project.

A. What is the expected net cash flow each year? (Hint: Cash flow equals net profit after taxes plus depreciation and amortization charges.)

B. What is the net present value of each project? On which project, if any, should PPI bid?

C. Suppose that PPI's primary business is quite cyclical, improving and declining with the economy, but that Job *A* is expected to be countercyclical. Might this have any bearing on your decision?

P16.10 **Cost of Capital.** Eureka Membership Warehouse, Inc., is a rapidly growing chain of retail outlets offering brand-name merchandise at discount prices. A security analyst's report issued by a national brokerage firm indicates that debt yielding 13 percent composes 25 percent of Eureka's overall capital structure. Furthermore, both earnings and dividends are expected to grow at a rate of 15 percent per year.

Currently, common stock in the company is priced at $30, and it should pay $1.50 per share in dividends during the coming year. This yield compares favorably with the 8 percent return currently available on risk-free securities and the 14 percent average for all common stocks, given the company's estimated beta of 2.

A. Calculate Eureka's component cost of equity using both the capital asset pricing model and the dividend yield plus expected growth model.

B. Assuming a 40 percent marginal federal-plus-state income tax rate, calculate Eureka's weighted average cost of capital.

CASE STUDY FOR CHAPTER 16

Investment Project Analysis at FlightSafety International, Inc.

FlightSafety International, Inc., trains more than 30,000 corporate, commercial, and military pilots per year and has found its niche business to be enormously profitable. Net profit margins have approached 30 percent of sales during the 1980s and early 1990s. It is the only company to have earned a spot on *Forbes's* annual list of the best Up & Comers in every year since the magazine started tracking such companies in 1979. Over this period, FlightSafety's profits have risen more than fivefold, and the company has racked up an average rate of return on common equity of 18 to 20 percent per year. Its stock was up from $7 a share (split-adjusted) in 1982 to more than $57 in 1991, a lofty 20 times estimated 1993 earnings. The company is expected to net roughly $100 million during 1993, on revenues of $330 million. Its 35 million NYSE-listed shares have a market value of roughly $1.75 billion. Among the 9,500 stockholders that have benefited from the company's amazing success is company founder, chairman, and president Albert Ueltschi—Ueltschi and his family own 34 percent of FlightSafety common stock.

What separates FlightSafety from other small companies that look good for a couple of years and then crash and burn is the quality of top management. Ueltschi is widely regarded as dedicated, highly intelligent, and honest. He started FlightSafety in 1951, while working as a pilot for Pan American Airways. Since 1946 he had served as the personal pilot to Pan Am's colorful founder, Juan Trippe, flying Trippe around in a converted B-23 military transport. During the early years of this association, Ueltschi noticed that other corporate CEOs were buying surplus military planes and converting them into corporate aircraft. He also noticed that many of the former military pilots who were signing on as corporate pilots had little or no training on the specific planes they were being hired to fly. Ueltschi reasoned that corporations would pay to rectify this dangerous situation.

Ueltschi opened an office next to Pan Am's LaGuardia terminal and began hiring moonlighting pilots from Pan Am and United to train corporate pilots. Actual flight instruction was done in the clients' aircraft. Additional instrument training was done on instrument trainers, rented by the hour from United Airlines. Early clients included Kodak, Burlington Industries, and National Distillers. Ueltschi poured all the profits back into the business, a practice he still abides by. During the past decade, the company has spent ever increasing amounts on new plant and equipment; current capital expenditures total roughly $100 million per year.

Today FlightSafety is the largest independent flight trainer in the United States. So complete is its grip on the market that 20 aircraft manufacturers, among them Gulfstream, Cessna, and Learjet, include its training with the price of a new plane. The company trains pilots on sophisticated flight simulators at training centers located adjacent to manufacturers' plants, military bases, and commercial airports. Flight simulators not only re-create the look, feel, and sound of flying specific planes but also simulate emergency flight conditions— such as wind shear or the loss of a hydraulic system—that one does not want to attempt with an actual plane. Training on a simulator is also significantly cheaper than training in an actual plane. FlightSafety's simulator time for a Boeing 737, for example, costs about $550 an hour. Operating costs for an actual 737 are about $3,000 an hour. The company, which now builds most of its own simulators at a cost of $8 million to $12 million each, is putting new ones into service at a rate of three per quarter.

To illustrate the company's capital budgeting process, assume that FlightSafety had built a given simulator for $8 million two years ago. The company uses straight-line depreciation over the simulator's projected 12-year life. Therefore, the used flight simulator has a present depreciated book value of $6.5 million; it has a current market value of $7.5 million (before taxes). If kept, the used simulator will last ten more years and produce an expected net cash flow before tax (CFBT) of $2.5 million per year. A new flight simulator costs $12 million to build but has greater capabilities and is expected to generate CFBT of $4 million per year over a useful life of 15 years. Assume that neither the new nor the used flight simulator has any salvage value at the end of its projected useful life, a marginal state-plus-federal tax rate of 40 percent, a current after-tax discount rate of 20 percent, and straight-line depreciation.

A. Calculate the expected *NPV* for retention of the used flight simulator equipment.
B. Calculate the expected *NPV* for construction of the new flight simulator equipment.
C. Based on the *NPV* criterion, should FlightSafety retain the used flight simulator equipment, build new equipment, or both? Why?

Selected References　Auerbach, Alan J. "On the Design and Reform of Capital-Gains Taxation." *American Economic Review* 82 (May 1992): 263–267.

Brandscomb, Lewis M. "Does America Need a Technology Policy?" *Harvard Business Review* 70 (March–April 1992): 24–31.

Frankel, Jeffrey A. "The Japanese Cost of Finance: A Survey." *Financial Management* 20 (Spring 1991): 95–127.

Frankel, Jeffrey A. "Measuring International Capital Mobility: A Review." *American Economic Review* 82 (May 1992): 197–202.

Givoly, Dan, and Carla Hyn. "The Valuation of the Deferred Tax Liability: Evidence from the Stock Market." *Accounting Review* 67 (April 1992): 394–410.

Gramlich, Edward M. "Setting National Priorities: 1992." *Journal of Economic Perspectives* 6 (Spring 1992): 3–12.

Guenther, David A. "Taxes and Organizational Form: A Comparison of Corporations and Master Limited Partnerships." *Accounting Review* 67 (January 1992): 17–45.

Harris, Milton, and Artur Raviv. "The Theory of Capital Structure." *Journal of Finance* 46 (March 1991): 297–355.

Howarth, Richard B., and Richard B. Norgaard. "Environmental Valuation under Sustainable Development." *American Economic Review* 82 (May 1992): 473–477.

Kaplan, Steven, and Michael S. Weisbach. "The Success of Acquisitions: Evidence from Divestitures." *Journal of Finance* 47 (March 1992): 107–138.

Mantrala, Murali, K. Prabttakant Sinha, and Andris A. Zoltners. "Impact of Resource Allocation Rules on Marketing Investment-Level Decisions and Profitability." *Journal of Marketing Research* 29 (May 1992): 162–175.

Myers, Mary D., Lawrence A. Gordon, and Michelle M. Hamer. "Post-Auditing Capital Assets and Firm Performance: An Empirical Investigation." *Managerial and Decision Economics* 12 (August 1991): 317–327.

Opler, Tim C. "Operating Performance in Leveraged Buyouts: Evidence from 1985–1989." *Financial Management* 21 (Spring 1992): 27–34.

Talmor, Eli, and Howard E. Thompson. "Technology, Dependent Investments, and Discounting Rules for Corporate Investment Decisions." *Managerial and Decision Economics* 13 (March–April 1992): 101–109.

Wheelwright, Steven C., and Kim B. Clark. "Creating Project Plans to Focus Product Development." *Harvard Business Review* 70 (March–April 1992): 70–82.

INTEREST FACTOR TABLES[1]

---

[1]These tables can be calculated using functions featured in *Lotus 1-2-3* or *Microsoft Excel* business application computer spreadsheet software.

TABLE A.1   Compound Sum of \$1: $FVIF_{i,N} = (1 + i)^N$

Period	1%	2%	3%	4%	5%	6%	7%	8%	9%	10%
1	1.0100	1.0200	1.0300	1.0400	1.0500	1.0600	1.0700	1.0800	1.0900	1.1000
2	1.0201	1.0404	1.0609	1.0816	1.1025	1.1236	1.1449	1.1664	1.1881	1.2100
3	1.0303	1.0612	1.0927	1.1249	1.1576	1.1910	1.2250	1.2597	1.2950	1.3310
4	1.0406	1.0824	1.1255	1.1699	1.2155	1.2625	1.3108	1.3605	1.4116	1.4641
5	1.0510	1.1041	1.1593	1.2167	1.2763	1.3382	1.4026	1.4693	1.5386	1.6105
6	1.0615	1.1262	1.1941	1.2653	1.3401	1.4185	1.5007	1.5869	1.6771	1.7716
7	1.0721	1.1487	1.2299	1.3159	1.4071	1.5036	1.6058	1.7138	1.8280	1.9487
8	1.0829	1.1717	1.2668	1.3686	1.4775	1.5938	1.7182	1.8509	1.9926	2.1436
9	1.0937	1.1951	1.3048	1.4233	1.5513	1.6895	1.8385	1.9990	2.1719	2.3579
10	1.1046	1.2190	1.3439	1.4802	1.6289	1.7908	1.9672	2.1589	2.3674	2.5937
11	1.1157	1.2434	1.3842	1.5395	1.7103	1.8983	2.1049	2.3316	2.5804	2.8531
12	1.1268	1.2682	1.4258	1.6010	1.7959	2.0122	2.2522	2.5182	2.8127	3.1384
13	1.1381	1.2936	1.4685	1.6651	1.8856	2.1329	2.4098	2.7196	3.0658	3.4523
14	1.1495	1.3195	1.5126	1.7317	1.9799	2.2609	2.5785	2.9372	3.3417	3.7975
15	1.1610	1.3459	1.5580	1.8009	2.0789	2.3966	2.7590	3.1722	3.6425	4.1772
16	1.1726	1.3728	1.6047	1.8730	2.1829	2.5404	2.9522	3.4259	3.9703	4.5950
17	1 1843	1.4002	1.6528	1.9479	2.2920	2.6928	3.1588	3.7000	4.3276	5.0545
18	1.1961	1.4282	1.7024	2.0258	2.4066	2.8543	3.3799	3.9960	4.7171	5.5599
19	1.2081	1.4568	1.7535	2.1068	2.5270	3.0256	3.6165	4.3157	5.1417	6.1159
20	1.2202	1.4859	1.8061	2.1911	2.6533	3.2071	3.8697	4.6610	5.6044	6.7275
21	1.2324	1.5157	1.8603	2.2788	2.7860	3.3996	4.1406	5.0338	6.1088	7.4002
22	1.2447	1.5460	1.9161	2.3699	2.9253	3.6035	4.4304	5.4365	6.6586	8.1403
23	1.2572	1.5769	1.9736	2.4647	3.0715	3.8197	4.7405	5.8715	7.2579	8.9543
24	1.2697	1.6084	2.0328	2.5633	3.2251	4.0489	5.0724	6.3412	7.9111	9.8497
25	1.2824	1.6406	2.0938	2.6658	3.3864	4.2919	5.4274	6.8485	8.6231	10.834
26	1.2953	1.6734	2.1566	2.7725	3.5557	4.5494	5.8074	7.3964	9.3992	11.918
27	1.3082	1.7069	2.2213	2.8834	3.7335	4.8223	6.2139	7.9881	10.245	13.110
28	1.3213	1.7410	2.2879	2.9987	3.9201	5.1117	6.6488	8.6271	11.167	14.421
29	1.3345	1.7758	2.3566	3.1187	4.1161	5.4184	7.1143	9.3173	12.172	15.863
30	1.3478	1.8114	2.4273	3.2434	4.3219	5.7435	7.6123	10.062	13.267	17.449
40	1.4889	2.2080	3.2620	4.8010	7.0400	10.285	14.974	21.724	31.409	45.259
50	1.6446	2.6916	4.3839	7.1067	11.467	18.420	29.457	46.901	74.357	117.39
60	1.8167	3.2810	5.8916	10.519	18.679	32.987	57.946	101.25	176.03	304.48

TABLE A.1 *continued*

Period	12%	14%	15%	16%	18%	20%	24%	28%	32%	36%
1	1.1200	1.1400	1.1500	1.1600	1.1800	1.2000	1.2400	1.2800	1.3200	1.3600
2	1.2544	1.2996	1.3225	1.3456	1.3924	1.4400	1.5376	1.6384	1.7424	1.8496
3	1.4049	1.4815	1.5209	1.5609	1.6430	1.7280	1.9066	2.0972	2.3000	2.5155
4	1.5735	1.6890	1.7490	1.8106	1.9388	2.0736	2.3642	2.6844	3.0360	3.4210
5	1.7623	1.9254	2.0114	2.1003	2.2878	2.4883	2.9316	3.4360	4.0075	4.6526
6	1.9738	2.1950	2.3131	2.4364	2.6996	2.9860	3.6352	4.3980	5.2899	6.3275
7	2.2107	2.5023	2.6600	2.8262	3.1855	3.5832	4.5077	5.6295	6.9826	8.6054
8	2.4760	2.8526	3.0590	3.2784	3.7589	4.2998	5.5895	7.2058	9.2170	11.703
9	2.7731	3.2519	3.5179	3.8030	4.4355	5.1598	6.9310	9.2234	12.166	15.916
10	3.1058	3.7072	4.0456	4.4114	5.2338	6.1917	8.5944	11.805	16.059	21.646
11	3.4785	4.2262	4.6524	5.1173	6.1759	7.4301	10.657	15.111	21.198	29.439
12	3.8960	4.8179	5.3502	5.9360	7.2876	8.9161	13.214	19.342	27.982	40.037
13	4.3635	5.4924	6.1528	6.8858	8.5994	10.699	16.386	24.758	36.937	54.451
14	4.8871	6.2613	7.0757	7.9875	10.147	12.839	20.319	31.691	48.756	74.053
15	5.4736	7.1379	8.1371	9.2655	11.973	15.407	25.195	40.564	64.358	100.71
16	6.1304	8.1372	9.3576	10.748	14.129	18.488	31.242	51.923	84.953	136.96
17	6.8660	9.2765	10.761	12.467	16.672	22.186	38.740	66.461	112.13	186.27
18	7.6900	10.575	12.375	14.462	19.673	26.623	48.038	85.070	148.02	253.33
19	8.6128	12.055	14.231	16.776	23.214	31.948	59.567	108.89	195.39	344.53
20	9.6463	13.743	16.366	19.460	27.393	38.337	73.864	139.37	257.91	468.57
21	10.803	15.667	18.821	22.574	32.323	46.005	91.591	178.40	340.44	637.26
22	12.100	17.861	21.644	26.186	38.142	55.206	113.57	228.35	449.39	866.67
23	13.552	20.361	24.891	30.376	45.007	66.247	140.83	292.30	593.19	1178.6
24	15.178	23.212	28.625	35.236	53.108	79.496	174.63	374.14	783.02	1602.9
25	17.000	26.461	32.918	40.874	62.668	95.396	216.54	478.90	1033.5	2180.0
26	19.040	30.166	37.856	47.414	73.948	114.47	268.51	612.99	1364.3	2964.9
27	21.324	34.389	43.535	55.000	87.259	137.37	332.95	784.63	1800.9	4032.2
28	23.883	39.204	50.065	63.800	102.96	164.84	412.86	1004.3	2377.2	5483.8
29	26.749	44.693	57.575	74.008	121.50	197.81	511.95	1285.5	3137.9	7458.0
30	29.959	50.950	66.211	85.849	143.37	237.37	634.81	1645.5	4142.0	10143.
40	93.050	188.88	267.86	378.72	750.37	1469.7	5455.9	19426.	66520.	*
50	289.00	700.23	1083.6	1670.7	3927.3	9100.4	46890.	*	*	*
60	897.59	2595.9	4383.9	7370.1	20555.	56347.	*	*	*	*

*FVIF > 99,999.

TABLE A.2 **Present Value of \$1:** $PVIF_{i,N} = 1/(1 + i)^N = 1/FVIF_{i,N}$

Period	1%	2%	3%	4%	5%	6%	7%	8%	9%	10%
1	.9901	.9804	.9709	.9615	.9524	.9434	.9346	.9259	.9174	.9091
2	.9803	.9612	.9426	.9246	.9070	.8900	.8734	.8573	.8417	.8264
3	.9706	.9423	.9151	.8890	.8638	.8396	.8163	.7938	.7722	.7513
4	.9610	.9238	.8885	.8548	.8227	.7921	.7629	.7350	.7084	.6830
5	.9515	.9057	.8626	.8219	.7835	.7473	.7130	.6806	.6499	.6209
6	.9420	.8880	.8375	.7903	.7462	.7050	.6663	.6302	.5963	.5645
7	.9327	.8706	.8131	.7599	.7107	.6651	.6227	.5835	.5470	.5132
8	.9235	.8535	.7894	.7307	.6768	.6274	.5820	.5403	.5019	.4665
9	.9143	.8368	.7664	.7026	.6446	.5919	.5439	.5002	.4604	.4241
10	.9053	.8203	.7441	.6756	.6139	.5584	.5083	.4632	.4224	.3855
11	.8963	.8043	.7224	.6496	.5847	.5268	.4751	.4289	.3875	.3505
12	.8874	.7885	.7014	.6246	.5568	.4970	.4440	.3971	.3555	.3186
13	.8787	.7730	.6810	.6006	.5303	.4688	.4150	.3677	.3262	.2897
14	.8700	.7579	.6611	.5775	.5051	.4423	.3878	.3405	.2992	.2633
15	.8613	.7430	.6419	.5553	.4810	.4173	.3624	.3152	.2745	.2394
16	.8528	.7284	.6232	.5339	.4581	.3936	.3387	.2919	.2519	.2176
17	.8444	.7142	.6050	.5134	.4363	.3714	.3166	.2703	.2311	.1978
18	.8360	.7002	.5874	.4936	.4155	.3503	.2959	.2502	.2120	.1799
19	.8277	.6864	.5703	.4746	.3957	.3305	.2765	.2317	.1945	.1635
20	.8195	.6730	.5537	.4564	.3769	.3118	.2584	.2145	.1784	.1486
21	.8114	.6598	.5375	.4388	.3589	.2942	.2415	.1987	.1637	.1351
22	.8034	.6468	.5219	.4220	.3418	.2775	.2257	.1839	.1502	.1228
23	.7954	.6342	.5067	.4057	.3256	.2618	.2109	.1703	.1378	.1117
24	.7876	.6217	.4919	.3901	.3101	.2470	.1971	.1577	.1264	.1015
25	.7798	.6095	.4776	.3751	.2953	.2330	.1842	.1460	.1160	.0923
26	.7720	.5976	.4637	.3607	.2812	.2198	.1722	.1352	.1064	.0839
27	.7644	.5859	.4502	.3468	.2678	.2074	.1609	.1252	.0976	.0763
28	.7568	.5744	.4371	.3335	.2551	.1956	.1504	.1159	.0895	.0693
29	.7493	.5631	.4243	.3207	.2429	.1846	.1406	.1073	.0822	.0630
30	.7419	.5521	.4120	.3083	.2314	.1741	.1314	.0994	.0754	.0573
35	.7059	.5000	.3554	.2534	.1813	.1301	.0937	.0676	.0490	.0356
40	.6717	.4529	.3066	.2083	.1420	.0972	.0668	.0460	.0318	.0221
45	.6391	.4102	.2644	.1712	.1113	.0727	.0476	.0313	.0207	.0137
50	.6080	.3715	.2281	.1407	.0872	.0543	.0339	.0213	.0134	.0085
55	.5785	.3365	.1968	.1157	.0683	.0406	.0242	.0145	.0087	.0053

TABLE A.2 *continued*

Period	12%	14%	15%	16%	18%	20%	24%	28%	32%	36%
1	.8929	.8772	.8696	.8621	.8475	.8333	.8065	.7813	.7576	.7353
2	.7972	.7695	.7561	.7432	.7182	.6944	.6504	.6104	.5739	.5407
3	.7118	.6750	.6575	.6407	.6086	.5787	.5245	.4768	.4348	.3975
4	.6355	.5921	.5718	.5523	.5158	.4823	.4230	.3725	.3294	.2923
5	.5674	.5194	.4972	.4761	.4371	.4019	.3411	.2910	.2495	.2149
6	.5066	.4556	.4323	.4104	.3704	.3349	.2751	.2274	.1890	.1580
7	.4523	.3996	.3759	.3538	.3139	.2791	.2218	.1776	.1432	.1162
8	.4039	.3506	.3269	.3050	.2660	.2326	.1789	.1388	.1085	.0854
9	.3606	.3075	.2843	.2630	.2255	.1938	.1443	.1084	.0822	.0628
10	.3220	.2697	.2472	.2267	.1911	.1615	.1164	.0847	.0623	.0462
11	.2875	.2366	.2149	.1954	.1619	.1346	.0938	.0662	.0472	.0340
12	.2567	.2076	.1869	.1685	.1372	.1122	.0757	.0517	.0357	.0250
13	.2292	.1821	.1625	.1452	.1163	.0935	.0610	.0404	.0271	.0184
14	.2046	.1597	.1413	.1252	.0985	.0779	.0492	.0316	.0205	.0135
15	.1827	.1401	.1229	.1079	.0835	.0649	.0397	.0247	.0155	.0099
16	.1631	.1229	.1069	.0930	.0708	.0541	.0320	.0193	.0118	.0073
17	.1456	.1078	.0929	.0802	.0600	.0451	.0258	.0150	.0089	.0054
18	.1300	.0946	.0808	.0691	.0508	.0376	.0208	.0118	.0068	.0039
19	.1161	.0829	.0703	.0596	.0431	.0313	.0168	.0092	.0051	.0029
20	.1037	.0728	.0611	.0514	.0365	.0261	.0135	.0072	.0039	.0021
21	.0926	.0638	.0531	.0443	.0309	.0217	.0109	.0056	.0029	.0016
22	.0826	.0560	.0462	.0382	.0262	.0181	.0088	.0044	.0022	.0012
23	.0738	.0491	.0402	.0329	.0222	.0151	.0071	.0034	.0017	.0008
24	.0659	.0431	.0349	.0284	.0188	.0126	.0057	.0027	.0013	.0006
25	.0588	.0378	.0304	.0245	.0160	.0105	.0046	.0021	.0010	.0005
26	.0525	.0331	.0264	.0211	.0135	.0087	.0037	.0016	.0007	.0003
27	.0469	.0291	.0230	.0182	.0115	.0073	.0030	.0013	.0006	.0002
28	.0419	.0255	.0200	.0157	.0097	.0061	.0024	.0010	.0004	.0002
29	.0374	.0224	.0174	.0135	.0082	.0051	.0020	.0008	.0003	.0001
30	.0334	.00196	.0151	.0116	.0070	.0042	.0016	.0006	.0002	.0001
35	.0189	.0102	.0075	.0055	.0030	.0017	.0005	.0002	.0001	*
40	.0107	.0053	.0037	.0026	.0013	.0007	.0002	.0001	*	*
45	.0061	.0027	.0019	.0013	.0006	.0003	.0001	*	*	*
50	.0035	.0014	.0009	.0006	.0003	.0001	*	*	*	*
55	.0020	.0007	.0005	.0003	.0001	*	*	*	*	*

*The factor is zero to four decimal places.

TABLE A.3   **Sum of an Annuity of $1 for *N* Periods**

$$FVIFA_{i,N} = \sum_{t=1}^{N} (1 + i)^{t-1}$$

$$= \frac{(1 + i)^N - 1}{i}$$

Number of Periods	1%	2%	3%	4%	5%	6%	7%	8%	9%	10%
1	1.0000	1.0000	1.0000	1.0000	1.0000	1.0000	1.0000	1.0000	1.0000	1.0000
2	2.0100	2.0200	2.0300	2.0400	2.0500	2.0600	2.0700	2.0800	2.0900	2.1000
3	3.0301	3.0604	3.0909	3.1216	3.1525	3.1836	3.2149	3.2464	3.2781	3.3100
4	4.0604	4.1216	4.1836	4.2465	4.3101	4.3746	4.4399	4.5061	4.5731	4.6410
5	5.1010	5.2040	5.3091	5.4163	5.5256	5.6371	5.7507	5.8666	5.9847	6.1051
6	6.1520	6.3081	6.4684	6.6330	6.8019	6.9753	7.1533	7.3359	7.5233	7.7156
7	7.2135	7.4343	7.6625	7.8983	8.1420	8.3938	8.6540	8.9228	9.2004	9.4872
8	8.2857	8.5830	8.8923	9.2142	9.5491	9.8975	10.259	10.636	11.028	11.435
9	9.3685	9.7546	10.159	10.582	11.026	11.491	11.978	12.487	13.021	13.579
10	10.462	10.949	11.463	12.006	12.577	13.180	13.816	14.486	15.192	15.937
11	11.566	12.168	12.807	13.486	14.206	14.971	15.783	16.645	17.560	18.531
12	12.682	13.412	14.192	15.025	15.917	16.869	17.888	18.977	20.140	21.384
13	13.809	14.680	15.617	16.626	17.713	18.882	20.140	21.495	22.953	24.522
14	14.947	15.973	17.086	18.291	19.598	21.015	22.550	24.214	26.019	27.975
15	16.096	17.293	18.598	20.023	21.578	23.276	25.129	27.152	29.360	31.772
16	17.257	18.639	20.156	21.824	23.657	25.672	27.888	30.324	33.003	35.949
17	18.430	20.012	21.761	23.697	25.840	28.212	30.840	33.750	36.973	40.544
18	19.614	21.412	23.414	25.645	28.132	30.905	33.999	37.450	41.301	45.599
19	20.810	22.840	25.116	27.671	30.539	33.760	37.379	41.446	46.018	51.159
20	22.019	24.297	26.870	29.778	33.066	36.785	40.995	45.762	51.160	57.275
21	23.239	25.783	28.676	31.969	35.719	39.992	44.865	50.422	56.764	64.002
22	24.471	27.299	30.536	34.248	38.505	43.392	49.005	55.456	62.873	71.402
23	25.716	28.845	32.452	36.617	41.430	46.995	53.436	60.893	69.531	79.543
24	26.973	30.421	34.426	39.082	44.502	50.815	58.176	66.764	76.789	88.497
25	28.243	32.030	36.459	41.645	47.727	54.864	63.249	73.105	84.700	98.347
26	29.525	33.670	38.553	44.311	51.113	59.156	68.676	79.954	93.323	109.18
27	30.820	35.344	40.709	47.084	54.669	63.705	74.483	87.350	102.72	121.09
28	32.129	37.051	42.930	49.967	58.402	68.528	80.697	95.338	112.96	134.20
29	33.450	38.792	45.218	52.966	62.322	73.639	87.346	103.96	124.13	148.63
30	34.784	40.568	47.575	56.084	66.438	79.058	94.460	113.28	136.30	164.49
40	48.886	60.402	75.401	95.025	120.79	154.76	199.63	259.05	337.88	442.59
50	64.463	84.579	112.79	152.66	209.34	290.33	406.52	573.76	815.08	1163.9
60	81.669	114.05	163.05	237.99	353.58	533.12	813.52	1253.2	1944.7	3034.8

TABLE A.3 *continued*

Number of Periods	12%	14%	15%	16%	18%	20%	24%	28%	32%	36%
1	1.0000	1.0000	1.0000	1.0000	1.0000	1.0000	1.0000	1.0000	1.0000	1.0000
2	2.1200	2.1400	2.1500	2.1600	2.1800	2.2000	2.2400	2.2800	2.3200	2.3600
3	3.3744	3.4396	3.4725	3.5056	3.5724	3.6400	3.7776	3.9184	4.0624	4.2096
4	4.7793	4.9211	4.9934	5.0665	5.2154	5.3680	5.6842	6.0156	6.3624	6.7251
5	6.3528	6.6101	6.7424	6.8771	7.1542	7.4416	8.0484	8.6999	9.3983	10.146
6	8.1152	8.5355	8.7537	8.9775	9.4420	9.9299	10.980	12.135	13.405	14.798
7	10.089	10.730	11.066	11.413	12.141	12.915	14.615	16.533	18.695	21.126
8	12.299	13.232	13.726	14.240	15.327	16.499	19.122	22.163	25.678	29.731
9	14.775	16.085	16.785	17.518	19.085	20.798	24.712	29.369	34.895	41.435
10	17.548	19.337	20.303	21.321	23.521	25.958	31.643	38.592	47.061	57.351
11	20.654	23.044	24.349	25.732	28.755	32.150	40.237	50.398	63.121	78.998
12	24.133	27.270	29.001	30.850	34.931	39.580	50.894	65.510	84.320	108.43
13	28.029	32.088	34.351	36.786	42.218	48.496	64.109	84.852	112.30	148.47
14	32.392	37.581	40.504	43.672	50.818	59.195	80.496	109.61	149.23	202.92
15	37.279	43.842	47.580	51.659	60.965	72.035	100.81	141.30	197.99	276.97
16	42.753	50.980	55.717	60.925	72.939	87.442	126.01	181.86	262.35	377.69
17	48.883	59.117	65.075	71.673	87.068	105.93	157.25	233.79	347.30	514.66
18	55.749	68.394	75.836	84.140	103.74	128.11	195.99	300.25	459.44	700.93
19	63.439	78.969	88.211	98.603	123.41	154.74	244.03	385.32	607.47	954.27
20	72.052	91.024	102.44	115.37	146.62	186.68	303.60	494.21	802.86	1298.8
21	81.698	104.76	118.81	134.84	174.02	225.02	377.46	633.59	1060.7	1767.3
22	92.502	120.43	137.63	157.41	206.34	271.03	469.05	811.99	1401.2	2404.6
23	104.60	138.29	159.27	183.60	244.48	326.23	582.62	1040.3	1850.6	3271.3
24	118.15	158.65	184.16	213.97	289.49	392.48	723.46	1332.6	2443.8	4449.9
25	133.33	181.87	212.79	249.21	342.60	471.98	898.09	1706.8	3226.8	6052.9
26	150.33	208.33	245.71	290.08	405.27	567.37	1114.6	2185.7	4260.4	8233.0
27	169.37	238.49	283.56	337.50	479.22	681.85	1383.1	2798.7	5624.7	11197.9
28	190.69	272.88	327.10	392.50	566.48	819.22	1716.0	3583.3	7425.6	15230.2
29	214.58	312.09	377.16	456.30	669.44	984.06	2128.9	4587.6	9802.9	20714.1
30	241.33	356.78	434.74	530.31	790.94	1181.8	2640.9	5873.2	12940.	28172.2
40	767.09	1342.0	1779.0	2360.7	4163.2	7343.8	22728.	69377.	*	*
50	2400.0	4994.5	7217.7	10435.	21813.	45497.	*	*	*	*
60	7471.6	18535.	29219.	46057.	*	*	*	*	*	*

*FVIFA > 99,999.

TABLE A.4   **Present Value of an Annuity of $1 for *N* Periods**

$$PVIFA_{i,N} = \sum_{t=1}^{N} \frac{1}{(1+i)^t} = \frac{1 - \dfrac{1}{(1+i)^N}}{i}$$

Number of Payments	1%	2%	3%	4%	5%	6%	7%	8%	9%
1	0.9901	0.9804	0.9709	0.9615	0.9524	0.9434	0.9346	0.9259	0.9174
2	1.9704	1.9416	1.9135	1.8861	1.8594	1.8334	1.8080	1.7833	1.7591
3	2.9410	2.8839	2.8286	2.7751	2.7232	2.6730	2.6243	2.5771	2.5313
4	3.9020	3.8077	3.7171	3.6299	3.5460	3.4651	3.3872	3.3121	3.2397
5	4.8534	4.7135	4.5797	4.4518	4.3295	4.2124	4.1002	3.9927	3.8897
6	5.7955	5.6014	5.4172	5.2421	5.0757	4.9173	4.7665	4.6229	4.4859
7	6.7282	6.4720	6.2303	6.0021	5.7864	5.5824	5.3893	5.2064	5.0330
8	7.6517	7.3255	7.0197	6.7327	6.4632	6.2098	5.9713	5.7466	5.5348
9	8.5660	8.1622	7.7861	7.4353	7.1078	6.8017	6.5152	6.2469	5.9952
10	9.4713	8.9826	8.5302	8.1109	7.7217	7.3601	7.0236	6.7101	6.4177
11	10.3676	9.7868	9.2526	8.7605	8.3064	7.8869	7.4987	7.1390	6.8052
12	11.2551	10.5753	9.9540	9.3851	8.8633	8.3838	7.9427	7.5361	7.1607
13	12.1337	11.3484	10.6350	9.9856	9.3936	8.8527	8.3577	7.9038	7.4869
14	13.0037	12.1062	11.2961	10.5631	9.8986	9.2950	8.7455	8.2442	7.7862
15	13.8651	12.8493	11.9379	11.1184	10.3797	9.7122	9.1079	8.5595	8.0607
16	14.7179	13.5777	12.5611	11.6523	10.8378	10.1059	9.4466	8.8514	8.3126
17	15.5623	14.2919	13.1661	12.1657	11.2741	10.4773	9.7632	9.1216	8.5436
18	16.3983	14.9920	13.7535	12.6593	11.6896	10.8276	10.0591	9.3719	8.7556
19	17.2260	15.6785	14.3238	13.1339	12.0853	11.1581	10.3356	9.6036	8.9501
20	18.0456	16.3514	14.8775	13.5903	12.4622	11.4699	10.5940	9.8181	9.1285
21	18.8570	17.0112	15.4150	14.0292	12.8212	11.7641	10.8355	10.0168	9.2922
22	19.6604	17.6580	15.9369	14.4511	13.1630	12.0416	11.0612	10.2007	9.4424
23	20.4558	18.2922	16.4436	14.8568	13.4886	12.3034	11.2722	10.3711	9.5802
24	21.2434	18.9139	16.9355	15.2470	13.7986	12.5504	11.4693	10.5288	9.7066
25	22.0232	19.5235	17.4131	15.6221	14.0939	12.7834	11.6536	10.6748	9.8226
26	22.7952	20.1210	17.8768	15.9828	14.3752	13.0032	11.8258	10.8100	9.9290
27	23.5596	20.7069	18.3270	16.3296	14.6430	13.2105	11.9867	10.9352	10.0266
28	24.3164	21.2813	18.7641	16.6631	14.8981	13.4062	12.1371	11.0511	10.1161
29	25.0658	21.8444	19.1885	16.9837	15.1411	13.5907	12.2777	11.1584	10.1983
30	25.8077	22.3965	19.6004	17.2920	15.3725	13.7648	12.4090	11.2578	10.2737
35	29.4086	24.9986	21.4872	18.6646	16.3742	14.4982	12.9477	11.6546	10.5668
40	32.8347	27.3555	23.1148	19.7928	17.1591	15.0463	13.3317	11.9246	10.7574
45	36.0945	29.4902	24.5187	20.7200	17.7741	15.4558	13.6055	12.1084	10.8812
50	39.1961	31.4236	25.7298	21.4822	18.2559	15.7619	13.8007	12.2335	10.9617
55	42.1472	33.1748	26.7744	22.1086	18.6335	15.9905	13.9399	12.3186	11.0140

TABLE A.4   *continued*

Number of Pay-ments	10%	12%	14%	15%	16%	18%	20%	24%	28%	32%
1	0.9091	0.8929	0.8772	0.8696	0.8621	0.8475	0.8333	0.8065	0.7813	0.7576
2	1.7355	1.6901	1.6467	1.6257	1.6052	1.5656	1.5278	1.4568	1.3916	1.3315
3	2.4869	2.4018	2.3216	2.2832	2.2459	2.1743	2.1065	1.9813	1.8684	1.7663
4	3.1699	3.0373	2.9137	2.8550	2.7982	2.6901	2.5887	2.4043	2.2410	2.0957
5	3.7908	3.6048	3.4331	3.3522	3.2743	3.1272	2.9906	2.7454	2.5320	2.3452
6	4.3553	4.1114	3.8887	3.7845	3.6847	3.4976	3.3255	3.0205	2.7594	2.5342
7	4.8684	4.5638	4.2883	4.1604	4.0386	3.8115	3.6046	3.2423	2.9370	2.6775
8	5.3349	4.9676	4.6389	4.4873	4.3436	4.0776	3.8372	3.4212	3.0758	2.7860
9	5.7590	5.3282	4.9464	4.7716	4.6065	4.3030	4.0310	3.5655	3.1842	2.8681
10	6.1446	5.6502	5.2161	5.0188	4.8332	4.4941	4.1925	3.6819	3.2689	2.9304
11	6.4951	5.9377	5.4527	5.2337	5.0286	4.6560	4.3271	3.7757	3.3351	2.9776
12	6.8137	6.1944	5.6603	5.4206	5.1971	4.7932	4.4392	3.8514	3.3868	3.0133
13	7.1034	6.4235	5.8424	5.5831	5.3423	4.9095	4.5327	3.9124	3.4272	3.0404
14	7.3667	6.6282	6.0021	5.7245	5.4675	5.0081	4.6106	3.9616	3.4587	3.0609
15	7.6061	6.8109	6.1422	5.8474	5.5755	5.0916	4.6755	4.0013	3.4834	3.0764
16	7.8237	6.9740	6.2651	5.9542	5.6685	5.1624	4.7296	4.0333	3.5026	3.0882
17	8.0216	7.1196	6.3729	6.0472	5.7487	5.2223	4.7746	4.0591	3.5177	3.0971
18	8.2014	7.2497	6.4674	6.1280	5.8178	5.2732	4.8122	4.0799	3.5294	3.1039
19	8.3649	7.3658	6.5504	6.1982	5.8775	5.3162	4.8435	4.0967	3.5386	3.1090
20	8.5136	7.4694	6.6231	6.2593	5.9288	5.3527	4.8696	4.1103	3.5458	3.1129
21	8.6487	7.5620	6.6870	6.3125	5.9731	5.3837	4.8913	4.1212	3.5514	3.1158
22	8.7715	7.6446	6.7429	6.3587	6.0113	5.4099	4.9094	4.1300	3.5558	3.1180
23	8.8832	7.7184	6.7921	6.3988	6.0442	5.4321	4.9245	4.1371	3.5592	3.1197
24	8.9847	7.7843	6.8351	6.4338	6.0726	5.4510	4.9371	4.1428	3.5619	3.1210
25	9.0770	7.8431	6.8729	6.4642	6.0971	5.4669	4.9476	4.1474	3.5640	3.1220
26	9.1609	7.8957	6.9061	6.4906	6.1182	5.4804	4.9563	4.1511	3.5656	3.1227
27	9.2372	7.9426	6.9352	6.5135	6.1364	5.4919	4.9636	4.1542	3.5669	3.1233
28	9.3066	7.9844	6.9607	6.5335	6.1520	5.5016	4.9697	4.1566	3.5679	3.1237
29	9.3696	8.0218	6.9830	6.5509	6.1656	5.5098	4.9747	4.1585	3.5687	3.1240
30	9.4269	8.0552	7.0027	6.5660	6.1772	5.5168	4.9789	4.1601	3.5693	3.1242
35	9.6442	8.1755	7.0700	6.6166	6.2153	5.5386	4.9915	4.1644	3.5708	3.1248
40	9.7791	8.2438	7.1050	6.6418	6.2335	5.5482	4.9966	4.1659	3.5712	3.1250
45	9.8628	8.2825	7.1232	6.6543	6.2421	5.5523	4.9986	4.1664	3.5714	3.1250
50	9.9148	8.3045	7.1327	6.6605	6.2463	5.5541	4.9995	4.1666	3.5714	3.1250
55	9.9471	8.3170	7.1376	6.6636	6.2482	5.5549	4.9998	4.1666	3.5714	3.1250

APPENDIX STATISTICAL TABLES

TABLE B.1

z	0.00	0.01	0.02	0.03	0.04	0.05	0.06	0.07	0.08	0.09
0.0	.0000	.0040	.0080	.0120	.0160	.0199	.0239	.0279	.0319	.0359
0.1	.0398	.0438	.0478	.0517	.0557	.0596	.0636	.0675	.0714	.0753
0.2	.0793	.0832	.0871	.0910	.0948	.0987	.1026	.1064	.1103	.1141
0.3	.1179	.1217	.1255	.1293	.1331	.1368	.1406	.1443	.1480	.1517
0.4	.1554	.1591	.1628	.1664	.1700	.1736	.1772	.1808	.1844	.1879
0.5	.1915	.1950	.1985	.2019	.2054	.2088	.2123	.2157	.2190	.2224
0.6	.2257	.2291	.2324	.2357	.2389	.2422	.2454	.2486	.2517	.2549
0.7	.2580	.2611	.2642	.2673	.2704	.2734	.2764	.2794	.2823	.2852
0.8	.2881	.2910	.2939	.2967	.2995	.3023	.3051	.3078	.3106	.3133
0.9	.3159	.3186	.3212	.3238	.3264	.3289	.3315	.3340	.3365	.3389
1.0	.3413	.3438	.3461	.3485	.3508	.3531	.3554	.3577	.3599	.3621
1.1	.3643	.3665	.3686	.3708	.3729	.3749	.3770	.3790	.3810	.3830
1.2	.3849	.3869	.3888	.3907	.3925	.3944	.3962	.3980	.3997	.4015
1.3	.4032	.4049	.4066	.4082	.4099	.4115	.4131	.4147	.4162	.4177
1.4	.4192	.4207	.4222	.4236	.4251	.4265	.4279	.4292	.4306	.4319
1.5	.4332	.4345	.4357	.4370	.4382	.4394	.4406	.4418	.4429	.4441
1.6	.4452	.4463	.4474	.4484	.4495	.4505	.4515	.4525	.4535	.4545
1.7	.4554	.4564	.4573	.4582	.4591	.4599	.4608	.4616	.4625	.4633
1.8	.4641	.4649	.4656	.4664	.4671	.4678	.4686	.4693	.4699	.4706
1.9	.4713	.4719	.4726	.4732	.4738	.4744	.4750	.4756	.4761	.4767
2.0	.4773	.4778	.4783	.4788	.4793	.4798	.4803	.4808	.4812	.4817
2.1	.4821	.4826	.4830	.4834	.4838	.4842	.4846	.4850	.4854	.4857
2.2	.4861	.4864	.4868	.4871	.4875	.4878	.4881	.4884	.4887	.4890
2.3	.4893	.4896	.4898	.4901	.4904	.4906	.4909	.4911	.4913	.4916
2.4	.4918	.4920	.4922	.4925	.4927	.4929	.4931	.4932	.4934	.4936
2.5	.4938	.4940	.4941	.4943	.4945	.4946	.4948	.4949	.4951	.4952
2.6	.4953	.4955	.4956	.4957	.4959	.4960	.4961	.4962	.4963	.4964
2.7	.4965	.4966	.4967	.4968	.4969	.4970	.4971	.4972	.4973	.4974
2.8	.4974	.4975	.4976	.4977	.4977	.4978	.4979	.4979	.4980	.4981
2.9	.4981	.4982	.4982	.4982	.4984	.4984	.4985	.4985	.4986	.4986
3.0	.4987	.4987	.4987	.4988	.4988	.4989	.4989	.4989	.4990	.4990

[1]z is the standardized variable, where $z = x - \mu/\sigma$ and x is the point of interest, μ is the mean, and σ is the standard deviation of a distribution. Thus, z measures the number of standard deviations between a point of interest x and the mean of a given distribution. In the table above, we indicate the percentage of the total area under the normal curve between x and μ. Thus, .3413 or 34.13% of the area under the normal curve lies between a point of interest and the mean when $z = 1.0$.

TABLE B.2 **Critical F Values at the 90 Percent Confidence Level ($\alpha = .10$)[2]**

Degrees of Freedom in the Numerator ($d.f. = k - 1$)

$d.f. = N - k$	1	2	3	4	5	6	7	8	9	10	12	15	20	24	30	40	60	120	∞
1	39.86	49.50	53.59	55.83	57.24	58.20	58.91	59.44	59.86	60.19	60.71	61.22	61.74	62.00	62.26	62.53	62.79	63.06	63.33
2	8.53	9.00	9.16	9.24	9.29	9.33	9.35	9.37	9.38	9.39	9.41	9.42	9.44	9.45	9.46	9.47	9.47	9.48	9.49
3	8.54	5.46	5.39	5.34	5.31	5.28	5.27	5.25	5.24	5.23	5.22	5.20	5.18	5.18	5.17	5.16	5.15	5.14	5.13
4	4.54	4.32	4.19	4.11	4.05	4.01	3.98	3.95	3.94	3.92	3.90	3.87	3.84	3.83	3.82	3.80	3.79	3.78	3.76
5	4.06	3.78	3.62	3.52	3.45	3.40	3.37	3.34	3.32	3.30	3.27	3.24	3.21	3.19	3.17	3.16	3.14	3.12	3.10
6	3.78	3.46	3.29	3.18	3.11	3.05	3.01	2.98	2.96	2.94	2.90	2.87	2.84	2.82	2.80	2.78	2.76	2.74	2.72
7	3.59	3.26	3.07	2.96	2.88	2.83	2.78	2.75	2.72	2.70	2.67	2.63	2.59	2.58	2.56	2.54	2.51	2.49	2.47
8	3.46	3.11	2.92	2.81	2.73	2.67	2.62	2.59	2.56	2.54	2.50	2.46	2.42	2.40	2.38	2.36	2.34	2.32	2.29
9	3.36	3.01	2.81	2.69	2.61	2.55	2.51	2.47	2.44	2.42	2.38	2.34	2.30	2.28	2.25	2.23	2.21	2.18	2.16
10	3.29	2.92	2.73	2.61	2.52	2.46	2.41	2.38	2.35	2.32	2.28	2.24	2.20	2.18	2.16	2.13	2.11	2.08	2.06
11	3.23	2.86	2.66	2.54	2.45	2.39	2.34	2.30	2.27	2.25	2.21	2.17	2.12	2.10	2.08	2.05	2.03	2.00	1.97
12	3.18	2.81	2.61	2.48	2.39	2.33	2.28	2.24	2.21	2.19	2.15	2.10	2.06	2.04	2.01	1.99	1.96	1.93	1.90
13	3.14	2.76	2.56	2.43	2.35	2.28	2.23	2.20	2.16	2.14	2.10	2.05	2.01	1.98	1.96	1.93	1.90	1.88	1.85
14	3.10	2.73	2.52	2.39	2.31	2.24	2.19	2.15	2.12	2.10	2.05	2.01	1.96	1.94	1.91	1.89	1.86	1.83	1.80
15	3.07	2.70	2.49	2.36	2.27	2.21	2.16	2.12	2.09	2.06	2.02	1.97	1.92	1.90	1.87	1.85	1.82	1.79	1.76
16	3.05	2.67	2.46	2.33	2.24	2.18	2.13	2.09	2.06	2.03	1.99	1.94	1.89	1.87	1.84	1.81	1.78	1.75	1.72
17	3.03	2.64	2.44	2.31	2.22	2.15	2.10	2.06	2.03	2.00	1.96	1.91	1.86	1.84	1.81	1.78	1.75	1.72	1.69
18	3.01	2.62	2.42	2.29	2.20	2.13	2.08	2.04	2.00	1.98	1.93	1.89	1.84	1.81	1.78	1.75	1.72	1.69	1.66
19	2.99	2.61	2.40	2.27	2.18	2.11	2.06	2.02	1.98	1.96	1.91	1.86	1.81	1.79	1.76	1.73	1.70	1.67	1.63
20	2.97	2.59	2.38	2.25	2.16	2.09	2.04	2.00	1.96	1.94	1.89	1.84	1.79	1.77	1.74	1.71	1.68	1.64	1.61
21	2.96	2.57	2.36	2.23	2.14	2.08	2.02	1.98	1.95	1.92	1.87	1.83	1.78	1.75	1.72	1.69	1.66	1.62	1.59
22	2.95	2.56	2.35	2.22	2.13	2.06	2.01	1.97	1.93	1.90	1.86	1.81	1.76	1.73	1.70	1.67	1.64	1.60	1.57
23	2.94	2.55	2.34	2.21	2.11	2.05	1.99	1.95	1.92	1.89	1.84	1.80	1.74	1.72	1.69	1.66	1.62	1.59	1.55
24	2.93	2.54	2.33	2.19	2.10	2.04	1.98	1.94	1.91	1.88	1.83	1.78	1.73	1.70	1.67	1.64	1.61	1.57	1.53
25	2.92	2.53	2.32	2.18	2.09	2.02	1.97	1.93	1.89	1.87	1.82	1.77	1.72	1.69	1.66	1.63	1.59	1.56	1.52
26	2.91	2.52	2.31	2.17	2.08	2.01	1.96	1.92	1.88	1.86	1.81	1.76	1.71	1.68	1.65	1.61	1.58	1.54	1.50
27	2.90	2.51	2.30	2.17	2.07	2.00	1.95	1.91	1.87	1.85	1.80	1.75	1.70	1.67	1.64	1.60	1.57	1.53	1.49
28	2.89	2.50	2.29	2.16	2.06	2.00	1.94	1.90	1.87	1.84	1.79	1.74	1.69	1.66	1.63	1.59	1.56	1.52	1.48
29	2.89	2.50	2.28	2.15	2.06	1.99	1.93	1.89	1.86	1.83	1.78	1.73	1.68	1.65	1.62	1.58	1.55	1.51	1.47
30	2.88	2.49	2.28	2.14	2.05	1.98	1.93	1.88	1.85	1.82	1.77	1.72	1.67	1.64	1.61	1.57	1.54	1.50	1.46
40	2.84	2.44	2.23	2.09	2.00	1.93	1.87	1.83	1.79	1.76	1.71	1.66	1.61	1.57	1.54	1.51	1.47	1.42	1.38
60	2.79	2.39	2.18	2.04	1.95	1.87	1.82	1.77	1.74	1.71	1.66	1.60	1.54	1.51	1.48	1.44	1.40	1.35	1.29
120	2.75	2.35	2.13	1.99	1.90	1.82	1.77	1.72	1.68	1.65	1.60	1.55	1.48	1.45	1.41	1.37	1.32	1.26	1.19
∞	2.71	2.30	2.08	1.94	1.85	1.77	1.72	1.67	1.63	1.60	1.55	1.49	1.42	1.38	1.34	1.30	1.24	1.17	1.00

Degrees of Freedom in the Denominator ($d.f. = N - k$)

Continued

[2]The F statistic provides evidence on whether or not a statistically significant proportion of the total variation in the dependent variable Y has been explained. The F statistic can be calculated in terms of the coefficient of determination as: $F_{k-1, n-k} = R^2/(k-1) \div (1-R^2)/n - k$, where R^2 is the coefficient of determination, k is the number of estimated coefficients in the regression model (including the intercept), and n is the number of data observations. When the critical F value is exceeded, we can conclude with a given level of confidence (e.g., $\alpha = 0.01$ or 90 percent confidence) that the regression equation, taken as a whole, significantly explains the variation in Y.

Source: Table 18 from *Biometrika Tables for Statisticians*, Volume 1, edited by E. S. Pearson and H. O. Hartley. By permission of the Biometrika Trustees.

TABLE B.2 **Critical *F* Values at the 95 Percent Confidence Level**

Degrees of Freedom in the Numerator (d.f. = k − 1)

	1	2	3	4	5	6	7	8	9	10	12	15	20	24	30	40	60	120	∞
1	161.4	199.5	215.7	224.6	230.2	234.0	236.8	238.9	240.5	241.9	243.9	245.9	248.0	249.1	250.1	251.1	252.2	253.3	254.3
2	18.51	19.00	19.16	19.25	19.30	19.33	19.35	19.37	19.38	19.40	19.41	19.43	19.45	19.45	19.46	19.47	19.48	19.49	19.50
3	10.13	9.55	9.28	9.12	9.01	8.94	8.89	8.85	8.81	8.79	8.74	8.70	8.66	8.64	8.62	8.59	8.57	8.55	8.53
4	7.71	6.94	6.59	6.39	6.26	6.16	6.09	6.04	6.00	5.96	5.91	5.86	5.80	5.77	5.75	5.72	5.69	5.66	5.63
5	6.61	5.79	5.41	5.19	5.05	4.95	4.88	4.82	4.77	4.74	4.68	4.62	4.56	4.53	4.50	4.46	4.43	4.40	4.36
6	5.99	5.14	4.76	4.53	4.39	4.28	4.21	4.15	4.10	4.06	4.00	3.94	3.87	3.84	3.81	3.77	3.74	3.70	3.67
7	5.59	4.74	4.35	4.12	3.97	3.87	3.79	3.73	3.68	3.64	3.57	3.51	3.44	3.41	3.38	3.34	3.30	3.27	3.23
8	5.32	4.46	4.07	3.84	3.69	3.58	3.50	3.44	3.39	3.35	3.28	3.22	3.15	3.12	3.08	3.04	3.01	2.97	2.93
9	5.12	4.26	3.86	3.63	3.48	3.37	3.29	3.23	3.18	3.14	3.07	3.01	2.94	2.90	2.86	2.83	2.79	2.75	2.71
10	4.96	4.10	3.71	3.48	3.33	3.22	3.14	3.07	3.02	2.98	2.91	2.85	2.77	2.74	2.70	2.66	2.62	2.58	2.54
11	4.84	3.98	3.59	3.36	3.20	3.09	3.01	2.95	2.90	2.85	2.79	2.72	2.65	2.61	2.57	2.53	2.49	2.45	2.40
12	4.75	3.89	3.49	3.26	3.11	3.00	2.91	2.85	2.80	2.75	2.69	2.62	2.54	2.51	2.47	2.43	2.38	2.34	2.30
13	4.67	3.81	3.41	3.18	3.03	2.92	2.83	2.77	2.71	2.67	2.60	2.53	2.46	2.42	2.38	2.34	2.30	2.25	2.21
14	4.60	3.74	3.34	3.11	2.96	2.85	2.76	2.70	2.65	2.60	2.53	2.46	2.39	2.35	2.31	2.27	2.22	2.18	2.13
15	4.54	3.68	3.29	3.06	2.90	2.79	2.71	2.64	2.59	2.54	2.48	2.40	2.33	2.29	2.25	2.20	2.16	2.11	2.07
16	4.49	3.63	3.24	3.01	2.85	2.74	2.66	2.59	2.54	2.49	2.42	2.35	2.28	2.24	2.19	2.15	2.11	2.06	2.01
17	4.45	3.59	3.20	2.96	2.81	2.70	2.61	2.55	2.49	2.45	2.38	2.31	2.23	2.19	2.15	2.10	2.06	2.01	1.96
18	4.41	3.55	3.16	2.93	2.77	2.66	2.58	2.51	2.46	2.41	2.34	2.27	2.19	2.15	2.11	2.06	2.02	1.97	1.92
19	4.38	3.52	3.13	2.90	2.74	2.63	2.54	2.48	2.42	2.38	2.31	2.23	2.16	2.11	2.07	2.03	1.98	1.93	1.88
20	4.35	3.49	3.10	2.87	2.71	2.60	2.51	2.45	2.39	2.35	2.28	2.20	2.12	2.08	2.04	1.99	1.95	1.90	1.84
21	4.32	3.47	3.07	2.84	2.68	2.57	2.49	2.42	2.37	2.32	2.25	2.18	2.10	2.05	2.01	1.96	1.92	1.87	1.81
22	4.30	3.44	3.05	2.82	2.66	2.55	2.46	2.40	2.34	2.30	2.23	2.15	2.07	2.03	1.98	1.94	1.89	1.84	1.78
23	4.28	3.42	3.03	2.80	2.64	2.53	2.44	2.37	2.32	2.27	2.20	2.13	2.05	2.01	1.96	1.91	1.86	1.81	1.76
24	4.26	3.40	3.01	2.78	2.62	2.51	2.42	2.36	2.30	2.25	2.18	2.11	2.03	1.98	1.94	1.89	1.84	1.79	1.73
25	4.24	3.39	2.99	2.76	2.60	2.49	2.40	2.34	2.28	2.24	2.16	2.09	2.01	1.96	1.92	1.87	1.82	1.77	1.71
26	4.23	3.37	2.98	2.74	2.59	2.47	2.39	2.32	2.27	2.22	2.15	2.07	1.99	1.95	1.90	1.85	1.80	1.75	1.69
27	4.21	3.35	2.96	2.73	2.57	2.46	2.37	2.31	2.25	2.20	2.13	2.06	1.97	1.93	1.88	1.84	1.79	1.73	1.67
28	4.20	3.34	2.95	2.71	2.56	2.45	2.36	2.29	2.24	2.19	2.12	2.04	1.96	1.91	1.87	1.82	1.77	1.71	1.65
29	4.18	3.33	2.93	2.70	2.55	2.43	2.35	2.28	2.22	2.18	2.10	2.03	1.94	1.90	1.85	1.81	1.75	1.70	1.64
30	4.17	3.32	2.92	2.69	2.53	2.42	2.33	2.27	2.21	2.16	2.09	2.01	1.93	1.89	1.84	1.79	1.74	1.68	1.62
40	4.08	3.23	2.84	2.61	2.45	2.34	2.25	2.18	2.12	2.08	2.00	1.92	1.84	1.79	1.74	1.69	1.64	1.58	1.51
60	4.00	3.15	2.76	2.53	2.37	2.25	2.17	2.10	2.04	1.99	1.92	1.84	1.75	1.70	1.65	1.59	1.53	1.47	1.39
120	3.92	3.07	2.68	2.45	2.29	2.17	2.09	2.02	1.96	1.91	1.83	1.75	1.66	1.61	1.55	1.50	1.43	1.35	1.25
∞	3.84	3.00	2.60	2.37	2.21	2.10	2.01	1.94	1.88	1.83	1.75	1.67	1.57	1.52	1.46	1.39	1.32	1.22	1.00

Degrees of Freedom in the Denominator (d.f. = N − k)

TABLE B.2 Critical *F* Values at the 99 Percent Confidence Level

d.f.	1	2	3	4	5	6	7	8	9	10	12	15	20	24	30	40	60	120	∞
1	4052	4999.5	5403	5625	5764	5859	5928	5982	6022	6056	6106	6157	6209	6235	6261	6287	6313	6339	6366
2	98.50	99.00	99.17	99.25	99.30	99.33	99.36	99.37	99.39	99.40	99.42	99.43	99.45	99.46	99.47	99.47	99.48	99.49	99.50
3	34.12	30.82	29.46	28.71	28.24	27.91	27.67	27.49	27.35	27.23	27.05	26.87	26.69	26.60	26.50	26.41	26.32	26.22	26.13
4	21.20	18.00	16.69	15.98	15.52	15.21	14.98	14.80	14.66	14.55	14.37	14.20	14.02	13.93	13.84	13.75	13.65	13.56	13.46
5	16.26	13.27	12.06	11.39	10.97	10.67	10.46	10.29	10.16	10.05	9.89	9.72	9.55	9.47	9.38	9.29	9.20	9.11	9.02
6	13.75	10.92	9.78	9.15	8.75	8.47	8.26	8.10	7.98	7.87	7.72	7.56	7.40	7.31	7.23	7.14	7.06	6.97	6.88
7	12.25	9.55	8.45	7.85	7.46	7.19	6.99	6.84	6.72	6.62	6.47	6.31	6.16	6.07	5.99	5.91	5.82	5.74	5.65
8	11.26	8.65	7.59	7.01	6.63	6.37	6.18	6.03	5.91	5.81	5.67	5.52	5.36	5.28	5.20	5.12	5.03	4.95	4.86
9	10.56	8.02	6.99	6.42	6.06	5.80	5.61	5.47	5.35	5.26	5.11	4.96	4.81	4.73	4.65	4.57	4.48	4.40	4.31
10	10.04	7.56	6.55	5.99	5.64	5.39	5.20	5.06	4.94	4.85	4.71	4.56	4.41	4.33	4.25	4.17	4.08	4.00	3.91
11	9.65	7.21	6.22	5.67	5.32	5.07	4.89	4.74	4.63	4.54	4.40	4.25	4.10	4.02	3.94	3.86	3.78	3.69	3.60
12	9.33	6.93	5.95	5.41	5.06	4.82	4.64	4.50	4.39	4.30	4.16	4.01	3.86	3.78	3.70	3.62	3.54	3.45	3.36
13	9.07	6.70	5.74	5.21	4.86	4.62	4.44	4.30	4.19	4.10	3.96	3.82	3.66	3.59	3.51	3.43	3.34	3.25	3.17
14	8.86	6.51	5.56	5.04	4.69	4.46	4.28	4.14	4.03	3.94	3.80	3.66	3.51	3.43	3.35	3.27	3.18	3.09	3.00
15	8.68	6.36	5.42	4.89	4.56	4.32	4.14	4.00	3.89	3.80	3.67	3.52	3.37	3.29	3.21	3.13	3.05	2.96	2.87
16	8.53	6.23	5.29	4.77	4.44	4.20	4.03	3.89	3.78	3.69	3.55	3.41	3.26	3.18	3.10	3.02	2.93	2.84	2.75
17	8.40	6.11	5.18	4.67	4.34	4.10	3.93	3.79	3.68	3.59	3.46	3.31	3.16	3.08	3.00	2.92	2.83	2.75	2.65
18	8.29	6.01	5.09	4.58	4.25	4.01	3.84	3.71	3.60	3.51	3.37	3.23	3.08	3.00	2.92	2.84	2.75	2.66	2.57
19	8.18	5.93	5.01	4.50	4.17	3.94	3.77	3.63	3.52	3.43	3.30	3.15	3.00	2.92	2.84	2.76	2.67	2.58	2.49
20	8.10	5.85	4.94	4.43	4.10	3.87	3.70	3.56	3.46	3.37	3.23	3.09	2.94	2.86	2.78	2.69	2.61	2.52	2.42
21	8.02	5.78	4.87	4.37	4.04	3.81	3.64	3.51	3.40	3.31	3.17	3.03	2.88	2.80	2.72	2.64	2.55	2.46	2.36
22	7.95	5.72	4.82	4.31	3.99	3.76	3.59	3.45	3.35	3.26	3.12	2.98	2.83	2.75	2.67	2.58	2.50	2.40	2.31
23	7.88	5.66	4.76	4.26	3.94	3.71	3.54	3.41	3.30	3.21	3.07	2.93	2.78	2.70	2.62	2.54	2.45	2.35	2.26
24	7.82	5.61	4.72	4.22	3.90	3.67	3.50	3.36	3.26	3.17	3.03	2.89	2.74	2.66	2.58	2.49	2.40	2.31	2.21
25	7.77	5.57	4.68	4.18	3.85	3.63	3.46	3.32	3.22	3.13	2.99	2.85	2.70	2.62	2.54	2.45	2.36	2.27	2.17
26	7.72	5.53	4.64	4.14	3.82	3.59	3.42	3.29	3.18	3.09	2.96	2.81	2.66	2.58	2.50	2.42	2.33	2.23	2.13
27	7.68	5.49	4.60	4.11	3.78	3.56	3.39	3.26	3.15	3.06	2.93	2.78	2.63	2.55	2.47	2.38	2.29	2.20	2.10
28	7.64	5.45	4.57	4.07	3.75	3.53	3.36	3.23	3.12	3.03	2.90	2.75	2.60	2.52	2.44	2.35	2.26	2.17	2.06
29	7.60	5.42	4.54	4.04	3.73	3.50	3.33	3.20	3.09	3.00	2.87	2.73	2.57	2.49	2.41	2.33	2.23	2.14	2.03
30	7.56	5.39	4.51	4.02	3.70	3.47	3.30	3.17	3.07	2.98	2.84	2.70	2.55	2.47	2.39	2.30	2.21	2.11	2.01
40	7.31	5.18	4.31	3.83	3.51	3.29	3.12	2.99	2.89	2.80	2.66	2.52	2.37	2.29	2.20	2.11	2.02	1.92	1.80
60	7.08	4.98	4.13	3.65	3.34	3.12	2.95	2.82	2.72	2.63	2.50	2.35	2.20	2.12	2.03	1.94	1.84	1.73	1.60
120	6.85	4.79	3.95	3.48	3.17	2.96	2.79	2.66	2.56	2.47	2.34	2.19	2.03	1.95	1.86	1.76	1.66	1.53	1.38
∞	6.63	4.61	3.78	3.32	3.02	2.80	2.64	2.51	2.41	2.32	2.18	2.04	1.88	1.79	1.70	1.59	1.47	1.32	1.00

Degrees of Freedom in the Denominator (d.f. = N − k)

TABLE B.3   Students' *t* Distribution[3]

Degrees of Freedom	Area in the Rejection Region (two-tail test)[a]												
	0.9	0.8	0.7	0.6	0.5	0.4	0.3	0.2	0.1	0.05	0.02	0.01	0.001
1	0.158	0.325	0.510	0.727	1.000	1.376	1.963	3.078	**6.314**	**12.706**	31.821	**63.657**	636.619
2	0.142	0.289	0.445	0.617	0.816	1.061	1.386	1.886	**2.920**	**4.303**	6.965	**9.925**	31.598
3	0.137	0.277	0.424	0.584	0.765	0.978	1.250	1.638	**2.353**	**3.182**	4.541	**5.841**	12.924
4	0.134	0.271	0.414	0.569	0.741	0.941	1.190	1.533	**2.132**	**2.776**	3.747	**4.604**	8.610
5	0.132	0.267	0.408	0.559	0.727	0.920	1.156	1.476	**2.015**	**2.571**	3.365	**4.032**	6.869
6	0.131	0.265	0.404	0.553	0.718	0.906	1.134	1.440	**1.943**	**2.447**	3.143	**3.707**	5.959
7	0.130	0.263	0.402	0.549	0.711	0.896	1.119	1.415	**1.895**	**2.365**	2.998	**3.499**	5.408
8	0.130	0.262	0.399	0.546	0.706	0.889	1.108	1.397	**1.860**	**2.306**	2.896	**3.355**	5.041
9	0.129	0.261	0.398	0.543	0.703	0.883	1.100	1.383	**1.833**	**2.262**	2.821	**3.250**	4.781
10	0.129	0.260	0.397	0.542	0.700	0.879	1.093	1.372	**1.812**	**2.228**	2.764	**3.169**	4.587
11	0.129	0.260	0.396	0.540	0.697	0.876	1.088	1.363	**1.796**	**2.201**	2.718	**3.106**	4.437
12	0.128	0.259	0.395	0.539	0.695	0.873	1.083	1.356	**1.782**	**2.179**	2.681	**3.055**	4.318
13	0.128	0.259	0.394	0.538	0.694	0.870	1.079	1.350	**1.771**	**2.160**	2.650	**3.012**	4.221
14	0.128	0.258	0.393	0.537	0.692	0.868	1.076	1.345	**1.761**	**2.145**	2.624	**2.977**	4.140
15	0.128	0.258	0.393	0.536	0.691	0.866	1.074	1.341	**1.753**	**2.131**	2.602	**2.947**	4.073
16	0.128	0.258	0.392	0.535	0.690	0.865	1.071	1.337	**1.746**	**2.120**	2.583	**2.921**	4.015
17	0.128	0.257	0.392	0.534	0.689	0.863	1.069	1.333	**1.740**	**2.110**	2.567	**2.898**	3.965
18	0.127	0.257	0.392	0.534	0.688	0.862	1.067	1.330	**1.734**	**2.101**	2.552	**2.878**	3.922
19	0.127	0.257	0.391	0.533	0.688	0.861	1.066	1.328	**1.729**	**2.093**	2.539	**2.861**	3.883
20	0.127	0.257	0.391	0.533	0.687	0.860	1.064	1.325	**1.725**	**2.086**	2.528	**2.845**	3.850
21	0.127	0.257	0.391	0.532	0.686	0.859	1.063	1.323	**1.721**	**2.080**	2.518	**2.831**	3.819
22	0.127	0.256	0.390	0.532	0.686	0.858	1.061	1.321	**1.717**	**2.074**	2.508	**2.819**	3.792
23	0.127	0.256	0.390	0.532	0.685	0.858	1.060	1.319	**1.714**	**2.069**	2.500	**2.807**	3.767
24	0.127	0.256	0.390	0.531	0.685	0.857	1.059	1.318	**1.711**	**2.064**	2.492	**2.797**	3.745
25	0.127	0.256	0.390	0.531	0.684	0.856	1.058	1.316	**1.708**	**2.060**	2.485	**2.787**	3.725
26	0.127	0.256	0.390	0.531	0.684	0.856	1.058	1.315	**1.706**	**2.056**	2.479	**2.779**	3.707
27	0.127	0.256	0.389	0.531	0.684	0.855	1.057	1.314	**1.703**	**2.052**	2.473	**2.771**	3.690
28	0.127	0.256	0.389	0.530	0.683	0.855	1.056	1.313	**1.701**	**2.048**	2.467	**2.763**	3.674
29	0.127	0.256	0.389	0.530	0.683	0.854	1.055	1.311	**1.699**	**2.045**	2.462	**2.756**	3.659
30	0.127	0.256	0.389	0.530	0.683	0.854	1.055	1.310	**1.697**	**2.042**	2.457	**2.750**	3.646
40	0.126	0.255	0.388	0.529	0.681	0.851	1.050	1.303	**1.684**	**2.021**	2.423	**2.704**	3.551
60	0.126	0.254	0.387	0.527	0.679	0.848	1.046	1.296	**1.671**	**2.000**	2.390	**2.660**	3.460
120	0.126	0.254	0.386	0.526	0.677	0.845	1.041	1.289	**1.658**	**1.980**	2.358	**2.617**	3.373
∞	0.126	0.253	0.385	0.524	0.674	0.842	1.036	1.282	**1.645**	**1.960**	2.326	**2.576**	3.291

[3]Columns in bold-face type indicate critical *t*-values for popular levels of significance for two-tail hypothesis testing. Thus, critical *t*-values for $\alpha = 0.1$ (90 percent confidence), $\alpha = 0.05$ (95 percent confidence), and $\alpha = 0.01$ (99 percent confidence) are highlighted. When the calculated *t*-statistic $= b/\sigma_b$ exceeds the relevant critical *t*-value, we can reject the hypothesis that there is no relationship between the dependent variable *Y* and a given independent variable *X*. For simple *t*-tests, the relevant number degrees of freedom (column row) is found as follows: $d.f. = N - k$, where *N* is the number of data observations and *k* is the number of estimated coefficients (including the intercept).

Source: Ya-lun Chou, *Probability and Statistics for Decision Making* (New York: Holt, Rinehart and Winston, 1972), p. 612. Reprinted by permission of the author.

SELECTED CHECK FIGURES FOR END-OF-CHAPTER PROBLEMS

2.1
B. $Q = 5$.

2.2
B. $Q = 5$.
C. $Q = 8$.

2.4
B. $ME = 5$, $NH = 3$, $VT = 2$.
C. Commission Income $= \$3,000$.

2.5
B. $I = 3$.
C. $I = 4$.

2.6
A. $Q = 500$, $P = \$500$, $\pi = \$150,000$.
B. $Q = 450$, $P = \$550$, $\pi = \$152,500$.

2.8
A. $Q = 6,000$, $MC = \$3,000$,
   $AC = \$3,000$, $P = \$3,600$,
   $\pi = \$3,600,000$.
B. $Q = 5,000$, $MC = \$2,600$,
   $AC = \$3,040$, $P = \$3,850$,
   $\pi = \$4,050,000$.

2.9
A. $Q = 400$, $P = \$6,000$,
   $\pi = \$400,000$.

B. $Q = 300$, $P = \$7,000$,
   $\pi = \$300,000$.
C. $\lambda = \$2,000$.
D. $\$100,000$.

2.10
B. $S = 4$, $M = 18$.
C. $\lambda = 0.00005$ Service.
D. $AC = \$30,000$ per unit.

3.3
A. $E(NC) = \$125$.

3.4
A. $E(\pi_{MA}) = \$1,000,000$,
   $E(\pi_{PS}) = \$750,000$.

3.5
A. $E(\pi_1) = \$500,000$,
   $E(\pi_2) = \$375,000$.
C. $\sigma_1 = \$300,000$, $\sigma_2 = \$125,000$.
D. $E(u_1) = 1,172$, $E(u_2) = 1,162.50$.

3.6
A. $E(CF_1) = \$10,000$,
   $E(CF_2) = \$10,000$.
B. $\sigma_1 = \$3,000$, $\sigma_2 = \$1,000$.
C. $NPV_1 = \$5,000$, $NPV_2 = \$7,500$.

3.7

A. $E(\pi_A) = \$150,000$, $\sigma_A = \$50,000$, $V_A = 0.33$, $E(\pi_{SF}) = \$200,000$, $\sigma_{SF} = \$140,000$, $V_{SF} = 0.7$.

B. $\alpha_A = 0.8$, $\alpha_{SF} = 0.85$.

3.8

A. $Pr = 40\%$.

3.9

A. $Pr = 50\%$.
B. $P = \$23.29$.
C. $Pr = 93.32\%$.

4.2

A. $P = \$10$.
B. $P = \$1$.
C. $P = \$4$, $Q = 300,000$.

4.5

A. $Q = 15,000$.
B. $Q = 22,500$.

4.6

B. $Q = 20,000$ passengers, $TR = \$2,000,000$.

4.7

B. If $P = \$50$, then $Q = 0$;
    If $P = \$60$, then $Q = 5,000,000$;
    If $P = \$70$, then $Q = 10,000,000$.
C. If $Q = 4,000,000$, $P = \$58$;
    If $Q = 6,000,000$, $P = \$62$;
    If $Q = 8,000,000$, $P = \$66$.

4.8

A. $Q = 2,500$, $MC = \$110$;
    $Q = 5,000$, $MC = \$120$;
    $Q = 7,500$, $MC = \$130$.
B. $MC = \$100$, $Q = 0$;
    $MC = \$125$, $Q = 6,250$;
    $MC = \$150$, $Q = 12,500$.
C. $Q = 12,500$.

4.9

B. $P = \$8$, $Q_C = 0$;
    $P = \$10$, $Q_C = 0$;
    $P = \$12$, $Q_C = 500$.
    $P = \$8$, $Q_P = 0$;
    $P = \$10$, $Q_P = 250$;
    $P = \$12$, $Q_P = 500$.

4.10

B. $P = \$1.50$, Shortage $= -50$;
    $P = \$2$, Surplus = Shortage $= 0$;
    $P = \$2.50$, Surplus $= +50$.
C. $P = \$2$, $Q_D = Q_S = 50,000,000$ bushels.

5.1

C. $G = 2$ units.

5.2

B. $S = 4$.
C. $G = 4$.
D. $G = 2$ and $S = 4$.

5.3

B. 20¢ per util.
C. $G = 1$, $P = \$10$;
    $G = 2$, $P = \$8$;
    $G = 3$, $P = \$6$;
    $G = 4$, $P = \$4$;
    $G = 5$, $P = \$2$.

5.5

A. $Q = 600$.
B. $P = \$3$.
C. $P = \$7.50$.
D. $Q = 1,500$.
E. $\epsilon_P = -2$.

5.6

A. $\epsilon_P = -4$.
B. $P = \$12,500$.

5.7

A. $E_P = -2$.
B. $E_{PX} = -2.67$.

5.8

A. $E_I = 6$.
B. $E_P = -8$.

5.9

A. $E_{PX} = 1.5$.
B. $E_P = -3$.
C. $\Delta P = \$20$.

5.10

A. $E_P = 2$.
B. $\Delta P = -\$2$.
C. $E_A = 1$.

6.3

A. $Q = 250,000 - 25P$.

6.4

A. Demand: $P = \$20 - \$0.005Q_D + \$10T$;
    Supply: $P = \$10 + \$0.005Q_S$.

6.5

C. $\epsilon_A = 1$.
D. $Pr = 50\%$.

7.1

A. $g = 32\%$.
B. $g = 28\%$.

7.2

B. $g = 0\%$.
C. $g = 11\%$.

7.3

A. $g = 10\%$.
B. $S_5 = \$104,715,000 + u$,
    $S_{10} = \$168,610,000 + u$.

7.4

A. $g = 7.4\%$.
B. $t = 2 + u$.

7.5

B. $A_t = 80 + u$.

7.6

B. $S_{t+1} = \$295,000 + u$.

7.7

B. $D_{t+1} = 375 + u$.

7.8

B. $S_{t+1} = 12,500 + u$.

7.9

B. Regular price: $TR = \$3,875 + u$,
    Special price: $TR = \$7,125 + u$.
C. Regular price: $\pi = \$1,450 + u$,
    Special price: $\pi = \$3,225 + u$.

7.10

$I = \$1,000 + u$ billion.
$GDP = \$7,000 + u$ billion.
$C = \$4,500 + u$ billion.
$T = \$1,400 + u$ billion.
$Y = \$5,600 + u$ billion.

8.1

C. $Y = 3$.

8.5

A. Bates = 3.75%, Belker = 4.5%,
    Coffey = 4%, Esterhaus = 3.33%.
B. Bates = \$8,000, Belker = \$5,000,
    Coffey = \$4,500, Esterhaus =
    \$3,750.

8.6

B. Inquiries = 4,000.

8.7

B. Attendants = 4.
C. Wage = \$80.

8.8

A. $MP_A = \$100 - A$.
B. $MRP_A = P_A$.
C. Advertising = 50.

8.9

A. $MRP_P = \$62,500$, $MRP_A = \$35,000$.

8.10

A. $\Delta Q/Q = -1.12\%$.
B. $\Delta Q/Q = -2.88\%$.

9.1

A. $X = 0$ to $X = 2$.
B. $X = 3$.
C. Minimum $AC = \$1.25$.
D. $MC = \$1.25$.

9.4

A. $\pi = \$175,000$.

9.5

A. $TC_A = \$9,000 + \$0.4Q$.
B. $TC_E = \$27,000 + \$0.4Q$.
C. $Q_{BE} = 45,000$.

9.6

A. $\Delta Q = 20,000$.
B. $E_P = -3$.

9.7

A. $Q_{BE} = 1,000$.
B. $\epsilon_C = 0.82$.

9.8

A. $Q_M = 60,000$;
    $Q_N = 55,000$;
    $Q_D = 162,500$.

9.9

A. $TC = \$450,000, AC = \$112.50$.
B.   Learning $= -\$5.50$, or 5%.

9.10

A. $\Delta Q_{BE} = 250,000$.
B. $\Delta DOL = 0.4$.
C. $\Delta \pi = \$1,000,000$.

10.4

C. $\% \Delta Q = 25\%$.

10.5

B.   \$1,193,000.

10.7

A. $AVC = \$50,000/Q + \$5 - \$0.01Q$
     $+ \$0.00001Q$;
     $MC = \$5 - \$0.02Q + \$0.00003Q^2$.
C.   1,250 to 1,750 units per week.

10.8

B. $Q = 10,000$.
C. $Q = 7,500$.

10.9

B. $Q_{MES} = 2,000,000$.

10.10

A. $Q_{BE} = 8,000$ or 10,000 units.
B. $Q = 8,944$.
C.   Potential Number of Efficient Com-
     petitors $= 10.7$ or 10.

11.2

A. $L = 4, K = 400, Q = 1$;
     $L = 16, K = 1,600, Q = 4$.
B. $\Delta MP_L = -0.0625$,
     $\Delta MP_K = -0.000625$.
C. $Q = 1,000$.
D. $MP_L = 0.25, MP_K = 0$.

11.3

C. $\pi = \$2,350$.

11.4

B. $A = 1, B = 4, L_F = 4, L_R = 0$,
     $L_{FC} = 0, C = \$240,000$.
C. $\Delta TC = -\$32,000$.
D. $\Delta C_A > \$120,000$.

11.5

B. $C = \$50,000,000, P = \$50,000,000$,
     $S_D = \$0, S_B = \$100,000,000$,

$S_C = \$25,000,000, S_A = \$0$,
$\pi = \$1,750,000$.

11.6

B. $I = 0.75, J = 0.25, L_I = 0$,
     $L_J = 0.05, L_L = 0, i = 0.0975$.
C. $\Delta R_J > -3\%$ or $\Delta R_I > 3\%$.
D.   Maximum cash $= 20\%$.

11.7

B. $E = 30, W = 40, S_H = 0, S_S = 0.15$,
     $S_P = 0, C = \$2,500$.
C. $\Delta P_W > \$12.50$.

11.8

B. $I = 120, C = 40, S_A = 0, S_B = 80$,
     $S_S = 0, \pi = \$18,000$.
C. $\pi = \$1,900$.
D. $\pi = \$2,900$.
E. $L_I = L_C = 0, V_A = \$50, V_B = \$0$,
     $V_S = \$50, \pi^* = \$18,000$.

11.9

B. $Q_1 = 5, Q_2 = 3, S_D = 0, S_A = 5$,
     $S_{AR} = 0, R = \$21,000$;
     $L_1 = L_2 = 0, V_D = \$125, V_A = \$0$,
     $V_{AR} = \$250, R^* = \$21,000$.

11.10

B. $Q_A = 0, Q_B = 2, Q_C = 2$,
     $S_L = S_P = 0, Q = 4$;
     $L_A = 0.625, L_B = L_C = 0$,
     $V_L = 0.125, V_P = 0.375, Q^* = 4$.
C. $MRP_P = \$56.25$.
D. $MRP_L = \$18.75$.

12.2

B. $P = MC = \$50$.
C. $P = \$75, Q = 3$;
     $P = \$100, Q = 6$.

12.3

B. $P = \$4, Q = 40$.
C.   Excess supply $= 15$.

12.4

A. $Q = 5,000, P = \$400$;
     $Q = 10,000, P = \$600$;
     $Q = 15,000, P = \$800$.
B. $P = \$200, Q = 0$;
     $P = \$500, Q = 7,500$;
     $P = \$1,000, Q = 20,000$.

12.5

C. $Q_S = 31,250,000.$

12.6

A. $Q = 50,000, \pi = -\$75,000.$
B. $Q = 200,000, \pi = \$300,000.$
C. $Q = 100,000, P = \$4, \pi = \$0.$

12.7

A. $P = \$200, Q = 100,000.$
B. $\pi = \$5,000,000,$ Margin $= 25\%.$

12.8

A. $Q = 1,000,000, P = \$10,$
$\pi = \$5,000,000.$
B. $P = MC = \$5, \pi = 0.$

12.9

A. $Q = 100,000, P = \$5,000,$
$\pi = \$50,000,000.$
B. $Q = 200,000, P = \$4,500, \pi = \$0.$

12.10

A. $Q = 150,000, P = \$3.50,$
$\pi = \$287,500.$
B. $Q = 100,000, P = \$1.50, \pi = \$0.$

13.3

B. $P = AC = \$14, Q = 6(000,000),$
$\pi = \$0.$
C. $P = AC = \$11, Q = 9(000,000),$
$\pi = \$0.$
D. $P = \$17, Q = 3(000,000),$
$\pi = \$9(000,000).$

13.4

A. $Q = 12, P = \$36$ million,
$\pi = \$88$ million, $\epsilon_P = -2.$
B. High-price/low-output:
$Q = 10, P = \$31$ million, $\pi = \$0;$
Low-price/high-output:
$Q = 20, P = \$26$ million, $\pi = \$0.$
C. $Q_2 = 16.2,$ high-price/low output;
$Q_2 = 23.4,$ low-price/high-output.

13.5

B. $A = 4, B = 1, C = 3,$
$\pi = \$50$ million.

13.6

A. $P = \$2, Q = 40,000.$
B. $P = \$3.60, Q = 24,000.$

13.7

C. $P = \$50, Q = 10(000),$
$\pi = \$150(000).$

13.8

A. $P_A > \$250, P_B > \$200.$

13.9

A. $P = \$4.50, Q = 7,000.$
B. $P = \$4.65, Q = 8,375.$

13.10

C. $Q_L = 40,000, P_L = \$23.$
D. $P = \$23, Q_M = 6,000, Q_N = 4,000.$

14.3

A. $\epsilon_P = -2.$
B. $P = \$20.$

14.4

A. $\epsilon_P = -5.$
B. Optimal Markup on Cost $= 25\%,$
$P = \$150.$

14.5

A. $E_P = -2.5.$
B. Optimal Markup on Price $= 40\%,$
$P = \$225.$

14.6

A. $P = \$2,875,000 + \epsilon.$
B. $P = \$2,701,000 + \epsilon.$

14.7

A. $\pi_1 = \$112,000, \pi_2 = \$104,000.$

14.8

A. $Q_W = 500, P_W = \$12,500,$
$Q_R = 1,000, P_R = \$30,000,$
$\pi = \$2,125,000.$
B. $\epsilon_{PW} = -5, \epsilon_{PR} = -1.5.$

14.9

A. $Q_S = Q_L = 20,000, P_S = \$10.40,$
$P_L = \$0.30.$
B. $Q_S = 150,000, P_S = \$32.50,$
$Q_L = 40,000, P_L = \$0.20.$

14.10

A. $Q = 10,000, P = \$850,$
$\pi = \$500,000.$
B. $P_T = \$600.$
C. $Q_{NA} = 8,000, P_{NA} = \$872.50,$
$Q_E = 6,000, P_E = \$645,$
$\pi = \$635,000.$

15.5

A. $A = 3, B = 2, C = 3, \pi = \$80.$
B. $P = \$20.$
C. $Q = 10.$
D. $40 or $50.

15.6

A. $Q_L = 400, P_L = \$10,000,$
    $Q_H = 2,500, P_H = \$7,500,$
    $\pi = \$3,250,000.$
B. $Q_L = 360, P_L = \$10,500,$
    $Q_H = 2,000, P_H = \$8,000,$
    $\pi = \$620,000.$
C. $\epsilon_{PL} = -2, \epsilon_{PH} = -3.$

15.7

A. $Q = 100,000, \pi = \$0.$
B. $Q = 100,000, \pi = \$0.$
C. $Q = 75,000, \pi = -\$437,500.$

15.8

A. $Q = 10,000, P = \$11,500,$
    $\pi = \$8,000,000.$
B. $Q = 9,000, P = \$11,730,$
    $\pi = \$3,630,000.$

15.9

A. $Q = 1,600, P_M = \$24, P_A = \$288,$
    $i = 12.5\%.$
B. $Q = 1,800, i = 12.25\%.$
C. $Q = 2,000, P_M = \$20.$

15.10

A. $Q_B = 50,000, P_B = \$5,$
    $Q_P = 500,000, P_P = \$85,$
    $\pi = \$10,250,000.$
B. Excess $B = 450,000.$
C. $Q = 200,000, \pi = \$3,500,000.$
D. $Q = 500,000, \pi = \$7,250,000.$

16.5

A. $NPV_{LB} = \$500,000,$
    $NPV_{SD} = \$600,000.$
B. $PI_{LB} = 1.25, PI_{SD} = 1.2.$

16.6

A. $E(CF_1) = \$1,000,000, \sigma_1 = \$200,000, V_1 = 0.2, E(CF_2) = \$900,000, \sigma_2 = \$360,000, V_2 = 0.4.$
B. $NPV_1 = \$1,192,500,$
    $NPV_2 = -\$362,640.$
C. $PI_1 = 1.40, PI_2 = 0.88.$

16.7

A. $E(CF_{A1}) = \$50,000, \sigma_{A1} = \$30,000, V_{A1} = 0.6;$
    $E(CF_{A2}) = \$50,000, \sigma_{A2} = \$20,000, V_{A2} = 0.4;$
    $E(CF_{B1}) = \$100,000, \sigma_{B1} = \$100,000, V_{B1} = 1;$
    $E(CF_{B2}) = \$100,000, \sigma_{B2} = \$50,000, V_{B2} = 0.5.$
B. $NPV_A = \$9,505, NPV_B = \$12,570.$
C. $PI_A = 1.13, PI_B = 1.08.$
D. $IRR_A = IRR_B = 21.6\%.$

16.8

A. $CF = \$8,000.$

16.9

A. Net cash inflow:
    $A = \$1,410,000, B = \$1,378,333,$
    $C = \$1,156,666.$
B. $NPV_A = \$444,180,$
    $NPV_B = \$159,924,$
    $NPV_C = \$497,927.$

16.10

A. $k_e = 20\%.$
B. $k = 16.95\%.$

INDEX

Note: Entries in boldface type indicate key glossary terms found defined in text margin on respective pages. Lowercase "n" following a page number indicates that the term is mentioned in a footnote on the respective page.